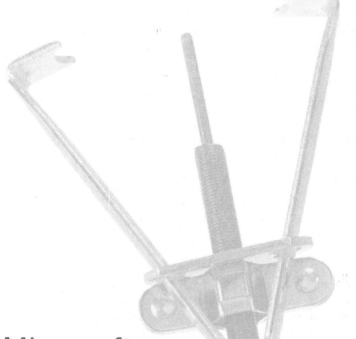

Microsoft®

WINDOWS® 2000
SCRIPTING
GUIDE

Automating System
Administration

The Microsoft® Windows® Resource Kit Scripting Team

PUBLISHED BY
Microsoft Press
A Division of Microsoft Corporation
One Microsoft Way
Redmond, Washington 98052-6399

Library of Congress Cataloging-in-Publication Data
Microsoft Windows 2000 Scripting Guide / Microsoft Corporation.
        p. cm.
    Includes index.
    ISBN 0-7356-1867-4
    1. Microsoft Windows (Computer file)   2. Operating systems (Computers)   I. Microsoft
Corporation.

    QA76.76.O63 M5241322525   2002
    005.4'4769--dc21   2002033719

Printed and bound in the United States of America.

2 3 4 5 6 7 8 9   QWT   8 7 6 5 4 3

Distributed in Canada by H.B. Fenn and Company Ltd.

A CIP catalogue record for this book is available from the British Library.

Microsoft Press books are available through booksellers and distributors worldwide. For further information about international editions, contact your local Microsoft Corporation office or contact Microsoft Press International directly at fax (425) 936-7329. Visit our Web site at www.microsoft.com/mspress. Send comments to *rkinput@microsoft.com*.

Active Directory, ActiveX, FrontPage, JScript, Microsoft, Microsoft Press, MSDN, MS-DOS, MSN, Notepad, SQL Server, Visual Basic, Visual Studio, Windows, Windows Media, Windows NT, and Win32 are registered trademarks of Microsoft Corporation in the United States and/or other countries. ActivePerl is a registered trademark of the ActiveState Corporation, Apple and Macintosh are registered trademarks of the Apple Corporation, IBM is a registered trademark of International Business Machines Corporation, and NetWare is a registered trademark of the Novell Corporation. Other product and company names mentioned herein may be the trademarks of their respective owners.

The example companies, organizations, products, domain names, e-mail addresses, logos, people, places, and events depicted herein are fictitious. No association with any real company, organization, product, domain name, e-mail address, logo, person, place, or event is intended or should be inferred.

Information in this document is subject to change without notice.

Microsoft may have patents or pending patent applications, trademarks, copyrights, or other intellectual property rights covering subject matter in this document. Except as expressly provided in any written license agreement from Microsoft, the furnishing of this document does not give you any license to these patents, trademarks, copyrights, or other intellectual property.

Acquisitions Editors: Juliana Aldous Atkinson, Martin Delre
Project Editor: Maureen Williams Zimmerman

Body Part No. X08-98407

Thank you to those who contributed to this book:

Microsoft Windows 2000 Scripting Guide

Book Writing Lead: Greg Stemp
Writers: Dean Tsaltas, Bob Wells, Ethan Wilansky
Technical Writing Manager: Peter Costantini

Book Editing Lead: Carolyn Eller
Editors: Anika Nelson, Scott Somohano, Nona Allison, Jim Becker, Bonnie Birger, Dale Callison, Justin Hall, Kate Robinson, Dee Teodoro, Scott Turnbull, Tom Winn, Krista Wall, Shawn Peck, Holly Viola
Editing Managers: Kate O'Leary, Jay Schram

Project Manager: Neil Orint

Production Lead: Jason Hershey
Production Specialists: Barbara Arend, Yong Ok Chung, Dean Prince
Documentation Tools Software Developers: Cornel Moiceanu, Steve Pyron

Indexer: Caroline Parks

Lead Graphic Designer: Gabriel Varela
Designers: Chris Blanton, Rochelle Parry
Art Production: Jon Billow

Test Lead: Richard Min
Testers: Matt Winberry, Ben Rangel

Windows Lab Administrators: Dave Meyer, Robert Thingwold

Special thanks for laying the groundwork for this book to:
Martin DelRe, Lola Gunter

A special recognition to the following technical experts for their exceptional contributions:
Alex Angelopolous, Mike Dutra, Mary Gray, Eric Lippert, Ryan Maas, Daryl Wray

A special thanks to the following technical experts who contributed to and supported this effort:
Muhammad Arrabi, John Biscevic, Andrew Clinick, David C. Winkler

Director, Windows Server User Assistance: Karen Forster
Resource Kit User Assistance Manager: Pilar Ackerman

Contents at a glance

PART I: Scripting Concepts and Technologies for System Administration 1

    CHAPTER 1   Introduction to Windows Script Technologies 3

    CHAPTER 2   VBScript Primer 15

    CHAPTER 3   WSH Primer 129

    CHAPTER 4   Script Runtime Primer 241

    CHAPTER 5   ADSI Scripting Primer 307

    CHAPTER 6   WMI Scripting Primer 427

PART II: Scripting Solutions for System Administration 547

    CHAPTER 7   Active Directory Users 549

    CHAPTER 8   Computer Assets 617

    CHAPTER 9   Computer Roles 689

    CHAPTER 10   Disks and File Systems 725

    CHAPTER 11   Files and Folders 767

    CHAPTER 12   Logs 841

    CHAPTER 13   Printing 881

    CHAPTER 14   Processes 937

    CHAPTER 15   Services 969

    CHAPTER 16   Registry 1015

PART III: Scripting for the Enterprise 1055

    CHAPTER 17   Creating Enterprise Scripts 1057

    CHAPTER 18   Scripting Guidelines 1149

INDEX..1191

Contents

Introduction xxvii

PART I: Scripting Concepts and Technologies for System Administration 1

    CHAPTER 1 Introduction to Windows Script Technologies 3

    CHAPTER 2 VBScript Primer 15

        VBScript Overview 17

            Working with Objects 18

                Connecting to Objects 19

                Creating an Object Reference 20

                Calling Methods 21

                Retrieving Properties 22

            Variables 23

            Constants 25

            Strings 26

                Strings as Variables 27

                Concatenating Strings 29

            Collections 30

                For Each 31

                Collections with Zero Items 33

            Looping 34

                For Next 34

            Making Decisions 37

                Taking Multiple Actions by Using If Then Else 38

            Arrays 39

            Input 41

Error Handling 43

    Using the Err Object 43

    Clearing Errors 46

VBScript Reference 47

  Working with Variables 49

    Initializing Variables 51

  Using Constants 53

    Defining Constants 54

    Using Intrinsic Constants 54

  VBScript Data Types 56

  Working with Dates and Times 59

    Retrieving Current Date and Time Values 60

    Verifying That a Value Is a Date 61

    Retrieving Specific Portions of a Date and Time Value 62

    Date Arithmetic 68

    Formatting Date and Time Values 70

  Working with Strings 73

    Manipulating Strings and String Lengths 74

    Searching for Text in a String 79

    Modifying String Case 81

  Working with Numbers 82

    Arithmetic Precedence 82

    Formatting Numbers 84

    Formatting Percentages 86

  Running Statements Multiple Times 87

    Do Loop 88

    Checking the Loop Condition 89

    Exiting a Loop 90

  Making Decisions 92

    Testing Multiple Conditions 92

    If Then ElseIf 93

    Select Case 96

Arrays 97
   Creating Arrays 98
   Creating Dynamic Arrays 100
   Converting a Delimited String to an Array 101
   Alternatives to Using Arrays 103
Error Handling 104
   Handling Run-Time Errors 106
   Toggling Error Handling 108
   Handling Errors in COM Objects 110
Procedures 111
   Calling a Procedure 112
   Functions 114
   Recursion 120
COM Objects 121
   The COM Process 122
   Binding 124
   Choosing a Method for Binding to an Automation Object 124
   Verifying Object References 126
   Unloading Objects from Memory 127

CHAPTER 3 WSH Primer **129**
 WSH Overview 130
 WSH Architecture 134
   Components of the WSH Environment 135
   How the Components of the WSH Environment Work Together 139
   WSH Object Model 140
 Running WSH Scripts 140
  Running Scripts from the Command Line 142
  Scheduling the Running of Scripts 146
  Other Methods of Running Scripts 146
 WSH Objects 147
  WScript Object 148
   Using COM Objects 150
   Handling Input and Output 154
   Working with Command-Line Arguments 162
   Controlling How a Script Runs 176
   Obtaining WSH Environment Information 179
   Handling Events 181

WshShell Object 181
    Running Programs 183
    Working with Shortcuts 191
    Working with Special Folders 195
    Environment Variables 197
    Logging an Event 201
    Reading From and Writing to the Local Registry 203
    Sending Keystrokes to a Program 206
    Retrieving and Changing a Script's Current Working Directory 211
    Displaying Timed Message Boxes 212
WshNetwork Object 219
    Managing Network Drives 221
    Managing Network Printers 224
    Obtaining User and Computer Information 226
WshController Object 227
    Running Scripts on Remote Computers 230
    Monitoring Status of Remotely Running Scripts 231
    Examining Errors Produced by Remotely Running Scripts 232
    Limitations of Remote WSH 234
Securing Scripts 234
Digitally Signing Scripts 235
    Enforcing the Use of Signed Scripts 236
    Programmatically Signing a Script 237
    Programmatically Verifying a Signed Script 237
Restricting the Ability to Run Scripts 238
    Disabling Windows Script Host 239

CHAPTER 4   Script Runtime Primer **241**
Script Runtime Overview 242
FileSystemObject 243
Managing Disk Drives 243
    Returning a Collection of Disk Drives 244
    Binding to a Specific Disk Drive 245
    Enumerating Disk Drive Properties 245
    Ensuring That a Drive is Ready 248

Managing Folders 249

    Binding to a Folder 249

    Verifying That a Folder Exists 250

    Creating a Folder 250

    Deleting a Folder 251

    Copying a Folder and Its Contents 252

    Moving a Folder and Its Contents 254

    Renaming a Folder 255

Using Folder Properties 256

    Enumerating Folder Properties 257

Managing Folder Attributes 258

    Changing Folder Attributes 261

    Enumerating the Files in a Folder 262

    Enumerating Subfolders 263

Managing Files 266

    Binding to a File 266

    Verifying That a File Exists 267

    Deleting a File 268

    Copying a File 270

    Moving a File 272

    Renaming a File 272

Retrieving File Properties 273

    Enumerating File Attributes 275

    Configuring File Attributes 276

    Parsing File Paths 277

    Retrieving the File Version 279

Reading and Writing Text Files 280

    Reading Text Files 285

    Writing to Text Files 292

Dictionary Object 296

    Creating a Dictionary 296

    Configuring Dictionary Properties 297

    Adding Key-Item Pairs to a Dictionary 298

Manipulating Keys and Items in a Dictionary 299
Determining the Number of Key-Item Pairs in a Dictionary 299
Enumerating Keys and Items in a Dictionary 300
Verifying the Existence of a Specific Key 301
Modifying an Item in a Dictionary 302
Removing Key-Item Pairs from a Dictionary 303

CHAPTER 5   ADSI Scripting Primer **307**
ADSI Overview 308
ADSI Scripting Fundamentals 309
Primary ADSI Scripting Tasks 310
Creating Directory Service Objects 310
Modifying Directory Service Objects 313
Reading Attributes of Directory Service Objects 315
Deleting Directory Service Objects 317
Comparing the Primary Scripting Tasks 319
Building ADSI Scripts 320
Step 1: Establishing a Connection 320
Step 2: Performing a Task 326
Step 3: Committing to Active Directory 331
Performing Multiple Scripting Tasks 332
Advanced ADSI Scripting Operations 336
Administering Multivalued Attributes 336
Modifying Multivalued Attributes 336
Reading Multivalued Attributes 344
Data Caching 346
Making Explicit Calls by Using the GetInfo Method 347
Making Explicit Calls by Using the GetInfoEx Method 348
Copying, Moving, and Renaming Objects 350
Copying Objects 350
Moving and Renaming Objects 354
Searching 358
Searching Active Directory 359
Optimizing Search Performance 378
Performing an Administrative Task Using a Result Set 382
Enumerating Active Directory Objects in Containers 386
Scripting Container Enumeration 386

Root Directory Service Entry 390
Scripting with rootDSE 391
Active Directory Architecture 393
Physical Architecture 393
Logical Structure 394
Classes and Attributes 395
Active Directory Replication and Indexing 406
Operational Attributes 412
ADSI Architecture 414
ADSI Layers 416
ADSI Interfaces 421

CHAPTER 6 WMI Scripting Primer **429**
WMI Overview 431
WMI Architecture 436
Managed Resources 438
WMI Infrastructure 439
WMI Consumers 445
WMI Security 445
WMI Namespace-Level Security 446
DCOM Security 447
Standard Windows Operating System Security 448
Common Information Model 448
Blueprint for Management 451
Namespaces 452
Class Categories 460
CIM Class Types 465
Components of a Class 468
Exploring the CIM Repository 481
WMI Scripting Library 482
WMI Scripting Library Object Model 482
SWbemLocator 486
SWbemServices 488
Writing WMI Scripts 494
Connecting to WMI Using the WMI Moniker 495
The "WinMgmts:" Prefix 496
WMI Security Settings 497
Using WMI Object Paths 503

Retrieving Managed Resources Using WMI Query Language 505

Returning All Properties of All Instances of a Class 507

Returning Selected Properties of All Instances of a Class 508

Returning All Properties of Selected Instances of a Class 509

Creating Targeted Queries Using AND or OR 514

Returning Selected Properties of Selected Instances of a Class 514

Creating Faster Queries by Using a Forward-only Enumerator 515

Working with Dates and Times 517

Converting WMI Dates to a Standard Date-Time Format 519

Converting a Standard Date to a WMI Date-Time Format 521

Creating Scripts Based on WMI Templates 525

Retrieving and Displaying Properties of a Managed Resource 525

Retrieving and Displaying All Properties of a Managed Resource 526

Writing Resource Properties 527

Calling Methods 529

Creating Resources 530

Deleting Resources 531

Monitoring Resources by Using WMI Event Notifications 532

Three Steps in a WMI Monitoring Script 535

How WMI Event Notification Works 538

Enhanced WMI Monitoring Scripts 541

PART II: Scripting Solutions for System Administration **547**

CHAPTER 7   Active Directory Users **549**

User Account Overview 551

Active Directory User Accounts 552

Active Directory User Account Objects 552

User Account Types 552

Identification Attributes 553

Creating User Accounts 555

Configuring User Account Passwords 558

Setting User Account Passwords 559

Changing User Account Passwords 560

Reading User Account Password Attributes 561

Displaying Password Attributes Accessible from
userAccountControl 563

Determining When a Password Was Last Set 564

Configuring User Account Password Attributes 565

    Changing Flags in the userAccountControl Attribute 565

    Configuring a Password Change at Next Logon Requirement 566

Managing User Accounts 567

    Enabling or Disabling a User Account 568

    Determining Whether an Account Is Enabled or Disabled 569

    Reading and Writing User Account Attributes 570

        Reading Attributes 573

        Writing Values to the Attributes 576

        Modifying a Multivalued Attribute 577

        Clearing Attributes 580

    Copying, Moving, and Renaming User Accounts 581

        Copying User Accounts 581

        Moving and Renaming User Accounts 584

Deleting User Accounts 588

Searching Active Directory for User Accounts 589

    Searching for an Attribute in a Container 593

    Limiting a Search for an Attribute in a Container to
User Account Types 596

    Searching for a User Account Attribute in a Container and
Its Subcontainers 598

    Verifying That an Attribute Is Unique in the Forest 600

    Searching for Empty Attribute Values 601

    Using Wildcards in Search Filters 606

    Searching for Multivalued Attributes 608

    Sorting the Result Set 610

    Modifying Multiple User Accounts by Using the Result Set from a Search ..611

Managing User Accounts by Enumeration 613

    Limiting Enumeration with Filters and Hints 614

CHAPTER 8 Computer Assets **617**

Computer Assets Overview 618

    Retrieving System Information 619

    Retrieving BIOS Information 623

        Retrieving Information About the BIOS 623

        Retrieving Identifying Information by Using the SMBIOS 628

Inventorying Computer Hardware 629
   Taking Inventory of Computer Hardware 632
   Identifying the Chassis Type of a Computer 634
Managing Operating Systems 637
   Identifying the Name and Version Number of the Operating System 637
   Retrieving the Properties of the Operating System 639
   Identifying the Latest Installed Service Pack 643
   Enumerating Installed Hot Fixes 645
Managing WMI Settings 646
   Enumerating WMI Settings 649
   Configuring WMI Settings 651
Managing Software 653
   Enumerating Software 654
      Enumerating Installed Software 655
      Enumerating Installed Software Features 658
   Installing, Upgrading, and Removing Software 659
      Installing Software on the Local Computer 660
      Installing Software on a Remote Computer 662
      Upgrading Software 664
      Removing Software 666
Managing Computer States 667
   Managing Computer Startups 667
      Enumerating Computer Startup Options 668
      Configuring Computer Startup Options 670
      Enumerating Computer Startup Commands 673
   Managing Computer Recovery Options 675
      Enumerating Computer Recovery Options 677
      Configuring Computer Recovery Options 679
      Querying the Event Log for Stop Events 680
   Shutting Down Computers and Logging Off Users 682
      Shutting Down a Computer 684
      Restarting a Computer 685
   Monitoring Changes in Computer Power Status 686

CHAPTER 9   Computer Roles **689**

Computer Roles Overview 690

Managing Computer Accounts 690

Retrieving Basic Logon and Computer Information 693

Creating Computer Accounts 694

Deleting Computer Accounts 698

Deleting Specified Computer Accounts 699

Modifying Computer Accounts 701

Enumerating Computer Account Attributes 701

Configuring the Computer Account Location Attribute 703

Renaming Computer Accounts 704

Moving Computer Accounts 705

Resetting Computer Account Passwords 706

Searching for Computer Accounts in Active Directory 707

Enumerating All the Computer Accounts in Active Directory 709

Locating Computer Accounts Based on Their Attributes 710

Managing Computer Roles 712

Identifying Computer Roles 713

Identifying the Role of a Computer Based on the Service It Provides 715

Identifying Active Directory–Specific Roles 716

Enumerating Domain Controllers 716

Identifying the Current Domain Controller for a Computer 718

Identifying Operations Master Roles 719

Identifying Global Catalog Servers 722

Enabling or Disabling Global Catalog Servers 723

CHAPTER 10   Disks and File Systems **725**

Disks and File Systems Overview 726

Managing and Monitoring Disk Drives 726

Managing Disk Partitions 730

Managing Logical Disk Drives 733

Identifying Drives and Drive Types 735

Changing Logical Disk Volume Names 737

Managing Disk Space 738

Enumerating Disk Space on a Computer 738

Enumerating Disk Space by User 739

Monitoring Free Disk Space in Real-Time 740

Managing Disk Quotas 742

   Managing Disk Quotas on the NTFS File System 742

      Enumerating Disk Quota Settings 744

      Enabling and Disabling Disk Quotas 745

      Configuring Default Disk Quota Settings 746

   Managing Disk Quotas for Individual Users 748

      Enumerating Disk Quotas 748

      Adding a New Disk Quota Entry 750

      Modifying a Disk Quota Entry 752

      Deleting a Disk Quota Entry 752

Managing File Systems 754

      Identifying the File System Type 754

      Enumerating NTFS Properties 755

      Modifying NTFS Properties 760

   Managing Page Files 762

      Monitoring Page File Use 764

      Configuring Page File Properties 765

CHAPTER 11   Files and Folders **767**

Files and Folders Overview 768

   Managing Files and Folders Using WMI 768

      Comparing WMI and the FileSystemObject 769

   Managing Files and Folders Using the Windows Shell Object 773

Folders and Folder Objects 775

   Enumerating Folders and Folder Properties 778

      Enumerating All the Folders on a Computer 780

      Enumerating the Subfolders of a Folder 781

      Enumerating a Specific Set of Folders 783

      Enumerating Folders by Date 784

      Enumerating Special Folders 787

      Enumerating the Items in a Special Folder 790

      Binding to a Folder by Using the Browse For Folder Dialog Box 791

   Managing Folders 794

      Renaming Folders 794

      Moving Folders by Using the Rename Method 795

      Copying Folders by Using WMI 796

      Copying Folders by Using the Shell Folder Object 797

Moving Folders by Using the Shell Folder Object 800

Deleting Folders 801

Compressing and Uncompressing Folders 802

Files and File Objects 804

Enumerating Files and File Properties 804

Retrieving Extended File Properties 806

Enumerating All the Files on a Computer 809

Using an Asynchronous Query to Enumerate
All the Files on a Computer 810

Enumerating All the Files in a Folder 811

Enumerating a Specific Set of Files 812

Managing Files 813

Renaming Files 813

Changing File Name Extensions 814

Copying Files 816

Deleting Files 817

Performing Actions on Files 818

Identifying Shell Object Verbs 820

Monitoring the File System 821

Monitoring File Creation 821

Monitoring File Deletion 822

Monitoring File Modification 824

Managing Shared Folders 825

Enumerating Shared Folders 826

Creating Shared Folders 828

Mapping Shared Folders to Local Folders 830

Deleting Shared Folders 832

Modifying Shared Folder Properties 833

Publishing Shared Folders in Active Directory 834

Managing Published Folders 836

Enumerating Published Folders 836

Searching for Published Folders in Active Directory 838

Deleting a Published Folder in Active Directory 839

CHAPTER 12   Logs **841**

Logs Overview 842

Managing Logs 842

Managing Event Logs 844

Retrieving Event Log Properties 845

Configuring Event Log Properties 850

Backing Up and Clearing Event Logs 852

Creating Unique File Names When Backing Up Event Logs 856

Querying Event Logs 857

Querying a Specific Event Log 861

Querying an Event Log for a Subset of Events 862

Retrieving Event Log Records from a Specified Day 863

Asynchronously Retrieving Event Log Statistics 865

Copying Events to a Database 867

Writing Events to Event Logs 870

Writing to Event Logs 871

Creating Detailed Event Log Entry Descriptions 872

Creating Custom Event Logs 874

Managing Plain-Text Logs 876

Parsing Comma-Separated-Values Logs 877

Parsing Fixed-Width Logs 879

CHAPTER 13   Printing **881**

Printing Overview 882

Monitoring Printers, Print Queues, and Print Jobs 885

Monitoring Printers 885

Monitoring Printer Status 887

Monitoring Printer Status in Real Time 888

Filtering Printer Status Displays 892

Monitoring Printer Status by Using a Temporary Event Subscription 893

Verifying the Status of the Print Service 896

Monitoring Printer Workloads 897

Reporting Print Queue Statistics 897

Monitoring Print Jobs 899

Monitoring Print Job Status 903

Monitoring the Time Print Jobs Spend in a Print Queue 905

Managing Printer Operations, Print Queues, and Print Jobs 906

Managing Printer Operations 906

Enumerating Printers and Print Capabilities 910

Pausing Printers 912

Resuming Printers 913

Managing Print Queues 913

Purging Print Queues 914

Managing Print Jobs 914

Pausing Print Jobs 915

Resuming Print Jobs 916

Configuring Printers and Print Jobs 917

Configuring Printer Properties 917

Configuring Printer Availability 918

Tracking Printer Locations 919

Enabling Printer Location Tracking 920

Configuring Printer Locations 921

Configuring Print Jobs 923

Configuring Print Job Properties 924

Managing Printer Connections on Client Computers 926

Enumerating Printer Connections 927

Adding and Deleting Printer Connections 928

Adding a Printer Connection by Using WSH 929

Removing a Printer Connection 930

Searching for Printers in Active Directory 930

Enumerating All the Published Printers in a Domain 931

Searching for Specific Printers in a Domain 932

CHAPTER 14 Processes **937**

Processes Overview 938

Managing Processes 939

Monitoring Processes 941

Monitoring Processes for Availability 942

Monitoring Processes for Reliability 943

Monitoring Processes for Performance 945

Displaying Current Process Performance Data 950

Enumerating Additional Process Properties 954

Determining Process Owners 955

Monitoring Threads 956

Creating and Terminating Processes 959
    Creating Processes 959
    Modifying Process Startup Options 961
    Terminating Processes 965

CHAPTER 15   Services **969**
    Services Overview 971
    Monitoring Services 973
        Monitoring Service Availability 974
        Monitoring Service Reliability 976
    Retrieving Service Properties 978
        Enumerating Service Properties 980
        Identifying the Services Running in a Process 983
    Changing Service State 987
        Determining Which Services Can Be Stopped or Paused 989
        Stopping or Pausing Services 990
        Starting or Resuming Services 991
    Enumerating Dependent and Antecedent Services 993
        Enumerating Dependent Services 994
        Enumerating Antecedent Services 997
        Stopping and Starting Dependent Services 998
    Configuring Services 1001
        Configuring Service Start Options 1003
        Configuring Error Control Codes for Autostart Services 1004
    Managing Service Accounts and Service Account Passwords 1006
        Configuring Service Accounts 1007
        Configuring Service Account Passwords 1009
    Installing and Removing Services 1010
        Installing Services 1011
        Removing Services 1013

CHAPTER 16   Registry ....** 1015**
    Registry Overview 1016
    Managing the Registry 1024
        Backing Up the Registry 1025
        Reading Entry Values and Types 1026
            Reading String-valued and DWORD-valued Entries 1027
            Reading a Multistring-valued Entry 1029

Reading an Expanded String-valued Entry 1030

Reading a Binary-valued Entry 1031

Changing String-valued and DWORD-valued Entries 1033

Creating Registry Subkeys and Entries 1035

Creating a Subkey 1035

Creating String-valued and DWORD-valued Entries 1036

Creating Multistring-valued Entries 1038

Creating Expanded String-valued Entries 1040

Enumerating Keys, Subkeys, and Entries 1041

Enumerating Subkeys of a Key or Subkey 1042

Enumerating Entry Names, Values, and Data Types 1043

Deleting Subkeys and Entries 1045

Deleting Registry Entries 1045

Deleting a Registry Subkey 1046

Checking Registry Subkey Access Rights 1047

Monitoring the Registry 1050

Monitoring Subtree-Level Events 1050

Monitoring Subkey-Level Events 1052

Monitoring Entry-Level Events 1053

PART III: Scripting for the Enterprise **1055**

CHAPTER 17   Creating Enterprise Scripts **1057**

Enterprise Scripts Overview 1059

Retrieving Arguments 1060

Retrieving Arguments from a Text File 1061

Using a Text File as a Command-Line Argument 1064

Retrieving Arguments from a Database 1067

Retrieving Arguments from an Active Directory Container 1070

Displaying Output 1072

Displaying Tabular Script Output in a Command Window 1073

Displaying Data by Using Internet Explorer 1077

Displaying Data in a Web Page 1081

Stopping a Script When Internet Explorer Is Closed 1085

Working with HTML Applications 1087

Displaying Script Output by Using the Tabular Data Control 1092

Sorting Data by Using the Tabular Data Control 1095

Filtering Data by Using the Tabular Data Control 1099

Sorting Data by Using a Disconnected Recordset 1101

Working with Databases 1103
   Connecting to a Database 1105
   Adding New Records to a Database 1107
   Finding Records in a Recordset 1109
   Updating Records in a Database 1112
   Deleting Selected Records from a Database 1114
   Deleting All Records in a Database Table 1116
Masking Passwords 1117
   Masking Passwords by Using Internet Explorer 1118
Sending E-Mail 1120
   Sending E-Mail from a Script 1122
   Sending E-Mail Without Installing the SMTP Service 1123
Tracking Script Progress 1125
   Tracking Script Progress by Using Internet Explorer 1126
   Tracking Dynamic Script Progress by Using Internet Explorer 1128
   Tracking Script Progress in a Command Window 1133
Managing Scheduled Tasks 1135
   Enumerating Scheduled Tasks 1137
   Creating Scheduled Tasks 1140
   Deleting Scheduled Tasks 1144

CHAPTER 18   Scripting Guidelines 1147
Overview of Scripting Guidelines 1148
Using Naming Conventions 1148
   Naming Scripts 1149
   Naming Variables 1151
   Naming Constants 1156
   Naming Functions and Procedures 1156
Constructing Scripts 1157
   Choosing a Script Construction 1158
   Creating a Script Template 1160
   Using Functions and Procedures 1161
Formatting Code 1164
   Using White Space 1164
   Setting Statement Breaks 1168
   Creating Scripts That Are Easier to Read 1170

Commenting Scripts 1175

   Adding Comments to a Script 1178

   Formatting Comments 1179

   Creating Script Headers 1179

   Creating Function and Procedure Headers 1180

   Creating Script Documentation by Using Comments 1181

   Using Comments as a Debugging Aid 1182

Debugging and Troubleshooting Scripts 1184

   Adding a Trace Routine to a Script 1184

   Incrementally Running a Script 1186

   Turning Off Error Handling as a Debugging Tool 1187

Testing Scripts 1188

INDEX...**1191**

Introduction

Welcome to the *Microsoft® Windows® 2000 Scripting Guide.*

As computers and computer networks continue to grow larger and more complex, system administrators continue to face new challenges. Not all that long ago, system administration was limited to managing a handful of computers (most located within the same general area), a relatively small number of user accounts, and a few applications, many of which had no knowledge of, or need for, a local area network.

Today, of course, system administrators often manage hundreds, and even thousands of computers, as well as a corresponding number of user accounts. These computers, many situated in remote locations, run scores of applications, and rely heavily on networks and networked resources including file servers, Dynamic Host Configuration Protocol (DHCP) and Domain Name System (DNS) servers, and shared printers. This has made it imperative for system administrators to find management solutions that:

- Can be tailored to meet the unique needs of the organization.

- Can operate against multiple computers, and against remote computers.

- Are quick, easy, and cost-effective.

Scripts provide all of these capabilities, and more. In addition, scripting requires no investment in hardware or software beyond a computer running Microsoft® Windows® 2000.

This book introduces you to the scripting technologies included in the Windows 2000 platform. It teaches you the basic concepts underlying such key scripting technologies as VBScript, Windows Script Host (WSH), Active Directory Service Interfaces (ADSI), and Windows Management Instrumentation (WMI). In addition, the book includes hundreds of pre-written scripts that carry out such routine, yet important, system administration tasks as: backing up and clearing event logs; monitoring process use; reading and writing to the registry; and managing user accounts, computer accounts, printers, and services. You can use these scripts as provided, or you can apply the principles of the Microsoft scripting technologies to modify them to meet your exact needs.

Compact Disc

The following contents are included on the *Windows 2000 Scripting Guide* companion CD:

- **Windows 2000 Scripting Guide (SagSAS.chm).** A searchable Help file containing the online version of the *Window 2000 Scripting Guide*.

- **CD-ROM Release Notes (Readme.txt).** The release notes for the contents of *Windows 2000 Scripting Guide* companion CD.

- **Script repository (Scripts.chm).** A searchable Help file containing scripts for use with WMI, ADSI, VBScript, and other Microsoft Scripting technologies.

- **Scriptomatic tool (Scriptomatic.hta).** A hypertext application you can use to write WMI scripts.

- **Scriptomatic documentation (Write WMI Scripts Like the Pros.doc).** Documentation for the Scriptomatic tool.

- **Windows Script 5.6 (Scripten.exe).** The installer for Microsoft® Visual Basic® Script Edition (VBScript) Version 5.6, JScript® Version 5.6, Windows Script Components, Windows Script Host 5.6, and Windows Script Runtime Version 5.6. These are the most recent versions of each technology at this writing and are covered in this book. Please note that this installer runs only on Windows 2000 operating systems.

- **Windows Script 5.6 Documentation (Scrdoc56en.exe).** A searchable reference and conceptual Help file for Windows Script 5.6.

- **Microsoft Word viewer.** If you do not have Microsoft® Word installed on your computer, install this viewer to see the Scriptomatic documentation.

- **Links to Microsoft Press.** Links to the Microsoft Press Support site, which you can search for Knowledge Base articles, and to the Microsoft Press product registration site, which you can use to register this book online.

Document Conventions

The following art symbols and text conventions are used throughout this book.

Scripting Diagram Symbols

Use the following table of symbols as a resource for understanding the scripting graphics included in this book.

Symbol	Meaning
	Object
	Method
	Property
	Event
	Collection object
	Item property of a collection object

Reader Alert Conventions

Reader alerts are used throughout this book to notify you of both supplementary and essential information. The following table explains the meaning of each alert.

Reader Alert	Meaning
Tip	Alerts you to supplementary information that is not essential to the completion of the task at hand.
Note	Alerts you to supplementary information.
Important	Alerts you to supplementary information that is essential to the completion of a task.
Caution	Alerts you to possible data loss, breaches of security, or other more serious problems.
Warning	Alerts you that failure to take or avoid a specific action might result in physical harm to you or to the hardware.

Command-line Style Conventions

The following style conventions are used in documenting scripting and command-line tasks throughout this book.

Element	Meaning
bold font	Characters that you type exactly as shown, including commands and parameters. User interface elements are also bold.
Italic font	Variables for which you supply a specific value. For example, *Filename.ext* can refer to any valid file name.
`Monospace font`	Code samples.
`Command`	Command that is typed at the command prompt.
`Syntax`	Syntax of script elements.
`Output`	Output from running a script.

Support Policy

Microsoft does not support the software supplied in the *Windows 2000 Scripting Guide*. Microsoft does not guarantee the performance of the scripting examples, job aids, or tools, bug fixes for the tools, or response times for answering questions. However, we do provide a way for customers who purchase the *Windows 2000 Scripting Guide* to report any problems with the software and receive feedback for such issues. You can do this by sending e-mail to rkinput@microsoft.com. This e-mail address is only for issues related to the *Windows 2000 Scripting Guide*. For issues related to the Windows 2000 operating systems, please refer to the support information included with your product.

Scripting Concepts and Technologies for System Administration

To write scripts for managing Microsoft® Windows®-based computers, you need a solid understanding of the scripting technologies included in the Microsoft® Windows® 2000 operating system. Part 1 of this book introduces key concepts for each of Microsoft's primary system administration scripting technologies, including: Microsoft® Visual Basic® Scripting Edition (VBScript); Windows Script Host (WSH); the Script Runtime library; Active Directory Service Interfaces (ADSI); and Windows Management Instrumentation (WMI).

In This Part

Introduction to Windows Script Technologies... 3
VBScript Primer..15
WSH Primer 129
Script Runtime Primer 241
ADSI Scripting Primer...307
WMI Scripting Primer 427

Introduction to Windows Script Technologies

This is a book about scripting for system administrators. If you are like many system administrators, you might be wondering why this book is targeted towards you. After all, scripting is not the sort of thing system administrators do. Everyone knows about scripting: scripting is hard; scripting is time-consuming; scripting requires you to learn all sorts of technical jargon and master a whole host of acronyms — WSH, WMI, ADSI, CDO, ADO, COM. System administrators have neither the time nor the requisite background to become script writers.

Or do they? One of the primary purposes of this book is to clear up misconceptions such as these. Is scripting hard? It can be. On the other hand, take a look at this script, which actually performs a useful system administration task:

```
Set objNetwork = CreateObject("WScript.Network")
objNetwork.MapNetworkDrive "X:", "\\atl-fs-01\public"
```

Even if you do not know the first thing about scripting and even if you are completely bewildered by line 1 of the script, you can still make an educated guess that this script must map drive X to the shared folder \\atl-fs-01\public. And that is exactly what it does. If you already understand system administration — that is, if you know what it means to map a drive and you understand the concept of shared folders and Universal Naming Convention (UNC) paths — the leap from mapping drives by using the graphical user interface (GUI) or a command-line tool to mapping drives by using a script is not very big.

Note

If you are already lost — because you are not sure what is meant by scripting in the first place— think of scripting in these terms:

Do you ever find yourself typing the same set of commands over and over to get a certain task done? Do you ever find yourself clicking the same set of buttons in the same sequence in the same wizard just to complete some chore — and then have to repeat the same process for, say, multiple computers or multiple user accounts?

Scripts help eliminate some of this repetitive work. A script is a file you create that describes the steps required to complete a task. After you create the script, you can "run" that script, and it will perform all of the steps for you, saving you a great deal of time and energy. You need only create the script once, and then you can reuse it any time you need to perform that task.

Admittedly, not all scripts are as simple and intuitive as the one just shown. But if you thumb through this book, you will find that the vast majority of scripts — almost all of which carry out useful system administration tasks — are no more than 15 or 20 lines long. And with a great many of those, you can read the code and figure out what is going on regardless of your level of scripting experience.

Does scripting take too much time? It can: If you write a script that is 500 lines long (and you probably never will), the typing alone will take some time. But it is important to balance the time it takes to write a script with the time that can be saved by *using* that script. For example, here is a script that backs up and clears all the event logs on a computer:

```
strComputer = "."
Set objWMIService = GetObject("winmgmts:" _
    & "{impersonationLevel=impersonate, (Backup, Security)}!\\" _
        & strComputer & "\root\cimv2")
Set colLogFiles = objWMIService.ExecQuery _
    ("Select * from Win32_NTEventLogFile")
For Each objLogfile in colLogFiles
    strBackupLog = objLogFile.BackupEventLog _
        ("c:\scripts\" & objLogFile.LogFileName & ".evt")
    objLogFile.ClearEventLog()
Next
```

Admittedly, this script is not as intuitive as the drive-mapping script. Furthermore, to write a script like this, you will need to learn a little bit about scripting in general, and about Windows Management Instrumentation (WMI) in particular. And then you still have to type it into Microsoft® Notepad, all 11 lines worth. This one might take you a little bit of time.

But think of it this way: How much time does it take you to manually back up and clear each event log on a computer. (And that assumes that you actually do this; the manual process can be so tedious and time-consuming that many system administrators simply forgo backing up and clearing event logs, even though they know this task should be done on a regular basis.) With a script, you can back up and clear event logs in a minute or two, depending on the size of those logs. And what if you take an extra half hour or so and add code that causes the script to back up and clear all the event logs on all your computers? You might have to invest a little time and energy in learning to script, but it will not be long before these scripts begin to pay for themselves.

Point conceded. But even though scripting does not have to be hard and does not have to be time-consuming, it still requires you to learn all the technical mumbo-jumbo, right? Sure, if you want to be an expert in scripting. But consider this script, which returns the names of all the services installed on a computer:

```
strComputer = "."
Set objWMIService = GetObject("winmgmts:" & _
    "{impersonationLevel=Impersonate}!\\" & strComputer & "\root\cimv2")
Set colItems = objWMIService.ExecQuery("Select * from Win32_Service")
For Each objItem in colItems
    Wscript.Echo objItem.Name
Next
```

Under the covers, this is a fairly complicated script. Among other things, it:

- Makes use of Automation object methods and properties.

- Utilizes Microsoft® Visual Basic® Scripting Edition (VBScript) constructs such as the For Each loop to iterate through the elements within a collection.

- Requires a COM (Common Object Model) moniker.

- Uses WMI object paths, namespaces, and classes.

- Executes a query string written in the WMI Query Language.

That is an awful lot to know and remember just to write a seven-line script. No wonder people think scripting is hard.

But the truth is, you do not have to fully understand COM and Automation to write a script like this. It does help to know about these things: As in any field, the more you know, the better off you are. But suppose what you really want is a script that returns the names of all the processes currently running on a computer instead of one that returns the names of all the installed services. Here is a script that does just that:

```
strComputer = "."
Set objWMIService = GetObject("winmgmts:" & _
    "{impersonationLevel=Impersonate}!\\" & strComputer & "\root\cimv2")
Set colItems = objWMIService.ExecQuery("Select * from Win32_Process")
For Each objItem in colItems
    Wscript.Echo objItem.Name
Next
```

What is so special about this script? Nothing. And that is the point. Look closely at the single item in boldface (Win32_Process). This is the only part of the process script that differs from the service script. Do you know anything more about COM monikers or WMI object paths than you did a minute ago? Probably not, and yet you can still take a basic script template and modify it to return useful information. Want to know the name of the video card installed on a computer? Try this script:

```
strComputer = "."
Set objWMIService = GetObject("winmgmts:" & _
    "{impersonationLevel=Impersonate}!\\" & strComputer & "\root\cimv2")
Set colItems = objWMIService.ExecQuery("Select * from Win32_VideoController")
For Each objItem in colItems
    Wscript.Echo objItem.Name
Next
```

Is it always this easy? No, not always. And these examples sidestep a few issues (such as, "How do I know to type in Win32_VideoController rather than, say, Win32_VideoCard?" or, "What if I want to know more than just the name of the video card?"). The point is not that you can start writing scripts without knowing anything; the point is that you can start writing scripts without knowing *everything*. If you want to master COM monikers and WMI object paths before you write your first script, that's fine. And if you prefer to just start writing scripts, perhaps by building on the examples in this book, that's fine too. You can always start writing and using scripts today, and then go back and learn about COM monikers and WMI object paths tomorrow.

How Did Scripting Acquire Such a Bad Reputation?

If scripting is so easy, then, how did it gain a reputation for being so hard? And if it is so valuable, why aren't more system administrators using it? After all, few system administrators knowingly turn their backs on something that will make their lives easier.

There are probably many reasons for this, but at least part of the problem dates back to the birth of the Microsoft® Windows® Script Technologies. Both VBScript and Microsoft® JScript® (the two scripting languages included with the Microsoft® Windows® operating system) began as a way to add client-side scripting to Web pages. This was great for Internet developers, but of little use to the typical system administrator. As a result, scripting came to be associated with Web page development. (Even today, many of the code samples in the official Microsoft documentation for VBScript show the code embedded in a Web page.)

Later on, Windows Script Host (WSH) was born. WSH provided a way for scripting languages and scripting technologies to be used outside Internet Explorer; in fact, WSH was aimed squarely at system administration. Nevertheless, scripting still failed to take the system administration world by storm.

Initially, this was probably due to a lack of documentation and a lack of proper positioning. It was difficult to find information about using VBScript or JScript as a tool for system administration; it was next-to-impossible to find information about technologies such as WMI or Active Directory Service Interfaces (ADSI). Even when these technologies were documented (typically in software development kits), the documentation was aimed at programmers; in fact, code samples were usually written in C++ rather than a scripting language. For example, suppose you are a typical system administrator (with substantial knowledge of Windows and minimal knowledge of programming). And suppose you looked up scripting on Microsoft's Web site and saw sample code that looked like this:

```
int main(int argc, char **argv)
{
  HRESULT hres;
  hres = CoInitializeEx(0, COINIT_MULTITHREADED); // Initialize COM.
  if (FAILED(hres))
  {
    cout << "Failed to initialize COM library. Error code = 0x"
         << hex << hres << endl;
    return 1;                     // Program has failed.
  }

  hres = CoInitializeSecurity(NULL, -1, NULL, NULL,
         RPC_C_AUTHN_LEVEL_CONNECT,
         RPC_C_IMP_LEVEL_IDENTIFY,
         NULL, EOAC_NONE, 0
         );
```

Needless to say, very few system administrators saw WMI or ADSI as a tool that would be useful for them.

Today, of course, there is no dearth of scripting-related literature; a recent search of a major online bookstore with the keyword "VBScript" returned 339 titles. That is the good news. The bad news is that most of those titles take one of two approaches: Either they continue to treat scripting as a tool for Web developers, or they focus almost exclusively on VBScript and WSH. There is no doubt that VBScript and WSH are important scripting technologies, but by themselves the two do not enable you to carry out many useful system administration tasks. Of the 339 scripting books found in the search, only a handful look at scripting as a tool for system administration, and only a few of those cover the key technologies — WMI and ADSI — in any depth. A system administrator who grabs a scripting book or two at random might still fail to understand that scripting can be extremely useful in managing Windows-based computers.

How This Book Helps

So is the *Microsoft® Windows® 2000 Scripting Guide* simply scripting book number 340, or does it somehow differ from its predecessors? In many ways, this book represents a new approach to scripting and system administration. In fact, at least four characteristics help distinguish this book from many of the other books on the market:

- **The focus is on scripting from the point of view of system administration.** This book includes many of the same chapters found in other scripting books; for example, it has a chapter devoted to VBScript. The difference is that the chapter is focused on the VBScript elements that are most useful to system administrators. System administrators need to work extensively with COM, so the VBScript chapter features detailed explanations of how to bind to and make use of COM objects within a script. System administrators have little use for calculating arctangents and cosines. Hence, these subjects are not covered at all, even though it is possible to make these calculations using VBScript.

- **This book is task-centered rather than script-centered.** In some respects, the scripts included in this book are an afterthought. Sometimes a book author will create a bunch of interesting scripts and then compose the text around those items. This book takes a very different approach: Instead of starting with scripts, the authors identified key tasks that system administrators must do on a routine basis. Only after those tasks were identified and categorized did they see whether the tasks could even be scripted. In that sense, this is not so much a book about scripting as it is a book about efficiently managing Windows-based computers. As it happens, the suggested ways to carry out these tasks all involve scripts. But the scripts could easily be removed from the book and replaced with command-line tool or GUI equivalents, and the book would still have value.

- **This book combines tutorial elements with practical elements.** Some books try to teach you scripting; thus they focus on conceptual notions and, at best, pay lip service to practical concerns. Others take the opposite approach. In those cases, the focus is on the practical: The books present a host of useful scripts, but make little effort to help you understand how the scripts work and how you might modify them. This book tries to combine the best of both worlds; for example, any time a useful system administration script is presented, the script is accompanied by a step-by-step explanation of how the script works and how it might be adapted to fit your individual needs.

- **This book recognizes that, the larger the organization, the more pressing the need to automate procedures.** If you are the system administrator for an organization that has a single computer, you might still find the scripts in this book useful. To be honest, though, you would probably find it faster and easier to manage your lone computer by using the GUI. If you have 100 computers, however, or 1,000 computers, the value of scripts and scripting suddenly skyrockets. In recognition of this fact, the book includes an entire chapter — "Creating Enterprise Scripts" — that discusses how the sample scripts in this book can be modified for use in organizations with many computers.

How Do You Know if This Book is for You?

Officially, this book was written for "system administrators in medium to large organizations who want to use scripting as a means to manage their Windows-based computers." That group (amorphous as it might be) will likely make up the bulk of the readership simply because 1) the book revolves around scripting system-administration tasks, and 2) system administrators in medium to large organizations are the people most likely to need to use scripts.

However, the book should be useful to anyone interested in learning how to script. The techniques discussed throughout the book, while focused on medium to large organizations, are likely to prove useful in small organizations as well. These techniques are typically used to carry out system administration tasks, but many of them can be adapted by application programmers or Web developers. The book does not discuss scripting as a method of managing Microsoft Exchange Server; however, Microsoft Exchange Server can be managed using WMI. Because of this, Exchange administrators might be interested not only in the chapter "WMI Scripting Primer" but also in the chapter "VBScript Primer," which discusses generic techniques for working with Automation objects.

This book also tries to provide information that will be useful to people with varying levels of scripting knowledge and experience. No scripting background is assumed, and if you read the book from cover to cover, you will start with the fundamental principles of scripting and gradually work your way through more complicated scenarios. But what if you already know VBScript but do not know much about ADSI? Skip directly to "ADSI Scripting Primer." What if you understand the basic principles of WMI but need to know how to create and terminate processes using WMI? Go right to the "Processes" chapter.

There is something for everyone in this book: No knowledge or experience is required, but that does not mean that the book does not occasionally discuss a task or technique that might be a bit more advanced. And what if you have already mastered every scripting technique ever created? In that case, the book will likely be useful as a reference tool; after all, even those who know everything about WMI have rarely taken the time to memorize all the class names, methods, and properties. For those people, the tables in the task-based chapters might well make up for the fact that some of the explanations are aimed at beginners instead of experts.

What Is in This Book

The *Windows 2000 Scripting Guide* is divided into three parts:

- **Conceptual chapters.** The conceptual chapters offer comprehensive primers on the primary scripting technologies from Microsoft, including Windows Script Host (WSH), VBScript, WMI, ADSI, and the Script Runtime library. These are tutorial-type chapters, all written from the standpoint of a system administrator, and all written under the assumption that the reader has little, if any, scripting experience.

- **Task-based chapters.** For the task-based chapters, core areas of system administration were identified, including such things as managing services, managing printers, and managing event logs. Within each of these core areas, 25 or so common tasks were also identified, such as starting and stopping services, changing service account passwords, and identifying the services running on a computer. Each task includes 1) a brief explanation of the task and why it is important, 2) a sample script that performs the task, and 3) a step-by-step explanation of how the script works and how you might modify it to fit your own needs.

- **Enterprise chapters.** The enterprise chapters cover a range of topics, including guidelines for setting up a scripting infrastructure and best practices to consider when writing scripts as part of an administrative team. These chapters also describe different ways to enterprise-enable a script, for example, writing a script that performs an action on all your domain controllers or on all your user accounts, or a script that accepts arguments from a text file or a database.

You do not have to begin on page 1 and read the entire book from start to finish. The book is designed so that you can skip around and read only the content that interests you. Are you less interested in a conceptual understanding of WMI than you are in learning how to manage services by using scripts? Then start off by reading the "Services" chapter; there is no reason to read all of the preceding chapters. If you are new to scripting, you might find it useful to read about VBScript and WMI first, but this is not a requirement. Consider this book to be a smorgasbord of scripting techniques: You are free to pick and choose as you please.

In fact, if you are as interested in using scripts as you are in writing them, you might want to start with the task-based chapters. Read a chapter, copy and run the scripts, and see what happens. If you then want to better understand how the scripts work or would like to modify them so that they better fit your individual needs, go back and read up on the conceptual information.

About the Scripts Used in This Book

Most of the people who saw draft copies of this book expressed surprise — and gratitude — that the scripts were so short; many were used to scripting books in which a sample script might cover two or three pages, and had no idea that scripting could be so simple.

Finding All the Pieces

Keeping the scripts simple does not mean that concepts such as error handling are ignored; script writers definitely have a need for error handling, they have a need for parsing command-line arguments, and they have a need for creating scripts that run against more than one computer (for example, against all their Dynamic Host Configuration Protocol [DHCP] servers or against all the computers with accounts in a particular Active Directory container). Because of that, these techniques are covered in considerable detail in "Creating Enterprise Scripts" and "Scripting Guidelines" in this book.

In other words, although this book does not include any 500-line scripts that make use of every possible scripting technique, all of these scripting techniques are demonstrated somewhere in the book. If you wanted to, you could easily take a number of the small sample scripts and stitch them together to create a 500-line production-level super script.

However, some people were shocked by the fact that the scripts were so bare-boned. For example, very few of the scripts in the book include error handling; why would you write a production-level system administration script without including things such as error handling?

The answer is simple: The scripts in this book were never intended to be production-level system administration scripts. Instead, they are included for educational purposes, to teach various scripting techniques and technologies. Most of them can be used as-is to carry out useful system administration tasks, but that is just a happy coincidence; this book and the script samples are designed to teach you how to write scripts to help you manage your computing infrastructure. They were never intended to be a management solution in and of themselves.

By leaving out such things as error handling, the scripts were kept as short as possible, and the focus remained on the task at hand. Consider the first script shown in this chapter, the one designed to map a network drive on the local computer:

```
Set objNetwork = CreateObject("WScript.Network")
objNetwork.MapNetworkDrive "X:", "\\atl-fs-01\public"
```

This script is about as simple as it can be, which is exactly the point: You do not have to study it very long before you say to yourself, "Oh, so that's how I map network drives using a script." Admittedly, in a production environment you might want to modify the script so that the user can specify any drive letter and any shared folder. This can be done, but you will need code for parsing command-line arguments. Likewise, the sample script will fail if drive X is already mapped to a shared folder. This can be accounted for too, but now you need code to check which drive letters are in use and then to prompt the user to enter a new drive letter. You might also need code that checks to make sure that the shared folder \\atl-fs-01\public actually exists. To account for all these activities would turn a 2-line script into a 22-line script; even worse, the whole idea of showing the script in the first place — demonstrating how to map network drives — would then be buried somewhere in the middle of a relatively large script.

Keeping the scripts short and simple also drives home the point that scripts do not have to be complicated to be useful. If you are creating a script that will be used by many different people throughout your organization, it might be advisable to include argument parsing and error handling. But what if this is a script that only you will use? In this case, you may not need these features. You should never feel compelled to do something in a script just because someone else did it that way. The only thing that matters is that the script carries out its appointed task.

A Note Regarding VBScript

All the scripts in this book were written using VBScript. The decision to use VBScript rather than another scripting language or combination of languages was based on three factors:

- With the possible exception of Perl, VBScript is the most popular language used for writing system administration scripts. It made sense to choose a language that many people are at least somewhat familiar with.

- Unlike Perl, VBScript (along with Jscript) is automatically installed on all Windows 2000–based computers. Thus there is nothing to buy and nothing to install.

- VBScript is easier to learn than Jscript. As a sort of added bonus, VBScript is very similar to Visual Basic, a programming language that many system administrators have a nodding acquaintance with.

In other words, VBScript is easy to use, requires no additional purchase, download, or installation, and has a large user base. This makes it ideal for introducing people to system administration scripting.

To be honest, though, in many ways the scripting language is irrelevant. By itself, VBScript offers very little support for system administration; VBScript is most useful when it works with WSH, WMI, ADSI, and other scripting technologies that offer extensive support for system administration. In this respect, it is similar to other scripting languages. The vast majority of the scripts in this book rely on WMI or ADSI; the scripting language is almost incidental. Do you prefer working in JScript or ActiveState ActivePerl? Great; all you have to do is learn how to connect to WMI or ADSI using those languages and then take it from there.

For example, here is a WMI script that retrieves and then displays the name of the BIOS installed on the computer. This script is written in VBScript.

```
strComputer = "."
Set objWMIService = GetObject("winmgmts:\\" _
    & strComputer & "\root\cimv2")
Set colItems = objWMIService.ExecQuery _
    ("Select * from Win32_BIOS")
For Each objItem in colItems
    Wscript.Echo objItem.Name
Next
```

Here is the same script, written in JScript. As you can see, the syntax and language conventions are different, but the key elements (shown in boldface) — connecting to WMI, retrieving information from the Win32_BIOS class, echoing the value of the BIOS name — are almost identical. In that respect, the language is largely a matter of individual choice; you can use WMI and VBScript to retrieve BIOS information, or you can use WMI and JScript to retrieve BIOS information.

```
var strComputer = ".";
var objWMIService = GetObject("winmgmts:\\\\" +
    strComputer + "\\root\\cimv2");
var colItems = objWMIService.ExecQuery
    ("Select * from Win32_BIOS");
var e = new Enumerator(colItems);
for (;!e.atEnd();e.moveNext()) { var objItem = e.item();
    WScript.Echo(objItem.Name);
}
```

 Note

In reality, there are some minor differences among scripting languages that affect what you can and cannot do with system administration scripts. However, these differences are not important to this discussion.

System Requirements

This book is targeted toward computers running any Microsoft® Windows® 2000 operating system (including Microsoft® Windows® 2000 Professional, and Microsoft® Windows® 2000 Server, Windows® 2000 Advanced Server, and Windows® 2000 Datacenter Server). In addition to having Windows 2000 installed, these computers should be running Windows Script Host version 5.6, which was released after Windows 2000. Some of the scripts in the book rely on features found only in version 5.6. For more information about WSH version 5.6, see "WSH Primer" in this book.

 Note

If you do not have WSH 5.6, an installation file for Windows 2000 is included on the compact disc that accompanies this book. If your computer is running an operating system other than Windows 2000, see the Windows Script Technologies link on the Web Resources page at http://www.microsoft.com/windows/reskits/webresources and click the Microsoft Windows Script 5.6 download link. If you are not sure which version of WSH you have on your computer, see "WSH Primer" in this book for information about determining the WSH version number.

If you are working with multiple operating systems, particularly Windows XP, it is also recommended that you install Windows 2000 Service Pack 2. Without this service pack, scripts running on a Windows 2000–based computer are unable to retrieve information from a Windows XP–based computer (although the Windows XP computers can retrieve information from the Windows 2000 computers).

In addition, most of these scripts require you to be logged on with administrative credentials; this is a requirement for most WMI and ADSI operations. If you want to run a script against a remote computer, you need to be an administrator both on your computer and on that local computer.

Beyond that, no fancy scripting tools, editors, or integrated development environments (IDEs) are required. As long as you have Notepad installed, you are ready to start writing scripts.

VBScript Primer

Microsoft® Visual Basic® Scripting Edition (VBScript) is an easy-to-use scripting language that enables system administrators to create powerful tools for managing their Microsoft® Windows®–based computers. In the first half of this chapter, the fundamental principles of VBScript are illustrated by the creation of a simple script for determining the amount of free disk space on drive C of a computer. This script will evolve throughout the chapter into a more sophisticated tool, one that can determine the amount of free space for any drive on any computer. The second half of this chapter then explores these fundamental principles of VBScript programming in more detail and touches on other VBScript constructs of interest to system administrators.

In This Chapter

VBScript Overview 17
   Working with Objects 18
   Variables 23
   Constants 25
   Strings 26
   Collections 30
   Looping 34
   Making Decisions 37
   Arrays 39
   Input 41
   Error Handling 43

VBScript Reference **47**

    Working with Variables 49

    Using Constants 53

    VBScript Data Types 56

    Working with Dates and Times 59

    Working with Strings 73

    Working with Numbers 82

    Running Statements Multiple Times 87

    Making Decisions 92

    Arrays 97

    Error Handling 104

    Procedures 111

    COM Objects 121

VBScript Overview

Microsoft® Visual Basic® Scripting Edition (VBScript) is often dismissed as being "just" a scripting language, the implication being that a scripting language is of little use to a system administrator faced with managing hundreds or even thousands of computers in an enterprise setting. Yet nothing could be further from the truth; when used in combination with technologies such as Windows Script Host (WSH), Windows Management Instrumentation (WMI), and Active Directory Service Interfaces (ASDI), VBScript becomes a powerful language for creating system administration tools. For example, using VBScript in combination with WMI and ADSI, you can write a script of 10,000 or so lines, complete with error handling, subroutines, and other advanced programming constructs. That single script can give you complete control over many aspects of your computing environment.

But what makes VBScript such a useful tool for system administrators is that you do not have to create such elaborate and complicated solutions. You can instead spend a few minutes typing a handful of lines of code into Notepad, and instantly create a custom solution to a particular problem.

For example, the three-line script in Listing 2.1 tells you how much free disk space is available on drive C of your computer.

Listing 2.1   Retrieving Free Disk Space Using VBScript

```
1   Set objWMIService = GetObject("winmgmts:")
2   Set objLogicalDisk = objWMIService.Get("Win32_LogicalDisk.DeviceID='c:'")
3   Wscript.Echo objLogicalDisk.FreeSpace
```

If you have been having problems with users filling up drive C on their computers, you now have a custom solution for identifying the computers running low on disk space, a solution developed using nothing more sophisticated than Notepad.

Of course, it might be that this script does not fully address your needs. For example, the script tells you the free space available only on your local computer; it cannot tell you how much free space is available on a remote computer. Likewise, the script reports the free space available only on drive C; it tells you nothing about free space available on drives D or E.

But if the script does not fully meet your needs, it can easily be modified, and without starting from scratch. This is another advantage of scripting in general and VBScript in particular: You can start with a very simple script and add to it as your needs change and as you become more proficient with the language. This chapter illustrates this process. It begins with the script shown in Listing 2.1, which reports the amount of free disk space on drive C. Subsequent sections in the chapter will take this simple three-line script and gradually add functionality to make it more useful in more situations. When this series of enhancements is complete, you will have a script that can:

- Retrieve free disk space information for any computer in your organization, including remote computers.

- Retrieve free disk space information from multiple computers.

- Retrieve free disk space information for all drives installed in a computer.

- Issue a notification only if a drive is low on disk space.

- Continue to function if a user types an invalid computer name, or if a computer is not available over the network.

As new features are added to the script, the VBScript constructs required to add this functionality are briefly explained. After the script has been completed, a reference section will cover these constructs (and others) in more detail.

Working with Objects

VBScript allows system administrators to create complex scripts using such advanced programming capabilities as branching, looping, error handling, and the calling of functions and subroutines. It does not, however, include intrinsic methods for performing system administration tasks. VBScript has built-in functions for determining the square root of a number or the ASCII value of a character, but no built-in methods for stopping services, retrieving events from event logs, or carrying out other tasks of interest to system administrators.

Fortunately, there are other ways to programmatically perform these tasks, primarily through the use of Automation objects. Automation objects are a subset of COM (Component Object Model), a standard way for applications (.exe files) or programming libraries (.dll files) to present their functionality as a series of objects. In turn, programmers (or script writers) can use these objects, and the functionality of the application or programming library, in their own projects. For example, a word processing application might expose its spell checker as an Automation object, thus providing a way for script writers to add spell checking to their projects.

The ability to work with Automation objects and to utilize the properties and methods of these objects makes VBScript a powerful tool for system administration. Admittedly, VBScript alone cannot read events from an event log; however, VBScript can use the functionality included within WMI to retrieve such events. VBScript has no intrinsic methods for creating user accounts; however, the language can use the functionality in ADSI to create such accounts. In fact, VBScript is often referred to as a glue language because one of its primary uses is to "glue" objects together. Rather than provide a seemingly infinite number of intrinsic functions devoted to system administration, VBScript instead provides a framework for using the methods and properties of Automation objects designed to carry out these tasks.

For example, the script in Listing 2.2 illustrates the importance of Automation objects within VBScript. This script reports the amount of free disk on drive C of the local computer. Furthermore, it does this using very little VBScript code. Instead, the script:

1. Connects to WMI (an Automation object) by using the VBScript GetObject method.

2. Uses the WMI Get method to retrieve information about drive C.

3. Uses the WSH Echo method to report the amount of free disk space on drive C.

As noted, there is very little VBScript code here. Instead, the primary purpose of VBScript in this example is to glue together the functionality of WMI and WSH.

Listing 2.2 Using Objects in VBScript

```
1  Set objWMIService = GetObject("winmgmts:")
2  Set objLogicalDisk = objWMIService.Get("Win32_LogicalDisk.DeviceID='c:'")
3  Wscript.Echo objLogicalDisk.FreeSpace
```

Connecting to Objects

Before you can do anything with the data in a database, you must first make a connection of some kind to that database. Likewise, before you can do anything with the methods or properties of an Automation object, you must first make a connection to that object, a process known as *binding*.

Binding to objects can be confusing, because VBScript and WSH both provide a GetObject and a CreateObject method for accessing objects. Furthermore, although the implementations are similar, there are some subtle differences that grow in importance as you become more proficient in scripting. These differences are discussed in more detail later in this chapter. For now, use the following rules-of-thumb without worrying about whether you are using the VBScript or the WSH method (although in most cases you will use the VBScript implementation):

- **Use GetObject to bind to either WMI or ADSI**. Both WMI and ADSI allow you to use a moniker when binding from VBScript. A moniker (discussed later in this chapter) is an intermediary object that makes it easy to bind to objects that do not exist in the file system namespace. ADSI exists in the Active Directory namespace, while WMI exists in its own namespace.

   Although it is possible (and sometimes required) to bind to WMI or ADSI using CreateObject, using GetObject and a moniker is typically faster and easier.

- **Use CreateObject to bind to all objects other than WMI or ADSI**. In general, CreateObject will be required to create new instances of such elements as the FileSystem object, the Dictionary object, and Internet Explorer. This is not a hard-and-fast rule, however. For example, you will often need to use CreateObject to create WMI objects other than SWbemServices (such as SWbemLocator).

Connecting to WSH

In line 1 of the script in Listing 2.2, the script binds to WMI by using the following code statement:

```
Set objWMIService = GetObject("winmgmts:")
```

This connects the script to the WMI SWbemServices object.

No similar binding string is used to connect to WSH. Instead, the Echo method is called without first binding to WSH. You are already connected to WSH because WSH is required to run a script written in VBScript.

Creating an Object Reference

With Automation, you do not work directly with an object itself. Instead, you create a reference to the object by using GetObject or CreateObject and then assign this reference to a variable. After the reference has been created, you can access the methods and properties of the object by using the variable rather than the object itself.

In the script in Listing 2.2, the GetObject method is used to assign the WMI SWbemServices object to the variable objWMIService. After the assignment has been made, all the properties of the SWbemServices object can be accessed through objWMIService. For example, in line 2 of the script, the Get method is used to retrieve the properties for drive C.

Anytime you create an object reference, you must use the Set keyword when assigning the reference to a variable. For example, the following line of code will result in a run-time error:

```
objWMIService = GetObject("winmgmts:")
```

To create the object reference, you must use the Set keyword like this:

```
Set objWMIService = GetObject("winmgmts:")
```

Set is a special VBScript statement that is used only when creating an object reference. If you use Set for other purposes, such as assigning a value to a variable, a run-time error will occur. For example, this line of code will fail because no object named 5 can be found on the computer:

```
Set x = 5
```

Calling Methods

Automation objects allow you to use their capabilities within your scripts. This enables you to create more powerful and more useful scripts than you could create if you were restricted to the functionality of the scripting language. For example, it is impossible to draw a chart or graph by using VBScript alone. Through Automation, however, you can borrow the capabilities of Microsoft Excel and easily add a chart or graph to, say, a Web page.

Automation objects typically expose both methods and properties. (However, there is no requirement for them to expose either.) Methods are equivalent to the actions that the object can perform. For example, although the script in Listing 2.2 is only three lines long, it uses Automation to access the methods of two different COM objects and thus performs two different actions. These two methods are:

- The Get method, available through the WMI SWbemServices object. This method retrieves information for the specified object.

- The Echo method, available through the WSH WScript object. This method displays information on the screen. If a script is running in a command window and thus under CScript.exe, this information is displayed within that command window. If the script is running under Wscript.exe, the information is displayed in a message box.

After you have created a reference to an object, you can call the methods of that object using *dot notation*. Dot notation is so named because you call a method by typing the name of the variable that references the object, a period (or dot), and the name of the method. (Depending on the method, you might also type method parameters.) Generally, dot notation uses the following syntax:

```
ObjectReference.MethodName
```

For example, in the following line of code, the SWbemServices Get method call is written in dot notation.

```
Set objLogicalDisk = objWMIService.Get("Win32_LogicalDisk.DeviceID='c:'")
```

The parts of the SWbemServices Get method call are shown in Table 2.1.

Table 2.1   Parts of the SWbemServices Get Method Call

Item	Description
ObjWMIService	Object reference.
.	Dot (separates the object reference and the name of the method).
Get	Method name.
("Win32_LogicalDisk.DeviceID='c:'")	Method parameter. For the Get method, this can be read as, "Get the instance of the Win32_LogicalDisk class where the DeviceID is equal to C:."

Note

Instead of using Wscript.Echo to display the amount of free disk space, you can use the VBScript function Msgbox:

```
Msgbox objLogicalDisk.FreeSpace
```

In this book, however, Wscript.Echo is used instead of Msgbox. This is because the Msgbox function always displays its information in a graphical dialog box. When this dialog box appears, the **OK** button must be clicked before the script can proceed. For system administration scripts that display a large amount of data, this would be extremely tedious; it would also prevent the script from running automatically. By contrast, Wscript.Echo displays information as lines within a command window, provided the script is running under CScript.

Retrieving Properties

Properties are the attributes associated with an object. They are particularly important in system administration scripting because many of the objects you use are virtual representations of actual objects. For example, in line 3 of Listing 2.2, the FreeSpace property is retrieved, using the same dot notation used to call methods.

```
objLogicalDisk.FreeSpace
```

With WMI, this object reference refers not to some amorphous programming construct but to an actual hard disk within the computer. The FreeSpace property is thus not just a property of an Automation object but also of drive C. In a sense, WMI creates a virtual mirror of an actual physical object. When you retrieve the properties of that virtual mirror, you also retrieve the properties of the physical object.

Variables

The script in Listing 2.2 works exactly as expected. When run, it reports the amount of free disk space on drive C. That does not mean that the script cannot be improved, however. For example, the FreeSpace property reports the number of bytes available on a drive. Because disk drive space is typically reported in gigabytes, the FreeSpace property often returns a value that is difficult to interpret. For example, Figure 2.1 shows the value reported for a drive with approximately 10 gigabytes of free disk space.

Figure 2.1   Free Disk Space Expressed in Bytes

Although it might be obvious from a glance that drive C has adequate disk space, it is far less obvious just how *much* disk space is actually available. System administrators might find it easier to interpret the data returned by this script if the data were reported as megabytes rather than bytes.

VBScript includes a full range of mathematical functions that enable you to perform such tasks as converting bytes to megabytes. In addition, VBScript also provides a construct — the variable — that can be used to store the results of those mathematical equations. In fact, variables provide a way to store any type of data while the script is running.

Variables represent portions of memory that are available to the script as it runs. You can think of computer memory, for these purposes, as being a series of cubbyholes. A variable would be one of these cubbyholes, with an identifying label attached. You can store any kind of data in this cubbyhole and VBScript will retrieve the data when it is needed. When you want to reference the data, VBScript simply looks up the memory address, and reports the information stored there.

In line 3 of Listing 2.3, a variable named FreeMegabytes is used to store the results of dividing FreeSpace by 10484576 (which converts bytes to megabytes). As soon as line 3 is run, the variable FreeMegabytes takes on the value of this equation. If you need to refer to the number of free megabytes of disk space anywhere else in the script, you do not have to repeat this equation; instead, you can simply reference the variable FreeMegabytes. This is shown in line 4, where the variable is echoed to the screen.

Listing 2.3   Using Variables

```
1   Set objWMIService = GetObject("winmgmts:")
2   Set objLogicalDisk = objWMIService.Get("Win32_LogicalDisk.DeviceID='c:'")
3   FreeMegaBytes = objLogicalDisk.FreeSpace / 1048576
4   Wscript.Echo FreeMegaBytes
```

When the script in Listing 2.3 runs, a dialog box similar to that shown in Figure 2.2 is displayed.

Figure 2.2   Free Disk Space Converted to Megabytes

 Note

Notice that the equation used the number 1048576 instead of 1,048,576 (with commas separating the thousands). You cannot use a comma or any other character to separate thousands in VBScript. Instead, you must run all the digits together. This is true for numbers hard-coded into the script as well as for numbers that are entered as command-line arguments or in response to a prompt.

Formatting Script Output

The value 10340.4458007813 (meaning 10,340 megabytes of free space) is probably more meaningful to the typical system administrator than the value 10842824704. However, the numbers after the decimal point are more of a distraction than they are useful information. Fortunately, VBScript provides several different ways to modify script output. For example, the Int function causes VBScript to display only the integer portion of a number, leaving off all digits following the decimal point. The Int function is shown in line 4 of Listing 2.4.

Listing 2.4   Formatting Output

```
1   Set objWMIService = GetObject("winmgmts:")
2   Set objLogicalDisk = objWMIService.Get("Win32_LogicalDisk.DeviceID='c:'")
3   FreeMegaBytes = objLogicalDisk.FreeSpace / 1048576
4   Wscript.Echo Int(FreeMegaBytes)
```

When the script in Listing 2.4 runs, a dialog box similar to that shown in Figure 2.3 appears. The Int function strips away all the digits following the decimal point, leaving only the integer portion of the original value. Additional formatting commands (covered later in this chapter) can be used to add a comma to the output, resulting in the displayed value 10,340.

Figure 2.3   Using the Int Function to Format Output

Constants

In the script in Listing 2.3, the amount of free megabytes is calculated by taking the value of the FreeSpace property and dividing it by the hard-coded value 1048576. (Hard-coded values such as this are often referred to as *literals* because they do not stand for something else but literally represent the value.)

In a small script such as this (particularly a small script written for your own use), hard-coding literal values usually does not pose much of a problem. However, in a larger script, particularly one used in an enterprise setting, literals can lead to at least two problems.

For one thing, in a small script it might be obvious that 1048576 is the value required to convert bytes (the value returned from the FreeSpace property) to megabytes. In a larger script, however, one that includes a number of mathematical equations, this might be less obvious. This is especially true in an enterprise setting, in which multiple administrators might use — and modify — the same script. You might know what the 1048576 represents, but another administrator charged with modifying the script might not.

The fact that scripts often need to be modified raises a second issue. Literal values not only can be confusing but can also require extra work for anyone modifying the script. Suppose this same procedure, converting kilobytes to megabytes, is used five or six times throughout a script. If you later decide to convert the value to gigabytes rather than megabytes, you will have to correctly modify each line of code where the conversion takes place or your script will no longer provide accurate results.

One way to work around the problems that can arise from the use of literals is to use constants instead. Constants are similar to variables in that they are places to store data. Unlike variables, however, after a constant has been defined (that is, after it has been assigned a value), it cannot be changed while the script is running. By assigning important items, such as the value required to convert bytes to megabytes, to a constant, you ensure that the value cannot be changed, inadvertently or otherwise.

In the script in Listing 2.5, a constant named CONVERSION_FACTOR is defined in line 1 and is assigned the value 1048576. Later in the script (line 4), the number of bytes of free disk space is converted to the number of megabytes of free disk space. Instead of the literal value 1048576, the constant CONVERSION_FACTOR is used. Both equations return the same result; however, the equation in Listing 2.5 is easier to read and understand.

Listing 2.5 Using Constants

```
1   Const CONVERSION_FACTOR = 1048576
2   Set objWMIService = GetObject("winmgmts:")
3   Set objLogicalDisk = objWMIService.Get("Win32_LogicalDisk.DeviceID='c:'")
4   FreeMegaBytes = objLogicalDisk.FreeSpace / CONVERSION_FACTOR
5   Wscript.Echo Int(FreeMegaBytes)
```

Another benefit to using constants is that they can be defined once and then used multiple times throughout the same script. For example, an expanded version of the script in Listing 2.5 might require you to convert bytes to megabytes several times during the running of the script. Rather than using the literal value in each equation, use the constant instead. If you later decide to convert bytes to gigabytes, you will have to change only the value of the constant; you will not have to change the value used in each equation.

Strings

As you write more sophisticated scripts, you will begin to encounter different types of data (a topic covered in more detail later in this chapter). In line 1 of Listing 2.5, for example, numeric data was used to assign the literal value 1048576 to the constant CONVERSION_FACTOR:

```
Const CONVERSION_FACTOR = 1048576
```

This line of code works because a numeric value is being assigned to the constant. Anytime you assign a numeric value to a variable or a constant, you simply type the equals sign followed by the value.

However, unexpected results occur if you try to assign an alphanumeric value (typically referred to as a string value) using this same approach. For example, the following code sample attempts to assign the string atl-dc-01 to the variable Computer and then echo the value of that variable:

```
Computer = atl-dc-01
Wscript.Echo Computer
```

When this script runs, however, the dialog box shown in Figure 2.4 appears.

Figure 2.4 Improperly Assigning String Data to a Variable

How did the value –1 get assigned to the variable Computer? When VBScript encounters a set of alphanumeric characters that is not surrounded by quotation marks, it assumes that these characters represent the name of a variable. If it sees a "stray" hyphen, it assumes that the hyphen represents a minus sign. As a result, VBScript interprets the line Computer = atl-dc-01 as "The variable Computer is to be assigned the value of the variable atl minus the value of the variable dc minus 01." Because atl and dc are viewed as new variables that have not been initialized, they are assigned the value 0. VBScript thus interprets this line of code as if it were written like this:

```
Computer = 0 - 0 - 1
```

As a result, the variable Computer receives the erroneous assignment –1.

When you assign a string value to a variable or a constant, you must enclose that value within quotation marks; this is the only way to ensure that VBScript treats the string as an alphanumeric value and not as a variable. For example, the following code sample correctly assigns the string atl-dc-01 to the variable Computer and then echoes the results:

```
Computer = "atl-dc-01"
Wscript.Echo Computer
```

When this script runs, the dialog box shown in Figure 2.5 appears.

Figure 2.5 Properly Assigning String Data to a Variable

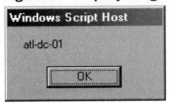

Strings as Variables

Strings are often used to assign values to variables. For example, the sample script in this chapter uses the following code to bind to WMI. (For information about binding to WMI, see "WMI Scripting Primer" in this book.)

```
Set objWMIService = GetObject("winmgmts:")
```

This code always connects you to the local computer. This is fine unless you are a system administrator responsible for managing a remote computer or two. In that case, you might want a script that can retrieve the free disk space from a remote computer. That would allow you to sit at your workstation and check the available disk space on any of the computers under your control.

When you are using WMI, it is possible to connect to a remote computer simply by including the computer name as part of the moniker passed to GetObject. For example, the following line of code binds to the WMI service on the remote computer atl-dc-01:

```
Set objWMIService = GetObject("winmgmts://atl-dc-01")
```

You can use the preceding code to write a script that binds to this one remote computer. In an enterprise setting, however, you might want a more flexible script, one that can bind to any remote computer.

One way to do this is to edit the script every time you run it, replacing one hard-coded computer name with another. A much better approach is to provide a way for the script to accept input as it runs, and thus operate against a computer whose name has been entered as a command-line argument.

User input methods will be discussed later in this chapter. Before that discussion takes place, however, it is important to understand how string values (such as computer names) can be assigned to a variable, and then used as part of the script code.

For example, in line 2 of Listing 2.6, the string value "atl-dc-01" is assigned to the variable Computer. In line 3, that variable is used to bind to the WMI service on the computer atl-dc-01. However, this is not done by hard-coding the value atl-dc-01 into the code, but instead by using the value of the variable Computer.

Listing 2.6   Using Strings

```
1   Const CONVERSION_FACTOR = 1048576
2   Computer = "atl-dc-01"
3   Set objWMIService = GetObject("winmgmts://" & Computer)
4   Set objLogicalDisk = objWMIService.Get("Win32_LogicalDisk.DeviceID='c:'")
5   FreeMegaBytes = objLogicalDisk.FreeSpace / CONVERSION_FACTOR
6   Wscript.Echo Int(FreeMegaBytes)
```

In a small demonstration script such as this, assigning the string to a variable actually requires more effort than hard-coding the value. However, this script does illustrate an important concept: You can assign a value to a variable, and then use that variable in place of a hard-coded value.

Why is that important? Imagine that this script was designed to retrieve free disk space from 100 computers. Instead of hard-coding separate WMI binding strings for each computer, you could create a single binding string using the variable Computer. Your script could then run that single line of code 100 times, each time replacing the value of Computer with a different computer name.

For the moment, however, you have to focus only on line 3 of Listing 2.6:

```
Set objWMIService = GetObject("winmgmts://" & Computer)
```

Here is how VBScript interprets that line of code:

1. It reads everything up to the second quotation mark. In other words:

   ```
   Set objWMIService = GetObject("winmgmts://"
   ```

2. It reads the ampersand (&), which essentially means, "Append whatever comes next to the string." What follows the ampersand is the variable Computer, which has been assigned the value atl-dc-01. VBScript will now see the line as being:

   ```
   Set objWMIService = GetObject("winmgmts://atl-dc-01"
   ```

3. It reads the closing parenthesis character. VBScript requires you to have an equal number of opening and closing parentheses. If the closing parenthesis is not included, you will receive an error message. VBScript now reads the line of code as:

   ```
   Set objWMIService = GetObject("winmgmts://atl-dc-01")
   ```

4. Having reached the end of the line, it runs the statement. In turn, the script will connect to the WMI service on atl-dc-01. To connect to the WMI service on a different computer, all you have to do is change the value of the variable Computer.

Concatenating Strings

Concatenation is the process of combining two or more strings into a single string. (You can also combine strings with numeric or date values.) Concatenation is often used to provide more readable or more meaningful output. For example, the script in Listing 2.4 returns the value 10340. This is very useful information, provided you know that the script is designed to return the number of megabytes of free disk space on drive C. But if you do not know what the script is designed to do, that output will be meaningless.

Among other things, concatenation helps you provide context for your script output. For example, rather than displaying the value 10340, you might want to display a message similar to "There are 10340 megabytes of free disk space." To do this, you must combine the following three items:

- "There are " — a simple string representing the start of the message.

- FreeMegabytes — the variable containing the number of free megabytes on the drive.

- " megabytes of free disk space." — a second string representing the end of the message.

As shown in lines 6 and 7 of Listing 2.7, you concatenate items in VBScript by using the ampersand (&).

Listing 2.7   Concatenating Strings

```
1   Const CONVERSION_FACTOR = 1048576
2   Computer = "atl-dc-01"
3   Set objWMIService = GetObject("winmgmts://" & Computer)
4   Set objLogicalDisk = objWMIService.Get("Win32_LogicalDisk.DeviceID='c:'")
5   FreeMegaBytes = objLogicalDisk.FreeSpace / CONVERSION_FACTOR
6   Wscript.Echo "There are " & Int(FreeMegaBytes) & _
7       " megabytes of free disk space."
```

 Note

The underscore (_) at the end of line 6 is known as the line continuation character and is used to indicate a statement break. This means that lines 6 and 7 should be treated as one line; the line was simply too long to fit in the allotted space. Statement breaks are covered in more detail later in this chapter.

Alternatively, you might have assigned the value "There are " to a variable named MessageStart and the value "megabytes of free disk space." to a variable named MessageEnd. You could then have concatenated the three variables like this:

```
Wscript.Echo MessageStart & Int(FreeMegabytes) & MessageEnd
```

If you look closely at lines 6 and 7, you will notice that blank spaces were hard-coded into the string values "There are " and " megabytes of free disk space." This is required because the ampersand does not insert any spaces between the items being concatenated. For example, suppose you leave out the blank spaces, like this:

```
Wscript.Echo "There are " & Int(FreeMegaBytes) & " megabytes of free disk
space."
```

In this case, the resulting message box will run the three values together, as shown in Figure 2.6.

Figure 2.6   Incorrectly Concatenating String Values

For simple forms of concatenation, you can work around this problem by using a comma rather than an ampersand when combining the values:

```
Wscript.Echo "There are ", Int(FreeMegaBytes), " megabytes of free disk space."
```

When the items are separated by a comma, a blank space is automatically inserted between the items. As a result, the message box is properly formatted, as shown in Figure 2.7.

Figure 2.7   Correctly Concatenating String Values

Collections

Up to this point in the chapter, the scripts have been designed to retrieve the amount of free space on drive C for a specified computer. Determining free space on a single drive is a common administrative task, particularly when you are working with user workstations that are likely to have only one hard drive. Because the intention was to retrieve free disk space for only drive C, the DeviceID (a property of the Win32_LogicalDisk class) was hard-coded into the script.

Of course, other computers, including most servers, are likely to have multiple drives. For these computers, determining the free space on drive C tells only part of the story; as a system administrator, you need to know the amount of free space on drive D, drive E, and any other drives installed on the computer.

However, this creates a problem: How do you know which drives are installed on a given computer? In theory, you could check for free space on drives C through Z. But if a computer does not have, say, a drive E, the script will fail. Although you can include code designed to handle these errors and prevent the script from failing, the resulting script will be extremely long, making it difficult to read and maintain. Such a script will also be extremely inefficient; even if a computer has only a single drive, the script will nonetheless attempt to retrieve the free space on the nonexistent drives D through Z.

Fortunately, Automation objects often return information in the form of collections. Like stamp collections or coin collections, Automation collections are simply a group of related objects. For example, the script in Listing 2.8 uses the WMI method InstancesOf (line 4) to return not just a specific drive but a collection consisting of all the logical disks installed on the computer. If the computer has four drives (C, D, E, and F), the collection will have four items, one for each drive.

Listing 2.8   Using Collections

```
1   Const CONVERSION_FACTOR = 1048576
2   Computer = "atl-dc-01"
3   Set objWMIService = GetObject("winmgmts://" & Computer)
4   Set colLogicalDisk = objWMIService.InstancesOf("Win32_LogicalDisk")
5   For Each objLogicalDisk In colLogicalDisk
6       FreeMegaBytes = objLogicalDisk.FreeSpace / CONVERSION_FACTOR
7       Wscript.Echo objLogicalDisk.DeviceID & " " & Int(FreeMegaBytes)
8   Next
```

Having information returned as a collection means you do not have to guess how many drives are installed on a computer. Instead, you simply ask for the collection (all the instances of disk drives installed on the computer). After the collection has been returned, you can use a For Each loop (also known as an iteration loop) to access each individual item in the collection.

For Each

The For Each statement provides a simple way to iterate through all the items in a collection. Unlike the For Next statement (discussed later in this chapter), For Each does not require you to know how many items are in the collection. Instead, it simply begins with the first item in the collection and continues until it has iterated through every item.

A typical For Each loop looks like this:

```
For Each objLogicalDisk In colLogicalDisk
    Wscript.Echo objLogicalDisk.DeviceID
Next
```

The individual items that make up this loop are described in Table 2.2.

Table 2.2 Components of the For Each Statement

Item	Description
objLogicalDisk	Variable name representing the individual disk drive instances.
colLogicalDisk	Variable name given to the collection of disk drives retrieved using WMI.
For Each objLogicalDisk in colLogicalDisk	Starts the loop. The basic syntax can be read as "For Each instance of an object in a collection of objects " do something. In this example, this can be read as "For each individual disk drive in the collection of disk drives installed on this computer ... "
Wscript.Echo objLogicalDisk.DeviceID	Commands carried out for each disk drive in the collection. (This example has only one command, but any number of lines of code are permitted between the For Each and Next statements.)
	Notice that individual disk drives are referenced using the variable objLogicalDisk and the appropriate property (in this case, DeviceID). The value of this property will change each time through the loop. For example, on a computer with drives C, D, and E, objLogicalDisk.DeviceID will equal C on the first iteration because C is the DeviceID for the first drive in the collection. On subsequent passes through the loop, objLogicalDisk.DeviceID will equal D and then E.
Next	Indicates the end of the loop.

When working with collections, you typically iterate through the entire collection rather than refer to a single item within the collection. For example, suppose your collection consists of disk drives C, D, E, F, and G, and you want to echo only the available drive space on drive G. To do this, you will have to set up a For Each loop and begin iterating through the set of disk drives. For each drive in the collection, you can check the drive letter, and echo the available space only for drive G.

Tip

There is no straightforward way to avoid iterating through the entire collection. However, you can make your scripts more efficient by limiting the number of items in the collection. For example, your WMI query can specify that data should be returned only for instances of the Win32_DiskDrive class in which the drive letter is equal to G. The script still returns a collection, and you still have to iterate all the items within that collection. In this case, however, the collection contains just one item, making that iteration much faster and more efficient.

Collections with Zero Items

It is possible for a collection to contain zero items. For example, consider this script sample, which returns the set of all tape drives installed on a computer:

```
Set objWMIService = GetObject("winmgmts:")
Set colTapeDrives = objWMIService.InstancesOf("Win32_TapeDrive")
For Each objTapeDrive In colTapeDrives
    Wscript.Echo objTapeDrive.Name
Next
```

If this script is run on a computer that does not have a tape drive, it will appear that nothing happened. In truth, the script will run as expected. However, because the computer does not have a tape drive, the resulting collection of all tape drives installed on the computer will have zero items in it.

When run on a computer without a tape drive, the script will:

1. Connect to the WMI service.

2. Retrieve the collection of tape drives installed on the computer.

3. Set up a For Each loop to iterate through the entire collection, echoing the name of each individual tape drive in the collection.

   However, because no items are in the collection, the For Each loop and any commands included within that loop are not actually run. Instead, the script skips the For Each loop and picks up with the first line following the Next statement. In this sample script, however, no lines of code follow the Next statement, meaning that the script simply stops.

There is no obvious way to tell whether the script actually ran. One way to improve this script is to use the Count property to determine how many items are in the collection. For example, this script sample uses the Count property to echo the number of tape drives installed on a computer:

```
Set objWMIService = GetObject("winmgmts:")
Set colTapeDrives = objWMIService.InstancesOf("Win32_TapeDrive")
Wscript.Echo colTapeDrives.Count
```

Your script can use the Count property to determine the number of items in the collection, and then do one of two things:

- Echo the item properties if one or more items are in the collection.

- Echo a message such as "No tape drives are installed on this computer." if the collection contains zero items.

This script might look like the following (the use of the If-Then-Else statement is explained later in this chapter):

```
Set objWMIService = GetObject("winmgmts:")
Set colTapeDrives = objWMIService.InstancesOf("Win32_TapeDrive")
If colTapeDrives.Count = 0 Then
    Wscript.Echo "No tape drives are installed on this computer."
Else
    For Each objTapeDrive In colTapeDrives
        Wscript.Echo objTapeDrive.Name
    Next
End If
```

Looping

Scripts that monitor or measure system resources typically need to collect data at periodic intervals. For example, it is unlikely that you would measure free disk space moments after installing a new hard disk and then never check again to be sure there was still space available on the disk. Instead, you are likely to check free disk space at regular intervals, perhaps once a week, once a day, or even once an hour, depending on the computer being monitored.

If there is a relatively long period of time between data collections, you might want to run the script as a scheduled task. This way, you can schedule the script to run every morning at 2:00 A.M., and you never need to give it a second thought.

However, using scheduled tasks is not always an option. For example, suppose you want to measure processor use on a computer every 10 seconds until you have collected 500 samples. Although you can create 500 scheduled tasks, one right after another, this is far more trouble than it is worth. A better approach is to run a single script that collects all 500 samples for you.

For Next

One way to get a single script to run the same set of commands over and over is to enclose those commands within a For Next loop, which allows you to run lines of code a specified number of times.

For example, the script shown in Listing 2.9 checks free disk space on a computer every hour for 12 hours. To do this, a For statement is used on line 5 to indicate that the enclosed code block should be run 12 times. Lines 6–10 include the code required to determine the amount of free space for each disk drive on the computer, and line 11 pauses the script for one hour (using a constant that pauses the script for 3,600,000 milliseconds). Line 12 is simply the Next statement, which marks the end of the loop.

When the script runs, a connection is made to the remote computer atl-dc-01. The script retrieves the free disk space information and then pauses for one hour. After that hour, the script returns to the first statement of the For Next loop and retrieves free disk space information for a second time. This continues until the disk space information has been retrieved 12 times. After that, the script runs the line of code following the Next statement. Because no lines of code follow that statement, the script completes.

Listing 2.9 Running Commands Multiple Times

```
1   Const CONVERSION_FACTOR = 1048576
2   Const ONE_HOUR = 3600000
3   Computer = "atl-dc-01"
4   Set objWMIService = GetObject("winmgmts://" & Computer)
5   For i = 1 to 12
6       Set colLogicalDisk = objWMIService.InstancesOf("Win32_LogicalDisk")
7       For Each objLogicalDisk In colLogicalDisk
8           FreeMegaBytes = objLogicalDisk.FreeSpace / CONVERSION_FACTOR
9           Wscript.Echo objLogicalDisk.DeviceID & " " & Int(FreeMegaBytes)
10      Next
11      Wscript.Sleep ONE_HOUR
12  Next
```

The For Next statement allows you to run a block of code a specific number of times. This should not be confused with a For Each statement. For Each is used to iterate through the individual items within a collection. For Next is used to run a particular set of statements a specified number of times.

To use a For Next statement, you must determine both a starting point and an ending point. Because For Next statements are typically designed to run a set of statements X number of times, you will generally start with 1 and end with X. Therefore, to do the same thing 10 times, you start with 1 and end with 10.

 Note

You can pick an arbitrary starting point (for example, 314 or 6,912) and then conclude with the appropriate end point (324 or 6,922). However, your code will be easier to read and maintain if you start with 1 and end with 10.

The For Next statement requires you to use a loop variable (also known as a counter) that keeps a running tally of how many times the code has run. For example, the variable i is used as the counter in the following code sample. The counter starts at 1 and runs the lines of code contained within the For Next statement block. After all the statements have run, the counter is automatically incremented by 1, meaning i is now equal to 2. The script loops back to the beginning of the For Next statement and checks to see whether the value 2 is still within the valid execution range. Because it is, the code within the For Next statement block runs a second time.

```
For i = 1 to 5
    Wscript.Echo i
Next
Wscript.Echo "For Next loop complete."
```

What happens when i is equal to 6? The script will loop back to the beginning of the For Next statement, and check to see if 6 is part of the valid execution range. Because it is not, the For Next statement will immediately stop, and running of the script will continue with the first line following the Next statement. In this case, that is the line that echoes the message "For Next loop complete."

The script output looks like this:

```
1
2
3
4
5
For Next loop complete.
```

Note

There are times when you want to run the same set of statements over and over; however, you might have no way of determining in advance how many times you need to run that code. For example, suppose you want to check free disk space once every hour and continue to run this check until disk space drops below a specified amount. In a case such as this, you want the script to start and continue to run until disk space has dropped below the threshold, regardless of how many iterations that requires. In these situations, you should use a Do Loop, discussed later in this chapter.

Making Decisions

One of the primary reasons for using scripts as a system administration tool is that scripts reduce the need for hands-on human intervention. The scripts introduced thus far in this chapter go a long way towards this goal; the version shown in Listing 2.8, for example, can connect to any computer (even a remote one), bind to the WMI service, and determine the amount of free disk space on each of the hard drives installed on that computer. By running this script on a regular basis, administrators can receive advance notification if any drive begins to run low on disk space.

However, it is still up to a system administrator to analyze the script output and determine whether a disk is running low on disk space. The script can be improved by examining the amount of free space and issuing a notification only if the free space has dropped below a specified level. With this approach, administrators are notified only if a disk is running out of space. No notification means that all the disks are in compliance and no action is required.

VBScript provides a number of programming constructs that allow scripts to "make decisions." This means a script can analyze a particular piece of data and then take a specified course of action based on the value of that data.

The simplest form of decision-making code is the If Then statement, which examines the value of a particular piece of data and compares it against a predetermined value (for example, if the amount of free disk space is less than 100 megabytes). If the statement is True (for example, if only 99 megabytes of disk space are available), the script carries out some action. If the statement is not true, no action is taken.

This simple type of decision-making is shown in Listing 2.10. In line 8, the script checks to see whether the amount of free space is less than 100 megabytes (by comparing the value with the constant WARNING_THRESHOLD). If this conditional statement is True (for example, if a drive has only 99 megabytes of free space), the statement immediately following the If-Then statement runs. In this script, that statement appears on line 9, which echoes the message that the drive is low on disk space.

If the conditional statement is False (for example, if the drive has 101 megabytes of free disk space), line 9 is not run. Instead, processing passes to line 10, which marks the end of the If Then code block, and the script continues with line 11.

Listing 2.10   Making Decisions

```
1   Const CONVERSION_FACTOR = 1048576
2   Const WARNING_THRESHOLD = 100
3   Computer = "atl-dc-01"
4   Set objWMIService = GetObject("winmgmts://" & Computer)
5   Set colLogicalDisk = objWMIService.InstancesOf("Win32_LogicalDisk")
6   For Each objLogicalDisk In colLogicalDisk
7       FreeMegaBytes = objLogicalDisk.FreeSpace / CONVERSION_FACTOR
8       If FreeMegaBytes < WARNING_THRESHOLD Then
9           Wscript.Echo objLogicalDisk.DeviceID & " is low on disk space."
10      End If
11  Next
```

Taking Multiple Actions by Using If Then Else

The script shown in Listing 2.10 displays a warning message if a disk drive is low on disk space. If a disk drive has adequate free space, however, no message of any kind is displayed. For a simple monitoring script this is probably acceptable. On the other hand, a user running this script would have no way of knowing whether the lack of output was because all the drives had adequate disk space, or whether the lack of output was because the script failed to run for some reason.

In other words, sometimes you want your script to evaluate a condition and then take a different course of action based on that evaluation. For example, you might want to echo a warning message if a drive is low on disk space and echo a "No problem" message if a drive has adequate disk space. This kind of approach can be implemented by using an If Then Else statement.

If-Then-Else statements work exactly as the name implies: **If** a condition is True (or False), **Then** take this course of action, **Else** take this course of action. If disk space is low, echo a warning message; otherwise, echo a "No problem" message.

An example of this is shown in Listing 2.11. In line 8, the amount of free disk space on a drive is compared against a warning threshold. If the conditional statement is True (that is, if the amount of free disk space is less than the warning threshold), then line 9 runs.

But what if the conditional statement is False? To handle this possibility, an Else statement is included on line 10. If the conditional statement is False, and the drive has adequate space, then line 11, the line immediately following the Else statement, runs instead.

Listing 2.11 Using an If-Then-Else Statement

```
1   Const CONVERSION_FACTOR = 1048576
2   Const WARNING_THRESHOLD = 100
3   Computer = "atl-dc-01"
4   Set objWMIService = GetObject("winmgmts://" & Computer)
5   Set colLogicalDisk = objWMIService.InstancesOf("Win32_LogicalDisk")
6   For Each objLogicalDisk In colLogicalDisk
7       FreeMegaBytes = objLogicalDisk.FreeSpace / CONVERSION_FACTOR
8       If FreeMegaBytes < WARNING_THRESHOLD Then
9           Wscript.Echo objLogicalDisk.DeviceID & " is low on disk space."
10      Else
11          Wscript.Echo objLogicalDisk.DeviceID & " has adequate disk space."
12      End If
13  Next
```

It is possible to construct more elaborate scenarios, scenarios that can take more than just two possible courses of action. Two different ways to construct these scenarios are discussed later in this chapter.

Arrays

Collections are an excellent way to package information because they allow you to work with any number of items, even if you do not know the details of any of those items. For example, the script introduced in Listing 2.8 allows you to retrieve the amount of free disk space for all the drives installed on a computer, even if you have no idea how many drives are installed on that computer. To carry out an action on each item in the collection, you simply use a For Each loop to iterate through the collection item by item.

Automation objects can create collections for you. However, you might have other information (information not returned from an Automation object) that might be easier to manipulate if you can iterate through the set of items one by one. Suppose you want to check the available disk space on three computers rather than just one. You can write the code to check the first computer, copy and paste the code, and then modify the pasted code to check free disk space on the second computer. You can repeat this process again to check for free disk space on the third computer.

Although this approach works, it can quickly become tedious, particularly if you need to check 100 computers. In addition, suppose you need to make a change in the code, perhaps to return not only the free space on the drive but also the total size of the drive. To make that change, you need to change all 100 instances of the code, a process that not only takes a long time to complete but greatly increases the likelihood that you will make an error somewhere along the way.

A better approach is to use a For Each loop to iterate through a collection of computers, checking for free disk space on each one. This can be done by placing the computer names in an array, a data structure that can be used in much the same way as a collection.

The script in Listing 2.12 places the names of three computers (atl-dc-01, atl-dc-02, and atl-dc-03) in an array and then uses a For Each loop to connect to and retrieve free disk space information from each computer. In line 3, the script creates an array named Computers by using the Array function and specifying the three computer names as the function parameters. (The names are enclosed in quotation marks because they are strings.) In line 4, a For Each loop us used to iterate through all the items in the Computers array.

Listing 2.12   Using an Array

```
1  Const CONVERSION_FACTOR = 1048576
2  Const WARNING_THRESHOLD = 100
3  Computers = Array("atl-dc-01", "atl-dc-02", "atl-dc-03")
4  For Each Computer In Computers
5      Set objWMIService = GetObject("winmgmts://" & Computer)
6      Set colLogicalDisk = objWMIService.InstancesOf("Win32_LogicalDisk")
7      For Each objLogicalDisk In colLogicalDisk
8          FreeMegaBytes = objLogicalDisk.FreeSpace / CONVERSION_FACTOR
9          If FreeMegaBytes < WARNING_THRESHOLD Then
10             Wscript.Echo Computer & " " & objLogicalDisk.DeviceID & _
11                 " is low on disk space."
12         End If
13     Next
14 Next
```

Although arrays are similar to collections, there is one primary difference. As a script writer, you have little control over collections. If you query WMI for a list of disk drives, you will get those disk drives back in whichever order WMI chooses. Furthermore, you will not be able to readily access individual drives without iterating through the entire collection.

By contrast, you can control the order of information in an array because you typically populate the array yourself. Furthermore, you have the ability to access individual items in an array without having to iterate through the entire set. This is because each item in an array is assigned an index number. In VBScript, the first item in an array is assigned index number 0, with subsequent items assigned index numbers 1, 2, 3, and so forth. The array created in Listing 2.12 therefore contains the items and index numbers shown in Table 2.3. Notice that the highest index number will always be 1 less than the number of items in the array.

Table 2.3   Index Numbers in an Array

Index Number	Item
0	atl-dc-01
1	atl-dc-02
2	atl-dc-03

You can use these index numbers to access individual items within the array. For example, this line of code will echo atl-dc-02, the value of item 1 (based on index number) in the array:

```
Wscript.Echo Computers(1)
```

To echo the value of a different item in the array, simply replace the value 1 with the appropriate index number.

Additional methods for creating arrays and for accessing the individual items within those arrays are discussed later in this chapter.

Input

The script in Listing 2.12 is designed for an organization in which the computing infrastructure is not expected to change. Needless to say, a static infrastructure such as this is the exception rather than the rule; most organizations have a more dynamic environment. Although there might be only three servers (atl-dc-01, atl-dc-02, atl-dc-03) that need monitoring today, there is no guarantee that only those three servers will need monitoring tomorrow.

Because of that, you might not want to hard-code computer names into a script. Hard-coding items such as computers names can lead to a pair of related problems:

- **Lack of flexibility**. The script in Listing 2.12 retrieves available disk space information only for the computers atl-dc-01, atl-dc-02, and atl-dc-03. If you need to retrieve free disk space for computer atl-dc-04, you will need to modify the script.

- **Frequent updating**. The script in Listing 2.12 was designed to retrieve free disk space information for a particular set of computers (for example, all the domain controllers in a particular location). Each time a new domain controller is added, or each time an existing domain controller is retired, the script will need to be updated. If this is the only script used in your organization, this might not pose much of a problem. If you use scores of scripts in your organization, however, you are likely to waste more time modifying scripts than you save by using those scripts in the first place.

There are a number of ways to enter information, such as server names, into a script. (For more information about these methods, see "Creating Enterprise Scripts" in this book.) Perhaps the easiest way is to have the user specify this information as command-line arguments each time the script is run.

An argument (also known as a parameter) is information supplied along with the command that actually runs the script. For example, suppose you typically start a script by typing the following at the command line:

```
cscript FreeDiskSpace.vbs
```

An argument is any information added to the end of that command. For example, this command has three arguments, one for each computer name:

```
cscript FreeDiskSpace.vbs atl-dc-01 atl-dc-02 atl-dc-03
```

In addition to supplying arguments, you must include code in the script that makes use of those arguments. This type of coding is covered in detail in the "WSH Primer" chapter of this book. A simple example is also shown in Listing 2.13. In line 9 of this script, a For Each loop is established to iterate through the set of arguments supplied when the script was started. In this script, each argument is successively assigned to the variable Computer and then used to connect to the WMI service on that computer (line 10). The first time the For Each loop runs, Computer will be assigned the value atl-dc-01. On subsequent iterations, Computer will be assigned the value atl-dc-02, and then atl-dc-03.

Listing 2.13   Getting User Input

```
1    Const CONVERSION_FACTOR = 1048576
2    Const WARNING_THRESHOLD = 100
3
4    If WScript.Arguments.Count = 0 Then
5        Wscript.Echo "Usage: FirstScript.vbs server1 [server2] [server3] ..."
6        WScript.Quit
7    End If
8
9    For Each Computer In WScript.Arguments
10       Set objWMIService = GetObject("winmgmts://" & Computer)
11       Set colLogicalDisk = objWMIService.InstancesOf("Win32_LogicalDisk")
12       For Each objLogicalDisk In colLogicalDisk
13           FreeMegaBytes = objLogicalDisk.FreeSpace / CONVERSION_FACTOR
14           If FreeMegaBytes < WARNING_THRESHOLD Then
15               Wscript.Echo Computer & " " & objLogicalDisk.DeviceID & _
16                   " is low on disk space."
17           End If
18       Next
19   Next
```

One benefit of using arguments is that they are automatically placed in a collection (Wscript.Arguments). This makes it easy to iterate through the arguments supplied to a script: You simply set up a For Each loop and iterate through each argument in the collection, exactly as you would iterate through the individual disk drives in a collection of disk drives.

Because arguments are placed in a collection, it is easy to verify how many arguments, if any, were supplied when starting a script. In line 4 of the script, Wscript.Arguments.Count is used to determine how many arguments were supplied (which will equal the number of items in the arguments collection). If Count equals 0, meaning no arguments were supplied, a set of usage instructions is displayed, and the script terminates (using the command WScript.Quit).

Error Handling

The script in Listing 2.13 has a potential flaw in it. Suppose the user enters an invalid server name as an argument. When the script attempts to connect to this nonexistent computer, it will fail with the error message, "The remote server machine does not exist or is unavailable."

Of course, flaws like this are inherent in all the scripts used so far in this chapter, including those in which the computer names are hard-coded. After all, the script cannot distinguish between an invalid name and a valid name for a computer that, for some reason, is not available over the network. For example, suppose you run the script in Listing 2.12, and the computer named atl-dc-01 is offline. At that point, the script fails. In turn, you fail to retrieve the free disk space not only on atl-dc-01 but also on atl-dc-02 and atl-dc-03, even if those computers are connected to the network and functioning properly. This occurs because the script will stop running before it even attempts to connect to atl-dc-02 or atl-dc-03.

The inability to connect to atl-dc-01 is an example of a run-time error, an error that occurs after the script has started. (By comparison, a syntax error, such as a misspelled command, is generated and the script stops running before any lines of code are actually processed.) To help protect against run-time errors, you can include the VBScript error-handling mechanism On Error Resume Next in your scripts.

Without error handling, a script stops immediately upon encountering a run-time error. With error handling, a script does not stop but instead attempts to run the next line. The script proceeds by skipping the lines that generate errors and running lines that do not.

Using the Err Object

On Error Resume Next allows your script to continue to function should a run-time error occur. There are at least two potential problems with this, however. For one thing, no error message is generated to let you know that an error occurred, so you will have no way of knowing where the script failed.

For another, you might prefer that a script *not* attempt to run every single line in the event of a run-time error. For example, consider a script that does the following:

1. Connects to a remote computer.
2. Copies a set of files from the local computer to the remote computer.
3. Deletes the original set of files from the local computer.

Suppose you run this script and the remote computer is not available. Here is what could happen.

1. The script attempts to connect to the remote computer and fails. However, On Error Resume Next ensures that the script continues to run.

2. The script attempts to copy files to the remote computer. This fails because the remote computer is not accessible.

3. The script deletes the files from the local computer. Unfortunately, this succeeds because the local computer *is* available. As a result, the files are deleted from the local computer but are not copied to the remote computer.

Fortunately, you can use the intrinsic VBScript Err object to determine whether an error occurred and, if so, take the appropriate action.

The Err object is automatically created each time you run a script. (There is only one Err object per script instance.) The Err object includes several properties, including the three shown in Table 2.4. Whenever your script encounters a run-time error, these properties are automatically filled in with information that identifies the error.

Table 2.4   Err Object Properties

Property	Description
Description	Description of the error. This can be used to inform the user that an error has occurred simply by echoing the value: `Wscript.Echo Err.Description`
Number	Integer uniquely identifying the error that occurred. The number might represent an intrinsic VBScript error number, or it might represent an error number derived from an Automation object. To determine where the error number came from, use the Source property.
Source	Class name or programmatic identifier (ProgID) of the object that caused the error. If VBScript caused the error, you typically see "Microsoft VBScript runtime error" as the source. If an Automation object is responsible for the error, you see the ProgID (for example, "Word.Application").

When a script is started, VBScript assigns the default value 0 (no error) to the Number property. If the script encounters an error, the value of the Number property will change accordingly. This enables you to periodically check to see whether your script has encountered any errors. For example, you might want your script to check error status after it attempts to connect to a remote computer. If Err.Number equals 0 (zero), no error occurred. If Err.Number does not equal 0, an error of some kind has occurred, and you can assume that the attempt to connect to the remote computer failed. As a result, your script can take action based on the fact that the remote computer was unavailable.

This type of error handling is implemented in the script in Listing 2.14. In line 1 of the script, On Error Resume Next enables error handling. In line 10, the script sets up a For Each loop to cycle through a list of server names. In line 11, the script attempts to connect, in turn, to each of these servers.

But what happens if one of these servers is not accessible? In line 11, the script tries to connect to one of these remote servers. If the connection is successful, no error is generated, meaning that Err.Number will remain 0. If the connection fails, however, an error will be generated and Err.Number will be changed to reflect the number corresponding to that error.

If the connection attempt in line 11 fails, On Error Resume Next ensures that the script next tries to run line 12. In line 12, the script checks the value of Err.Number. If the value is anything but 0 (meaning that an error occurred), the script echoes Err.Description and then restarts the loop with the next server name. If the value is 0, this means that the connection succeeded. The script will then retrieve the free disk space on the computer in question.

Listing 2.14 Handling Errors

```
1    On Error Resume Next
2    Const CONVERSION_FACTOR = 1048576
3    Const WARNING_THRESHOLD = 100
4
5    If WScript.Arguments.Count = 0 Then
6        Wscript.Echo "Usage: FirstScript.vbs server1 [server2] [server3] ..."
7        WScript.Quit
8    End If
9
10   For Each Computer In WScript.Arguments
11       Set objWMIService = GetObject("winmgmts://" & Computer)
12       If Err.Number <> 0 Then
13           Wscript.Echo Computer & " " & Err.Description
14           Err.Clear
15       Else
16           Set colLogicalDisk = _
17               objWMIService.InstancesOf("Win32_LogicalDisk")
18           For Each objLogicalDisk In colLogicalDisk
19               FreeMegaBytes = objLogicalDisk.FreeSpace / CONVERSION_FACTOR
20               If FreeMegaBytes < WARNING_THRESHOLD Then
21                   Wscript.Echo Computer & " " & objLogicalDisk.DeviceID & _
22                       " is low on disk space."
23               End If
24           Next
25       End If
26   Next
```

If you run the script in Listing 2.14 and one of the servers is not accessible, the properties of the Err object will be populated as shown in Table 2.5.

Table 2.5   Values Assigned to Err Object Properties

Property	Value
Err.Description	The remote server machine does not exist or is unavailable
Err.Number	462
Err.Source	Microsoft VBScript run-time error

Clearing Errors

Line 14 of the script in Listing 2.14 uses the Clear method to explicitly reset the properties of the Err object. This is important, because otherwise these properties change only when a new error occurs. When no error occurs, the property values remain the same. This might cause your script to take inappropriate action based on the mistaken notion that another error has occurred.

Here is what can happen if you do not explicitly reset the properties of the Err object. When a script begins, the Err object has the default number 0 and empty source and description properties. If the script cannot connect to the computer atl-dc-01, the Err object properties are set as shown in Table 2.5.

This works as expected. However, what happens when the computer iterates through the loop and attempts to connect to atl-dc-02? In this case, the attempt succeeds, and no error is generated. However, the Err object still contains the property values shown in Table 2.5. Why? Because the Err object is not updated unless an error occurs. Next the script checks the error number and sees 462, the value left over from the failed attempt to connect to atl-dc-01. Because 462 is not equal to 0, the script takes action based on the incorrect assumption that an error occurred and atl-dc-02 must therefore be inaccessible. This same problem occurs when the script attempts to retrieve free disk space on atl-dc-03.

The Clear method overcomes this problem by resetting the properties of the Err object back to the default values. (Number is 0; source and description are empty.) Because the values have been reset, they will correctly reflect the fact that no error occurred when the script attempts to retrieve free disk space for atl-dc-02.

VBScript Reference

The first half of this chapter introduced you to basic concepts underlying VBScript and gave you an idea of the kinds of tasks that can be accomplished using VBScript, particularly when the language is used in conjunction with ADSI or WMI. The second half of the chapter is a more standard reference work, focusing on VBScript methods and functions considered the most useful to system administrators. This is not an exhaustive list of all the things you can do with VBScript; if you need such a list, see the VBScript link on the Web Resources page at http://www.microsoft.com/windows/reskits/webresources. Instead, this section of the chapter targets a subset of VBScript functions and methods and attempts to place them in a context useful to anyone writing system administration scripts.

Statement Breaks in VBScript

Many scripting and programming languages make no attempt to match the code that is run with the actual physical lines typed into the text editor. For example, although the following Microsoft® JScript® sample covers nine physical lines of type, JScript treats it as a single code statement. This is because, for the most part, JScript does not recognize the end of a line of code until it sees the termination character (in this case, the semicolon). The actual physical lines of type taken up by the code are irrelevant.

```
var
objWMI

=

new
Enumerator
(GetObject("winmgmts:")

.

InstancesOf("Win32_process"))

;
```

By contrast, a similar code statement written in VBScript will generate a syntax error:

```
Set
objWMI

=

(GetObject("winmgmts:")

.

InstancesOf("Win32_process"))
```

This is because VBScript uses the carriage return instead of a special line termination character. To end a statement in VBScript, you do not have to type in a semicolon or other special character; you simply press ENTER.

In general, the lack of a required statement termination character simplifies script writing in VBScript. There is, however, one complication: To enhance readability, it is recommended that you limit the length of any single line of code to 80 characters. (In fact, some text editors will not allow a line to extend past 80 characters.) What happens, then, if you have a line of code that contains 100 characters?

Although it might seem like the obvious solution, you cannot split a statement into multiple lines simply by entering a carriage return. For example, the following code snippet returns a run-time error in VBScript because a statement was split by using ENTER.

```
strMessageToDisplay = strUserFirstName, strUserMiddleInitial, strUserLastName,
strCurrentStatus
Wscript.Echo strMessageToDisplay
```

You cannot split a statement into multiple lines in VBScript by pressing ENTER because VBScript sees a carriage return as marking the end of a statement. In the preceding example, VBScript interprets the first line as the first statement in the script. Next it interprets the second line as the second statement in the script, and the error occurs because strCurrentStatus is not a valid VBScript command.

Instead, use the underscore (_) to indicate that a statement is continued on the next line. In the revised version of the script, a blank space and an underscore indicate that the statement that was started on line 1 is continued on line 2. To make it more apparent that line 2 is a continuation of line 1, line 2 is also indented four spaces. (This was done for the sake of readability, but you do not have to indent continued lines.)

```
strMessageToDisplay = strUserFirstName, strUserMiddleInitial, strUserLastName, _
    strCurrentStatus
Wscript.Echo strMessageToDisplay
```

Line continuation is more complex when you try to split a statement inside a set of quotation marks. For example, suppose you split a WMI statement using a blank space and an underscore:

```
Set colServiceList = GetObject("winmgmts:").ExecQuery("SELECT * FROM _
    Win32_Service WHERE State = 'Stopped' AND StartMode = 'Auto' ")
```

If you run this script, you will encounter a run-time error because the line continuation character has been placed inside a set of quotation marks (and is therefore considered part of the string). To split this statement:

1. Close the first line with quotation marks, and then insert the blank space and the underscore.

2. Use an ampersand at the beginning of the second line. This indicates that line two is a continuation of the interrupted string in line 1.

3. Add quotation marks before continuing the statement.

    These quotation marks indicate that this line should be included as part of the quoted string started on the previous line. Without the quotation marks, the script engine would interpret the continued line — Win32_Service — as a VBScript statement. Because this is not a valid VBScript statement, an error would occur.

The revised statement looks like this:

```
Set colServiceList = GetObject("winmgmts:").ExecQuery("SELECT * FROM " _
    & "Win32_Service WHERE State = 'Stopped' AND StartMode = 'Auto' ")
```

When splitting statements in this fashion, be careful to insert spaces in the proper location. In the preceding sample, a blank space was added after the word "FROM" and before the closing quotation marks. If the blank space is left out, the string is interpreted incorrectly (notice how the words "FROM" and "Win32_Service" run together), and an error results:

```
"SELECT * FROMWin32_Service WHERE State = 'Stopped' AND StartMode = 'Auto' "
```

Working with Variables

Variables are named locations within computer memory that can be used to store data. Most scripting languages allow implicit declaration of variables, enabling you to use a variable without formally declaring your intention to use that variable. For example, you can run the following script without encountering an error of any kind, even though the first line in the script assigns a value to the variable sngDegreesCelsius. Even though this variable has not been declared (meaning that VBScript has not been informed of its existence), the value 11 is assigned to the variable.

```
sngDegreesCelsius = 11
sngDegreesFahrenheit = ConvertToFahrenheit(sngDegreesCelsius)
Wscript.Echo sngDegreesFahrenheit

Function ConvertToFahrenheit(ByVal sngDegreesCelsius)
    ConvertToFahrenheit = (sngDegreesCelsius * (9/5)) + 32
End Function
```

Implicit variable declaration can make writing scripts faster and easier; at the same time, however, it can lead to subtle errors that are difficult to diagnose and fix.

To illustrate, the previous script converts 11° Celsius to Fahrenheit (51.8°). The following script should do the same thing, but it echoes the value 32 instead.

```
sngDegreesCelsius = 11
sngDegreesFahrenheit = ConvertToFahrenheit(sngDegreesCelsius)
Wscript.Echo sngDegreesFahrenheit

Function ConvertToFahrenheit(ByVal sngDegreesCelsius)
    ConvertToFahrenheit = (sngDegresCelsius * (9/5)) + 32
End Function
```

The preceding script provides an incorrect answer because of a typographical error. Instead of typing **sngDegreesCelsius** in line 6, the script writer typed **sngDegresCelsius**, leaving out one of the two e's in Degrees. As a result, the equation uses the value of sngDegresCelsius instead of sngDegreesCelsius. Because sngDegresCelsius has never been assigned a value, it is treated as an Empty variable with the value 0. Consequently, 0 is multiplied by 9/5, resulting in 0. The script then adds 32 to that 0 and returns an incorrect answer.

Mistakes like this can be difficult to catch. The syntax is correct, so no error message will be generated. You expected to get a numeric value other than 11, and you got one. When embedded inside a much larger script, this typographical error can be very difficult to find and correct.

Declaring Variables in VBScript

To help avoid problems like this, you can explicitly declare all your variables. When explicit variable declaration is in effect, any variables that are not specifically declared in the script will result in a run-time error.

For example, in the following script the explicit declaration of variables is forced by the use of the VBScript Option Explicit statement, and each variable is then declared using a Dim statement:

```
Option Explicit
Dim sngDegreesCelsius
Dim sngDegreesFahrenehit

sngDegreesCelsius = 11
sngDegreesFahrenheit = ConvertToFahrenheit(sngDegreesCelsius)
Wscript.Echo sngDegreesFahrenheit

Function ConvertToFahrenheit(ByVal sngDegreesCelsius)
    ConvertToFahrenheit = (sngDegresCelsius * (9/5)) + 32
End Function
```

When the preceding script runs, the scripting host encounters an undeclared variable. As a result, the script halts execution and displays an error message similar to this:

```
C:\Scripts\TempConvert.vbs(10, 5) Microsoft VBScript runtime error: Variable is
undefined:
'sngDegresCelsius'
```

To declare variables in VBScript:

1. Use the **Option Explicit** statement to force variables to be declared. This must be the first noncommented, non-white-space line in the script.

2. Use a separate **Dim** statement to declare each variable used in your script. Although you can declare multiple variables with a single Dim statement, limiting each statement to a single variable declaration allows you to add a brief inline comment that explains the purpose of the variable, as shown in the following sample:

```
Option Explicit
Dim intFirstNumber        ' First number in our simple equation
Dim intSecondNumber       ' Second number in our simple equation
Dim intTotal              ' Sum of intFirstNumber and intSecondNumber
```

Initializing Variables

Initializing a variable simply means assigning a beginning (initial) value to that variable. For example, the following lines of code initialize two variables, setting the value of X to 100 and the value of Y to *abcde*:

```
X = 100
Y = "abcde"
```

If you create a variable but do not initialize it (that is, you do not assign it a value), the variable will take on one of two default values:

- If the variable is used as a string, the value will be *Empty*.
- If the variable is used as a number, the value will be 0.

For example, the following script creates two variables (X and Y), but does not initialize either variable:

```
Dim X
Dim Y
Wscript.Echo X & Y
Wscript.Echo X + Y
```

In line 3 of the script, the two variables are used as strings. (The & operator is used to combine two strings.) When this line runs, the message box shown in Figure 2.8 appears. Because the two variables are Empty, combining the two strings means combining nothing with nothing. As a result, the message box displays an empty string.

Figure 2.8 Combining Two Uninitialized Variables

In line 4 of the script, the two variables are used as numbers. Numeric variables that have not been initialized are automatically assigned the value 0. Thus, this line of the script echoes the sum of 0 + 0, as shown in Figure 2.9.

Figure 2.9   Adding Two Uninitialized Variables

Using the Equals Sign in VBScript

In VBScript, the equals sign (=) has a subtly different meaning than it does in arithmetic. In arithmetic, the equation X = 2 + 2 is read:

"X equals 2 plus 2."

In VBScript, however, this same statement is read:

"X is assigned the value of 2 plus 2."

In the preceding example, there is not much difference; either way, X gets assigned the value 4. But consider the following script, which uses a loop to count from 1 to 10:

```
For i = 1 to 10
    X = X + 1
Next
```

The second line in this script would appear to be a mathematical impossibility: How can X be equal to X plus 1? The reason why this is a perfectly valid VBScript statement is that it is not an example of a mathematical equation but is instead an example of a variable (X) being assigned a new value. The statement is actually read:

"X is assigned the current value of X plus 1."

In other words, if X is currently 3, when this statement runs X will be assigned the value 4, that is, 3 (the current value) plus 1.

The fact that the equals sign is actually an *assignment* sign is also useful in constructing strings. For example, the following script constructs a message from multiple string values:

```
Message = "This "
Message = Message & "is a "
Message = Message & "test message."
Wscript.Echo Message
```

When the script runs, the message box shown in Figure 2.10 appears.

Figure 2.10   Concatenated Message

Using Constants

Constants represent values that cannot change while a script is running. For example, suppose you have a script that converts Japanese yen to U.S. dollars. Assuming the current exchange rate is 1 yen for every 0.00888759 dollars, you can hard-code the literal value into the script, like the following:

```
curConvertedPrice = curPriceInYen * 0.00888759
```

Although this approach works, it does pose some potential problems:

- Another administrator editing your script might not understand what 0.00888759 represents.

- Exchange rates change frequently. By using the literal value, you must search the script for each occurrence of the literal value and then change this value every time the exchange rate changes. If you overlook one such occurrence, your script will no longer provide accurate information.

- Every time you type a literal value, you risk making a mistake that can affect your calculations. For example, inadvertently typing 0.0888759 will drastically affect the equation. One thousand yen converted using the correct rate of 0.00888759 is a little less than $9. The same thousand yen converted using the incorrect rate of 0.0888759 is approximately $89.

To help overcome these problems, use constants rather than literal values. Constants have a number of advantages over literal values. Constants:

- Can be given meaningful names. Rather than use a cryptic value such as 0.00888759, you can use a meaningful name such as YEN_TO_DOLLARS_EXCHANGE_RATE.

- Are easy to modify. If the exchange rate changes, you have to modify only the single statement where the value of the constant is defined.

- Are less prone to typing mistakes because the value (which might be something along the lines of 0.00888759) has to be entered only once. In addition, constants must be predefined the same way variables are predeclared. If you use the Option Explicit statement in VBScript, any mistyped constant name will generate an error.

- Cannot be changed, inadvertently or otherwise. After a constant has been defined, any attempt by the script to change its value will generate an error.

- Are useful for string values as well as for numeric values. For example, suppose you have a standard message that is repeatedly echoed to users when a script runs. Rather than type the message multiple times, define it once as a constant. If you need to change the message, you need to change it only in one location.

Defining Constants

Constants are defined in VBScript by using the Const statement followed by the name and value of the constant. When you define a constant, you must assign it a literal value; you cannot assign a value to a constant by using a variable, another constant, or a function. For example, the following code sample, which attempts to define a constant using the variable NumberOfDepartments, will generate an "Expected literal constant" error:

```
NumberOfDepartments = 20
Const NUMBER_OF_DEPARTMENTS = NumberOfDepartments
```

Instead, assign the constant the literal value 20:

```
Const NUMBER_OF_DEPARTMENTS = 20
```

Using Intrinsic Constants

VBScript includes a number of intrinsic constants that can be used to construct message boxes, format output, or carry out other activities. To improve the readability of your scripts, you might want to use these intrinsic constants rather than their numeric equivalents.

For example, the following script sample uses a pair of numeric values to display a message box and then determine which button in that message box was clicked. Although the script works, anyone not familiar with VBScript values would have difficulty reading and editing the script. They must know that 260 means, "Create a message box with a **Yes** button and a **No** button, with the second button being the default button," and that the number 7 means, "The user clicked the **No** button."

```
ConfirmDelete = MsgBox ("Are you sure you want to delete these files?", _
    260, "Delete all files")
If ConfirmDelete = 7 then
    Wscript.Quit
End If
```

The following revised version of this script uses VBScript intrinsic constants (VbYesNo, VBDefaultButton2, and VbNo) instead of literal values. This makes the script easier to read and understand.

```
ConfirmDelete = MsgBox ("Are you sure you want to delete these files?", _
    VbYesNo OR VBDefaultButton2, "Delete all files")
If ConfirmDelete = VbNo then
    Wscript.Quit
End If
```

Using intrinsic constants also helps prevent your scripts from breaking each time the scripting language is updated. The VBScript constants are unlikely to change; there is little chance that the constant VbYesNo will be changed to something like VbNoYes. However, the *value* of those constants can conceivably change the next time VBScript is updated. Using constants can also make it easier to migrate scripts to another language should the need arise. For example, VBScript uses the value –1 to represent True. In Visual Basic .NET, however, True equals 1. It will be much easier to convert a script that uses the constant True than a script that uses the hard-coded value –1.

Most likely you will repeatedly find yourself using two intrinsic constants:

- **VbCrLf**. This is equivalent to pressing the ENTER key and is typically used to format output for display. For example, this statement creates a message that displays a line of text, a blank line, and then a second line of text:

```
Wscript.Echo "This is the first line of text." & VbCrLF & VbCrLF & _
    "This is the second line of text."
```

When the preceding script is run using Wscript, a message box similar to the one shown in Figure 2.11 is displayed.

Figure 2. 11   Messages Separated by Using VbCrLf

- **VbTab**. This is equivalent to pressing the TAB key. For example, this statement creates three tab-separated columns:

```
Wscript.Echo " 1" & VbTab & " 2" & VbTab & " 3"
Wscript.Echo "A" & VbTab & "B" & VbTab & "C"
Wscript.Echo "D" & VbTab & "E" & VbTab & "F"
```

When the preceding script runs under Cscript, the following output appears in the command window:

```
1        2        3
A        B        C
D        E        F
```

Scripts written in VBScript have access only to the intrinsic constants defined in VBScript, and do not have native access to the intrinsic constants found in WMI, ADSI, the Script Runtime library, or other external Automation objects. When you write scripts using VBScript, you can use intrinsic VBScript constants such as VbCrLf or VbYesNo without defining those constants. However, to use intrinsic WMI or ADSI constants, you must explicitly define the value of those constants.

For example, the Script Runtime Drive object includes the intrinsic constant Fixed to indicate a fixed disk drive. Automation languages that have access to the Script Runtime constants can use Fixed without explicitly defining a value for it.

Because VBScript does not have access to this constant, any attempt to use this constant without first defining it will cause the script either to fail or to provide inaccurate information. For example, the following script will run, but it will not identify any fixed disks on your computer:

```
Set objFSO = CreateObject("Scripting.FileSystemObject")
Set colDiskDrives = objFSO.Drives
For Each objDiskDrive in colDiskDrives
    If objDiskDrive.DriveType = Fixed then
        Wscript.Echo objDiskDrive.DriveLetter
    End if
Next
```

The script fails because VBScript does not know that Fixed is a constant that has the value 2. Instead of treating Fixed as a constant, VBScript treats Fixed as a variable. Until you assign a value to a variable, that variable is Empty. In this example, then, VBScript looks for disk drives where the DriveType property is equal to 0 rather than equal to 2. Because VBScript cannot find any drives with this property, the script does not return any data.

To make this script work, you must create your own constant named Fixed and explicitly assign it the value 2. This is shown in the following example:

```
Const Fixed = 2
Set objFSO = CreateObject("Scripting.FileSystemObject")
Set colDiskDrives = objFSO.Drives
For Each objDiskDrive in colDiskDrives
    If objDiskDrive.DriveType = Fixed then
        Wscript.Echo objDiskDrive.DriveLetter
    End if
Next
```

VBScript Data Types

VBScript is a *typeless* language. This means that variables cannot be restricted to a single data type. VBScript does not allow you to specify in advance that a particular variable can hold only a particular kind of data. Instead, VBScript uses a single kind of variable, known as a *variant*, which can store any kind of data.

By contrast, a programming language such as C++ is considered strongly typed because you must specify in advance the type of data that can be stored in a variable. Your code will generate an error if you attempt to store any other kind of data in that variable. If you specify that a variable can only contain numeric data, the program will crash if you try to store alphabetic data in that variable.

Variants can make writing scripts easier; you can declare and use variables without considering the type of data being stored in them. However, variants can introduce a new set of problems into a script if you do not understand the process of type coercion.

Working with Type Coercion

Scripting languages appear typeless only to the script writer. Internally, scripting languages must still work with data types. For example, when presented with a simple statement such as `c = a + b`, the scripting language must derive typed values for both a and b. In other words, it must take those two variants and create typed values such as integer or string. After it has derived the typed values, the scripting language can then perform the operation.

The process of deriving typed values is known as *type coercion* because the variant value is "coerced" into temporarily storing a new, typed, value. Type coercion is based on specific rules about how and when to coerce variants into different data types, and, for the most part, VBScript handles type conversions without any problem.

However, type coercion can lead to trouble, as shown in the following:

```
intFirstNumber = InputBox("Please enter the first number:")
intSecondNumber = InputBox("Please enter the second number:")
intTotal = intFirstNumber + intSecondNumber
Wscript.Echo intTotal
```

If you run the script and enter 4 as the first number and 2 as the second number, the computer echoes back "42" as the answer to 4 + 2, rather than the expected answer of 6.

This is because the addition operator is valid both for numbers and for strings. VBScript is given two values (4 and 2), with no way to know which data type these values represent. With no other information available, VBScript uses type coercion to convert the two variables to string data.

By contrast, the following script snippet returns the correct value (2) if you enter the numbers 4 and 2. This is because the division operator works only with numbers, so VBScript uses type coercion to correctly convert the two values to numeric data.

```
intFirstNumber = InputBox("Please enter the first number:")
intSecondNumber = InputBox("Please enter the second number:")
intTotal = intFirstNumber / intSecondNumber
Wscript.Echo intTotal
```

To avoid the problems that can occur with type coercion, explicitly declare data types when performing operations, a process referred to as *casting type values*. For example, the following script uses the VBScript function CInt (convert to integer) to convert the input variables to integers before adding them:

```
intFirstNumber = CInt(InputBox("Please enter the first number:"))
intSecondNumber = CInt(InputBox("Please enter the second number:"))
intTotal = intFirstNumber + intSecondNumber
Wscript.Echo intTotal
```

Table 2.6 lists the type conversion functions used in VBScript.

Table 2.6   VBScript Type Conversion Functions

Function	Description
CBool	Converts any nonzero value to True and 0 (zero) to False.
CByte	Converts an expression to a Byte value.
CCur	Converts an expression to a Currency value.
CDate	Converts an expression to a Date value.
CDbl	Converts an expression to a Double value.
CInt	Converts an expression to an Integer value. If the fractional part of the expression is .5, CInt will round the value to the nearest even number. For example, 3.5 will be rounded to 4, and 6.5 will be rounded to 6.
CLng	Converts an expression to a Long value.
CSng	Converts an expression to a Single value.
CStr	Converts an expression to a String value.

Working with Empty Variables and Null Variables

Understanding the difference between an Empty variable and a Null variable can make an equally big difference in the success or failure of your scripts. An Empty variable is a variable that has not been initialized. For example, in a statement such as `Dim curBonus`, the variable is considered "empty" until you set curBonus equal to a value. An Empty variable is coerced into having the value 0 when used as a number and coerced into having the value "" (zero-length text string) when used as a string.

By contrast, a Null variable is a variable that has not had a valid value assigned to it. Typically, Null variables are derived from database operations. Suppose you query a database, retrieve the current bonus field for a particular employee, and assign that value to the variable curBonus. If no bonus has been assigned, the value of curBonus will be Null. Note that while curBonus *could* be 0, you do not know for sure if it *is* 0. You cannot assume that the value is 0; in this case, the user might actually have a $5,000 bonus, but this value has not been entered into the database yet. This is why VBScript draws a distinction between Empty variables and Null variables.

The difference between an Empty variable and a Null variable is apparent when doing mathematical operations. For example, in the following script snippet, the value of curBonus is set to Empty, and then curBonus is added to curBaseSalary (50,000). The net result: 50,000 + 0 = 50,000.

```
curBonus = Empty
curBaseSalary = 50000
curTotalCompensation = curBaseSalary + curBonus
Wscript.Echo TotalCompensation
```

In the revised version of this script, the same operation is performed, this time setting curBonus to Null. When you run the calculation, however, you do not get 50,000 (that is, 50,000 + 0). Instead, the answer is null. Anytime a Null variable is used in a mathematical equation, the end result is always null. This is because you do not know the actual value of a Null variable. You cannot substitute 0 because you do not know whether the value of that variable really is 0. Because you do not know the value, you do not know what the result would be if you used that value in a calculation. Thus, the answer has to be Null. (Think of Null as meaning, "I do not know.")

```
curBonus = Null
curBaseSalary = 50000
curTotalCompensation = curBaseSalary + curBonus
Wscript.Echo TotalCompensation
```

Null values can be a problem when working with databases and when using ADSI to retrieve data from Active Directory. Fortunately, you can use the IsNull method to ensure that a variable is not Null. For example, the following script checks the value of the variable curBonus. If curBonus is Null, the value 0 is explicitly assigned to the variable. This allows the variable to be used in the calculation. Alternatively, you can choose not to perform the calculation but instead echo a message like, "No bonus information available for this employee."

```
curBonus = Null
curBaseSalary = 50000
If IsNull(curBonus) Then
    CurBonus = 0
End If
curTotalCompensation = curBaseSalary + curBonus
Wscript.Echo curTotalCompensation
```

Working with Dates and Times

Dates and times play important roles in system administration. For example, when working with event logs you will often want to extract a set of records based on a specific time period (all the events that occurred yesterday, all the events that occurred last week, all the events that occurred last month). To determine such things as service reliability, you need to take the date and time a service started and the date and time the service stopped, and then use the difference to calculate the service uptime. To ensure that your scripts are running as scheduled, you need to log the date and time that a script ran and the date and time that it finished. It is difficult to underestimate the importance of dates and times in managing your computing infrastructure.

VBScript provides several different ways for you to retrieve date and time values. It also provides several methods for performing date arithmetic — that is, calculating such things as the amount of time that elapsed between two events or determining whether the date 180 days from today falls on a weekend.

 Note

The date and time formats used in VBScript are very different from the date and time formats used in WMI. For information about the WMI date and time formats and how they can be converted to the VBScript format, see "WMI Scripting Primer" in this book.

Retrieving Current Date and Time Values

The ability to determine the current date or the current time is a useful task in system administration scripting. Many scripts, including those that write to log files or those that write to databases, need to include the current date or time as part of the data written. Scripts that need to take action on specific days or at specific times need to be able to determine the current date and time. Scripts designed to work with a range of dates (for example, retrieve all the error events written to the event log in the past two weeks) need to be able to identify the current date or time to use as a starting point.

VBScript includes three functions that can be used to identify the current date, the current time or both:

- **Now** — retrieves both the date and the time.

- **Date** — retrieves the current date.

- **Time** — returns the current time.

For example, the following script retrieves date and time information by using Now, Date, and Time and then displays the results of all the functions in a single message box:

```
DateInfo = DateInfo & Now & VbCrLf
DateInfo = DateInfo & Date & VbCrLf
DateInfo = DateInfo & Time & VbCrLf
Wscript.Echo DateInfo
```

When the preceding script runs, a message box similar to the one shown in Figure 2.12 appears.

Figure 2.12   Date and Time Information by Using Now, Date, and Time Functions

Verifying That a Value Is a Date

In working with dates, it is important to know whether a particular value is actually a date or not. This is especially true when making WMI queries or when working with databases; your script will fail if it attempts to use an invalid date in these situations.

The IsDate function can tell you whether a supplied value is a date. IsDate returns False (0) if the value is not a date and True (−1) if the value is a date. Date values can be passed using either of the following:

- **Date literals**. These are date values enclosed within pound signs (#). This is the recommended way of using dates in scripts because it eliminates the possibility that VBScript will misinterpret the value as being something other than a date. A date literal might look like this:

    `#9/3/2002#`

- **Date and time formats recognized by your system settings**. For example, if your system is set for English (United States), these values are recognized as valid dates:

    - 6/6/2002

    - 6,1,2002

    - 6-1-2002

    However, this value is not recognized as a valid date:

    - 6.1.2002

    If you change your settings to German (Austria), all four values are recognized as dates.

 Note

To check valid date formats for your computer, open the Regional and Language Options control panel, click **Customize**, and then click **Date**.

The following script creates an array of values and then enumerates each item in the array. The script then uses IsDate to determine whether the item represents a valid date and echoes the value and a message indicating that this is actually a date.

```
DateArray = Array("6/1/2002", "June 1, 2002",  "6", "6/1")
For Each dtmDate in DateArray
    If IsDate(dtmDate) = 0 Then
        Wscript.Echo dtmDate & " is not a valid date."
    Else
        Wscript.Echo dtmDate & " is a valid date."
    End If
Next
```

When the preceding script runs under CScript, the following information appears in the command window:

```
6/1/2002 is a valid date.
June 1, 2002 is a valid date.
6 is not a valid date.
6/1 is a valid date.
```

 Note

> Why is 6/1 a valid date? When using the IsDate function, VBScript tries to construct a plausible date from the value given to it. When it sees a statement that can be interpreted as Month/Day, it automatically appends the current year, resulting in Month/Day/Year. In the preceding script, which was run in the year 2002, that means a value of 6/1/2002, which is a valid date.

Retrieving Specific Portions of a Date and Time Value

Often times you are interested in only a portion of a date or time. For example, you might have a backup script that performs a full backup on Sundays and a partial backup every other day of the week. Likewise, you might have a script that retrieves event log events every day, but on the 15th and 30th of each month also clears the event log.

VBScript provides two ways to retrieve specific portions of a date or time. The DatePart function is a generic function that can retrieve any portion of a date or time value. In addition, VBScript also includes several functions, such as Day, Month, and Year, that allow you to retrieve a specific part of a date or time.

The DatePart function can be used to return a specific part of a date or time value. This function requires two items: the date to be parsed and one of the parameters shown in Table 2.7.

Table 2.7   DatePart Parameters

Parameter	Description
yyyy	Year. Returns the year from the date-time value.
q	Quarter. Returns the quarter — 1, 2, 3, or 4 — from the date-time value.
m	Month. Returns the month of the year using the following values: 1 — January 2 — February 3 — March 4 — April 5 — May 6 — June 7 — July 8 — August 9 — September 10 — October 11 — November 12 — December
y	Day of Year. Returns the day number, with January 1 being 1 and December 31 being 365 (366 during leap years). For example, February 1 returns 32 because it is the 32nd day of the year.
d	Day. Returns the day of the month. For example, both April 17 and August 17 return 17.
w	Weekday. Returns the day of the week using the following values: 1 — Sunday 2 — Monday 3 — Tuesday 4 — Wednesday 5 — Thursday 6 — Friday 7 — Saturday You can specify that the day of the week start on a day other than Sunday. For more information, see "Retrieving Specific Portions of a Date and Time Value " later in this chapter.
ww	Week of Year. Returns the week number, with the week of January 1 typically being week 1 and the week of December 31 being week 52. However, you have several options for specifying which is the first week in the year. These options, in turn, affect the other week numbers. For details, see "Retrieving Specific Portions of a Date and Time Value " later in this chapter.
h	Hour. Returns the hour from the date-time value using 24-hour format. For example, 2:00 P.M. is returned as 14, and 6:00 P.M. is returned as 18. Times between midnight and 1:00 A.M. are returned as 0. Midnight (12:00 A.M.) is also returned as 0.
n	Minute. Returns the minutes from the date-time value.
s	Second. Returns the seconds from the date-time value.

To use the DatePart function, you can create a variable and assign it the DatePart value. For example, the following line of code extracts the year from the current date and assigns it to the variable CurrentYear:

```
CurrentYear = DatePart("yyyy", Date)
```

In the preceding example, the two parameters are:

- **"yyyy"** — Indicates that the year should be returned from the specified date. This parameter must be enclosed in quotation marks.

- **Date** — Indicates that the date to be parsed should be the current date. You can also enclose a valid date within quotation marks (for example, "6/1/2002") or use a variable that has been assigned a date. For example, these two lines of code return the value 1977:

```
DateToCheck = #8/15/1977#
CurrentYear = DatePart("yyyy" , DateToCheck)
```

> **Note**
> When assigning a date to a variable, enclose the date using date literals (#).
> This ensures that VBScript views the value as a date, and not as a number
> or string. Alternatively, you can use the CDate function.

The script shown in Listing 2.15 parses the current date and time, and then displays each date time component.

Listing 2.15   Using the DatePart Function

```
1   Wscript.Echo Now
2   Wscript.Echo "Year: " & DatePart("yyyy" , Now)
3   Wscript.Echo "Quarter: " & DatePart("q", Now)
4   Wscript.Echo "Month: " & DatePart("m" , Now)
5   Wscript.Echo "Day of Year: " & DatePart("y" , Now)
6   Wscript.Echo "Day: " & DatePart("d" , Now)
7   Wscript.Echo "Weekday: " & DatePart("w" , Now)
8   Wscript.Echo "Week of Year: " & DatePart("ww" , Now)
9   Wscript.Echo "Hour: " & DatePart("h", Now)
10  Wscript.Echo "Minute: " & DatePart("n" , Now)
11  Wscript.Echo "Seconds: " & DatePart("s" , Now)
```

When the preceding script was run on January 17, 2002, at 11:40:27 A.M., the following output was returned:

```
1/17/2002 11:40:27 AM
Year: 2002
Quarter: 1
Month: 1
Day of Year: 17
Day: 17
Weekday: 5
Week of Year: 3
Hour: 11
Minute: 40
Seconds: 27
```

No error will be generated if you pass incomplete data to DatePart, but you might not get the expected results. For example, this line of code returns the value 1899:

```
Wscript.Echo DatePart("yyyy", "8:00 AM")
```

This line of code returns 0:

```
Wscript.Echo DatePart("h", "12/1/2002")
```

Configuring DatePart Options

By default, VBScript considers the first week of the year to be the week in which January 1 occurs. However, the DatePart function includes an optional parameter that can be used to set the first week of the year to one of the values shown in Table 2.8.

Table 2.8   Parameters for Setting the First Week of the Year

Constant	Value	Description
vbUseSystem	0	Uses the National Language Support API to determine the first full week based on the regional and language settings.
vbFirstJan1	1	Sets the first week as the week in which January 1 occurs.
vbFirstFourDays	2	Sets the first week as the first week to have at least four days in it.
VbFirstFullWeek	3	Sets the first week as the first week that begins on a Sunday.

To use this parameter, call the DatePart function followed by the "ww" parameter, the date for which the week number is being determined, and the appropriate constant. The following script shows how the different constants can affect the week number assigned to a particular date.

```
TestDate = "1/6/2003"
Wscript.Echo ProjectedDate
Wscript.Echo "Week of Year: " & DatePart("ww" , TestDate)
Wscript.Echo "Week of Year: " & DatePart("ww" , TestDate, vbFirstJan1)
Wscript.Echo "Week of Year: " & DatePart("ww" , TestDate, vbFirstFourDays)
Wscript.Echo "Week of Year: " & DatePart("ww" , TestDate, vbFirstFullWeek)
```

When the preceding script runs under CScript, the following output appears in the command window:

```
1/6/2003
Week of Year: 2
Week of Year: 2
Week of Year: 2
Week of Year: 1
```

As shown in Figure 2.13, January 6, 2003, does not fall in the same week as January 1, nor does it fall in the first week to have four days. However, it does fall during the first week to start with a Sunday.

Figure 2.13   January 6, 2003

Other Functions for Retrieving Portions of a Date

In addition to the DatePart function, the functions shown in Table 2.9 can also retrieve portions of a date-time value. DatePart can retrieve values such as day of the year and week of the year that cannot be retrieved any other way. However, DatePart does have parameters, such as "n" for minute, that are difficult to remember and can make your code harder to read and maintain than the stand-alone equivalent. For example, although these two lines of code return the same value (the minute), the second line leaves little doubt as to its purpose:

```
Wscript.Echo DatePart("n", Now)
Wscript.Echo Minute(Now)
```

Table 2.9 Functions for Retrieving Portions of a Date

Function	Description
Day	Returns the day for the specified date-time value.
Hour	Returns the hour for the specified date-time value.
Minute	Returns the minute for the specified date-time value.
Month	Returns the month for the specified date-time value.
Second	Returns the second for the specified date-time value.
Weekday	Returns the day of the week for the specified date-time value. Return values are: 1 — Sunday 2 — Monday 3 — Tuesday 4 — Wednesday 5 — Thursday 6 — Friday 7 — Saturday
Year	Returns the year for the specified date-time value.

To use one of the stand-alone functions, simply call the function, passing the appropriate date-time value as the sole parameter. For example, the following code passes the current date and time to each stand-alone date function:

```
CurrentDate = Now
Wscript.Echo "Year: " & VbTab & VbTab & Year(CurrentDate)
Wscript.Echo "Month: " & VbTab & VbTab & Month(CurrentDate)
Wscript.Echo "Day: " & VbTab & VbTab & Day(CurrentDate)
Wscript.Echo "Weekday: " & VbTab & Weekday(CurrentDate)
Wscript.Echo "Hour: " & VbTab & VbTab & Hour(CurrentDate)
Wscript.Echo "Minute: " & VbTab & Minute(CurrentDate)
Wscript.Echo "Second: " & VbTab & Second(CurrentDate)
```

When the preceding script is run using CScript, the following output appears in the command window:

```
Year:       2002
Month:      1
Day:        31
Weekday:    5
Hour:       14
Minute:     20
Second:     41
```

Date Arithmetic

Individual dates are an important consideration is system administration. Equally important, however, are ranges of dates and intervals between dates. In system administration, you will often need to make projections based on a specified date and a specified interval. For example, you might need to know which date is 180 days from today. Alternatively, you might have two dates or times and need to calculate the difference between them. If a service started on February 1, 2002, at 6:00 A.M. and then shut down on July 17, 2002, at 3:30 P.M., you might want to calculate how long the service ran before stopping.

VBScript provides two functions, DateDiff and DateAdd, which enable you to perform date arithmetic.

Determining the Interval Between Two Dates or Times

Calculating the amount of time that elapsed between two events is a common system administration task. For example, using WMI, you can determine the date and time that a computer started. By subtracting that value from the current date and time, you can calculate the system uptime, the amount of time the computer has been running since its last reboot.

The DateDiff function is used to calculate time intervals such as this. DateDiff requires three parameters:

- The date or time interval (for example, the number of days between two events or the number of hours between two events). DateDiff accepts the same date parameters as DatePart. These parameters are shown in Table 2.9.

- The date of the first event.

- The date of the second event.

For example, the script shown in Listing 2.16 calculates the number of days between the current date and July 1, 2002. To calculate a different interval, simply substitute the appropriate parameter. For example, to calculate the number of weeks between the two dates, replace the "d" parameter with the "w" parameter.

Listing 2.16   Determining Time Intervals

```
1  Wscript.Echo "Date: " & Date
2  Wscript.Echo "Days Until July 1: " & DateDiff("d", Date, "7/1/2002")
```

When the script is run using Cscript, the following output is returned:

```
Date: 1/8/2002
Days Until July 1: 174
```

 Note

Depending on the dates you use, you might get a negative number. For example, the difference between January 18, 2002, and July 1, 2002, is 164 days. If you reverse the order of the two dates, however, DateDiff will return the value –164. If you do not want negative values, you can use Abs, the VBScript absolute value function: Abs(DateDiff("d", "7/1/2002", "1/18/2002"). The absolute value function always returns a positive (unsigned) value.

With DateDiff, you might get different results depending on whether you use the "w" or the "ww" parameter. The "w" parameter calculates the number of weeks between the two dates, based on the day of the week when the first date occurs. For example, January 18, 2002, occurred on a Friday. With the "w" parameter, DateDiff calculates the number of Fridays between the two dates, not counting the initial Friday. For the interval January 18, 2002, to July 1, 2002, the "w" parameter counts 23 weeks.

The "ww" parameter, however, counts the number of Sundays between the two dates, again not counting the initial date. In this case, there are 24 Sundays between the two dates, meaning that the "w" and "ww" parameters return different values.

 Note

You might also get unexpected results when calculating the number of years between events. For example, the time between December 31, 2001, and January 1, 2002, is 1 day. However, because it covers two different years, DateDiff will tell you that there is 1 year between the two days. Because of that, you might want to return the number of days between two events and then divide by 365 to determine the number of years between the two.

DateDiff is also a useful tool for monitoring how long it takes for your scripts to run. To time the running of a script, set a variable to Now before the script runs any code. This variable will thus hold the time that the script started. At the end of the script, subtract this value from Now, and echo the results.

For example, the following script tracks how long it takes to retrieve and display the free disk space for all the disk drives on the local computer.

```
Start = Now
Set objWMIService = GetObject("winmgmts://")
Set colLogicalDisk = objWMIService.InstancesOf("Win32_LogicalDisk")
For Each objLogicalDisk In colLogicalDisk
    Wscript.Echo objLogicalDisk.DeviceID & " " & objLogicalDisk.FreeSpace
Next
Wscript.Echo DateDiff("s", Start, Now)
```

Projecting Dates Based on a Specified Time Interval

DateDiff can tell you the interval between two dates; however, there will be times when you *know* the interval but need to calculate either the starting date or the end date. For example, suppose you want to retrieve all the event log events that were recorded in the past 45 days. You know the interval: 45 days. You also know the end date: today. What you do not know is the beginning date.

The DateAdd function projects a date forward or backward from a specified starting point; in a sense, it is almost the reverse of the DateDiff function. With DateAdd, you specify the following three parameters:

- The time interval (again using the values shown in Table 2.9). For example, to calculate 180 days from today, use the "d" parameter.

- The time value (for example, 180 to indicate 180 days). To work backward from the starting date (for example, to determine the date 45 days ago), use a negative number. To project forward in time, use a positive number.

- The starting date.

For example, the script shown in Listing 2.17 calculates the date that falls 180 days from the current date.

Listing 2.17   Projecting Dates

```
1  Wscript.Echo "Date: " & Date
2  Wscript.Echo "180 Days From Today: " & DateAdd("d", 180, Date)
```

When the script shown in Listing 2.17 was run on January 8, 2002, the following output was returned:

```
Date: 1/8/2002
180 Days From Today: 7/7/2002
```

Formatting Date and Time Values

By default, VBScript displays the output of the Now, Date, and Time functions using the same date-time settings used by the operating system. For computers running the American English version of Windows, output will look similar to that shown in Table 2.10.

Table 2.10   Default Date-Time Output

Function	Sample Output
Now	6/30/02 9:01:47 PM
Date	6/30/02
Time	9:01:47 PM

However, you are not limited to these default formats. Instead, VBScript includes several constants (shown in Table 2.11) that can be used along with the FormatDateTime function to display date-time values in alternate ways.

Table 2.11   FormatDateTime Settings

Constant	Value
vbGeneralDate	0
vbLongDate	1
vbShortDate	2
vbLongTime	3
vbShortTime	4

The following script displays the current date and time using each of the date-formatting constants:

```
CurrentDate = Now
Wscript.Echo "General date: " & FormatDateTime(CurrentDate, vbGeneralDate)
Wscript.Echo "Long date: " & FormatDateTime(CurrentDate, vbLongDate)
Wscript.Echo "Short date: " & FormatDateTime(CurrentDate, vbShortDate)
Wscript.Echo "Long time: " & FormatDateTime(CurrentDate, vbLongTime)
Wscript.Echo "Short time: " & FormatDateTime(CurrentDate, vbShortTime)
```

When the preceding script runs under CScript, the following output appears in the command window:

```
General date: 1/31/2002 3:29:37 PM
Long date: Thursday, January 31, 2002
Short date: 1/31/2002
Long time: 3:29:37 PM
Short time: 15:29
```

Although these are the only date-time formats predefined in VBScript, you can use the various date and time functions to create your own formats. For example, the following lines of code display the date using just the month and year (8/2002):

```
Wscript.Echo Month(Now) & "/" & Year(Now)
```

Formatting Days of the Week and Months of the Year

The WeekdayDay and Month functions allow you to retrieve just the day of the week or just the month from a specified date. When you use these functions, the data is returned as an integer. These values are summarized in Table 2.12.

Table 2.12   Weekday and Month Return Values

Value	Day of the Week	Month
1	Sunday	January
2	Monday	February
3	Tuesday	March
4	Wednesday	April
5	Thursday	May
6	Friday	June
7	Saturday	July
8	–	August
9	–	September
10	–	October
11	–	November
12	–	December

Both WeekdayName and MonthName require you to first use the Day or Month function to retrieve the integer value for the day or the month. You cannot use either WeekdayName or MonthName directly with a date. For example, this code will fail because the function cannot determine the integer value to use for the month:

```
Wscript.Echo MonthName("9/19/2002")
```

To determine MonthName, you must first use the Month function:

```
MonthValue = Month("9/19/2002")
Wscript.Echo MonthName(MonthValue)
```

Alternatively, you can nest the two functions in a single line of code:

```
Wscript.Echo MonthName(Month("9/19/2002"))
```

The WeekdayName and MonthName functions are described in more detail in Table 2.13.

Table 2.13 Date Formatting Functions

Function	Description

WeekdayName	Returns the actual name of the day rather than the number of the day. (For example, WeekdayName returns the value Tuesday rather than the value 3.) WeekdayName requires only one parameter, the day of the date being evaluated. This means you must nest the WeekdayName and Day functions like this:
	
	`Wscript.Echo WeekDayName(Day("9/1/2002"))`
	
	The preceding code returns the string "Sunday" because September 1, 2002, occurred on a Sunday. WeekdayName also accepts an optional parameter to abbreviate the name of the day. By setting this parameter to True, WeekdayName will return a three-letter abbreviation for the day. For example, this command returns the value "Sun":
	
	`Wscript.Echo WeekDayName(Day("9/1/2002") True)`

MonthName	Returns the actual name of the month rather than the number of the month. (For example, MonthName returns the value September rather than the value 9.) MonthName requires only one parameter, the month of the date being evaluated. This means you must nest the MonthName and Month functions like this:
	
	`Wscript.Echo MonthName(Month("9/1/2002"))`
	
	The preceding code returns the string "September". MonthName also accepts an optional parameter to abbreviate the name of the month. When this parameter is set to True, MonthName will return a three-letter abbreviation for the month. For example, this command returns the value "Sep":
	
	`Wscript.Echo MonthName(Month("9/1/2002") , True)`

Working with Strings

Many system administration scripts are designed to return information about managed items, including such things as the services running on a remote server, the hardware installed on a client workstation, or the events recorded in the event logs on a domain controller. Much of the information returned from these managed objects comes back in the form of string data, data composed of any combination of alphabetic and numeric values. For example, if you query an event log for information about an event description, you might get back a string similar to this:

```
Security policy in the Group policy objects has been applied successfully.
```

In other words, there is nothing particularly special about strings; strings are just bits of text, the same kind of text you create when typing in a text editor.

Although strings are a simple enough concept, working with string data can be tricky, especially when 1) that data is returned from a COM object and 2) you need to store that data in a database or display it on the screen. This is because you have no control over how the returned data is packaged; it might be oddly formatted (for example, all uppercase letters), or it might be too long or too short to fit the allocated space. (For example, your database field might be sized to accept no more than 20 characters, but the returned string might contain 30 characters.)

Because of this, it is important for you to be able to manipulate string data; you might want to shorten (or, in some cases, lengthen) the size of a string, you might want to reformat a string, and sometimes you might even want to search within a string and extract only a specified portion of the text. To help you carry out these tasks, VBScript provides a number of functions for manipulating strings.

Manipulating Strings and String Lengths

Many times you want to work with only a portion of a string value. For example, Windows Script Host (WSH) has a property, FullName, which tells you whether a script is running under CScript or WScript. This can be useful information because you are likely to have certain scripts that should be, or in some cases can only be, run under CScript. However, the FullName property returns not just the name of the script host but the full path to the script host executable file. Typically these paths are:

```
C:\Windows\Cscript.exe
C:\Windows\Wscript.exe.
```

Of course, most of the time you are not interested in the full path but only the name of the script host; after all, the full path will vary depending on the drive and the directory where Windows is installed. Because of this, you need a method for retrieving only the last eight characters (cscript.exe or wscript.exe) of the path string.

At other times, the length of a string is very important. This is particularly true when it comes to formatting output either to display in a command window or to save to a text file. For example, the following script retrieves a collection of files stored in C:\Windows and displays the file name, file size, and last access time for each one:

```
Set FSO = CreateObject("Scripting.FileSystemObject")
Set Folder = FSO.GetFolder("C:\Windows")
Set FileList = Folder.Files
For Each File in FileList
    Wscript.Echo File.Name & VbTab & File.Size & File.DateLastModified
Next
```

When the preceding script runs, output similar to the following appears. As you can see, it is very difficult to make immediate sense of this output.

```
PCL5EMS.X12    46618/3/00 9:07:50 AM
SchedLog.Txt   1778412/17/00 7:51:40 PM
Straw Mat.bmp   5905/11/98 8:01:00 PM
Bubbles.bmp   21185/11/98 8:01:00 PM
Carved Stone.bmp   5825/11/98 8:01:00 PM
HKLM   3711/12/99 8:27:20 AM
LT Win Modem.log   207512/3/01 9:30:16 PM
```

When placed in tabular format, with well-defined columns, the data is much easier to read and to analyze:

```
PCL5EMS.X12                                       4661     8/3/00 9:07:50 AM
SchedLog.Txt                                      17784   12/17/00 7:51:40 PM
Straw Mat.bmp                                     590      5/11/98 8:01:00 PM
Bubbles.bmp                                       2118     5/11/98 8:01:00 PM
Carved Stone.bmp                                  582      5/11/98 8:01:00 PM
HKLM                                              371      1/12/99 8:27:20 AM
LT Win Modem.log                                  2075    12/3/01 9:30:16 PM
```

To create tabular output such as this, you need to be able to take string values and manipulate them in various ways. For example, in the preceding output, the file name begins in the first character position, and the file size begins in the 51st character position (digits have been added to make it easier to identify character positions):

```
12345678901234567890123456789012345678901234567890 1
PCL5EMS.X12                                       4661     8/3/00 9:07:50 AM
```

To create this output, you need to:

1.   Calculate the length of the file name. (For example, PCL5EMS.X12 is 11 characters long.)

2.   Subtract the length of the file name (11 characters) from the total space allocated for the file name (50 characters).

3.   Append enough blank spaces (50 minus 11, or 39 blank spaces) to ensure that the length of the file name equals the total space allocated.

This works very well for short file names. But what if you had a file name of 75 characters? In that case, you would need to truncate the string, taking only the first 50 characters and leaving off the rest.

Fortunately, VBScript includes a number of functions that allow you to manipulate strings. For example, you can calculate the length of a string and add blank spaces to pad the length, or use functions that return only a specified number of characters, beginning either from the start of the string and working forward or from the end of the string and working back (or even from some point in the middle and working in either direction).

Some of the more commonly used functions for manipulating strings are shown in Table 2.14.

Table 2.14   String Manipulation Functions

Function	Description

Len	Returns the number of characters in a string. This is particularly useful when formatting data for on-screen display. Suppose you allow 20 characters for a particular column. To ensure that columns line up correctly, you need to determine the number of characters in the string and then add or subtract characters as needed until the string is 20 characters long.
	
	The following two lines of code returns the value 22 because 22 characters are in the string *This is a test string*.
	
	```TestString = "This is a test string."```
	```Wscript.Echo Len(TestString)```

Left	Returns the specified number of characters from the string, starting with the first character and working forward toward the end of the string (from left to right). You must supply two parameters: the string and the number of characters to return.
	
	The following two lines of code return the string *Thi* because these are the first three characters in the string *This is a test string*.
	
	```TestString = "This is a test string."```
	```Wscript.Echo Left(TestString, 3)```

Right	Returns the specified number of characters from the string, starting with the last character and working backward toward the beginning of the string (from right to left). You must supply two parameters: the string and the number of characters to return.
	
	The following two lines of code return the string *ng.* because these are the last three characters in the string *This is a test string*.
	
	```TestString = "This is a test string."```
	```Wscript.Echo Right(TestString, 3)```

Mid	Returns the specified number of characters from the string, starting with a designated character position and working toward the end of the string (from left to right). You must supply three parameters: the string, the starting character position (for example, 5 to start counting from the fifth character in the string), and the number of characters to return.
	
	The following two lines of code return the string *is_* (with the underscore representing a blank space) because these are the characters that hold positions 6, 7, and 8 in the string *This is a test string*.
	
	```TestString = "This is a test string."```
	```Wscript.Echo Mid(TestString, 6, 3)```

(continued)

Table 2.14 String Manipulation Functions *(continued)*

Function	Description
Space	Inserts the specified number of blank spaces into a string. For example, the following line of code inserts 10 blank spaces between "This is a" and "test string." The end result is the string "This is a test string." ```Wscript.Echo "This is a" & Space(10) _\n & "test string."```
LTrim	Removes any blank spaces that appear at the beginning of a string. (These are typically referred to as leading spaces.) For example, the following code transforms the string " This is a test string. " into "This is a test string. " ```TestString = " This is a test string. "\nWscript.Echo LTrim(TestString)```
RTrim	Removes any blank spaces that appear at the end of a string. (These are typically referred to as trailing spaces.) For example, the following code transforms the string " This is a test string. " into " This is a test string." ```TestString = " This is a test string. "\nWscript.Echo RTrim(TestString)```
Trim	Removes both the leading and trailing spaces from a string. For example, the following code transforms the string " This is a test string. " into "This is a test string." ```TestString = " This is a test string. "\nWscript.Echo Trim(TestString)```

Creating Tabular Output

The string manipulation functions are particularly useful in creating tabular output, output in which items are displayed in aligned columns. An example of this is shown in the following script, which uses the Len and Space functions to create a table showing two services and their current state. The script in Listing 2.18 does the following:

1. Sets the value of four variables, two representing the names of services and two representing service states.

2. For the first service variable, uses the Len function to determine the number of characters in the string and saves this value to the variable NameLength. For example, Alerter has seven characters in its name, so the value 7 is saved to NameLength.

3. Subtracts the value of NameLength from 20, the number of spaces allocated for displaying the service name, and stores the difference in the variable SpacesToAdd. For the Alerter service, this value would be 13: 20 − 7.

4. Sets the value of the variable DisplayName to the name of the service plus as many blank spaces as needed to make the name 20 characters long. For example, the Alerter service requires 13 blank spaces (the value stored in SpacesToAdd) to make the name 20 characters long. These blank spaces are added using the Space function.

The DisplayName for the Alerter service looks like this (the hyphens indicate blank spaces):

```
Alerter-------------
```

5. Echoes the DisplayName and the service state.

6. Repeats the process for the next two variables.

Listing 2.18   Creating Tabular Output

```
1    Service1 = "Alerter"
2    State1 = "Running"
3    Service2 = "DHCP Client"
4    State2 = "Stopped"
5
6    NameLength = Len(Service1)
7    SpacesToAdd = 20 - NameLength
8    DisplayName = Service1 & Space(SpacesToAdd)
9    Wscript.Echo DisplayName & State1
10
11   Display = ""
12
13   NameLength = Len(Service2)
14   SpacesToAdd = 20 - NameLength
15   DisplayName = Service2 & Space(SpacesToAdd)
16   Wscript.Echo DisplayName & State2
```

When this script runs under CScript, the following output appears in the command window:

```
Alerter             Running
DHCP Client         Stopped
```

Formatting Text for Message Boxes

If you prefer using message boxes to display data, you will discover that it is much harder, if not impossible, to display data in aligned columns. This is because of a difference in the fonts used in a command window and the fonts used in a message box. The command window uses a nonproportional font, which means that all characters (including spaces) are the same width. As shown in Figure 2.14, the letters i, j, and l take up the same amount of space as the letters m, v, and w in a nonproportional font.

Figure 2.14   Letters Displayed in Nonproportional Font

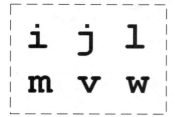

By contrast, message boxes typically use a proportional font, which means that characters vary in width. As shown in Figure 2.15, the letters i, j, and l take up far less space than the letters m, v, and w in a proportional font.

Figure 2.15   Letters Displayed in Proportional Font

Because of the differences in character widths, you cannot specify that a column should begin at, say, the 20th character space, and assume that all the column items will line up.

Searching for Text in a String

As noted previously, you do not always have control over the text returned to you when running a script. For example, suppose your script opens log files on a computer and checks to see whether a particular action succeeded or failed. In most cases, the log file will contain far more text than simply the word *Succeeded* or *Failed*. Instead, the log might look like this:

```
MSI: False - MSP: True - CMW: False
MSISW: REINSTALL=all REINSTALLMODE=vomus /QB /L*V+ C:\WINNT\DEBUG
    \officexp_sp1.log
MSPSW: REBOOT=ReallySuppress /QB- /L*V+ C:\WINDOWS\DEBUG\officexp_sp1.log
InstallFile Result: [0] and Success: True
Client Maint Wiz: PROPLUS detected
```

To determine the success or failure of the activity, your script will need to read in all the text and programmatically search for the relevant piece of information (in this example, the phrase "Success: True").

The InStr function provides a way to search for the presence of a string within another string. In practical terms, this allows you to create scripts that perform tasks such as reading through a log file and reporting back only if a line contains a specific error code. For example, imagine a plain-text log file that contains hundreds of lines like this:

```
6/1/2002    File a.doc successfully copied
6/1/2002    File b.doc successfully copied
6/1/2002    Error: File c.doc could not be copied
6/1/2002    File d.doc successfully copied
```

Rather than manually read through this log looking for errors, you can create a script that reads each line in the log file, echoing back any lines that contain the word Error. This provides a quick and easy way for you to extract only the operations that failed and thus need your attention.

Note

The InStr function is designed to carry out simple string manipulation. If you need to carry out more complex types of operation, you need to use the VBScript Regular Expressions object. This use of this object is beyond the scope of this book; for more information, see the VBScript link on the Web Resources page at http://www.microsoft.com/windows/reskits/webresources.

InStr works by reporting back the character position where the substring is first found. For example, suppose you are looking for the letters *ment* in the word *developmental*. InStr returns the value 8 because the letters *ment* are found beginning in the eighth character position, as shown in Figure 2.16.

Figure 2.16 Character Positions in the Word *Developmental*

By contrast, if you searched for the letters *mant*, InStr would return 0, indicating that the substring could not be found.

InStr requires two parameters: the string being searched and the string being searched for (the substring). For example, the following line of code searches for the letters *ment* in the word *developmental*:

```
Wscript.Echo InStr("ment", "developmental")
```

For longer strings, you can set variables equal to the string values and then use those variables as InStr parameters. For example, the following script searches for the words *test* and *strong* in the sentence, "This is a test string being searched for two different words."

```
TestString = "This is a test string being searched for two different words."
PresentString = "test"
AbsentString = "strong"
Wscript.Echo InStr(PresentString, TestString)
Wscript.Echo InStr(AbsentString, TestString)
```

When the preceding script runs, the values 11 and 0 will be returned. The value 11 indicates that the word *test* can be found beginning with the eleventh character. The value 0 indicates that the word *strong* could not be found anywhere within the string being searched.

Modifying String Case

Font control is not a strong point of VBScript. Regardless of whether you are displaying output in the command window or in a message box, you have no ability to control such font characteristics as style, size, and color. In fact, about the only thing you can do with fonts is modify the case; that is, you can configure a character (or set of characters) to be either uppercase or lowercase.

Modifying string case can be useful in displaying information. By changing case as needed, you can either ensure a consistent look to a data display (for example, all items shown in lowercase letters) or, alternatively, draw attention to specific items. For example, in this hypothetical output it is easy to see which server requires immediate attention:

```
Server          Status
atl-dc-01       Healthy
atl-dc-02       Healthy
ATL-DC-03       ERROR
atl-dc-04       Healthy
```

Modifying the case is also useful for data entry. For example, to ensure that users enter states using an all-uppercase format (WA, OR, CA), you can simply take the value they enter, regardless of case, and convert it to all uppercase letters.

The two functions that allow you to modify string case are described in Table 2.15.

Table 2.15 Functions for Modifying String Case

Function	Description
LCase	Converts all the alphabetic characters in a string to their lowercase equivalents. The following lines of code convert the string *Arlene Huff* to the all-lowercase string *arlene huff*. ``` UserName = "Arlene Huff" Wscript.Echo LCase(UserName) ```
UCase	Converts all the alphabetic characters in a string to their uppercase equivalents. The following lines of code convert the string *Arlene Huff* to the all-uppercase string *ARLENE HUFF*. ``` UserName = "Arlene Huff" Wscript.Echo UCase(UserName) ```

Working with Numbers

Much of system administration revolves around numbers: How much memory is available on this computer? How many services are paused on that computer? How many failed logons have been recorded in the event log? How much processor time is being used on our domain controllers?

This type of numeric information can easily be returned using scripts; for example, you can use WMI to answer all of the preceding questions. As explained in the first half of this chapter, however, this information does not always come back in a format that is useful for system administrators. Free disk space is reported in bytes; a disk drive with approximately 10 gigabytes of free disk space might show 10,842,824,704 bytes of free disk space. Processor use is reported in 100-nanosecond increments; the maximum length and width of the paper that can be used on a printer is reported in tenths of a millimeter.

Fortunately, VBScript provides a number of functions that allow you to manipulate numbers, including functions for performing mathematical calculations and functions for formatting numeric output.

Arithmetic Precedence

Most of the calculations you carry out as a system administrator are likely to be simple ones, such as dividing bytes by 1,024 to convert the value to kilobytes. On occasion, however, you might need to carry out a calculation that involves more than one operator (for example, a calculation that adds two numbers and then divides that value). Because of that, it is important to understand arithmetic precedence.

VBScript does not treat the arithmetic operators (addition, subtraction, multiplication, and division) equally. Instead, when given an equation, VBScript always performs the math operations in this order:

1. Division

2. Multiplication

3. Addition

4. Subtraction

Why does that matter to you? Consider the following script, which adds two numbers, multiplies them by a third, subtracts a fourth, and then divides by a fifth:

```
Wscript.Echo 1 + 2 * 3 - 4 / 5
```

When this script runs, the value 6.2 is echoed to the screen. Here is how that value is derived.

1. Because division takes precedence over all the other operations, the first thing VBScript does is divide 4 by 5, yielding .8. To VBScript, the equation now looks like this:

   ```
   1 + 2 * 3 - .8
   ```

2. Next it multiplies 2 and 3, yielding 6. Now the equation looks like this:

   ```
   1 + 6 - .8
   ```

3. Because addition is next in the order of precedence, it adds 1 and 6, yielding 7, and resulting in this equation:

   ```
   7 - .8
   ```

4. Finally it subtracts .8 from 7, giving the final answer 6.2.

Of course, this might not be the answer, or the equation, you expected. Instead, you might have preferred that VBScript:

1. Add 1 + 2.

2. Multiply that value by 3.

3. Subtract 4.

4. Divide the total by 5.

For this to happen, you need to use parentheses to indicate the preferred order of precedence. Parentheses always take precedence, regardless of the arithmetic operator being used. Because of this, your equation should be rewritten to ensure that the steps are carried out in the proper order. (When multiple parentheses are used, the equation within the innermost parentheses is evaluated first and the equation in the outermost parentheses evaluated last.)

```
Wscript.Echo (((1 + 2) * 3) - 4) / 5
```

Formatting Numbers

On its own, VBScript does not always format numbers in easy-to-read fashion. For example, one of the first scripts used in this chapter returned the free disk space on a hard drive. The value returned was 10842824704. This value is accurate but difficult to read; it would be much better to have the free space reported like this: 10,842,824,704.

Likewise, a calculation performed earlier in this chapter returned the value 10340.4458007813. Rarely, if ever, will you require that type of precision when performing system administration tasks. Instead, it would be better to have the value returned as 10,340 or 10,340.45. These numbers not only are easier to read but also require less room to display. This is an important consideration when creating tabular output to be displayed on the screen.

The FormatNumber function allows you to control how numbers are displayed in script output. FormatNumber requires you to specify the number to be formatted, followed by any or all of the parameters described in Table 2.16. For example, this line of code displays the number 37.874 with no decimal places (that is, the value 37 will be displayed):

```
Wscript.Echo FormatNumber(37.874, 0)
```

Table 2.16 FormatNumber Parameters

Parameter	Description
Number of digits after the decimal point.	FormatNumber does not simply delete digits. Instead, it rounds the number to the closest value. For example, if you decide to display 11.6 with no decimal places, the value 12 will be displayed. By contrast, 19.2 is displayed as 19. If you use the value −1, the number of digits after the decimal point will be based on the regional and language options for the computer.
Use leading zero.	Values are: −1 — True. Use the leading 0. 0 — False. −2 — Use the setting configured in the regional and language options for the computer.
Place negative numbers in parentheses.	Values are: −1 — True. Put negative numbers in parentheses. 0 — False. Do not put negative numbers in parentheses. −2 — Use the setting configured in the regional and language options for the computer.
Group digits.	Values are: −1 — True. Group digits using the group separator. 0 — False. Do not group digits. −2 — Use the setting configured in the regional and language options for the computer.

To help make your scripts easier to read and maintain, you might want to use constants in place of the literal values. For example, in this script it is not readily apparent what the 0 means:

```
Wscript.Echo FormatNumber(37.874, 0)
```

Using a constant makes the script easier to understand:

```
Const NoDecimalPlaces = 0
Wscript.Echo FormatNumber(37.874, NoDecimalPlaces)
```

Because each of the FormatNumber parameters is optional you, can perform such tasks as grouping digits without specifying values for the other parameters. However, the parameter for grouping digits must still be the fifth item in the parameter list (after the number to be formatted and the other three optional parameters). To ensure that the parameters maintain the correct order, you can do one of the following:

- Use a "blank" parameter (that is, simply insert a comma without including a value).

- Use the default value by setting each unused parameter to False.

- Use the default value by setting each unused parameter to a constant that has been set to False.

For example, in this script constants are assigned the appropriate values, and then used to format the result of 1 / −7:

```
Const Decimals = 3
Const LeadingZero = True
Const UseParentheses = True
Const Default = False
NumberToFormat = 1 / -7
Wscript.Echo NumberToFormat
Wscript.Echo FormatNumber(NumberToFormat, Decimals)
Wscript.Echo FormatNumber(NumberToFormat, Default, LeadingZero)
Wscript.Echo FormatNumber(NumberToFormat, Default, Default, UseParentheses)
```

When the preceding script runs under CScript, the following output appears in the command window:

```
-0.142857142857143
-0.143
-0.14
(0.14)
```

The following script snippet shows different ways to format the value returned when multiplying 33 by 454:

```
Const GroupDigits = True
Const Default = False
Const NoDecimals = 0
NumberToFormat = 33 * 454
Wscript.Echo NumberToFormat
Wscript.Echo FormatNumber(NumberToFormat, Default, Default, Default,
GroupDigits)
Wscript.Echo FormatNumber _
    (NumberToFormat, NoDecimals , Default, Default, GroupDigits)
```

When the preceding script runs under CScript, the following output appears in the command window:

```
14982
14,982.00
14,982
```

Formatting Percentages

Sometimes raw numbers are not as meaningful as percentages. For example, event logs have a maximum size that can vary from computer to computer. Because of that, simply knowing the current size of an event log (a property that can be retrieved by using WMI) will not tell you whether the log is nearly full and should be backed up and cleared. In this case, it might be more useful to know the maximum allowed size (another property available through WMI) as well as the current size. This lets you determine what percentage of the event log is "full" and what percentage is still available.

If you are going to retrieve numbers as percentages, it is a good idea to also report those numbers as percentages. For example, suppose you have an event log with a maximum size of 5,000,000 bytes and a current size of 3,127,354 bytes. To determine how full the event log is, you can divide 3,127,354 by 5,000,000. When you do the calculation, the value .6254708 is returned. To lessen the possibility of confusion, it is better to have this value returned as a percentage (63%).

The FormatPercent function converts a number to a percentage; in effect, this means multiplying the number by 100 and then appending a percent symbol. However, FormatPercent also accepts the same optional parameters as FormatNumber. These parameters allow you to:

- Specify the number of digits to be displayed after the decimal point.

- Place a leading 0 in front of fractional values (numbers less than 1 but greater than –1).

- Display negative values in parentheses.

- Group digits using a group separator (allowing you to display a value as 6,500,000% rather than 6500000%).

The syntax for the FormatPercent function is identical to that for FormatNumber: You supply the value to be formatted, followed by zero or more parameters. As with FormatNumber, the order in which the parameters are presented is crucial. For example, the leading 0 must always be the second parameter following the value being formatted. If you do not want to specify a value for the first parameter (number of digits following the decimal point), use False as a placeholder for that parameter.

The following script divides 1 by 7 and echoes the result. The script then uses FormatPercent to display the result as a percentage, with no decimal places.

```
Const NoDecimals = 0
NumberToFormat = 1 / 7
Wscript.Echo NumberToFormat
Wscript.Echo FormatPercent(NumberToFormat, NoDecimals)
```

When the preceding script is run under CScript, the following output appears in the command window:

```
0.142857142857143
14%
```

Running Statements Multiple Times

One reason system administration is so difficult and so time-consuming is that computing environments are dynamic. This means that system administrators find themselves doing the same tasks over and over. For example, the fact that a computer has adequate hard disk space today is no guarantee that it will have adequate hard disk space a month from now, a week from now, or even an hour from now. Because there is no guarantee, you must check hard disk space repeatedly. Likewise, when monitoring processor use, you might want to check this value every 10 seconds for the next 5 minutes. Trying to perform this task manually would be very difficult, extremely tedious, and prone to error.

Of course, scripts get neither tired nor bored, nor are scripts apt to start making errors the more often they have to repeat a task. This makes a script the perfect vehicle for carrying out the same activity over and over. With VBScript, repetitive tasks can be performed by means of a Do loop within your code.

Do Loop

The Do loop allows you to repeatedly run a set of statements until a specified condition has been met. For example, you might want to periodically monitor free disk space until the amount of free disk space falls below a specified value. Likewise, you might want to run some sort of disk cleanup process as long as available memory remains above a certain level; if memory drops below that level, you might end the cleanup process as a way to regain memory. The Do loop allows you to run loops for an indefinite number of times. (The For Next loop, by contrast, requires that the loop be run a specific number of times.)

VBScript supports two types of Do loops: Do Until and Do While. The Do Until loop continues running a loop *until* a specific condition is met. This generally means that the loop runs until the loop condition becomes True. For example, the following script uses the FileSystemObject to open a text file and then read in the text file line by line. To do this, the code for reading the text file is placed in a loop that will continue to run *until* the end of the file (the text stream) has been reached. In the following script, the loop condition has the following syntax:

```
Do Until objTextFile.AtEndOfStream
```

This is read as, "Continue looping until the end of the file is reached."

```
Const ForReading = 1
Set objFSO = CreateObject("Scripting.FileSystemObject")
Set objTextFile = objFSO.OpenTextFile _
    ("c:\test.txt", ForReading)
Do Until objTextFile.AtEndOfStream
    strNextLine = objTextFile.Readline
    Wscript.Echo strNextLine
Loop
```

When the preceding script runs, the loop condition is checked each time to see whether the end of the file has been reached. If it has, the loop will not run. If it has not, the loop will run, and the next line of the file will be read.

By contrast, the Do While loop runs as long as the condition has not been met (that is, as long as it is False). The following script uses the syntax:

```
Do While Not objTextFile.AtEndOfStream
```

This is read as, "Continue looping as long as the end of the text file has not been reached." If the text file still has unread lines, this loop will continue to run.

```
Const ForReading = 1
Set objFSO = CreateObject("Scripting.FileSystemObject")
Set objTextFile = objFSO.OpenTextFile _
    ("c:\test.txt", ForReading)
Do While Not objTextFile.AtEndOfStream
    strNextLine = objTextFile.Readline
    Wscript.Echo strNextLine
Loop
```

Creating Endless Loops

As you might expect, it is possible to create an endless loop, one that never stops running. (If the condition is never met, the loop will continue to run forever.) This is often a mistake on the part of the script writer. However, suppose you have a script that alerts you each time an error event is recorded in the event log. You do not want that loop to stop after the first alert has been sent; instead, you would want the loop to continue and allow you to continue to receive these notifications.

To create a loop that runs forever, you simply specify a loop condition that will never be met. For example, in the following script fragment, the loop is designed to run until LoopVariable is equal to 0. Because the script does nothing to change the value of LoopVariable, this condition will never be met, and the loop will continue to run indefinitely.

```
LoopVariable = 1
Do Until LoopVariable = 0
    FreeMegaBytes = objLogicalDisk.FreeSpace / CONVERSION_FACTOR
    If FreeMegaBytes < WARNING_THRESHOLD Then
        Wscript.Echo Computer & " " & objLogicalDisk.DeviceID & _
            " is low on disk space."
    End If
Loop
```

The only way stop this loop is to stop the script.

Checking the Loop Condition

VBScript allows you to check the loop condition in one of two places: either before the loop begins or after the loop has concluded. This can make a difference in whether the loop is run. If you want to run the loop *only* if the condition has been met, check the condition before the loop is run. If you want ensure that the loop always runs at least one time, regardless of whether the condition has been met, check the condition after the loop has been run.

The following script sample illustrates the difference between the two methods for checking loop conditions. After setting a variable named LoopVariable to 1, the script sets up two loops. In the first loop, the condition is checked before the loop runs; this is done by using the following syntax:

```
Do Until LoopVariable = 1
```

The second loop uses this syntax, which does not check the condition until after the loop has been run:

```
Loop Until LoopVariable = 1
```

The script itself looks like this:

```
LoopVariable = 1
Do Until LoopVariable  = 1
    Wscript.Echo "Script entered loop 1."
Loop
Do
    Wscript.Echo "Script entered loop 2."
Loop Until LoopVariable  = 1
```

When the preceding script runs, the following output appears on the screen:

```
Script entered loop 2.
```

As you can see, loop 2 ran a single time, while loop 1 did not run at all.

Why the difference? In the first loop, the condition (is LoopVariable equal to 1?) is tested before the loop begins. Because LoopVariable equals 1, the Do loop is skipped altogether.

In the second loop, however, the condition is not tested until after the loop has begun. Because scripts are processed sequentially, line by line, VBScript does the following:

1. Sets up the Do loop.

2. Echoes the message "Script entered loop 2."

3. Checks to see whether the condition (is LoopVariable equal to 1?) is True. Because it is, the loop stops, but only after it has run one time.

With the Loop Until construct, the loop will always run at least one time. If that is not your intention, use the Do Until construct.

Exiting a Loop

After you have entered a Do loop, VBScript will, by default, process each line of code within that loop. In most cases, that is exactly what you want it to do. However, there might be times when you want to exit a loop immediately, without running every line of code. In that event, you can use the Exit Do statement to immediately stop processing of the loop.

For example, the following script has been designed to cause an error (dividing 5 by 0). The loop condition states, "Run this loop until an Err occurs" (Err <> 0). That might lead you to believe that the loop will stop as soon as the script attempts to divide 5 by 0.

```
On Error Resume Next
Do Until Err <> 0
    X = 5/0
    Wscript.Echo "The result of the equation is " & X & "."
Loop
```

When you run the script, however, you see the dialog box shown in Figure 2.17.

Figure 2.17 Erroneous Message Box

Why? When the script encountered the divide by 0 error, it did not exit the loop, even though the loop condition specified, "Run this loop until an error occurs." Instead, it continued processing the remaining statements in the loop. This is because the loop condition, in this example, is tested only before the loop is running. As a result, the dialog box echoes the message, "The result of the equation is " and the result of the equation, which happens to be Null. After processing this statement, the script loops around, checks the error condition, and *then* exits the loop.

If you need to stop a loop before the loop actually completes, use the Exit Do statement. In the following script the error condition is checked within the loop itself. If an error has occurred, an error message is displayed, and the Exit Do command is used to stop the loop. If no error has occurred, the result of the equation is displayed.

```
On Error Resume Next
Do Until Err <> 0
    X = 5/0
    If Err <> 0 Then
        Wscript.Echo "An error has occurred."
        Exit Do
    End If
        Wscript.Echo "The result of the equation is " & X & "."
Loop
```

When the preceding script runs, the message box shown in Figure 2.18 appears. As you can see, the script stopped the loop before processing the statement that would have displayed the equation result.

Figure 2.18 Message Box Indicating That an Error Has Occurred

Making Decisions

Typically, VBScript runs a script in sequential order, running line 1, then line 2, and then line 3, continuing until it runs the last line and then automatically completes.

In general, this makes script writing easier; after a script has started, you can rely on VBScript to run each line in the proper order and then stop the script and release any memory that was allocated to run the script. At the same time, however, the fact that VBScript runs every line in a script introduces a complication: What happens if there are lines in the script that you do not want to run?

For example, suppose you have a script that backs up a set of files to a remote computer and then deletes the original files from the local computer. Provided there are no problems, you want the script to run each line. But what if the remote computer is unavailable? In that case, if the script runs each line, it will try to back up the files. This will fail because the remote computer is not available. It then deletes the original files, even though the backup was not successful. Unfortunately, the delete operation succeeds, and you lose the files.

In a case such as this, you want the script to check the condition — is the remote computer available? — and proceed *only* if the condition is True. This type of decision-making can be implemented by using If Then or Select case statements.

Testing Multiple Conditions

The scripts used in the first half of this chapter made a decision based on a single condition: If the amount of free disk space was less than a specified amount, an alert was triggered:

```
If FreeMegaBytes < WARNING_THRESHOLD Then
    Wscript.Echo objLogicalDisk.DeviceID & " is low on disk space."
End If
```

There might be times, however, when you want to take action only if two or more conditions are met. For example, you might want immediate notification if your e-mail servers start running out of disk space. For other servers, you might not need immediate notification. Instead, you can simply check the log at some point to verify that these servers have adequate disk space.

In a situation such as this, you want an alert to be triggered only if two conditions are true: the amount of free disk space has dropped below the specified level *and* the server in question is an e-mail server. You can test for multiple conditions by using the logical operator And.

In the following script fragment, an alert is triggered only if free disk space has fallen below the threshold *and* the computer in question is an e-mail server. If either of these two conditions is not true (that is, either there is adequate disk space or the computer is not an e-mail server), no alert will be triggered.

```
If FreeMegaBytes < WARNING_THRESHOLD And ServerType = "Email" Then
    Wscript.Echo objLogicalDisk.DeviceID & " is low on disk space."
End If
```

On other occasions, you might want to take action if any one of a specified set of conditions is true. For example, you might want an alert if free disk space has fallen below a specified threshold or if available memory has fallen below a specified threshold. The decision matrix for this type of script is shown in Table 2.17.

Table 2.17   Decision Matrix

Adequate Disk Space?	Adequate Memory?	Trigger Alert?
Yes	Yes	No
Yes	No	Yes
No	Yes	Yes
No	No	Yes

To make this type of decision, use the logical Or operator, as shown in this code snippet:

```
If FreeMegaBytes < WARNING_THRESHOLD Or AvailableMemory < MEMORY_THRESHOLD Then
    Wscript.Echo "Computer is low on disk space or memory."
End If
```

The logical Or operator returns True if *either* condition is true (or if both conditions are true). In the preceding example, if FreeMegabytes is less than the warning threshold *or* if Available Memory is less than the memory threshold, the condition is true, and the warning message is echoed. Thus, the warning is displayed if the computer is running low on memory, even if free disk space is adequate.

If Then ElseIf

System administrators often work in an either-or world: Either a computer has enough disk space or it does not; either a computer has enough available memory or it does not. In situations in which there are only two possible conditions — either a computer has enough free disk space or it does not — the If Then Else construction allows you to test the condition and choose a course of action, with a minimal amount of coding.

At other times, however, there can be more than two possible conditions. For example, you might assess maintenance requirements for disk drives by using the following criteria:

- A drive with less than 100 megabytes of free space requires immediate attention.

- A drive with less than 250 megabytes of free space but more than 100 megabytes of free space should be looked at as time allows.

- A drive with more than 250 megabytes of free space requires no attention at this time.

To evaluate multiple possibilities, you can use an If Then ElseIf statement. With an If Then ElseIf statement in your script, the script checks for the first condition (for example, x = 1). If true, the script takes the specified action and then exits the If Then construct.

But what if the condition is false and x does not equal 1? In that event, the script can check for a second condition by using a syntax similar to this:

```
ElseIf x = 2 Then
```

You can continue inserting ElseIf statements until you have exhausted all the possible values for x. (Actually, to ensure that you have all the possible values covered, your last statement should be simply an Else statement. The Else statement can be translated as, "If none of the preceding conditions are true, then take this action.")

For example, the following lines of code echo a message depending on whether:

- FreeMegabytes is less than or equal to 100.

- FreeMegabytes is greater than 100 but less than 250.

- FreeMegabytes is equal to or greater than 250.

```
If FreeMegabytes <= 100 Then
    Wscript.Echo Computer.Name & " requires immediate attention."
ElseIf FreeMegabytes < 250 Then
    Wscript.Echo Computer.Name & " should be looked at as soon as possible."
Else
    Wscript.Echo Computer.Name & " requires no attention at this time."
End If
```

When evaluating multiple possibilities using either an If Then ElseIf or a Select Case statement (discussed in the next section of this chapter), VBScript checks each condition until it finds a True statement. At that point it takes action without evaluating any of the other conditions. That means it is very important to properly order your conditional statements.

For example, consider the following script sample:

```
x = 5
If x < 20 Then
    Wscript.Echo "X is between 11 and 20."
ElseIf x < 11 Then
    Wscript.Echo "X is between 0 and 10."
Else
    Wscript.Echo "X equals 0."
End If
```

Figure 2.19 shows the message box that is displayed when you run this script.

Figure 2.19 Incorrectly Ordering Conditional Statements

Why is the incorrect result? The first condition checked in the If Then ElseIf statement is this: Is X less than 20? Because that happens to be true, VBScript echoes the message, "X is between 11 and 20" and then immediately exits the statement block. The script never checks to see whether X is less than 11 because processing ends as soon as a True statement is found.

To get the script to work properly, the conditions must be reordered like this:

```
x = 5
If x = 0 Then
    Wscript.Echo "X equals 0."
ElseIf x < 11 Then
    Wscript.Echo "X is between 0 and 10."
Else
    Wscript.Echo "X is between 11 and 20."
End If
```

It is generally a good idea to always include an Else statement as the last statement within the If Then block; this enables your script to account for *all* conditions, not just the ones specified in the ElseIf statement. For example, consider the following script snippet, which matches a job ID number with a job title:

```
If JobID = 1 Then
    Wscript.Echo "This user is a manager."
ElseIf JobID = 2 Then
    Wscript.Echo "This user is not a manager."
End If
```

The preceding script works fine as long as each user has been assigned a job ID of 1 or 2. But what if the user was assigned a job ID of 3, or not assigned a job ID? By adding an Else statement, you can account for any job ID that is not 1 or 2:

```
If JobID = 1 Then
    Wscript.Echo "This user is a manager."
ElseIf JobID = 2 Then
    Wscript.Echo "This user is not a manager."
Else
    Wscript.Echo "This user has not been assigned a valid job ID."
End If
```

Select Case

The Select Case statement provides a more readable alternative to the If Then ElseIf statement. If you have a script that evaluates more than three conditions, you will typically find it faster and easier to use Select Case rather than If Then ElseIf. For example, the following code sample uses the Select Case statement to evaluate the printer status codes that can be returned by using WMI:

```
Select Case PrinterStatus
    Case 1 strCurrentState = "Other"
    Case 2 strCurrentState = "Unknown"
    Case 3 strCurrentState = "Idle"
    Case 4 strCurrentState = "Printing"
    Case 5 strCurrentState = "Warming Up"
End Select
```

By comparison, the task written using an If Then ElseIf statement is almost twice as long, and more difficult to read:

```
If PrinterStatus = 1 Then
    strCurrentState = "Other"
ElseIf PrinterStatus = 2 Then
    strCurrentState = "Unknown"
ElseIf PrinterStatus = 3 Then
    strCurrentState = "Idle"
ElseIf PrinterStatus = 4 Then
    strCurrentState = "Printing"
ElseIf PrinterStatus = 5 Then
    strCurrentState = "Warming Up"
End Select
```

To use a Select Case statement, do the following:

1. Start the statement block with Select Case, followed by the name of the variable being evaluated.

2. For each potential value, use a Case statement followed by the potential value, and then by any code that should be run if the statement is true. For example, if you want to echo an error message if the value is equal to 99, use a code statement similar to the following:

```
Case 99 Wscript.Echo "An error has occurred."
```

3. Close the statement block with End Select.

You can also use a Case Else statement to account for all other possibilities:

```
Select Case PrinterStatus
    Case 1 strCurrentState = "Other"
    Case 2 strCurrentState = "Unknown"
    Case 3 strCurrentState = "Idle"
    Case 4 strCurrentState = "Printing"
    Case 5 strCurrentState = "Warming Up"
    Case Else strCurrentState = "Status cannot be determined."
End Select
```

In addition, you can place the Case statement on one line, followed by the lines of code that should be run if the statement is True. For example:

```
Case 1
    strCurrentState = "Other"
    Wscript.Echo strCurrentState
Case 2
```

Arrays

Scripts are probably most useful when you need to carry out the same task multiple times. For example, if you own one computer, it is just as quick and just as easy to open the Services snap-in to see which services are installed as it would be to write a script to retrieve the same information. If you have 100 computers, however, you will likely prefer using a script to retrieve service information as opposed to manually retrieving this information.

Of course, if a script is to run against 100 different computers, it needs a way to store those computer names and a way to keep track of which computers it has retrieved service information from and which computers it has not. One common way to store related bits of information (such as a list of computer names) is in an array, a special type of variable that can be used to store (and later retrieve) multiple values.

 Note

A full discussion of arrays, including the use of multidimensional arrays, is beyond the scope of this chapter. This chapter focuses on those aspects of arrays most commonly used in system administration scripts.

Creating Arrays

The easiest way to create an array is to use the Array function. As easy as this is, however, there are two things to keep in mind when using the Array function. First, the Array function can be used only to create one-dimensional arrays. Second, this function requires you to know in advance each of the items to be placed in the array. In system administration tasks that usually is not the case: After all, one of the primary reasons you write a script is to determine these items (which services are installed on a computer, which computers are in a specified organizational unit, which printers are being managed by a particular print server. Only then could you place them in an array.

Nevertheless, at times you will know the items in advance, and thus will be able to use the Array function. For example, the script used in the first half of this chapter assumed that you needed to run the script against exactly three computers. This might occur in your organization as well: If you have eight e-mail servers, you might want to hard-code all eight computer names into a script.

To put items in an array, use the Array function. With this function, you simply assign a list of values to a variable. For example, the following code statement assigns four domain controllers to an array variable named Computers:

```
Computers = Array("atl-dc-01", "atl-dc-02", "atl-dc-03", "atl-dc-04")
```

Declaring and Populating Arrays

Of course, there is a very good chance that you will not know, in advance, the items to be stored in an array. For example, your script might read in computer names from a text file, or might populate an array using the names of files found in a folder. In either case, you will not know the actual array items, or even how many items there are, until the script is run.

VBScript allows you to designate a variable as being an array without using the Array function and without immediately populating that array. To do this, you must use a Dim statement and must indicate the maximum number of items the array can hold. This can be a little confusing because the dimension of the array is based on the highest allowed index number rather than the actual number of items. Because the first item in an array is actually item 0 rather than item 1, the maximum number used in the Dim statement must always be the maximum number minus 1. If your array will contain 9 items, the Dim statement must show the maximum number as 8 (9 − 1).

For example, this command creates an array variable named arrTestArray and indicates that the array can contain a maximum of 4 items (4 − 1 = 3):

```
Dim arrTestArray(3)
```

After you have declared an array, you can populate it by assigning a value to the appropriate item. For example, this line of code assigns the value "A" to item 0, the first item in the array:

```
arrTestArray(0) = "A"
```

This simple script creates an array named arrTestArray and assigns values to each of the four items:

```
Dim arrTestArray(3)
arrTestArray(0) = "A"
arrTestArray(1) = "B"
arrTestArray(2) = "C"
arrTestArray(3) = "D"
```

So far, so good. But what if you guessed wrong when originally declaring the array? What if arrTestArray will actually contain five items rather than four? If that is the case, an error will be generated when you try to assign a fifth item to the array; an array cannot contain more items than the maximum number assigned to it. For example, this sample script creates a four-item array and then attempts to assign a value to a fifth item:

```
Dim arrTestArray(3)
arrTestArray(0) = "A"
arrTestArray(1) = "B"
arrTestArray(2) = "C"
arrTestArray(3) = "D"
arrTestArray(4) = "E"
```

When the preceding script runs, a "Subscript out of range" error is generated.

In a situation such as this, you have two options:

- You can allocate more space to the array than you will need. For example, you might declare, in advance, that arrTestArray will contain a maximum of 1,000 items. That provides adequate storage space for the array. However, it also wastes memory, and hundreds of items in the array might have no value at all.

- You can create a dynamic array.

Creating Dynamic Arrays

A dynamic array offers two advantages to script writers:

- You do not have to specify the maximum size of the array in advance.

- The size of the array can change during the course of the script.

For example, you might have a script that reads computer names from a text file. Rather than guess at the number of names in the text file, you can use a dynamic array to store these names. That way, you can create an array, read in the first name, and store it as the first item in the array. If a second name happens to be in the file, you can resize the array and then read in and store the second name. You can then repeat this process until every name has been read and stored.

To create a dynamic array, you must do two things. First, when you declare the array, do not specify a maximum size. Instead, simply use empty parentheses, like this:

```
Dim arrTestArray()
```

Second, before you add a new item to the array, use the ReDim Preserve statement and increment the size of the array by 1. The ReDim Preserve statement performs two tasks:

- The ReDim portion resizes the array.

- The Preserve portion ensures that no data is lost when the array is resized. This is important. If you simply use the ReDim statement by itself, all the data in your array will be lost when the array is resized.

For example, the following code sample creates a dynamic array named arrTestArray. The script creates a variable named intSize and assigns this the value 0. The script then uses the resultant line of code (intSize = 0) to resize arrTestArray so that it accepts one element (1 − 1 = 0).

After the script has assigned a value to the first element (item 0) in the array, ReDim Preserve is used to resize the array so that it accepts two elements (intSize + 1). A value is then assigned to the second element:

```
Dim arrTestArray()
intSize = 0
ReDim Preserve arrTestArray(intSize)
arrTestArray(intSize) = "A"
ReDim Preserve arrTestArray(intSize + 1)
arrTestArray(intSize + 1) = "B"
```

To illustrate how you might use ReDim Preserve in an actual system administration script, the following code sample retrieves a list of all the services installed on a computer and stores those service names in a dynamic array. To perform this task, the script must:

1. Create a dynamic array named arrTestArray.

2. Create a variable named intSize and assign this variable the value 0.

3. Connect to the WMI service and retrieve a list of the installed services.

4. For each service in the returned collection:

   a. Use the ReDim Preserve statement to set the size of arrTestArray to the value stored in intSize. For the first service in the collection, intSize is equal to 0. The array arrTestArray will thus have a size of 0, meaning it can contain one element.

   b. Assign the name of the service (objService.DisplayName) to the array element just created.

   c. Increment the size of intSize. For example, after the first element has been assigned a value, intSize will be changed to 1 (the original value, 0, plus 1).

   d. Repeat the step for the remaining services in the collection. For the second service, ReDim Preserve sets the size of the array to 1, allowing two elements to be contained within the array. For the third service, ReDim Preserve sets the size to 2, allowing three elements to be stored in the array.

```
Dim arrTestArray()
intSize = 0

strComputer = "."
Set objWMIService = GetObject("winmgmts:" _
    & "{impersonationLevel=impersonate}!\\" & strComputer & "\root\cimv2")
Set colRunningServices = objWMIService.ExecQuery _
    ("SELECT * FROM Win32_Service")

For Each objService in colRunningServices
    ReDim Preserve arrTestArray(intSize)
    arrTestArray(intSize) = objService.DisplayName
    intSize = intSize + 1
Next
```

Converting a Delimited String to an Array

To make administrative data readily accessible to a wide variety of applications (including scripts), this data is often saved in plain-text files and in delimited format. *Delimited* simply means that a unique character separates the individual fields for each record in the file. This character is known as a delimiter and is typically the comma. These files are often referred to as comma-separated-values files because the individual values are separated by commas.

For example, a log file that lists the name of a server, the name of an event log on that server, and the number of error events that were recorded in that event log might look like this:

```
atl-dc-01,DNS Server,13
atl-dc-01,System,14
atl-dc-02,Security,3
alt-dc-02,Application,22
```

One advantage of delimited files is that they can be imported into applications that can automatically parse each line into a single record with multiple fields. For example, an application such as Microsoft Excel or Microsoft Access would parse the sample file like the example shown in Table 2.18.

Table 2.18   Parsing a Sample Data File into Fields

Field 1	Field 2	Field 3
atl-dc-01	DNS Server	13
atl-dc-01	System	4
atl-dc-02	Security	3
atl-dc-02	Application	22

The Split function can be used to convert a delimited string to an array. This is done by passing the function two parameters:

- The delimited text string.

- The delimiter.

For example, in the following script the delimited text string is the variable TestString, and the comma serves as the delimiter:

```
TestString = " atl-dc-01,DNS Server,13"
TestArray = Split(TestString , ",")
For i = LBound(TestArray) to UBound(TestArray)
    Wscript.Echo TestArray(i)
Next
```

When this script is run under CScript, the individual data fields are echoed to the screen:

```
atl-dc-01
DNS Server
13
```

Alternatives to Using Arrays

Arrays provide a quick and easy way to track one-dimensional data. When you have multidimensional data, however, it can become difficult to keep track of the various subscripts; it can also become exceedingly complex to try to sort the data. Because of that, if you do have multidimensional data you might want to consider one of the these alternatives:

- **Dictionary object**. The Dictionary object is part of the Script Runtime library and provides a way for you to easily store, retrieve, and modify array-like data. For more information about the Dictionary object, see "Script Runtime Primer" in this book.

- **Disconnected recordset**. A disconnected recordset is a temporary database that is not tied to an actual physical database. Instead, the recordset is constructed in memory and is deleted when the script finishes. Like the Dictionary object, the disconnected recordset allows you to refer to items by name rather than by an index number. Equally important, a disconnected recordset has access to the same methods and properties as a standard recordset, including the ability to sort records. For example, the following code sample sorts a one-dimensional array:

```
For i = LBound(SampleArray) to UBound(SampleArray)
    For j = LBound(SampleArray) to UBound(SampleArray)
        If j = UBound(SampleArray) Then
        Else
            If SampleArray(j) > SampleArray(j + 1) Then
                TempValue = SampleArray(j + 1)
                SampleArray(j + 1) = SampleArray(j)
                SampleArray(j) = TempValue
            End If
        End If
    Next
Next
```

By contrast, this single line of code sorts a disconnected recordset by field name (in this case, FileSize):

```
DisconnectedRecordset.Sort = "FileSize"
```

For more information about disconnected recordsets, see "Creating Enterprise Scripts" in this book.

Error Handling

VBScript provides a relatively simple method for handling run-time errors within a script. Run-time errors represent any errors that are not caught by the compiler and thus manifest themselves only after the script has started running. For example, the following script generates a syntax error because the command Wscript.Echo is mistyped and the compiler is unable to interpret the line. Before a script actually runs, the scripting engine reads each line to verify that the syntax is correct; no lines of code are actually run until this checking verifies that the syntax of all the lines of code is correct. Because of that, an error message will be displayed, even though the misspelled command does not occur until line 3 in the script:

```
Wscript.Echo "Line 1."
Wscript.Echo "Line 2."
W script.Echo "Line 3."
```

Instead of the message boxes for lines 1 and 2, the error message shown in Figure 2.20 appears. This error is generated because line 3 appears to reference an invalid command named W.

Figure 2.20   Syntax Error Message

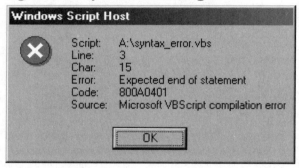

By contrast, the following script will display two message boxes before encountering an error (the misspelling of Wscript.Echo). This is because, as far as the compiler is concerned, line 3 is typed correctly. The compiler has no way of knowing that Eho is not a valid Wscript property and thus does not flag this as an error. VBScript cannot determine the properties and methods of a COM object in advance (that is, before a particular line of code runs).

```
Wscript.Echo "Line 1."
Wscript.Echo "Line 2."
Wscript.Eho "Line 3."
```

When line 3 of the script is actually run, the error message shown in Figure 2.21 appears. You might notice that this error message lists the source as a Microsoft VBScript run-time error rather than as a compilation error.

Figure 2.21 Runtime Error Message

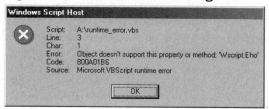

Not all run-time errors involve typographical errors within the script. For example, this line of code is syntactically and typographically correct. However, it will also generate a run-time error if the remote computer named InaccessibleComputer is not available over the network:

```
Set Computer = GetObject("winmgmts:\\InaccessibleComputer")
```

This means that run-time errors are bound to occur, if only because of activities beyond your control. (The network goes down, a computer is shut down, another administrator deletes a user account.) With VBScript, you have three options for handling errors. The advantages and disadvantages of each of these options are summarized in Table 2.19.

Table 2.19 Advantages and Disadvantages of Error Handling Options

Option	Advantages	Disadvantages
Allow the script to fail.	▪ Requires no work of any kind on the part of the script writer. By default, all scripts will fail when they encounter a run-time error. ▪ In many cases, running part of a script might be worse than not running a script at all. For example, if you have a script that backs up files to a remote computer and then deletes the original files, you would probably prefer that the script fail if the backup cannot take place. You would not want the backup portion to fail but then have the delete portion succeed.	▪ Allowing the script to fail at some arbitrary point could leave your computer in an unstable state. ▪ Some failures need not be fatal. For example, suppose a monitoring script is designed to retrieve information from 100 computers. If computer 1 is inaccessible, the script will fail and no information will be returned, even though the other 99 computers are up and running.
Have the script ignore all errors.	▪ Scripts will continue to run without interruption. ▪ Scripts can complete a major share of their tasks, even if a problem arises. For example, a script might be able to successfully copy 99 of 100 files, even if one file could not be copied. ▪ End users will not be presented with error messages that they must respond to.	▪ Difficult to debug problems because no message is displayed indicating that an error occurred, nor is any clue given as to where the error might have taken place. ▪ Can leave a computer in an uncertain state, wherein some actions have been carried out while others have not.

(continued)

Table 2.19   Advantages and Disadvantages of Error Handling Options *(continued)*

Option	Advantages	Disadvantages
Write code to respond to errors as they occur.	▪ Allows you to create meaningful error messages. ▪ Allows you to create code that attempts to address the error that occurred. For example, if a script is unable to connect to a remote computer, it might try to make that connection again before terminating.	▪ Requires extra work on the part of the script writer. The script writer must anticipate where errors are likely to occur and then include the code to respond appropriately.

Handling Run-Time Errors

For the most part, to handle a run-time error simply means, "If an error occurs, do not allow the script to fail, but do something else instead." Typically the "something else" that you can do is one of the following:

- You can ignore the error and proceed with the next line of the script.

- You can *trap* the error and include code that responds to the error in some way (for example, by displaying an error message to the user).

Both of these methods for handling errors are implemented by including the On Error Resume Next statement within the script. When running under On Error Resume Next, a script will not fail when encountering a run-time error. Instead, the script will ignore the line of code where the error occurred and will attempt to process the next line of code. This will continue until every line of code has been either ignored (because an error occurred) or processed.

Ignoring All Errors

By far the simplest form of error handling is the type that instructs a script to ignore all errors and continue running until every line of code has been processed. To create a script that ignores all errors and continues to run, place the On Error Resume Next statement at the beginning of the script. For example, the following script attempts to use a nonexistent WSH method (Wscript.X); none of the lines of code can thus run successfully. However, the script will actually run without generating an error message because of the On Error Resume Next statement:

```
On Error Resume Next
Wscript.X "Testing 1-2-3."
Wscript.X "Testing 4-5-6"
Wscript.X "Testing 7-8-9"
```

Note that error handling does not begin until VBScript processes the On Error Resume Next statement. For example, the following script will generate a run-time error because On Error Resume Next is not implemented until the error has already occurred:

```
Wscript.Echo "Line 1."
Wscript.Echo "Line 2."
Wscript.Eho "Line 3."
On Error Resume Next
Wscript.Echo "Line 4."
```

To ensure that error handling is in place before an error occurs, put the On Error Resume Next statement near the beginning of your script:

```
On Error Resume Next
Wscript.Echo "Line 1."
Wscript.Echo "Line 2."
Wscript.Eho "Line 3."
Wscript.Echo "Line 4."
```

When the preceding script is run under CScript, the following output appears in the command window. When the script host encountered the run-time error generated by Wscript.Eho, it simply skipped that line and continued with the rest of the script:

```
Line 1.
Line 2.
Line 4.
```

Responding to Errors

Instead of having your script ignore errors, you can create code that periodically checks the error condition and then takes some sort of action. For this purpose, you might create code that:

1. Checks to see whether the value of the Err object is not equal to 0. (If Err is equal to 0, that means that no run-time error has occurred.)

2. Takes some sort of action (for example, displaying the value of Err.Number and Err.Description).

3. Resets the value of the Err object to 0. This is very important because, as noted previously in this chapter, the Err object does not automatically reset itself each time the error condition is checked.

For example, the following script sample first attempts to connect to the WMI service. If this connection attempt fails (that is, if Err does not equal 0), a message box is displayed showing the error number and description. After displaying the error message, the script then clears the Err object.

The script then attempts to return a list of all the services installed on a computer. This line of code will fail because the ExecQuery method has been misspelled as ExcQuery. After running this line of code, the script will again check the error condition. If Err does not equal 0, a message box will be displayed showing the error number and description. After displaying the error message, the script then clears the Err object.

```
On Error Resume Next
Set Computer = GetObject("winmgmts:")
If Err <> 0 Then
    Wscript.Echo Err.Number & " -- " &  Err.Description
    Err.Clear
End If
Set ServiceList = Computer.ExcQuery("SELECT * FROM Win32_Service")
If Err <> 0 Then
    Wscript.Echo Err.Number & " -- " &  Err.Description
    Err.Clear
End If
```

When this script is run under WScript, the message box in Figure 2.22 is displayed:

Figure 2.22   WMI Error Message

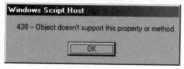

Toggling Error Handling

At times you might want to implement error handling in one portion of a script but not in another portion. In other words, sometimes you might want to trap errors, while other times you might prefer to simply let the script fail.

You can toggle error handling on and off by:

- Using the On Error Resume Next statement to turn error handling on.

- Using the On Error GoTo 0 statement to turn error handling off. After this statement has been run, error handling will not take place until another On Error Resume Next statement has been encountered.

For example, in the following script, error handling is implemented in the first line. In the second line, an error occurs because Wscript.Echo has been misspelled. However, because error handling has been implemented, the script will continue to run. Error handling is turned off in line 3, using On Error GoTo 0, and then reimplemented in line 5. Because no errors occur while error handling is off, the script will run without failing.

```
On Error Resume Next
Wscript.Eco "A"
On Error GoTo 0
Wscript.Echo "B"
On Error Resume Next
Wscript.Eco "C"
Wscript.Echo "D"
```

When the preceding script is run under Cscript, the following data is displayed in the command window. The values "A" and "B" are the only values echoed to the screen because those are the only lines of code that could be run without generating an error.

```
A
B
```

The following sample script shows a slightly revised version of the same script. In this case, error handling is turned on and then off, but this time an error occurs while error handling is off.

```
On Error Resume Next
Wscript.Eco "A"
On Error GoTo 0
Wscript.Eco "B"
On Error Resume Next
Wscript.Eco "C"
Wscript.Echo "D"
```

When this script is run under Cscript, the following error message is displayed in the command window:

```
C:\Documents and Settings\gstemp\Desktop\Scripts\x.vbs(4, 1) Microsoft VBScript
runtime error: Object doesn't support this property or method: 'Wscript.Eco'
```

In this case, the script fails to run line 2 (with the misspelling of Wscript.Echo) but continues to run because error handling has been implemented. In line 3, however, error handling been turned off. As a result, the misspelling in line 4 causes the script to fail, generating a run-time error and the resultant error message.

Handling Errors in COM Objects

One issue that complicates error handling is the fact that system administration scripts typically make use of COM objects. If an error occurs with the COM object itself, VBScript will be aware of the error. However, VBScript might have no knowledge of what actually caused the error. For example, in the following script, WMI attempts to bind to a nonexistent printer named TestPrinter. Not surprisingly, this raises an error. You might expect, therefore, to be able to trap the error number and description and echo that to the screen:

```
On Error Resume Next
Set Test = GetObject _
    ("Winmgmts:root\cimv2:Win32_Printer.Name='TestPrinter'")
Wscript.Echo Err.Number & VbTab & Err.Description
```

When the script runs, however, you get neither a standard four-digit VBScript error number nor any error description. Instead, you get the cryptic message box shown in Figure 2.23.

Figure 2.23   COM Object Error Number and Description

The problem is that the error occurred within WMI, and the error details are not available to VBScript. VBScript receives notice that an error occurred, and in most scripts that type of notice might be sufficient. In other scripts, however, or when you are developing and debugging a new script, you might find detailed error information much more useful.

Many COM objects provide their own mechanisms for trapping error information. For example, WMI allows you to create an error object, SWbemLastError, and then retrieve the following information:

- Method being called when the error occurred.

- Parameter responsible for generating the error.

- Name of the WMI provider where the error occurred.

The following script uses the SWbemLastError object to retrieve error information from within WMI and then display that information in a message box.

```
On Error Resume Next
Set Test = GetObject _
    ("Winmgmts:root\cimv2:Win32_Printer.Name='TestPrinter'")
Set WMI_Error = CreateObject("WbemScripting.SwbemLastError")
Wscript.Echo WMI_Error.Operation & VbTab & _
    WMI_Error.ParameterInfo & VbTab & WMI_Error.ProviderName
```

When the preceding script runs, the message box in Figure 2.24 appears.

Figure 2.24 Message Box Using SWbemLastError

When working with SWbemLastError, you must create the error object *following* the line of code where you believe an error could occur. For example, the following script will not return any error information because the SWbemLastError object was created before the error occurred:

```
On Error Resume Next
Set WMI_Error = CreateObject("WbemScripting.SwbemLastError")
Set Test = GetObject _
    ("Winmgmts:root\cimv2:Win32_Printer.Name='TestPrinter'")
Wscript.Echo WMI_Error.Operation & VbTab & _
    WMI_Error.ParameterInfo & VbTab & WMI_Error.ProviderName
```

Procedures

The first few system administration scripts you write are likely to be simple scripts that carry out a single task and then stop. For example, you might have a script that connects to a computer, retrieves a list of the services running on that computer, and then ends. You might have a second script that connects to a computer and starts a selected set of services, and a third that connects to a computer and stops a selected set of services.

As you become more proficient with scripting, you might begin to write more complex scripts, perhaps by combining several simple scripts. Instead of having three separate scripts for managing services, you might create a single service management script that can perform three different tasks depending on the command-line parameters entered. For example:

- If you include **/info** on the command line, the script retrieves service information.

- If you include **/start** on the command line, the script starts a selected set of services.

- If you include **/stop** on the command line, the script stops a selected set of services.

As your scripts become more complex, you might find it beneficial to place portions of the code within a procedure. Procedures are lines of code that carry out a specific task. For example, your service management script might have three procedures: one to retrieve service information, one to start selected services, and one to stop selected services. Placing code within procedures makes it easy to identify and to isolate the tasks carried out by the script. This enhances the readability and maintainability of the script and also makes it easy to copy and paste the code into scripts that carry out similar activities.

Procedures are also useful for scripts that need to carry out the same task over and over. For example, you might want to echo a message each time an error occurs within a script. To do this, you can include the message display code at every point in the script where an error might occur. Of course, this requires extra work, not only to write the original code but to maintain it as well; if you ever decide to change the displayed message, you will have to locate and change each instance within the code.

A better approach is to create a procedure that displays the message and then *call* that procedure each time an error occurs. As a result, you have to write — and maintain — only a single instance of the display code.

VBScript allows you to create two types of procedures:

- **Subroutines**. Code that is run but typically does not return a value. For example, you might create a subroutine to display error messages.

- **Functions**. Code that is run and returns a value. Functions are often used to carry out mathematical equations. For example, you might pass free disk space to a function, and the function will, in turn, convert the free space from bytes to gigabytes and then return that value.

Calling a Procedure

In general, VBScript processes each line of code in succession. Procedures are an exception to this rule. Neither subroutines nor functions are run unless they have been specifically invoked somewhere in the script. If a procedure has not been invoked, the procedure is simply skipped, regardless of where it appears within the script.

For example, the following script includes a subroutine embedded in the middle of the code. However, this subroutine is never actually called.

```
Wscript.Echo "A"
Sub EchoLine2
    Wscript.Echo "B"
End Sub
Wscript.Echo "C"
```

When the preceding script runs under CScript, the following output appears in the command window. Because the subroutine was never called, the subroutine and all the code inside it was skipped and not run:

```
A
C
```

The flow of the script goes like this:

1. The script runs line 1 and echoes the message "A".

2. The script parses line 2 and sees that it marks the beginning of a subroutine. Because the subroutine has not been called, the script skips lines 2, 3, and 4.

3. The script runs line 5, the first line following the end of the subroutine, and echoes the message "C". The script then automatically stops without ever running the subroutine.

To ensure that a subroutine runs, it must be called. This is done using a statement that consists solely of the subroutine name. For example, the following script echoes the message "A", calls the subroutine named EchoLineB, and then echoes the message "C".

```
Wscript.Echo "A"
EchoLine2
Wscript.Echo "C"
Wscript.Quit
Sub EchoLineB
    Wscript.Echo "B"
End Sub
```

When the preceding script runs under CScript, the following output appears in the command window:

```
A
B
C
```

The flow of the script goes like this:

1. The script runs line 1, and echoes the message "A".

2. The script runs line 2, which is a call to the subroutine named EchoLineB.

3. The script skips to line 5, where the subroutine begins. It skips all the intervening lines, including line 4, which would have caused the script to stop.

4. The script runs line 6, the only line within the subroutine, which echoes the message "B".

5. The script runs line 7, which marks the end of the subroutine. Because the subroutine has ended, control of the script returns to the line immediately following the line (line 2) where the subroutine was called.

6. The script runs line 3 and echoes the message "C".

7. The script runs line 4 and stops.

Procedures can be placed anywhere within a script, with no degradation of performance. However, the placement of procedures can affect the ease with which a script can be read and maintained. For more information about placing procedures within a script, see "Scripting Guidelines" in this book.

In the following script, an error-handling procedure is used to display any WMI errors that might occur. Throughout the script the Err object is checked. If the value is anything but 0, this means an error occurred; the ErrorHandler subroutine is called, and the appropriate error message is displayed.

```
On Error Resume Next
Set objWMIService = GetObject("winmgmts:root\cimv2")
If Err <> 0 Then
    ErrorHandler
End If
Set colPrinters = objWMIService.ExecQuery _
    ("SELECT * FROM Win32_Printer WHERE Name='TestPrinter'")
If Err <> 0 Then
    ErrorHandler
End If
For Each objPrinter in colPrinters
    Wscript.Echo objPrinter.Name
Next
Sub ErrorHandler
    Select Case Hex(Err.Number)
        Case "80041001"
            Wscript.Echo "The call failed."
        Case "80041002"
            Wscript.Echo "The object could not be found."
        Case "80041010"
            Wscript.Echo "The specified class is not valid."
        Case "8004103A"
            Wscript.Echo "The specified object path was invalid."
        Case "80041048"
            Wscript.Echo "The specified class is not supported."
        Case Else
            Wscript.Echo "An unknown error occurred."
    End Select
    Err.Clear
End Sub
```

Functions

Like subroutines, functions provide a way for you to use one section of code multiple times within a script. Unlike subroutines, however, functions are designed to return a value of some kind. This is not necessarily a hard-and-fast rule; VBScript does nothing to ensure that a function always returns a value and that a subroutine never returns a value. However, the scripting language is designed to make it easier to return values using functions.

In fact, when you create a function, VBScript automatically declares and initializes a variable that has the same name as the function. This variable is designed to hold the value derived by the function. Although there is no requirement that you use this variable, doing so makes it very clear that the value in question was derived by the function of the same name.

For example, the following script includes the statement Wscript.Echo ThisDate. ThisDate also happens to be the name of a function that retrieves the current date. In this script, notice that:

- The Wscript.Echo statement actually performs two tasks.

  - First it calls the function ThisDate. The function, in turn, sets the value of the special variable ThisDate to the current date.

  - After the function has completed, Wscript.Echo then echoes the value of this special variable.

- Option Explicit is used, and the variable ThisDate is never declared. However, no error occurs because VBScript internally declares and initializes this function variable for you.

```
Option Explicit
Wscript.Echo ThisDate
Function ThisDate
    ThisDate = Date
End Function
```

Note that this approach works only for a function, and not for a subroutine. The following code generates a run-time error because VBScript is unable to assign the date to the name of a subroutine:

```
Wscript.Echo ThisDate
Sub ThisDate
    ThisDate = Date
End Sub
```

Passing Parameters to Functions

Functions are often used to carry out a mathematical equation and then return the result of this equation. For example, you might use a function to convert bytes to megabytes or convert pounds to kilograms.

For a function to carry out a mathematical equation, you must supply the function with the appropriate numbers. For example, if you want a function to add the numbers 1 and 2, you must supply the functions with those two values. The numbers 1 and 2 are known as parameters (or arguments), and the process of supplying a function with parameters is typically referred to as *passing* those values.

To pass parameters to a function, simply include those values in the function call. For example, this line of code calls the function AddTwoNumbers, passing the values 1 and 2:

```
AddTwoNumbers(1 , 2)
```

In addition to including the parameters within the function call, the function itself must make allowances for those parameters. This is done by including the appropriate number of variables in the Function statement. This line of code, for example, creates a function that accepts three parameters:

```
Function AddThreeNumbers(x, y, z)
```

If the number of parameters in the Function call does not match the number of parameters in the Function statement, an error will occur. For example, this script generates a "Wrong number of arguments" error. Why? Because two values are passed to the function, but the Function statement does not allow for any parameters:

```
x = 5
y = 10
Wscript.Echo AddTwoNumbers(x, y)
Function AddTwoNumbers
    AddTwoNumbers = a + b
End Function
```

To correct this problem, include space for two parameters within the Function statement:

```
x = 5
y = 10
Wscript.Echo AddTwoNumbers(x, y)
Function AddTwoNumbers(a, b)
    AddTwoNumbers = a + b
End Function
```

You might have noticed that the parameters used in the Function call (x and y) have different names from the parameters used in the Function statement (a and b). VBScript does not require the parameter names to be identical; if it did, this would limit your ability to call the function from multiple points within a script. (Although this would be possible, you would always have to assign new values to variables x and y before calling the function. This could be a problem if you did not want to assign new values to x and y.)

Instead, VBScript simply relies on the order of the parameters. Because x is the first parameter in the function call, the value of x is assigned to a, the first parameter in the Function statement. Likewise, the value of y, the second parameter in the Function call, is assigned to b, the second parameter in the Function statement.

To show how a function might be used in an actual system administration script, the following
sample retrieves the amount of free disk space on drive C of a computer and then calls a function
named FreeMegabytes. This function converts the free space from bytes to megabytes and
returns that value. This new value is then echoed to the screen:

```
Set objWMIService = GetObject("winmgmts:")
Set objLogicalDisk = objWMIService.Get("Win32_LogicalDisk.DeviceID='c:'")
Wscript.Echo FreeMegaBytes(objLogicalDisk.FreeSpace)
Function FreeMegabytes(FreeBytes)
    FreeMegabytes =  FreeBytes / 1048576
    FreeMegabytes = Int(FreeMegabytes)
End Function
```

Note when working with functions that each time VBScript sees the name of a function, it will
attempt to call that function. This means that even though there is a special variable named, in
this case, FreeMegabytes, you do not have access to that variable except when calling the
function. For example, in the following script, the FreeMegaBytes function is called, and the free
space displayed. In the next line, the script then attempts to echo the value of the FreeMegabytes
variable.

```
Set objWMIService = GetObject("winmgmts:")
Set objLogicalDisk = objWMIService.Get("Win32_LogicalDisk.DeviceID='c:'")
Wscript.Echo FreeMegaBytes(objLogicalDisk.FreeSpace)
Wscript.Echo "Free space: " & FreeMegaBytes
Function FreeMegabytes(FreeBytes)
    FreeMegabytes =  FreeBytes / 1048576
    FreeMegabytes = Int(FreeMegabytes)
End Function
```

When the script runs, the error message shown Figure 2.25 appears. This happens because
VBScript does not echo the value of the FreeMegaBytes variable. Instead, it tries to call the
function FreeMegaBytes. This call fails because the function requires you to supply the number
of free bytes.

Figure 2.25   Error Message for Improperly Accessing a Function Variable

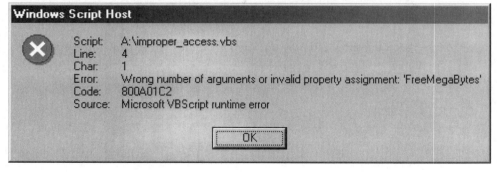

If you need to refer to the value derived from a function without calling that function, save the value in a separate variable. For example, in this script, the value returned from the FreeMegabytes function is saved in the variable AvailableSpace. This variable can be used at any time without calling the function.

```
Set objWMIService = GetObject("winmgmts:")
Set objLogicalDisk = objWMIService.Get("Win32_LogicalDisk.DeviceID='c:'")
AvailableSpace = FreeMegaBytes(objLogicalDisk.FreeSpace)
Wscript.Echo "Free space: " & AvailableSpace
Function FreeMegabytes(FreeBytes)
    FreeMegabytes =  FreeBytes / 1048576
    FreeMegabytes = Int(FreeMegabytes)
End Function
```

Passing Parameters by Value or by Reference

The values passed to a function are rarely hard-coded into a script; instead, values are typically passed to a function by using a variable. For example, the following two lines of code set the value of the variable x to 100 and then pass the variable to a function named ModifyValue:

```
x = 100
Wscript.Echo ModifyValue(x)
```

The value of x at the time the function is called is 100. The value of x at the time the function finishes running depends on two things: whether the function actually modifies the value in some way and whether the function was called by value or by reference.

To explain the difference between passing variables by value or by reference, consider the following script, which sets the value of x to 100 and then, within the function itself, changes the value of x to 99:

```
x = 100
Wscript.Echo ModifyValue(x) & VbTab & x
Function ModifyValue(x)
    ModifyValue = x / 25
    x = 99
End Function
```

When the preceding script runs, the message box shown in Figure 2.26 appears. As you can see, the variable x was divided by 25 and then was reassigned the new value 99.

Figure 2.26 Assigning a New Value Within a Function

In many scripts, the fact that the function changed the value of x makes no difference. However, what if you need to use the original value of x later in your script? In that case, the fact that the function changed the value of x makes a very big difference.

By default, VBScript passes variables by reference. This means that the function receives a reference to the variable's location in memory, and thus performs its calculations using the variable itself. Depending on the function, this can change the value of the variable.

To ensure that your variables are not changed by a function, pass the variables by value. With this approach, VBScript does not pass a reference to the actual variable; instead, it merely passes the value of that variable. Because the function does not have access to the variable itself, it cannot change the value of that variable.

To pass a variable by value, include the ByVal keyword within the name of the function. For example, this script passes the variable x by value to the function ModifyValue:

```
x = 100
Wscript.Echo ModifyValue(x) & VbTab & x
Function ModifyValue(ByVal x)
    ModifyValue = x / 25
    x = 99
End Function
```

When the preceding script runs, the message box shown in Figure 2.27 appears. Notice that the value of the variable x remains unchanged, even though the function appears to have set the value of x to 99. What really happened is that the function set the value of a *copy* of x to 99. Within the function itself, x now equals 99. As soon as the function ends, however, this temporary copy of x disappears. Meanwhile, the real x has retained its original value.

Figure 2.27   Passing a Variable by Value

You can pass some variables to a function by value and other variables to the same function by reference (using the ByRef keyword). For example, this line of code passes the variable x by value and the variable y by reference:

```
Function TestFunction(ByVal x, ByRef y)
```

In this function, it is possible for the value of y to be changed after the function finishes. However, the value of x will remain unchanged.

Recursion

Recursion is a programming technique in which a subroutine or a function calls itself. You have probably seen photographs of a person staring into a mirror. In turn, his or her reflection is staring into a mirror located in the background, which reflects the person in the mirror staring into the mirror, and so on. This is the basic idea behind recursion: Subroutine A calls subroutine A, which calls subroutine A, which calls subroutine A, and so on.

Although the concept of recursion might seem a bit bizarre, it actually has important uses in system administration scripting. For example, suppose you want to enumerate all the files in a shared folder. You can easily connect to the shared root folder and list all the files, but what happens if the shared root folder has subfolders? And what happens if those subfolders contain other subfolders? Recursion allows you to enumerate all items and subitems, even if you have no advance knowledge of the folder structure.

For example, the folder structure shown in Figure 2.28 shows a root folder, Scripts, and main subfolders, Subfolder 1 and Subfolder 2. Each of those subfolders contains other subfolders.

Figure 2.28   Sample Folder Structure

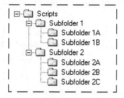

To enumerate all the folders shown in this figure, you will have to start with the Scripts folder, return a list of subfolders, bind to each subfolder, return a list of subfolders within those folders, and so on.

To perform this task, you can use a script similar to the following. This script uses a function named ShowSubFolders that is called over and over until every folder and subfolder has been enumerated.

```
Set FSO = CreateObject("Scripting.FileSystemObject")
ShowSubfolders FSO.GetFolder("C:\Scripts")
Sub ShowSubFolders(Folder)
    For Each Subfolder in Folder.SubFolders
        Wscript.Echo Subfolder.Path
        ShowSubFolders Subfolder
    Next
End Sub
```

The function ShowSubFolders does the following:

1. Retrieves a collection consisting of all the subfolders of the root folder, C:\Scripts. This collection has two items: Subfolder1 and Subfolder 2.

2. Takes the first item in the collection, Subfolder 1, and echoes the folder path. It then uses the name of that folder as a parameter passed to itself. In other words, it now runs the function ShowSubFolders using Subfolder 1 as the parameter.

3. Retrieves a collection consisting of all the subfolders of Subfolder 1. This collection has two items: Subfolder1A and Subfolder 1B.

4. Takes the first item in the collection, Subfolder 1A, and echoes the folder path. It then uses the name of that folder as a parameter passed to itself. In other words, it now runs the function ShowSubFolders using Subfolder 1A as the parameter.

5. Because Subfolder 1A has no subfolders, control passes to the next item in the collection, Subfolder 1B. The function calls itself using Subfolder 1B as the parameter.

6. Because Subfolder 1B has no subfolders, the function has finishes recursing through Subfolder 1. It thus returns to the second item in the original collection (subfolders of C:\Scripts), and repeats the entire process.

When the script runs, the following output appears:

```
C:\scripts\Subfolder 1
C:\scripts\Subfolder 1\Subfolder 1A
C:\scripts\Subfolder 1\Subfolder 1B
C:\scripts\Subfolder 2
C:\scripts\Subfolder 2\Subfolder 2A
C:\scripts\Subfolder 2\Subfolder 2B
C:\scripts\Subfolder 2\Subfolder 2C
```

Recursion is an extremely powerful technique for exploring data stored in a tree structure, including Active Directory as well as the file system.

COM Objects

The Component Object Model (COM) provides a standard way for applications (.exe files) or libraries (.dll files) to make their functionality available to any COM-compliant application or script. That is the textbook definition of COM. What COM really does, however, is make it possible for nonprogrammers to write scripts for managing Windows operating systems. COM provides a mechanism for translating script code into commands that can be acted on by the operating system. Without COM, anyone hoping to automate system administration would have to master not only a high-level programming language such as C++ or Visual Basic but also all of the Windows Application Programming Interfaces (APIs). In effect, COM brings Windows programming to the masses.

COM components are files (typically .exe or .dll files) that contain definitions of the objects the component has available for use. (These definitions are known as *classes*.) When you create a COM object in a script (a process known as *instantiation*), you are creating an instance, or copy, of one of the classes contained within the COM component. After the instance has been created, you can then take advantage of the properties, methods, and events exposed by the object.

Objects that make their functionality available through COM are known as COM servers. Applications or scripts that make use of that functionality are referred to as COM clients. For example, when you write a script that uses WMI, WMI is the COM server and your script is the COM client. COM servers can be implemented in one of two ways:

- **Out-of-process servers**. Out-of-process servers are typically implemented in executable files and run in a different process than the script. For example, when you start a script, an instance of Wscript.exe begins to run. If you next instantiate a Microsoft Word object, you are then working with two processes: Wscript.exe and the Winword.exe process in which the Microsoft Word object runs.

- **In-process servers**. Libraries (.dll files) are known as in-process servers because they run in the same process as the application or script that called them. For example, when you call the FileSystemObject from within a script, no new process is created. This is because the FileSystemObject (which is found in the Scrrun.dll library) is an in-process server and thus runs in the same process as the script. In-process servers typically run faster than out-of-process servers because the operating system does not have to cross process boundaries (from the script process to the object process and then back) to access the object's methods and properties.

As noted previously in this chapter, VBScript works with a subset of objects known as Automation objects. All COM objects must support one or more *interfaces*, which are simply the avenues by which a COM client can access the COM server. Any object that supports the IDispatch interface is known as an Automation object. Because not all COM objects support the IDispatch interface, VBScript cannot access all of the COM objects on your computer.

The COM Process

As a script writer, you have to know only how to create a reference to an Automation object. You do not have to worry about how to locate and load the object because the Windows operating system takes care of that for you. Nevertheless, it is still useful for you to understand what happens between the time when the script runs your CreateObject command and the time when the object itself is available for use.

What is especially useful to understand is that there is no magic here; in fact, the process is relatively simple. When you install an application or a library that contains object classes, that application or library registers itself with the operating system, a procedure that enables the operating system to know:

- That a new COM server is available for use.

- The object classes that the new COM server makes available.

The registration process includes adding a number of subkeys to HKEY_CLASSES_ROOT in the registry. Among the subkeys that are added is one that specifies the Programmatic Identifier (ProgID) for each new object class. The ProgID is a short text string that identifies the name given to each object class. In addition, the ProgID is the parameter used in the CreateObject and GetObject calls to specify the object you want to create. For example, in the following line of code, the ProgID is Excel.Application:

```
Set TestObject = CreateObject("Excel.Application")
```

The ProgID is all the information the operating system needs to locate and instantiate the COM object.

Creating a New Object

When a CreateObject call runs, the script engine parses out the ProgID and passes that to a COM API. This API actually creates the object reference. For example, in this line of code, the string Scripting.FileSystemObject is passed to the COM API:

```
Set TestObject = CreateObject("Scripting.FileSystemObject")
```

The COM API searches the HKEY_CLASSES_ROOT portion of the registry for a subkey with the same name as the ProgID. If such a subkey is found, the API then looks for a subkey named CLSID.

The CLSID subkey maintains a globally unique identifier (GUID) for the Automation object being created. The GUID will look something like this:

{172BDDF8-CEEA-11D1-8B05-00600806D9B6}

The GUID is the way that the operating system tracks and uses COM objects. The ProgID is simply an alias that is easier for script writers to remember.

After the GUID is discovered, the HKEY_LOCAL_MACHINE\Software\Classes\CLSID portion of the registry is searched for a subkey with the same name as the GUID. When the operating system finds this subkey, it examines the contents for additional subkeys that store the information needed to locate the executable file or library file for the object (in the case of the FileSystemObject, C:\Windows\System32\Scrrun.dll). The COM API loads the application or library, creates the object, and then returns an object reference to the calling script.

Server Mode

When an object is created from an executable file, the application is started in a special mode known as Server mode or Embedded mode. This means that although the application is running and fully functional, there is no graphical user interface and nothing is visible on the screen. (You can, however, use Task Manager to verify that the process is running.) Server mode allows you to carry out actions without a user seeing, and possibly interfering with, those actions.

Although server mode is often useful in system administration scripting, sometimes you might want a user interface (for example, if you are displaying data in Internet Explorer). If so, you will need to use the appropriate command for that COM object to make the application appear on screen. For example, the following script creates an instance of Internet Explorer and then uses the Visible command to allow the user to see the application:

```
Set IE = CreateObject("InternetExplorer.Application")
IE.Visible = True
```

Binding

Binding refers to the way that a script or an application accesses a COM object. When you create an object reference to an Automation object, VBScript must verify that the object exists and that any methods or properties you attempt to access are valid and are called correctly. This process of connecting to and verifying an object and its methods and properties is known as binding.

COM supports two types of binding: early and late. With early binding, an object, its methods, and its properties are checked when the application is compiled. If there are any problems, compilation will fail. Early binding is faster than late binding because the object is verified before the application runs. In addition, early binding provides access to the object's type library, which contains information about the methods and properties of the object. The information in the type library can then be included within the compiled code and thus be available whenever the application needs it.

Because VBScript is not a compiled language, it does not support early binding. Instead, you must use late binding, in which binding does not occur until the script actually runs. With late binding, the script must access the registry to obtain information about the object, its methods, and its properties. Because VBScript does not have access to the object's type library, it must perform a similar lookup any time it accesses the object or attempts to use one of the object's methods or properties. In addition, any incorrect calls to the object will not be found until the script actually runs.

Choosing a Method for Binding to an Automation Object

Binding to an Automation object is actually quite easy; the hardest part involves knowing how to bind to that object (that is, do you use the GetObject method or the CreateObject method?). For the most part, this depends on the object you are binding to; however, some general guidelines for binding to Automation objects are listed in Table 2.20.

Table 2.20   Methods for Binding to Automation Objects

To Perform This Task ...	Use This Method ...
Bind to WMI or ADSI.	VBScript GetObject and the appropriate moniker. A moniker is an intermediate object that makes it possible to locate, activate, and create a reference to Automation objects. Both WMI and ADSI are accessed using monikers; this allows your script to locate WMI and ADSI objects without having to know the physical location of these objects. Monikers are typically used to bind to COM objects that reside outside the file system. `Set TestObject = GetObject("winmgmts:")`
Bind to a new instance of an Automation object.	VBScript CreateObject and the appropriate ProgID. `Set TestObject = CreateObject("Word.Application")`
Bind to an existing instance of an Automation object.	VBscript GetObject and the appropriate ProgID. `Set TestObject = GetObject("Word.Application")`
Bind to an Automation object by using an existing file.	VBScript GetObject and the appropriate file path. `Set TestObject = GetObject("c:\scripts\test.xls")`

Bind to a new instance of an Automation object, with the ability to receive event notifications from that object.	Wscript CreateObject, the appropriate ProgID, and an event mapping variable.
	
	`Set TestObject = Wscript.CreateObject _`
	`    ("Word.Application", "Word")`

Bind to an existing instance of an Automation object, with the ability to receive event notifications from that object.	Wscript GetObject, the appropriate ProgID, and an event mapping variable.
	
	`Set TestObject = Wscript.GetObject _`
	`    ("Word.Application", "Word")`

Bind to a new instance of an Automation object on a remote computer.	VBScript CreateObject, the appropriate ProgID, and the name of the remote computer.
	
	`Set TestObject = CreateObject _`
	`    ("Word.Application", "atl-dc-01")`

Verifying Object References

The IsObject function allows you to verify that you were able to obtain an object reference. If the GetObject or CreateObject call succeeds, IsObject will return True (−1). If the GetObject or CreateObject call fails, IsObject will return False (0). For example, the following code uses CreateObject to try to obtain an object reference (assigned to the variable TestObject) to a nonexistent object. Because the object call fails, TestObject is not assigned an object reference, and IsObject returns 0.

```
On Error Resume Next
Set TestObject = CreateObject("Fake.Object")
Wscript.Echo IsObject(TestObject)
```

Unfortunately, VBScript assumes that once an object reference has been established, that reference will remain valid for the lifetime of the script. That is generally not a problem, particularly for ADSI and WMI, which are unlikely to disappear while the script is running.

The same cannot be said for other Automation objects, however. For example, consider the following script, which starts an instance of Microsoft Word, immediately stops that instance, and then uses IsObject to test whether the object reference is still valid:

```
Set TestObject = CreateObject("Word.Application")
TestObject.Quit
Wscript.Echo IsObject(TestObject)
```

When the script runs, IsObject reports that TestObject is still an object because TestObject is still an object reference; it just no longer points to a running instance of Microsoft Word.

There are two ways to work around this problem. One approach is to use WMI to verify that the process (in this case, Winword.exe) is still running. Although this method will work, it requires you to repeatedly query the set of running processes on the computer, something that will slow your script. In addition, matters can get complicated if multiple instances of Winword.exe are running because there is no straightforward method for identifying the instance of Winword.exe that you created and that your object reference refers to. To avoid possible problems (such as a script that inadvertently deletes text from the wrong Word document), your script should use the same instance of Winword.exe all the way through.

A better approach is to add eventing to your script. With this approach, your script can receive notification when specified events occur with your Automation object. For example, should Word quit unexpectedly, notice can be sent to your script that the Word object is no longer available. Your script can then take the appropriate action.

For more information about adding eventing to a script, see "Creating Enterprise Scripts" in this book.

Unloading Objects from Memory

In-process servers (that is, Automation objects encapsulated in .dll files) will automatically unload themselves from memory when the calling script completes. This is because these objects run in the same process as the script; when the script process ends and is thus removed from memory, any in-process servers will also be stopped and removed from memory. For example, the following script creates an instance of the FileSystemObject and then displays a message box. As soon as you dismiss the message box, both the script and the FileSystemObject are removed from memory.

```
Set TestObject = CreateObject("Scripting.FileSystemObject")
Wscript.Echo "Click here to end the script."
```

This is not true, however, for out-of-process servers, Automation objects that run in a different process than the script itself. For example, the following script creates an instance of Microsoft Word and then displays a message box. When you dismiss the message box, the script process is unloaded from memory.

```
Set TestObject = CreateObject("Word.Application")
Wscript.Echo "Click here to end the script."
```

However, the Microsoft Word process (Winword.exe) will continue to run and remain in memory, even though it is not visible on the screen. This is because there is no inherent tie between the script process and the Word process; anything you do to the script process does not affect the Word process and vice versa. You can verify that the process is still running and verify the amount of memory it is still allocated by using Task Manager, as shown in Figure 2.29.

Figure 2.29   Automation Object Running After a Script Has Completed

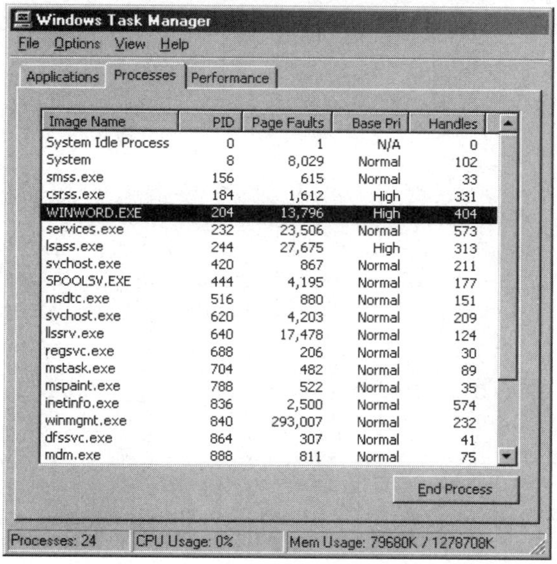

With out-of-process servers, you will typically have to use the method built into the object to explicitly unload it from memory. (You will need to check the documentation for the object to determine that method.) Microsoft Word, for example, is unloaded from memory by using the Quit method. The following script creates an instance of Microsoft Word and then immediately unloads that instance using the Quit method.

```
Set TestObject = CreateObject("Word.Application")
TestObject.Quit
```

If you run the preceding script and then check the processes running on the computer, you will not see Winword.exe (unless, of course, you had multiple copies of Winword.exe running).

Nothing Keyword

VBscript includes the Nothing keyword, which can be used to disassociate an object reference and an object. After an object variable is set to Nothing, the variable no longer maintains an object reference and thus cannot be used to control the object. For example, the following code creates an instance of Microsoft Word, sets the object variable to TestObject, and then tries to use TestObject to quit Word and unload the object from memory.

```
Set TestObject = CreateObject("Word.Application")
Set TestObject = Nothing
TestObject.Quit
```

When this script runs, the error message shown in Figure 2.30 appears. The script fails because TestObject no longer represents a valid reference.

Figure 2.30   Working with an Invalid Object Reference

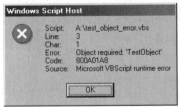

Setting an object variable to Nothing releases a small amount of memory but does not unload the object itself from memory. Because of that, there is generally no reason to set an object variable to Nothing; in effect, object variables (and all other variables, for that matter) are set to Nothing when the script completes. For example, in the following script the last line of code is superfluous: It sets the object variable TestVariable to Nothing, but that would occur anyway as soon as the script ended.

```
Set TestObject = CreateObject("Scripting.FileSystemObject")
Set TestObject = Nothing
```

CHAPTER 3

WSH Primer

Windows Script Host (WSH), a feature of the Microsoft® Windows® 2000 family of operating systems, is a powerful multi-language scripting environment ideal for automating system administration tasks. Scripts running in the WSH environment can leverage the power of WSH objects and other COM-based technologies that support Automation, such as Windows Management Instrumentation (WMI) and Active Directory Service Interfaces (ADSI), to manage the Windows subsystems that are central to many system administration tasks.

In This Chapter

WSH Overview **130**
WSH Architecture **134**
Running WSH Scripts.. **140**
    Running Scripts from the Command Line 142
    Scheduling the Running of Scripts 146
    Other Methods of Running Scripts 146
WSH Objects.. **147**
    WScript Object... 148
    WshShell Object 181
    WshNetwork Object 219
    WshController Object 227
Securing Scripts.. **234**
    Digitally Signing Scripts 235
    Restricting the Ability to Run Scripts 238

WSH Overview

The first time people encounter Windows Script Host (WSH), they often express some confusion. What exactly is WSH? Is it a language, like VBScript or JScript? No; although WSH enables you to run programs written in these languages, it is not a language itself. Is it an object model, like WMI or ADSI? No; WSH does provide a simple object model, but providing an object model is not its primary purpose.

So then what *is* WSH? As the name implies, WSH is a script host. A script host is a program that provides an environment in which users can execute scripts in a variety of languages, languages that use a variety of object models to perform tasks.

You are probably already familiar with other script hosts. Microsoft® Internet Explorer, for example, enables users to execute scripts that use the Dynamic HTML object model. Shell programs (such as C Shell, Bourne Shell and Korn Shell) enable you to write scripts that use an object model capable of manipulating the file system. Even the command prompt can be thought of as a scripting environment because it can run scripts written in the "batch file" language.

WSH is an unusual script host in that it was designed to be general-purpose. Unlike most of the scripting tools mentioned above, WSH imposes restrictions on neither the language used to write scripts nor the object models used by scripts.

WSH capabilities can be divided into four major areas. These areas, which will be discussed in detail throughout the remainder of this chapter, include:

- The ability to intrinsically carry out system administration tasks
- The ability to use COM objects to carry out system administration tasks
- The ability to add standard programming features to WSH-compatible scripting languages
- The ability to run command-line tools

The ability to intrinsically carry out system administration tasks

In many ways, this might be the least important of the WSH capabilities. WSH is primarily a scripting runtime; it provides the environment in which scripts can run, in much the same way that the command processor provides the environment in which batch files can run.

However, even though WSH primarily serves as the conduit through which other scripting languages and technologies operate, it is still possible to use "pure" WSH scripts to carry out system administration tasks. You can use WSH to do such things as map and unmap network drives, and add and remove printer connections. For example, this simple two-line script maps drive X to the network share \\atl-fs-01\public:

```
Set objNetwork = CreateObject("WScript.Network")
objNetwork.MapNetworkDrive "X:", "\\atl-fs-01\public"
```

The ability to use COM objects to carry out system administration tasks

As noted, WSH can be used to map network drives and to add printer connections. Beyond that, however, few system administration tasks can be carried out using WSH alone. You cannot use WSH to take inventory of computer hardware or to determine the software that is installed on a computer. You cannot use WSH to manage disk quotas or to list the members of the Enterprise Administrators group in the Active Directory® directory service.

But even though WSH has no intrinsic methods for carrying out these tasks, you can still perform system administration chores by using a WSH script. This is possible because WSH allows you to use COM (Component Object Model) objects within your scripts.

COM objects are a standard way for applications (.exe files) or programming libraries (.dll files) to present their capabilities as a series of objects. In turn, WSH can *bind* (connect) to these objects and harness these capabilities.

For example, WSH provides no methods for managing services on a computer. However, WMI — which is made up of a series of COM objects — *can* be used to manage services; WMI can perform such tasks as retrieve service properties, start and stop services, and configure service settings. Rather than provide its own methods for managing services, WSH can instead use the methods available through WMI.

In fact, WSH can access any COM object that supports *Automation*. Automation refers to a standard way of accessing a COM object. For the most part, scripting languages can access only COM objects using Automation; full-featured programming languages, such as C++, can access COM in additional ways. On the typical Windows-based computer, scores of Automation objects are available to manage everything from services to software to disk quotas to Active Directory. Because WSH can access all these objects, you can write scripts to manage everything from services to software to disk quotas to Active Directory.

For example, this WSH script uses ADSI to create a user account in Active Directory:

```
Set objOU = Wscript.GetObject("LDAP://OU=management,dc=fabrikam,dc=com")
Set objUser = objOU.Create("User", "cn=MyerKen")
objUser.Put "sAMAccountName", "myerken"
objUser.SetInfo
```

The ability to add standard programming features to WSH-compatible scripting languages

Applications vary widely both in what they are intended to do and in how they go about doing it; Calculator, for example, bears little resemblance to Ipconfig.exe, which bears even less resemblance to Microsoft® Word. Despite these wide variations, however, applications share some basic attributes. Many applications provide for input and output: They allow users to enter data, and they provide a method for displaying data to users. Many applications can read and write to the registry. Many applications accept command-line arguments that affect how the application runs or what the application does. This is true even of graphical applications: For example, the following command, which uses the /n argument, starts Microsoft Word without loading a blank document:

```
winword.exe /n
```

These same standard features are needed in system administration scripts; for example, how valuable would scripting be if a script could not display information? As it turns out, WSH can be used to add many of these standard features to a script: WSH can provide for input and output, it can read and write to the registry, and it can allow a script to accept command-line arguments. This ensures that any WSH-compatible language will be able to use these features, even if the language itself has no intrinsic support for them.

For example, suppose you need a script that can delete any folder from a computer; whenever you ran the script, you would pass the name of the folder to be deleted as a command-line argument:

```
deletefolder.vbs c:\scripts
```

You can use the FileSystemObject to delete folders, and you can write the script using the VBScript scripting language. But how do you handle command-line arguments? After all, neither the FileSystemObject nor VBScript have any knowledge of command-line arguments or how to use them.

Fortunately, you can use WSH to handle command-line arguments. For example, the following script actually uses three technologies:

- Line 1 uses VBScript to instantiate the FileSystemObject (although this could also have been done using WSH).

- Line 2 uses WSH to read the value of the command-line argument and assign it to a variable.

- Line 3 uses the FileSystemObject to delete the specified folder.

```
Set objFSO = Wscript.CreateObject("Scripting.FileSystemObject")
strFolder = Wscript.Arguments.Item(0)
objFSO.DeleteFolder(strFolder)
```

This same script can be easily rewritten in Jscript, PythonScript or any other WSH-compatible scripting language. Do these languages support the use of command-line arguments? It does not matter; because they are WSH-compatible, you can use WSH to provide this capability.

The ability to run command-line tools

Obviously, WSH is not required to run command-line tools; command-line tools can be run as stand-alone programs or can be called from batch files. However, WSH is extremely useful if you want to add "intelligence" to these tools or batch files. For example, suppose you want to map a drive only if a user logs on from the fabrikam domain. If the user is from the fabrikam domain, you want to use the net use command to map drive X to \\atl-fs-01\public. If the user is not from the fabrikam domain, you do not want the script to do anything.

Can this be done from within a batch file? Yes, although the solution is not particularly straightforward. (You need to figure out how to get the domain name, how to pipe that name into the script, and how to use the shell language to take action based on the value of that name.) By contrast, this simple six-line script will accomplish the same task:

```
Set objNetwork = Wscript.CreateObject("Wscript.Network")
Set objShell = WScript.CreateObject("WScript.Shell")
strDomain = objNetwork.DomainName
If strDomain = "fabrikam" Then
    objShell.Run "net use x: \\atl-fs-01"
End If
```

In other words, not only can you run command-line tools from within your WSH scripts, but you can also augment those tools with capabilities that would be very difficult to replicate in a batch file.

WSH vs. Cmd.exe

At this point, it might be useful to briefly compare WSH and Cmd.exe, the command-line interpreter found in Windows. Both are scripting environments: WSH allows you to run WSH scripts; Cmd.exe allows you to run batch files (sometimes referred to as shell scripts). Both WSH and Cmd.exe require interaction with scripting languages and scripting tools: It is difficult to write useful scripts with nothing more than WSH, and it is difficult to write useful batch files with nothing more than the shell language.

This is where the differences between the two runtimes become more apparent. WSH provides access to a large number of sophisticated scripting languages; Cmd.exe limits you largely to the simplistic syntax of the batch file language. The only tools available to Cmd.exe are command-line utilities; WSH not only offers access to these same utilities but provides access to Automation objects as well. The scripting tools available to Cmd.exe represent a very small subset of the tools available to WSH. These differences make WSH a superior scripting environment.

Does this mean that you should throw away all your command-line tools and batch files and switch exclusively to WSH? Of course not — if you have a solution that works, there is no reason to get rid of it. But for problems that batch files and command-line tools cannot solve, WSH, with its access to the myriad capabilities of VBScript, JScript, WMI, ADSI, and other Automation objects, might provide the solution you have been looking for.

A Note About WSH Versions

The sample scripts in this chapter were authored and tested with WSH version 5.6. Some of the WSH functionality described is available only under WSH version 5.6 or later. Therefore, you should determine which version of WSH you currently have installed on your computer; if it is earlier than version 5.6, you should upgrade it before proceeding with the chapter.

 Note

Of course, the added functionality found in WSH 5.6 makes it a very worthwhile upgrade regardless of whether you intend to test the scripts found in this chapter.

To display the version of WSH installed on a computer, type **cscript** at the command prompt and then press ENTER. If you have WSH 5.6 installed, you should see output similar to this:

```
C:\WINDOWS>cscript
Microsoft (R) Windows Script Host Version 5.6
Copyright (C) Microsoft Corporation 1996-2000. All rights reserved.
```

You can also retrieve this information using the following script:

```
Wscript.Echo Wscript.Version
```

For information about downloading WSH version 5.6, go to the Windows Script Technologies link on the Web Resources page at http://www.microsoft.com/windows/reskits/webresources.

WSH Architecture

When you learn how to drive a car, you do not need to first become an expert on the internal combustion engine or fluid dynamics. If you can distinguish between the gas and the brake pedal and figure out how the steering wheel works, you probably will be able to get from Point A to Point B.

And that is perfectly fine, assuming that after you get to Point B you will get out of the car and never drive again. But what if you want to drive on a regular basis? In that case, it helps to understand a little bit about how cars work, and why they might not work. You should know that cars require gas, that tires require air, and that batteries will run down if the lights are left on. If you do not understand these basic principles of cars, you are likely headed for some unpleasant surprises.

The same is true of scripting. If all you want to do is use a script to stop the Alerter service on the local computer, there is no need to read this book and to memorize the ins and outs of scripting. Instead, just copy and run the following:

```
strComputer = "."
Set objWMIService = GetObject("winmgmts:" _
    & "{impersonationLevel=impersonate}!\\" & strComputer & "\root\cimv2")
Set colServices = objWMIService.ExecQuery _
    ("SELECT * FROM Win32_Service WHERE Name = 'Alerter'")
For Each objService in colServices
    errReturnCode = objService.StopService()
Next
```

But what happens if you want to stop a different service, or you want to stop a service on a remote computer? What happens if you want to *start* the Alerter service? If you want to modify existing scripts or if you want to create your own scripts, you need to understand how scripting works. This understanding requires at least a passing familiarity with the WSH architecture.

Components of the WSH Environment

WSH has a modular architecture: It is made up of separate parts, each responsible for performing a specific function. This modularity gives WSH two important capabilities: it can make use of multiple scripting languages and it can leverage COM objects.

Figure 3.1 illustrates the major components of the WSH environment and their interactions. The WSH environment includes script files, script hosts, scripting language engines, and COM objects. In this diagram, the shaded boxes represent the items that are installed when you install WSH 5.6. The major components shown in this diagram, and the ways in which they interact, are explained in subsequent sections of this chapter.

Figure 3.1   Major Components of the WSH Environment

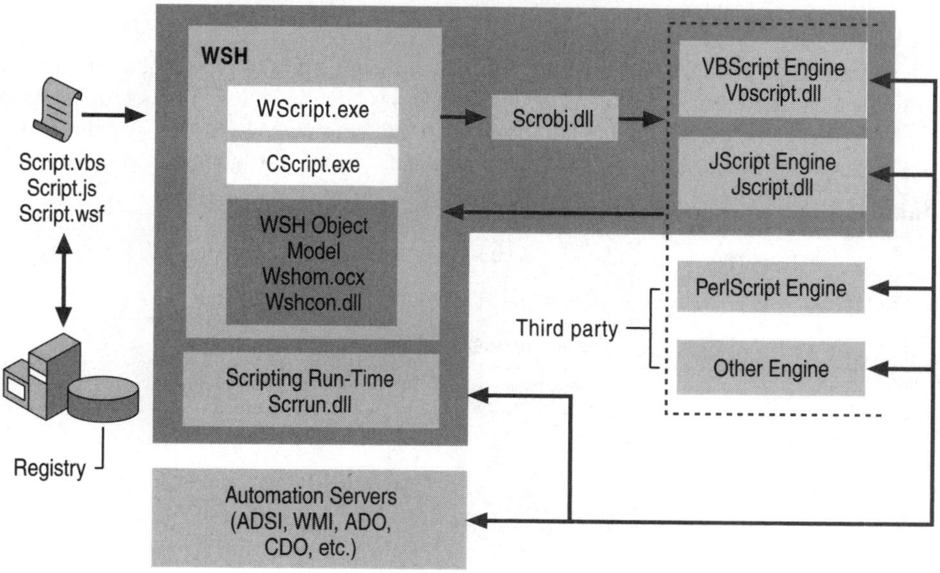

Script Files

You create WSH script files to automate system administration tasks. Script files (more commonly referred to simply as scripts) are plain-text files that contain instructions describing how to accomplish a task or set of tasks. (*Plain-text* means that the files cannot include any special formatting characters.) For example, the following script will fail because line 2 uses "smart quotes." Because these are not standard characters, WSH cannot interpret them, and the script fails with the error message, "Invalid character."

```
Wscript.Echo "This line is correct."
Wscript.Echo "This line is incorrect."
```

This is important to keep in mind because most word processing applications use special formatting characters by default. This means that word processing applications do not make the best environment for creating scripts: It is too easy to save a script with special formatting characters that will prevent the script from running. Instead, text editors designed to work with plain text (such as Notepad) are the best tools for creating WSH scripts. Because these editors typically do not support special formatting characters, there is less chance that you will inadvertently include such a character in your script.

 Note

You should also avoid the temptation of creating scripts in a word processor and then copying and pasting the code into a text editor; there is no guarantee that the pasted lines of code will actually be in plain-text format. These problems can be especially difficult to diagnose because the code might *look* as though it is in plain-text format. In reality, the code might still contain special characters that will cause the script to fail.

The instructions included in a script can be written in any WSH-compliant scripting language for which a corresponding scripting language engine has been installed. You should save the file with the file-name extension that corresponds to that language. Table 3.1 lists three example script files along with the language that corresponds to their file-name extensions.

Table 3.1   Script File Name Extensions

File Extension	Sample File Name	Scripting Language
.VBS	EnumPrinters.vbs	VBScript
.JS	EnumProcesses.js	JScript
.PLS	EnumDisks.pls	PerlScript

In other words, if you are writing a script using VBScript, save the file with the .vbs file name extension. If you are writing a script using JScript, save the file with the .js file name extension.

 Note

It is possible to run scripts even if you use a nonstandard file name extension (such as .xyz). This is explained later in this chapter.

After you have typed your script into Notepad and saved it, it is ready to run. This is one of the primary advantages of scripting: you do not need to create any supporting files nor run the script through a compilation process; instead, you simply write it, save it, and run it. For example, type the following two lines of code into Notepad:

```
Set objNetwork = Wscript.CreateObject("Wscript.Network")
Wscript.Echo objNetwork.ComputerName
```

Save the file with the .vbs file name extension, and you have a script that returns the name of the local computer.

Script Hosts

The script host initiates and coordinates the running of your script; it reads your script file and interacts with components of the WSH environment and any COM objects required by the script. It is also the responsibility of the script host to determine which language engine to use when running the script. For example, if the script has a .vbs extension, the script host will load the VBScript language engine and begin working with that engine to execute the code.

The WSH environment includes two script hosts: the console-based CScript and the GUI-based WScript. The two script hosts provide nearly identical capabilities, and in most cases, it does not matter which of the script hosts you use to run your scripts.

The two exceptions lie in how you interact with a script; that is, how you get information into a script (input) and how the script displays information it has retrieved (output). In general, CScript receives input from the command prompt and displays output in a command window. WScript, by contrast, receives input through a graphical dialog box and displays output in a graphical message box.

Otherwise, the two script hosts are largely identical: If you have a script that does not require user interaction, you can run that script under either CScript or WScript. For example, the following script maps a network drive. Because it neither requires input nor displays output, it runs exactly the same under either script host:

```
Set objNetwork = Wscript.CreateObject("WScript.Network")
objNetwork.MapNetworkDrive "g:", "\\atl-fs-01\Sales"
```

On the other hand, the following script — which displays a series of messages — runs much differently under CScript (where the messages are displayed as individual lines within a command window) and WScript (where the messages are displayed as a series of message boxes). If you are interested in seeing the difference for yourself, copy the script into Notepad, save it with a .vbs file extension, and then run it under both CScript and WScript. (For more information about running scripts under a script host, see "Running WSH Scripts" later in this chapter.)

```
Wscript.Echo "Line 1."
Wscript.Echo "Line 2."
Wscript.Echo "Line 3."
Wscript.Echo "Line 4."
```

Scripting Language Engines

Although the script host is responsible for initiating and coordinating the running of a script, it is not capable of interpreting any scripting language. The WSH environment separates the logic necessary to interpret a given scripting language from the script host.

It is this separation that enables WSH to be a multi-language scripting environment. This is because WSH does not attempt to "speak" VBScript, JScript, ActivePerl, Rexx, Python, or any other scripting language. Instead, it is up to the language engine to translate a script into commands that WSH can understand. You can write a WSH script in VBScript because the VBScript language engine can translate the code in your scripts into commands that WSH can understand and act upon. You cannot write a WSH script in C++ because there is no language engine that can translate C++ code into WSH commands.

When a scripting language engine is installed, at least one mapping is recorded in the registry. The mapping associates a file name extension with the dynamic link library (DLL) that implements the scripting language engine. The script host usually determines the language used in a script by examining the file name extension and then checking the registry to determine the corresponding scripting language engine.

 Note

You can force the script host to use the scripting language engine of your choice by specifying the //E: command-line option. (See Table 3.2.) This option allows you to use any file name extension on your script files, regardless of the scripting language in which they are written.

COM Objects

WSH includes the WScript object and three COM-based objects: WshShell, WshNetwork, and WshController. Although they are included with the WSH environment, you use them in your scripts in the same way you use other COM objects.

The WSH COM objects possess neither the depth nor the breadth of the system administration capabilities found in WMI or ADSI. Nevertheless, you are likely to find these objects useful in several situations:

- If you need to carry out a task that cannot be carried out using another Automation object. For example, the WshNetwork object allows you to map network drives; this capability is not available in either WMI or ADSI.

- If you have down-level clients that are not running WMI or ADSI. For example, ADSI might be the preferred method to retrieve the name of the local computer, but ADSI did not ship with Windows 98. For Windows 98 computers, you can use the WshNetwork object to retrieve the name of the local computer.

- If you need to run a script on a remote computer, and neither WMI nor ADSI is capable of carrying out this task remotely. In that case, you can use the WshController object to run the script on the remote computer.

How the Components of the WSH Environment Work Together

Components in the WSH environment must interact with one another to run scripts. These interactions include the following:

Script Host and Script File   When a script host is invoked to run a script, it begins by examining the file-name extension of the script file. The script host searches the registry to determine the scripting language engine that corresponds to the extension and then loads the script file in preparation for interpreting its instructions. All this happens before a single line of code is actually executed.

Script Host and Scripting Language Engine   After determining the language used in the script, the script host works with the corresponding scripting language engine to interpret the instructions in the script. The script host communicates with the scripting language engine through the *Windows Script Interfaces*. The entire script is read and checked for syntax errors before any code is executed. For example, the following script has an error in line 3; the syntax of the If…Then statement is incorrect:

```
Wscript.Echo "Line 1."
Wscript.Echo "Line 2."
If x = 1
    Wscript.Echo "X is equal to 1."
End If
```

You might expect that the script would execute lines 1 and 2 — and thus display two messages — before encountering the error on line 3. Instead, the error is caught in the pre-execution syntax check. Instead of displaying two messages, the script displays the error message "Expected 'Then'."

WScript Library and COM Objects   When instructions within a script indicate that a COM object is to be used, the built-in WScript library interacts with the COM runtime on behalf of the script.

Note

Many scripting languages provide the ability to interact with COM objects directly, in which case WScript is not part of the interaction. Because this chapter is about WSH, the examples use the WScript CreateObject and GetObject methods. However, VBScript also enables you to bind to COM objects and has a slightly easier syntax. Consequently, the VBScript functions are used in nearly all the other scripts in this book. For a more thorough comparison of the two functions, see "VBScript Primer" in this book.

WSH Object Model

People typically speak of WSH as though it were a single item. In truth, however, WSH is made up of multiple components. For example, the WSH environment includes a built-in object, WScript, and three COM objects: WshShell, WshNetwork, and WshController. Together, WScript, WshShell, WshNetwork, and WshController are referred to as the WSH objects. Your scripts access the capabilities of these objects through the WSH Object Model.

Figure 3.2 presents the WSH Object Model. Each of the items detailed in the diagram will be discussed at some point in this chapter.

Running WSH Scripts

If you were to ask a group of people how to start Microsoft Word, you would likely get a number of different answers. After all, you can start Word by clicking the Start menu and then clicking **Microsoft Word**, or by typing **winword.exe** in the **Run** dialog box. Some people might start Word from the command prompt, some from the Quick Launch bar, and others by using a keyboard shortcut. You can also start Word implicitly, by double-clicking a file with the .doc file name extension. Regardless of the method employed, in each case the end result is the same: Microsoft Word will run. Whether or not one method is better than another depends on such factors as convenience, personal preference, and individual needs (for example, whether you want a specific document to be loaded when Word starts).

Figure 3.2 WSH Object Model Diagram

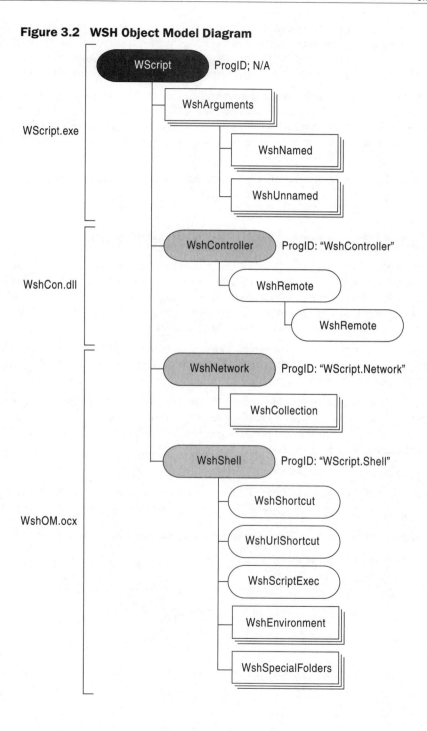

While you are working through the examples in this chapter, it is recommended that you run the scripts from the command line using CScript (unless otherwise indicated). Often times it makes no difference which script host you use to run a script. However, many system administration scripts should be run under CScript, the console-based script host, for at least two reasons.

For one, running your scripts under CScript enables them to run an external program and retrieve the output from the program. Perhaps more important, though, returned data is displayed in a command window rather than in a serious of message boxes. This is particularly useful for scripts that might return hundreds of items of data, such as scripts that retrieve events from the event logs.

The next few sections of this chapter will discuss the ins and outs of running scripts in more detail.

Running Scripts from the Command Line

Although this might be the age of the graphical user interface, many system administrators are still more comfortable working from the command prompt than within the GUI. This is not a problem with WSH; you can run scripts from the command prompt or from the GUI. Not only do you not lose any capabilities by choosing the command prompt over the GUI, but running scripts from the command line and under CScript also has at least two benefits:

- It is easier to pass arguments to the script. These arguments might be used by the script itself (for example, you might pass the name of a folder to be deleted), or the script host might use them when running the script.

- It is easier to cancel a script running under CScript. When a script runs from the command prompt, you can cancel the script either by pressing CTRL+C or by closing the command window in which it is running. If a script is running under WScript, the only way to cancel it is to terminate the Wscript.exe process.

You can run script files from the command line in one of two ways:

- Type the name of the script, including its file name extension, at the command prompt:

    `HardwareAudit.vbs`

- Type the name of one of the script hosts followed by the name of the script:

    `cscript HardwareAudit.vbs`

    `wscript HardwareAudit.vbs`

When you use the first method, the command interpreter must determine which script host to call. If you do not specify either CScript or WScript, the script will run under the default script host as configured on the computer. When you use the second method, you explicitly specify the script host under which the script should be run. The command interpreter runs cscript.exe or wscript.exe, whichever was specified, passing it the script file HardwareAudit.vbs.

Script Host Options

Both CScript and WScript accept a number of options that either affect how the script host will run a script or modify some aspect of the WSH environment. The two script hosts share a common set of options; CScript also has a few options, most notably //logo and //nologo, which have no effect in WScript.

When WSH is first installed, WScript is configured as the default script host. (If you do not specify either CScript or WScript when starting a script, WSH runs scripts using the default script host.) To set the default script host to CScript, type the following at the command prompt:

```
cscript //H:cscript
```

To reset WScript as the default script host, type this:

```
wscript //H:wscript
```

Table 3.2 lists a number of the more commonly used WSH options.

Table 3.2 Script Host Options

Parameter	Description
//B	Batch mode; suppresses display of user prompts and script errors. For example, if your script includes messages displayed using Wscript.Echo, these messages will not appear when the script runs in Batch mode. Batch mode also suppresses the use of VBScript functions such as Msgbox. The default is Interactive mode.
//D	Turns on the Microsoft Script Debugger if this program is installed. The Script Debugger ships as part of Windows 2000, although it is not installed by default. The Script Debugger does not ship with Windows XP . If the Script Debugger is not installed, no error will occur. Instead, the script will simply run.

(continued)

Table 3.2   Script Host Options *(continued)*

Parameter	Description

//E:engine	Executes the script with the specified script engine. Among other things, this allows you to run scripts that use a custom file name extension. Without the //E argument, you can run only scripts that use registered file name extensions. For example, if you try to run this command:
	
	`cscript test.admin`
	
	You will receive this error message:
	
	`Input Error: There is no script engine for file extension ".admin".`
	
	To run a script that uses a custom file extension, include the //E argument:
	
	`Cscript //E:vbscript test.admin`
	
	One advantage of using nonstandard file name extensions is that it guards against accidentally double-clicking a script and thus running something you really did not want to run.
	
	This does not create a permanent association between the .admin file name extension and VBScript. Each time you run a script that uses a .admin file name extension, you will need to use the //E argument.

//H:CScript -or- //H:WScript	Registers Cscript.exe or Wscript.exe as the default application for running scripts. When WSH is initially installed, WScript is set as the default script host.
//I	Interactive mode; allows display of user prompts and script errors. This is the default mode and is the opposite of Batch mode.

//logo	Displays a logo when the script runs under CScript (this is the default setting for WSH). The logo, which appears prior to any of the output from the script, looks like this:
	
	`Microsoft (R) Windows Script Host Version 5.6`
	`Copyright (C) Microsoft Corporation 1996-2000. All rights reserved.`

//nologo	Prevents display of the logo at run time (by default, the logo is displayed). The //nologo option is often used for scripts whose output is redirected to a text file. Suppressing the logo ensures that this information does not appear within the text file. This makes it easier to write scripts that parse the information found in the text file or that import the contents of the file to a database, because these scripts do not have to account for the logo.
//S	Saves the Timeout and Logo options for this user. For example, this command ensures that the logo will be suppressed anytime a script runs under CScript: `cscript //nologo //S` You can also modify these settings by right-clicking a script file and then clicking **Properties**.

(continued)

Table 3.2 Script Host Options *(continued)*

Parameter	Description
//T:nn	Determines the maximum number of seconds the script can run. (The default is no limit.) The //T parameter prevents excessive execution of scripts by setting a timer. When execution time exceeds the specified value, the script host interrupts the script engine and terminates the process.
//X	Starts the program in the Microsoft Script Debugger. If the Script Debugger is not installed, the script simply runs.
//?	Displays a brief description of command parameters (the usage information). The usage information is similar to the information presented in this table, although with less explanation. For example, here is the usage information for the //E argument: `//E:engine Use engine for executing script`

Redirecting Script Output to a Text File

Sometimes you run a script because you need to do something right away. For example, you might need to check the status of a particular service or the amount of free space on a particular hard drive. Other times you run a script with the intention of going back and analyzing the data later; for example, you might run a script that retrieves a list of all the software installed on all your domain controllers. Sometime in the future, you will examine that list and determine whether your domain controllers have been properly configured.

If your script retrieves data that needs to be accessed later on, it is a good idea to save this data, perhaps in a database or a text file. It is possible to include code within a script that saves data in either of these formats. If a script is designed to always save data, it is best to include the code to carry out that procedure.

But what if there are times when you want to save the output from a script and other times when, using that same script, you prefer to view that output on the screen? If you use Wscript.Echo to display data, you actually have two choices: display the data on the screen or write the data to a text file. If you choose to write the data to a text file, all you have to do is run the script using one of the two command-line redirection characters.

The command interpreter provides two ways to redirect output from the screen to a file. (That is, output is saved to a file instead of being displayed on the screen.) If you use the > character followed by a file name, output will be saved in a text file, overwriting anything that might already be saved in that file. For example, this command saves the output of a script to the file c:\scripts\services.txt:

```
cscript service_info.vbs > c:\scripts\services.txt
```

The >> characters *append* data to the specified file; new output from the script is added to anything already in the file:

```
cscript service_info.vbs >> c:\scripts\services.txt
```

You might also want to use the //nologo option, to ensure that the logo is not included within the text file:

```
cscript //nologo service_info.vbs > c:\scripts\services.txt
```

When you redirect the output of the script, no messages of any kind appear in the command window. Instead, all output, including error messages, is redirected to the text file.

Scheduling the Running of Scripts

Tasks that you script often need to be done repeatedly according to a prescribed schedule. You can use the Windows 2000 Task Scheduler or At.exe to schedule the running of these scripts. The scripts still run under one of the script hosts, but they run at the designated times without your interaction.

The ability to run scripts without the need for any human intervention is one of the major advantages scripting has over other administrative tools. For example, suppose you have a script that runs once a week and backs up and clears the event logs on all your domain controllers. There is no need for you to remember to manually run this script each week, and no need for you to arrange for someone else to run this script should you be out of the office. Instead, the script can be scheduled to run once a week, and it can do so without any need for human intervention. As an added bonus, the script can be scheduled to run during off-hours, thus minimizing any disruption to users.

You can also use WMI to create, delete, and manage scheduled tasks. (For more information about scheduling the running of scripts using WMI, see "Creating Enterprise Scripts" in this book.) For example, this script creates a scheduled task that runs a script named Monitor.vbs every Monday, Wednesday, and Friday at 12:30 P.M.

```
Set Service = GetObject("winmgmts:")
Set objNewJob = Service.Get("Win32_ScheduledJob")
errJobCreated = objNewJob.Create _
    ("cscript c:\scripts\monitor.vbs", "********123000.000000-420", _
        True , 1 OR 4 OR 16, , , JobID)
Wscript.Echo errJobCreated
```

Other Methods of Running Scripts

For the most part, system administrators either run scripts from the command line or schedule scripts to run periodically. However, a number of other methods are available for running scripts.

Running Scripts on Remote Computers. The WshController object, a COM object included with WSH, allows your scripts to run other WSH-based scripts on remote computers. For more information about the WshController object, see "WSHController Object" later in this chapter.

Running Scripts from Windows Explorer. You can run a WSH script by double-clicking the script file in Windows Explorer. This will cause the script to run using the default script host. If the default script host is CScript, a command window will open and the script will run. However, the command window will close as soon as the script finishes running. This means that any output generated by the script will disappear as soon as the script finishes and the command window closes.

Running Scripts from the Context-Sensitive Menu. You can run a WSH script by right-clicking the script file in Windows Explorer and selecting the appropriate option: **Open with Command Prompt** if CScript is your default script host or **Open** if WScript is your default script host.

Running Scripts by using Drag and Drop. You can run a script by dragging one or more files or folders onto the script file in Windows Explorer. The script runs under the default host, and the full path to each file or folder dropped onto the script file is passed to the script host as a command-line argument.

For example, this script echoes the path name of each file or folder dropped onto it:

```
For Each strArgument in Wscript.Arguments
    Wscript.Echo strArgument
Next
```

This method is commonly used for passing a list of file names as arguments to a script that performs an action on a set of files. For example, you might drag several files onto a script, and the script, in turn, might copy each of those files to a remote server.

The command interpreter limits the number of characters that can be passed by a program (or script) and all of its arguments to roughly 2048 characters. If you use the drag-and-drop feature to provide arguments to a script, be sure the total number of characters does not exceed the 2048 limit. The total number of characters can be determined by adding the length of the script's fully qualified path and file name, the length of each argument, and any white space used to separate each argument.

WSH Objects

The WSH environment includes the built-in WScript object and three COM objects: WshShell, WshNetwork, and WshController. Your scripts can use these objects to help automate system administration tasks.

The WSH objects provide your scripts with functionality that might not be available elsewhere, including the ability to work with command-line arguments, control script execution, and run scripts on remote computers. This means that the scripting language does not have to supply these elements. VBScript, for example, does not include any methods for working with command-line arguments. However, you can still use command-line arguments with VBScript by using the argument capabilities built into WSH.

WSH and the WSH objects do not include all the things system administrators might want to do; far from it. In addition, even tasks that are covered by the WSH objects are often better handled by using technologies such as WMI and ADSI.

For example, the WshShell object has a method named RegRead that allows your scripts to read a fixed registry entry. This method works fine if you know in advance the registry entry the script needs to read. Suppose you want to determine the wallpaper that the user is displaying. In a very specific situation such as that, a simple little WSH script such as this will suffice:

```
Set WshShell = WScript.CreateObject("WScript.Shell")
strWallpaper = WshShell.RegRead "HKCU\Control Panel\Desktop\Wallpaper"
Wscript.Echo strWallpaper
```

But what if you have a more open-ended task, such as enumerating all of the entries within a given subkey? In a case such as that, WSH is of little use. Instead, you should use the WMI StdRegistry provider to enumerate the entries of a subkey. The StdRegistry provider gives your scripts more complete and more flexible methods for managing the registry than the WshShell object.

In addition, WMI, for the most part, works exactly the same on remote computers as it does on the local computer. WSH, by contrast, is designed to work only on the local computer. To run WSH scripts remotely, you must use the WshController object and actually create two scripts: the script to be run and the script that allows that script to run remotely. (The WshController object is discussed in detail later in this chapter.)

Nevertheless, there are still times when you might want to use WSH rather than WMI. For example, "pure" WSH scripts are more likely to be supported by Windows NT 4.0-based and Windows 98-based computers. WSH is included with both those operating systems; however, neither WMI nor ADSI shipped with Windows NT 4.0 or Windows 98. If you need to support these older operating systems, WSH might allow you to write a single script that will run on all your computers rather than requiring you to write separate scripts for each platform.

WScript Object

The WScript object provides a wide range of capabilities to WSH scripts regardless of the language in which that script is written. As such, the WScript object ensures that a WSH-compliant language will always be able to carry out such key tasks as binding to COM objects and parsing command-line arguments.

Depending on the scripting language you use and the task you have chosen, you might or might not need to use the WScript object. For example, VBScript includes a GetObject function that allows your script to bind to COM objects. Because the syntax of the VBScript GetObject function is slightly simpler, you will likely use it rather than the WScript equivalent.

On the other hand, VBScript does not include functions for parsing command-line arguments. Fortunately, you can still use command-line arguments within VBScript; you simply make use of the argument parsing functionality provided by the WScript object. This ability to mix and match methods from WSH with methods and functions from the scripting language is one primary advantages of using WSH as a scripting environment.

Figure 3.3 shows the properties and methods of the WScript object as well as the properties and methods of the WshArguments, WshUnnamed, and WshNamed collections, all of which are accessed through the WScript object.

Figure 3.3   WScript Object Model

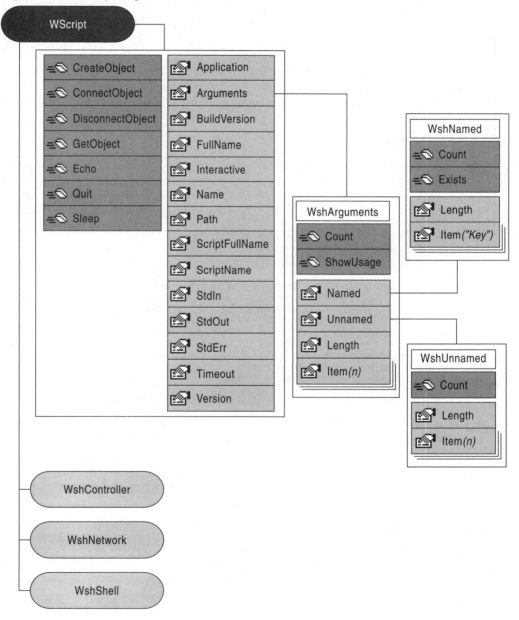

Accessing the WScript Object

The WScript object is available to all WSH scripts without the script needing to bind to the object. No call to the WScript CreateObject method is required prior to using WScript properties and methods. This means you can use WSH functions such as Echo or Sleep without having to bind to the WScript object; as a result, this single line of code is a perfectly valid WSH script:

```
Wscript.Echo "No binding required."
```

The WScript object is always available for one reason: CreateObject and GetObject are methods found within this object. If the WScript object were not always available, neither CreateObject nor GetObject would be. Thus, you would not be able to bind to any COM object (including the WScript object).

WScript Capabilities

The primary purpose of the WScript object is to provide your script with basic functionality as opposed to carrying out a particular system administration task. In other words, you will not find the capability to manage services or event logs; instead, you will find capabilities that enable you to bind to other objects that *can* be used to manage services or event logs.

Table 3.3 lists the capabilities provided by the WScript object, along with the methods and properties that your scripts can use to access this functionality. Each of these methods and properties is explained in more detail in subsequent sections of this chapter.

Table 3.3   Capabilities Provided by the WScript Object

Category	Methods or Properties
Using COM objects	CreateObject, GetObject
Handling input and output	Echo, StdOut, StdIn, StdErr
Working with command-line arguments	Arguments
Controlling script execution	Quit, Sleep, Timeout, Interactive
Obtaining WSH environment info	Application, BuildVersion, FullName, Name, Path, ScriptFullName, ScriptName, Version
Handling events	CreateObject, GetObject, ConnectObject, DisconnectObject

Using COM Objects

If you have a question about practically anything — sports, history, science, gardening — it is likely that you can find the answer at the public library. However, this does not mean that you can walk into the library, pick out a book at random, and expect to find the answer. Instead, answers to specific questions are found in specific books, and you need to locate the correct book if you want to have your question answered.

The same thing applies to COM objects. There is likely to be a COM object that can be used to script most of your system administration needs. However, you cannot use just any COM object; COM objects have specific, oftentimes unique capabilities. By the same token, you cannot simply start using a COM object, just as you cannot start reading a book without first finding that book. (The one exception is the WScript object, which you *can* simply start using.) Instead, before a script can use a COM object, it must first bind to that object. The WScript object provides two methods for creating COM objects: CreateObject and GetObject.

Creating a New Instance of a COM Object

To create a new instance of a COM object, a script can call the WScript CreateObject method and pass it the Programmatic Identifier (ProgID) of the COM object by using the following syntax:

```
WScript.CreateObject("ProgID")
```

To continue the analogy with the library, the ProgID is roughly equivalent to the call number assigned to a book. If you go to the library and give the librarian the call number, he or she can locate the book for you. Likewise, if you pass the scripting host a ProgID, the scripting host can look in the registry and locate the COM object you want to create. ProgIDs are unique to each COM object, just as call numbers are unique to each book.

How do you know the correct ProgID for a given COM object? Unfortunately, there is no simple answer to that question; your best course of action is to look at the documentation that accompanies the object. All ProgIDs are stored in the HKEY_CLASSES_ROOT portion of the registry, as shown in Figure 3.4. However, this listing is of only limited use because not all of these ProgIDs can be accessed using scripts.

Figure 3.4   ProgIDs in the Registry

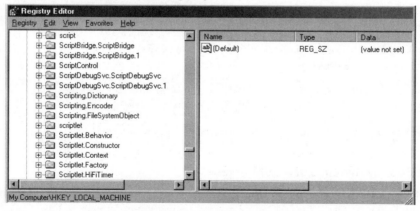

To be able to use a newly created object, the script needs to store a reference to the object in a variable by using the following syntax:

```
Set objVariable = WScript.CreateObject ("ProgID")
```

After a reference to the object is stored in a variable, the script can call a method or access a property of the object by using dot notation. (Dot notation is discussed in the "VBScript Primer" chapter of this book.)

Scripts call methods by using the following syntax:

```
objVariable.MethodName
```

Scripts access properties by using the same syntax:

```
objVariable.PropertyName
```

The script in Listing 3.1 creates a new instance of the ADSI System Information object (using the ProgID ADSystemInfo), stores a reference to it in the objSysInfo variable, and then displays the Domain Name System (DNS) domain name for the logged-on user.

Listing 3.1   Using a COM Object

```
1   Set objSysInfo = Wscript.CreateObject("ADSystemInfo")
2   Wscript.Echo "Domain DNS name: " & objSysInfo.DomainDNSName
```

As shown in Figure 3.5, only two portions of the code statement must change when you create different COM objects: the ProgID, and the name of the reference variable (if your script must reference multiple COM objects).

Figure 3.5   Elements of a Statement That Creates a COM Object

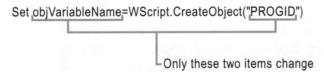

```
Set objVariableName=WScript.CreateObject("PROGID")
```

└Only these two items change

For example, the following lines of code bind to various COM objects. From line to line, the only item that changes is the ProgID:

```
Set objReference = Wscript.CreateObject("Word.Application")
Set objReference = Wscript.CreateObject("InternetExplorer.Application")
Set objReference = Wscript.CreateObject("Scripting.Dictionary")
Set objReference = Wscript.CreateObject("Wscript.Network")
```

Attaching to an Existing Instance of a COM Object

If the COM object you want to use is already running, you can use that existing object rather than create a new instance. The WScript GetObject method lets you reference and use a previously instantiated object instead of creating a new one.

When you write scripts that use WMI or ADSI, you will typically use the GetObject method; this is because both WMI and ADSI are always available. (For example, you can stop the WMI service, but if you run a script that uses WMI, the service will automatically restart.) Although there are exceptions, a typical WMI script might start like this:

```
Set objWMIService = Wscript.GetObject("winmgmts:")
```

When you are writing scripts that use the WSH objects, you will usually use the CreateObject method because the WSH objects are not usually preinstantiated.

Comparing VBScript CreateObject and GetObject Functions with WSH

The VBScript language also provides CreateObject and GetObject functions. The VBScript CreateObject function and the WScript CreateObject method both instantiate COM objects when they are called with a single parameter, the ProgID of the COM object to instantiate. For example, these two lines of code — the first using the VBScript version of CreateObject and the second using the WSH version — are functionally identical; both instantiate an instance of the FileSystemObject:

```
Set objFSO = CreateObject("Scripting.FileSystemObject")
Set objFSO = Wscript.CreateObject("Scripting.FileSystemObject")
```

Both versions of CreateObject can also accept a second parameter; however, each interprets this second parameter in a completely different way. Consider these two lines of code. The first line uses VBScript, and the second uses WSH:

```
Set objExcel = CreateObject("Excel.Application", "Parameter2")
Set objExcel = Wscript.CreateObject("Excel.Application", "Parameter2")
```

The VBScript CreateObject function interprets the second parameter as a remote computer name and tries to create the COM object on that remote computer; in this example, it tries to instantiate an instance of Microsoft Excel on a remote computer named Parameter2. The WScript CreateObject method interprets a second parameter as a subroutine prefix to be used in handling events from the object. The two GetObject functions are similarly related.

To simply create a COM object, you can use either the VBScript function or the WScript CreateObject method. After the object has been created, there are no differences in capabilities; all the methods and properties of the object available using Wscript CreateObject are also available using VBScript CreateObject. Furthermore, these properties and methods are all called in identical fashion.

On the other hand, if you want to use the remote object creation or event-handling capabilities, you need to choose the method or function that provides that additional functionality. For more information about the VBScript CreateObject and GetObject functions, see "VBScript Primer" in this book.

Handling Input and Output

Scripts have to interact with users. Output, for example, is a key element of many system administration scripts: A script that parses event logs for specific entries should display any entries it finds. Likewise, scripts need to be able to prompt users for input and then make use of that input. Suppose you write a script that retrieves information about the connectivity between two computers. You need to provide users with a simple way to specify the two computers being checked for connectivity.

WSH provides a means for interacting with users and, perhaps more important, provides a way to receive input from and direct output to the command window. Among other things, this allows you to create VBScript scripts that can run as command-line utilities, accepting input from the command prompt and displaying output within a command window. This is more useful than it might first seem, because VBScript has no intrinsic methods for receiving input from or directing output to the command window.

The WScript Echo method provides a simple way to display messages. It accepts an item (a string, a number, a date) as its only parameter and displays that item as a message to the user. The script in Listing 3.2 uses the WScript Echo method to display the version of WSH installed on the computer on which the script runs.

Listing 3.2   Displaying the Version of WSH on a Computer

```
1    Wscript.Echo "The version of WSH on this computer is: " & WScript.Version
```

In addition, the WScript object has properties that enable your scripts to access three objects that provide input and output functionality: StdOut, StdIn, and StdErr. These objects provide their own methods and properties for working with input and output, which are shown in Figure 3.6. In general, only scripts run under CScript can access StdOut, StdIn, and StdErr.

Displaying Messages to Script Users

One of the primary purposes of system administration scripting is to answer questions. How much free hard disk space is available on this server? Which user account is Internet Information Service running under? Available memory is quite low on this mail server; what processes are running and using up the memory?

For a script to answer questions such as these, it must retrieve the answers and have a way to communicate those answers back to you. Although scripts can save retrieved information in text files or databases, it is more common to have the script display that information on the screen. WSH can display information by using the Echo method.

Figure 3.6   Methods and Properties of the TextStream Objects

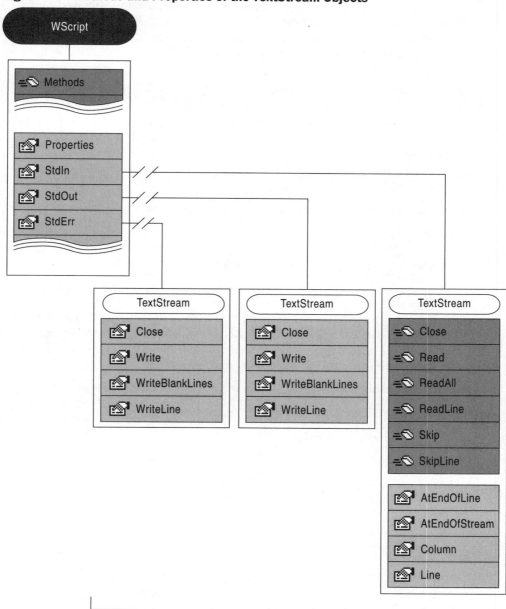

ScrRun.dll
Script Runtime
TextStream objects

The WScript Echo method takes one or more items as parameters and displays those items to the user. If a script is run under CScript, the items are displayed in the command window. If a script is run under WScript, the items appear in message boxes. The Echo method can display almost any kind of data, including strings, numbers, dates and times, and even the results of mathematical calculations. For example, this line of code displays the value 4, the result of adding 2 and 2:

```
Wscript.Echo 2 + 2
```

The Echo method is easy to implement; you simply call the method, followed by the information you want to display on the screen. To display the value of a variable, specify the variable name as the parameter:

```
Wscript.Echo strMyVariable
```

This also holds true for VBScript variables such as Now and Time:

```
Wscript.Echo Now
```

To display a string, simply enclose it in quotation marks:

```
Wscript.Echo "This is my string."
```

In fact, the only real trick to working with Wscript.Echo is understanding the difference between what happens when a script using this method runs under CScript and what happens when that same script runs under WScript. For example, consider the script in Listing 3.3, which displays three status messages by using the WScript.Echo method.

Listing 3.3   Using the Echo Method to Display Three User Messages

```
1   Wscript.Echo "Examining System Drives"
2   Wscript.Echo "Determining Free Drive Space"
3   Wscript.Echo "Mapping Network Drives"
```

When run under CScript, the script displays the following in a command window — all at once, without stopping or requiring any user interaction.

```
Examining System Drives
Determining Free Drive Space
Mapping Network Drives
```

When run under WScript, however, the script creates three separate message boxes, as shown in Figure 3.7. The message boxes are presented one at a time, and each requires a user to click the OK button before the next one can be displayed.

Figure 3.7   Three Separate Message Boxes Produced by the Echo Method Running Under WScript

Under WScript, each call to the WScript.Echo method results in the creation of a new message box. Depending on the script, this can be very important. If your script simply returns the amount of free disk space on drive C, the fact that this information is displayed in a message box rather than in the command window might be irrelevant. Suppose, however, that the script returns a list of all the services installed on a computer. Using WScript, you would need to respond to 100 or so message boxes, one for each service. In addition, as each message box was dismissed, that piece of information would disappear from the screen.

Under CScript, not only is the information displayed in the command window without the need for any user intervention (such as dismissing message boxes), but all the information also remains on the screen until the command window is dismissed. This allows you to copy the data and paste it into another application.

Getting Text into and out of Scripts

Command-line tools (including batch files) typically interact with three standard input and output streams. These are known as Standard In (StdIn), Standard Out (StdOut), and Standard Error (StdErr). Unless you specify otherwise, the command processor assumes that input will be received from the keyboard (StdIn) and output (StdOut) and error messages (StdErr) should be sent to the command window.

StdIn, StdOut, and StdErr (available only when your scripts run under CScript) provide your scripts with access to each of these streams. These streams serve several important purposes:

- They provide a way to display output in a command window.

- They provide a way for users to type input from a command prompt and have that input read by a script.

- They provide a way for scripts to access output and standard error information generated by a script, a batch file, or a command-line tool.

Displaying Output Using StdOut

StdOut can be used to display output within a command window. StdOut includes the properties shown in Table 3.4.

Table 3.4   StdOut Methods

Method	Description

Write	Writes the supplied characters to the screen but does not append a carriage return/linefeed. For example, this script uses the Write method four times:
	
	```\nWscript.StdOut.Write "ABCD"\nWscript.StdOut.Write "EFGHIJKLMN"\nWscript.StdOut.Write "OPQRSTUV"\nWscript.StdOut.Write "WXYZ"\n```
	
	When this script is run, the following output appears in the command window:
	
	```\nABCDEFGHIJKLMNOPQRSTUVWXYZ\n```

WriteLine	Similar to Wscript.Echo, WriteLine writes the supplied characters to the screen and then appends a carriage return/linefeed (as though a user had pressed ENTER). For example, this script uses the WriteLine method four times:
	
	```\nWscript.StdOut.WriteLine "ABCD"\nWscript.StdOut.WriteLine "EFGHIJKLMN"\nWscript.StdOut.WriteLine "OPQRSTUV"\nWscript.StdOut.WriteLine "WXYZ"\n```
	
	When this script is run, the following output appears in the command window:
	
	```\nABCD\nEFGHIJKLMN\nOPQRSTUV\nWXYZ\n```

WriteBlankLines	Inserts a blank line in the output, as though a user had pressed ENTER twice without typing any characters. WriteBlankLines accepts a single parameter: the number of blank lines to insert.
	
	For example, this script uses WriteBlankLines to insert first 1 and then 2 blanks lines in the output:
	
	```\nWscript.StdOut.WriteLine "ABCD"\nWscript.StdOut.WriteBlankLines 1\nWscript.StdOut.WriteLine "EFGHIJKLMN"\nWscript.StdOut.WriteLine "OPQRSTUV"\nWscript.StdOut.WriteBlankLines 2\nWscript.StdOut.WriteLine "WXYZ"\n```
	
	When this script is run, the following output appears in the command window:
	
	```\nABCD\n\nEFGHIJKLMN\nOPQRSTUV\n\n\nWXYZ\n```

The script in Listing 3.4 displays a message in the command window by using the Write and WriteLine methods of the StdOut TextStream object.

Listing 3.4   Using the Write and WriteLine Methods to Display Messages in the Command Window

```
1   Set objNetwork = Wscript.CreateObject("Wscript.Network")
2   Set objStdOut = WScript.StdOut
3   objStdOut.Write "User: "
4   objStdOut.Write objNetwork.UserDomain
5   objStdOut.Write "\"
6   objStdOut.Write objNetwork.UserName
7   objStdOut.WriteBlankLines(1)
8   objStdOut.WriteLine objNetwork.ComputerName
9   objStdOut.Write "Information retrieved."
10  objStdOut.Close
```

The following is output from the script in Listing 3.4:

```
User: FABRIKAM\kenmyer

atl-wk-01
Information retrieved.
```

By contrast, here is what output from the same script would look like if Wscript.Echo were substituted for the StdOut methods:

```
User:
FABRIKAM
\
kenmyer

atl-wk-01
Information retrieved.
```

Reading Input by Using StdIn

One way to provide a script with input is to use arguments (discussed later in this chapter). For example, the following command runs a script named DeleteUser.vbs, passing as an argument the name of the user account to be deleted:

```
cscript DeleteUser.vbs kenmyer
```

Arguments provide a quick and easy way to add input to a script. On the other hand, arguments require the user running the script to know which arguments need to be supplied and to know how to supply them. Instead of requiring users to memorize the syntax for your scripts, you can prompt users to supply the correct information after the script has started. For example:

```
C:\Scripts\cscript DeleteUser.vbs
Please enter the name of the user account to be deleted: _
```

StdIn can be used to read information entered at the command line. StdIn includes the methods and properties shown in Table 3.5.

Table 3.5   StdIn Methods and Properties

Method/Property	Description

Read	Reads the specified number of characters and then stops. For example, the following reads and echoes 3 characters at a time from StdIn until the entire line has been read:
	
	``
	Do Until Wscript.StdIn.AtEndOfLine
	    strInput = Wscript.StdIn.Read(3)
	    Wscript.Echo strInput
	Loop
	``
	
	If StdIn consists of the string "abcdefghijklmnopqrstuvwxyz", output from the script will look like this:
	
	``
	abc
	def
	ghi
	jkl
	mno
	pqr
	stu
	vwx
	yz
	``

ReadLine	Reads one line from StdIn and then stops before reaching the newline character. ReadLine is particularly useful for reading input typed by users because it reads all the characters typed by the user before he or she pressed ENTER: ``` strInput = Wscript.StdIn.ReadLine Wscript.Echo strInput ``` If StdIn consists of the string "abcdefghijklmnopqrstuvwxyz", output from the script will look like this: ``` abcdefghijklmnopqrstuvwxyz ``` ReadLine is also useful for reading the output generated by a spawned command-line tool. For more information about this, see "Running Programs" later in this chapter.
ReadAll	Used only for reading the output generated by a spawned command-line tool, batch file, or shell command.

(continued)

Table 3.5 StdIn Methods and Properties *(continued)*

Method/Property	Description

Skip	Skips the specified number of characters and then stops. For example, this script skips the first 23 characters in StdIn and then reads any remaining characters one at a time:
	
	``
	Wscript.StdIn.Skip(23)
	Do Until Wscript.StdIn.AtEndOfLine
	    strInput = Wscript.StdIn.Read(1)
	    Wscript.Echo strInput
	Loop
	``
	
	If StdIn consists of the string "abcdefghijklmnopqrstuvwxyz", output from the script will look like this:
	
	``
	x
	y
	z
	``

SkipLine	Used to skip a line when reading the output generated by a spawned command-line tool, batch file, or shell command.

AtEndOfLine	Boolean value indicating whether the end of a line has been reached. When the Read method is used to retrieve input typed by a user, this property — when True — informs the script that the entire line has been read.
	
	``
	Do Until Wscript.StdIn.AtEndOfLine
	    strInput = Wscript.StdIn.Read(1)
	    Wscript.Echo strInput
	Loop
	``

AtEndOfStream	Boolean value indicating whether the end of the stream has been reached. Used only for reading the output generated by a spawned command-line tool, batch file, or shell command.

You can use StdIn to retrieve information from the user. To obtain input from the user, you do the following:

1. Use the Write method to display a prompt on screen (such as, "Please enter your name:"). The Write method is used to ensure that the prompt and the response are included on the same line. Your screen will look similar to this, with the underscore representing the command prompt cursor:

   ```
   C:\Scripts> Please enter your name: _
   ```

2. Use the ReadLine method to read anything the user types at the command prompt, and store this information in a variable. Information is read until the user presses ENTER. For example, if you type **Ken Myer** and then press ENTER, the value Ken Myer will be stored in the variable.

   ReadLine can read as many as 254 characters typed at the command prompt.

For instance, suppose you create a script that converts numbers from decimal to hexadecimal. You need to prompt the user to enter the decimal value to convert. The script in Listing 3.5 uses the ReadLine method of the WScript StdIn object to retrieve a decimal value from the user and store it in the strDecimal variable. The VBScript Hex function is used to convert the decimal value to hexadecimal, and the WriteLine method of the WScript StdOut object is used to display the results.

Listing 3.5   Convert Between Decimal and Hexadecimal

```
1  Wscript.StdOut.Write "Enter a Decimal Number: "
2  strDecimal = Wscript.StdIn.ReadLine
3
4  Wscript.StdOut.WriteLine strDecimal & " is equal to " & _
5      Hex(strDecimal) & " in hex."
```

When run under CScript, the interaction between the script and the user looks similar to this:

```
C:\Scripts>cscript test.vbs
Microsoft (R) Windows Script Host Version 5.6
Copyright (C) Microsoft Corporation 1996-2001. All rights reserved.

Enter a Decimal Number: 256
256 is equal to 100 in hex.
```

Working with Command-Line Arguments

Command-line arguments are values that you enter at the command line when you run a script. If you have worked with command-line tools, you are already familiar with the concept of arguments. For example, when you run Ping.exe, you must supply, at a minimum, the name or the Internet Protocol (IP) address of the computer being pinged as a command-line argument:

```
ping 192.168.1.1
```

Providing values to a script by means of the command line is convenient in cases in which you expect the values to be different each time the script runs. If the values were hard coded within the script, changing the values would require you to edit the script. Using command-line arguments saves time in these cases.

Again, this is no different from working with command-line tools. Ping.exe uses command-line arguments to provide flexibility: This way, you can attempt to ping any computer anywhere. If Ping.exe did not accept command-line arguments, you would either need a separate version of the program for each computer you wanted to ping, or you would have to edit and recompile the source code any time you wanted to ping a different computer.

Command-line arguments are stored in the WshArguments collection, which you access through the Arguments property of the WScript object as shown in Figure 3.8. In addition to storing all command-line arguments in the WshArguments collection, WSH automatically filters each argument into the WshNamed or WshUnnamed collection based on the format of the argument.

Figure 3.8 WSH Command-Line Argument Collections

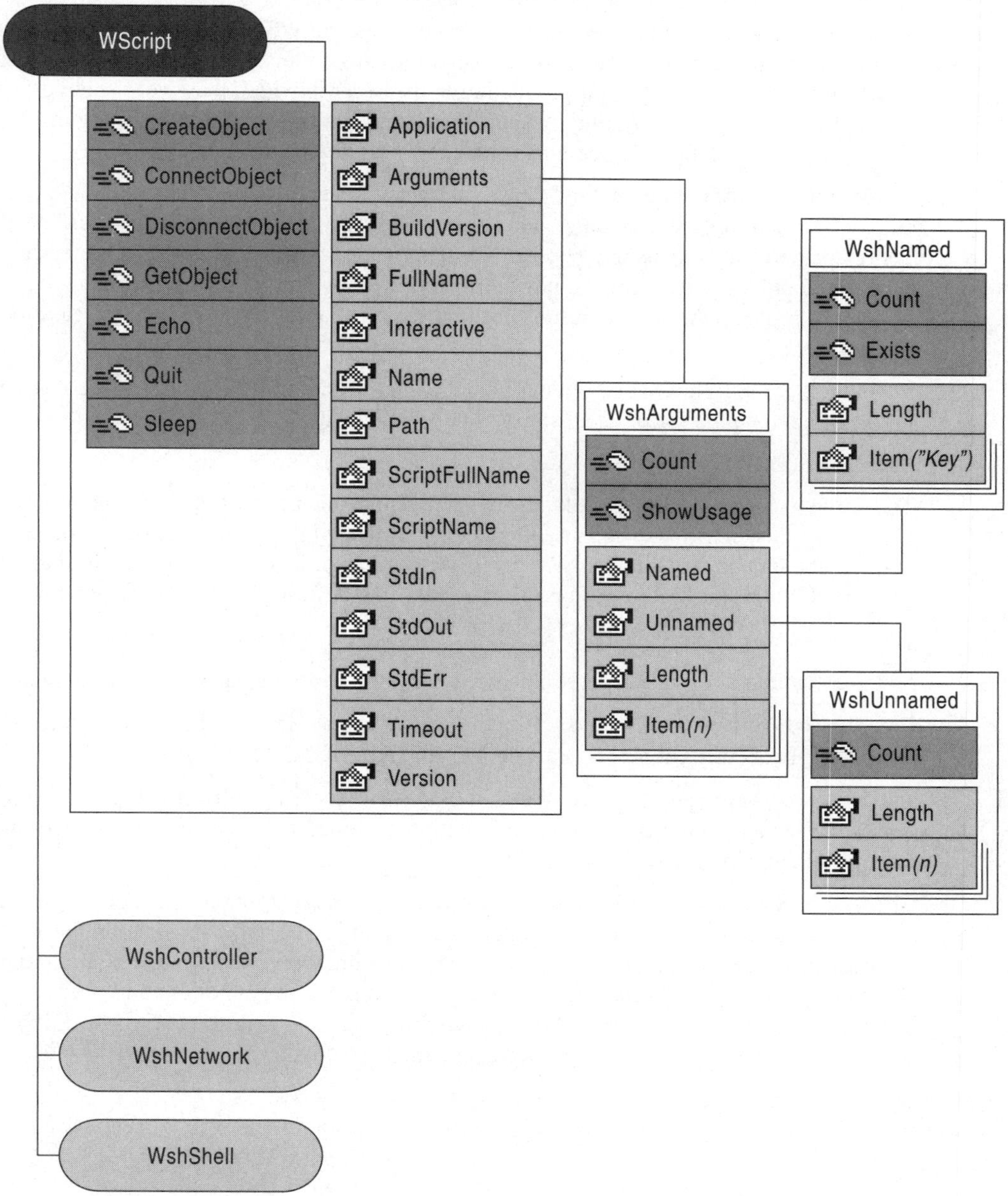

How Command-Line Arguments Are Stored and Filtered

When you run a script with command-line arguments, the WSH runtime stores these values in a location in memory represented by the WshArguments collection. The WSH runtime stores the arguments in the WshArguments collection in the order in which they were entered on the command line: WScript.Arguments.Item(0) contains the first command-line argument, WScript.Arguments.Item(1) contains the second argument, and so on.

In addition to storing all command-line arguments in the WshArguments collection, WSH automatically filters the command-line arguments into one of two subcollections: WshNamed or WshUnnamed. Arguments that conform to /name:value format are stored in the WshNamed collection, and arguments that do not follow the /name:value format are stored in the WshUnnamed collection. The purpose behind filtering arguments will become clear later in this section.

For example, the following command runs the ServerStats.vbs script and passes three command-line arguments to the script: /s:atl-dc-01, /u:admin, and perf.

```
cscript serverstats.vbs  /s:atl-dc-01  /u:admin  perf
```

The command-line arguments follow the script name and are separated by one or more spaces. Because of this, command-line arguments that contain white space must be enclosed in quotation marks to be treated as a single argument. For example, in this command, the third argument contains a blank space. As a result, the entire argument must be enclosed in quotation marks:

```
cscript serverstats.vbs  /s:atl-dc-01  /u:admin  "perf monitor"
```

Without the quotation marks, perf and monitor would be treated as separate arguments.

Figure 3.9 illustrates the contents of the three argument collections having run status.vbs with the three command-line arguments /s:atl-dc-01, /u:admin, and perf.

All command-line arguments are stored in the WshArguments collection exactly as they are typed on the command line. Count and Length return the total number of command-line arguments entered on the command line.

The WshNamed filtered collection contains the two named arguments. Named arguments are arguments that consist of two parts: a name and a value. The name must be prefaced with a forward slash, and a colon must separate the name from the value. The slash prefix and the colon separator are fixed and cannot be changed. For example, you cannot use a hyphen in place of the slash; the following command will *not* pass Server as a named argument; instead, it will treat -Server:atl-dc-01 as the value of a single unnamed argument:

```
cscript  serverstats.vbs  -Server:atl-dc-01
```

Figure 3.9   Mechanics of the WSH Argument Collections

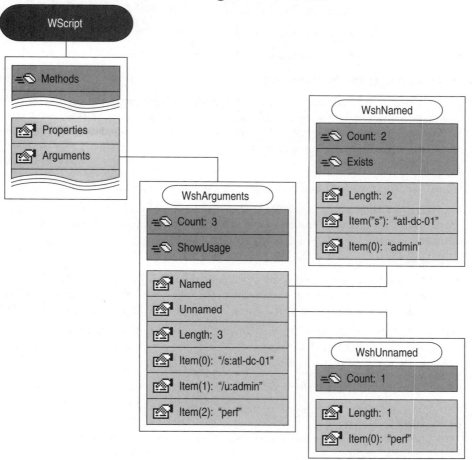

C:> cscript status.vbs /s:atl-dc-01 /u:admin perf

If you examine Figure 3.9 closely, you will see that named arguments are modified before they are stored in the WshNamed collection. The name portion of the argument becomes the index, or key, and is used with the WshNamed Item property to identify the argument to retrieve. The name is also used with the WshNamed Exists method to check whether a named argument was provided to the script at run time. The slash prefix and the colon separator are discarded, and only the value portion of the named argument is stored in the Item property of the WshNamed collection. Like WshArguments, the WshNamed Count method and Length property return the number of filtered arguments in the WshNamed collection.

The WshUnnamed filtered collection contains the one unnamed argument: perf. The WshUnnamed Count method and Length property return the number of filtered arguments in the WshUnnamed collection.

There are three ways to access command-line arguments:

- You can access the entire set of arguments using the WshArguments collection.
- You can access the arguments that have names using the WshNamed collection.
- You can access the arguments that have no names using the WshUnnamed collection.

Using the Default Arguments Collection

As described in the preceding topic, all command-line arguments are stored in the default arguments collection, WshArguments. The WshArguments collection is accessed through the WScript Arguments property. WshArguments provides two methods and four properties to read and work with command-line arguments.

Methods

Count. Returns the total number of arguments in the WshArguments collection.

ShowUsage. Echoes usage instructions about the script. This is constructed from information provided in the <runtime> section of a Windows Script File (.wsf). Windows Script Files are not discussed in this book.

Properties

Named. Provides access to the WshNamed collection. WshNamed is a filtered collection of arguments, where each argument conforms to the following format: /name:value. Command-line arguments that conform to the /name:value format are called named arguments in WSH.

Unnamed. Provides access to the WshUnnamed collection. WshUnnamed is a filtered collection of arguments, drawn from WshArguments, that do not conform to the /name:value format. Windows Script Host refers to these as unnamed arguments.

Length. Returns the total number of arguments in the WshArguments collection.

> **Note**
>
> You might have noticed that the Length property is identical to the Count method. Length was provided to maintain a level of consistency with the ECMAScript Language Specification, Standard ECMA-262, which JScript is based on. Although either Count or Length can be used to determine the number of arguments passed to VBScript, you must use Length with JScript. Any attempt to use Count with JScript will result in a run-time error.

Item(n). Retrieves the element from the WshArguments collection that corresponds to the index number enclosed in parentheses.

The following command runs a fictitious script named GetEvents.vbs with three arguments:

```
cscript getevents.vbs atl-dc-01 "Directory Service" 1130
```

WSH stores the three arguments in the WshArguments collection in the order in which they were entered, and exactly as they were typed on the command line. To read the three arguments, you use the WScript Arguments property in combination with the WshArguments Item property as shown here:

```
ServerName = WScript.Arguments.Item(0)
EventLog = WScript.Arguments.Item(1)
EventID = WScript.Arguments.Item(2)
```

Because collections are zero-based, WScript.Arguments.Item(0) points to the first argument in the WshArguments collection. WScript.Arguments.Item(1) points to the second argument, which is enclosed inside quotation marks because the argument, Directory Services, contains a space. Omitting the quotation marks would cause the two words to be treated as separate arguments, which would lead to errors because incorrect values would be assigned to the EventLog and EventID variables. WScript.Arguments.Item(2) points to the third argument.

The collection looks like the one shown in Table 3.6.

Table 3.6 Sample WSH Arguments Collection

Item	Value
0	atl-dc-01
1	Directory Service
2	1130

If the fictitious script employed additional arguments, WScript.Arguments.Item(3) would point to the fourth argument, WScript.Arguments.Item(4) would point to the fifth argument, and so on.

There is no fixed limit on the number of arguments that can be stored in the WshArguments collection. However, the entire command line, which includes the host name, host options, script name, and script arguments, cannot exceed the maximum command-line length. Exceeding the maximum command-line length generally is not a problem unless you use the WSH Drag and Drop feature to populate WshArguments. The maximum command-line length also applies to WSH Drag and Drop.

You can reduce the amount of typing necessary to access each argument by setting a reference to the WshArguments collection by way of the WScript Arguments property. Use the VBScript Set keyword followed by the variable name you want to use to access the WshArguments collection. Set is required because collections are standard COM objects. The following example is functionally equivalent to the preceding example despite some syntactical differences.

```
Set args = WScript.Arguments
ServerName = args.Item(0)
EventLog = args.Item(1)
EventID = args.Item(2)
```

The previous three examples assume GetEvents.vbs is always passed three command-line arguments. While omitting any kind of argument verification might be OK for a quick ad hoc script, failing to perform some level of verification can lead to error-prone scripts, especially when the script is shared with other users.

The following command runs the fictitious GetEvents.vbs script without any arguments.

```
cscript getevents.vbs
```

Running GetEvents.vbs without arguments using one of the three previous examples would result in the following run-time error:

```
C:\Scripts\GetEvents.vbs(2, 1) Microsoft VBScript runtime error: Subscript out of
range
```

Any attempt at using the Item property to access an argument that does not exist will result in a Subscript out of range run-time error. Listing 3.6 demonstrates how to use the WshArguments Count method to verify that the correct number of command-line arguments is provided to the script at run time.

Listing 3.6   Using Count to Verify the Number of Arguments Used

```
1   If WScript.Arguments.Count = 3 Then
2       ServerName = WScript.Arguments.Item(0)
3       EventLog = WScript.Arguments.Item(1)
4       EventID = WScript.Arguments.Item(2)
5   Else
6       Wscript.Echo "Usage: GetEvents.vbs ServerName EventLog EventID"
7       Wscript.Quit
8   End If
```

In Line 1 of Listing 3.6, the script uses the WshArguments Count method to obtain the number of command-line arguments in the WshArguments collection. If the value is equal to 3, the script initializes the ServerName, EventLog, and EventID variables with the three arguments in the WshArguments collection. Otherwise, the script echoes usage instructions and immediately exits.

Unnamed Command-Line Arguments

Unnamed arguments are entered on the command line as values only, without an associated name. At times the order of your arguments might be irrelevant; for example, a script might require you to type in three computer names, and it makes no difference which computer the script runs against first. Otherwise, unnamed arguments must be entered in the order that the script requires.

You might want to use unnamed arguments when your script:

- Accepts only one or two command-line arguments. If your script accepts only the name of a folder as its sole command-line argument, there is no reason to make this a named argument.

- Accepts arguments that are all of the same type and are each used in the same way within your script. For example, you might have a script that backs up and clears event logs on all computers whose names are entered as command-line arguments. Because all the arguments are the same (names of servers), and because the order is probably irrelevant, there is no reason to use named arguments.

When you run a script with unnamed command-line arguments, the WSH runtime stores the arguments in the WshArguments collection in the order in which they were entered on the command line. The arguments can then be referenced in the script using index numbers that represent the order in which they were entered. The sequence of index numbers begins with 0.

The script in Listing 3.7 uses the unnamed command-line arguments collection to retrieve and display the command-line arguments provided to it.

Listing 3.7   Retrieving Command-Line Arguments Using the Arguments Collection

```
1   strServer = WScript.Arguments.Item(0)
2   strPacketSize = WScript.Arguments.Item(1)
3   strTimeout = WScript.Arguments.Item(2)
4
5   Wscript.Echo "Pinging Server: " & strServer
6   Wscript.Echo "Packet Size: " & strPacketSize
7   Wscript.Echo "Timeout: " & strTimeout
```

The following command runs the script with the command-line arguments entered in the order required by the script.

EchoUnnamedArgs.vbs DCServer01 100 5000

This command produces the following output:

```
Pinging Server: DCServer01
Packet Size: 100
Timeout: 5000
```

This command runs the same script with the command-line arguments entered in the wrong order.

EchoUnnamedArgs.vbs 100 DCServer01 5000

This command produces the following output:

```
Pinging Server: 100
Packet Size: DCServer01
Timeout: 5000
```

The output from the first command is correct but the output from the second command is incorrect. Because the script is written using unnamed arguments, the order in which the command-line arguments are entered is crucial for the script to work properly. If the script actually tried to run Ping.exe, the procedure would fail because there is no server named 100 and no such thing as a packet size of DCServer01.

Named Command-Line Arguments

As the preceding example showed, the order in which unnamed arguments are entered can make the difference between a script that runs successfully and a script that does not. This places a considerable burden on administrators running the script; not only must they supply the correct arguments, but they must also supply them in the correct order. One mistake will likely cause the script to fail.

To make it easier for people to run scripts that use multiple arguments, you can use named arguments instead. Named arguments are entered on the command line as values with associated names. They can be entered in any order.

A named argument begins with a slash (/), and the name and the value are separated by a colon (:). The following command runs a script named ServerTest.vbs with two named arguments:

```
ServerTest.vbs /Server:HRServer01 /Timeout:3000
```

The name of the first argument is Server, and its value is HRServer01. The name of the second argument is Timeout, and its value is 3000. These arguments could also be entered in the reverse order, as follows:

```
ServerTest.vbs /Timeout:3000 /Server:HRServer01
```

When you run a script with named command-line arguments, each argument's name and value are stored in the WshNamed collection.

The script in Listing 3.8 uses the named command-line arguments collection to retrieve and display the command-line arguments it receives in the command window.

Listing 3.8   Retrieving Command-Line Arguments Using the Named Arguments Collection

```
1   Set colNamedArguments = WScript.Arguments.Named
2
3   strServer = colNamedArguments.Item("Server")
4   strPacketSize = colNamedArguments.Item("PacketSize")
5   strTimeout = colNamedArguments.Item("Timeout")
6   Wscript.Echo "Server Name: " & strServer
7   Wscript.Echo "Packet Size: " & strPacketSize
8   Wscript.Echo "Timeout (ms): " & strTimeout
```

The following command runs the script with three named arguments.

```
EchoNamedArgs.vbs /Server:HRServer01 /PacketSize:300 /Timeout:8000
```

This command produces the following output:

```
Server Name: HRServer01
Packet Size: 300
Timeout (ms): 8000
```

This command runs the same script with the order of the named arguments changed.

EchoNamedArgs.vbs /Timeout:8000 /PacketSize:300 /Server:HRServer01

This command produces the following output:

```
Server Name: HRServer01
Packet Size: 300
Timeout (ms): 8000
```

The output from the first command and the second command is the same. You can enter named arguments in any order without affecting the outcome of the script.

Named arguments are also useful when you want to include optional parameters within your scripts. The script in Listing 3.9 is similar to the script in Listing 3.8, but the PacketSize argument is an optional argument. If the script user does not enter a packet size, the script uses a default packet size.

The script uses the Exists method to check whether the user entered an argument named PacketSize. If the result of the test is True, the script proceeds to line 7. If the result of the test is False, the script proceeds to line 9, where the PacketSize variable is set to 100, using the DEFAULT_PACKET_SIZE constant.

Listing 3.9   Retrieving Command-Line Arguments and Using Default Argument Values

```
1   Const DEFAULT_PACKET_SIZE = 100
2
3   Set colNamedArguments = WScript.Arguments.Named
4
5   strServer = colNamedArguments.Item("Server")
6   If colNamedArguments.Exists("PacketSize") Then
7       strPacketSize = colNamedArguments.Item("PacketSize")
8   Else
9       strPacketSize = DEFAULT_PACKET_SIZE
10  End If
11  strTimeout = colNamedArguments.Item("Timeout")
12
13  Wscript.Echo "Server Name: " & strServer
14  If colNamedArguments.Exists("PacketSize") Then
15      Wscript.Echo "Packet Size :" & strPacketSize
16  Else
17      Wscript.Echo "Packet Size [default]: " & strPacketSize
18  End If
19  Wscript.Echo "Timeout (ms): " & strTimeout
```

Using Both Unnamed and Named Arguments

In most cases, you should not use both named and unnamed arguments in the same script. Using both types of arguments makes the required command-line syntax more difficult to remember. If your script accepts two or fewer arguments or multiple arguments of the same type, you might want to use unnamed arguments. If your script accepts three arguments of distinct types or has optional arguments, you should probably use named arguments.

Occasionally, however, it can be useful to mix named and unnamed arguments in a script. For example, if you have a script that has one required argument and a number of optional arguments, you can use an unnamed argument for the required argument and named arguments for all of the optional arguments. The following command contains a required server name (HRServer01) plus three optional arguments. In this command, the unnamed argument must be listed first, or the script will likely fail.

```
CheckServer.vbs HRServer01 /timeout:200 /logfile:serverlog.txt /verbose:true
```

Verifying Command-Line Arguments

Many of your scripts will require you to enter the required number and types of command-line arguments for the scripts to run correctly. You might need to perform two verifications on command-line arguments:

- Number of arguments entered is within the acceptable range

- Required arguments have been entered

Verifying the Number of Arguments Entered

Some scripts require a specific number of command-line arguments. For example, suppose you have a script that copies files from one computer to another. This script likely requires two, and only two, command-line arguments: the name of the source computer and the name of the target computer. Trying to run this script with one command-line argument or with three command-line arguments would not make any sense; there would be no way for the script to correctly determine the source and target computers.

In a situation such as this, one of the first things the script should do is verify that two command-line arguments were entered. This requires little effort on your part because arguments are returned as part of a collection, and collections typically include a Count property. The purpose of the Count property is to tell you how many items are in the collection. If Wscript.Arguments.Count equals 2, two arguments are in the collection.

The script in Listing 3.10 verifies the number of command-line arguments entered. The script accepts up to four arguments, any two of which are optional. Therefore, the user must enter at least two but no more than four arguments.

Listing 3.10   Verifying the Number of Command-Line Arguments Entered

```
1   iNumberOfArguments = WScript.Arguments.Count
2   If iNumberOfArguments >= 2 And iNumberOfArguments <= 4 Then
3       Wscript.Echo iNumberOfArguments & " arguments entered. " & _
4           "This is a valid number."
5   Else
6       Wscript.Echo "Error: invalid number of arguments entered. " & _
7           "Please enter 2, 3, or 4 arguments."
8       Wscript.Quit
9   End If
```

In line 1 of Listing 3.10, the script uses WScript.Arguments.Count to determine the number of command-line arguments entered. The script stores this value in the iNumberOfArguments variable.

In line 2, the script uses iNumberOfArguments >=2 And iNumberOfArguments <=4 to test whether the user entered 2, 3, or 4 arguments:

- If the result of the test is True, the script proceeds to line 3 and uses the Echo method to display a message indicating that the correct number of arguments was entered.

- If the result of the test is False, the script proceeds to line 6 and uses the Echo method to display an error message indicating that the wrong number of arguments was entered.

The following command tries to run the script with more than four arguments.

CheckNumArgs.vbs HRServer01 RASServer01 SQLServer01 1000 300

This command produces the following output:

```
Error:   invalid number of arguments entered. Please enter 2, 3, or 4 arguments.
```

The output informs you that you have entered the wrong number of arguments. You are told that you should have entered between two, three, or four arguments instead of the five you entered.

This command runs the script with three arguments, an acceptable number for the script.

CheckNumArgs.vbs HRServer01 1000 300

This command produces the following output:

```
3 arguments entered. This is a valid number.
```

The output validates the fact that you have entered the correct number of arguments and that, as a result, the script is proceeding as expected. The script then displays the number of arguments you entered.

Verifying That All Required Arguments Are Entered

When you use command-line arguments in a script, the script should check to ensure that any required arguments have been entered before it proceeds. Unfortunately, WSH does not allow you to specify that an argument is required, and then notify you if the argument is not found. For example, if you run a command-line tool without a required argument, the tool typically will not run; instead, it displays usage instructions. Your scripts can do the same thing, but it is up to you to write code that checks the arguments collection and ensures that all the required arguments are present.

If you need to use required arguments in a script, it is recommended that you use named arguments. One advantage of using named arguments is that you can then use the Exists method to check whether an argument has been provided. For example, this line of code checks whether an argument named FolderName is present in the arguments collection. If the argument exists, the value –1 (True) will be echoed to the screen. Otherwise, the value 0 (False) will be displayed:

```
Wscript.Echo colNamedArguments.Exists("FolderName")
```

Suppose you enter the correct number of arguments but omit a required argument. The script in Listing 3.11 builds on the script in Listing 3.10. It uses the WshNamed collection Exists method to ensure that the named argument, Server, is among the arguments that you entered. In line 4, the script uses Not colNamedArgument.Exists("Server") to test whether the user has entered the named argument Server:

- If the test reveals that the argument was not entered, the script proceeds to line 5. There the script uses the Echo method to display a message indicating that the named argument Server is required for the script to run. In line 6, Wscript.Quit is used to stop the script from running because the required argument, Server, was not entered.

- If the test reveals that the argument was entered, the script proceeds to line 7.

  In lines 9 and 10, the script uses colNamedArguments.Item("Server") to retrieve the value of the Server named argument entered by the user. The script then displays a message constructed from this value. The message tells the user the value they entered for the Server named argument.

Listing 3.11 Verifying That All Required Arguments Are Entered

```
1   iNumberOfArguments = WScript.Arguments.Count
2   Set colNamedArguments = WScript.Arguments.Named
3
4   If Not colNamedArguments.Exists("Server") Then
5       Wscript.Echo "Usage: /Server:<servername> is required."
6       Wscript.Quit
7   ElseIf iNumberOfArguments >= 2 Or iNumberOfArguments <= 4 Then
8       Wscript.Echo iNumberOfArguments & " arguments entered"
9       Wscript.Echo "including Server Name: " & _
10          colNamedArguments.Item("Server")
11  Else
12      Wscript.Echo "Usage: Please enter between 2 and 4 arguments."
13      Wscript.Quit
14  End If
```

The following command tries to run the script without including the Server named argument.

CheckReqArgs.vbs 1000 300

This command produces the following output:

```
Usage: /Server:<servername> is required.
```

The output reflects the fact that you have not entered the Server named argument, which is required, by displaying a usage message.

This command runs the script with the required argument and an acceptable number of arguments.

CheckReqArgs.vbs /Server:HRServer01 1000 300

This command produces the following output:

```
3 arguments entered
including Server Name: HRServer01
```

The output reflects the fact that you have entered the correct number of arguments, including the required Server named argument. The script displays the value entered for the Server argument to reinforce the fact that this required argument was actually entered.

Controlling How a Script Runs

When you run a script, the commands in the script are typically executed in the order in which they appear in the script file. There are no pauses in the running of the script, and the script ends only after the last command is completed.

The WScript object provides two properties (Timeout and Interactive) and two methods (Sleep and Quit) that enable you to alter how a script runs. A script can use these properties and methods to cause itself to:

- Pause for a specified length of time.

- Immediately stop running.

- Stop running after a specified length of time.

Pausing a Script

Most of the time, WSH attempts to complete a script as quickly as possible; as soon as WSH finishes executing the first line of code, it begins executing the second line of code. More often than not, this is the desired behavior: In general, the faster a script can complete its tasks, the better.

There are times, however, when you do not want a script to run as quickly as possible. For example, suppose you need to monitor processor use on a computer. To do this, you might want to record processor use every 10 seconds until you have collected 100 measurements. In this case, you do not want the script to take these 100 measurements as quickly as it can. Instead, you want it to take the first measurement and then wait 10 seconds before taking the second measurement.

A script can force itself to pause by calling the WScript Sleep method. The Sleep method accepts a single parameter that indicates how long, in milliseconds, to pause the script. (There are 1,000 milliseconds in a second and 60,000 milliseconds in a minute.)

You will need to use the Sleep method in your scripts when:

- Your script must wait for an event to occur before continuing to run.

- You want your script to periodically check the status of a system parameter (for example, checking processor usage every 10 seconds).

- Your script is interacting with a user and you want to slow the interaction to a usable speed. For example, when displaying events retrieved from an event log, you might want to insert a pause, giving the user time to read the first event before displaying the next event.

The script in Listing 3.12 checks the amount of free space on all the disk drives on a computer. The script then pauses for 5 minutes (300,000 milliseconds) and then checks free disk space again.

Listing 3.12   Using the Sleep Method to Pause a Script

```
1   strComputer = "."
2   Set objWMIService = GetObject("winmgmts:" _
3       & "{impersonationLevel=impersonate}!\\" & strComputer & "\root\cimv2")
4   Do While True
5       Set colDisks = objWMIService.ExecQuery _
6           ("SELECT * FROM Win32_LogicalDisk")
7       For Each objDisk in colDisks
8           Wscript.Echo "DeviceID: " & objDisk.DeviceID
9           Wscript.Echo "Free Disk Space: " & objDisk.FreeSpace
10      Next
11      Wscript.Sleep 300000
12  Loop
```

> **Note**
>
> The preceding script is designed to run indefinitely. To stop the script, you will need to terminate the process under which it is running.

Quitting a Script

In general, scripts begin by executing line 1 and continue to run until each line in the script has been executed. (This is not entirely true, but it will do for the purposes of this discussion. In reality, some lines of code — such as those in a particular function — might be skipped rather than executed.) After each line of code has been executed, the script automatically terminates itself. For example, this simple little script echoes three numbers to the screen and then quits. The script does not include any special instructions telling it to quit; it automatically terminates after executing the last line:

```
Wscript.Echo "1"
Wscript.Echo "2"
Wscript.Echo "3"
```

Most of the time, this is exactly what you want a script to do. However, there might be occasions when you want a script to terminate *before* every line of code has been executed. For example, suppose you have a script that requires two command-line arguments: a source computer and a target computer. At the very beginning of the script, you check to see whether two (and only two) arguments have been supplied. If they have, the script continues.

But what if they have not? What if the user supplied only one argument, or what if the user supplied four arguments? In that case, there is no reason to proceed; after all, the script is likely to fail and could leave one or more computers in an indeterminate state. In this case, the best course of action might be to echo a message stating that the user must supply two command-line arguments, and then immediately terminate the script, regardless of how many lines of code remain unexecuted.

A script can force itself to stop running before it reaches its last command by calling the Quit method. This can be done using a single line of code:

```
Wscript.Quit
```

When a script executes the Quit method, it immediately terminates. For example, this script echoes three messages and then quits. The last three Wscript.Echo commands will never execute:

```
Wscript.Echo "1"
Wscript.Echo "2"
Wscript.Echo "3"
Wscript.Quit
Wscript.Echo "4"
Wscript.Echo "5"
Wscript.Echo "6"
```

Setting a Time-out Value for a Script

It is good practice to set the time-out value on any script, but it is particularly important if the script is liable to run into issues that might force it to run indefinitely.

For example, suppose you have a script that must first connect to a remote computer. What if this connection cannot be made? In that case, you might include code that tells the script to wait 60 seconds after a failed connection and then try again. The script will continue in this loop until the connection is made.

But what if the remote computer has been permanently removed from the network? In that case, the script could theoretically run forever, taking up computer processing cycles and using up network bandwidth as it tries to make a connection that can no longer be made. In a situation such as that, it might be beneficial to set the Timeout property. This instructs the script to run only for a set amount of time. If it cannot complete its task when the time period expires, the script simply terminates.

The WScript Timeout property sets a time period, in seconds, after which a script will stop running. (By default, WSH does not time out the running of a script.) Setting a Timeout ensures that no script will run forever.

The script in Listing 3.13 sets a time-out value of 5 seconds. If the script has not finished executing 5 seconds after it starts, the script will automatically terminate. Because the script includes a 60-second pause (line 2), the timeout will always expire before the script completes. As a result, line 3, which echoes a message to the screen, will never run.

Listing 3.13 Setting the Time-out Value of a Script

```
1   Wscript.Timeout = 5
2   Wscript.Sleep 60000
3   Wscript.Echo "Script is finished."
```

Obtaining WSH Environment Information

The WScript object has a number of properties that provide information about the script host being used and the script being run. This *metadata* includes the information shown in Table 3.7.

Table 3.7   WSH Environment Properties

Property	Description
ScriptFullName	Full path of the currently running script (for example, C:\Scripts\Monitor.vbs).
ScriptName	File name of the currently running script (for example, Monitor.vbs).
Version	WSH version number (for example, 5.6).
Build	WSH build number. The full version number of Windows Script Host consists of the product release version number followed by the build version number. For example, if the Windows Script Host product release version number is 5.6, and the build version number is 6626, the full version number is 5.6.6626. The build number is perhaps most useful if you are testing beta copies of WSH. Otherwise, the version number will typically suffice.
Name	Always returns *Windows Script Host*.
FullName	Full path to the script host (either Wscript.exe or CScript.exe).
Path	Full path to the folder where the script host is located. Does not include the file name (Wscript.exe or Cscript.exe).

This metadata can be extremely useful. For example, the version number can be used to verify that a computer has the correct version of WSH installed; if you have a script that requires WSH 5.6, the script can first check the version number and then terminate if Version is not 5.6. For example:

```
If Wscript.Version <> "5.6" Then
    Wscript.Echo "This script must be run under WSH 5.6."
    Wscript.Quit
End If
```

Likewise, you might have a script that makes extensive use of Wscript.Echo. In that case, you probably do not want to run the script under WScript; this can result in hundreds of message boxes that must be responded to. Consequently, your script might check to see which script host it is running under and then terminate if the host is not CScript.

You can determine the script host by using the FullName property and using the VBScript function Right to check the last 11 characters. (To ensure that the check is done correctly, you should also convert these 11 characters to uppercase using the UCase function.) If the last 11 characters equal WSCRIPT.EXE, the script is running under WScript. If the last 11 characters are CSCRIPT.EXE, the script is running under CScript.

 Note

Why the last 11 characters? The value of ScriptFullName will vary depending on where WSH has been installed; it might be C:\Winnt\System32\CScript.exe, or it might be E:\Windows\System32\Wscript.exe. However, the last 11 characters in the path will always be either Wscript.exe or Cscript.exe.

For example, the following script snippet checks the script host and then displays a message and terminates if the host is WSCRIPT.EXE:

```
If UCase(Right(Wscript.FullName, 11)) = "WSCRIPT.EXE" Then
    Wscript.Echo "This script must be run under CScript."
    Wscript.Quit
End If
```

The script in Listing 3.14 displays the available WSH environment properties by retrieving them and echoing them to the screen.

Listing 3.14   Displaying Information About the WSH Environment

```
1  Wscript.Echo "Script Full Name: " & Wscript.ScriptFullName
2  Wscript.Echo "Script Name: " & Wscript.ScriptName
3  Wscript.Echo "Version: " & WScript.Version
4  Wscript.Echo "Build: " & Wscript.BuildVersion
5  Wscript.Echo "Name: " & Wscript.Name
6  Wscript.Echo "Full Name: " & Wscript.FullName
7  Wscript.Echo "Path: " & Wscript.Path
```

The following is typical output from the script:

```
Script Full Name: C:\scripts\wsh_info.vbs
Script Name: wsh_info.vbs
Version: 5.6
Build: 6626
Name: Windows Script Host
Full Name: C:\WINDOWS\System32\CScript.exe
Path: C:\WINDOWS\System32
```

Handling Events

Windows is an event-based operating system. Events generated within Windows are often the result of a user action such as the click of an OK button or the movement of a mouse. Typically, most of the actions performed by a Windows program are the result of handling these user-generated events. For example, when you start an application such as Microsoft Word, the application loads and then waits for you to do something (for example, type something on the keyboard or select something with the mouse). Word will wait indefinitely until you trigger an event that it can respond to.

The event mechanism also enables software components to communicate with one another. When an occurrence takes place in one component (firing component), another component (handling component) is notified of the occurrence. The handling component can respond by performing some action.

Event handling mechanism used by WSH is not commonly employed in system administration scripts. Scripts tend to be procedure-driven; that is, after they have been set in motion, they run on their own, neither looking for nor responding to outside events.

 Note

The ability to monitor resources and respond to changes in these resources is extremely important. However, this type of event handling is best done using WMI.

Event handling can be important in scripts that automate Windows GUI applications, and such scripts are sometimes useful to system administrators. For example, WSH scripts can use Microsoft Internet Explorer to provide a GUI interface for users. Simple examples of this can be found in the chapter "Creating Enterprise Scripts" in this book.

WshShell Object

The shell is the component of Windows that presents users with an interface to the operating system and provides familiar elements of the Windows desktop experience, including Windows Explorer, the Start menu, shortcuts, and desktop themes.

The WshShell object gives your scripts the ability to work with the Windows shell. Your scripts can use the WshShell object to perform a number of system administration tasks, including running programs, reading from and writing to the registry, and creating shortcuts.

Figure 3.10 shows the properties and methods of the WshShell object.

Figure 3.10 WshShell Object Model

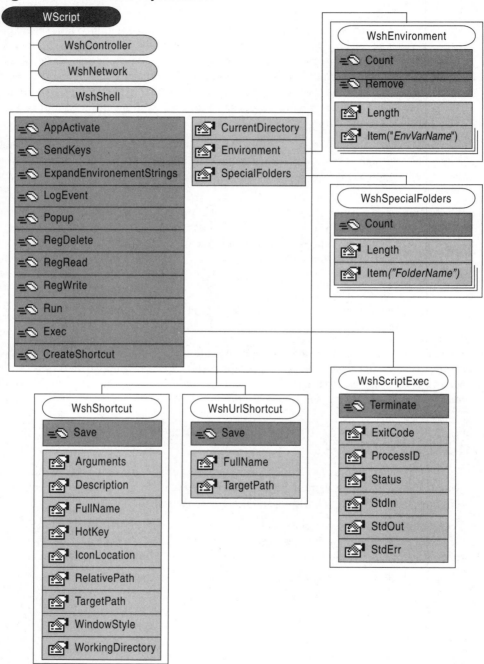

Accessing the WshShell Object

The WshShell object is a COM object, and using the following code statement can create an instance of the object:

```
Set objShell = WScript.CreateObject("WScript.Shell")
```

WshShell Capabilities

The WshShell object enables your script to automate tasks in a number of categories related to the Windows shell. Table 3.8 lists these categories along with the methods and properties of the WshShell object that your scripts can use to access this functionality.

Table 3.8   Capabilities Provided by the WshShell Object

Category	Method or Property
Running Programs	Run, Exec
Working with Special Folders	SpecialFolders
Working with Shortcuts	CreateShortcut
Working with Environment Variables	Environment, ExpandEnvironmentStrings
Working with the Event Log	LogEvent
Working with the Registry	RegRead, RegWrite, RegDelete
Sending Keystrokes to an Application	AppActivate, SendKeys
Obtaining a Script's Current Directory	CurrentDirectory
Creating Timed Dialog Boxes	Popup

Running Programs

One of the most important lessons to learn about scripting is this: Scripting is not the answer to all your system administration needs.

For one thing, scripting does not provide 100 percent coverage for all the administrative tasks that can be performed under Windows. For example, you can use scripts to create shared folders. But what if you want to set the offline folder options for that share? This procedure cannot be scripted using WSH or WMI. Instead, you must configure offline folder options using either the GUI or the Net.exe command.

For another, there is no reason to write a script if a tool already exists that fills your needs. Suppose you want to see the list of files that are stored in a folder on the local computer. You can spend the time creating a script to return this information. Alternatively, you can simply type **dir** at the command prompt and be done with it.

Using WSH scripts to help automate tasks does not require that you abandon the command-line tools or batch scripts that you currently use. If you have a batch script that performs well at a given task, there is no reason to create a WSH script that performs the same task.

On the other hand, you might want to augment the capabilities of a batch script with capabilities available only in the WSH scripting environment. For example, you might have a disk cleanup utility that you want to run only if free disk space falls below a specified level. It is possible to create a batch file that can determine free disk space and then decide whether to run the cleanup utility; however, the procedure for creating such a batch file is not particularly straightforward. By contrast, this same task can be accomplished quite easily in WSH: You can use the FileSystemObject or WMI to determine the free disk space and then either run or not run the disk cleanup utility.

One of the advantages of using WSH is that you do not have to choose WSH *or* choose batch files and command-line tools. The two approaches are not at odds with one another; instead, they complement one another. For example, you can use the WshShell Run and Exec methods in scripts to incorporate existing batch files or command-line tools.

Although running command-line tools and running batch scripts are important uses of the Run and Exec methods, these methods are not restricted to running a particular type of program. The Run and Exec methods enable your scripts to run any Windows program, including GUI applications. In addition, you can also run other scripts from within a script.

Comparing Run and Exec

The fact that there are two ways to run programs from a script leads to an obvious question: which method should you use in your scripts? The answer to that question depends on the script and what it needs to accomplish.

A script can use either the Run method or the Exec method to run a program in a manner similar to using the Run dialog box from the Start menu. Regardless of the method used, the program starts, and runs in a new process.

However, when you use the Run method, your script will not have access to the standard input, output, and error streams generated by the program being run. A script cannot use the Run method to run a command-line tool and retrieve its output.

For example, suppose you want to run Ping.exe and then examine the output to see whether the computer could be successfully contacted. This cannot be done using the Run command. Instead, you would need to ping the computer, save the results of the ping command to a text file, open the text file, read the results, and then parse those results to determine the success or failure of the command.

The following script uses the Run method to call Ping.exe, redirecting the output to a temporary file. The script opens and reads the text file, checks to see whether the command succeeded (by determining whether any of the lines of output begin with the word Reply), and then closes and deletes the temporary file:

```
Set objFSO = Wscript.CreateObject("Scripting.FileSystemObject")
Set objShell = Wscript.CreateObject("Wscript.Shell")
objName = objFSO.GetTempName
objTempFile = objName
objShell.Run "cmd /c ping -n 3 -w 1000 157.59.0.1 >" & objTempFile, 0, True
Set objTextFile = objFSO.OpenTextFile(objTempFile, 1)
Do While objTextFile.AtEndOfStream <> True
    strText = objTextFile.ReadLine
    If Instr(strText, "Reply") > 0 Then
        Wscript.Echo "Reply received."
        Exit Do
    End If
Loop
objTextFile.Close
objFSO.DeleteFile(objTempFile)
```

Although this approach works, it is somewhat complicated. If you need access to command-line output, you should use the Exec method instead. The following script also parses the output generated by Ping.exe. However, it does so by using the Exec method and by directly reading the output. There is no need to create, open, read, and delete a temporary file, and the script is only 9 lines long, compared with the 15 lines required to perform this same task using the Run method:

```
Set objShell = WScript.CreateObject("WScript.Shell")
Set objExecObject = objShell.Exec("cmd /c ping -n 3 -w 1000 157.59.0.1")
Do While Not objExecObject.StdOut.AtEndOfStream
    strText = objExecObject.StdOut.ReadLine()
    If Instr(strText, "Reply") > 0 Then
        Wscript.Echo "Reply received."
        Exit Do
    End If
Loop
```

In many respects, this makes the Exec method a better choice than the Run method. However, the Run method is still useful in a number of situations:

- You might want to run the application in a specified window type, such as a minimized window. Exec offers no control over window style; Run offers the options listed in Table 3.9.

- You might need to run a script on computers that do not have WSH 5.6 installed. Exec is supported only on WSH 5.6.

- You might want to wait for the application being called to finish running before the script resumes. This can be done with either Run or Exec but requires less coding with Run.

Running Programs

The Run method accepts three parameters. The first and only required parameter is the name of the program you want to run. If the program is in the same folder as the script, or if it is located within the computer path, you need enter only the name (for example, Calc.exe). Otherwise, enter the full path to the program (C:\Admin\Monitoring\DiskSpace.exe).

The second parameter is an integer that indicates the window style with which the program should begin (assuming the program has a window). The window style determines such things as whether a window will be the active window or be maximized. Table 3.9 lists the integers that Run accepts as a second parameter as well as the corresponding the window styles.

Table 3.9   Integers Accepted by the Run Method for the Window Style

Integer	Window Style Description
0	Hides the window and activates another window.
1	Activates and displays a window. If the window is minimized or maximized, the system restores it to its original size and position. An application should specify this flag when displaying the window for the first time.
2	Activates the window and displays it as a minimized window.
3	Activates the window and displays it as a maximized window.
4	Displays a window in its most recent size and position. The active window remains active.
5	Activates the window and displays it in its current size and position.
6	Minimizes the specified window and activates the next top-level window in the Z order. The Z order is nothing more than the list detailing the order in which windows are to be activated. If you press ALT+TAB, you will see a graphical representation of the Z list.
7	Displays the window as a minimized window. The active window remains active.
8	Displays the window in its current state. The active window remains active.
9	Activates and displays the window. If the window is minimized or maximized, the system restores it to its original size and position. An application should specify this flag when restoring a minimized window.
10	Sets the show-state based on the state of the program that started the application.

For example, the script in Listing 3.15 starts Notepad. In line 1, the script sets the MAXIMIZE_WINDOW constant to 3, which represents an activated and maximized window style. In line 3, the script uses the WshShell Run method to start Notepad, passing it the MAXIMIZE_WINDOW constant so that the program runs in a maximized window.

Listing 3.15   Running a Program Using the Run Method

```
1   Const MAXIMIZE_WINDOW = 3
2   Set objShell = WScript.CreateObject("WScript.Shell")
3   objShell.Run "notepad.exe", MAXIMIZE_WINDOW
```

 Note

Not all applications respond to the window style options. For example,
Control Panel (Control.exe) always opens in the same way, regardless of the
window style specified in the script.

The Run method also accepts a Boolean value as a third parameter that determines whether the
script pauses until the called program is finished running or instead continues with the next
command in the script. If this value is set to False (the default), the Run method simply issues the
command to run the program but does not check to ensure that the program actually ran. If the
third parameter is set to True, the script will wait for the program to finish running, return the
integer exit code provided by the program, and then continue with the next line of the script.

If you set this value to False, you can run multiple programs at the same time; the script will start
program A and then immediately start program B, even though program A is still running. This
can enable your scripts to complete faster. However, it can also lead to possible problems: For
example, what if program B cannot be run until program A has finished? If you are worried about
possible "collisions" between programs, set this value to True. In that case, program B will not
start until program A has concluded.

For example, this script runs Calculator and then waits until Calculator has been closed before
proceeding. If Calculator is never closed, line 3 of this script will never execute:

```
Set objShell = WScript.CreateObject("WScript.Shell")
objShell.Run("calc.exe"),1,True
Wscript.Echo "Script completed."
```

 Note

WSH keeps track of the specific instance of a program started using Run.
For example, suppose you run the preceding script and then manually start a
second instance of Calculator. If you close this second instance, the script
will not respond. Instead, it will continue to wait until the initial instance of
Calculator, the one started using Run, has been closed.

Running Command-Line Tools

Although both Run and Exec are well suited for running GUI programs from scripts, you are unlikely to call many GUI programs from within a script. After all, the basic idea behind most system administration scripts is to carry out a task without the need for any human intervention. Because GUI applications typically require human intervention, about the best you can do within a script is open the application; you are very limited in what you can do with the application after it has been opened.

This is not true for command-line tools, however. Most command-line tools are designed to run in automated fashion; after they have been started, there is no need for any human intervention. The tools start, perform their appointed task, and then terminate.

Both the Run method and the Exec method can be used to run command-line tools, although in either case you should use a slightly different syntax from the one used to run GUI tools. When you run a command-line tool using either of these methods, you should always preface the tool name with one of the following:

- %comspec% /k
- %comspec% /c

The %comspec% variable is an environment variable that specifies the command-line processor. By using %comspec%, you can create scripts that run on both Windows 98 computers (where the command-line processor is Command.exe) and on Windows 2000 computers (where the command-line processor is named Cmd.exe).

The %comspec% variable is not required; however, it does provide a way for a the command window in which a tool runs to remain on the screen. (By default, a command window opens, the tool runs, and then the command window closes as soon as the tool finishes. This means that you might not have time to view the output generated by that tool.)

Including %comspec% is also the only way to run command-line commands such as dir. This script will *not* run the dir command. Instead, you will receive an error message stating that dir could not be found. (This is because dir is not a stand-alone tool; there is, for example, no program named dir.exe.)

```
Set objShell = WScript.CreateObject("WScript.Shell")
objShell.Run("dir"), 1, True
```

However, this script, which first starts the command interpreter, *will* run the dir command:

```
Set objShell = WScript.CreateObject("WScript.Shell")
objShell.Run("%comspec% /K dir"), 1, True
```

The /k and /c parameters allow you to specify whether the command window will remain open after the script completes or whether it will be closed. If you want the window to remain open so that you can view the script output, use the /k parameter. If you want the window to close (as you might with a logon script), use the /c parameter.

For example, the following script runs the Cacls.exe tool, which, in this instance, displays permission settings for the folder C:\Scripts. The script leaves the command window open so that the results can be viewed:

```
Set objShell = WScript.CreateObject("WScript.Shell")
objShell.Run("%comspec% /K cacls.exe c:\scripts"), 1, True
```

By contrast, this script runs the Sc.exe tool and stops the Alerter service. As soon as the script completes, the command window closes:

```
Set objShell = WScript.CreateObject("WScript.Shell")
objShell.Run("%comspec% /c sc.exe stop alerter"), 1, True
```

Using Spaces in Command-Line Parameters

If a parameter passed to a command-line tool includes a space, that parameter must be enclosed in quotation marks. For example, to use Sc.exe to determine the keyname for the Upload Manager service, you need to use the following syntax:

```
sc.exe getkeyname "Upload Manager"
```

To use this same command within a script, you must also include quotation marks around the parameter. However, this is not entirely straightforward. For example, you might try placing quotation marks around Upload Manager, like this:

```
Set objShell = WScript.CreateObject("WScript.Shell")
objShell.Run("%comspec% /k sc.exe getkeyname "Upload Manager""), 1, True
```

When you run this script, you do not get the keyname for Upload Manager. Instead, you get the error message shown in Figure 3.11.

Figure 3.11 Incorrectly Specifying the Run Parameter

At first, this error message might seem nonsensical; after all, it says that the script expected to see a right parenthesis, and your code *has* a right parenthesis. As it turns out, though, the problem lies not with the parentheses but with the quotation marks. WSH correctly sees the first set of quotation marks (the ones right before %comspec%) as marking the start of the command string being passed to the Run method. However, it sees the second set of quotation marks (the ones right before the word Upload) as marking the end of the command string. To WSH, this is the command you are trying to execute:

```
objShell.Run("%comspec% /k sc.exe getkeyname ""
```

Because the syntax is not correct (a right parenthesis is required immediately after the second set of quotation marks), the script fails.

Anytime you need to include quotation marks as part of the command string, you must use a *pair* of quotation marks. For example:

```
Set objShell = WScript.CreateObject("WScript.Shell")
objShell.Run("%comspec% /k sc.exe getkeyname ""Upload Manager"""), 1, True
```

In this script:

1. A single set of quotation marks is used to begin the command string.

2. A pair of quotation marks is used with Upload Manager. This will cause "Upload Manager" (with the surrounding quotation marks) to be included as part of a command string.

3. A single set of quotation marks is used to end the command string. In this example, that results in three quotation marks appearing, one right after another.

Running a Program and Directly Accessing Its Output

To run a program and use its output, a script can use the WshShell Exec method. The WshShell Exec method returns a WshScriptExec object that provides access to the program's standard output, standard input, and standard error streams. Your scripts can retrieve the output that results from running a program by accessing the program's standard output stream (StdOut).

The script in Listing 3.16 runs the command-line tool, Ipconfig.exe, which retrieves information about the networking configuration of a computer, including the IP address currently assigned to that computer. The script captures the output of the tool and filters it line by line, displaying only lines that include the word Address.

Listing 3.16 Running an Application and Using Its Output

```
1   Set objShell = WScript.CreateObject("WScript.Shell")
2   Set objExecObject = objShell.Exec("%comspec% /c ipconfig.exe")
3
4   Do Until objExecObject.StdOut.AtEndOfStream
5       strLine = objExecObject.StdOut.ReadLine()
6       strIP = Instr(strLine,"Address")
7       If strIP <> 0 Then
8           Wscript.Echo strLine
9       End If
10  Loop
```

In line 2 of Listing 3.16, the script uses the Exec method to run the Ipconfig.exe command-line tool. The output generated by Opconfig.exe will be stored in the object reference named objExecObject.

In line 4, the script sets up a loop that will continue until the end of the program's standard output stream is reached. The script checks for the end of the stream by using the AtEndOfStream property of the StdOut TextStream object.

In line 5, the script reads a line of the program's output and stores it in the strLine variable.

In line 6, the script uses the VBScript Instr function to determine whether the word *Address* is stored in strLine. If the word *Address* is found, the script displays the line using the Echo method on line 8.

When you run Ipconfig.exe, you receive output similar to this:

```
Windows IP Configuration

Ethernet adapter Local Area Connection 2:

        Connection-specific DNS Suffix . : fabrikam.com
        IP Address. . . . . . . . . . . : 192.168.248.248
        Subnet Mask . . . . . . . . . . : 255.255.252.0
        Default Gateway . . . . . . . . : 192.168.248.1
```

When you run the preceding script, you receive output only for those lines that contain the word Address:

```
        IP Address. . . . . . . . . . . : 192.168.248.248
```

This enables you to run a command-line tool, check its output, and then have your script proceed accordingly.

Working with Shortcuts

Shortcuts are links to local or network programs, files, folders, computers, or Internet addresses. Each shortcut is a file with either an .lnk or a .url extension. The two extensions correspond to the two types of shortcuts: standard shortcuts and Uniform Resource Locator (URL) shortcuts. Standard shortcuts can link to local or network programs, files, folders, or computers, while URL shortcuts link only to entities that can be referenced by a URL — most commonly, Web pages.

Shortcuts are used in a number of places within the Windows shell, particularly within menus and toolbars. The Start menu, the Programs menu, the Quick Launch bar, and the SendTo menu, for example, consist of a group of shortcuts located in special folders. The shortcuts that appear on the Quick Launch bar are located in the following folder:

```
C:\Documents and Settings\{user profile name}\Application Data\Microsoft\Internet
Explorer\Quick Launch
```

Your scripts can make use of shortcuts to customize the menus and the desktops of your users; for example, you can create a script that provides different menu options to different groups of users within your organization.

The properties of the WSH Shortcut object are shown in Table 3.10.

Table 3.10   WSH Shortcut Properties

Property	Description
Arguments	Additional command-line arguments that can be used when starting the application.
Description	Description given to the shortcut.
FullName	Read-only property that returns the complete path to the target application.
HotKey	Keyboard shortcut: a combination of keys that, when held down together, will start the application. Keyboard shortcuts typically consist of one of the following keys plus a letter (a–z), number (0–9), or function key (F1–F12): ▪ ALT ▪ CTRL ▪ SHIFT For example, to set the keyboard shortcut to the CTRL key and the 9 key, use this value: `CTRL + 9` If the key combination you select is already in use, it will be overwritten and will be applied to the new shortcut created by your script.
IconLocation	Allows you to specify an icon and an icon index for the shortcut. If no location is specified, the default icon for the application is used.
TargetPath	Complete path to the target application. You must specify the full path, including the drive letter or UNC path. When setting a TargetPath, WSH will accept the value entered. It will not check to ensure that the path is correct.
WindowStyle	Specifies the initial window type for the application. Valid styles are the same as those shown for the Run method and are listed in Table 3.9.
WorkingDirectory	Specifies the working directory for the application.

Creating Standard Shortcuts

Creating a standard shortcut involves three steps:

1. Create an instance of the WshShortcut object by calling CreateShortcut(), passing as the sole parameter the path for the new shortcut file. Although shortcuts can be created anywhere within the file system, they are typically created within special folders such as AllUsersDesktop and StartMenu. Special folders are discussed later in this chapter.

2. Set the properties of the WshShortcut object.

3. Call the WshShortcut Save method. If you do not call the Save method, the shortcut will not actually be created.

The script in Listing 3.17 creates a shortcut to the Internet Information Services (IIS) manager on the desktop. The shortcut is visible to all users of the computer and can be opened either by double-clicking it or by using the key combination **CTRL+SHIFT+I**.

Listing 3.17 Creating a Desktop Shortcut

```
1  Set objShell = WScript.CreateObject("WScript.Shell")
2  strDesktopFolder = objShell.SpecialFolders("AllUsersDesktop")
3  Set objShortCut = objShell.CreateShortcut(strDesktopFolder & _
4      "\IIS Manager.lnk")
5  objShortCut.TargetPath = "%SystemRoot%\System32\Inetsrv\iis.msc"
6  objShortCut.Description = "Run the Internet Information Services Manager."
7  objShortCut.HotKey = "Ctrl+Shift+I"
8  objShortCut.Save
```

In line 2 of Listing 3.17, the WshShell SpecialFolders property retrieves the directory path to the Desktop special folder. This path is stored in the strDesktopFolder variable.

In lines 3–4, the CreateShortcut method creates a shortcut file named IISManager.lnk in the Desktop folder.

In lines 5–7, the script sets the TargetPath, Description, and HotKey properties of the WshShortcut object.

In line 8, the script creates the actual shortcut by calling the WshShortcut Save method.

 Note

An icon will be created on the desktop even if you do not set any properties, but the icon will not be a functional shortcut; if you double-click it, nothing will happen. (You will not even receive an error message.) To create a functional shortcut, you must set the TargetPath property. If the TargetPath property is not set, double-clicking the shortcut will not do anything.

Creating URL Shortcuts

Creating a URL Shortcut involves three similar steps:

1. Create an instance of the WshUrlShortcut object by calling CreateShortcut, passing as the sole parameter the URL for the new shortcut file.

2. Set the properties of the WshUrlShortcut object.

3. Call the WshUrlShortcut Save method.

The script in Listing 3.18 creates a shortcut to the MSDN® Web site on the desktop. The shortcut is visible only to users who run the script. This is because the shortcut is created in the Desktop folder for the current user and not in the AllUsersDesktop folder.

Listing 3.18 Creating a Desktop URL Shortcut

```
1  Set objShell = WScript.CreateObject("WScript.Shell")
2  strDesktopFld = objShell.SpecialFolders("Desktop")
3  Set objURLShortcut = objShell.CreateShortcut(strDesktopFld & "\MSDN.url")
4  objURLShortcut.TargetPath = "http://msdn.microsoft.com"
5  objURLShortcut.Save
```

Adding an Item to the Quick Launch Bar

The script in Listing 3.19 uses a URL shortcut to create a Quick Launch button that opens the Microsoft® TechNet Web site. The Quick Launch button is visible only to users who run the script because the shortcut is created in the personal Quick Launch bar for the user.

Listing 3.19 Creating a Quick Launch Button to Open the TechNet Online Web Site

```
1  Set objShell = WScript.CreateObject("WScript.Shell")
2  Set colEnvironmentVariables = objShell.Environment("Volatile")
3
4  strQLFolder = colEnvironmentVariables.Item("APPDATA") & _
5      "\Microsoft\Internet Explorer\Quick Launch"
6
7  Set objURLShortcut = objShell.CreateShortcut(strQLFolder & "\TechNet.url")
8  objURLShortcut.TargetPath = "http://www.microsoft.com/technet"
9  objURLShortcut.Save
```

Deleting Shortcuts

Shortcuts are files that can be deleted in the same way you delete any other file. For example, the following script deletes the shortcut created in Listing 3.18:

```
Set objShell = WScript.CreateObject("WScript.Shell")
Set colEnvironmentVariables = objShell.Environment("Volatile")
Set objFSO = CreateObject("Scripting.FileSystemObject")

strQLFolder = colEnvironmentVariables.Item("APPDATA") & _
    "\Microsoft\Internet Explorer\Quick Launch\TechNet.URL"
objFSO.DeleteFile(strQLFolder)
```

For more information about working with files in WSH scripts, see "Script Runtime Primer" in this book.

Working with Special Folders

Special folders are folders that are — or at least potentially can be — present on all Windows computers; these include the My Documents, Fonts, and Start Menu folders. There are two types of special folders: those that map to standard directories and those that do not. The Favorites folder, for example, maps to a standard directory; the My Computer folder does not.

The WScript SpecialFolders collection contains the full path to each of the special folders that map to a standard directory. Table 3.11 lists the identifiers and the contents of each of the special folders in the SpecialFolders collection.

Table 3.11   Special Folders Identifier

Identifier	Folder Contents
AllUsersDesktop	Shortcuts that appear on the desktop for all users
AllUsersStartMenu	Shortcuts that appear on the Start menu for all users
AllUsersPrograms	Shortcuts that appear on the Programs menu for all users
AllUsersStartup	Shortcuts to programs that are run on startup for all users
Desktop	Shortcuts that appear on the desktop for the current user
Favorites	Shortcuts saved as favorites by the current user
Fonts	Fonts installed on the system
MyDocuments	Current user's documents
NetHood	Objects that appear in Network Neighborhood
PrintHood	Printer links
Recent	Shortcuts to current user's recently opened documents
SendTo	Shortcuts to applications that show up as possible send-to targets when a user right-clicks on a file in Windows Explorer
StartMenu	Shortcuts that appear in the current user's start menu
Startup	Shortcuts to applications that run automatically when the current user logs on to the system
Templates	Application template files specific to the current user

To determine the location of any folder, retrieve the value of the SpecialFolders.Item property, specifying the name of one of the identifiers shown in Table 3.11.

Note

The SpecialFolders collection enables your script to determine the path of any special folder that maps to a standard directory but does not enable your script to manipulate that folder or its contents. You must use a mechanism such as the FileSystemObject to actually work with the contents of the special folders. For more information about using the FileSystemObject in your scripts, see "Script Runtime Primer" in this book.

Retrieving the Location of Special Folders

The script in Listing 3.20 determines the location of the Fonts special folder. The script echoes the location of the Fonts folder.

Listing 3.20   Determining the Location of the Fonts Folder

```
1   Set objShell = WScript.CreateObject("WScript.Shell")
2   strFontDirectoryPath = objShell.SpecialFolders.Item("Fonts")
3   Wscript.Echo "Font Directory Path: " & strFontDirectoryPath
```

Creating a Shortcut in a Special Folder

When you install an application, that application often associates itself with a particular file type. For example, when you install the Microsoft® FrontPage® Web site creation and management tool, FrontPage associates itself with all .htm files. If you right-click on a .htm file and click **Edit**, the file will open in FrontPage.

Of course, there might be times when you simply want to view the .htm file in Notepad. Recognizing this fact, Windows includes a special folder named SendTo. The SendTo option presents a menu of applications or locations to which you can send the selected file. You can add to the options available in the SendTo menu by adding shortcuts to the SendTo special folder. The next time you want to open an .htm file (or any file) in Notepad, you can simply right-click the file, select **SendTo**, and then click **Notepad**.

The script in Listing 3.21 creates a shortcut to the Notepad application in the SendTo special folder, thus adding Notepad to the SendTo menu.

Listing 3.21   Adding the Notepad Application to the SendTo Menu

```
1   Set objShell = WScript.CreateObject("WScript.Shell")
2   strSendToFolder = objShell.SpecialFolders("SendTo")
3   strPathToNotepad = objShell.ExpandEnvironmentStrings _
4       ("%SystemRoot%/system32/notepad.exe")
5
6   Set objShortcut = objShell.CreateShortcut(strSendToFolder & _
7       "\notepad.lnk")
8   objShortcut.TargetPath = strPathToNotepad
9   objShortcut.Save
```

Environment Variables

Environment variables are a set of string values associated with a process. The Windows Shell process has a number of environment variables associated with it that contain useful information that you can use within your scripts, including:

- Directories searched by the shell to locate programs (the path).

- Number of processors, processor manufacturer, and processor architecture of the computer.

- User profile location.

- Temporary directory locations.

When a user logs on to Windows, the shell process starts and obtains its initial environment variables by loading both the computer-specific (system) and user-specific (user) environment variables from the registry.

In addition to the computer-specific and user-specific environment variables loaded from the registry, additional process environment variables are generated dynamically during each logon.

Table 3.12 lists a description of each type of environment variable and its location in the registry.

Table 3.12 Types of Environment Variables and Their Storage Locations

Type	Description	Registry Location
User	Applies to the user currently logged on to the computer and is saved between logoffs and restarts	HKCU\Environment
System	Applies to all users of the computer and is saved between logoffs and restarts	HKLM\System\CurrentControlSet\Control\Session Manager\Environment
Volatile	Applies to current logon session and is not saved between logoffs and restarts	HKCU\VolatileEnvironment
Process	Applies to current process and might be passed to child processes	Not stored in the registry

The Environment property of the WshShell object returns a WshEnvironment collection object that gives your scripts the ability to retrieve, create, and modify environment variables. The WshEnvironment collection provides access to all four types of environment variables: system, user, process, and volatile.

Retrieving Environment Variables

To retrieve a collection of environment variables of a specific type, your script must access the WshShell Environment property and provide a string parameter that represents the desired type of environment variable: system, user, process, or volatile. Your script can then use the resulting WshEnvironment collection to access the values of those environment variables by name.

The environment variables that can be retrieved using WSH are shown in Table 3.13.

Table 3.13 WSH Environment Variables

Name	System	User	Process	Process (Windows 98/ ME only)
NUMBER_OF_PROCESSORS	●		●	
PROCESSOR_ARCHITECTURE	●		●	
PROCESSOR_IDENTIFIER	●		●	
PROCESSOR_LEVEL	●		●	
PROCESSOR_REVISION	●		●	
OS	●		●	
COMSPEC	●		●	●
HOMEDRIVE			●	
HOMEPATH			●	
PATH	●	●	●	●
PATHEXT	●		●	
PROMPT			●	●
SYSTEMDRIVE			●	
SYSTEMROOT			●	
WINDIR	●		●	●
TEMP		●	●	●
TMP		●	●	●

The environment variables shown in the preceding table are present on all Windows computers. However, you might also have additional user-specific or computer-specific environment variables, which can also be accessed through a script. If you do not know the names of these variables, you can obtain a complete list of the variables (and their values) by typing **set** from the command prompt.

The script in Listing 3.22 retrieves both the user-specific and computer-specific PATH environment variables.

Listing 3.22 Displaying User-specific and Computer-specific PATH Environment Variables

```
1  Set objShell = WScript.CreateObject("WScript.Shell")
2  Set colSystemEnvVars = objShell.Environment("System")
3  Set colUserEnvVars = objShell.Environment("User")
4  Wscript.Echo "Computer-specific PATH Environment Variable"
5  Wscript.Echo colSystemEnvVars("PATH")
6  Wscript.Echo "User-specific PATH Environment Variable"
7  Wscript.Echo colUserEnvVars("PATH")
```

When the preceding script runs under CScript, output similar to the following appears in the command window:

```
Computer-specific PATH Environment Variable
%SystemRoot%\system32;%SystemRoot%;%SystemRoot%\system32\WBEM;C:\Program Files\M
icrosoft.NET\FrameworkSDK\Bin\;C:\Program Files\Microsoft Visual Studio.NET\Vc7\
bin\;C:\Program Files\Microsoft Visual Studio.NET\Common7\IDE\;C:\WINNT\Microsof
t.NET\Framework\v1.0.2914\;C:\Program Files\Microsoft Visual Studio.NET\Vc7\bin\
;C:\Program Files\Microsoft Visual Studio.NET\Common7\IDE\;
C:\MSSQL7\BINN;C:\Program Files\Support Tools\;C:\Program Files\
Resource Kit\C:\PROGRA~1\CA\Common\SCANEN~1;C:\PROGRA~1\CA\eTrust\ANTIVI~1
User-specific PATH Environment Variable
C:\Perl\bin;C:\Perl\bin;C:\Perl\bin\
```

Creating Environment Variables

To create a new environment variable, your script must start with the same first step required for retrieving the values of environment variables: It must obtain a reference to a collection of environment variables of one of the four types (user, system, process, or volatile).

After your script has a reference to the collection corresponding to the type of environment variable being created, it can then store a new string value in the corresponding collection location.

Storing the string value creates the new environment variable. The new index becomes the name of the new environment variable, and the corresponding string becomes its initial value. For example, this line of code creates an environment variable named MyVariable, with the initial value 0:

```
colUsrEnvVars("MyVariable") = 0
```

You can write scripts that create process or volatile environment variables, but neither of these types is saved between logons and reboots. You can also create a volatile type, which is stored in the registry and lasts for a logon session; this type of environment variable can be used as a mechanism for communicating information between two scripts that both run during a single logon session. However, you will likely find that creating system or user types is more useful because these environment variables are saved between logon sessions and computer reboots.

The script in Listing 3.23 creates a user environment variable named APP_VARIABLE and sets its initial value to "Installed." The script then retrieves the value of the new APP_VARIABLE environment variable to confirm that it was created.

Listing 3.23 Creating a User-specific Environment Variable

```
1  Set objShell = WScript.CreateObject("WScript.Shell")
2  Set colUsrEnvVars = objShell.Environment("USER")
3  colUsrEnvVars("APP_VARIABLE") = "Installed"
4  Wscript.Echo colUsrEnvVars("APP_VARIABLE")
```

Modifying Environment Variables

To modify an environment variable, your script must use steps similar to those used to create a new environment variable. It must obtain a reference to a collection of environment variables of one of the four types (user, system, process, or volatile) and store that reference in a variable.

After your script has a reference to the collection corresponding to the type of environment variable being modified, it can then reference the name of the environment variable to modify and store a string value in the corresponding collection location, overwriting the string previously located in that location.

The script in Listing 3.24 modifies the value of a user-specific environment variable named APP_VARIABLE by changing the value to *Upgraded*.

Listing 3.24 Modifying a User-specific Environment Variable

```
1  Set objShell = WScript.CreateObject("WScript.Shell")
2  Set colUsrEnvVars = objShell.Environment("USER")
3  strCurrentValue = colUsrEnvVars("APP_VARIABLE")
4  colUsrEnvVars("APP_VARIABLE") = "Upgraded"
5  Wscript.Echo colUsrEnvVars("APP_VARIABLE")
```

Expanding Environment Variables

When constructing environment variables or configuration strings to be used in the registry or elsewhere, you might want to incorporate the current value of an existing environment variable within those variables or strings. For example, if a script needs access to the temporary folder, you need to somehow indicate that, for this user on this computer, the temporary folder can be found in C:\Temp.

However, you would not want to hard-code the value of that environment variable in your configuration string, as it might change in the future and your script would no longer be valid. Although the temporary folder might be C:\Temp today, there is no reason why that cannot be changed to something else (for example, C:\Temporary Folder) tomorrow. Because of that, it is better to use an environment variable to dynamically retrieve the location of the temporary folder rather than hard-coding in the value and hoping that it never changes.

To refer to the *value* of environment variables within configuration strings, you must use the WshShell ExpandEnvironmentStrings method.

This method accepts, as a parameter, a string with an embedded environment variable name enclosed in percentage symbols (%) and returns a string in which the environment variable name and percentage symbols (%) have been replaced with the value of the corresponding environment variable.

The script in Listing 3.25 shows the difference between echoing the value of an environment variable and echoing the *expanded* value of an environment variable.

Listing 3.25 Creating and Displaying an Environment Variable That Incorporates Existing Environment Variables

```
1   Set objShell = WScript.CreateObject("WScript.Shell")
2   Set colEnvVars = objShell.Environment("User")
3   Wscript.Echo "Temporary folder (Unexpanded):"
4   Wscript.Echo colEnvVars("TEMP") & vbCrLf
5   Wscript.Echo "Temporary folder (Expanded)"
6   Wscript.Echo objShell.ExpandEnvironmentStrings("%TEMP%")
```

When run under Cscript, output similar to the following appears in the command window:

```
Temporary folder (Unexpanded):
%USERPROFILE%\Local Settings\Temp

Temporary folder (Expanded)
C:\DOCUME~1\kmyer\LOCALS~1\Temp
```

Logging an Event

Troubleshooting applications and services is simplified if these applications and services log important events to event logs. Your scripts will also be easier to troubleshoot if they do the same.

The WshShell object provides the LogEvent method for logging events to the Application event log. The LogEvent method enables you to write to the event log from within your scripts.

 Note

If you want to read and process event log information from within your scripts, you need to use WMI. For more information about using WMI to work with event logs, see "Logs" in this book.

LogEvent has two required parameters. The first parameter of the LogEvent method is an integer that specifies the type of event you would like your script to log. Table 3.14 lists the available event types and their corresponding integer values.

Table 3.14   Event Types and Integer Values

Value	Event Type
0	SUCCESS
1	ERROR
2	WARNING
4	INFORMATION
8	AUDIT_SUCCESS
16	AUDIT_FAILURE

The second parameter your scripts need to supply to the LogEvent method is a string containing the message to log. You also have the option to supply a computer name as the third parameter, in which case the event will be logged in the Application log on that computer instead of the computer on which the script is running. (This parameter is ignored on Windows 95- and Windows 98-based computers.) Remote logging is useful for scripts designed to run on a number of different computers: Instead of being logged locally, all events generated by these scripts can be logged to a central computer.

The script in Listing 3.26 logs an event of each of the types listed in Table 3.14 along with a corresponding description.

Listing 3.26   Logging Events to the Application Log

```
1   Set objShell = WScript.CreateObject("Wscript.Shell")
2   objShell.LogEvent 0,"Test Success Event"
3   objShell.LogEvent 1,"Test Error Event"
4   objShell.LogEvent 2,"Test Warning Event"
5   objShell.LogEvent 4, "Test Information Event"
6   objShell.LogEvent 8, "Test Success Audit Event"
7   objShell.LogEvent 16, "Test Failure Audit Event"
```

The LogEvent method can record events only in the Application event log. In addition, you cannot specify a unique source or a unique event code: All events are automatically given the source Windows Script Host and an event code corresponding to the event type (for example, all Success events will have an event code of 0).

Reading From and Writing to the Local Registry

As a general rule, it is best to manage the registry using system tools such as Regedit.exe; although not foolproof, these tools have built-in safeguards that help minimize the damage that can be caused by incorrectly configuring a registry entry. On the other hand, it is also true that many of these registry tools cannot be automated and are designed to work on only one computer at a time (typically the local computer). It is one thing to say that you should use Regedit.exe to manage the registry; it is quite another to have an urgent security bulletin recommending that you change a registry entry on all 1,000 of your domain controllers as quickly as possible. In situations in which system tools are not fast enough or efficient enough, the WshShell object provides methods for reading from, writing to, and deleting from the registry.

   Caution

Changing the registry with a script can easily propagate errors. The scripting tools bypass safeguards, allowing settings that can damage your system, or even require you to reinstall Windows. Before scripting changes to the registry, test your script thoroughly and back up the registry on every computer on which you will make changes. For more information about scripting changes to the registry, see the Registry Reference on the *Microsoft Windows 2000 Server Resource Kit* companion CD or at http://www.microsoft.com/reskit.

Reading a Registry Entry

The registry is the primary configuration database for the Windows operating system; the ability of an operating system component to run, and to run correctly, often depends on the configuration of one or more settings within the registry.

As a system administrator, you spend a considerable amount of time checking values set within the registry. For example, in the event of computer problems, support personnel will often ask you to verify specific registry settings. This can be done directly, using a tool such as Regedit.exe, or it can be done programmatically, using the WshShell RegRead method.

For the most part, the RegRead method requires you to do just two things: 1) Create an instance of the WScript Shell object and 2) call the RegRead method, specifying the registry entry you wand to read. For example, the version number of the Windows operating system is stored in HKLM\Software\Microsoft\Windows NT\CurrentVersion\CurrentVersion. You can retrieve this value by using the following code:

```
Set objShell = WScript.CreateObject("WScript.Shell")
sngVersion = objShell.RegRead _
    ("HKLM\Software\Microsoft\Windows NT\CurrentVersion\CurrentVersion")
Wscript.Echo sngVersion
```

Registry Data Types

Each value stored in the registry has a particular data type. Table 3.15 lists the subset of registry types that WSH supports and the corresponding VBScript-compatible types into which the RegRead method translates corresponding registry values.

Table 3.15   Registry Data Types and Associated Script Data Types

Name	Data Type	Script Data Type
REG_SZ	String	Converted to String
REG_DWORD	Number	Converted to Integer
REG_BINARY	Binary Value	Converted to VBArray of Integers
REG_EXPAND_SZ	Expandable String	Converted to String
REG_MULTI_SZ	Array of Strings	Converted to VBArray of Strings

The data types listed in Table 3.15 are the ones most commonly used in the registry. If your script attempts to use the RegRead method to retrieve the value of a registry entry with an unsupported data type, the call will result in an error.

 Note

Unfortunately, WSH does not provide a way for you to verify the data type of a registry entry before you attempt to read it. However, you can use WMI to verify data types.

The script in Listing 3.27 uses the RegRead method to read the value of a multistring registry entry. Because this is a multistring value, the information is returned as an array, and a For Each loop is used to report each item in that array.

Listing 3.27   Reading a Multistring Value from the Registry

```
1   Set objShell = WScript.CreateObject("WScript.Shell")
2   arrValues = objShell.RegRead _
3       ("HKLM\SYSTEM\CurrentControlSet\Services\EventLog\Security\Sources")
4   For Each strValue In arrValues
5       Wscript.Echo strValue
6   Next
```

When the preceding script is run under CScript, output similar to the following is displayed in the command window:

```
Spooler
Security Account Manager
SC Manager
NetDDE Object
LSA
DS
Security
```

Creating or Modifying a Registry Entry

Your scripts can use the RegWrite method to create a new registry entry or modify an existing one. The RegWrite method accepts three parameters: the registry entry to create or modify, the value to assign to the entry, and (optionally) the data type of the entry.

The script in Listing 3.28 uses the RegWrite method to create a DWORD entry (and set the value to 56) in the registry.

Listing 3.28 Creating a DWORD Value in the Registry

```
1  Set objShell = WScript.CreateObject("WScript.Shell")
2  objShell.RegWrite "HKCU\TestKey\Version", 56, "REG_DWORD"
```

 Note

The WshShell RegWrite method does not support writing the REG_MULTI_SZ data type.

Deleting a Registry Entry

Your scripts can use the RegDelete method to delete registry subkeys or entries. The RegDelete method accepts a single parameter that specifies the subkey or entry to delete. Deleting a subkey deletes all the entries in that subkey.

The script in Listing 3.29 uses the RegDelete method to delete a DWORD value in the registry.

Listing 3.29 Deleting a DWORD Value in the Registry

```
1  Set objShell = WScript.CreateObject("WScript.Shell")
2  objShell.RegDelete "HKCU\TestKey\Version"
```

Sending Keystrokes to a Program

By providing scripts with access to most COM objects, WSH enables you to automate applications that have a COM-based object model. Unfortunately, some applications, especially older ones, do not have a COM-based object model. To automate these applications, WSH provides a way to send keystrokes to these applications.

When you use the WshShell SendKeys method to send keystrokes to an application, your script mimics a human typing on the keyboard. To send a single keyboard character, you pass SendKeys the character itself as a string argument. For example, "x" to send the letter *x*. To send a space, send the string " ". This is exactly what a user would do if he or she was working with the application: to type the letter x, the user would simply press the x key on the keyboard.

When you use the SendKeys method, special keys that do not have a direct text representation (for example, CTRL or ALT) are represented by special characters. Table 3.16 lists these SendKeys representations for commonly used keys.

Table 3.16 SendKeys Representations of Common Keys

Key	SendKeys Representation
BACKSPACE	{BACKSPACE}, {BS}, or {BKSP}
BREAK	{BREAK}
CAPS LOCK	{CAPSLOCK}
DEL or DELETE	{DELETE} or {DEL}
DOWN ARROW	{DOWN}
END	{END}
ENTER	{ENTER} or ~
ESC	{ESC}
HELP	{HELP}
HOME	{HOME}
INS or INSERT	{INSERT} or {INS}
LEFT ARROW	{LEFT}
NUM LOCK	{NUMLOCK}
PAGE DOWN	{PGDN}
PAGE UP	{PGUP}
PRINT SCREEN	{PRTSC}

(continued)

Table 3.16   SendKeys Representations of Common Keys *(continued)*

Key	SendKeys Representation
RIGHT ARROW	{RIGHT}
SCROLL LOCK	{SCROLLLOCK}
TAB	{TAB}
UP ARROW	{UP}
SHIFT	+
CONTROL	^
ALT	%
BACKSPACE	{BACKSPACE}, {BS}, or {BKSP}

All function keys, like F1, are represented by the button name contained within braces — for example, {F1} for the F1 button and {F2} for the F2 button.

For example, the following script starts Notepad and then types the sentence, "This is a test."

```
Set objShell = WScript.CreateObject("WScript.Shell")
objShell.Run "Notepad.exe"
Do Until Success = True
    Success = objShell.AppActivate("Notepad")
    Wscript.Sleep 1000
Loop
objShell.SendKeys "This is a test."
```

When the script runs, Notepad will open, and the sample sentence will be typed in, as shown in Figure 3.12.

Figure 3.12   Controlling Notepad by Using SendKeys

> **Note**
>
> You can send repeated keystrokes by using the SendKeys method. For example, to send the letter *a* ten times, you send the string "{a 10}". You must include a space between the keystroke and the number. SendKeys allows you to send only repeated single keystrokes. You cannot send multiple characters using repeated keystrokes; for example, this command will fail: {dog 10}.

You should be aware that sending keystrokes to an application is not the optimal method for automating a procedure. If you have an application in your enterprise that you need to automate and it has no COM-based object model, you might consider this technique. However, you should first examine whether other methods exist for automating that particular application.

Although SendKeys can be used effectively, there are several potential problems with this approach:

- The script might have difficulty determining which window to send the keystrokes to.

- Because the application runs in GUI mode, a user might close the application prematurely. Unfortunately, this will not terminate the script, and the script could end up sending keystrokes to the wrong application.

- The script might have difficulty synchronizing with the application.

This timing issue is especially troublesome, simply because scripts tend to run much faster than GUI applications. For example, this simple script, which starts Calculator and then tries to type the number 2 into the application, is coded correctly but will likely fail when run (Calculator will start, but the number 2 will not be entered):

```
Set objShell = WScript.CreateObject("WScript.Shell")
objShell.Run "Calc.exe"
objShell.AppActivate "Calculator"
objShell.SendKeys "2"
```

The script fails not because of a syntax issue but because of a timing issue. As quickly as it can, the script issues commands to:

1. Start Calculator.

2. Switch the focus to Calculator (using the AppActivate method).

3. Send the number 2 to Calculator.

Unfortunately, the script runs faster than Calculator can load. As a result, the number 2 is sent, and the script terminates, before Calculator can finish loading and start accepting keystrokes.

There are at least two ways of working around this problem. First, you might be able to estimate how long it will take an application to load and then pause the script for that amount of time. For example, in this script the Run method is called, and then the script pauses for 5 seconds, giving Calculator time to load:

```
Set objShell = WScript.CreateObject("WScript.Shell")
objShell.Run "Calc.exe"
Wscript.Sleep 5000
objShell.AppActivate "Calculator"
objShell.SendKeys "2"
```

Of course, is some cases it might be difficult to estimate how long it will take before an application is loaded and ready to accept keystrokes. In that case, you can call the AppActivate method and check the return value.

Using AppActivate

Before sending keystrokes to an application, you must first ensure that the application is running and that the focus is on the application (that is, the application is running in the active window). You can use the AppActivate method to set the focus on an application. The AppActivate method brings the specified window to the foreground so that you can then start using the WshShell SendKeys method to send keystrokes to the application.

The AppActivate method takes a single parameter that can be either a string containing the title of the application as it appears in the title bar or the process ID of the application. The AppActivate method returns a Boolean value that indicates whether the procedure call has been successful. If the value is False, AppActivate has failed, usually because it was unable to find the application (possibly because that application had not finished loading).

You can place your script in a loop, periodically calling AppActivate until the return value is True. At that point, the application is loaded and prepared to accept keystrokes.

For example, this script checks the return value for AppActivate. If this value is False, the script pauses for 1 second and then checks the value again. This continues until the return value is True, meaning that the application is loaded and ready for use. At that point, the script continues.

```
Set objShell = WScript.CreateObject("WScript.Shell")
objShell.Run "Calc.exe"
Do Until Success = True
    Success = objShell.AppActivate("Calculator")
    Wscript.Sleep 1000
Loop
objShell.SendKeys "2"
```

When the script is determining which application to activate, the given title is compared to the title of each window visible on-screen. If no exact match exists, the AppActivate method sets the focus to the first window whose title begins with the given text. If a window still cannot be found, the first window whose title string *ends* with the text is given the focus. The partial matching with the leading and trailing text of title bars ensures that AppActivate works with applications, such as Notepad, that display the name of the currently opened document on the title bar. (For example, when you first start Notepad, the window title is **Untitled - Notepad**, not **Notepad**.)

This means that when setting the focus to the Calculator, you can use one of the following lines of code:

```
objShell.AppActivate "Calculator"
objShell.AppActivate "Calc"
objShell.AppActivate "C"
```

Of course, this shortcut method of referring to a window can cause problems. For example, suppose you use this line of code:

```
objShell.AppActivate "Calc"
```

If you happen to be working on a Microsoft Word document named Calculations.doc, the keystrokes might be sent to the Word document instead of Calculator.

The script in Listing 3.30 demonstrates a more practical use of the SendKeys method: It starts and sets focus to the Microsoft Management Console (MMC) and then sends keystrokes that cause the **Add/Remove Snap-in** and **Add Standalone Snap-in** dialog boxes to be displayed. The script automates the first part of the common task of constructing custom MMC snap-in tools.

Listing 3.30   Sending Keystrokes to a GUI Application

```
1   Const iNormalFocus = 1
2   Set objShell = WScript.CreateObject("WScript.Shell")
3   objShell.Run "mmc.exe",iNormalFocus
4
5   Wscript.Sleep 300
6
7   objShell.AppActivate "Console1"
8   Wscript.Sleep 100
9   objShell.SendKeys "^m"
10  Wscript.Sleep 100
11  objShell.SendKeys "{TAB}"
12  Wscript.Sleep 100
13  objShell.SendKeys "{TAB}"
14  Wscript.Sleep 100
15  objShell.SendKeys "{ENTER}"
```

Retrieving and Changing a Script's Current Working Directory

The working directory for a script is initially set to the directory from which the script is started. This is not necessarily the directory where the script file is located. If you are working in the C:\Temp directory, for example, and you type **c:\scripts\report.vbs** to run the Report.vbs script, the working directory is C:\Temp, even though the actual script file, Report.vbs, is located in the C:\Scripts directory.

The WshShell object provides the CurrentDirectory property to allow your scripts to determine or modify their current working directory.

There are a number of reasons why you might need to know — and possibly change — the current working directory of a script. For example:

- You want your script to create a log file in the same folder as the script.

- You want to determine whether the script has been run locally or from across the network. (The current working directory will start with two backslashes [\\] instead of a drive letter such as C if it has been run from across the network.)

To retrieve the current directory for a script, create an instance of the WshShell object, and then echo the value of the CurrentDirectory property. To configure the working directory, simply assign a new value to this property.

The script in Listing 3.31 uses the CurrentDirectory property to both retrieve and set a script's working directory. If the specified working directory does not exist, the script will fail.

Listing 3.31   Setting and Retrieving a Script's Current Working Directory

```
1  Set objShell = WScript.CreateObject("WScript.Shell")
2
3  Wscript.Echo "Initial Working Directory:"
4  Wscript.Echo objShell.CurrentDirectory
5
6  objShell.CurrentDirectory = "C:\"
7
8  Wscript.Echo "Working Directory After Change:"
9  Wscript.Echo objShell.CurrentDirectory
```

If the preceding script is started from the folder C:\Temp, the following output will appear in the command window:

```
Initial Working Directory:
C:\Temp
Working Directory After Change:
C:\
```

Displaying Timed Message Boxes

In a perfect world, each time you ran a script the script would encounter optimal conditions and be able to quickly and easily complete its appointed task. In the real world, of course, things do not always work quite so smoothly. Sometimes you will run a script and encounter a decision point; for example, you might try to connect to a remote computer, only to find that the connection cannot be made. When that occurs, a decision must be made: Should the script try again, should it ignore the problem, or should it simply give up?

Depending on your needs, you might make the decision ahead of time and include code that instructs the script what to do: If you cannot make the connection, try again. At other times, you might prefer to be notified that a problem occurred and then make the decision yourself. If so, you need a way to be notified that a decision needs to be made, as well as a way to make that decision.

Your script can use the WshShell Popup method to display a message box with a variety of buttons and return a value that indicates which of the buttons the user clicked. For example, you can display a message box with Yes and No buttons, and your script can take the appropriate action based on the button clicked by the user: Try to make the connection if the user clicks **Yes**; terminate the script if the user clicks **No**.

In addition to providing users with multiple-choice options, you can also supply the Popup method with a parameter that forces it to time out after a given number of seconds as well as change the icon and title of the message box. By contrast, Wscript.Echo message boxes do not have an icon and always have the title **Windows Script Host**.

A sample message box created using the Popup method is shown in Figure 3.13.

Figure 3.13   Message Box Created by the Popup Method

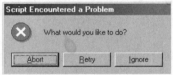

Comparing the Echo and Popup Methods

If you run your script under Wscript, you can use Wscript.Echo instead of the WshShellPopup method to display messages in a message box. However, with Wscript.Echo, users can only click the OK button or do nothing. Wscript.Echo does not enable you to present users with multiple choices.

In addition, your script is paused while the Wscript.Echo message is displayed. Only after the user clicks the OK button does the script proceed. In cases where no user acknowledges the message, Wscript.Echo pauses your script indefinitely or until it times out (if a time-out has been set). If you want your script to display messages in GUI message boxes as it progresses, but continue regardless of whether a user clicks the OK button, you cannot use Wscript.Echo.

As shown in Figure 3.14, the message box displayed by Wscript.Echo has a single OK button. The user can either do nothing and keep the script waiting or click the OK button, allowing the script to continue.

Figure 3.14   Message Box Produced by Using Wscript.Echo Under WScript

 Note

Unlike Wscript.Echo, the Popup method always displays a message box, regardless of whether a script is running under CScript or WScript.

Creating a Message Box That Times Out

The script in Listing 3.32 uses the WScript Popup method to create three messages in message boxes, each of which has a single OK button. Each message box will be displayed on the screen for a maximum of 5 seconds. If no one has clicked the **OK** button after 5 seconds, the message box will automatically dismiss itself from the screen.

Listing 3.32   Displaying Timed Progress Message Boxes

```
1  Const TIMEOUT = 5
2  Set objShell = WScript.CreateObject("WScript.Shell")
3
4  objShell.Popup "Disk Report Complete", TIMEOUT
5  objShell.Popup "Memory Report Complete", TIMEOUT
6  objShell.Popup "CPU Report Complete", TIMEOUT
```

Timed message boxes are useful in at least two instances. For one, they enable you to provide a sort of graphical progress indicator without interrupting the flow of the script. For example, the script shown in Listing 3.32 can be incorporated within a script that actually generates a disk report, a memory report, and a CPU report.

As each report is completed, you might want to display a message box notifying users of the current status. If this message box were displayed using the Echo method, the message box would remain on the screen, and the script would remain paused until someone clicked **OK**. With the Popup method, the message remains on the screen either until someone clicks **OK** or until the time-out period expires. In the preceding script, the message appears — and the script pauses — for no more than 5 seconds before continuing.

Along similar lines, you might want to give users the opportunity to make a decision but, if no decision is immediately forthcoming, allow the script to follow a default course of action. For example, you might have a script that carries out a number of activities and then copies a set of files across the network. Because this copying procedure might take considerable time and bandwidth, you can display a pop-up message box asking the user whether he or she wants to proceed with the copying. The message can could be displayed for a minute or so; if there is no response, the script can automatically begin copying files.

Choosing Icons and Buttons

The WshShell Popup method enables you to create message boxes with various sets of buttons and icons. For example, you can create a message box with **Yes** and **No** buttons or a message box with the button set **Abort, Retry, Ignore**. In addition, you can determine which button a user clicked and then take appropriate action based on the user choice. This helps differentiate the Popup method from the Echo method; message boxes displayed using Echo have *only* an **OK** button.

You specify both the button set and the icon by providing the Popup method with a fourth parameter. This parameter accepts a combination of predefined constants that specify the button set and the icon the message box should use.

Table 3.17 lists the icons available to use with the Popup method along with their corresponding constants.

Table 3.17   Constants for Icons

Icon	Constant Name	Constant Value
STOP	vbCritical	16
QUESTION MARK	vbQuestion	32
EXCLAMATION MARK	vbExclamation	48
INFORMATION	vbInformation	64

Table 3.18 lists the button sets available to use with the Popup method along with their corresponding constants.

Table 3.18   Constants for Button Sets

Button Set	Constant Name	Constant Value
OK	vbOKOnly	0
OK and CANCEL	vbOKCancel	1
ABORT, RETRY and IGNORE	vbAbortRetryIgnore	2
YES, NO and CANCEL	vbYesNoCancel	3
YES and NO	vbYesNo	4
RETRY and CANCEL	vbRetryCancel	5

Although you can use either the constant names or the constant values within a script, using the constant names makes it much easier to understand the code. For example, it is relatively easy to see that the following line of code creates a pop-up message box with **Yes** and **No** buttons. (This message box also has a time-out value of 10 seconds and the title Popup Example.)

```
objShell.Popup "Stop Icon / Abort, Retry and Ignore Buttons", _
    10, "Popup Example", vbYesNo
```

To display both an icon and a button set, use two constants (joined by a plus sign) in the code:

```
objShell.Popup "Stop Icon / Abort, Retry and Ignore Buttons", _
    10, "Popup Example", vbCritical + vbYesNo
```

The script in Listing 3.33 displays a series of message boxes, each of which has a different icon and button set. If you click any button on a message box, the next message box will be displayed; otherwise, the script displays each message box for five seconds.

Listing 3.33   Displaying Combinations of Icons and Button Sets

```
1   Const TIMEOUT = 5
2   Const POPUP_TITLE = "Icons and Buttons"
3   Set objShell = WScript.CreateObject("WScript.Shell")
4   objShell.Popup "Stop Icon / Abort, Retry and Ignore Buttons", _
5       TIMEOUT, POPUP_TITLE, vbCritical+vbAbortRetryIgnore
6
7   objShell.Popup "Question Mark Icon / Yes, No and Cancel Buttons", _
8       TIMEOUT, POPUP_TITLE, vbQuestion+vbYesNoCancel
9
10  objShell.Popup "Exclamation Mark Icon / Yes and No Buttons", _
11      TIMEOUT, POPUP_TITLE, vbExclamation+vbYesNo
12
13  objShell.Popup "Information Icon / Retry and Cancel Buttons", _
14      TIMEOUT, POPUP_TITLE, vbInformation+vbRetryCancel
```

In lines 4–14, the WshShell Popup method is called four times in succession to display pop-up message boxes with various icons and button sets. The third parameter passed to Popup is always the POPUP_TITLE constant and results in each pop-up message box having **Icons and Buttons** as its title. The fourth parameter is passed various constants representing both the icon and the button set to be used. Note that the constants are combined by using the plus (+) operator.

Choosing the Default Button

The WshShell Popup method lets you specify the default button when you create a message box. The default button is the button that has focus and will be chosen if the user presses ENTER.

It is not unusual for users to reflexively press ENTER any time a message box is displayed. Because of that, some care should be taken when choosing the default button. For example, you might choose the button that, 9 times out of 10, users will select anyway. Or you might choose the button that is the "safest" should a user press ENTER without realizing what they are doing. For example, your message box might prompt the user, "Are you sure you want to delete all the files on this hard drive?" In a case such as this, you might want to configure **No** as the default button. That way, no damage will be done if a user accidentally presses ENTER.

You can specify which button to make the default by adding another constant to the fourth parameter of the Popup method. Table 3.19 lists the constants you can use to set the default button in a message box. If you try to set the second or third button as the default when the message box does not have a second or third button, the default button constant you specify will be ignored and the left button will be set as the default.

Table 3.19 Constants for Default Button Locations

Default Button	Constant Name	Constant Value
LEFT	vbDefaultButton1	0
MIDDLE	vbDefaultButton2	256
RIGHT	vbDefaultButton3	512

The script in Listing 3.34 displays two message boxes in succession. Both message boxes use the Abort, Retry, Ignore button set. The first message box does not specify the default button, so the leftmost button, Abort, is automatically selected as the default. The second message box uses the vbDefaultButton2 constant to make Retry the default button.

Listing 3.34   Setting Retry as the Default Button

```
1  Const TIMEOUT = 5
2  Set objShell = WScript.CreateObject("WScript.Shell")
3
4  objShell.Popup "Abort, Retry, Ignore. No Default Specified." _
5      ,TIMEOUT,,vbAbortRetryIgnore
6
7  objShell.Popup "Abort, Retry, Ignore. Retry Set as Default." _
8      ,TIMEOUT,,vbAbortRetryIgnore+vbDefaultButton2
```

Retrieving User Input

One of the advantages of using the Popup method rather than the Echo method is that you can give users the chance to make a choice: Yes, I want to try again; no, I would rather just quit. This means that the script needs to determine which button a user has clicked. The Popup method returns an integer that you can compare with a set of constants to determine which button was clicked. If a message box times out, the Popup method returns –1.

Table 3.20 lists the values you can use to identify which button a user has clicked. If the return value of the Popup method is equal to one of these constants, the user has clicked the associated button. Within a script, you can check either for the value of the constant or for the constant itself. For example, these two lines of code both check to see whether the OK button was clicked:

```
If intClicked = 1
If intClicked = vbOK
```

Table 3.20   Button Constants

Value	Constant	Button Clicked
1	VbOK	OK
2	VbCancel	Cancel
3	VbAbort	Abort
4	VbRetry	Retry
5	VbIgnore	Ignore
6	VbYes	Yes
7	VbNo	No

The script in Listing 3.35 displays a message box that uses the Yes, No button set to determine whether the user would like more detailed information.

The script uses the FileSystemObject to present the user with information about the host the script is running under. The script determines and displays the version of the script host file and uses the Popup method to allow the user to decide whether or not they would like to see more details about the file.

Listing 3.35   Retrieving User Input from a Message Box

```
1   Const TIMEOUT = 7
2   Set objShell = WScript.CreateObject("WScript.Shell")
3   Set objFS = WScript.CreateObject("Scripting.FileSystemObject")
4
5   strPath = Wscript.FullName
6   strFileVersion = objFS.GetFileVersion(strPath)
7
8   iRetVal = objShell.Popup(Wscript.FullName & vbCrLf & _
9       "File Version: " & _
10      strFileVersion & vbCrLf & _
11      "Would you like more details?" _
12      ,TIMEOUT,"More Info?",vbYesNo + vbQuestion)
13
14  Select Case iRetVal
15      Case vbYes
16          Set objFile = objFS.GetFile(strPath)
17          objShell.Popup WScript.FullName & vbCrLf & vbCrLf & _
18            "File Version: " & strFileVersion & vbCrLf & _
19            "File Size: " & Round((objFile.Size/1024),2) & _
20              " KB" & vbCrLf & _
21              "Date Created: " & objFile.DateCreated & vbCrLf & _
22              "Date Last Modified: " & objFile.DateLastModified & _
23              vbCrLf,TIMEOUT
24          Wscript.Quit
25      Case vbNo
26          Wscript.Quit
27      Case -1
28          WScript.StdOut.WriteLine "Popup timed out."
29          Wscript.Quit
30  End Select
```

WshNetwork Object

The WshNetwork object provides your scripts with the ability to work with network drives and printers. It also provides your scripts with access to the name of the computer they are currently running on, as well as the domain and user names of the account under which they are running. This makes WshNetwork extremely useful in scripts that take actions based on such information as the name of the user logging on or the domain in which the user account resides.

The WshNetwork object can be used to accomplish some of the same tasks as the net.exe command-line tool. For example, the **net name** command returns the name of the user and the computer; the **net use** command is used to map and unmap network drives. These similarities make WshNetwork useful for converting legacy batch files and logon scripts that use net.exe to a WSH-based solution.

Table 3.21 lists the capabilities provided by the WshNetwork object, along with the methods and properties that your scripts can use to access this functionality.

Table 3.21 Capabilities Provided by the WshNetwork Object

Category	Method or Property
Working with network drives	MapNetworkDrive
	EnumNetworkDrives
	RemoveNetworkDrive
Working with network printers	AddPrinterConnection
	AddWindowsPrinterConnection
	EnumPrinterConnections
	SetDefaultPrinter
	RemovePrinterConnection
Obtaining information about the currently logged-on user	ComputerName
	UserDomain
	UserName

WshNetwork is part of the Windows Script Host Object Model, wshom.ocx. The object model for the WshNetwork object is shown in Figure 3.15. In addition to the methods and properties provided by the WshNetwork object, WshNetwork also exposes a WshCollection object. The WshCollection object is not created using CreateObject but is automatically created and returned by the WshNetwork object's EnumNetworkDrives and EnumPrinterConnections methods.

Figure 3.15 shows the properties and methods of the WshNetwork object.

Figure 3.15   WshNetwork Object Model

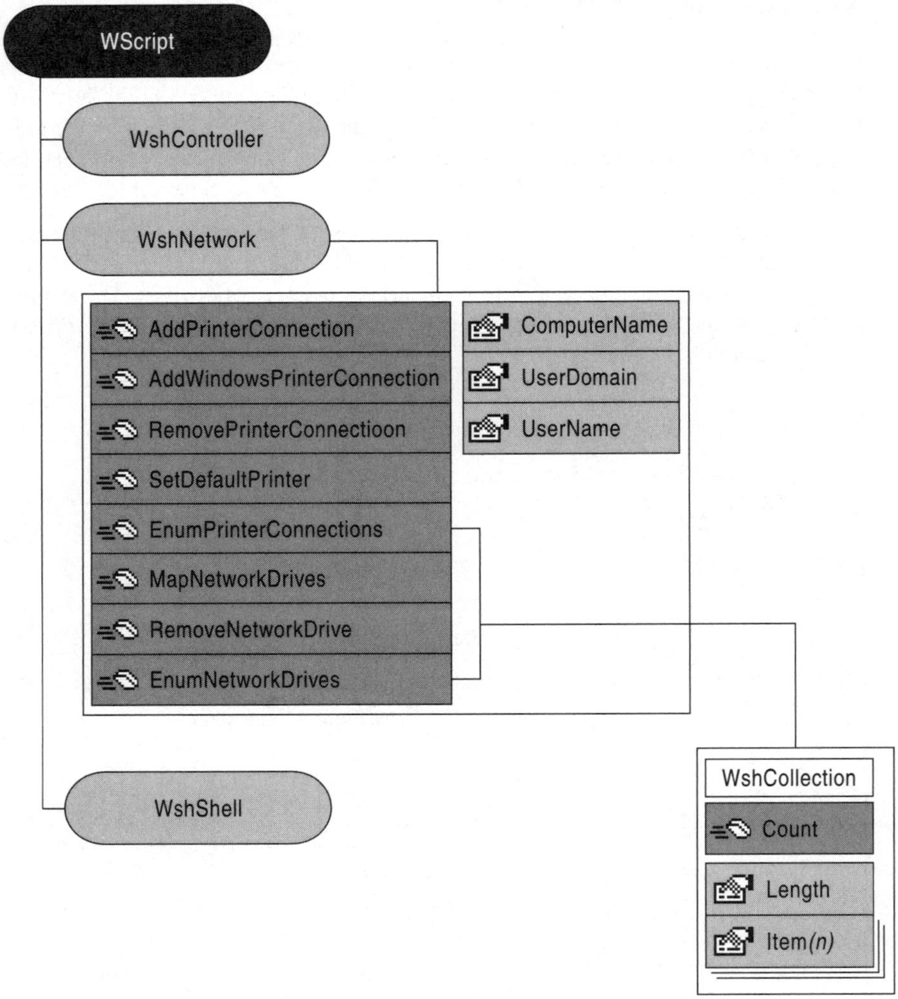

Accessing the WshNetwork Object

The WshNetwork object is a COM object, and an instance of the object can be created by the following code statement:

```
Set objNetwork = WScript.CreateObject("WScript.Network")
```

Managing Network Drives

Network drives remain an important part of the computing infrastructure. Users prefer mapped network drives to Universal Naming Convention (UNC) path names; it is easier to remember that financial records are stored on drive X than to remember that financial records are stored on \\atl-fs-01\departments\accounting\admin\financial_records\2002_archive. Administrators prefer mapped network drives as well; if financial records need to be moved to a new server, it is far easier to remap drive X than to expect users to memorize the new location.

Your scripts can use the methods in this section to manage network drive connections as part of a logon script or in any WSH script that has a need to connect to or disconnect from a network share. In fact, this represents one area where WSH has system administration capability not found in WMI. While both WSH and WMI let you enumerate mapped network drives (WMI by using the Win32_MappedLogicalDisk class), only WSH enables you to create and delete drive mappings.

WshNetwork provides three methods to work with network drive connections: MapNetworkDrive, RemoveNetworkDrive, and EnumNetworkDrives. You can use the three methods to manage network connections as part of a user's logon script or in any WSH script that needs to connect to or disconnect from a network share.

Mapping a Network Drive

You map a local drive letter to a shared folder using the WshNetwork object's MapNetworkDrive method. You can use MapNetworkDrive to connect directly to a shared folder or any child folder beneath a shared folder. MapNetworkDrive has two mandatory and three optional arguments, defined in Table 3.22.

Table 3.22   MapNetworkDrive Arguments

Argument	Type	Required	Default	Description
LocalName	String	●	None	The drive letter, followed by a colon, assigned to the mapped network drive, e.g., "H:".
RemoteName	String	●	None	The shared folder's UNC name, e.g., "\\ServerName\ShareName" or "\\ServerName\ShareName\FolderName".
UpdateProfile	Boolean		False	Boolean value indicating whether the mapping information is stored in the current user's profile. The value True updates the current user's profile; False does not.
UserName	String		None	Maps the network drive using the credentials of someone other than the current user.
Password	String		None	Password for the user identified by the UserName argument.

The following example demonstrates how MapNetworkDrive can be used in a user's logon script to connect to two network shares.

```
Set objNetwork = Wscript.CreateObject("WScript.Network")
objNetwork.MapNetworkDrive "G:", "\\atl-fs-01\Sales"
objNetwork.MapNetworkDrive "H:", "\\atl-fs-01\Users$\lewjudy"
```

Drive G is mapped to the Sales share on the file server named atl-fs-01. Drive H is mapped to the user's home directory located directly beneath the hidden share named Users$ on atl-fs-01.

By default, MapNetworkDrive uses the access token of the current user to validate permissions prior to making the connection; you cannot map a drive to a folder unless you have permission to access that folder. In administrative scripts, it might be necessary to supply an alternate or elevated set of credentials to successfully connect to a share. You can use the optional UserName and Password arguments to supply a set of credentials that are used in lieu of the current user's access token. After the connection is established, the supplied credentials govern access to the network drive for the duration of the connection.

Two common conditions can cause MapNetworkDrive to fail:

- The user running the script might not have sufficient permissions to connect to the target share.

- The local drive letter might already be in use.

Left unchecked, both conditions can result in run-time errors. To avoid permissions-related or password-related issues, your best defense is to trap and handle the error using VBScript's On Error Resume Next statement. To handle a local drive letter that is already in use, you can forcibly disconnect the mapped drive or locate and use a different drive letter.

Unmapping a Network Drive

Your scripts can use the RemoveNetworkDrive method to unmap a network drive. If the network drive has a mapping between a local drive letter and the remote UNC path, the method requires the local drive letter as its single parameter.

If the network drive does not have a mapping between a local drive letter and the remote UNC path, the method requires the remote UNC path as its single parameter.

The script in Listing 3.36 unmaps a drive G.

Listing 3.36 Unmapping a Network Drive

```
1  Set objNetwork = WScript.CreateObject("Wscript.Network")
2  objNetwork.RemoveNetworkDrive "G:"
```

In addition to the mandatory parameter that specifies the mapped drive to be removed, the MapNetworkDrive method accepts two additional, optional, parameters:

- A Boolean value that, if set to True, specifies that the method should unmap the drive regardless of whether it is currently in use. If the value is set to True, the user will no longer be able to save data to that drive, even if he or she has already opened a document from there. Instead, the user will have to save the document to an alternate location.

- A Boolean value that, if set to True, specifies that the method should remove the drive mapping from the profile of the user.

Listing Current Network Drives

Your scripts can use the EnumNetworkDrives method to retrieve a list of the current mapped network drives on a computer.

The EnumNetworkDrives method returns a collection that holds pairs of items: network drive local names and their associated UNC names. The collection is zero-indexed; the even-numbered items in the collection are the local drive names, and the odd-numbered items are the associated UNC paths.

A sample network drive collection is shown in Table 3.23. In this sample collection, drive D (index number 0) maps to \\atl-fs-01\users\kmyer (index number 1).

Table 3.23 Sample Network Drive Collection

Index Number	Value
0	D:
1	\\atl-fs-01\users\kmyer
2	E:
3	\\atl-fs-02\accounting
4	F:
5	\\atl-fs-03\public

A script can retrieve both pieces of information about each mapped network drive by iterating through the collection returned by EnumNetworkDrives and retrieving two items from the collection during each iteration. An example of this is shown in Listing 3.37.

Listing 3.37 Listing Current Network Drives

```
1   Set objNetwork = WScript.CreateObject("WScript.Network")
2   Set colDrives = objNetwork.EnumNetworkDrives
3   For i = 0 to colDrives.Count-1 Step 2
4      Wscript.Echo colDrives.Item(i) & vbTab & colDrives.Item (i + 1)
5   Next
```

Managing Network Printers

Managing printer connections on user computers is an important part of system administration. When a new printer comes online, you do not have to send instructions on how to connect to this device; instead, you can simply include code in a logon script that automatically makes this connection for a user. Likewise, when a printer is removed from the network, you can remove the printer connection, preventing the problems likely to arise when users try to print to a printer that no longer exists.

The WshNetwork object provides methods that enable your scripts to add or remove printer connections, to set the default printer, and to list the current printer connections on a computer.

Adding Printer Connections

Two WshNetwork methods enable your scripts to add printer connections: AddWindowsPrinterConnection and AddPrinterConnection.

The AddWindowsPrinterConnection method enables a script to add a Windows-based printer connection (like using the Control Panel Add Printer Wizard), while the AddPrinterConnection method enables a script to add an MS-DOS®-based printer connection.

Adding Windows-based Printer Connections

When used to add a Windows-based printer connection to a Windows NT–based operating system such as Windows 2000, Windows XP, or Windows NT, the AddWindowsPrinterConnection method accepts, as its only required parameter, the UNC path of the printer.

The script in Listing 3.38 adds a connection to the network printer with the UNC path \\HRServer01\Printer1.

Listing 3.38 Adding a Windows-based printer connection (Windows NT–based operating system)

```
1   Set objNetwork = Wscript.CreateObject("WScript.Network")
2   objNetwork.AddWindowsPrinterConnection "\\HRServer01\Printer1"
```

When used to add a Windows-based printer connection to Windows 95, Windows 98, or Windows Me, the AddWindowsPrinterConnection method requires two parameters: the UNC path of the printer and the name of the printer driver (which must already be installed on the computer). In addition, when used with these operating systems, the method accepts a third, optional, parameter that specifies the local port through which the printer should be made available.

Adding MS-DOS-based printer connections

The AddPrinterConnection method enables a script to add an MS-DOS-based printer connection. The method takes two required parameters: the local port through which the printer will be available and the UNC path of the network printer.

The AddPrinterConnection method also lets you add the mapping to the user profile. If you want to do this, set the updateProfile Boolean argument to True. The user name and the password parameters let you connect to the specified printer by using another user's credentials.

Unlike the AddWindowsPrinterConnection method, the AddPrinterConnection method requires you to specify a port name.

Removing a Printer Connection

To remove a printer connection, use the RemovePrinterConnection method.

```
WshNetwork.RemovePrinterConnection(printerName, [forced], [updateProfile])
```

The first argument identifies the shared printer. The other two optional arguments let you specify:

- Whether the disconnection should be forced, even if the printer is in use.
- Whether the user profile should be updated to reflect the disconnection.

The RemovePrinterConnection method removes both Windows and MS-DOS-based printer connections. If the printer was connected using AddPrinterConnection, the printerName argument must be the same as the printer's local port. If the printer was set up using the AddWindowsPrinterConnection method or was added manually through the Add Printer wizard, the printerName argument must be the printer's UNC name.

For example, this command removes the connection to the printer \\atl-ps-01\colorprinter.

```
Set objNetwork = WScript.CreateObject("WScript.Network")
objNetwork.RemovePrinterConnection "\\atl-ps-01\colorprinter"
```

Enumerating the Available Printers

To obtain a list of the printers set up on a computer, you use code similar to that used to list the mapped network drives.

You use the EnumPrinterConnections method to obtain a WshCollection object where each network printer is made up of two elements in the collection. The even-positioned item contains the printer's local name or port. The odd-positioned item contains the UNC name. As shown in Listing 3.39, you can use a For Next loop with the step value 2 to collect all the information you need.

Listing 3.39 Enumerating Available Printers

```
1  Set objNetwork = WScript.CreateObject("WScript.Network")
2  Set colPrinters = objNetwork.EnumPrinterConnections
3  For i = 0 to colPrinters.Count -1 Step 2
4    Wscript.Echo colPrinters.Item(i) & vbTab & colPrinters.Item (i + 1)
5  Next
```

When run under CScript, output similar to this is displayed in the command window:

```
LPT1:   Art Department Printer
XRX00034716DD75 \\atl-prn-xrx\plotter
XRX0000AA622E89 \\atl-prn-xrx\colorprinter
```

Setting the Default Printer

Many users print documents by clicking the printer icon within their application; in most cases that means that documents are automatically sent to the user's default printer. By assigning different users different default printers, you can help divide the print load among your print devices and ensure that documents are printed quickly and efficiently.

The SetDefaultPrinter method lets you assign a specific printer the role of the default printer. SetDefaultPrinter uses the following syntax:

```
WshNetwork.SetDefaultPrinter(printerName)
```

The printerName parameter is the UNC name of the printer. (If the printer is a local printer, you can also use a port name such as LPT1.) This script sets the printer \\atl-ps-01\colorprinter as the default:

```
Set objNetwork = WScript.CreateObject("WScript.Network")
objNetwork.SetDefaultPrinter("\\atl-ps-01\colorprinter")
```

The SetDefaultPrinter method cannot retrieve the current default printer.

Obtaining User and Computer Information

The WshNetwork object has three read-only properties that your scripts can use to obtain information about the computer they are running on and the user account under which they are running. These properties are ComputerName, UserDomain, and UserName.

Depending on your needs, you should consider using ADSI to return this same information. WSH is able to return only the SAM account name of a user or computer (for example, kenmyer). ADSI, however, is able to return the distinguished name for these same objects. (For example, cn=ken myer,ou=Human Resources,dc=fabrikam,dc=com.) Using the distinguished name, the script can then directly bind to the object in Active Directory and perform such tasks as enumerate the groups that the user belongs to. With the SAM account name, the script would need to search Active Directory, determine the distinguished name, and then bind to the object.

There might be times, however, when simply knowing the user name, computer name, or domain name is sufficient information for your script to perform its tasks. In those instances, the WshNetwork object will likely suffice. In addition, WSH is installed by default on Windows 98 and Windows NT 4.0 computers, while ADSI is not. Because of this, WSH might be your only option when supporting computers such as those running Windows NT 4.0.

The WshNetwork object is often used in logon scripts that map different network drives, depending on the domain of the user running the script. The script in Listing 3.40 maps drive N to \\fileserver01\accounting if the user's domain is ACT or maps drive N to \\fileserver01\development if the user's domain is DEV.

Listing 3.40 Mapping a Network Drive According to User Domain

```
1   Set objNetwork = WScript.CreateObject("WScript.Network")
2   strUserDomain = objNetwork.UserDomain
3
4   If strUserDomain = "ACCOUNTING" Then
5       objNetwork.MapNetworkDrive "N:", "\\fileserver01\accounting", True
6   ElseIf strUserDomain = "DEVELOPMENT" Then
7       objNetwork.MapNetworkDrive "N:", "\\fileserver01\development", True
8   Else
9       Wscript.Echo "User " & objNetwork.UserName & _
10          "not in ACCOUNTING or DEVELOPMENT. N: not mapped."
11  End If
```

WshController Object

One limitation of WSH has always been the fact that scripts could only be run locally; they could not be run against remote computers. For instance, suppose you want to use a script to add printer connections to a number of computers. You would have to run that script on each of those computers; historically, you could not run a script on Computer A and get it to add a printer connection to Computer B. Because of that, WSH has primarily been relegated to use in logon scripts.

Clearly, it would be useful to automate the running of a script on remote computers and on multiple computers. The WshController object, introduced in WSH 5.6, provides that capability.

The WshController object allows you to create a *controller script* that can run *worker scripts* against remote computers. The controller script initiates, monitors, and, if necessary, terminates the worker script. The worker script, meanwhile, is simply the script that carries out the administrative task — for example, adding a printer connection or mapping a network drive.

The worker scripts do not have to be located on the same computer as the controller script, although their location must be specified relative to the computer on which the controller script runs. For instance, you can create a controller script that accesses a worker script in a shared folder on another computer and runs that worker script on yet another computer.

The WshController object provides communication among all the local and remote computers involved. The script that runs on the remote computer is never saved to disk on the remote computer. Instead, the WshController object starts the script within a WSH process in the memory of the remote computer.

Figure 3.16 shows a list of all the objects, events, methods, and properties your scripts can make use of when using the WshController object to run scripts on remote computers.

Figure 3.16   WshController Object Model

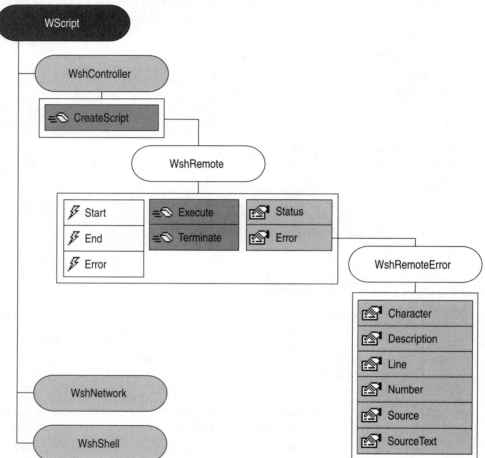

Accessing the WshController Object

The WshController object is a COM object, and an instance of the object can be created by the following code statement:

```
Set objController = WScript.CreateObject("WshController")
```

Note

The ProgID of the WshController object does not follow the same naming convention as the WshNetwork (WScript.Network) and WshShell (WScript.Shell) objects. The ProgID of the WshController object has no dot (.) and does not begin with WScript. It is simply the name of the object: WshController.

Setup Required to Run Scripts Remotely

Before you can use the WshController object to run scripts on remote computers, you must first ensure that your environment is configured as follows:

- Both the local and target remote computers must be running WSH version 5.6.

- You must add a string-valued entry (REG_SZ) named **Remote** to the registry subkey HKEY_LOCAL_ MACHINE\SOFTWARE\Microsoft\Windows Script Host\Settings and set its value to 1 on all target remote computers. You do not need to add this entry to the registry of the local computer from which you run the controller script.

Caution

Changing the registry with a script can easily propagate errors. The scripting tools bypass safeguards, allowing settings that can damage your system, or even require you to reinstall Windows. Before scripting changes to the registry, test your script thoroughly and back up the registry on every computer on which you will make changes. For more information about scripting changes to the registry, see the Registry Reference on the *Windows 2000 Server Resource Kit* companion CD or at http://www.microsoft.com/reskit.

The script in Listing 3.41 uses the WMI Registry Provider to add the **Remote** entry and set its value to 1 on the computer specified in the strComputer variable.

Listing 3.41 Adding a Registry Entry to Enable Running Scripts Remotely

```
1  Const HKEY_LOCAL_MACHINE = &H80000002
2  strComputer = "RemoteComputerName"
3
4  Set objRegProv = GetObject("winmgmts:{impersonationLevel=Impersonate}" & _
5                   "!\\" & strComputer & "\root\default:StdRegProv")
6
7  strKeyPath = "SOFTWARE\Microsoft\Windows Script Host\Settings"
8  objRegProv.SetStringValue HKEY_LOCAL_MACHINE,strKeyPath,"Remote","1"
```

The user running the controlling script on the local computer must be a member of the local administrators group of each target remote computer.

WshController Capabilities

The WshController object enables you to run scripts on remote computers, monitor the status of remotely running scripts, and examine errors produced by these scripts. Table 3.24 lists these categories along with the methods, properties, and events of the WshController object, the WshRemote object, and the WshRemoteError object that your scripts can use to access this functionality.

Table 3.24   Capabilities Provided by the WshController Object

Task Category	Method, Property, or Event
Running Scripts on Remote Computers	CreateScript, Execute, Terminate
Monitoring Status of Remotely Running Scripts	Status, Start, End, Error (event)
Examining Errors Produced by Remotely Running Scripts	Error (event), Error (property), Character, Description, Line, Number, Source, SourceText

Running Scripts on Remote Computers

The WshController object provides you with the ability to run scripts on remote computers. The WshController object has a single method, CreateScript, which returns a WshRemote object.

In turn, the WshRemote object can then be used to run the worker script. The worker script is not run as a result of the call to CreateScript. Instead, the WshRemote object Execute method is used to actually run the script on the remote computer.

The script in Listing 3.42 runs the hypothetical worker script MapNetworkDrive.vbs on the remote computer, RASServer01. Although the location of the worker script can be specified using either a local file path or a UNC path, because no path is specified in Listing 3.42, this means the worker script must be located in the same directory as the controller script.

Listing 3.42   Running a Local Script on a Remote Computer

```
1   strRemoteComputer = "RASServer01"
2   strWorkerScript = "MapNetworkDrive.vbs"
3   Set objWshController = WScript.CreateObject("WshController")
4   Set objRemoteScript = _
5   objWshController.CreateScript(strWorkerScript, strRemoteComputer)
6   objRemoteScript.Execute
7
8   Do While Not objRemoteScript.Status = 2
9       Wscript.Sleep(100)
10      Wscript.Echo "Remote script not yet complete."
11  Loop
```

Note

Remote access is not an interactive process, which means that remotely run scripts cannot display any GUI elements on the remote computer. If you run a remote script that displays a GUI element, the script might fail or produce indeterminate results. For example, suppose your script displays a message box that the user must respond to. Because the script runs in a hidden window, the user will never be able to see, and thus never be able to respond to, that message box. As a result, the script will hang, waiting for user input that will never be provided.

Monitoring Status of Remotely Running Scripts

Running scripts on remote computers is most useful if you can be sure that the scripts actually ran successfully. You can do so by using the WshRemote object and monitoring events that are generated when the remote script runs.

The WshRemote object (created when you call the CreateScript method) has a property named Status that monitors the status of the worker script associated with the object. The Status property can take on one of three values:

- **0** indicates that the remote script has not yet started to run.

- **1** indicates that the remote script is currently running.

- **2** indicates that the remote script has finished running.

In addition to the WshRemote object Status property, three events are triggered when certain things happen with the remote script. Having your script handle these events allows you to monitor the running of the remote script. The three events are:

- **Start.** This event is triggered when the remote script starts executing.

- **End.** This event is triggered when the remote script is finished executing.

- **Error.** This event is triggered only if the remote script encounters a problem. If the Error event is triggered, you can access the WshRemoteError object as a property of the WshRemote object and retrieve information about the error that occurred.

The script in Listing 3.43 has three subroutines (Remote_Start, Remote_Error, and Remote_End) that respond to the three events Start, Error, and End. The subroutines are called if and when each of the events takes place. In turn, each subroutine simply displays a message indicating that the corresponding event has taken place.

The call to ConnectObject in line 7 of Listing 3.43 causes the script to handle the events. Note that the string "Remote_", passed as the second parameter to the ConnectObject method, determines the first part of the names of the event-handling subroutines; the last part of the names is determined by the particular event the subroutine handles.

Listing 3.43 Monitoring a Remotely Running Script

```
1    strRemoteComputer = "RASServer01"
2    strWorkerScript = "CreateTextFilMapNetworkDrive.vbs"
3
4    Set objWshController = WScript.CreateObject("WshController")
5    Set objRemoteScript =_
6       objWshController.CreateScript(strWorkerScript, strRemoteComputer)
7    Wscript.ConnectObject objRemoteScript, "Remote_"
8    objRemoteScript.Execute
9
```

(continued)

Listing 3.43   Monitoring a Remotely Running Script *(continued)*

```
10   Do While Not objRemoteScript.Status = 2
11      Wscript.Sleep(100)
12   Loop
13
14   Sub Remote_Start
15      Wscript.Echo "Started Running Remote Script."
16   End Sub
17
18   Sub Remote_Error
19      Wscript.Echo "Error Running Remote Script."
20      objRemoteScript.Terminate
21      Wscript.Quit
22   End Sub
23
24   Sub Remote_End
25      Wscript.Echo "Finished Running Remote Script."
26   End Sub
```

If everything works as expected, only the Start and End events will be triggered when you run the script in Listing 3.43. When the script runs, you will receive messages indicating that the remote script started and ended. If an error occurs, however, you will receive a simple message stating that an error occurred. For information about retrieving more details about errors, see "Examining Errors Produced by Remotely Running Scripts", which follows.

Examining Errors Produced by Remotely Running Scripts

Knowing that a remotely executing script has encountered an error is important. However, once you know the error has occurred, you next need to determine the cause and correct the problem. If an error occurs in a remotely executing script, the WshRemoteError object can be accessed as a property of the WshRemote object. The WshRemoteError object includes a number of properties that describe the error that occurred and can help you troubleshoot the problem. These properties are shown in Table 3.25.

Table 3.25   Properties of the WshRemoteError Object

Property	Description
Character	Returns the character position in the line where the error occurred. For example, in this simple script, the semicolon is an invalid character. Because the semicolon is the 14th character in the line, the Character property is 14: `Wscript.Echo ;`
Description	Brief description of the error.

(continued)

Table 3.25 Properties of the WshRemoteError Object *(continued)*

Property	Description
Line	Line number of the script in which the error occurred.
Number	Error code associated with the error.
Source	Identifies the COM object that reported the error.
SourceText	Contains the line of code that generated the error. The SourceText cannot always be retrieved; in that case, an empty string will be returned.

The script in Listing 3.44 includes a subroutine that handles the Error event. Unlike the script in Listing 3.43, which simply displayed a message indicating that an error occurred, this script uses the WshRemote object Error property to retrieve an instance of the WshRemoteError object. The script then displays all of the properties of the WshRemoteError object, providing you with a great deal of information that is useful for troubleshooting the problem.

Listing 3.44 Examining Errors Produced by a Script Running Remotely

```
 1  strRemoteComputer = "RASServer01"
 2  strWorkerScript = "CreateTestFile.vbs"
 3
 4  Set objWshController = WScript.CreateObject("WshController")
 5  Set objRemoteScript =_
 6      objWshController.CreateScript(strWorkerScript, strRemoteComputer)
 7  Wscript.ConnectObject objRemoteScript, "Remote_"
 8  objRemoteScript.Execute
 9
10  Do While Not objRemoteScript.Status = 2
11      Wscript.Sleep(100)
12  Loop
13
14
15  Sub Remote_Error
16      Wscript.Echo "Error Running Remote Script."
17      Set objError = objRemoteScript.Error
18      Wscript.Echo "Character    :" & objError.Character
19      Wscript.Echo "Description :" & objError.Description
20      Wscript.Echo "Line        :" & objError.Line
21      Wscript.Echo "Number      :" & objError.Number
22      Wscript.Echo "Source      :" & objError.Source
23      Wscript.Echo "Source Text :" & objError.SourceText
24      objRemoteScript.Terminate
25      Wscript.Quit
26  End Sub
```

Limitations of Remote WSH

Remote WSH has two important limitations. First, there is no easy way to retrieve the output from a remotely run script. Second, remotely run scripts cannot access shared folders using the credentials of the user who ran the controller script.

To work around the first problem, you can create a text file that holds the results of your worker script. You might create the file on a shared folder on each of the remote computers you are running the worker scripts on and then retrieve the files and store them in a central location. To learn about creating text files and accessing them by using UNC paths, see "Script Runtime Primer" in this book.

However, there is no way around the second problem, at least not without creating potential security vulnerabilities.

Securing Scripts

Security is always a primary concern for system administrators; this is as true for scripts and scripting as it is for anything else. After all, no one wants a repeat of the ILOVEYOU virus, a script that, largely without warning, managed to wreak havoc worldwide.

WSH 5.6 includes a number of measures designed to guard against problems such as this. The ILOVEYOU virus succeeded not so much by exploiting a flaw in Windows Script Host as it did by exploiting a flaw in human nature: people are innately curious about anything that is given to them. Faced with the decision "Do you want to run this script?" and with no other information to go on, many people opted to run the script.

WSH 5.6 can help users make more intelligent choices. For example, when a user tries to run a script, WSH can be configured to display a dialog box that says, in effect, "We do not know who wrote this script, and we have no guarantee that it is safe to run. Are you sure you want to proceed?" Alternatively, system administrators can relieve users of the need to make choices at all. Instead, WSH can be configured so that users can only run scripts that have been pre-approved and digitally-signed.

This section of the chapter examines several techniques that can be used to enhance script security, including:

- Signing scripts with digital signatures.
- Restricting the ability of a user to run a script.
- Disabling Windows Script Host.

Important

Security obviously applies to items other than scripts. It is true that hackers often use scripts to ply their trade, simply because these plain-text files are easy to write and easy to distribute. However, scripts are not the only security threat faced by system administrators; after all, executable files and batch files have been misused as well. The techniques discussed in this chapter can be a useful part of any security plan, but they are by no means an entire security plan in and of themselves.

Digitally Signing Scripts

Digital signatures (introduced with WSH 5.6) provide a way for you to verify who authored a script, as well as a way to guarantee that a script has not been altered since it was written and signed. This does not necessarily mean that the script is "safe;" after all, virus writers can obtain digital signatures, too. However, digital signatures do provide two measures of protection:

- You can specify which script authors are to be trusted and which ones are not. For example, you can specify that only scripts signed using a certificate issued by trusted authorities can be run in your organization. If you list Verisign as the only trusted authority, then only scripts signed with a certificate issued by Verisign will be considered safe and will be able to run. (Of course, if a hacker has obtained a certificate from Verisign, then any scripts he or she writes will be considered safe, whether they actually are or not.)

- You can be assured that the script has not been changed since the time it was written and signed. If you know that the script ThirdPartyScript.vbs is safe to use within your organization, you can distribute that script with the knowledge that no one can modify the script without violating the digital signature. When a script is signed, a "hash" is derived and used to verify the signature. If the script has been modified in any way, the hash will be invalid, and the script will be reported as having been altered in some way.

When a script is signed, the digital signature is appended to the end of the file as a set of comments. Adding the signature as commented lines ensures that the script can still be run using previous versions of WSH (these versions will see the additional lines as comments rather than as a digital signature). A signature might look like this:

```
'' SIG '' Begin signature block
'' SIG '' MIIC8AYJKoZIhvcNAQcCoIIC4TCCAtOCAQExDjAMBggq
'' SIG '' hkiG9w0CBQUAMGYGCisGAQQBgjcCAQSgWDBWMDIGCisG
'' SIG '' AQQBgjcCAR4wJAIBAQQQTvApFpkntU2P5azhDxfrqwIB
'' SIG '' AAIBAAIBAAIBAAIBADAgMAwGCCqGSIb3DQIFBQAEEPC2
'' SIG '' QdSn0Xnjl7nT/Xwadl2gggF6MIIBdjCCASCgAwIBAgIQ
'' SIG '' NeMgQmXo1o1F8M6hs6TX1jANBgkqhkiG9w0BAQQFADAW
'' SIG '' MRQwEgYDVQQDEwtSb290IEFnZW5jeTAeFw0wMDEyMjEy
```

(continued)

(continued)

```
'' SIG ''  MzUxMTJaFw0zOTEyMzEyMzU5NTlaMBUxEzARBgNVBAMT
'' SIG ''  Ck15IENvbXBhbnkwXDANBgkqhkiG9w0BAQEFAANLADBI
'' SIG ''  AkEAx/bBOOqOzdHk2EfxXloUaGo9PtI/HSJ9LQSXkhF7
'' SIG ''  neEf4Qy+oyA7NImnOacI+1HDCOAPeKgGJIvaFcZs0BuM
'' SIG ''  iQIDAQABo0swSTBHBgNVHQEEQDA+gBAS5AktBh0dTwCN
'' SIG ''  YSHcFmRjoRgwFjEUMBIGA1UEAxMLUm9vdCBBZ2VuY3mC
'' SIG ''  EAY3bACqAGSKEc+41KpcNfQwDQYJKoZIhvcNAQEEBQAD
'' SIG ''  QQA6/fIIDKycSp2DdBT/A3iUSxoiu2BqmEEpVoGKE5yY
'' SIG ''  CA3MDWuI29RRvgNJ2oQasb8rZiD5dEexGK3rWEQGV6r+
'' SIG ''  MYHhMIHeAgEBMCowFjEUMBIGA1UEAxMLUm9vdCBBZ2Vu
'' SIG ''  Y3kCEDXjIEJl6NaNRfDOobOk19YwDAYIKoZIhvcNAgUF
'' SIG ''  AKBOMBAGCisGAQQBgjcCAQwxAjAAMBkGCSqGSIb3DQEJ
'' SIG ''  AzEMBgorBgEEAYI3AgEEMB8GCSqGSIb3DQEJBDESBBCV
'' SIG ''  t6owbn7YLnkAnCqiDdINMA0GCSqGSIb3DQEBAQUABECe
'' SIG ''  xmfNlmrIls2kFkyhXOWKicnpOk5iW4twTRNAc4LAkO8M
'' SIG ''  uk0ZBCBgR5XC8F7slEMfWCG9R7129EUF4vFhZToK
'' SIG ''  End signature block
```

Enforcing the Use of Signed Scripts

To configure security settings for signed and unsigned scripts, you need to modify the registry key HKEY_LOCAL_MACHINE\Software\Microsoft\Windows Script Host\Settings\TrustPolicy. Valid values for this key are:

- **0**. All scripts run without any sort of warning. This is the default setting.

- **1**. Before a script is run, a Security Warning dialog box is displayed showing the security status of the script (signed and verified, signed but not verified, unsigned). The user has the option of running any of these scripts, regardless of their security status. The user can also click a button to view the details of the certificate used to sign the script.

- **2**. Before a script is run, the signature is verified, and a check is made to ensure that the script is coming from a trusted author (someone known to the certification authority). After this verification, the script runs automatically, without giving the user the option to view that signature. If the script is unsigned or the signature cannot be verified, the script will not run, and the user will not be given the option of running the script at their own risk. Instead, the user will receive the following message:

```
Execution of the Windows Script Host Failed. (No signature was present in
the subject.)
```

Programmatically Signing a Script

WSH 5.6 includes the Scripting.Signer object that allows you to digitally sign a script using another script. To do this you need to:

- Create an instance of the Scripting.Signer object.

- Use the SignFile method, specifying both the file name of the script to be signed and the name of the digital certificate to be used to sign the script.

For example, this script uses the IT Department certificate to sign the script C:\Scripts\CreateUsers.vbs.

```
set objSigner = WScript.CreateObject("Scripting.Signer")
objSigner.SignFile "C:\Scripts\CreateUsers.vbs", "IT Department"
```

You can also digitally sign a number of scripts at the same time. This script loops through and signs all the files found in the C:\Scripts folder. (The assumption is that the only scripts are stored in C:\Scripts.)

```
set objSigner = WScript.CreateObject("Scripting.Signer")
Set objFSO = WScript.CreateObject("Scripting.FileSystemObject")
Set objFolder = objFSO.GetFolder("c:\scripts")
Set colListOfFiles = objFolder.Files
For each objFile in colListOfFiles
    objSigner.SignFile objFile.Name, "IT Department"
Next
```

Programmatically Verifying a Signed Script

The Scripting.Signer object can also be used to programmatically verify the digital signature on a script. To do this, you need to use the VerifyFile method, along with two arguments:

- The file name of the script whose signature is to be verified.

- A Boolean value indicating whether or not you want the **Security Warning** dialog box to appear in case the signature cannot be verified. If this value is set to False, the dialog box will not appear. If the value is set to True, however, a dialog box will be displayed, warning you that the script signature could not be verified, and asking you whether or not you still want to run the script.

The following script verifies the signature on the file C:\Scripts\CreateUsers.vbs, and suppresses the **Security Warning** dialog box. The script will return one of two values: True means that the digital signature has been verified, False means either that the script has not been signed or the signature could not be verified.

```
set objSigner = WScript.CreateObject("Scripting.Signer")
blnShowGUI = False

blnIsSigned = objSigner.VerifyFile("C:\Scripts\CreateUsers.vbs", blnShowGUI)
    If blnIsSigned then
        WScript.Echo objFile.Name & " has been signed."
    Else
        WScript.Echo objFile.Name & " has not been signed."
    End If
End If
```

Alternatively, you might want to use the VerifyFile method to verify the digital signatures on a number of scripts. For example, this script verifies the digital signatures on all the scripts found in the C:\Scripts folder.

```
set objSigner = WScript.CreateObject("Scripting.Signer")
blnShowGUI = False

Set objFSO = CreateObject("Scripting.FileSystemObject")
Set objFolder = objFSO.GetFolder("C:\Scripts")
Set colListOfFiles = objFolder.Files
For each objFile in colListOfFiles
    blnIsSigned = objSigner.VerifyFile(objFile.Name, blnShowGUI)
    If blnIsSigned then
        WScript.Echo objFile.Name & " has been signed."
    Else
        WScript.Echo objFile.Name & " has not been signed."
    End If
Next
```

Restricting the Ability to Run Scripts

By default, double-clicking a .VBS file will immediately run the script. If you modify the registry, however, you can prevent the script from running immediately; instead, a warning box (complete with a customized message) will be displayed.

This does not prevent the user from running the script; he or she can click **Open With**, locate Wscript.exe or Cscript.exe, and then run the script. Alternatively, the script can be started from the command line by specifying the script host:

```
wscript.exe DeleteFiles.vbs
```

```
cscript.exe DeleteFiles.vbs
```

However, this approach does provide an extra layer of protection by giving users the option to cancel a script before it runs. Without this option, a script that is double-clicked will run without warning.

The following batch file can be used to modify the registry and force a warning box to appear whenever a user double-clicks a .VBS file. This batch file:

1. Uses Reg.exe (found in the Windows 2000 Support Tools) to copy the registry tree HKEY_CLASSES_ROOT\VBSFile\Shell to HKEY_CLASSES_ROOT\VBSFile\bkupShell. Backing up this key rather than deleting it enables you to easily restore standard functionality if necessary.

2. Deletes HKEY_CLASSES_ROOT\VBSFile\Shell.

3. Adds a new entry (NoOpen) to HKEY_CLASSES_ROOT\VBSFile, and sets the value of the entry to the desired warning message. In this sample script, the message — which is limited to 140 characters — is "Do not run this file unless it has been approved by Information Services."

```
reg copy HKCR\VBSFile\Shell HKCR\VBSFile\bkupShell /s /f
reg delete HKCR\VBSFile\Shell /f
reg add HKCR\VBSfile\ /v NoOpen /t REG_SZ /d "Do not run this file unless it has
been approved by Information Services."
```

To restore standard functionality, use this batch file:

```
reg copy HKCR\VBSFile\bkupShell HKCR\VBSFile\Shell /s /f
reg delete HKCR\VBSFile\bkupShell /f
reg delete HKCR\VBSFile /v NoOpen /f
```

Similar steps can be undertaken to restrict the use of other scripting file types, including .VBE, .JS, .JSE, and .WSF files.

 Important
Configuring scripts to display a message box when started could create problems with logon or logoff scripts. Instead of running each time a user logs on, your logon script will display the message box instead. To work around this problem, call the logon script from a batch file instead.

Disabling Windows Script Host

In more desperate circumstances, you can disable Windows Script Host; this will prevent users from running any scripts (including VBScript and JScript scripts) that rely on WSJ.

To disable Windows Script Host, create one of the following two registry entries (REG_DWORD) and set the value to 0 (you need to create the entry, because it does not exist by default). To disable WSH for a particular user, create this entry:

```
HKEY_CURRENT_USER\Software\Microsoft\Windows Script Host\Settings\Enabled
```

To disable WSH for all users of a particular computer, create this entry:

```
HKEY_CURRENT_USER\Software\Microsoft\Windows Script Host\Settings\Enabled
```

When enforced, the following message will be displayed any time a user attempts to run a WSH script:

```
Windows Script Host access is disabled on this machine. Contact your
administrator for details.
```

This message box appear even if the user attempts to start the script from a batch file or using a designated script host (for example, by typing **cscript.exe c:\scripts\myscript.vbs** at the command prompt).

CHAPTER 4

Script Runtime Primer

File system management is a key part of system administration, and yet neither Windows Script Host (WSH) nor Microsoft® Visual Basic® Scripting Edition (VBScript) provides many capabilities in that area. Fortunately, you can use the Script Runtime library to manage such key file system components as disk drives, folders, and files. In addition, the Script Runtime library provides methods for reading from and writing to text files, for creating "dictionaries" (used to manage data within a script), and for encoding scripts.

In This Chapter

Script Runtime Overview 242

FileSystemObject 243

   Managing Disk Drives 243

   Managing Folders 249

   Using Folder Properties 269

   Managing Folder Attributes 271

   Managing Files 279

   Retrieving File Properties 286

   Reading and Writing Text Files 293

Dictionary Object 310

   Creating a Dictionary 310

   Manipulating Keys and Items in a Dictionary 313

Script Runtime Overview

The two primary Microsoft scripting languages, Microsoft® Visual Basic® Scripting Edition (VBScript) and Microsoft® JScript®, were originally developed as client-side scripting languages for Microsoft® Internet Explorer. Because of this, a number of limitations were specifically built into each language. For example, neither VBScript nor JScript has inherent methods for performing file management tasks such as copying, moving, or deleting files. This was done to protect consumers: Most visitors to a Web site would not appreciate having a script on a Web page begin deleting files from their hard drives.

However, scripting began to rapidly evolve from a client-side technology used primarily for such things as HTML "rollovers" (for example, changing the color of a font when you pass the mouse over a hyperlink). With the advent of Active Server Pages, Web developers required the ability to perform file management on the server. With the advent of Windows Script Host (WSH), system administrators required the ability to perform file management outside the Web browser.

In response to these needs, Microsoft released the Script Runtime library. The Script Runtime library is a single dynamic-link library (DLL), scrrun.dll, that provides script writers with a number of file system management capabilities, including the ability to:

- Retrieve information about the file system, including disk drives, files, and folders.
- Copy, move, and delete files and folders.
- Create, read from, and write to text files.

In addition to these file management capabilities, the Script Runtime library also features the ability to create dictionaries (data structures that function similar to collections) and to encode scripts, effectively shielding the code from prying eyes.

 Note

This chapter discusses the FileSystemObject (used for file management) and the Dictionary object, but not the Script Encoder object.

The Script Runtime library is a part of Windows® 2000. The Script Runtime library is also installed anytime you install or upgrade a number of Microsoft applications, including the following:

- Windows Script Host
- VBScript
- Internet Explorer
- Microsoft Office

FileSystemObject

As the name implies, the FileSystemObject (FSO) is designed to help you manage the file system. The FileSystemObject allows you to retrieve information about essential file system elements, including disk drives, folders, and files; it also includes methods that allow you to perform common administrative tasks, such as copying, deleting, and moving files and folders. In addition, the FileSystemObject enables you to read from and write to text files.

It is worth noting that the name *FileSystemObject* is a bit of a misnomer, simply because the FileSystemObject actually includes a number of objects, each designed for a specific purpose. The individual objects that make up the FileSystemObject are listed in Table 4.1.

Table 4.1 Objects That Make Up the FileSystemObject

Object	Description
Drive	Represents a drive or collection of drives on the system.
File	Represents a file or collection of files in the file system.
Folder	Represents a folder or collection of folders in the file system.
TextStream	Represents a stream of text that is read from, written to, or appended to a text file.

Each of these objects will be examined in detail in this chapter.

Managing Disk Drives

Disk drive management is an important part of system administration. As a system administrator, it is important for you to know the disk drives that are installed on a computer; it is equally important for you to know the characteristics of those disk drives, including such things as the drive type (floppy disk, hard disk, CD-ROM), drive size, and the amount of free disk space available on each drive.

As a script writer, you have two primary options for managing disk drives: the FileSystemObject and Windows Management Instrumentation (WMI). In general, WMI is the preferred technology for scripts that manage disk drives, for several reasons:

- WMI can return a number of properties that cannot be obtained by using the FileSystemObject, including physical characteristics such as heads, sectors, and cylinders.

- WMI can return a targeted set of drives (for example, only hard drives).

  The FileSystemObject cannot return a targeted set of drives. Instead, the FileSystemObject requires the script to return a collection of all the drives and then iterate through the collection to pick out the drives of interest. (You can, however, use the FileSystemObject to return an individual drive simply by specifying the appropriate drive letter.)

- WMI can be used to return drive information from remote computers.

  The FileSystemObject cannot be run on remote computers unless it is used in conjunction with the WshController object.

Although WMI might be the preferred technology for returning disk drive information, there are at least two good reasons to be familiar with the FileSystemObject. First, you might have older computers running an operating system that does not have WMI installed. (For example, Microsoft® Windows® 98 did not ship with WMI, although it is possible to download and install WMI on this operating system.)

Second, and perhaps most important, script writers have typically used the FileSystemObject whenever they wrote a script requiring disk drive information. Because of that, you are likely to encounter the FileSystemObject when reading scripts written by other script writers.

Returning a Collection of Disk Drives

Before you can manage disk drives on a computer, you need to know which disk drives are actually available on that computer. The FileSystemObject allows you to return a collection of all the drives installed on a computer, including removable drives and mapped network drives (in other words, any drive with a drive letter).

To return this collection, create an instance of the FileSystemObject, and then create a reference to the Drives property. After the collection has been returned, you can use a For Each loop to iterate through the collection.

For example, the script in Listing 4.1 returns a collection of all the drives installed on a computer and then echoes the drive letter for each drive in the collection.

Listing 4.1   Enumerating All the Drives on a Computer

```
1  Set objFSO = CreateObject("Scripting.FileSystemObject")
2  Set colDrives = objFSO.Drives
3  For Each objDrive in colDrives
4      Wscript.Echo "Drive letter: " & objDrive.DriveLetter
5  Next
```

For a complete list of drive properties available using the FileSystemObject, see Table 4.2 later in this chapter.

Binding to a Specific Disk Drive

If you know in advance which drive you want to bind to (for example, drive C, or the shared folder \\accounting\receivables), you can use the GetDrive method to bind directly to the drive. This allows you to retrieve information for a specific drive, without having to return and iterate through an entire collection.

The GetDrive method requires a single parameter: the driver letter of the drive or the UNC path to the shared folder. To specify a drive letter, you can use any of the following formats:

- C

- C:

- C:\

The script shown in Listing 4.2 creates an instance of the FileSystemObject, uses the GetDrive method to bind directly to drive C, and then echoes the amount of available space on the drive.

Listing 4.2 Binding to a Single Drive

```
1  Set objFSO = CreateObject("Scripting.FileSystemObject")
2  Set objDrive = objFSO.GetDrive("C:")
3  Wscript.Echo "Available space: " & objDrive.AvailableSpace
```

Notice that no For Each loop is required to retrieve the drive properties. This is because the script returns an individual drive object rather than a collection of drive objects. Therefore, there is no collection to iterate through.

Enumerating Disk Drive Properties

The Drives collection is typically used for inventory or monitoring purposes; as a system administrator, you need to know what drives are available on a computer, as well as details such as the drive serial number and the amount of free space on the drive. After you have returned a drives collection or an individual drive object, you can retrieve any of the properties shown in Table 4.2.

Table 4.2   Disk Drive Properties Available by Using the FileSystemObject

Property	Description
AvailableSpace	Reports the amount of free space on the drive, in bytes. To report the amount of available space in kilobytes, divide this value by 1,024. To report the amount of available space in megabytes, divide this value by 1,048,576 (1,024 * 1,024). The AvailableSpace property reports the amount of space available to the user running the script. If disk quotas are in use on the drive, this value might be less than the total amount of free space available on the drive.
DriveLetter	Drive letter assigned to the drive. The drive letter does not include the trailing colon; thus, a floppy disk drive will be reported as A rather than A:.
DriveType	Integer value indicating the type of drive. Values include: 1 — Removable drive 2 — Fixed drive (hard disk) 3 — Mapped network drive 4 — CD-ROM drive 5 — RAM disk
FreeSpace	Reports the amount of free space on the drive, in bytes. To report the amount of free space in kilobytes, divide this value by 1,024. To report the amount of free space in megabytes, divide this value by 1,048,576 (1,024 * 1,024). Unlike the AvailableSpace property, FreeSpace reports the total amount of free space available on the drive, regardless of whether disk quotas have been enabled.
FileSystem	Type of file system used on the drive (FAT, FAT 32, NTFS).
IsReady	Indicates whether a drive is accessible. This value will be False for floppy disk drives or CD-ROM drives where no medium is inserted.
Path	Path to the drive. For local drives, this will be the drive letter and the trailing colon (for example, A:). For mapped network drives, this will be the Universal Naming Convention (UNC) path for the drive (for example, \\Server1\SharedFolder).
RootFolder	Path to the root folder on the drive.
SerialNumber	Serial number assigned to the drive by the manufacturer. For floppy disk drives or mapped network drives, this value will typically be 0.
ShareName	Share name assigned to a mapped network drive.
TotalSize	Reports the total size of the drive, in bytes. To report the total size in kilobytes, divide this value by 1,024. To report the total size in megabytes, divide this value by 1,048,576 (1,024 * 1,024).
VolumeName	Volume name (if any) assigned to the drive.

To enumerate the drives installed on a computer, create an instance of the FileSystemObject, create a reference to the Drives property, and then use a For Each loop to iterate through the set of drives. For each drive in the collection, you can echo any or all of the individual drive object properties shown in Table 4.2.

The script in Listing 4.3 echoes all the drive properties for every drive installed on a computer.

Listing 4.3   Enumerating Disk Drive Properties

```
1   Set objFSO = CreateObject("Scripting.FileSystemObject")
2   Set colDrives = objFSO.Drives
3   For Each objDrive in colDrives
4       Wscript.Echo "Available space: " & objDrive.AvailableSpace
5       Wscript.Echo "Drive letter: " & objDrive.DriveLetter
6       Wscript.Echo "Drive type: " & objDrive.DriveType
7       Wscript.Echo "File system: " & objDrive.FileSystem
8       Wscript.Echo "Is ready: " & objDrive.IsReady
9       Wscript.Echo "Path: " & objDrive.Path
10      Wscript.Echo "Root folder: " & objDrive.RootFolder
11      Wscript.Echo "Serial number: " & objDrive.SerialNumber
12      Wscript.Echo "Share name: " & objDrive.ShareName
13      Wscript.Echo "Total size: " & objDrive.TotalSize
14      Wscript.Echo "Volume name: " & objDrive.VolumeName
15  Next
```

When the script in Listing 4.3 runs under CScript, information similar to the following appears in the command window:

```
Available space: 10234975744
Drive letter: C
Drive type: 2
File system: NTFS
Free space: 10234975744
Is ready: True
Path: C:
Root folder: C:\
Serial number: 1343555846
Share name:
Total size: 20398661632
Volume name: Hard Drive
```

Ensuring That a Drive is Ready

The script in Listing 4.3 has a potential flaw in it: If there is no floppy disk in the floppy disk drive that is being checked or no CD in the CD-ROM drive, the script will fail with a "Drive not ready" error. Drives that are not ready create problems for scripts that use the FileSystemObject; although the FileSystemObject can identify the existence of those drives, your script will fail if it attempts to access disk drive properties such as AvailableSpace or FreeSpace.

If a drive is not ready (which typically means that a disk has not been inserted into a drive that uses removable disks), you can retrieve only the following four drive properties:

- DriveLetter
- DriveType
- IsReady
- ShareName

Any attempt to retrieve the properties of another drive will trigger an error. Fortunately, the IsReady property allows the script to check whether a drive is ready before attempting to retrieve any of the properties that can trigger an error. The IsReady property returns a Boolean value; if the value is True, the drive is ready, and you can retrieve all the properties of the drive. If the value is False, the drive is not ready, and you can return only DriveLetter, DriveType, IsReady, and ShareName.

The script in Listing 4.4 returns a collection of disk drives installed on a computer. For each drive, the script uses the IsReady property to ensure that the drive is ready. If it is, the script echoes the drive letter and the amount of free space. If the drive is not ready, the script echoes only the drive letter, one of the four properties that can be accessed even if a drive is not ready.

Listing 4.4   Verifying That a Drive is Ready

```
1   Set objFSO = CreateObject("Scripting.FileSystemObject")
2   Set colDrives = objFSO.Drives
3   For Each objDrive in colDrives
4       If objDrive.IsReady = True Then
5           Wscript.Echo "Drive letter: " & objDrive.DriveLetter
6           Wscript.Echo "Free space: " & objDrive.FreeSpace
7       Else
8           Wscript.Echo "Drive letter: " & objDrive.DriveLetter
9       End If
10  Next
```

Note

This problem does not occur with WMI. If there is no disk in drive A or no CD in the CD-ROM drive, the script does not fail. Instead, WMI simply reports the amount of free space as Null.

Managing Folders

Disk drive properties such as FreeSpace and TotalSize provide global information that is important to system administrators. However, disk drive information is necessary, but not sufficient, for managing a file system. Although it is important to know which drive a file is stored on, you also need to know the folder in which that file is stored. In addition, many other system management tasks take place at the folder level: Folders are copied, folders are moved, folders are deleted, folder contents are enumerated.

The FileSystemObject can return detailed information about the folders on a disk drive. In addition, the FileSystemObject provides a number of methods for carrying out such tasks as copying, moving, and deleting folders, and for enumerating the files and subfolders within a folder.

Binding to a Folder

In the Windows Shell, folders are Component Object Model (COM) objects. This means that, before you can access the properties of an individual folder, you must create an object reference to that folder, a process commonly referred to as binding. You can bind to a folder by creating an instance of the FileSystemObject and then using the GetFolder method to connect to the folder.

When using the GetFolder method, you must:

- **Specify the path name to the folder.** The path can be referenced by either a local path or a UNC path (for example, \\accounting\receivables). However, you cannot use wildcards within the path name. In addition, you cannot create a single object reference that binds to multiple folders at the same time. A code statement similar to the following results in a compilation error:

```
objFSO.GetFolder("C:\FSO", "C:\Scripts")
```

If you need to work with multiple folders, you either need to use WMI (which can return a collection of folders) or create a separate object reference for each folder.

- **Use the Set keyword when assigning the path to a variable.** The Set keyword is required because it indicates that the variable in question is an object reference.

For example, the script in Listing 4.5 binds to the folder C:\FSO.

Listing 4.5   Binding to a Folder

```
1  Set objFSO = CreateObject("Scripting.FileSystemObject")
2  Set objFolder = objFSO.GetFolder("C:\FSO")
```

Although wildcard characters are not allowed, you can use the dot (.) to bind to the current folder, dot-dot (..) to bind to the parent folder of the current folder, and the backslash (\) to bind to the root folder. For example, the following code statement binds to the current folder:

```
Set objFolder = objFSO.GetFolder(".")
```

Verifying That a Folder Exists

Most folder operations, including copying, moving, and deleting, require the specified folder to exist before the operation can be carried out; after all, a script cannot copy, move, or delete a folder that does not exist. If the script attempts to bind to a nonexistent folder, the script will fail with a "Path not found" error.

To avoid this problem, you can use the FolderExists method to verify that a folder exists before attempting to bind to it. FolderExists takes a single parameter (the path name to the folder) and returns a Boolean value: True if the folder exists, False if the folder does not.

For example, in the script in Listing 4.6, the FolderExists method is used to verify the existence of the folder C:\FSO. If FolderExists equals True, the script uses the GetFolder method to bind to the folder. If FolderExists is False, the script echoes the message "Folder does not exist."

Listing 4.6   Verifying the Existence of a Folder

```
1   Set objFSO = CreateObject("Scripting.FileSystemObject")
2   If objFSO.FolderExists("C:\FSO") Then
3       Set objFolder = objFSO.GetFolder("C:\FSO")
4       Wscript.Echo "Folder binding complete."
5   Else
6       Wscript.Echo "Folder does not exist.•
7   End If
```

Creating a Folder

It is unlikely that you will ever sit down, implement your file system infrastructure (that is, your folders and subfolders), and then never have to touch that infrastructure again. Instead, a file system tends to be dynamic: because of ever-changing needs, existing folders might be deleted and new folders might be created. For example, if your organization provides users with storage space on file servers, you need to create a new folder each time a new user account is created.

The FileSystemObject gives script writers the ability to programmatically create folders, a capability that can make your scripts even more powerful and more useful. For example, the script in Listing 4.6 checks to see whether a specified folder exists. If the folder exists, the script uses the GetFolder method to bind to the folder. If the folder does not exist, the script echoes a message to that effect.

Although this approach prevents the script from crashing, you might prefer that your script create the folder rather than simply report that the folder does not exist. To do this, create an instance of the FileSystemObject, and then call the CreateFolder method, passing the complete path to the new folder as the sole parameter. For example, the script in Listing 4.7 creates a new folder named C:\FSO.

Listing 4.7   Creating a New Folder

```
1  Set objFSO = CreateObject("Scripting.FileSystemObject")
2  Set objFolder = objFSO.CreateFolder("C:\FSO")
```

If the folder already exists, a "File exists" error will occur. Because of that, you might want to check for the existence of the folder before trying to create (or, in that case, re-create) it.

 Note

The FileSystemObject can only create folders on the local computer. If you need to create folders on a remote computer, you will need to use the WshController object. Alternatively, you can create a folder locally and then use WMI to move that folder to the remote computer. (The folder must be created and then moved because WMI does not have a method for creating folders.)

Deleting a Folder

From time to time, folders need to be deleted. For example, you might have a file server that includes a folder for each individual user. When a user leaves the organization, the folder belonging to that user should be deleted; this helps ensure that the orphaned folder does not use up valuable disk space. Likewise, you might have a script that stores temporary files within a folder. Before the script finishes, you might want to delete that folder and thus remove all the temporary files.

The DeleteFolder method provides a way to delete a folder and all its contents. The DeleteFolder method requires a single parameter: the path of the folder to be deleted. For example, the script in Listing 4.8 deletes the folder C:\FSO and everything in it.

Listing 4.8   Deleting a Folder

```
1  Set objFSO = CreateObject("Scripting.FileSystemObject")
2  objFSO.DeleteFolder("C:\FSO")
```

The DeleteFolder method deletes all items immediately; it does not ask for confirmation of any kind or send the items to the Recycle Bin.

Using Wildcards to Delete Folders

One of the main advantages of using scripts as a management tool is that scripts can operate on multiple items at the same time. For example, rather than delete a series of folders one by one, you can use scripts to delete a set of folders in a single operation.

The FileSystemObject allows you to use wildcard characters to delete a specific set of folders. For example, suppose you have the folder structure shown in Figure 4.1 and you want to delete all the subfolders beginning with the letter S.

Figure 4.1   Sample Folder Structure

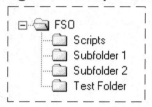

This can be done by using the following command; when run against the sample folder structure, the command deletes the folders Scripts, Subfolder1, and Subfolder2:

```
objFSO.DeleteFolder("C:\FSO\S*")
```

This command deletes all the subfolders beginning with the letters Su, meaning only Subfolder1 and Subfolder2 will be deleted:

```
objFSO.DeleteFolder("C:\FSO\Su*")
```

Wildcard characters can appear only in the final part of the path parameter. For example, this command, which features a wildcard character in the middle of the path parameter, generates a "Path not found" error:

```
objFSO.DeleteFolder("C:\*\Subfolder1")
```

Copying a Folder and Its Contents

The ability to copy a folder, and every item contained within that folder, is important in system administration. Sometimes you need to copy folders in order to create backups; by having the same folder on Computer A that you have on Computer B, you are less likely to experience data loss should Computer B unexpectedly fail. At other times, you might want to deploy all the files contained in a particular folder to a large number of computers. Using a script to copy this folder to each computer is far more efficient than performing the task manually.

The CopyFolder method allows you to copy a folder and its contents to another location. When used without any wildcard characters, the CopyFolder method functions like the Xcopy /E command: It copies all the files and all the subfolders, including any empty subfolders. The CopyFolder method requires two parameters:

- **Source folder** (the folder being copied). This folder can be specified either as a local path (C:\Scripts) or as a UNC path (\\helpdesk\scripts).

- **Destination folder** (the folder that will hold the copied information). This folder can also be specified either as a local path or as a UNC path. If the destination folder does not exist, the script automatically creates the folder.

In addition, the CopyFolder method accepts an optional third parameter, Overwrite. When this parameter is set to True, the default setting, the script overwrites any existing folders in the destination folder. For example, if you are copying a folder named Scripts, and the destination already contains a folder by that name, the destination folder will be replaced by the newly copied information. By setting this parameter to False, the script will not overwrite existing information and instead generates a run-time error.

 Note

> The CopyFolder method stops the moment it encounters an error, even if the script contains an On Error Resume Next statement. For example, suppose the script has 100 subfolders to copy, and CopyFolder successfully copies 3 of those subfolders before encountering an error. At that point, the CopyFolder method ends and the script fails; the script will not even attempt to copy the remaining 97 subfolders.

The script in Listing 4.9 uses the CopyFolder method to copy the contents of C:\Scripts to C:\FSO, overwriting any existing files in the destination folder. Note that this will not result in a folder named C:\FSO\Scripts; instead, the folder C:\FSO will simply contain the same files and folders as C:\Scripts. To create a folder named C:\FSO\Scripts, you would need to specify C:\FSO\Scripts as the destination folder.

Listing 4.9   Copying a Folder

```
1  Const OverWriteFiles = True
2  Set objFSO = CreateObject("Scripting.FileSystemObject")
3  objFSO.CopyFolder "C:\Scripts" , "C:\FSO" , OverWriteFiles
```

 Note

> Because CopyFolder is a single operation, there is no way to track its progress; you simply have to wait until the operation has finished. If you want to monitor the progress of the copy command, you should use the Shell Application object instead. This object is discussed in "Files and Folders" in this book.

Using Wildcards to Copy Folders

The CopyFolder command copies the files stored in a folder as well as the files stored in any subfolders of that folder. This can be a problem; after all, what if you want to copy only the files in C:\FSO and not all the files stored in C:\FSO\Subfolder1, C:\FSO\Subfolder2, and C:\FSO\Subfolder3?

Unfortunately, there is no straightforward method for copying the files in a parent folder without also copying the files stored in child folders. You can use wildcard characters to limit the set of subfolders that are copied; for example, the following command copies only those folders that start with the letters *log*. However, when you use wildcard characters, no files other than those in the specified folders will be copied, not even files that begin with the letters *log*:

```
objFSO.CopyFolder "C:\Scripts\Log*" , "C:\Archive", True
```

When the preceding line of code is run, the folders C:\Scripts\Logs and C:\Scripts\Logfiles are copied, along with all the files stored within those folders. However, the files within the C:\Scripts folder are not copied.

When you use the CopyFolder method, you cannot copy only the files in a folder without also copying the files in any subfolders. To copy only the files and not the subfolders, use the CopyFile method instead. (This method is discussed later in this chapter.)

Moving a Folder and Its Contents

When you copy a folder from one location to another, you end up with duplicate copies of the information. Sometimes that is exactly what you want. On other occasions, however, you do not want two copies of the information; instead, you want to move the sole copy from Computer A to Computer B, or from hard disk C to hard disk D.

Moves such as this are often done to free disk space on a particular drive; for example, you might periodically move seldom-accessed folders to an archive drive. Alternatively, you might have a monitoring script that logs information to the local computer. When monitoring is complete, you might want that information uploaded to a central monitoring station and then deleted from the local computer. That way, the local computer will be prepared for the next round of monitoring.

The MoveFolder method accepts two parameters:

- **Source folder** (the folder to be moved). This folder can be specified either as a local path or as a UNC path.

- **Destination folder** (the location where the folder is to be moved). This folder can be specified either as a local path or as a UNC path.

If the destination folder does not exist, the source folder will be moved. If the destination folder already exists, however, the move operation will fail. You cannot use MoveFolder to overwrite an existing folder.

The script in Listing 4.10 moves the local folder, C:\Scripts, to the shared folder \\helpdesk\management.

Listing 4.10 Moving a Folder

```
1  Set objFSO = CreateObject("Scripting.FileSystemObject")
2  objFSO.MoveFolder "C:\Scripts" , "\\helpdesk\management"
```

Note that the MoveFolder method cannot perform any sort of rollback should the script fail. For example, suppose a network connection fails before a script has been able to move all the files from one computer to another. In a case such as that, you will end up with some files on Computer A, some files on Computer B, and possibly even a file or two lost in transit. However, there is no way for MoveFolder to roll back the failed transactions and restore the two computers to their previous states.

Because of that, you might want to use two methods, CopyFolder and DeleteFolder, when transferring folders and their contents across the network. You can use CopyFolder to copy the folder from Computer A to Computer B. If the copy operation succeeds, you can then use DeleteFolder to delete the folder on Computer A. If the operation fails, you can cancel the delete command and rest assured that the folder and all its contents are still safely stored on Computer A.

Renaming a Folder

The FileSystemObject does not include a method, such as RenameFolder, that provides an obvious way to rename a folder. However, you can rename a folder by using the MoveFolder method and maintaining the same relative location. For example, suppose you have a folder with the following path:

`C:\Scripts\PerformanceMonitoring\Servers\Domain Controllers\Current Logs`

If you rename the folder by using the Rename command in Windows Explorer, the path remains identical except for the endpoint, the folder itself:

`C:\Scripts\PerformanceMonitoring\Servers\Domain Controllers\`**`Archived Logs`**

The MoveFolder method enables you to achieve the same end result by moving the folder from C:\Scripts\PerformanceMonitoring\Servers\Domain Controllers\Current Logs to C:\Scripts\PerformanceMonitoring\Servers\Domain Controllers\Archived Logs. The net result is exactly the same as that of using Windows Explorer to rename the folder.

For example, the script in Listing 4.11 uses MoveFolder to rename the folder C:\FSO\Samples to C:\FSO\Scripts. Before the script runs, Samples is the only subfolder in C:\FSO. After the script runs, Scripts is the only subfolder in C:\FSO. Furthermore, Scripts contains all the files and subfolders previously contained in Samples.

Listing 4.11 Renaming a Folder Using the MoveFolder Method

```
1  Set objFSO = CreateObject("Scripting.FileSystemObject")
2  objFSO.MoveFolder "C:\FSO\Samples" , "C:\FSO\Scripts"
```

Using Folder Properties

Because folders are COM objects, they have properties that can be retrieved and enumerated. To retrieve detailed information about a specified folder, you can use the Folder object, one of the components of the FileSystemObject. The properties of the Folder object are listed in Table 4.3.

Table 4.3   Folder Properties

Property	Description
Attributes	Bitmap containing the attributes for the folder. For more information, see "Managing Folder Attributes" later in this chapter.
DateCreated	Date that the folder was created.
DateLastAccessed	Date of the last time a user accessed the contents of the folder.
DateLastModified	Date of the last time a user modified the properties of the folder.
Drive	Drive letter and trailing colon (for example, C:) representing the drive on which the folder is stored.
Files	Collection containing a file object for each file stored in the folder.
IsRootFolder	Boolean value indicating whether the folder is a root folder (such as C:\).
Name	Folder name, not including path information. For example, the Name of the folder C:\Windows\System32 is System32.
ParentFolder	Name of the folder in which this folder is stored. For example, the ParentFolder of C:\Windows\System32 is Windows; the ParentFolder of C:\Scripts is C:\.
Path	Full path of the folder (for example, C:\Windows\System32).
ShortName	MS-DOS®–style name of the folder, using the 8.3 naming convention. For example, the folder C:\Windows\Program Files might have the ShortName Progra~1.
ShortPath	MS-DOS–style path to the folder, using the 8.3 naming convention. For example, the folder C:\Windows\Program Files might have the ShortName C:\Windows\Progra~1.
Size	Total size, in bytes, of the contents of the folder. This includes the files stored within the folder as well as all the files stored within any subfolders of the folder.
SubFolders	Collection of all the top-level subfolders contained within this folder. Subfolders contained within these subfolders are not included in the collection.
Type	String describing the folder type. This is almost always "File Folder".

Enumerating Folder Properties

To retrieve the properties of a folder, a script must:

1. Create an instance of the FileSystemObject.

2. Use the GetFolder method to bind to an individual folder.

3. Echo (or otherwise manipulate) the properties shown in Table 4.3.

When working with folder properties, note that the Files property and the Subfolders property both return collections rather than a single item. In addition, the Attributes property is returned as a bitmap value. A more detailed explanation of how to work with each of these properties is provided in subsequent sections of this chapter.

The script in Listing 4.12 uses the GetFolder method to bind to the folder C:\FSO and then echoes a number of properties for that folder.

Listing 4.12   Binding to a Specific Folder Using the GetFolder Method

```
1   Set objFSO = CreateObject("Scripting.FileSystemObject")
2   Set objFolder = objFSO.GetFolder("C:\FSO")
3   Wscript.Echo "Date created: " & objFolder.DateCreated
4   Wscript.Echo "Date last accessed: " & objFolder.DateLastAccessed
5   Wscript.Echo "Date last modified: " & objFolder.DateLastModified
6   Wscript.Echo "Drive: " & objFolder.Drive
7   Wscript.Echo "Is root folder: " & objFolder.IsRootFolder
8   Wscript.Echo "Name: " & objFolder.Name
9   Wscript.Echo "Parent folder: " & objFolder.ParentFolder
10  Wscript.Echo "Path: " & objFolder.Path
11  Wscript.Echo "Short name: " & objFolder.ShortName
12  Wscript.Echo "Short path: " & objFolder.ShortPath
13  Wscript.Echo "Size: " & objFolder.Size
14  Wscript.Echo "Type: " & objFolder.Type
```

When this script runs under CScript, output similar to the following appears in the command window:

```
Date created: 2/7/2002 10:27:50 AM
Date last accessed: 2/13/2002 8:57:18 AM
Date last modified: 2/13/2002 8:57:18 AM
Drive: C:
Is root folder: False
Name: FSO
Parent folder: C:\
Path: C:\FSO
Short name: FSO
Short path: C:\FSO
Size: 0
Type: File Folder
```

Managing Folder Attributes

File systems typically support the concept of attributes, information about a file or folder that goes beyond the folder name and size. For example, if you right-click a folder in Windows Explorer and then click **Properties**, you can access the attributes for that folder. Figure 4.2 shows a folder with the following attributes set:

- Read-only

- Hidden

- Ready for archiving

- Compressed

Figure 4.2   Folder Attributes in Windows Explorer

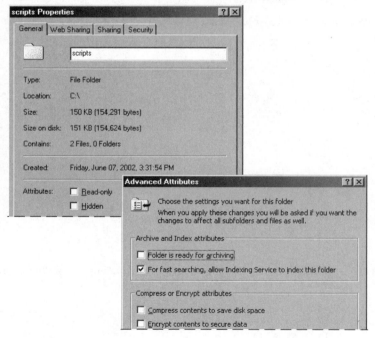

The FileSystemObject can be used to return several important attributes of a folder. These attributes, and their FileSystemObject values, are listed in Table 4.4.

Table 4.4   Folder Attributes Used by the FileSystemObject

Constant	Value	Description
Hidden	2	Indicates that the folder is hidden, and not visible by default in My Computer or Windows Explorer.
System	4	Indicates that the folder is a System folder. In general, it is a good idea not to modify the properties of a system folder.
Directory	16	Standard value applied to all folders. All folders accessed by the FileSystemObject will have, at a minimum, the bit value 16.
Archive	32	Archive bit used by backup programs to determine the files and folders that need to be backed up. Enabling the archive bit will ensure that the folder is backed up during the next incremental backup. Disabling the archive bit will prevent the folder from being backed up during the next incremental backup.
Compressed	2048	Indicates whether Windows compression has been used on the folder.

The values listed in Table 4.4 are the only values that can be retrieved or configured by using the FileSystemObject. Although this seems simple enough, the data returned to you by the FileSystemObject can be confusing at first. For example, if you echo the value of the Attributes property for a folder, you might see a value like 20, a value that does not appear in the list of valid attribute values.

In addition, you will receive only a single value, even if a folder has all possible attributes (that is, it is a hidden, compressed system folder ready for archiving). In a case such as this, your script will not display the values 2, 4, 16, 32, and 2048 but instead will display the value 2102. This is because attribute values are always returned in the form of a bitmap.

 Note

With attributes, the term *bitmap* refers to the way data is stored and returned. It should not be confused with bitmap images, such as .BMP files.

Working with Bitmaps

A bitmap is like a set of switches that can be either on or off. If a particular switch is off, that switch has the value 0. If the switch is on, at least in the case of a folder object, it has one of the values shown in Table 4.4. The value of the bitmap is equal to the sum of all the switches.

For example, a highly simplified illustration of a folder object bitmap is shown in Figure 4.3. In this example, only one individual switch, Directory, is on. Directory has the value 16. Because the other switches are off, each has the value 0. The total value for the bitmap is thus 16. If you queried the Attributes value for this folder, the script would return 16.

Figure 4.3   First Sample Bitmap Representation

| Hidden | Archive | Directory | System | Compressed |

By comparison, the folder object shown in Figure 4.4 has three switches activated: Hidden (with the value 2), Directory (with the value 16), and Compressed (with the value 2048). The value for this bitmap would thus be 2 + 16 + 2048, or 2066. This is also the value that would be returned by a script querying this folder for its Attributes value.

Figure 4.4   Second Sample Bitmap Representation

| Hidden | Archive | Directory | System | Compressed |

Bitmaps are designed so that there is only one possible way to achieve a given value. The only way for a folder attribute to return the value 2066 is for it to be a hidden and compressed folder. It is mathematically impossible to return a 2066 with any other combination of attributes.

This design enables you to take the return value and determine which switches have been set and which ones have not; in turn, this allows you to determine the attributes of the folder. If you receive the return value 2066, you know that the only way to receive that value is to have a hidden and compressed folder.

Fortunately, you do not have to perform any sort of mathematical calculations to derive the individual attributes. Instead, you can use the logical AND operator to determine whether an individual switch is on or off. For example, the following code sample checks to see whether the folder is hidden; if it is, the script echoes the message "Hidden folder."

```
If objFolder.Attributes AND 2 Then
    Wscript.Echo "Hidden folder."
End If
```

Although the If Then statement might appear a bit strange, it makes a little more sense when read like this: "If the attributes switch with the value 2 is on, then …." Likewise, this statement would read, "If the attributes switch with the value 16 is on, then …."

```
If objFolder.Attributes AND 16 Then
```

The script in Listing 4.13 binds to the folder C:\FSO and then echoes the folder attributes.

Listing 4.13 Enumerating Folder Attributes

```
1   Set objFSO = CreateObject("Scripting.FileSystemObject")
2   Set objFolder = objFSO.GetFolder("C:\FSO")
3   If objFolder.Attributes AND 2 Then
4       Wscript.Echo "Hidden folder."
5   End If
6   If objFolder.Attributes AND 4 Then
7       Wscript.Echo "System folder."
8   End If
9   If objFolder.Attributes AND 16 Then
10      Wscript.Echo "Folder."
11  End If
12  If objFolder.Attributes AND 32 Then
13      Wscript.Echo "Archive bit set."
14  End If
15  If objFolder.Attributes AND 2048 Then
16      Wscript.Echo "Compressed folder."
17  End If
```

Changing Folder Attributes

As explained in "Working with Bitmaps," individual folder attributes can be likened to switches. If the switch for Hidden is on, the folder is a hidden folder. If the switch for Hidden is off, the folder is not a hidden folder.

This analogy can be carried further by noting that light switches are typically under your control: you can choose to turn them on, or you can choose to turn them off. The same thing is true of folder attributes: as with other switches, you can turn these attribute switches on, or you can turn them off.

You can use scripts to toggle these switches on or off (for example, to hide or unhide a folder). The easiest way to change folder attributes is to use the following procedure:

1. Use the GetFolder method to bind to the folder.

2. Check for the value of the attribute you want to change.

    For example, if you want to unhide a folder, check to see whether the folder is hidden.

3. If the folder is hidden, use the logical operator XOR to toggle the switch and change it to not hidden. If the folder is not hidden, be careful *not* to use XOR. If you do, the switch will be toggled, and the folder will end up hidden.

For example, the script in Listing 4.14 uses the AND operator to check whether the switch with the value 2 (hidden folder) has been set on the folder C:\FSO. If it has, the script then uses the XOR operator to turn the switch off and unhide the folder.

Listing 4.14   Changing Folder Attributes

```
1  Set objFSO = CreateObject("Scripting.FileSystemObject")
2  Set objFolder = objFSO.GetFolder("C:\FSO")
3  If objFolder.Attributes AND 2 Then
4      objFolder.Attributes = objFolder.Attributes XOR 2
5  End If
```

Enumerating the Files in a Folder

Except for a few rare cases, folders exist solely to act as storage areas for files. Sometimes these folders are required by the operating system; for example, the operating system expects to find certain files in certain folders. In other cases, folders are created as a way to help system administrators manage their computers, or as a way to help users manage their documents. System administrators might place their scripts in a folder named Scripts and their trouble-shooting tools in a folder named Diagnostic Tools; users might place their budget spreadsheets in a folder named Budgets and their payroll information in a folder named Timecards.

Of course, the fact that a folder exists is often of limited use; you must also know what files are stored within that folder. Administrators need to know whether a particular script is stored in C:\Scripts; users need to know whether a particular spreadsheet is stored in C:\Budgets.

The Folder object includes a Files property that returns a collection of all the files stored in a folder. To retrieve this collection, a script must:

1. Create an instance of the FileSystemObject.

2. Use the GetFolder method to bind to the appropriate folder.

3. Set an object reference to the Files property of the folder.

4. Use a For Each loop to enumerate all the files and their properties. (File properties available using the FileSystemObject are shown in Table 4.5.) The script does not have to bind to each file individually in order to access the file properties.

For example, the script in Listing 4.15 retrieves a collection of files found in the folder C:\FSO and then echoes the name and size (in bytes) of each file.

Listing 4.15   Retrieving Properties for Each File in a Folder

```
1  Set objFSO = CreateObject("Scripting.FileSystemObject")
2  Set objFolder = objFSO.GetFolder("C:\FSO")
3  Set colFiles = objFolder.Files
4  For Each objFile in colFiles
5      Wscript.Echo objFile.Name, objFile.Size
6  Next
```

As with most collections, you have no control over the order in which information is returned; that is, you cannot specify that files be sorted by name, by size, or by any other criteria. If you want to sort the file collection in a particular way, you need to copy the collection to an array, a Dictionary, or a disconnected recordset and then sort the items. For more information on arrays, see "VBScript Primer" in this book. For information on disconnected recordsets, see "Creating Enterprise Scripts" in this book.

Enumerating Subfolders

In addition to knowing which files are stored in a folder, you need to know which subfolders are stored in a folder; this allows you to develop a complete picture of the folder infrastructure. The Folder object includes a Subfolders property that returns a collection consisting of the top-level subfolders for a folder.

Top-level subfolders are those folders contained directly within a folder; subfolders contained within those subfolders are not part of the collection. For example, in the sample folder structure shown in Figure 4.5, only Subfolder 1 and Subfolder 2 are top-level subfolders of the folder Scripts. As a result, only Subfolder 1 and Subfolder 2 are returned as part of the Subfolders property.

Figure 4.5 Sample Folder Structure

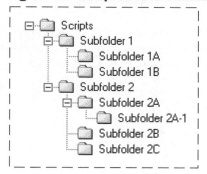

To obtain a subfolder collection, a script must:

1. Create an instance of the FileSystemObject.

2. Use the GetFolder method to bind to a folder.

3. Create an object reference to the Subfolders property. This is required because collections are considered objects.

After you have obtained the object reference to the collection, you can then use a For Each loop to enumerate each of the subfolders in that collection. The script in Listing 4.16 binds to the folder C:\FSO and then echoes the name and size of each subfolder. In addition to the folder name, you can echo any of the folder properties shown in Table 4.3.

Listing 4.16 Enumerating Subfolders

```
1  Set objFSO = CreateObject("Scripting.FileSystemObject")
2  Set objFolder = objFSO.GetFolder("C:\FSO")
3  Set colSubfolders = objFolder.Subfolders
4  For Each objSubfolder in colSubfolders
5      Wscript.Echo objSubfolder.Name, objSubfolder.Size
6  Next
```

Enumerating Subfolders Within Subfolders

Depending on how your file system has been designed, simply knowing the top-level subfolders of a folder might provide sufficient information to map the folder infrastructure. In most file systems, however, folders are nested within folders that are, in turn, nested within other folders. The Subfolders collection can tell you that the folder C:\Accounting contains two subfolders: 2001 and 2002. However, it cannot tell which subfolders, if any, are contained within C:\Accounting\2001 and C:\Accounting\2002.

Fortunately, you can use recursion to enumerate all the subfolders within a set of subfolders. For example, the Subfolders collection, as shown in Listing 4.16, returns only the two top-level subfolders (Subfolder 1 and Subfolder 2) in the folder structure shown in Figure 4.6.

Figure 4.6 Sample Folder Structure

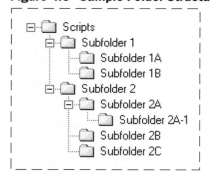

To return the complete set of subfolders (for example, Subfolder 1A and Subfolder 1B), you need to use a *recursive* function, a function that can call itself. For more information about recursion, see "VBScript Primer" in this book.

An example of a script that can enumerate all the subfolders of a folder (as well as any subfolders within those subfolders) is shown in Listing 4.17. This script:

1.   Creates an instance of the FileSystemObject.

2.   Uses the GetFolder method to bind to the folder C:\Scripts.

     GetFolder is used to return a folder object for C:\Scripts. In turn, the path C:\Scripts is passed as a parameter to the recursive subroutine ShowSubfolders. This subroutine will enumerate all the subfolders of C:\Scripts, as well as any subfolders within those subfolders.

3.   Retrieves a collection consisting of all the subfolders of the folder C:\Scripts. This collection has two items: Subfolder1 and Subfolder 2.

4.   Echoes the folder path of the first item in the collection, Subfolder 1. The subroutine then uses the name of that folder as a parameter passed to itself. In other words, the script now runs the subroutine ShowSubFolders using Subfolder 1 as the parameter.

5.   Retrieves a collection consisting of all the subfolders of Subfolder 1. This collection has two items: Subfolder1A and Subfolder 1B.

6.   Echoes the folder path of the first item in the collection, Subfolder 1A. The subroutine then uses the name of that folder as a parameter passed to itself. In other words, it now runs the function ShowSubFolders using Subfolder 1A as the parameter.

7.   Passes control to the next item in the collection, Subfolder 1B. This occurs because Subfolder 1A has no subfolders. The subroutine calls itself using Subfolder 1B as the parameter.

8.   Finishes recursing through Subfolder 1. This occurs because Subfolder 1B has no subfolders. The script then returns to the second item (Subfolder 2) in the original collection, and repeats the entire process.

Listing 4.17   Recursively Enumerating Subfolders

```
1   Set FSO = CreateObject("Scripting.FileSystemObject")
2   ShowSubfolders FSO.GetFolder("C:\Scripts")
3   Sub ShowSubFolders(Folder)
4       For Each Subfolder in Folder.SubFolders
5           Wscript.Echo Subfolder.Path
6           ShowSubFolders Subfolder
7       Next
8   End Sub
```

When this script runs under CScript, the following output appears in the command window:

```
C:\scripts\Subfolder 1
C:\scripts\Subfolder 1\Subfolder 1A
C:\scripts\Subfolder 1\Subfolder 1B
C:\scripts\Subfolder 2
C:\scripts\Subfolder 2\Subfolder 2A
C:\scripts\Subfolder 2\Subfolder 2A\Subfolder 2A-1
C:\scripts\Subfolder 2\Subfolder 2B
C:\scripts\Subfolder 2\Subfolder 2C
```

To return a complete list of all the folders on a hard disk, begin the search in the root folder of the drive (for example, C:\).

Managing Files

Managing a file system ultimately requires managing the individual files stored within that file system. As a system administrator, it is your job to keep track of the files stored on a computer. For example, you need to know whether the correct diagnostic tools have been copied to a server. You need to know whether certain files (such as games or media files) are being stored on a file server, despite an organizational policy that forbids users to store such files. You need to know whether files have been stored on a computer for months without being accessed and thus are serving no purpose other than using up valuable hard disk space.

In addition to keeping track of these files, you must dynamically manage them as well: Files need to be copied, files need to be moved, files need to be renamed, files need to be deleted. The FileSystemObject provides methods that can help you carry out all these administrative tasks.

Binding to a File

The FileSystemObject provides a number of methods, such as the CopyFile and DeleteFile methods, that allow a script to act on a file without creating an instance of the File object. Other tasks, however, require the File object. For example, to retrieve a list of file properties, a script must first bind to that file and then retrieve the properties.

The GetFile method allows you to bind to an individual file. To do this, you create an instance of the FileSystemObject and then create an instance of the File object. When using the GetFile method in a script, you must:

- **Specify the path to the file.** The path can be referenced by using either a local path or a UNC path (for example, \\accounting\receivables\scriptlog.txt). However, you cannot use wildcards within the path, nor can you specify multiple files. GetFile can bind to only a single file at a time.

- **Use the Set keyword when assigning the path to a variable.** The Set keyword is required because it indicates that the specified variable is an object reference.

For example, the script in Listing 4.18 binds to the file C:\FSO\ScriptLog.txt.

Listing 4.18   Binding to a File

```
1  Set objFSO = CreateObject("Scripting.FileSystemObject")
2  objFSO.GetFile("C:\FSO\ScriptLog.txt")
```

In general, it is a good idea to pass the absolute path as the GetFile parameter; this ensures that the script will always be able to locate the file in question. However, it is possible to use relative paths. For example, the following code sample will work provided that ScriptLog.txt is in the same folder as the script attempting to bind to it:

```
objFSO.GetFile("ScriptLog.txt")
```

Likewise, the next code sample will work if ScriptLog.txt is in the parent folder of the script attempting to bind to it:

```
objFSO.GetFile(".\ScriptLog.txt")
```

Please note, however, that the FileSystemObject will not use the path environment variable to search for files. For example, you can start Calculator from the command prompt by typing **calc.exe**, regardless of the current drive or directory, because the operating system searches all folders in the path to locate the file. This does not happen with the GetFile method. The following code sample will fail unless the script is running in the C:\Windows\System32 folder, the same folder where calc.exe is located:

```
objFSO.GetFile("calc.exe")
```

Verifying That a File Exists

Sometimes it is important simply to know whether a file exists. This might be done as part of a software inventory; for example, you might want to check all your mail servers and see whether a particular script file is present.

Knowing whether a file exists is also important when using scripts to carry out file system management tasks; as you might expect, attempting to copy, move, delete, or otherwise manipulate a file that does not exist will generate a run-time error. To avoid this kind of error, you can use the FileExists method to verify the existence of the file. The FileExists method requires a single parameter (the path to the file) and returns a Boolean value: True if the file exists; False if it does not.

The script in Listing 4.19 uses the FileExists method to verify the existence of the file C:\FSO\ScriptLog.txt. If the file exists, the script uses the GetFile method to bind to the file. If the file does not exist, the script echoes the message, "File does not exist."

Listing 4.19   Verifying the Existence of a File

```
1  Set objFSO = CreateObject("Scripting.FileSystemObject")
2  If objFSO.FileExists("C:\FSO\ScriptLog.txt") Then
3      Set objFile = objFSO.GetFile("C:\FSO\ScriptLog.txt")
4  Else
5      Wscript.Echo "File does not exist.•
6  End If
```

You cannot use wildcard characters to verify whether a particular set of files (such as .txt files) exists in a folder, nor can you use wildcards to verify whether any files at all exist in a folder. For example, the following code sample does not result in an error but always returns the value False, regardless of how many files are in the folder:

```
WScript.Echo objFSO.FileExists("C:\FSO\*.*")
```

If you need to verify the existence of a file based on some criteria other than the path, you have two options:

- Use the GetFolder object to bind to the folder, retrieve the Files property, and then iterate through the collection of files looking for the files of interest. For example, you could enumerate all the files and file name extensions, and keep track of how many have the .doc extension.

- Use WMI. WMI allows you to create more targeted queries, such as selecting all the files with the .doc file name extension. You can then use the Count method to determine the number of items in the collection returned to you. If Count is greater than 0, at least one file was found with the .doc extension.

Deleting a File

The ability to delete files by using the FileSystemObject enables you to create scripts that can automatically perform tasks such as disk cleanup operations. For example, you might have a script that periodically searches for and deletes all temporary files (files with the .tmp file name extension). Alternatively, the script might delete files based on some other criteria, such as those that have not been accessed in the past six months, or those with a particular file name extension (such as .bmp or .mp3).

You can delete a file by creating an instance of the FileSystemObject and then calling the DeleteFile method, passing the path to the file as the parameter. For example, the script in Listing 4.20 deletes the file C:\FSO\ScriptLog.txt.

Listing 4.20 Deleting a File

```
1   Set objFSO = CreateObject("Scripting.FileSystemObject")
2   objFSO.DeleteFile("C:\FSO\ScriptLog.txt")
```

By default, the DeleteFile method will not delete a read-only file; if fact, a run-time error will occur if you attempt to delete such a file. To avoid errors, and to delete read-only files, add the optional Force parameter. When the Force parameter is set to True, the DeleteFile method can delete any file. For example, this line of code deletes the file ScriptLog.txt, even if that file is marked as read-only:

```
objFSO.DeleteFile("C:\FSO\ScriptLog.txt", True)
```

Deleting a Set of Files

There might be occasions when you require a script to delete a single, specified file. More likely, though, you will want to use scripts to delete multiple files. For example, at the end of the week, you might want to delete a set of log files that has been archived or delete all the temporary files that have been created but not removed.

Wildcard characters allow you to delete a set of files within a single folder. However, you cannot use the DeleteFile method to directly delete files from multiple folders. Instead, your script needs to iterate through the folders and use the DeleteFile method to individually delete the files in each folder. To delete files from multiple folders in a single operation (for example, to delete all the .TMP files stored anywhere on a computer), you should use WMI instead of the FileSystemObject.

To delete a set of files, call the DeleteFile method, supplying the path of the folder and the wildcard string required to delete files based on name or file name extension. For example, this line of code deletes all the .doc files in the C:\FSO folder:

```
objFSO.DeleteFile("C:\FSO\*.doc")
```

This line of code deletes all the files with the letters *log* somewhere in the file name:

```
objFSO.DeleteFile("C:\FSO\*log.* ")
```

As noted previously, the DeleteFile method does not delete any documents marked as read-only. If a script attempts to delete a read-only document, a run-time error will occur, and the DeleteFile method will stop, even if the script uses the On Error Resume Next statement. For example, suppose you are trying to delete 1,000 .txt files, and one of those files is marked as read-only. As soon as the script attempts to delete that file, an error will occur, and the DeleteFile method will stop. The script will make no attempt to delete any other files, even though none of them are read-only.

Because of that, you can use an optional second parameter, Force, that can be set to True. When the Force parameter is set to True, the DeleteFile method can delete read-only documents. When the Force parameter is set to False (the default value), the DeleteFile method cannot delete read-only documents.

The script in Listing 4.21 deletes all the .txt files in the folder C:\FSO. To ensure that all files, including read-only files, are deleted, the Force parameter is set to True using the constant DeleteReadOnly.

Listing 4.21   Deleting a Set of Files

```
1   Const DeleteReadOnly = True
2   Set objFSO = CreateObject("Scripting.FileSystemObject")
3   objFSO.DeleteFile("C:\FSO\*.txt"), DeleteReadOnly
```

Tip

What if you want to delete all files *except* those marked as read-only? In that case, you can retrieve the complete set of files by using the Folder object Files property. You can then cycle through the collection, check to see whether each individual file is read-only, and, if it is not, delete the file.

Copying a File

Copying files, either from one folder to another on a single computer or from one computer to another, is a common administrative task. For example, you might want to copy a new monitoring script to all your servers or replace an outdated DLL with a newer version. The CopyFile method provides a way to perform these tasks programmatically.

The CopyFile method has two required parameters and one optional parameter:

- **Source** (required). Path to the file being copied. This can be either a path on the local computer or a UNC path to a remote computer.

- **Destination** (required). Path to the location where the file is to be copied. This can also be a local path or a UNC path.

To specify that the file keep the same name in its destination location, put a trailing forward slash after the destination folder:

```
objFSO.CopyFile "C:\FSO\ScriptLog.txt" , "D:\Archive\"
```

To give the file a new name in its destination location, specify a full file name as the destination:

```
objFSO.CopyFile "C:\FSO\ScriptLog.txt" , "D:\Archive\NewFileName.txt"
```

If the destination folder does not exist, it will automatically be created.

- **Overwrite** (optional). By default, the CopyFile method will not copy a file if a file by that same name exists in the destination location. This can be a problem; among other things, this prevents you from replacing an older version of a file with a newer version. To allow the CopyFile method to copy over existing files, set the optional Overwrite parameter to True.

The script in Listing 4.22 copies C:\FSO\ScriptLog.txt to the folder D:\Archive. This operation results in the existence of two files:

- The original file, C:\FSO\ScriptLog.txt.

- The copied file, D:\Archive\ScriptLog.txt.

To ensure that the procedure will be carried out even if D:\Archive\ScriptLog.txt exists, the Overwrite parameter is set to True by using the constant OverWriteExisting.

Listing 4.22   Copying a File

```
1  Const OverwriteExisting = True
2  Set objFSO = CreateObject("Scripting.FileSystemObject")
3  objFSO.CopyFile "C:\FSO\ScriptLog.txt" , "D:\Archive\", OverwriteExisting
```

When specifying the destination folder, it is important to include the trailing backslash (for example, D:\Archive\). If the backslash is there, CopyFile will copy the file into the Archive folder. If the backslash is not there, CopyFile will try to create a new file named D:\Archive. If the folder D:\Archive already exists, a "Permission denied error" will be generated, and the copy procedure will fail.

The CopyFile method will also fail if you attempt to overwrite an existing read-only file, even if you have set the OverWrite parameter to True. To copy over a read-only file, you must first delete the file and then call the CopyFile method.

Copying a Set of Files

Wildcard characters provide a way to copy an entire set of files as long as these files are all in the same folder. You can copy a set of files using the same parameters used to copy a single file, but you must include a wildcard as part of the source parameter. For example, the script in Listing 4.23 copies all the .txt files found in C:\FSO to D:\Archive.

Listing 4.23   Copying a Set of Files

```
1  Const OverwriteExisting = True
2  Set objFSO = CreateObject("Scripting.FileSystemObject")
3  objFSO.CopyFile "C:\FSO\*.txt" , "D:\Archive\" , OverwriteExisting
```

Using wildcards with the CopyFile method allows you to copy all the files in a folder without copying any subfolders in that folder; the CopyFolder method, by contrast, copies both files and subfolders. The following code statement copies all the files in the C:\FSO folder without copying any subfolders:

```
objFSO.CopyFile "C:\FSO\*.*" , "D:\Archive\"
```

Moving a File

Instead of copying a file, you might want to move it. For example, if a disk is running low on space, you might want to move a file to a new location. If a computer is changing roles, you might want to move certain diagnostic tools to its replacement. In either case, you do not want two or more copies of the file; you want one copy of the file, stored in a new place.

The MoveFile method enables you to move a file from one location to another. The MoveFile method works exactly like the CopyFile method: You create an instance of the FileSystemObject, call the MoveFile method, and pass two parameters:

- The complete path to the file to be moved.

- The complete path to the new location, making sure to include the trailing backslash.

For example, the script in Listing 4.24 moves C:\FSO\ScriptLog.log to the Archive folder on drive D.

Listing 4.24   Moving a File

```
1  Set objFSO = CreateObject("Scripting.FileSystemObject")
2  objFSO.MoveFile "C:\FSO\ScriptLog.log" , "D:\Archive\"
```

Moving a Set of Files

You can also use wildcard characters to move multiple files in a single operation. For example, to move all the files in the FSO folder that begin with the letters *data*, use the following parameter:

```
C:\FSO\Data*.*
```

Wildcard characters are especially useful for moving all the files of a particular type because file types are usually denoted by file name extensions. For example, the script in Listing 4.25 moves all the log files (with the .log file name extension) from the FSO folder on drive C to the Archive folder on drive D.

Listing 4.25   Moving a Set of Files

```
1  Set objFSO = CreateObject("Scripting.FileSystemObject")
2  objFSO.MoveFile "C:\FSO\*.log" , "D:\Archive\"
```

Renaming a File

The FileSystemObject does not include a direct method for renaming a file. However, in much the same way that a folder can be renamed using the MoveFolder method, files can be renamed using the MoveFile method. To rename a file, call the MoveFile method but leave the file in its current folder.

For example, the script in Listing 4.26 renames ScriptLog.txt to BackupLog.txt. Technically, the script actually moves C:\FSO\ScriptLog.txt to a new path: C:\FSO\BackupLog.txt. The net result, however, is that the file named ScriptLog.txt is now named BackupLog.txt.

Listing 4.26   Renaming a File Using the MoveFile Method

```
1  Set objFSO = CreateObject("Scripting.FileSystemObject")
2  objFSO.MoveFile "C:\FSO\ScriptLog.txt" , "C:\FSO\BackupLog.txt"
```

Retrieving File Properties

Files have a number of properties that are extremely useful for managing a file system. For example, the DateLastAccessed property tells you the date when someone last opened the file. This property can be used to identify files that are taking up disk space yet are never used. Similarly, the Size property tells you the size of a file in bytes. This helps you to better analyze disk usage; you can tell whether a single file might be using up more than its fair share of storage space.

Traditionally, system administrators have accessed file properties by using either Windows Explorer or command-line tools. Although these tools can return information about the files on a computer, they are not always designed to save this data or to act on it. In addition, many of these tools have only a limited ability to be automated, making it more difficult for system administrators to periodically sweep their hard drives and search for files that meet specific criteria.

Fortunately, detailed information about any file on a computer can also be retrieved by using the FileSystemObject; among other things, this allows you to automate the process of querying the file system for information about a file or group of files. A complete list of properties available through the File object is shown in Table 4.5.

Table 4.5   File Object Properties

Property	Description
Attributes	Bitmap containing the attributes for the file.
DateCreated	Date that the file was created.
DateLastAccessed	Date of the last time a user accessed the file.
DateLastModified	Date of the last time a user modified the file.
Drive	Drive letter and trailing colon (for example, C:) representing the drive on which the file is stored.
Name	File name, not including path information. For example, the Name of the file C:\Windows\System32\Scrrun.dll is Scrrun.dll.

(continued)

Table 4.5   File Object Properties *(continued)*

Property	Description
ParentFolder	Name of the folder in which the file is stored. For example, the ParentFolder of C:\Windows\System32\Scrrun.dll is Windows.
Path	Full path of the file (for example, C:\Windows\System32\Scrrun.dll).
ShortName	MS-DOS–style name of the file, using the 8.3 naming convention. For example, the file C:\MySpreadsheet.xls might have the ShortName MySpre~1.xls.
ShortPath	MS-DOS–style path to the file, using the 8.3 naming convention. For example, the file C:\Windows\Program Files\MyScript.vbs might have the ShortName C:\Windows\Progra~1\MyScript.vbs.
Size	Total size, in bytes, of the contents of the file.
Type	String describing the file type, as recorded in the registry (for example, "Microsoft Word Document").

To access file properties, a script must:

1. Create an instance of the FileSystemObject.

2. Use the GetFile method to create an object reference to a particular file. The script must pass the path of the file as the GetFile parameter.

3. Echo (or otherwise manipulate) the appropriate file properties.

For example, the script in Listing 4.27 uses the GetFile method to bind to the file C:\Windows\System32\Scrrun.dll and then echoes a number of the file properties.

Listing 4.27   Enumerating File Properties

```
1   Set objFSO = CreateObject("Scripting.FileSystemObject")
2   Set objFile = objFSO.GetFile("c:\windows\system32\scrrun.dll")
3   Wscript.Echo "Date created: " & objFile.DateCreated
4   Wscript.Echo "Date last accessed: " & objFile.DateLastAccessed
5   Wscript.Echo "Date last modified: " & objFile.DateLastModified
6   Wscript.Echo "Drive: " & objFile.Drive
7   Wscript.Echo "Name: " & objFile.Name
8   Wscript.Echo "Parent folder: " & objFile.ParentFolder
9   Wscript.Echo "Path: " & objFile.Path
10  Wscript.Echo "Short name: " & objFile.ShortName
11  Wscript.Echo "Short path: " & objFile.ShortPath
12  Wscript.Echo "Size: " & objFile.Size
13  Wscript.Echo "Type: " & objFile.Type
```

When this script runs under CScript, output similar to the following appears in the command window:

```
Date created: 10/29/2001 10:35:36 AM
Date last accessed: 2/14/2002 1:55:44 PM
Date last modified: 8/23/2001 4:00:00 AM
Drive: c:
Name: scrrun.dll
Parent folder: C:\Windows\system32
Path: C:\Windows\system32\scrrun.dll
Short name: scrrun.dll
Short path: C:\Windows\system32\scrrun.dll
Size: 147483
Type: Application Extension
```

Enumerating File Attributes

Like folders, files also have attributes that can be retrieved and configured using the FileSystemObject. Also like folders, file attributes are returned as a bitmap value. (For more information on bitmap values and how to use them, see "Managing Folder Attributes" earlier in this chapter.) File attributes can include any or all of the values shown in Table 4.6.

Table 4.6   File Attributes Used by the FileSystemObject

Constant	Value	Description
Normal	0	File with no attributes set.
Read-only	1	File can be read but cannot be modified.
Hidden	2	File is hidden from view in Windows Explorer or My Computer.
System	4	File is needed by the operating system.
Archive	32	File is flagged as requiring backup.
Alias	64	File is a shortcut to another file.
Compressed	2048	File has been compressed.

To retrieve the attributes of a file, use the GetFile method to bind to the file. After you have created an object reference to the file, you can use the logical AND operator to determine the file attributes. If the file does not have any attributes configured, the Attributes value will be 0.

For example, the script in Listing 4.28 binds to the file C:\FSO\ScriptLog.txt and then checks for the presence of each attribute that can be retrieved using the FileSystemObject.

Listing 4.28   Enumerating File Attributes

```
1   Set objFSO = CreateObject("Scripting.FileSystemObject")
2   Set objFile = objFSO.GetFile("C:\FSO\ScriptLog.txt")
3   If objFile.Attributes AND 0 Then
4       Wscript.Echo "No attributes set."
5   End If
6   If objFile.Attributes AND 1 Then
7       Wscript.Echo "Read-only."
8   End If
9   If objFile.Attributes AND 2 Then
10      Wscript.Echo "Hidden file."
11  End If
12  If objFile.Attributes AND 4 Then
13      Wscript.Echo "System file."
14  End If
15  If objFile.Attributes AND 32 Then
16      Wscript.Echo "Archive bit set."
17  End If
18  If objFile.Attributes AND 64 Then
19      Wscript.Echo "Link or shortcut."
20  End If
21  If objFile.Attributes AND 2048 Then
22      Wscript.Echo "Compressed file."
23  End If
```

Configuring File Attributes

In addition to enumerating file attributes, the FileSystemObject provides a way to configure the following attributes:

- ReadOnly
- Hidden
- System
- Archive

To configure a file attribute, the script should use the following procedure:

1.   Use the GetFile method to bind to the file.

2. Check for the attribute you want to change.

   For example, if you want to make a file read-only, check to see whether the file has already been marked read-only.

3. If the file is not read-only, use the logical operator XOR to toggle the switch. This will mark the file as read-only. If the file is already read-only, be careful *not* to use XOR. If you do, the switch will be toggled, and the read-only attribute will be removed.

The script in Listing 4.29 uses the AND operator to check whether the switch with the value 1 (read-only) has been set on the file C:\FSO\TestScript.vbs. If the file is not read-only, the script uses the XOR operator to turn the switch on and mark the file as read-only.

Listing 4.29   Configuring File Attributes

```
1  Set objFSO = CreateObject("Scripting.FileSystemObject")
2  Set objFile = objFSO.GetFile("C:\FSO\TestScript.vbs")
3  If objFile.Attributes AND 1 Then
4      objFile.Attributes = objFile.Attributes XOR 1
5  End If
```

You can also simultaneously remove the ReadOnly, Hidden, System, and Archive attributes by using the following code statement:

```
objFile.Attributes = objFile.Attributes AND 0
```

Parsing File Paths

A path is a hierarchical series of names that allow you to pinpoint the exact location of a file or folder. In that respect, paths are similar to street addresses: they provide information that tells you precisely where to locate an object. A street address such as One Main Street, Redmond, WA, tells you precisely where to find a particular residence. Likewise, the path C:\FSO\Scripts\ScriptLog.txt tells you precisely where to locate a particular file. Just as only one building can be located at One Main Street, Redmond, WA, only one file can be located at C:\FSO\Scripts\ScriptLog.txt.

Complete paths such as C:\FSO\Scripts\ScriptLog.txt are very important because they provide the only way to uniquely identify a file or folder location. Because of that, there will be times when your script will need the complete path.

At other times, however, you might want only a portion of the path. For example, you might want to extract only the file name or only the file name extension. To allow you to parse paths and extract individual path components, the FileSystemObject provides the methods listed in Table 4.7.

Table 4.7   Methods for Parsing File Paths

Method	Description
GetAbsolutePathName	Returns the complete path of the file (for example, C:\FSO\Scripts\Scriptlog.txt).
GetParentFolderName	Returns the path of the folder where the file is stored (for example, C:\FSO\Scripts).
GetFileName	Returns the name of the file, minus any path information (for example, ScriptLog.txt).
GetBaseName	Returns the base name of the file, the file name minus the file name extension (for example, ScriptLog).
GetExtensionName	Returns the file name extension (for example, txt).

The script in Listing 4.30 parses the path for the file ScriptLog.txt. This script works only if ScriptLog.txt is in the same folder as the script doing the parsing. If the two files are stored in different folders, you must pass the complete path to the GetFile method (for example, C:\FSO\Scripts\ScriptLog.txt).

Listing 4.30   Parsing File Paths

```
1  Set objFSO = CreateObject("Scripting.FileSystemObject")
2  Set objFile = objFSO.GetFile("ScriptLog.txt")
3  Wscript.Echo "Absolute path: " & objFSO.GetAbsolutePathName(objFile)
4  Wscript.Echo •Parent folder: • & objFSO.GetParentFolderName(objFile)
5  Wscript.Echo "File name: " & objFSO.GetFileName(objFile)
6  Wscript.Echo "Base name: " & objFSO.GetBaseName(objFile)
7  Wscript.Echo "Extension name: " & objFSO.GetExtensionName(objFile)
```

When this script is run under CScript, output similar to the following appears in the command window:

```
Absolute path: C:\FSO\Scripts\ScriptLog.txt
Parent folder: C:\FSO\Scripts
File name: ScriptLog.txt
Base name: ScriptLog
Extension name: txt
```

Retrieving the File Version

File versions that are incompatible or out-of-date can create considerable problems for system administrators. For example, a script that runs fine on Computer A, where version 2.0 of a particular DLL has been installed, might fail on Computer B, which has version 1.0 of that DLL installed.

These problems can be difficult to troubleshoot, because you are likely to get back an error saying that the object does not support a particular property or method. This is because the version of the object installed on Computer B does not support the new property or method. If you try to debug the script on Computer A, you will have difficulty finding the problem because the version of the object installed on Computer A *does* support the property or method in question.

The GetFileVersion method allows you to retrieve version information from a file. To use this method, a script must:

1. Create an instance of the FileSystemObject.
2. Call the GetFileVersion method, passing the path to the file as the sole parameter.

For example, the script in Listing 4.31 retrieves the file version for Scrrun.dll.

Listing 4.31 Retrieving File Versions

```
1  Set objFSO = CreateObject("Scripting.FileSystemObject")
2  Wscript.Echo objFSO.GetFileVersion("c:\windows\system32\scrrun.dll")
```

When this script runs on a Windows 2000-based computer with WSH 5.6 installed, the message box shown in Figure 4.7 appears.

Figure 4.7 Version Number for Scrrun.dll

Version numbers are typically displayed in four parts, such as 5.6.0.6626, rather than a single number (such as version 1 or version 5). Version number 5.6.0.6626 contains the following parts:

- **5** — The major file part.
- **6** — The minor file part. The major and minor parts together represent the way a version is typically referred to. In conversation, you would likely refer to version 5.6 rather than version 5.6.0.6626.
- **0** — The build part. This is typically 0.
- **6626** — The private file part.

Not all files types support versioning. Executable files and DLLs typically support versioning; plain-text files, including scripts, typically do not.

Reading and Writing Text Files

One of the more powerful tools available to system administrators is the text file. This might seem hard to believe in an age of high-resolution graphics and multi-user databases. Nevertheless, simple text files, such as those created in Notepad, remain a key element in system administration. Text files are lightweight and low maintenance: They use up very little disk space and require no additional software of any kind to be installed on the computer. Text files are easy to work with and are extremely portable: A text file created by using a script can be copied and viewed on almost any computer in the world, including computers that do not run a Windows operating system.

In addition to their convenience, text files provide a quick, easy, and standardized way to get data both into a script and out of a script. Text files can be used to hold arguments that would otherwise need to be typed at the command line or hard-coded into a script; rather than typing 100 server names at the command line, a script can simply read those names from a text file. Likewise, text files provide a quick and easy way to store data retrieved from a script. This data could be written directly to a database; however, that requires additional configuration on the server, additional coding in the script, and additional overhead when the script runs. Instead, data can be saved to a text file and then later imported into a database.

The FileSystemObject provides a number of methods for both reading from and writing to text files.

Creating Text Files

The FileSystemObject allows you to either work with existing text files or create new text files from scratch. To create a brand-new text file, simply create an instance of the FileSystemObject and call the CreateTexFile method, passing the complete path name as the method parameter.

For example, the script in Listing 4.32 creates a new text file named ScriptLog.txt in the C:\FSO folder.

Listing 4.32   Creating a Text File

```
1  Set objFSO = CreateObject("Scripting.FileSystemObject")
2  Set objFile = objFSO.CreateTextFile("C:\FSO\ScriptLog.txt")
```

If the file does not exist, the CreateTextFile method creates it. If the file does exist, the CreateTextFile method will overwrite the existing file and replace it with the new, blank file. If you prefer that the existing file not be overwritten, you can include the optional Overwrite parameter. When this parameter is False, existing files are not overwritten; when this parameter is True (the default value), existing files are overwritten. For example, the following code sample does not overwrite the file C:\FSO\ScriptLog.txt if that file already exists:

```
Set objFile = objFSO.CreateTextFile("C:\FSO\ScriptLog.txt", False)
```

If you set the Overwrite parameter to False and the file already exists, a run-time error will occur. Because of that, you might want to check for the existence of the file and then, if the file exists, take some other action, such as allowing the user to specify an alternative file name for the new file.

Creating File Names Within the Script

One way to avoid the problems that can occur if a file already exists is to allow the script to generate a unique file name. Because the file name generator does not create meaningful file names, this is probably not a good approach for naming log files and other files that you might need to refer to in the future. However, it does provide a way to ensure unique file names for scripts that require a temporary file. For example, you might have your script save data in HTML or XML format, have that data displayed in a Web browser, and then have this temporary file deleted as soon as the Web browser is closed. In a situation such as that, you can use the GetTempFile name method to generate a unique file name.

To generate a unique file name, a script must create an instance of the FileSystemObject and then call the GetTempName method (with no parameters). For example, the script in Listing 4.33 uses a For Next loop to create 10 random file names.

Listing 4.33   Creating a File Name

```
1  Set objFSO = CreateObject("Scripting.FileSystemObject")
2  For i = 1 to 10
3      strTempFile = objFSO.GetTempName
4      Wscript.Echo strTempFile
5  Next
```

When this script is run under Cscript, output similar to the following appears in the command window:

```
rad646E9.tmp
radEC50C.tmp
rad0C40A.tmp
radE866E.tmp
rad77F3D.tmp
rad19970.tmp
rad7A21A.tmp
radB9DDC.tmp
rad84930.tmp
rad92199.tmp
```

Note

The file names generated by GetTempName are not guaranteed to be unique, partly because of the algorithm used to generate the names and partly because there are only a finite number of possible names; file names are limited to eight characters, and the first three characters are always *rad*. For example, in a test script that created 10,000 file names, one right after another, 9,894 names were unique. The remaining 106 were duplicates (53 pairs of duplicated names).

The demonstration script in Listing 4.34 uses the GetTempName method to create a file. The script must:

1. Create an instance of the FileSystemObject.

2. Set a variable named strPath to the folder where the file will be created (C:\FSO).

3. Use the GetTempName method to generate a unique file name.

4. Use the BuildPath method to combine the folder name and file name and create a full path for the temporary file. The full path is stored in the variable strFullName.

5. Call the CreateTextFile method, using strFullName as the method parameter.

6. Close the file immediately after creating it. In a production environment, you would most likely write data to the file before closing it.

Listing 4.34   Creating and Naming a Text File

```
1  Set objFSO = CreateObject("Scripting.FileSystemObject")
2  strPath = "C:\FSO"
3  strFileName = objFSO.GetTempName
4  strFullName = objFSO.BuildPath(strPath, strFileName)
5  Set objFile = objFSO.CreateTextFile(strFullName)
6  objFile.Close
```

Opening Text Files

Working with text files is a three-step process. Before you can do anything else, you must open the text file. This can be done either by opening an existing file or by creating a new text file. (When you create a new file, that file is automatically opened and ready for use.) Either approach returns a reference to the TextStream object.

After you have a reference to the TextStream object, you can either read from or write to the file. However, you cannot simultaneously read from and write to the same file. In other words, you cannot open a file, read the contents, and then write additional data to the file, all in the same operation. Instead, you must read the contents, close the file, and then reopen and write the additional data.

When you open an existing text file, the file can be opened either for reading or for writing. When you create a new text file, the file is open only for writing, if for no other reason than that there is no content to read.

Finally, you should always close a text file. Although this is not required (the file will generally be closed as soon as the script terminates), it is good programming practice.

To open a text file:

1. Create an instance of the FileSystemObject.

2. Use the OpenTextFile method to open the text file. The OpenTextFile method requires two parameters: the path to the file and one of the following values:

   - **For reading (parameter value = 1, constant = ForReading).** Files opened in this mode can only be read from. To write to the file, you must open it a second time by using either the ForWriting or ForAppending mode.

   - **For writing (parameter value 2, constant = ForWriting).** Files opened in this mode will have new data replace any existing data. (That is, existing data will be deleted and the new data added.) Use this method to replace an existing file with a new set of data.

   - **For appending (parameter value 8, constant = ForAppending).** Files opened in this mode will have new data appended to the end of the file. Use this method to add data to an existing file.

You must use the appropriate parameter when opening the file. For example, if you open a file for reading and then attempt to write to the file, you will receive a "Bad file mode" error. You will also receive this error if you attempt to open anything other than a plain-text file. (It is worth noting that both HTML and XML files are plain-text files.)

You can use either the parameter value (for example, 1 for reading) or you can create a constant and set the value appropriately. For example, both of these methods will open a file for reading:

```
Const ForReading = 1
Set objFSO = CreateObject("Scripting.FileSystemObject")
Set objFile = objFSO.OpenTextFile("C:\FSO\ScriptLog.txt", ForReading)
Set objFile2 = objFSO.OpenTextFile("C:\FSO\ScriptLog2.txt", 1)
```

However, you cannot use the constants without first defining them. This is due to the fact that VBScript does not have intrinsic access to COM object constants. The following script sample will fail and return an "Invalid procedure call or argument" error because the ForReading constant has not been explicitly defined. Because it has not been defined, ForReading is automatically assigned the value 0, and 0 is not a valid parameter for OpenTextFile.

```
Set objFSO = CreateObject("Scripting.FileSystemObject")
Set objFile = objFSO.OpenTextFile("C:\FSO\ScriptLog.txt", ForReading)
```

The script in Listing 4.35 opens C:\FSO\ScriptLog.txt for reading, using the user-defined constant ForReading to represent the value 1.

Listing 4.35 Opening a Text File for Reading

```
1  Const ForReading = 1
2  Set objFSO = CreateObject("Scripting.FileSystemObject")
3  Set objFile = objFSO.OpenTextFile("C:\FSO\ScriptLog.txt", ForReading)
```

Closing Text Files

Any text files opened by a script are automatically closed when the script ends. Because of this, you do not have to explicitly close text files any time you open them. Nevertheless, it is a good idea to always close text files when you are finished with them. Not only is this good programming practice, but problems will occur if you try to do one of the following without first closing the file:

- **Delete the file.** As noted previously in this chapter, you might occasionally write scripts that create a temporary file, use that file for some purpose, and then delete the file before the script terminates. If you attempt to delete an open file, however, you will encounter an "Access denied" error because the operating system will not allow you to delete an open file.

- **Reread the file.** There might be times when you need to read the same file multiple times within a script. For example, you might open a text file, save the entire contents of the file to a string variable, and then search that string for the existence of a particular error code. If the code is found, you might then read the file on a line-by-line basis, extracting each line where the error was recorded.

If you try to read an open file multiple times, however, you either will not receive the expected results or will encounter a run-time error. For example, the following script reads a text file, echoes the contents of that file back to the screen, and then attempts to repeat the procedure:

```
Set objFSO = CreateObject("Scripting.FileSystemObject")
Set objFile = objFSO.OpenTextFile("C:\FSO\ScriptLog.txt", 1)
Wscript.Echo "Reading file the first time:"
strContents = objFile.ReadAll
Wscript.Echo strContents
Wscript.Echo "Reading file the second time:"
Do While objFile.AtEndOfStream = False
    strLine = objFile.ReadLine
    Wscript.Echo strLine
Loop
```

When this script is run under Cscript, the following output appears in the command window:

```
Reading file the first time:
File line 1.
File line 2.
File line 3.
Reading file the second time:
```

The first time the file was read, the contents were stored in the variable strContents. The second time the file was read, however, no data was echoed to the screen. This is because the end of the file had already been reached, and there was no more data left to read. To reread the file, you must close the file and then reopen it. You cannot read to the end of a file and then jump back to the beginning.

The TextStreamObject Close method is used to close a text file. For example, the script shown in Listing 4.36 creates an instance of the FileSystemObject, opens a text file (C:\FSO\ScriptLog.txt), and then immediately closes the file. To access the file contents, you need to call the OpenTextFile method a second time and reopen the file.

Listing 4.36   Opening and Closing a Text File

```
1  Set objFSO = CreateObject("Scripting.FileSystemObject")
2  Set objFile = objFSO.OpenTextFile("C:\FSO\ScriptLog.txt", 1)
3  objFile.Close
```

Reading Text Files

Reading data from a text file is a standard procedure used in many enterprise scripts. You might use this capability to:

- **Read in command-line arguments.** For example, a text file might contain a list of computers, with the script designed to read in the list and then run against each of those computers.

- **Programmatically search a log file for specified conditions.** For example, you might search a log file for any operations marked Error.

- **Add the contents of a log file to a database.** For example, you might have a service or an application that saves information in plain-text format. You could write a script that reads in the text file and then copies the relevant information to a database.

The FileSystemObject can be used to read the contents of a text file. When using the FileSystemObject, keep the following limitations in mind:

- **The FSO can read only ASCII text files.** You cannot use the FSO to read Unicode files or to read binary file formats such as Microsoft Word or Microsoft Excel.

- **The FileSystemObject reads a text file in one direction: from the beginning to the end of the text file.** In addition, the FSO reads only line by line. If you need to go back to a previous line, you must return to the beginning of the file and read forward to the required line.

- **You cannot open a file for simultaneous reading and writing.** If you open a file for reading, you must open the file a second time if you want to modify the contents. If you attempt to read a file after opening it in write mode, you will receive a "bad file mode" error.

The file-reading methods available through the FileSystemObject are listed in Table 4.8. The examples shown in the table are based on a text file of services and service properties that looks similar to this:

```
Alerter,Share Process,Running,Auto,LocalSystem,
AppMgmt,Share Process,Running,Manual,LocalSystem,
Ati HotKey Poller,Own Process,Stopped,Auto,LocalSystem,
```

Table 4.8   Read Methods Available to the FileSystemObject

Method	Description
Read	Reads the specified number of characters and then stops. For example, the following command would read the first 12 characters of the first line ("Alerter,Shar") into the variable strText and then stop: ```strText = objTextFile.Read(12)```
ReadLine	Reads one line from a text file and then stops before reaching the newline character. For example, the following command would read the first line ("Alerter,Share Process,Running,Auto,LocalSystem") into the variable strText and then stop: ```strText = objTextFile.ReadLine``` To read an entire text file on a line-by-line basis, place the ReadLine function within a loop.
ReadAll	Reads the entire contents of a text file into a variable.
Skip	Skips the specified number of characters and then stops. For example, the following command would skip the first 12 characters. Any subsequent read operations would begin with the 13th character and continue from there ("e Process,Running,Auto,LocalSystem"): ```objTextFile.Skip(12)```

SkipLine	Skips an entire line in a text file. For example, this code reads the first and third lines of a text file, skipping the second line:
	
	```strText = objTextFile.Readline```
	```objTextFile.SkipLine```
	```strText = objTextFile.Readline```

Verifying the Size of a File

Windows will sometimes create text files that are empty — that is, files that contain no characters and have a file size of 0 bytes. This often occurs with log files, which remain empty until a problem is recorded there. For example, if problems occur with a user logon (such as a user attempting to log on with an incorrect password or user account), those problems will be recorded in the Netlogon.log file. Until such a problem occurs, however, the Netlogon.log file remains empty.

Empty files represent a problem for script writers, because a VBScript run-time error will occur if you attempt to read such a file. If you try to read an empty file, an error message similar to the one shown in Figure 4.8 appears.

Figure 4.8   Empty File Error Message

If there is a chance that a file might be empty, you can avoid errors by checking the file size before attempting to read the file. To do this, the script must:

1.   Create an instance of the FileSystemObject.

2.   Use the GetFile method to bind to the file.

3.   Use the Size property to ensure that the file is not empty before attempting open it.

The script in Listing 4.37 binds to the file C:\Windows\Netlogon.log. The script checks the size of the file; if the size is greater than 0, the script opens and reads the file. If the file size is 0, the script echoes the message "The file is empty."

Listing 4.37   Verifying the Size of a File

```
1   Set objFSO = CreateObject("Scripting.FileSystemObject")
2   Set objFile = objFSO.GetFile("C:\Windows\Netlogon.log")
3   If objFile.Size > 0 Then
4       Set objReadFile = objFSO.OpenTextFile("C:\Windows\Netlogon.log", 1)
5       strContents = objReadFile.ReadAll
6       Wscript.Echo strContents
7       objReadFile.Close
8   Else
9       Wscript.Echo "The file is empty."
10  End If
```

Reading an Entire Text File

The ReadAll method provides the easiest way to read a text file: You simply call the method, and the entire text file is read and stored in a variable. Having the contents of the text file stored in a single variable can be useful in a number of situations. For example, if you want to search the file for a particular item (such as an error code), it is easier to search a single string than to search the file line by line.

Likewise, if you want to concatenate (combine) text files, the ReadAll method provides the quickest and easiest method. For example, suppose you have a set of daily log files that you want to combine into a single weekly log file. To do that, a script can:

1. Open the text file for Monday and use ReadAll to store the entire contents in a variable.

2. Open the weekly log file for appending, and write the contents of the variable to the file. This is possible because any formatting (such as line breaks or tabs) that is read in from the Monday file is preserved in the variable.

3. Repeat steps 1 and 2 until the entire set of daily files has been copied into the weekly log.

 Note

Although it is easier to search a single string, it is not necessarily faster. The ReadAll method took less than a second to search a 388-KB test file of approximately 6,000 lines. Reading and searching the file on a line-by-line basis also took less than a second.

To use the ReadAll method, open a text file for reading and then call ReadAll. (No parameters are needed.) For example, the script in Listing 4.38 opens the file C:\FSO\ScriptLog, reads in the contents of the file, and stores that data in the variable strContents. The script then echoes the value of strContents, which happens to be the contents of the text file as well.

Listing 4.38   Reading a Text File Using the ReadAll Method

```
1  Const ForReading = 1
2  Set objFSO = CreateObject("Scripting.FileSystemObject")
3  Set objFile = objFSO.OpenTextFile("C:\FSO\ScriptLog.txt", ForReading)
4  strContents = objFile.ReadAll
5  Wscript.Echo strContents
6  objFile.Close
```

Reading a Text File Line by Line

For system administration purposes, text files typically serve as flat-file databases, with each line of the file representing a single record in the database. For example, scripts often read in a list of server names and then carry out an action against each of those servers. In those instances, the text will look something like the following:

```
atl-dc-01
atl-dc-02
atl-dc-03
atl-dc-04
```

When a text file is being used as a flat-file database, a script will typically read each record (line) individually and then perform some action with that record. For example, a script (using the preceding sample text file) might read in the name of the first computer, connect to it, and carry out some action. The script would then read in the name of the second computer, connect to it, and carry out that same action. This process would continue until all the records (lines) in the text file have been read.

The ReadLine method allows a script to read individual lines in a text file. To use this method, open the text file, and then set up a Do Loop that continues until the AtEndOfStream property is True. (This simply means that you have reached the end of the file.) Within the Do Loop, call the ReadLine method, store the contents of the first line in a variable, and then perform some action. When the script loops around, it will automatically drop down a line and read the second line of the file into the variable. This will continue until each line has been read (or until the script specifically exits the loop).

For example, the script shown in Listing 4.39 opens the file C:\FSO\ServerList.txt and then reads the entire file line by line, echoing the contents of each line to the screen.

Listing 4.39   Reading a Text File Using the ReadLine Method

```
1  Set objFSO = CreateObject("Scripting.FileSystemObject")
2  Set objFile = objFSO.OpenTextFile("C:\FSO\ServerList.txt", 1)
3  Do Until objFile.AtEndOfStream
4      strLine = objFile.ReadLine
5      Wscript.Echo strLine
6  Loop
7  objFile.Close
```

"Reading" a Text File from the Bottom to the Top

As noted previously, the FileSystemObject can read a text file only from the beginning to the end; you cannot start at the end and work your way backwards. This can sometimes be a problem when working with log files. Most log files store data in chronological order: The first line in the log is the first event that was recorded, the second line is the second event that was recorded, and so on. This means that the most recent entries, the ones you are perhaps most interested in, are always located at the very end of the file.

There might be times when you want to display information in reverse chronological order — that is, with the most recent records displayed first and the oldest records displayed last. Although you cannot read a text file from the bottom to the top, you can still display the information in reverse chronological order. To do this, a script must:

1. Create an array to hold each line of the text file.

2. Use the ReadLine method to read each line of the text file and store each line as a separate element in the array.

3. Display the contents of the array on screen, starting with the last element in the array (the most recent record in the log file) and ending with the first element in the array (the oldest log file).

For example, the script in Listing 4.40 reads in the file C:\FSO\ScriptLog.txt, storing each line as an element in the array arrFileLines. After the entire file has been read, the contents are echoed to the screen, beginning with the last element in the array. To do this, the For Loop begins with the last element (the upper bound of the array) and incrementally works down to the first element (the lower bound).

Listing 4.40   "Reading" a Text File from the Bottom to the Top

```
1   Dim arrFileLines()
2   i = 0
3   Set objFSO = CreateObject("Scripting.FileSystemObject")
4   Set objFile = objFSO.OpenTextFile("C:\FSO\ScriptLog.txt", 1)
5   Do Until objFile.AtEndOfStream
6       Redim Preserve arrFileLines(i)
7       arrFileLines(i) = objFile.ReadLine
8       i = i + 1
9   Loop
10  objFile.Close
11  For l = Ubound(arrFileLines) to LBound(arrFileLines) Step -1
12      Wscript.Echo arrFileLines(l)
13  Next
```

If the contents of C:\FSO\ScriptLog.txt look like this:

```
6/19/2002    Success
6/20/2002    Failure
6/21/2002    Failure
6/22/2002    Failure
6/23/2002    Success
```

The following information will be echoed to the screen:

```
6/23/2002    Success
6/22/2002    Failure
6/21/2002    Failure
6/20/2002    Failure
6/19/2002    Success
```

Reading a Text File Character by Character

In a fixed-width text file, fields are delimited by length: Field 1 might consist of the first 15 characters on a line, Field 2 might consist of the next 10 characters, and so on. Thus a fixed-width text file might look like the following:

```
Server                  Value            Status
atl-dc-01               19345            OK
atl-printserver-02      00042            OK
atl-win2kpro-05         00000            Failed
```

In some cases, you might want to retrieve only the values, or only the status information. The value information, to pick one, is easy to identify: Values always begin with the 26th character on a line and extend no more than 5 characters. To retrieve these values, you need to read only the 26th, 27th, 28th, 29th, and 30th characters on each line.

The Read method allows you to read only a specified number of characters. Its sole parameter is the number of characters to be read. For example, the following code sample reads the next 7 characters in the text file and stores those 7 characters in the variable strCharacters:

```
strCharacters = objFile.Read(7)
```

By using the Skip and SkipLine methods, you can retrieve selected characters from a text file. For example, the script in Listing 4.41 reads only the sixth character in each line of a text file. To do this, the script must:

1. Skip the first five characters in a line, using Skip(5).

2. Read the sixth character, using Read(1).

3. Skip to the next line of the file.

Listing 4.41   Reading a Fixed-Width Text File

```
1   Set objFSO = CreateObject("Scripting.FileSystemObject")
2   Set objFile = objFSO.OpenTextFile("C:\FSO\ScriptLog.txt", 1)
3   Do Until objFile.AtEndOfStream
4       objFile.Skip(5)
5       strCharacters = objFile.Read(1)
6       Wscript.Echo strCharacters
7       objFile.SkipLine
8   Loop
```

To better illustrate how this script works, suppose the file C:\FSO\ScriptLog.txt looks like the following:

```
XXXXX1XXXXXXXXXXXXXX
XXXXX2XXXXXXXXXXXXXXXXXX
XXXXX3XXXXXXXXXXXX
XXXXX4XXXXXXXXXXXXXXXXXXXXXXXXXX
```

For each line in this file, the first five characters are X's, the sixth character is a number, and the remaining characters are a random number of X's. When the script in Listing 4.41 runs, the script will:

1. Open the text file and begin to read the first line.

2. Skip the first five characters.

3. Use the Read method to read the sixth character.

4. Echo that character to the screen.

5. Skip to the next line and repeat the process until all the lines have been read.

When the script is run under CScript, the following output appears in the command window:

```
1
2
3
4
```

Writing to Text Files

Writing data to a text file is another powerful aid in writing system administration scripts. Text files provide a way for you to permanently save data retrieved by a script; this data can be saved either instead of or in addition to being displayed on the screen. Text files also provide a way for you to keep a log of the actions carried out by a script. This can be especially useful when creating and debugging scripts. By having the script record its actions in a text file, you can later review the log to determine which procedures the script actually carried out and which ones it did not.

The FileSystemObject gives you the ability to write data to a text file. To write data using the FSO, a script must do the following:

1. Create an instance of the FileSystemObject.

2. Use the OpenTextFile method to open the text file. You can open the text file in one of two ways:

    ▪   **For writing (parameter value 2, constant = ForWriting).** Files opened in this mode will have new data replace any existing data in its entirety. (That is, existing data will be deleted and the new data added.) Use this mode to replace an existing file with a new set of data.

    ▪   **For appending (parameter value 8, constant = ForAppending).** Files opened in this mode will have new data appended to the end of the file. Use this mode to add data to an existing file.

3. Use either the Write, WriteLine, or WriteBlankLines method to write to the file.

4. Close the text file.

The three methods for writing to a text file are shown in Table 4.9.

Table 4.9 Write Methods Available to the FileSystemObject

Method	Description

Write	Writes data to a text file without appending a carriage-return/newline character at the end. For example, this code writes two separate strings to a text file:
	
	```\nobjFile.Write ("This is line 1.")\nobjFile.Write ("This is line 2.")\n```
	
	The resulting text file looks like this:
	
	```\nThis is line 1.This is line 2.\n```

WriteLine	Writes data to a text file, appending a carriage-return/newline character at the end of each operation. For example, this code writes two separate strings to a text file:
	
	```\nobjFile.WriteLine ("This is line 1.")\nobjFile.WriteLine ("This is line 2.")\n```
	
	The resulting text file looks like this:
	
	```\nThis is line 1.\nThis is line 2.\n```

WriteBlankLines	Writes a blank line to a text file. For example, this code writes two separate strings to a text file, separating the two with one blank line:
	
	```\nobjFile.Writeline ("This is line 1.")\nobjFile.WriteBlankLines(1)\nobjFile.Writeline ("This is line 2.")\n```
	
	The resulting text file looks like this:
	
	```\nThis is line 1.\n\nThis is line 2.\n```

In addition to the methods shown in Table 4.9, the VBScript constant VbTab can be useful in writing data to text files. VbTab inserts a tab between characters. To create a tab-separated data file, use code similar to the following:

```
objTextFile.WriteLine(objService.DisplayName & vbTab & objService.State)
```

One weakness with the FileSystemObject is that it cannot be used to directly modify specific lines in a text file; for example, you cannot write code that says, in effect, "Skip down to the fifth line in this file, make a change, and then save the new file." To modify line 5 in a 10-line text file, a script must instead:

1. Read in the entire 10-line file.

2. Write lines 1–4 back to the file.

3. Write the modified line 5 to the file.

4. Write lines 6–10 back to the file.

Overwriting Existing Data

In system administration, simplicity is often a virtue. For example, suppose you have a script that runs every night, retrieving events from the event logs on your domain controllers, writing those events to a database, and recording which computers were successfully contacted and which ones were not. For historical purposes, you might want to keep track of every success and every failure over the next year. This might be especially useful for a new script just being put into use, or for a network with suspect connectivity or other problems that crop up on a recurring basis.

On the other hand, you might simply want to know what happened the *last* time the script ran. In other words, you do not want a log file that contains data for the past 365 days. Instead, you want a log file that contains only the most recent information. That allows you to open the file and quickly verify whether or not the script ran as expected.

When you open a text file in ForWriting mode, any new data you write to the file replaces all the existing data in that file. For example, suppose you have the complete works of Shakespeare stored in a single text file. Suppose you then run a script that opens the file in ForWriting mode and writes the single letter *a* to the file. After the file has been written and closed, it will consist only of the letter *a*. All the previously saved data will be gone.

The script in Listing 4.42 opens the text file C:\FSO\ScriptLog.txt in ForWriting mode and then writes the current date and time to the file. Each time this script is run, the old date and time are replaced by the new date and time. The text file will never contain more than a single date-time value.

Listing 4.42   Overwriting Existing Data

```
1  Const ForWriting = 2
2  Set objFSO = CreateObject("Scripting.FileSystemObject")
3  Set objFile = objFSO.OpenTextFile("C:\FSO\ScriptLog.txt", ForWriting)
4  objFile.Write Now
5  objFile.Close
```

Appending New Data to Existing Data

Some scripts are designed to run at regularly scheduled intervals and then collect and save a specific kind of data. These scripts are often used to analyze trends and to look for usage over time. In these instances, you typically do not want to overwrite existing data with new data.

For example, suppose you have a script that monitors processor usage. At any given point in time, processor usage could be anywhere from 0 percent to 100 percent by itself, that single data point is meaningless. To get a complete picture of how much a processor is being utilized, you need to repeatedly measure and record processor usage. If you measure processor use every few seconds and get back data like 99 percent, 17 percent, 92 percent, 90 percent, 79 percent, 88 percent, 91 percent, you can assume processor use is very high. However, this can only be determined by comparing processor use over time.

By opening a text file in ForAppending mode, you can ensure that existing data is not overwritten by any new data; instead, that new data is appended to the bottom of the text file. For example, the script in Listing 4.43 opens a text file and writes the current date and time to the file. Because the file is opened for appending, the current date and time is simply added to the bottom of the file. If you run the script several times, you will end up with a text file similar to this:

```
6/25/2002 8:49:47 AM
6/25/2002 8:49:48 AM
6/25/2002 8:50:33 AM
6/25/2002 8:50:35 AM
```

Listing 4.43 Appending Data to a Text File

```
1  Const ForAppending = 8
2  Set objFSO = CreateObject("Scripting.FileSystemObject")
3  Set objFile = objFSO.OpenTextFile("C:\FSO\ScriptLog.txt", ForAppending)
4  objFile.WriteLine Now
5  objFile.Close
```

The script uses the WriteLine method to ensure that each new date and time entry is written to a separate line. If the script used the Write method instead, the entries would run together, and the text file would look like this:

```
6/25/2002 8:49:47 AM6/25/2002 8:49:48 AM6/25/2002 8:50:33 AM6/25/2002 8:50:35 AM
```

Dictionary Object

Scripts often retrieve information from an outside source, such as a text file or a database. After this information has been retrieved, it needs to be stored in memory so that the script can act upon it. Information such as this can be stored in individual variables (one variable for each bit of information) or in an array. Alternatively, information can also be stored in a Dictionary object.

The Dictionary object functions as an associative array; that is, it stores values in key-item pairs. This is different from an array, which uses a numeric index to store values. For example, a one-dimensional array consisting of state capitals might look like this:

- 0 — Olympia
- 1 — Salem
- 2 — Sacramento

By contrast, a Dictionary containing state capitals might look like this:

- Washington — Olympia
- Oregon — Salem
- California — Sacramento

If your command-line arguments consist of single-item entries, such as computer names, you can use an array to hold the item names. However, the Dictionary object does offer several advantages over arrays. In particular, the Dictionary object does not require a script to:

- Specify (or modify) the number of elements being stored. With an array, you must specify the size in advance, or repeatedly resize the array as new elements are added.

- Know the index number assigned to a particular element. Any element in a Dictionary can be accessed either by key or by item.

This makes Dictionaries an ideal tool for system administration scripts that need to retrieve information such as server names from an outside source and then store that information in memory for later use.

Creating a Dictionary

Because the Dictionary is a COM object, it must be instantiated in the same fashion as any other COM Object. The following code statement creates an instance of the Dictionary object:

```
Set objDictionary = CreateObject("Scripting.Dictionary")
```

After the Dictionary object has been created, you can then configure Dictionary properties and add elements to the Dictionary.

Configuring Dictionary Properties

The Dictionary object has only one configurable property, Compare Mode, which plays an important role in determining which keys can be added and which ones cannot. (It is also important in verifying which keys are present in a Dictionary and which ones are not.) By default, a Dictionary is created in binary mode, which means each key in the Dictionary is based on its ASCII value. This is important because the ASCII value of an uppercase letter is different from the ASCII value of that same lowercase letter. In binary mode, both of these services can be added to the Dictionary as individual keys:

- alerter

- ALERTER

In other words, with binary mode, you can inadvertently add multiple entries for the same item. Binary mode dictionaries can also be difficult to search. For example, if you try to verify the existence of the key *Alerter*, you will be told that the key does not exist; that is because no key exists with that same pattern of uppercase and lowercase letters. As a result, you might end up adding yet another key for this same item.

When a Dictionary is configured in text mode, uppercase and lowercase letters are treated identically. This helps eliminate duplicate keys; you cannot add a key for *ALERTER* if a key for *alerter* already exists. It is also much easier to verify the existence of a key; searching for either *alerter* or *ALERTer* will find the key named *Alerter*.

To configure the Dictionary mode, create an instance of the Dictionary object and then set the CompareMode property to one of the following values:

- **0** — Sets the mode to binary. This is the default value.

- **1** — Sets the mode to text.

For example, the script in Listing 4.44 sets the Dictionary to text mode.

Listing 4.44   Configuring the Dictionary Object

```
1  Const TextMode = 1
2  Set objDictionary = CreateObject("Scripting.Dictionary")
3  objDictionary.CompareMode = TextMode
```

You cannot change the CompareMode property of a Dictionary if that Dictionary contains any elements. This is because the binary mode allows you to differentiate between keys based solely on uppercase and lowercase letters. For example, each of these keys can be in the same Dictionary as long as the Dictionary is in binary mode:

- apple

- Apple

- APPLE

In text mode, however, these three keys are considered identical. If you had these elements in a binary Dictionary and were able to reconfigure that Dictionary in text mode, the Dictionary would suddenly contain three duplicate keys, and it would fail. If you must reconfigure the Dictionary mode, you first need to remove all items from the Dictionary.

Adding Key-Item Pairs to a Dictionary

After you have created an instance of the Dictionary object, you can use the Add method to add key-item pairs to the dictionary. The Add method requires two parameters, which must be supplied in the following order and separated by a comma:

- Key name
- Item value

For example, the script in Listing 4.45 creates a Dictionary object and then adds the key-item pairs shown in Table 4.10.

Table 4.10   Sample Key-Item Pairs

Key	Item
Printer 1	Printing
Printer 2	Offline
Printer 3	Printing

Listing 4.45   Adding Key-Item Pairs to a Dictionary

```
1  Set objDictionary = CreateObject("Scripting.Dictionary")
2  objDictionary.Add "Printer 1", "Printing"
3  objDictionary.Add "Printer 2", "Offline"
4  objDictionary.Add "Printer 3", "Printing"
```

Dictionary keys must be unique. For example, the following two script statements will generate a run-time error because, after the first line is interpreted, the key "Printer 1" will already be in the Dictionary:

```
objDictionary.Add "Printer 1", "Printing"
objDictionary.Add "Printer 1", "Offline"
```

Inadvertently Adding a Key to a Dictionary

One potential problem in using the Dictionary object is that any attempt to reference an element that is not contained in the Dictionary does not result in an error. Instead, the nonexistent element is added to the Dictionary. Consider the following script sample, which creates a Dictionary, adds three key-item pairs to the Dictionary, and then attempts to echo the value of a nonexistent item, Printer 4:

```
Set objDictionary = CreateObject("Scripting.Dictionary")
objDictionary.Add "Printer 1", "Printing"
objDictionary.Add "Printer 2", "Offline"
objDictionary.Add "Printer 3", "Printing"
Wscript.Echo objDictionary.Item("Printer 4")
```

When the script tries to echo the value of the nonexistent item, no run-time error occurs. Instead, the new key, Printer 4, is added to the Dictionary, along with the item value Null. As a result, the message box shown in Figure 4.9 appears.

Figure 4.9   Message Resulting from Inadvertently Adding a Key to a Dictionary

To avoid this problem, check for the existence of a key before trying to access the value of the item.

Manipulating Keys and Items in a Dictionary

By itself, a Dictionary is of little use; a Dictionary is valuable only when you can access, enumerate, and modify the keys and items within that Dictionary. After you have created a Dictionary, you will probably want to do such things as:

- Determine how many key-item pairs are in that Dictionary.

- Enumerate the keys and/or items within the Dictionary.

- Determine whether or not a specific key exists in the Dictionary.

- Modify the value of a key or an item in the Dictionary.

- Remove key-item pairs from the Dictionary.

All of these tasks can be carried out by using the methods and properties provided by the Script Runtime library.

Determining the Number of Key-Item Pairs in a Dictionary

Like most collections, the Dictionary object has a Count property that returns the number of key-item pairs in the collection. The script in Listing 4.46 creates an instance of the Dictionary object, adds three key-item pairs, and then echoes the value of the Count property.

Listing 4.46   Determining the Number of Key-Item Pairs in a Dictionary

```
1   Set objDictionary = CreateObject("Scripting.Dictionary")
2   objDictionary.Add "Printer 1", "Printing"
3   objDictionary.Add "Printer 2", "Offline"
4   objDictionary.Add "Printer 3", "Printing"
5   Wscript.Echo objDictionary.Count
```

When this script runs, the value 3 (the number of key-item pairs in the collection) will be echoed to the screen.

Enumerating Keys and Items in a Dictionary

A Dictionary is designed to serve as a temporary repository for information. Any data placed in a Dictionary is not intended for permanent storage; it is simply placed in the Dictionary temporarily and then later recalled for use within the script. For example, a list of server names might be placed in the Dictionary. Later the script might need to connect to each of these servers and retrieve a specified piece of information. As a result, the information stored in the Dictionary will have to be recalled each time the script needs to connect to a new server.

The Keys and Items methods can be used to return arrays consisting of, respectively, all the keys and all the items in a Dictionary. After you have called one of these methods, you can use a For Each loop to enumerate all the keys or items in the array.

For example, the script in Listing 4.47 creates a simple Dictionary with three keys and three items. After the Dictionary has been created, the script uses the Keys method to enumerate all the keys in the Dictionary and the Items method to enumerate all the items in the Dictionary.

Listing 4.47   Enumerating Keys and Items in a Dictionary

```
1    Set objDictionary = CreateObject("Scripting.Dictionary")
2    objDictionary.Add "Printer 1", "Printing"
3    objDictionary.Add "Printer 2", "Offline"
4    objDictionary.Add "Printer 3", "Printing"
5
6    colKeys = objDictionary.Keys
7    For Each strKey in colKeys
8        Wscript.Echo strKey
9    Next
10
11   colItems = objDictionary.Items
12   For Each strItem in colItems
13       Wscript.Echo strItem
14   Next
```

When this script is run under CScript, the following output appears in the command window:

```
Printer 1
Printer 2
Printer 3
Printing
Offline
Printing
```

To display the value of a specific item, use the Item method. For example, the following code statement displays the item value (Printing) associated with the key Printer 3:

```
Wscript.Echo objDictionary.Item("Printer 3")
```

Verifying the Existence of a Specific Key

One of the major advantages the Dictionary object has over an array or a standard collection is that you can quickly verify the existence of a particular key. For example, suppose you have a list of files installed on a computer and want to search that list to ensure that a particular set of DLLs has been installed. With either a collection or an array, there is no way to verify the existence of any one file without methodically looping through the entire set and checking each item individually.

With a Dictionary, however, you can use the Exists method to verify the existence of any given key. The Exists method takes a single parameter (the name of the key) and then returns a Boolean value: True if the key is in the Dictionary, False if it is not.

For example, the script in Listing 4.48 creates a Dictionary object and adds three elements: Printer 1, Printer 2, and Printer 3. The script then checks for the existence of a key named Printer 4 and echoes back the results of that check.

Listing 4.48 Verifying the Existence of a Dictionary Key

```
1  Set objDictionary = CreateObject("Scripting.Dictionary")
2  objDictionary.Add "Printer 1", "Printing"
3  objDictionary.Add "Printer 2", "Offline"
4  objDictionary.Add "Printer 3", "Printing"
5  If objDictionary.Exists("Printer 4") Then
6      Wscript.Echo "Printer 4 is in the Dictionary."
7  Else
8      Wscript.Echo "Printer 4 is not in the Dictionary."
9  End If
```

When this script runs, the message "Printer 4 is not in the Dictionary" is echoed to the screen.

Modifying an Item in a Dictionary

Items added to a Dictionary are not set in stone; in fact, you can modify the value of an item at any time. This allows you to do record keeping within a script. For example, your Dictionary might list the names of servers being targeted by the script. Each time the script is run against a server, the value of that Dictionary item can be changed to indicate whether the script succeeded. Right before the script terminates, it can then print a status report showing you a list of successes and failures.

The script shown in Listing 4.49 creates a Dictionary with three keys: servers atl-dc-01, atl-dc-02, and atl-dc-03. In each case, the item value for the key has been set to "No status." This is done to indicate that status information on the server has not been obtained. The item values are then echoed to the screen.

After the Dictionary has been created, the item value for each of the three keys is changed by using the Item method, with the key name passed as the parameter. For example, the following code statement sets the item value for the key atl-dc-01 to "Available":

```
objDictionary.Item("atl-dc-01") = "Available"
```

After the three item values have been changed, the new item values are echoed to the screen.

Listing 4.49   Modifying the Value of a Dictionary Item

```
1   Set objDictionary = CreateObject("Scripting.Dictionary")
2   objDictionary.Add "atl-dc-01", "No status"
3   objDictionary.Add "atl-dc-02", "No status"
4   objDictionary.Add "atl-dc-03", "No status"
5
6   colKeys = objDictionary.Keys
7   For Each strKey in colKeys
8       Wscript.Echo strKey, objDictionary.Item(strKey)
9   Next
10
11  objDictionary.Item("atl-dc-01") = "Available"
12  objDictionary.Item("atl-dc-02") = "Available"
13  objDictionary.Item("atl-dc-03") = "Unavailable"
14
15  colKeys = objDictionary.Keys
16  For Each strKey in colKeys
17      Wscript.Echo strKey, objDictionary.Item(strKey)
18  Next
```

When the script is run under CScript, the following information appears in the command window:

```
atl-dc-01 No status
atl-dc-02 No status
atl-dc-03 No status
atl-dc-01 Available
atl-dc-02 Available
atl-dc-03 Unavailable
```

Removing Key-Item Pairs from a Dictionary

Key-Item pairs can also be removed from a Dictionary. The Script Runtime library provides two methods for removing key-item pairs from a Dictionary:

- **RemoveAll**, which removes all the key-item pairs in a Dictionary.
- **Remove**, which removes a specified key-item pair from the Dictionary.

Removing All Key-Item Pairs from a Dictionary

You might have scripts, particularly monitoring scripts, that perform some action, store the information in a Dictionary, and then either display the data or save the data to a text file or database. At that point, the script might pause for several minutes and then run a second time, gathering updated information. This pattern might continue indefinitely.

If you are using a Dictionary as a temporary storehouse for the gathered data, you will likely want to clear the Dictionary before you begin gathering the next set of data. To do that, you can simply use the RemoveAll method, which removes all the key-item pairs from the specified Dictionary.

For example, the script in Listing 4.50 creates a Dictionary with three elements. After displaying the Dictionary keys, the script deletes each key-item pair in the Dictionary by using the RemoveAll method in the following code statement:

```
objDictionary.RemoveAll
```

To verify that the elements were removed, the script then echoes the Dictionary keys again.

Listing 4.50   Removing All the Key-Item Pairs in a Dictionary

```
1   Set objDictionary = CreateObject("Scripting.Dictionary")
2   objDictionary.Add "Printer 1", "Printing"
3   objDictionary.Add "Printer 2", "Offline"
4   objDictionary.Add "Printer 3", "Printing"
5   colKeys = objDictionary.Keys
6   Wscript.Echo "First run: "
```

(continued)

Listing 4.50   Removing All the Key-Item Pairs in a Dictionary *(continued)*

```
7   For Each strKey in colKeys
8       Wscript.Echo strKey
9   Next
10  objDictionary.RemoveAll
11  colKeys = objDictionary.Keys
12  Wscript.Echo VbCrLf & "Second run: "
13  For Each strKey in colKeys
14      Wscript.Echo strKey
15  Next
```

When this script is run under the WSH CScript host, the following output appears in the command window. As you can see, the second time through the dictionary is empty and contains no keys (this is not an error, because collections are allowed to contain 0 items):

```
First run:
Printer 1
Printer 2
Printer 3

Second run:
```

Removing a Specific Key-Item Pair from a Dictionary

Instead of removing all the key-item pairs from a Dictionary, you might at times want to remove only a single key and item. For example, suppose you have a script that retrieves event-log events from a series of computers. The script is designed to try each computer in succession and to keep track of successes and failures. For each failed attempt to contact a computer, the script tries again, continuing on until all the computers have been contacted and all the event-log events retrieved.

In this scenario, you might have a Dictionary consisting of the following keys:

```
atl-dc-01
atl-dc-02
atl-dc-03
atl-dc-04
atl-dc-05
```

When the script runs, it might be unable to contact computers atl-dc-03 and atl-dc-04. In that case, the script must attempt to contact these computers again. However, how will the script know which computers have been contacted and which ones have not?

One way to solve this problem is to simply remove successful contacts from the Dictionary; after the first iteration, the Dictionary will then consist only of the following elements.

```
atl-dc-03
atl-dc-04
```

Each time a computer is contacted, the corresponding Dictionary element is removed. When the Dictionary no longer contains any elements, that means that all the computers have been contacted and the script can then complete.

To remove a Dictionary element, use the Remove method, passing the key name as the only parameter. For example, the following code statement removes the key atl-dc-02 (and its associated item):

```
objDictionary.Remove("atl-dc-02")
```

The script in Listing 4.51 creates a Dictionary with three elements and then echoes the Dictionary keys. The script then removes the Printer 2 key and echoes the Dictionary keys again.

Listing 4.51 Removing a Specified Key-Item Pair from a Dictionary

```
1   Set objDictionary = CreateObject("Scripting.Dictionary")
2   objDictionary.Add "Printer 1", "Printing"
3   objDictionary.Add "Printer 2", "Offline"
4   objDictionary.Add "Printer 3", "Printing"
5   colKeys = objDictionary.Keys
6   Wscript.Echo "First run: "
7   For Each strKey in colKeys
8       Wscript.Echo strKey
9   Next
10  objDictionary.Remove("Printer 2")
11  colKeys = objDictionary.Keys
12  Wscript.Echo VbCrLf & "Second run: "
13  For Each strKey in colKeys
14      Wscript.Echo strKey
15  Next
```

When this script is run under CScript, the following output appears in the command window:

```
First run:
Printer 1
Printer 2
Printer 3

Second run:
Printer 1
Printer 3
```

At the end of the second iteration, the key Printer 2 is no longer present in the Dictionary.

CHAPTER 5

ADSI Scripting Primer

Administering a directory service often involves numerous repetitive tasks such as creating, deleting, and modifying users, groups, organizational units, computers, and other directory resources. Performing these steps manually by using graphical user interface (GUI) tools is time-consuming, tedious, and error prone. A key to reducing time consumption, tedium, and errors when administering a directory is automating repetitive tasks by using scripts.

Active Directory Service Interfaces (ADSI) is the technology that allows you to create custom scripts to administer directories. ADSI-enabled scripts are capable of performing a wide range of administrative tasks involving network directories such as the Active Directory® directory service.

In This Chapter

ADSI Overview 309
ADSI Scripting Fundamentals..310
   Primary ADSI Scripting Tasks 311
   Comparing the Primary Scripting Tasks 320
   Building ADSI Scripts 321
   Performing Multiple Scripting Tasks...333
Advanced ADSI Scripting Operations 337
   Administering Multivalued Attributes 337
   Data Caching..347
   Copying, Moving, and Renaming Objects...351
   Searching..359
   Enumerating Active Directory Objects in Containers.....................................387
   Root Directory Service Entry..391
Active Directory Architecture...394
   Physical Architecture 394
   Logical Structure 395
ADSI Architecture 415
   ADSI Layers..417
   ADSI Interfaces...422

ADSI Overview

Obtaining the skills necessary to successfully script directory administration tasks is not difficult. In fact, of all the required scripting skills, scripting with Active Directory Service Interfaces (ADSI) is perhaps the easiest to master. This is largely a result of the consistent and uniform approach ADSI brings to directory services management.

An Introductory Example

Consider the following scenario: It is Friday morning, and you plan to have a great weekend followed by a weeklong vacation. You then receive an urgent e-mail message from your boss telling you that a group of consultants will be working in the lab starting Monday morning. Their task is to load-test their application by logging on to this application using 1,000 different user accounts. The application is tightly integrated with Active Directory.

Your task is to set up an Active Directory domain on a computer running Microsoft® Windows® 2000 and create 1,000 user accounts in the Users container of the new domain. Installing Microsoft® Windows® 2000 Advanced Server and Active Directory is simple because you already have automated installation procedures in place.

But how are you going to create 1,000 user accounts and still get all of your daily work done before your planned hiatus? This is one of the many times that ADSI scripting can help you accomplish a potentially tedious and lengthy task. The script in Listing 5.1 creates 1,000 user accounts named UserNo1 – UserNo1000.

Listing 5.1   Creating 1,000 Active Directory User Accounts

```
1   Set objRootDSE = GetObject("LDAP://rootDSE")
2   Set objContainer = GetObject("LDAP://cn=Users," & _
3       objRootDSE.Get("defaultNamingContext"))
4
5   For i = 1 To 1000
6       Set objLeaf = objContainer.Create("User", "cn=UserNo" & i)
7       objLeaf.Put "sAMAccountName", "UserNo" & i
8       objLeaf.SetInfo
9   Next
10  Wscript.Echo "1000 Users created."
```

 Caution

Do not run the script in Listing 5.1 in a production domain. By default, the script creates 1,000 user accounts in the current logon domain.

It might take this script up to five minutes to run if a slow domain controller is servicing the request. Even this amount of delay is minuscule compared with how long it would take you to create 1,000 user accounts manually.

Directory Service Management

The script in Listing 5.1 is powerful but represents only a single task, creating user accounts. Using ADSI scripts, you can complete countless Active Directory administration tasks. Simply put, Active Directory administration involves managing the life cycle of directory objects from initial creation (as demonstrated in Listing 5.1) to deletion. Active Directory includes objects such as user accounts, groups, computers, and sites. The four common task categories and some example tasks involved in the life cycle of objects are:

1. **Create.** Creating user accounts, groups, organizational units (OUs), computer accounts, sites, subnets, published printers, and shared folders.

2. **Modify.** Adding a telephone number to a user account, deleting a member from a group, resetting a password, disabling a computer account, and delegating control of an OU or a site to a user or group.

3. **Read.** Reading the full name of a user account, reading a list of group members or a list of users in an OU, and reading operating system information from computer account objects.

4. **Delete.** Deleting objects that are no longer in use, such as user accounts, groups, and OUs.

What makes using ADSI scripts a powerful and efficient way to manage Active Directory is the consistent approach ADSI provides for performing similar tasks on different types of objects. This consistency carries over from one major task category to the next. For example, you use the same basic approach to create a user, group, OU, or almost any object stored in Active Directory.

The same is true for modifying and reading Active Directory objects: You use the same basic steps to modify and read objects without regard to the target object's type. Finally, you use the same steps to delete objects, again regardless of the target object's type.

ADSI Scripting Fundamentals

Examining script examples from each of the major task categories — create, modify, read, and delete — will give you a better understanding of ADSI scripting. Throughout this section, you will observe the relative ease with which a variety of tasks are carried out and the consistent approach used to perform the same task on different object types.

Primary ADSI Scripting Tasks

The primary scripting tasks — create, modify, read, and delete — are simple to complete with scripts. Simplicity might suggest that these tasks are limited in scope, but in reality they play a significant role in managing almost any directory service. Thus, they are the four most useful tasks in directory service management.

Creating Directory Service Objects

Listing 5.1 showed how to create 1,000 user accounts. To simplify matters, the following section takes a more modest approach by creating one OU, one user account, and one group.

Creating Active Directory objects involves four basic steps:

1. Connect to the Active Directory container that will store the new object.

2. Create the object.

3. Set the object's mandatory attributes, if necessary.

4. Commit the new object to Active Directory.

The goal of the three scripts in this section is to create an OU named HR (Human Resources department), a user account named MyerKen in the HR OU, and a group named Atl-Users, also in the HR OU.

Creating an OU

The script in Listing 5.2 creates an OU named HR in the na.fabrikam.com domain. All mandatory attributes of an OU are automatically assigned a value by Active Directory. Therefore, the step that sets mandatory attributes does not appear in Listing 5.2.

To carry out this task, the script performs the following steps:

1. Connect to the na.fabrikam.com domain container.

2. Create an OU object named HR.

3. Commit the new OU to Active Directory.

Listing 5.2   Creating an OU

```
1   Set objDomain = GetObject("LDAP://dc=NA,dc=fabrikam,dc=com")
2   Set objOU = objDomain.Create("organizationalUnit", "ou=HR")
3   objOU.SetInfo
```

Creating a User Account

The script in Listing 5.3 creates a user account named MyerKen in the OU named HR. The HR OU is located in the na.fabrkam.com domain. To carry out this task, the script performs the following steps:

1. Connect to the HR OU container in the na.fabrikam.com domain.

HR is the OU that was created by running the script appearing in Listing 5.2.

2. Create a user account named MyerKen.

Using an uppercase letter for the first letter of the last and first name is not necessary. However, the case is preserved when the object is saved to Active Directory. Therefore, users will be able to distinguish the last name from the first name when searching Active Directory.

3. Set the sAMAccountName mandatory attribute to the value myerken.

There is no need to capitalize the first letter of the last and first name for this attribute's value because, typically, users do not perform user account searches on the sAMAccountName attribute.

4. Commit the new user account to Active Directory.

Listing 5.3 Creating a User Account

```
1  Set objOU = GetObject("LDAP://ou=HR,dc=NA,dc=fabrikam,dc=com")
2  Set objUser = objOU.Create("user", "cn=MyerKen")
3  objUser.Put "sAMAccountName", "myerken"
4  objUser.SetInfo
```

Creating a Group

The script in Listing 5.4 creates a global group named Atl-Users in the OU named HR, located in the na.fabrikam.com domain. To carry out this task, the script performs the following steps:

1. Connect to the HR OU container in the na.fabrikam.com domain.

2. Create a group named Atl-Users.

By default, the script creates a global group.

3.   Set the sAMAccountName mandatory attribute to a value of Atl-Users.

Like creating a user account, creating a security group requires a single mandatory attribute, sAMAccountName.

4.   Commit the new group account to Active Directory.

Listing 5.4   Creating a Group

```
1   Set objOU = GetObject("LDAP://ou=HR,dc=NA,dc=fabrikam,dc=com")
2   Set objGroup = objOU.Create("group", "cn=Atl-Users")
3   objGroup.Put "sAMAccountName", "Atl-Users"
4   objGroup.SetInfo
```

Important observations about the scripts in this section are:

- They perform the same basic steps: They connect to an Active Directory container, create an object, set the object's mandatory attributes (if necessary), and commit the object to Active Directory.

- They use the same method (Create) without regard to the class of the object being created.

- The script parameters are the only parts of the scripts that are different. Each script contains the class name (organizationalUnit, user, and group) identifying the type of object to create and the object's corresponding attributes (the new object's name and the user's and group's mandatory sAMAccountName attribute).

The steps for creating an OU (Listing 5.2), a user account (Listing 5.3), and a group (Listing 5.4) are strikingly similar, as the three preceding code listings demonstrate. This similarity extends to creating all types of directory objects. This consistency will become even clearer by examining each code line in each listing.

To create an object, the script first connects to a container, a process called *binding*. Binding occurs on the first line of each listing. In Listing 5.2, the script binds to the domain to create an OU. When creating an object in a domain, think of the domain as simply a container that can hold objects, just as an OU is a container that can hold objects. In Listing 5.3 and Listing 5.4, both scripts bind to an OU to create objects within it. The code in Listing 5.3 creates a user account object, and the code in Listing 5.4 creates a group object.

After binding to a container, the script performs the task of creating an object. To create an object, you must specify two parameters, the object's class and name. In Listing 5.2, the script creates an OU by specifying the organizationalUnit class and the name, ou=HR. In Listing 5.3, the script creates a user account by specifying the user class and the name, cn=MyerKen. In Listing 5.4, the script creates a group by specifying the group class and the name, cn=Atl-Users. You will see these parameter pairs on line 3 of each listing. For information about how to determine an object's class and name, see "ADSI Interfaces" later in this chapter.

Before committing an object to the directory, you must first set any mandatory attributes defined for an object. There are no mandatory attributes that the script needs to set for creating an OU. Therefore, this step does not occur in Listing 5.2. However, line 4 in both Listing 5.3 and Listing 5.4 sets a mandatory attribute (sAMAccountName) for a user account and a group object. The script assigns the mandatory attribute to the object by specifying the mandatory attribute's name and its value. In Listing 5.3, the value is myerken; and in Listing 5.4, the value is Atl-Users. For information about how to determine the mandatory attributes of an object, see "Active Directory Architecture" later in this chapter.

The last step in creating an object is committing (saving) the object to the directory. This final step is the last script line in each listing. Modify, read, and delete tasks also exhibit similar uniformity, as the next sections demonstrate.

Modifying Directory Service Objects

Modifying an object is equivalent to writing an attribute to an existing object in Active Directory. If an attribute contains a value, modifying it will clear the existing value and replace it with a different value.

Typically, the type of modification you make to an object will depend on the type of object you want to modify and various characteristics of the attribute — for example, whether the attribute holds a single value or multiple values. For simplicity, however, the following task descriptions illustrate how to write a single value to the same attribute in three different objects.

Modifying attributes of Active Directory objects involves three basic steps:

1. Connect to the Active Directory object you want to modify.

2. Modify one or more of the object's attributes.

3. Commit the change to Active Directory.

The goal of the three scripts in this section is to write an attribute to each of the objects created in "Creating Directory Service Objects" earlier in this chapter. The objects include the HR OU, the MyerKen user account, and the Atl-Users global group. The description attribute is contained in all three of these objects, so it is used as the attribute to modify.

Modifying an Attribute of an OU

The script in Listing 5.5 modifies the description attribute of the OU named HR in the na.fabrikam.com domain. The description attribute is assigned the value Human Resources. To carry out this task, the script performs the following steps:

1. Connect to the HR OU object in the na.fabrikam.com domain.

   In contrast with the create task, the HR OU is referred to as an object rather than a container because the task completed in this script is to write an attribute of an object.

2. Modify the object's attributes by assigning the description attribute the value Human Resources.

3. Commit the change to the OU in Active Directory.

Listing 5.5   Writing the description Attribute to an OU

```
1   Set objOU = GetObject("LDAP://ou=HR,dc=NA,dc=fabrikam,dc=com")
2   objOU.Put "description", "Human Resources"
3   objOU.SetInfo
```

Modifying an Attribute of a User Account

The script in Listing 5.6 modifies the description attribute of the user account named MyerKen in the HR OU of the na.fabrikam.com domain. The description attribute is assigned the value HR employee. To carry out this task, the script performs the following steps:

1. Connect to the MyerKen user account object in the HR OU of the na.fabrikam.com domain.

2. Modify the object's attributes by assigning the description attribute the value HR employee.

3. Commit the change to the user account in Active Directory.

Listing 5.6   Writing the description Attribute to a User Account

```
1   Set objUser = _
2       GetObject("LDAP://cn=MyerKen,ou=HR,dc=NA,dc=fabrikam,dc=com")
3   objUser.Put "description", "HR employee"
4   objUser.SetInfo
```

Modifying an Attribute of a Group

The script in Listing 5.7 modifies the description attribute of the group account named Atl-Users in the HR OU of the na.fabrikam.com domain. The description attribute is assigned the value of Atlanta users. To carry out this task, the script performs the following steps:

1. Connect to the Atl-Users group in the HR OU of the na.fabrikam.com domain.

2. Modify the object's attributes by assigning the description attribute the value Atlanta users.

3. Commit the change to the group in Active Directory.

Listing 5.7   Writing the description Attribute to a Group

```
1   Set objOU = GetObject _
2       ("LDAP://cn=Atl-Users,ou=HR,dc=NA,dc=fabrikam,dc=com")
3   objOU.Put "description", "Atlanta users"
4   objOU.SetInfo
```

Important observations about the scripts in this section are:

- They perform the same basic steps: They connect to an Active Directory object, modify an attribute of the object, and write the change to the corresponding Active Directory object.

- They use the same method (Put) without regard to the class of object being modified.

Reading Attributes of Directory Service Objects

The preceding sections described how to create an OU, a user account, and a group, and set the description attribute on each of these objects. The next common task is to read an attribute of each object.

Reading an Active Directory object's attributes involves two simple steps:

1. Connect to the Active Directory object you want to read.

2. Read one or more of the object's attributes.

The goal of the three scripts in this section will be to read the description attribute of the HR OU, the MyerKen user account, and the Atl-Users group and display their values on the screen.

 Important

Command window output generated by the CScript script host follows each script example that echoes information to the screen. If you run these scripts, be sure you use CScript because some of the scripts contain a significant amount of output. This makes WScript an inappropriate scripting host for running these scripts.

Reading an Attribute of an OU

The script in Listing 5.8 reads and displays the description attribute of the OU named HR in the na.fabrikam.com domain. To carry out this task, the script performs the following steps:

1. Connect to the HR OU object in the na.fabrikam.com domain.

2. Read the object's description attribute.

Listing 5.8   Reading the description Attribute of an OU

```
1   Set objOU = GetObject("LDAP://ou=HR,dc=NA,dc=fabrikam,dc=com")
2   Wscript.Echo objOU.Get("description")
```

When this script runs in the na.fabrikam.com domain, it echoes the description of the HR OU to the command window, as shown:

```
Human Resources
```

Reading an Attribute of a User Account

The script in Listing 5.9 reads and displays the description attribute of the user account named MyerKen, located in the HR OU of the na.fabrikam.com domain.

1. Connect to the MyerKen user account object in the HR OU of the na.fabrikam.com domain.

2. Read the object's description attribute.

Listing 5.9   Reading the description Attribute of a User Account

```
1  Set objUser = _
2     GetObject("LDAP://cn=MyerKen,ou=HR,dc=NA,dc=fabrikam,dc=com")
3  Wscript.Echo objUser.Get("description")
```

When this script runs in the na.fabrikam.com domain, it echoes the description of the user account to the command window, as shown:

```
HR employee
```

Reading an Attribute of a Group

The script in Listing 5.10 reads and displays the description attribute of a global group named Atl-Users, located in the HR OU of the na.fabrikam.com domain.

1. Connect to the Atl-Users group in the HR OU of the na.fabrikam.com domain.

2. Read the object's description attribute.

Listing 5.10   Reading the description Attribute of a Group

```
1  Set objGroup = _
2     GetObject("LDAP://cn=Atl-Users,ou=HR,dc=NA,dc=fabrikam,dc=com")
3  Wscript.Echo objGroup.Get("description")
```

When this script runs in the na.fabrikam.com domain, it echoes the description of the group to the command window, as shown:

```
Atlanta users
```

Important observations about the scripts in this section:

- They perform the same basic steps: They connect to an Active Directory object and read an attribute of the object.

- They use the same method (Get) without regard to the class of object being read.

As demonstrated in this section, the process for reading attributes is uniform from one object to the next. In fact, within a particular task, the steps you follow from one object to the next are consistent. This consistency empowers you to write scripts that can read thousands of attributes from the many objects stored in Active Directory.

Deleting Directory Service Objects

In the life cycle of an object, the final management task is deletion. All of the preceding code examples started by performing a task to create or act on the OU named HR. This task, however, starts in reverse order by demonstrating how to delete a group, then a user account, and then an OU. This reverse approach is necessary because, when you use the Delete method in an ADSI script, you cannot delete an OU without first removing the objects (called leaf objects) within it.

If you use the Delete method to delete an OU before all leaf objects are removed, Windows Script Host (WSH) displays a message similar to the following:

```
C:\DeleteOu.vbs(2, 1) (null): The directory service can perform the requested
operation only on a leaf object.
```

It might not be entirely clear why the error message reads, "The directory service can perform the requested operation only on a leaf object." It is true that an OU is a container object. However, when an OU is empty, the Delete method can delete an OU because, from the script's perspective, an empty OU is considered a leaf object.

This error message is avoided in the following examples because the first script removes the Atl-Users group and the second script removes the MyerKen user account before the third script deletes the HR OU.

Deleting Active Directory objects involves two simple steps:

1. Connect to the Active Directory container where the object is stored.

2. Delete the object.

Deleting a Group

The script in Listing 5.11 deletes the Atl-Users group from the HR OU in the na.fabrikam.com domain.

1. Connect to the HR OU container in the na.fabrikam.com domain.

   The OU is referred to as a container rather than an object because the task completed in this script is to delete an object within a container.

2. Delete the Atl-Users group from the HR OU in Active Directory.

Listing 5.11   Deleting a Group

```
1  Set objOU = GetObject("LDAP://ou=HR,dc=NA,dc=fabrikam,dc=com")
2  objOU.Delete "group", "cn=Atl-Users"
```

Deleting a User Account

The script in Listing 5.12 deletes the MyerKen user account from the HR OU in the na.fabrikam.com domain.

1. Connect to the HR OU container in the na.fabrikam.com domain.

2. Delete the MyerKen user account from the HR OU in Active Directory.

Listing 5.12   Deleting a User Account

```
1  Set objOU = GetObject("LDAP://ou=HR,dc=NA,dc=fabrikam,dc=com")
2  objOU.Delete "user", "cn=MyerKen"
```

Deleting an OU

The script in Listing 5.13 deletes the HR OU from the na.fabrikam.com domain.

1. Connect to the na.fabrikam.com domain container.

2. Delete the HR OU from the na.fabrikam.com domain in Active Directory.

Listing 5.13   Deleting an OU

```
1  Set objDomain = GetObject("LDAP://dc=NA,dc=fabrikam,dc=com")
2  objDomain.Delete "organizationalUnit", "ou=HR"
```

Important observations about the scripts in this section are:

- They perform the same two steps: They connect to an Active Directory container and delete an object in the container.

- They use the same method (Delete) without regard to the class of object being deleted.

Comparing the Primary Scripting Tasks

You have now seen the four primary categories of directory administration tasks (creating, reading, modifying, and deleting). The script examples demonstrate how simply and consistently you can complete these tasks using ADSI scripts. Figure 5.1 summarizes each major task category and the set of ADSI scripting steps involved in completing each task.

Figure 5.1   Comparison of Steps in Completing Primary ADSI Scripting Tasks

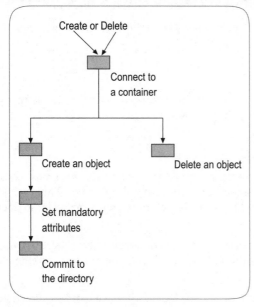

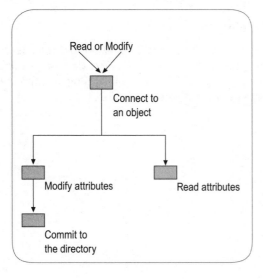

Figure 5.1 and the twelve scripts preceding it illustrate the following rules about ADSI scripting:

1. Regardless of the task at hand, step 1 is connecting (binding) to an object or container.

2. The Create method creates an Active Directory object.

3. The Delete method deletes an Active Directory object.

4. The Put method modifies or writes an Active Directory object's attributes.

5. The Get method reads an Active Directory object's attributes.

6. The SetInfo method commits new and modified objects to Active Directory.

7. The parameters used with Create, Delete, Put, and Get are always the same.

Building ADSI Scripts

The following sections examine the main steps of the preceding script examples so that you have a better understanding of how to construct your own ADSI scripts.

Step 1: Establishing a Connection

Figure 5.1 and all of the preceding listings demonstrated that the first step you must take to complete any scripted directory management task is connecting to an object. This initial step is referred to as *binding to the directory*. Binding to the directory prepares the script to operate on an object.

When creating or deleting an object, you must bind to the container object where a leaf object will be created or deleted. When reading or modifying an object, you must bind to the object that you want to read or modify.

Because the first part of this chapter focuses on Active Directory, the examples shown here demonstrate how an ADSI script binds to Active Directory.

Choosing a Directory Service Object for a Binding Operation

To determine which directory service object to specify in a binding operation, consider the task you want to complete (create, delete, read, or modify), the type of object (leaf or container), and, if the object is a container, whether it is empty. Figure 5.2 shows a data flow diagram to help you determine which directory service object to use for a binding operation.

Figure 5.2   How To Determine Which Directory Service Object to Use for a Binding Operation

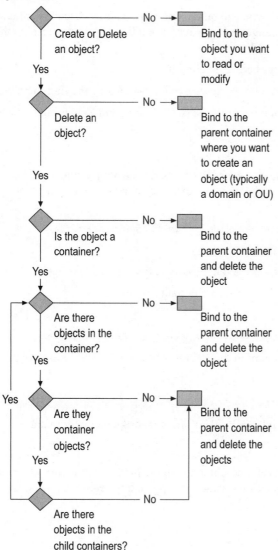

The data flow diagram does not show the following two tasks that can also be scripted:

- Deleting a container that is not empty.

  Using the DeleteObject method, you can quickly and irreversibly delete a container that is not empty. This is potentially dangerous, so exercise caution before performing this type of delete operation.

- Moving objects from a container before deleting it.

  You might need to delete a container but preserve its contents by moving them elsewhere.

For information about how to script object moves, see "Moving and Renaming Objects" later in this chapter.

Performing a Binding Operation

To bind to an Active Directory object, you use the VBScript GetObject function, the prefix LDAP: followed by two slashes, and the path to a directory object. The binding statements in four of the previous listings are:

- ```
  Set objDomain = GetObject("LDAP://dc=NA,dc=fabrikam,dc=com")
  ```

  Binds to the na.fabrikam.com domain.

- ```
  Set objOU = GetObject("LDAP://ou=HR,dc=NA,dc=fabrikam,dc=com")
  ```

  Binds to the HR OU in the na.fabrikam.com domain.

- ```
  Set objUser = _
      GetObject("LDAP://cn=MyerKen,ou=HR,dc=NA,dc=fabrikam,dc=com")
  ```

  Binds to the MyerKen user account in the HR OU of the na.fabrikam.com domain.

- ```
  Set objGroup = _
      GetObject("LDAP://cn=Atl-Users,ou=HR,dc=NA,dc=fabrikam,dc=com")
  ```

  Binds to the Atl-Users group in the HR OU of the na.fabrikam.com domain.

ADsPath

In ADSI terminology, the LDAP: prefix combined with the path to a directory object is called an *ADsPath*. The binding code examples appearing in the preceding section show ADsPath strings enclosed in parentheses.

Specifying the provider

The first part of the ADsPath identifies an ADSI provider. ADSI scripts use providers to communicate with different types of directory services. For example, ADSI scripts use the ADSI Lightweight Directory Access Protocol (LDAP) provider (Adsldp.dll) to communicate with Active Directory and other LDAP version 2.0–compliant and version 3.0–compliant directory services. To communicate with the local Security Accounts Manager (SAM) database, ADSI scripts use the ADSI WinNT provider (Adsnt.dll). The LDAP: prefix at the beginning of the ADsPath identifies the ADSI LDAP provider as the appropriate provider for completing the binding operation.

 Note

ADSI provider identifiers are case sensitive.

The VBScript GetObject function uses the provider identifier to locate and load the appropriate ADSI provider dynamic-link library into memory. Once the provider is loaded into memory, the second part of the ADsPath, the path to the directory object, tells the provider which object to bind to in the directory.

Specifying the directory object's path

The second part of the ADsPath is the path to the target object in the directory. ADSI supports several object path formats; the path format used in all of the preceding scripting examples is referred to as an object's *distinguished name* (DN). This is just one of a number of identifiers that you can use to build an object's ADsPath. For more information about ADSI identifiers and how to use them to refer to objects in Active Directory, see "Root Directory Service Entry" later in this chapter.

Every object stored in Active Directory has a distinguished name. Think of an object's distinguished name as the LDAP version of a file's fully qualified path. Every file has a fully qualified path that consists of a device name, followed by zero or more folder names, followed by the file name. Likewise, objects are located within Active Directory according to a hierarchical path. The full path to the object is defined by the object's distinguished name.

Similar to a file path that contains multiple folder names separated by backslashes, an object's distinguished name contains a series of attribute=value pairs separated by commas. Each attribute=value pair in an object's distinguished name is analogous to a single folder in a file's fully qualified path.

The attribute part of each attribute=value pair identifies an attribute type, which is defined in RFC 2247 and RFC 2253 and is based on the class of object. For example, the attribute type for a user account (User class) is CN, and the attribute type for an organizational unit (organizationalUnit class) is OU.

 Note

With the exception of the Domain Controllers container, the attribute type of the default containers directly below an Active Directory domain, such as the Computers, Users, and Built-in containers, is CN rather than OU.

The value part of each attribute=value pair is the name you provide when you create the object. Consider the MyerKen user account located in the HR OU of the na.fabrikam.com domain. Table 5.1 shows the object class from which each component of the DN is derived, along with its attribute type and value.

Table 5.1   Object Class, Naming Attributes, and Values

Object Class	Attribute Types	Value
User	CN	MyerKen
organizationalUnit	OU	HR
domain	DC	NA
domain	DC	fabrikam
domain	DC	com

The entire string of attribute=value pairs represents the path from an object to the root of the directory tree. Following each attribute=value pair from left to right moves you up through the directory hierarchy, as shown in Figure 5.3.

Figure 5.3   Example Directory Hierarchy and the DN of a User Account Object

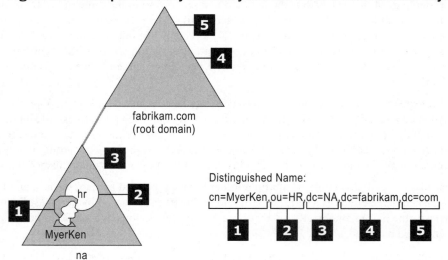

The MyerKen user account is located in the HR OU in the NA child domain. The parent domain of NA is fabrikam.com. Fabrikam.com is the root domain of the Active Directory hierarchy. Thus, the binding string (ADsPath) to this object is:

```
"LDAP://cn=MyerKen,ou=HR,dc=NA,dc=fabrikam,dc=com"
```

 Note

The binding string used in Listing 5.1 is a little different from the other listings because it employs a special ADSI feature called rootDSE. Ultimately, though, the binding string in Listing 5.1 also resolves to a distinguished name. For information about the rootDSE feature, see "Root Directory Service Entry" later in this chapter.

Creating an Object Reference to the Directory Object

The last part of the binding step to explore is the code on the left side of the assignment operator (equal sign), the VBScript Set keyword followed by a variable name that you provide. For example, the variable names objDomain, objOU, objUser, and objGroup appear in the earlier listings.

In contrast with simple string and numeric assignment statements, you must use the VBScript Set statement to associate an object reference with (or assign it to) a variable. The Set statement appears in the binding step because the GetObject function requires this in order to return a reference to an object.

In the case of ADSI, the object reference returned by GetObject is a virtual representation of the Active Directory object defined by the ADsPath in the binding step. The Set statement assigns the object reference to the variable following the Set keyword. For example, the objUser variable appearing in earlier listings is a virtual representation of the MyerKen user account object. Think of the variable as the script's pointer, or reference, to the virtual representation of the Active Directory object. The script then uses the variable to manage the referenced object.

Now that you have determined the object to bind to and have completed step 1 (binding to the object) you can perform a task against the object.

Step 2: Performing a Task

Creating and deleting objects by using a script are straightforward. After the script binds to a container object, you can either create or delete objects in the container. Reading and writing objects from a script are equally straightforward. After the script binds to an object, you can perform either a read or a write operation on the object.

When you call the Create, Put (modify), or Get (read) method to perform a task on a directory object, these operations do not occur against Active Directory. Instead, they are performed locally in a special area of memory called the *local property cache*. The local property cache contains one or more attributes of an Active Directory object. In contrast, the Delete method acts upon the object in Active Directory. A small number of other methods also operate in this way.

Any changes you make are initially made only on the locally cached objects. To apply the changes to the actual objects in Active Directory, you need to call the SetInfo method.

Task Code

If you review all of the listings shown in each task section, you will notice that the task code of each script contains the name of the object variable that you initialized in the binding step, a dot, and the name of the task, as shown in the following list:

- `objVariableName.Create`

  To **create** an object in the container specified by *objVariableName*

- `objVariableName.Get`

  To **read** an attribute of the object specified by *objVariableName*

- `objVariableName.Put`

  To **modify** or **write** an attribute of the object specified by *objVariableName*

- `objVariableName.Delete`

  To **delete** an object in the container specified by *objVariableName*

The Create and Delete names are easy to remember because they are synonymous with the task. Use Get to read an attribute, and use Put to modify or write an attribute. In ADSI scripting, these tasks are called *methods*. Methods perform a task against an object.

Method Parameters

Each method — Create, Get, Put, and Delete — uses syntax specific to the task at hand. The task of creating an object requires you to define the type of object you want to create and give the object a name. On the other hand, the task of reading an attribute requires you to name the attribute you want to read. The required items that a method expects are called the method's *parameters.*

Create parameters

The Create method requires two parameters, the class name and the *relative distinguished name* of the object you want to create. A relative distinguished name is the part of an object's name that identifies an object as unique within the container where it is located. A relative distinguished name consists of a naming attribute and a value to be assigned to the object.

Consider the following examples from previous listings:

- ```
Set objOU = objDomain.Create("organizationalUnit", "ou=HR")
```

  Creates an OU

  The class name is organizationalUnit, the naming attribute is ou, and the value assigned to the object is HR. Thus, the relative distinguished name is ou=HR.

- ```
Set objUser = objOU.Create("user", "cn=MyerKen")
```

  Creates a user account

  The class name is user, the naming attribute is cn, and the value assigned to the object is MyerKen. Thus, the relative distinguished name is cn=MyerKen.

- ```
Set objGroup = objOU.Create("group", "cn=Atl-Users")
```

  Creates a group

  The class name is group, the naming attribute is cn, and the value assigned to the object is Atl-Users. Thus, the relative distinguished name is cn=Atl-Users.

Like the binding string, the Create method requires the VBScript **Set** statement and a variable to serve as a reference to the object created by the method. The object is created in local memory.

 **Important**

If you write a script to create an object or modify an attribute and the changes requested in the script are not reflected in Active Directory, verify that you included the SetInfo method call in your script.
```

Just as binding to an object or a container in Active Directory creates an object reference (virtual representation of an object) in local memory, the Create method also creates a virtual representation of an object in local memory. The difference is that the object did not come from Active Directory. Instead, it was created locally by the script, separate from a binding string. The Create method provides an object reference to the local object. You use this object reference to modify the object and ultimately to commit the object to Active Directory.

Figure 5.4 shows the pieces of the three create methods in the previous listings:

Figure 5.4   Comparison of Three Create Method Calls

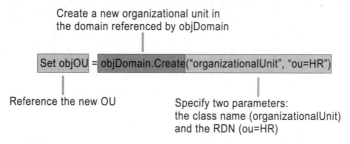

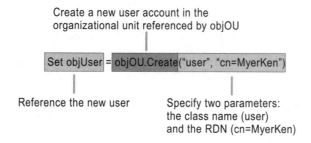

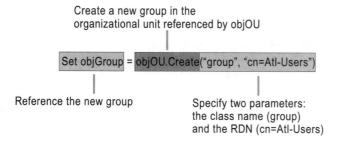

Modify parameters

The Put method requires two parameters: the name of the attribute (its lDAPDisplayName) and the value you will assign the attribute.

ADSI expects a certain type of attribute name, called the lDAPDisplayName, for completing read and write operations. Attributes are assigned a number of names, but the lDAPDisplayName is common to most ADSI scripts.

Consider the following examples from previous listings:

- `objOU.Put "description", "Human Resources"`

  Writes an attribute of an OU

  The lDAPDisplayName of the attribute to modify is description, and the value assigned to the attribute is Human Resources.

- `objUser.Put "description", "HR employee"`

  Writes an attribute of a user account

  The lDAPDisplayName of the attribute to modify is description, and the value assigned to the attribute is HR employee.

- `objOU.Put "description", "Atlanta users"`

  Writes an attribute of a group

  The lDAPDisplayName of the attribute to modify is description, and the value assigned to the attribute is Atlanta users.

The write operation also appears in the Create task scripts when an object being created contains one or more mandatory attributes that must be assigned values before the object is committed to the directory. Objects cannot be created without configuring those mandatory attributes to which values are not automatically assigned by Active Directory.

The following examples from previous listings illustrate writing a manatory attribute:

- `objUser.Put "sAMAccountName", "myerken"`

  Writes a mandatory attribute (sAMAccountName) of a user account

- `objUser.Put "sAMAccountName", "atl-users"`

  Writes a mandatory attribute (sAMAccountName) of a group

Mandatory attributes are defined in Active Directory. For information about how to determine the mandatory attributes of an object, see "Active Directory Architecture" later in this chapter.

Read parameters

The Get method (read task) requires a single parameter, the lDAPDisplayName of the attribute to read. In line 2 of Listing 5.8 and line 3 of Listing 5.9 and Listing 5.10, the description attribute was read.

The goal of Listing 5.8 through Listing 5.10 was to read and display the value of an attribute. Therefore, VBScript's Wscript.Echo statement appears with the call to the Get method to display information on the screen, as shown in the following examples from previous listings:

- `Wscript.Echo objOU.Get("description")`

  Reads and displays the description attribute of an OU

- `Wscript.Echo objUser.Get("description")`

  Reads and displays the description attribute of a user account

- `Wscript.Echo objGroup.Get("description")`

  Reads and displays the description attribute of a group

Delete parameters

Like the Create method, the Delete method requires two parameters: the type of object you want to delete and the relative distinguished name of the object.

These parameters are illustrated in the following examples from previous listings:

- `objOU.Delete "group", "cn=Atl-Users"`

  Deletes a group

  The class name is group, and the relative distinguished name of the object to delete is cn=Atl-Users.

- `objOU.Delete "user", "cn=MyerKen"`

  Deletes a user account

  The class name is user, and the relative distinguished name of the object to delete is cn=MyerKen.

- `objDomain.Delete "organizationalUnit", "ou=HR"`

  Deletes an OU

  The class name is organizationalUnit, and the relative distinguished name of the object to delete is ou=HR.

Step 3: Committing to Active Directory

Anytime you make a change, whether by creating an object or by writing a value to an attribute, you must save the changes to the directory by calling the SetInfo method. An ADSI script will run properly even if you do not commit changes, but if you do not commit changes, anything that the script did in the local property cache is lost after the script ends. For more information about the local property cache, see "Step 2: Performing a Task" in the preceding section.

The act of saving an object to the directory is called *committing*. Committing an object to Active Directory is analogous to saving a document that you created in a word processing application. The act of saving the document writes the data in memory to a location on your hard disk, just as the act of calling the SetInfo method writes the data in memory (the local property cache) to Active Directory.

The code for committing an object to the directory includes the variable name of the object, a dot, and the SetInfo method call. Previously, you learned that Create, Get, Put, and Delete are method calls to complete a task. SetInfo is simply another method call whose sole task is to save objects or attributes to a directory service. Notice that this method call is the last line in all script examples in the previous Create and Modify task sections.

The code listings in "Reading Attributes of Directory Service Objects" earlier in this chapter do not contain the SetInfo method because these tasks simply bind to an object in Active Directory and read an attribute of an object. The object is not modified, so there is no need to save any changes to Active Directory. This is analogous to reading a word processing document without making any changes to it. While you can save the document to the disk, there is no reason to do so.

The code listings in "Deleting Directory Service Objects" earlier in this chapter do not contain the SetInfo method because the Delete method deletes objects from Active Directory immediately.

Performing Multiple Scripting Tasks

Each of the previous code examples demonstrated one of the primary ADSI scripting task categories by completing a single task — creating one object, deleting one object, writing one attribute, and reading one attribute. It is more common, however, to perform more than a single task in an ADSI script.

Large scripts start from a discrete set of tasks and tie them together to meet some larger administrative goal. Think about each script task as a building block. Each building block is useful in itself, but properly cementing the blocks together creates a larger, more functional structure, just as tying scripting tasks together makes a more robust and useful script.

When you are presented with a large, sophisticated script, you might be able to run it right away. But if you try to use it as a learning tool, it will be difficult to know where to start unless the script is broken down into its component parts. Therefore, consider documenting your scripts carefully so that other administrators can understand the purpose of your scripts and troubleshoot them when necessary.

Many production scripts include a significant amount of code that has nothing directly to do with ADSI —one reason why you might have found other scripts hard to follow. The ADSI scripts included with the *Microsoft® Windows® 2000 Server Resource Kit* highlight this point. For example, the Resource Kit's ListDCs.vbs ADSI script is 454 lines long. Of the 454 lines, more than 400 lines have nothing to with ADSI. Why are they there? They are there because ListDCs.vbs is designed to be a general-purpose utility much like a command-line executable. As such, the script includes routines to parse command line arguments, format output, and handle errors. Although the routines are important to ListDCs.vbs, they are not part of ADSI technology. Admittedly, there are times when it is necessary to use some non-ADSI code in an ADSI script. The script code in this chapter, however, avoids non-ADSI scripting code as much as possible so that you can clearly see what ADSI scripting *is*.

To successfully create a script that writes and reads multiple attributes of an Active Directory object, you combine tasks described earlier in this chapter:

1. **Bind to the object.** This task requires you to know the path to the object in order to create script code that binds to the object.

2. **Write or modify attributes.** This task requires you to know certain characteristics of the attributes you want to write or modify. For example, you must know each attribute's lDAPDisplayName. To complete this task, you must save changes to Active Directory.

3. **Read attributes.** Reading attributes requires knowledge of the same information needed to write or modify attributes.

Complete the procedures in this section to perform write and read operations against an Active Directory user account object.

Preliminary Steps

1. Start Notepad, and save a file to the C:\scripts folder named **ModifyUser.vbs**.

   As you read this section, copy and paste the appropriate code lines into ModifyUser.vbs.

2. Verify that you have previously created the MyerKen user account object in Active Directory. If not, create the user account in an OU or the Users container of the Active Directory domain to which you are connected.

Binding to a User Account Object

Complete one of the following steps to add the appropriate binding code line into ModifyUser.vbs:

- If the account object is located in the HR OU of the na.fabrikam.com domain, start with the following code statement:

```
Set objUser = _
    GetObject("LDAP://cn=MyerKen,ou=HR,dc=NA,dc=fabrikam,dc=com")
```

  If you have created an OU of a different name and you do not have a domain named na.fabrikam.com, use the code in this step but change the DN to the Active Directory container where for the test account named MyerKen. For example, if your domain is named contoso.com and the OU that contains the MyerKen user account is named Test, the code statement is:

```
Set objUser = _
    GetObject("LDAP://cn=MyerKen,ou=Test,dc=contoso,dc=com")
```

- If you have created a test user account named MyerKen in the Users container in an Active Directory domain to which you are currently connected, start with the following code statement:

```
Set objRootDSE = GetObject("LDAP://rootDSE")
Set objUser = GetObject("LDAP://cn=MyerKen,cn=Users," & _
    objRootDSE.Get("defaultNamingContext"))
```

This code is similar to the code in Listing 5.1 that is used to bind to Active Directory.

Writing or Modifying Attributes

To complete this procedure, you need to determine the lDAPDisplayNames of the attributes you want to write to the user account object. Figure 5.5 shows the General Properties page of the MyerKen user account and the corresponding lDAPDisplayName of each attribute that appears as a label on the page.

Figure 5.5   General Properties Page of the MyerKen User Account Object

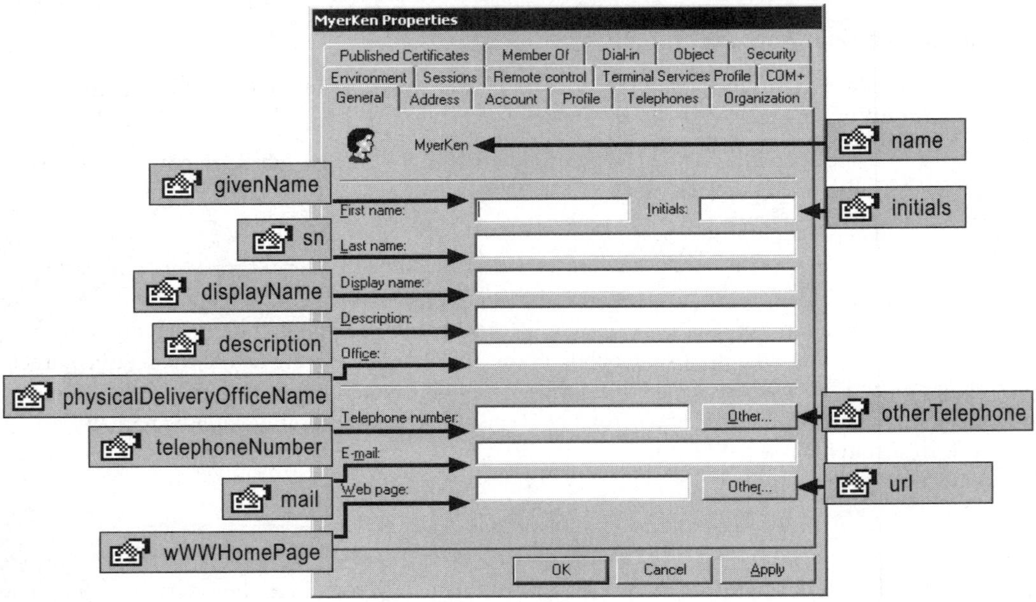

Notice that there is no attribute with an lDAPDisplayName of First name or Last name. Thus the labels on the property pages of an Active Directory object are an unreliable information source for determining lDAPDisplayNames.

There are other ways you can refer to an Active Directory object's attributes in ADSI scripts, but the most consistent approach is by using their lDAPDisplayName. This is also the only way that enables you to write an attribute using the Put method.

To keep this procedure as straightforward as possible, the attributes that can contain more than one value (called multivalued attributes) will not be modified in the script. These are the otherTelephone and url attributes. For information about writing and reading multivalued attributes, see "Administering Multivalued Attributes" later in this chapter.

1. To create code that writes or modifies attributes of a user account object, place the following code below the lines of code that bind to the user account object:

```
objUser.Put "givenName", "Ken"
objUser.Put "initials", "E."
objUser.Put "sn", "Myer"
objUser.Put "displayName", "Myer, Ken"
objUser.Put "description", "HR employee"
objUser.Put "physicalDeliveryOfficeName", "Room 4358"
objUser.Put "telephoneNumber", "(425) 707-9790"
objUser.Put "mail", "myerken@fabrikam.com"
objUser.Put "wWWHomePage", "http://www.fabrikam.com"
```

2. To create code that saves the modifications back to the corresponding object in Active Directory, place the following code statement below the lines of code in the previous step:

```
objUser.SetInfo
```

Reading and Displaying the Modified Attributes

After the script modifies the user account object in Active Directory, you can either review the settings on the General Properties page of the MyerKen user account or add to the ADSI script so that it reads and displays the modifications.

- To create code that reads the attributes modified in the Writing or Modifying Attributes procedure, copy and paste the following code into ModifyUser.vbs below the line of code containing the SetInfo method call:

```
strGivenName = objUser.Get("givenName")
strInitials = objUser.Get("initials")
strSn = objUser.Get("sn")
strDisplayName = objUser.Get("displayName")
strPhysicalDeliveryOfficeName = _
    objUser.Get("physicalDeliveryOfficeName")
strTelephoneNumber = objUser.Get("telephoneNumber")
strMail = objUser.Get("mail")
strWwwHomePage = objUser.Get("wWWHomePage")
```

- To create code that displays the modified attributes, copy and paste the following code into ModifyUser.vbs below the lines of code in the preceding step:

```
Wscript.Echo "givenName: " & strGivenName
Wscript.Echo "initials: " & strInitials
Wscript.Echo "sn: " & strSn
Wscript.Echo "displayName: " & strDisplayName
Wscript.Echo "physicalDeliveryOfficeName: " & _
    strPhysicalDeliveryOfficeName
Wscript.Echo "telephoneNumber: " & strTelephoneNumber
Wscript.Echo "mail: " & strMail
```

Advanced ADSI Scripting Operations

There are a number of Active Directory administration tasks that go beyond performing basic create, modify, read, and delete operations. Some of the other administrative tasks you can perform with ADSI scripts are:

- Administering multivalued attributes.
- Copying, moving, and renaming objects.
- Data caching.
- Searching.
- Enumerating Active Directory objects in containers.
- Using the Root Directory Service Entry.

Administering Multivalued Attributes

The scripts earlier in this chapter, including the procedures in "Performing Multiple Scripting Tasks," demonstrated how to read and write single-valued attributes. However, single-valued attributes cannot hold multiple records that are required for storing certain types of information. Multivalued attributes accommodate list type information. The attribute that contains a list of bridgehead servers configured in a domain, the attribute that contains a list of members in a group, and the attribute that contains a list of secondary telephone numbers for a user account are all examples of multivalued attributes.

 Note

For information about how to determine whether an attribute is single-valued or multivalued, see "Active Directory Architecture" later in this chapter.

Modifying and reading a multivalued attribute is similar to modifying and reading a single-valued attribute: the script binds to an object, uses a method to perform the modify or read task on an attribute, and, for the modify task, uses the SetInfo method to commit the change to Active Directory.

Modifying Multivalued Attributes

When an attribute can contain multiple values or entries, there are a number of possible modifications:

- **Clear all entries.** Clearing all entries removes the attribute from the target object. From the perspective of an ADSI script, when the attribute contains no values it is no longer a part of the object.

- **Update all entries.** Updating all entries removes any existing entries and then writes one or more new entries to the attribute.

- **Append an entry.** Appending an entry adds one or more values to the attribute while preserving any existing entries.

- **Delete an entry.** Deleting an entry removes one or more values from the attribute while preserving any other existing entries.

Regardless of the type of multivalued attribute modification you want to make, you can use the PutEx method to make the modification. When you call the PutEx method in a script, the first parameter (also known as an *argument*) of the method designates the type of update you want to make, the second argument designates the attribute to be modified, and the third argument designates the values to set. Table 5.2 shows the arguments of the PutEx method.

Table 5.2 PutEx Arguments

Argument	Type	Required	Default	Description
Control Code	Integer (long)	Yes	None	The value 1 clears all entries, the value 2 updates all entries, the value 3 appends one or more entries, and the value 4 deletes one or more entries.
Attribute	String	Yes	None	The lDAPDisplayName of the attribute to be modified.
Value	Variant (array)	Yes	None	To update, append, or delete entries, surround each value with quotes and, if specifying multiple values, delimit each value with a comma. To clear an attribute, set this parameter to 0.

Tip

To make your ADSI scripts easier to read, use constants to designate the values of the PutEx control code parameter. The constants are:

- ADS_PROPERTY_CLEAR = 1
- ADS_PROPERTY_UPDATE = 2
- ADS_PROPERTY_APPEND = 3
- ADS_PROPERTY_DELETE = 4

One or more of these constants appears in all scripts in this chapter that use the PutEx method.

Modifying multivalued attributes of Active Directory objects involves three basic steps. Note that defining a constant for the control code parameter is optional, so it does not appear in the following steps.

1. Bind to the Active Directory object you want to modify.

2. Perform clear, update, add, or delete operations on one or more of an object's multivalued attributes.

3. Commit the change to Active Directory.

The goal of the first four scripts that appear in this section is to manage group membership by modifying the member multivalued attribute of the Atl-Users global group. The attribute will be modified by updating all members, adding a member, deleting a member, and clearing all members, in that order. The fifth script in this section shows how to update multivalued attributes of a user account object. The purpose of this script is to demonstrate how administering multivalued attributes is similar from one object to the next.

Restrictions in performing modifications by using the PutEx method

PutEx does not allow you to add duplicate entries to a multivalued attribute. For example, you cannot add duplicate telephone numbers to the otherTelephone attribute of a user account object or add duplicate user accounts to the member attribute of a group object. PutEx does not report an error if a script attempts to add a duplicate entry. However, when the SetInfo method is called, the script will fail and report that the object already exists.

PutEx will report an error if you attempt any attribute modification and specify a nonexistent object for an object-dependent entry. That is, if the entry a script attempts to add specifies an Active Directory object that does not exist, the script will end and report that there is no such object on the server. For example, if a script attempts to add the distinguished name of a user account to a Group but the user account object does not exist, the script will fail.

PutEx also does not require an entry to be present to attempt a delete operation. If a script specifies a nonexistent value to delete, PutEx will run normally but will not report an error. However, when the SetInfo method is called, the script will fail and report that the server is unwilling to process the request.

In the following listings, all PutEx operations are committed by a single SetInfo method call. However, whenever you perform more than one operation on the same multivalued attribute, commit the change for each operation before continuing to the next operation. Consider the following code example:

```
objUser.PutEx ADS_PROPERTY_DELETE, "otherTelephone", Array("707-9790")
objUser.PutEx ADS_PROPERTY_APPEND, "otherTelephone", Array("707-9799")
objUser.SetInfo
```

The number 707-9799 is added as an entry to the otherTelephone attribute when SetInfo is called, but the number 707-9790 is not deleted. To commit both changes to the directory, use this code instead:

```
objUser.PutEx ADS_PROPERTY_DELETE, "otherTelephone", Array("707-9790")
objUser.SetInfo
objUser.PutEx ADS_PROPERTY_APPEND, "otherTelephone", Array("707-9799")
objUser.SetInfo
```

Another important nuance of using PutEx is that the order of the entries stored in multivalued attributes is not guaranteed. Therefore, whenever you write scripts that operate on multivalued attributes, do not depend on a specific ordering of entries.

Clearing multivalued and single-valued attributes with the PutEx method

Using the PutEx method to clear attributes applies to both single and multivalued attributes. It is important for single-valued attributes because the Put method cannot completely clear an attribute. For example, you cannot specify NULL or "" for an attribute's value when calling Put. In addition, although the following code will work to update the telephoneNumber attribute, the resulting telephoneNumber attribute is not empty. Instead, it contains a single space.

```
objUser.Put "telephoneNumber", " "
```

Therefore, PutEx is the only method capable of completely clearing one or more entries from an attribute.

Updating a Multivalued Attribute of a Group

The script in Listing 5.14 modifies the member attribute of the group named Atl-Users. The member attribute is updated so that it contains two members. To carry out this task, the script performs the following steps:

1. Set the ADS_PROPERTY_UPDATE constant equal to the control code parameter used by the PutEx method to indicate this mode of modification (used in lines 5–9).

   This control code replaces any existing entries in a multivalued attribute.

2. Bind to the Atl-Users group in the HR OU of the na.fabrikam.com domain.

3. Update the object's member attribute by assigning the distinguished names of the MyerKen and LewJudy user accounts to it. Because PutEx is designed to work with multiple attributes, the two user accounts must be passed to the method in an array.

    Notice that the MyerKen user account is located in the HR OU and the LewJudy user account is located in the Sales OU, both in the na.fabrikam.com domain.

4. Commit the change to the group in Active Directory.

    Because an update operation is specified in the script, any existing members of the Atl-Users group are removed.

Listing 5.14   Updating the member Attribute of a Group

```
1   Const ADS_PROPERTY_UPDATE = 2
2   Set objGroup = GetObject _
3       ("LDAP://cn=Atl-Users,ou=HR,dc=NA,dc=fabrikam,dc=com")
4
5   objGroup.PutEx ADS_PROPERTY_UPDATE, _
6       "member", Array("cn=MyerKen,ou=HR,dc=NA,dc=fabrikam,dc=com", _
7           "cn=LewJudy,ou=Sales,dc=NA,dc=fabrikam,dc=com")
8
9   objGroup.SetInfo
```

Appending an Entry to a Multivalued Attribute of a Group

The script in Listing 5.15 appends an entry to the member attribute of the group named Atl-Users. Assuming that the script in Listing 5.14 has been run, the script in Listing 5.15 appends an entry to the member attribute so that it contains a third member. To carry out this task, the script performs the following steps:

1. Set the ADS_PROPERTY_APPEND constant equal to the control code parameter used by the PutEx method to indicate this mode of modification (used in lines 5–8).

    This control code adds one or more entries to a multivalued attribute.

2. Bind to the Atl-Users group in the HR OU of the na.fabrikam.com domain.

3. Append an entry to the object's member attribute by specifying the ADS_PROPERTY_APPEND constant, the member attribute, and the distinguished name of the YoungRob user account object.

    Notice that the YoungRob user account is located in the R&D OU in the na.fabrikam.com domain.

4.   Commit the change to the group in Active Directory.

Because an append operation is specified in the script, any existing members of the Atl-Users group are preserved.

Listing 5.15   Appending an Entry to the member Attribute of a Group

```
1  Const ADS_PROPERTY_APPEND = 3
2  Set objGroup = GetObject _
3      ("LDAP://cn=Atl-Users,ou=HR,dc=NA,dc=fabrikam,dc=com")
4
5  objGroup.PutEx ADS_PROPERTY_APPEND, _
6      "member", Array("cn=YoungRob,ou=R&D,dc=NA,dc=fabrikam,dc=com")
7
8  objGroup.SetInfo
```

Deleting an Entry from a Multivalued Attribute of a Group

The script in Listing 5.16 deletes an entry from the member attribute of the group named Atl-Users. Assuming that the scripts in Listing 5.14 and Listing 5.15 are run, the script in Listing 5.16 deletes an entry from the member attribute so that only two members remain. To carry out this task, the script performs the following steps:

1.   Set the ADS_PROPERTY_DELETE constant equal to the control code parameter used by the PutEx method to indicate this mode of modification (used in lines 5–8).

This control code deletes one or more entries from a multivalued attribute.

2.   Bind to the Atl-Users group in the HR OU of the na.fabrikam.com domain.

3.   Delete an entry from the object's member attribute by specifying the ADS_PROPERTY_DELETE constant, the member attribute, and the distinguished name of the MyerKen user account object.

4.   Commit the change to the group in Active Directory.

Because a delete operation is specified in the script, any existing members of the Atl-Users group are preserved except for the MyerKen user account.

Listing 5.16   Deleting an Entry from the member Attribute of a Group

```
1  Const ADS_PROPERTY_DELETE = 4
2  Set objGroup = GetObject _
3      ("LDAP://cn=Atl-Users,OU=HR,dc=NA,dc=fabrikam,dc=com")
4
5  objGroup.PutEx ADS_PROPERTY_DELETE, _
6      "member", Array("cn=MyerKen,ou=HR,dc=NA,dc=fabrikam,dc=com")
7
8  objGroup.SetInfo
```

Clearing a Multivalued Attribute of a Group

The script in Listing 5.17 clears the member attribute of the group named Atl-Users. To carry out this task, the script performs the following steps:

1. Set the ADS_PROPERTY_CLEAR constant equal to the control code parameter used by the PutEx method to indicate this mode of modification (used in line 5).

    This control code clears a multivalued attribute so that, from the script's perspective, the attribute is empty and thus is no longer associated with the object.

2. Bind to the Atl-Users group in the HR OU of the na.fabrikam.com domain.

3. Clear the object's member attribute so that it is empty.

    Notice that the last parameter is set to 0. This value is necessary and must be specified in order to successfully clear an attribute.

4. Commit the change to the group in Active Directory.

Listing 5.17   Clearing the member Attribute of a Group

```
1  Const ADS_PROPERTY_CLEAR = 1
2  Set objGroup = GetObject _
3     ("LDAP://cn=Atl-Users,ou=HR,dc=NA,dc=fabrikam,dc=com")
4
5  objGroup.PutEx ADS_PROPERTY_CLEAR,"member", 0
6
7  objGroup.SetInfo
```

Updating Multivalued Attributes of a User Account

Regardless of the Active Directory object, the way that you modify the multivalued attributes of an object is the same. To demonstrate this uniformity, the script in Listing 5.18 updates the url and otherTelephone multivalued attributes of the MyerKen user account. To carry out this task, the script performs the following steps:

1. Set the ADS_PROPERTY_UPDATE constant equal to the control code parameter used by the PutEx method to indicate this mode of modification (used in lines 5–10 and lines 12 and 13).

2. Bind to the MyerKen user account in the HR OU of the na.fabrikam.com domain.

3. Update the object's url and otherTelephone attributes by assigning values to them.

   Notice that the values for the url attribute are in the form of Web addresses and that the values for the otherTelephone attribute are in the form of telephone numbers. However, unlike the member attribute of a group object, these attributes are not limited to specific string formats. In other words, you can insert values that do not comply with any defined format for a url or a telephone number.

4. Commit the change to the group in Active Directory.

   Because an update operation is specified in the script, any existing values for these two attributes are removed.

Listing 5.18 Updating the url and otherTelephone Attributes of a User Account

```
1    Const ADS_PROPERTY_UPDATE = 2
2    Set objGroup = GetObject _
3       ("LDAP://cn=MyerKen,ou=HR,dc=NA,dc=fabrikam,dc=com")
4
5    objGroup.PutEx ADS_PROPERTY_UPDATE, _
6       "url", Array("http://www.microsoft.com", _
7            "http://www.fabrikam.com/na","http://www.contoso.com")
8
9    objGroup.PutEx ADS_PROPERTY_UPDATE, _
10      "otherTelephone", Array("707-9790", "707-9791", "707-9792")
11
12   objGroup.SetInfo
```

Important observations about the scripts in this section are:

- They perform the same basic steps: They bind to an Active Directory object, modify a multivalued attribute of the object, and write the change to the corresponding Active Directory object.

- They use the same method (PutEx) without regard to the class of object being modified.

  The PutEx method is similar to the Put method except that it requires a control code parameter to specify the type of modify operation.

Reading Multivalued Attributes

Because a multivalued attribute of an object can contain more than one value, you use the GetEx method to retrieve all values of the attribute. The information retrieved from GetEx is returned in the form of a variant array. An *array* is a data structure containing one or more values, and a *variant* is a data structure containing any data type, such as a string or an integer. Thus a *variant array* is a data structure containing one or more values of any type.

 Important

The Get method can also return entries in a multivalued attribute, but as a general rule, use Get for single-valued attributes only. For more information, see the section "Data Caching."

To display the values in an array, you must add script code that is able to iterate through the array of values. Use the VBScript For Each statement to accomplish this task.

Even with the additional scripting code (that is, the For Each statement) that you must add to read a multivalued attribute, reading this type of attribute involves the same two steps outlined in "Reading Attributes of Directory Service Objects" earlier in this chapter:

1. Connect to the Active Directory object you want to read.

2. Read one or more of the object's attributes.

   The difference in this step is that you use the GetEx method instead of the Get method to complete the read operation and you use a For Each statement to display each value contained in the attribute.

The goal of the scripts in this section is to read and display the member attribute of the Atl-Users group and the url and otherTelephone attributes of the MyerKen user account. These attributes were modified in "Modifying Multivalued Attributes" earlier in this chapter.

Reading a Multivalued Attribute of a Group

The script in Listing 5.19 reads and displays the entries in the member attribute of the Atl-Users group. If you ran the scripts in the preceding section, the member attribute is now empty. Therefore, rerun the script in Listing 5.14 before running this script.

1. Connect to the Atl-Users group in the HR OU of the na.fabrikam.com domain.

2. Use a For Each statement to read and display the object's member attribute.

Listing 5.19   Reading the member Attribute of an OU

```
1   Set objGroup = GetObject _
2       ("LDAP://cn=Atl-Users,ou=HR,dc=NA,dc=fabrikam,dc=com")
3
4   For Each Member in objGroup.GetEx("member")
5       Wscript.Echo Member
6   Next
```

When this script runs in the na.fabrikam.com domain, it echoes the members of the Atl-Users group to the command window, as shown:

```
CN=LewJudy,OU=Sales,dc=NA,DC=fabrikam,DC=com
CN=MyerKen,OU=HR,dc=NA,DC=fabrikam,DC=com
```

Reading Multivalued Attributes of a User Account

The script in Listing 5.20 reads and displays the entries in the url and otherTelephone attributes of the MyerKen user account.

1. Connect to the MyerKen user account in the HR OU of the na.fabrikam.com domain.

2. Use a For Each statement to read and display the object's url attribute.

3. Use another For Each statement to read and display the object's otherTelephone attribute.

Listing 5.20   Reading the url and otherTelephone Attributes of a User Account

```
1   Set objGroup = GetObject _
2       ("LDAP://cn=MyerKen,ou=HR,dc=NA,dc=fabrikam,dc=com")
3
4   For Each url in objGroup.GetEx("url")
5       Wscript.Echo url
6   Next
7
8   For Each otherTelephone in objGroup.GetEx("otherTelephone")
9       Wscript.Echo otherTelephone
10  Next
```

When this script runs in the na.fabrikam.com domain, it echoes the url and otherTelephone attributes of the MyerKen user account to the command window, as shown:

```
http://www.contoso.com
http://www.fabrikam.com/na
http://www.microsoft.com
707-9792
707-9791
707-9790
```

Important observations about the scripts in this section are:

- They perform the same basic steps: they bind to an Active Directory object and use a For Each statement to read the entries contained in multivalued attributes.

- They use the same method (GetEx) without regard to the class of object being read.

  The GetEx method is similar to the Get method except that you must use a For Each statement to read and display an attribute's values.

Data Caching

Thus far, little has been said about how ADSI scripts use the local property cache to complete read operations. You know from the preceding sections that you use either the Get or the GetEx method to perform read operations. Behind the scenes, both of these methods make implicit calls to the GetInfo method to retrieve attributes from Active Directory and load them into the local property cache. You can make an explicit call to GetInfo or use another method, GetInfoEx, to take control of the data loaded into the local property cache. For more information about the local property cache, see "Step 2: Performing a Task" earlier in this chapter.

Understanding how these four method calls interact with the local property cache will help you avoid accidentally overwriting values, and it can also help you make scripts operate more efficiently.

How the Get Method Retrieves Attributes

The Get method retrieves the value or values of attributes from the local property cache as either a string or a variant array, depending on the type of attribute and its contents:

- **Single-valued attributes.** Get returns a string value.

- **Multivalued attributes containing a single entry.** Get returns a string value.

- **Multivalued attributes containing more than one entry.** Get returns a variant array of values.

 Important

An attribute that does not contain a value is not considered by ADSI to be associated with an Active Directory object. Therefore, empty attributes are never downloaded to the local property cache.

All of the preceding examples suggest that you should always use Get for single-valued attributes and GetEx for multivalued attributes. Following this rule will simplify the scripting process because then you will not have to determine whether the values are returned as a string or a variant array. However, if you do know whether your target attribute is single-valued or multivalued and you know how many values an attribute contains, using Get is slightly more efficient than GetEx.

If the attribute is not already loaded into the local property cache, the Get method implicitly calls the GetInfo method. As a result, GetInfo loads most attributes into the local property cache, with the exception of operational attributes and attributes that have already been downloaded to the cache.

Operational attributes are attributes whose values are not stored in a directory service but are calculated by the domain controller when they are requested. For example, canonicalName is an operational attribute. Operational attributes are synonymous with constructed attributes.

If you use the Get method again in a script, the specific attribute requested will be retrieved from the property cache without any additional calls to the GetInfo method. Therefore, attribute values that already exist in the local property cache will not be overwritten by an implicit call to the GetInfo method.

How the GetEx Method Retrieves Attributes

The GetEx method always returns the value or values of the specified attribute from the property cache in a variant array. Thus, you must always use a statement such as For Each to read even a single-valued attribute. However, if you do not know whether an attribute is single-valued or multivalued, GetEx can be easier to use than Get because all returned data is packaged in a variant array. This means you can handle all attribute data using the same approach.

If the attribute is not already loaded into the local property cache, the GetEx method implicitly calls the GetInfo method to load all attributes of an object. Attribute values that already exist in the local property cache will not be overwritten by the implicit call to the GetInfo method.

Making Explicit Calls by Using the GetInfo Method

You can explicitly call the GetInfo method to load or refresh the local property cache. When called explicitly, this method retrieves all attributes (except for operational attributes) associated with an object from Active Directory and loads them into the local property cache. Call the GetInfo method if you need to be sure that the attribute values in the local property cache are the same as the attribute values of the corresponding Active Directory object.

The syntax for the GetInfo method is:

`object.GetInfo`

The script in Listing 5.21 downloads most attributes of a group object named Atl-Users.

1. Bind to the Atl-Users group in the HR OU of the na.fabrikam.com domain.

2. Use the GetInfo method to explicitly download most of the group's attributes into the local property cache.

Listing 5.21 Making an Explicit Call to GetInfo

```
1  Set objGroup = _
2     GetObject("LDAP://cn=Atl-Users,ou=HR,dc=NA,dc=fabrikam,dc=com")
3  objGroup.GetInfo
```

Exercise caution when explicitly calling the GetInfo method because any modification made to attributes in the local property cache are lost if the SetInfo method is not called before the local property cache is refreshed with GetInfo. For example, line 2 of the following code writes the value Human Resources to the description attribute in the local property cache. Line 3 then commits the value to the description attribute of the HR OU in Active Directory.

```
1  Set objOU = GetObject("LDAP://ou=HR,dc=NA,dc=fabrikam,dc=com")
2  objOU.Put "description", "Human Resources"
3  objOU.SetInfo
```

However, you might add the GetInfo method in the following way:

```
1  Set objOU = GetObject("LDAP://ou=HR,dc=NA,dc=fabrikam,dc=com")
2  objOU.Put "description", "Human Resources"
3  objOU.GetInfo
4  objOU.SetInfo
```

Line 2 still writes the value Human Resources to the description attribute, but then line 3 refreshes the local property cache, thereby overwriting the value Human Resources in the cache. In contrast, if GetInfo is called implicitly (using Get or GetEx), attribute values already in the local property cache are not overwritten. The only exception to this is if you use Get or GetEx to download the specific attribute that you are modifying in the previous step. This, of course, defeats the purpose of modifying the attribute.

Making Explicit Calls by Using the GetInfoEx Method

Rather than download most attributes of an object, you can selectively load or refresh the local property cache with a specific attribute or set of attributes by using the GetInfoEx method. In addition, you must use this method to download operational attributes.

Using GetInfoEx is an ideal approach to working with attributes if you want to minimize the load placed on the domain controller servicing the request and the minimize network traffic that results from downloading attributes.

The syntax for this method is:

object.**GetInfoEx** *Attributes,* **0**

The Attributes parameter of GetInfoEx is an array containing the lDAPDisplayName of each attribute. The second parameter (0) is reserved and must be specified when calling the GetInfoEx method.

You can initialize a variable with an array containing the lDAPDisplayName of one or more attributes and then use that variable in the GetInfoEx call. The script in Listing 5.22 downloads two attributes, description and dnsHostName, of a computer object named SEA-SQL-01.

1. Bind to the SEA-SQL-01 computer in the Computers container of the na.fabrikam.com domain.

2. Initialize a variable named arrAttributes with an array containing the lDAPDisplayName of two attributes, description and dnsHostName (line 3).

3. Use the GetInfoEx method to explicitly download attributes specified in the arrAttributes variable into the local property cache (line 4).

The attributes downloaded are the two specified in the arrAttributes variable in line 3.

Listing 5.22 Making an Explicit Call to GetInfoEx

```
1   Set objComputer = GetObject _
2       ("LDAP://cn=SEA-SQL-01,cn=Computers,dc=NA,dc=fabrikam,dc=com")
3   arrAttributes = Array("description", "dnsHostName")
4   objComputer.GetInfoEx arrAttributes, 0
```

As with the GetInfo method, you must exercise caution when combining the GetInfoEx method with a script that modifies the attributes that GetInfoEx downloads. Modifications to attributes are lost if the SetInfo method is not called before the local property cache is refreshed with GetInfoEx.

For example, lines 3 and 4 of the following code write values to the description and dnsHostName attributes in the local property cache. However, the values are overwritten when these attributes are refreshed using the GetInfoEx method in line 7. When the SetInfo method is called in line 8, the values of the two attributes downloaded by GetInfoEx are written back to Active Directory instead of the values assigned in lines 3 and 4.

```
1   Set objComputer = GetObject _
2       ("LDAP://cn=SEA-SQL-01,cn=Computers,dc=NA,dc=fabrikam,dc=com")
3   objComputer.Put "description", "SQL Computer 1"
4   objComputer.Put "dnsHostName", "sea-sql-01.na.fabrikam.com"
5
6   arrAttributes = Array("description", "dnsHostName")
7   objComputer.GetInfoEx arrAttributes, 0
8   objComputer.SetInfo
```

By moving line 8 (the SetInfo method call) up to line 5, the two attributes written to the local property cache by the Put method calls are committed to Active Directory. When GetInfoEx selectively refreshes the cache in line 7, the values match those previously written to the cache by the Put method calls.

Copying, Moving, and Renaming Objects

In the management life cycle of Active Directory objects, common tasks not part of the four primary administrative tasks (create, delete, read, and modify) include copying, moving, and renaming. For example, you can copy objects to speed object creation, move objects if you need to delete a container but preserve its contents, and rename objects to comply with new company naming standards.

Copying Objects

To copy an object, you need a source object from which to make a copy. You must also determine which attributes of the source object you want to duplicate in the target object (the copy).

To copy an object, you simply combine some of the primary tasks covered earlier in this chapter:

1. Complete the create task to create the target object.

    For task details, see "Creating Directory Service Objects" earlier in this chapter.

2. Complete the read task to obtain attributes from the source object that should be copied to the target object.

    For task details, see "Reading Attributes of Directory Service Objects" and "Reading Multivalued Attributes" earlier in this chapter.

3. Complete the modify task to write selected attributes to the target object.

    For task details, see "Modifying Directory Service Objects" and "Modifying Multivalued Attributes" earlier in this chapter.

The goal of the scripts in this section is to demonstrate how to copy objects. The first example copies a source computer object to a target computer object. This example demonstrates that ADSI scripts work with other Active Directory objects besides users, groups, and OUs. The second example copies a source user account to a target user account. This example demonstrates how to copy both single-valued and multivalued attributes.

Copying a Computer Account

The script in Listing 5.23 copies selected attributes from a computer account named SEA-PM-01 to a new computer account named SEA-SQL-01. The account to be used as a template (SEA-PM-01) is located in the Computers container of the na.fabrikam.com domain. When the new computer account (SEA-SQL-01) is created, it will also be located in the Computers container.

1. Bind to the Computers container in the na.fabrikam.com domain.

    Notice that the Computers container has the attribute type CN. Except for the Domain Controllers container, all built-in containers directly below an Active Directory domain have the attribute type CN rather than OU.

2. Create a computer object named sea-sql-01.

3. Set the sAMAccountName mandatory attribute to the value sea-sql-01.

4. Commit the new computer object to Active Directory.

    This step completes the task of creating the new computer object.

5. Bind to the SEA-PM-01 computer object in the Computers container of the na.fabrikam.com domain.

    This computer object serves as the template object from which attributes are derived for the copy operation.

6. Create an array named arrAttributes that contains the lDAPDisplayNames of the optional attributes that will be applied to the new computer object.

7. Use a For Each statement to loop through the lDAPDisplayNames of the attributes specified in the array.

    a. Read each attribute from the computer object serving as the template.

        This step completes the task of reading the template computer object.

    b. Write the attributes to the new computer object.

8. Commit the change to the new computer object in Active Directory.

    This step completes the task of modifying the new computer object. Notice that it was not necessary to bind again to the new computer object. The binding operation completed in line 2 provided the necessary connection to the new computer object.

Listing 5.23 Copying a Computer Object

```
1   Set objCompt = GetObject("LDAP://cn=Computers,dc=NA,dc=fabrikam,dc=com")
2   Set objComptCopy = objCompt.Create("computer", "cn=SEA-SQL-01")
3   objComptCopy.Put "sAMAccountName", "sea-sql-01"
4   objComptCopy.SetInfo
5
6   Set objComptTemplate = _
7       GetObject("LDAP://cn=SEA-PM-01,cn=Computers,dc=NA,dc=fabrikam,dc=com")
8   arrAttributes = Array("description", "location")
9
10  For Each strAttrib in arrAttributes
11      strValue = objComptTemplate.Get(strAttrib)
12      objComptCopy.Put strAttrib, strValue
13  Next
14
15  objComptCopy.SetInfo
```

Listing 5.23 demonstrated how to copy two attributes from one object to another. However, many more attributes can be copied. The purpose of the preceding listing was simply to show how you can perform a copy operation by writing attributes from one object to another. In fact, you can copy both single-valued and multivalued attributes from one object to another, as the next listing demonstrates.

Copying a User Account

The script in Listing 5.24 copies selected single-valued and multivalued attributes from a user account named HuffArlene to a new user account named BarrAdam. The user account to be used as a template (HuffArlene) is located in the HR OU of the na.fabrikam.com domain. When the new user account (BarrAdam) is created, it will also be located in the HR OU.

1. Set the ADS_PROPERTY_UPDATE constant equal to the control code parameter used by the PutEx method to indicate this mode of modification (used in line 21).

2. Bind to the HR OU in the na.fabrikam.com domain.

3. Create a user account named BarrAdam.

4. Set the sAMAccountName mandatory attribute to the value barradam.

5. Commit the new user account to Active Directory.

6. Bind to the HuffArlene user account in the HR OU of the na.fabrikam.com domain.

7. Create an array named arrSVAttributes that contains the lDAPDisplayNames of the optional single-valued attributes that will be applied to the new user account.

8. Create another array named arrMVAttributes that contains the lDAPDisplayNames of the optional multivalued attributes that will be applied to the new user account.

9. Use a For Each statement to iterate through the lDAPDisplayNames of the attributes specified in the arrSVAttributes array.

    Within the loop, use the Get method to read each attribute from the template user account and use the Put method to write it to the new user account.

10. Use another For Each statement to iterate through the lDAPDisplayNames of the attributes specified in the arrMVAttributes array.

Within the loop, use the GetEx method to read each attribute from the template user account and use the PutEx method to write it to the new user account.

11. Commit the changes to the new user account in Active Directory.

Listing 5.24   Copying a User Account

```
1   Const ADS_PROPERTY_UPDATE = 2
2   Set objOU = GetObject("LDAP://OU=HR,dc=NA,dc=fabrikam,dc=com")
3   Set objUserCopy = objOU.Create("user", "cn=BarrAdam")
4   objUserCopy.Put "sAMAccountName", "barradam"
5   objUserCopy.SetInfo
6
7   Set objUserTemplate = _
8       GetObject("LDAP://cn=HuffArlene,ou=HR,dc=NA,dc=fabrikam,dc=com")
9
10  arrSVAttributes = Array("description", "department", _
11      "company", "wWWHomePage")
12  arrMVAttributes = Array("url", "otherTelephone")
13
14  For Each strAttrib in arrSVAttributes
15      strValue = objUserTemplate.Get(strAttrib)
16      objUserCopy.Put strAttrib, strValue
17  Next
18
19  For Each strAttrib in arrMVAttributes
20      arrValue = objUserTemplate.GetEx(strAttrib)
21      objUserCopy.PutEx ADS_PROPERTY_UPDATE, strAttrib, arrValue
22  Next
23
24  objUserCopy.SetInfo
```

Important observations about the scripts in this section are:

- Copying an Active Directory object involves the following three tasks: Create an object, read attributes from a different object, and write the attributes to the new object.

- No method is available to the LDAP provider for directly performing the copy task.

Moving and Renaming Objects

The move and rename tasks use the same method, MoveHere, to complete their respective operations. Unlike the copy task, the move and rename tasks are relatively simple to complete with an ADSI script. The MoveHere method supports the following Active Directory move and rename operations:

- Moving an object to a different container within the same domain
- Renaming an object within the same container
- Renaming and moving an object to a different container within the same domain
- Moving an object to another domain
- Renaming an object while moving it to another domain

You cannot use the MoveHere method to move an object to another forest.

General Conditions for Cross-Domain Moves

There are some object-specific restrictions to making cross-domain moves. However, moving an object to other domains within the same forest is possible when the following general conditions are met:

- The destination domain is running in native mode.
- Both the destination and the source domain use Kerberos authentication.
- The move operation must be completed from the source domain to the destination, or target, domain. If you attempt to move an object while logged on to the destination domain, the following message will appear:

```
(null): Inappropriate authentication
```

- To move an object from one domain to another, you must have permission to remove the object from the source domain and add the object to the target domain.
- Only leaf objects can be moved. Therefore, if the object is a container, make sure it is empty before attempting to move it to another domain.
- Security principals, such as users, groups, and computers cannot be moved to another domain if they are members of one or more global groups. They must first be removed from all global groups.

When you call the MoveHere method in a script, the first parameter of the method designates the ADsPath of the move or rename operation. The DN in the ADsPath designates where the object currently resides. The second argument designates the relative distinguished name of the object to be moved or the new name of the object to be renamed. If your intention is simply to move and not rename the object, the second parameter can be specified as vbNullString. Table 5.3 shows the arguments of the MoveHere method.

Table 5.3   MoveHere Arguments

Argument	Type	Required	Default	Description
ADsPath	string	Yes	None	The name of the provider and the DN of the source object to move or rename.
RelativeDistinguish edName	string	Yes	None	The cn=name attribute of the user account object to be moved or the new name of the user account to be renamed. If you are not renaming the account, you can specify vbNullString instead.

Regardless of the move or rename task you want to complete, both tasks involve two simple steps:

1. Bind to the Active Directory container that is the target of the object move or rename operation.

2. Move or rename the object.

   Like the Delete method, the MoveHere method acts immediately upon Active Directory. Therefore, there is no need to call the SetInfo method to complete a rename or move operation.

The goal of the three scripts in this section is to rename a published printer, move a group from one OU to another within the same domain, and move an OU from one domain to another. These three objects and tasks provide a good sampling of what can be done with the MoveHere method. For more information about how to complete object-specific move operations, see the ADSI task-based chapters in this book.

Renaming a Published Printer

The script in Listing 5.25 renames the Printer1 printer to HRPrn1. After the rename operation, the printer remains in the HR OU of the na.fabrikam.com domain.

1. Bind to the HR OU container in the na.fabrikam.com domain.

    This binding operation designates the HR OU as the target container of the rename operation.

2. Rename the Printer1 printer to HRPrn1.

    The first parameter of the MoveHere method specifies the ADsPath of the object to be renamed, the LDAP provider and the DN of Printer1. The second parameter specifies the new name for the printer.

Listing 5.25 Renaming a Published Printer

```
1   Set objOU = GetObject("LDAP://ou=HR,dc=NA,dc=fabrikam,dc=com")
2
3   objOU.MoveHere _
4       "LDAP://cn=Printer1,ou=HR,dc=NA,dc=fabrikam,dc=com", "cn=HRPrn1"
```

Moving a Group from One Container to Another

The script in Listing 5.26 moves the Atl-Users group from the HR OU to the Users container of the na.fabrikam.com domain. Note that the Atl-Users group is not modified in any way. All members of the group remain, and the group is not renamed.

1. Bind to the Users container in the na.fabrikam.com domain.

    This binding operation designates the Users container as the target container of the move operation.

2. Move the Atl-Users group from the HR OU to the Users container within the same domain.

The first parameter of the MoveHere method specifies the ADsPath of the object to be moved, the LDAP provider and the DN of the Atl-Users group. The second parameter specifies vbNullString because the group is not renamed during the move operation. Alternatively, you can specify the relative distinguished name (cn=Atl-Users) for the second parameter.

Listing 5.26 Moving a Group Within the Same Domain

```
1  Set objOU = GetObject("LDAP://cn=Users,dc=NA,dc=fabrikam,dc=com")
2
3  objOU.MoveHere "LDAP://cn=Atl-Users,ou=HR,dc=NA,dc=fabrikam,dc=com", _
4    vbNullString
```

> **Tip**
>
> It is easy to get confused about whether you specify the target or source container in the binding step. To remember that it is the target container that you specify in the binding step, ask yourself, "Where do I want the object to go?" After you have answered that question, specify that location in the binding step.

Moving an OU from One Domain to Another

The script in Listing 5.27 moves the Management OU from the fabrikam.com domain to the na.fabrikam.com domain.

1. Bind to the na.fabrikam.com domain.

This binding operation designates the na.fabrikam.com domain as the target container of the move operation.

2. Move the Management OU from the fabrikam.com domain to the na.fabrikam.com domain.

Listing 5.27 Performing a Cross-Domain Move of an OU

```
1  Set objDomain = GetObject("LDAP://dc=NA,dc=fabrikam,dc=com")
2
3  objDomain.MoveHere "LDAP://ou=Management,dc=fabrikam,dc=com", _
4    vbNullString
```

While the script in Listing 5.27 might appear useful, it is of limited use in its current form. A cross-domain move works only for leaf objects. Therefore, the OU must be empty before it can be moved. However, if you have assigned a number of attributes to the OU, it might make sense to move all of the objects in the container to the other domain, then move the OU, and finally move all of the objects back into the OU. For information about moving specific types of objects, such as user accounts, see the corresponding ADSI task-based chapter.

Important observations about the scripts in this section are:

- They perform the same basic steps: They bind to a target container and then call the MoveHere method to move or rename an object.

- They use the same method (MoveHere) without regard to the class of object or the operation (move or rename).

Searching

Although searching Active Directory is a useful administrative task in itself, it becomes even more powerful when the results of a search are combined with other administrative tasks. For example, you can search for all the user accounts in a domain and then use the results of the search to modify attributes that should be the same for all users, or verify that an Active Directory object does not already exist before attempting to create it.

The query technology available to VBScript is ActiveX® Data Objects (ADO). ADO uses the ADSI OLE DB provider to read information from Active Directory. OLE DB is a set of interfaces that provide access to all types of databases, including the Active Directory database. The information returned to ADO by the ADSI OLE DB provider is read-only. Thus, you cannot use ADO to modify the result set returned by a query. However, as the preceding paragraph explains, after the result set is returned, you can use ADSI methods to perform administrative tasks that go beyond returning a result set.

Returning a result set typically involves three ADO objects:

- **Connection.** This object provides a link between the ADSI script and Active Directory by loading the ADSI OLE DB provider.

- **Command.** This object enables the script to initiate a query against Active Directory and control various aspects of the search, such as the sort order.

- **RecordSet**. This object receives the query results from the Command object.

Searching Active Directory

The goal of performing a search is to return a result set containing zero or more records. A result set containing no records is useful if you are verifying that an object is not present before attempting to create it.

Searching for Active Directory objects involves the following steps:

1. Create an ADO Connection object and use the Open method of the object to access Active Directory with the ADSI OLE DB provider.

2. Create an ADO Command object, and assign the Command object's ActiveConnection property to the Connection object.

    This step is necessary because the Command object holds both the connection and the query string to run against Active Directory.

3. Assign a search request (query string) to the CommandText property of the Command object.

    You can use either SQL syntax or LDAP search dialect for the query string. All of the examples in this chapter use LDAP search dialect. For information about the SQL dialect for performing an Active Directory search, see the Active Directory Programmer's Guide link on the Web Resources page at http://www.microsoft.com/windows/reskits/webresources.

4. Using the Execute method of the Command object, run the query and store the results in a RecordSet object.

5. Using properties of the RecordSet object, read information in the result set.

6. Using the Connection object Close method, close the Connection.

    This final step is optional, but it is good practice to remove objects from memory when a script has finished using them. In much larger scripts that take time to complete, removing unused objects from memory saves resources.

The goal of the scripts in this section is to demonstrate how to construct Active Directory searches by using ADO and the ADSI OLE DB provider. In each case, the script includes the six steps just described for searching Active Directory.

Creating a Simple Search Script

The script in Listing 5.28 returns a result set containing the name of all objects in the na.fabrikam.com domain.

To carry out this task, the script performs the following steps:

1. Create an ADO Connection object to access Active Directory by using the ADSI OLE DB provider.

    Line 1 creates a Connection object in memory, and line 2 opens the Connection object using the ADSI OLE DB provider. Notice that the name of the ADSI OLE DB provider that you use in all ADSI search scripts is ADsDSOObject. This is called the ProgID (Program ID) of the provider.

2. Create an ADO Command object in memory, and assign the Command object's ActiveConnection property to the Connection object (lines 4 and 5).

3. Assign the query string to the CommandText property of the Command object.

    Line 8, which continues line 7, specifies the search base, the attribute to return, and the search scope.

    - The search base, surrounded by angle brackets (< >), specifies the start of the search — the ADsPath to the na.fabrikam.com domain.

    - The attribute to return, which appears after two semicolons, specifies the lDAPDisplayName of each attribute that the query should return. In this case, a single attribute, name, is specified. If more than one attribute is specified, separate each attribute with a comma.

    - The search scope, appearing at the end of the query string, specifies where to perform the query — subtree, which performs the search of the entire hierarchy, starting from the search base na.fabrikam.com.

4. Run the query by calling the Execute method of the Command object and assigning the return value to the RecordSet object (line 9).

    The query string returns records containing a single field, the name field.

5. Use a While Wend statement to display each record in objRecordSet. Use the MoveNext method of the RecordSet object to move to the next record.

6. Close the Connection object.

Listing 5.28   Searching for the Names of All Objects in the Domain

```
1    Set objConnection = CreateObject("ADODB.Connection")
2    objConnection.Open "Provider=ADsDSOObject;"
3
4    Set objCommand = CreateObject("ADODB.Command")
5    objCommand.ActiveConnection = objConnection
6
7    objCommand.CommandText = _
8        "<LDAP://dc=NA,dc=fabrikam,dc=com>;;name;subtree"
9    Set objRecordSet = objCommand.Execute
10
11   While Not objRecordSet.EOF
12       Wscript.Echo objRecordSet.Fields("name")
13       objRecordSet.MoveNext
14   Wend
15
16   objConnection.Close
```

When this script runs in the na.fabrikam.com domain, it echoes the name of each object in the domain to the command window, as shown in the following abbreviated result set:

```
na
Builtin
Administrators
Users
...
S-1-5-11
Program Data
Microsoft
```

The information returned by running the script in Listing 5.28 is of limited use for the following reasons:

- The names of all objects in the na.fabrikam.com domain are returned.
- There is no indication of where in the domain hierarchy the objects exist.
- There is no indication of the type of objects in the result set.
- The result set might be too large or too small, depending on the requirements of your search.

To make the result set more useful, you can change the script by:

Modifying the query string. In the query string, you can specify the attributes to return and the part of the directory that is searched (the search base). You can also implement filters and specify the scope of the search.

Specifying additional search options by using the Command object. Using the Command object lets you control many aspects of the search, such as the sort order of the query, the size limit of the result set, how long the script waits for results, and other options.

 Note

For a complete list of search options and other properties supported by ADO and available from the ADSI OLE DB Provider, see the Active Directory Programmer's Guide link on the Web Resources page at http://www.microsoft.com/windows/reskits/webresources.

The goal of the next eight scripts in this section is to show examples of how you can change the query string, specify additional Command object properties, and modify the script language in other ways to fine-tune the results of a search.

Scripting the Attributes to Be Returned by the Search

Listing 5.28 demonstrated how to return a single value, that of the name attribute. Returning additional attributes can make the result set more useful. For example, by adding the distinguishedName attribute to the result set, you can determine where objects are located in Active Directory.

The script in Listing 5.29 returns a result set containing both the name and the distinguishedName of all objects in the na.fabrikam.com domain. The steps in this listing are exactly the same as those in the preceding listing; therefore, the steps are not repeated here.

To expand the result set, the following modifications were made to the script:

1. Include the distinguishedName attribute in the query string (line 8).

2. Echo the value of the distinguishedName attribute to the command window (lines 14 and 15).

Listing 5.29 Searching for the Names and DNs of All Objects in the Domain

```
1   Set objConnection = CreateObject("ADODB.Connection")
2   objConnection.Open "Provider=ADsDSOObject;"
3
4   Set objCommand = CreateObject("ADODB.Command")
5   objCommand.ActiveConnection = objConnection
6
7   objCommand.CommandText = _
8       "<LDAP://dc=NA,dc=fabrikam,dc=com>;;distinguishedName,name;subtree"
9
10  Set objRecordSet = objCommand.Execute
11
12  While Not objRecordSet.EOF
13      Wscript.Echo objRecordSet.Fields("Name")
14      Wscript.Echo "[" & _
15          objRecordSet.Fields("distinguishedName") & "]"
16      objRecordSet.MoveNext
17  Wend
18
19  objConnection.Close
```

When this script runs in the na.fabrikam.com domain, it echoes the name and DN of each object in the domain to the command window, as shown in the following abbreviated result set:

```
na
[dc=NA,DC=fabrikam,DC=com]
Builtin
[CN=Builtin,dc=NA,DC=fabrikam,DC=com]
Administrators
[CN=Administrators,CN=Builtin,dc=NA,DC=fabrikam,DC=com]
Users
[CN=Users,CN=Builtin,dc=NA,DC=fabrikam,DC=com]
...
S-1-5-11
[CN=S-1-5-11,CN=ForeignSecurityPrincipals,dc=NA,DC=fabrikam,DC=com]
Program Data
[CN=Program Data,dc=NA,DC=fabrikam,DC=com]
Microsoft
[CN=Microsoft,CN=Program Data,dc=NA,DC=fabrikam,DC=com]
```

Limiting a Search to a Specific Type of Object

Suppose you are interested in a result set containing only a certain type of object, such as a computer, printer, user account, or group. To limit a search to a specific type of object, you can specify either the objectClass or objectCategory search filter property in the query string.

Each Active Directory object contains a single-valued objectCategory attribute. This attribute is the DN of the class from which the object is derived. For example, the objectCategory of a group object is cn=Group,cn=Schema,cn=Configuration,dc=fabrikam,dc=com. To return only group objects in the result set, you include the filter property (objectCategory=Group) in the filter portion of the search string.

Each Active Directory object also contains a multivalued objectClass attribute. This attribute contains an ordered list of the entire class hierarchy from which the Active Directory object is derived. The objectClass filter property lets you limit the query to objects matching any one of the values stored in the objectClass multivalued attribute. For example, to return all user and computer objects, you can specify (objectClass=user). This returns both user and computer objects because in the Active Directory hierarchy, the computer class is a child class of the user class.

Because the objectCategory attribute contains a single value, it is better suited for performing searches. Therefore, whenever possible, use the objectCategory filter property instead of objectClass for performing searches containing potentially large result sets.

Note

For information about Active Directory classes and the class hierarchy, see "Active Directory Architecture" later in this chapter.

Listing 5.30 demonstrates how to return a result set containing a certain category of object — the Computer category. The script returns both the name and the distinguishedName of computer objects in the na.fabrikam.com domain. The steps in this listing are exactly the same as those in the preceding listings in this section; therefore, the steps are not repeated here.

To limit the result set to computer objects in the domain, the following modification was made to the script:

- Include the objectCategory filter in the query string, and set its value to return all computer objects (line 8).

Listing 5.30   Searching for the Names and DNs of Computer Objects in the Domain

```
1    Set objConnection = CreateObject("ADODB.Connection")
2    objConnection.Open "Provider=ADsDSOObject;"
3
4    Set objCommand = CreateObject("ADODB.Command")
5    objCommand.ActiveConnection = objConnection
6
7    objCommand.CommandText = _
8       "<LDAP://dc=NA,dc=fabrikam,dc=com>;(objectCategory=computer)" & _
9          ";distinguishedName,name;subtree"
10
11   Set objRecordSet = objCommand.Execute
12
13   While Not objRecordSet.EOF
14       Wscript.Echo objRecordSet.Fields("Name")
15       Wscript.Echo "[" & _
16           objRecordSet.Fields("distinguishedName") & "]"
17       objRecordSet.MoveNext
18   Wend
19
20   objConnection.Close
```

When this script runs in the na.fabrikam.com domain, it echoes the name and DN of each computer object in the domain to the command window, as shown in the following abbreviated result set:

```
SEA-DC-02
[CN=SEA-DC-02,OU=Domain Controllers,dc=NA,DC=fabrikam,DC=com]
SEA-DC-03
[CN=SEA-DC-02,OU=Domain Controllers,dc=NA,DC=fabrikam,DC=com]
...
SEA-PM-01
[CN=SEA-PM-01,cn=Computers,dc=NA,DC=fabrikam,DC=com]
SEA-SQL-01
[CN=SEA-SQL-01,cn=Computers,dc=NA,DC=fabrikam,DC=com]
```

Filter properties can be combined, and wildcards are supported. For details about the search filter syntax, see the Active Directory Programmer's Guide link on the Web Resources page at http://www.microsoft.com/windows/reskits/webresources and perform a search on the phrase, "Search Filter Syntax." For object-specific search examples, see the ADSI task-based chapters in this book.

Specifying the Global Catalog in the Search Base

Suppose you want to return the names and DNs of all computers in the forest. To accomplish this task, you can query the Global Catalog server in the root domain because the name and distinguishedName attributes are two attributes that are located in the Global Catalog server by default. Global catalog servers contain a partial attribute set of every object in the domain. To query the Global Catalog in the forest, change the LDAP moniker in the search base portion of the query string to GC and change the DN to the root domain. Therefore, the ADsPath changes from

```
<LDAP://dc=NA,dc=fabrikam,dc=com>
```

to

```
<GC://dc=NA,dc=fabrikam,dc=com>
```

Listing 5.31 demonstrates how to return a result set containing information about all computer objects in the forest.

To expand the result set to all computer objects in the forest, the following modification was made to the script:

- Use the GC moniker in the search base (ADsPath) of the query string, and change the DN to the root domain, fabrikam.com (line 8).

Listing 5.31   Searching for the Names and DNs of All Computer Objects in the Forest

```
1   Set objConnection = CreateObject("ADODB.Connection")
2   objConnection.Open "Provider=ADsDSOObject;"
3
4   Set objCommand = CreateObject("ADODB.Command")
5   objCommand.ActiveConnection = objConnection
6
7   objCommand.CommandText = _
8       "<GC://dc=fabrikam,dc=com>;(objectCategory=computer)" & _
9           ";distinguishedName,name;subtree"
10
11  Set objRecordSet = objCommand.Execute
12
13  While Not objRecordSet.EOF
14      Wscript.Echo objRecordSet.Fields("Name")
15      Wscript.Echo "[" & _
16          objRecordSet.Fields("distinguishedName") & "]"
17      objRecordSet.MoveNext
18  Wend
19
20  objConnection.Close
```

When this script runs in the fabrikam.com root domain, it echoes the name and DN of each computer object in the forest to the command window, as shown in the following abbreviated result set:

```
SEA-DC-01
[CN=SEA-DC-01,OU=Domain Controllers,DC=fabrikam,DC=com]
SEA-DC-04
[CN=SEA-DC-04,OU=Domain Controllers,DC=fabrikam,DC=com]
SEA-DC-02
[CN=SEA-DC-02,OU=Domain Controllers,dc=NA,DC=fabrikam,DC=com]
SEA-DC-03
[CN=SEA-DC-03,OU=Domain Controllers,dc=NA,DC=fabrikam,DC=com]
...
SEA-PM-01
[CN=SEA-PM-01,cn=Computers,dc=NA,DC=fabrikam,DC=com]
SEA-SQL-01
[CN=SEA-SQL-01,cn=Computers,dc=NA,DC=fabrikam,DC=com]
```

Using Referral Chasing to Expand the Result Set

If you want to return a complete result set containing one or more attributes that are not in the Global Catalog, you must use referral chasing. When a domain controller in a parent domain, such as the root domain, builds its result set, it passes a list of child domains back to the client computer running the script. The client computer then contacts each of the child domains so that they can build their result sets to satisfy the query. This process is called *referral chasing*.

Referral chasing increases network traffic and processing load on the domain controllers servicing the request. Network traffic is increased because, in contrast with a Global Catalog search, the client must contact a domain controller in each child domain and each domain controller servicing the request must respond with a result set.

You can explicitly enable referral chasing by setting the Chase Referrals property of the Command object to ADS_CHASE_REFERRALS_SUBORDINATE (a constant with the value &h20). Listing 5.32 demonstrates how to return a result set that uses referral chasing to retrieve attributes from a domain and its child domains. With the exception of four minor additions, the steps in this listing are similar to the previous listings in this section.

To support referral chasing, the following modifications were made to the script:

1. Set the ADS_CHASE_REFERRALS_SUBORDINATE constant for referral chasing (line 1).

2. Enable referral chasing by setting the Chase Referrals property of the ADO Command object to ADS_CHASE_REFERRALS_SUBORDINATE. This instructs the server to send a list of referrals back to the client so that child domains can also process the result set (lines 8 and 9).

3. Include the isCriticalSystemObject attribute in the query string to demonstrate retrieving a value not contained in the Global Catalog (line 13).

4. Echo the value of isCriticalSystemObject to the command window (lines 19 and 20).

Listing 5.32 Using Referral Chasing to Perform a Search

```
1   ADS_CHASE_REFERRALS_SUBORDINATE = &h20
2   Set objConnection = CreateObject("ADODB.Connection")
3   objConnection.Open "Provider=ADsDSOObject;"
4
5   Set objCommand = CreateObject("ADODB.Command")
6   objCommand.ActiveConnection = objConnection
7
8   objCommand.Properties("Chase Referrals") = _
9       ADS_CHASE_REFERRALS_SUBORDINATE
10
11  objCommand.CommandText = _
12      "<LDAP://dc=fabrikam,dc=com>;(objectCategory=computer);" & _
13          "distinguishedName,name,isCriticalSystemObject;subtree"
14
15  Set objRecordSet = objCommand.Execute
16
17  While Not objRecordSet.EOF
18      Wscript.Echo objRecordSet.Fields("Name")
19      Wscript.Echo "isCriticalSystemObject: " & _
20          objRecordSet.Fields("isCriticalSystemObject")
21      Wscript.Echo "[" & _
22          objRecordSet.Fields("distinguishedName") & "]"
23      objRecordSet.MoveNext
24  Wend
25
26  objConnection.Close
```

When this script runs in the fabrikam.com root domain, it echoes the name, the DN, and the Boolean value of isCriticalSystemObject of each computer object in the forest to the command window, as shown in the following abbreviated result set:

```
SEA-DC-01
isCriticalSystemObject: True
[CN=SEA-DC-01,OU=Domain Controllers,DC=fabrikam,DC=com]
SEA-DC-04
isCriticalSystemObject: True
[CN=SEA-DC-04,OU=Domain Controllers,DC=fabrikam,DC=com]
SEA-DC-02
isCriticalSystemObject: True
[CN=SEA-DC-02,OU=Domain Controllers,dc=NA,DC=fabrikam,DC=com]
SEA-DC-03
isCriticalSystemObject: True
[CN=SEA-DC-03,OU=Domain Controllers,dc=NA,DC=fabrikam,DC=com]
...
SEA-PM-01
isCriticalSystemObject: False
[CN=SEA-PM-01,cn=Computers,dc=NA,DC=fabrikam,DC=com]
SEA-SQL-01
isCriticalSystemObject: False
[CN=SEA-SQL-01,cn=Computers,dc=NA,DC=fabrikam,DC=com]
```

Controlling the Scope of a Search

Suppose you are interested in limiting a result to attributes of computer objects in the Computers container of a particular domain. Suppose as well that additional child containers in the Computers container contain objects. To limit a search to a specific container, such as the Computers container, you can modify the DN specified in the ADsPath (the search base) as follows:

```
cn=Computers,dc=NA,dc=fabrikam,dc=com
```

A possible query string might look like this:

```
"<GC://cn=Computers,dc=NA,dc=fabrikam,dc=com>" & _
    ";(objectCategory=computer)" & _
        ";distinguishedName,name;subtree"
```

This query string instructs the script to retrieve the DN and name of all computer objects in the Computers container of the na.fabrikam.com domain. However, because subtree is specified at the end of the query string, the result set will also include any computer objects in child containers of the Computers container. To limit the search to just the Computers container, you can specify a different search scope.

The search scope is the last part of the query string; options for search scope are base, onelevel, and subtree:

Base.   Searches only the DN specified in the search base. For example, a query for the name attribute with the search base <GC://cn=Computers,dc=NA,dc=fabrikam,dc=com> and no search filter returns the name value of the container, Computers. No child objects of the Computers container are searched.

Onelevel.   Searches the immediate children of the specified search base. For example, a query for the name attribute with the search base <GC://cn=Computers,dc=NA,dc=fabrikam,dc=com> and the (objectCategory=computer) search filter returns the name values of all computer objects in the Computers container. Any child containers in the Computers container are not searched.

Subtree.   Searches the entire subtree, including the object specified in the search base. Examples of this search scope appear in all previous search examples. This is the default scope option: If you do not specify a scope option in the query, subtree is used.

The script in Listing 5.33 demonstrates how to return a result set containing the name and distinguishedName of all computer objects in the Computers container. Subcontainers of the Computers container are not searched.

To limit the search scope:

- Specify the Computers container in the na.fabrikam.com domain as the search base.
- Specify onelevel as the search scope.

Listing 5.33   Limiting the Scope of a Search

```
1    Set objConnection = CreateObject("ADODB.Connection")
2    objConnection.Open "Provider=ADsDSOObject;"
3
4    Set objCommand = CreateObject("ADODB.Command")
5    objCommand.ActiveConnection = objConnection
6
7    objCommand.CommandText = _
8        "<GC://cn=Computers,dc=NA,dc=fabrikam,dc=com>" & _
9          ";(objectCategory=computer)" & _
10            ";distinguishedName,name;onelevel"
11
12   Set objRecordSet = objCommand.Execute
13
14   While Not objRecordSet.EOF
15       Wscript.Echo objRecordSet.Fields("Name")
16       Wscript.Echo "[" & _
17           objRecordSet.Fields("distinguishedName") & "]"
18       objRecordSet.MoveNext
19   Wend
20
21   objConnection.Close
```

When this script runs in the na.fabrikam.com domain, it echoes the name and the DN of computer objects in the Computers container to the command window, as shown in the following abbreviated result set:

```
SEA-PM-01
[CN=SEA-PM-01,cn=Computers,dc=NA,DC=fabrikam,DC=com]
SEA-SQL-01
[CN=SEA-SQL-01,cn=Computers,dc=NA,DC=fabrikam,DC=com]
...
```

Sorting the Results of a Search

If you want the server to sort the result set before it is sent to the client, you can include the Sort On property of the command object in the ADSI script. The Sort On property instructs the server to perform the sort operation before the data is returned.

You assign the Sort On property the lDAPDisplayName of an attribute. The attribute should contain a meaningful value for the search. For example, you can search on the name attribute to sort a result set alphanumerically or search on the whenCreated attribute to sort a result set chronologically.

 Note

> The Sort On property cannot sort on an attribute stored as a distinguished name. If you attempt to sort on this type of attribute, an empty result set is returned.

Listing 5.34 demonstrates how to instruct the server to sort a result set containing information about all computer objects in the forest. The result set includes the name, distinguishedName, and whenCreated attributes of each computer object in the forest. The script instructs the server to sort on the whenCreated attribute. Therefore, the result set contains all computer objects in the forest, from first created to last created.

To sort the result set, the following modifications were made to the script:

1. Assign the whenCreated attribute to the Sort On property of the Command object (line 7).

2. Include the whenCreated attribute in the query string so that its value will be part of the result set (line 11).

   Notice that the script uses the GC moniker in the query string. This works properly because all three attributes are contained in the Global Catalog.

3. Echo the value of the whenCreated attribute to the command window (line 19).

Listing 5.34 Sorting Computer Objects in the Domain Based on Creation Date

```
1    Set objConnection = CreateObject("ADODB.Connection")
2    objConnection.Open "Provider=ADsDSOObject;"
3
4    Set objCommand = CreateObject("ADODB.Command")
5    objCommand.ActiveConnection = objConnection
6
7    objCommand.Properties("Sort On") = "whenCreated"
8
9    objCommand.CommandText = _
10       "<GC://dc=fabrikam,dc=com>;(objectCategory=Computer);" & _
11          "distinguishedName,name,whenCreated;subtree"
12
13   Set objRecordSet = objCommand.Execute
14
15   While Not objRecordSet.EOF
16       Wscript.Echo objRecordSet.Fields("Name")
17       Wscript.Echo "[" & _
18          objRecordSet.Fields("distinguishedName") & "]"
19       Wscript.Echo objRecordSet.Fields("whenCreated") & VbCrLf
20       objRecordSet.MoveNext
21   Wend
22
23   objConnection.Close
```

When this script runs in the na.fabrikam.com domain, it echoes the name, DN, and whenCreated attributes of each computer object in the domain to the command window. The result set is returned by the server in ascending order (oldest to newest object creation date) based on the whenCreated attribute, as shown in the following abbreviated result set:

```
SEA-DC-01
[CN=SEA-DC-01,OU=Domain Controllers,DC=fabrikam,DC=com]
8/14/2002 9:59:12 AM

SEA-DC-02
[CN=SEA-DC-02,OU=Domain Controllers,dc=NA,DC=fabrikam,DC=com]
8/21/2002 1:53:24 PM

SEA-DC-03
[CN=SEA-DC-03,OU=Domain Controllers,dc=NA,DC=fabrikam,DC=com]
8/27/2002 9:53:24 AM

SEA-PM-01
[CN=SEA-PM-01,cn=Computers,dc=NA,DC=fabrikam,DC=com]
8/27/2002 11:53:24 AM


. . .


SEA-SQL-01
[CN=SEA-SQL-01,cn=Computers,dc=NA,DC=fabrikam,DC=com]
8/27/2002 4:06:30 PM

SEA-DC-04
[CN=SEA-DC-04,OU=Domain Controllers,DC=fabrikam,DC=com]
9/03/2002 2:00:03 PM
```

Retrieving Multivalued Attributes from a Search

A number of Active Directory objects contain multivalued attributes. The entries in multivalued attributes can also be part of a result set. For example, you might want to return a list of group members (both user accounts and groups) from the member attribute of groups.

The script in Listing 5.35 returns a result set containing the name and distinguishedName single-valued attributes and the member multivalued attribute for each group in the na.fabrikam.com domain.

To include a multivalued attribute in the result set, the following modifications were made to the script:

1. Include the (objectCategory=Group) filter in the query string to limit the result set to group objects (line 8). Also, include the member multivalued attribute in the query string so that its value is part of the result set (line 9).

    For this script to return group memberships, a global catalog server must be configured in the na.fabrikam.com domain. This is required because the script uses the GC moniker and the distinguished name of the na.fabrikam.com domain for the search base.

    If no global catalog server is in the na.fabrikam.com domain, you must use the LDAP moniker instead.

2. Initialize a variable named arrMembers with the contents of the member attribute contained in the fields property of the RecordSet object (line 19).

3. Using the VBScript IsArray function, test whether the member attribute is an array (line 22).

This result is false if the member attribute of the group is empty and true if one or more members are listed in the group.

- If IsArray is true, use a For Each statement to echo each member of the group to the command window (lines 23–25).

- If IsArray is false, echo the word *None* to the command window (line 27).

Listing 5.35 Searching for the Names and DNs of All Objects in the Domain

```
1   Set objConnection = CreateObject("ADODB.Connection")
2   objConnection.Open "Provider=ADsDSOObject;"
3
4   Set objCommand = CreateObject("ADODB.Command")
5   objCommand.ActiveConnection = objConnection
6
7   objCommand.CommandText = _
8     "<GC://dc=NA,dc=fabrikam,dc=com>;(objectCategory=Group);" & _
9       "distinguishedName,name,member;subtree"
10
11  Set objRecordSet = objCommand.Execute
12
13  While Not objRecordSet.EOF
14      Wscript.Echo objRecordSet.Fields("Name")
15      Wscript.Echo "[" & _
16          objRecordSet.Fields("distinguishedName") & "]"
17
18      Wscript.Echo "Group Member(s):"
19      arrMembers = objRecordSet.Fields("member")
21
22      If IsArray(objRecordSet.Fields("member")) Then
23          For Each strMember in arrMembers
24              Wscript.Echo vbTab & strMember
25          Next
26      Else
27          Wscript.Echo vbTab & "None"
28      End If
29      Wscript.Echo VbCrLf
30      objRecordSet.MoveNext
31  Wend
32
33  objConnection.Close
```

When this script runs in the na.fabrikam.com domain, it echoes the name, DN, and members of each group object in the domain to the command window, as shown in the following abbreviated result set:

```
Administrators
[CN=Administrators,CN=Builtin,DC=na,DC=fabrikam,DC=com]
Group Member(s):
    CN=Enterprise Admins,CN=Users,DC=fabrikam,DC=com
    CN=Domain Admins,CN=Users,DC=na,DC=fabrikam,DC=com
    CN=Administrator,CN=Users,DC=na,DC=fabrikam,DC=com


Users
[CN=Users,CN=Builtin,DC=na,DC=fabrikam,DC=com]
Group Member(s):
    CN=Domain Users,CN=Users,DC=na,DC=fabrikam,DC=com
    CN=S-1-5-11,CN=ForeignSecurityPrincipals,DC=na,DC=fabrikam,DC=com
    CN=S-1-5-4,CN=ForeignSecurityPrincipals,DC=na,DC=fabrikam,DC=com


. . .


Pre-Windows 2000 Compatible Access
[CN=Pre-Windows 2000 Compatible Access,CN=Builtin,DC=na,DC=fabrikam,DC=com]
Group Member(s):
    None


Atl-Users
[CN=Atl-Users,CN=Users,DC=na,DC=fabrikam,DC=com]
Group Member(s):
    CN=LewJudy,OU=Sales,DC=na,DC=fabrikam,DC=com
    CN=HuffArlene,OU=HR,DC=na,DC=fabrikam,DC=com
    CN=MyerKen,OU=HR,DC=na,DC=fabrikam,DC=com
```

Using Range Limits When Retrieving Multivalued Attributes

If a multivalued attribute contains many records, you can request a group of records in the attribute (rather than retrieve them all at once) by specifying Range Limits. This more evenly distributes the processing load placed on a domain controller servicing the request and, as a result, can improve the performance of the search operation. Also, if a multivalued attribute contains more than 1,000 entries, you must specify range limits, or the result set might not be complete.

The script in Listing 5.36 returns a result set containing the first 1,000 entries in the member multivalued attribute for the Atl-Users group in the na.fabrikam.com domain.

 Note

This script will fail if there are fewer than 1,000 members in the Atl-Users group. There must always be more members than the upper limit of the range (in this case, 999).

To specify range limits in a result set, the following modifications are made to the script:

1. Include the Range keyword in the query string to limit the result set to a certain number of entries contained in the member attribute (line 9). The range 0–999 returns the first 1,000 entries in the member attribute of the Atl-Users group.

2. Echo the phrase, "First 1000 Members:" to the screen (line 13).

   This phrase will appear ahead of the entries that are returned from the member attribute of the Atl-Users group.

3. Initialize a variable named arrMembers with the contents of the member attribute contained in the fields property of the RecordSet object. Within the fields property, specify a range limit that instructs the script to return the first 1,000 records (line 14).

   You must specify the Range Limit in the Fields property of the RecordSet object exactly as it was specified in the query string.

Listing 5.36 Searching for Group Membership Using Range Limits

```
1   Set objConnection = CreateObject("ADODB.Connection")
2   objConnection.Open "Provider=ADsDSOObject;"
3
4   Set objCommand = CreateObject("ADODB.Command")
5   objCommand.ActiveConnection = objConnection
6
7   objCommand.CommandText = _
8       "<LDAP://cn=Atl-Users,cn=Users,dc=NA,dc=fabrikam,dc=com>;;" & _
9           "member;Range=0-999;base"
10
11  Set objRecordSet = objCommand.Execute
12
13  Wscript.Echo "First 1000 Member(s):"
14  arrMembers = objRecordSet.Fields("member;Range=0-999")
15
16  For Each strMember in arrMembers
17      Wscript.Echo vbTab & strMember
18  Next
19
21  objConnection.Close
```

When this script runs in the na.fabrikam.com domain, it echoes a list containing the first 1,000 members in the Atl-Users Group to the command window, as shown in the following abbreviated result set:

```
First 1000 Member(s):
        CN=UserNo988,CN=Users,DC=na,DC=fabrikam,DC=com
        CN=UserNo987,CN=Users,DC=na,DC=fabrikam,DC=com
        CN=UserNo986,CN=Users,DC=na,DC=fabrikam,DC=com
            . . .
        CN=HuffArlene,OU=HR,DC=na,DC=fabrikam,DC=com
        CN=MyerKen,OU=HR,DC=na,DC=fabrikam,DC=com
```

Important observations about the scripts in this section are:

- They perform the same basic steps:

    1. Create an ADO Connection object using the ADSI OLE DB provider.

    2. Create an ADO Command object, and associate it with the Connection object.

    3. Use the Command object to build a query string.

    4. Create a RecordSet object to run the query and store the result set.

    5. Use the RecordSet object to read each record in the RecordSet.

    6. Close the connection.

- With the exception of Listing 5.36, inside the While Wend statement the scripts echo the records in the result set to the command window. This step is not necessary in Listing 5.36 because the example script returns a single record containing the entries in the member attribute of the Atl-Users group.

Displaying a result set is the most rudimentary task that can be completed with a search operation. For other tasks that can be completed as a result of a search operation, see "Performing an Administrative Task Using a Result Set" later in this chapter.

Optimizing Search Performance

Optimizing a search operation requires knowledge of Active Directory to construct efficient query strings and an understanding of performance-related properties of the Command object. A search operation is also affected by how efficiently you use objects in a script.

Consolidating Query Strings

When writing a script that performs many search operations, consider consolidating the search operations. For example, write a query that returns a result set containing multiple attributes rather than create two separate queries that return attributes from the same object. Consolidating search operations reduces the load placed on the domain controller or domain controllers servicing the search request.

Limiting the Result Set

Narrow the scope of your search operation as much as possible. For example, if you want a result set containing all objects in an OU but you are not concerned about objects outside the OU, specify a search base that starts in the container you want to search. Also, if you are interested only in the objects within the OU but not child containers of the OU, limit the scope of the search to onelevel.

Use search filters to further narrow the search. For example, specify (objectCategory=*class type*), where *class type* is the type of object you want in the result set. Also, use objectCategory rather than objectClass because objectCategory is single-valued and ideal for servicing search requests. Unlike the objectClass attribute, objectCategory is replicated to the Global Catalog and indexed.

Specify filters, such as (cn=SEA*), so that the result set is limited to objects beginning with the letters *SEA*. However, if you do use the * wildcard, use it only at the end of the string. Specifying the wildcard at the beginning or in the middle of a value requires more processing on the domain controller servicing the request.

Combine filters to further refine the search. For example, the following filter limits a search to all computer objects starting with *SEA*:

```
(&(objectCategory=computer)(cn=SEA*))
```

You can also limit the number of entries returned by a multivalued attribute containing many entries by specifying a range limit. For an example of how to implement range limits in a search operation, see Listing 5.36 in "Searching Active Directory" earlier in this chapter.

Specifying Additional Command Object Properties

Certain Command object properties control various aspects of the search operation. These properties are especially useful for handling large result sets. Table 5.4 shows some of the options of the Command object that control a search operation.

Table 5.4   Options for Improving Performance for Large Result Sets

Option	Description	Default	Syntax
Page Size (paging)	Instructs the domain controller to process a certain number of records and return them to the client before continuing the search.	Disabled	`objCommand.Properties _` `    ("Page Size")= `*`Records`* where *Records* is the number of records the domain controller should return before continuing the search.
Size Limit	Specifies the size of the result set. If the server reaches the size specified by the Size Limit property, the result set is returned to the client and the search operation is considered complete.	1,000 records	`objCommand.Properties _` `    ("Size Limit")= `*`Records`* where *Records* is the number of records the domain controller should return before completing the search. The default size limit of a search is 1,000 records.
Time Limit	Specifies the time that the domain controller will search before returning a result set. If the server reaches the time limit, the search is ended.	None	`objCommand.Properties _` `    ("Time Limit")= `*`Time`* where *Time* is the maximum amount of time (in seconds) that the domain controller should perform a search operation.
Timeout	Specifies the amount of time the client waits for a result set before terminating the search request.	None	`objCommand.Properties _` `    ("Timeout")= `*`Time`* where *Timeout* is the maximum amount of time (in seconds) that the client waits before terminating a search request.

(continued)

Table 5.4   Options for Improving Performance for Large Result Sets *(continued)*

Option	Description	Default	Syntax

Cache Results (caching)	Specifies whether the result set should be cached to the client. For very large result sets, disabling caching will reduce memory consumption on the client.	True	`objCommand.Properties _`
			`   ("Cache Results"=`
			`Boolean`
			
			If set to False, caching is disabled. If set to True, caching is enabled.

Asynchronous	Specifies whether the server should send a result set a record at a time (asynchronously) or wait until the search operation completes (synchronously).	False	`objCommand.Properties _`
			`   ("Asynchronous"= Boolean`
			
			If set to True, results are sent asynchronously. If set to False, results are sent synchronously.

See the ADSI task-based chapters in this book for script examples that use filter combinations, range limits, and properties of the Command object to complete object-specific search operations.

Using the Global Catalog to Perform Search Operations

When all attributes in a search operation are contained in the Global Catalog, use the GC prefix in the search base rather than LDAP. This is especially important when you want to return a result set from more than one domain. If you use the Global Catalog, a single domain controller can service the request. If you do not use the Global Catalog, you must enable referral chasing to get a complete result set from multiple domains. Referral chasing is not efficient and should be avoided whenever possible.

If you need to sort a result set, sort on attributes that are both indexed and in the Global Catalog. For information about how to determine which attributes are in the Global Catalog and are indexed, see "Active Directory Architecture" later in this chapter.

Minimize Object Creation (Instantiation)

Create a Connection object only once, and reuse it in the same script. Do not clear the Connection object from memory until you have completed all operations that use it. This rule also applies to other types of objects. For example, if you bind to an object in Active Directory, do not bind again to the object in the same script. Instead, reuse the object that is already in memory.

Performing an Administrative Task Using a Result Set

The ADSI OLE DB provider gains read-only access to Active Directory. Therefore, you cannot use ADO to modify Active Directory directly. However, you can use the result set returned by a search operation to perform administrative tasks using a combination of ADO and ADSI methods. For example, you can:

- Search for the sAMAccountName attribute of an object in a domain and, if the result set is empty, use the Create method to create the object.

  For an example of how to complete this task, see "Active Directory Users" in this book.

- Search for all computer objects using the objectCategory attribute and then use the Put method to modify an attribute of each object.

- Search for all objects whose description attribute designates that the object is owned by a specific department and then use the MoveHere method to consolidate all objects in a container.

The goal of the two scripts in this section is to demonstrate how to use a result set returned by a search operation to perform an administrative task.

Modifying an Attribute in Multiple Objects

The script in Listing 5.37 modifies the location attribute to Atlanta, Georgia, for all computers in a domain whose name begins with ATL. The steps to complete this task are a combination of the steps described in "Searching" and "Modifying Directory Service Objects" earlier in this chapter; therefore, the steps are summarized here.

1. Using ADO, query Active Directory for all computer objects starting with the name ATL.

    - In line 9, two filters are combined, (objectCategory=Computer) and (cn=ATL*). The second filter uses the asterisk wildcard to find all computers whose name starts with ATL.

    - In line 10, ADsPath is the attribute returned for each computer in the result set.

2. Use a While Wend statement and the MoveNext method to read each record in the result set.

   a. For each record in the result set, bind to the corresponding object in Active Directory, write the location attribute to the object, and then commit the object to Active Directory (lines 15–18).

   b. Show the number of records modified by echoing the value of the RecordSet object's RecordCount property to the command window (lines 21 and 22).

Listing 5.37   Modifying Multiple Computer Objects Using the Result Set Returned by a Search

```
1   Set objConnection = CreateObject("ADODB.Connection")
2   objConnection.Open "Provider=ADsDSOObject;"
3
4   Set objCommand = CreateObject("ADODB.Command")
5   objCommand.ActiveConnection = objConnection
6
7   objCommand.CommandText = _
8      "<LDAP://dc=NA,dc=fabrikam,dc=com>;" & _
9         "(&(objectCategory=Computer)(cn=ATL*));" & _
10           "ADsPath;subtree"
11
12  Set objRecordSet = objCommand.Execute
13
14  While Not objRecordSet.EOF
15      strADsPath = objRecordSet.Fields("ADsPath")
16      Set objComputer = GetObject(strADsPath)
17      objComputer.Put "location", "Atlanta, Georgia"
18      objComputer.SetInfo
19      objRecordSet.MoveNext
20  Wend
21  Wscript.Echo objRecordSet.RecordCount & " computers objects modified."
22
23  objConnection.Close
```

Moving Objects Containing a Certain Value for an Attribute

The script in Listing 5.38 moves user account objects to the HR OU if their department attribute is set to Human Resources. The steps to complete this task are a combination of the steps described in "Searching" and "Moving and Renaming Objects" earlier in this chapter; therefore, the steps are summarized here.

1. Using ADO, query Active Directory for all user account objects with a department attribute value of Human Resources.

    ▪ On lines 9 and 10, three filters are combined: (objectCategory=person), (objectClass=user), and (department=Human Resources). Take note of how ampersands and parentheses are used to combine the filters. The script uses both objectCategory and objectClass so that all user account types that are security principals are returned by the query. For more information about why this filter combination is necessary, see "Active Directory Users" in this book.

    ▪ On line 10, return the ADsPath, distinguishedName, and name attributes of each user account that matches the filter properties and scope. All of these attributes are used later in the script.

2. Bind to the target OU of the move operation (line 14).

    Note that this binding operation could have been completed inside the While Wend statement that starts on line 16. However, it is more efficient to perform a binding operation once and reuse it as many times as necessary in the script.

3. Use a While Wend statement to read each record in the result set (line 16).

    a. Initialize the strADsPath variable with the field containing the ADsPath.

    b. Initialize two variables, strDNRecord and strDNCompare. The strDNRecord contains the value of the distinguishedName attribute returned by the query. The strDNCompare attribute contains a distinguishedName that is constructed from the name field returned by the query and the path to the HR OU. Use the strDNCompare variable to determine whether the user account specified by strDNRecord is currently located in the HR OU.

c.   If the user account is not already in the HR OU, (that is, strDNRecord is not equal to strDNCompare), use the MoveHere method to move the object into the that OU. Then echo the distinguishedName of the user account before it was moved and state that it was moved. Otherwise, echo the distinguishedName of the user account in the HR OU and state that it was not moved.

Listing 5.38   Moving Multiple User Accounts Using the Result Set Returned by a Search

```
1    Set objConnection = CreateObject("ADODB.Connection")
2    objConnection.Open "Provider=ADsDSOObject;"
3
4    Set objCommand = CreateObject("ADODB.Command")
5    objCommand.ActiveConnection = objConnection
6
7    objCommand.CommandText = _
8       "<LDAP://dc=NA,dc=fabrikam,dc=com>;" & _
9          "(&(&(objectCategory=person)(objectClass=user)" & _
10            "(department=Human Resources)));" & _
11                "ADsPath,distinguishedName,name;subtree"
12
13   Set objRecordSet = objCommand.Execute
14
15   Set objOU = GetObject("LDAP://ou=HR,dc=NA,dc=fabrikam,dc=com")
16
17   While Not objRecordSet.EOF
18       strADsPath = objRecordSet.Fields("ADsPath")
19
20       strDNRecord=LCase(objRecordSet.Fields("distinguishedName"))
21       strDNCompare=LCase("cn=" & objRecordSet.Fields("name") & _
22           ",ou=HR,dc=NA,dc=fabrikam,dc=com")
23
24       If strDNRecord <> strDNCompare Then
25           objOU.MoveHere strADsPath, vbNullString
26           Wscript.Echo objRecordSet.Fields("distinguishedName") & " Moved."
27       Else
28           Wscript.Echo objRecordSet.Fields("distinguishedName") & " Not Moved."
29       End If
30       objRecordSet.MoveNext
31   Wend
32
33   objConnection.Close
```

Important observations about the scripts in this section are:

- Both scripts perform the same basic steps: They use ADO to create a Connection, a Command, and a RecordSet object, and then they read each record in the RecordSet object.
- Using the information in the result set, both scripts perform an administrative task.

Enumerating Active Directory Objects in Containers

Using ADO and the ADSI OLE DB provider is not the only way to return results from a container. You can also enumerate the contents of a container, such as a domain or an OU. Enumeration is the process of returning a list of objects in a container.

Enumeration in ADSI is not as sophisticated as in ADO and is not as efficient for retrieving information about a large number of objects. However, container enumeration does provide limited capabilities, and writing scripts that enumerate containers is simpler than writing scripts that perform a search operation against Active Directory.

Scripting Container Enumeration

Enumerating the contents of an Active Directory container typically involves three basic steps:

1. Bind to an Active Directory container to be enumerated.

   Typically, the container is an OU.

2. Limit the result set with the Filter property.

   This step is optional but should be used if you need to limit the type of objects enumerated in a container of many objects.

3. Create a loop to perform an administrative task against the objects in the container.

Enumerating the Contents of a Container

The script in Listing 5.39 enumerates the Configuration container and echoes the names of the child containers to the command window. The Configuration container is located in the fabrikam.com root domain. The script involves the following steps:

1. Bind to the Configuration container in the root domain.

2. Use a For Each statement to echo the names of each child container in the Configuration container.

Listing 5.39   Enumerating the Configuration Container for Names of Objects Within It

```
1  Set objConfiguration = GetObject _
2      ("LDAP://cn=Configuration,dc=fabrikam,dc=com")
3
4  For Each objContainer in objConfiguration
5      Wscript.Echo objContainer.Name
6  Next
```

When the script runs in the fabrikam.com forest, it echoes the name of each child container of the Configuration container to the command window, as shown:

```
CN=DisplaySpecifiers
CN=Extended-Rights
CN=ForestUpdates
CN=LostAndFoundConfig
CN=Partitions
CN=Physical Locations
CN=Services
CN=Sites
CN=WellKnown Security Principals
```

The script works from any domain in the forest.

Enumerating a Container to Perform an Administrative Task

The script in Listing 5.40 enumerates the Partitions container, which is located in the Configuration container of the fabrikam.com root domain. During enumeration, two entries in the upnSuffixes multivalued attribute are updated and the script echoes all values in the attribute to the command window.

This script demonstrates container enumeration combined with writing and reading a multivalued attribute. For more information about multivalued attributes, see "Administering Multivalued Attributes" earlier in this chapter.

1. Set the ADS_PROPERTY_APPEND constant equal to the control code parameter used by the PutEx method to indicate this mode of modification (used in lines 5–7).

2. Bind to the Partitions container in the Configuration container of the root domain.

3. Add entries to the upnSuffixes attribute.

4. Use a For Each statement to echo the entries in the Partitions container's upnSuffixes attribute.

Listing 5.40   Enumerating the Partitions Container to Write and Read the upnSuffixes Attribute

```
1    Const ADS_PROPERTY_APPEND = 3
2    Set objPartitions = GetObject _
3        ("LDAP://cn=Partitions,cn=Configuration,dc=fabrikam,dc=com")
4
5    objPartitions.PutEx ADS_PROPERTY_APPEND, upnSuffixes", _
6        Array("sa.fabrikam.com","corp.fabrikam.com")
7    objPartitions.SetInfo
8
9    For Each Suffix in objPartitions.GetEx("upnSuffixes")
10       Wscript.Echo Suffix
11   Next
```

When this script runs in the fabrikam.com root domain, it inserts two entries in the upnSuffixes attribute and then echoes all entries in the upnSuffixes attribute to the command window, as shown:

```
corp.fabrikam.com
sa.fabrikam.com
```

By default, the script in Listing 5.40 works only if your user account is a member of the Domain Admins global group or the Enterprise Admins universal group in the root domain. Both of these groups are granted the right to update attributes in the partitions container.

Limiting Container Enumeration to a Specific Object Type

The script in Listing 5.41 enumerates the Users container of the na.fabrikam.com root domain and uses the Filter method to limit the enumeration to all user account objects. The script then echoes the value of the primaryGroupID attribute and all entries in the memberOf attribute to the command window. For information about the Filter method, see "ADSI Interfaces" later in this chapter.

1. Use the On Error Resume Next statement.

    This statement can be used to catch (or suppress) any run-time error; however, you should use it only if you are testing for and addressing errors that might occur when the script runs. In this case, the script uses the On Error Resume Next statement to catch the ADSI error that is generated if an attribute cannot be found in the local property cache.

2. Set the E_ADS_PROPERTY_NOT_FOUND constant equal to the ADSI error code generated if the memberOf attribute cannot be found in the local property cache (used in line 15).

3. Bind to the Users container in the na.fabrikam.com domain.

4. Set the Filter property to return user account objects (line 6).

5. Use a For Each statement to echo information about each user account. Inside the loop, do the following:

   a. Using the Get method, echo the value of the primaryGroupID single-valued attribute to the command window (line11).

   b. Using the GetEx method, initialize the arrMemberOf variable with the entries in the memberOf multivalued attribute (line 13).

   If the memberOf attribute is present, the script does not raise the error number corresponding to E_ADS_PROPERTY_NOT_FOUND. Therefore, echo each entry in the arrMemberOf variable to the command window (lines 15–18).

   Otherwise, echo a message stating that the memberOf attribute is empty, and clear the error code (lines 19–21).

Listing 5.41   Limiting Container Enumeration to User Accounts by Using the Filter Property

```
1    On Error Resume Next
2    Const E_ADS_PROPERTY_NOT_FOUND   = &h8000500D
3    Set objOU = GetObject _
4        ("LDAP://cn=Users,dc=NA,dc=fabrikam,dc=com")
5
6    ObjOU.Filter= Array("user")
7
8    For Each objUser in objOU
9        Wscript.Echo objUser.cn & " is a member of: "
10       Wscript.Echo vbTab & "Primary Group ID: " & _
11            objUser.Get("primaryGroupID")
12
13       arrMemberOf = objUser.GetEx("memberOf")
14
15       If Err.Number <>  E_ADS_PROPERTY_NOT_FOUND Then
16           For Each Group in arrMemberOf
17               Wscript.Echo vbTab & Group
18           Next
19       Else
20           Wscript.Echo vbTab & "memberOf attribute is not set"
21           Err.Clear
22       End If
23       Wscript.Echo VbCrLf
24   Next
```

When this script runs in the na.fabrikam.com root domain, it echoes the primaryGroupID attribute and the entries in the memberOf attribute of user accounts to the command window, as shown in the following abbreviated list:

```
Administrator is a member of:
        Primary Group ID: 513
        CN=Group Policy Creator Owners,CN=Users,DC=na,DC=fabrikam,DC=com
        CN=Domain Admins,CN=Users,DC=na,DC=fabrikam,DC=com
        CN=Print Operators,CN=Builtin,DC=na,DC=fabrikam,DC=com
        CN=Administrators,CN=Builtin,DC=na,DC=fabrikam,DC=com

FABRIKAM$ is a member of:
        Primary Group ID: 513
        memberOf attribute is not set

Guest is a member of:
        Primary Group ID: 514
        CN=Guests,CN=Builtin,DC=na,DC=fabrikam,DC=com
...
```

Root Directory Service Entry

An element important to building an ADsPath to an object is the Root Directory Service Entry (rootDSE). The *rootDSE* is defined as the root of the directory, and it is a useful feature of ADSI because it allows a script to derive important information about the root directory. In turn, this enables you to stay away from hard-coding distinguished names when constructing an ADsPath.

Up to this point, all of the script examples in this chapter use a feature of ADSI called serverless binding. *Serverless binding* means that the name of a domain controller is not hard-coded into the ADsPath. Instead, ADSI locates a domain controller in the default domain that can service the binding request. Typically, when you run a script, the default domain is your current logon domain and, depending on the configuration of Active Directory, a domain controller at a local site will service the request.

Serverless binding is an important step toward making ADSI scripts function efficiently within the forest. However, because all of the script examples in this chapter thus far use hard-coded distinguished names in the ADsPath, the scripts function only within the fabrikam.com forest. In every case, rootDSE can be used to make the scripts function in Active Directory forests other than fabrikam.com.

Scripting with rootDSE

Using rootDSE involves three basic steps.

1. Bind to rootDSE.

2. Use the Get method to read an attribute of rootDSE.

3. Use the attribute returned by rootDSE to construct an ADsPath and bind to a container or an object in the directory.

    Steps 2 and 3 are often combined to reduce the length of the script.

The goal of the four scripts in this section is to demonstrate how to use rootDSE to bind to the current domain, the root domain, the configuration container, and the schema container. Using rootDSE to form an ADsPath to the current domain, the root domain, and the configuration container is useful for the previous script examples in this chapter. Using rootDSE to form an ADsPath to the schema container is useful for the scripts appearing in the upcoming section "Active Directory Architecture."

Binding to the Current Domain

The script in Listing 5.42 binds to the current domain by using the defaultNamingContext attribute of rootDSE. The current domain is the domain where the client is logged on. This example is particularly useful for the numerous listings in this chapter that access the current domain. By modifying the binding string, you can also use this example for binding to a common container such as the Users container, an OU, or any leaf object in the domain. To carry out this task, the script performs the following steps:

1. Bind to the rootDSE.

2. Construct an ADsPath to the current domain.

3. Use the strADsPath variable in the binding operation.

Listing 5.42 Constructing an ADsPath to the Current Domain with rootDSE

```
1  Set objRootDSE = GetObject("LDAP://rootDSE")
2  strADsPath = "LDAP://" & objRootDSE.Get("defaultNamingContext")
3  Set objDomain = GetObject(strADsPath)
```

In the na.fabrikam.com domain, the strADsPath variable contains:

```
LDAP://DC=na,DC=fabrikam,DC=com
```

Binding to the Root Domain

The script in Listing 5.43 binds to the root domain. Regardless of which domain the client is logged on to, the root domain in the forest is returned.

Listing 5.43   Constructing an ADsPath to the Root Domain with rootDSE

```
1   Set objRootDSE = GetObject("LDAP://rootDSE")
2   strADsPath = "LDAP://" & objRootDSE.Get("rootDomainNamingContext")
3   Set objRootDomain = GetObject(strADsPath)
```

In any domain in the fabrikam.com forest, the strADsPath variable contains:

```
LDAP://DC=fabrikam,DC=com
```

Binding to the Configuration Container

The script in Listing 5.44 binds to the configuration container in the forest.

Listing 5.44   Constructing an ADsPath to the Configuration Container with rootDSE

```
1   Set objRootDSE = GetObject("LDAP://rootDSE")
2   strADsPath = "LDAP://" & objRootDSE.Get("configurationNamingContext")
3   Set objConfiguration = GetObject(strADsPath)
```

In any domain in the fabrikam.com forest, the strADsPath variable contains:

```
LDAP://CN=Configuration,DC=fabrikam,DC=com
```

Binding to the Schema Container

The script in Listing 5.45 binds to the schema container in the forest.

Listing 5.45   Constructing an ADsPath to the Schema Container with rootDSE

```
1   Set objRootDSE = GetObject("LDAP://rootDSE")
2   strADsPath = "LDAP://" & objRootDSE.Get("schemaNamingContext")
3   Set objSchema = GetObject(strADsPath)
```

In any domain in the fabrikam.com forest, the strADsPath variable contains:

```
LDAP://CN=Schema,CN=Configuration,DC=fabrikam,DC=com
```

 Note

For a complete list of rootDSE properties, see the Active Directory Programmer's Guide link on the Web Resources page at http://www.microsoft.com/windows/reskits/webresources.

Active Directory Architecture

Having a general understanding of Active Directory physical architecture and logical structure will help you successfully create ADSI scripts to complete directory management tasks. For example, knowing how to determine the attributes that can be assigned to an object will aid you in writing attributes to the object. Also, knowing which attributes are stored in the Global Catalog and which are indexed will aid you in writing efficient search scripts.

Active Directory physical architecture includes the Active Directory store and the components that make the store accessible. Active Directory logical structure defines how the directory is managed using ADSI and other tools, such as various Microsoft Management Command window (MMC) snap-ins.

Physical Architecture

An important aspect of managing Active Directory with ADSI scripts is understanding the two primary parts of Active Directory, the Active Directory store and the components (DLLs) that make the directory accessible. These two parts of Active Directory work together to provide the foundation of Windows 2000 Server family distributed networks.

The Active Directory store provides secure, searchable, hierarchical storage of objects contained in a network, including users, computers, printers, and applications. The objects in the Active Directory store contain identity and location information to describe network resources. The Active Directory store is contained in a file named the Windows NT® Directory Services Directory Information Tree, Ntds.dit.

The Active Directory components that make the information in the store accessible to users and applications are the:

- **Extensible Storage Engine**. Writes and reads data from the Active Directory store (Ntds.dit). The Extensible Storage Engine (ESE) performs each write operation as a discrete transaction. ESE protects Ntds.dit by using Active Directory log files to provide transaction rollback and database recovery capabilities.

- **Database Layer**. Provides an object-oriented, hierarchical view of the data contained in the Active Directory store.

- **Directory System Agent**. ADSI providers and other interface components use the Directory System Agent (DSA) to establish a connection with the database layer and ultimately the Active Directory store. The DSA acts as a gatekeeper by ensuring that client operations on the objects in the Active Directory store comply with the rules that define each object. For example, the DSA will not allow script operations that attempt to write a value that is too long for a field or a script operation that does not specify all mandatory attributes of an object when it is created.

  The DSA is also integral to directory replication from one domain controller to another.

- **Lightweight Directory Access Protocol**. The protocol layer to LDAP-compliant directory services such as Active Directory. LDAP is the language used by the client and the server to communicate with LDAP-compliant directories. The Active Directory store is compliant with both version 2 and version 3 of the LDAP protocol (LDAP v2 and LDAP v3). The LDAP layer component in Active Directory is LDAP v3.

Logical Structure

Promoting a computer running Windows 2000 Server to a domain controller installs Active Directory on the computer. The Active Directory store is contained on each domain controller in the domain. Before the promotion process completes, you must specify the relationship of the new domain controller to the network. The domain controller can be configured to create a domain or to become part of an existing domain.

To make Active Directory scalable from a single-server network to a network containing thousands of servers, Active Directory is designed to contain many domains. All domains are interconnected to form a hierarchy. A single branch in the hierarchy is called a *tree,* and all the trees in the hierarchy are collectively called a *forest.*

Classes and Attributes

Each Active Directory forest contains a schema. The schema is the library from which all objects are created in Active Directory. You can think of the schema as a template repository whose templates are categorized as either classes or attributes. Classes are used by Active Directory to create objects in the forest. Classes contain references to the attributes in the schema; thus, the objects created from classes contain attributes. Objects created from classes are logical representations of objects in the network, such as a user or a printer. Figure 5.6 shows the relationship between attributes and classes in the schema and the objects they create (instantiate) in Active Directory.

Figure 5.6   Attribute, Class, and Instantiated Object Relationships

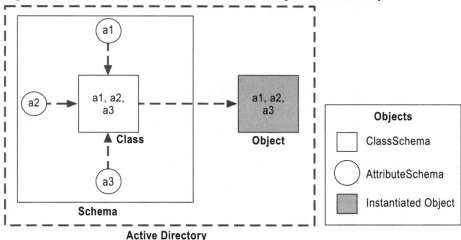

The process of creating an object from a class is called *instantiation,* and an object created from a class is called an *instance.* Each class defines a type of object that can be created in the forest. Attributes contained in a class serve to describe the class. For example, the computer class contains a cn attribute whose value is **Computer** and an lDAPDisplayName attribute whose value is **computer**. Each attribute of a class has a purpose in the directory. For instance, as you have seen, the LDAP provider uses the lDAPDisplayName attribute in ADSI scripts to access objects.

Mandatory and Optional Attributes

Classes also include the systemMustContain and systemMayContain attributes. These attributes define which attributes an object of this class must have (mandatory attributes) and which additional attributes it can have (optional attributes) when it is instantiated. Optional attributes can be set at the same time as the mandatory attributes (when an object is created) or later.

Listing 5.46 shows a script that reads any mandatory and optional attributes assigned to the computer class. To carry out this task, the script performs the following steps:

1. Use the On Error Resume Next statement.

2. Set the E_ADS_PROPERTY_NOT_FOUND constant equal to the ADSI error code generated if either the systemMustContain or systemMayContain attribute is not found in the local property cache (used in lines 10 and 21).

3. Use rootDSE to determine the value of the schemaNamingContext attribute.

    For more information about rootDSE, see "Root Directory Service Entry" earlier in this chapter.

4. Bind to the computer class in the schema container using the GetObject function and the LDAP provider.

5. Initialize the arrMandatoryAttributes variable with the systemMustContain attribute (line 9).

    ▪ If initializing the variable returns the error code equal to E_ADS_PROPERTY_NOT_FOUND, echo to the command window that no mandatory attributes were found.

    ▪ Otherwise, use a For Each statement to read and display the name of each mandatory attribute in the computer class.

6. Initialize the arrOptionalAttributes variable with the systemMayContain attribute (line 20).

- If initializing the variable returns the error code equal to E_ADS_PROPERTY_NOT_FOUND, echo to the command window that no optional attributes were found.

- Otherwise, use a For Each statement to read and display the name of each optional attribute in the computer class.

Listing 5.46   Reading the Mandatory and Optional Attributes of the Computer Class

```
1    On Error Resume Next
2    Const E_ADS_PROPERTY_NOT_FOUND   = &h8000500D
3    strClassName = "cn=Computer"
4
5    Set objRootDSE = GetObject("LDAP://rootDSE")
6    Set objSchemaClass = GetObject("LDAP://" & strClassName & "," & _
7        objRootDSE.Get("schemaNamingContext"))
8
9    arrMandatoryAttributes = objSchemaClass.GetEx("systemMustContain")
10   If Err.Number =  E_ADS_PROPERTY_NOT_FOUND Then
11       Wscript.Echo "No mandatory attributes"
12       Err.Clear
13   Else
14       Wscript.Echo "Mandatory (Must-Contain) attributes"
15       For Each strAttribute in arrMandatoryAttributes
16           Wscript.Echo strAttribute
17       Next
18   End If
19
20   arrOptionalAttributes = objSchemaClass.GetEx("systemMayContain")
21   If Err.Number =  E_ADS_PROPERTY_NOT_FOUND Then
22       Wscript.Echo "No optional attributes"
23       Err.Clear
24   Else
25       Wscript.Echo VbCrLf & "Optional (May-Contain) attributes"
26       For Each strAttribute in arrOptionalAttributes
27           Wscript.Echo strAttribute
28       Next
29   End If
```

When the script runs, it echoes a message indicating that there are no mandatory attributes and then it echoes a list showing the entries in the systemMayContain attribute of the computer class, as shown in the following abbreviated list:

```
No mandatory attributes

Optional (May-Contain) attributes
volumeCount
siteGUID
rIDSetReferences
...
dNSHostName
defaultLocalPolicyObject
cn
catalogs
```

When you create a computer object you must specify a value for the sAMAccountName attribute because it is a mandatory attribute of the computer class. However, running the preceding script suggests that the computer class does not contain any mandatory attributes. The script is not incorrect. The computer class, like many other classes, inherits attributes from other classes by means of direct inheritance or through the Active Directory class hierarchy. The sAMAccountName attribute is mandatory, but is not defined in the computer class.

Class Inheritance and Categorization

Not only is the Active Directory hierarchical in structure (domains are interconnected by trees and trees are interconnected to form a forest), but so are the classes in the schema. Inheritance from one class to another means that some attributes defined for a class are inherited, whereas others are applied directly to the class. Ultimately, the object that is instantiated from the class can contain all of the attributes of the class.

Understanding the differences between class categories will help you determine how objects are used in the forest. In the case of the computer object, the object inherits attributes from the user class. Moving up the class hierarchy, attributes are inherited from the organizationalPerson, person, and top classes. Notice that the user class contains attributes directly applied by the mailRecipient and securityPrincipal classes. The securityPrincipal class contains the sAMAccountName attribute, which is mandatory for all classes that inherit this attribute. Thus, the computer class contains the sAMAccountName attribute through inheritance.

Other distinctions about objects can be drawn by understanding the class hierarchy and inheritance. For example, the contact class is not a securityPrincipal because the securityPrincipal auxiliary class is not applied to the contact class and the contact class does not inherit the attributes of this auxiliary class. Therefore, if you want to create a user account type that is a security principal, you know from the class relationship that a contact object is not a security principal.

Classes are categorized as abstract, structural, auxiliary, or 88. This categorization is stored as an integer in the objectClassCategory attribute of each class.

- **Abstract classes**. Classes of this type provide attributes that flow through the hierarchy, but they cannot be used to instantiate an object. The objectClassCategory attribute for this type of class has the value 2.

- **Auxiliary classes**. Classes of this type provide attributes that extend a structural class, but they cannot be used to form a structural class by themselves or instantiate an object. The objectClassCategory attribute for this type of class has the value 3.

- **Structural classes**. Classes of this type can be instantiated into objects and can contain additional attributes that are not inherited from the other class types. The objectClassCategory attribute for this type of class has the value 1.

- **88**. Classes of this type were defined before there was a specification to classify class categories. Therefore, they are not required to be categorized as abstract, auxiliary, or structural and instead are assigned the value 88. Classes assigned this value behave like structural classes in that they can be instantiated into objects. However, you should view 88 classes as abstract classes because the objects that they create are not typically used to perform Active Directory tasks or to populate the Active Directory store. The objectClassCategory attribute for this type of class has the value 0.

Active Directory complies with the X.500 standard, and therefore must maintain these class categories as defined in the X.500 1993 specification. Any classes defined before the 1993 specification comply with the X.500 1988 specification, which does not contain a categorization requirement. Thus, the 88 category includes all classes defined before there was a categorization requirement.

The script shown in Listing 5.47 reads the objectClassCategory attribute of the classes Top, Mail-Recepient, Security-Principal, Person, Organizational-Person, Contact, User, Computer, and Organizational-Unit. To perform this task the script must:

1. Initialize a variable with an array containing the common names of the classes.

    The common name of each class, not the value of the lDAPDisplayName attribute, is provided to the part of the GetObject function appearing on line 9. GetObject uses the common name of the attribute to build the distinguished name for binding to a class in the schema container.

2. Use rootDSE to determine the value of the schemaNamingContext attribute.

    For more information about rootDSE, see "Root Directory Service Entry" earlier in this chapter.

3. Use a For Each statement to bind to each class in the schema container using the GetObject function and the LDAP provider.

4. Initialize the intClassCategory variable with the integer value of the objectClassCategory attribute.

5. Use a Select Case statement to test the value of the intClassCategory variable and display a message indicating the class type of each class.

Listing 5.47   Reading the objectClassCategory Attribute of Several Classes

```
1   arrClassNames = Array _
2     ("cn=top","cn=mail-Recipient", "cn=security-Principal", _
3       "cn=person", "cn=Organizational-Person", _
4         "cn=contact", "cn=user", "cn=computer", "cn=organizational-Unit")
5
6   Set objRootDSE = GetObject("LDAP://rootDSE")
7   For Each ClassName in arrClassNames
8       Set objSchemaClass = GetObject("LDAP://" & ClassName & "," & _
9       objRootDSE.Get("schemaNamingContext"))
10
11      intClassCategory = objSchemaClass.Get("objectClassCategory")
12      WScript.STDOUT.Write ClassName & " is "
13      Select Case intClassCategory
14          Case 0
15              Wscript.Echo "88"
16          Case 1
17              Wscript.Echo "structural"
18          Case 2
19              Wscript.Echo "abstract"
20          Case 3
21              Wscript.Echo "auxiliary"
22      End Select
23   Next
```

When the script runs, it echoes the class categories of selected classes to the command window, as shown in the following list:

```
cn=top is abstract
cn=mail-Recipient is auxiliary
cn=security-Principal is auxiliary
cn=person is 88
cn=Organizational-Person is 88
cn=contact is structural
cn=user is structural
cn=computer is structural
cn=organizational-Unit is structural
```

The systemAuxiliaryClass attribute of each class lists any auxiliary classes applied directly to a class. The script in Listing 5.48 reads the systemAuxiliaryClass attribute of several classes:

1. Specify the On Error Resume Next statement, and set the E_ADS_PROPERTY_NOT_FOUND constant to determine later in the script whether the systemAuxiliaryClass is empty.

2. Initialize a variable with an array containing the common names of the classes used in the previous task.

3. Use rootDSE to determine the value of the schemaNamingContext attribute.

4. Use a For Each statement to bind to each class in the schema container, using the GetObject function and the LDAP provider.

5. Initialize the arrSystemAuxiliaryClass variable with the systemAuxiliaryClass attribute (lines 15 and 16).

- If initializing the variable returns the error code equal to E_ADS_PROPERTY_NOT_FOUND, echo to the command window that no system auxiliary classes are applied directly to the class.

- Otherwise, use a For Each statement to read and display a list of auxiliary classes assigned directly to the class.

Listing 5.48   Reading the systemAuxiliaryClass Attribute of Several Classes

```
1   On Error Resume Next
2   Const E_ADS_PROPERTY_NOT_FOUND  = &h8000500D
3   arrClassNames = Array _
4     ("cn=top","cn=mail-Recipient", "cn=security-Principal", _
5       "cn=person", "cn=Organizational-Person", _
6         "cn=contact", "cn=user", "cn=computer", "cn=organizational-Unit")
7
8   Set objRootDSE = GetObject("LDAP://rootDSE")
9   For Each ClassName in arrClassNames
10      Set objSchemaClass = GetObject("LDAP://" & ClassName & "," & _
11      objRootDSE.Get("schemaNamingContext"))
12
13      arrSystemAuxiliaryClass = _
14      objSchemaClass.GetEx("systemAuxiliaryClass")
15
16      If Err.Number = E_ADS_PROPERTY_NOT_FOUND Then
17          Wscript.Echo "No auxiliary classes" & _
18              " assigned to " & ClassName
19          Err.Clear
20      Else
21          Wscript.Echo "Auxiliary classes in " & ClassName & ":"
22          For Each strAuxiliaryClass in arrSystemAuxiliaryClass
23              Wscript.Echo vbTab & strAuxiliaryClass
24          Next
25        Wscript.Echo
26      End If
27  Next
```

When this script runs it echoes a message indicating that the mailRecipient auxiliary class is applied to the contact and user classes and that the securityPrincipal auxiliary class is also applied to the user class, as shown in the following list:

```
No auxiliary classes assigned to cn=top.
No auxiliary classes assigned to cn=mail-Recipient.
No auxiliary classes assigned to cn=security-Principal.
No auxiliary classes assigned to cn=person.
No auxiliary classes assigned to cn=Organizational-Person.
Auxiliary classes in cn=contact:
        mailRecipient

Auxiliary classes in cn=user:
        securityPrincipal
        mailRecipient

No auxiliary classes assigned to cn=computer.
No auxiliary classes assigned to cn=organizational-Unit.
```

Understanding class inheritance will help you write search scripts that return the expected set of objects. For example, if you perform a search for all objects whose objectClass attribute contains user, you might be surprised to find that objects instantiated from the computer class are returned in the result set. The computer class inherits the attributes of the user class and all other classes above it in the hierarchy. Therefore, you have to modify the search to exclude computer objects from the result set. For more information about searching using ADSI, see "Searching Active Directory" earlier in this chapter.

You can use a script to view class relationships. The subClassOf attribute shows the parent class from which a class is derived. The steps for reading an attribute are similar to the preceding two listings, so scripting steps are not included here. Listing 5.49 shows how to determine the parent class of the Computer class.

Listing 5.49   Reading the subClassOf Attribute of a Class

```
1  strClassName = "cn=computer"
2
3  Set objRootDSE = GetObject("LDAP://rootDSE")
4  Set objSchemaClass = GetObject("LDAP://" & strClassName & "," & _
5      objRootDSE.Get("schemaNamingContext"))
6
7  strSubClassOf = objSchemaClass.Get("subClassOf")
8  Wscript.Echo "The " & strClassName & _
9      " class is a child of the " & strSubClassOf & " class."
```

When this script runs, it echoes a message indicating that the user class is the parent of the computer class, as shown:

```
The cn=computer class is a child of the user class.
```

Snap-ins For Viewing and Configuring User Account Attributes, Classes, and Objects

As demonstrated in the preceding section, scripts can be used to view information about classes and attributes. You can also examine all of the classes and attributes in the schema using the MMC Active Directory Schema snap-in or the ADSI Edit snap-in. Knowing how to use these tools will make the process of writing scripts easier to achieve. The Active Directory Schema snap-in provides a graphical interface to the classes and attributes in the schema. The ADSI Edit snap-in provides a graphical interface to all objects in Active Directory, including the schema.

Active Directory Schema snap-in

The command window tree in the Active Directory Schema Snap-in provides two lists:

- Class list, which contains all the classes in an Active Directory schema

- Attributes list, which contains all the attributes in the schema

From the Class list, you can learn which attributes are contained in a particular class and the hierarchical relationships of the class, such as the parent class, auxiliary classes, and possible superiors of the class. The attributes of a class include information such as whether the attribute is mandatory or optional and the lDAPDisplayName of the attribute. The lDAPDisplayName is the name you will use to identify most attributes in an ADSI script.

From the Attribute list, you can learn about the characteristics of an attribute, such as whether an attribute is replicated to the Global Catalog, whether it is single or multivalued, and whether the attribute is a Unicode string (string), integer, or other data type. Knowing the characteristics of an attribute is critical to managing the objects that contain the attributes derived from the associated class.

▶ **To load the Active Directory Schema snap-in**

1. From a command prompt, type **regsvr32 schmmgmt** to register the snap-in.

   This step must be completed only once on each computer where the snap-in will be loaded.

2. Start MMC by typing **MMC** at the command prompt or from the **Run** menu.

3. From the **File** menu, click **Add/Remove Snap-in**, and then click **Add**.

4. From the **Add Standalone Snap-in** dialog box, click **Active Directory Schema**, and then click **Add**.

ADSI Edit snap-in

The ADSI Edit snap-in lets you view information about the objects created in Active Directory and lets you view the schema. However, many find the presentation of the schema provided by the Active Directory Schema Snap-in easier to use.

After loading the ADSI Edit snap-in, you can choose where in Active Directory to connect. The default connection points are:

- **LDAP://*domain_controller_name*/Domain.** This view provides information about the objects in the domain. Use this view to read information about attributes that are or can be assigned to Active Directory objects in the domain.

- **LDAP://*domain_controller_name*/Configuration.** This view provides information about the objects that are used to construct Active Directory, such as the sites and services of the domain.

- **LDAP://*domain_controller_name*/RootDSE.** This view provides information about the attributes contained in the RootDSE object. For information about how to use this object, see "Root Directory Services Entry" earlier in this chapter.

- **LDAP://*domain_controller_name*/Schema.** This view provides information about the objects and classes in the Active Directory schema.

 Note

You can also establish a connection with the Global Catalog from this snap-in and view information about the attributes replicated to the Global Catalog.

▶ **To load the ADSI Edit snap-in and connect to the domain**

1. Install the Support tools (SupTools.msi) from the Windows 2000 Server family installation CD-ROM.

   The Support Tools are located in the Support\Tools folder on the installation CD-ROM.

2. Start MMC by typing **MMC** at the command prompt or from the **Run** menu.

3. From the **File** menu, click **Add/Remove Snap-in**, and then click **Add**.

4. From the **Add Standalone Snap-in** dialog box, click **ADSI Edit**, and then click **Add**.

5. In the command window tree, right-click the **ADSI Edit** item, and then click **Connect to**.

6. Accept the defaults appearing in the **Connection Settings** dialog box to connect to the domain, and then click **OK**.

Active Directory Replication and Indexing

Active Directory is well suited for handling a large number of read and search operations, and a significantly smaller number of changes and updates. The data in Active Directory is replicated, meaning that updates occurring to the Active Directory on one domain controller are sent to other domain controllers in the network. Because the data is replicated, Active Directory is not well suited for dynamic data that frequently changes — for example, CPU utilization and Internet stock prices.

Note

However, you can retrieve frequently changing data, such as computer system performance and event logging information, by using WMI. For more information about WMI, see "WMI Scripting Primer" in this book.

A critical part of managing Active Directory with ADSI scripts is knowing where directory objects are replicated. Active Directory is divided into partitions to reduce replication. Partitions are either fully replicated (full replicas) or partially replicated (partial replicas). *Full replicas* are partitions that are replicated to every domain controller in the forest and can be read or written to from any domain controller. *Partial replicas* are read-only partitions that contain a subset of data contained in Active Directory.

Partitions Replicated on Domain Controllers

The three full replicas found on each domain controller are the:

- **Schema partition.** This partition contains all of the classes and attributes defined in the forest.

- **Configuration partition.** This partition contains system information that all domain controllers must store — this includes information about the various partitions, forest-wide services, sites, and well-known security principals in the forest.

- **Domain Directory partition.** This partition contains all of the objects created in a particular domain and is replicated to every domain controller within a domain. Unlike the other two types of partitions, which are full replicas, this partition is different for each domain.

Note

Other replicas might be present on domain controllers.

Attributes Replicated to the Global Catalog

All domain controllers designated as Global Catalog servers contain a partial replica of all other domain directory partitions in the forest. This partial replica, appropriately named the Global Catalog, contains all of the objects in the domain directory partition, but only a subset of the attributes of these objects. Knowing which attributes are contained in the Global Catalog is critical to creating scripts that perform search operations efficiently. For example, if you write a script to request an attribute that is not in the Global Catalog and you want the script to return results from more than one domain, you must use referral chasing. Referral chasing increases network congestion and can cause the script to respond slowly. For information about referral chasing, see "Searching Active Directory" earlier in this chapter.

To avoid referral chasing, read attributes that are contained in the Global Catalog. By doing so, you ensure that the script contacts a single domain controller designated as a Global Catalog server to fulfill the request of the script.

The isMemberOfPartialAttributeSet attribute contains a True or False value indicating whether an attribute is replicated to the Global Catalog. Listing 5.50 shows how to determine whether an attribute is replicated to the Global Catalog.

1. Initialize a variable named strAttributeName with the common name of an attribute.

   In this example, the script tests the given-name attribute. To test other attributes, simply initialize the attribute with the common name of a different attribute.

2. Use rootDSE to determine the value of the schemaNamingContext attribute.

3. Bind to the attribute in the schema container using the GetObject function and the LDAP provider.

4. Initialize the blnInGC variable with the Boolean value contained in the isMemberOfPartialAttributeSet attribute.

- If blnInGC is True, echo to the command window that the attribute is replicated to the Global Catalog.

- Otherwise, echo to the command window that the attribute is not replicated to the Global Catalog.

Listing 5.50 Reading the isMemberOfPartialAttributeSet Attribute of an Attribute

```
1   strAttributeName = "cn=given-name"
2
3   Set objRootDSE = GetObject("LDAP://rootDSE")
4   Set objSchemaAttribute = GetObject("LDAP://" & strAttributeName & "," & _
5       objRootDSE.Get("schemaNamingContext"))
6
7   blnInGC = objSchemaAttribute.Get("isMemberOfPartialAttributeSet")
8   If blnInGC Then
9       Wscript.Echo strAttributeName & _
10          " is replicated to the Global Catalog."
11      Else
12          Wscript.Echo "The " & strAttributeName & _
13              " is not replicated to the Global Catalog."
14  End If
```

When this script runs, it echoes a message indicating that the attribute is contained in the Global Catalog, as shown:

```
cn=given-name is replicated to the Global Catalog.
```

After you have determined that an attribute is in the Global Catalog, you specify GC instead of LDAP when constructing a query string. For information about creating a query string that uses the Global Catalog, see "Searching Active Directory" earlier in this chapter.

In Listing 5.50, you might have noticed that the script searches for an attribute (isMemberOfPartialAttributeSet) in an attribute (givenName or cn=given-name). This illustrates the fact that attributes can contain attributes. In fact, if you view the schema from a tool such as the ADSI Edit snap-in, you will see that attributes and classes are viewed as objects. As you know, Active Directory objects contain attributes.

Indexed Attributes

Another important aspect to consider when performing a search operation is whether the attribute to be sorted is indexed. Indexed attributes are already sorted, which reduces the processing requirements placed on a domain controller when you perform a search operation that includes sorting the result set. For information about enabling a sort operation in a search, see "Searching Active Directory" earlier in this chapter.

The searchFlags attribute contains an integer value indicating, among other things, whether an attribute is indexed. Listing 5.51 shows how to determine whether an attribute is indexed. This script is similar to Listing 5.50, so only steps that differ are shown here.

1. Set the IS_INDEXED constant to determine later in the script whether an attribute is indexed.

2. Use rootDSE to determine the value of the schemaNamingContext attribute.

3. Initialize the intSearchFlags variable with the integer value contained in the searchFlags attribute (line 8).

4. Use rootDSE to determine the value of the schemaNamingContext attribute.

5. Use the AND operator to evaluate the value of IS_INDEXED against the first bit in the searchFlags attribute.

   - If the first bit in the searchFlags attribute is on, echo to the command window that the attribute is indexed.

   - Otherwise, echo to the command window that the attribute is not indexed.

Listing 5.51 Reading the searchFlags Attribute to Determine Whether an Attribute Is Indexed

```
1   Const IS_INDEXED = 1
2   strAttributeName = "cn=given-name"
3
4   Set objRootDSE = GetObject("LDAP://rootDSE")
5   Set objSchemaAttribute = GetObject("LDAP://" & strAttributeName & "," & _
6       objRootDSE.Get("schemaNamingContext"))
7
8   intSearchFlags = objSchemaAttribute.Get("searchFlags")
9   If IS_INDEXED AND intSearchFlags Then
10      Wscript.Echo strAttributeName & " is indexed."
11  Else
12      Wscript.Echo strAttributeName & " not indexed."
13  End If
```

When this script runs, it echoes a message indicating that the given-name attribute is indexed, as shown:

```
cn=given-name is indexed.
```

Attributes That Are Both Replicated to the Global Catalog and Indexed

Ideally, search operations should use attributes that are both replicated to the global catalog and indexed. To retrieve a result set containing all attributes that meet both of these criteria by default, it is more efficient to perform a search operation than it is to bind to each attribute individually. For more information about performing efficient search operations, see "Optimizing Search Performance" earlier in this chapter.

 Caution

You can configure attributes in the schema to be replicated to the Global Catalog or to be indexed by using a tool such as the Active Directory Schema snap-in. However, you must be cautious about how you modify the schema because improper modifications can damage Active Directory or severely affect network and server performance.

Listing 5.52 shows how to perform a search operation to retrieve a result set of all attributes that are both replicated to the Global Catalog and indexed. The steps to complete this task are similar to the search tasks shown earlier in this chapter; therefore, steps are summarized.

1. Set the IS_INDEXED constant to determine later in the script whether an attribute is indexed.

2. Use rootDSE to determine the value of the schemaNamingContext attribute and initialize the strADsPath variable.

3. Using ADO, query Active Directory for all AttributeSchema objects and return the lDAPDisplayName, isMemberOfPartialAttributeSet, and searchFlags attributes of the objects.

   The objectCategory=AttributeSchema returns objects in the schema that are defined as attributes.

4. Use a While Wend statement to read each record in the result set.

5. For each record in the result set, determine both whether the attribute is contained in the Global Catalog — isMemberOfPartialAttributeSet = True — and whether the attribute is indexed — first bit of the searchFlags attribute is on (lines 20 and 21).

If both conditions are true, display the lDAPDisplayName of the attribute (stored in the strAttribute variable).

Listing 5.52   Locating Attributes That Are in the Global Catalog and Indexed

```
1    Const IS_INDEXED = 1
2
3    Set objConnection = CreateObject("ADODB.Connection")
4    objConnection.Open "Provider=ADsDSOObject;"
5
6    Set objCommand = CreateObject("ADODB.Command")
7    objCommand.ActiveConnection = objConnection
8
9    Set objRootDSE = GetObject("LDAP://rootDSE")
10   strADsPath = "<LDAP://" & objRootDSE.Get("schemaNamingContext") & ">"
11   objCommand.CommandText = strADsPath & _
12       ";(objectCategory=AttributeSchema);" & _
13         "lDAPDisplayName,isMemberOfPartialAttributeSet,searchFlags;onelevel"
14
15   Set objRecordSet = objCommand.Execute
16   Wscript.Echo "Attributes in Global Catalog and indexed: "
17   While NOT objRecordSet.EOF
18       strAttribute = objRecordSet.Fields("lDAPDisplayName")
19       If objRecordSet.Fields("isMemberOfPartialAttributeSet") AND _
20          (IS_INDEXED AND objRecordSet.Fields("searchFlags")) Then
21               Wscript.Echo strAttribute
22       End If
23       objRecordSet.MoveNext
24   Wend
25
26   objConnection.Close
```

When this script runs, it echoes the lDAPDisplayName of the attributes that are both contained in the Global Catalog and indexed, as shown in the following abbreviated result set:

```
Attributes in Global Catalog and indexed:
AltSecurityIdentities
cn
displayName
mail
...
name
sAMAccountName
sAMAccountType
servicePrincipalName
sIDHistory
sn
```

Operational Attributes

Not all attribute values are stored in a directory service. Instead, attribute values that are not contained in the directory can be calculated when a request for the attribute is made. This type of attribute is called *operational*. Note that this type of attribute is defined in the schema but it does not contain a value in the directory. Instead, the domain controller that processes a request for an operational attribute calculates the attribute's value to answer the client request.

It is critical that you know which attributes are operational because, unlike the other attributes of an object, operational attributes are not downloaded to the local property cache unless you make an explicit call to the GetInfo or GetInfoEx method. For more information about how to use these methods, see "Data Caching" earlier in this chapter.

The script in Listing 5.53 determines which attributes in the schema are operational. It accomplishes this task by reading the systemFlags attribute of each AttributeSchema object. The steps to complete this task are similar to those for Listing 5.52; therefore, these steps are summarized.

1. Set the ADS_SYSTEMFLAG_ATTR_IS_CONSTRUCTED constant to determine later in the script whether an attribute is operational.

2. Use rootDSE to determine the value of the schemaNamingContext attribute and initialize the strADsPath variable.

3. Using ADO, query Active Directory for all AttributeSchema objects and return the lDAPDisplayName and systemFlags attributes of the objects.

4. Use a While Wend statement to read each record in the result set.

5. For each record in the result set, determine whether the attribute is operational, indicated by whether the third bit of the searchFlags attribute is on (lines 19 and 20).

   ■ If the searchFlags attribute is on, display the lDAPDisplayName of the attribute (stored in the strAttribute variable).

Listing 5.53 Determining Which Attributes Are Operational

```
1   Const ADS_SYSTEMFLAG_ATTR_IS_CONSTRUCTED = &h4
2
3   Set objConnection = CreateObject("ADODB.Connection")
4   objConnection.Open "Provider=ADsDSOObject;"
5
6   Set objCommand = CreateObject("ADODB.Command")
7   objCommand.ActiveConnection = objConnection
8
9   Set objRootDSE = GetObject("LDAP://rootDSE")
10  strADsPath = "<LDAP://" & objRootDSE.Get("schemaNamingContext") & ">"
11  objCommand.CommandText = strADsPath & _
12      ";(objectCategory=AttributeSchema);" & _
13          "lDAPDisplayName,systemFlags;onelevel"
14
15  Set objRecordSet = objCommand.Execute
16  Wscript.Echo "Constructed Attributes: "
17  While NOT objRecordSet.EOF
18      strAttribute = objRecordSet.Fields("lDAPDisplayName")
19      If ADS_SYSTEMFLAG_ATTR_IS_CONSTRUCTED AND _
20          objRecordSet.Fields("systemFlags") Then
21              Wscript.Echo strAttribute
22              objRecordSet.MoveNext
23      End If
24  Wend
25
26  objConnection.Close
```

When this script runs, it echoes a list of operational attributes, as shown in the following abbreviated result set:

```
Constructed Attributes:
allowedAttributes
allowedAttributesEffective
allowedChildClasses
allowedChildClassesEffective
aNR
attributeTypes
canonicalName
createTimeStamp
...
```

ADSI Architecture

Understanding architectural aspects of Active Directory is a critical part of writing ADSI scripts that perform a wide variety of tasks efficiently. In fact, the schema of the underlying directory service ultimately defines the rules for using ADSI to programmatically administer the directory. For example, an ADSI script that creates an object in Active Directory must also write mandatory attributes defined for the object that are not automatically set by the directory.

Another critical part of writing ADSI scripts is having an understanding of the ADSI object model, the ADSI file and logical components, the various ADSI providers available for directory access, and the interfaces that make performing tasks possible.

ADSI Object Model

ADSI is a collection of dynamic-link libraries (DLLs) that are used by client applications such as Windows Script Host (WSH) and Active Directory Users and Computers to administer directory services such as Active Directory.

When you perform a binding operation in an ADSI script, the script uses the moniker in the ADsPath to load the proper ADSI provider DLL. For example, specifying the LDAP moniker loads the LDAP provider, (Adsidp.dll). The ADSI provider DLL creates or instantiates a Component Object Model (COM) object. The COM object is given the name you provide as a reference in the Set statement, for example, objUser, objGroup, or objDomain.

Each instantiated object contains interfaces. An *interface* is a grouping of related methods. As all of the preceding listings demonstrated, methods allow you to perform administrative tasks upon a directory. For example, you used the Create, Put, Get, and Delete methods to perform create, write, read, and delete tasks in Active Directory. All of these methods are contained in a single interface named IADs. Figure 5.7 shows the relationship between a binding operation, a provider, a COM object, its interfaces, and a directory.

Figure 5.7   Creating a COM Object Representation of a Directory Object

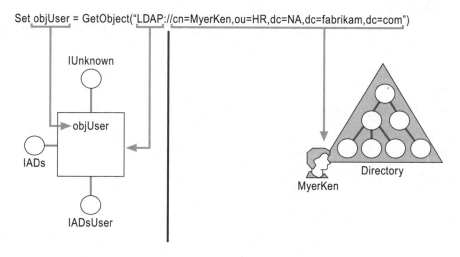

Set objUser = GetObject("LDAP://cn=MyerKen,ou=HR,dc=NA,dc=fabrikam,dc=com")

In Figure 5.7, the LDAP provider instantiates a COM object. The provider determines that MyerKen in the HR OU of the na.fabrikam.com domain is a user account object, so it creates a COM object with the appropriate interfaces for interacting with a user account object. Only three interfaces, IADs, IADsUser, and IUnknown appear in the figure. IADs and IADsUser are the two interfaces that you are most likely to use from an ADSI script to interact with an Active Directory user account object. The IUnknown interface is attached to every COM object and is the base interface for all other interfaces.

The Set statement in Figure 5.7 provides a reference to the object and names the object objUser.

ADSI Installation Components

ADSI resides in the *systemroot*\System32 folder of Microsoft® Windows NT®–based client computers. The file names are ActiveDS.dll, ActiveDS.tlb, and DLLs starting with the ads prefix, such as Adsldp.dll. An installation of ADSI also updates some DLLs, such as Wldap32.dll.

ADSI is a system component on computers running Windows 2000 and Microsoft® Windows® XP operating systems. Therefore, you do not have to install it separately from the operating system. In contrast, ADSI is not a system component on computers running Microsoft® Windows® 95, Windows® 98, Windows® Millenium Edition (Me), or Windows NT 4.0. This means you must install it to use it on these computers. For information about how you can install ADSI on client computers, see the Active Directory Service Interfaces link on the Web Resources page at http://www.microsoft.com/windows/reskits/webresources.

ADSI Layers

The ADSI architecture can be visualized as consisting of five layers, as shown in Figure 5.8. From the bottom of the figure up, the layers are:

- Directory or Namespace
- ADSI Provider
- ADSI Router and Registry
- Property Cache
- ADSI application

Figure 5.8   ADSI Architecture

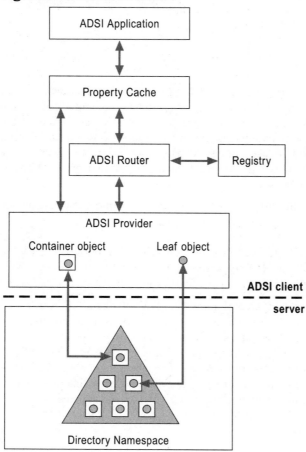

The five layers appearing in Figure 5.8 reside in two places. The lowest layer, the directory or namespace, resides on computers running directory services accessible by ADSI, and the other three layers reside on client computers.

Directory Namespace

A directory service stores information about all resources on a network and makes the information accessible to users and applications. The directory is the physical database where information about the network is stored.

A *namespace* is an area where a name can be resolved. For example, the Domain Name System (DNS) namespace is a tree of domains where host names and IP addresses are contained. Name resolution allows computers to use the DNS namespace to resolve host names to IP addresses and IP addresses to host names. Similarly, a directory namespace is a defined area where a network name (directory element) can be resolved into an object regardless of where it resides within the namespace. In the case of Active Directory, the namespace is the forest and Active Directory provides name resolution services.

Any network names in Active Directory can be resolved into objects. For example, directory elements such as domains, user accounts, groups, OUs, and computers can all be resolved into objects. In turn, the object contains properties that you can manage using ADSI scripts. For example, after you have obtained a domain object using a script, you can create OUs; after you have obtained an OU object in a script, you can create user accounts, groups, and other objects.

Providers

ADSI is not part of the directory service itself, but it provides the interfaces to interact with the directory namespace. You can use ADSI to access all of the following directory namespaces:

- LDAP directories, including Active Directory
- Security Accounts Manager (SAM) databases, in both local workstations and Windows NT domains
- Internet Information Services (IIS) metabase
- Novell NetWare Directory Services (NDS)
- NetWare Bindery

ADSI providers access the directory namespace and create virtual representations of objects that you then administer with ADSI interfaces. In the suite of ADSI DLLs, there is a subset of provider DLLs that access various directory services, as shown in Table 5.5.

Table 5.5   ADSI Providers and the Directory Services They Access

Provider	To Access
LDAP provider	LDAP Version 2– and Version 3–based directories, including Active Directory.
GC provider	The Global Catalog on Active Directory domain controllers designated as Global Catalog servers. The GC provider is similar to the LDAP provider but uses TCP port number 3268 to access the Global Catalog.
ADSI OLE DB provider	Active Directory to perform search operations.
WinNT provider	Windows NT domains and Windows NT/Windows 2000/Windows XP local account databases.
IIS provider	The Internet Information Services (IIS) metabase.
NDS provider	Novell NetWare Directory Services.
NWCOMPAT provider	The Novell Netware Bindery.

ADSI providers act as the intermediaries between a directory namespace and an ADSI application, such as an ADSI script. All of the listings in this chapter bind to Active Directory using the LDAP provider or the GC provider.

 Note

Provider names are case sensitive. All ADSI providers listed are uppercase except for the WinNT provider, which is a mixture of uppercase and lowercase. Also, unlike the other providers listed, the IIS provider is not categorized as a system provider.

Binding to a directory varies from one provider to the next. However, the binding syntax always begins with the name of the provider, followed by a colon, two forward slashes, and a path distinctive to the type of directory you are binding to.

As explained in "Step 1: Establishing a Connection" earlier in this chapter, the ADsPath is the name of the provider combined with the path to a directory object. The ADsPath syntax from one provider to the next is unique to avoid naming conflicts from one directory namespace to the next. The following list shows ADsPath syntax examples for many of the ADSI providers:

- **LDAP provider path to a domain controller in the na.fabrikam.com domain**: LDAP://dc=NA,dc=fabrikam,dc=com. Notice that the example does not specify a server name, just a domain name. This method of binding is called *serverless binding*. It is a good idea to use serverless binding whenever possible so that the script is not tied to completing a bind operation to a specific domain controller.

- **GC provider path to a global catalog server in the na.fabrikam.com domain**: GC://dc=NA,dc=fabrikam,dc=com.

- **WinNT provider path to a domain controller in the na.fabrikam.com domain:** WinNT://NA.

- **IIS provider path to the IIS server sea-dc-01.na.fabrikam.com:** IIS://sea-dc-01.na.fabrikam.com.

- **NDS provider path to a directory server in the na.fabrikam.com domain:** NDS://server01/o=org01/dc=com/dc=fabrikam/dc=na.

- **NWCOMPAT provider to a bindery server:** NWCOMPAT://server01.

The ADSI OLE DB provider uses the same ADsPath syntax as the LDAP and GC providers but with additional parameters to control what is returned by a search operation. For more information, see "Searching Active Directory" earlier in this chapter.

Tip

Use rootDSE to avoid hard-coding distinguished names into the ADsPath of an Active Directory bind operation. For more information about rootDSE, see "Root Directory Service Entry" earlier in this chapter.

There is a special provider called the ADSI namespace provider. You can use this provider to return a list of all providers installed on a client computer, as shown in Listing 5.54.

Listing 5.54   Displaying a List of Installed ADSI Providers

```
1   Set objProvider = GetObject("ADs:")
2   For Each Provider In objProvider
3       Wscript.Echo Provider.Name
4   Next
```

When this script runs, it echoes the name of each installed provider, as shown in the following list that was generated from a Windows 2000 Professional computer:

```
WinNT:
NWCOMPAT:
NDS:
LDAP:
IIS:
```

Caution

Although the ADSI WinNT provider can be used to manage a subset of objects and attributes in Active Directory, using the WinNT provider to manage Active Directory is not recommended because it can have adverse effects on a script's performance and resiliency.

Router

When a script calls the GetObject function, the ADSI router receives the request, identifies the provider being requested, searches the registry for information about the provider, and then loads the provider into local memory. The router identifies the provider by matching the provider name (its ProgID) with its ProgID as listed in the registry. The provider then passes the requested named element back to the ADSI router, and the router creates the ADSI object that is then passed back to the calling script.

The ADSI Router is responsible for creating many of the ADSI core objects and the corresponding interfaces used to manage elements in ADSI-supported directories. After object creation (completing the binding operation), object management, such as reading and writing object attributes, is undertaken directly between the ADSI application and the provider.

Property Cache

Immediately following the binding operation, a region of local memory is set aside to hold a virtual representation of an Active Directory object. The Active Directory object and its attributes are not downloaded to the property cache during the binding operation. This is important because the Active Directory object can contain hundreds of attributes, most of which you will not need to manage in a single script. For more information about the local property cache, see "Data Caching" earlier in this chapter.

ADSI-Enabled Applications

This is the top layer of ADSI, and is where you interact with the rest of the architecture. All of the listings in this chapter demonstrate how to use WSH and VBScript to create scripts that interact with ADSI. Many other applications depend on ADSI, such as the Active Directory Users and Computers and ADSI Edit snap-ins. These GUI-based applications can help you manage directories and gain a further understanding of how directories operate.

ADSI Interfaces

Each interface contains a set of methods you use to programmatically administer directories. Methods either perform an action or identify something about the object to which they are attached. Methods that perform an action are always referred to as *methods,* and methods that describe an object are often called *properties*.

A common convention for showing an interface and its method or property is *interfacename*::*methodname* or *interfacename*::*propertyname*. For example, the GetEx method of the IADs core interface is written as IADs::GetEx.

Whether an interface is available to administer a directory service is dependent on the provider being used. Providers do not implement all interfaces. For example, the LDAP provider does not implement the IADsADSystemInfo interface because this interface is specifically designed to retrieve information about a client computer and the currently logged-on user in an Active Directory domain. In contrast, the LDAP provider is specifically designed to interact on domain controllers with Active Directory and other LDAP-compliant directories.

 Note

To use the IADsADSystemInfo interface, the computer must be running Windows 2000 or an operating system in the Windows XP family and the interface must be created separately from the binding operation.

In addition, providers do not necessarily implement all methods within an interface. For example, the LDAP provider does not implement the CopyHere method of the IADsContainer interface. Instead, you must use other techniques to perform a copy operation.

For a list of the interfaces supported by each system provider, go to the Active Directory Programmer's Guide link on the Web Resources page at http://www.microsoft.com/windows/reskits/webresources and search for the topic "Provider Support of ADSI Interfaces."

Categorizing Interfaces

Interface categorizations make it easier to locate the appropriate interface for a particular task. Table 5.6 shows the interface categories, a general description of their purposes, and the interfaces within each category that are implemented by the LDAP provider.

Table 5.6   Interfaces Implemented by the LDAP Provider

Categories	LDAP Provider–Specific Purpose	Interfaces
Core	General-purpose interfaces for interacting with almost any object in a directory. You are likely to use these interfaces most of the time in ADSI scripts.	IADs, IADsContainer, IADsNamespaces, IADsOpenDSObject
Schema	Interfaces for managing and extending a directory's schema.	IADsClass, IADsProperty, IADsSyntax
Property Cache	Interfaces for interacting with the local property cache.	IADsPropertyEntry, IADsPropertyList, IADsPropertyValue, IADsPropertyValue2
Persistent Object	Interfaces for interacting with a specific type of object or a logical grouping of attributes.	IADsGroup, IADsLocality, IADsMembers, IADsO, IADsOU, IADsPrintQueue, IADsUser
Dynamic Object	Interface for interacting with a print queue published to the directory.	IADsPrintQueueOperations
Security	Interfaces that interact with DACLs assigned to directory objects.	IADsAccessControlEntry, IADsAccessControlList, IADsSecurityDescriptor
Non-Automation	Interfaces that provide low-level access to directory objects. These interfaces are not available to scripting languages such as VBScript.	IDirectoryObject, IDirectorySearch
Extension	Interface for adding methods and other functions to existing objects.	IADsExtension
Utility	Interfaces that provide helper functions.	IADsDeleteOps, IADsPathname, IADsObjectOptions
Data Type	Interface for interpreting attributes that are stored as large integer (64-bit) data types.	IADsLargeInteger

LDAP Provider Objects and Their Interfaces

Grouping interfaces by the objects that they support simplifies the process of determining the properties and methods that are implemented for an object. For a table showing the ADSI object types generated by the LDAP provider, such as generic object (GenObject) and User, and the ADSI interfaces supported by each object, see the Active Directory Programmer's Guide link on the Web Resources page at http://www.microsoft.com/windows/reskits/webresources and search for the topic "ADSI Objects of LDAP." For tables implemented by the other system providers, search for the following topics:

- "ADSI Objects for WinNT"
- "ADSI Objects for NDS"
- "ADSI Objects of NWCOMPAT"

The core interfaces, IADs and IADsContainer, are the two interfaces you are most likely to encounter when working with COM objects instantiated by the ADSI system providers. Interfaces implemented by the LDAP or WinNT provider to perform specialized tasks, such as changing a user account password or reading an attribute stored as a large integer, appear in the ADSI task-based chapters in this book.

IADs Properties

The six read-only properties in the IADs interface let you uniquely identify every object in the directory.

- **IADs::ADsPath.** Returns a string containing the fully qualified path of the object in the directory. The path uniquely identifies the object in the directory and can be used to retrieve the object as long as the object is not moved.
- **IADs::Class.** Returns a string containing the name of the schema class of the object.
- **IADs::GUID.** Returns a string containing the globally unique identifier (GUID) of the object.

  You can use the GUID returned by this property to bind directly to the object. If you choose to do this, however, the ADsPath property will return a GUID ADsPath.
- **IADs::Name.** Returns a string containing the relative name of the object within the underlying directory service. This name distinguishes the object from its siblings.

- **IADs::Parent.** Returns a string containing the ADsPath of the parent object.

  Although concatenating the Parent property to the Name property in an ADSI script might sometimes return the object's ADsPath, it is not guaranteed to return valid results. Use the object's ADsPath property to retrieve the actual ADsPath.

- **IADs::Schema.** Returns a string containing the schema class of the object.

  You can use the string returned by this property to bind to the schema class object. After you have bound to the schema class object, you can determine the mandatory and optional attributes defined for objects based on the schema. For more information about mandatory and optional attributes, see "Classes and Attributes" earlier in this chapter.

The script in Listing 5.55 displays information about the na.fabrikam.com domain using the IADs properties collection.

Listing 5.55   Displaying Information About a Domain Using IADs Properties

```
1   Set objDomain = GetObject("LDAP://dc=NA,dc=fabrikam,dc=com")
2   Wscript.Echo "ADsPath:" & objDomain.ADsPath
3   Wscript.Echo "Class:" & objDomain.Class
4   Wscript.Echo "GUID:" & objDomain.GUID
5   Wscript.Echo "Name:" & objDomain.Name
6   Wscript.Echo "Parent:" & objDomain.Parent
7   Wscript.Echo "Schema:" & objDomain.Schema
```

When this script runs, it echoes IADs properties in the domain object, as shown in the following list:

```
ADsPath:LDAP://dc=NA,dc=fabrikam,dc=com
Class:domainDNS
GUID:618a1da520255a41ab778f5dc1d8da4d
Name:dc=NA
Parent:LDAP://dc=fabrikam,dc=com
Schema:LDAP://schema/domainDNS
```

IADsContainer Property

The one read-only property in IADsContainer lets you read the object classes specified in the Filter method.

- **IADsContainer::Filter.** This property returns the class of objects being filtered in a container enumeration.

  IADsContainer::Filter is also considered a method because you use it to set the Filter property on a container object to be enumerated. Therefore, to separate the property from the method, the property is referred to as get_Filter because it reads the value of the filter. The method is referred to as put_Filter because it sets or writes the value of the filter.

The other two properties of IADsContainer, IADsContainer::Count and IADsContainer::Hints, are not implemented in the LDAP provider.

The script in Listing 5.56 displays the Filter property in the container enumeration of the HR OU. Note that you must assign a value to the Filter property by using the Filter method, as shown in line 2 of the listing.

Listing 5.56   Displaying the Filtered Property

```
1  Set objOU = GetObject("LDAP://OU=HR,dc=NA,dc=fabrikam,dc=com")
2  ObjOU.Filter= Array("Computer", "User")
3  Wscript.Echo "Object Filters:"
4  For each strObject in objOU.Filter
5      Wscript.Echo vbTab & strObject
6  Next
```

When this script runs, it echoes the IADsContainer::Filter property in the HR OU, as shown in the following list:

```
Object Filters:
        Computer
        User
```

For information about IADsContainer methods, see the following sections earlier in this chapter:

- **IADsContainer::Filter (put_Filter).** "Enumerating Active Directory Objects in Containers"

- **IADsContainer::get__NewEnum**. "Enumerating Active Directory Objects in Containers"

  This method allows a script to enumerate through a container of objects. Every script in "Enumerating Active Directory Objects in Containers" implicitly calls this method to perform enumeration tasks with the VBScript For Each statement. Therefore, no explicit call to this method appears in the scripts.

- **IADsContainer::Create**. "Creating Directory Service Objects"

- **IADsContainer::Delete**. "Deleting Directory Service Objects"

- **IADsContainer::MoveHere**. "Moving and Renaming Objects"

One method of IADsContainer that requires some explanation beyond referring to sections earlier in this chapter is:

- **IADsContainer::GetObject**. This method retrieves an IADs reference to an object in a container.

After you have used the VBScript GetObject function to bind to a container, you can then use the IADs::GetObject method to retrieve an object from the container. However, for simplicity, you will usually complete a single GetObject function call to bind directly to an object in a container instead of performing the binding operation in two steps.

WMI Scripting Primer

Windows Management Instrumentation (WMI) is the primary management technology for Microsoft® Windows® operating systems. It enables consistent and uniform management, control, and monitoring of systems throughout your enterprise. Based on industry standards, WMI allows system administrators to query, change, and monitor configuration settings on desktop and server systems, applications, networks, and other enterprise components. System administrators can write scripts that use the WMI Scripting Library to work with WMI and create a wide range of systems management and monitoring scripts.

In This Chapter

WMI Overview...**431**

WMI Architecture...**436**

    Managed Resources...438

    WMI Infrastructure...439

    WMI Consumers..445

    WMI Security..445

Common Information Model **448**

    Blueprint for Management...451

    Exploring the CIM Repository 481

WMI Scripting Library **482**

    WMI Scripting Library Object Model 482

Writing WMI Scripts...**494**

Connecting to WMI Using the WMI Moniker...495

Retrieving Managed Resources Using WMI Query Language...............................505

Working with Dates and Times 517

Creating Scripts Based on WMI Templates..525

Monitoring Resources by Using WMI Event Notifications 532

WMI Overview

Windows Management Instrumentation (WMI) makes managing Windows-based computers much more convenient than it has been in the past. WMI provides you with a consistent way to access comprehensive system management information and was designed, from the beginning, to work across networks. For system administrators managing Windows-based computers, understanding WMI is as important and useful as understanding the Active Directory® directory service.

WMI provides a consistent model of the managed environment. For each manageable resource, there is a corresponding WMI class. You can think of a WMI class as a succinct description of the properties of a managed resource and the actions that WMI can perform to manage that resource.

 Note

What is a managed resource? For the purposes of this chapter, a managed resource is any object — computer hardware, computer software, a service, a user account, and so on — that can be managed by using WMI.

Consider how you had to manage and monitor Windows-based workstations and servers in the past. You had to use a number of different administrative tools to administer various resources, including disk drives, event logs, files, folders, file systems, networking components, operating system settings, performance data, printers, processes, registry settings, security, services, shares, users, and groups.

With WMI, instead of learning how to use all of these different administrative tools, you need to learn only how to write scripts that use the WMI scripting library. The scripting library lets you work with WMI classes that correspond to managed resources. After you understand this model and how to make use of it, you can apply what you have learned to manage any resource that has a corresponding WMI class. This is one of the primary benefits of using WMI: You can use the same approach to manage resources as disparate as disk drives, event logs, and installed software.

WMI conforms to industry standards overseen by the Distributed Management Task Force (DMTF). The DMTF is an industry organization that works with key technology vendors, including Microsoft, as well as affiliated standards groups to define interoperable management solutions. The architecture of WMI is based on ideas described in the DMTF Web-Based Enterprise Management (WBEM) initiative.

WMI was originally released in 1998 as an add-on component with Microsoft® Windows NT® 4.0 with Service Pack 4. WMI is now an integral part of the Windows family of operating systems, including Microsoft Windows 2000 and Microsoft® Windows® XP.

Capabilities of WMI

Using Windows Script Host (WSH) and Microsoft® Visual Basic® Scripting Edition (VBScript), Microsoft® JScript®, or any scripting language that supports COM Automation (for example, ActivePerl from ActiveState Corporation), you can write WMI scripts that automate the management of the following aspects of your enterprise:

- **Computers based on Windows XP Professional and Windows 2000**

    You can write scripts to manage event logs, file systems, printers, processes, registry settings, scheduled tasks, security, services, shared folders, and numerous other operating system components and configuration settings.

- **Networks**

    You can create WMI-based scripts to manage network services such as Domain Name System (DNS), client-side network settings (for example, configuring a computer to use a static IP address or to obtain an IP address from a Dynamic Host Configuration Protocol [DHCP] server), and Simple Network Management Protocol (SNMP)–enabled devices.

- **Real-time health monitoring**

    You can write scripts that use WMI event subscriptions to monitor and respond to the creation of event log entries, modifications to the file system or the registry, and other real-time operating system changes. Conceptually, event subscriptions and notifications perform the same function in WMI as traps do in SNMP.

- **Windows .NET enterprise server applications**

    You can write scripts to manage Microsoft Application Center, Operations Manager, Systems Management Server, Exchange Server, and SQL Server.

In some cases, the capabilities found in WMI replicate capabilities found in command-line tools or GUI applications. In other cases, however, WMI provides management capabilities not readily available anywhere else. For example, before WMI the seemingly trivial task of retrieving the total amount of physical memory installed in a remote Windows-based computer could not be scripted, at least not without using a third-party tool. In fact, prior to WMI the only operating system tool that enabled you to determine the amount of memory installed in a computer was the System Properties dialog box. Although this approach works fine for manually retrieving the memory configuration on the local computer, it cannot be used to automatically retrieve the memory configuration, or to obtain memory information from a remote computer.

Using WMI, however, you can retrieve the amount of physical memory installed on any computer (or at least any computer you have administrator rights to) by using the simple WMI script in Listing 6.1.

 Note

Admittedly, the script might not look all that simple at first glance. As you will discover, however, much of the script is boilerplate code that can be used, unchanged, in any WMI script that retrieves information about a managed resource.

Listing 6.1   Retrieving and Displaying Total Physical Memory

```
1   strComputer = "."
2
3   Set objSWbemServices = GetObject("winmgmts:\\" & strComputer)
4   Set colSWbemObjectSet = _
5       objSWbemServices.InstancesOf("Win32_LogicalMemoryConfiguration")
6
7   For Each objSWbemObject In colSWbemObjectSet
8       Wscript.Echo "Total Physical Memory (kb): " & _
9           objSWbemObject.TotalPhysicalMemory
10  Next
```

If you run this script under CScript, you should see the number of kilobytes of physical memory installed on the target computer displayed in the command window. The following is typical output from the script:

```
Total Physical Memory (kb): 261676
```

So how did the script determine the amount of memory installed on the computer? If you look at the boldfaced items in the code, you will see that the script performed two tasks:

1. It connected to a WMI class named **Win32_LogicalMemoryConfiguration**.

    WMI classes represent the managed resources on a computer. As the name implies, Win32_LogicalMemoryConfiguration allows you to retrieve information about the memory configuration on a computer.

2. It echoed the value of a property named **TotalPhysicalMemory**.

    WMI classes — which are typically virtual representations of real, live items — have properties that mimic the properties of the real, live item. By looking at the memory configuration on a computer, you can determine the total amount of memory installed. Likewise, the Win32_LogicalMemoryConfiguration class has a property that can be used to determine the total amount of memory installed on a computer. The properties of a WMI class are typically the same as the properties of the actual item. Disk drives have properties such as heads, sectors, and cylinders. The Win32_DiskDrive class has properties such as TotalHeads, TotalSectors, and TotalCylinders.

In addition to physical memory, Windows-based computers also support the concept of virtual memory. Not too surprisingly, the Win32_LogicalMemoryConfiguration class also has a property that corresponds to the virtual memory on a computer: TotalVirtualMemory. If you want to know the total amount of virtual memory on a computer, you can use the script shown in Listing 6.2. The single item in boldface (the property name) is the only real difference between this script and the script that returned the total physical memory installed on a computer. (The script also echoes the phrase, "Total Virtual Memory (kb)" as opposed to "Total Physical Memory (kb).")

Listing 6.2 Retrieving and Displaying Total Virtual Memory

```
1   strComputer = "."
2
3   Set objSWbemServices = GetObject("winmgmts:\\" & strComputer)
4   Set colSWbemObjectSet = _
5       objSWbemServices.InstancesOf("Win32_LogicalMemoryConfiguration")
6
7   For Each objSWbemObject In colSWbemObjectSet
8       Wscript.Echo "Total Virtual Memory (kb): " & _
9           objSWbemObject.TotalVirtualMemory
10  Next
```

Of course, WMI can be used to do more than just return information about the memory configuration on a computer, For example, the script in Listing 6.3 retrieves and displays the name, state, and startup type for all of the services installed on a computer.

Listing 6.3 Retrieving and Displaying Information About Services

```
1   strComputer = "."
2
3   Set objSWbemServices = GetObject("winmgmts:\\" & strComputer)
4   Set colSWbemObjectSet = objSWbemServices.InstancesOf("Win32_Service")
5
6   For Each objSWbemObject In colSWbemObjectSet
7       Wscript.Echo "Display Name: " & objSWbemObject.DisplayName & vbCrLf & _
8                    "   State:      " & objSWbemObject.State        & vbCrLf & _
9                    "   Start Mode: " & objSWbemObject.StartMode
10  Next
```

Running this script under CScript produces output similar to the following (only partial output is shown):

```
Display Name: MSSQLServerADHelper
    State:      Stopped
    Start Mode: Manual
Display Name: Network DDE
    State:      Stopped
    Start Mode: Disabled
Display Name: Network DDE DSDM
    State:      Stopped
    Start Mode: Disabled
Display Name: Net Logon
    State:      Running
    Start Mode: Auto
```

If you look closely at the script in Listing 6.3, you should notice two things:

1. Instead of using the class Win32_LogicalMemoryConfiguration, this script uses a class named **Win32_Service**. Why? Because it is returning information about services, not about memory configuration. If the script was returning information about a computer monitor, it would use the class Win32_DesktopMonitor. The class name will always change to reflect the managed resource.

2. The properties echoed in this script differ from the properties echoed in the previous scripts. Why? Because services have properties that differ from memory configuration properties. Services have properties such as display name and start mode; memory does not. The properties will always change to reflect the managed resource.

If you are beginning to detect a pattern here, you have already taken a big step toward learning how to write WMI scripts. WMI scripts that retrieve information about managed resources are almost identical; you can take a basic script template, type the appropriate class name and class properties, and retrieve information for nearly all managed resources. (In fact, a template that lets you do this is provided later in this chapter.)

As you will see throughout this chapter, WMI scripts typically involve three steps:

1. They connect to the WMI service.

2. They retrieve some information about WMI classes.

3. They do something with that information (for example, echo it to the screen).

To a large extent, all WMI scripts follow this same pattern. For example, suppose you want to write a script to retrieve and display records from the Windows event logs. Reusing some of the code from Listing 6.1, you can easily create a script that carries out this task, as demonstrated in Listing 6.4. In this listing, the starting point for each of the three steps of a typical WMI script is denoted by the boldfaced numerals 1, 2, and 3: 1) Connect to the WMI service; 2) retrieve information; 3) display that information.

  Note
> Before you run Listing 6.4, be aware that this script can take a long time to
> run if your event logs contain thousands of records.

Listing 6.4   Retrieving and Displaying Windows Event Log Records

```
1   strComputer = "."
2
3   Set objSWbemServices = GetObject("winmgmts:\\" & strComputer)
4   Set colSWbemObjectSet = objSWbemServices.InstancesOf("Win32_NTLogEvent")
5   For Each objSWbemObject In colSWbemObjectSet
6       Wscript.Echo "Log File:        " & objSWbemObject.LogFile        & vbCrLf & _
7                    "Record Number:   " & objSWbemObject.RecordNumber   & vbCrLf & _
8                    "Type:            " & objSWbemObject.Type           & vbCrLf & _
```

(continued)

Listing 6.4 Retrieving and Displaying Windows Event Log Records *(continued)*

```
 9                  "Time Generated:  " & objSWbemObject.TimeGenerated & vbCrLf & _
10                  "Source:          " & objSWbemObject.SourceName      & vbCrLf & _
11                  "Category:        " & objSWbemObject.Category         & vbCrLf & _
12                  "Category String: " & objSWbemObject.CategoryString   & vbCrLf & _
13                  "Event:           " & objSWbemObject.EventCode        & vbCrLf & _
14                  "User:            " & objSWbemObject.User             & vbCrLf & _
15                  "Computer:        " & objSWbemObject.ComputerName     & vbCrLf & _
16                  "Message:         " & objSWbemObject.Message          & vbCrLf
17  Next
```

WMI Architecture

The first few pages of this chapter were designed to drive home one important point: WMI scripting does not have to be hard. In fact, WMI scripting can be very easy: As you have seen, you can take a basic script template and, by making only minor changes here and there, create hundreds of scripts that can retrieve information about any managed object on a computer.

All of this is true. However, it is also true that the opening section of this chapter sidestepped some important issues. For example, everyone appreciates the fact that WMI provides the Win32_NTLogEvent class, enabling you to retrieve events from event logs. However, how are you supposed to know that there *is* such a class as Win32_NTLogEvent? No one denies the value of having the Win32_Service class include properties such as Name, Description, and State, but how are you supposed to know these properties are included in the class? The fact that you can write hundreds of scripts using the same basic template is extremely useful, but only if you know what elements to plug in to that template.

In fact, in many respects scripting is the easy part of managing computers with WMI; the hard part involves figuring out what can and cannot be managed. The task-based chapters in this book can help you in that respect; if you want to manage files and folders, the "Files and Folders" chapter will provide detailed information about the appropriate WMI classes (and their methods and properties). But what if you want to manage video cards, desktop monitors, or network adapters? Although these items can be managed by using WMI, there is no handy reference to the appropriate classes (and their methods and properties) in this book.

Does this mean you can manage only the items referenced in this book? Of course not; in fact, you can manage anything WMI can manage, provided you understand how WMI works. After you understand how, and where, WMI stores information, you can easily determine the answer to such questions as 1) Which classes are available to me, 2) What are the names of these classes, and 3) Which properties and methods can be used with each class?

This section and the following section regarding the Common Information Model (CIM) provide in-depth coverage of the WMI architecture, starting you on your way toward a better understanding of this powerful administration tool. This section begins by examining the three primary layers of WMI (shown in Figure 6.1):

1.   Consumers

2.   WMI infrastructure

3.   Managed resources

The section concludes by introducing the topic of WMI security. Although security is not an architectural layer like consumers, the WMI infrastructure, and managed resources, it is important to understand how WMI handles security before you begin writing and deploying scripts.

Figure 6.1   WMI Architecture

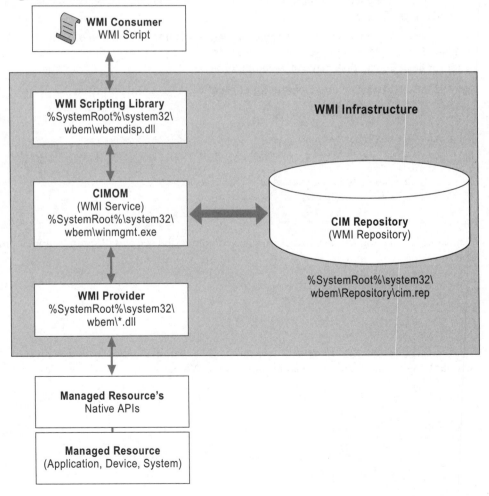

Managed Resources

Managed resources are the fundamental layer in the WMI architecture. A managed resource is any logical or physical component that can be accessed and managed by using WMI. Windows resources that can be managed by using WMI include the computer system, disks, peripheral devices, event logs, files, folders, file systems, networking components, operating system subsystems, performance counters, printers, processes, registry settings, security, services, shared folders, SAM users and groups, Active Directory, Windows Installer, Windows Driver Model (WDM) device drivers, and SNMP Management Information Base (MIB) data.

A WMI-managed resource communicates with WMI through a provider. As you begin to write scripts to interact with WMI-managed resources, you will often see the term *instance* used to refer to a virtual representation of the managed resource in the running script. According to the WMI SDK, an instance is "a representation of a real-world managed object that belongs to a particular class."

In more concrete terms, an instance represents an actual implementation of something WMI can manage. For example, suppose you run the script shown in Listing 6.5, which returns the drive letter for each logical disk drive on a computer.

Listing 6.5   Retrieving and Displaying Logical Disk Drive Information

```
1    strComputer = "."
2
3    Set objSWbemServices = GetObject("winmgmts:\\" & strComputer)
4    Set colSWbemObjectSet = objSWbemServices.InstancesOf("Win32_LogicalDisk")
5
6    For Each objSWbemObject In colSWbemObjectSet
7        Wscript.Echo objSWbemObject.DeviceID
8    Next
```

Depending on the logical disk drives on your computer, the script will return output similar to this:

```
A:
C:
D:
E:
```

Each of these drive letters represents two things: 1) a real, live logical disk drive installed (or mapped) on the computer and 2) an instance of the Win32_LogicalDiskDrive class.

Note

But what if there are no instances of a class? For example, suppose you run a script that returns information about all the tape drives on a computer, only no tape drives are on the computer. Will that generate an error? No; after all, Win32_TapeDrive is a valid WMI class. It just happens that no actual tape drives (no *instances* of the class) are installed on the computer.

WMI Infrastructure

The WMI infrastructure is the middle layer in the architectural model. WMI consists of three primary components: the Common Information Model Object Manager (CIMOM), also known as the WMI service; the Common Information Model (CIM) repository, also known as the WMI repository; and WMI providers. Together these three components provide the infrastructure through which configuration and management data is defined, exposed, accessed, and retrieved.

Note

A related component, the WMI Scripting Library, is discussed later in this chapter.

WMI Providers

WMI providers act as an intermediary between the CIMOM and a managed resource. Providers request information from and send instructions to WMI-managed resources on behalf of consumer applications and scripts. For example, Listing 6.1 and Listing 6.3 use the built-in Win32® provider to retrieve memory and service-related information. Listing 6.4 uses the built-in Event Log provider to retrieve records from the Windows event logs.

Providers hide the implementation details unique to a particular managed resource by exposing the managed resource to the WMI infrastructure using a standards-based, uniform access model. WMI providers communicate with their respective managed resources by using the native application programming interfaces (APIs) of the managed resource, and communicate with the CIMOM by using WMI programming interfaces. For example, the built-in Event Log provider calls Win32 Event Log APIs to access event logs.

Why does this matter to you? To create an application that manages Windows subsystems, you typically use the Win32 APIs. Without WMI, you would need to call these APIs yourself. This creates at least two problems. First, Win32 APIs cannot be called from a script; as a result, you must use a programming language such as C++ or Visual Basic to manage these resources. Having to use a programming language such as C++ eliminates the benefits available through scripting:

- Scripts can be written in a matter of minutes.

- Scripts can be written using nothing more powerful than Notepad.

- Scripts can be written without requiring header files, compilers, and other items more commonly used by developers than by system administrators.

Second, the Win32 APIs do not necessarily work in a consistent manner; just because you learn how to program the Event Log APIs does not mean you have a head start in learning how to program the Win32 Service APIs. One of the difficulties in programming management applications in Windows is that different APIs must be accessed and used in different ways.

WMI providers help solve both of these problems. For one thing, you do not have to worry about calling the Win32 APIs; WMI will do that for you. Likewise, you do not have to worry about differences between various APIs; again, you use a standard set of WMI commands, and WMI will translate those commands into commands that the APIs understand. The WMI providers give you a simple and consistent way to access the Win32 APIs, even if you never realize that you *are* accessing the Win32 APIs.

Of course, WMI is not just for system administrators. Software developers can leverage the extensible architecture of WMI to develop and integrate add-on providers that expose the management functions unique to their products. The Exchange Server 2000 provider, which monitors Exchange connector status, is one such example. Likewise, Application Center, Operations Manager, Systems Management Server, Internet Information Server, and SQL Server all include WMI providers.

Providers are generally implemented as dynamic-link libraries (DLLs) residing in the *systemroot*\System32\Wbem directory. WMI includes many built-in providers for the Windows 2000 and Windows XP operating systems. The built-in providers, also known as standard providers, supply data and management functions from well-known operating system sources such as the Win32 subsystem, event logs, performance counters, and the registry. Table 6.1 lists several of the standard WMI providers included with Windows 2000 and Windows XP.

Table 6.1   Partial List of Standard WMI Providers

Provider	DLL	Namespace	Description
Active Directory	dsprov.dll	root\directory\ldap	Maps Active Directory objects to WMI
Event Log	ntevt.dll	root\cimv2	Manages Windows event logs (for example, reads, backs up, clears, copies, deletes, monitors, renames, compresses, and uncompresses event log files and changes event log settings)
Performance Counter	wbemperf.dll	root\cimv2	Provides access to raw performance data
Registry	stdprov.dll	root\default	Reads, writes, enumerates, monitors, creates, and deletes registry keys and values
SNMP	snmpincl.dll	root\snmp	Provides access to SNMP MIB data and traps from SNMP-managed devices

(continued)

Table 6.1   Partial List of Standard WMI Providers *(continued)*

Provider	DLL	Namespace	Description
WDM	wmiprov.dll	root\wmi	Provides access to information about WDM device drivers
Win32	cimwin32.dll	root\cimv2	Provides information about the computer, disks, peripheral devices, files, folders, file systems, networking components, operating system, printers, processes, security, services, shares, SAM users and groups, and more
Windows Installer	msiprov.dll	root\cimv2	Provides access to information about installed software

Windows XP includes many additional standard providers. For a complete list of standard providers, see the WMI Providers reference in the WMI Software Developers Kit (SDK) documentation. For information about downloading WMI SDK, see the Microsoft Windows Management Instrumentation (WMI) SDK link on the Web Resources page at http://www.microsoft.com/windows/reskits/webresources.

CIMOM

The CIMOM (pronounced see-mom) handles the interaction between consumers and providers. The term comes from the Web-Based Enterprise Management (WBEM) initiative and the Common Information Model (CIM) specification maintained by the Distributed Management Task Force (DMTF).

The CIMOM acts as the WMI information broker. All WMI requests and data flow through the CIMOM. When you write a WMI script, the script is directed to the CIMOM. However, the CIMOM does not directly handle your request. For example, suppose you request a list of all the services installed on a computer. The CIMOM will not actually retrieve the list of services for you. Instead, it will locate the appropriate WMI provider and ask the provider to retrieve the list. When the list has been retrieved, it will be handed back to the CIMOM, and the CIMOM will then return the information to you.

The WMI service (winmgmt.exe) provides the role of the CIMOM on Windows XP. It runs under the control of the generic services host process, svchost.exe.

 Note

On computers running Windows 2000 or Windows NT 4.0 with Service Pack 4 (SP4), the WMI service runs as a separate service process. On computers running Microsoft® Windows® Millennium Edition (ME), Windows® 98, or Windows® 95 OSR 2.5, WMI runs as a standard executable process.

The WMI service is similar to most operating system services; for example, it can be stopped and started using these commands:

```
net stop winmgmt

net start winmgmt
```

One interesting note: Suppose the WMI service is stopped, and you run a script or an application that requires WMI. In that case, the service will automatically restart itself.

In addition to providing the common interface through which consumers access WMI, the CIMOM provides the following core services to the WMI infrastructure:

- **Provider registration.** WMI providers register location and capability information with the CIMOM. The CIMOM stores this information in the CIM repository.

- **Request routing.** The CIMOM uses the provider registration information to route consumer requests to the appropriate provider. When a script requests information from a CIM class (such as Win32_Service or Win32_LogicalMemoryConfiguration), the CIMOM takes the query and forwards it to the provider capable of filling the request.

- **Remote access.** Consumers access remote WMI-enabled systems by connecting to the CIMOM on the remote system. After a connection is established, consumers can perform the same operations that can be performed locally. This is a key point: With only a few minor exceptions, anything WMI can do on the local computer it can do just as easily on a remote computer.

- **Security.** The CIMOM controls access to WMI-managed resources by validating each user access token before the user is permitted to connect to WMI on either the local computer or a remote computer.

- **Query processing.** Allows a consumer to issue queries against any WMI-managed resource by using the WMI Query Language (WQL). For example, you can query the event logs for all events matching a specific Event ID that occurred during the past 24 hours. The CIMOM performs the evaluation of the query in cases where providers do not natively support query operations.

- **Event processing.** Allows a consumer to subscribe to events that represent a change to a WMI-managed resource. For example, you can subscribe to an event that fires when the amount of space on a logical disk drive drops below an acceptable threshold. The CIMOM polls the managed resource at an interval you specify and generates an event notification when the subscription is satisfied.

Management applications, administrative tools, and scripts make requests to the CIMOM to retrieve data, subscribe to events, or to perform some other management-related task. The CIMOM retrieves the provider and class information necessary to service consumer requests from the CIM repository. The CIMOM uses the information obtained from the CIM repository to hand off consumer requests to the appropriate WMI provider.

CIM Repository

WMI is based on the idea that configuration and management information from different sources can be uniformly represented with a schema. The CIM repository holds the schema, also called the object repository or class store, that models the managed environment and defines every piece of data exposed by WMI. The schema is based on the DMTF Common Information Model standard.

Similar to the Active Directory schema, the CIM is built on the concept of *classes*. A class is a blueprint of a WMI-manageable resource. However, unlike Active Directory classes, which represent static objects that can be created and stored in the directory, CIM classes usually represent dynamic resources. Instances of resources are not stored in the CIM repository but are dynamically retrieved by a provider based on a consumer request. This means that the term *repository* is somewhat misleading in the context of the CIM. Although the CIM is a repository and is capable of storing static data, its primary role is storing the blueprints for managed resources.

The reason for this is simple: The operational state for most WMI-managed resources changes frequently and therefore must be read on demand to ensure that the most up-to-date information is retrieved. For example, WMI classes can be used to retrieve all the events from all the event logs on a computer and information about all the files stored on a computer. Storing all this information and keeping track of all the changes made to it would not be the most effective use of computer resources. Instead, it is faster and more efficient to dynamically retrieve the information each time it is needed.

Note

Admittedly, retrieving information each time it is needed will occasionally cause queries to run slowly. For example, if you *did* need to enumerate all the files on a computer, this would take some time, simply because WMI would have to locate every file and retrieve information about it. However, the fact that a query such as this might run a bit slowly must be balanced against the computing resources required for and the complications involved in keeping an up-to-date copy of every managed object in the repository.

Even though most instances must be retrieved dynamically, a typical WMI query will still be completed in a matter of seconds. (For example, it typically takes 1 to 2 seconds to return a list of all the services installed on a computer.)

Like Active Directory classes, CIM classes are organized hierarchically and child classes inherit from parent classes. The DMTF maintains the set of core and common base classes from which system and application software developers, such as those at Microsoft Corporation, derive and create system-specific or application-specific extension classes. For example, the Win32_Process class is derived from the CIM_Process class (which, in turn, is derived from CIM_LogicalElement and CIM_ManagedSystemElement).

Classes are grouped into *namespaces*, logical groups representing a specific area of management. For example, the root\cimv2 namespace includes most of the classes that represent resources commonly associated with a computer and an operating system. The classes used in the preceding scripts (Win32_LogicalMemoryConfiguration, Win32_Service, and Win32_NTLogEvent) reside in the root\cimv2 namespace and are just three of hundreds of classes defined in the various CIM namespaces.

 Note
Namespaces are also important in WMI security, a topic discussed later in this chapter.

CIM classes include both properties and methods. Properties describe the configuration and state of a WMI-managed resource; methods are executable functions that perform actions on the WMI-managed resource associated with the corresponding class.

In Windows 2000 and Windows NT 4.0 with SP4, the CIM is stored in *systemroot*\System32\Wbem\Respository\cim.rep. In Windows Millennium Edition (Me), Windows 98, and Windows 95 OSR 2.5 operating systems, the CIM repository is stored in *%windir%*\System\Wbem\Repository\cim.rep.

In Windows XP, the CIM repository resides in the *systemroot*\System32\Wbem\Repository\FS directory and consists of the following four files:

- **Index.btr.** Binary-tree (btree) index file.
- **Index.map.** Transaction control file.
- **Objects.data.** CIM repository where managed resource definitions are stored.
- **Objects.map.** Transaction control file.

Although the CIM is based on object-oriented design principles, you do not need to become an expert on information modeling or schema design to be productive using WMI and writing WMI-based scripts. However, it is important that you understand the basic structure and organization of the CIM repository and how to navigate and interpret its contents.

WMI Consumers

WMI consumers are the final layer in the WMI infrastructure. A consumer can be a script, an enterprise management application, a Web-based application, or some other administrative tool that accesses and controls management information available through the WMI infrastructure.

WMI consumers do not have to be complicated. The following three-line script, which returns the amount of free disk space on drive C, is an example of a WMI consumer:

```
Set objSWbemServices = GetObject("winmgmts:")
Set objDisk = objSWbemServices.Get("Win32_LogicalDisk.DeviceID='C:'")
Wscript.Echo objDisk.FreeSpace
```

 Note

Many management applications serve dual roles as both WMI consumer and WMI provider. Such is the case with several Microsoft management products, such as Application Center, Operations Manager, and Systems Management Server.

WMI Security

WMI is an extremely powerful technology for system administration. It is also a versatile technology: It is just as easy to run scripts against remote computers as it is to run scripts against the local computer. Furthermore, WMI scripts can be written using nothing more powerful (or expensive) than Notepad. This makes WMI the perfect technology for system administrators. It would also appear to make WMI the perfect technology for someone else: hackers. After all, how hard would it be to create a script that methodically shuts down each computer in your organization, one by one?

In truth, it would be easy to write such a script; however, successfully *running* this script would be far more difficult. This is because security is an important part of the WMI infrastructure; in fact, WMI has been specifically designed to prevent people from carrying out activities such as this (either inadvertently or otherwise).

For example, suppose a hacker tried to shut down one of your computers using WMI. This attempt will fail. Why? Because only an administrator can run a script against a remote computer. Unless the hacker is an administrator on the computer, he or she will not be able to shut it down by using WMI. (And of course, if the hacker *is* an administrator, he or she can cause plenty of trouble without bothering to write a script.)

But what if the hacker e-mails a shutdown script to users and somehow tricks these users into shutting down their local computers? Even this is likely to fail: For the most part, running a WMI script that actually *does* something requires you to be an administrator and to have specific privileges. In most organizations, users do not have the right to shut down a computer; therefore, if they inadvertently run a script that tries to shut down their computer, the script will fail. Why? Because, by default, WMI can carry out only those tasks that the person running the script can carry out.

WMI security is an extension of the security subsystem built into Windows operating systems. WMI security includes:

- WMI namespace-level security.

- Distributed COM (DCOM) security.

- Standard Windows NT–based Windows operating system security.

WMI Namespace-Level Security

Before a user is allowed to connect to WMI, on either the local computer or a remote computer, the access token for the user account is validated against permissions applied to and stored in the CIM repository.

By default, the built-in Administrators security group is granted full control of WMI and the entire CIM repository on both local and remote computers. All other users, by way of the Everyone group, are granted Enable Account, Execute Methods, and Provider Write on the local computer only. Table 6.2 lists the available WMI permissions, which are configured on the Security tab in the WMI Control MMC Snap-in, *systemroot*\System32\Wmimgmt.msc.

 Note

On computers running Windows NT 4.0 SP4, Windows 98, and Windows 95 OSR 2.5, the WMI Control application is named Wbemcntl.exe. Wbemcntl.exe is located in the *systemroot*\System32\Wbem directory on Windows NT 4.0 SP4.

Table 6.2   WMI Namespace Permissions

Permission	Description	Administrators	Everyone
Execute Methods	Lets a user call methods in the specific namespace. However, the provider checks to ensure that the user has the right to perform these tasks. For example, a user cannot run a script that stops a service unless the user has the right to stop that service.	●	●
Full Write	Lets users create or modify a namespace, a system class, or an instance.	●	

(continued)

Table 6.2   WMI Namespace Permissions *(continued)*

Permission	Description	Administrators	Everyone
Partial Write	Lets users create or modify any static class or any instance of non-system classes.	●	
Provider Write	Lets users write classes and instances to WMI providers.	●	●
Enable Account	Grants read permissions to a WMI namespace. This allows users to run scripts that retrieve data, but only on the local computer.	●	●
Remote Enable	Lets a user access a WMI namespace from a remote computer. By default, this right is granted only to administrators; regular users cannot retrieve any WMI-related information from a remote computer.	●	
Read Security	Lets the user read (but not modify) the security descriptor for a WMI namespace.	●	
Edit Security	Lets the user modify the security descriptor for a WMI namespace.	●	

WMI permissions are applied at the namespace level and apply to all classes within the namespace. These permissions also apply — potentially — to child namespaces based on inheritance. By default, permissions are explicitly applied to the root namespace only and inherited by all other child namespaces.

Security is checked only when a user connects to the CIMOM. As a result, any changes made to the WMI permissions while a user is connected will not affect that user until he or she establishes a new connection. If you have the Full Write permission when you begin running a script, you (in the context of that script) will continue to have that permission until the script completes. However, if you start a new script, any new permissions will be applied to that particular script.

By default, WMI scripts run in the security context of the user running the script.

DCOM Security

DCOM, the architecture underlying the interaction of the WMI scripting library with the WMI service, provides a mechanism known as impersonation. Impersonation enables you to specify whom the WMI service should act as when carrying out a task.

The default, and the recommended, impersonation level is Impersonate. This enables the WMI service to act on your behalf, using your credentials. You can also give the WMI service the right to contact other DCOM-based services and enable them to use your credentials. This level of impersonation is known as Delegate and has some security risks associated with it.

What kind of security risks? By default, DCOM supports only single-hop impersonation. Suppose you run a script on Computer A, and that script needs to retrieve information from Computer B. The script can impersonate you on the "single hop" between computers A and B. But what if Computer B needs to retrieve information from a third computer? By default, the script cannot impersonate you on this "double hop" from Computer A to Computer B to Computer C. Because of this, the script will fail.

It is possible to allow Computer B to also use your credentials; for that matter, you can also allow computers C, D, and E to use your credentials. This is where the security risk occurs. With single-hop security, you are limited to working with at most two computers. As a result, any problems can be confined to computers A and B. With delegation, and with multi-hop security, problems can spread to many computers.

The different DCOM security levels are discussed in more detail in the "Writing WMI Scripts" section of this chapter. That section will also discuss additional safeguards that help reduce the potential risks associated with delegation.

Standard Windows Operating System Security

In addition to WMI and DCOM-specific security settings, WMI also respects standard operating system settings. For example, suppose someone has set NTFS permissions on a folder that prohibit you from writing to that folder. If you run a WMI script that attempts to copy a file to that folder, the script will fail with an "Access denied" error because you (and therefore WMI, which is impersonating you) do not have write access to the folder. WMI will not override operating system security in any way.

 Note

What if you need to copy files to this folder? In that case, you have to either modify the NTFS permissions or run the script under the credentials of a user who *is* allowed to copy files to the folder.

Common Information Model

If you are going to build a house, you need to know how to read and interpret an architectural drawing. If you are going to build an electronic device, you need to know how to read and interpret a schematic diagram. And if you are going to write WMI scripts, you need to know how to interpret the WMI blueprint for management: the CIM repository.

The CIM repository is the WMI schema that stores the class definitions that model WMI-managed resources.

To emphasize the importance of the CIM and CIM classes, consider the scripts in Listing 6.6 and Listing 6.7. Listing 6.6, a slightly enhanced version of Listing 6.3, returns information about the services installed on a computer.

Listing 6.6   Retrieving Service Information Using WMI and VBScript

```
1   strComputer = "."
2
3   Set objSWbemServices = GetObject("winmgmts:\\" & strComputer)
4   Set colServices = objSWbemServices.InstancesOf("Win32_Service")
5
6   For Each objService In colServices
7       Wscript.Echo "Name:          " & objService.Name        & vbCrLf & _
8                    "Display Name: " & objService.DisplayName & vbCrLf & _
9                    "Description: " & objService.Description & vbCrLf & _
10                   "Path Name:   " & objService.PathName     & vbCrLf & _
11                   "Start Mode:  " & objService.StartMode    & vbCrLf & _
12                   "State:       " & objService.State        & vbCrLf
13  Next
```

Listing 6.7, meanwhile, is another variation of the same basic script, this time using the Win32_OperatingSystem class. As you might expect, it returns information about the operating system currently in use on a computer.

Listing 6.7   Retrieving Operating System Information Using WMI and VBScript

```
1   strComputer = "."
2
3   Set objSWbemServices = GetObject("winmgmts:\\" & strComputer)
4   Set colOperatingSystems = objSWbemServices.InstancesOf("Win32_OperatingSystem")
5
6   For Each objOperatingSystem In colOperatingSystems
7       Wscript.Echo "Name:              " & objOperatingSystem.Name        & vbCrLf & _
8           "Caption:         " & objOperatingSystem.Caption         & vbCrLf & _
9           "CurrentTimeZone: " & objOperatingSystem.CurrentTimeZone & vbCrLf & _
10          "LastBootUpTime:  " & objOperatingSystem.LastBootUpTime  & vbCrLf & _
11          "LocalDateTime:   " & objOperatingSystem.LocalDateTime   & vbCrLf & _
12          "Locale:          " & objOperatingSystem.Locale          & vbCrLf & _
13          "Manufacturer:    " & objOperatingSystem.Manufacturer    & vbCrLf & _
14          "OSType:          " & objOperatingSystem. OSType         & vbCrLf & _
15          "Version:         " & objOperatingSystem.Version         & vbCrLf & _
16          "Service Pack:    " & objOperatingSystem.ServicePackMajorVersion & _
17          "." & objOperatingSystem.ServicePackMinorVersion         & vbCrLf & _
18          "Windows Directory: " & objOperatingSystem.WindowsDirectory
19  Next
```

There are only two differences between these scripts: the class name identifying the WMI-managed resource and the property values reported for each class. For example, the services script reports values for properties such as DisplayName, StartMode, and State; the operating system script reports values for properties such as LastBootUpTime, Version, and ServicePackMajorVersion.

The fact that the same script template can be used to retrieve total physical memory, services, event log records, processes, and operating system information demonstrates the important role CIM classes play in WMI scripting. After you know how to write a script to manage one type of WMI-managed resource, you can use the same basic technique to manage other resources.

Of course, knowing a managed resource class name and its corresponding properties is only part of the story. Before you can tap the full power of WMI scripting, you need to know a little bit more about the structure of the CIM repository and WMI classes for two important reasons:

- Understanding how to navigate the CIM repository will help you determine the computer and software resources exposed through WMI.

- Understanding how to interpret a managed resource blueprint (class definition) will help you understand the tasks that can be performed on the managed resource.

Both points are true regardless of the WMI tool you use: Whether you use the WMI scripting library or an enterprise management application, you need to know how to navigate the CIM repository and interpret WMI classes.

A less obvious yet equally important reason to learn about the CIM repository is that the CIM repository is an excellent source of documentation for WMI-managed resources. If you need detailed information about a WMI class, you can use the WMI SDK. But what if you do not need detailed information about a WMI class? Suppose you want to know only whether a specific class, method, or property is supported on the version of Windows you are managing. You can check the CIM repository of the target computer.

For example, suppose you see this script in the Script Center on Microsoft TechNet:

```
Const JOIN_DOMAIN = 1
Const ACCT_CREATE = 2
Set objNetwork = CreateObject("Wscript.Network")
strComputer = objNetwork.ComputerName
Set objComputerSystem = GetObject _
    ("winmgmts:{impersonationLevel=Impersonate}!\\" & strComputer & _
        "\root\cimv2:Win32_ComputerSystem.Name='" & strComputer & "'")
ReturnValue = objComputerSystem.JoinDomainOrWorkGroup _
    ("FABRIKAM", "password", "FABRIKAM\shenalan", NULL, JOIN_DOMAIN+ACCT_CREATE)
```

You want to know whether the script will run on Windows 2000–based computers. As it turns out, it does not, because the Win32_ComputerSystem class does not support the JoinDomainOrWorkGroup method on Windows 2000. The JoinDomainOrWorkGroup method was added to the Win32_ComputerSystem class in the version of WMI included with Windows XP.

But how would you find this out, other than trying the script and having it fail? One way is by using the collection of WMI tools described in "Exploring the CIM Repository" later in this chapter. A more powerful and flexible approach is to use the WMI scripting library. One useful property of WMI is the fact that you can use the WMI scripting library to learn about WMI itself. In the same way you write WMI scripts to retrieve information about managed resources, you can write WMI scripts to learn many interesting details about WMI itself. For instance, you can write WMI scripts that list all of the namespaces and classes in the CIM repository. You can write scripts to list all of the providers installed on a WMI-enabled computer. You can even write WMI scripts to retrieve managed resource class definitions.

Whether you choose to use existing tools or create your own, you need a basic understanding of the structure of the CIM repository and its contents, as well as knowledge of how to interpret managed resource class definitions. The next section takes a closer look at the WMI blueprint for management — the CIM repository.

Blueprint for Management

WMI is based on the idea that configuration and management information from different sources can be uniformly represented with a schema, and that the CIM repository is the schema for WMI. Think of a schema as a blueprint or model that represents something that exists in the real world. Much like an architectural drawing models a physical structure such as a house, the CIM models the hardware, operating system, and software that make up a computer. The CIM is the data model for WMI.

 Note

> As noted previously, although the CIM repository stores some data, its primary purpose is to model the managed environment. The CIM is not designed to store the volumes of management information it defines. Instead, most of the data is dynamically retrieved, on demand, from a WMI provider. The exception is WMI operational data. WMI operational data, such as namespace information, provider registration information, managed resource class definitions, and permanent event subscriptions, *is* stored in the CIM repository.

Figure 6.2 provides a conceptual view of the internal structure and organization of the CIM repository. As illustrated in Figure 6.2, the CIM uses classes to create the data model. The CIM contains far more classes than the eleven shown in the diagram. It is important to understand that the CIM repository is the class store that defines the WMI managed environment and every manageable resource exposed through WMI.

There are three important CIM concepts illustrated in Figure 6.2 that help explain how to successfully navigate and interpret the WMI schema:

1. The CIM repository is divided into multiple namespaces.

2. Each namespace can contain one or more of the following groups of classes:

    -   System classes

    -   Core and common classes

    -   Extension classes

3. There are three primary class types: abstract, static, and dynamic. A fourth class type, known as an association class, is also supported.

    -   An *abstract class* is a template used to derive (define) new abstract and nonabstract classes and cannot be used to retrieve instances of managed resources.

    -   A *static class* defines data physically stored in the CIM repository — the most common of which is WMI configuration and operational data.

    -   A *dynamic class* is a class that models a WMI-managed resource that is dynamically retrieved from a provider.

    -   An *association class* is an abstract, static, or dynamic class that describes a relationship between two classes or managed resources.

The next section of this chapter examines each of these concepts in more detail.

Namespaces

CIM classes are organized into *namespaces*. Namespaces are the partitioning mechanism employed by the CIM to control the scope and visibility of managed resource class definitions. Each namespace in the CIM contains a logical group of related classes representing a specific technology or area of management.

Namespaces are roughly equivalent to folders on a disk drive. Like folders, namespaces provide a place to store related information; a folder named Scripts is likely to contain scripts and a namespace named MicrosoftActiveDirectory is likely to contains WMI classes used to manage Active Directory. Both folders and namespaces help you to uniquely identify an item. You can have only one file on a computer named C:\Scripts\WMI_Script.vbs; likewise, you can have only one WMI class named root\cimv2:Win32_Process.

 Note

One difference between folders and WMI namespaces is that folders are often deeply nested; for example, it is common to have folders such as C:\Program Files\Microsoft Office\Office\Office10. By contrast, namespaces rarely go more than three levels deep; the vast majority of classes useful in system administration scripts reside in the root\cimv2 namespace, a namespace nested only two levels deep.

Figure 6.2   Structural View of the CIM Repository — the WMI Schema

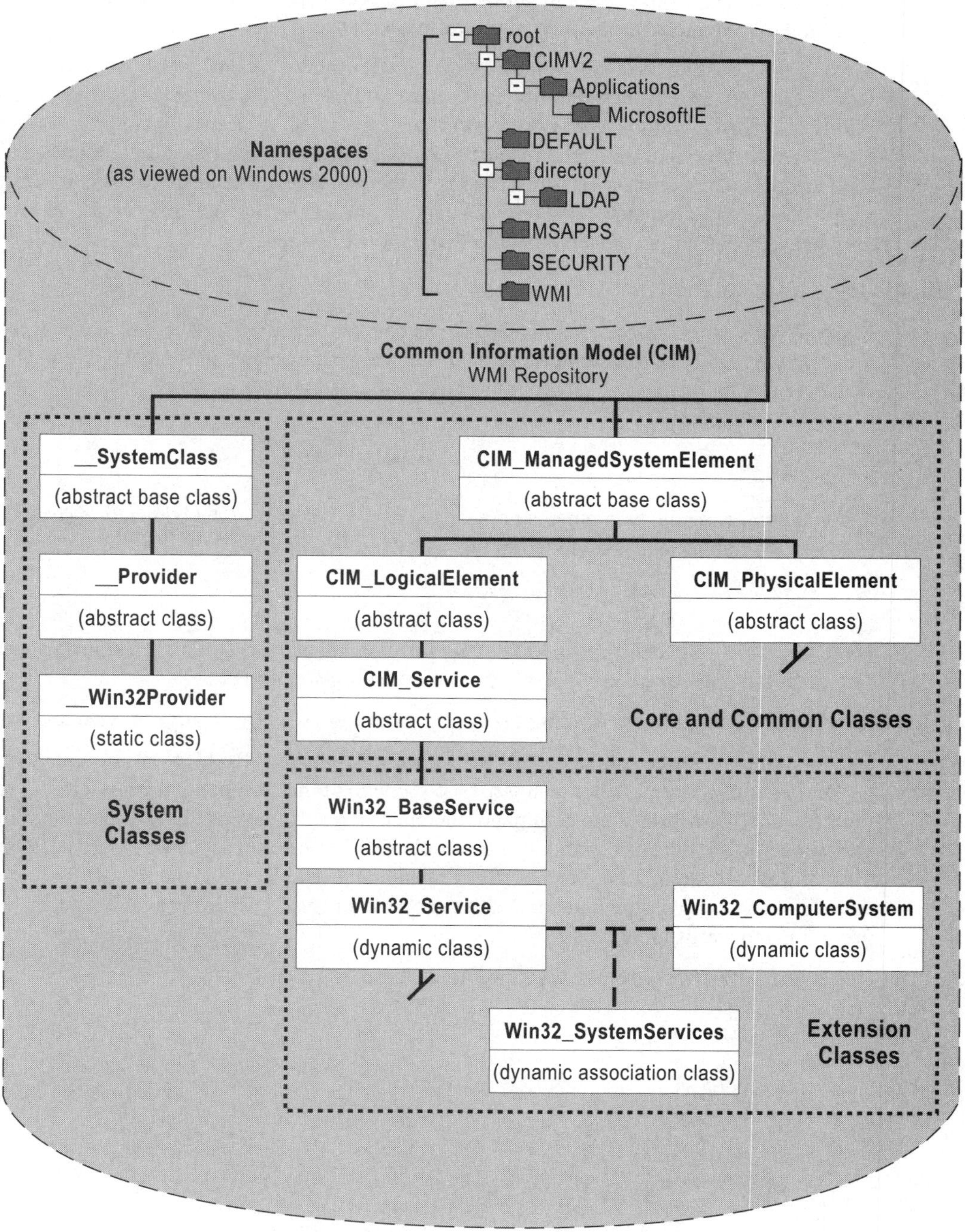

All classes within a namespace must have a unique class name, and classes in one namespace cannot be derived from classes in another namespace. This is why you will find identical system, core, and common classes defined in multiple namespaces.

Most of the classes that model Windows-managed resources reside in the root\cimv2 namespace. However, root\cimv2 is not the only namespace you need to be aware of, as suggested in Figure 6.2. Although the Event Log, Performance Counter, Windows Installer, and Win32 providers all store their managed resource class definitions in the root\cimv2 namespace, the Registry provider stores its class definitions in the root\default namespace. This means that scripts that use the Registry provider will differ from scripts that use the Event Log provider, if only because the scripts must connect to different namespaces.

Specifying a Namespace

Every WMI script connects to a namespace as part of the initial connection step. For example, the following line of code connects to the root\cimv2 namespace on the local computer. (The connection is made on the local computer because no computer name is specified in the connection string.)

```
Set objSWbemServices = GetObject("winmgmts:root\cimv2")
```

A connection is made even when a namespace is not included in the connection string. For example, no namespace is included in the following line of code.

```
Set objSWbemServices = GetObject("winmgmts:")
```

If the target namespace is not specified, the script connects to the default scripting namespace. The default namespace is defined by the following registry entry:

HKEY_LOCAL_MACHINE\SOFTWARE\Microsoft\WBEM\Scripting\Default Namespace

The default namespace setting is to WMI scripting what the %PATH% environment variable is to the operating system. When you issue a command at the command prompt without specifying the fully qualified path of the command, the operating system uses the %PATH% environment variable to locate the corresponding executable file. For example, you do not have to type **C:\Windows\System32\calc.exe** to start Calculator. Why? Because the System32 folder is in the path. You can simply type **Calc.exe**, and the operating system will check the path, find the program, and start Calculator.

If the operating system cannot find the file, an error is generated.

Similarly, when you retrieve a managed resource in a WMI script, the WMI Service (winmgmts) searches for the managed resource blueprint (class definition) in the default namespace if no namespace is specified. If the WMI service cannot find the managed resource class definition in the default namespace, it generates a WBEM_E_INVALID_CLASS (0x80041010) error.

Note

Don't confuse the Default Namespace setting with the root\DEFAULT namespace. They are unrelated unless, of course, you set root\DEFAULT as your default namespace.

There is at least one difference between %PATH% and namespaces, however. The path can include multiple locations, even folders on different drives. The default namespace, by contrast, refers to a single location.

The root\cimv2 namespace is initially configured as the default namespace for scripting; however, the default scripting namespace can easily be changed. Because of this, you should always identify the namespace of a managed resource in your WMI scripts rather than assume that the default is root\cimv2. The following code snippet shows how to specify a namespace when connecting to WMI. In addition to specifying the namespace, the script also uses a variable, strComputer, to represent the name of the computer that the script should run against.

```
strComputer = "."
Set objSWbemServices = GetObject("winmgmts:\\" & strComputer & "\root\cimv2")
```

Note

Why was strComputer set to the value dot (".")? In WMI scripting, the first part of the object path is always the name of the computer. If no computer name is specified or if a dot is found, the script runs against the local computer. Setting strComputer to dot does two things: 1) It causes the script to run against the local computer, and 2) it provides a placeholder that makes it easy to modify the script to run against a remote computer. For example, to run the script against a computer named WebServer, simply set the value of strComputer to WebServer:

```
strComputer = "WebServer"
```

Adding the target namespace to the connection string tells the CIMOM where to look for the managed resource class definition in the CIM, much as a fully qualified path tells the operating system exactly where to look for a file. When you specify the target namespace, the script does not first check the default namespace setting in the registry. Instead, it connects directly to the specified location.

 Note

> You might think that WMI could just search all its namespaces until it located the desired class. This cannot be done, however, because different namespaces can have classes with the same name. For example, WMI includes both a class named root\cimv2__Event and one named root\default__Event.

Managing the Default Namespace for Scripting

You can use the WMI scripting library in combination with the Win32_WMISetting class to read and change the default namespace for scripting, as demonstrated in Listing 6.8 and Listing 6.9. Win32_WMISetting is a dynamic class that models operational parameters for the WMI service. The writable property representing the default namespace for scripting is ASPScriptDefaultNamespace.

Listing 6.8 uses the same three WMI scripting steps — connect, retrieve, and display — that have been used all along, with one noticeable change. As recommended earlier, it specifies the fully qualified namespace for the Win32_WMISetting class in the WMI connection string passed to the VBScript GetObject function. Not only does this example follow the namespace recommendation in Listing 6.8, but this chapter will use qualified namespaces from this point forward. Doing this will help you avoid invalid class errors in your WMI scripts.

Listing 6.8   Retrieving the Default Namespace for Scripting Using WMI and VBScript

```
1  strComputer = "."
2
3  Set objSWbemServices = _
4      GetObject("winmgmts:\\" & strComputer & "\root\cimv2")
5  Set colWMISettings = objSWbemServices.InstancesOf("Win32_WMISetting")
6
7  For Each objWMISetting in colWMISettings
8      Wscript.Echo "Default namespace for scripting: " & _
9                  objWMISetting.ASPScriptDefaultNamespace
10 Next
```

If you run this script under CScript on your local computer, you should see the default namespace of the local computer displayed in the command window, as in the following output.

```
Default namespace for scripting: root\cimv2
```

To set the default namespace for scripting, you can perform the same scripting steps as in Listing 6.8 with one important change: Rather than use the WMI to read a property of a managed object , you use WMI to:

1. Set the property value.

2. Call the SWbemObject Put_ method to commit the change to the WMI-managed resource.

    The set and commit operations are performed inside the For Each loop because the InstancesOf method always returns an SWbemObjectSet collection. This is true even when there is only one instance of the target WMI-managed resource, as is the case with Win32_WMISetting.

Listing 6.9   Setting the Default Namespace for Scripting

```
1   strComputer = "."
2
3   Set objSWbemServices = _
4       GetObject("winmgmts:\\" & strComputer & "\root\cimv2")
5   Set colWMISettings = objSWbemServices.InstancesOf("Win32_WMISetting")
6
7   For Each objWMISetting in colWMISettings
8           objWMISetting.ASPScriptDefaultNamespace = "root\cimv2"
9           objWMISetting.Put_
10  Next
```

Listing Namespaces

Thus far the scripts in this chapter have used the same WMI scripting technique to retrieve instances of dynamic WMI-managed resources. For example, the same script template was used to retrieve total physical memory, services, and event log records. In Listing 6.6 through Listing 6.8, the same template was used to retrieve services, operating system information, and the default namespace for scripting. As it turns out, you can use the same WMI scripting technique to retrieve namespace information from the CIM. The only change you need to make to the script is the target class name.

Namespace information is stored inside the CIM as static instances of the __NAMESPACE class. The __NAMESPACE class is an example of the static class type defined earlier. Unlike dynamic managed resources that are retrieved on demand from a provider, static class instances are stored in and retrieved directly from the CIM without the use of a WMI provider. Listing 6.10 uses the __NAMESPACE class to retrieve and echo all of the namespaces directly beneath the root namespace.

Listing 6.10   Retrieving CIM Namespaces Using WMI and VBScript

```
1   strComputer = "."
2
3   Set objSWbemServices = GetObject("winmgmts:\\" & strComputer & "\root")
4   Set colNameSpaces = objSWbemServices.InstancesOf("__NAMESPACE")
5
6   For Each objNameSpace In colNameSpaces
7       Wscript.Echo objNameSpace.Name
8   Next
```

The following output is the result of running the script on a Windows 2000–based computer:

```
DEFAULT
SECURITY
CIMV2
WMI
directory
```

The list of namespaces will vary based on the versions of both Windows and WMI installed on the target computer, and any WMI-enabled applications installed on the computer. For example, these namespaces are found on Windows XP with Microsoft® Office XP and the .NET Framework installed:

```
SECURITY
RSOP
Cli
WMI
CIMV2
MSAPPS10
Policy
Microsoft
DEFAULT
directory
subscription
NetFrameworkv1
```

Listing 6.10 does not provide a complete picture of all of the namespaces available on the target computer. It retrieves and displays only the namespaces beneath a single specified namespace (in this case, root). To display all of the namespaces on a local or remote WMI-enabled computer, you need to modify Listing 6.10 to recursively connect to and enumerate each namespace. Fortunately, this is not as difficult as you might think, as shown in Listing 6.11.

Changing Listing 6.10 into a recursive namespace script primarily involves implementing the body of the original script inside a subroutine and providing a mechanism to call the subroutine for each namespace instance retrieved from the CIM. Listing 6.11 accomplishes this by performing the following steps:

1. Initializes the variable strComputer with the name of the target computer.

2. Calls the recursive subroutine, EnumNameSpaces, and passes the subroutine a string identifying the initial namespace as "root". The body of the EnumNameSpaces subroutine is identical to Listing 6.10 with one important change. The subroutine:

   a. Begins by echoing the value of the subroutine's single argument, strNameSpace.

      The variable strNameSpace identifies the namespace used in the connection string each time the subroutine is called. The first time the subroutine is called, strNameSpace is equal to "root".

   b. Uses the VBScript GetObject function to connect to the namespace identified by the subroutine's strNameSpace argument.

   c. After establishing a connection to the WMI service and namespace on the target computer, the subroutine retrieves all namespace instances immediately beneath the namespace referenced by strNameSpace.

   d. Using a For Each loop, the subroutine enumerates the namespace instances immediately beneath the currently connected namespace. However, instead of the script simply echoing the names of the child (or sub) namespaces, each child (or sub) namespace name is concatenated with the current namespace name. This name is then passed to a new invocation of the EnumNameSpaces subroutine.

Substeps a through d are repeated until all namespace instances are enumerated.

Listing 6.11 Retrieving All CIM Namespaces

```
1   strComputer = "."
2   Call EnumNameSpaces("root")
3
4   Sub EnumNameSpaces(strNameSpace)
5       Wscript.Echo strNameSpace
6       Set objSWbemServices = _
7           GetObject("winmgmts:\\" & strComputer & "\" & strNameSpace)
8       Set colNameSpaces = objSWbemServices.InstancesOf("__NAMESPACE")
9       For Each objNameSpace In colNameSpaces
10          Call EnumNameSpaces(strNameSpace & "\" & objNameSpace.Name)
11      Next
12  End Sub
```

The following is output generated from running the script on a Windows 2000 Advanced Server computer:

```
root
root\DEFAULT
root\SECURITY
root\CIMV2
root\CIMV2\Applications
root\CIMV2\Applications\MicrosoftIE
root\CIMV2\ms_409
root\WMI
root\directory
root\directory\LDAP
root\directory\LDAP\ms_409
root\MicrosoftNLB
root\MicrosoftNLB\ms_409
```

Class Categories

As illustrated earlier in Figure 6.2, three general categories of classes are used to construct the CIM: system, core and common, and extension.

System Classes

System classes are classes that support internal WMI configuration and operations, such as namespace configuration, namespace security, provider registration, and event subscriptions and notifications. When browsing the CIM, you can easily identify system classes by the two underscores prefacing each system class name. For example, the __SystemClass, __Provider, and __Win32Provider classes shown in Figure 6.2 are system classes. The __NAMESPACE class examined in the preceding section is another example of a system class.

System classes are either abstract or static. Abstract system classes are templates used to derive (define) other abstract or static system classes. Static system classes define WMI configuration and operational data that is physically stored in the CIM repository. For example, the __Win32Provider system class defines provider registration information stored in the CIM. The CIMOM uses the provider registration information stored in the CIM to map requests for dynamic managed resources to the appropriate provider.

As demonstrated with the __NAMESPACE system class earlier, you can use the same WMI scripting technique to retrieve static instances of system classes stored in the CIM. Listing 6.12, for example, retrieves and displays all of the __Win32Provider instances registered in the root\cimv2 namespace.

Listing 6.12   Retrieving Win32 Providers Registered in the root\cimv2 Namespace

```
1  strComputer = "."
2
3  Set objSWbemServices = _
4      GetObject("winmgmts:\\" & strComputer & "\root\cimv2")
5  Set colWin32Providers = objSWbemServices.InstancesOf("__Win32Provider")
6
7  For Each objWin32Provider In colWin32Providers
8      Wscript.Echo objWin32Provider.Name
9  Next
```

When the script runs on a Windows 2000–based computer, it returns the following provider names:

```
CIMWin32
WBEMCORE
MS_Power_Management_Event_Provider
MS_NT_EVENTLOG_PROVIDER
MS_NT_EVENTLOG_EVENT_PROVIDER
SECRCW32
MSIProv
NT5_GenericPerfProvider_V1
```

It is unlikely you will use system classes in your WMI scripts, with one exception: WMI monitoring scripts. WMI monitoring scripts are scripts that subscribe to WMI events and provide real-time notification that something of interest has happened with a WMI-managed resource. WMI event subscriptions and notifications are covered later in this chapter.

It is useful to know what system classes are, however, if for no other reason than the fact that tools that browse the CIM repository will return these classes. Understanding the difference between system classes and other classes helps you determine which classes are likely to be useful to you and which ones are not.

Core and Common Classes

The core and common classes serve two roles. First, they represent the abstract classes from which system and application software developers can derive and create technology-specific extension classes. Second, they define resources common to particular management areas, but independent of a particular technology or implementation; in theory, these are resources that any operating system (not just Windows) is likely to support. The DMTF defines and maintains the set of core and common classes, which can be identified by the CIM_ prefix. The four classes prefaced with CIM_ in Figure 6.2 are core and common classes.

Of the approximately 275 core and common classes defined in the root\cimv2 namespace, all are abstract classes, with a few exceptions. You will rarely use core and common classes (classes prefaced with CIM_) in your WMI scripts because you cannot retrieve instances of abstract classes; abstract classes can be used only as a basis for new classes. Because 271 of the core and common classes are abstract, these classes are used primarily by software developers to create technology-specific extension classes. These classes serve as the basis for the scores of Win32_ classes used to manage computers running the Windows operating system.

Just four of the 275 core and common classes are dynamic classes rather than abstract classes. These four classes, which use the Win32 Provider (cimwin32.dll) to retrieve instances of managed resources, are CIM_DataFile, CIM_DirectoryContainsFile, CIM_ProcessExecutable, and CIM_VideoControllerResolution. This means you can actually use these classes to retrieve information about managed resources. For example, this script returns information about all the possible video modes supported by the video controllers on a computer:

```
strComputer = "."
Set objSWbemServices = GetObject("winmgmts:\\" & strComputer & "\root\cimv2")
Set colVideoControllers = _
    objSWbemServices.InstancesOf("CIM_VideoControllerResolution")
For Each objVideoController In colVideoControllers
    Wscript.Echo objVideoController.HorizontalResolution
    Wscript.Echo objVideoController.VerticalResolution
    Wscript.Echo objVideoController.NumberOfColors
    Wscript.Echo objVideoController.RefreshRate
Next
```

Extension Classes

Extension classes are technology-specific classes created by system and application software developers. The Win32_BaseService, Win32_Service, Win32_SystemServices, and Win32_ComputerSystem classes shown in Figure 6.2 are Microsoft extension classes. Microsoft extension classes in the root\cimv2 namespace can be identified by the Win32_ prefix.

However, you should not conclude that all Microsoft extension class names begin with Win32_; they do not. For example, the StdRegProv class defined in the root\DEFAULT namespace is not prefaced with Win32_, even though the StdRegProv class is a Microsoft extension class for registry management tasks.

In the latest version of WMI, about 463 Win32 extension classes are defined in the root\cimv2 namespace. Of the 463 Win32 classes, 68 are abstract classes and the remaining 395 are dynamic. Extension classes are the primary category of classes you will use in your WMI scripts.

 Note

The class statistics are intended only to illustrate general CIM concepts. Your numbers will differ based on several factors, including Windows version, WMI version, and installed software.

Listing Classes in a Namespace

In addition to listing namespaces, you can write a script to retrieve all of the classes defined within a namespace. Listing 6.13, for example, lists all classes defined in the root\cimv2 namespace. However, unlike the previous scripts that used the SWbemServices InstancesOf method, Listing 6.13 uses a different method, SubclassesOf, which is also provided by the SWbemServices object.

As the name suggests, SubclassesOf returns all of the child (or sub) classes of a specified parent (super) class, or of a specified namespace when no parent class is provided. Like InstancesOf, SubclassesOf returns all of the subclasses in the form of an SWbemObjectSet collection, where each item in the collection is an SWbemObject representing a single class.

A new element is introduced in Listing 6.13: the objClass.Path_.Path property echoed in the body of the For Each loop. Like other For Each loops used in this chapter, this one enumerates each object in the collection returned by the SubclassesOf method. In this case, each object represents a discrete class in the root\cimv2 namespace.

However, in contrast with previous scripts that displayed properties defined by a managed resource blueprint (class definition), Path_ is a property provided by the SWbemObject. To understand this, you have to think about the context in which the script is using SWbemObject. In this case, you are not accessing an instance of a managed resource (for example, a service named Alerter or a process named Notepad.exe). Instead, you are accessing the managed resource class definition.

When you use SWbemObject to access an instance of a managed resource, you are more likely to access properties and methods defined by the blueprint for the managed resource (the class definition). When you use SWbemObject to get detailed *class* information, such as supported properties, methods, and qualifiers, you use properties and methods provided by SWbemObject itself. Path_ is one such property.

Path_ actually references another WMI scripting library object named SWbemObjectPath, which provides the Path property. The SWbemObjectPath Path property contains the fully qualified path to the class referenced by SWbemObject (objClass in Listing 6.13).

Listing 6.13   Retrieving All Classes Defined in the root\cimv2 Namespace

```
1  strComputer = "."
2
3  Set objSWbemServices = _
4      GetObject("winmgmts:\\" & strComputer & "\root\cimv2")
5  Set colClasses = objSWbemServices.SubclassesOf()
6
7  For Each objClass In colClasses
8      Wscript.Echo objClass.Path_.Path
9  Next
```

Running Listing 6.13 on a Windows 2000-based computer displays a long list of 636 classes, some of which are shown in the following output.

```
\\ATL-WIN2K-01\ROOT\CIMV2:Win32_NTEventlogFile
\\ATL-WIN2K-01\ROOT\CIMV2:Win32_NTLogEvent
\\ATL-WIN2K-01\ROOT\CIMV2:Win32_NTLogEventLog
\\ATL-WIN2K-01\ROOT\CIMV2:Win32_NTLogEventUser
\\ATL-WIN2K-01\ROOT\CIMV2:Win32_NTLogEventComputer
\\ATL-WIN2K-01\ROOT\CIMV2:Win32_SID
\\ATL-WIN2K-01\ROOT\CIMV2:Win32_AccountSID
\\ATL-WIN2K-01\ROOT\CIMV2:Win32_SecuritySetting
\\ATL-WIN2K-01\ROOT\CIMV2:Win32_SecuritySettingOfObject
\\ATL-WIN2K-01\ROOT\CIMV2:Win32_SecuritySettingOwner
\\ATL-WIN2K-01\ROOT\CIMV2:Win32_SecuritySettingGroup
\\ATL-WIN2K-01\ROOT\CIMV2:Win32_SecuritySettingAccess
\\ATL-WIN2K-01\ROOT\CIMV2:Win32_SecuritySettingAuditing
\\ATL-WIN2K-01\ROOT\CIMV2:Win32_Trustee
\\ATL-WIN2K-01\ROOT\CIMV2:Win32_ACE
\\ATL-WIN2K-01\ROOT\CIMV2:Win32_SecurityDescriptor
\\ATL-WIN2K-01\ROOT\CIMV2:Win32_LogicalFileSecuritySetting
```

You can modify Listing 6.13 to list classes in other namespaces by changing the target namespace of the script. You can also use Listing 6.13 in combination with the findstr.exe command to search for classes. The Findstr.exe command is a command-line tool that searches for strings in files.

Suppose, for example, you need to know whether the new Windows XP Win32_TSSessionSetting class is supported on the version of Windows you are running. You can use the following command to determine whether this class exists in the root\cimv2 namespace. This command retrieves the classes found in the root\cimv2 namespace and "pipes" that output to Findstr.exe. Findstr.exe then searches the output and reports any instances of the string "Win32_TSSessionSetting".

```
cscript GetClasses.vbs |findstr /I "win32_tssessionsetting"
```

When the command runs on a Windows XP-based computer, the following output is returned:

```
\\ATL-WINXP-01\ROOT\cimv2:Win32_TSSessionSettingError
\\ATL-WINXP-01\ROOT\cimv2:Win32_TSSessionSetting
```

When the command runs on a Windows 2000-based computer, no data is returned. This means that the Win32_TSSessionSetting class is not supported in Windows 2000.

Here are a few additional scenarios you can try.

- List all system classes in the root\cimv2 namespace:

  ```
  cscript GetClasses.vbs |findstr /I "__"
  ```

- List all core and common classes in the root\cimv2 namespace:

  ```
  cscript GetClasses.vbs |findstr /I "CIM_"
  ```

- List all Win32 extension classes in the root\cimv2 namespace:

  ```
  cscript GetClasses.vbs |findstr /I "Win32_"
  ```

- List all classes in the root\cimv2 namespace that contain the string "process":

  ```
  cscript GetClasses.vbs |findstr /I "process"
  ```

CIM Class Types

It should be obvious at this point that classes are the basic building blocks in the CIM repository. WMI configuration information and WMI-managed resources are defined by one or more classes. Similar to the Active Directory schema, CIM classes are organized hierarchically such that child classes inherit properties, methods, and qualifiers from parent classes. (Properties, methods, and qualifiers will be covered in the next section of this chapter.)

For example, the Win32_Service dynamic class is inherited from the Win32_BaseService abstract class, which is inherited from the CIM_Service abstract class, which is inherited from the CIM_LogicalElement abstract class, which is inherited from the CIM_ManagedSystemElement abstract class, as illustrated in Figure 6.2. It is the sum of the classes in a class hierarchy that ultimately defines a managed resource.

Table 6.3 compares the non-system properties found in each of these classes. As you can see, child classes inherit all the properties from their parent class and typically include additional properties as well. Of course, this is why a software developer creates a new child class in the first place: because an existing class has many of the properties needed but not *all* of the properties needed. Rather than modify an existing class, the developer creates a new child class and adds properties to that child class.

Table 6.3   Comparing Parent and Child Class Properties

CIM_ManagedSystemElement and CIM_LogicalElement	CIM_Service	Win32_BaseService	Win32_Service
Caption	Caption	Caption	Caption
Description	Description	Description	Description
InstallDate	InstallDate	InstallDate	InstallDate
Name	Name	Name	Name
Status	Status	Status	Status
	CreationClassName	CreationClassName	CreationClassName
	Description	Description	Description
	Name	Name	Name
	Started	Started	Started
	StartMode	StartMode	StartMode
	Status	Status	Status
	SystemCreationClass Name	SystemCreation ClassName	SystemCreation ClassName
	SystemName	SystemName	SystemName
		AcceptPause	AcceptPause
		AcceptStop	AcceptStop
		DesktopInteract	DesktopInteract
		DisplayName	DisplayName
		ErrorControl	ErrorControl
		ExitCode	ExitCode
		PathName	PathName
		ServiceSpecificExit Code	ServiceSpecific ExitCode
		ServiceType	ServiceType
		StartName	StartName
		State	State

(continued)

Table 6.3   Comparing Parent and Child Class Properties *(continued)*

CIM_ManagedSystemElement and CIM_LogicalElement	CIM_Service	Win32_BaseService	Win32_Service
		TagID	TagID
			Checkpoint
			ProcessID
			WaitHint

Does this mean that you can use Win32_BaseService to return information about services? No; Win32_BaseService is an abstract class, meaning that it is designed to serve as a template for other classes, not to return data.

Abstract Classes

An *abstract class* is a template used to define new classes. Like abstract classes in the Active Directory schema, CIM abstract classes serve as base classes for other abstract, static, and dynamic classes. Most WMI-managed resource class definitions are built (or derived) from one or more abstract classes.

You can identify an abstract class by examining the *Abstract* qualifier. An abstract class must define the Abstract qualifier and set the Abstract qualifier value to true.

The most common use of the abstract class type is to define core and common classes. Abstract classes are rarely used in WMI scripts because you cannot retrieve instances of abstract classes.

Static Classes

A *static class* defines data that is physically stored in the CIM repository. Static classes have instances just like dynamic classes; however, instances of static classes are stored in the CIM repository. Likewise, static class instances are retrieved directly from the CIM. They do not use a provider.

You can identify a static class by examining the class qualifiers. However, unlike abstract and dynamic class types that are identified by the presence of a specific qualifier, static classes are identified by the absence of the Abstract and Dynamic qualifiers. In other words, if a class has neither an Abstract nor a Dynamic qualifier, the class is a static class.

The most common use of the static class type is in the definition of system classes. Static classes are rarely used in WMI scripts.

Dynamic Classes

A *dynamic class* is a class that models a WMI-managed resource that is dynamically retrieved from a provider.

You can identify a dynamic class by examining the *Dynamic* qualifier. A dynamic class must define the Dynamic qualifier and set the Dynamic qualifier value to true.

The dynamic class type is typically used to define extension classes. Dynamic classes are the most common type of classes used in WMI scripts.

Association Classes

A fourth class type, known as an association class, is also supported. An *association class* is an abstract, static, or dynamic class that describes a relationship between two classes or managed resources. The Win32_SystemServices class, shown in Figure 6.2, is an example of a dynamic association class that describes the relationship between a computer and the services running on the computer.

You can identify an association class by examining the *Association* qualifier. An abstract, static, or dynamic association class must define the Association qualifier and set the Association qualifier value to true.

Components of a Class

Every hardware and software resource that is manageable through WMI is defined by a class. A class is a blueprint (or template) for a discrete WMI-managed resource, and all instances of the resource use the blueprint. These means, for example, that all services (which are instances of the Win32_Service class) will have the same properties. This does not mean that they will have the same property *values*; for example, Alerter has the Name Alerter, while the WMI service has the Name Winmgmt. However, all services have a Name property.

 Note

This is true even if no value has been configured for a property. For example, all services have the Description property, although there is no requirement that all services actually have a description. If a property is valid but has not been configured, WMI will return the value Null. This prevents a script from crashing should it encounter a property with no configured value.

Classes represent the things computers have. Because computers have disks, event logs, files, folders, memory, printers, processes, processors, services, and so on, WMI has classes for disks, event logs, files, folders, memory, printers, processes, processors, services, and so on. Although there are exceptions (such as __Event abstract system classes), most classes that are used in scripting can be directly tied to real things.

These blueprints consist of *properties*, *methods*, and *qualifiers*. Before examining properties, methods, and qualifiers, it is useful to learn where managed resource class definitions originate.

Suppose Microsoft decides to create a new WMI provider that system administrators can use to manage and monitor Microsoft DNS servers. At a minimum, the DNS provider development team would need to create two files: a provider and something called a Managed Object Format (MOF) file.

The provider is the dynamic-link library (DLL) that acts as the intermediary between the WMI infrastructure and the underlying managed resource — the Microsoft DNS server in this case. The provider services WMI requests by calling the native APIs of the managed resource.

The MOF file contains the class definitions that describe the capabilities provided by the DNS provider. The MOF file describes the capabilities of the DNS provider, using classes that model resources commonly associated with a DNS server. DNS servers have such things as zones and resource records; thus, you might expect to see classes such as MicrosoftDNS_Zone and MicrosoftDNS_ResourceRecord defined in the MOF file. Each class defined in the DNS MOF file defines the data (properties) associated with a specific DNS-related resource and the actions (methods) you can perform on that resource. For example, a resource record has a time-to-live (TTL) property. Therefore, you might expect the MicrosoftDNS_ResourceRecord class to have a property such as TTL.

When the DNS provider is installed, the DNS provider DLL is registered with the operating system and WMI, and the DNS MOF file undergoes a compilation process. This loads the DNS provider class definitions into the CIM repository. At this point, the DNS provider can be used by any WMI-enabled consumer, including scripts.

As it turns out, this story is true: Microsoft developed a new DNS provider that can be downloaded for Windows 2000. However, the story is not as important as the fact that managed resource class definitions originate in MOF files. MOF files are to WMI what MIB files are to SNMP.

MOF files are text files based on the MOF language created and maintained by the DMTF. The class definition of every managed resource follows a well-defined structure and syntax, as illustrated in Figure 6.3.

Every managed resource class definition consists of *properties*, *methods*, and *qualifiers*. This definition is applied to all instances of a class and determines what can and cannot be done to an instance. For example, with services you can specify actions that will be taken should the service fail (restart the service, restart the computer, run a program, or take no action). These recovery options are not specified anywhere with the class definition. That means that they cannot be managed by using a script.

Properties

Properties are like nouns that describe a managed resource. Classes use properties to describe things such as the identity, configuration, and state of a managed resource. Services, for example, have a name, display name, description, startup type, and status. The Win32_Service class has the same properties.

Figure 6.3   Structure of a Managed Resource Class Definition

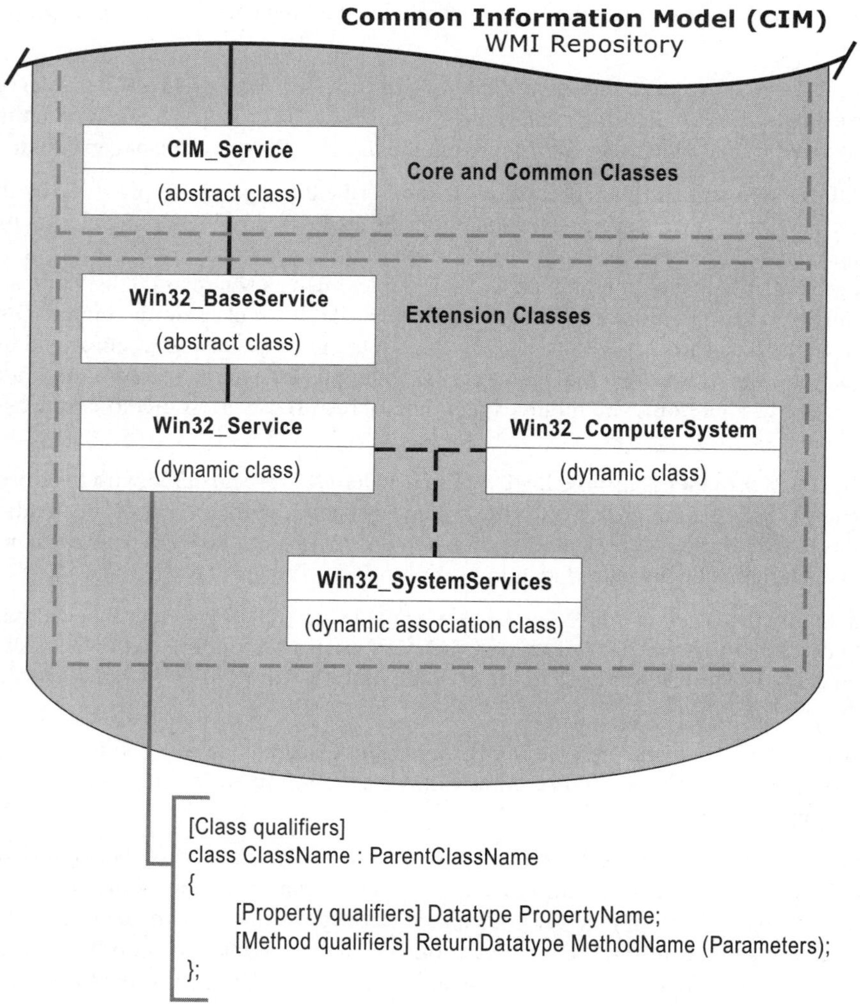

Each property has a name, a type, and optional property qualifiers. You use the property name in combination with the WMI scripting library SWbemObject to access a property, as demonstrated in Listing 6.1. For example, assuming that objService represents an instance of an installed service, these lines of code echo the service name and the description:

```
Wscript.Echo objService.Name
Wscript.Echo objService.Description
```

In the MOF file itself, a property definition looks similar to this, with the name, data type, and qualifier (in this case, the Read qualifier) indicated in boldface:

```
[read : ToSubclass,MappingStrings{"Win32API|Service
Structures|SERVICE_STATUS|dwControlsAccepted|SERVICE_ACCEPT_PAUSE_CONTINUE"} :
ToSubclass] boolean AcceptPause;
```

Methods

Methods are like verbs that perform an action on a managed resource. Think of the methods of the Win32_Service class in these terms: What can you do with services? You can start services, stop services, pause services, and resume services. As it turns out, there are methods that allow you to start, stop, pause, and resume services.

Each method has a name, a return type, optional parameters, and optional method qualifiers. As with properties, you use the method name in combination with SWbemObject to call a method. For example, this line of code stops the service represented by objService. The error code of the operation will be stored in the variable errReturn and then echoed to the screen (in general, the value 0 means that an operation succeeded, and anything else means the script failed):

```
errReturn = obService.StopService()
Wscript.Echo errReturn
```

Not all classes define methods. In Windows 2000, you will find methods implemented in classes such as Win32_Service, Win32_NTEventLogFile, and Win32_Process. In Windows XP, methods are implemented in a number of additional classes, including both new (Win32_DiskQuota) and existing (Win32_Printer) classes.

In the MOF file, a method definition looks similar to this one. The boldface items indicate the fact that the method is implemented (meaning it can be used in scripts), the return codes (ValueMap) used by the method, and the name of the method.

```
[Implemented,ValueMap{"0", "1", "2", "3", "4", "5", "6", "7", "8", "9", "10",
"11", "12", "13", "14", "15", "16", "17", "18", "19", "20", "21", "22", "23",
"24", ".."} : ToSubclass,MappingStrings{"Win32API|Service
Functions|ControlService|dwControl|SERVICE_CONTROL_CONTINUE"} : ToSubclass]
uint32 ResumeService();
```

Qualifiers

Qualifiers are like adjectives that provide additional information about the class, property, or method to which they apply. For example, the Dynamic qualifier answers the question, "What type of class is Win32_Service?" As you begin to write WMI scripts that do more than simply retrieve information (such as modify properties or call methods), qualifiers become increasingly important. This is because they define the operational characteristics of the property you are updating or the method you are calling.

So what kind of information do qualifiers provide? As it turns out, there are three types of qualifiers, providing three types of information.

Class qualifiers

Class qualifiers provide operational information about a class:

- The Abstract, Dynamic, and Association qualifiers tell you the class type.

- The Provider qualifier tells you the provider that services the class. For example, the Provider qualifier for the Win32_Service class tells you that the class uses the CIMWin32 provider (cimwin32.dll). On the other hand, the Win32_NTLogEvent class uses the MS_NT_EVENTLOG_PROVIDER provider (ntevt.dll) as indicated by the Win32_NTLogEvent class Provider qualifier.

- The EnumPrivileges qualifier informs you of special privileges required to use the class. For example, the Win32_NTLogEvent class EnumPrivileges qualifier tells you that SeSecurityPrivilege must be enabled before the Win32_NTLogEvent class can be used to manage the Security log. If this privilege is not specified in the script, the script will not be able to manage the Security event log.

The definition for the Win32_NTLogEvent class in ntevt.mof shows the class type (dynamic), the provider name, and required privileges, all shown in boldface:

```
[Dynamic, Provider ("MS_NT_EVENTLOG_PROVIDER") :
ToInstance, EnumPrivileges{"SeSecurityPrivilege"} :
ToSubclass, Locale(1033) :
ToInstance, UUID("{8502C57C-5FBB-11D2-AAC1-006008C78BC7}") :
ToInstance]
class Win32_NTLogEvent
```

Property qualifiers

Property qualifiers provide information about each property. For example:

- The CIMType qualifier tells you the property data type. WMI supports a number of data types, including strings, integers, dates and times, arrays, and Boolean values.

  Does it really matter which data type a property is? In the simple examples presented thus far in this chapter, no. However, suppose you connect to the Win32_Printer class and retrieve the value of the Capabilities property. This property stores values as an array; consequently, simply echoing the property value (like this) results in a "Type mismatch" error:

```
Wscript.Echo objPrinter.Capabilities
```

  Instead, you have to loop through the individual elements in the array, like this:

```
For Each intCapability in objPrinter.Capabilities
    Wscript.Echo intCapability
Next
```

- The Read qualifier indicates whether the property is readable.

- The Write qualifier indicates whether you can modify the property value. For example, the Win32_WMISetting ASPScriptDefaultNamespace property modified in Listing 6.9 is marked as writable. This means that you can change the value of the property. On the other hand, all of the Win32_Service properties shown in previous scripts are defined as read-only; that is, they do not define the Write qualifier. In general, this means that these properties cannot be configured using a script. (The only exceptions are those properties where the class provides a method that can configure the values. For example, you can use the ChangeStartMode method to change the start mode for a service, even though the StartMode property is read-only.)

- The Key qualifier indicates that the property is the class key and is used to identify unique instances of a managed resource in a collection of identical resources. DeviceID is a key property in the Win32_LogicalDisk class. Why? Because device IDs must be unique; a computer can have no more than one C drive. Size is not a key property, because there is no reason why a single computer cannot have multiple drives all the same size.

Method qualifiers

Method qualifiers provide information about each method. For example:

- The Implemented qualifier indicates that the method has an implementation supplied by a provider. This is important because WMI classes often include methods that are valid but do not actually work (because they have not been implemented). For example, a number of hardware classes include a method named SetPowerState that is a valid method but has not been implemented. Therefore, it cannot actually be used to set the power state of an object.

- The ValueMap qualifier defines a set of permissible values for a method parameter or return type.

- The Privileges qualifier informs you of special privileges required to call the method.

 Note
There are many more qualifiers than those mentioned here. For a complete list, see the WMI Qualifiers topic in the WMI SDK. For information about how to download the WMI SDK, see the Microsoft Windows Management Instrumentation (WMI) SDK link on the Web Resources page at http://www.microsoft.com/windows/reskits/webresources.

Comparing Classes with Managed Resources

Classes determine what you can and cannot do with WMI. If you have a class for services, you can manage services; if you do not have a class for services, you cannot. Consequently, it is important to know which classes are available on a given computer.

Properties and methods are important because the versions of WMI differ among operating systems; the Win32_ComputerSystem class in Windows XP has many new properties and methods not supported by the Win32_ComputerSystem class in Windows 2000. You have to know these details because, unlike Active Directory Service Interfaces (ADSI), the WMI properties and methods must be available on the target computer in order for a script to work.

> **Note**
>
> ADSI works as long as ADSI is installed on your computer. The target computer does not have to have the same version of ADSI as you do; in fact, it does not have to have ADSI at all. With WMI, however, this is different. You cannot retrieve information from a remote computer unless both your computer and the remote computer have WMI installed. Similarly, the methods and properties defined in a managed resource's class definition must exist on the remote computer for a script to work. For example, the Win32_Printer class in Windows XP has a method named CancelAllJobs that can purge a print queue. However, this method cannot be used against a Windows 2000-based computer because the Win32_Printer class in Windows 2000 does not support CancelAllJobs. The method must be present on the target computer.

How do you determine whether a property or a method is supported on a remote Windows-based computer? You examine the class definition.

Retrieving Class Definitions

You can use the WMI scripting library to retrieve managed resource class definitions in two different ways:

- You can use the SWbemObject Qualifiers_, Properties_, and Methods_ properties to retrieve class information.

- You can use the SWbemObject GetObjectText_ method to retrieve the class definition formatted in MOF syntax.

Using the SWbemObject Properties_, Methods_, and Qualifiers_ properties

Listing 6.14, Listing 6.15, and Listing 6.16 demonstrate how to use the Properties_, Methods_, and Qualifiers_ properties of SWbemObject to retrieve information about the Win32_Service class. All three scripts employ the same basic approach, although there are some differences.

Listing 6.14 begins by initializing three variables: strComputer, strNameSpace, and strClass. The value assigned to strComputer is the target computer. The value assigned to strNameSpace is the namespace to connect to, and the value assigned to strClass is the name of the class whose properties are to be retrieved and displayed.

Separating the three values into multiple variables makes it easy to reuse the script for other computers, namespaces, and classes. In fact, you can easily turn these scripts into command-line scripts by using the WSH Arguments collection. This allows a user to retrieve information about any computer, namespace, or class simply by specifying the appropriate information as a command-line argument. For more information about WSH arguments, see "WSH Primer" in this book.

Next the script uses the VBScript GetObject function to connect to the WMI Service on the target computer. You might have noticed something different about the connection string passed to GetObject. In addition to the target namespace, the class name is also specified. This has a profound impact on what GetObject and the WMI scripting library return. Rather than return a reference to an SWbemServices object, as was the case in the previous scripts, GetObject returns a reference to an SWbemObject representing the target class. How? The answer lies in something called an *object path*. Although object paths are covered in detail later in this chapter, a quick explanation will help you understand what is going on in these scripts.

Every WMI class and every instance of a WMI-managed resource has an object path. An object path is very similar to the file paths associated with files and folders. A file has a fully qualified path that consists of a device name, followed by zero or more directory names, followed by the file name. Likewise, every class and managed resource has an object path that consists of the computer name, followed by the namespace, followed by the managed resource class name, followed by the class key property and the key property value, as shown here. (Note that the square brackets serve only to delimit the four permissible parts of an object path; they are not part of the object path.)

```
[\\ComputerName] [\Namespace] [:ClassName] [.KeyProperty='Value']
```

When you use all or part of an object path in the connection string passed to GetObject, the object path you use determines the type of reference returned. For example, if you include only the computer name portion of an object path, you get back an SWbemServices object reference connected to the default namespace. If you include the computer name or the namespace or both, you also get a reference to an SWbemServices object. If you include the computer name, namespace, and class name, you get back a reference to an SWbemObject representing the class. And if you include all four parts, you get back an SWbemObject representing the managed resource instance identified by the class, key, and value.

The object path elements and the objects returned are summarized in Table 6.4.

Table 6.4   Object Path Elements and Objects Returned

Items Specified in Object Path	Object Returned

Computer name:
 	
```Set objSWbemServices = _```
```GetObject("winmgmts:\\WebServer")```
	SWbemServices (connected to the default namespace)

Computer name and/or namespace:
 	
```Set objSWbemServices = _```
```GetObject("winmgmts:\\WebServer\root\cimv2")```
	SWbemServices (connected to the specified namespace root\cimv2)

(continued)

Table 6.4 Object Path Elements and Objects Returned *(continued)*

Items Specified in Object Path	Object Returned

Computer name, namespace, class name:
 	
`Set objSWbemObject = GetObject _`
`("winmgmts:\\WebServer\root\cimv2:Win32_Service")`
	SWbemObject (representing the class Win32_Service)

Computer name, namespace, class name, key property:
 	
`Set objSWbemObject = GetObject _`
`("winmgmts:\\WebServer\root\cimv2:" & _`
`"Win32_Service.Name='Alerter'")`
	SWbemObject (representing the specific instance, the service named Alerter)

The remainder of the script is reasonably straightforward. After echoing a simple header identifying the class name whose properties are going to be displayed, the script uses the SWbemObject reference (objClass) to access the SWbemObject Properties_ property (objClass.Properties_). The Properties_ property references an SWbemPropertySet, which is the collection of properties for the class. Each property in the collection is an SWbemProperty (objClassProperty) object, which is used to read and echo each property name.

Listing 6.14 Using SWbemObject Properties_ to Retrieve Win32_Service Properties

```
1   strComputer = "."
2   strNameSpace = "root\cimv2"
3   strClass = "Win32_Service"
4
5   Set objClass = GetObject("winmgmts:\\" & strComputer & _
6                           "\" & strNameSpace & ":" & strClass)
7
8   Wscript.Echo strClass & " Class Properties"
9   Wscript.Echo " — — — — — — — — — — — — — — "
10
11  For Each objClassProperty In objClass.Properties_
12      Wscript.Echo objClassProperty.Name
13  Next
```

The following is output displaying the names of the 25 properties defined (or inherited) by the Win32_Service class.

```
Win32_Service Class Properties
- - - - - - - - - - - - - - -
AcceptPause
AcceptStop
Caption
CheckPoint
CreationClassName
Description
DesktopInteract
DisplayName
ErrorControl
ExitCode
InstallDate
Name
PathName
ProcessId
ServiceSpecificExitCode
ServiceType
Started
StartMode
StartName
State
Status
SystemCreationClassName
SystemName
TagId
WaitHint
```

Listing 6.15 is identical to Listing 6.14, with one exception: The For Each loop enumerates the SWbemMethodSet collection and displays the Name property for each SWbemMethod (objClassMethod) in the SWbemMethodSet collection.

Listing 6.15   Using SWbemObject Methods_ to Retrieve Win32_Service Methods

```
1   strComputer = "."
2   strNameSpace = "root\cimv2"
3   strClass = "Win32_Service"
4
5   Set objClass = GetObject("winmgmts:\\" & strComputer & _
6                            "\" & strNameSpace & ":" & strClass)
7
8   Wscript.Echo strClass & " Class Methods"
9   Wscript.Echo " - - - - - - - - - - - - -"
10
11  For Each objClassMethod In objClass.Methods_
12      Wscript.Echo objClassMethod.Name
13  Next
```

The following output displays the names of the 10 methods defined (or inherited) by the Win32_Service class.

```
Win32_Service Class Methods
- - - - - - - - - - - - - -
StartService
StopService
PauseService
ResumeService
InterrogateService
UserControlService
Create
Change
ChangeStartMode
Delete
```

Listing 6.16 is identical to Listing 6.14 and Listing 6.15, with three exceptions:

- The For Each loop enumerates the SWbemQualifierSet collection (by way of the Qualifiers_ property) and echoes the Name property for each SWbemQualifier (objClassQualifier) in the collection.

- Because class qualifiers are part of the class definition and qualifiers have values, Listing 6.16 also retrieves and echoes the Value property for each SWbemQualifier in the collection.

- Because a qualifier can have multiple values stored in an array, Listing 6.16 must account for this prior to reading the value of a qualifier. Not doing so would result in a run-time error if the script tried to read an array-based qualifier as a "regular" variable. The Win32_NTLogEvent EnumPrivileges qualifier is an example of an array-based qualifier (although only one value, the privilege SeSecurityPrivilege, is stored in the array).

    This checking is done by using the VBScript function VarType to determine the data type of the variable.

Listing 6.16   Using SWbemObject Qualifiers_ to Retrieve Win32_Service Class Qualifiers

```
1   strComputer = "."
2   strNameSpace = "root\cimv2"
3   strClass = "Win32_Service"
4
5   Set objClass = GetObject("winmgmts:\\" & strComputer & _
6                        "\" & strNameSpace & ":" & strClass)
7
8   Wscript.Echo strClass & " Class Qualifiers"
9   Wscript.Echo " - - - - - - - - - - - - - - - "
10
```

(continued)

Listing 6.16   Using SWbemObject Qualifiers_ to Retrieve Win32_Service Class Qualifiers *(continued)*

```
11   For Each objClassQualifier In objClass.Qualifiers_
12       If VarType(objClassQualifier.Value) = (vbVariant + vbArray) Then
13           strQualifier = objClassQualifier.Name & " = " & _
14                           Join(objClassQualifier.Value, ",")
15       Else
16           strQualifier = objClassQualifier.Name & " = " & _
17                           objClassQualifier.Value
18       End If
19       Wscript.Echo strQualifier
20       strQualifier = ""
21   Next
```

The following output displays the names and values of the five class qualifiers defined (or inherited) by the Win32_Service class.

```
Win32_Service Class Qualifiers
– – – – – – – – – – – – – – –
dynamic = True
Locale = 1033
provider = CIMWin32
SupportsUpdate = True
UUID = {8502C4D9-5FBB-11D2-AAC1-006008C78BC7}
```

As you might have noticed, Listing 6.14 and Listing 6.15 do not show you the property and method qualifiers. This was done to keep the scripts to a size that could be easily explained.

Using the SWbemObject GetObjectText_ method

Earlier it was noted that you can retrieve managed resource class definitions directly from the MOF file in which the class is defined. For example, if you want to look up the Win32_Service class, look in the *systemroot*\System32\Wbem\Cimwin32.mof file. However, using MOF files directly comes with a price. You must examine every class in a class hierarchy to obtain the complete blueprint for the managed resource.

For example, if you want to look up Win32_Service, you have to examine all five classes in the Win32_Service class hierarchy to get the complete picture. This is tedious at best. An easier approach to obtaining the MOF representation of a class is to use the WMI scripting library SWbemObject GetObjectText_ method, as demonstrated in Listing 6.17.

Unlike Listing 6.14 through Listing 6.16, Listing 6.17 uses the SWbemServices Get method rather than GetObject to retrieve the class. The Get method must be used so the wbemFlagUseAmendedQuailifiers flag can be enabled. Enabling this flag tells WMI to return the entire managed resource blueprint (class definition) rather than just the local definition. In other words, the information returned includes only the three properties unique to Win32_Service, and no information is returned for all the properties and methods inherited from other classes.

The Get method returns a reference to an SWbemObject (objClass) representing the target class, which is used to call the GetObjectText_ method. The GetObjectText_ method returns the MOF representation for the class. Had GetObjectText_ been used without enabling the wbemFlagUseAmendedQuailifiers flag, the method would have only returned those properties, methods, and qualifiers defined by Win32_Service; inherited properties and methods would have been omitted.

Listing 6.17   Using SWbemObject GetObjectText_ to Retrieve the MOF Representation of the Win32_Service Class

```
1   strComputer = "."
2   strNameSpace = "root\cimv2"
3   strClass = "Win32_Service"
4
5   Const wbemFlagUseAmendedQualifiers = &h20000
6
7   Set objSWbemServices = _
8       GetObject("winmgmts:\\" & strComputer & "\" & strNameSpace)
9   Set objClass = objSWbemServices.Get(strClass, wbemFlagUseAmendedQualifiers)
10  strMOF = objClass.GetObjectText_
11
12  Wscript.Echo strMOF
```

The output from the script will be similar to this partial output:

```
[dynamic: ToInstance, provider("CIMWin32"): ToInstance, Locale(1033): Amended,
UUID("{8502C4D9-5FBB-11D2-AAC1-006008C78BC7}"): ToInstance, Description("The
Win32_Service class represents a service on a Win32 computer system. A service
application conforms to the interface rules of the Service Control Manager (SCM)
and can be started by a user automatically at system boot through the Services
control panel utility, or by an application that uses the service functions
included in the Win32 API. Services can execute even when no user is logged on to
the system."): ToSubClass Amended]
class Win32_Service : Win32_BaseService
{
    [Description("The Caption property is a short textual description (one-line
string) of the object."): ToSubClass Amended] string Caption;
```

There is a caveat to using GetObjectText_, however: The method does not return information about inherited qualifiers included in the MOF file. This can present a problem if you want to use GetObjectText_ to determine a Key property when the Key qualifier is defined in a parent class.

Exploring the CIM Repository

Browsing the CIM repository is probably the best way to learn about the available classes and about the methods and properties available through those classes. As you have seen, you can use scripts to explore the CIM repository. However, you are not limited to using scripts to carry out this task; in fact, you can use a number of different tools to browse the WMI classes in the CIM repository that correspond to WMI-managed resources.

WMI Tester

WMI Tester (Wbemtest.exe) is a general-purpose graphical tool you can use to interact with the WMI infrastructure. You can use WMI Tester to browse the CIM schema and examine managed resource class definitions. WMI Tester can also be used to perform the same actions your WMI-based scripts perform, such as retrieving instances of managed resources and running queries. Because WMI Tester is part of the default WMI installation on all WMI-enabled computers, Wbemtest.exe is an excellent and readily available WMI learning and troubleshooting tool.

CIM Studio

CIM Studio, part of the WMI SDK and WMI Administrative Tools, provides a Web-based interface you can use to interact with the WMI infrastructure. As with WMI Tester, you can use CIM Studio to browse the CIM schema, view class definitions, and retrieve instances of managed resources. The superior user interface of CIM Studio makes it easy to view class relationships and associations, and CIM Studio provides a rudimentary search facility — two features not available with the WMI Tester tool. To use CIM Studio, you must download and install the WMI SDK or the WMI Administrative Tools. The WMI Administrative Tools can be obtained from the Microsoft.com Download Center.

Resource Kit scripts

The *Microsoft Windows 2000 Server Resource Kit* includes dozens of scripts that leverage the power of WMI. Three of those scripts, EnumClasses.vbs, EnumInstances.vbs, and EnumNamespaces.vbs, are general-purpose scripts that can be used to browse the CIM schema, view class definitions, and retrieve instances of managed resources.

WMI Scripting Library

The WMI scripting library provides the set of automation objects through which scripting languages, such as VBScript, JScript, and ActiveState ActivePerl access the WMI infrastructure. The WMI scripting library is implemented in a single automation component named wbemdisp.dll that physically resides in the *systemroot*\System32\Wbem directory.

WMI Scripting Library Object Model

The WMI scripting library consists of 19 Automation objects, 16 of which are illustrated in the WMI scripting library object model diagram shown in Figure 6.4. In many ways, you can compare the Automation objects in the WMI scripting library with the core interfaces provided by ADSI. The ADSI core interfaces, IADs and IADsContainer, provide a consistent approach to managing objects in Active Directory, irrespective of the object class and attributes. Similarly, the Automation objects in the WMI scripting library provide a consistent and uniform scripting model for WMI-managed resources.

It is important to understand the relationship between the Automation objects in the WMI scripting library (wbemdisp.dll) and the managed resource class definitions that reside in the CIM repository (cim.rep). As previously explained, managed resource class definitions are the blueprints for the computer resources exposed through WMI. In addition to defining the resources that can be managed, the blueprints define the methods and properties unique to each managed resource.

The WMI scripting library, on the other hand, provides a general-purpose set of Automation objects that scripts can use to authenticate and connect to WMI, giving the scripts to access instances of WMI-managed resources. After you obtain an instance of a WMI-managed resource using the WMI scripting library, you can access the methods and properties defined by the class definition of the managed resource — as if the methods and properties were part of the WMI scripting library itself.

 Note

The lines in Figure 6.4 point to the object that is obtained by calling a method (or accessing a property) of the originating object. For example, calling the SWbemLocator ConnectServer method returns an SWbemServices object. Calling the SWbemServices InstancesOf method returns an SWbemObjectSet collection. On the other hand, calling the SWbemServices Get method returns an SWbemObject.

Figure 6.4   WMI Scripting Library Object Model

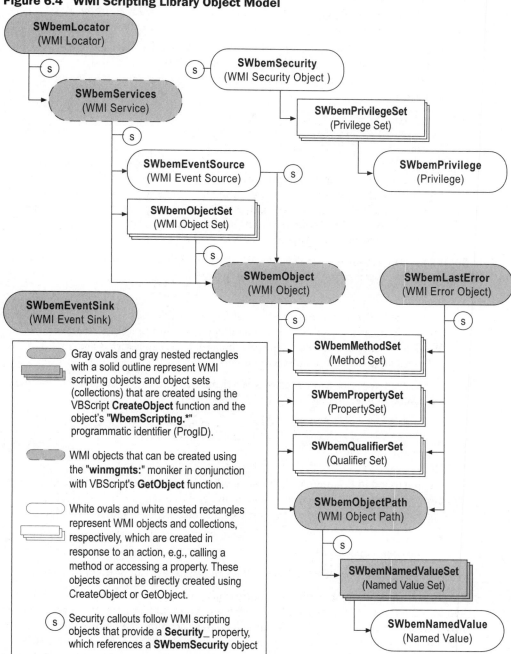

The WMI scripting library object model diagram provides a great deal of insight into the mechanics of how WMI scripting works. For example, consider all of the WMI scripts presented thus far. Each script performs three basic steps common to many WMI scripts.

1. Each script starts by connecting to the WMI service on a target computer. The scripts use the VBScript GetObject function combined with a WMI connection string consisting of the WMI moniker "winmgmts:" followed by a WMI object path to the target computer and a namespace.

```
strComputer = "."
Set objSWbemServices = GetObject("winmgmts:\\" & strComputer &
"\root\cimv2")
```

Connecting to WMI in this way returns a reference to the SWbemServices object shown in Figure 6.4. After you obtain a reference to an SWbemServices object, you can call one of the object methods. The method you call depends on the type of WMI script you are creating. For more information about WMI script types, see "Creating Scripts Based on WMI Templates" later in this chapter.

2. Each script retrieves instances of a WMI-managed resource using the InstancesOf method.

```
Set colSWbemObjectSet = objSWbemServices.InstancesOf("Win32_Service")
```

InstancesOf always returns an SWbemObjectSet collection. As shown by the line between the SWbemServices and SWbemObjectSet objects in Figure 6.4, this is one of the three WMI scripting library object types SWbemServices can return. (The other two are SWbemObject and SWbemEventSource.)

3. Each script accesses properties of a WMI-managed resource by enumerating the instances in the SWbemObjectSet.

```
For Each objSWbemObject In colSWbemObjectSet
    Wscript.Echo "Name: " & objSWbemObject.Name
Next
```

As illustrated in Figure 6.4, each managed resource instance in an SWbemObjectSet collection is represented by an SWbemObject. For example, if your SWbemObjectSet consists of a collection of all the services installed on a computer, two things will be true:

- Each item in the collection will be an SWbemObject. (This is true for any SWbemObjectSet.)

- Each object in the collection will be an instance of an installed service.

You can think of the WMI scripting library object model as your road map to WMI scripting. As you become more proficient with WMI scripting, you will learn that WMI provides multiple ways to script the same task. For example, you have seen the SWbemServices InstancesOf method used a number of times to retrieve instances of WMI-managed resources. You can use the SWbemServices ExecQuery method to do the same thing, as you will see later in this chapter.

Interpreting the WMI Scripting Library Object Model

What else does the WMI scripting library object model tell you? The object model tells you that the SWbemLocator, SWbemSink, SWbemObjectPath, SWbemNamedValueSet, and SWbemLastError objects are created using the CreateObject function. On the other hand, SWbemServices and SWbemObject can be created using the GetObject function combined with the WMI moniker and a WMI object path.

The object model also tells you that seven of the objects in the WMI scripting library expose an SWbemSecurity object, as indicated by the circle S call-out immediately beneath or to the right of the object.

Of the nineteen Automation objects in the WMI scripting library, the two most important WMI scripting objects are SWbemServices and SWbemObject. SWbemServices represents an authenticated connection to a WMI namespace on a local or remote computer. Additionally, SWbemServices plays an important role in two of the most powerful scripting features found in WMI: query and event processing.

SWbemObject is the multiple-identity object that masquerades as the managed resource you have requested. For example, if you retrieve instances of the Win32_Process managed resource, SWbemObject takes on an identity modeled after the Win32_Process class definition. In other words, each returned object will have the properties of an actual process currently running on the computer. Likewise, if you retrieve instances of the Win32_Service managed resource, SWbemObject takes on an identity modeled after the Win32_Service class. You use SWbemObject to call the methods and access the properties defined in the managed resource class definition.

The discussion that follows examines the role that the primary WMI scripting library Automation objects play in WMI scripting. As you read about each WMI scripting object and review the accompanying scripts, take a moment to examine the relationship of each object with adjacent objects in the object model diagram. After you have a basic understanding of the role of each object and how it interacts with other objects in the WMI scripting library, you will be well on your way to becoming proficient in WMI scripting.

Variable Naming Conventions

In the example scripts that accompany the WMI scripting library object descriptions, the variable names used to reference each WMI automation object follow a consistent naming convention. Each variable is named according to the Automation object name in the WMI scripting library and is prefaced with "obj" (to indicate an object reference) or "col" (to indicate a collection object reference). For example, a variable that references an SWbemServices object is named objSWbemServices. A variable that references an SWbemObject is named objSWbemObject. And a variable that references an SWbemObjectSet is named colSWbemObjectSet.

This information is important because it helps you understand the type of WMI object you are working with at any given point in a WMI script. In addition, following a consistent naming convention makes your code easier to read and to maintain. However, the object reference variable names can be whatever you choose. If you prefer variable names such as x and y, that is fine. There is no requirement stating that you must name a reference to an SWbemServices object objSWbemServices. For example, these two script snippets are functionally identical; they simply use different variable names:

```
strComputer = "."
Set objSWbemServices = GetObject("winmgmts:\\" & strComputer & "\root\cimv2")
```

```
strComputer = "."
Set x = GetObject("winmgmts:\\" & strComputer & "\root\cimv2")
```

 Note

The following discussion does not attempt to cover every method and property provided by each Automation object in the WMI scripting library. However, this information can be found in the WMI Software Development Kit. For information about how to download the WMI SDK, see the Microsoft Windows Management Instrumentation (WMI) SDK link on the Web Resources page at http://www.microsoft.com/windows/reskits/webresources.

SWbemLocator

At the top of the WMI scripting library object model is the SWbemLocator object. SWbemLocator is used to establish an authenticated connection to a WMI namespace, much as the VBScript GetObject function and the WMI moniker "winmgmts:" are used to establish an authenticated connection to WMI. However, SWbemLocator is designed to address two specific scripting scenarios that cannot be performed using GetObject and the WMI moniker. You must use SWbemLocator if you need to:

- Provide user and password credentials to connect to WMI on a remote computer. The WMI moniker used with the GetObject function does not include a mechanism for specifying credentials. Most WMI activities (including all of those carried out on remote computers) require administrator rights. If you typically log on using a regular user account instead of an administrator account, you will not be able to perform most WMI tasks unless you run the script under alternate credentials.

- Connect to WMI if you are running a WMI script from within a Web page. You cannot use the GetObject function when running scripts embedded within an HTML page because Internet Explorer disallows the use of GetObject for security reasons.

In addition, you might want to use SWbemLocator to connect to WMI if you find the WMI connection string used with GetObject confusing or difficult.

You use CreateObject rather than GetObject to create a reference to SWbemLocator. To create the reference, you must pass the CreateObject function the SWbemLocator programmatic identifier (ProgID) "WbemScripting.SWbemLocator", as shown on line 2 in the following script sample. After you obtain a reference to an SWbemLocator object, you call the ConnectServer method to connect to WMI and obtain a reference to an SWbemServices object. This is demonstrated on line 3 of the following script.

```
strComputer = "."
Set objSWbemLocator = CreateObject("WbemScripting.SWbemLocator")
Set objSWbemServices = objSWbemLocator.ConnectServer(strComputer, "root\cimv2")
Set colSWbemObjectSet = objSWbemServices.InstancesOf("Win32_Service")
For Each objSWbemObject In colSWbemObjectSet
    Wscript.Echo "Name: " & objSWbemObject.Name
Next
```

Lines 2 and 3 in the previous example are functionally identical to all of the GetObject examples you have seen thus far. ConnectServer is the only method provided by the SWbemLocator object.

To run a script under alternate credentials, include the user name and password as additional parameters passed to ConnectServer. For example, this script runs under the credentials of a user named kenmyer, with the password homerj.

```
strComputer = "atl-dc-01"
Set objSWbemLocator = CreateObject("WbemScripting.SWbemLocator")
Set objSWbemServices = objSWbemLocator.ConnectServer _
    (strComputer, "root\cimv2", "kenmyer", "homerj")
Set colSWbemObjectSet = objSWbemServices.InstancesOf("Win32_Service")
For Each objSWbemObject In colSWbemObjectSet
    Wscript.Echo "Name: " & objSWbemObject.Name
Next
```

You can also use the Domain\User Name format to specify a user name. For example:

```
"fabrikam\kenmyer"
```

WMI scripts that connect to the WMI service on the local computer always connect using the security context of the logged on user. You cannot use the SWbemLocator ConnectServer method to specify user and password credentials for a local connection.

You should avoid hard-coding passwords in scripts. Instead, you can use the WScript StdOut and StdIn properties to prompt for and retrieve the password just before it is needed. If you are running Windows XP Professional, you can mask password input by using the ScriptPW object.

For example, this script uses StdOut to prompt the user for the administrator password, and then uses StdIn to read the value typed by the user and assign it to the variable strPassword. Because this script uses StdIn and StdOut, it must be run under CScript.

```
strComputer = "atl-dc-01"
Wscript.StdOut.Write "Please enter the administrator password: "
strPassword = Wscript.StdIn.ReadLine
Set objSWbemLocator = CreateObject("WbemScripting.SWbemLocator")
Set objSWbemServices = objSWbemLocator.ConnectServer _
    (strComputer, "root\cimv2", "administrator", strPassword)
Set colSWbemObjectSet = objSWbemServices.InstancesOf("Win32_Service")
For Each objSWbemObject In colSWbemObjectSet
    Wscript.Echo "Name: " & objSWbemObject.Name
Next
```

SWbemServices

SWbemServices serves two primary roles. First, the SWbemServices object represents an authenticated connection to a WMI namespace on a target computer. Second, SWbemServices is the Automation object you use to retrieve WMI-managed resources. You can obtain a reference to an SWbemServices object in either of two ways:

- As demonstrated in most of the WMI scripts presented thus far, you can use the VBScript GetObject function in combination with the WMI moniker "winmgmts:". The following example is the simplest form of a WMI connection. The example connects to the default namespace (typically root\cimv2) on the local computer:

```
Set objSWbemServices = GetObject("winmgmts:")
```

- You can also use the SWbemLocator object ConnectServer method to obtain a reference to an SWbemServices object. For more information, see "SWbemLocator" earlier in this section.

After you obtain a reference to an SWbemServices object, you use the object reference to call 1 of 18 methods available using SWbemServices. SWbemServices can return one of three different WMI scripting library objects (SWbemObjectSet, SWbemObject, or SWbemEventSource), depending on the method you call. Knowing the type of object each method returns will help you determine the next step your script must take. For example, if you get back an SWbemObjectSet, you must enumerate the collection to access each SWbemObject in the collection. If you get back an SWbemObject, you can immediately access the object methods and properties without enumerating the collection first.

SWbemServices methods and their return types are described in Table 6.5.

Table 6.5   SWbemServices Methods

Method Name	Default Mode	Return Type	Description
AssociatorsOf	Semisynchronous	SWbemObjectSet	Retrieves the instances of managed resources that are associated with a specified resource through one or more association classes. You provide the object path for the originating endpoint, and AssociatorsOf returns the managed resources at the opposite endpoint. The AssociatorsOf method performs the same function that the ASSOCIATORS OF WQL query performs.
Delete	Synchronous (cannot be changed)	None	Deletes an instance of a managed resource (or a class definition from the CIM repository).
ExecMethod	Synchronous (cannot be changed)	SWbemObject	Provides an alternative way to execute a method defined by a managed resource class definition. Primarily used in situations in which the scripting language does not support out parameters. For example, JScript does not support out parameters.
ExecNotificationQuery	Semisynchronous	SWbemEventSource	Executes an event subscription query to receive events. An event subscription query is a query that defines a change to the managed environment that you want to monitor. When the change occurs, the WMI infrastructure delivers an event describing the change to the calling script.
ExecQuery	Semisynchronous	SWbemObjectSet	Executes a query to retrieve a collection of instances of WMI-managed resources (or class definitions). ExecQuery can be used to retrieve a filtered collection of instances that match criteria you define in the query passed to ExecQuery.
Get	Synchronous (cannot be changed)	SWbemObject	Retrieves a single instance of a managed resource (or class definition) based on an object path.

(continued)

Table 6.5   SWbemServices Methods *(continued)*

Method Name	Default Mode	Return Type	Description
InstancesOf	Semisynchronous	SWbemObjectSet	Retrieves all the instances of a managed resource based on a class name. By default, InstancesOf performs a deep retrieval. That is, InstancesOf retrieves the instances of the resource identified by the class name passed to the method and also retrieves all the instances of all the resources that are subclasses (defined beneath) of the target class.
ReferencesTo	Semisynchronous	SWbemObjectSet	Returns all of the associations that reference a specified resource. The best way to understand ReferencesTo is to compare it with the AssociatorsOf method. AssociatorsOf returns the dynamic resources that are at the opposite end of an association. ReferencesTo returns the association itself. The ReferencesTo method performs the same function that the REFERENCES OF WQL query performs.
SubclassesOf	Semisynchronous	SWbemObjectSet	Retrieves all the subclasses of a specified class from the CIM repository.

Table 6.5 lists only 9 of the 18 methods of SWbemServices; the remaining 9 methods are the asynchronous counterparts. The asynchronous methods have similar names; however, each asynchronous method name is appended with the suffix *Async*. For example, the asynchronous version of ExecNotificationQuery is named ExecNotificationQueryAsync.

SWbemServices modes of operation

SWbemServices supports three modes of operation: synchronous, asynchronous, and semisynchronous.

Synchronous. In synchronous mode, your script blocks (pauses) until the SWbemServices method completes. Not only does your script wait, but in cases in which WMI retrieves instances of managed resources, WMI builds the entire SWbemObjectSet in memory before the first byte of data is returned to the calling script. This can have an adverse effect on the script performance and on the computer running the script. For example, synchronously retrieving thousands of events from the Windows 2000 Event Logs can take a long time and use a lot of memory. For these reasons, synchronous operations are not recommended except for the three methods (Delete, ExecMethod, and Get) that are synchronous by default. These methods do not return large data sets, so semisynchronous operation is not required.

Note

Changing the run-time behavior of a semisynchronous method to synchronous is possible but not recommended. Doing so can result in WMI scripts that appear to hang when retrieving large data sets such as all the instances of CIM_DataFile or Win32_NTLogEvent.

Asynchronous. In asynchronous mode, your script calls one of the nine asynchronous methods and returns immediately. That is, as soon as the asynchronous method is called, your script resumes running the next line of code. To use an asynchronous method, your script must first create an SWbemSink object and a special subroutine called an event handler. WMI performs the asynchronous operation and notifies the script by calling the event handler subroutine when the operation is complete.

Semisynchronous. Semisynchronous mode is a compromise between synchronous and asynchronous. Semisynchronous operations offer better performance than synchronous operations, yet they do not require the extra knowledge and scripting steps necessary to handle asynchronous operations. This is the default operation type for most WMI queries.

In semisynchronous mode, your script calls one of the six data retrieval methods and returns immediately. WMI retrieves the managed resources in the background as your script continues to run. As the resources are retrieved, they are immediately returned to your script by way of an SWbemObjectSet. You can begin to access the managed resources without waiting for the entire collection to be assembled.

There is a caveat to semisynchronous operations when you are working with managed resources that have many instances (many meaning greater than 1,000), such as CIM_DataFile and Win32_NTLogEvent. The caveat is a result of how WMI handles instances of managed resources. For each instance of a managed resource, WMI creates and caches an SWbemObject object. When a large number of instances exist for a managed resource, instance retrieval can monopolize available resources, reducing the performance of both the script and the computer.

To work around the problem, you can optimize semisynchronous method calls using the wbemFlagForwardOnly flag. The wbemFlagForwardOnly flag, combined with the wbemFlagReturnImmediately flag (the default semisynchronous flag), tells WMI to return a forward-only SWbemObjectSet, which eliminates the large data set performance problem. However, using the wbemFlagForwardOnly flag comes with a cost. A forward-only SWbemObjectSet can be enumerated only once. After each SWbemObject in a forward-only SWbemObjectSet is accessed, the memory allocated to the instance is released.

With the exception of the Delete, ExecMethod, Get, and nine asynchronous methods, semisynchronous is the default and recommended mode of operation.

Using SWbemServices methods

The methods most often used in system administration scripts are InstancesOf, ExecQuery, Get, and ExecNotificationQuery. Although often used, InstancesOf is not necessarily the recommended way to retrieve information (although it is arguably the easiest way). This will be discussed in more detail later in this chapter.

InstancesOf

You have already seen the InstancesOf method used numerous times throughout this chapter. At this time, it is important to clarify something said earlier. Earlier it was stated that you cannot retrieve instances of abstract classes, such as CIM_Service. And while that is true, the default behavior of InstancesOf might lead you to think otherwise.

By default, InstancesOf performs a deep retrieval. That is, InstancesOf retrieves all instances of the managed resource you identify and all instances of all the subclasses defined beneath the target class. For example, the following script retrieves all of the resources modeled by all of the dynamic classes defined beneath the CIM_Service abstract class.

```
strComputer = "."
Set objSWbemServices = GetObject("winmgmts:\\" & strComputer & "\root\cimv2")
Set colSWbemObjectSet = objSWbemServices.InstancesOf("CIM_Service")
For Each objSWbemObject In colSWbemObjectSet
    Wscript.Echo "Object Path: " & objSWbemObject.Path_.Path
Next
```

If you run this script, you will get information back. However, this information will not be limited to the services installed on a computer. Instead, it will include information from all child classes of CIM_Service, including Win32_SystemDriver and Win32_ApplicationService.

ExecQuery

Like the InstancesOf method, the ExecQuery method always returns an SWbemObjectSet collection. Thus your WMI script must enumerate the collection ExecQuery returns in order to access each managed resource instance in the collection, as shown here:

```
strComputer = "."
Set objSWbemServices = GetObject("winmgmts:\\" & strComputer & "\root\cimv2")
Set colSWbemObjectSet = objSWbemServices.ExecQuery _
   ("SELECT * FROM Win32_Service")
For Each objSWbemObject In colSWbemObjectSet
    Wscript.Echo "Name: " & objSWbemObject.Name
Next
```

Other SWbemServices methods that return an SWbemObjectSet include AssociatorsOf, ReferencesTo, and SubclassesOf.

Get

Unlike the ExecQuery and InstancesOf methods, the Get method always returns an SWbemObject representing a specific instance of a WMI-managed resource (or single class definition, as shown earlier). To obtain a specific instance of a WMI-managed resource using the Get method, you must tell Get the instance to retrieve by passing the method the object path, as shown in the following script.

```
strComputer = "."
Set objSWbemServices = GetObject("winmgmts:\\" & strComputer & "\root\cimv2")

Set objSWbemObject = objSWbemServices.Get("Win32_Service.Name='Messenger'")

Wscript.Echo "Name:          " & objSWbemObject.Name        & vbCrLf & _
             "Display Name: " & objSWbemObject.DisplayName & vbCrLf & _
             "Start Mode:   " & objSWbemObject.StartMode   & vbCrLf & _
             "State:        " & objSWbemObject.State
```

SWbemObjectSet

An SWbemObjectSet is a collection of zero or more SWbemObject objects. Each SWbemObject in a SWbemObjectSet can represent one of two things:

- An instance of a WMI-managed resource.

- An instance of a class definition.

For the most part, the only thing you will ever do with an SWbemObjectSet is enumerate all the objects contained within the collection itself. However, SWbemObjectSet does include a property — Count — that can be useful in system administration scripting. As the name implies, Count tells you the number of items in the collection. For example, this script retrieves a collection of all the services installed on a computer and then echoes the total number of services found:

```
strComputer = "."
Set objSWbemServices = GetObject("winmgmts:\\" & strComputer & "\root\cimv2")
Set colSWbemObjectSet = objSWbemServices.InstancesOf("Win32_Service")
Wscript.Echo "Services installed on target computer: " & colSWbemObjectSet.Count
```

What makes Count useful is that it can tell you whether a specific instance is available on a computer. For example, this script retrieves a collection of all the services on a computer that have the Name W3SVC. If the Count is 0 (and it is valid for collections to have no instances), that means the W3SVC service is not installed on the computer.

```
strComputer = "."
Set objSWbemServices = GetObject("winmgmts:\\" & strComputer & "\root\cimv2")
Set colSWbemObjectSet = objSWbemServices.ExecQuery _
    ("SELECT * FROM Win32_Service WHERE Name='w3svc'")
If colSWbemObjectSet.Count = 0 Then
    Wscript.Echo "W3SVC service is not installed on target computer."
Else
    For Each objSWbemObject In colSWbemObjectSet
        ' Perform task on World Wide Web Publishing service.
    Next
End If
```

One thing to be careful of when using Count is that WMI does not keep a running tally of the number of items in a collection. If you request Count for a collection, WMI cannot instantly respond with a number; instead, it must literally count the items, enumerating the entire collection. For a collection that has relatively few items, such as services, this enumeration likely takes less than a second. Counting the number of events in an event log collection, however, can take considerably longer.

And then suppose you want to display the property values for every event in the collection. If so, WMI will have to enumerate the entire collection a second time.

Writing WMI Scripts

One point that has been reiterated throughout this chapter is that most WMI scripts follow a simple three-step pattern. In general, WMI scripts:

1. Connect to the WMI service.

2. Retrieve a WMI object or collection of objects.

3. Perform some sort of task on the object or objects. Until now, this task has largely been confined to reporting property values. However, you can also do such things as run methods, configure property values, and create or delete instances.

To become proficient in writing WMI scripts, you need to understand the nuances of these three steps. The preceding section of this chapter was a bit more theoretical in nature: It provided useful background information for understanding what WMI is and what it can do. This portion of the chapter takes a more practical approach; in particular, it provides a detailed look at the three steps used in most WMI scripts. This is done by:

- Explaining the use of the WMI moniker, a versatile method for connecting to the WMI service.

- Explaining the use of ExecQuery, an SWbemServices method that provides an alternative (and typically better and faster) way to retrieve WMI data.

- Providing a series of templates that can serve as the basis for scripts that carry out common tasks such as retrieving information, configuring property values, executing methods, and creating or deleting instances.

In addition to detailing the three steps in a typical WMI script, this section also looks at two other important elements in script writing: working with WMI dates and times, and monitoring events.

Connecting to WMI Using the WMI Moniker

The WMI scripting library provides two distinct mechanisms you can use to establish a connection to WMI on a local or remote computer: the SWbemLocator object (part of the WMI scripting library) and the WMI moniker, "winmgmts:". Other than general usage and syntax differences, the capability that separates the two connection mechanisms is that SWbemLocator lets you specify user and password credentials to be used to establish the connection, and the WMI moniker does not. SWbemLocator is discussed in more detail in the "WMI Scripting Library" section of this chapter.

The WMI moniker enables you use just one line of code to concisely describe a WMI object or collection of WMI objects to manage. However, with power comes the difficulty of constructing complex WMI moniker strings. The following sections of this chapter decipher the components you can use to construct WMI monikers and look at some best practices for writing WMI scripts that use WMI monikers.

The "WinMgmts:" Prefix

WMI monikers can consist of three parts: one mandatory component and two optional components. The mandatory component is the "winmgmts:" prefix. All WMI monikers must begin with `"winmgmts:"` as shown here:

```
Set objSWbemServices = GetObject("winmgmts:")
```

The moniker in this code is the string "winmgmts:", which is passed to the GetObject function. Although in this example the string is entered using all lowercase letters, you can use whatever case you like; that is, "WinMgmts:", "WINMGMTS:", and "winmgmts:" all produce the same result.

Specifying a moniker that consists only of the "winmgmts:" prefix is the most basic form of WMI moniker you can use. The result is always a reference to an SWbemServices object, which represents a connection to the Windows Management Instrumentation service on the local computer. Under the covers, the "winmgmts:" moniker:

1. Retrieves the WMI CLSID from the registry subkey HKCR\WINMGMTS\CLSID. The CLSID ({172BDDF8-CEEA-11D1-8B05-00600806D9B6}) is the identifier used by the operating system to map WMI to the appropriate COM object.

2. Retrieves the value from a second registry entry, HKCR\CLSID \{172BDDF8-CEEA-11D1-8B05-00600806D9B6}\InProcServer32. This value (typically C:\Windows\System32\wbem\wbemdisp.dll) indicates the path to the COM object that exposes the SWbemServices object.

3. Loads Wbemdisp.dll, the DLL containing the WMI scripting library that exposes SWbemServices.

After you have obtained a reference to SWbemServices, you can then invoke one of the object methods as shown here:

```
Set objSWbemServices = GetObject("winmgmts:")
Set colSWbemObjectSet = objSWbemServices.InstancesOf("Win32_LogicalDisk")
```

In this example, a reference variable named objSWbemServices is initialized using the "winmgmts:" moniker. This reference variable is subsequently used to invoke the InstancesOf method provided by the SWbemServices object.

Although the preceding example is perfectly acceptable, you do not have to use two lines of code to retrieve all Win32_LogicalDisk instances. This can also be done with the following single line of script:

```
Set colSWbemObjectSet = GetObject("winmgmts:").InstancesOf("Win32_LogicalDisk")
```

In this case, a user-defined variable (objSWbemServices in the example preceding this one) is not used to explicitly reference the SWbemServices object commonly returned by GetObject and the WMI moniker. Instead, the "winmgmts:" moniker creates an SWbemServices reference in memory and immediately uses the unnamed, memory based reference to call the SWbemServices InstancesOf method.

In the end, both examples produce identical results in the form of an SWbemObjectSet collection containing all instances of the Win32_LogicalDisk class on the local computer. You can also call the ExecQuery method or any other method provided by the SWbemServices object. In fact, if the objective of your script is to simply enumerate and echo all Win32_LogicalDisk instances, you can get by with as little as the following:

```
For Each objDisk In GetObject("winmgmts:").InstancesOf("Win32_LogicalDisk")
    Wscript.Echo objDisk.DeviceID
Next
```

In this case, user-defined variables are not used to reference SWbemServices or SWbemObjectSet. Both objects are still created, but only in memory and without an explicit object reference. By using the most basic WMI moniker, and by understanding the relationship of the moniker with the WMI scripting library, you can begin to construct concise yet powerful WMI statements.

WMI Security Settings

The second, and typically optional, part of WMI monikers is the security settings component. The security settings component has been a source of confusion for many system administrators. This is primarily because of the impersonationLevel setting, which behaves differently depending on the version of WMI installed on a target computer.

The optional security settings component lets you specify several different security settings that are used to connect to and communicate with WMI. The security settings you can control as part of the moniker string include:

- Impersonation level, expressed as "winmgmts:{impersonationLevel=Value}".

- Authentication level, expressed as "winmgmts:{authenticationLevel=Value}".

- Authenticating authority, expressed as "winmgmts:{authority=ntlmdomain:DomainName}" or "winmgmts:{authority=kerberos:DomainName\ServerName}".

- Privileges to grant or deny, expressed as "winmgmts:{(Security, !RemoteShutdown)}".

Impersonation Level

The first two settings, impersonationLevel and authenticationLevel, are not specific to WMI but rather are derived from DCOM, which WMI uses to access the WMI infrastructure on remote computers. In the context of WMI, impersonation governs the degree to which your script will allow a remote WMI service to carry out tasks on your behalf. DCOM supports four levels of impersonation: Anonymous, Identify, Impersonate, and Delegate. These levels are defined in Table 6.6.

Table 6.6   DCOM Impersonation Levels

Value	Description
Anonymous	Hides the credentials of the caller. WMI does not actually support this impersonation level; if a script specifies impersonationLevel=Anonymous, WMI will silently upgrade the impersonation level to Identify. This is in some ways a meaningless exercise, however, because scripts using the Identify level are likely to fail.
Identify	Enables objects to query the credentials of the caller. Scripts using this impersonation level are likely to fail; the Identify level typically lets you do no more than check access control lists. You will not be able to run scripts against remote computers using Identify.
Impersonate	Enables objects to use the credentials of the caller. It is recommended that you use this impersonation level with WMI scripts. When you do so, the WMI script will use your user credentials; as a result, it will be able to perform any tasks that you are able to perform.
Delegate	Enables objects to permit other objects to use the credentials of the caller. Delegation allows a script to use your credentials on a remote computer and then enables that remote computer to use your credentials on another remote computer. While you can use this impersonation level within WMI scripts, you should do so only if necessary because it might pose a security risk. You cannot use the Delegate impersonation level unless all the user accounts and computer accounts involved in the transaction have all been marked as **Trusted for delegation** in Active Directory. This helps minimize the security risks. Although a remote computer can use your credentials, it can do so only if both it and any other computers involved in the transaction are trusted for delegation.

As noted, Anonymous impersonation hides your credentials and Identify permits a remote object to query your credentials, but the remote object cannot impersonate your security context. (In other words, although the remote object knows who you are, it cannot "pretend" to be you.) WMI scripts accessing remote computers using one of these two settings will generally fail. In fact, most scripts run on the local computer using one of these two settings will also fail.

Impersonate permits the remote WMI service to use your security context to perform the requested operation. A remote WMI request that uses the Impersonate setting typically succeeds, provided your credentials have sufficient privileges to perform the intended operation. In other words, you cannot use WMI to perform an action (remotely or otherwise) that you do not have permission to perform outside WMI.

Setting impersonationLevel to Delegate permits the remote WMI service to pass your credentials on to other objects and is generally considered a security risk.

The confusion surrounding the impersonationLevel setting has to do with the default impersonation behavior, which differs based on the version of WMI installed on the target computer. WMI versions prior to version 1.5 use Identify as the default impersonationLevel setting. This forces WMI scripts that connect to remote computers to include impersonationLevel=Impersonate as part of any moniker string. With the release of WMI version 1.5 in Windows 2000, Microsoft changed the default impersonationLevel setting to Impersonate. This is a registry-based setting that can be managed by means of the following entry:

`HKEY_LOCAL_MACHINE\SOFTWARE\Microsoft\WBEM\Scripting\Default Impersonation Level`

If your WMI scripts connect only to computers with WMI version 1.5 or later, the change eliminates the need to explicitly set impersonationLevel. However, by omitting impersonationLevel=Impersonate, scripts accessing computers with an earlier release of WMI fail. For backward and — potentially — forward compatibility, you should always explicitly set impersonationLevel.

Authentication Level

The authenticationLevel setting enables you to request the level of DCOM authentication and privacy to be used throughout a connection. Settings range from no authentication to per-packet encrypted authentication. The seven permissible moniker settings include Default, None, Connect, Call, Pkt, PktIntegrity, and PktPrivacy, each described in Table 6.7. Specifying an authenticationLevel is more of a request than a command because there is no guarantee that the setting will be honored. For example, local connections always use authenticationLevel=PktPrivacy.

Table 6.7   DCOM Authentication Levels

Value	Description
None	Does not use any authentication. All security settings are ignored.
Default	Uses a standard security negotiation to select an authentication level. This is the recommended setting because the client involved in the transaction will be negotiated to the authentication level specified by the server. DCOM will not select the value None during a negotiation session.
Connect	Authenticates the credentials of the client only when the client tries to connect to the server. After a connection has been made, no additional authentication checks take place.

(continued)

Table 6.7 DCOM Authentication Levels *(continued)*

Value	Description
Call	Authenticates the credentials of the client only at the beginning of each call, when the server receives the request. The packet headers are signed, but the data packets exchanged between the client and the server are neither signed nor encrypted.
Pkt	Authenticates that all data packets are received from the expected client. Similar to Call; packet headers are signed but not encrypted. Packets themselves are neither signed nor encrypted.
PktIntegrity	Authenticates and verifies that none of the data packets transferred between the client and the server have been modified. Every data packet is signed, ensuring that the packets have not been modified during transit. None of the data packets are encrypted.
PktPrivacy	Authenticates all previous impersonation levels and signs and encrypts each data packet. This ensures that all communication between the client and the server is confidential.

Authority Setting

The authority setting allows you to specify the security package that is used to authenticate your WMI connection. You can specify standard NTLM or Kerberos authentication. To use NTLM, set the authority setting to "authority=ntlmdomain:DomainName" where DomainName identifies a valid NTLM domain name. To use Kerberos, specify "authority=kerberos:DomainName\ServerName". You cannot include the authority setting in WMI monikers that access the local computer.

Privileges

The final security setting is privilege overrides. This setting allows you to grant or revoke privileges as part of a WMI moniker string. For example, you might grant yourself the Security privilege to successfully query the Windows NT/2000 Security Log. Privileges you can grant or revoke are shown in Table 6.8.

Table 6.8 Privileges and Descriptions

Privilege	Description
CreateToken	Required to create a primary token.
AssignPrimaryToken	Required to assign the primary token of a process.
LockMemory	Required to lock physical pages in memory.
IncreaseQuota	Required to increase the quota assigned to a process.
MachineAccount	Required to create a computer account.
Tcb	Identifies its holder as part of the trusted computer base. Some trusted, protected subsystems are granted this privilege.

(continued)

Table 6.8 Privileges and Descriptions *(continued)*

Privilege	Description
Security	Required to perform a number of security-related functions, such as controlling and viewing audit messages. This privilege identifies its holder as a security operator.
TakeOwnership	Required to take ownership of an object without being granted discretionary access. This privilege allows the owner value to be set only to those values that the holder might legitimately assign as the owner of an object.
LoadDriver	Required to load or unload a device driver.
SystemProfile	Required to gather profiling information for the entire system.
SystemTime	Required to modify the system time.
ProfileSingleProcess	Required to gather profiling information for a single process.
IncreaseBasePriority	Required to increase the base priority of a process.
CreatePagefile	Required to create a paging file.
CreatePermanent	Required to create a permanent object.
Backup	Required to perform backup operations.
Restore	Required to perform restore operations. This privilege lets you set any valid user or group SID as the owner of an object.
Shutdown	Required to shut down a local computer.
Debug	Required to debug a process.
Audit	Required to generate audit-log entries.
SystemEnvironment	Required to modify the nonvolatile RAM of systems that use this type of memory to store configuration information.
ChangeNotify	Required to receive notifications of changes to files or directories. This privilege also causes the system to skip all traversal access checks. It is enabled by default for all users.
RemoteShutdown	Required to shut down a computer using a network request.
Undock	Required to remove a computer from its docking station.
SyncAgent	Required to synchronize directory service data.
EnableDelegation	Required to enable computer and user accounts to be trusted for delegation.

In addition to granting privileges, you can also disable privileges by prefacing the privilege name with an exclamation mark (!).

 Note

Disabling a privilege means that the script, or anything running in the script process, cannot carry out a particular action. For example, if you disable the Shutdown privilege, neither the script nor any anything running in the script process can shut down the computer. This provides an additional layer of security: It prevents the script from doing anything you do not want it to do.

The privileges to be enabled on a connection are specified by including the name of the privilege within parentheses. If the privilege is to be disabled, it is preceded by an exclamation mark. The following moniker string enables the LockMemory privilege and disables the IncreaseQuota privilege:

```
Set objSWbemServices = GetObject _
    ("winmgmts:{impersonationLevel=impersonate,(LockMemory, !IncreaseQuota)}")
```

Granting privileges within a script does not confer those privileges upon the user. For example, suppose you try to run a script that includes the Shutdown privilege. If you do not already have the Shutdown privilege, the script will fail; as is always the case with WMI, you are not allowed to use a script to carry out a task that you would otherwise not be able to perform. To carry out a task that requires a privilege such as Shutdown or Backup, two things must be true:

- The script must specify the privilege in the connection string.
- You must already possess the privilege.

Including Security Settings in Moniker Strings

The general format you use when including security settings in WMI monikers is as follows:

```
Set objSWbemServices = GetObject("winmgmts:"         & _
                    "{SecuritySetting1=Value,"       & _
                    "SecuritySetting2=Value,"        & _
                    "(Privilege1,!Privilege2)}")
```

Here you can see that the security settings component immediately follows the colon in the "winmgmts:" prefix and is enclosed inside braces. Multiple settings must be comma delimited, and override privileges are further separated inside parentheses and also comma delimited.

Using WMI Object Paths

The third component of WMI monikers is the WMI object path. Like the security settings component, the object path component is optional. However, the object path provides a great deal of flexibility, including the ability to identify remote computers. Because of this, chances are good you will use WMI object paths whether or not you realize it. You use the WMI object path to uniquely identify one or more of the following target resources:

- Remote computer. If the computer is not specified in the object path, the script will connect to the WMI service on the local computer. For example, this moniker does not include a computer name, so it runs on the local computer:

```
Set objSWbemServices = GetObject("winmgmts:")
```

This moniker connects to the WMI service on a remote computer named atl-dc-01:

```
Set objSWbemServices = GetObject("winmgmts:\\atl-dc-01")
```

Computer names are typically specified using the NetBIOS name of the computer. However, computer names can also be specified using a DNS name (for example, atl-dc-01.fabrikam.com) or an IP address (for example, 192.168.1.1).

- WMI namespace. If not specified, the default namespace is used. This moniker connects to the default namespace on a remote computer named atl-dc-01:

```
Set objSWbemServices = GetObject("winmgmts:\\atl-dc-01")
```

This moniker connects to the root\default namespace on atl-dc-01:

```
Set objSWbemServices = GetObject("winmgmts:\\atl-dc-01\root\default")
```

- WMI class within a namespace. If a class is specified within a moniker, it must be separated from the computer name and the namespace by a colon. For example, this moniker binds directly to the Win32_OperatingSystem class:

```
Set objSWbemObject = GetObject _
    ("winmgmts:\\atl-dc-01\root\cimv2:Win32_OperatingSystem")
```

- Specific instance or instances of a WMI class within a namespace. This moniker connects directly to the WMI instance representing drive C. To bind directly to an instance, you must include the key property (defined in the "Key properties" section of this chapter) in the object path:

```
Set objSWbemObject = GetObject _
    ("winmgmts:\\atl-dc-01\root\cimv2:Win32_LogicalDisk.DeviceID='C:'")
```

Formatting Object Paths

In an object path, the computer name and the WMI namespace are separated using either forward slashes or back slashes. Both of these are valid object paths:

```
\\WebServer\root\cimv2
```

```
//WebServer/root/cimv2
```

 Note

> In fact, you can even mix forward and back slashes within the same object path. This is not recommended because the code will likely confuse anyone reading or editing it. However, this is a valid object path:
> `\\Webserver/root/cimv2`.

If a WMI class is to be included in the object path, the class name must be separated from the namespace by a colon (:). For example, this object path connects to the Win32_Printer class:

```
\\WebServer\root\cimv2:Win32_Printer
```

 Note

> You will rarely use an object path like the preceding one within a system administration script. This is because the path binds you to the class itself and not instances of the class. In the preceding example, you cannot return information about any printers installed on the computer; you can only return information about the Win32_Printer class. However, this type of binding is occasionally used to create new objects — for example, to create a new shared folder, you connect directly to the Win32_Share class and then call the Create method.

To bind directly to an instance of a class (for example, to bind to a particular service), you must include the class name, a dot (.), the key property of the class, and the value of that property. This object path returns only one object, representing the Alerter service:

```
\\WebServer\root\cimv2:Win32_Service.Name='Alerter'
```

Key properties

A key property is a property that can be used to uniquely identify an instance. Name is a key property of Win32_Service because all services must have unique names. StartMode is not a unique property of a service because all services could, at least in theory, have the same start mode.

In other words, a connection string such as the following will fail because StartMode is not a key property of the Win32_Service class:

```
Set colServices = GetObject _
    ("winmgmts:\\.\root\cimv2\Win32_Service.StartMode='Auto'")
```

If you attempt to run the preceding script, you will receive an "Invalid syntax" error.

 Note

But what if you only need to return a list of services that have a StartMode of Auto? To do this, you can use the ExecQuery method, explained in the "Retrieving Managed Resources Using WMI Query Language" section of this chapter.

Classes typically have only one key property, although there are some exceptions. The Win32_NTLogEvent class has two key properties: Logfile and RecordNumber. This is because RecordNumber alone does not uniquely identify an event recorded in the event logs: Both the Application event log and the Security event log can have a record with a RecordNumber of 555. To uniquely identify an event log record, you need to specify both key properties in the object path:

```
\\WebServer\root\cimv2:Win32_NTLogEvent.Logfile='Application',RecordNumber=555
```

Retrieving Managed Resources Using WMI Query Language

Querying WMI is the process of issuing a request for data or events that match some predefined criteria. For example, a WMI data query can request all services with a StartMode of Auto that are in a Stopped state. A WMI event query can request to be notified when a running service stops or a stopped service starts. Because the WMI query processor is an integral part of the WMI service, system administrators can query WMI for any piece of data defined in the CIM.

WMI queries provide a more efficient mechanism for retrieving object instances and instance data than the InstancesOf method. WMI queries return only those instances and data that match the query, whereas InstancesOf always returns all object instances of a specified class. Also, queries are processed on the target computer identified in the object path rather than on the source computer running the WMI script. Therefore, WMI queries can significantly reduce the amount of network traffic that would otherwise be encountered by less efficient data retrieval mechanisms such as InstancesOf.

To query WMI, a system administrator constructs a query string using the WMI Query Language (WQL). The query string defines the criteria that must be satisfied to result in a successful match. After the query string is defined, the query is submitted to the WMI service using one of several methods provided by the SWbemServices object. Object instances that satisfy the query are returned to the script in the form of an SWbemObjectSet collection.

WQL is a subset of the ANSI Structured Query Language (SQL) commonly used in database applications. For the most part, WQL can be used only to retrieve information; WQL does not support such SQL functions as UPDATE and DELETE. In addition, WQL does not let you specify a sort order for the data that is returned; you are limited to the sort order imposed on the data by WMI. (However, there are workarounds for this limitation. For examples, see "Creating Enterprise Scripts" in this book.)

Using WQL (and the ExecQuery method) rather than InstancesOf provides you with the flexibility to create scripts that return only the items that are of interest to you. For example, you can use a basic WQL query to return all properties of all instances of a given class; this is the same information that is returned by the InstancesOf method. However, you can also create targeted queries using WQL, queries that do such things as:

- Return only selected properties of all the instances of a class.

- Return all the properties of selected instances of a class.

- Return selected properties of selected instances of a class.

Creating targeted queries will sometimes noticeably increase the speed with which data is returned. (It is obviously much faster to return only those events in the Application event log that have EventCode 0 than to return all the events in all the event logs.) Targeted queries also make it easier to work with the returned data. For example, suppose you want only events from the Application event log with EventCode 0. Using a targeted query will return *only* those items. By contrast, InstancesOf would return all the events, and you would have to individually examine each one and determine whether it 1) came from the Application event log and 2) has EventCode 0. Although this can be done, it is less efficient and requires additional coding on your part.

Targeted queries can also cut down on the amount of data that is returned, an important consideration for scripts that run over the network. Table 6.9 shows some relative figures for different query types. (These different types are explained in subsequent sections of this chapter.) As you can see, there can be a considerable difference in the amount of data returned by the various query types.

Table 6.9   Comparing WMI Data Queries

Query	Bytes Returned
objSWbemServices.InstancesOf("Win32_Service")	157,398
objSWbemServices.ExecQuery("SELECT * FROM Win32_Service")	156,222
objSWbemServices.ExecQuery("SELECT Name FROM Win32_Service")	86,294

(continued)

Table 6.9   Comparing WMI Data Queries (continued)

Query	Bytes Returned
objSWbemServices.ExecQuery("SELECT StartMode FROM Win32_Service")	88,116
objSWbemServices.ExecQuery _ ("SELECT StartMode FROM Win32_Service WHERE State='Running'")	52,546
objSWbemServices.ExecQuery _ ("SELECT StartMode, State FROM Win32_Service WHERE State='Running'")	56,314
objSWbemServices.ExecQuery _ ("SELECT * FROM Win32_Service WHERE Name='WinMgmt'")	27,852
objSWbemServices.Get("Win32_Service.Name='WinMgmt'")	14,860

 Note

This does not necessarily mean that the queries that return the least amount of data represent the best approach. These queries return smaller amounts of data because they either do not return all the properties of the services or they do not return the properties of all of the services (or both). If you need all of the properties of all of the services, most of these queries will not serve your needs. The point is that you can create faster and more efficient queries *if* you do not need all of the properties of all of the instances of a given class.

Returning All Properties of All Instances of a Class

The simplest WQL query is one that retrieves all properties of all instances of a class. This is done simply by:

1.   Using the asterisk (*) to indicate that all properties should be retrieved.

2.   Specifying the name of the class.

For example, this query returns all properties of all services installed on a computer:

```
"SELECT * FROM Win32_Service"
```

The advantage of using a SELECT * query is that it is quick and easy; the disadvantage is that it might return far more data than you need. In some cases, the difference might be negligible. For example, a query that returns all properties of all physical disk drives installed on a computer returned 808 bytes of data; a query that specified only the Name property returned 145 bytes of data. The SELECT * query completed in less than 2 seconds; the SELECT Name query completed in less than 1 second. In practical terms, there is no real difference between the scripts.

In other cases, however, the difference can be more dramatic. A script that returned all properties of all threads running on a computer required approximately 7 seconds to complete and returned 105 kilobytes (KB) of data. A script that returned only the thread handle required less than 1 second to complete and returned 6 KB of data. Although the time difference is not substantial, the difference in the amount of data might be important, particularly if you are running the script across the network.

The script in Listing 6.18 includes a standard WQL query that returns all properties of all services installed on a computer.

Listing 6.18   Returning All Properties of All Instances of a Class

```
1    strComputer = "."
2    Set objSWbemServices = _
3        GetObject("winmgmts:\\" & strComputer & "\root\cimv2")
4
5    Set colServices = _
6        objSWbemServices.ExecQuery("SELECT * FROM Win32_Service")
7
8    For Each objService In colServices
9        Wscript.Echo objService.Name
10   Next
```

Returning Selected Properties of All Instances of a Class

As noted in the preceding section, you can create a script that runs faster and returns less extraneous data (that is, data that is not needed by the script) by using a query that requests only specific properties from a class. To do this, you replace the asterisk in a standard WQL query with the names of the properties to be returned. For example, this query returns only the Name property for all the instances of the Win32_Service class:

```
"SELECT Name FROM Win32_Service"
```

If you want to return multiple properties, separate the property names with commas. This query returns the Name and State properties from Win32_Service:

```
"SELECT Name, State FROM Win32_Service"
```

What does it mean to return only selected properties? Consider this script, which requests only the Name property from Win32_Service but then attempts to echo the value of the State property as well:

```
strComputer = "."
Set objSWbemServices = GetObject("winmgmts:\\" & strComputer & "\root\cimv2")

Set colServices = objSWbemServices.ExecQuery("SELECT Name FROM Win32_Service")

For Each objService In colServices
    Wscript.Echo objService.Name, objService.State
Next
```

If you try to run this script under CScript, the following error message will appear in the command window:

```
Microsoft VBScript runtime error: Object doesn't support this property or method:
'objService.State'
```

Why? State is indeed a valid property of the Win32_Service class, but you did not ask for it. Therefore, State is not included within the collection of services and properties returned to you. The script acts against the returned collection, not against the Win32_Service class.

There is one exception to this: The key property for a class is always returned, even if it is not specified in the WQL query. For example, Name is the key property for the Win32_Service class. The following script retrieves only the State property from the Win32_Service class, but then attempts to display Name as well as State.

```
strComputer = "."
Set objSWbemServices = GetObject("winmgmts:\\" & strComputer & "\root\cimv2")

Set colServices = objSWbemServices.ExecQuery("SELECT State FROM Win32_Service")

For Each objService In colServices
    Wscript.Echo objService.Name, objService.State
Next
```

If you run this script under Cscript, it will not fail. Instead, output similar to the following appears in the command window:

```
Alerter Stopped
ALG Stopped
AppMgmt Stopped
Ati HotKey Poller Stopped
AudioSrv Running
BITS Running
```

Returning All Properties of Selected Instances of a Class

The two WQL query types demonstrated so far return information for each instance of the specified class. However, you will often want to work with only a subset of instances. For example, you might want information only about services that are stopped, or only about hard disks (and not floppy disk drives or CD-ROM drives). In a situation like this, it can be inconvenient to return all the instances of a class. If you returned a list of all the services, you would need to individually check each one to see whether it was stopped before you echoed information about the service. Although this kind of checking can be included within a script, you never want to write more code than absolutely required. More code means more chances for making a mistake.

At other times, returning all instances of a class rather than selected instances of a class can make a significant difference. For example, consider a Windows 2000–based test computer with approximately 48,000 events recorded in its three event logs (Application, System, and Security). A script designed to return only the 4,000 events recorded in the System event log completed its task in 18 seconds.

And how long did it take to return all the events from all the event logs? No one knows. After 14 minutes, and after returning 41,592 events, the script exhausted available memory and crashed.

 Note

It is bad enough that the script could not complete its task. Even worse, however, is the fact that, although the script stops, WMI continues running the query. In this case, that brought the entire system to a near-standstill. The only way to stop a "runaway" query such as this is to stop and then restart the WMI service.

In this case, returning only the events in the System event log made a dramatic difference. Likewise, a script that returned only those instances in the System event log that had EventCode 532 completed in just a few seconds.

To return a selected set of instances, you need to append a WHERE clause to the SELECT query. The generic representation of such a query looks like this:

```
"SELECT * FROM ClassName WHERE PropertyName = PropertyValue"
```

 Note

This generic representation is not entirely accurate. You are not restricted to using only the equals sign (=). You can also use other operators, such as less than (<), greater than (>), and not equal to (<>).

For example, this query returns only events recorded in the System event log:

```
"SELECT * FROM Win32_NTLogEvent WHERE Logfile = 'System'"
```

In the preceding query:

- **Win32_NTLogEvent** is the WMI class being queried.

- **Logfile** is the class property.

- **System** is the value of the Logfile property. Only events that have a Logfile property equal to System are returned by the query.

When writing queries that use WHERE clauses, you must correctly format the property value. The formatting you use will vary depending on whether the value is a string, a number, a Boolean value, or a variable.

Using Strings in WHERE Clauses

You might have noticed that, in the preceding query, the value (System) was enclosed within single quote marks. This is required anytime the value of the WHERE clause is a string. For example, the following script returns the names of all of the services on a computer that are stopped. In this query:

- **Win32_Service** is the WMI class being queried.

- **State** is the class property.

- **Stopped** is the value of the State property. Because Stopped is a string value, it is enclosed in single quote marks.

```
strComputer = "."
Set objSWbemServices = GetObject("winmgmts:\\" & strComputer & "\root\cimv2")

Set colServices = objSWbemServices.ExecQuery _
    ("SELECT * FROM Win32_Service WHERE State = 'Stopped'")

For Each objService In colServices
    Wscript.Echo objService.Name
Next
```

Using Numbers and Boolean Values in WHERE Clauses

When you use numbers or Boolean values (such as True or False) in a WHERE clause, these values should not be enclosed in single quote marks. For example, the following script returns the names of all of the services on a computer that are capable of being paused. In this query:

- **Win32_Service** is the WMI class being queried.

- **AcceptPause** is the class property.

- **True** is the value of the AcceptPause property. Because True is a Boolean value, it is not enclosed in quotation marks.

```
strComputer = "."
Set objSWbemServices = GetObject("winmgmts:\\" & strComputer & "\root\cimv2")

Set colServices = objSWbemServices.ExecQuery _
    ("SELECT * FROM Win32_Service WHERE AcceptPause = True")

For Each objService In colServices
    Wscript.Echo objService.Name
Next
```

Using Variables in WHERE Clauses

One approach to writing scripts is to hard-code values as needed. For example, if you want to return a list of all the services that are stopped, you can hard-code the query into the script:

```
Set colServices = objSWbemServices.ExecQuery _
    ("SELECT * FROM Win32_Service WHERE State = 'Stopped'")
```

But what if you there are times when want to see a list of all the services that are running *or* a list of all the services that are paused? One way to handle this problem is to create separate scripts to return each data set. If services can be running, stopped, paused, or resuming, you need four scripts, one for each state.

Alternatively, you can create a single script that returns information about services based on service state. When the user runs the script, he or she simply supplies the desired state, perhaps as a command-line argument, and the script does the rest.

The most efficient way to do this is to store the supplied value in a variable and then reference the variable within the WQL query. Essentially, you need the query to do this:

```
Select all the properties from the Win32_Service class where the State is equal
to the value stored in this variable.
```

This is easy enough to write in pseudo code. But how do you translate the pseudo code into an actual WQL query?

Here is how:

1. Write the query in the usual fashion, stopping where the variable must be inserted. For example, suppose you are modifying the following query:

    ```
    "SELECT * FROM Win32_Service WHERE State = 'Stopped'".
    ```

    You write the first part of the query up to the word *Stopped*, including the single quotation mark. (Why write the query up to the word *Stopped*? Because, in this example, you want to replace the hard-coded value with the variable name.) Your query will look like this:

    ```
    "SELECT * FROM Win32_Service WHERE State = '
    ```

2. Insert a set of quotation marks to indicate that the string is being cut off at this point, and then insert a space and an ampersand (&). The ampersand indicates that you are appending something to the string. Your query will now look like this:

    ```
    "SELECT * FROM Win32_Service WHERE State ='" &
    ```

3. Insert the name of the variable (in this example, strState), and then add an ampersand, a space, and a second set of quotation marks. This indicates that there is additional text to be appended after the variable name. Your query should look like this:

```
"SELECT * FROM Win32_Service WHERE State = '" & strState & "
```

4. Add the rest of the query string. If you recall, the original query string was:

```
"SELECT * FROM Win32_Service WHERE State = 'Stopped'"
```

You have now replaced the word *Stopped* with the variable name and have only the last single quotation mark and the last quotation mark remaining. Add these to the end of the string, making the final query look like this:

```
"SELECT * FROM Win32_Service WHERE State ='" & strState & "'"
```

This is what the query looks like within a script that lets you specify a service state as a command-line argument. Assuming that you named the script ServiceState.vbs and you wanted a list of running services, you start the script using this command:

cscript servicestate.vbs running

```
strState = Wscript.Arguments.Item(0)

strComputer = "."
Set objSWbemServices = GetObject("winmgmts:\\" & strComputer & "\root\cimv2")

Set colServices = objSWbemServices.ExecQuery _
    ("SELECT * FROM Win32_Service WHERE State = '" & strState & "'")

For Each objService In colServices
    Wscript.Echo objService.Name
Next
```

Admittedly, this can be a little confusing. You will likely find it easier if you follow the same approach each time: Start by creating a query with a hard-coded value, and then replace the hard-coded value with the variable name and the appropriate quotation marks and ampersands.

You can use the following pattern (with a space following each element):

Quotation marks — Ampersand — Variable name — Ampersand — Quotation marks

Or:

```
" & strVariableName & "
```

Creating Targeted Queries Using AND or OR

By using the AND and OR keywords, you can create more complex queries, queries that either narrow or expand the range of a query that uses a WHERE clause.

The AND keyword lets you limit the scope of a query. For example, suppose you want a list of autostart services that are stopped. This query requires two parameters in the WHERE clause: the State property, which must be equal to Stopped, and the StartMode, which must be equal to Auto. To create a query such as this, include both parameters, separating them with the AND keyword. In this query, an instance will be returned only if it meets both criteria.

```
strComputer = "."
Set objSWbemServices = GetObject("winmgmts:\\" & strComputer & "\root\cimv2")

Set colServices = objSWbemServices.ExecQuery _
   ("SELECT * FROM Win32_Service WHERE State = 'Stopped' AND StartMode = 'Auto'")

For Each objService In colServices
    Wscript.Echo objService.Name
Next
```

The OR keyword, by contrast, allows you to expand the scope of a query. For example, suppose you need a list of services that are either stopped *or* paused. In this case there are two criteria, but a service needs to meet only one of these to qualify: Either it needs to be stopped or it needs to be paused.

To create a query such as this, separate the two parameters with the OR keyword. In this query, an instance will be returned as long as it is either stopped or paused.

```
strComputer = "."
Set objSWbemServices = GetObject("winmgmts:\\" & strComputer & "\root\cimv2")

Set colServices = objSWbemServices.ExecQuery _
    ("SELECT * FROM Win32_Service WHERE State = 'Stopped' OR State = 'Paused'")

For Each objService In colServices
    Wscript.Echo objService.Name
Next
```

Returning Selected Properties of Selected Instances of a Class

You also have the option of returning only selected properties of selected classes. To do this, you must:

- Specify the properties to be returned.
- Include a WHERE clause to limit the instances returned.

In other words, this type of query combines two query types — returning selected properties and returning selected instances — explored earlier in this chapter.

For example, this script returns only the name and the state of services that can be paused:

```
strComputer = "."
Set objSWbemServices = GetObject("winmgmts:\\" & strComputer & "\root\cimv2")

Set colServices = objSWbemServices.ExecQuery _
    ("SELECT Name, State FROM Win32_Service WHERE AcceptPause = True")

For Each objService In colServices
    Wscript.Echo objService.Name, objService.State
Next
```

Creating Faster Queries by Using a Forward-only Enumerator

In some cases, you can speed up a query by using a *forward-only enumerator*. For example, on a Windows 2000–based test computer, a script that returned 10,000 events from the event logs required 47 seconds to complete. A script using a forward-only enumerator required just 28 seconds to complete. Admittedly, the time differential (19 seconds) might not appear that large. However, suppose the script had to perform the same task on all 50 of your domain controllers. In a situation like that, 19 seconds times 50 domain controllers results in a large difference between the two scripts.

A forward-only enumerator requires you to provide three parameters to ExecQuery. The first parameter is the WQL query. The second parameter represents the query language; this should either be left blank or set to "WQL". (At this point in time, WQL is the only query language that can be used with WMI.) The third parameter is the value 48. This value represents the combination of two "flags," numbers that can be combined to act as a single parameter to a method. These flags are:

- **wbemFlagReturnImmediately (decimal value 16).** This is the default setting that causes ExecQuery to run semisynchronously. As explained earlier in this chapter, in semisynchronous mode, the script starts the query and can immediately begin working with the SWbemObjectSet that is returned while instances are still being retrieved. This is the default behavior for most WMI queries (in other words, although you do not have to specify it in the script, wbemFlagReturnImmediately is enabled on most queries).

- **wbemFlagForwardOnly (decimal value 32).** This flag causes the script to use a forward-only enumerator.

Forward-only enumerators typically run faster than other queries and use less memory. However, with a forward-only enumerator, as soon as an object is enumerated it is released from memory. This frees memory and enables the query to run faster, but the objects can be enumerated only once; after that, they are no longer available. This means that you can use a forward-only enumerator to return instances and echo their values to the screen only once. As soon as the enumeration is finished (that is, as soon as the For Each loop completes), no instances remain in memory. As a result, an error occurs if you try to enumerate the instances a second time.

The following script uses a forward-only enumerator to return events from the event logs. Notice that the parameter following the SELECT query is left blank.

```
Const wbemFlagReturnImmediately = 16
Const wbemFlagForwardOnly = 32

strComputer = "."
Set objSWbemServices = _
    GetObject("winmgmts:{(Security)}\\" & strComputer & "\root\cimv2")

Set colNTLogEvents = objSWbemServices.ExecQuery _
    ("SELECT * FROM Win32_NTLogEvent", , _
    wbemFlagReturnImmediately + wbemFlagForwardOnly)

For Each objNTLogEvent In colNTLogEvents
    Wscript.Echo "Log File:         " & objNTLogEvent.LogFile         & vbCrLf & _
                 "Record Number:    " & objNTLogEvent.RecordNumber    & vbCrLf & _
                 "Type:             " & objNTLogEvent.Type            & vbCrLf & _
                 "Time Generated:   " & objNTLogEvent.TimeGenerated   & vbCrLf & _
                 "Source:           " & objNTLogEvent.SourceName      & vbCrLf & _
                 "Category:         " & objNTLogEvent.Category        & vbCrLf & _
                 "Category String:  " & objNTLogEvent.CategoryString  & vbCrLf & _
                 "Event:            " & objNTLogEvent.EventCode       & vbCrLf & _
                 "User:             " & objNTLogEvent.User            & vbCrLf & _
                 "Computer:         " & objNTLogEvent.ComputerName    & vbCrLf & _
                 "Message:          " & objNTLogEvent.Message         & vbCrLf
Next
```

You cannot use the SWbemObjectSet Count property when using a forward-only enumerator. For example, suppose you inserted the following statement after the ExecQuery call in the previous script.

```
Wscript.Echo colNTLogEvents.Count
```

If you try to run the revised script, the following error message will appear in the command window:

```
SWbemObjectSet: Unspecified error
```

Why? The answer lies in the way Count works. Because Count performs an enumeration to determine the number of items in the collection, reading the Count property would exhaust your one-time enumeration of the forward-only enumerator. As such, Count is not a supported property for any SWbemObjectSet that is returned using the forward only flag.

Working with Dates and Times

One of the more confusing aspects of WMI is the way WMI handles dates and times. For example, consider this simple script, which returns the date that the operating system was installed on a computer:

```
strComputer = "."
Set objSWbemServices = GetObject("winmgmts:\\" & strComputer & "\root\cimv2")
Set colOS = objSWbemServices.ExecQuery("SELECT * FROM Win32_OperatingSystem")
For Each objOS in colOS
    Wscript.Echo objOS.InstallDate
Next
```

When this script is run under CScript, output similar to the following appears in the command window:

```
20011224113047.000000-480
```

This is not a misprint; 20011224113047.000000–480 really *is* the date that the operating system was installed on the computer. In fact, this value indicates that the operating system was installed on December 24, 2001. The date is correct; the problem lies not with the date but with the fact that the date is displayed in the Universal Time Coordinate (UTC) format.

In the UTC format, dates are displayed as yyyymmddHHMMSS.xxxxxx±UUU, where:

- **yyyy** represents the year.

- **mm** represents the month.

- **dd** represents the day.

- **HH** represents the hour (in 24-hour format).

- **MM** represents the minutes.

- **SS** represents the seconds.

- **xxxxxx** represents the milliseconds.

- **±UUU** represents the difference, in minutes, between the local time zone and Greenwich Mean Time (GMT).

Consequently, the value 20011224113047.000000–480 is translated like this:

- **2001** is the year.

- **12** is the month (December).

- **24** is the day.

- **11** is the hour of the day (in 24-hour format).

- **30** is the minutes.

- **47** is the seconds.

- **000000** is the milliseconds.

- **–480** is the number of minutes different from Greenwich Mean Time.

Needless to say, the UTC format creates a number of problems for both script writers and script users. For one thing, it is difficult to determine dates and times at a glance. For another, it is not exactly a straightforward process to query for items based on date-time values. Suppose you want to retrieve a list of all the folders on a computer that were created after September 3, 2002. This seems like a simple enough task; after all, the Win32_Directory class includes a CreationDate property that specifies the date the folder was created.

Unfortunately, you cannot simply ask WMI to return a list of folders created after 9/3/2002. This script, which attempts to do just that, will run, but will not return any data.

```
dtmTargetDate = #9/3/2002#

strComputer = "."
Set objSWbemServices = GetObject("winmgmts:\\" & strComputer & "\root\cimv2")

Set colDirectories = objSWbemServices.ExecQuery _
  ("SELECT * FROM Win32_Directory WHERE CreationDate > '" & dtmTargetDate & "'")

For Each objDirectory In colDirectories
    Wscript.Echo objDirectory.Name
Next
```

Instead, you have to pass WMI the date using UTC format:

```
dtmTargetDate = "20020903000000.000000-480"

strComputer = "."
Set objSWbemServices = GetObject("winmgmts:\\" & strComputer & "\root\cimv2")

Set colDirectories = objSWBemServices.ExecQuery _
  ("SELECT * FROM Win32_Directory WHERE CreationDate > '" & dtmTargetDate & "'")

For Each objDirectory In colDirectories
    Wscript.Echo objDirectory.Name
Next
```

Because dates are very important in system administration, and because WMI is the technology of choice for most system administration tasks, it is important for script writers to be able to carry out two tasks:

- Convert WMI dates to a standard date-time format.

- Convert a standard date to a WMI date-time format.

Converting WMI Dates to a Standard Date-Time Format

Although UTC dates are intimidating at first glance, they are relatively easy to convert to a standard date-time format. This is because 1) VBScript treats UTC dates as strings, meaning that they can be manipulated using VBScript string functions and 2) UTC dates use a standard fixed-width format. The year will always take up the first four character positions in a UTC string, the month will always take up the next two character positions, and so forth. These character positions are described in Table 6.10.

Table 6.10 Character Positions of a UTC Date-Time Value

Character Positions	Description	Sample Value
1–4	Four digits representing the year (such as 2001 or 2002).	2002
5–6	Two digits representing the month. For example, January is represented by the digits 01; November, by the digits 11.	10
7–8	Two digits representing the day of the month. For example, the 5th day is represented by the digits 05; the 23rd day by the digits 23.	18
9–14	Six zeros representing the hours, minutes, and seconds of the day (in 24-hour format). If you prefer, you can specify values other than 0 to create more finely targeted searches. For example, to search for folders created after 1:47 P.M. on a given day, set these characters to 134700, where 13 represents the hours (1:00 P.M. in 24-hour format), 47 represents the minutes, and 00 represents the seconds.	000000
15	A period (.).	.
16–21	Six zeros representing the milliseconds.	000000
22–25	The number of minutes difference between your local time and Greenwich mean time.	–480

To convert a UTC date to a standard date-time format, you simply select the desired date-time components (such a month, day, and year) and construct a date-time string of your own. For example, with the UTC value 20020710113047.000000–420, you need to:

1. Extract the month (07).

2. Extract the day (10).

3. Extract the year (2002).

4. Combine them into a standard date format: 07/10/2002.

You can extract the individual date components using VBScript functions such as Left and Mid. (These functions are explained in more detail in "VBScript Primer" in this book.) For example, to extract the day (character positions 7 and 8), you use code similar to this, in which dtmInstallDate is a variable used to represent the date being converted:

```
Mid(dtmInstallDate, 7 ,2)
```

VBScript interprets this line of code as follows: Take the string dtmInstallDate, start in the seventh character position, and return two values (characters 7 and 8). In the date 20020710113047.000000–420, characters 7 and 8 are 10, the tenth day of the month.

The following function converts a UTC date to a standard date by:

1. Extracting the month.

2. Appending a backslash (/).

3. Extracting the day.

4. Appending a backslash.

5. Extracting the year.

6. Adding a space.

7. Extracting the hour.

8. Appending a colon (:).

9. Extracting the minutes.

10. Appending a colon.

11. Extracting the seconds.

12. Converting the resultant string to a date using the CDate function.

```
WMIDateStringToDate = CDate(Mid(dtmInstallDate, 5, 2) & "/" & _
    Mid(dtmInstallDate, 7, 2) & "/" & Left(dtmInstallDate, 4) _
        & " " & Mid (dtmInstallDate, 9, 2) & ":" & _
            Mid(dtmInstallDate, 11, 2) & ":" & Mid(dtmInstallDate, _
                13, 2))
```

If passed the UTC value 20020219145216.000000–480, the function returns this date:

2/19/02 2:52:16 PM

The script shown in Listing 6.19 retrieves the date that the operating system was installed on a computer. This value is not echoed in UTC format; instead, it is passed to a function named WMIDateStringToDate. This function converts the UTC value to a standard date-time format. This standard date is then echoed to the screen.

Listing 6.19   Converting a UTC Value to a Standard Date-Time Value

```
1   strComputer = "."
2   Set objSWbemServices = GetObject("winmgmts:\\" & strComputer & "\root\cimv2")
3   Set objOS = objSWbemServices.ExecQuery("SELECT * FROM Win32_OperatingSystem")
4   For Each strOS in objOS
5       dtmInstallDate = strOS.InstallDate
6       strReturn = WMIDateStringToDate(dtmInstallDate)
7       Wscript.Echo strReturn
8   Next
9   Function WMIDateStringToDate(dtmInstallDate)
10      WMIDateStringToDate = CDate(Mid(dtmInstallDate, 5, 2) & "/" & _
11          Mid(dtmInstallDate, 7, 2) & "/" & Left(dtmInstallDate, 4) _
12          & " " & Mid (dtmInstallDate, 9, 2) & ":" & _
13              Mid(dtmInstallDate, 11, 2) & ":" & Mid(dtmInstallDate, _
14                  13, 2))
15  End Function
```

Converting a Standard Date to a WMI Date-Time Format

As noted previously, you cannot use standard date-time formats — such as 10/18/2002 — when writing WMI queries. Instead, you need to convert any dates used in your queries to UTC format. This requires two steps: 1) You must determine the offset (difference in minutes) between your time zone and Greenwich Mean Time, and 2) you must convert 10/18/2002 to a UTC value.

Determining the Offset from Greenwich Mean Time

Admittedly, WMI makes it difficult to work with dates and times; fortunately, WMI at least makes it easy to determine the offset between your time zone and Greenwich Mean Time. The WMI class Win32_TimeZone includes a property — Bias — that returns the GMT offset. The script in Listing 6.20 shows how this property is retrieved.

Listing 6.20   Determining the Offset from Greenwich Mean Time

```
1   strComputer = "."
2   Set objSWbemServices = GetObject("winmgmts:" _
3       & "{impersonationLevel=impersonate}!\\" & strComputer & "\root\cimv2")
4   Set colTimeZone = objSWbemServices.ExecQuery _
5       ("SELECT * FROM Win32_TimeZone")
6   For Each objTimeZone in colTimeZone
7       Wscript.Echo "Offset: "& objTimeZone.Bias
8   Next
```

When the preceding script runs under CScript on a computer operating on Pacific daylight time, the following value is echoed to the command window:

```
Offset: -480
```

Converting a Date to a UTC Value

After you determine the GMT offset, you must then convert a standard date such as 10/18/2002 to a UTC date. To convert a standard date to a UTC date, you can use VBScript date functions such as Year, Month, and Day to isolate the individual components that make up a UTC date. (See Table 6.10 for details.) After you have individual values for these components, you can concatenate them in the same manner as you would any other string value.

UTC dates are treated as strings because the GMT offset must be appended to the end. If the date were seen as a number, this value:

```
20011018113047.000000-480
```

Would be erroneously treated as a mathematical equation (parentheses added for clarity):

```
(20011018113047.000000) - (480)
```

For example, in the date 10/18/2002, the individual components are:

- **Year**: 2002
- **Month**: 10
- **Day**: 18

The script would need to combine these three values, the string "113047.000000" (representing the time, including milliseconds), and the GMT offset to derive a UTC date. For example, (parentheses again added for clarity):

```
(2002) & (10) & (18) & (113047.000000) & (-480)
```

 Note

You can use the VBScript functions Hour, Minute, and Second to convert the time portion of a UTC date. Thus, a time such as 11:30:47 A.M. would be converted to 113047.

There is one complicating factor. The month *must* take up positions 5 and 6 in the string; the day must take up positions 7 and 8. This is no problem with month 10 and day 18. But how do you get July 5 (month 7, day 5) to fill up the requisite positions?

The answer is to add a leading zero to each value, thus changing the 7 to 07 and the 5 to 05. To do this, use the VBScript Len function to check the length (number of characters) in the month and the day. If the length is 1 (meaning that there is just one character), add a leading zero. Thus:

```
If Len(dtmMonth) = 1 Then
    dtmMonth = "0" & dtmMonth
End If
```

The script shown in Listing 6.21 converts the current date to a UTC date. The script first determines the GMT offset and then converts the date to UTC format. When appending the time value (000000.000000), the script uses the function CStr; this ensures that the value is appended as a string and not as a number.

Listing 6.21 Converting the Current Date to a UTC Date

```
1   strComputer = "."
2   Set objSWbemServices = GetObject("winmgmts:" _
3       & "{impersonationLevel=impersonate}!\\" & strComputer & "\root\cimv2")
4   Set colTimeZone = objSWbemServices.ExecQuery _
5       ("SELECT * FROM Win32_TimeZone")
6   For Each objTimeZone in colTimeZone
7       strBias = objTimeZone.Bias
8   Next
9
10  dtmCurrentDate = Date
11  dtmTargetDate = Year(dtmCurrentDate)
12
13  dtmMonth = Month(dtmCurrentDate)
14  If Len(dtmMonth) = 1 Then
15      dtmMonth = "0" & dtmMonth
16  End If
17
18  dtmTargetDate = dtmTargetDate & dtmMonth
19
20  dtmDay = Day(dtmCurrentDate)
21  If Len(dtmDay) = 1 Then
22      dtmDay = "0" & dtmDay
23  End If
24
25  dtmTargetDate = dtmTargetDate & dtmDay & "000000.000000"
26  dtmTargetDate = dtmTargetDate & Cstr(strBias)
```

The script in Listing 6.22 demonstrates a more practical use of these conversions. The script determines the GMT offset, and then converts a specified current date (in this case, 10/18/2002) to UTC date-time format. After the date has been converted, that value is used to search a computer and returns a list of all the folders that were created after 10/18/2002.

Listing 6.22 Retrieving Folders Based on Creation Date

```
1   strComputer = "."
2   Set objSWbemServices = GetObject("winmgmts:" _
3       & "{impersonationLevel=impersonate}!\\" & strComputer & "\root\cimv2")
4   Set colTimeZone = objSWbemServices.ExecQuery _
5       ("SELECT * FROM Win32_TimeZone")
6   For Each objTimeZone in colTimeZone
7       strBias = objTimeZone.Bias
8   Next
9
10  dtmCurrentDate = "10/18/2002"
11  dtmTargetDate = Year(dtmCurrentDate)
12
13  dtmMonth = Month(dtmCurrentDate)
14  If Len(dtmMonth) = 1 Then
15      dtmMonth = "0" & dtmMonth
16  End If
17
18  dtmTargetDate = dtmTargetDate & dtmMonth
19
20  dtmDay = Day(dtmCurrentDate)
21  If Len(dtmDay) = 1 Then
22      dtmDay = "0" & dtmDay
23  End If
24
25  dtmTargetDate = dtmTargetDate & dtmDay & "000000.000000"
26  dtmTargetDate = dtmTargetDate & Cstr(strBias)
27
28  Set colFolders = objSWbemServices.ExecQuery _
29      ("SELECT * FROM Win32_Directory WHERE CreationDate < '" & _
30          dtmtargetDate & "'")
31  For Each objFolder in colFolders
32      Wscript.Echo objFolder.Name
33  Next
```

Creating Scripts Based on WMI Templates

WMI has a reputation for being very difficult to learn and even more difficult to use. In many respects, this reputation has been acquired not so much because WMI really *is* difficult but simply because it is so big. WMI can be used to manage computer hardware, computer software, and nearly everything in between; the assumption is that any technology that encompasses so many different elements *must* be difficult.

In reality, though, many of the system administration tasks that can be performed by using WMI follow one of a handful of standard approaches. For example, you have already seen how a template can serve as the basis for scripts that return information about almost any managed resource. In the opening pages of this chapter, the same basic script — with one or two minor modifications — was used to return information about items as disparate as installed memory, services, and events recorded in the event logs.

The following sections of this chapter present basic script templates that can be used to:

- Retrieve and display the properties of a managed resource.

- Configure the property values of a managed resource.

- Call the methods of a WMI class.

- Create new instances of managed resources.

- Delete existing instances of managed resources.

 Note

All of the script templates are designed to work on the local computer; this is done by setting the value of the variable strComputer to a dot ("."). To run a script against a remote computer, simply set the value of strComputer to the name of the remote computer. For example, this line of code causes a script to run against a computer named atl-dc-01:

```
strComputer = "atl-dc-01"
```

Retrieving and Displaying Properties of a Managed Resource

WMI is perhaps best suited for returning information about a computer; there are literally hundreds of WMI classes that provide information on everything from the services installed on a computer to the events recorded in the event logs to attached peripherals such as printers, monitors, and disk drives.

The amount — and variety — of information that can be returned by using WMI is, in itself, enough to make scripting an important tool for system administration. What makes the technology even more valuable, however, is the fact that the same basic approach can be used to return information regardless of the source. For example, the script template shown in Listing 6.23 returns information about the services installed on a computer. However, this template can easily be adapted to return information about any other managed resource on the computer.

Listing 6.23   Template for Retrieving and Displaying Resource Properties

```
1   strComputer = "."
2   strNamespace = "\root\cimv2"
3   strClassName = "Win32_Service"
4
5   Set objSWbemServices = GetObject("winmgmts:" _
6       & "{impersonationLevel=impersonate}!\\" & strComputer & strNamespace)
7
8   Set colInstances = objSWbemServices.ExecQuery _
9       ("SELECT * FROM" & strClassName)
10  For Each objInstance in colInstances
11      Wscript.Echo "Caption "       & objInstance.Caption
12      Wscript.Echo "Description " & objInstance.Description
13  Next
```

To use this template with other WMI classes:

1. Set the value of strClassName to the appropriate WMI class.

2. If necessary, set the value of strNamespace to the appropriate WMI namespace.

3. Replace the statements within the For Each loop that echo the properties and their values. Remove the following lines and replace them with the appropriate lines of code for the property values being displayed.

```
Wscript.Echo "Caption "       & objInstance.Caption
Wscript.Echo "Description " & objInstance.Description
```

Retrieving and Displaying All Properties of a Managed Resource

One limitation of the script shown in Listing 6.23 is that it requires you to know, in advance, the names of all of the properties that you want to retrieve and display. However, what if you want to display values for all the properties of a class but you either do not know the property names or do not want to type the 40 or 50 lines of code required to display each property value? In that case, you can use the script in Listing 6.24, which automatically retrieves and displays the values of each property found in a class.

Listing 6.24 Template for Retrieving and Displaying All Properties of a Resource

```
1    strComputer = "."
2    strNamespace = "\root\cimv2"
3    strClassName = "Win32_Process"
4
5
6    Set objSWbemServices = _
7        GetObject("winmgmts:{impersonationLevel=impersonate}!\\" &_
8            strComputer & strNamespace)
9
10   Set colInstances = objSWbemServices.ExecQuery("SELECT * FROM " &_
11       strClassName)
12
13   Wscript.Echo "Properties of Instances of Class " & strClassName
14   Wscript.Echo "===================================================="
15
16   iCount = 0
17   For Each objInstance in colInstances
18       iCount = iCount + 1
19       Set colProperties = objInstance.Properties_
20
21       Wscript.Echo vbCrLf
22       Wscript.Echo "*******************"
23       Wscript.Echo "INSTANCE NUMBER: " & iCount
24       Wscript.Echo "*******************"
25       Wscript.Echo vbCrLf
26
27       For Each objProperty in colProperties
28           Wscript.Echo objProperty.Name & " : " & objProperty.Value
29       Next
30       Wscript.Sleep(2000)
31   Next
```

To use this template with other WMI classes:

1. Set the value of strClassName to the appropriate WMI class.

2. If necessary, set the value of strNamespace to the appropriate WMI namespace.

Writing Resource Properties

In Windows 2000, WMI is primarily a read-only technology; you use it mainly to retrieve information about managed resources. However, some WMI properties are read/write. This means you can use a script not only to retrieve the values of these properties but also to configure those values.

For example, the script in Listing 6.25 retrieves all instances of the Win32_OSRecoveryConfiguration class. (In this case, the class contains only a single instance.) The script provides new values for properties such as DebugInfoType and DebugFilePath and then applies the changes (and thus configures operating system recovery options) by using the Put_ method. If you do not call the Put_ method, the changes will not be applied.

 Note

This template works only for properties that are writable. Attempting to change a read-only property will result in an error.

Listing 6.25   Template for Writing Resource Properties

```
1   strComputer = "."
2   strClassName = "Win32_OSRecoveryConfiguration"
3   strNamespace = "\root\cimv2"
4
5   Set objSWbemServices = GetObject("winmgmts:" _
6       & "{impersonationLevel=impersonate}!\\" & strComputer & strNamespace)
7   Set colInstances = objSWbemServices.ExecQuery _
8       ("SELECT * FROM " & strClassName)
9   For Each objInstance in colInstances
10      objInstance.DebugInfoType = 1
11      objInstance.DebugFilePath = "c:\scripts\memory.dmp"
12      objInstance.OverWriteExistingDebugFile = False
13      objInstance.Put_
14  Next
```

To use this template with other WMI classes and to configure other WMI properties:

1. Set the value of strClassName to the name of the WMI class.

2. If necessary, set the value of strNamespace to the appropriate WMI namespace.

3. Replace the statements within the For Each loop that configure new property values. Remove the following lines, and replace them with the appropriate lines of code for the properties being modified:

```
objInstance.DebugInfoType = 1
objInstance.DebugFilePath = "c:\scripts\memory.dmp"
objInstance.OverWriteExistingDebugFile = False
```

Calling Methods

Methods enable a script to carry out actions. For example, the Win32_Service class includes methods that let you perform such tasks as starting and stopping services; the Win32_NTEventLogfile class includes methods for backing up and clearing event logs; the Win32_OperatingSystem class includes methods for shutting down or rebooting a computer.

Listing 6.26 provides a template that can be used to write scripts that call WMI methods. This particular script uses the StopService method of the Win32_Service class to stop the Alerter service on the local computer.

Listing 6.26   Template for Calling Methods

```
1   strComputer = "."
2   strNamespace = "\root\cimv2"
3   strClassName = "Win32_Service"
4   strKeyName = "Name"
5   strKeyValue = "Alerter"
6
7   Set objSWbemServices = GetObject("winmgmts:" &_
8       "{impersonationLevel=impersonate}!\\" & strComputer & strNamespace)
9   Set colInstances = objSWbemServices.ExecQuery _
10      ("SELECT * FROM " & strClassName & " WHERE " & strKeyName & " = '" &_
11       strKeyValue & "'")
12  For Each objInstance in colInstances
13       objInstance.StopService()
14  Next
```

To use this template with other WMI classes:

1. Set the value of strClassName to the appropriate WMI class.

2. If necessary, set the value of strNamespace to the appropriate WMI namespace.

3. Set the value of strKeyName to the name of the property that forms the basis of the WHERE clause.

4. Set the value of strKeyValue to the appropriate value for this property.

5. Replace the statement within the For Each loop that calls the method. Remove the following line, and replace it with the appropriate line of code for the method being called. If necessary, you must also include the appropriate method parameters.

```
objInstance.StopService()
```

Creating Resources

Some WMI classes (including Win32_Share and Win32_Process) include a Create method. If a class includes the Create method, that method can be used to create such things as a new shared folder or a new process.

Creating a new resource requires you to use the Get method to bind to the actual WMI class (rather than retrieve instances of the class). After you have an object representing the class, use the SpawnInstance_ method to create a new, "blank," instance of the class. Configure properties for the instance, and then call the Create method.

The script template in Listing 6.27 uses the Create method to create a new shared folder.

Listing 6.27   Template for Creating Resources

```
1   strComputer = "."
2   strNamespace = "\root\cimv2"
3   strClassName = "Win32_Share"
4
5   Set objSWbemServices = GetObject("winmgmts:" _
6       & "{impersonationLevel=impersonate}!\\" & strComputer & strNamespace)
7
8   Set objNewShare = objSWbemServices.Get(strClassName)
9   Set objInParams = _ objNewShare.Methods_("Create").InParameters.SpawnInstance_()
10
11  objInParams.Properties_.Item("Description") = "New Share Description"
12  objInParams.Properties_.Item("Name") = "New Share Name"
13  objInParams.Properties_.Item("Path") = "C:\scripts\shared"
14  objInParams.Properties_.Item("Type") = 0
15
16  objNewShare.ExecMethod_ "Create", objInParams
```

To use this template with other WMI classes:

1. Set the value of strClassName to the appropriate WMI class.

2. If necessary, set the value of strNamespace to the appropriate WMI namespace.

3. Replace the statements within the For Each loop that configure the values for the new share. Remove the following lines, and replace them with the appropriate lines of code for the object being created:

```
objInParams.Properties_.Item("Description") = "New Share Description"
objInParams.Properties_.Item("Name") = "New Share Name"
objInParams.Properties_.Item("Path") = "C:\scripts\shared"
objInParams.Properties_.Item("Type") = 0
```

Deleting Resources

The Delete method lets you delete instances of a managed resource. Not all WMI classes support the Delete method; those that do include Win32_Directory, CIM_DataFile, Win32_Share, and Win32_ScheduledJob. This means that you can use scripts to delete files, folders, shared folders, or scheduled tasks.

To delete a managed resource, retrieve the instance to be deleted, and then call the Delete method. The script template in Listing 6.28 demonstrates this operation by deleting the shared folder named "New Share Name."

Listing 6.28 Template for Deleting Resources

```
1   strComputer = "."
2   strNamespace = "\root\cimv2"
3   strClassName = "Win32_Share"
4   strKeyName   = "Name"
5   strKeyValue = "New Share Name"
6
7   Set objSWbemServices = GetObject("winmgmts:" _
8       & "{impersonationLevel=impersonate}!\\" & strComputer & strNamespace)
9
10  Set objInstance = objSWbemServices.Get(strClassName & "."    &_
11                                          strKeyName  & "='" &_
12                                          strKeyValue & "'")
13  objInstance.Delete
```

To use this template to delete other managed resources:

1. Set the value of strClassName to the appropriate WMI class.
2. If necessary, set the value of strNamespace to the appropriate WMI namespace.
3. Set the value of strKeyName to the name of the key property for the class.
4. Set the value of strKeyValue to the appropriate value.

Monitoring Resources by Using WMI Event Notifications

System administrators spend a great deal of their time fixing problems. Unfortunately, by the time a system administrator is alerted to a problem, the problem might already be disrupting the work of other employees. In turn, this can cost the organization money, in the form of lost productivity.

By using WMI event notifications, you can monitor the state of any WMI-managed resource and respond to an issue much earlier, perhaps before it is even noticed by your users.

For example, instead of waiting for a problem related to insufficient free disk space on a server to be brought to your attention, you can set up a WMI event notification that notifies you by e-mail when the free disk space on a server falls below a specified value. By knowing about the *potential* problem before it occurs, you can solve it before any productivity is lost — in this case, perhaps by archiving some of the data on the hard disk or by installing an additional hard disk.

If WMI event notifications did not exist, you *could* use a WMI script that retrieves the properties of a WMI-managed resource to monitor the state of that resource. In that case, you would need to repeatedly run a script that checks the amount of free space on a hard disk. The script would have to be scheduled to run whenever a given interval of time has elapsed. If you set too short an interval, the script will run very frequently and consume valuable computing resources. If you set too long an interval, the script might notify you of potential trouble only after this has already become an actual problem for users.

The WMI event notification mechanism was designed to overcome these issues, providing you with an efficient way of monitoring WMI-managed resources.

Scripts that monitor WMI-managed resources look similar to other WMI scripts. For example, the script in Listing 6.29 monitors the processes on a computer and displays a message if a process named Notepad.exe is started on that computer. As you can see, the script is only a few lines long and has a number of elements identical to scripts used to this point in the chapter.

If you run this script under CScript, you will likely notice that the script starts running but does not seem to finish; although it appears to have stopped running, you are not returned to the command prompt. This is the expected behavior; the script has started and is simply waiting for an instance of Notepad to be created.

Now start a new instance of Notepad. The script will display the following output and then end:

```
An instance of notepad.exe just started.
```

This is exactly what the script was designed to do. It waits until an instance of Notepad is created, it reports the fact that this instance was just created, and then it stops.

Listing 6.29   Monitoring the Notepad.exe Process

```
1   strComputer = "."
2   Set objSWbemServices = GetObject("winmgmts:" &_
3       "{impersonationLevel=impersonate}!" &_
4       "\\" & strComputer & "\root\cimv2")
5
6   Set objEventSource = objSWbemServices.ExecNotificationQuery( _
7       "SELECT * FROM __InstanceCreationEvent " &_
8       "WITHIN 10 " &_
9       "WHERE TargetInstance " &_
10      "ISA 'Win32_Process' " &_
11      "AND TargetInstance.Name = 'notepad.exe'")
12
13  Set objEventObject = objEventSource.NextEvent()
14  Wscript.Echo "An instance of notepad.exe just started."
```

Lines 1 through 4 of the script are typical of most WMI scripts. They establish a connection to the root\cimv2 namespace on the computer specified in the strComputer variable.

In lines 6 through 11, a notification query is made using the ExecNotificationQuery method. The WMI Query Language (WQL) for the query is built up in lines 7 through 11. The WQL is similar to the WQL used to retrieve instances of CIM classes, but two new keywords are used: WITHIN and ISA. These keywords are discussed in more detail later in this chapter.

In line 13, the NextEvent method is used to pause the script and wait for the event described by the notification query to occur.

Line 14 displays a message after the event has occurred. The script then automatically terminates.

The script in Listing 6.29 might look a little complicated, at least at first glance. However, like other WMI scripts in this chapter, this script can be modified to work with a different WMI-managed resource by making only a few modifications.

For example, the script in Listing 6.30 monitors the services on a computer and displays a message if the state of the Alerter service changes. Enter and run the script in the same way you did the script shown in Listing 6.29. Start or stop the Alerter service by typing **net start alerter** or **net stop alerter** in a command window. The following message should be displayed:

```
The status of the alerter service just changed.
```

Listing 6.30   Monitoring the Alerter Service

```
1   strComputer = "."
2   Set objSWbemServices = GetObject("winmgmts:" &_
3       "{impersonationLevel=impersonate}!" &_
4       "\\" & strComputer & "\root\cimv2")
5
6   Set objEventSource = objSWbemServices.ExecNotificationQuery( _
7       "SELECT * FROM __InstanceModificationEvent " &_
8       "WITHIN 10 " &_
9       "WHERE TargetInstance " &_
10      "ISA 'Win32_Service' " &_
11      "AND TargetInstance.Name = 'alerter'")
12
13  Set objEventObject = objEventSource.NextEvent()
14  Wscript.Echo "The status of the alerter service just changed."
```

Compare this script with the one in Listing 6.29. The elements that differ between the two scripts are highlighted in Listing 6.30. There are four differences between the two scripts:

1. **The type of event monitored.**

   `__InstanceCreationEvent` was changed to `__InstanceModificationEvent` on line 7.

   The script in Listing 6.29 displays a message when a new instance of Notepad is created. To do this, it registers to receive events of type __InstanceCreationEvent. This event occurs whenever a new instance of a managed object is created.

   The script in Listing 6.30 displays a message when the state of the Alerter service is modified. To do this, it registers to receive events of type __InstanceModificationEvent. This event occurs whenever an existing instance of a managed object is modified.

2. **The WMI class of the resource being monitored.**

   `Win32_Process` was changed to `Win32_Service` on line 10.

   The script in Listing 6.29 monitors a process, so it requires a reference to the Win32_Process WMI class. The script in Listing 6.30 monitors a service and therefore requires a reference to Win32_Service.

3. **The value of the Name property specifying the instance of interest.**

`notepad.exe` was changed to `alerter` on line 11.

The Win32_Process and Win32_Service WMI classes each include a Name property. In the script in Listing 6.29, the name of the process monitored is notepad.exe; in Listing 6.30, the name of the service monitored is alerter. The values of properties other than the Name property could have been used instead. For example, suppose you want to know only whether a service that is currently stopped has been modified in some way. In that case, you would use this code:

```
TargetInstance.State = 'Stopped'
```

4. **The message displayed when the specified event is received.**

`"An instance of notepad.exe just started."` was changed to `"The status of the alerter service just changed."` on line 14.

Three Steps in a WMI Monitoring Script

Just as there are three primary steps in a WMI script that retrieves and displays the properties of a managed resource, there are three steps in a WMI monitoring script.

1. A connection is made to a WMI namespace on a computer.

The first step is the same as the first step in most WMI scripts. A connection is made to the namespace where the WMI class corresponding to the resource being monitored is located.

```
strComputer = "."
Set objSWbemServices = GetObject("winmgmts:" &_
    "{impersonationLevel=impersonate}!" &_
    "\\" & strComputer & "\root\cimv2")
```

2. A notification query is issued.

In the second step, a notification query is issued using WQL. The query looks similar to the WQL statements used previously in this chapter, although there are several new elements, such as WITHIN and ISA.

```
Set objEventSource = objSWbemServices.ExecNotificationQuery( _
    "SELECT * FROM __InstanceModificationEvent " &_
    "WITHIN 10 " &_
    "WHERE TargetInstance " &_
    "ISA 'Win32_Service' " &_
    "AND TargetInstance.Name = 'alerter'")
```

3. The event is received and some action performed.

In the third step, the NextEvent method is called, which causes the script to pause and wait for an event before proceeding to the next line. After the event is received, the script proceeds to the next line, which is a message that informs the user that a particular event occurred.

```
Set objEventObject = objEventSource.NextEvent()
Wscript.Echo "The status of the alerter service was just changed."
```

Despite the similarities, however, there are some important differences between a standard WMI query and an event notification query.

Event notification queries use event classes

Instead of selecting instances from a WMI class that represents a managed resource, the WQL event query selects instances from an event class. The __InstanceModificationEvent class, as its name makes clear, represents the event that occurs when an instance is modified. There are also event classes that represent the events that occur when an instance is created or deleted: __InstanceDeletionEvent and __InstanceModificationEvent. Each of these three classes derives from the more general __InstanceOperationEvent class, a class containing events generated whenever an instance is created, deleted, or modified.

Event notification queries use the WITHIN keyword

Because the Win32_Service class does not have a corresponding WMI event provider, the WITHIN keyword must be used to signify that the WMI polling mechanism should be used with a polling interval of 10 seconds. In other words, every 10 seconds the CIM repository is checked to see whether any new changes have been made to the Alerter service. At most, you are notified within 10 seconds if the Alerter service is modified.

Theoretically, some events can be missed, depending on the polling interval. For example, suppose you are checking every 30 seconds to see whether a new instance of Notepad has been created. If a user starts Notepad and then immediately closes it, this event will likely not be reported.

This is because of the way the polling mechanism works. Suppose you create an event subscription that checks every 30 seconds to see whether Notepad has been started. WMI will begin by taking a snapshot of the specified class; in this case, it will record the state of all the processes running on the computer. Thirty seconds later, WMI will take a second snapshot of the Win32_Process class and then compare this with the previous snapshot. Suppose the first snapshot had only two processes:

```
Calc.exe
Word.exe
```

And suppose the second snapshot has three processes:

```
Calc.exe
Word.exe
Notepad.exe
```

In this case, it is obvious that Notepad has been created. However, if Notepad was started and then immediately stopped, it would not appear in the second snapshot. As far as WMI is concerned, the event never occurred.

This snapshot approach also explains why it is not recommended that you use WMI to monitor changes to all the files on a hard disk: The resultant snapshots would be huge, and comparing the two snapshots would require considerable computer resources. Items such as processes and services can be more readily monitored because there are far fewer of them on a computer.

 Note

So why can you monitor changes to the event logs, even though event logs typically have thousands of events stored in them? You can do that because there is an event provider for event logs that will watch for and notify you of changes as they happen. WMI does not need to use the snapshot method to monitor event logs. However, no such event provider exists for files or folders.

If you do not include the WITHIN clause when the resource being monitored does not have a corresponding event provider, you will receive the following error message:

```
'WITHIN' clause must be used in this query due to lack of event providers
```

Event notification queries use the TargetInstance object

It is unlikely that you will find it useful to be notified of the creation of every instance of every WMI class. Instead, you need a way to request the specific instances you are interested in. Using TargetInstance provides a way to make reference to the instances you would like the query to return.

TargetInstance is an object, created in response to an event, that has the same properties (and values) of the object that triggered the event. For example, if the Alerter service is stopped, the TargetInstance object will be an instance of the Win32_Service class that has the name Alerter and the state Stopped (plus any other properties of the Alerter service).

In addition to TargetInstance, there is also a WMI object known as PreviousInstance. As the name suggests, this object maintains the properties and values of the object *before* the event occurred. In this example, PreviousInstance would be an instance of the Win32_Service class that has the name Alerter and the state Running.

 Note

Where did PreviousInstance come from? Remember that WMI is taking, and comparing, two snapshots of the specified class. PreviousInstance represents objects found in the previous snapshot; TargetInstance, objects found in the current snapshot.

Knowing both the current and the previous state of an instance allows you to tell *what* changed when an object was modified. As a very simple example, a script can echo the values of all of the PreviousInstance and all of the TargetInstance properties. You can then compare those values to see any and all changes that were made to an object.

Event notification queries use the ISA keyword

The ISA keyword enables you to check whether a particular instance belongs to a certain class. The ISA keyword is roughly equivalent to the equals sign. However, you cannot say that the TargetInstance *equals* the Win32_Service class; it does not. Instead, the TargetInstance is an instance of the Win32_Service class. Thus, it *is a* Win32_Service instance.

How WMI Event Notification Works

Just as there is a WMI class that represents each type of system resource that can be managed using WMI, there is a WMI class that represents each type of WMI event. When an event that can be monitored by WMI occurs, an instance of the corresponding WMI event class is created. A *WMI event* occurs when that instance is created.

There are three major types of WMI event classes, all of which are derived from the __Event WMI class: Intrinsic Events, Extrinsic Events, and Timer Events. Intrinsic Events, in turn, are represented by three distinct classes derived from the __Event class: __NamespaceOperationEvent, __InstanceOperationEvent, and __ClassOperationEvent.

 Note

Timer events are seldom, if ever, used in system administration scripts and are not discussed in this chapter.

The __Event-derived classes must be present in each namespace that includes resources that can be monitored using WMI. The hierarchy of __Event-derived classes in the \root\default namespace is shown in Figure 6.5.

Figure 6.5   Event Class Hierarchy

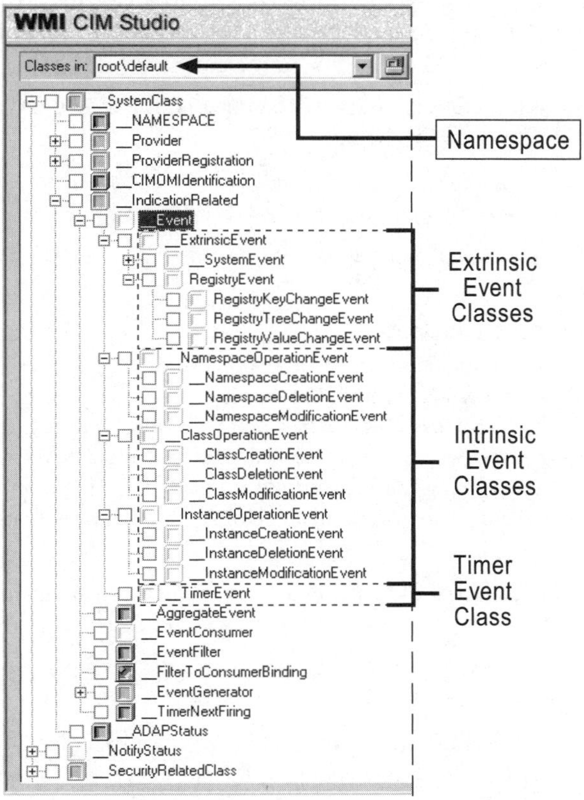

Intrinsic Events

Intrinsic events are used to monitor a resource represented by a class in the CIM repository. Each resource is represented by an *instance* of a class. This means that monitoring a resource using WMI actually involves monitoring the instances that correspond to the resource.

Intrinsic events can also be used to monitor changes to a namespace or class in the repository. However, monitoring changes to namespaces or classes is of limited value to system administrators.

An intrinsic event is represented by an instance of a class derived from __InstanceOperationEvent, __NamespaceOperationEvent, or __ClassOperationEvent. Any changes to instances in WMI are represented by the __InstanceOperationEvent class and the classes derived from it: __InstanceCreationEvent, __InstanceModificationEvent, and __InstanceDeletionEvent.

Monitoring resources using WMI involves monitoring instances and all changes to instances are represented by __InstanceOperationEvent and the classes derived from it. This means that monitoring resources ultimately involves monitoring instances of __InstanceOperationEvent-derived classes.

You register interest in instances of one of these classes by issuing a notification query expressed in WQL. The query uses syntax similar to the following:

```
SELECT * FROM __InstanceOperationEventOrDerivedClass WITHIN PollingInterval WHERE
TargetInstance ISA WMIClassName AND TargetInstance.WMIClassPropertyName = Value
```

The __InstanceOperationEvent-derived classes you register interest in depend on the event you want to monitor.

Creation of a resource: __InstanceCreationEvent

Suppose you are interested in receiving a notification if Notepad is run on a certain computer. When Notepad runs, a corresponding process is created. Processes can be managed by using WMI and are represented by the Win32_Process class. When Notepad starts running, a corresponding instance of the Win32_Process class becomes available through WMI. If you have registered your interest in this event (by issuing the appropriate event notification query), the availability of this instance results in the creation of an instance of the __InstanceCreationEvent class.

Notification queries that request notification of the creation of a resource and use intrinsic events all use syntax similar to the following:

```
SELECT * FROM __InstanceCreationEvent WITHIN PollingInterval WHERE TargetInstance
ISA 'Win32_Process' and TargetInstance.Name = 'notepad.exe'
```

Modification of a resource: __InstanceModificationEvent

Suppose you suspect that a management application you are using is erroneously changing the startup type of a service on one of your servers. You want to write a WMI script to monitor any modifications made to the configuration of the service. As soon as a modification is made to a service, its corresponding TargetInstance reflects the modification.

If you register your interest in this event, a modification to the configuration of the service results in the creation of an instance of the __InstanceModificationEvent class.

Notification queries that request notification of the modification of a resource and use intrinsic events all use syntax similar to the following:

```
SELECT * FROM __InstanceModificationEvent WITHIN PollingInterval WHERE
TargetInstance ISA 'Win32_Service' and TargetInstance.Name = 'alerter'
```

Deletion of a resource: __InstanceDeletionEvent

If you want to ensure that a particular antivirus scanner program continues to run on a computer, you can write a script that monitors the processes on the computer to determine whether any of them stop.

Notification queries that request notification of the deletion of a resource and use intrinsic events all use syntax similar to the following:

```
SELECT * FROM __InstanceDeletionEvent WHERE TargetInstance ISA 'Win32_Process'
and TargetInstance.Name = 'notepad.exe'
```

Extrinsic Events

Extrinsic events are used to monitor a resource that is not represented by a class in the CIM repository. For example, to monitor whether a process modifies an entry in the registry, you make use of extrinsic events. There is no WMI class that represents a registry entry, so you cannot use intrinsic events. (If you are interested in learning how to write scripts to monitor registry keys, subkeys, and entries, see "Registry" in this book.)

Scripts that make use of extrinsic events follow the same three steps as scripts that use intrinsic events. However, when you register to receive extrinsic events, you will not refer to an event class derived from __InstanceOperationEvent, __ClassOperationEvent, or __NamespaceOperationEvent in your event notification query. Instead, you will refer to a class derived from the __ExtrinsicEvent class.

Unlike intrinsic events, extrinsic events must have an associated WMI event provider.

Enhanced WMI Monitoring Scripts

As previously explained, the WMI monitoring scripts presented in the introduction to this section can be easily adapted to monitor any WMI-managed resource. However, these scripts do have some limitations. In particular, they can only:

- Specify the instance monitored with the value of a single property.

- Handle a single event.

- Handle a single type of event: creation, modification, or deletion.

- Monitor a single type of resource.

- Continue monitoring a resource as long as they are running. If the script stops for any reason, monitoring stops as well.

The following example scripts demonstrate how you can change the type of monitoring script presented in the introduction in order to overcome each of these limitations.

Targeting a Particular Resource

You can be more specific about the resource to monitor by enhancing the WHERE clause. The query in Listing 6.31 specifies that the Device ID property must have the value CPU0 and also specifies that the Load Percentage property must have a value greater than 90. You can include additional constraints on the values of any of the properties of the class, making use of the AND and OR keywords to combine the constraints.

Listing 6.31   Monitoring the First CPU for 90 Percent Load

```
1   Set objSWbemServices = _
2       GetObject("winmgmts:{impersonationLevel=impersonate}!\\.\root\cimv2")
3
4   strWQL = "SELECT * FROM __InstanceModificationEvent " &_
5           "WITHIN 5 " &_
```

(continued)

Listing 6.31   Monitoring the First CPU for 90 Percent Load *(continued)*

```
 6            "WHERE TargetInstance ISA 'Win32_Processor' " &_
 7            "AND TargetInstance.DeviceID='CPU0' " &_
 8            "AND TargetInstance.LoadPercentage > 90"
 9
10  Set objEventSource = objSWbemServices.ExecNotificationQuery(strWQL)
11  Set objEventObject = objEventSource.NextEvent()
12  Wscript.Echo "Load Percentage on CPU0 exceeded 90%."
```

Handling More than One Event

The scripts in Listing 6.29 and Listing 6.30 stop running after receiving a single event. You might want to have a script that continues to receive events even after the first event occurs. This requires only a minor modification to the scripts in Listing 6.29 and Listing 6.30. Simply encapsulate the call to the NextEvent method and the event notification message within an endless loop. Setting the condition statement for the loop to True ensures that the loop will never end.

So how do you stop the script when you no longer need it? If the script is running under CScript, either press CTRL+C or close the command window in which the script is running. If the script is running under WScript, you can terminate the Wscript.exe process by using Task Manager.

Listing 6.32   Continually Monitoring the First CPU for 90 Percent Load

```
 1  strComputer = "."
 2  Set objSWbemServices = _
 3      GetObject("winmgmts:\\" & strComputer & "\root\cimv2")
 4
 5  strWQL = "SELECT * FROM __InstanceModificationEvent " & _
 6          "WITHIN 5 " & _
 7          "WHERE TargetInstance ISA 'Win32_Processor' " & _
 8          "AND TargetInstance.DeviceID='CPU0' " & _
 9          "AND TargetInstance.LoadPercentage > 90"
10
11  Set objSWbemEventSource = objSWbemServices.ExecNotificationQuery(strWQL)
12
13  While True
14      Set objSWbemObject = objSWbemEventSource.NextEvent()
15      WScript.Echo "Load Percentage on CPU0 exceeded 90%."
16  Wend
```

Handling More than One Type of Event

The script in Listing 6.29 handled only instance creation events; the script in Listing 6.30 handled only instance modification events. Suppose you want to know when a new instance of Notepad is started, when the priority of a running instance of Notepad is changed, or when an instance of Notepad is deleted. In other words, suppose you want to be notified when any changes involving Notepad occur. You can write three separate scripts, one for each event type, but there is an easier way to do it.

The __InstanceCreationEvent, __InstanceModificationEvent, and __InstanceDeletionEvent classes are all derived from the __InstanceOperationEvent class. Creation, modification, and deletion are just special cases of the more general action — operation. If you handle instance operation events in your script by specifying the __InstanceOperationEvent class in your WQL notification query (line 7), your script will receive creation, modification, and deletion events.

You can also add code to determine which of the three possibilities actually occurred in a particular case. You do this by examining the class of the event object (line 14) and then deciding how to proceed based on the event that occurred, as shown in Listing 6.33.

Listing 6.33   Monitoring the Creation, Modification, and Deletion of Notepad.exe

```
1   strComputer = "."
2   Set objSWbemServices = GetObject("winmgmts:" &_
3       "{impersonationLevel=impersonate}!" &_
4       "\\" & strComputer & "\root\cimv2")
5
6   Set objEventSource = objSWbemServices.ExecNotificationQuery( _
7       "SELECT * FROM __InstanceOperationEvent " &_
8       "WITHIN 1 " &_
9       "WHERE TargetInstance " &_
10      "ISA 'Win32_Process' " &_
11      "AND TargetInstance.Name = 'notepad.exe'")
12
13  Set objEventObject = objEventSource.NextEvent()
14  Select Case objEventObject.Path_.Class
15      Case "__InstanceCreationEvent"
16          Wscript.Echo "An instance of notepad.exe was just started."
17      Case "__InstanceDeletionEvent"
18          Wscript.Echo "An instance of notepad.exe was just stopped."
19      Case "__InstanceModificationEvent"
20          Wscript.Echo "An instance of notepad.exe was just modified."
21  End Select
```

Monitoring More than One Type of Managed Resource

The script in Listing 6.29 monitors a process and the script in Listing 6.30 monitors a service. It seems that each managed resource requires a separate script. As it turns out, however, you can create a single script that monitors two different types of resources. To do so, you have to make two modifications to scripts like those in Listing 6.29 and Listing 6.30, as shown in Listing 6.34.

First you have to modify the WQL by using logical ORs to register for notifications from each of the different resource types (lines 12–14).

Second you have to add code that examines the class of the TargetInstance, retrieved from the event object, to determine which of the resources the event came from, and then proceed accordingly (lines 17–22).

Listing 6.34   Monitoring Both the W3SVC Service and the Notepad.exe Process

```
1   strComputer = "."
2   Set objSWbemServices = _
3       GetObject("winmgmts:\\" & strComputer & "\root\cimv2")
4
5   Set objSWbemEventSource = objSWbemServices.ExecNotificationQuery( _
6       "SELECT * FROM __InstanceModificationEvent " & _
7       "WITHIN 1 " & _
8       "WHERE (TargetInstance " & _
9       "ISA 'Win32_Process' " & _
10      "AND TargetInstance.Name = 'notepad.exe') " & _
11      "OR (TargetInstance " & _
12      "ISA 'Win32_Service' " & _
13      "AND TargetInstance.Name='w3svc')")
14
15  Set objSWbemObject = objSWbemEventSource.NextEvent()
16  Select Case objSWbemObject.TargetInstance.Path_.Class
17      Case "Win32_Process"
18          WScript.Echo "An instance of notepad.exe was just modified."
19      Case "Win32_Service"
20          WScript.Echo "The state of the W3SVC service was just modified."
21  End Select
```

Monitoring Events by Using a Permanent Event Subscription

The WMI monitoring scripts presented to this point use temporary event subscriptions, which exist only as long as the scripts are running. If you want to monitor resources without perpetually running a script, you need to set up a permanent event subscription.

Suppose you want to monitor the free disk space available on the busiest Microsoft Exchange servers in your enterprise. You can write a script with a temporary event subscription. However, what if the process running the script terminates? What if someone reboots one of the servers and the script fails to restart?

Clearly, it would be useful to have a solution that is more permanent (and hence more reliable) than subscriptions tied to a running process. Permanent event subscriptions provide this more permanent solution. These event subscriptions are stored in the CIM repository; canceling a subscription involves deleting it from the CIM repository. There is no associated process that, if stopped, will interrupt the subscription.

The process of handling an event can be divided into two distinct subprocesses: 1) deciding which events to handle and 2) describing the actions to be taken in response to the event. There are WMI classes that correspond to each of these subprocesses. The __EventFilter class represents the process of deciding which events to handle, and the __EventConsumer class represents the process of describing the actions to be taken in response to particular events.

Three steps are involved in setting up a permanent event subscription:

1. Create an __EventFilter class.

2. Create a class derived from __EventConsumer.

3. Associate the two classes with each other by creating a __FilterToConsumerBinding class.

In practice, creating the __EventFilter class is fairly straightforward. However, creating the __EventConsumer class (and the required associated WMI provider) is beyond the scope of this chapter. Fortunately, WMI provides prebuilt __EventConsumer classes that you can use. Before you can use the prebuilt __EventConsumer classes, you must register them in the CIM repository by using the mofcomp.exe tool.

The __EventFilter Class

Creating an instance of an __EventFilter class involves retrieving the class itself from the CIM repository by using the Get method and then calling the SpawnInstance_ method to create a "blank" instance of the class and storing a reference to it. After you have a reference to an instance of the class, you need to set the properties of the class and then use the Put_ method to actually store the instance in the CIM repository.

The most important property of __EventFilter class is its Query property. The Query property must be set to the WQL notification query that describes the events for which the instance of the __EventFilter class should filter, as shown in Listing 6.35.

Listing 6.35 Creating an Instance of the __EventFilter Class

```
1   strComputer = "."
2   Set objSWbemServices = GetObject("winmgmts:" _
3       & "{impersonationLevel=impersonate}!\\" & strComputer & "\root\cimv2")
4
5   Set objEventFilterClass = objSWbemServices.Get("__EventFilter")
6   Set objEventFilter = objEventFilterClass.SpawnInstance_()
7
8   objEventFilter.Name = "WebServiceStateModFilter"
9   objEventFilter.QueryLanguage = "WQL"
10  objEventFilter.Query = "SELECT * FROM __InstanceModificationEvent " &_
11                         "WITHIN 600 WHERE TargetInstance " &_
12                         "ISA 'Win32_Service' " &_
13                         "AND TargetInstance.Name = 'W3SVC'"
14
15  objEventFilter.Put_()
16
```

The Prebuilt __EventConsumer Classes

As mentioned previously, creating an __EventConsumer-derived class is beyond the scope of this chapter. However, WMI includes a number of prebuilt consumer classes that you can use. These standard consumer classes are listed and described in Table 6.11.

Table 6.11 Standard Event Consumer Classes

Class	Description
ActiveScriptEventConsumer	Runs a script when an event is delivered to it
SMTPEventConsumer	Sends an e-mail message by using SMTP when an event is delivered to it
CommandLineEventConsumer	Runs a program in the local system context when an event is delivered to it
NTEventLogEventConsumer	Logs a message to the Windows event log when an event is delivered to it
LogFileEventConsumer	Writes strings to a text file when an event is delivered to it
ScriptingStandardConsumerSetting	Provides registration data common to all instances of the ActiveScriptEventConsumer consumer

The standard consumer classes are not available for use until they have been registered in the CIM repository. For example, you will need to run the following command to register the ActiveScriptEventConsumer, which will be used in Listing 6.36.

```
mofcomp -N:root\cimv2 %SYSTEMROOT%\system32\wbem\scrcons.mof
```

Assuming the command completes successfully, you should see output similar to the following:

```
Parsing MOF file: C:\WINNT2\system32\wbem\scrcons.mof
MOF file has been successfully parsed
Storing data in the repository...
Done!
```

Registration needs to be performed only once unless the information about ActiveScriptEventConsumer that was added to the CIM repository is explicitly removed.

Following registration of a standard consumer class, creating an instance of this class uses code similar to that used in Listing 6.35 (where an instance of the __EventFilter class was created), as shown in Listing 6.36.

Listing 6.36 Creating an Instance of the __EventConsumer Class

```
1  strComputer = "."
2  strComputer = "."
3  Set objSWbemServices = GetObject("winmgmts:" _
4      & "{impersonationLevel=impersonate}!\\" & strComputer & "\root\cimv2")
```

(continued)

Listing 6.36 Creating an Instance of the __EventConsumer Class *(continued)*

```
5
6  Set objConsumerClass = objSWbemServices.Get("ActiveScriptEventConsumer")
7  Set objConsumer = objConsumerClass.SpawnInstance_()
8
9  objConsumer.Name = "RunResponseScript"
10 objConsumer.ScriptFileName = "C:\scripts\response.vbs"
11 objConsumer.ScriptEngine = "VBScript"
12
13 objConsumer.Put_()
```

The __FilterToConsumerBinding Class

The purpose of the __FilterToConsumerBinding class is to associate an __EventFilter with an __EventConsumer. After that association is established, any events that the __EventFilter instance intercepts are handed off to the __EventConsumer instance so that it can act upon them.

Creating an instance of the __FilterToConsumerBinding class requires the same steps as creating instances of the __EventFilter and __EventConsumer classes. The two properties of the class that need to be set are Filter and Consumer, which are the relative object paths of the __EventFilter and __EventConsumer classes being associated, as shown in Listing 6.37.

Listing 6.37 Creating an Instance of the __FilterToConsumerBinding Class

```
1  strComputer = "."
2  Set objSWbemServices = GetObject("winmgmts:" _
3      & "{impersonationLevel=impersonate}!\\" & strComputer & "\root\cimv2")
4
5  Set objBindingClass = objSWbemServices.Get("__FilterToConsumerBinding")
6  Set objBindingInstance = objBindingClass.SpawnInstance_()
7
8  objBindingInstance.Filter = "WebServiceStateModFilter"
9  objBindingInstance.Consumer = "RunResponseScript"
10
11 objBindingInstance.Put_()
```

After the __EventFilter-derived and __EventConsumer-derived instances have been created in the CIM repository and have been bound together by the __FilterToConsumerBinding class, the final step is to create the script that will run in response to a Web service status modification. This can simply be a script that displays a message when invoked by the Active Script Event Consumer.

Scripting Solutions for System Administration

System administration encompasses many different tasks in many different areas. Part 2 of this book examines scripting technologies useful in managing core elements of a computing infrastructure, including such items as printers, services, Active Directory user accounts, and computer hardware. Each chapter features a number of tasks routinely required of system administrators, such as stopping and starting services, managing disk quotas, and taking a hardware inventory. Each task includes a brief description, a script that performs the task, a step-by-step analysis of how the script works, and a discussion of how the script can be modified to meet your individual needs.

In This Part

Active Directory Users 549
Computer Assets...617
Computer Roles..689
Disks and File Systems...725
Files and Folders..767
Logs..841
Printing 881
Processes 937
Services 969
Registry.. 1015

C H A P T E R   7

Active Directory Users

Managing user data is a critical function in any organization. Using graphical user interface tools for one user or one task at a time, in all but the smallest companies, can be a costly and time-consuming exercise. Through scripting, you can manage the entire life cycle of all the individual users accounts in an enterprise efficiently, accurately, and cost effectively. To help you automate user account management tasks locally and remotely, the Microsoft® Windows® 2000 family of operating systems provide a variety of scripting tools.

In This Chapter

User Account Overview..551
Active Directory User Accounts 552
    Active Directory User Account Objects...552
Creating User Accounts..555
    Configuring User Account Passwords 558
    Reading User Account Password Attributes...561
    Configuring User Account Password Attributes 565
Managing User Accounts 567
    Reading and Writing User Account Attributes..570
    Copying, Moving, and Renaming User Accounts 581
Deleting User Accounts...588
Searching Active Directory for User Accounts 589
    Searching for an Attribute in a Container...593
    Limiting a Search for an Attribute in a Container to User Account Types............596
    Searching for a User Account Attribute in a Container and Its Subcontainers....598
    Verifying That an Attribute Is Unique in the Forest...600

Searching for Empty Attribute Values..601

Using Wildcards in Search Filters 606

Searching for Multivalued Attributes...608

Sorting the Result Set...610

Modifying Multiple User Accounts by Using the Result Set from a Search..........611

Managing User Accounts by Enumeration...613

User Account Overview

Managing user accounts is a fundamental task common to all enterprises that deploy the Active Directory® directory service. Although you can manage Active Directory user accounts by using graphical user interface (GUI) tools such as Active Directory Users and Computers, you might find this approach less than ideal in large, distributed environments. Active Directory user accounts consist of more than 250 attributes. Management of the many attributes exposed through the standard user account properties pages can be time-consuming and error-prone when performed manually.

Suppose user accounts are created manually for each user in an organization. A request is made to create a user account for a new user named Ken Myer. When the request is received, one administrator manually creates the user account and uses the "first name, first initial of the last name" notation to name the user account **KenM**. Another administrator sees the same request for user account creation and uses the "first name, dot, last name" notation to name the user account **Ken.Myer**. While both naming conventions are appropriate, they are inconsistent and, in this example, lead to the creation of two user accounts for the same user. Using a script, you can specifically define the naming policy for user accounts. If both administrators attempt to create the Ken Myer user account, only the first administrator's effort will succeed (the second attempt will fail because the account already exists). A single, uniformly named user account is created for the user because the naming convention for all user accounts is the same.

Errors can be introduced in a number of ways, such as by not following naming conventions or by mistyping initial passwords. Creating Active Directory user accounts that follow naming and configuration guidelines is further complicated by the hundreds of user account attributes available in each Active Directory user account. Unofrtunately, to reduce the amount of time it takes to create user accounts, system administrators commonly take shortcuts by leaving out a number of useful attributes (such as phone number or office location) when creating user accounts.

The most significant challenges in creating Active Directory user accounts are complying with naming conventions and consistently configuring user account attributes properly for all users. Scripting user account creation is an ideal way to maintain consistency while making the account creation process rapid and relatively error free.

The scripting solutions presented in this chapter, which use ADSI and Microsoft® Visual Basic® Scripting Edition (VBScript), provide an alternative to the GUI-based approach to user account management and thus reduce the amount of time and potential for error generally associated with manual entry of user data. Furthermore, as you become comfortable using the techniques that follow, you can create a wide range of highly customized script-based tools that address your organization's specific needs.

Active Directory User Accounts

Consider the life cycle of an Active Directory user account. Common user account administrative tasks that occur over the lifetime of a user account include creating the user account, setting the user account's initial password, enabling the user account, and configuring the user account's attributes. Scripts can be used to automate all of these user account management tasks.

To maintain control of user accounts on an ongoing basis, you can create scripts to audit user accounts, generate reports, verify common settings, and change user account settings as necessary. Other common management tasks that can be scripted include copying, moving, and renaming user accounts.

If you need to locate multiple user accounts that reside in different organizational units or domains, you can use scripts to search for the user accounts in Active Directory. Finally, when an employee leaves the company, you can disable the employee's user account for a fixed amount of time and delete the user account once you are certain the account is no longer needed. All of the steps in the life cycle of a user account can be automated using scripts.

Active Directory User Account Objects

Learning to automate Active Directory user operations begins with a basic understanding of each type of Active Directory object, each object's attributes, and the tasks commonly associated with each type of object.

A user account object, like all objects in Active Directory, is derived from a *class*. A class can be thought of as a template that defines what an object can or must contain. Just as a word processing template defines the content of a document created from it, a class defines the content of an object created from it.

User Account Types

In most cases, a user account is created so that a person or a program, such as a service, can log on to a computer or a domain. To access resources in an Active Directory forest, each user or application must have an account in Active Directory. Domain controllers running Windows 2000 use accounts to verify that the user or application has permission to use a resource.

Active Directory defines two types of user account objects: User and Contact.

User Account

The User account is the primary Active Directory object type used to represent users. Users can be people who log on to the network or services that must log on in order to run. An Active Directory User account is a security principal that the Windows 2000 security subsystem recognizes.

When a user logs on to the domain, the domain controller verifies the user's password by comparing it with the corresponding user account object in the Active Directory database. If the password presented matches the password stored in the corresponding Active Directory user account object, the domain controller produces an access token, which is subsequently used to verify access to computing resources throughout the forest.

Contact Account

The Contact user account object type is used to represent human users for address book, distribution list, and e-mail purposes; however, a contact account is not a security principal. A Contact account has no security context and therefore cannot be used to log on to a domain or to control access to computing resources.

Identification Attributes

All Active Directory user account object types are identified by several attributes defined in the Active Directory schema. All user account object types have names in the form of cn (common name), name, distinguishedName, and objectGUID. For example, a user account object created for a user named Ken Myer and stored in the Management organizational unit (OU) of the na.fabrikam.com domain could be assigned the following names:

- **cn and name:** MyerKen

  When you create the user account, you must give the object a name. The name you provide is the *relative distinguished name* of the object and must be unique in the current container. The value you provide is assigned to the user's cn (Common-Name) and name (RDN) attributes.

- **distinguishedName:** cn=MyerKen,ou=Management,dc=na,dc=fabrikam,dc=com

  The value of a user account's distinguishedName (Obj-Dist-Name) attribute is constructed from the user's relative distinguished name and the relative distinguished name of each parent all the way to the root of the directory. Because a user account's distinguishedName is automatically generated, you cannot explicitly set its value. However, an object's distinguishedName changes when the object is moved or renamed. If the MyerKen account is moved to the Finance OU, the new distinguishedName for the account will be this:

  cn=MyerKen,ou=Finance,dc=na,dc=fabrikam,dc=com

- **objectGUID:** 77 22 D5 1D B8 65 67 4F A9 C2 10 19 D1 D7 4E 9E (hexadecimal value)

  Active Directory assigns a unique value to the objectGUID attribute for each object when it is created. The objectGUID is a unique 128-bit structure used by the system to identify the object. The objectGUID does not change even if a user account object is moved or renamed. You will rarely, if ever, need to use the objectGUID when writing scripts to manage users and user accounts.

Security Principal Naming Attributes

Because the user account object type is a security principal, it has additional naming attributes, such as sAMAccountName, userPrincipalName, and objectSid. The security principal naming attributes are critical for the Windows 2000 security system to recognize user accounts. The MyerKen user account mentioned in the preceding example could be assigned the following security naming attributes:

- **sAMAccountName:** myerken

  This mandatory attribute is used to log on to the domain from computers running versions of Windows earlier than Windows 2000 and by other computers running the LAN Manager client redirector. This value must be unique in the domain and must be no longer than 20 characters.

- **userPrincipalName (UPN):** MyerKen@fabrikam.com

  This attribute can be used to log on to the domain from computers running Windows 2000 or Microsoft® Windows® XP. The UPN is assigned an e-mail style value to simplify logon to the domain. For consistency and ease of use, consider making the UPN the same as the user's e-mail address.

- **objectSid:** 01 05 00 00 00 00 00 05 15 00 00 00 83 3D 2B 46 67 FD 7C 30 F8 9F B4 74 6B 04 00 00 (hexadecimal value)

  The domain security authority, an operating system component of Windows 2000, assigns a unique value to the objectSid attribute for user account types that are security principals. When a user logs on to the domain, the security system assigns the value in the objectSid to the user's access token. The access token identifies the user account to the Windows 2000 security infrastructure.

User account types that are security principals also contain security attributes. These attributes define account and password characteristics that help to maintain domain security. For example, the accountExpires attribute can define a date when a user account will automatically expire. This ensures that a user will not be able to access the network with this user account after the expiration date.

All user account types contain address book attributes that provide supplementary information to identify user accounts. For example, the displayName attribute contains a friendly name for each user account. This name appears in the directory to assist users in identifying other users in the network.

Creating User Accounts

Creating user accounts is a fundamental task for any organization supporting computer users. In most network environments, each employee is assigned a user account that must be used in order to access local and network computing resources.

As shown in the following code sample, it takes only a few lines of code to create a user account. To create a user account, the script needs only to contain a valid path to the Active Directory container where a user account should be created, as well as two mandatory attributes of the user class, the common name (cn attribute) and the SAM account name (sAMAccountName attribute). For example, this code creates a user account with the common name MyerKen:

```
Set objOU = GetObject("LDAP://ou=Management,dc=NA,dc=fabrikam,dc=com")
Set objUser = objOU.Create("User", "cn=MyerKen")
objUser.Put "sAMAccountName", "myerken"
objUser.SetInfo
```

The system automatically generates a GUID and a security identifier (SID) for the user account object, as well as the optional attributes listed in Table 7.1.

Table 7.1   Default Settings for User Account Object Optional Attributes

Attribute	Default Setting
pwdLastSet	User must change password at next logon
userAccountControl	Password Not Required
userAccountControl	Account Disabled

The user account is a member of the Domain Users group by default. However, after the user account is created, no password is assigned and the account is disabled.

 Note

There are over forty attributes that contain values when a user account is created. To see the attributes that contain values for user accounts, you can use the ADSI Edit snap-in.

Choosing a container for user account creation

User account objects are typically created in an OU that was itself created after Active Directory has been installed. You can also create user account objects in built-in containers, such as the Users container or domain containers, but this approach is not recommended. The Users container is primarily designed and used for migrating user accounts from domains other than Active Directory domains, such as Windows NT® 4.0 domains. Creating user account objects in OUs provides for a more organized, and thus easier to manage, directory structure.

If you create user accounts in a built-in container, you must use a naming attribute for the parent container of **cn**. Conversely, if you create a user account in an OU, you must use a naming attribute for the parent container of **ou**. The following examples show the difference between the distinguishedName attributes of two user accounts created in the na.fabrikam.com domain.

- distinguishedName attribute of the AkersKim user account in the Users built-in container:

```
"cn=AkersKim,cn=Users,dc=NA,dc=fabrikam,dc=com"
```

- distinguishedName attribute of the MyerKen user account in the Management OU:

```
"cn=MyerKen,ou=Management,dc=NA,dc=fabrikam,dc=com"
```

Specifying a valid path for user account creation

When you create a user account object, you must specify both a path in Active Directory to the container where you want the object to be created and the cn for the user account object to give the user account object a unique identity in Active Directory.

The cn is the relative distinguished name of the user account object. The relative distinguished name is the unique name within the container where the object is created.

The combination of the path and the cn is the distinguishedName attribute of a user account object. The distinguishedName attribute is a unique name in Active Directory.

Verifying a unique name when creating a user account in the domain

The sAMAccountName attribute for a user account object must be unique throughout the domain. Thus, a script used to create user accounts should check that the sAMAccountName is unique before attempting to create the account. There are many ways to verify that a sAMAccountName is unique. For example, you can query Active Directory to verify the uniqueness of a sAMAccountName, or, without querying Active Directory, you can trap certain script errors that indicate an attempt to create a duplicate sAMAccountName. For information about verifying user account uniqueness, see "Searching Active Directory for User Accounts" later in this chapter.

The relative distinguished name must also be unique but only in the target container where the user account is created. For example, if a user account object with the cn MyerKen is in the Management OU, you cannot create another user account in the Management OU with the cn MyerKen. However, you can create another user account with the cn MyerKen in a different OU, proved this user has a unique sAMAccountName.

To create a user account object in Active Directory, use the Create method of the IADsContainer interface. Table 7.2 shows the arguments of this method.

Table 7.2   Arguments of the Create Method

Argument	Type	Required	Default	Description
Class	string	Yes	None	The class type. In this case, "User".
cn	string (specified as cn = string)	Yes	None	The cn of the object to create. In this case, the object is a user account.

Scripting Steps

Listing 7.1 contains a script that creates an Active Directory user account object but does not check whether a user account name is unique before attempting to create the account. To carry out this task, the script performs the following steps:

1. Bind to the OU (Management) by using the GetObject function and the LDAP provider.

   A reference (objOU) to the OU is created in local memory. Because an OU is a container, the objOU reference exposes the ADSI IADsContainer interface. IADsContainer is the ADSI interface that provides the Create method. As its name implies, the Create method is used to create objects in Active Directory.

2. Create the object, and set the object's mandatory attributes in the local property cache.

   The first mandatory attribute, the object's relative distinguished name, is listed as the second parameter of the Create method on line 2. (The first parameter — User — specifies the type of object being created by the method.) The mandatory user attribute, sAMAccountName, is then added to the user account object on line 3.

3. Commit the new object to Active Directory.

   The SetInfo method commits the new user account object to Active Directory.

Listing 7.1   Creating a User Account in Active Directory

```
1   Set objOU = GetObject("LDAP://ou=Management,dc=NA,dc=fabrikam,dc=com")
2   Set objUser = objOU.Create("User", "cn=MyerKen")
3   objUser.Put "sAMAccountName", "myerken"
4   objUser.SetInfo
```

The user account MyerKen is created in the Management OU of the na.fabrikam.com domain. The name and cn attribute of the user account object is MyerKen; the sAMAccountName of the user account is MyerKen. There is no assigned password for this user account, and the account is disabled.

Configuring User Account Passwords

User account passwords provide a critical barrier against unauthorized access to computing resources. In most network environments, it is unacceptable to create user accounts without initial passwords. Doing so leaves the user account vulnerable to initial logon by an unauthorized user. After all, to log on to a domain, you only need two things: a valid user account and the password for that user account. If the account does not have a password, the unauthorized user needs only to guess the user account name to obtain network access.

Therefore, the next step in the life cycle of creating user accounts is assigning an initial password. You can assign initial passwords to user accounts immediately after creating them, and you can configure other password attributes to control whether the user will be required to change the password at initial logon.

 Note

By default, user accounts are disabled when they are created unless they are specifically enabled in the script. For information about enabling a user account object with a script, see "Enabling or Disabling a User Account" later in this chapter.

The unicodePwd attribute of each user account object contains the password. The password is an octet string stored in Unicode format and encoded with one-way format (OWF). The operating system can read the password, but you cannot use a script to decode the password to plain text. If a user forgets his or her password, there is no way for you to query the system and retrieve that password.

You can, however, use a script to set or change a password. The two methods in the IADsUser interface for assigning passwords to user accounts are SetPassword and ChangePassword. The SetPassword method is used to reset a forgotten password or to set a password immediately after a user account is created. The SetPassword method requires administrator credentials, and the method performs a replace operation.

The ChangePassword method enables users to change their password. Unlike SetPassword, ChangePassword requires the current password and a new value in order to assign a new password. This is because the ChangePassword method must perform both a delete and an add operation. The delete operation requires the current password, and the add operation requires the new password.

Table 7.3 and Table 7.4 in the following task sections contain the arguments that must be included when the SetPassword or ChangePassword method is called.

A password cannot be assigned until after you use the SetInfo method to commit a user account to Active Directory. In contrast, other user account attributes, such as the streetAddress attribute, can be stored in the local property cache before the user account is committed to Active Directory.

 Note

In contrast with Active Directory user accounts, strict password policy configured for local user accounts on Windows 2000 nondomain controllers requires that SetPassword be called prior to SetInfo.

Regardless of which password assignment method you employ in your scripts, the password you assign must comply with password policies or the script will fail. If, for example, the **Minimum password length** policy setting is five characters and you attempt to assign a password that is three characters long, the following error message appears:

```
The password does not meet the password policy requirements. Check the minimum
password length, password complexity and password history requirements.
```

Setting User Account Passwords

After creating a user account, you should set a password that a user will enter to log on to the network. If the password policies in the domain dictate that a password is required, you will have to set a password because Active Directory does not automatically add a password to a user account when it is created.

Table 7.3 shows the argument of the SetPassword method.

Table 7.3 Argument of the SetPassword Method

Argument	Type	Required	Default	Description
NewPassword	string	Yes	None	New password value

Scripting Steps

Listing 7.2 contains a script that sets a user account password to a specified value. To carry out this task, the script performs the following steps:

1. Bind to the user account object by using the GetObject function and the LDAP provider.

2. Use the SetPassword method to set the user account's password to the specified value.

Listing 7.2 Setting a User Account Password

```
1  Set objUser = GetObject _
2    ("LDAP://cn=MyerKen,ou=Management,dc=NA,dc=fabrikam,dc=com")
3  objUser.SetPassword "i5A2sj*!"
```

After the user account is enabled, a user can log on as MyerKen in the na.fabrikam.com domain with the password i5A2sj*!. The password is case sensitive when the user logs on from a computer running a Windows NT–based operating system but is not case sensitive when the user logs on from computers running other Windows operating systems, such as Windows 98. For Windows NT–based computers, a password of **PASSWORD** is not the same as a password of **password**.

 Tip

Listing 7.2 shows the basic script structure required to set a user account password. However, you can improve on this script by using the Arguments property of the Windows Script Host (WSH) WScript object to receive parameters, such as the user account name and the OU where the user account resides. For more information about using the Arguments property, see "WSH Primer" in this book.

Changing User Account Passwords

Password policies configured at the domain level by using Group Policy objects (GPOs) can dictate when users must change their passwords. Concern about unauthorized access and the need to configure more secure passwords are two reasons why users might need to preempt password policies and change their passwords immediately. The ChangePassword method allows you to create a script that users can employ to change their own passwords.

Table 7.4 shows the arguments of the ChangePassword method.

Table 7.4   Arguments of the ChangePassword Method

Argument	Type	Required	Default	Description
OldPassword	string	Yes	None	Current password value
NewPassword	string	Yes	None	New password value

Scripting Steps

Listing 7.3 contains a script that changes a user account password. To carry out this task, the script performs the following steps:

1.   Bind to the user account object by using the GetObject function and the LDAP provider.

2. Use the ChangePassword method to specify the current password and to change the password to the specified value.

The current password is the first parameter that the ChangePassword method receives. The current password specified in the script must be the same as the password currently assigned to the user, or the script will fail.

The second parameter represents the new password to be assigned to the user account.

Listing 7.3   Changing a User Account Password

```
1  Set objUser = GetObject _
2      ("LDAP://cn=MyerKen,ou=Management,dc=NA,dc=fabrikam,dc=com")
3  objUser.ChangePassword "i5A2sj*!", "jl3R86df"
```

Reading User Account Password Attributes

A number of password attributes affect how users are able to manage their passwords. Reading password attributes of user accounts is useful for identifying potential security holes. For example, a script can help you determine which users have not reset their passwords in the past 30 days.

 Note

You can make the regular changing of passwords a domain-wide requirement by configuring a password policy setting in a GPO linked to the domain. Domain-level password attributes apply to all user accounts in the domain.

Password attributes in each user account object appear in Table 7.5.

Table 7.5   Password Attributes in Each User Account

Attribute Name	User Account Setting	Data Type
pwdLastSet	Password Last Changed	Large Integer/Date Time
userAccountControl	Password Required	Integer: ADS_UF_PASSWD_NOTREQD flag Value: 0x0020
userAccountControl	Cannot Change Password	Integer: ADS_UF_PASSWD_CANT_CHANGE flag Value: 0x0040
userAccountControl	Password Never Expires	Integer: ADS_UF_DONT_EXPIRE_PASSWD flag Value: 0x1000

(continued)

Table 7.5   Password Attributes in Each User Account *(continued)*

Attribute Name	User Account Setting	Data Type
userAccountControl	Store password using reversible encryption	Integer: ADS_UF_ENCRYPTED_TEXT_PASSWORD_ALLOWED flag Value: 0x0080
userAccountControl	Password Expired	Integer: ADS_UF_PASSWORD_EXPIRED flag Value: 0x80000

Password attributes that are part of each Active Directory user account object can be viewed and, in some cases, configured by using scripts. Table 7.5 shows password attributes contained in each Active Directory user account object.All password attributes appearing in Table 7.5 are stored in the userAccountControl attribute of a user object except for the pwdLastSet attribute. The userAccountControl attribute is a 4-byte (32-bit) data structure that contains flags for configuring other user account settings, such as the flag that controls whether a user account is enabled or disabled.

The userAccountControl is a type of integer wherein each bit in its value represents a unique setting. This type of integer is called a *bit field*. Because each bit in a bit field represents a different setting, simply examining the integer's value as a whole number is of little use. You must examine the individual bit that corresponds to the setting you are interested in reading.

To help you identify which bit to check, programming libraries such as ADSI often include predefined constants that map the bits in a bit field to friendly names. The constants serve as bit masks, each of which is used to test whether certain bits are set in the bit field.

The set of constants that represent bit masks for properties of the userAccountControl attribute is included in the ADS_USER_FLAG_ENUM enumeration. An *enumeration* in this context is simply one or more constants grouped together according to their usage. The specific constant that represents a user account's *Password never expires* option is ADS_UF_DONT_EXPIRE_PASSWD, which is defined as 0x10000, or &h10000 in VBScript.

For example, to determine whether a user account expires, you examine the state (1 or 0) of the ADS_UF_DONT_EXPIRE_PASSWD bit in the userAccountControl attribute. To accomplish this task, you must first read the userAccountControl attribute from a user account object. This attribute contains this and other settings. Then, you use the bitwise AND operator along with the setting's bit mask to extract the corresponding bit values from the bit field.

Values of the Flags in the userAccountControl Attribute

Most of the password-related flags in the userAccountControl attribute can be displayed by reading the integer value of the attribute returned by the LDAP provider and IADs. Other password flags require alternative methods. Table 7.6 lists password flags in the userAccountControl attribute and the attributes that contain values corresponding to these flags.

Table 7.6 Flags in userAccountControl and Attributes to Read Using ADSI

Setting	Flag	Attribute to Read
Password Required	ADS_UF_PASSWD_NOTREQD	userAccountControl
Password Never Expires	ADS_UF_DONT_EXPIRE_PASSWD	userAccountControl
Store password using reversible encryption	ADS_UF_ENCRYPTED_TEXT_PASSWORD_ALLOWED	userAccountControl
The password has expired	ADS_UF_PASSWORD_EXPIRED	userFlags
User cannot change password	ADS_UF_PASSWD_CANT_CHANGE	nTSecurityDescriptor

The pwdLastSet attribute is a large integer and does not appear in an easily readable format when IADs is used. Therefore, use the IADsUser interface (accessible from the LDAP provider) to display this value.

Displaying Password Attributes Accessible from userAccountControl

The LDAP provider can read the value of the userAccountControl attribute to determine:

- Whether a password is required.
- Whether the **Password never expires** option is enabled or disabled.
- Whether the **Store password using reversible encryption** option is enabled or disabled.

Scripting Steps

Listing 7.4 contains a script that displays the state of password flags in the userAccountControl attribute and the pwdLastSet attribute of a user account. To carry out this task, the script performs the following steps:

1. Create a Dictionary object to hold the value of the flags directly available from the userAccountControl attribute.

2. Define the name and the value of each flag in the Dictionary object.

3. Bind to the user account object by using the GetObject function and the LDAP provider.

4. Create the intUAC variable, and initialize it to the integer value of the userAccountControl attribute.

5. Create a loop, and use the bitwise AND operator to evaluate each flag value against the value of the userAccountControl attribute.

6. Display each flag name and whether it is enabled or disabled.

Listing 7.4   Displaying Password Attributes Available from the LDAP Provider and the userAccountControl Attribute

```
1   Set objHash = CreateObject("Scripting.Dictionary")
2   objHash.Add "ADS_UF_PASSWD_NOTREQD", &h00020
3   objHash.Add "ADS_UF_ENCRYPTED_TEXT_PASSWORD_ALLOWED", &h0080
4   objHash.Add "ADS_UF_DONT_EXPIRE_PASSWD", &h10000
5
6   Set objUser = GetObject _
7       ("LDAP://cn=MyerKen,ou=Management,dc=NA,dc=fabrikam,dc=com")
8   intUAC = objUser.Get("userAccountControl")
9
10  For Each Key In objHash.Keys
11      If objHash(Key) And intUAC Then
12          Wscript.Echo Key & " is enabled"
13      Else
14          Wscript.Echo Key & " is disabled"
15      End If
16  Next
```

Determining When a Password Was Last Set

To determine when a password will expire, it is important to know when the password was last set. Determining when a password was last set requires that you read the pwdLastSet attribute.

You can use the PasswordLastChanged property of the IADsUser interface to determine the last time that a user changed his or her user account password.

Scripting Steps

Listing 7.5 contains a script that checks the exact date and time when a user account password was last changed. To carry out this task, the script performs the following steps:

1. Bind to the user account object by using the GetObject function and the LDAP provider.

2. Create a variable, and initialize it to the value returned by the PasswordLastChanged property of the IADsUser interface.

3. Display the date and time when the password was last set.

Listing 7.5   Determining When a Password Was Last Set

```
1   Set objUser = GetObject _
2       ("LDAP://cn=MyerKen,ou=Management,dc=NA,dc=fabrikam,dc=com")
3   dtmValue = objUser.PasswordLastChanged
4   Wscript.Echo "Password was last set: " & dtmValue
```

Configuring User Account Password Attributes

The topic "Reading User Account Password Attributes" demonstrated how to read the password attributes associated with a user account object. Reading these values is an excellent way to begin troubleshooting problems that might be related to a user account object's password attributes. If the issue is password related, configuring password attributes is the next important step.

You can configure password attributes to increase network security in a number of ways — for example, by requiring users to change their passwords regularly or by enforcing the use of passwords. Configuring password attributes can also help maintain the proper operation of service accounts by keeping service account passwords from expiring.

How you configure password attributes of a user account from ADSI varies depending on the attribute:

- **Use the XOR bitwise operator** to configure the flags in the userAccountControl attribute that correspond to the following settings:

    - **Password required**

    - **Password never expires**

    - **Store password using reversible encryption**

- **Set pwdLastSet to 0 or –1** to enable or disable the **User must change password at next logon** option.

Changing Flags in the userAccountControl Attribute

To enable any of the flags directly available from the userAccountControl attribute (see Table 7.6), use the XOR bitwise operator. Listing 7.6 contains a script that demonstrates how to evaluate and set a password flag in the userAccountControl attribute.

Scripting Steps

Listing 7.6 contains a script that disables the ADS_UF_ENCRYPTED_TEXT_PASSWORD_ALLOWED flag using the XOR operator. To carry out this task, the script performs the following steps:

1. Set a constant to the value of the ADS_UF_ENCRYPTED_TEXT_PASSWORD_ALLOWED flag in the userAccountControl attribute.

2. Bind to the user account object by using the GetObject function and the LDAP provider.

3. Create a variable, and initialize it to the integer value of the userAccountControl attribute.

4. Use the bitwise AND operator to determine whether the flag is enabled.

5. If the flag is enabled, use the XOR bitwise operator to disable it in the userAccountControl attribute of the user account object.

6. Commit the change to the user account object in the local property cache to Active Directory.

Listing 7.6   Disabling a Password-Related Flag in userAccountControl

```
1   Const ADS_UF_ENCRYPTED_TEXT_PASSWORD_ALLOWED = &H80
2
3   Set objUser = GetObject _
4       ("LDAP://cn=MyerKen,ou=Management,dc=NA,dc=fabrikam,dc=com")
5   intUAC = objUser.Get("userAccountControl")
6
7   If intUAC AND _
8       ADS_UF_ENCRYPTED_TEXT_PASSWORD_ALLOWED Then
9       objUser.Put "userAccountControl", intUAC XOR _
10          ADS_UF_ENCRYPTED_TEXT_PASSWORD_ALLOWED
11      objUser.SetInfo
12  End If
```

Configuring a Password Change at Next Logon Requirement

For security, you might want users to change their passwords at next logon. You can accomplish this task by enabling the **User must change password at next logon** option. Selecting this option is important to ensure that users change their passwords to something that only they know.

The pwdLastSet attribute controls the value of the ADS_UF_PASSWORD_EXPIRED flag in the userAccountControl attribute. When set to 0, the pwdLastSet attribute enables the ADS_UF_PASSWORD_EXPIRED flag. When this flag is enabled, the current password is expired and the **User must change password at next logon** option is enabled.

Active Directory automatically enables this flag (expires the password) when a new user account is created but not when the SetPassword method is used to set a user's password. Therefore, if you run an ADSI script that uses the SetPassword method, you should also enable the **User must change password at next logon** option from the script.

Scripting Steps

Enabling and disabling the **User must change password at next logon** option are done in opposite fashion.

Enabling the User must change password at next logon option

Listing 7.7 contains a script that enables the **User must change password at next logon** option. To carry out this task, the script performs the following steps:

1. Bind to the user account object by using the GetObject function and the LDAP provider.

2. Set the pwdLastSet attribute to 0 to enable the **User must change password at next logon** option.

3. Commit the change to the user account object in the local property cache to Active Directory.

Listing 7.7 Enabling the User must change password at next logon Option

```
1   Set objUser = GetObject _
2       ("LDAP://cn=MyerKen,ou=Management,dc=NA,dc=fabrikam,dc=com")
3   objUser.Put "pwdLastSet", 0
4   objUser.SetInfo
```

Disabling the User must change password at next logon option

To disable this option, simply change the 0 in line 3 of Listing 7.7 to –1, as shown in Listing 7.8.

Listing 7.8 Disabling the User must change password at next logon Option

```
1   Set objUser = GetObject _
2       ("LDAP://cn=MyerKen,ou=Management,dc=NA,dc=fabrikam,dc=com")
3   objUser.Put "pwdLastSet", -1
4   objUser.SetInfo
```

Managing User Accounts

After you create a user account, assign it a password, and configure password attributes for it, the next important step in preparing the account for user access is to enable it. By default, a user account is disabled if you create a user account and specify only the sAMAccountName mandatory attribute. A user cannot log on with the user account until you specifically enable it.

For security, you might want to disable an enabled user account if the user of the account will not be logging on to the network for an extended period of time or if, after a period of user account inactivity, you will be reassigning an existing user account to another user.

For both security and troubleshooting, it is useful to check user accounts for their enabled or disabled status. A user account that you specifically disabled should stay that way until it will be used again. Otherwise, a dormant user account that is enabled increases the vulnerability of your network to unauthorized access. Using a script, you can periodically check the status of user accounts that should be disabled. If a user is having trouble logging on to the network, you can use a script to determine whether the user account is enabled.

Using the ADS_UF_ACCOUNTDISABLE flag, you can display or configure the disabled status of a user account. This flag contains the decimal value 2 when an account is disabled and 0 when it is enabled. The ADS_UF_ACCOUNTDISABLE flag is stored in the userAccountControl attribute of each user account object.

For a list of attributes that are enabled automatically when a user account is created, see "Creating User Accounts" earlier in this chapter.

Enabling or Disabling a User Account

You can use scripts to either enable or disable a user account. This is done by toggling the value of the ADS_UF_ACCOUNTDISABLE flag in the userAccountControl attribute.

The scripts for enabling or disabling a user account are similar.

Scripting Steps

Listing 7.9 contains a script that sets the ADS_UF_ACCOUNTDISABLE flag to 0 to enable a user account. To carry out this task, the script performs the following steps:

1. Set the ADS_UF_ACCOUNTDISABLE constant equal to the disabled flag in the userAccountControl attribute (used on line 8).

2. Bind to the user account object by using the GetObject function and the LDAP provider.

3. Create a variable, and initialize it to the integer value of the userAccountControl attribute.

4. Use the bitwise AND operator to determine whether the flag is enabled.

5. If the flag is enabled, use the XOR bitwise operator to disable it in the userAccountControl attribute of the user account object, thereby enabling the user account.

6. Commit the change to the user account object in the local property cache to Active Directory.

Listing 7.9   Enabling a User Account by Modifying the ADS_UF_ACCOUNTDISABLE Flag

```
1   Const ADS_UF_ACCOUNTDISABLE = 2
2
3   Set objUser = GetObject _
4       ("LDAP://cn=MyerKen,ou=Management,dc=NA,dc=fabrikam,dc=com")
5   intUAC = objUser.Get("userAccountControl")
6
7   If intUAC AND ADS_UF_ACCOUNTDISABLE Then
8       objUser.Put "userAccountControl", intUAC XOR ADS_UF_ACCOUNTDISABLE
9       objUser.SetInfo
10  End If
```

Listing 7.10 contains a script that disables a user account. To carry out this task, the script performs the following steps:

1. Set the ADS_UF_ACCOUNTDISABLE constant equal to the disabled flag in the userAccountControl attribute (used on line 7).

2. Bind to the user account object by using the GetObject function and the LDAP provider.

3. Create a variable, and initialize it to the integer value of the userAccountControl attribute.

4. Use the bitwise OR operator to enable ADS_UF_ACCOUNTDISABLE in the userAccountControl attribute, thereby disabling the user account.

5. Commit the change to the user account object in the local property cache to Active Directory.

Listing 7.10 Disabling a User Account by Modifying the ADS_UF_ACCOUNTDISABLE Flag

```
1  Const ADS_UF_ACCOUNTDISABLE = 2
2
3  Set objUser = GetObject _
4      ("LDAP://cn=MyerKen,ou=Management,dc=NA,dc=fabrikam,dc=com")
5  intUAC = objUser.Get("userAccountControl")
6
7  objUser.Put "userAccountControl", intUAC OR ADS_UF_ACCOUNTDISABLE
8  objUser.SetInfo
```

Determining Whether an Account Is Enabled or Disabled

If a user is having trouble logging on to the network, it might be because his or her user account has been disabled. Because of this, checking the status of the disabled flag (ADS_UF_ACCOUNTDISABLE) in the userAccountControl attribute is an important preliminary troubleshooting step. If the account is disabled, you can be reasonably sure that the user's trouble logging on is associated with the disabled status of the user account. It is also a useful security precaution to periodically check that user accounts that should be disabled are in fact disabled.

Scripting Steps

Listing 7.11 contains a script that reads the userAccountControl attribute to determine whether a user account is enabled or disabled. To carry out this task, the script performs the following steps:

1. Set the ADS_UF_ACCOUNTDISABLE constant equal to the disabled flag in the userAccountControl attribute.

2. Bind to the user account object by using the GetObject function and the LDAP provider.

3. Create a variable and initialize it to the integer value of the userAccountControl attribute.

4. Use the bitwise AND operator to determine whether the flag is enabled.

5. Display a message indicating whether the account is enabled or disabled.

Listing 7.11   Checking the Value of the ADS_UF_ACCOUNTDISABLE Flag

```
1   Const ADS_UF_ACCOUNTDISABLE = 2
2
3   Set objUser = GetObject _
4       ("LDAP://cn=MyerKen,ou=Management,dc=NA,dc=fabrikam,dc=com")
5   intUAC = objUser.Get("userAccountControl")
6
7   If intUAC AND ADS_UF_ACCOUNTDISABLE Then
8       Wscript.Echo "The account is disabled"
9   Else
10      Wscript.Echo "The account is enabled"
11  End If
```

Reading and Writing User Account Attributes

The two primary interfaces for managing Active Directory user accounts are IADs and IADsUser. IADs is a core interface and can be used to manage many types of objects in Active Directory, not just user accounts. In contrast, IADsUser is a persistent interface that is specifically limited to managing user account objects. The attributes of a user account object available from IADsUser are represented as properties of the interface. For example, the pwdLastSet attribute of a user account is represented by the PasswordLastChanged property of IADsUser. IADs has a small set of methods that use the lDAPDisplayNames of attributes to manage user accounts and other types of object in Active Directory. Therefore, to retrieve the first name of a user account, IADs reads the lDAPDisplayName, givenName.

It might seem sensible to use IADsUser for all of your user account management tasks, because the property names are intuitive and easier to remember than the lDAPDisplayNames of the attributes. However, the IADsUser interface does not provide access to most of the attributes of a user account and is limited to managing user account objects. IADs, on the other hand, can read all attributes of all Active Directory object. Thus, your comfort with managing user account attributes from the IADs core interface will make it easier to understand how to manage many other types of Active Directory objects.

Managing the attributes of a user account object involves reading and writing to those attributes. The key to using the IADs core interface to manage attributes of user account objects is knowing how to find the following characteristics of each attribute:

- **lDAPDisplayName of an attribute.** Use the Active Directory Schema snap-in to determine the lDAPDisplayNames of attributes to determine the names of the attributes associated with the User class. For information about installing the Active Directory Schema snap-in, see "ADSI Scripting Primer" in this book.

- **Data type of the attribute.** Some data types are simple to read, such as attributes stored as strings. Other attributes might require some manipulation in VBScript in order to read them, such as octet string and large integer data types.

  If an attribute cannot be easily displayed by using the LDAP provider and VBScript, determine whether you can read the attribute with a persistent interface such as IADsUser or by using the WinNT provider.

- **Number of entries an attribute can hold.** Attributes are either single-valued, containing a single entry; or multivalued, containing one or more entries. Use the Get and Put methods of IADs to manage single-valued attributes and use the GetEx and PutEx methods of IADs to manage multivalued attributes. To clear entries from both single-valued and multivalued attributes, use the PutEx method.

 Note

In rare instances, an attribute might be defined as multivalued but only be capable of holding a single value. In this case, you can use the Get and Put methods of IADs to manage them. In the remainder of this section, any multivalued attribute that holds a maximum of one entry is noted.

When modifying values using either Put or PutEx, you will need to specify the type of operation being performed (clear, update, append, or delete). These operations are listed in Table 7.7.

Table 7.7   Put and PutEx Operations

Constant	Value	Description
ADS_PROPERTY_CLEAR	1	Clears the value (or values) from the specified attribute.
ADS_PROPERTY_UPDATE	2	Replaces the value in the specified attribute with new values.
ADS_PROPERTY_APPEND	3	Appends a new value to the value (or values) in the specified attribute.
ADS_PROPERTY_DELETE	4	Deletes the value (or values) from the specified attribute.

Administering the General Properties Page

The General tab appears first by default when you view the Properties dialog box of a user account object. This tab contains attributes that are commonly used to identify particular users in the directory. The information on this page is available to all Active Directory users when they access the properties of a user account by browsing the directory from Windows Explorer.

The General properties page is shown in this chapter to demonstrate methods for reading and writing user account attributes. These same methods can be used for reading and writing the user account attributes found on the other properties pages.

The lDAPDisplayName of each attribute is commonly used to read and write entries to the General properties page. Therefore, it is important for you to be able to identify these attributes by name. The labels appearing on the property pages are often different from the lDAPDisplayNames of their corresponding attributes. On the General properties page, only two labels are the same as their lDAPDisplayNames: the Description label (with the lDAPDisplayName *description*) and the Initials label (with the lDAPDisplayName *initials*). Figure 7.1 shows the General properties page of the MyerKen user account and the lDAPDisplayNames as they appear in the Active Directory schema for each user interface label on this page.

Figure 7.1   User Account Attributes on the General Properties Page

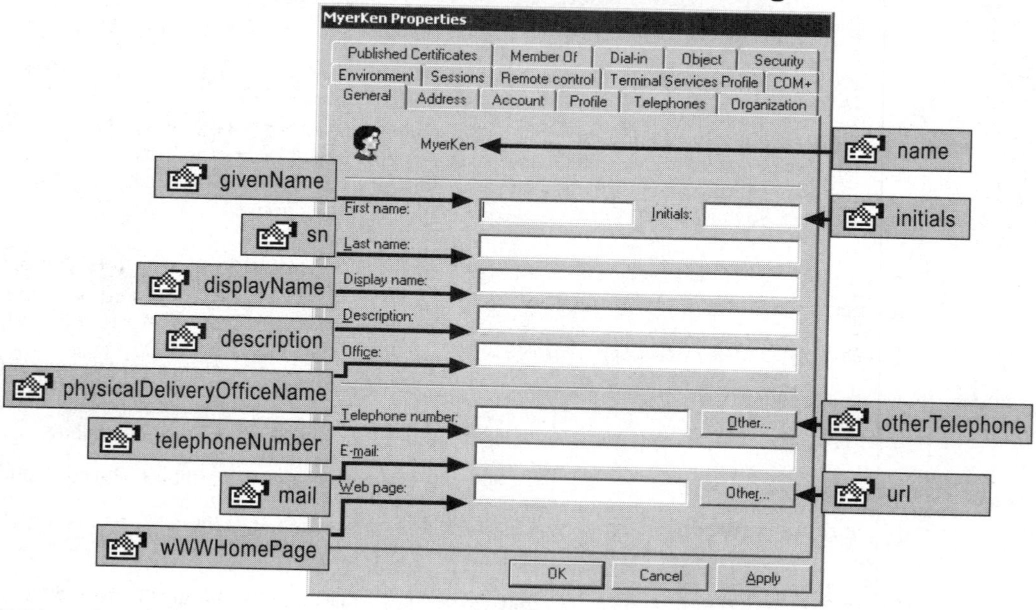

Table 7.8 lists selected properties of the attributes appearing on the General properties page of a user account object.

Table 7.8   User Account Attributes on the General Properties Page and Selected Attribute Definitions

lDAPDisplayName	Single-valued or Multivalued	Indexed	Data Type	In Global Catalog
givenName	Single-valued	Yes	String	Yes
initials	Single-valued	No	String	No
sn	Single-valued	Yes	String	Yes
displayName	Single-valued	Yes	String	Yes

(continued)

Table 7.8   User Account Attributes on the General Properties Page and Selected Attribute Definitions *(continued)*

IDAPDisplayName	Single-valued or Multivalued	Indexed	Data Type	In Global Catalog
description	Multivalued	No	String	Yes
physicalDeliveryOffice Name	Single-valued	Yes	String	No
telephoneNumber	Single-valued	No	String	Yes
otherTelephone	Multivalued	No	String	No
mail	Single-valued	Yes	String	Yes
wWWHomePage	Single-valued	No	String	No
url	Multivalued	No	String	No

The cn/name attribute, MyerKen, that appears near the top of Figure 7.1 does not appear in Table 7.8 because this attribute is automatically created when the user account object is created, and it cannot be changed by simply modifying the cn/name attribute. Modifying this attribute is equivalent to renaming the user account object. For information about renaming a user account, see "Moving and Renaming User Accounts" later in this chapter.

Reading Attributes

As shown in Table 7.8, the General properties page contains both single-valued and multivalued attributes. Use the Get method of IADs to return all single-valued attributes, and use the GetEx method of IADs to return entries assigned to multivalued attributes.

For example, the following lines of code use the Get method to return the givenName and the GetEx method to return the otherTelephone value:

```
strGivenName = objUser.Get("givenName")
strOtherTelephone = objUser.GetEx("otherTelephone")
```

Using the correct method is very important. If you use the GetEx method to retrieve a single-valued attribute (such as givenName), you will generate a "Data type mismatch" error. If you use the Get method to retrieve a multivalued attribute (such as otherTelephones), no error will be generated. However, no data will be retrieved, either.

Scripting Steps

Listing 7.12 contains a script that reads entries assigned to single-valued and multivalued attributes that appear on the General properties page of a user account object. To carry out this task, the script performs the following steps:

1. Use the On Error Resume Next statement to bypass the ADSI error generated when an attribute cannot be found in the local property cache.

    A discussion of this ADSI error follows the script.

2. Bind to the user account object by using the GetObject function and the LDAP provider.

3. Use the GetInfo method to initialize the local cache with attributes of the user account object.

   This step is not required, but it ensures that the most up-to-date attribute values of the ADSI object are retrieved.

4. Use the Get method to retrieve values from single-valued attributes.

   What happens if no value exists for a specified attribute? For example, suppose no value has been configured for physicalDeliveryOfficeName. When the script calls the Get method on a nonexistent attribute, an error is generated. More information about this behavior follows the script.

5. Use the GetEx method to retrieve entries assigned to multivalued attributes.

   The GetEx method returns an array.

   The same type of error generated for the Get method is also generated for the GetEx method for multivalued attributes that are not part of the user account object being evaluated.

6. Display each single-valued attribute's lDAPDisplayName and value.

7. Using a For Each loop, display each multivalued attribute's lDAPDisplayName and value.

Listing 7.12   Reading Attributes on the General Properties Page

```
1    On Error Resume Next
2    Set objUser = GetObject _
3        ("LDAP://cn=MyerKen,ou=Management,dc=NA,dc=fabrikam,dc=com")
4    objUser.GetInfo
5
6    strGivenName = objUser.Get("givenName")
7    strInitials = objUser.Get("initials")
8    strSn = objUser.Get("sn")
9    strDisplayName = objUser.Get("displayName")
10   strPhysicalDeliveryOfficeName = _
11       objUser.Get("physicalDeliveryOfficeName")
12   strTelephoneNumber = objUser.Get("telephoneNumber")
13   strMail = objUser.Get("mail")
14   strWwwHomePage = objUser.Get("wWWHomePage")
15
16   strDescription = objUser.GetEx("description")
17   strOtherTelephone = objUser.GetEx("otherTelephone")
18   strUrl = objUser.GetEx("url")
19
20   Wscript.Echo "givenName: " & strGivenName
21   Wscript.Echo "initials: " & strInitials
22   Wscript.Echo "sn: " & strSn
23   Wscript.Echo "displayName: " & strDisplayName
24   Wscript.Echo "physicalDeliveryOfficeName: " & _
25       strPhysicalDeliveryOfficeName
```

(continued)

Listing 7.12 Reading Attributes on the General Properties Page *(continued)*

```
26   Wscript.Echo "telephoneNumber: " & strTelephoneNumber
27   Wscript.Echo "mail: " & strMail
28   Wscript.Echo "wWWHomePage: " & strWwwHomePage
29
30   For Each strValue in strDescription
31      Wscript.Echo "description: " & strValue
32   Next
33   For Each strValue in strOtherTelephone
34      Wscript.Echo "otherTelephone: " & strValue
35   Next
36   For Each strValue in strUrl
37      Wscript.Echo "url: " & strValue
38   Next
```

If any of the attributes do not contain values and the On Error Resume Next statement is not present, the script returns the following ADSI error message when the Get or GetEx method attempts to read values of the nonexistent attributes:

```
Active Directory: The directory property cannot be found in the cache.
```

If an attribute does not contain a value, the attribute does not exist according to LDAP specifications. This results in an ADSI error with an error code of &h8000500D.

You can avoid this error in the following ways:

- Place the On Error Resume Next statement at the top of the script, as shown in line 1 of Listing 7.12.

- Use the On Error Resume Next statement to test for the &h8000500D error code. If there is an error, display the attribute's name and a message stating that there is no value. Otherwise, display the attribute's name and value.

For information about error handling, see "VBScript Primer" and "Creating Enterprise Scripts" in this book.

 Note

You can use the properties of the IADsUser interface to return values and avoid errors generated when an attribute is not in the property cache. However, not all attributes appearing on the General properties page have corresponding properties in the IADsUser interface. Therefore, using the IADs interface and implementing error handling in your scripts is the preferred method of reading and writing attribute values.

Writing Values to the Attributes

Using scripts to configure user accounts is a good way to ensure a consistent attribute format and uniform attribute content among user accounts. For example, the script can dictate whether the displayName attribute should contain each user's givenName, initial, and sn in that order (for example, Ken E. Myer) or, alternatively, the sn, a comma, and the givenName (for example, Myer, Ken). Even if you make a mistake when configuring user account attributes with scripts, the mistake is uniform and likely to be easier to fix than the variety of mistakes common to manual entry.

The methods for writing single-valued and multivalued attributes are different. Use the Put method of IADs to assign single-valued entries, and use the PutEx method with the ADS_PROPERTY_UPDATE control code to write multivalued entries.

Scripting Steps

Listing 7.13 contains a script that writes values to the attributes appearing on the General properties page. Any existing entries are replaced with new entries specified in the script. To carry out this task, the script performs the following steps:

1. Set the ADS_PROPERTY_UPDATE constant equal to the control code parameter used by the PutEx method to indicate this mode of modification (used in lines 14–19).

   This control code replaces any existing entries in a multivalued attribute.

2. Bind to the user account object by using the GetObject function and the LDAP provider.

3. Use the Put method of IADs to update all single-valued attributes in the local property cache. Any existing entries in the local property cache are replaced.

   The Put method uses the attribute's lDAPDisplayName to identify the target attribute.

4. Use the PutEx method of IADs to update all multivalued attributes.

   Because ADS_PROPERTY_UPDATE is specified when PutEx is called, any existing entries are replaced in the local property cache.

5. Use SetInfo to commit the entries assigned to the user account object in the local property cache to Active Directory.

Listing 7.13 Writing Values to Attributes

```
1   Const ADS_PROPERTY_UPDATE = 2
2   Set objUser = GetObject _
3       ("LDAP://cn=MyerKen,ou=Management,dc=NA,dc=fabrikam,dc=com")
4
5   objUser.Put "givenName", "Ken"
6   objUser.Put "initials", "E."
7   objUser.Put "sn", "Myer"
8   objUser.Put "displayName", "Myer, Ken"
9   objUser.Put "physicalDeliveryOfficeName", "Room 4358"
10  objUser.Put "telephoneNumber", "(425) 707-9795"
11  objUser.Put "mail", "MyerKen@fabrikam.com"
12  objUser.Put "wWWHomePage", "http://www.fabrikam.com"
13
14  objUser.PutEx ADS_PROPERTY_UPDATE, _
15      "description", Array("Management staff")
16  objUser.PutEx ADS_PROPERTY_UPDATE, _
17      "otherTelephone", Array("(425) 707-9794", "(425) 707-9790")
18  objUser.PutEx ADS_PROPERTY_UPDATE, _
19      "url", Array("http://www.fabrikam.com/management")
20
21  objUser.SetInfo
```

You can use the Put method to write values to single-valued or multivalued attributes. As shown in Listing 7.13, there is no need to retrieve existing entries from attributes to assign new entries. This method replaces any existing entries. Therefore, if you need to log the values stored in existing attributes, retrieve the current entries using the Get method and store the values in a log file prior to using the Put method.

To confirm that an entry has been assigned, use the GetInfo (or GetInfoEx) method to retrieve the assigned entry or entries from Active Directory.

Modifying a Multivalued Attribute

The PutEx method can modify assigned entries in multivalued attributes by specifying either append or delete operations as the first argument of the method. The append control code (ADS_PROPERTY_APPEND) adds to the entries already stored in a multivalued attribute, and the delete control code (ADS_PROPERTY_DELETE) removes specified entries from the multivalued attribute.

Using PutEx to perform modifications to multivalued attributes is efficient because a single trip to the server is all that is required to perform modifications. ADSI does not check Active Directory first to modify the entries in multivalued attributes. When a modification request is received using the SetInfo method, the control code is sent with the modification request and Active Directory performs the identified action.

To confirm that an entry has been modified, use the GetInfo (or GetInfoEx) method to retrieve the modified entry or entries from Active Directory.

 Note

> Even though the description attribute is multivalued, it behaves like a single-valued attribute when performing append or delete operations because it can contain a maximum of one entry. This is to allow for pre-Active Directory compatibility, and this attribute behaves as a single-valued attribute only for security principals such as the user account object.

Scripting Steps

There are multiple ways to modify a multivalued attribute:

- Adding an entry to a multivalued attribute
- Removing an entry assigned to a multivalued attribute

Adding an entry to a multivalued attribute

Listing 7.14 contains a script that demonstrates how to add an entry to a multivalued attribute on the General properties page. To carry out this task, the script performs the following steps:

1. Set the ADS_PROPERTY_APPEND constant equal to the control code parameter used by the PutEx method to indicate the mode of modification (used on line 6).

   This control code appends an entry to a multivalued attribute.

2. Bind to the user account object by using the GetObject function and the LDAP provider.

3. Use the PutEx method of IADs to append the http://www.fabrikam.com/policy entry to the url attribute.

   If the http://www.fabrikam.com/policy entry is already assigned to the multivalued attribute, PutEx does not add a duplicate entry.

4. Commit the change to the user account object in the local property cache to Active Directory.

Listing 7.14   Appending an Entry to a Multivalued Attribute

```
1   Const ADS_PROPERTY_APPEND = 3
2
3   Set objUser = GetObject _
4       ("LDAP://cn=MyerKen,ou=Management,dc=NA,dc=fabrikam,dc=com")
5
6   objUser.PutEx ADS_PROPERTY_APPEND, _
7       "url", Array("http://www.fabrikam.com/policy")
8
9   objUser.SetInfo
```

Removing an entry assigned to a multivalued attribute

Listing 7.15 contains a script that demonstrates how to use the delete operation of PutEx to remove an entry assigned to a multivalued attribute on the General properties page. To carry out this task, the script performs the following steps:

1. Set the ADS_PROPERTY_DELETE constant to the control code parameter used by the PutEx method to indicate the mode of modification (used on lines 6–9).

   This control code deletes an entry from a multivalued attribute.

2. Bind to the user account object by using the GetObject function and the LDAP provider.

3. Use the PutEx method of IADs to delete the (425) 707-9790 entry in the otherTelephone attribute.

   The script in Listing 7.13 added this value to the otherTelephone multivalued attribute by using the PutEx and the ADS_PROPERTY_UPDATE control code. If the (425) 707-9790 entry was not previously assigned to the multivalued attribute, PutEx simply ignores the delete operation.

4. Commit the change to the user account object in the local property cache to Active Directory.

Listing 7.15   Deleting an Entry in a Multivalued Attribute

```
1   Const ADS_PROPERTY_DELETE = 4
2
3   Set objUser = GetObject _
4       ("LDAP://cn=MyerKen,ou=Management,dc=NA,dc=fabrikam,dc=com")
5
6   objUser.PutEx ADS_PROPERTY_DELETE, _
7       "otherTelephone", Array("(425) 707-9790")
8   objUser.PutEx ADS_PROPERTY_DELETE, _
9       "initials", Array("E.")
10
11  objUser.SetInfo
```

In Listing 7.13 through Listing 7.15, all PutEx operations are committed using a single SetInfo method call. However, whenever you perform more than one operation on the same multivalued attribute, you must commit the change for each operation before continuing to the next operation. Consider the following code example:

```
objUser.PutEx ADS_PROPERTY_DELETE, "otherTelephone", Array("(425) 707-9790")
objUser.PutEx ADS_PROPERTY_APPEND, "otherTelephone", Array("(425) 707-9791")
objUser.SetInfo
```

The number (425) 707-9791 is added as an entry to the otherTelephone attribute when SetInfo is called, but the number (425) 707-9790 is not deleted.

Another important nuance of using PutEx is that the order of the entries stored in multivalued attributes is not guaranteed. For example, suppose you enter three telephone numbers: (425) 707-9791, (425) 707-9792, and (425) 707-9793. If you write a script that returns these phone numbers, the data might be returned in this order instead: (425) 707-9792, (425) 707-9791, and (425) 707-9793.

Therefore, whenever you write scripts that operate on multivalued attributes, do not depend on a specific ordering of entries.

Clearing Attributes

Using the PutEx method with the clear control code (ADS_PROPERTY_CLEAR) applies to both single-valued and multivalued attributes. This control code deletes all existing entries. It is important for single-valued attributes because the Put method cannot completely clear an attribute. For example, you cannot specify NULL or "" for an attribute's value when calling Put. In addition, while the following code will work to update the telephoneNumber attribute, the telephoneNumber attribute is not empty. Instead, it contains a single space:

```
objUser.Put "telephoneNumber", " "
```

To Active Directory, this means that the user actually *has* a phone number, regardless of whether it is valid phone number. If you search Active Directory for all users without a phone number (that is, all users for whom the telephoneNumber attribute is null), this user will not be included in the returned data.

Therefore, PutEx is the only method capable of completely clearing one or more entries from an attribute.

Scripting Steps

Listing 7.16 contains a script that demonstrates how to remove an entry in a single-valued attribute and all entries in a multivalued attribute. To carry out this task, the script performs the following steps:

1. Set the ADS_PROPERTY_CLEAR constant equal to the control code parameter used by the PutEx method to indicate the mode of modification (used on lines 6 and 7).

    This control code removes entries from single-valued and multivalued attributes.

2. Bind to the user account object by using the GetObject function and the LDAP provider.

3. Use the PutEx method of IADs to remove the entry assigned to the initials single-valued attribute.

   If no entry is assigned to the attribute, PutEx simply ignores the remove operation.

4. Use the PutEx method of IADs to remove any entries assigned to the otherTelephone attribute.

   If no entries are assigned to the attribute, PutEx simply ignores the remove operation.

5. Commit the change to the user account object in the local property cache to Active Directory.

Listing 7.16   Removing Entries in Selected Single-valued and Multivalued Attributes

```
1   Const ADS_PROPERTY_CLEAR = 1
2
3   Set objUser = GetObject _
4       ("LDAP://cn=MyerKen,ou=Management,dc=NA,dc=fabrikam,dc=com")
5
6   objUser.PutEx ADS_PROPERTY_CLEAR, "initials", 0
7   objUser.PutEx ADS_PROPERTY_CLEAR, "otherTelephone", 0
8
9   objUser.SetInfo
```

Copying, Moving, and Renaming User Accounts

Copying and moving user accounts are relatively common administrative tasks. While it is not necessary to copy a user account in order to create a new one, it saves time because common attributes can be copied from an existing user account to a new user account.

Moving user accounts is an important task for managing changes within an organization. For example, if a user is promoted, it might be necessary to move the user's account to another OU. A user account name might need to be changed if a user's last name (sn attribute) changes or if a new employee takes over for an employee who has left the company.

Copying User Accounts

User account attributes are often similar from one account to the next. For example, organization policies might specify that all user accounts in the human resources department should be members of the HR global group, have HR Department listed in the department attribute, and have the same URL specified in the wWWHomePage attribute.

If you create user accounts that contain many configured attributes, and those attributes are similar from one user account to the next, you can copy selected attributes from an existing user account to a newly created one. To streamline this process further, consider creating a template user account that contains mandatory attributes and the optional attributes that are similar from one user account to the next. For example, create a user account named HRUser, configure optional attributes, and then use this template user account to create user accounts for employees of the human resources department. Keep the template user account disabled so that no one can log on with this user account.

The Active Directory Users and Computers console provides a copy user feature that you can access by right-clicking an existing user account. This feature copies a set of optional attributes by default. You cannot control which attributes are copied to the new user account. ADSI does not contain a method specifically designed to duplicate this capability by using the WinNT or LDAP providers. However, you can create a script that uses ADSI to copy selected attributes of existing user accounts after creating new user accounts.

To do this, the script reads selected attributes from the template account and then configures the new user account with those same values. For example, suppose the wWWHomePage attribute in the template account is configured as http://www.fabrikam.com. The script reads this value and then configures the wWWHomePage attribute for the new user account to also be http://www.fabrikam.com.

Scripting Steps

Listing 7.17 contains a script that creates a new user account and then copies selected attributes from a template user account to the new user account. To carry out this task, the script performs the following steps:

1. Bind to the target container, the HR OU, by using the GetObject function and the LDAP provider.

2. Create the new user account, and set the object's mandatory attributes in the local property cache.

3. Commit the new object to the Active Directory.

4. Bind to the template user account object by using the GetObject function and the LDAP provider.

5. Create an array that contains all of the optional attributes that will be applied to the new user account.

6. Use the GetInfoEx method of IADs to copy selected attributes to the local property cache.

It is not necessary to use GetInfoEx, because the Get method called later in the script will perform an implicit GetInfo call that copies all the attributes of the user account object into the local property cache. However, because an array is created in the script for writing selected attributes to the new user account, you can also use the array and the GetInfoEx method to selectively copy attributes to the local property cache.

7. Create a loop to get each value of the attributes defined in the array and to write that value to the new user account in the local property cache.

8. Commit the change to the user account object in the local property cache to Active Directory.

Listing 7.17   Copying the Attributes from One User Account to Another

```
1   Set objOU = GetObject("LDAP://ou=HR,dc=NA,dc=fabrikam,dc=com")
2   Set objUser = objOU.Create("User", "cn=BarrAdam")
3   objUser.Put "sAMAccountName", "barradam"
4   objUser.SetInfo
5
6   Set objUserTemplate = _
7       GetObject("LDAP://cn=HRUser,ou=HR,dc=fabrikam,dc=com")
8   arrAttributes = _
9       Array("description", "wWWHomePage", "department", "company")
10  objUserTemplate.GetInfoEx arrAttributes, 0
11
12  For Each strAttrib in arrAttributes
13      strValue = objUserTemplate.Get(strAttrib)
14      objUser.Put strAttrib, strValue
15  Next
16
17  objUser.SetInfo
```

Another way of completing the copy user account task is by using the schema attribute of IADs to determine which attributes of the user class are optional, then check the template user account to determine which of these attributes contain values. For those that do contain values, write those values to the new user account object. This approach does not require you to define the specific attributes you want assigned to the new user account.

Moving and Renaming User Accounts

When an employee changes roles within the organization, it might be necessary to move the employee's user account to another OU within the same domain, or even from one domain to another. A user account might need to be renamed if, for example, user account naming conventions are changed, an employee changes his or her name, or a new employee replaces an existing employee.

How you move or rename a user account depends on where you plan to move it. Using ADSI, you can move or rename a user account using the MoveHere method of IADsContainer. The MoveHere method supports the following move and rename operations:

- Moving a user account to a different container within the same domain
- Renaming a user account within the same container
- Renaming and moving a user account to a different container within the same domain
- Moving a user account to another domain
- Renaming an account while moving it to another domain

You cannot use the MoveHere method to move a user account to another forest.

Preparing a User Account for a Cross-Domain Move

Moving user accounts to other domains within the same forest is possible when the following conditions are met:

- The destination domain is running in native mode.
- Both the destination and the source domain use Kerberos authentication.
- The move operation must be completed from the source domain to the destination, or target, domain. If you attempt to move a user while logged on to the destination domain, the following message will appear:

```
(null): Inappropriate authentication
```

To move a user from one domain to another, you must have permission to remove a user from the source domain and add a user to the target domain. For example, a user with administrator credentials in a root domain can move a user to a child domain because the user is a member of the Enterprise Admins group. However, a user with administrator credentials in a child domain cannot move a user to a parent domain because the user does not have permission, by default, to add user accounts to the parent domain.

- The user account to be moved must not be a member of a global group in the source domain, or the move operation will fail. Therefore, you must remove the user from any global groups before attempting the move.

By default, a user account is made a member of the Domain Users global group. This group is also configured as the Primary group for compatibility with Macintosh clients and POSIX-compliant applications.

You cannot remove a group configured as the Primary group. Therefore, make the user a member of a Universal group, configure that group as primary, and then remove the user's membership in any global groups. If you do not remove the user account from all global groups, the move operation will fail and the following message will appear:

```
(null): The server is unwilling to process the request.
```

After the move is completed, the moved user account is automatically made a member of the Domain Users global group in the target domain. Membership in any Universal groups is automatically revoked.

The MoveHere method allows you to create a script to move or rename a user account. Table 7.9 shows the arguments of the MoveHere method.

Table 7.9   Arguments of the MoveHere Method

Argument	Type	Required	Default	Description
Source container	string	Yes	None	The name of the provider and the distinguishedName attribute of the target container.
RelativeDistinguish edName	string	Yes	None	The cn=name attribute of the user account object to be moved or the new name of the user account to be renamed. If you are not renaming the account, you can specify vbNullString instead.

To use the MoveHere method, the script must first bind to the target (destination) container where the user account should be moved or renamed. The target container is not an argument of the MoveHere method.

Scripting Steps

The scripting steps for each type of move operation are similar.

Moving a user account to a different container within the same domain

Listing 7.18 contains a script that moves a user account from one OU to another OU within the same domain. To carry out this task, the script performs the following steps:

1. Bind to the target OU by using the GetObject function and the LDAP provider.

2. Use the MoveHere method of IADsContainer to move the user account from the HR OU to the Sales OU.

Listing 7.18 Moving a User Account to a Different OU Within the Same Domain

```
1   Set objOU = GetObject("LDAP://ou=Sales,dc=NA,dc=fabrikam,dc=com")
2
3   objOU.MoveHere _
4       "LDAP://cn=BarrAdam,ou=HR,dc=NA,dc=fabrikam,dc=com", "cn=barradam"
```

Line 4 of Listing 7.18 shows that the BarrAdam user account is moved but not renamed. The second argument of the MoveHere method, the relative distinguished name, is identical to the relative distinguished name portion of the distinguishedName specified in the first argument (cn=BarrAdam). Therefore, the second argument can be written as vbNullString rather than the actual RDN:

```
"LDAP://cn=BarrAdam,ou=HR,dc=NA,dc=fabrikam,dc=com", vbNullString
```

Renaming a user account within the same container

Renaming a user account is similar to moving a user account. The difference is that the second argument of the MoveHere method is a name other than the relative distinguished name originally assigned to the user account. Also, you can rename a user account without moving it to another container.

Listing 7.19 contains a script that renames a user account from within the OU in which it currently resides. To carry out this task, the script performs the following steps:

1. Bind to the target OU by using the GetObject function and the LDAP provider.

2. Use the MoveHere method of IADsContainer to rename the user account to LewJudy in its current container.

Listing 7.19 Renaming a User Account Within the Same OU

```
1   Set objOU = GetObject("LDAP://ou=Sales,dc=NA,dc=fabrikam,dc=com")
2
3   objOU.MoveHere _
4       "LDAP://cn=BarrAdam,ou=Sales,dc=NA,dc=fabrikam,dc=com", "cn=LewJudy"
```

Renaming and moving a user account to a different container within the same domain

You can perform a rename operation while simultaneously moving the user account to another location. Simply change the target container specified on line 1 of Listing 7.19 to a different OU.

Listing 7.20 contains a script that renames a user account and moves it to a different OU. To carry out this task, the script performs the following steps:

1. Bind to the target OU by using the GetObject function and the LDAP provider.

2. Use the MoveHere method of IADsContainer to rename the user account and move it to the Management OU.

Listing 7.20   Renaming and Moving a User Account to a Different OU

```
1  Set objOU = GetObject("LDAP://ou=Management,dc=NA,dc=fabrikam,dc=com")
2
3  objOU.MoveHere _
4     "LDAP://cn=LewJudy,ou=Sales,dc=NA,dc=fabrikam,dc=com", _
5        "cn=AckermanPilar"
```

Moving a user account to another domain

There are times when a user account might have to be moved to another domain within the forest — for example, if a user is moving to another location within the company and that location contains a different domain in the forest. It might also be necessary to move user accounts if the forest is being expanded into additional child domains or consolidated into a smaller number of domains.

Before moving a user account to another domain in the forest, you must make sure that all of the conditions outlined in the introduction to this section are met. Once these conditions are met, writing a script to move a user account to another domain is similar to moving a user account to another OU within the same domain.

Listing 7.21 contains a script that moves a user account to an OU in a child domain. To carry out this task, the script performs the following steps:

1. Bind to the target OU by using the GetObject function and the LDAP provider.

2. Use the MoveHere method of IADsContainer to rename the user account and move it to the Management OU.

Listing 7.21   Moving a User Account to an OU in a Different Domain

```
1  Set objOU = GetObject("LDAP://ou=Management,dc=NA,dc=fabrikam,dc=com")
2
3  objOU.MoveHere _
4     "LDAP://cn=AckermanPilar,ou=Management,dc=fabrikam,dc=com", _
5        vbNullString
```

If you need to move an OU or another container (and all of the objects within the container) to a different domain in the forest, use the Movetree.exe command-line tool. For information about this tool, install the Windows Support Tools from the \Support\Tools folder on the Windows 2000 Server installation CD. Following installation, from a command prompt, type **movetree /?** for syntax and Movetree examples.

Deleting User Accounts

Deleting a user account object in Active Directory is the final step in the life cycle of a user account. Deleting a user account clears all of its attributes and tombstones the account in Active Directory. The object remains marked with a tombstone until the cleanup process permanently removes it. Once deleted, there is no way to recover the user account.

To delete a user account by using an ADSI script, you must use the Delete method of the IADsContainer interface. Like IADs, IADsContainer is a core interface. IADsContainer is used to create, delete, and manage objects contained inside other objects. In this case, the user account object is contained in either an OU or one of the built-in containers, such as the Users container.

Table 7.10 shows the arguments of the Delete method.

Table 7.10   Arguments of the Delete Method

Argument	Type	Required	Default	Description
Class	string	Yes	None	Name of the schema class object to delete
Relative Distinguished Name	string	Yes	None	Value of the object's name attribute

Scripting Steps

Listing 7.22 contains a script that deletes a user account from an OU. To carry out this task, the script performs the following steps:

1. Bind to the OU from which the object will be deleted by using the GetObject function and the LDAP provider.

2. Call the Delete method of the IADsContainer interface.

Listing 7.22   Deleting an Active Directory User Account

```
1  Set objOU = GetObject("LDAP://ou=Management,dc=NA,dc=fabrikam,dc=com")
2  objOU.Delete "User", "cn=MyerKen"
```

The user is immediately deleted from Active Directory. You do not need to call SetInfo to commit the change.

Searching Active Directory for User Accounts

A critical part of scripting user account management is searching the Active Directory database. Some of the user account management tasks that involve searching Active Directory include:

- Verifying that a user account does not already exist before attempting to create one.

- Finding all user account objects that do not contain a value for a particular attribute.

- Reading the value of an attribute from all user accounts before modifying the value.

- Setting an attribute of all user account objects that meet a specific criterion to the same value.

The query interfaces available to VBScript are the ActiveX® Data Object (ADO) interfaces. These interfaces use OLE DB to read information from the Active Directory database. The information returned by the ADO interfaces is read-only; you cannot use ADO from VBScript to modify the result set returned by a query. However, after the result set is returned, you can use ADSI interfaces and methods to modify values and then write the values back to the Active Directory database. For an illustration of this technique, see "Modifying Multiple User Accounts by Using the Result Set from a Search," later in this section.

A typical query using ADO almost always includes three objects:

- Connection

- Command

- RecordSet

All of the tasks in this section use these objects to search the Active Directory.

The Connection object loads the OLE DB provider, ADsDSOObject, to establish a link to the Active Directory database through the ADSI search interface, IDirectorySearch.

After the link is established, the Command object initiates the query. The query passes through ADsDSOObject to IDirectorySearch, which then uses an LDAP query function to query the Active Directory database. The RecordSet object receives the data returned from the query.

The CommandText property of the Command object is used to specify the query to run against Active Directory. The CommandText property uses either LDAP or SQL dialect to define the query. With one exception, all examples in this section use the LDAP search dialect to assign a query string to the CommandText property. For information about the SQL dialect for performing an Active Directory search, see the Active Directory Programmer's Guide link on the Web Resources page at http://www.microsoft.com/windows/reskits/webresources.

LDAP search dialect consists of four parts:

- Search base
- One or more search filters
- One or more attributes
- Search scope

Search base specifies where in Active Directory to begin the search. Search filters specify the criteria for the search. Attributes specify the data that should be returned, and search scope specifies where in the Active Directory database to start and finish the search.

 Note

For more information about constructing and running queries of the Active Directory database, see "ADSI Scripting Primer" in this book.

Search Base

The search base of a query string consists of three parts: angle brackets surrounding the expressions, a moniker, and a distinguishedName. The syntax for the search base is:

```
<moniker://distinguishedName>
```

The moniker is either LDAP or GC, and the distinguishedName specifies the starting point of the search. For example, if you want to query the contents of the Management OU in the na.fabrikam.com domain for attributes contained in the global catalog, the search base is:

```
<GC://ou=Management,dc=NA,dc=fabrikam,dc=com>
```

Using the LDAP moniker instructs the query to perform a search using a full replica of the Active Directory database in a domain and, depending on the query, possibly all subdomains. In contrast, using the GC moniker instructs the query to search a global catalog server, which contains a partial replica of its domain and all of its child domains. Consequently, if you query a global catalog server in the root domain, the query contains data from all domains in the forest. Therefore, if all attributes that you want to query are contained in the global catalog, it is more efficient to query this data source than to search one or more full replicas of the Active Directory database in the forest.

Rather then hard code the search base into a query string, you can retrieve the rootDomainNamingContext from the RootDSE object. For information about retrieving this value using a script, see "ADSI Scripting Primer" in this book.

Filters

Search filters are an optional but important part of the LDAP search dialect used by the OLE DB provider to query the Active Directory database. A search filter consists of the name of a filter property, an operator, and a value. Each search filter is enclosed in parentheses, and search filters can be combined.

When combining search filters, preface the filter clause with an AND operator (&), an OR operator (|), or a NOT operator (!) and surround the entire filter clause in parentheses. There are a number of user account search filter examples in the remainder of this section. For more details about search filter syntax, see "ADSI Scripting Primer" in this book.

To limit a search to a specific type of object, specify either the objectClass or objectCategory search filter property. Table 7.11 shows the relationship between the user account types and the objectCategory and objectClass properties.

Table 7.11   User Account Types and the Values of objectCategory and objectClass

Account Type	objectCategory	objectClass
User Account	person	Top:person;organizationalPerson;user
contact	person	Top:person;organizationalPerson;contact

The objectCategory property lets you limit the query to all user account types that were derived from a class whose defaultObjectCategory attribute is person. The objectClass property lets you limit the query to objects matching any one of the values stored in the objectClass multivalued attribute.

Before determining which filter property to use or whether both filter properties are necessary, it is important to understand which objects are returned by each filter property and value combination. Consider the following example of an OU named R&D with two user account types: User1 (user account) and ContactUser1 (contact account). Table 7.12 shows search filters that use the objectCategory and objectClass properties to limit a search to user account types.

Table 7.12   Values Returned by Filter Properties

Filters	Returns
(objectCategory = person)	User1, ContactUser1
(objectClass = top), (objectClass = person), or (objectClass = organizationalPerson)	User1, ContactUser1
(objectClass = user)	User1
(objectClass = contact)	ContactUser1

If a computer object also existed in the R&D OU, the search filter examples in rows 2 and 3 would return the computer object. This is because the objectClass attribute of a computer object is Top:person;organizationalPerson;user;computer.

The objectCategory attribute is the better choice for most searches involving user objects, not only because it limits the search to user account types but because the objectCategory filter is single-valued, indexed, and stored in the global catalog. For more information about performing efficient searches, see "ADSI Scripting Primer" in this book.

The third row in Table 7.12 shows a filter example that limits the search to the user, the user account type that is a security principal. Another way to accomplish this is to specify a filter that uses both the objectCategory and objectClass properties, as shown in the following example:

```
(&(objectCategory=person)(objectClass=user))
```

Because the objectCategory attribute is indexed and in the global catalog, using this filter first should provide an efficient method of limiting the results before the objectClass filter is evaluated. However, to use the objectCategory attribute stored in the global catalog, you must use the GC moniker in the search base.

Other attributes of user account types are commonly specified in a search filter for limiting the result set returned from a user account type query. For example, you can search on a specific sAMAccountName value to verify that a particular name does not exist in the domain. A filter to return a sAMAccountName of MyerKen is as follows: (sAMAccountName = myerken). You must specify the lDAPDisplayName of an attribute to use it in a search filter.

Search filters also support wildcards such as the * (ANY operator). See "Using Wildcards in Search Filters" later in this section for code examples that contain wildcards, and see "ADSI Scripting Primer" in this book for more information about wildcards in search filters.

Attributes

The second to last part of a query that uses LDAP search dialect contains the attributes that the query should return.

Specify attributes to return by using their lDAPDisplayName. Separate each attribute by a comma, and separate the entire set of attributes from the rest of the query string by semicolons. The following code sample specifies the name, initials, sn, and mail attributes:

```
;name, initials, sn, mail;
```

Search Scope

The search scope is the last part of the query string; options for search scope are base, onelevel, or subtree:

Base.   This option searches the dn specified in the search base. For example, a query for the name attribute with a search base of `<GC://ou=Management,dc=NA,dc=fabrikam,dc=com>` and no search filter returns the name value of the OU, Management. No child objects of the Management OU are searched.

Onelevel.   This option searches the immediate children of the specified search base. For example, a query for the name attribute with a search base of `<GC://ou=Management,dc=NA,dc=fabrikam,dc=com>` and no search filter returns the name values of all objects in the Management OU. Any child containers in the Management OU are not searched, but the names of the child containers are included in the result set.

Subtree.   This option searches the entire subtree, including the object specified in the search base. For example, a query for the name attribute with a search base of `<GC://ou=Management,dc=NA,dc=fabrikam,dc=com>` and no search filter returns the name values of the all objects in the Management OU and the name of the Management OU itself. All child containers in the Management OU are also searched for their name values. This is the default scope option; if you do not specify a scope option in the query, subtree is used.

 Note

The search scope can also be specified as a parameter of the Command object's property collection, but when LDAP search dialect is used, it is more commonly assigned as part of the CommandText property.

Searching for an Attribute in a Container

Most searching tasks start with checking objects in a container for the value of an attribute. For example, you might want to identify all objects in a container by retrieving the value of their distinguishedName or name attributes.

Scripting Steps

You can use either LDAP search dialect or SQL syntax to search for attributes in a container.

Using LDAP search dialect to perform a search to display all names in an OU

Listing 7.23 contains a script that uses LDAP search dialect to display the value of an attribute assigned to all objects in an OU. To carry out this task, the script performs the following steps:

1. Create an ADO Connection object to access the Active Directory database by using the ADSI OLE DB provider.

    Line 1 creates a connection object using ADO, and line 2 opens the connection using the ADSI OLE DB provider.

2. Create an ADO Command object, and assign the ADO connection to it.

    This step is necessary because the Command object holds both the connection and the query string to run against the Active Directory database.

3. Assign the query string to the CommandText property of the ADO Command object. The string uses LDAP search dialect.

Line 8 specifies the search base, the attribute to return, and the search scope.

   a. The search base, surrounded by angle brackets (< >), specifies the LDAP moniker to query — the Management OU in the na.fabrikam.com domain.

   b. The attribute to return, which appears after two semicolons, specifies the lDAPDisplayName of the attribute that the query should return — the name attribute.

   c. The search scope, appearing at the end of the query string, specifies where to perform the query — onelevel, which performs the search in the Management OU. The contents of any child OUs of the management OU are not searched.

4. Run the query by assigning the Execute method to the Command object and storing the return value in the RecordSet object, objRecordSet.

The query string returns records containing a single field, the name field.

5. Use a While Wend statement to display each record in objRecordSet. Use the MoveNext method of the RecordSet object to move to the next record.

6. Close the connection object.

This final step is optional, but it is good practice to remove objects from memory when a script has finished using them. In much larger scripts that take time to complete, removing unused objects from memory saves resources and helps ensure that a script will not be using computing resources unnecessarily.

Listing 7.23   Performing a Search to Display All Names in an OU

```
1    Set objConnection = CreateObject("ADODB.Connection")
2    objConnection.Open "Provider=ADsDSOObject;"
3
4    Set objCommand = CreateObject("ADODB.Command")
5    objCommand.ActiveConnection = objConnection
6
7    objCommand.CommandText = _
8        "<LDAP://ou=Management,dc=NA,dc=fabrikam,dc=com>;;name;onelevel"
9    Set objRecordSet = objCommand.Execute
10
11   While Not objRecordset.EOF
12       Wscript.Echo objRecordset.Fields("name")
13       objRecordset.MoveNext
14   Wend
15
16   objConnection.Close
```

Listing 7.23 is intentionally simple to show the fundamental components of a search routine that uses ADO to search the Active Directory database.

Using SQL syntax to perform a search to display all names in an OU

To use SQL syntax to duplicate the results of the query statement in Listing 7.23, specify the search scope as a property of the Command object and use SQL syntax in place of line 8.

Listing 7.24 contains a script that uses SQL syntax to display the value of an attribute assigned to objects in an OU. To carry out this, task the script performs the following steps:

1. Set the ADS_SCOPE_ONELEVEL constant.

   This constant is part of the ADS_SCOPEENUM enumeration, which specifies the search scope of a query.

2. Create an ADO Connection object to access the Active Directory database by using the ADSI OLE DB provider.

3. Create an ADO Command object, and assign the ADO connection to it.

4. Set the ADO Command object's searchscope property to ADS_SCOPE_ONELEVEL.

   This limits the search to a single container, excluding the parent object. The scope is specified in this way because it is not possible to specify the search scope in the SQL dialect.

5. Assign the query string to the CommandText property of the ADO Command object. The string uses SQL dialect.

6. Run the query by assigning the Execute method to the Command object and storing the return value in the RecordSet object, objRecordSet.

   The query string returns records containing a single field, the name field.

7. Use a While Wend statement to display each record in objRecordSet. Use the MoveNext method of the RecordSet object to move to the next record.

8. Close the connection object.

Listing 7.24   Using SQL Syntax to Perform a Search to Display All Names in an OU

```
1   Const ADS_SCOPE_ONELEVEL = 1
2
3   Set objConnection = CreateObject("ADODB.Connection")
4   objConnection.Open "Provider=ADsDSOObject;"
5
6   Set objCommand = CreateObject("ADODB.Command")
7   objCommand.ActiveConnection = objConnection
8   objCommand.Properties("searchscope") = ADS_SCOPE_ONELEVEL
9
10  objCommand.CommandText = _
11      "SELECT name FROM 'LDAP://ou=Management,dc=NA,dc=fabrikam,dc=com'"
12
```

(continued)

Listing 7.24   Using SQL Syntax to Perform a Search to Display All Names in an OU
(continued)

```
13   Set objRecordSet = objCommand.Execute
14
15   While Not objRecordset.EOF
16       Wscript.Echo objRecordset.Fields("name")
17       objRecordset.MoveNext
18   Wend
19
20   objConnection.Close
```

The remaining tasks in this section show script examples that use LDAP search dialect. For more information about using SQL search dialect to perform an Active Directory search, see the Active Directory Programmer's Guide link on the Web Resources page at http://www.microsoft.com/windows/reskits/webresources.

Limiting a Search for an Attribute in a Container to User Account Types

The search in the preceding section is not limited to user account types in the Management OU. The name attributes of other objects, such as computers and OUs, are also found. To specify criteria to limit your search, you add one or more search filters to your query statement.

Scripting Steps

Listing 7.25 contains a script that uses LDAP search dialect to limit a result set to the value of an attribute assigned to a specific type of user account in an OU. To carry out this task, the script performs the following steps:

1. Create an ADO Connection object to access the Active Directory database by using the ADSI OLE DB provider.

2. Create an ADO Command object, and assign the ADO connection to it.

3. Assign the query string to the CommandText property of the ADO Command object. The string uses LDAP search dialect.

Lines 8–10 specify the search base, two search filters, the attribute to return, and the search scope.

The first search filter limits the query to all objects that are assigned the defaultObjectCategory of person. The objectCategory property of the LDAP search dialect maps to the defaultObjectCategory of an object's class.

The second search filter limits the query to all user account types whose objectClass attribute is user. Anything returned by the query must satisfy both filter conditions because the search filters are prefaced with the ampersand (&), which is the AND operator.

4. Run the query by assigning the Execute method to the Command object and storing the return value in the RecordSet object, objRecordSet.

The query string returns records containing a single field, the name field.

5. Use a While Wend statement to display each record in objRecordSet. Use the MoveNext method of the RecordSet object to move to the next record.

6. Close the Connection object.

Listing 7.25 Performing a Search to Display the Names of User Account Types That Are Security Principals in an OU

```
1   Set objConnection = CreateObject("ADODB.Connection")
2   objConnection.Open "Provider=ADsDSOObject;"
3
4   Set objCommand = CreateObject("ADODB.Command")
5   objCommand.ActiveConnection = objConnection
6
7   objCommand.CommandText = _
8       "<LDAP://ou=Management,dc=NA,dc=fabrikam,dc=com>;" & _
9           "(&(objectCategory=person)(objectClass=user));" & _
10              "name;onelevel"
11
12  Set objRecordSet = objCommand.Execute
13
14  While Not objRecordset.EOF
15      Wscript.Echo objRecordset.Fields("name")
16      objRecordset.MoveNext
17  Wend
18
19  objConnection.Close
```

Searching for a User Account Attribute in a Container and Its Subcontainers

The script in Listing 7.25 is limited to returning the name attribute of objects in the Management OU. If there are child OUs of the Management OU, objects within the child OUs are not searched for the value of their name attribute. To find all objects meeting the criteria of the search in the Management OU and all child OUs, change the search scope from onelevel (line 10 in Listing 7.25) to subtree.

To expand the search to all objects in the domain, modify the search base to the domain and specify subtree as the search scope. The LDAP search dialect as it would appear in a script for this search is the following:

```
objCommand.CommandText = _
    "<LDAP://dc=NA,dc=fabrikam,dc=com>;" & _
        "(&(objectCategory=person)(objectClass=user));" & _
            "name;subtree"
```

Using the LDAP moniker in the LDAP search dialect of the preceding example limits the search to the contents of the na.fabrikam.com domain by default. Any child domains of na.fabrikam.com are not searched. This default behavior can be changed, but if the attributes that should be returned by the script are in the global catalog, a better option is to use the GC moniker to bind to the global catalog instead of the domain.

Unlike the domain, the global catalog contains a partial attribute list of all objects in its domain and all child domains. Therefore, if you bind to a global catalog server in the root domain, you can perform a forest-wide search from a single global catalog server.

Scripting Steps

Listing 7.26 contains a script that uses LDAP search dialect to limit a result set to the values of an attribute assigned to a specific type of user account in a forest. To carry out this task, the script performs the following steps:

1. Create an ADO Connection object to access the Active Directory database by using the ADSI OLE DB provider.

2. Create an ADO Command object, and assign the ADO connection to it.

3. Assign the query string to the CommandText property of the ADO Command object. The string uses LDAP search dialect.

Lines 8–10 specify the search base, two search filters, the attribute to return, and the search scope.

The search base binds to the global catalog because the name attribute is contained in the global catalog, and the global catalog in the root domain contains a partial replica of all objects in the forest.

4. Run the query by assigning the Execute method to the Command object and storing the return value in the RecordSet object, objRecordSet.

5. Use a While Wend statement to display each record in objRecordSet. Use the MoveNext method of the RecordSet object to move to the next record.

6. Close the Connection object.

Listing 7.26 Performing a Search to Display the Names of User Account Types That Are Security Principals in a Forest

```
1   Set objConnection = CreateObject("ADODB.Connection")
2   objConnection.Open "Provider=ADsDSOObject;"
3
4   Set objCommand = CreateObject("ADODB.Command")
5   objCommand.ActiveConnection = objConnection
6
7   objCommand.CommandText = _
8    "<GC://dc=fabrikam,dc=com>;" & _
9        "(&(objectCategory=person)(objectClass=user));" & _
10           "name;subtree"
11
12  Set objRecordSet = objCommand.Execute
13
14  While Not objRecordset.EOF
15      Wscript.Echo objRecordset.Fields("name")
16      objRecordset.MoveNext
17  Wend
18
19  objConnection.Close
```

Verifying That an Attribute Is Unique in the Forest

The sAMAccountName attribute must be unique among all security principal objects within a forest. If you are using a script to create a user account in a domain, one way to verify that the sAMAccountName has not already been used is to search for the sAMAccountName attribute in the forest.

Scripting Steps

Listing 7.27 contains a script that uses LDAP search dialect to verify that a user account with a particular sAMAccountName does not already exist. To carry out this task, the script performs the following steps:

1. Create an ADO Connection object to access the Active Directory database by using the ADSI OLE DB provider.

2. Create an ADO Command object, and assign the ADO connection to it.

3. Assign the query string to the CommandText property of the ADO Command object. The string uses LDAP search dialect.

   Lines 8–11 specify the search base, two search filters, the attribute to return, and the search scope.

   The search filter on line 10 limits the query to a sAMAccountName of myerken.

4. The first part of line 11 requests two attributes, sAMAccountName and the distinguishedName. The distinguishedName is specified so that the output of the script displays the exact location of the user account object with the specified sAMAccountName.

5. Run the query by assigning the Execute method to the Command object and storing the return value in the RecordSet object, objRecordSet.

   If the RecordCount property of the RecordSet object is 0, display a message stating that the sAMAccountName is not in use.

   If the RecordCount property is not 0, use a While Wend statement to display each record in objRecordSet. Use the MoveNext method of the RecordSet object to move to the next record.

   A sAMAccountName value can be used only once in a forest. However, it is possible that user account types can exist in the LostAndFound container in a domain. A user account in this container does not prevent you from creating a duplicate user account type with the sAMAccountName. However, if the sAMAccountName is in use in another container, the While Wend statement will display both the sAMAccountName in LostAndFound and the sAMAccountName in the other container.

6. Close the Connection object.

Listing 7.27 Performing a Search to Determine Whether a User Account Name Is in Use

```
1   Set objConnection = CreateObject("ADODB.Connection")
2   objConnection.Open "Provider=ADsDSOObject;"
3
4   Set objCommand = CreateObject("ADODB.Command")
5   objCommand.ActiveConnection = objConnection
6
7   objCommand.CommandText = _
8       "<GC://dc=fabrikam,dc=com>;" & _
9           "(&(objectCategory=person)(objectClass=user)" & _
10              "(sAMAccountName=myerken));" & _
11                  "sAMAccountName, distinguishedName;subtree"
12
13  Set objRecordSet = objCommand.Execute
14
15  If objRecordSet.RecordCount = 0 Then
16      Wscript.Echo "The sAMAccountName is not in use."
17  Else
18      While Not objRecordset.EOF
19          Wscript.Echo "sAMAccountName = " & _
20          objRecordset.Fields("sAMAccountName")
21          Wscript.Echo "distinguishedName = " & _
22          objRecordset.Fields("distinguishedName")
23          objRecordset.MoveNext
24      Wend
25  End If
26
27  objConnection.Close
```

Searching for Empty Attribute Values

Determining whether an attribute does not have a value is a common searching task. For example, company policy might dictate that each user account must contain an office telephone number or an e-mail address. Thus, searching for all user accounts that are missing these values will help you determine which accounts are not in compliance with company policy.

Scripting Steps

Two scripting approaches for finding attributes that do not contain a value are as follows:

- Using the not present operator of a search filter (!*attribute_name*=*) to test for the absence of an attribute

- Using the VBScript IsNull function to test for the absence of an attribute

Using the Not Present operator of a search filter

Listing 7.28 contains a script that uses a filter to find all user accounts in the forest that do not contain a value for an attribute. To carry out this task, the script performs the following steps:

1. Create an ADO Connection object to access the Active Directory database by using the ADSI OLE DB provider.

2. Create an ADO Command object, and assign the ADO connection to it.

3. Assign the query string to the CommandText property of the ADO Command object. The string uses LDAP search dialect.

   Line 8 specifies the search base using the GC moniker to query the global catalog server in the Active Directory root domain, fabrikam.com, because the mail attribute in the search filter and the distinguishedName attribute are replicated to the global catalog.

   Line 9 specifies the search filter for the query. The filter, which uses the objectCategory property, limits the query to user account types, including contact accounts. The mail filter limits the query to all user account types whose mail attribute does not contain a value.

   Line 10 specifies the attribute of the objects to return, the distinguishedName attribute, and the scope of the search.

4. Run the query by assigning the Execute method to the Command object and storing the return value in the RecordSet object, objRecordSet.

5. Use an If Then Else statement to determine whether the recordset is empty by checking the EOF (end of file) property of the RecordSet object. If EOF is true, display a message stating that all user accounts contain a value for the mail attribute; otherwise, display each record that does not contain a value for the mail attribute.

6. To display the records, use a While Wend statement to loop through all of the records in the RecordSet object. For each record, display the distinguishedName values stored in the Fields collection of the RecordSet object.

7. Move to the next record in the recordset by using the MoveNext method of the RecordSet object. When all records are processed, end the loop.

8. Close the Connection object.

Listing 7.28   Using the Not Present Operator to Display All User Accounts with an Empty Attribute

```
1   Set objConnection = CreateObject("ADODB.Connection")
2   objConnection.Open "Provider=ADsDSOObject;"
3
4   Set objCommand = CreateObject("ADODB.Command")
5   objCommand.ActiveConnection = objConnection
6
7   objCommand.CommandText = _
8       "<GC://dc=fabrikam,dc=com>;" & _
9           "(&(objectCategory=person)(!mail=*));" & _
10              "distinguishedName;subtree"
11
12  Set objRecordSet = objCommand.Execute
13
14  If objRecordset.EOF Then
15     Wscript.Echo _
16        "All user accounts contain a value for the mail attribute."
17  Else
18     Wscript.Echo "User account(s) without a mail value:"
19     While Not objRecordset.EOF
20        Wscript.Echo objRecordset.Fields("distinguishedName")
21           objRecordset.MoveNext
22     Wend
23  End If
24
25  objConnection.Close
```

Using the IsNull function to find attributes without values

You can also determine whether an attribute is empty by using the IsNull VBScript function to find the user account types that do not contain values in the mail attribute.

Listing 7.29 contains a script that uses the VBScript IsNull function to determine which user accounts in the forest do not contain a value for an attribute. To carry out this task, the script performs the following steps:

1. Create an ADO Connection object to access the Active Directory database by using the ADSI OLE DB provider.

2. Create an ADO Command object, and assign the ADO connection to it.

3. Assign the query string to the CommandText property of the ADO Command object. The string uses LDAP search dialect.

    Line 9 specifies the search filter for the query. The filter using the objectCategory property limits the query to user account types, including contact accounts. However, a search filter to limit the search to user account types without a mail attribute is not specified.

    Line 10 specifies the attributes of the objects to return, the distinguishedName and mail attributes, and the scope of the search. The mail attribute is returned by the search so that the script can later test whether any value is contained in the attribute.

4. Run the query by assigning the Execute method to the Command object and storing the return value in the RecordSet object, objRecordSet.

5. Initialize the variable blnNoEmptyMailAttribute to True. This variable will remain true unless a single record is found that does not contain the mail attribute.

6. Use a While Wend statement to loop through all of the records in the RecordSet object. For each record, test whether the mail attribute is empty by using the VBScript IsNull function.

7. If a mail attribute is empty, set the blnNoEmptyMailAttribute to False and then display the distinguishedName value of the user account.

8. Move to the next record in the recordset by using the MoveNext method of the RecordSet object. When all records are processed, end the loop.

9. When all records are tested, use an If Then statement to test whether blnNoEmptyMailAttribute is true. If it is true, display a message stating that all user accounts contain a value for the mail attribute.

10. Close the Connection object.

Listing 7.29   Using IsNull to Display All User Accounts with an Empty Attribute

```
1    Set objConnection = CreateObject("ADODB.Connection")
2    objConnection.Open "Provider=ADsDSOObject;"
3
4    Set objCommand = CreateObject("ADODB.Command")
5    objCommand.ActiveConnection = objConnection
6
7    objCommand.CommandText = _
8      "<GC://dc=fabrikam,dc=com>;" & _
9        "(objectCategory=person);" & _
10            "distinguishedName,mail;subtree"
11
12   Set objRecordSet = objCommand.Execute
13   blnNoEmptyMailAttribute = True
14   While Not objRecordset.EOF
15       If IsNull(objRecordset.Fields("mail")) Then
16           blnNoEmptyMailAttribute = False
17           Wscript.Echo objRecordset.Fields("distinguishedName")
18       End If
19       objRecordset.MoveNext
20       If blnNoEmptyMailAttribute Then
21           Wscript.Echo _
22               "All user accounts contain a value for the mail attribute."
23       End If
24   Wend
25
26   objConnection.Close
```

This approach does not require that the script use an ! (NOT operator) in the search filter. The NOT operator requires additional processing by the domain controller servicing the search request. However, because the filter does not limit the user accounts to those that do not contain a mail attribute, all user account types are returned by the query. The client must then test all of the records to determine whether the mail attribute is empty. This approach increases network traffic because the server returns all user account records, and it increases the processing requirements placed on the client computer running the script because the client computer must read each record to determine whether IsNull is true.

The scripts in Listing 7.28 and Listing 7.29 demonstrate that performance optimization is an important consideration when writing scripts to search Active Directory. For more information about optimizing scripts that search Active Directory, see "ADSI Scripting Primer" in this book.

Using Wildcards in Search Filters

It is often necessary to locate all attributes that contain similar but not identical values so that these values can be modified. For example, you might need to locate all user accounts that start with the same network path in their user profile path, or user accounts with the same area code specified for their telephoneNumber attribute.

Scripting Steps

Listing 7.30 contains a script that finds all user accounts in the forest that contain a similar value for an attribute. To carry out this task, the script performs the following steps:

1. Create an ADO Connection object to access the Active Directory database by using the ADSI OLE DB provider.

2. Create an ADO Command object, and assign the ADO connection to it.

3. Assign the query string to the CommandText property of the ADO Command object. The string uses LDAP search dialect.

   Line 8 specifies the search base by using the GC moniker to query the global catalog server in the Active Directory root domain, fabrikam.com, because the telephoneNumber and distinguishedName attributes are replicated to the global catalog.

   Line 9 specifies the search filters for the query. The objectCategory filter limits the query to all user account types. The telephoneNumber filter uses the any operator to limit the query to telephoneNumber attribute values starting with 707.

   Line 10 specifies the attributes of the objects to return, the distinguishedName and telephoneNumber attributes, and the scope of the search.

4. Run the query by assigning the Execute method to the Command object and storing the return value in the RecordSet object, objRecordSet.

5. Use an If Then Else statement to determine whether the recordset is empty by checking the EOF property of the RecordSet object. If EOF is true, display a message stating that no user accounts were found with the specified area code. Otherwise, display each record that starts with 707 for the telephoneNumber attribute.

6. To display the records, use a While Wend statement to loop through all of the records in the RecordSet object. For each record, display the distinguishedName and telephoneNumber values stored in the Fields collection of the RecordSet object.

7. Move to the next record in the recordset by using the MoveNext method of the RecordSet object. When all records are processed, end the loop.

8. Close the Connection object.

Listing 7.30 Searching for User Accounts That Contain a Similar Value in an Attribute

```
1   Set objConnection = CreateObject("ADODB.Connection")
2   objConnection.Open "Provider=ADsDSOObject;"
3
4   Set objCommand = CreateObject("ADODB.Command")
5   objCommand.ActiveConnection = objConnection
6
7   objCommand.CommandText = _
8       "<GC://dc=fabrikam,dc=com>;" & _
9           "(&(objectCategory=person)(telephoneNumber=707*));" & _
10              "distinguishedName,telephoneNumber;subtree"
11
12  Set objRecordSet = objCommand.Execute
13
14  If objRecordset.EOF Then
15      Wscript.Echo _
16          "No user accounts found with this area code."
17  Else
18      Wscript.Echo "User account(s) with the specified area code:"
19      While Not objRecordset.EOF
20      Wscript.Echo objRecordset.Fields("distinguishedName") & ": " & _
21          objRecordset.Fields("telephoneNumber")
22      objRecordset.MoveNext
23      Wend
24  End If
25
26  objConnection.Close
```

The example shown in Listing 7.30 uses a search filter that performs post-wildcard matching on an indexed attribute. In this example, post-wildcard matching means that all telephoneNumber attribute values that start with 707 are returned. Pre-wildcard matching, such as (telephoneNumber=*707-9794), and mid-wildcard matching, such as (telephoneNumber=425*9794), should not be performed against a potentially large result set. This is because the server performs significantly more processing to return such a result set than to return a result set from a post-wildcard match. If you must perform a pre- or mid-wildcard match, consider limiting the search to a smaller search base and search scope.

Searching for Multivalued Attributes

At times it might be necessary to search for multivalued attributes. For example, you might want a list of user accounts with URLs listed in the url multivalued attribute, or you might want to retrieve a list of direct reports listed in the directReports multivalued attribute for user accounts in a particular OU.

Multivalued attributes are not indexed and not located in the global catalog, so searches for this type of attribute should be limited in scope.

Scripting Steps

Listing 7.31 contains a script that finds all user accounts in an OU that contain values in a multivalued attribute. To carry out this task, the script performs the following steps:

1. Create an ADO Connection object to access the Active Directory database by using the ADSI OLE DB provider.

2. Create an ADO Command object, and assign the ADO connection to it.

3. Assign the query string to the CommandText property of the ADO Command object. The string uses LDAP search dialect.

   Line 8 specifies the search base using the LDAP moniker to query a domain controller in the na.fabrikam.com domain because the otherTelephone attribute is not replicated to the global catalog. The search base has been intentionally limited to the Management OU because not only is the otherTelephone attribute not in the global catalog, but it is not an indexed attribute, either. Limiting the result set by specifying the Management OU as the search base avoids overburdening the domain controller with an intensive search request.

   Line 9 specifies the objectCategory=person and otherTelephone=* search filters to limit the result set to all user account types that contain values for the otherTelephone attribute. This does not exclude the contact account type, which can contain a value for the otherTelephone attribute. User account types without a value for the otherTelephone attribute are not returned by the query because the * (ANY operator) means that the attribute must be present — that is, it must contain a value.

   Line 10 specifies the attributes of the objects to return, the cn and otherTelephone attributes, and the scope of the search. The search scope has been limited to onelevel so that only user accounts in the Management OU are searched and child OUs are not.

4. Run the query by assigning the Execute method to the Command object and storing the return value in the RecordSet object, objRecordSet.

5. Use a While Wend statement to loop through all of the records in the RecordSet object.

6. Display the cn value, a single-valued attribute stored in the Fields collection of the RecordSet object.

7. Use a For Each loop to read each value stored in the otherTelephone field of the RecordSet object and then display the values.

   The end of line 16 shows that the Value property of the Fields collection is specified. The Value property is the default property and does not need to be specified when single-valued attributes are displayed. However, it is required for this script to display the values contained in the otherTelephone multivalued attribute.

8. Move to the next record in the recordset by using the MoveNext method of the RecordSet object. When all records are processed, end the loop.

9. Close the Connection object.

Listing 7.31 Searching for User Accounts Containing a Particular Multivalued Attribute

```
1   Set objConnection = CreateObject("ADODB.Connection")
2   objConnection.Open "Provider=ADsDSOObject;"
3
4   Set objCommand = CreateObject("ADODB.Command")
5   objCommand.ActiveConnection = objConnection
6
7   objCommand.CommandText = _
8       "<LDAP://ou=Management,dc=NA,dc=fabrikam,dc=com>;" & _
9           "(&(objectCategory=person)(otherTelephone=*));" & _
10              "cn,otherTelephone;onelevel"
11
12  Set objRecordSet = objCommand.Execute
13
14  While Not objRecordset.EOF
15      Wscript.Echo objRecordset.Fields("cn") & VbCr
16      For Each varRecord in objRecordset.Fields("otherTelephone").Value
17          Wscript.stdOut.Write varRecord & " "
18      Next
19      Wscript.Echo VbCrLf
20      objRecordset.MoveNext
21  Wend
22
23  objConnection.Close
```

Sorting the Result Set

Sorting a large result set can be useful, particularly when you need to group similar values together in an easy-to-read list. Ideally, you should perform searches on indexed attributes because the server performs the sort operation while it is building the result set. Otherwise, the server must generate the entire result set before performing a sort operation. To instruct the server to perform a sort operation, set the Sort On property of the Command object to the attribute you want to sort. If multiple attributes are defined for the sort operation, separate each one with a comma.

Even though the physicalDeliveryOfficeName attribute that appears in Listing 7.32 is not in the global catalog, it is an indexed attribute. Therefore, the server can efficiently sort the result set.

An interesting caveat to searching the directory with referral chasing and sorting enabled is that each domain controller performs the search operation independently. Therefore, the result set is returned in separately sorted blocks. That is, the result set for the root domain will be sorted, and then the result set for each child domain will be sorted. Conversely, a search of the global catalog with sorting enabled returns a single sorted list to the client computer. To obtain a single sorted result set in this way, the attribute must be replicated to the global catalog.

Scripting Steps

Listing 7.32 contains a script that lists all user account types in a domain and the value of an attribute that is not contained in the global catalog. Sorting is enabled on an indexed attribute. To carry out this task, the script performs the following steps:

1. Create an ADO Connection object to access the Active Directory database by using the ADSI OLE DB provider.

2. Create an ADO Command object, and assign the ADO connection to it.

3. Sort the result set by physicalDeliveryOfficeName by setting the Sort On property of the Command object equal to the attribute's lDAPDisplayName.

4. Assign the query string to the CommandText property of the ADO Command object. The string uses LDAP search dialect.

5. Run the query by assigning the Execute method to the Command object and storing the return value in the RecordSet object, objRecordSet.

6. Use a While Wend statement to loop through all of the records in the RecordSet object and display the value of the distinguishedName and physicalDeliveryOfficeName attributes.

7. Move to the next record in the recordset by using the MoveNext method of the RecordSet object. When all records are processed, end the loop.

8. Close the Connection object.

Listing 7.32   Sorting a Result Set from a Search of the Active Directory

```
1    Set objConnection = CreateObject("ADODB.Connection")
2    objConnection.Open "Provider=ADsDSOObject;"
3
4    Set objCommand = CreateObject("ADODB.Command")
5    objCommand.ActiveConnection = objConnection
6
7    objCommand.Properties("Sort On") = "physicalDeliveryOfficeName"
8
9    objCommand.CommandText = _
10       "<LDAP://dc=NA,dc=fabrikam,dc=com>;" & _
11          "(objectCategory=person);" & _
12             "distinguishedName,physicalDeliveryOfficeName;subtree"
13
14   Set objRecordSet = objCommand.Execute
15
16   While Not objRecordset.EOF
17      Wscript.Echo objRecordset.Fields("distinguishedName") & ": " & _
18           objRecordset.Fields("physicalDeliveryOfficeName")
19      objRecordset.MoveNext
20   Wend
21
22   objConnection.Close
```

Modifying Multiple User Accounts by Using the Result Set from a Search

The need to modify attributes for a specific set of accounts is frequently the reason for performing a search in the first place. For example, you might want to modify an attribute in user accounts so that the value is identical in the accounts retrieved by the search request.

The result set returned by the ADSI OLE DB provider is read-only. Therefore, to modify the data returned in the result set, you must use a different provider and a different interface, such as the LDAP provider and the IADs core interface.

To modify the contents of a result set, configure the search to request the ADsPath attribute. The value of the ADsPath attribute is the binding string passed to the GetObject function. The GetObject function loads the user object in the local property cache. Once the user object is in the property cache, you can write to it using an interface such as IADs.

Scripting Steps

Listing 7.33 contains a script that retrieves a result set and then modifies an attribute in user account objects. To carry out this task, the script performs the following steps:

1. Create an ADO Connection object to access the Active Directory database by using the ADSI OLE DB provider.

2. Create an ADO Command object, and assign the ADO connection to it.

3. Assign the query string to the CommandText property of the ADO Command object. The string uses LDAP search dialect. The search request returns the value of the ADsPath attribute.

4. Run the query by assigning the Execute method to the Command object and storing the return value in the RecordSet object, objRecordSet.

5. Use a While Wend statement to loop through all of the records in the RecordSet object.

6. In the loop, initialize the strADsPath variable to hold the ADsPath value. This value is the LDAP binding string.

7. Bind to the user account object, specified in the strADsPath variable, by using the GetObject function and the LDAP provider.

8. Use the Put method of IADs to update the company attribute, contained in the local property cache, to Fabrikam.

9. Use SetInfo to commit the company value assigned to the user account object in the local property cache to Active Directory.

10. Move to the next record in the recordset by using the MoveNext method of the RecordSet object. When all records are processed, end the loop.

11. Use the RecordCount property of the RecordSet object to display the number of user accounts that were modified.

12. Close the Connection object.

Listing 7.33   Modifying Multiple User Accounts Using the Result Set Returned by a Search

```
1   Set objConnection = CreateObject("ADODB.Connection")
2   objConnection.Open "Provider=ADsDSOObject;"
3
4   Set objCommand = CreateObject("ADODB.Command")
5   objCommand.ActiveConnection = objConnection
6
7   objCommand.CommandText = _
8       "<LDAP://dc=NA,dc=fabrikam,dc=com>;" & _
9           "(&(objectCategory=person)(objectClass=user));" & _
10              "ADsPath;subtree"
11
```

(continued)

Listing 7.33   Modifying Multiple User Accounts Using the Result Set Returned by a Search *(continued)*

```
12   Set objRecordSet = objCommand.Execute
13
14   While Not objRecordset.EOF
15       strADsPath = objRecordset.Fields("ADsPath")
16       Set objUser = GetObject(strADsPath)
17       objUser.Put "company", "Fabrikam"
18       objUser.SetInfo
19       objRecordset.MoveNext
20   Wend
21
22   Wscript.Echo objRecordSet.RecordCount & " user accounts modified."
23
24   objConnection.Close
```

Managing User Accounts by Enumeration

Another way to manage multiple user accounts is to enumerate a container's contents by using the IADsContainer interface. Enumeration is the process of returning a list of objects in a container.

IADsContainer is a multipurpose interface that is used to complete a number of user account management tasks, such as:

- Using the Create method of IADsContainer to create a user account (demonstrated in "Creating User Accounts" earlier in this chapter)

- Using the MoveHere method to move and rename a user account (demonstrated in "Moving and Renaming User Accounts" earlier in this chapter).

- Using the Delete method of IADsContainer to remove a user account (demonstrated in "Deleting User Accounts" earlier in this chapter.

Combining these methods and the methods of the IADs interface with the ability of the IADsContainer interface to enumerate a container allows you to manage multiple user accounts.

Limiting Enumeration with Filters and Hints

The Filter and Hints properties of IADsContainer allow limiting the number of objects returned by enumeration. The filter property is similar to the search filters discussed earlier in "Searching Active Directory for User Accounts." Unlike search filters, the Filter property of IADsContainer requires the client to filter objects rather than the server. The Hints property is equivalent to the attributes requested in a search query. For example, you can use the Hints property to instruct IADsContainer to return only the cn or the ADsPath of an object.

IADsContainer also provides methods, including Create, MoveHere, and Delete (discussed earlier in this chapter), which can be used to perform account management tasks on enumerated objects.

Because IADsContainer enumeration loads all objects from a container into the local property cache, using enumeration for a large number of objects can affect client performance. Therefore, to retrieve the contents of a container with many objects, use the ADO OLEDB provider to perform a search.

Scripting Steps

Listing 7.34 contains a script that enumerates a container and then modifies an attribute in user account objects. To carry out this task, the script performs the following steps:

1. Bind to the target container, the Management OU, by using the GetObject function and the LDAP provider.

2. Set the Filter property of the IADsContainer interface to return user account objects.

    Contact account types are not returned by this filter.

3. Use a For Each loop to assign each object stored in the objOU container object to the objUser variable.

4. Display the value of the IADs name property for each user account in the enumeration.

5. Use the Put method of IADs to update the company single-valued attribute in the local property cache to Fabrikam.

6. Use SetInfo to commit the company value assigned to the user account object in the local property cache to Active Directory.

7. Use the Get method of IADs to read the value of the company attribute for each user object.

8. Repeat the loop for each object in the enumeration.

Listing 7.34   Modifying Multiple User Accounts in a Container by Using Enumeration

```
1   Set objOU = GetObject("LDAP://ou=Management,dc=NA,dc=fabrikam,dc=com")
2
3   objOU.Filter = Array("user")
4
5   For Each objUser In objOU
6       Wscript.Echo "Modified " & objUser.Name
7       objUser.Put "company", "Fabrikam"
8       objUser.SetInfo
9       Wscript.Echo "The new company name is: " & _
10          objUser.Get("company")
11  Next
```

CHAPTER 8

Computer Assets

Computers must be managed as physical assets; this involves such key tasks as taking inventory of computer hardware, identifying the operating system and other software installed on a computer, and configuring such things as computer startup and recovery options. Scripting provides a single-source method that can facilitate computer management in your organization.

In This Chapter

Computer Assets Overview..**619**

    Retrieving System Information..620

    Retrieving BIOS Information...624

    Inventorying Computer Hardware..630

Managing Operating Systems...**638**

    Identifying the Name and Version Number of the Operating System.................638

    Retrieving the Properties of the Operating System...........................640

    Identifying the Latest Installed Service Pack.........................644

    Enumerating Installed Hot Fixes..646

Managing WMI Settings..**647**

Managing Software...**654**

    Enumerating Software..655

    Installing, Upgrading, and Removing Software.....................660

Managing Computer States..**668**

    Managing Computer Startups...668

    Managing Computer Recovery Options..................................676

    Shutting Down Computers and Logging Off Users...............683

    Monitoring Changes in Computer Power Status....................687

Computer Assets Overview

In most organizations, computers represent a sizable portion of the physical assets that must be managed. Because of this, many organizations have adopted asset management techniques as a way to maintain and manage computers.

Asset management is the process of maintaining, upgrading, and operating physical assets in a cost-effective manner. Effective asset management requires a detailed, accurate report of the physical assets under your control, including:

- The number and type of resources available.

- The location of these resources.

- The current status of these resources.

This data provides a clear picture of the resources available, how they have been distributed, and how they are being used. The data can then be used to create a more equitable (and less expensive) distribution of existing resources and to plan for future needs.

Unfortunately, maintaining up-to-date information about the computers in an organization can be difficult. Unlike other assets, computers often change configuration: A new hard disk might be installed, additional memory added, software upgraded or removed. In addition, computers are often moved to new locations. The number and type of changes that computers can undergo require you to inventory these items on a regular basis; inventorying computer hardware once or twice a year will probably not supply an accurate picture of the computing resources available in your organization.

On the other hand, performing a computer inventory can be very time-consuming. Although some information can be collected by a visual inspection, many components and peripherals are hidden inside the computer case. In many organizations, support technicians must physically log on to each computer to conduct an inventory. After they are logged on, they typically require a variety of third-party software tools to determine the configuration.

Scripting provides a way to inventory the required information and to ensure that the inventory is updated on a regular basis. Scripts can automatically retrieve detailed information about the computers in the enterprise, including such things as:

- The configuration of each computer.

- Unique identifiers, such as asset tags and serial numbers.

- The physical hardware installed on each computer.

- Software installed on each computer.

By using a script to conduct the inventory, you can efficiently maintain up-to-date information that enables you to manage computers as assets. Furthermore, you can do this without requiring support technicians to physically log on to each computer and without purchasing and deploying multiple tools. Instead, a single script can be used to obtain a complete inventory of every computer in the organization.

Retrieving System Information

Most computer management activities, including troubleshooting computer problems, installing new software, and applying Group Policy, require comprehensive information about how a computer has been configured. This information includes such things as the:

- Operating system installed on a computer.

- Amount of memory installed on a computer.

- Amount of disk space available on a computer.

The System Information snap-in has long been the tool of choice for system administrators needing comprehensive information about a computer, the hardware installed on that computer, and the software running on that computer. The System Information snap-in and a sample of the kind of information it can return are shown in Figure 8.1.

Figure 8.1   System Information Snap-in

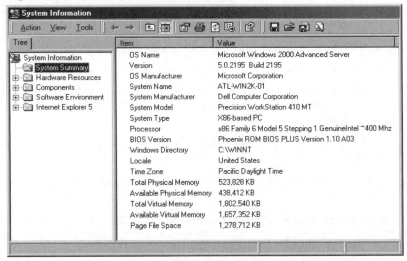

Although the System Information snap-in is a useful tool, it does have limitations that make it a less than optimal choice for performing inventories. In particular, this tool:

- Is designed to work on a single computer at a time, and it works best when run against the local computer rather than a remote computer.

- Cannot be automated or customized.

- Does not lend itself to enterprise-wide retrieval and storage of computer information.

- Does not allow for exporting data directly into a database.

  Although it is possible to manually export the data from within System Information, the resulting text file uses a free-form style of formatting that makes it difficult to parse the information and save it to a database.

- Does not allow you to customize data retrieval to meet your needs. In fact, the amount of data returned from System Information is often more than is needed for routine administrative tasks.

To overcome these limitations, system administrators have typically turned to third-party tools. Depending on your needs, however, you can save considerable cost by creating custom Windows Management Instrumentation (WMI) scripts that replicate the full functionality of the System Information snap-in. Using a WMI script provides a number of advantages over the System Information snap-in:

- Scripts can be run against a single computer or against multiple computers.

- Scripts can be used to automate data collection.

  For example, a script can be scheduled to run on a group of computers at a specific date and time.

- Scripts can be customized to return only the desired data.

- Scripts can be customized to collect data not retrieved by System Information.

  For example, although System Information can retrieve the name and version number of the operating system, it cannot retrieve more detailed information such as the set of hot fixes that have been applied to the computer.

- Scripts can save data in a standard text file format (such as tab-delimited or comma-delimited), or directly to a database.

Table 8.1 lists the data fields found on the System Information Summary tab and the equivalent WMI classes and properties.

Table 8.1   System Information Fields and Equivalent WMI Classes and Properties

System Information Field	WMI Class and Property
OS Name	Win32_OperatingSystem.Name
OS Version	Win32_OperatingSystem.Version
Service Pack	Win32_OperatingSystem.ServicePackMajorVersion
	Win32_OperatingSystem.ServicePackMinorVersion
OS Manufacturer	Win32_OperatingSystem.Manufacturer

(continued)

Table 8.1   System Information Fields and Equivalent WMI Classes and Properties
(continued)

System Information Field	WMI Class and Property
System Name	Win32_ComputerSystem.Name
System Manufacturer	Win32_ComputerSystem.Manufacturer
System Model	Win32_ComputerSystem.Model
System Type	Win32_Processor.Architecture
Processor	Win32_Processor.Description
BIOS Version	Win32_BIOS.Version
Windows Directory	Win32_OperatingSystem.WindowsDirectory
Locale	Win32_OperatingSystem.Locale
Time Zone	Win32_ComputerSystem.TimeZone
Total Physical Memory	Win32_ComputerSystem.PhsyicalMemory
Available Physical Memory	Win32_OperatingSystem.FreePhysicalMemory
Total Virtual Memory	Win32_OperatingSystem.TotalVirtualMemory
Available Virtual Memory	Win32_OperatingSystem.AvailableVirtualMemory
Page File Space	Win32_OperatingSystem.SizeStoredInPagingFiles

Scripting Steps

Listing 8.1 contains a script that retrieves the specified system information for a computer. To carry out this task, the script must perform the following steps:

1. Create a variable to specify the computer name.

2. Use a GetObject call to connect to the WMI namespace root\cimv2, and set the impersonation level to "impersonate."

3. Use the ExecQuery method to query the Win32_OperatingSystem class.

    This query returns a collection consisting of all the operating systems installed on the computer.

4. For each item in the collection, echo the desired property values.

5. Repeat steps 3 and 4, substituting the other desired WMI classes.

Separate calls are required because WMI allows you to connect to only a single class at a time.

Listing 8.1   Retrieving System Information

```
1   strComputer = "."
2   Set objWMIService = GetObject("winmgmts:" _
3       & "{impersonationLevel=impersonate}!\\" & strComputer & "\root\cimv2")
4   Set colSettings = objWMIService.ExecQuery _
5       ("SELECT * FROM Win32_OperatingSystem")
6   For Each objOperatingSystem in colSettings
7       Wscript.Echo "OS Name: " & objOperatingSystem.Name
8       Wscript.Echo "Version: " & objOperatingSystem.Version
9       Wscript.Echo "Service Pack: " & _
10          objOperatingSystem.ServicePackMajorVersion _
11              & "." & objOperatingSystem.ServicePackMinorVersion
12      Wscript.Echo "OS Manufacturer: " & objOperatingSystem.Manufacturer
13      Wscript.Echo "Windows Directory: " & _
14          objOperatingSystem.WindowsDirectory
15      Wscript.Echo "Locale: " & objOperatingSystem.Locale
16      Wscript.Echo "Available Physical Memory: " & _
17          objOperatingSystem.FreePhysicalMemory
18      Wscript.Echo "Total Virtual Memory: " & _
19          objOperatingSystem.TotalVirtualMemorySize
20      Wscript.Echo "Available Virtual Memory: " & _
21          objOperatingSystem.FreeVirtualMemory
22      Wscript.Echo "OS Name: " & objOperatingSystem.SizeStoredInPagingFiles
23  Next
24  Set colSettings = objWMIService.ExecQuery _
25      ("SELECT * FROM Win32_ComputerSystem")
26  For Each objComputer in colSettings
27      Wscript.Echo "System Name: " & objComputer.Name
28      Wscript.Echo "System Manufacturer: " & objComputer.Manufacturer
29      Wscript.Echo "System Model: " & objComputer.Model
30      Wscript.Echo "Time Zone: " & objComputer.CurrentTimeZone
31      Wscript.Echo "Total Physical Memory: " & _
32          objComputer.TotalPhysicalMemory
33  Next
```

(continued)

Listing 8.1   Retrieving System Information *(continued)*

```
34   Set colSettings = objWMIService.ExecQuery _
35       ("SELECT * FROM Win32_Processor")
36   For Each objProcessor in colSettings
37       Wscript.Echo "System Type: " & objProcessor.Architecture
38       Wscript.Echo "Processor: " & objProcessor.Description
39   Next
40   Set colSettings = objWMIService.ExecQuery _
41       ("SELECT * FROM Win32_BIOS")
42   For Each objBIOS in colSettings
43       Wscript.Echo "BIOS Version: " & objBIOS.Version
44   Next
```

Retrieving BIOS Information

The BIOS provides an interface between the operating system and the computer hardware; it also contains information regarding a computer and how it has been configured. The information contained in the BIOS is important both for identifying a computer and for determining the hardware that can be installed on it. In addition, the BIOS, which is located on a computer chip, supports peripheral equipment and manages internal services such as the computer date and time.

Besides the standard BIOS required by all computers, most computers also adhere to the System Management BIOS (SMBIOS) specification. The SMBIOS specification enables computer manufacturers and BIOS and software developers to provide support for managed systems. This specification includes standardized methods for querying the BIOS to retrieve information about items such as the number of processors installed on a computer, the amount and type of memory installed on a computer, and information about the BIOS used on a computer. BIOS information such as this does not compete with the information that can be returned using a scripting technology such as WMI; instead, the two complement one another. In fact, WMI can be used to return a number of key properties about the BIOS itself.

Retrieving Information About the BIOS

Each computer has a BIOS that is used to configure basic computer settings, including fundamental properties such as whether a password is required to start the computer and how memory can be configured. The BIOS also helps determine which hardware can be installed on a computer. For example, before you can add a new CPU or a new motherboard to a computer, you must make sure the computer has the correct version of the BIOS.

BIOS manufacturers routinely issue BIOS upgrades that enable a computer to support new classes of hardware or that add features to the computer. Before installing such an upgrade, you must know which version of a BIOS has been installed on a computer. Attempting to add hardware to a computer that does not support this hardware can cause serious problems. Problems can also occur if you attempt to install a BIOS upgrade on a computer that does not use that particular BIOS to begin with.

 Note

> The make and model of a computer are not always indicative of which BIOS has been installed on that computer. Two seemingly identical computers from the same manufacturer might use different BIOS.

You can use the Win32_BIOS class to enumerate the properties of the BIOS installed in your computer. Table 8.2 lists some of the more commonly used properties of the Win32_BIOS class, including properties related to the installed version of SMBIOS.

Table 8.2   Win32_BIOS Properties

Property	Description
BIOSCharacteristics	Array of BIOS characteristics supported by the computer as defined by the SMBIOS Reference Specification. The possible values for this property are: 3 – BIOS characteristics not supported 4 – ISA is supported 6 – EISA is supported 7 – PCI is supported 8 – PC Card (PCMCIA) is supported 9 – Plug and Play is supported 10 – APM is supported 11 – BIOS is upgradable (flash) 15 – Boot from CD is supported 16 – Selectable boot is supported 17 – BIOS ROM is socketed 18 – Boot from PC card (PCMCIA) is supported 32 – ACPI supported 34 – AGP is supported

(continued)

Table 8.2   Win32_BIOS Properties *(continued)*

Property	Description
BuildNumber	Internal identifier for the BIOS.
CurrentLanguage	Name of the current BIOS language.
InstallableLanguages	Number of languages available for installation on this computer.
Manufacturer	Manufacturer of the BIOS.
Name	Name used to identify the BIOS.
PrimaryBIOS	Indicates whether this is the primary BIOS of the computer.
ReleaseDate	Release date of the BIOS. Dates are in the Universal Time Coordinate (UTC) format yyyymmddHHMMSS.xxxxxx-UUU, where: • yyyy represents the year • mm represents the month • dd represents the day • HH represents the hour (in 24-hour time format) • MM represents the minutes • SS represents the seconds • xxxxxx represents the milliseconds • UUU represents the number of minutes to be subtracted from the current time in order to calculate Greenwich Mean Time For example, a BIOS released on October 31, 2002, at 10:45:39 A.M. Pacific time looks like this: `20021031104539.000000-480`
SerialNumber	Serial number assigned to the BIOS by the manufacturer.
SMBIOSVersion	BIOS version as reported by SMBIOS.
SMBIOSMajorVersion	Major SMBIOS version number.
SMBIOSMinorVersion	Minor SMBIOS version number.
SMBIOSPresent	Indicates whether the SMBIOS is available on this computer.
Version	Version of the BIOS.

Some, but not all, of this information is also available through the System Information snap-in, as shown in Figure 8.2.

Figure 8.2   Win32_BIOS Properties and System Information

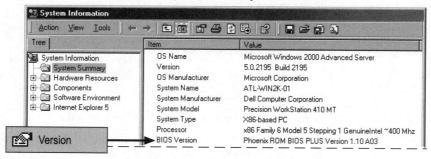

Scripting Steps

Listing 8.2 contains a script that retrieves BIOS information for a computer. To carry out this task, the script must perform the following steps:

1. Create a variable to specify the computer name.

2. Use a GetObject call to connect to the WMI namespace root\cimv2, and set the impersonation level to "impersonate."

3. Use the ExecQuery method to query the Win32_BIOS class.

   This query returns a collection consisting of a single object representing the BIOS installed on the computer.

4. For each BIOS in the collection, echo the retrieved values.

Because the BIOS characteristics are contained within an array, a For Each loop must be used to loop through each element in the array.

Listing 8.2 Retrieving BIOS Information

```
1   strComputer = "."
2   Set objWMIService = GetObject("winmgmts:" _
3       & "{impersonationLevel=impersonate}!\\" & strComputer & "\root\cimv2")
4   Set colBIOS = objWMIService.ExecQuery _
5       ("SELECT * FROM Win32_BIOS")
6   For Each objBIOS in colBIOS
7       Wscript.Echo "Build Number: " & objBIOS.BuildNumber
8       Wscript.Echo "Current Language: " & objBIOS.CurrentLanguage
9       Wscript.Echo "Installable Languages: " & objBIOS.InstallableLanguages
10      Wscript.Echo "Manufacturer: " & objBIOS.Manufacturer
11      Wscript.Echo "Name: " & objBIOS.Name
12      Wscript.Echo "Primary BIOS: " & objBIOS.PrimaryBIOS
13      Wscript.Echo "Release Date: " & objBIOS.ReleaseDate
14      Wscript.Echo "Serial Number: " & objBIOS.SerialNumber
15      Wscript.Echo "SMBIOS Version: " & objBIOS.SMBIOSBIOSVersion
16      Wscript.Echo "SMBIOS Major Version: " & objBIOS.SMBIOSMajorVersion
17      Wscript.Echo "SMBIOS Minor Version: " & objBIOS.SMBIOSMinorVersion
18      Wscript.Echo "SMBIOS Present: " & objBIOS.SMBIOSPresent
19      Wscript.Echo "Status: " & objBIOS.Status
20      Wscript.Echo "Version: " & objBIOS.Version
21      For Each intCharacteristic in objBIOS.BiosCharacteristics
22          Wscript.Echo "BIOS Characteristics: " & intCharacteristic
23      Next
24  Next
```

Retrieving Identifying Information by Using the SMBIOS

Computers are typically identified by name. This practice provides a convenient way to distinguish one computer from another, but it is not always sufficient for uniquely identifying computers; after all, computer names are easily, and often, changed. To track individual computers, you should always use a more immutable identifier, such as the serial number or the asset tag number.

The SMBIOS specification enables manufacturers to store extended information in the BIOS, including unique identifiers such as the serial number and the asset tag number. Retrieving the serial number or the asset tag number can help identify a specific computer. For example, each computer has a unique serial number that does not change unless the BIOS is replaced. Because you are far less likely to replace a BIOS than to rename a computer, the BIOS serial number provides a good way to identify computers.

Identifying information such as serial number and asset tag can be retrieved from a computer by using the WMI Win32_SystemEnclosure class.

 Note

A number of third-party tools can also retrieve extended BIOS information. However, most of these tools are hardware-specific; before the SMBIOS specifications were completed, many hardware manufacturers stored the serial number and asset tag in nonstandard formats. The Win32_SystemEnclosure class can generally retrieve this information, even if it has been stored in a nonstandard way.

Table 8.3 lists the SMBIOS-related properties of the Win32_SystemEnclosure class.

Table 8.3   Win32_SystemEnclosure Properties

Property	Description
PartNumber	Part number assigned by the organization responsible for producing or manufacturing the computer.
SerialNumber	Manufacturer-allocated number used to identify the computer.
SKU	Stock-keeping unit number for the computer.
SMBIOSAssetTag	Asset tag number of the computer.

Scripting Steps

Listing 8.3 contains a script that retrieves identifying information for a computer. To carry out this task, the script must perform the following steps:

1. Create a variable to specify the computer name.

2. Use a GetObject call to connect to the WMI namespace root\cimv2, and set the impersonation level to "impersonate."

3. Use the ExecQuery method to query the Win32_SystemEnclosure class.

   This query returns a collection consisting of the physical properties of the computer and its housing.

4. Echo the values for PartNumber, SerialNumber, and SMBIOSAssetTag.

Listing 8.3 Retrieving Identifying Information

```
1   strComputer = "."
2   Set objWMIService = GetObject("winmgmts:" _
3       & "{impersonationLevel=impersonate}!\\" & strComputer & "\root\cimv2")
4   Set colSMBIOS = objWMIService.ExecQuery _
5       ("SELECT * FROM Win32_SystemEnclosure")
6   For Each objSMBIOS in colSMBIOS
7       Wscript.Echo "Part Number: " & objSMBIOS.PartNumber
8       Wscript.Echo "Serial Number: " & objSMBIOS.SerialNumber
9       Wscript.Echo "Asset Tag: " & objSMBIOS.SMBIOSAssetTag
10  Next
```

Inventorying Computer Hardware

The inventory process helps determine the number of computers in your organization and how these computers have been configured. This type of information can be very useful in a number of situations:

- Preparing to upgrade to a new operating system or a new software package.

  The inventory helps determine which computers have hardware that is compatible with the new produc. It also helps you determine whether these computers have sufficient hardware resources to run the new product.

- Planning the information technology budget.

  The inventory helps determine which computers have adequate hardware to last through the next budget period and which computers require hardware upgrades or need to be replaced.

- Replacing computers in an organization.

  The inventory helps determine which hardware can be used elsewhere in the organization and which hardware cannot.

- Taking help desk calls from users.

  The inventory helps determine the hardware configuration of a user's computer. This kind of information is important for help desk personnel trying to remotely diagnose and resolve computer problems.

WMI contains many classes that enable you to retrieve detailed information about computer hardware. For example, Table 8.4 lists hardware categories that can be retrieved either by using the System Information snap-in or by using the equivalent WMI classes.

Table 8.4   System Information Categories and Their WMI Equivalents

System Information Category	WMI Class
CD-ROM	Win32_CDRomDrive
Sound Device	Win32_SoundDevice
Display	Win32_VideoController
Infrared	Win32_InfraredDevice
Keyboard	Win32_Keyboard
Pointing Device	Win32_PointingDevice
Modem	Win32_POTSModem
Network Adapter	Win32_NetworkAdapter
Serial Ports	Win32_SerialPort
Parallel Ports	Win32_ParallelPort
Drives	Win32_DiskDrive
SCSI	Win32_SCSIController
Printers	Win32_Printer
USB	Win32_USBController

In addition to the classes listed in Table 8.4, a number of other WMI classes are useful in taking inventory of computer hardware. WMI classes exist for almost all hardware components on a computer. (However, there are proprietary hardware devices that do not support WMI.) Some of these classes are listed in Table 8.5.

Table 8.5   Additional WMI Classes for Retrieving Hardware Information

WMI Class	Description
Win32_Baseboard	Provides information about the computer motherboard (also known as the baseboard or system board). The motherboard contains the bus, the processor and coprocessor sockets, memory sockets, keyboard controller, and other electrical components.
Win32_Bus	Provides information about the internal bus. The bus allows the computer to transfer data between the central processing unit, system memory, and peripheral buses.
Win32_DesktopMonitor	Provides information about the monitor or display device used by the computer.
Win32_Fan	Provides information about fans, including the CPU cooling device, installed in the computer.
Win32_PhysicalMemory	Provides information regarding physical memory devices installed in the computer.
Win32_PNPEntity	Provides information about all Plug and Play devices installed in the computer. Plug and Play devices are hardware devices that conform to the Plug and Play standard, allowing them to be installed on a computer without the need for manual configuration.
Win32_Processor	Provides information about each processor installed on a computer.

The information available through the various WMI classes is almost identical to the hardware information available using graphical user interface (GUI) tools. For example, Figure 8.3 compares the Win32_PointingDevice class with the data available in the System Information snap-in.

Figure 8.3   Win32_PointingDevice and System Information

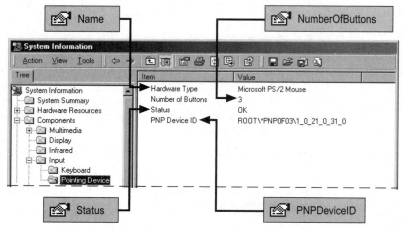

Taking Inventory of Computer Hardware

Although different hardware settings must be accessed through different WMI classes, the scripting approach is identical in each case:

1. Your script connects to the WMI service on the computer to be inventoried.

2. Your script connects to the appropriate WMI class.

    For example, if you want a list of CD-ROM drives, you should connect to the Win32_CDROMDrive class. If you want information about display adapters, you should connect to the Win32_VideoController class.

3. For each item in the returned collection (that is, each installed CD-ROM drive or each installed display adapter), retrieve the desired properties.

One nice feature of WMI is the fact that no error condition occurs if you attempt to enumerate hardware that does not exist. For example, suppose you are trying to inventory tape drives, and no tape drive exists on a particular computer. This is not a problem; you will still receive a collection of the tape drives on that computer. The only difference is that the collection will have no items in it.

Of course, you do not receive any "official" notice that the computer does not have any tape drives; you have to infer this from the fact that no tape drive information was returned. To help verify that the computer does not have any tape drives, you can use the Count property to check the number of items in the collection. If the Count is 0, you can echo the message, No tape drives were found in this computer. If the Count is greater than 0, you can then report the property values for each tape drive.

The following code sample uses the Count property to identify zero-item collections:

```
If colTapeDrives.Count = 0 Then
    Wscript.Echo "No tape drives were found in this computer."
Else
    For Each objTapeDrive in colTapeDrives
        Wscript.Echo objTapeDrive.Name
    Next
End If
```

Scripting Steps

Listing 8.4 contains a script that retrieves the hardware inventory for a computer. In this script, information is retrieved for only a single hardware category: the pointing device. To retrieve information about additional hardware categories, the script would need to connect to each additional hardware class (for example, Win32_SoundDevice) and retrieve the appropriate property values.

To carry out this task, the script must perform the following steps:

1. Create a variable to specify the computer name.

2. Use a GetObject call to connect to the WMI namespace root\cimv2, and set the impersonation level to "impersonate."

3. Use the ExecQuery method to query the Win32_PointingDevice class.

This query returns a collection of all the pointing devices (mice, trackballs, and similar hardware) installed on the computer.

4. For each pointing device in the collection, echo the values for the hardware type, number of buttons, pointing device status, and Plug and Play device ID.

 Note

In a production script, you would probably save the inventory information from multiple computers to a database or text file rather than echoing it to the screen. For more information about saving data, see "Creating Enterprise Scripts" in this book.

Listing 8.4   Inventorying Computer Hardware

```
1   strComputer = "."
2   Set objWMIService = GetObject("winmgmts:" _
3       & "{impersonationLevel=impersonate}!\\" & strComputer & "\root\cimv2")
4   Set colMice = objWMIService.ExecQuery _
5       ("SELECT * FROM Win32_PointingDevice")
6   For Each objMouse in colMice
7       Wscript.Echo "Hardware Type: " & objMouse.HardwareType
8       Wscript.Echo "Number of Buttons: " & objMouse.NumberOfButtons
9       Wscript.Echo "Status: " & objMouse.Status
10      Wscript.Echo "PNP Device ID: " & objMouse.PNPDeviceID
11  Next
```

Identifying the Chassis Type of a Computer

The chassis is the physical container that houses the components of a computer. Chassis types include the tower configuration, desktop computer, notebook computer, and handheld computer.

At first glance, it might seem that the chassis type is interesting information but of minimal use to system administrators. In truth, however, knowing the physical design of the chassis provides valuable information for system administrators. After all, the physical design is a key factor in determining the type of hardware you can install on the computer; for example, disk drives that can be installed on a desktop computer are unlikely to fit in a subnotebook computer.

Knowing the chassis type of a computer can also be important for:

- **Applying Group Policy.** Group Policy is often applied differently to computers with some chassis types. For example, software is typically installed in full on notebook computers rather than simply installed on first use. This ensures that a mobile user has available all the features of the software package.

- **Planning hardware upgrades.** A computer that is going to be upgraded must be able to support the intended upgrade. Hard disks and network adapters designed for desktop computers do not work on notebook computers.

- **Planning hardware moves.** If space is limited, you might prefer moving a mini-tower computer to a particular area rather than a full tower computer.

Traditionally, the only way to identify the chassis type has been by visual inspection. However, the Win32_SystemEnclosure class can be used to determine the chassis type of a computer. Chassis types are stored as an array consisting of one or more of the values shown in Table 8.6.

Table 8.6   Computer Chassis Values

Value	Description
1	Other
2	Unknown
3	Desktop
4	Low Profile Desktop
5	Pizza Box
6	Mini Tower
7	Tower
8	Portable
9	Laptop
10	Notebook
11	Hand Held
12	Docking Station
13	All in One
14	Sub Notebook
15	Space-Saving
16	Lunch Box
17	Main System Chassis
18	Expansion Chassis
19	Sub Chassis
20	Bus Expansion Chassis
21	Peripheral Chassis
22	Storage Chassis
23	Rack Mount Chassis
24	Sealed-Case PC

Scripting Steps

Listing 8.5 contains a script that identifies computer chassis type. To carry out this task, the script must perform the following steps:

1. Create a variable to specify the computer name.

2. Use a GetObject call to connect to the WMI namespace root\cimv2, and set the impersonation level to "impersonate."

3. Use the ExecQuery method to query the Win32_SystemEnclosure class.

   This query returns a collection consisting of the physical properties of the computer and its housing.

4. For each set of physical properties in the collection, echo the chassis type.

   To do this, you must set up a For-Next loop to echo the values for the chassis type. The For-Next loop is required because the chassis type is stored as an array.

Listing 8.5   Identifying Computer Chassis Type

```
1   strComputer = "."
2   Set objWMIService = GetObject("winmgmts:" _
3       & "{impersonationLevel=impersonate}!\\" & strComputer & "\root\cimv2")
4   Set colChassis = objWMIService.ExecQuery _
5       ("SELECT * FROM Win32_SystemEnclosure")
6   For Each objChassis in colChassis
7       For Each intType in objChassis.ChassisTypes
8           Wscript.Echo intType
9       Next
10  Next
```

When the script in Listing 8.5 runs, the chassis type is reported as an integer. For example, if the computer has a mini-tower configuration, the value 6 is echoed to the screen. In a production script, a Select Case statement should be used to echo back string values as shown in the following code sample:

```
Case 6
Wscript.Echo "This computer is configured as a mini-tower."
```

Managing Operating Systems

Many management activities require you to know which version of the Windows operating system is installed on a computer. Among other things, this knowledge helps you ensure that:

- Service packs, hot fixes, and other operating system upgrades are applied to all computers requiring these updates.

- Software installations and upgrades are targeted only toward computers with operating systems that support the software.

- Support personnel can better answer questions and respond to problems.

Scripts can identify the operating system installed on a computer and can provide additional details about that operating system, including such things as build number and language. Scripts can also identify service packs, hot fixes, and other operating system upgrades that have been installed since the operating system was first configured.

Identifying the Name and Version Number of the Operating System

Operating systems vary in the capabilities they support; newer operating systems typically support more features and have more capabilities than older operating systems. For example, scripts that run on a Windows 2000 operating system might not run on an earlier version of Windows. This is because many new WMI classes were introduced in Windows 2000.

You can use the WMI Win32_OperatingSystem class to return both the name and the version number of the operating system running on a computer. For example, the following information is returned from a computer running Windows 2000 Professional:

```
Microsoft Windows 2000 Professional 5.0.2600
```

The kind of information you need to collect can affect whether you need to retrieve both the name and the version number. To distinguish between products with different names, you can retrieve either the product name or the version number. To distinguish between products with the same version number, you must retrieve the name.

Table 8.7 lists the names and version numbers for a selected subset of Windows operating systems.

Table 8.7   Windows Operating System Names and Version Numbers

Name	Version Number
Microsoft Windows 2000 Professional	5.0.2195
Microsoft Windows 2000 Server	5.0.2195
Microsoft® Windows® XP Home Edition	5.1.2600
Microsoft® Windows® XP Professional	5.1.2600

The properties of the WMI Win32_OperatingSystem class used to retrieve the operating system name and version number of each operating system installed on a computer are listed in Table 8.8.

Table 8.8   Win32_OperatingSystem Properties

Property	Description
Caption	Name of the operating system.
Version	Version number of the operating system.

Scripting Steps

Listing 8.6 contains a script that identifies the name and version number of the operating system installed on a computer. To carry out this task, the script must perform the following steps:

1. Create a variable to specify the computer name.

2. Use a GetObject call to connect to the WMI namespace root\cimv2, and set the impersonation level to "impersonate."

3. Use the ExecQuery method to query the Win32_OperatingSystem class.

   This query returns a collection consisting of all the operating systems installed on the computer.

4. For each operating system in the collection, echo the name and version number.

Listing 8.6   Identifying the Name and Version Number of the Operating System

```
1  strComputer = "."
2  Set objWMIService = GetObject("winmgmts:" _
3      & "{impersonationLevel=impersonate}!\\" & strComputer & "\root\cimv2")
4  Set colOperatingSystems = objWMIService.ExecQuery _
5      ("SELECT * FROM Win32_OperatingSystem")
6  For Each objOperatingSystem in colOperatingSystems
7      Wscript.Echo objOperatingSystem.Caption, objOperatingSystem.Version
8  Next
```

Retrieving the Properties of the Operating System

Even though the operating systems on two different computers might have the same name and version number, those two operating systems can still differ. They might be configured with different language settings, support different encryption levels, or have different client licensing requirements.

Many differences between similar computers are reflected in the detailed property settings of their operating systems. These property settings can greatly affect the way each computer should be managed. For example, you might send a different technician to work on a computer running a Japanese version of a Windows 2000 operating system than you would send to work on a computer running a French version.

The WMI Win32_OperatingSystem class can be used to retrieve details of the operating system installed on a computer.

 Important

Unfortunately, WMI can retrieve information only about the operating system currently being used by a computer. For example, suppose you have a dual-boot computer with Windows XP and Windows 2000 installed, and the computer is currently running under Windows XP. If you run a script to return information about the operating system, only information for Windows XP will be returned.

Some of the more commonly used properties from this class are listed in Table 8.9.

Table 8.9   Win32_OperatingSystem Properties

Property	Description
BootDevice	Name of the disk drive from which the Win32 operating system boots.
BuildNumber	Build number of the operating system. The build number can be used for more precise versioning information than product release version numbers. For example, 2195 is the build number for the released version of Windows 2000.
BuildType	Type of build used for the operating system. The two primary build types are retail (the build purchased through a software vendor), and checked (test versions of the operating system that include special code to aid in debugging).
Caption	Name of the operating system.

(continued)

Table 8.9   Win32_OperatingSystem Properties *(continued)*

Property	Description
CodeSet	Code page value used by the operating system.
	A code page contains a character table used by the operating system to translate strings for different languages. The American National Standards Institute (ANSI) lists values that represent defined code pages. If the operating system does not use an ANSI code page, this member will be set to 0. The CodeSet string can use up to six characters to define the code page value. For example, the code page value for US English is 1252.
CountryCode	Code for the country/region used by the operating system.
	Values are based on international phone dialing prefixes (also referred to as IBM country/region codes). The property can use up to six characters to define the country/region code value. For example, the country code for the United States is 1.
Debug	Operating system is a checked (debugged) build.
	Checked builds provide error checking, argument verification, and system debugging code. Additional code in a checked binary generates a kernel debugger error message and breaks into the debugger. This helps to immediately determine the cause and location of the error. Performance suffers in the checked build because of the additional code that must be executed. In general, checked builds should be used on test computers, not production computers.
InstallDate	Date the operating system was installed, in UTC format.
NumberOfLicensedUsers	Number of user licenses for the operating system. If unlimited, this is returned as 0. If unknown, this is usually returned as –1.
Organization	Company name of the registered user of the operating system.
OSProductSuite	Installed and licensed system product additions to the operating system. Values include the following: 1 – Small Business Server 2 – Enterprise Server 4 – Back Office Server 8 – Communication Server 16 – Terminal Server 32 – Small Business Server (restricted) 64 – Embedded NT 128 – Data Center

(continued)

Table 8.9   Win32_OperatingSystem Properties *(continued)*

Property	Description
OSType	Type of operating system. The most common values include: 16 = WIN95 17 = WIN98 18 = WINNT 19 = WINCE The value 18 (WINNT) is returned as the OsType for Windows 2000 and Windows XP.
Primary	Boolean value that indicates whether this is the primary operating system. This property is meaningful only on multiple-boot computers that have more than one operating system installed.
RegisteredUser	Name of the registered user of the operating system.
SerialNumber	Serial identification number of the operating system.
Version	Version number of the operating system (for example, 4.0).

Scripting Steps

Listing 8.7 contains a script that retrieves the properties of the operating system currently in use on a computer. To carry out this task, the script must perform the following steps:

1. Create a variable to specify the computer name.

2. Use a GetObject call to connect to the WMI namespace root\cimv2, and set the impersonation level to "impersonate."

3. Use the ExecQuery method to query the Win32_OperatingSystem class.

This query returns a collection consisting of the operating system currently in use on the computer.

4. For the only operating system in the collection, echo the values for the specified properties.

Listing 8.7   Retrieving the Properties of the Operating System

```
1   strComputer = "."
2   Set objWMIService = GetObject("winmgmts:" _
3       & "{impersonationLevel=impersonate}!\\" & strComputer & "\root\cimv2")
4   Set colOperatingSystems = objWMIService.ExecQuery _
5       ("SELECT * FROM Win32_OperatingSystem")
6   For Each objOperatingSystem in colOperatingSystems
7       Wscript.Echo "Boot Device: " & objOperatingSystem.BootDevice
8       Wscript.Echo "Build Number: " & objOperatingSystem.BuildNumber
9       Wscript.Echo "Build Type: " & objOperatingSystem.BuildType
10      Wscript.Echo "Caption: " & objOperatingSystem.Caption
11      Wscript.Echo "Code Set: " & objOperatingSystem.CodeSet
12      Wscript.Echo "Country Code: " & objOperatingSystem.CountryCode
13      Wscript.Echo "Debug: " & objOperatingSystem.Debug
14      Wscript.Echo "Install Date: " & objOperatingSystem.InstallDate
15      Wscript.Echo "Licensed Users: " & _
16          objOperatingSystem.NumberOfLicensedUsers
17      Wscript.Echo "Organization: " & objOperatingSystem.Organization
18      Wscript.Echo "OS Language: " & objOperatingSystem.OSLanguage
19      Wscript.Echo "OS Product Suite: " & objOperatingSystem.OSProductSuite
20      Wscript.Echo "OS Type: " & objOperatingSystem.OSType
21      Wscript.Echo "Primary: " & objOperatingSystem.Primary
22      Wscript.Echo "Registered User: " & objOperatingSystem.RegisteredUser
23      Wscript.Echo "Serial Number: " & objOperatingSystem.SerialNumber
24      Wscript.Echo "Version: " & objOperatingSystem.Version
25  Next
```

Identifying the Latest Installed Service Pack

Service packs represent changes that have been made to the base operating system since the time the operating system was first released. These changes can include fixes to known problems, updates to device drivers, new tools, and enhanced functionality.

Knowing which service packs have been installed on a computer is important for several reasons. For example:

- Many hot fixes or software updates cannot be installed unless a particular service pack has previously been installed on a computer.

  Hot fixes (code fixes released to address specific problems in the operating system) are generally tied to a service pack, meaning the service pack must be installed before the hot fix can be applied. Before you can apply hot fixes or other software updates, you might need to know whether a particular service pack has been installed on a computer.

- Technical support personnel (including those from Microsoft Product Support Service) need to know which service packs have been installed when troubleshooting problems.

Service packs are released on an as-needed basis and are cumulative. For example, when Service Pack 3 for a version of Windows is released, it contains all the updates that were included in Service Packs 1 and 2. Installing Service Pack 3 provides all the benefits of the new service pack as well as those of the first two service packs.

The version number of the latest service pack installed on a computer can be retrieved using the Win32_OperatingSystem class. The Win32_OperatingSystem class cannot retrieve the version number of previously installed service packs. However, because all the fixes and functionality found in previous service packs are included in the latest service pack, you will be able to determine the actual code base of the operating system. The code base consists of the operating system (for example, Windows 2000 Professional 5.0.2195) plus any service packs that have been used to upgrade that operating system.

 Note

If it is important for auditing purposes to know whether previous service packs were installed, you can use WMI to query the System Event Log for all instances of event 4359. An event with this event code is written to the System Event Log each time a service pack or hot fix is installed.

Two service pack–related properties are available through the Win32_OperatingSystem class. These two properties are shown in Table 8.10.

Table 8.10 Win32_OperatingSystem Service Pack Properties

Property	Description
ServicePackMajorVersion	Major version of the latest service pack installed on the computer. If the latest service pack is 4 or 4a, the major version is 4. If no service pack has been installed, this value is 0.
ServicePackMinorVersion	Minor version of the latest service pack installed on the computer. If the latest service pack is 4a, the minor version is a. If the latest service pack is 4, there is no minor version. To ensure that you identify the proper service pack, you must check both the major version and the minor version.

Scripting Steps

Listing 8.8 contains a script that identifies the latest service pack installed on a computer. To carry out this task, the script must perform the following steps:

1. Create a variable to specify the computer name.

2. Use a GetObject call to connect to the WMI namespace root\cimv2, and set the impersonation level to "impersonate."

3. Use the ExecQuery method to query the Win32_OperatingSystem class.

   This query returns a collection consisting of the operating system currently in use on the computer.

4. Echo the values of the service pack major version and the service pack minor version.

Listing 8.8 Identifying the Latest Installed Service Pack

```
1  strComputer = "."
2  Set objWMIService = GetObject("winmgmts:" _
3      & "{impersonationLevel=impersonate}!\\" & strComputer & "\root\cimv2")
4  Set colOperatingSystems = objWMIService.ExecQuery _
5      ("SELECT * FROM Win32_OperatingSystem")
6  For Each objOperatingSystem in colOperatingSystems
7      Wscript.Echo objOperatingSystem.ServicePackMajorVersion _
8          & "." & objOperatingSystem.ServicePackMinorVersion
9  Next
```

Enumerating Installed Hot Fixes

A hot fix is a temporary operating system patch produced by the Quick Fix Engineering group at Microsoft. Like service packs, hot fixes represent changes that have been made to a version of Windows after the operating system has been released.

Unlike service packs, hot fixes are not intended for blanket installation on all computers. Instead, they are developed to address very specific problems, often for specific computer configurations. For example, the hot fix Q278438 should be installed only on computers running the Japanese version of Windows 2000 and Adobe PageMaker 6.53 and using a PostScript printer.

In addition, hot fixes represent independent installations that do not depend on other released hot fixes. For example, a hypothetical hot fix 4 would not include the bug fixes and functionality included in hot fixes 1, 2, and 3. In most cases, there would also be no requirement that you install hot fixes 1, 2, and 3 before installing hot fix 4. This makes enumeration of individual hot fixes an important administrative task: to know the exact configuration of a computer, you need to know not only which service packs have been installed but also which individual hot fixes have been installed.

The Win32_QuickFixEngineering class enables you to enumerate all the hot fixes that have been installed on a computer. Table 8.11 lists some of the hot fix properties that can be returned using the Win32_QuickFixEngineering class.

Table 8.11   Win32_QuickFixEngineering Properties

Property	Description
CSName	Local name of the computer system.
Description	Description of the hot fix.
HotFixID	Unique identifier associated with a particular hot fix.
InstallDate	Date the hot fix was installed.
InstalledBy	Person who installed the update.

Scripting Steps

Listing 8.9 contains a script that enumerates the installed hot fixes on a computer. To carry out this task, the script must perform the following steps:

1. Create a variable to specify the computer name.

2. Use a GetObject call to connect to the WMI namespace root\cimv2, and set the impersonation level to "impersonate."

3. Use the ExecQuery method to query the Win32_QuickFixEngineering class.

   This query returns a collection consisting of all the hot fixes installed on the computer.

4. For each hot fix installed on the computer, echo the values for properties such as hot fix description, hot fix ID, and the date the hot fix was installed.

Listing 8.9   Enumerating Installed Hot Fixes

```
1   strComputer = "."
2   Set objWMIService = GetObject("winmgmts:" _
3       & "{impersonationLevel=impersonate}!\\" & strComputer & "\root\cimv2")
4   Set colQuickFixes = objWMIService.ExecQuery _
5       ("SELECT * FROM Win32_QuickFixEngineering")
6   For Each objQuickFix in colQuickFixes
7       Wscript.Echo "Computer: " & objQuickFix.CSName
8       Wscript.Echo "Description: " & objQuickFix.Description
9       Wscript.Echo "Hot Fix ID: " & objQuickFix.HotFixID
10      Wscript.Echo "Installation Date: " & objQuickFix.InstallDate
11      Wscript.Echo "Installed By: " & objQuickFix.InstalledBy
12  Next
```

Managing WMI Settings

WMI is an example of a *self-instrumented* service. This simply means that you can use WMI scripts to monitor, configure, and control the WMI service. In fact, WMI scripts can be used to enumerate and configure the following items:

- Logging level, file size, and logging folder for the WMI service

- Backup interval for the WMI repository

- WMI time-out values

- Default WMI namespace

The WMI service exposes many of its properties through the Win32_WMISetting class. You can write scripts to return information regarding the configuration of WMI on a computer, such as the error logging level, the location of the WMI repository, or a list of .mof files that will automatically be reinstalled if the repository becomes corrupted.

Table 8.12 includes some of the more commonly used properties found in the Win32_WMISetting class.

Table 8.12 Win32_WMISetting Properties

Property	Description
ASPScriptDefaultNamespace	Default script namespace. Contains the namespace used by calls from the WMI Scripting API if one is not specified by the caller. On most computers, the default namespace is root\cimV2.
AutoRecoverMOFs	List of fully qualified Managed Object Format (MOF) file names used to initialize or recover the WMI repository. The list determines the order in which MOF files are compiled.
BackupInterval	Length of time that will elapse between backups of the WMI database.
BackupLastTime	Time that the last backup of the WMI repository was performed.
BuildVersion	Version information for the currently installed WMI service. For Windows 2000, the build version is 1085.0005.
DatabaseDirectory	Directory path for the WMI repository.
EnableEvents	Indicates whether or not the WMI event subsystem is enabled.
HighThresholdOnClientObjects	Maximum rate at which provider-created objects can be delivered to clients. To accommodate speed differentials between providers and clients, WMI holds objects in queues before delivering them to consumers. WMI slows down the addition of new objects into the queue when the low threshold is reached. If this does not help, and high threshold (specified by this property) is reached, WMI accepts no more objects from providers and returns an out-of-memory error to the clients.
HighThresholdOnEvents	Maximum rate at which events are to be delivered to clients. To accommodate speed differentials between providers and clients, WMI queues events before delivering them to consumers. WMI slows down the addition of new events into the queue when the low threshold is reached. If this does not help, and high threshold (specified by this property) is reached, WMI accepts no more events from providers and returns an out-of-memory error to the clients.

(continued)

Table 8.12   Win32_WMISetting Properties *(continued)*

Property	Description
LoggingDirectory	Directory path to the WMI system log files.
LoggingLevel	Indicates whether event logging is enabled and the level of logging used. Values include: 0 – No logging 1 – Error logging 2 – Verbose error logging
LowThresholdOnClientObjects	Rate at which WMI starts to slow the creation of new objects created for clients. To accommodate speed differentials between providers and clients, WMI holds objects in queues before delivering them to consumers. If the rate of requests for objects grows out of control, WMI gradually slows down the creation of new objects to match the rate used by the client. This slowdown starts when the rate at which objects are being created exceeds the value of this property. The slowdown continues until equilibrium is achieved or the high threshold is reached.
LowThresholdOnEvents	Rate at which WMI starts to slow the delivery of new events. To accommodate speed differentials between providers and clients, WMI queues events before delivering them to consumers. If the queue grows out of control, WMI slows down the delivery of events gradually to get them in line with the rate used by the client. This slowdown starts when the rate at which events are generated exceeds the value of this property. The slowdown continues until either the equilibrium is achieved or the high threshold is reached.
MaxLogFileSize	Maximum size of the log files produced by the WMI service.
MaxWaitOnClientObjects	Amount of time a newly created object waits to be used by the client before it is discarded and an error value is returned.
MaxWaitOnEvents	Amount of time for which an event sent to a client is queued before being discarded.
MOFSelfInstallDirectory	Directory path for applications that install MOF files to the WMI repository. WMI automatically compiles any MOF files placed in this directory and, depending on its success, moves the MOF to a subdirectory labeled good or bad.

Enumerating WMI Settings

Knowing how WMI is configured on a computer can be very useful when you are debugging scripts or troubleshooting problems with the WMI service itself. For example, many WMI scripts are written under the assumption that root\cimv2 is the default namespace on the target computer. As a result, script writers who need to access a class in root\cimv2 often fail to include the namespace in the GetObject moniker, as shown in the following code sample:

```
Set colServices = GetObject("winmgmts:").ExecQuery _
    ("SELECT * FROM Win32_Service")
```

If root\cimv2 is not the default namespace on the target computer, this script will fail. To prevent this from happening, the namespace root\cimv2 must be included in the moniker, as shown in the following code sample:

```
Set colServices = GetObject("winmgmts:root\cimv2").ExecQuery _
    ("SELECT * FROM Win32_Service")
```

If the default namespace on the target computer is different from the namespace assumed by a script, the script will fail. On top of that, the user will be presented with the somewhat misleading error message "Invalid class." In truth, the failure is not because the class is invalid but because the class cannot be found in the default namespace. This is a difficult problem to troubleshoot, because you are likely to investigate possible problems with the class rather than problems with the namespace that was (or, in this case, was not) specified.

You can use the Win32_WMISetting class to determine how WMI has been configured on a computer. Configuration details such as the default namespace or the WMI build number can be useful in troubleshooting script problems. These settings also provide important administrative information such as how, or even whether, WMI errors are logged on a computer and which WMI providers will automatically be reloaded if you need to rebuild the WMI repository.

Scripting Steps

Listing 8.10 contains a script that enumerates WMI settings on a computer. To carry out this task, the script must perform the following steps:

1. Create a variable to specify the computer name.

2. Use a GetObject call to connect to the WMI namespace root\cimv2, and set the impersonation level to "impersonate."

3. Use the ExecQuery method to query the Win32_WMISetting class.

This query returns a collection consisting of the WMI configuration settings for the computer.

4. For each group of WMI settings in the collection, echo the value of the specified property.

Because the autorecover MOFs are stored in an array, a For Each loop must be used to enumerate each MOF.

Listing 8.10 Enumerating WMI Settings

```
1   strComputer = "."
2   Set objWMIService = GetObject("winmgmts:" _
3       & "{impersonationLevel=impersonate}!\\" & strComputer & "\root\cimv2")
4   Set colWMISettings = objWMIService.ExecQuery _
5       ("SELECT * FROM Win32_WMISetting")
6   For Each objWMISetting in colWMISettings
7       Wscript.Echo "Default namespace: " & _
8           objWMISetting.ASPScriptDefaultNamespace
9       Wscript.Echo "Backup interval: " & objWMISetting.BackupInterval
10      Wscript.Echo "Last backup: " & objWMISetting.BackupLastTime
11      Wscript.Echo "Build version: " & objWMISetting.BuildVersion
12      Wscript.Echo "Repository directory: " & _
13          objWMISetting.DatabaseDirectory
14      Wscript.Echo "Enable events: " & objWMISetting.EnableEvents
15      Wscript.Echo "High threshold on client objects: " & _
16          objWMISetting.HighThresholdOnClientObjects
17      Wscript.Echo "High threshold on events: " & _
18          objWMISetting.HighThresholdOnEvents
19      Wscript.Echo "Installation folder: " & _
20          objWMISetting.InstallationDirectory
21      Wscript.Echo "Logging folder: " & objWMISetting.LoggingDirectory
22      Wscript.Echo "Logging level: " & objWMISetting.LoggingLevel
23      Wscript.Echo "Low threshold on client objects: " & _
24          objWMISetting.LowThresholdOnClientObjects
25      Wscript.Echo "Low threshold on events: " & _
26          objWMISetting.LowThresholdOnEvents
27      Wscript.Echo "Maximum log file size: " & objWMISetting.MaxLogFileSize
28      Wscript.Echo "Maximum wait time on client objects: " & _
29          objWMISetting.MaxWaitOnClientObjects
30      Wscript.Echo "Maximum wait time on events: " & _
31          objWMISetting.MaxWaitOnEvents
32      Wscript.Echo "MOF Self-install folder: " & _
33          objWMISetting.MofSelfInstallDirectory
34      For Each strMOF in objWMISetting.AutorecoverMofs
35          Wscript.Echo "Autorecover MOF: " & strMOF
36      Next
37  Next
```

Configuring WMI Settings

The default WMI settings are adequate for most computers and most purposes. Under special circumstances, however, you might want to modify the WMI settings on a computer or a group of computers.

For example, a developer might want to configure WMI to log all errors for the purpose of collecting information that could help in debugging applications that use WMI. A system administrator might want to change the default namespace on the company's DNS servers from root\cimv2 to root\MicrosoftDNS. Using a script to change settings such as these is much faster than visiting each computer and manually reconfiguring the WMI service.

You can use the Win32_WMISetting class to reconfigure many of the WMI properties on a computer. Several of the configurable WMI settings are shown in Table 8.13.

Table 8.13 Configurable WMI Settings in the Win32_WMISetting Class

Property	Description
ASPScriptDefaultNamespace	Default script namespace. The default is root\cimv2. You must specify the entire namespace path, including root.
BackupInterval	Length of time that will elapse between backups of the WMI database. The default is 30 minutes.
EnableEvents	Boolean value indicating whether the WMI event subsystem is enabled. By default, EnableEvents is set to True.
HighThresholdOnClientObjects	Maximum rate at which provider-created objects can be delivered to clients. The default value is 20,000,000 objects per second.
HighThresholdOnEvents	Maximum rate at which events are to be delivered to clients. The default value is 2,000,000 event objects per second.
LoggingDirectory	Directory path to the WMI system log files. The default is *systemroot*\WBEM\Logs.
LoggingLevel	Indicates whether event logging is enabled and the verbosity level of logging used. By default, logging is disabled (set to 0). Values include: 0 – No logging 1 – Error logging 2 – Verbose error logging
LowThresholdOnClientObjects	Rate at which WMI starts to slow the creation of new objects created for clients. The default value is 10,000,000 objects per second.
LowThresholdOnEvents	Rate at which WMI starts to slow the delivery of new events. The default value is 1,000,000 event objects per second.

(continued)

Table 8.13   Configurable WMI Settings in the Win32_WMISetting Class *(continued)*

Property	Description
MaxLogFileSize	Maximum size of the log files produced by the WMI service. The default value is 65536 KB.
MaxWaitOnClientObjects	Amount of time a newly created object waits to be used by the client before it is discarded and an error value is returned. The default value is 60,000 milliseconds (60 seconds).
MaxWaitOnEvents	Amount of time for which an event sent to a client is queued before being discarded. The default value is 2,000 milliseconds (2 seconds).

Scripting Steps

Listing 8.11 contains a script that configures WMI settings on a computer. To carry out this task the script must perform the following steps:

1. Create a variable to specify the computer name.

2. Use a GetObject call to connect to the WMI namespace root\cimv2 and set the impersonation level to "impersonate."

3. Use a GetObject call to connect to the Win32_WMISetting class.

4. Set the BackupInterval property to 60 minutes.

5. Set the LoggingLevel to 2 (verbose).

6. Use the Put_ method to apply the changes.

Listing 8.11   Configuring WMI Settings

```
1   strComputer = "."
2   Set objWMIService = GetObject("winmgmts:" _
3       & "{impersonationLevel=impersonate}!\\" & strComputer & "\root\cimv2")
4   Set colWMISettings = objWMIService.ExecQuery _
5       ("SELECT * FROM Win32_WMISetting")
6   For Each objWMISetting in colWMISettings
7       objWMISetting.BackupInterval = 60
8       objWMISetting.LoggingLevel = 2
9       objWMISetting.Put_
10  Next
```

Managing Software

The *software life cycle* provides an administrative framework for managing software within your organization. In the software life cycle, software is:

- Installed
- Maintained
- Upgraded
- Removed

WMI scripts can be used to install, upgrade, or remove software. Although the Software Installation and Maintenance component of Group Policy remains the preferred method for carrying out these activities, there are occasions when a scripted deployment offers advantages over Group Policy. For example, software deployment changes made by using Software Installation and Maintenance take effect only when a computer is restarted or when a user logs on, not as part of the regular Group Policy refresh. This is done to prevent loss of data; for example, any number of problems could arise if a user were in the middle of editing a document with Microsoft Word at the very moment that a new Group Policy object began to remove Word from the computer.

 Note

A WMI script can also attempt to remove an application while that application is currently in use, which can lead to similar problems. Because of this, you might want to use the Win32_Process class to determine which applications are running before you install, upgrade, or remove software using WMI. For more information about the Win32_Process class, see "Processes" in this book.

A computer that is never restarted will never have this new Group Policy applied, and the software will never be installed, upgraded, or removed. WMI, by contrast, allows you to install, upgrade, or remove software without requiring a computer to be restarted or requiring a user to log off and then log back on.

WMI scripts can also carry out tasks such as taking inventory of all the software installed on a computer. Because Software Installation and Maintenance is not designed to perform tasks such as these, administrators have had to purchase and use third-party software to do such things as software inventory.

In addition, WMI enables you to monitor and manage the use of software in your organization, provided the software was installed by using the Windows Installer. Windows Installer, introduced in Windows 2000, represents a new and improved way to install software by using .msi files known as packages. These packages contain all the information necessary to set up an application in every conceivable situation. In addition, Windows Installer maintains a database on each computer detailing the software and software features that have been installed on that computer. WMI has the ability to access this database and report back on the software and software features present on a computer.

Enumerating Software

Taking inventory of the software installed on a computer is as important as taking inventory of the hardware installed on a computer. A software inventory helps you:

- Understand how computers are being used in your organization.

- Prevent problems associated with users running unauthorized software or software that is incompatible with other software used in your organization.

- Ensure compliance with software licensing agreements.

In the past, administrators taking software inventories had to purchase third-party tools or use a *brute force* approach to taking inventory. With the brute force approach, *all* the .exe and .com files on a computer (any files that potentially represent executable files for software programs) are retrieved. In most cases, this is far more information than you can use. For example, on a typical Windows 2000 Professional–based computer running Microsoft Office and several other software applications, the brute force approach returns 1,742 .exe files. The amount of data returned, and the fact that the only information returned is the file name, can make it hard to determine the actual (and perhaps most meaningful) software products that have been installed on the computer. Among the problems you face when trying to analyze this data are the following:

- Applications such as Microsoft Word are difficult to distinguish from self-extracting archive files or system files that might also have the .exe extension. In fact, the vast majority of the file names returned are operating system files that are essentially meaningless in an inventory. Very rarely will you be concerned with knowing whether or not Calc.exe or Attrib.exe is installed on all your computers.

  In addition, having an executable file on your computer does not mean that the application has been installed. You could have a file named Winword.exe yet not have Microsoft Word installed.

- File names might not provide enough information to identify a software program. Many executable file names have no obvious relationship to the name of the software. For example, is it a good thing or a bad thing that the files Qwinsta.exe and W32mkde.exe were found on your file server?

- Although a list of 1,742 files might be manageable when working with a single computer, when working with multiple computers the brute force method can result in a huge amount of data.

The WMI Win32_Product and Win32_SoftwareFeature classes allow you to enumerate the software and software features that have been installed on a computer using Windows Installer. Limiting enumeration to software installed by Windows Installer does not provide a complete inventory of the applications installed on a computer. However, this approach does offer several advantages over the brute force method:

- Data retrieval is held to a minimum.

  On the same Windows 2000–based test computer, a script listing only items that were installed using .msi files returned 77 records instead of the 1,742 items returned using the brute force approach.

- Data retrieval is limited to manageable software (software installed using Windows Installer).

- Data retrieval can include important details such as the software version number and a more meaningful description of the software (for example, Microsoft® Visual Studio® instead of Mse.exe).

- Data retrieval can include other items (such as scripts, templates, and help files) that were installed using Windows Installer but that do not have executable files. This can be extremely useful in organizations that have adopted the Windows Installer format and Group Policy as a way to push documents to user workstations.

Enumerating Installed Software

Knowing the software packages that have been installed on a computer is useful for many reasons. Among other things, this knowledge helps you:

- Gain insight into what the computer is used for. A computer that does not have a word processor installed is probably not used for writing memos or other documents.

- Ensuring that only licensed software, and only approved software, is in use in your organization. If your organization has decided to standardize on Microsoft Excel, it is very useful, for both support and legal reasons, to know whether anyone has installed a different spreadsheet program on a computer.

- Tracking the progress of software deployment projects (for example, the number of people who have installed this new application and the number of people who have not).

- Planning for future software needs.

These activities cannot be carried out using Group Policy because the Software Installation and Maintenance component does not provide information on the software installed on a computer; it only makes that software available for installation. For example, although the Software Installation and Maintenance component can publish a software package, it provides no way to track which users install that package. This makes it difficult to analyze actual software use or to make projections for future software needs.

The WMI Win32_Product class enables you to enumerate the software installed on a computer, provided the software was installed by using the Windows Installer. Selected properties available through the Win32_Product class are shown in Table 8.14.

Table 8.14   Win32_Product Properties

Property	Description
Caption	Short description of the object.
Description	Object description.
IdentifyingNumber	Product identification, such as a serial number on software.
InstallLocation	Location of the installed product.
InstallState	Installed state of the product. Values include: −6 − Bad configuration −2 − Invalid argument −1 − Unknown package 1 − Advertised 2 − Absent 6 − Installed
Name	Commonly used product name.
PackageCache	Location of the locally cached package for this product.
SKUNumber	Product SKU (stock-keeping unit) information.
Vendor	Name of the product's supplier.
Version	Product version information.

Scripting Steps

Listing 8.12 contains a script that enumerates the software installed on a computer and then saves the information to a text file. To carry out this task, the script must perform the following steps:

1. Create an instance of the FileSystem Object.

   This object will be used to write the retrieved software information to a text file.

2. Create the text file C:\Scripts\Software.tsv.

3. Write the field headers to the text file in tab-separated-values format.

   The VBScript constant VbTab is used to insert a tab character between each field header. The tab-separated-values format is used because software property values sometimes contain commas. If they do, these extra commas can make it difficult to parse a text file saved in comma-separated-values format.

4. Create a variable to specify the computer name.

5. Use a GetObject call to connect to the WMI namespace root\cimv2, and set the impersonation level to "impersonate."

6. Use the ExecQuery method to query the Win32_Product class.

    This query returns a collection consisting of all the software products installed on the computer.

7. For each software product installed on the computer, retrieve the property values for the application and write those values to the text file, separating each value using a tab character.

8. Close the text file.

Listing 8.12 Enumerating Installed Software

```
1   Set objFSO = CreateObject("Scripting.FileSystemObject")
2   Set objTextFile = objFSO.CreateTextFile("c:\scripts\software.tsv", True)
3   strComputer = "."
4   Set objWMIService = GetObject("winmgmts:" _
5       & "{impersonationLevel=impersonate}!\\" & strComputer & "\root\cimv2")
6   Set colSoftware = objWMIService.ExecQuery _
7       ("SELECT * FROM Win32_Product")
8   objTextFile.WriteLine "Caption" & vbtab & _
9       "Description" & vbtab & "Identifying Number" & vbtab & _
10      "Install Date" & vbtab & "Install Location" & vbtab & _
11      "Install State" & vbtab & "Name" & vbtab & _
12      "Package Cache" & vbtab & "SKU Number" & vbtab & "Vendor" & vbtab _
13          & "Version"
14  For Each objSoftware in colSoftware
15      objTextFile.WriteLine objSoftware.Caption & vbtab & _
16      objSoftware.Description & vbtab & _
17      objSoftware.IdentifyingNumber & vbtab & _
18      objSoftware.InstallLocation & vbtab & _
19      objSoftware.InstallState & vbtab & _
20      objSoftware.Name & vbtab & _
21      objSoftware.PackageCache & vbtab & _
22      objSoftware.SKUNumber & vbtab & _
23      objSoftware.Vendor & vbtab & _
24      objSoftware.Version
25  Next
26  objTextFile.Close
```

Enumerating Installed Software Features

Because much of the software developed today allows the user to choose which features to install, enumerating only the software packages might not provide a complete picture of the software installed on that computer. To obtain more detailed information about the software installed on a computer, you might need to enumerate the installed features of each software package, including such things as a dictionary, clip art, and design templates.

You can retrieve a list of software features by using the Win32_SoftwareFeature class. Some of the primary properties of this class are listed in Table 8.15.

Table 8.15 Win32_SoftwareFeature Properties

Property	Description
Accesses	Number of times the software feature has been used.
Attributes	Feature execution option. Values include: 0 — Install components locally if possible. 1 — Install components to run from the source CD/server if possible. 2 — Follow the remote execution option of the parent feature.
Caption	Short textual description of the object.
Description	Textual description of the object. In practice, this will often return the same value as Caption.
IdentifyingNumber	Product identification, such as a serial number.
InstallDate	Date the feature was installed.
InstallState	Installed state of the product. Values include: −6 — Bad configuration −2 — Invalid argument −1 — Unknown package 1 — Advertised 2 — Absent 3 — Local 4 — Source
LastUse	Date and time the software feature was last used. If the application has never been used, this date will typically be January 1, 1980.
Name	Label by which the object is known.
ProductName	Commonly used product name.
Vendor	Name of the product's supplier.
Version	Product version information.

Scripting Steps

Listing 8.13 contains a script that enumerates the software features installed on a computer. To carry out this task, the script must perform the following steps:

1. Create a variable to specify the computer name.

2. Use a GetObject call to connect to the WMI namespace root\cimv2, and set the impersonation level to "impersonate."

3. Use the ExecQuery method to query the Win32_SoftwareFeature class.

   This query returns a collection consisting of all the software features for all the software products installed on the computer.

4. For each feature in the collection, echo the appropriate properties.

Listing 8.13   Enumerating Installed Software Features

```
1   strComputer = "."
2   Set objWMIService = GetObject("winmgmts:" _
3       & "{impersonationLevel=impersonate}!\\" & strComputer & "\root\cimv2")
4   Set colFeatures = objWMIService.ExecQuery _
5       ("SELECT * FROM Win32_SoftwareFeature")
6   For each objFeature in colFeatures
7       Wscript.Echo "Accesses: " & objFeature.Accesses
8       Wscript.Echo "Attributes: " & objFeature.Attributes
9       Wscript.Echo "Caption: " & objFeature.Caption
10      Wscript.Echo "Description: " & objFeature.Description
11      Wscript.Echo "Identifying Number: " & objFeature.IdentifyingNumber
12      Wscript.Echo "Install Date: " & objFeature.InstallDate
13      Wscript.Echo "Install State: " & objFeature.InstallState
14      Wscript.Echo "Last Use: " & objFeature.LastUse
15      Wscript.Echo "Name: " & objFeature.Name
16      Wscript.Echo "Product Name: " & objFeature.ProductName
17      Wscript.Echo "Vendor: " & objFeature.Vendor
18      Wscript.Echo "Version: " & objFeature.Version
19  Next
```

Installing, Upgrading, and Removing Software

As part of the software life cycle, software must be installed, upgraded, and removed. These activities can be carried out using Software Installation and Maintenance. Sometimes, however, you might need to perform these actions without using Group Policy. For example, you might want to install, upgrade, or remove software:

- Without restarting the computer or without logging the user off and back on.

  The Software Installation and Maintenance component policies are refreshed only when a computer restarts or a user logs on. These policies are not affected by the automatic Group Policy refresh rate. If they were, you could encounter a scenario in which Group Policy attempts to remove an application while it is being used.

- On only one or two computers.

  Creating a Group Policy object (GPO) to manage software installation and maintenance on a single computer involves more administrative overhead than performing the activity directly on the computer. Applying Group Policy to a single computer would require you to:

  1. Create the Group Policy object.
  2. Create a security group.
  3. Add the computer as the sole member of the security group.
  4. Create a filter to ensure that the GPO is applied only to the new security group.
  5. Apply the GPO.

WMI provides the Win32_Product Install, Uninstall, and Upgrade methods to perform these tasks without using Group Policy and without restarting the computers.

Installing Software on the Local Computer

The ability to install software without using Group Policy can be an enormous boon to administrators; this allows you to install software without requiring user interaction and without requiring the user to log off and log on or the computer to restart. In addition, a WMI script can help ensure a successful installation by doing such things as checking for available memory or available disk space before beginning the installation process. If there is not enough memory or disk space on the target computer, your script can terminate without installing the software. This prevents any problems that can occur from attempting to install software on computers not capable of running that software.

The Win32_Product class includes an Install method that can be used to install software on the local computer. (In other words, the script physically resides on the computer where the software will be installed.) Software can also be installed on remote computers; however, because remote installation might require some additional configuration, the remote installation process is discussed in the next section of this chapter.

Regardless of whether the software is installed locally or remotely, the Install method requires three parameters:

- **PackageLocation.** Path to the Installer package, which is relative to the computer on which the software is being installed and which can be referenced using a Universal Naming Convention (UNC) path.

- **Options.** Command-line options required for installing the software. If no options are required, this parameter should be left blank.

- **AllUsers.** Boolean value that indicates whether the software should be available to all the users on a computer or just the currently logged-on user.

  - If set to True, the software will be installed under the All Users profile.

  - If set to False, the software will be installed under the profile of the user whose credentials are being used to run the script. For example, if the script is running under the Administrator account, the software will be installed under the Administrator profile and thus will not be accessible to other users.

Scripting Steps

Listing 8.14 contains a script that installs software for all users on a computer. To carry out this task, the script must perform the following steps:

1. Create a constant ALL_USERS and assign it the value True. This constant is used to install the software in the All Users profile.

2. Use a GetObject call to connect to the WMI service.

3. Retrieve an instance of the Win32_Product class.

4. Use the Install method to install the Windows Installer package. This method requires the following three parameters:

   - **C:\Scripts\Database.msi** — The location of the software package being installed

   - **Null** — Indicates that no command-line options are required to install the product

   - **ALL_USERS** — Constant (with the value True) that installs the software under the All Users profile

Listing 8.14 Installing Software

```
1  Const ALL_USERS = True
2  Set objService = GetObject("winmgmts:")
3  Set objSoftware = objService.Get("Win32_Product")
4  errReturn = objSoftware.Install("c:\scripts\database.msi", , ALL_USERS)
```

Installing Software on a Remote Computer

Installing software remotely frees technical support personnel for other duties (such as installing new hardware) that cannot be carried out remotely. Remote software installation also enables you to install software from a central site, without having to copy the scripts and the Installer packages to each computer. Although you can use WMI to install software on remote computers, you must be aware of the potential security issues involved in performing these remote installations.

When you use the Win32_Product class to install software on a remote computer, you might receive an `Access denied` error message, even though you have full administrative rights to the remote computer. This can occur in a scenario with three computers involved, as follows:

- You are running a script from your computer (Computer A).

- The script is designed to install software on a second computer (Computer B).

- The Windows Installer package for the software to be installed is stored on a third computer (Computer C).

The Access Denied error message occurs because of the way distributed security works in Windows 2000. When your script (running on Computer A) begins the software installation process, it connects to Computer B by using your user credentials. Assuming you are an administrator, you can perform any operation you want on Computer B. This is known as *single-hop* security because the security credentials used to start the script from your computer are being used on one remote computer (a single hop from your computer to the remote computer). If the installation process requires no more than two computers, then the software can be installed on a remote computer using the same procedure used to install software on the local computer.

However, suppose the Windows Installer package is located on a third computer, Computer C. To access the package, the WMI service on Computer B must connect to Computer C. This involves *multihop* security:

1. Computer A passes the script credentials to Computer B.

2. Computer B must then present security credentials to Computer C in order to access the Windows Installer package.

The problem occurs in step 2, when you might expect the script to present your security credentials. (This is multihop security because the credentials must pass through several points.) By default, multihop security is not supported in WMI scripting. This means that Computer B does not pass your security credentials on to Computer C. Instead, the WMI service makes this network connection using the LocalSystem account of Computer B. Because a LocalSystem account has no network credentials, it is denied access to the computer storing the Windows Installer package (Computer C). Because the package cannot be retrieved, the script fails.

By default, you can use your security credentials to connect to a remote computer. However, without additional configuration, that remote computer cannot use your security credentials to connect to a third computer. Default security is limited to a single hop.

There are several ways to work around this problem:

- Run the script using delegation, which allows remote Computer B to pass your user credentials to Computer C.

- Copy the Windows Installer package to the remote computer, and then install the software, referencing the local path. The script copies the Windows Installer package from Computer A to Computer B, installs the software, and then deletes the package. Security is then limited to a single hop.

  This method works, but it creates additional network traffic as the Windows Installer package is copied between computers.

- Allow the computer hosting the Windows Installer share to accept Null sessions.

  This method is not recommended because allowing a computer to accept Null sessions is a potential security risk: It opens the door for anyone on the network to connect to a computer.

Trusting Users and Computers for Delegation

To implement multihop security, you must do the following:

- Make sure that all the computers involved in the procedure have been trusted for delegation. This is a property of the Active Directory® directory service computer account.

- Make sure the user account that will be employed in the operation is also configured for delegation.

You can use Active Directory Users and Computers to trust both users and computers for delegation.

Scripting Steps

Listing 8.15 contains a script that installs software on a remote computer. Because this script installs software that is stored locally (and not on a third computer), delegation is not required.

To carry out this task, the script must perform the following steps:

1. Create a variable to specify the name of the remote computer (atl-dc-02).

2. Use a GetObject call to connect to the WMI namespace root\cimv2, and set the impersonation level to "impersonate."

3. Retrieve an instance of the Win32_Product class on the remote computer.

4. Install the software, referencing the local path where the Windows Installer package is stored.

5. Echo the success or failure of the installation.

Listing 8.15   Installing Software on a Remote Computer

```
1  strComputer = "atl-dc-02"
2  Set objWMIService = GetObject("winmgmts:" _
3      & "{impersonationLevel=impersonate}!\\" & strComputer & "\root\cimv2")
4  Set objSoftware = objWMIService.Get("Win32_Product")
5  errReturn = objSoftware.Install("c:\scripts\database.msi",,True)
6  Wscript.Echo errReturn
```

Upgrading Software

As new versions of a software package are released, you might need to upgrade existing copies of that software. These upgrades can be carried out using the Win32_Product Upgrade method.

The Upgrade method works only under the following conditions:

- It is used only with a software upgrade package.

  Upgrade packages are .msi files specifically designed to upgrade a previous version of the software. If you attempt to use a standard Windows Installer package with the Upgrade method, you will receive an error message 1636:

  This patch package could not be opened. Contact the application vendor to verify that this is a valid Windows Installer patch package.

- A previous version of the product is already installed.

  The Upgrade method will fail if a previous version of the software is not found. For example, to upgrade a computer from version 1 to version 2 of an application, version 1 must first be installed on that computer. If it is not, the upgrade will fail, and version 2 will not be installed.

In turn, the Upgrade method requires two parameters:

- **PackageLocation.** Path to the Windows Installer upgrade package, relative to the computer on which the software is being installed. The path can be referenced using UNC paths or mapped network drives.

- **Options.** Command-line options required for installing the software. If no options are required, this parameter should be left blank.

Scripting Steps

Listing 8.16 contains a script that upgrades an application called Personnel Database on a computer. To carry out this task, the script must perform the following steps:

1. Create a variable to specify the computer name.

2. Use a GetObject call to connect to the WMI namespace root\cimv2, and set the impersonation level to "impersonate."

3. Use the ExecQuery method to query the Win32_Product class.

   Because the upgrade is targeted toward a particular piece of software, include a WHERE clause to limit data retrieval to installed applications with the name Personnel Database. Without this clause, the Upgrade method would be applied (unsuccessfully) to each application installed on the computer.

4. For each instance of Personnel Database in the collection, call the Upgrade method, specifying the path to the Installer file. This path must be relative to the computer on which the upgrade will take place.

> **Note**
>
> If you are upgrading software on a remote computer and the Installer file is located on a third computer, you need to reference the UNC path to the file and use delegation to allow the computer being upgraded to connect over the network and retrieve that file. For information about using delegation, see "Installing Software on a Remote Computer" earlier in this chapter.

Listing 8.16   Upgrading Software

```
1   strComputer = "."
2   Set objWMIService = GetObject("winmgmts:" _
3       & "{impersonationLevel=impersonate}!\\" & strComputer & "\root\cimv2")
4   Set colSoftware = objWMIService.ExecQuery _
5       ("SELECT * FROM Win32_Product WHERE Name = 'Personnel Database'")
6   For Each objSoftware in colSoftware
7       errReturn = objSoftware.Upgrade("c:\scripts\database2.msi")
8   Next
```

Removing Software

Software installation is rarely permanent; instead, software is typically removed at some point in time, and for any number of reasons:

- The functionality supplied by the software is no longer needed.
- The software is being replaced by a competing software package.
- The software is installed on the wrong computer.
- The software is not licensed for use in the organization.

The Win32_Product Uninstall method can be used to remove software from a computer. The Uninstall method can be used either on the local computer or on a remote computer, and without delegation. This is because no multihop security operations are involved. Instead, the software is simply removed from the computer.

Although the Uninstall method can remove software from a computer, it does not override Group Policy. For example, if Microsoft Excel has been installed on a computer, you can use the Uninstall method to remove it. However, if Microsoft Excel is available to the user through Group Policy, the user will be able to reinstall the application.

Scripting Steps

Listing 8.17 contains a script that deletes software on a computer. To carry out this task, the script must perform the following steps:

1. Create a variable to specify the computer name.

2. Use a GetObject call to connect to the WMI namespace root\cimv2, and set the impersonation level to "impersonate."

3. Use the ExecQuery method to query the Win32_Product class.

   Because only one software package is to be deleted, include a WHERE clause to limit data retrieval to installed applications with the name Personnel Database. Otherwise, the script would remove all the software installed on the computer.

4. For each instance of Personnel Database in the collection, call the Uninstall method to remove the software.

Listing 8.17   Removing Software

```
1   strComputer = "."
2   Set objWMIService = GetObject("winmgmts:" _
3       & "{impersonationLevel=impersonate}!\\" & strComputer & "\root\cimv2")
4   Set colSoftware = objWMIService.ExecQuery _
5       ("SELECT * FROM Win32_Product WHERE Name = 'Personnel database'")
6   For Each objSoftware in colSoftware
7       objSoftware.Uninstall()
8   Next
```

Managing Computer States

Computers are dynamic entities. The exact configuration and set of resources available on a system are constantly changing. Software is installed and then removed; files are created and deleted; memory is allocated and then released.

Many of these dynamic changes, such as the creation and deletion of temporary files, are of little interest to administrators. Others, however, are of considerable interest. For example, administrators need to know when computers are shut down and restarted. After all, if a server shuts down unexpectedly, the resources provided by that server will be unavailable until it has been restarted.

Likewise, administrators need to know when computers switch from regular power sources to backup power sources. A computer that switches to battery power will be operational only as long as the battery lasts. Steps must be taken to correct the problem before the battery runs out and the computer shuts down.

In addition, administrators typically configure computers so that specific actions are carried out in specific situations. If the power fails, you might want to ensure that a multiple-boot computer is restarted by using a specific operating system. If a server encounters an unrecoverable error, you might want to ensure that a detailed record is made of what the computer was doing at the time the error occurred.

WMI provides a number of classes, properties, and methods that enable administrators to monitor, configure, and, in some cases, trigger changes in computer state. In particular, you can:

- Manage and configure computer startup settings.
- Manage and configure computer recovery settings.
- Monitor computer shutdowns, and remotely shut down or restart a computer.
- Monitor changes in computer power status (for example, a computer that switches from its primary power source to battery power).

Managing Computer Startups

Multiple operating systems can be installed on a single computer. Although servers are rarely configured in this way, workstations occasionally have multiple operating systems installed. For example, developers often do work on multi-boot computers for convenience in testing applications on different platforms. Workstations might need multiple operating systems if users need an application that runs only under a previous version of Windows. In addition, workstations are likely to have both the Windows operating system and the Windows Recovery Console installed.

As a system administrator, it is important to know:

- Which operating systems have been installed on a computer.
- Which operating system is loaded by default each time the computer is started.
- Whether users are given enough time to load an alternate operating system during startup.

This information enables you to know what will happen to a computer anytime it is restarted.

The Windows Startup Process

When you start a Windows-based computer, it loads the operating system by using the following process:

1. The computer runs a power-on self test (POST) that determines the amount of real memory installed on the computer and verifies the presence of required hardware components such as the keyboard.

2. NTLDR, the bootstrap loader for the operating system, reads the file Boot.ini and displays the bootstrap loader screen, which is based on information found in Boot.ini.

   The screen display looks similar to the following:

```
Please select the operating system to start:
Windows 2000 Professional
Windows 2000 Professional Recovery Console
Use ↓ and ↑ to move the highlight to your choice.
Press ENTER to choose.
Seconds until highlighted choice will be started automatically: 29
For troubleshooting and advanced startup options for Windows 2000, press F8.
```

3. NTLDR counts down the seconds. (By default, a user has 30 seconds in which to choose an operating system.)

4. If the user does not select an entry before the counter reaches 0, NTLDR loads the default operating system specified in Boot.ini.

Enumerating Computer Startup Options

The computer startup options include such key items as:

- The default operating system to be loaded by a computer.
- Alternate operating systems installed on a computer.
- The time-out period during which a user can select an alternate operating system.

The Win32_ComputerSystem class can be used to enumerate the startup properties for a computer. The properties available through this class are shown in Table 8.16.

Table 8.16   Win32_ComputerSystem Properties for Enumerating Startup Options

Property	Description
AutomaticResetBootOption	Boolean value indicating whether the automatic restart option is enabled.
AutomaticResetCapability	Boolean value indicating whether the computer is capable of automatic restart.
BootupState	Value indicating the current startup mode of the computer. Fail-safe boot (also called SafeBoot) bypasses the user's startup files. This property must have a value. Values are: ▪ Normal boot ▪ Safe mode ▪ Safe mode with network support
SystemStartupDelay	Time to delay (in seconds) before starting the operating system.
SystemStartupOptions	Array containing the options for starting up the Win32® computer system. On a multiple-boot computer with both Windows XP and Windows 2000 Advanced Server installed, the SystemStartupOptions might look like this: `"\"Microsoft Windows XP Professional\" /fastdetect","\"Microsoft Windows 2000 Advanced Server\" /fastdetect"`
SystemStartupSetting	Index of the default operating system, as determined by the Boot.ini file. This value is calculated so that it usually returns 0 because during startup the selected operating system is physically moved to the top of the list. (This is how the computer determines which value is the default.)

Scripting Steps

Listing 8.18 contains a script that enumerates the startup options on a computer. To carry out this task, the script must perform the following steps:

1.   Create a variable to specify the computer name.

2.   Use a GetObject call to connect to the WMI namespace root\cimv2, and set the impersonation level to "impersonate."

3. Use the ExecQuery method to query the Win32_ComputerSystem class.

4. Echo the value of each startup option in the collection.

Listing 8.18 Enumerating Startup Options

```
1   strComputer = "."
2   Set objWMIService = GetObject("winmgmts:" _
3       & "{impersonationLevel=impersonate}!\\" & strComputer & "\root\cimv2")
4   Set colStartupCommands = objWMIService.ExecQuery _
5       ("SELECT * FROM Win32_ComputerSystem")
6   For Each objStartupCommand in colStartupCommands
7       Wscript.Echo "Reset Boot Enabled: " & _
8           objStartupCommand.AutomaticResetBootOption
9       Wscript.Echo "Reset Boot Possible: " & _
10          objStartupCommand.AutomaticResetCapability
11      Wscript.Echo "Boot State: " & objStartupCommand.BootupState
12      Wscript.Echo "Startup Delay: " & objStartupCommand.SystemStartupDelay
13      For Each strOption in objStartupCommand.SystemStartupOptions
14          Wscript.Echo "Startup Options: " & strOption
15      Next
16      Wscript.Echo "Startup Setting: " & _
17          objStartupCommand.SystemStartupSetting
18  Next
```

Configuring Computer Startup Options

Administrators can control both the default operating system loaded by a computer and the amount of time that users are given to choose an alternate operating system when the computer starts. This allows administrators to:

- Specify the default operating system on computers that have multiple operating systems installed.

- Minimize (or maximize) the amount of time it takes for a computer to start.

  If the operating system wait time is set to 0 seconds, the computer automatically loads the default operating system without giving the user an opportunity to choose an alternate system. This can help prevent users from choosing a valid but typically inappropriate operating system such as the Windows 2000 Recovery Console. It also helps the computer start faster because the computer does not have to wait for 30 seconds before it begins to load the operating system.

The selection of the operating system to be loaded when a computer starts is based on the information stored in the Boot.ini file. The Boot.ini file includes two sections:

- **Boot loader.** Specifies the default operating system and the number of seconds NTLDR will wait before loading the default system.

  On a typical Windows-based computer, the Boot loader section looks similar to the following:

```
[boot loader]
timeout=30
default=multi(0)disk(0)rdisk(0)partition(1)\WINNT
```

- **Operating systems.** Specifies the operating systems that can be loaded.

  On a server running Windows 2000, the Operating systems section might look similar to the following:

```
[operating systems]
multi(0)disk(0)rdisk(0)partition(1)\WINNT="Microsoft Windows 2000 Server"
/fastdetect
```

The Win32_ComputerSystem class allows you to programmatically configure the time-out value or the default operating system by setting the properties shown in Table 8.17.

Table 8.17 Win32_ComputerSystem Properties for Configuring Startup Options

Property	Description
SystemStartupDelay	Specifies the number of seconds to wait before NTLDR loads the default operating system.
SystemStartupSetting	Specifies the index value of the operating system to be set as the default. The first operating system listed is item 0, with additional operating systems numbered consecutively.
	For example, in the following Boot.ini, there are two operating systems: Microsoft Windows XP Professional (with the index value 0), and Microsoft Windows 2000 Professional (with the index value 1).
	<code>[operating systems] multi(0)disk(0)rdisk(0)partition(1)\WINDOWS="Microsoft Windows XP Professional" /fastdetect C:\WINNT="Microsoft Windows 2000 Professional"</code>
	If you specify an incorrect value (for example, if you specify index 4 when only two operating systems are included), the script will fail with an out-of-range error.

The relationship between the Win32_ComputerSystem properties and the Windows graphical user interface are shown in Figure 8.4.

Figure 8.4   Startup Options and the Startup and Recovery Page

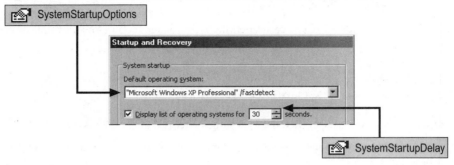

> ### Note
>
> You cannot use WMI to add or remove items to or from the Operating Systems portion of Boot.ini. This must be done by directly editing Boot.ini.

Scripting Steps

Listing 8.19 contains a script that configures the system startup delay on a computer. To carry out this task, the script must perform the following steps:

1. Create a variable to specify the computer name.

2. Use a GetObject call to connect to the WMI namespace root\cimv2, and set the impersonation level to "impersonate."

3. Use the ExecQuery method to query the Win32_ComputerSystem class.

4. For each computer in the collection, set the SystemStartupDelay to 10 seconds.

5. Use the Put_ method to apply the changes.

Listing 8.19   Configuring the System Startup Delay

```
1   strComputer = "."
2   Set objWMIService = GetObject("winmgmts:" _
3       & "{impersonationLevel=impersonate}!\\" & strComputer & "\root\cimv2")
4   Set colStartupCommands = objWMIService.ExecQuery _
5       ("SELECT * FROM Win32_ComputerSystem")
6   For Each objStartupCommand in colStartupCommands
7       objStartupCommand.SystemStartupDelay = 10
8       objStartupCommand.Put_
9   Next
```

After running this script, the Boot.ini will look similar to the following:

```
[boot loader]
timeout=10
default=multi(0)disk(0)rdisk(0)partition(1)\WINNT
```

Enumerating Computer Startup Commands

Computer startup does not end after the operating system has been loaded. Instead, the Windows operating system can be configured so that startup commands are run each time Windows starts. Startup commands are stored in the registry or as part of the user profile and are used to automatically start specified scripts or applications each time Windows is loaded.

In most cases, autostart programs are useful; they ensure that certain applications, such as antivirus tools, are automatically started and run each time Windows is loaded. However, autostart programs also can be responsible for problems such as:

- Computers that take an exceptionally long time to start. This might be the result of a large number of applications that must be started each time Windows starts.

- Applications that are represented in the Taskbar or in Task Manager, even though the user did not start them. Although these applications do not necessarily cause problems, they can result in help desk calls from users who are confused as to where these programs came from and why they are running.

- Computers experiencing problems even when they seem idle. These problems are often traced to startup commands that are running when no one is aware that they are running.

Identifying the applications and scripts that automatically run at startup is an important but difficult administrative task, because startup commands can be stored in many different locations:

- HKLM\Software\Microsoft\Windows\CurrentVersion\Run

- HKLM\Software\Microsoft\Windows\CurrentVersion\RunOnce

- HKCU\Software\Microsoft\Windows\CurrentVersion\Run

- HKCU\Software\Microsoft\Windows\CurrentVersion\RunOnce

- HKU*ProgID*\Software\Microsoft\Windows\CurrentVersion\Run

- *systemdrive*\Documents and Settings\All Users\Start Menu\Programs\Startup

- *systemdrive*\Documents and Settings*username*\Start Menu\Programs\Startup

You can use the WMI Win32_StartupCommand class to enumerate autostart programs regardless of where the information is stored. A partial set of properties available through the Win32_StartupCommand class is shown in Table 8.18.

Table 8.18   Win32_StartupCommand Properties

Property	Description
Command	Command run by the startup command. For example, "c:\windows\notepad.exe myfile.txt".
Description	Description of the startup command.
Location	Path to where the startup command resides in the file system or the registry. For example: HKLM\SOFTWARE\Microsoft\Windows\CurrentVersion\Run
Name	File name of the startup command.
User	User profile under which this startup command will run.

Scripting Steps

Listing 8.20 contains a script that enumerates the startup commands on a computer. To carry out this task, the script must perform the following steps:

1. Create a variable to specify the computer name.

2. Use a GetObject call to connect to the WMI namespace root\cimv2, and set the impersonation level to "impersonate."

3. Use the ExecQuery method to query the Win32_StartupCommand class.

    This query returns a collection consisting of all the startup commands on the computer.

4. For each startup command in the collection, echo the property values.

Listing 8.20   Enumerating Computer Startup Commands

```
1    strComputer = "."
2    Set objWMIService = GetObject("winmgmts:" _
3        & "{impersonationLevel=impersonate}!\\" & strComputer & "\root\cimv2")
4    Set colStartupCommands = objWMIService.ExecQuery _
5        ("SELECT * FROM Win32_StartupCommand")
6    For Each objStartupCommand in colStartupCommands
7        Wscript.Echo "Command: " & objStartupCommand.Command
8        Wscript.Echo "Description: " & objStartupCommand.Description
9        Wscript.Echo "Location: " & objStartupCommand.Location
10       Wscript.Echo "Name: " & objStartupCommand.Name
11       Wscript.Echo "SettingID: " & objStartupCommand.SettingID
12       Wscript.Echo "User: " & objStartupCommand.User
13   Next
```

Managing Computer Recovery Options

Occasionally a computer encounters an error condition from which it cannot recover. This condition is called a stop event because the computer stops processing when the error occurs. In addition to halting all processing, the computer displays a special kind of error message known as a stop message.

A stop message is often called a stop error or blue screen. The blue screen refers to the fact that the stop message changes the display to a solid blue character-mode background that contains the error message. The message itself consists of the following items:

- Unique identifier.

- Series of four hexadecimal numbers that identify error parameters.

- Symbolic name for the error condition.

- Additional information related to the problem.

For example, a stop message header might look similar to the following:

```
         DSR CTS
*** STOP:  0x0000000A (0x00000000, 0x0000001a, 0x00000000, 0x00000000)
IRQL_NOT_LESS_OR_EQUAL
P4-0300 irql:1f  SYSVER: 0xf000030e
Dll Base DateStmp - Name          Dll Base DateStmp - Name
80100000 2e53fe55 - ntoskrnl.exe    80400000 2e53eba6 - hal.dll
```

Besides displaying this message, a computer can be configured to take additional actions after a stop event. For example, you can configure a computer to automatically restart after a stop event, or to save a *memory dump*, a file containing the complete contents of the system memory at the time the stop event occurred. This file can be extremely useful to Microsoft support personnel helping you troubleshoot and resolve the problem.

The WMI Win32_OSRecoveryConfiguration class allows you to both retrieve and configure the recovery options for a computer. A subset of properties available through the Win32_OSRecoveryConfiguration class is shown in Table 8.19. Unless otherwise noted, each of these properties can be modified programmatically.

Table 8.19   Win32_OSRecoveryConfiguration Properties

Property	Description
AutoReboot	Boolean value that indicates whether the system will automatically reboot during a recovery operation.
DebugPathFile	Full path to the debug file. A debug file is created with the memory state of the computer after a computer failure. For example: "C:\Windows\Memory.dmp".
KernelOnlyDump	Specifies that only kernel debug information will be written to the debug log file. If True, only the state of the kernel is written to a file in the event of a system failure. If False, the system will try to log the state of the memory and any devices that can provide information about the system when it failed.
MiniDumpDirectory	Folder where small memory dump files will be recorded and accumulated. For example, "%systemroot%\MiniDump".
Name	Name of the operating system, along with information regarding the file path and disk drive where the operating system has been installed. For example, a Windows 2000 Professional computer might have a name similar to this: "Microsoft Windows 2000 Professional|C:\WINNT|\Device\Harddisk0\Partition1" This property is read-only.
OverWriteExistingDebugFile	New log file will overwrite an existing one. If this property is False, each new log file will be saved under a unique file name.
SendAdminAlert	Alert message will be sent to the system administrator in the event of an operating system failure.
WriteDebugInfo	Debugging information is to be written to a log file.
WriteToSystemLog	Events will be written to a system log.

The relationship between the Win32_OSRecoveryConfiguration properties and the Windows graphical user interface is shown in Figure 8.5.

Figure 8.5   Win32_OSRecoveryConfiguration and the Startup and Recovery Page

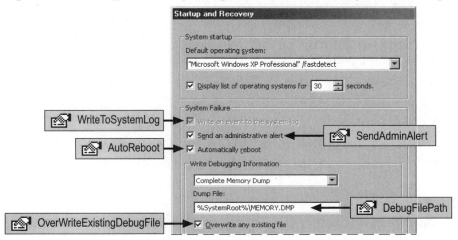

Enumerating Computer Recovery Options

Although system administrators often overlook the recovery options, this information can be extremely useful when developing a computer management plan for your organization. For example, the recovery options let you know which troubleshooting aids (such as a debug file) will be available if the computer encounters a stop error. Likewise, these options tell you whether a computer will automatically restart during a recovery operation; if it does not, you will have to manually restart it if problems occur. Knowing how these options are configured can also help you estimate how long the recovery process takes and give you a better idea of how long it will be before a given computer will be available if it encounters an unrecoverable error.

 Note

The actual time required to create a memory dump file depends on several factors, including the amount of memory installed on a computer and the type of dump file being created. At least, however, you know that it will take much longer to write a complete memory dump file than it will to write a small memory dump file.

You can use the Win32_OSRecoveryConfiguration class to enumerate the recovery options for a computer.

Scripting Steps

Listing 8.21 contains a script that enumerates the recovery configuration options for a computer. To carry out this task, the script must perform the following steps:

1. Create a variable to specify the computer name.

2. Use a GetObject call to connect to the WMI namespace root\cimv2, and set the impersonation level to "impersonate."

3. Use the ExecQuery method to query the Win32_OSRecoveryConfiguration class.

    This query returns a collection consisting of the operating system recovery operation settings for the computer.

4. For each set of recovery options in the collection, echo the specified property value.

Listing 8.21   Enumerating the Recovery Configuration Options for a Computer

```
1   strComputer = "."
2   Set objWMIService = GetObject("winmgmts:" _
3       & "{impersonationLevel=impersonate}!\\" & strComputer & "\root\cimv2")
4   Set colRecoveryOptions = objWMIService.ExecQuery _
5       ("SELECT * FROM Win32_OSRecoveryConfiguration")
6   For Each objOption in colRecoveryOptions
7       Wscript.Echo "Auto reboot: " & objOption.AutoReboot
8       Wscript.Echo "Debug File Path: " & objOption.DebugFilePath
9       Wscript.Echo "Kernel Dump Only: " & objOption.KernelDumpOnly
10      Wscript.Echo "Name: " & objOption.Name
11      Wscript.Echo "Overwrite Existing Debug File: " & _
12          objOption.OverwriteExistingDebugFile
13      Wscript.Echo "Send Administrative Alert: " & objOption.SendAdminAlert
14      Wscript.Echo "Write Debug Information: " & objOption.WriteDebugInfo
15      Wscript.Echo "Write to System Log: " & objOption.WriteToSystemLog
16  Next
```

Configuring Computer Recovery Options

You can configure a computer to take specific actions if it encounters an unrecoverable error condition. The actions you specify affect how long it takes to restart a computer and how much information will be available for diagnosing the cause of the error condition. This enables you to balance the need for recording information about the error condition (which can take a considerable amount of time, depending on how much memory is installed on the computer) with the need to have the computer operational as soon as possible.

You can control the amount of time required to restore a computer to full functionality by configuring the type of memory dump file that is written when the computer encounters an unrecoverable error condition. The different memory dump types vary greatly in the size of the file they generate; in turn, this affects the time it takes to write the file and the time it takes to restart the computer. (File sizes are also affected by the amount of memory installed on a computer.) Table 8.20 shows the relative sizes of the memory dump files on a Windows 2000–based computer with 512 MB of RAM.

Table 8.20   Relative Sizes of Memory Dump Files

Recovery Option	Size of Dump File
Complete memory dump	512 MB
Kernel memory dump	244 MB
Small memory dump	64 KB

In addition to specifying the type of memory dump file to be generated, you can control other recovery options such as:

- The folder in which memory dump files are stored.

- Whether error condition events are saved in the System Event log.

- Whether each new memory dump file is given a unique file name or whether new files overwrite existing memory dump files.

The Win32_OSRecoveryConfiguration class can be used to configure the recovery options for a computer. The properties available through this class are shown in Table 8.19.

Scripting Steps

Listing 8.22 contains a script that modifies the recovery configuration on a computer. To carry out this task, the script must perform the following steps:

1. Create a variable to specify the computer name.

2. Use a GetObject call to connect to the WMI namespace root\cimv2, and set the impersonation level to "impersonate."

3. Use the ExecQuery method to query the Win32_OSRecoveryConfiguration class.

   This query returns a collection consisting of all the operating system recovery settings for the computer.

4. For each set of recovery options in the collection, set the DebugFilePath to C:\Scripts\Memory.dmp.

5. For each set of recovery options in the collection, configure the OverWriteExistingDebugFile property to False.

   If a debug file is found, it will not be overwritten.

6. Use the Put_ method to apply the changes.

Listing 8.22   Modifying the Recovery Configuration on a Computer

```
1   strComputer = "."
2   Set objWMIService = GetObject("winmgmts:" _
3       & "{impersonationLevel=impersonate}!\\" & strComputer & "\root\cimv2")
4   Set colRecoveryOptions = objWMIService.ExecQuery _
5       ("SELECT * FROM Win32_OSRecoveryConfiguration")
6   For Each objOption in colRecoveryOptions
7       objOption.DebugFilePath = "c:\scripts\memory.dmp"
8       objOption.OverWriteExistingDebugFile = False
9       objOption.Put_
10  Next
```

Querying the Event Log for Stop Events

Tracking stop events and the details about those stop events can help you determine whether a particular problem is endemic to one computer or if it is occurring on other computers in your organization. Because stop events are recorded in the System Event log, you can create a script that periodically queries the System Event log on a computer or set of computers and checks to see whether any stop events have occurred.

Each time a stop event occurs, a record is saved with the following parameters:

- **EventType** = Information

- **EventCode** = 1001

- **SourceName** = Save Dump

The event description will look similar to the following:

```
The computer has rebooted from a bugcheck. The bugcheck was: 0x000000e2
(0x00000000, 0x00000000, 0x00000000, 0x00000000). Microsoft Windows 2000
[v15.2195]. A dump was saved in: C:\WINNT\MEMORY.DMP.
```

You can use the Win32_NTLogEvent class to periodically query the System Event Log and retrieve the details of each stop event.

Scripting Steps

Listing 8.23 contains a script that queries the System Event Log for all stop events. To carry out this task, the script must perform the following steps:

1. Create a variable to specify the computer name.

2. Use a GetObject call to connect to the WMI namespace root\cimv2, and set the impersonation level to "impersonate."

3. Use the ExecQuery method to query the Win32_NTEventLog class.

   Include a WHERE clause to limit the records retrieved only to those events found in the System Event Log that have the source name Save Dump.

4. For each record in the collection, echo the time the event occurred and the event message.

Listing 8.23   Querying the System Event Log for Stop Events

```
1   strComputer = "."
2   Set objWMIService = GetObject("winmgmts:" _
3       & "{impersonationLevel=impersonate}!\\" & strComputer & "\root\cimv2")
4   Set colLoggedEvents = objWMIService.ExecQuery _
5       ("SELECT * FROM Win32_NTLogEvent WHERE Logfile = 'System'" _
6           & " AND SourceName = 'SaveDump'")
7   For Each objEvent in colLoggedEvents
8       Wscript.Echo "Event date: " & objEvent.TimeGenerated
9       Wscript.Echo "Description: " & objEvent.Message
10  Next
```

Generating a Stop Event

Before you configure recovery options on a production computer, it is helpful to know the actual impact of these options. In particular, you will want to know the size of the dump file that will be generated and how much time it takes the computer to create the dump file and restart. To see what happens to a particular computer if a stop event occurs, you can add an entry to the registry and manually generate a stop event.

 Caution

Changing the registry with a script can easily propagate errors. The scripting tools bypass safeguards, allowing settings that can damage your system, or even require you to reinstall Windows. Before scripting changes to the registry, test your script thoroughly and back up the registry on every computer on which you will make changes. For more information about scripting changes to the registry, see the Registry Reference on the *Microsoft Windows 2000 Server Resource Kit* companion CD or at http://www.microsoft.com/reskit.

▶ **To add an entry to the registry**

1. Start Regedit.exe.

2. Navigate to the subkey HKLM\System\CurrentControlSet\Services\i8024prt\Parameters.

3. Select the Parameters subkey, and then click **Add Value** from the **Edit** menu.

4. In the **Add Value** dialog box, in the **Value Name** box type **CrashOnCtrlScroll**, in the **Data Type** box select **Reg_DWORD**, and then click **OK**.

5. Double-click the **CrashOnCtrlScroll** entry. In the **DWORD** Editor dialog box, type **1** in the **Data** box and then click **OK**.

6. Close Regedit.exe, and restart your computer.

After the computer has restarted, you can generate a stop event.

▶ **To manually generate a stop event**

▪ Press and hold the **right Ctrl key** (the left Ctrl key will not allow you to generate a stop event), and then press the **Scroll Lock** key twice.

A stop event will occur, and a stop error will be displayed with the following message:

```
*** STOP: 0x000000E2 (0x00000000, 0x00000000, 0x00000000, 0x00000000)
The end-user manually generated the crashdump.
```

After generating a stop event, the computer will be inoperable until it has been restarted. After the restart, complete functionality will be restored.

Shutting Down Computers and Logging Off Users

For more efficient management of computers in an organization, administrators need the ability to remotely shut down or restart a computer, or to remotely log off a user. The ability to carry out these tasks allows administrators to install software, reconfigure computer settings, remove computers from the network, and perform other tasks without having to manually shut down or restart each computer.

For example, to perform a network upgrade, you might need to shut down all the computers running on a particular network segment. To force a Group Policy upgrade, you need to log users off their computers. If a computer virus is present anywhere in your organization, you might want to shut down as many computers as possible, before the virus has an opportunity to spread. The ability to shut down and restart computers and to log off users programmatically instead of manually can be an enormous time-saver.

Shutdowns, restarts, and logoffs can be performed using the Win32Shutdown method of the Win32_OperatingSystem class along with one of the parameters shown in Table 8.21.

Table 8.21   Win32Shutdown Method Parameters

Value	Description
0	**Logoff.** Logs the user off the computer. Logging off stops all processes associated with the security context of the process that called the exit function, logs the current user off the system, and displays the logon dialog box.
1	**Shutdown.** Shuts down the computer to a point where it is safe to turn off the power. (All file buffers are flushed to disk, and all running processes are stopped.) Users see the message, `It is now safe to turn off your computer.` During shutdown the system sends a message to each running application. The applications perform any cleanup while processing the message and return True to indicate that they can be terminated.
2	**Reboot.** Shuts down and then restarts the computer.
4	**Forced logoff.** Logs the user off the computer immediately and does not notify applications that the logon session is ending. This can result in a loss of data.
5	**Forced shutdown.** Shuts down the computer to a point where it is safe to turn off the power. (All file buffers are flushed to disk, and all running processes are stopped.) Users see the message, `It is now safe to turn off your computer.` When the forced shutdown approach is used, all services, including WMI, are shut down immediately. Because of this, you will not be able to receive a return value if you are running the script against a remote computer.
6	**Forced reboot.** Shuts down and then restarts the computer. When the forced reboot approach is used, all services, including WMI, are shut down immediately. Because of this, you will not be able to receive a return value if you are running the script against a remote computer.
8	**Power off.** Shuts down the computer and turns off the power (if supported by the computer in question).
12	**Forced power off.** Shuts down the computer and turns off the power (if supported by the computer in question). When the forced power off approach is used, all services, including WMI, are shut down immediately. Because of this, you will not be able to receive a return value if you are running the script against a remote computer.

> **Note**
>
> The Win32Shutdown method does not have a parameter for locking a workstation, leaving the user logged on. However, workstations can be locked from the command line by using the following command:
>
> `%windir%\System32\rundll32.exe user32.dll,LockWorkStation`

To shut down a computer, your script must include the Shutdown privilege. For more information about including privileges within a WMI script, see "WMI Scripting Primer" in this book.

Shutting Down a Computer

Computers occasionally need to be removed from the network, perhaps for scheduled maintenance, because the computer is not functioning correctly, or to complete a configuration process. For example, if a DHCP server is handing out erroneous IP addresses, you might want to shut the computer down until a service technician can be dispatched to fix the problem. If you suspect that a security breach has occurred, you might need to shut down certain servers to ensure that they cannot be accessed until the security issue has been resolved. Some configuration operations (such as changing a computer name) require you to restart the computer before the change takes effect.

A computer can be shut down using the Win32Shutdown method, specifying **1** as the parameter value. Passing 1 as a parameter indicates that the computer should be shut down. Other parameters specify different actions, such as restarting the computer or logging off the user. For a complete list of parameter values, see Table 8.21.

For computers that support the ability to be programmatically powered off, you can specify **8** as the parameter value. Passing 8 as the parameter shuts down the computer and also turns off the power.

Scripting Steps

Listing 8.24 contains a script that shuts down a computer. To carry out this task, the script must perform the following steps:

1. Create a constant named SHUTDOWN and set the value to 1.

   This constant specifies that the computer should be shut down.

2. Create a variable to specify the computer name.

   In Listing 8.24, the computer name is set to "." which will result in the local computer being shut down. To shut down a remote computer, simply set the variable to the appropriate computer name.

3. Use a GetObject call to connect to the WMI namespace root\cimv2, and set the impersonation level to "impersonate."

4. Use to the ExecQuery method to return a collection consisting of all instances of the Win32_OperatingSystem class.

   The Shutdown privilege must be specified as part of the GetObject moniker. If it is not, the script will fail and the computer will not be shut down. The Shutdown privilege is required to shut down a computer by using WMI. However, including the privilege within the moniker does not ensure that the script will succeed. In addition to inclusion of the privilege within the moniker, the user under whose credentials the script is running must also have permission to shut down the computer.

5. For each operating system in the collection, use the Win32Shutdown method, specifying the constant SHUTDOWN (with the value 1) for the method parameter.

To shut down, but not power off, the computer, use the value 1 as the method parameter. Other values will result in other actions. For example, the value 0 will log the user off but will not shut down the computer.

Listing 8.24 Shutting Down a Computer

```
1   Const SHUTDOWN = 1
2   strComputer = "."
3   Set objWMIService = GetObject("winmgmts: {(Shutdown)}" _
4       & "{impersonationLevel=impersonate}!\\" & strComputer & "\root\cimv2")
5   Set colOperatingSystems = objWMIService.ExecQuery _
6       ("SELECT * FROM Win32_OperatingSystem")
7   For Each objOperatingSystem in colOperatingSystems
8       ObjOperatingSystem.Win32Shutdown(SHUTDOWN)
9   Next
```

When the script in Listing 8.24 runs, the computer is shut down, the user is logged off, all processes are stopped, and the screen displays the message:

```
"It is now safe to shut down your computer."
```

However, the computer remains powered on unless manually turned off.

Restarting a Computer

The ability to programmatically restart a computer allows administrators to perform many computer management tasks remotely. For example, if you create a script to install software or make a configuration change that requires restarting a computer, you can include the restart command in the script and perform the entire operation remotely.

The Win32_OperatingSystem class includes a Reboot method that can be used to restart a computer. Like the Win32Shutdown method, the Reboot method requires the user whose security credentials are being used by the script to possess the Shutdown privilege. In addition, the Shutdown privilege must be explicitly included in the script moniker.

Scripting Steps

Listing 8.25 contains a script that restarts a computer. To carry out this task, the script must perform the following steps:

1. Use a GetObject call to connect to the Win32_OperatingSystem class. This call returns a collection consisting of the operating system currently in use on the computer.

   Because restarting a computer requires the Shutdown privilege, this privilege must be included as part of the moniker.

2. For each operating system in the collection, use the Reboot method to restart the computer.

Listing 8.25   Restarting a Computer

```
1  strComputer = "."
2  Set objWMIService = GetObject("winmgmts:" _
3      & "{impersonationLevel=impersonate,(Shutdown)}!\\" & _
4          strComputer & "\root\cimv2")
5  Set colOperatingSystems = objWMIService.ExecQuery _
6      ("SELECT * FROM Win32_OperatingSystem")
7  For Each objOperatingSystem in colOperatingSystems
8      objOperatingSystem.Reboot()
9  Next
```

Monitoring Changes in Computer Power Status

Changes in power status often indicate that a problem has occurred with a computer or with another managed device. If a server suddenly switches from AC power to an uninterruptible power supply, this change can indicate that an electrical problem of some kind has occurred, either with the computer itself or with the electrical system in the room in which the computer is kept.

Administrators need to monitor these changes in power status and be notified of such changes immediately. This enables them to take action before the device loses power entirely. (Uninterruptible power supply systems, for example, might run for only 15 minutes or so before shutting down.)

The Win32_PowerManagementEvent class can be used to monitor changes in power status on a computer. These changes can include a switch from one power source to another as well as a change in computer power state (for example, entering or exiting Suspend mode).

The Win32_PowerManagementEvent class has only two properties: EventType, used to indicate the type of power change event that occurred, and OEMEventType, which is used by some original equipment manufacturers to define additional power change events. The values for the EventType property are shown in Table 8.22.

Table 8.22   Win32_PowerManagementEvent Event Types

EventType Value	Description
4	**Entering Suspend.** Indicates that the computer is about to enter the suspended state.
	While suspended, the computer appears to be off; however, it can be "awakened" in response to various events, including user input (such as moving the mouse or pressing a key on the keyboard). While the computer is suspended, power consumption is reduced to one of several levels depending on how the system is to be used. The lower the level of power consumption, the more time it takes the system to return to the working state.
	When the computer enters the suspend state, the desktop is locked, and you must press **CTRL+ALT+DELETE** and provide a valid user name and password to resume operations.
7	**Resume from Suspend.** Indicates that a ResumeSuspend message has been sent, enabling the computer to return to its regular power state.
10	**Power Status Change.** Indicates a change in the power status of the computer, such as a switch from battery power to AC, or from AC to an uninterruptible power supply. The system also broadcasts this event when remaining battery power slips below the threshold specified by the user or if the battery power changes by a specified percentage.
11	**OEM Event.** Indicates that an Advanced Power Management (APM) BIOS has sent an OEM event.
	The value of the event will be captured in the OEMEventCode property. Because some APM BIOS implementations do not provide OEM event notifications, this event might never be broadcast on some computers.
	APM is the legacy power management scheme that was first widely supported in Windows 95. Although still supported in Windows 2000 and Windows XP, APM has been largely superseded by ACPI (Advanced Configuration and Power Interface).
18	**Resume Automatic.** Indicates that the computer has awakened in response to an event. If the system detects user activity (such as a mouse click), the ResumeSuspend message will be broadcast, letting applications know that they can resume full interactivity with the user.

Scripting Steps

Listing 8.26 contains a script that monitors changes in power status on a computer. To carry out this task, the script must perform the following steps:

1.   Use a GetObject call and an ExecNotification query to monitor for changes in power status.

   This query looks for new instances of the Win32_PowerManagementEvent class.

2.   When a power change event occurs, echo the event type.

Listing 8.26   Monitoring Changes in Power Status

```
1   Set colMonitoredEvents = GetObject("winmgmts:")._
2       ExecNotificationQuery("SELECT * FROM Win32_PowerManagementEvent")
3   Do
4       Set strLatestEvent = colMonitoredEvents.NextEvent
5       Wscript.Echo strLatestEvent.EventType
6   Loop
```

Computer Roles

Computers play different roles in the IT infrastructure. It is important for system administrators to know the role played by any computer; after all, the techniques used to manage a workstation are usually quite different from those used to manage a domain controller. Scripting provides a way for administrators to easily identify computers and their roles, and to modify those roles as needed.

In This Chapter

Computer Roles Overview **690**

Managing Computer Accounts **690**

Retrieving Basic Logon and Computer Information 693

Creating Computer Accounts 694

Deleting Computer Accounts.. 698

Deleting Specified Computer Accounts 699

Modifying Computer Accounts 701

Searching for Computer Accounts in Active Directory....................................... 707

Managing Computer Roles **712**

Identifying Computer Roles 713

Identifying the Role of a Computer Based on the Service It Provides................. 715

Identifying Active Directory–Specific Roles.. 716

Computer Roles Overview

In enterprise settings, computers are not just pieces of hardware used to type memos or prepare spreadsheets; computers are dynamic role players that are largely responsible for ensuring that the IT infrastructure runs at peak efficiency. System administrators might supervise the network, but computers are responsible for carrying out such key tasks as authenticating user logons, handing out IP addresses, and maintaining the integrity of the Active Directory® directory service.

Of course, no entity could be entrusted with such important duties without having to undergo authentication itself; after all, you would not want users to take any old computer and configure it to be a domain controller or a global catalog server. Instead, computers are security principals within Active Directory. To have full access to network resources, computers must have valid accounts within Active Directory. In turn, the fact that computers are security principals and role players charges system administrators with:

- Creating, managing, and deleting computer accounts in Active Directory.

- Managing the roles played by computers. These management tasks include such things as identifying the roles played by a single computer, enumerating all the key role players in Active Directory, and changing computer roles as circumstances dictate.

By using both Windows Management Instrumentation (WMI) and Active Directory Service Interfaces (ADSI), you can create scripts that help you manage computers as dynamic role players.

Managing Computer Accounts

In Active Directory, computers are security principals, just like users. This means that computers must also have accounts and passwords, just like other security principals. To be fully authenticated by Active Directory, a user must not only have a valid user account, but he or she must also log on to the domain from a computer that has a valid computer account. If a user attempts to log on from an unauthorized computer, authentication will fail and the user will be denied access to important Active Directory capabilities such as Group Policy, roaming user profiles, remote installation, Quality of Service (QoS) networking, DNS, and applications that use Active Directory as a data store.

You cannot create computer accounts for computers running Microsoft® Windows® 95, Microsoft® Windows® 98, Microsoft® Windows® Millennium Edition, and Microsoft® Windows® XP Home Edition because these operating systems do not adhere to Active Directory security requirements. As a result, computers running these operating systems cannot join a domain, and users logging on from these computers will not have access to the complete range of Active Directory resources and services.

Attributes of an Active Directory Computer Account

Each computer account in Active Directory is an instance of the Computer class. This class has six mandatory attributes. (Attributes are also referred to as properties.) Mandatory attributes are properties that each account must have; you cannot create a computer account in Active Directory unless that account has each of the following attributes:

- Common-Name
- SAM-Account-Name
- Instance-Type
- NT-Security-Descriptor
- Object-Category
- Object-Class

 Note

When you create a computer account, you need to specify that the account is for a computer and provide the Common-Name and the SAM-Account-Name. The other mandatory attributes will automatically be created for you.

In addition to the six mandatory attributes, the Computer class has scores of optional attributes that are inherited from the User class. These attributes vary in usefulness. Some, such as computer location, are extremely useful to administrators; by configuring the computer location attribute, administrators can use Active Directory as a way to identify the physical location of every computer in the organization.

Other attributes are meaningless when applied to a computer; for example, computers do not have user profile paths or home phone numbers (although Active Directory does not prevent you from assigning a user profile path or a home phone number to a computer). Although these might seem nonsensical, the Computer class possesses these attributes simply because the class was derived from the User class. As such, the Computer class inherited all the attributes found in the User class.

A subset of the attributes useful for working with computer accounts are listed in Table 9.1. All of these attributes are available after the computer account has been created.

Table 9.1 Attributes of the ADSI Active Directory Computer Account

Attribute	Description
accountDisabled	Boolean value indicating whether the account is enabled for use.
canonicalName	Name of the computer in canonical form (for example, Server5.fabrikam.com).
cn	Common name of the computer (for example, Server5).
company	Name of the company responsible for the computer. This attribute can be useful in large organizations that encompass multiple companies.
department	Name of the department responsible for the computer.
description	Description of the computer. The description often includes information about the roles played by the computer.
distinguishedName	Distinguished name of the computer (in the format, CN=Server5, OU=Finance, DC=fabrikam, DC=com).
division	Name of the division responsible for the computer.
dnsHostName	Name of the computer as registered with the DNS server.
location	Physical location of the computer (often in the format Building Name/Floor Number/Room Number).
name	Name of the computer.
operatingSystem	Name of the operating system (such as Windows® 2000 Professional).
operatingSystemServicePack	ID string for the latest service pack installed on the computer (for example, SP4 indicates that the last service pack installed was service pack 4).
operatingSystemVersion	Version number for the operating system (for example, 5.0).
sAMAccountName	Logon name used to support clients and servers from a previous version of Windows (such as Microsoft® Windows NT® 4.0 and earlier, Windows 95, and Windows 98). The value of the sAMccountName attribute must be less than 20 characters to support computers running these operating systems.
whenChanged	Date the computer account was last modified.
whenCreated	Date the computer account was initially created.

Retrieving Basic Logon and Computer Information

Logon scripts often require basic information about a user and his or her computer. For example, if you know the user name, you can connect to the user account object in Active Directory and determine the groups that the user belongs to. In turn, you can then make certain resources available to that user, depending on group membership. Of course, your ability to do that hinges on your ability to determine the name of the user who just logged on.

Likewise, if you know the computer name or the site name, you can map appropriate drives ahead of time for users. For example, a computer located at site A might have drives mapped to file server A, while a computer located at site B might have drives mapped to file server B.

Some of this information (user name, computer name, and domain name) can be returned using the Windows Script Host (WSH) Network object. However, there are at least two limitations to the Network object.

- The Network object returns only the user logon name (for example, kenmeyer). By itself, this name cannot be used to bind to the user account object in Active Directory. Instead, you need a distinguished name similar to CN=KenMeyer, OU=Management, DC=Fabrikam, DC=com. The same is true for computers.

- The Network object can return only the names of the user, the domain, and the computer; it cannot provide information about items such as the forest name or the site.

If you need this additional information, or if you need to bind to the user or computer account in Active Directory, you can instead use the IADsADSystemInfo interface, an ADSI interface implemented in the ADSystemInfo object (Activeds.dll). This object returns the attributes shown in Table 9.2.

Table 9.2 Attributes of the ADSystemInfo Object

Attribute	Description
UserName	Distinguished name for the logged-on user. The distinguished name is in the form CN=KenMeyer, OU=Management, DC=Fabrikam, DC=com.
ComputerName	Distinguished name for the computer account.
SiteName	Site in which the computer account is located.
DomainShortName	"Short name" for the domain. For example, the name na is returned for the domain na.fabrikam.com.
DomainDNSName	DNS name for the domain (for example, na.fabrikam.com).

(continued)

Table 9.2   Attributes of the ADSystemInfo Object *(continued)*

Attribute	Description
ForestDNSName	DNS name for the forest (for example, fabrikam.com).
PDCRoleOwner	Distinguished name of the directory service agent that serves as the primary domain controller (PDC) emulator.
SchemaRoleOwner	Distinguished name of the directory service agent that serves as the schema master.
IsNativeMode	Boolean value that indicates whether the domain is in native mode.

Scripting Steps

Listing 9.1 contains a script that uses ADSystemInfo to return basic information about a computer and computer account. To carry out this task, the script must perform the following steps:

1. Create an instance of the ADSystemInfo object.

2. Echo the values of ADSystemInfo attributes such as user name, computer name, and site name.

Listing 9.1   Retrieving Basic Computer Information Using ADSystemInfo

```
1   Set objSysInfo = CreateObject("ADSystemInfo")
2   Wscript.Echo "User name: " & objSysInfo.UserName
3   Wscript.Echo "Computer name: " & objSysInfo.ComputerName
4   Wscript.Echo "Site name: " & objSysInfo.SiteName
5   Wscript.Echo "Domain short name: " & objSysInfo.DomainShortName
6   Wscript.Echo "Domain DNS name: " & objSysInfo.DomainDNSName
7   Wscript.Echo "Forest DNS name: " & objSysInfo.ForestDNSName
8   Wscript.Echo "PDC role owner: " & objSysInfo.PDCRoleOwner
9   Wscript.Echo "Schema role owner: " & objSysInfo.SchemaRoleOwner
10  Wscript.Echo "Domain is in native mode: " & objSysInfo.IsNativeMode
```

Creating Computer Accounts

For a computer in your organization to have full access to Active Directory resources, it must have a corresponding computer account in Active Directory. Computers that do not have accounts in Active Directory and do not belong to a domain have limited access to resources and cannot be managed by using Group Policy or software installation and maintenance.

Table 9.3 lists the Microsoft Windows operating systems and indicates whether a computer running a given operating system requires a computer account in Active Directory.

Table 9.3   Operating Systems and Computer Account Requirements

Operating System	Computer Account Required
Windows XP Home Edition	
Windows XP Professional	●
Windows XP 64-Bit Edition	●
Windows 2000 Professional	●
Windows 2000 Server	●
Windows 2000 Advanced Server	●
Windows 2000 Datacenter Server	●
Windows NT Server 4.0	●
Windows NT Server 4.0, Terminal Server Edition	●
Windows NT Server 4.0, Enterprise Edition	●
Windows NT Workstation 4.0	●
Windows NT Server 3.51	●
Windows NT Workstation 3.51	●
Windows Millennium Edition	
Windows 98	
Windows 95	
Windows 3.1	

Computer accounts can be created programmatically by using ADSI (and, more specifically, by using the IADs interface). To create a large number of computer accounts in a single operation, you can write a script that reads relevant information (computer name, computer location, and so forth) from a text file or a database, and then creates an account for each new computer. Using this kind of script is much quicker than manually creating each computer account by using Active Directory Users and Computers.

Note

For information about reading data from a database, see "Creating Enterprise Scripts" in this book.

When you create a computer account, you need to specify only the common name and the Security Accounts Manager (SAM) account name; the other mandatory attributes are automatically created for you.

However, if you specify only those two items, the account will initially be disabled. For a computer account to be enabled, you must also set the appropriate flags in the userAccountControl attribute. The userAccountControl attribute determines a number of different account attributes, including whether an account is enabled or disabled and whether an account requires a password. By setting two flags (ADS_UF_PASSWD_NOTREQD and ADS_UF_WORKSTATION_TRUST_ACCOUNT), the account will be enabled upon creation.

Setting Flags in the userAccountControl Attribute

For the purposes of this chapter, consider the userAccountControl attribute to be a control panel with a series of switches. These switches can be set to on or off. If a switch is set to on, the attribute controlled by that switch (the flag within the userAccountControl attribute) is also on. For example, if the ADS_UF_WORKSTATION_TRUST_ACCOUNT switch is on, that means that the account is a trusted workstation account. If the switch is off, the account is *not* a trusted workstation account. For a computer account to be enabled, both the ADS_UF_PASSWD_NOTREQD and ADS_UF_WORKSTATION_TRUST_ACCOUNT switches must be on.

Each flag within the userAccountControl attribute is assigned a value; for example, ADS_UF_PASSWD_NOTREQD is assigned the value &h0020 and ADS_UF_WORKSTATION_TRUST_ACCOUNT is assigned the value &h1000. These values correspond to the switches in the hypothetical control panel. When the userAccountControl attribute is assigned the value &h0020, it effectively flips the switch for ADS_UF_PASSWD_NOTREQD. Likewise, assigning the value &h1000 flips the switch for ADS_UF_WORKSTATION_TRUST_ACCOUNT.

If you are wondering how the userAccountControl attribute can be assigned multiple values, it is because the userAccountControl attribute contains multiple switches (flags).

For a more technical explanation of both the userAccountControl attribute and setting flags within that control, see "Active Directory Users" in this book.

Scripting Steps

Listing 9.2 contains a script that creates a computer account in Active Directory. To carry out this task, the script must perform the following steps:

1. Create a variable named strComputer, and set the value to the name of the computer account to be created.

2. Create a constant named ADS_UF_PASSWD_NOTREQD and set the value to &h0020.

3. Create a constant named ADS_UF_WORKSTATION_TRUST_ACCOUNT and set the value to &h1000.

   These two constants are used to configure flags in the userAccountControl property and enable the new computer account. You can create a computer account merely by specifying a value for the sAMAccountName attribute. In that case, however, the account will be created but will not be enabled, and thus cannot be used immediately.

4. Bind to the Computers container in Active Directory. The new account will be created in this container. To create the account in an organizational unit (OU), bind to the appropriate OU instead.

5. Use the Create method to create the new account in the local cache. The Create method requires the following two parameters:

   - **"Computer"** — indicating the type of account to be created.

   - **"cn="** & strComputer — indicating that the cn for the computer should be configured to the value of the variable strComputer.

6. Use the Put method to set the value of the sAMAccountName attribute to the name of the computer and append a dollar sign ($) (in this case, atl-pro-001$).

7. Use the Put method to enable the ADS_UF_PASSWD_NOTREQD and ADS_UF_WORKSTATION_TRUST_ACCOUNT flags in the userAccountControl property. This will enable the new computer account.

8. Use the SetInfo method to apply the changes in the local cache to Active Directory. In turn, this will create the new account.

Listing 9.2   Creating a Computer Account in Active Directory

```
1   strComputer = "atl-pro-001"
2   Const ADS_UF_PASSWD_NOTREQD = &h0020
3   Const ADS_UF_WORKSTATION_TRUST_ACCOUNT = &h1000
4   Set objRootDSE = GetObject("LDAP://rootDSE")
5   Set objContainer = GetObject("LDAP://cn=Computers," & _
6       objRootDSE.Get("defaultNamingContext"))
7   Set objComputer = objContainer.Create("Computer", "cn=" & strComputer)
8   objComputer.Put "sAMAccountName", strComputer & "$"
9   objComputer.Put "userAccountControl", _
10      ADS_UF_PASSWD_NOTREQD Or ADS_UF_WORKSTATION_TRUST_ACCOUNT
11  objComputer.SetInfo
```

Using the New Computer Account

After the account has been created, the computer in question must still be joined to the domain. This can be done only by someone who has the right to join a computer to the domain and who has access rights to the newly created computer account. By default, only administrators have access to the computer account; consequently, only an administrator can join the computer to the domain.

Deleting Computer Accounts

When a computer is no longer used within an organization, you might want to delete its corresponding computer account from Active Directory. Retaining accounts that are not tied to a specific computer can complicate computer management in the following ways:

- The organization will appear to be responsible for more computers than it actually has.

- The one-to-one correspondence between the computers listed in the computer inventory and the computer accounts shown in Active Directory will no longer exist.

- Automated scripts that attempt to run against every computer account in an Active Directory container will encounter problems because the script will try to access computers that no longer exist.

The ADSI IADsDeleteOps interface enables you to programmatically delete computer accounts from Active Directory.

 Note

When you programmatically delete a computer account, no confirmation box will appear (although you can write code that displays such a confirmation box before actually carrying out the DeleteObject method). Instead, the account object is deleted as soon as the DeleteObject method is called.

Scripting Steps

Listing 9.3 contains a script that deletes a computer account from Active Directory. To carry out this task, the script must perform the following steps:

1. Use a GetObject call to connect to Workstation4, a computer account located in the Computers container in fabrikam.com.

2. Use the DeleteObject method with the required parameter (0) to remove the account.

   The value (0) is the only value that can be used as the parameter for the DeleteObject method.

Listing 9.3 Deleting a Computer Account

```
1  set objComputer = GetObject _
2      ("LDAP://CN=Workstation4, CN=Computers, DC=fabrikam, DC=com")
3  objComputer.DeleteObject (0)
```

Deleting Specified Computer Accounts

If all you need to do is delete a single computer account, it is probably faster — and easier — to delete it by using Active Directory Users and Computers. Creating a script to delete a single computer account is probably more trouble than it is worth; scripts are far more useful when they are used to delete multiple computer accounts based on specified criteria.

For example, your organization might have made the decision to require all computers to use the Windows 2000 operating system. To help ensure compliance with this new requirement, you might give departments a specific period of time in which to complete the upgrade. At the end of that time period, you might then delete the accounts for any computer not running Windows 2000. Deleting these accounts will help prevent users from using an unauthorized operating system to gain access to network resources.

You can delete specified computer accounts by writing a script that:

1. Searches Active Directory for all computer accounts meeting specified criteria. For example, you can search for all computers running Windows 2000 or Windows NT 4.0.

2. Returns a recordset consisting of all the computer accounts meeting the criteria.

3. Individually bind to and delete each account in the recordset.

Scripting Steps

Listing 9.4 contains a script that deletes specified computer accounts from Active Directory. To carry out this task, the script must perform the following steps:

1. Create a constant named ADS_SCOPE_SUBTREE and set the value to 2.

   This constant is used to specify a search that begins in the Active Directory root and then proceeds to search all the child containers as well.

2. Create an instance of the Active Directory connection object (ADODB.Connection).

3. Create an instance of the Active Directory command object (ADODB.Command).

   The command object allows you to issue queries and other database commands through the Active Directory connection.

4. Set the Provider property of the connection object to the Active Directory provider (ADsDSOObject), the OLE database provider for ADSI.

5. Set the active connection to the Active Directory connection.

6. Set the command text for the Active Directory command object to the Structured Query Language (SQL) query that retrieves the specified computer accounts from fabrikam.com.

   In this script, the SQL query is `"SELECT distinguishedName, operatingSystemVersion FROM 'LDAP://DC=fabrikam,DC=com' WHERE objectClass='computer' AND operatingSystemversion = '4.0'"`.

7. Specify values for page size, time-out, search scope, and caching.

   Although this step is optional, it can improve the performance of your script in a domain with thousands of computers.

8. Execute the SQL query.

   This query returns a recordset consisting of all the computer accounts for all computers currently running the Windows NT 4.0 operating system.

9. When the set of computers is returned, use the MoveFirst method to move to the first computer in the recordset.

10. For each computer in the recordset, set the value of the variable strComputer to the distinguished name for the computer account.

11. Use a second GetObject call to bind to the computer account. You must individually bind to each account because items in an ActiveX Data Object (ADO) recordset are read-only.

12. After binding to the individual computer account, use the DeleteObject method to delete the account from Active Directory.

Listing 9.4   Deleting Specified Computer Accounts

```
1   Const ADS_SCOPE_SUBTREE = 2
2   Set objConnection = CreateObject("ADODB.Connection")
3   Set objCommand =    CreateObject("ADODB.Command")
4   objConnection.Provider = "ADsDSOObject"
5   objConnection.Open "Active Directory Provider"
6   Set objCommand.ActiveConnection = objConnection
7   objCommand.CommandText = _
8       "SELECT distinguishedName, operatingSystemVersion FROM " _
9           & "'LDAP://DC=fabrikam,DC=com' WHERE objectClass='computer' " _
10              & "AND operatingSystemVersion = '4.0'"
11  objCommand.Properties("Page Size") = 1000
12  objCommand.Properties("Timeout") = 30
13  objCommand.Properties("Searchscope") = ADS_SCOPE_SUBTREE
14  objCommand.Properties("Cache Results") = False
15  Set objRecordSet = objCommand.Execute
16  objRecordSet.MoveFirst
17  Do Until objRecordSet.EOF
18      strComputer = objRecordSet.Fields("distinguishedName").Value
19      Set objComputer = GetObject("LDAP://" & strComputer & "")
20      objComputer.DeleteObject (0)
21      objRecordSet.MoveNext
22  Loop
```

Modifying Computer Accounts

Computer account attributes often need to be modified. For example, because many computer accounts are created before the computers are actually assigned to users, attributes such as Description, Department, and Location cannot be configured at the time the account is created. In addition, the ownership of a computer can be transferred to a new user or department, or a computer might be physically moved to a new location. In such circumstances, the computer account attributes need to be modified.

You can use the ADSI Put and SetInfo methods to modify these attributes at any time. In addition to modifying account attributes, you can also create scripts that:

- Rename computer accounts.

- Move computer accounts to new Active Directory containers.

- Reset computer account passwords.

Enumerating Computer Account Attributes

By retrieving and reviewing computer account attributes you can do such things as identify the computers owned by each department, or compile a list of the computers that are located in a particular location (city, building, floor, room). This information is very useful in a number of situations, from planning new equipment allocations to making preparations to move a group of users from one building to another.

You can use the ADSI IADs Get method to retrieve the attributes of any computer account in Active Directory. You simply bind to the appropriate computer account and then echo the value of the desired attributes.

Creating a script to return computer account attributes is easy, but there is one caveat you must be aware of. Although you can retrieve any attribute by using ADSI, a problem can occur if any of these attributes have a null value (that is, if no value has been assigned to the attribute). For example, suppose you create a computer account and assign values only to the mandatory attributes. In that instance, all the optional attributes, including such properties as Location and Description, will have a null value, which means no value has been assigned to the attribute.

Although a script can retrieve attributes with null values, an error will occur if you attempt to do things such as assign that value to a variable or echo the value to the screen. For example, if you attempt to report the value, you will receive the following error message:

```
The property could not be found in the cache.
```

To avoid getting this error, your script must do two things:

1. Include the On Error Resume Next statement at the beginning of the script. This will prevent the script from failing if an attribute has a null value.

2. Check each retrieved attribute to ensure that the value is not null before attempting to do anything else with it. For example, before echoing the value of the computer account Location attribute, check to ensure that the computer actually has a location.

You can check for null values by using the function IsNull in Microsoft® Visual Basic® Scripting Edition (VBScript). The following code sample tests to see if the value assigned to the variable strLocation is null. If it is, a message is echoed.

```
If IsNull(strLocation) Then
    Wscript.Echo "The location has not been configured for this computer."
Else
    Wscript.Echo "Location: " & strLocation
End If
```

Scripting Steps

Listing 9.5 contains a script that enumerates the values of two attributes of a computer account. To carry out this task, the script must perform the following steps:

1. Include the On Error Resume Next statement. This will prevent the script from failing if the value of either the Location or Description attribute is null.

2. Use a GetObject call to bind to the computer account.

3. Use the Get method to retrieve the computer location.

4. Use the IsNull function to check whether a value has been configured for the Location attribute, and do one of the following:

   - If no location has been configured, echo a message stating that the Location attribute has not been configured.

   - If a location has been configured, echo the value of the Location attribute.

5. To retrieve the computer description, repeat steps 2 and 3, using the Get method to retrieve the Description attribute and then echoing the value of that attribute. If the value is null, echo the message "The description has not been configured for this computer."

This same approach can be used to retrieve additional computer account attributes.

Listing 9.5   Enumerating Computer Account Attributes

```
1   On Error Resume Next
2   Set objComputer = GetObject _
3       ("LDAP://CN=atl-dc-01, CN=Computers, DC=fabrikam, DC=com")
4   objProperty = objComputer.Get("Location")
5   If IsNull(objProperty) Then
6       Wscript.Echo "The location has not been set for this computer."
7   Else
8       Wscript.Echo "Location: " & objProperty
9       objProperty = Null
10  End If
```

(continued)

Listing 9.5   Enumerating Computer Account Attributes *(continued)*

```
11  objProperty = objComputer.Get("Description")
12  If IsNull(objProperty) Then
13      Wscript.Echo "The description has not been set for this computer."
14  Else
15      Wscript.Echo "Description: " & objProperty
16      objProperty = Null
17  End If
```

Configuring the Computer Account Location Attribute

The computer account Location attribute is crucial for administrative tasks that depend on knowing the physical location of individual or multiple computers. For example, knowing the physical location of individual computers enables you to dispatch service technicians to those computers. If a computer is no longer accessible over the network, you can use the Location attribute for the computer account to determine the actual physical location of the computer.

Location information can also help in identifying and diagnosing problems across the network. For example, if you observe that four computers having similar problems are located in the same general area, you might speculate that the problem is not with the computers themselves, but with the network infrastructure.

In addition, configuring the location for a computer allows you to use Active Directory printer location tracking. Printer location tracking enables users to quickly locate printers in their immediate proximity. To enable printer location tracking, you must develop a domain-wide naming scheme and use that scheme to specify the locations of all your printers and all your computers.

For more information about Active Directory printer location tracking, see "Printing" in this book.

You can use ADSI to configure the Location attribute for a computer account. Although the Location attribute for an individual computer can be easily changed by using Active Directory Users and Computers, scripts can be particularly useful if a large group of computers changes location at the same time (for example, when an entire department moves from one building to another).

Scripting Steps

Listing 9.6 contains a script that changes the value of the Location attribute for a computer. To carry out this task, the script must perform the following steps:

1. Use a GetObject call to bind to the desired computer.

2. Use the Put method to set the value of the Location attribute to Building 37, Floor 2, Room 2133.

3. Use the SetInfo method to write the changes to the computer account.

Listing 9.6   Changing the Computer Account Location Attribute

```
1   Set objComputer = GetObject _
2       ("LDAP://CN=atl-dc-01, CN=Computers, DC=fabrikam, DC=com")
3   objComputer.Put "Location" , "Building 37, Floor 2, Room 2133"
4   objComputer.SetInfo
```

Renaming Computer Accounts

If you rename a computer for any reason, you must also rename the computer account. Although it is generally best to rename both the computer and the computer account at the same time, this is not always possible. For example, a computer might be transferred to a new department and thus need be renamed to reflect departmental standards. If the new user does not have the right to rename the computer account in Active Directory, however, a discrepancy will exist between the computer name and the computer account name. This is not an unusual scenario; many organizations place strict limits on the modifications users can make to any object stored in Active Directory.

In a situation such as this, a person with the right to rename the computer account will have to rename the computer account to match the new computer name.

You can rename a computer account by using the ADSI MoveHere method. Using the MoveHere method, the script binds to a computer account and then moves the account. Rather than moving the account to a new OU or another new container, however, the script leaves the account in the same OU, but "moves" it to a new account name.

For example, to rename a computer account named ComputerA in the Finance OU, you "move" the computer account to a new account named ComputerB, also located in the Finance OU. This has the same effect as renaming the account. The account named ComputerA disappears, and the information previously stored in that account is now stored in the new account named ComputerB.

Scripting Steps

Listing 9.7 contains a script that renames a computer account. To carry out this task, the script must perform the following steps:

1. Use a GetObject call to bind to the Active Directory container in which the computer account is stored.

2. Use the MoveHere method with the following two parameters:

    - The object to be renamed ("LDAP://CN=Workstation4, OU=Finance, DC=fabrikam, DC=com").

    - The new common name for the object ("CN=Workstation5").

Listing 9.7   Renaming a Computer Account

```
1   Set objNewOU = GetObject("LDAP://OU=Finance, DC=fabrikam, DC=com")
2   Set objMoveComputer = objNewOU.MoveHere _
3       ("LDAP://CN=Workstation4, OU=Finance, DC=fabrikam, DC=com", _
4           "CN=Workstation5")
```

When this script is run, the computer account Workstation4 is renamed to Workstation5. The account remains in the Finance OU.

Moving Computer Accounts

Occasionally it is necessary to move computer accounts to reflect changes in organizational or managerial structure, to account for a transfer of equipment ownership, or to facilitate the application of Group Policy.

For example, many organizations place all new computer accounts in the Computers container in Active Directory. However, having all the computer accounts in the Computers container makes it difficult to know which computers belong to which departments. In addition, Group Policy cannot be applied to the Computers container because it is not an OU. Keeping all computer accounts in the same container also limits your ability to delegate administrative control of those accounts. If all computer accounts are stored in the Computers container, you cannot give the Finance Department system administrator control over accounts in his department without also giving that administrator control over *all* the accounts in that container.

For these reasons, computer accounts are typically moved out of the Computers container as soon as the computers are given to particular users or departments. Moving accounts to the appropriate Active Directory OU helps reflect the actual distribution of resources within the organization and allows for delegation of administration. For example, the Finance Department can use one set of policies to manage their computers, while the Human Resources Department can use a separate set of policies to manage their computers.

Accounts can be moved from one Active Directory container to another programmatically by using ADSI.

Scripting Steps

Listing 9.8 contains a script that moves a computer account to a different OU. To carry out this task, the script must perform the following steps:

1. Use a GetObject call to bind to the Active Directory container to which the computer account will be moved. In this example, the container is the Finance OU in fabrikam.com.

   This first step illustrates one important difference between renaming a computer account and moving a computer account: When you rename a computer account, you bind to the Active Directory container in which the account currently resides. When you move a computer account, you bind to the container to which the account will be moved.

2. Use the MoveHere method with the following two parameters:

- Distinguished name of the account to be moved (LDAP://CN=Server4, CN=Computers, DC=fabrikam, DC=com).

- Common name to be given to the account in the new container. Keeping the common name the same (CN=Workstation4) ensures that the account will be moved without being renamed.

Listing 9.8 Moving Computer Accounts

```
1  Set objNewOU = GetObject("LDAP://OU=Finance, DC=fabrikam, DC=com")
2  Set objMoveComputer = objNewOU.MoveHere _
3      ("LDAP://CN=Workstation4, CN=Computers, DC=fabrikam, DC=com", _
4          "CN=Workstation4")
```

Resetting Computer Account Passwords

Each computer account has a password that must match a password stored in Active Directory. If the two passwords do not match, Active Directory cannot authenticate the computer. If this occurs, the computer account password must be reset by a system administrator. Resetting the password returns both the password stored on the computer and the password stored in Active Directory to the default value, and enables the computer to be authenticated.

When a computer account is created, the passwords for both the account and the secure channel (a special communication channel used to communicate with a domain controller) are set to *%computername%$*. For example, a new computer named Server7 would be given an initial password of Server7$. After the computer has joined the domain, a unique password is generated to replace *%computername%$*. Thereafter, a new password for both the computer account and the secure channel is automatically generated every 30 days.

Although these passwords generally match, certain situations can cause them to differ. For example, Active Directory replication problems might cause one of the passwords to be changed but not the other one. Or, a computer might be offline for an extended period of time. During that time, the Active Directory password might have been changed; with the computer offline, however, the local password could not have been changed accordingly. In either case, Active Directory would be unable to authenticate the computer and the user unable to log on to the network. Instead, a user attempting to log on would be presented with the following error message:

```
The session setup from the computer DomainMember failed to authenticate. The name
of the account referenced in the security database is DomainMember$. The
following error occurred: Access is denied.
```

If this occurs, a system administrator must reset the password for the computer account, which can be done using the ADSI IADsUser interface.

Scripting Steps

Listing 9.9 contains a script that resets a computer account password. To carry out this task, the script must perform the following steps:

1. Use a GetObject call to bind to the computer account in Active Directory.

2. Use the SetPassword method to reset the password to the original computer password: the computer name, with a dollar sign ($) appended to it.

Listing 9.9   Resetting a Computer Account Password

```
1  Set objComputer = GetObject _
2      ("LDAP://CN=atl-dc-01,CN=Computers,DC=fabrikam,DC=COM")
3  objComputer.SetPassword "atl-dc-01$"
```

Searching for Computer Accounts in Active Directory

Active Directory is more than a repository for resources such as accounts, shared printers, and public folders. It is also a searchable database that allows users and administrators to quickly locate these resources. Because computer accounts are stored in Active Directory, you can take advantage of the Active Directory searching capabilities to locate any computer in your organization.

Active Directory supports the following two primary search types:

- **Basic enumeration**. Lists all the computer accounts in a specified domain, OU, or other Active Directory container. For example, a SQL command similar to the following retrieves a list of all the computers in fabrikam.com:

```
Select Name from 'LDAP://DC=fabrikam,DC=com' where objectClass = 'computer'
```

- **Filtered search**. Returns only the computer accounts that have a specified value for an attribute. For example, you might search for all computers located in a particular building or owned by a particular department. The following SQL command retrieves all the computers owned by the Finance Department:

```
Select Name from 'LDAP://DC=fabrikam,DC=com' where objectClass='computer'
and Department = 'Finance'
```

The filtered search capabilities of Active Directory allow you to write scripts that can run against a specified set of computers even if you do not know the names of those computers. For example, if the Human Resources department moves to a new building, you can retrieve a list of computers for which the value of the Department attribute is equal to Human Resources, and then change the value of the Location attribute. Likewise, you can search Active Directory for a list of all the domain controllers in the domain and then run a monitoring or inventory script against those computers.

When you conduct a search, a recordset is returned that includes each of the computers that meet the search criteria. For more information about working with recordsets, see "Creating Enterprise Scripts" in this book.

Facilitating a Search in Active Directory

Following are some tips that can facilitate Active Directory searches. For more information about searching in Active Directory, see "ADSI Scripting Primer" in this book.

Target the scope of the search appropriately.

Large Active Directory domains can contain thousands of computers. Instead of searching through all of Active Directory to find the computers of interest, search only the container in which the computer accounts are likely to be stored (for example, in the Finance OU).

Set a search page size.

Some searches can returns thousands of objects. A return of the entire recordset in one operation can noticeably degrade the performance of the server, the client, and the network. If you expect your search to return a large number of objects, specify a search page size to allow the server to return information in more manageable chunks. For example, rather than return 50,000 records all at once, a search with a page size of 500 allows the computer to return just the first 500 records when the search is completed, and each subsequent set of 500 records only when requested.

Include a time-out value.

When you conduct a search of Active Directory, your search request is queued and the server attempts to satisfy the request as soon as possible. If the server is extremely busy, the request can be delayed or the search can be slow. You can specify a time-out value to make the script wait a set amount of time (for example, 30 seconds) for a reply from the server, and then automatically terminates if no reply is received.

Limit the number of attributes retrieved.

If you need only the common name for each computer, do not retrieve the entire set of attributes. Scripts returning fewer attributes run faster and minimize the amount of data that must be transmitted across the network.

Use a search filter.

Instead of returning a list of all the computers, return only the computers that meet specific criteria (for example, only the computers located in a particular building or only the computers with a particular version of the operating system installed).

Enumerating All the Computer Accounts in Active Directory

All computers running Windows NT, Windows 2000, and Windows XP Professional in a domain must have accounts in Active Directory. Because of this, Active Directory contains a list of all the computers in your organization that run one of these operating systems. Any time you need such a list (perhaps for inventory or planning purposes), you can retrieve this information by using ADSI to enumerate all the computer accounts in Active Directory.

Note

In large organizations, Active Directory can contain thousands of computer accounts. Any operation that attempts to enumerate all the accounts can take a considerable amount of time to be completed. Because of that, you might want to conduct large searches at a time when user and network activity is low.

Scripting Steps

Listing 9.10 contains a script that enumerates all the computer accounts in Active Directory. To carry out this task, the script must perform the following steps:

1. Create a constant named ADS_SCOPE_SUBTREE and set the value to 2.

   This constant is used to specify a search that begins in the Active Directory root and then proceeds to search all the child containers as well.

2. Create an instance of the Active Directory connection object (ADODB.Connection).

3. Create an instance of the Active Directory command object (ADODB.Command).

   The command object allows you to issue queries and other database commands through the Active Directory connection.

4. Set the Provider property of the connection object to the Active Directory provider (ADsDSOObject), the OLE database provider for ADSI.

5. Set the active connection to the Active Directory connection.

6. Set the command text for the Active Directory command object to the SQL query that retrieves all the computers from fabrikam.com.

   In this script, the SQL query is `"Select Name, Location from 'LDAP://DC=fabrikam,DC=com' where objectClass='computer'"`.

7. Specify values for page size, time-out, search scope, and caching.

   Although this step is optional, it can improve the performance of your script in a domain with thousands of computers.

8. Execute the SQL query.

   This query returns a recordset consisting of all the computer accounts in Active Directory.

9. When the set of computers is returned, use the MoveFirst method to move to the first computer in the recordset.

10. For each computer in the recordset, echo the computer name and location.

Listing 9.10   Enumerating All the Computer Accounts in Active Directory

```
1   Const ADS_SCOPE_SUBTREE = 2
2   Set objConnection = CreateObject("ADODB.Connection")
3   Set objCommand =   CreateObject("ADODB.Command")
4   objConnection.Provider = "ADsDSOObject"
5   objConnection.Open "Active Directory Provider"
6   Set objCommand.ActiveConnection = objConnection
7   objCommand.CommandText = _
8       "SELECT Name, Location FROM 'LDAP://DC=fabrikam,DC=com' " _
9           & "WHERE objectClass='computer'"
10  objCommand.Properties("Page Size") = 1000
11  objCommand.Properties("Timeout") = 30
12  objCommand.Properties("Searchscope") = ADS_SCOPE_SUBTREE
13  objCommand.Properties("Cache Results") = False
14  Set objRecordSet = objCommand.Execute
15  objRecordSet.MoveFirst
16  Do Until objRecordSet.EOF
17      Wscript.Echo "Computer Name: " & objRecordSet.Fields("Name").Value
18      Wscript.Echo "Location: " & objRecordSet.Fields("Location").Value
19      objRecordSet.MoveNext
20  Loop
```

Locating Computer Accounts Based on Their Attributes

There are times when you need a list of specific computer accounts rather than a list of all the computer accounts in Active Directory. For example, you might want a list of all the computers located in a particular building, all the computers running a specific version of the Windows operating system, or all the computers whose computer accounts have been created in the past 30 days.

To obtain such a list, you can use a filtered search. Because each computer account has a number of attributes associated with it, you can create a search that returns only the computer accounts for which specific attributes meet specific criteria.

For example, the Department property is an attribute of the computer account. To return a list of all the computers that belong to a specific department, you can create a query that limits data retrieval only to those accounts for which the attribute value is equal to a specific value (for example, Department = "Finance"). For a list of attributes to use for searching, see Table 9.1.

> ☑ **Note**
>
> Most computer account attributes, such as Department, are optional and do not require values to be specified at the time the computer account is created. However, in order for you to be able to search by using a specific attribute, the desired accounts must have a value for that attribute. If you do not require administrators to specify the department when creating a computer account, you will have no way to search for computers based on the Department attribute. To avoid this problem, you can design a script that creates an account only if a complete set of values is assigned to the attributes.

Scripting Steps

Listing 9.11 contains a script that locates computers based on computer account attributes. To carry out this task, the script must perform the following steps:

1. Create a constant named ADS_SCOPE_SUBTREE and set the value to 2.

    This constant is used to specify a search that begins in the Active Directory root and then proceeds to search all the child containers as well.

2. Create an instance of the Active Directory connection object (ADODB.Connection).

3. Create an instance of the Active Directory command object (ADODB.Command).

    The command object allows you to issue queries and other database commands through the Active Directory connection.

4. Set the Provider property of the connection object to the Active Directory provider (ADsDSOObject), the OLE database provider for ADSI.

5. Set the active connection to the Active Directory connection.

6. Set the command text for the Active Directory command object to the SQL query that retrieves all the computers from fabrikam.com.

    To limit the number of computers retrieved, an additional clause is included that limits the search to computers that have a value of 5.0 (2195) for their operatingSystemVersion attributes. This is the version number for Windows 2000.

7. Specify values for page size, time-out, search scope, and caching.

    Although optional, this step can improve the performance of your script in a domain with thousands of computer accounts.

8. Execute the SQL query.

   This query returns a collection of all the computers in Active Directory with an operating system of version 5.0 (2195).

9. When the set of computers is returned, use the MoveFirst method to move to the first computer in the recordset.

10. For each computer in the recordset, echo the computer name and location.

Listing 9.11   Locating Computers Based on Computer Account Attributes

```
1   Const ADS_SCOPE_SUBTREE = 2
2   Set objConnection = CreateObject("ADODB.Connection")
3   Set objCommand =   CreateObject("ADODB.Command")
4   objConnection.Provider = "ADsDSOObject"
5   objConnection.Open "Active Directory Provider"
6   Set objCommand.ActiveConnection = objConnection
7   objCommand.CommandText = _
8       "SELECT Name, Location, operatingSystemVersion FROM " _
9           & "'LDAP://DC=fabrikam,DC=com' WHERE objectClass='computer' " _
10              & "and operatingSystemVersion = '5.0 (2195)'"
11  objCommand.Properties("Page Size") = 1000
12  objCommand.Properties("Timeout") = 30
13  objCommand.Properties("Searchscope") = ADS_SCOPE_SUBTREE
14  objCommand.Properties("Cache Results") = False
15  Set objRecordSet = objCommand.Execute
16  objRecordSet.MoveFirst
17  Do Until objRecordSet.EOF
18      Wscript.Echo "Computer Name: " & objRecordSet.Fields("Name").Value
19      Wscript.Echo "Location: " & objRecordSet.Fields("Location").Value
20      objRecordSet.MoveNext
21  Loop
```

Managing Computer Roles

One of the primary goals of system administrators is to continually reduce the need for system administration. For example, system administrators could manually edit host files, thus enabling users to access resources over the intranet and the Internet. Alternatively, system administrators can use DNS and allow computers to carry out this task. System administrators could visit each individual computer in the organization and use a known user name and password to log users on the network; alternatively, they can rely on Active Directory and allow domain controllers to authenticate users.

What this means, of course, is that computers are dynamic role players largely responsible for keeping a network functioning. This also means that all computers are not alike: some are workstations, some are member servers, and some are domain controllers. Others take on additional roles; these computers might be responsible for key services such as DNS or DHCP, or they might hold important Active Directory roles such as global catalog server or PDC emulator. Scripting provides a way for you to identify the various roles played by a computer, and also allows you to change those roles as needed.

Identifying Computer Roles

It is important to know whether a computer is part of a domain because this helps determine the means by which a computer can be managed. Computers that do not belong to a domain and do not have accounts in Active Directory cannot be managed by using Group Policy or software installation and maintenance.

For example, a single domain-level Group Policy can be applied to computers that are members of a domain. Stand-alone computers, by contrast, must be managed on an individual basis by using local Group Policy. Domain membership also affects the availability of resources for anyone using that computer.

The role that a computer plays within a domain (workstation, server, or domain controller) also impacts the management of that computer. For example, when you use scripts that automatically install software or configure a computer, you need to know the computer role because:

- Some software is designed for installation on workstations but not on servers.

- Some services need to be configured by using a particular service account if they are being installed on a member server, but not if they are being installed on a domain controller.

- Some software installation programs might automatically reboot the computer, and you might prefer that certain computers not be taken offline.

In these instances, verifying a computer's role before you install software or configure a service helps ensure that you install the correct software on the computer or use the correct service account for the role of the computer.

The DomainRole property of the Win32_ComputerSystem class can be used to identify the basic role of a computer and its membership in a domain. This property returns one of the values shown in Table 9.4.

Table 9.4   DomainRole Property Values

Value	Description
0	Stand-alone workstation (the computer is not a member of a domain)
1	Member workstation
2	Stand-alone server (the computer is not a member of a domain)
3	Member server

(continued)

Table 9.4   DomainRole Property Values *(continued)*

Value	Description
4	Backup domain controller
5	Primary domain controller

Scripting Steps

Listing 9.12 contains a script that identifies the basic role of a computer. To carry out this task, the script must perform the following steps:

1. Create a variable to specify the computer name.

2. Use a GetObject call to connect to the WMI namespace root\cimv2 on the computer, and set the impersonation level to Impersonate.

3. Use the ExecQuery method to query the Win32_ComputerSystem class.

4. Retrieve the value of the DomainRole property.

5. Convert the value of the DomainRole property to a string value, and then echo that result.

   This step is required because the DomainRole property is stored as an integer (for example, the value 0 for the DomainRole property means that the computer is a stand-alone workstation). This step converts the integer to the appropriate string value.

Listing 9.12   Identifying the Basic Role of a Computer

```
1   strComputer = "."
2   Set objWMIService = GetObject("winmgmts:" _
3       & "{impersonationLevel=impersonate}!\\" & strComputer & "\root\cimv2")
4   Set colComputers = objWMIService.ExecQuery _
5       ("SELECT * FROM Win32_ComputerSystem")
6   For Each objComputer in colComputers
7       Select Case objComputer.DomainRole
8           Case 0
9               strComputerRole = "Standalone Workstation"
10          Case 1
11              strComputerRole = "Member Workstation"
12          Case 2
13              strComputerRole = "Standalone Server"
14          Case 3
15              strComputerRole = "Member Server"
16          Case 4
17              strComputerRole = "Backup Domain Controller"
18          Case 5
19              strComputerRole = "Primary Domain Controller"
20      End Select
21      Wscript.Echo strComputerRole
22  Next
```

Identifying the Role of a Computer Based on the Service It Provides

The way in which you manage a specific computer depends greatly on the role that computer plays. For example, you generally monitor different aspects of a DNS server than a DHCP server. Although no single property can tell you whether a particular computer is a database server, an e-mail server, or a multimedia server, you can often identify the role a computer plays by identifying the services installed on it.

In large organizations, only one of the major services (such as e-mail) is likely to be installed on a single computer. It would be unusual for a mail server to also perform as a server for Microsoft® Windows Media® technologies player files. Because of this, identifying a service installed on a computer can help identify the computer's role in the network. If the Microsoft® Exchange Server service is installed and running on a computer, it is generally safe to assume that this computer functions as a mail server.

You can use the WMI Win32_Service class to enumerate the services installed on a computer. In addition, you can use this class to determine whether those services are currently running and to return any other required information about that service and how it has been configured.

Note

For more information about managing services using WMI, see "Services" in this book.

Scripting Steps

Listing 9.13 contains a script that identifies computer roles based on services installed on the computer. To carry out this task, the script must perform the following steps:

1. Create a variable to specify the computer name.

2. Use a GetObject call to connect to the WMI namespace root\cimv2 on the computer, and set the impersonation level to Impersonate.

3. Use the ExecQuery method to query the Win32_Service class.

   To limit the number of services returned, a Where clause is used to restrict data retrieval to those services with a registry name of MSSQLServer.

4. Use the Count property to determine the number of services returned.

   The Count property provides a quick way to determine whether any instances of Microsoft®
   SQL Server™ are installed on the computer. If the value of the Count property is 0, SQL
   Server is not installed. If the Count is greater than 0, SQL Server is installed.

5. Based on the value of the Count property, echo a string reporting whether SQL Server is
   installed.

   If the service is installed, the script also echoes the current service state, that is, whether the
   service is running, paused, stopped, or resuming operation.

Listing 9.13   Identifying Computer Roles Based on Services

```
1    strComputer = "."
2    Set objWMIService = GetObject("winmgmts:" _
3        & "{impersonationLevel=impersonate}!\\" & strComputer & "\root\cimv2")
4    Set colServices = objWMIService.ExecQuery _
5        ("SELECT * FROM Win32_Service WHERE Name = 'MSSQLServer'")
6    If colServices.Count > 0 Then
7        For Each objService in colServices
8            Wscript.Echo "SQL Server is " & objService.State & "."
9        Next
10   Else
11       Wscript.Echo "SQL Server is not installed on this computer."
12   End If
```

Identifying Active Directory–Specific Roles

Several computer roles (available only to domain controllers) are contingent upon membership in
an Active Directory domain, including the operations master roles (also known as flexible single
master operations, or FSMO, roles) and the global catalog server role. Because Active Directory
relies on these roles to carry out operations, it is vital for system administrators to know which
computers perform operations master roles or function as global catalog servers.

You can use ADSI to determine the Active Directory roles played by a given computer.
Depending on your needs, you can do this by searching Active Directory for computers that
perform specific roles or by using ADSI to bind to a computer and enumerate the roles that the
computer performs.

Enumerating Domain Controllers

The script shown in Listing 9.12 can connect to a specified computer and tell you whether that
computer is a domain controller. What the script cannot do, however, is tell which other
computers are domain controllers. To do that, the script would need to connect to every computer
and determine the computer role.

A better way to obtain a list of all your domain controllers is to retrieve that information from Active Directory. Active Directory includes a Configuration partition that maintains information about the structure of the directory service. This information includes such things as the names of all the domains in the forest and the names of all the domain controllers and global catalog servers. To retrieve a list of domain controllers, you can search the Configuration container for all instances of the nTDSDSA object class. This class represents the Directory Services Agent, the process that provides access to the Active Directory database itself. All domain controllers are members of this class.

Scripting Steps

Listing 9.14 contains a script that enumerates all the domain controllers in Active Directory. To carry out this task, the script must perform the following steps:

1. Create a constant named ADS_SCOPE_SUBTREE and set the value to 2.

   This constant is used to specify a search that begins in the Active Directory root and then proceeds to search all the child containers as well.

2. Create an instance of the Active Directory connection object (ADODB.Connection).

3. Create an instance of the Active Directory command object (ADODB.Command).

   The command object allows you to issue queries and other database commands through the Active Directory connection.

4. Set the Provider property of the connection object to the Active Directory provider (ADsDSOObject), which is the OLE database provider for ADSI.

5. Set the active connection to the Active Directory connection.

6. Set the command text for the Active Directory command object to the SQL query that retrieves all the domain controllers from fabrikam.com.

   The SQL query that retrieves the list of domain controllers is `Select distinguishedName from ' LDAP://cn=Configuration,DC=fabrikam,DC=com' where objectClass='nTDSDSA`.

7. Specify values for page size, time-out, search scope, and caching.

   Although optional, specifying these values can improve the performance of your script in a domain with thousands of computer accounts.

8. Execute the SQL query.

9. When the set of domain controllers is returned, use the MoveFirst method to move to the first computer in the recordset.

10. For each domain controller in the recordset, echo the computer name.

Listing 9.14   Enumerating Domain Controllers

```
1   Const ADS_SCOPE_SUBTREE = 2
2   Set objConnection = CreateObject("ADODB.Connection")
3   Set objCommand =    CreateObject("ADODB.Command")
4   objConnection.Provider = "ADsDSOObject"
5   objConnection.Open "Active Directory Provider"
6   Set objCommand.ActiveConnection = objConnection
7   objCommand.CommandText = _
8       "SELECT distinguishedName FROM " _
9           & "'LDAP://cn=Configuration,DC=fabrikam,DC=com' " _
10              & "WHERE objectClass='nTDSDSA'"
11  objCommand.Properties("Page Size") = 1000
12  objCommand.Properties("Timeout") = 30
13  objCommand.Properties("Searchscope") = ADS_SCOPE_SUBTREE
14  objCommand.Properties("Cache Results") = False
15  Set objRecordSet = objCommand.Execute
16  objRecordSet.MoveFirst
17  Do Until objRecordSet.EOF
18      Wscript.Echo "Computer Name: " & _
19          objRecordSet.Fields("distinguishedName").Value
20      objRecordSet.MoveNext
21  Loop
```

Identifying the Current Domain Controller for a Computer

There are often times when it is useful to know which domain controller was used to authenticate a computer. For example, if users are having difficulty accessing resources, you might want to identify the domain controller that processed the initial authentication. If it seems to be taking an inordinately long time for certain users to log on to the network, you might want to check and see if the same domain controller is processing those logons. To periodically check the validity of your Active Directory topology, you might want to see which domain controllers are being used by the computers at a particular site.

To identify the domain controller used to authenticate a computer, you can use the LDAP provider and bind to rootDSE. When you bind to rootDSE, you are bound to the directory service root. This is why rootDSE is often used as a way to bind to the domain; you can bind to your domain without having to hard-code the domain name within a script.

However, rootDSE is also used to return information about the directory server itself. For example, the dnsHostName attribute tells you the name of the current domain controller for the computer. The serverName attribute returns the distinguished name of the current domain controller.

This script must be run locally; you cannot use it to identify the domain controller for a remote computer. If you want to monitor the domain controllers being used to authenticate user logons, you could use this code as part of a logon script. That way, each time a user logs on, information about the user and the domain controller could be stored in a database.

Scripting Steps

Listing 9.15 contains a script that identifies the current domain controller for a computer. To carry out this task, the script must perform the following steps:

1. Use the LDAP provider to bind to the Active Directory root.

2. Use the Get method to retrieve the value of the dnsHostName attribute, and store that value in a variable named objDC.

3. Echo the value of the variable objDC.

Listing 9.15 Identifying the Current Domain Controller

```
1   Set objDomain = GetObject("LDAP://RootDSE")
2   objDC = objDomain.Get("dnsHostName")
3   Wscript.Echo objDC
```

Identifying Operations Master Roles

Active Directory includes five operations master roles (also known as flexible single master operation or FSMO) that delegate particular responsibilities to particular computers.

Understanding operations master roles and knowing which computers hold these roles is very important. If an operations master role holder is unavailable, you cannot carry out certain Active Directory activities. For example, in order to modify the schema, the schema master must be available. To know if the schema master is available, you need to know which computer holds this role.

In addition, before you assign a computer certain roles, you need to determine whether that computer holds a conflicting role. For example, in a multidomain forest, the infrastructure master must never be placed on a global catalog server. If a given domain controller is the infrastructure master, you must not promote that domain controller to a global catalog server.

To help identify operations master role holders, you can use the searching capabilities available through ADSI. The five operations master roles and their associated ADSI object class are listed in Table 9.5. The object classes are used to search Active Directory for the operations master role holder. The search connects to the object class and then retrieves the value of the FSMORoleOwner attribute.

Table 9.5 ADSI Object Classes and Operations Master Roles

ADSI Object Class	Operations Master Role
domainDNS	**Primary domain controller (PDC) emulator.** Serves two essential functions. First, it acts as a primary domain controller to provide compatibility with Windows NT domains. Second, password changes performed within a domain are replicated immediately to the PDC emulator. This ensures that new password changes take effect right away. If a user is unable to log on to a domain due to a password error, the authenticating domain controller contacts the PDC emulator to see if the user's password has been changed but not yet replicated throughout the domain. If the PDC has a new password, that password is used to authenticate the user. The PDC emulator is often referred to as the primary domain controller.
rIDManager	**RID master.** Replenishes the relative IDs (RIDs) for domain controllers. When a new security principal such as a user or computer account is created, the domain controller used to create the security principal assigns the new object a security identifier (SID). A SID consists of two parts: an identification number that is given to all the objects created in that domain and a unique RID. Together, the two parts uniquely identify any object in the domain. Each domain controller is allocated 512 RIDs. When a domain controller has approximately 100 RIDs remaining, it contacts the RID master and requests an additional 512 RIDs to replenish its supply. If the RID master is unavailable and a domain controller runs out of relative IDs, you will no longer be able to use that computer to create new Active Directory objects.
infrastructureUpdate	**Infrastructure master.** Synchronizes group-to-user references. The infrastructure master is particularly important in a scenario such as this: a user from domain A is a member of a security group in domain B. If you rename the user account, the security group membership is not updated until replication occurs. The infrastructure master is responsible for identifying and correcting issues such as this. If the infrastructure master fails, you can transfer the role to another domain controller. However, you must ensure that the previous infrastructure master never comes back online.
dMD	**Schema master.** Updates the schema for the forest. (There is only one schema master per forest.) You must connect to the schema master in order to update the schema. If the schema master fails, you can transfer the role to another domain controller. However, you must ensure that the previous schema master never comes back online.
crossRefContainer	**Domain naming master.** Adds or removes a domain from the forest. (There is only one domain naming master per forest.) You cannot add or remove a domain unless the domain naming master is available. If the domain naming master fails, you can transfer the role to another domain controller. However, you must ensure that the previous domain naming master never comes back online.

Scripting Steps

Listing 9.16 contains a script that identifies operations master roles in Active Directory. To carry out this task, the script must perform the following steps:

1. Create an instance of the Active Directory connection object (ADODB.Connection).

2. Set the Provider property of the connection object to the Active Directory provider (ADsDSOObject). This is the OLE database provider for ADSI.

3. Set the active connection to the Active Directory connection.

4. Create a command string that searches Active Directory from the root down (LDAP://DC=fabrikam, DC=com). The command string must specify the object class to search for (domainDNS) and the attribute to return (FSMORoleOwner).

   To search for a different operations master role holder, replace domainDNS with the appropriate object class. For example, to locate the RID manager, set the object class to rIDManager.

5. Execute the search command.

6. Retrieve the value of the operations master role holder. This value will be returned as a globally unique identifier (GUID).

7. Connect to the operations master role holder, using the GUID as part of the connection string.

8. Echo the DNS host name of the operations master role holder.

Listing 9.16   Identifying FSMO Roles

```
1   Set objADOConnection = CreateObject("ADODB.Connection")
2   objADOConnection.Provider = "ADSDSOObject"
3   objADOConnection.Open "ADs Provider"
4   strADOQueryString = _
5       "<LDAP://DC=fabrikam,DC=com>;(&(objectClass=domainDNS)" _
6           & "(fSMORoleOwner=*));adspath;subtree"
7   Set RSObj = objADOConnection.Execute(strADOQueryString)
8   Set objFSMO = GetObject(RSObj.Fields(0).Value)
9   Set objNTDS = GetObject("LDAP://" & objFSMO.fSMORoleOwner)
10  Set objComputer = GetObject(objNTDS.Parent)
11  WScript.Echo "The Primary Domain Controller FSMO is: " & _
12      objComputer.dnsHostName
```

Identifying Global Catalog Servers

Knowing which computers in your organization are global catalog servers is very helpful for administering Active Directory efficiently.

Because global catalog servers are required for user authentication, it is important to have an adequate number of global catalog servers at a site to handle the volume of authentication requests and a quick connection to handle each request efficiently. If a remote office does not have its own global catalog server and is connected over a slow network link, authentication of the site's users will be slow.

However, having too many global catalog servers can slow down your network by creating unnecessary replication traffic. Global catalog servers contain information about every item in the forest and can generate a considerable amount of replication data. A remote office that has its own global catalog servers and is connected over a slow network link can provide efficient authentication to its local users, but it might have trouble communicating with other sites because of the quantity of replication data moving across the network link.

You can identify global catalog servers by using ADSI.

Scripting Steps

Listing 9.17 contains a script that identifies global catalog servers by using ADSI. To carry out this task, the script must perform the following steps:

1. Use a GetObject call to bind to the root of the directory information tree on a domain controller (rootDSE).

   The rootDSE is a well-known and reliable location on every domain controller. You can use rootDSE to get distinguished names for the domain container, schema container, and configuration container, as well as other information about the server and the contents of its directory information tree.

2. Use the Get method to retrieve the value of the dsServiceName attribute.

   This attribute represents the distinguished name of the NTDS Settings object for the directory server.

3. Use a second GetObject call to connect to the NTDS Settings object.

   The NTDS settings represent the data in Active Directory that define a computer as a domain controller.

4. Use the Get method to retrieve the value of the Options attribute. The Options attribute represents different things depending on the object. For the NTDS Settings object, the Options attribute indicates whether the computer has been enabled as a global catalog server.

   - If the value is True, echo "This computer is a global catalog server."

   - If the value is False, echo "This computer is not a global catalog server."

Listing 9.17   Identifying Global Catalog Servers

```
1   On Error Resume Next
2   Set objRoot = GetObject("LDAP://atl-dc-01/RootDSE")
3   objDSServiceDN = objRoot.Get("dsServiceName")
4   Set objDSRoot = GetObject("LDAP://atl-dc-02/" & objDSServiceDN )
5   blnCurrentOptions = objDSRoot.Get("options")
6   If blnCurrentOptions Then
7       Wscript.Echo "This computer is a global catalog server."
8   Else
9       Wscript.Echo "This computer is not a global catalog server."
10  End If
```

Enabling or Disabling Global Catalog Servers

As the number of computers in your organization increases or decreases, you might need to enable or disable the global catalog service on domain controllers. For example, if the only global catalog server in a site fails, you can enable a different global catalog server. If a single site has more global catalog servers than it needs (resulting in excessive replication traffic), you can disable the global catalog service on one or more computers.

You can enable and or disable domain controllers as global catalog servers by using ADSI.

Scripting Steps

The scripts for enabling or disabling a global catalog server are very similar.

Enabling a Global Catalog Server

Listing 9.18 contains a script that enables a computer to act as a global catalog server. To carry out this task, the script must perform the following steps:

1. Use a GetObject call to bind to RootDSE on the domain controller you want to enable as a global catalog server.

2. Use the Get method to obtain the value of the dsServiceName attribute.

   The dsServiceName attribute represents the distinguished name for the NTDS Settings object for this domain controller.

3. Use a second GetObject call to connect to the NTDS Settings object.

   The NTDS settings represent the data in the Active Directory that define a computer as a domain controller.

4. Set the value of the Options attribute to 1.

   The Options attribute represents different things depending on the object. For the NTDS Settings object, the Options attribute indicates whether the computer has been enabled as a global catalog server.

5. Use the SetInfo method to apply the changes to Active Directory.

Listing 9.18   Enabling a Global Catalog Server

```
1   On Error Resume Next
2   Set objRoot = GetObject("LDAP://atl-dc-01/RootDSE")
3   objDSServiceDN = objRoot.Get("dsServiceName")
4   Set objDSRoot = GetObject("LDAP://atl-dc-01/" & objDSServiceDN )
5   blnCurrentOptions = objDSRoot.Get("Options")
6   objDSRoot.Put "options" , 1
7   objDSRoot.Setinfo
```

Disabling a Global Catalog Server

To disable a global catalog server, use the same code as shown in Listing 9.18, but set the value of the Options attribute to 0, as shown in Listing 9.19.

Listing 9.19   Disabling a Global Catalog Server

```
1   On Error Resume Next
2   Set objRoot = GetObject("LDAP://atl-dc-01/RootDSE")
3   objDSServiceDN = objRoot.Get("dsServiceName")
4   Set objDSRoot = GetObject("LDAP://atl-dc-01/" & objDSServiceDN )
5   blnCurrentOptions = objDSRoot.Get("Options")
6   objDSRoot.Put "options" , 0
7   objDSRoot.Setinfo
```

Disks and File Systems

On any given day, an organization can generate a staggering amount of data. Maintaining the physical disks and logical disk drives that contain this data is a critical task. System administrators must ensure the preservation of important data for future use, guarantee that users have access to data, and provide adequate free disk space for users to carry out their daily duties. Scripts can be powerful tools that assist system administrators in managing disks, file systems, and other parts of the storage management infrastructure.

In This Chapter

Disks and File Systems Overview **726**

Managing and Monitoring Disk Drives...**726**

    Managing Disk Partitions 730

    Managing Logical Disk Drives 733

    Managing Disk Space 738

Managing Disk Quotas **742**

    Managing Disk Quotas on the NTFS File System...742

    Managing Disk Quotas for Individual Users 748

Managing File Systems **754**

    Managing Page Files...762

Disks and File Systems Overview

Not too long ago, the idea of storage management would have been nonsensical to most system administrators. In the early days of the personal computer, very few computers had hard disks and even fewer needed them. Considering that both the operating system and an application could fit on a floppy drive, the primary task in storage management lay in ensuring that there was always a box of floppy disks in the storeroom.

Needless to say, things have changed considerably in the past 15 years or so. Storage management is now one of the more important duties charged to system administrators, administrators who must manage and monitor hundreds, thousands, and maybe even tens of thousands of disk drives, all with different capacities and characteristics. System administrators must deal with multiple file systems; they must ensure that all users have adequate disk space; and they must impose quotas, if necessary, to ensure that users do not exceed their allotted disk space. System administrators must also quickly identify and repair problems with disks or file systems before those problems affect scores of users.

Because storage management is a huge undertaking, Microsoft provides several scripting solutions that make it easier for system administrators to manage disks and file systems throughout an organization. You can use these scripts on computers running Microsoft® Windows® 2000 operating systems.

Managing and Monitoring Disk Drives

Physical hard disk drives are the primary storage medium for information in any computing environment. Although organizations often use devices such as tape drives and compact disc drives for archiving data, these devices are not suited for day-to-day storage of user data. Only physical hard disks offer the speed and ease of use required for storing data and for running applications and the operating system.

To efficiently manage data, it is important to have a detailed inventory of all your physical disks, their capabilities, and their capacities. You can use the Win32_DiskDrive class to derive this type of inventory. As shown in Table 10.1, you can use the Win32_DiskDrive class to enumerate the disk drives installed on a computer and to return data such as the type of interface used by the drive, the drive manufacturer and model number, and the number of tracks, cylinders, sectors, and heads that compose the drive hardware.

Table 10.1   Win32_DiskDrive Properties

Property	Description
BytesPerSector	Number of bytes in each sector for the physical disk drive.
Capabilities	Array of capabilities of the disk drive. Values include: 0 — Unknown 1 — Other 2 — Sequential Access 3 — Random Access 4 — Supports Writing 5 — Encryption 6 — Compression 7 — Supports Removable Media 8 — Manual Cleaning 9 — Automatic Cleaning 10 — SMART Notification 11 — Supports Dual-Sided Media 12 — Ejection Prior to Drive Dismount Not Required
CompressionMethod	Algorithm or tool used by the device to support compression.
Description	Description of the disk drive.
DeviceID	Unique identifier of the disk drive with other devices on the system.
Index	Physical drive number of the given drive. A value of 0xFF indicates that the given drive does not map to a physical drive.
InterfaceType	Interface type of physical disk drive, typically IDE or SCSI.
Manufacturer	Name of the disk drive manufacturer.
MediaType	Type of media used or accessed by this device. Values are: ▪ Removable media ▪ Fixed hard disk ▪ Unknown
Model	Manufacturer's model number of the disk drive.
Name	Label by which the disk drive is known.
Partitions	Number of partitions on the physical disk drive that are recognized by the operating system.

(continued)

Table 10.1   Win32_DiskDrive Properties *(continued)*

Property	Description
PNPDeviceID	Plug and Play device identifier of the logical device.
SCSIBus	SCSI bus number of the disk drive.
SCSILogicalUnit	SCSI logical unit number (LUN) of the disk drive.
SCSIPort	SCSI port number of the disk drive.
SCSITargetId	SCSI identifier number of the disk drive.
SectorsPerTrack	Number of sectors in each track for the physical disk drive.
Signature	Unique identifier for a disk drive.
Size	Size of the disk drive. Disk drive size is calculated by multiplying the total number of cylinders, the tracks in each cylinder, the sectors in each track, and the bytes in each sector.
SystemName	Name of the computer where the disk is installed.
TotalCylinders	Total number of cylinders on the physical disk drive.
TotalHeads	Total number of heads on the disk drive.
TotalSectors	Total number of sectors on the physical disk drive.
TotalTracks	Total number of tracks on the physical disk drive.
TracksPerCylinder	Number of tracks in each cylinder on the physical disk drive.

 Note

The values reported for TotalCylinders, TotalHeads, TotalSectors, TotalTracks, and TracksPerCylinder are obtained through extended functions of BIOS interrupt 13h. These values might be inaccurate if the drive uses a translation scheme to support high capacity disk sizes. Consult the manufacturer for accurate drive specifications.

Scripting Steps

Listing 10.1 contains a script that enumerates the properties of all the physical drives installed on a computer. To carry out this task, the script must perform the following steps:

1. Create a variable to specify the computer name.

2. Use a GetObject call to connect to the Windows Management Instrumentation (WMI) namespace root\cimv2, and set the impersonation level to "impersonate."

3. Use the ExecQuery method to query the Win32_DiskDrive class.

   This query returns a collection consisting of all the disk drives installed on the computer.

4. For each disk drive in the collection, echo the values of selected drive properties, including DeviceID (drive letter) and partitions, and total cylinders, heads, sectors, and tracks.

Because the drive capabilities are returned as an array, a For Each loop is used to enumerate each capability.

Listing 10.1   Enumerating Physical Disk Drive Properties

```
1   strComputer = "."
2   Set objWMIService = GetObject("winmgmts:" _
3       & "{impersonationLevel=impersonate}!\\" & strComputer & "\root\cimv2")
4   Set colDiskDrives = objWMIService.ExecQuery _
5       ("SELECT * FROM Win32_DiskDrive")
6   For each objDiskDrive in colDiskDrives
7       Wscript.Echo "Bytes Per Sector: " & _
8           objDiskDrive.BytesPerSector
9       For Each strCapability in objDiskDrive.Capabilities
10          Wscript.Echo "Capabilities: " & strCapability
11      Next
12      Wscript.Echo "Caption: " & objDiskDrive.Caption
13      Wscript.Echo "Device ID: " & objDiskDrive.DeviceID
14      Wscript.Echo "Index: " & objDiskDrive.Index
15      Wscript.Echo "Interface Type: " & objDiskDrive.InterfaceType
16      Wscript.Echo "Manufacturer: " & objDiskDrive.Manufacturer
17      Wscript.Echo "Media Loaded: " & objDiskDrive.MediaLoaded
18      Wscript.Echo "Media Type: " & objDiskDrive.MediaType
19      Wscript.Echo "Model: " & objDiskDrive.Model
20      Wscript.Echo "Name: " & objDiskDrive.Name
21      Wscript.Echo "Partitions: " & objDiskDrive.Partitions
22      Wscript.Echo "PNP DeviceID: " & objDiskDrive.PNPDeviceID
23      Wscript.Echo "SCSI Bus: " & objDiskDrive.SCSIBus
24      Wscript.Echo "SCSI Logical Unit: " & _
25          objDiskDrive.SCSILogicalUnit
26      Wscript.Echo "SCSI Port: " & objDiskDrive.SCSIPort
27      Wscript.Echo "SCSI TargetId: " & objDiskDrive.SCSITargetId
28      Wscript.Echo "Sectors Per Track: " & _
29          objDiskDrive.SectorsPerTrack
30      Wscript.Echo "Size: " & objDiskDrive.Size
31      Wscript.Echo "Status: " & objDiskDrive.Status
32      Wscript.Echo "Total Cylinders: " & _
33          objDiskDrive.TotalCylinders
34      Wscript.Echo "Total Heads: " & objDiskDrive.TotalHeads
35      Wscript.Echo "Total Sectors: " & objDiskDrive.TotalSectors
36      Wscript.Echo "Total Tracks: " & objDiskDrive.TotalTracks
37      Wscript.Echo "Tracks Per Cylinder: " & _
38          objDiskDrive.TracksPerCylinder
39  Next
```

Managing Disk Partitions

A partition is a structural division of a physical disk drive. Although a drive can contain a single partition, larger volumes are often divided into multiple partitions. This is why you might have drives C, D, and E even though your computer has only a single physical hard disk.

The Windows 2000 operating system supports the following partition types:

- **Primary partition**. This is the only type of partition that can have an operating system installed. Each drive can have as many as four primary partitions, each assigned a different drive letter.

- **Extended partition**. An additional partition that can be subdivided into multiple logical drives, each assigned a unique drive letter. A drive can have only one extended partition; however, you can divide this partition into multiple logical drives. This enables a disk to have more than just the four allowed primary partitions.

- **System partition**. Any primary partition containing an operating system.

Partitions can tell you how a physical disk drive is actually being used. By examining the physical partitions on a disk, you can determine the following types of things:

- How the disk has been divided into logical drives.

- If there is unpartitioned space available on the disk. This can be determined by subtracting the size of all the partitions on a disk from the size of the disk itself.

- If you can boot the computer from that disk (that is, does the disk contain a boot partition).

All these questions can be resolved by using the Win32_DiskPartition class. A subset of partition properties available through this class is shown in Table 10.2.

Table 10.2   Win32_DiskPartition Properties

Property	Description
BlockSize	Size (in bytes) of the blocks that form this partition.
Bootable	Boolean value indicating whether the computer can be booted from this partition.
BootPartition	Boolean value that indicates whether the partition is the active partition. The operating system uses the active partition when booting from a hard disk.
DeviceID	Unique identifier that differentiates the disk drive and partition from the rest of the system.
DiskIndex	Index number of the disk containing this partition.

(continued)

Table 10.2   Win32_DiskPartition Properties *(continued)*

Property	Description
Index	Index number of the partition.
Name	Label by which the object is known.
NumberOfBlocks	Total number of consecutive blocks, each block being the size of the value contained in the BlockSize property. The total size of the disk can be calculated by multiplying the value of the BlockSize property by the value of this property. If the value of BlockSize is 1, this property is the total size of the disk.
PrimaryPartition	Boolean value indicating whether this is the primary partition on the computer.
Size	Total size of the partition in bytes.
StartingOffset	Starting offset (in bytes) of the partition.
SystemName	Name of the computer where the partition is installed.
Type	Type of the partition. Values are: • Unused • 12-bit FAT • Xenix Type 1 • Xenix Type 2 • 16-bit FAT • Extended Partition • MS-DOS® V4 Huge • Installable File System • PowerPC Reference Platform • UNIX • NTFS file system • Win95 with Extended Int 13 • Extended with Extended Int 13 • Logical Disk Manager • Unknown

Scripting Steps

Listing 10.2 contains a script that enumerates the properties of all the disk partitions on a computer. To carry out this task, the script must perform the following steps:

1. Create a variable to specify the computer name.

2. Use a GetObject call to connect to the WMI namespace root\cimv2, and set the impersonation level to "impersonate."

3. Use the ExecQuery method to query the Win32_DiskPartition class.

   This query returns a collection consisting of all the disk partitions on all the disk drives installed on the computer.

4. For each disk partition in the collection, echo the value of properties such as the DeviceID, the partition size, and whether the partition is bootable.

Listing 10.2   Enumerating Disk Partition Properties

```
1   strComputer = "."
2   Set objWMIService = GetObject("winmgmts:" _
3       & "{impersonationLevel=impersonate}!\\" & strComputer & "\root\cimv2")
4   Set colDiskPartitions = objWMIService.ExecQuery _
5       ("SELECT * FROM Win32_DiskPartition")
6   For each objPartition in colDiskPartitions
7       Wscript.Echo "Block Size: " & objPartition.BlockSize
8       Wscript.Echo "Bootable: " & objPartition.Bootable
9       Wscript.Echo "Boot Partition: " & objPartition.BootPartition
10      Wscript.Echo "Description: " & objPartition.Description
11      Wscript.Echo "Device ID: " & objPartition.DeviceID
12      Wscript.Echo "Disk Index: " & objPartition.DiskIndex
13      Wscript.Echo "Index: " & objPartition.Index
14      Wscript.Echo "Name: " & objPartition.Name
15      Wscript.Echo "Number Of Blocks: " & _
16          objPartition.NumberOfBlocks
17      Wscript.Echo "Primary Partition: " & _
18          objPartition.PrimaryPartition
19      Wscript.Echo "Size: " & objPartition.Size
20      Wscript.Echo "Starting Offset: " & _
21          objPartition.StartingOffset
22      Wscript.Echo "Type: " & objPartition.Type
23  Next
```

Managing Logical Disk Drives

A physical disk drive is the cornerstone of any storage management system. However, after a physical disk drive has been installed, neither users nor system administrators typically deal with the hardware directly. Instead, both users and system administrators interact with the logical drives that have been created on the disk.

A logical drive is a subdivision of a partition that has been assigned its own drive letter. (It is possible to have a partition that has *not* been assigned a drive letter.) When you talk about drive C or drive D, you are referring to a logical drive rather than to a physical disk drive. Likewise, when you save a document to drive E, you are saving it to the logical drive. Physical disks compose the hardware that makes up a drive, including such components as heads, sectors, and cylinders. Logical drives, by contrast, have properties such as disk space, available disk space, and drive letters.

The properties of a logical drive can be retrieved using the Win32_LogicalDisk class. A subset of properties available through this class is shown in Table 10.3.

 Note

The Win32_LogicalDisk class can be used only to enumerate the properties of local disk drives. However, you can use the Win32_MappedLogicalDisk class to enumerate the properties of mapped network drives.

Table 10.3   Win32_LogicalDisk Properties

Property	Description
Compressed	Indicates whether the logical volume exists as a single compressed entity, such as a DoubleSpace volume. If file-based compression is supported (such as on NTFS), this property is False.
DeviceID	Unique identifier of the logical disk from other devices on the system.
DriveType	Numeric value corresponding to the type of disk drive this logical disk represents. Values are: 0 – Unknown 1 – No Root Directory 2 – Removable Disk 3 – Local Disk 4 – Network Drive 5 – Compact Disc 6 – RAM Disk
FileSystem	File system on the logical disk.

(continued)

Table 10.3 Win32_LogicalDisk Properties *(continued)*

Property	Description
FreeSpace	Space available on the logical disk.
MaximumComponentLength	Maximum length of a file name component (the portion of a file name between backslashes) supported by the Win32 drive. The value can indicate that long names are supported by the specified file system.
MediaType	Type of media currently present in the logical drive. The value might not be exact for removable drives if there is no media currently in the drive. Values include (but are not limited to): 0 — Format is unknown 1 — 5.25-inch floppy disk (1.2Mb, 512 bytes/sector) 2 — 3.5-inch floppy disk (1.44Mb, 512 bytes/sector) 3 — 3.5-inch floppy disk (2.88Mb, 512 bytes/sector) 4 — 3.5-inch floppy disk (20.8Mb, 512 bytes/sector) 11 — Removable media other than floppy 12 — Fixed hard disk media 20 — 3.5-inch floppy disk (128Mb, 512 bytes/sector) 21 — 3.5-inch floppy disk (230Mb, 512 bytes/sector)
Name	Label by which the object is known.
Size	Size of the disk drive.
SupportsFileBasedCompression	Indicates whether the logical disk partition supports file-based compression, such as is the case with NTFS. This property is False when the Compressed property is True.
SystemName	Name of the computer where the drive is installed.
VolumeName	Volume name of the logical disk. (Maximum 32 characters.)
VolumeSerialNumber	Volume serial number of the logical disk. (Maximum 11 characters.)

Scripting Steps

Listing 10.3 contains a script that enumerates the properties of all the logical disk drives on a computer. To carry out this task, the script must perform the following steps:

1. Create a variable to specify the computer name.

2. Use a GetObject call to connect to the WMI namespace root\cimv2, and set the impersonation level to "impersonate."

3. Use the ExecQuery method to query the Win32_LogicalDisk class.

   This query returns a collection consisting of all the logical disk drives installed on the computer.

4. For each logical disk drive in the collection, echo the drive properties, including the DeviceID, the type of file system installed on the drive, the drive type, and the amount of free space available on the drive.

Listing 10.3   Enumerating Logical Disk Drive Properties

```
1   strComputer = "."
2   Set objWMIService = GetObject("winmgmts:" _
3       & "{impersonationLevel=impersonate}!\\" & strComputer & "\root\cimv2")
4   Set colDisks = objWMIService.ExecQuery _
5       ("SELECT * FROM Win32_LogicalDisk")
6   For each objDisk in colDisks
7       Wscript.Echo "Compressed: " & objDisk.Compressed
8       Wscript.Echo "Description: " & objDisk.Description
9       Wscript.Echo "Device ID: " & objDisk.DeviceID
10      Wscript.Echo "Drive Type: " & objDisk.DriveType
11      Wscript.Echo "FileSystem: " & objDisk.FileSystem
12      Wscript.Echo "FreeSpace: " & objDisk.FreeSpace
13      Wscript.Echo "MediaType: " & objDisk.MediaType
14      Wscript.Echo "Name: " & objDisk.Name
15      Wscript.Echo "Size: " & objDisk.Size
16      Wscript.Echo "SupportsFileBasedCompression: " & _
17          objDisk.SupportsFileBasedCompression
18      Wscript.Echo "SystemName: " & objDisk.SystemName
19      Wscript.Echo "VolumeName: " & objDisk.VolumeName
20      Wscript.Echo "VolumeSerialNumber: " & _
21          objDisk.VolumeSerialNumber
22  Next
```

Identifying Drives and Drive Types

Enterprise scripting often involves configuring hardware and software on remote computers; in turn, this requires you to know, in advance, the type of disk drives installed on a computer. For example, a script that installs an application on drive E works only if drive E is a hard disk. If drive E happens to represent a floppy disk or a CD-ROM drive, the script fails.

Fortunately, you can use the Win32_LogicalDisk class to verify the drive type for each disk drive installed on a computer.

Scripting Steps

Listing 10.4 contains a script that identifies the drives and drive types installed on a computer. To carry out this task, the script must perform the following steps:

1. Create a variable to specify the computer name.

2. Use a GetObject call to connect to the WMI namespace root\cimv2, and set the impersonation level to "impersonate."

3. Use the ExecQuery method to query the Win32_LogicalDisk class.

This query returns a collection consisting of all the logical disk drives (including hard disks, floppy disks, and compact discs) installed on the computer.

4. For each logical disk drive in the collection, echo the DeviceID (the drive letter) and the drive type.

The Win32_LogicalDisk class returns the value of the DriveType property as an integer. Therefore, a series of Select Case statements is used to convert the value to a text string. For example, if the DriveType is equal to 3, the string "Local hard disk" is echoed to the screen.

Listing 10.4   Identifying Drives and Drive Types

```
1   strComputer = "."
2   Set objWMIService = GetObject("winmgmts:" _
3       & "{impersonationLevel=impersonate}!\\" & strComputer & "\root\cimv2")
4   Set colDisks = objWMIService.ExecQuery _
5       ("SELECT * FROM Win32_LogicalDisk")
6   For Each objDisk in colDisks
7       Wscript.Echo "DeviceID: "& objDisk.DeviceID
8       Select Case objDisk.DriveType
9           Case 1
10              Wscript.Echo "No root directory."
11          Case 2
12              Wscript.Echo "DriveType: Removable drive."
13          Case 3
14              Wscript.Echo "DriveType: Local hard disk."
15          Case 4
16              Wscript.Echo "DriveType: Network disk."
17          Case 5
18              Wscript.Echo "DriveType: Compact disk."
19          Case 6
20              Wscript.Echo "DriveType: RAM disk."
21          Case Else
22              Wscript.Echo "Drive type could not be determined."
23      End Select
24  Next
```

Changing Logical Disk Volume Names

Using drive letters as the sole means of identifying a logical drive can cause confusion. Drive letters can vary not only from computer to computer (depending on how many drives are installed on each computer), but can also vary over time on an individual computer. For example, a computer might have a removable drive connected, and thus have drives A, B, C, D, and E. Later, the drive might be disconnected and the computer would then have drives A, B, C, and D.

One way to work around this problem is to use volume names (also referred to as volume labels) to help differentiate logical drives. For example, a computer might have the following logical drives:

- Drive C (system drive)

- Drive D (applications drive)

- Drive E (data drive)

Instead of referring to these as drives C, D, and E, you can give them the volume names System, Applications, and Data. This makes it easier to identify the individual drives, particularly if other computers in the organization are configured in a different manner, for example, with drive D hosting data and drive E hosting applications. Using a consistent naming scheme across the organization helps facilitate administration and makes it easier for users who might use a different computer each time they log on.

You can use the Win32_LogicalDisk class to rename volumes on a computer. When renaming volumes, consider the following issues:

- Volume names are limited to 32 characters.

- You cannot change the volume label on a removable drive.

- Volume names do not have to be unique on a computer. Therefore, if you specify the incorrect drive when using scripts to change volume names, you could inadvertently give every volume on the computer the same name.

Scripting Steps

Listing 10.5 contains a script that changes the name of a volume. To carry out this task, the script must perform the following steps:

1. Create a variable to specify the computer name.

2. Use a GetObject call to connect to the WMI namespace root\cimv2 and set the impersonation level to "impersonate."

3. Use the ExecQuery method to query the Win32_DiskDrive class.

   To ensure that only drive C receives the name change, a Where clause is included to limit data retrieval to those drives with a DeviceID of C. The query thus returns a collection consisting of only those logical disk drives with a DeviceID of C.

4. For the only disk drive in the collection, set the VolumeName property to "Finance Volume".

5. Use the Put_ method to apply the changes and rename the volume.

Listing 10.5   Changing Volume Names

```
1  strComputer = "."
2  Set objWMIService = GetObject("winmgmts:" _
3      & "{impersonationLevel=impersonate}!\\" & strComputer & "\root\cimv2")
4  Set colDrives = objWMIService.ExecQuery _
5      ("SELECT * FROM Win32_LogicalDisk WHERE DeviceID = 'C:'")
6  For Each objDrive in colDrives
7      objDrive.VolumeName = "Finance Volume"
8      objDrive.Put_
9  Next
```

Managing Disk Space

In storage management, it is crucial to ensure that there is enough disk space available to meet user needs. Users need room to store their documents, and you should not allow servers to fail because of an out-of-disk-space error. In addition, tracking disk space usage is important in planning for future needs.

Enumerating Disk Space on a Computer

You can use the Win32_LogicalDisk class to enumerate the available disk space on any computer in your organization.

Scripting Steps

Listing 10.6 contains a script that enumerates the free space on all the hard disk drives on a computer. To carry out this task, the script must perform the following steps:

1. Create a constant named LOCAL_HARD_DISK and set the value to 3. This constant limits data retrieval to local hard disks (DriveType = 3).

2. Create a variable to specify the computer name.

3. Use a GetObject call to connect to the WMI namespace root\cimv2, and set the impersonation level to "impersonate."

4. Use the ExecQuery method to query the Win32_LogicalDisk class.

   Because free space is typically a concern only on local hard disks (as opposed to floppy disks or compact discs), a Where clause is included to limit data retrieval to local hard disks (DriveType = LOCAL_HARD_DISK). This results in a collection of all the hard disks installed on the computer.

5. For each logical disk drive in the collection, echo the DeviceID and the value of the FreeSpace property.

Listing 10.6   Enumerating Free Disk Space

```
1  Const HARD_DISK = 3
2  strComputer = "."
3  Set objWMIService = GetObject("winmgmts:" _
4      & "{impersonationLevel=impersonate}!\\" & strComputer & "\root\cimv2")
5  Set colDisks = objWMIService.ExecQuery _
6      ("SELECT * FROM Win32_LogicalDisk WHERE DriveType = " _
7          & HARD_DISK & "")
8  For Each objDisk in colDisks
9      Wscript.Echo "Device ID: " & objDisk.DeviceID
10     Wscript.Echo "Free Disk Space: " & objDisk.FreeSpace
11 Next
```

Enumerating Disk Space by User

Tracking disk space use by user is an important administrative task. It helps ensure that users are allocated sufficient disk space, and it also ensures that no single user takes up a disproportionate share of the available space.

If you use NTFS disk quotas, NTFS tracks the amount of disk space consumed by each user on a volume. To gain a better understanding of how disk space is being apportioned on a computer, you can enable disk quotas on a volume and allow NTFS to enumerate disk space use by user. After quotas have been enabled, you can retrieve the disk space use enumeration by using the DiskQuotaControl Automation object. This use of this object is explained in more detail in the "Managing Disk Quotas on the NTFS File System" section of this chapter.

 Tip

Enabling disk quotas does not mean you have to limit the amount of disk space available to users. If you are primarily concerned with assessing disk space use, enable quotas but allocate each user an unlimited amount of disk space. Alternatively, you can enable quotas, retrieve an NTFS-generated disk space use report, and then disable the quotas again.

Scripting Steps

Listing 10.7 contains a script that uses disk quotas to enumerate disk space use by user. To carry out this task, the script must perform the following steps:

1. Create an instance of the DiskQuota1 object.

2. Use the Initialize method to indicate that the new quota entry should be added to drive C. This will return a collection of all users with disk quota entries on drive C.

   The Initialize method requires the following two parameters:

   - The drive letter of the drive where quotas are being enumerated (in this case, C).

   - The value True, indicating that the drive should be initialized for read/write access. By setting this value to False, you can enumerate disk quota entries on the volume but you cannot make any changes (read-only).

3. For each user in the collection of disk quota entries, echo the values of the LogonName and QuotaUsed properties.

Listing 10.7   Using Disk Quotas to Enumerate Disk Space by User

```
1  Set colDiskQuotas = CreateObject("Microsoft.DiskQuota.1")
2  colDiskQuotas.Initialize "C:\", True
3  For Each objUser in colDiskQuotas
4      Wscript.Echo "Logon name: " & objUser.LogonName
5      Wscript.Echo "Quota used: " & objUser.QuotaUsed
6  Next
```

Monitoring Free Disk Space in Real-Time

If disk space is used at a fairly predictable rate, you do not have to constantly monitor the free space on a disk. Instead, you might check free space once or twice a day and then use that data to predict when available space might become scarce.

However, disk use might not always be predictable. On some servers, the amount of data added to the drive might vary widely from day to day. If these servers carry out critical functions in your organization, you might prefer to be notified immediately if disk space runs low. Instead of finding out tomorrow morning that the mail server is almost out of disk space, you might want to be informed the moment available space drops below a specified level.

To receive these immediate notifications, you can use a temporary event consumer to monitor available disk space. You can specify a threshold, such as 100 megabytes (MB) of free space, and receive immediate notification if available disk space on the computer falls below that threshold.

Scripting Steps

Listing 10.8 contains a script that monitors the free disk space on a computer. To carry out this task, the script must perform the following steps:

1. Create a constant named LOCAL_HARD_DISK and set the value to 3.

This ensures that the query responds only to changes to the hard disks installed on the computer.

2. Create a variable to specify the computer name.

3. Use a GetObject call to connect to the WMI namespace root\cimv2, and set the impersonation level to "impersonate."

4. Use the ExecNotificationQuery method to register for event notifications. In this case, notification is requested any time there is a modification to the Win32_LogicalDisk class. The Within 30 clause specifies that events will be checked every 30 seconds, which means you will receive a notice no later than 30 seconds after a disk runs low on disk space.

5. Create a Do loop to allow for continuous monitoring.

6. Each time notification is received (by means of the NextEvent method), check to see if the event involves a hard disk. If it does, proceed to step 7. If it does not, proceed to step 8.

7. If the event involved a change to a hard disk and the available space on the disk is now less than 100,000,000 bytes, echo the message "Hard disk space has fallen below 100,000,000 bytes." In a production-level script, of course, you might send an e-mail or a network alert rather than simply echo a message to the screen.

8. Loop around and continue monitoring.

Listing 10.8   Monitoring Free Disk Space

```
1   Const LOCAL_HARD_DISK = 3
2   strComputer = "."
3   Set objWMIService = GetObject("winmgmts:" _
4       & "{impersonationLevel=impersonate}!\\" & strComputer & "\root\cimv2")
5   Set colMonitoredDisks = objWMIService.ExecNotificationQuery _
6       ("Select * from __instancemodificationevent within 30 where " _
7           & "TargetInstance isa 'Win32_LogicalDisk'")
8   i = 0
9   Do While i = 0
10      Set objDiskChange = colMonitoredDisks.NextEvent
11      If objDiskChange.TargetInstance.DriveType = LOCAL_HARD_DISK Then
12          If objDiskChange.TargetInstance.Size < 100000000 Then
13              Wscript.Echo "Hard disk space is below 100000000 bytes."
14          End If
15      End If
16  Loop
```

Managing Disk Quotas

Storing user data on central file servers offers a number of conveniences: the data is easy to locate, easy to transfer to another user, and easy to back up. However, centralized data storage does pose one problem: How do you prevent a single user from using up all the available disk space? As more and more users have gained access to the Internet, this problem has become even more severe, with many users downloading music and video files, expecting to store that data on the central file server. Disk quotas, introduced in the Windows 2000 operating systems, provide a way for administrators to monitor and control disk space use on servers.

With disk quotas, you can set limits on a user's disk space. If a user exceeds his or her quota, you can record this fact in the System event log, or you can set the system to deny the user the ability to store additional information. You can also customize quotas; this allows you to allocate larger amounts of disk space to users (such as graphic artists) who require additional storage.

Disk quotas also enable you to:

- Track disk use on a per-user, per-volume basis, and thus better plan for storage allocation.

- Manage storage resources more effectively by requiring users to periodically delete unneeded files.

- Decrease backup and restoration times by limiting the amount of data that needs to be backed up and restored.

Managing Disk Quotas on the NTFS File System

Disk quotas are an integral part of the NTFS file system. When a file or a folder is created on a volume formatted with NTFS, that item is assigned an owner (typically the user who created the item). NTFS obtains the user ID of the file owner and stores that information in the file or folder's Standard Information attribute. This attribute tallies all the disk space allocated to the file or folder. NTFS then locates the quota entry for that user and determines whether the new allocation of disk space causes the user to exceed the assigned quota. If it does, NTFS then takes the appropriate steps, which can include logging an entry in the System event log or preventing the user from creating the file or folder. As the file or folder changes size, NTFS updates the quota control entry to reflect the total disk space used by the user.

Disk quotas are not configured on a computer-wide basis, but are instead tied to individual NTFS volumes. Each drive has separate quota settings, and the actions you take on one volume do not affect the other volumes.

For example, a computer might have a single hard disk divided into three volumes: drives C, D, and E. Each of these drives has separate quota settings. You could enable disk quotas on drives C and D, but disable them on drive E. Likewise, you could grant users 50 MB of disk space on drive C and 100 MB of disk space on drive D.

When managing disk quotas on a computer, the actions you take on one volume do not affect the other volumes in any way. If you allocate User A 50 MB of disk space on drive C, this does not also give User A 50 MB of disk space on drives D and E. If you disable disk quotas on drive D, quotas remain enabled on drives C and E.

In addition to allocating disk space, you can specify a quota warning level, the amount of disk space use that triggers an alert (an event recorded in the System event log informing you that a user is nearing the quota). You can also determine which of the following actions the system takes if a user exceeds the quota:

- Take no action at all.

- Record an event in the System event log.

- Deny the user the right to store additional data until he or she has removed enough files to get back under the quota.

The Windows 2000 operating systems include an Automation object — the DiskQuotaControl object — that can be used to create and manage disk quotas on a volume. The one limitation of this object is that it must be used locally. You must run the script on the computer where the disk quota entry is created, and you cannot use the DiskQuotaControl object to create quota entries or manage quota settings on remote volumes.

 Note

You can use the WshController object to run the script on a remote computer, and thus create quota entries on a remote computer. For more information about the WshController object, see "WSH Primer" in this book.

In addition, the DiskQuotaControl object can retrieve information only for one volume at a time. After creating an instance of the object, you must use the Initialize method and pass it the drive letter of the volume you want to work with. (You cannot return a collection consisting of all the volumes on the computer and then manage the quota settings for each of these volumes all at once.) For example, the following code sample allows you to work with disk quotas on drive C:

```
Set colDiskQuotas = CreateObject("Microsoft.DiskQuota.1")
colDiskQuotas.Initialize "C:\", True
```

To work with a second volume (such as drive D), you will have to call the Initialize method a second time, passing the drive letter of the new volume.

```
colDiskQuotas.Initialize "D:\", True
```

After calling this method, you will be able to work only with disk quotas on drive D. To work with quotas on drive C again, you would need to call the Initialize method a third time, once again passing the method the drive letter for drive C.

Enumerating Disk Quota Settings

Keeping track of the quota settings on all volumes on a computer is an important administrative task. You need to know whether disk quotas have been enabled, and you need to know both the default quota and the actions the system takes if a user exceeds the quota. This information can be retrieved by using the DiskQuotaControl. Table 10.4 lists a subset of key properties for this object. All of these properties are read/write, meaning that scripts can be used to both configure and enumerate these settings.

Table 10.4   DiskQuotaControl Properties

Property	Description
DefaultQuotaLimit	Default limit (in bytes) set for quotas on this particular volume. If the DefaultQuotaLimit is -1, no quota limit has been set.
DefaultQuotaThreshold	Default warning limit (in bytes) set for quotas on this particular volume. If the DefaultQuotaThreshold is -1, no warning limit has been set.
LogQuotaLimit	Indicates whether or not events are written to the event log if users exceed their quotas.
QuotaState	Level of quota management set for this particular volume. Values are: 0 – Quota management is not enabled on this volume. 1 – Quotas are enabled on this volume, but are not enforced. Users are allowed to exceed their quota limit. 2 – Quotas are tracked and enforced on this volume. Users are not allowed to exceed their quota limit.
LogQuotaThreshold	Indicates that events are written to the event log when the warning limit is exceeded.

Scripting Steps

Listing 10.9 contains a script that enumerates the disk quota settings for drive C on a computer. To carry out this task, the script must perform the following steps:

1. Create an instance of the DiskQuota1 object.

2. Use the Initialize method to indicate that quota settings should be enumerated for drive C.

    The Initialize method requires the following two parameters:

    *   The drive letter of the drive (in this case, C).

    *   The value True, indicating that the drive should be initialized for read/write access. By setting this value to False, you can enumerate disk quota settings on the volume but you cannot make any changes (read-only).

3. Echo the values of the disk quota settings.

   Because the quota state is returned as an integer (0 if quotas are disabled, 1 if quotas are enabled but not enforced, and 2 if quotas are enabled and enforced), an If Then construct is used to echo the appropriate message (for example, "Quota state: Disabled" if the value of the QuotaState property is 0).

Listing 10.9   Enumerating Disk Quota Settings

```
1   Set colDiskQuotas = CreateObject("Microsoft.DiskQuota.1")
2   colDiskQuotas.Initialize "C:\", True
3   If colDiskQuotas.QuotaState = 2 Then
4       Wscript.Echo "Quota state: Enabled and enforced"
5   ElseIf colDiskQuotas.QuotaState = 1 Then
6       Wscript.Echo "Quota state: Enabled but not enforced"
7   Else
8       Wscript.Echo "Quota state: Disabled"
9   End If
10  Wscript.Echo "Default quota limit: " & colDiskQuotas.DefaultQuotaLimit
11  Wscript.Echo "Default warning limit: " & _
12      colDiskQuotas.DefaultQuotaThreshold
13  Wscript.Echo "Record quota violations in event log: " & _
14      colDiskQuotas.LogQuotaLimit
15  Wscript.Echo "Record warnings in event log: " & _
16      colDiskQuotas.LogQuotaThreshold
```

Enabling and Disabling Disk Quotas

You can enable and disable disk quotas on a volume by toggling the value of the DiskQuotaControl QuotaState property. When the value of the QuotaState property is set to 2, quotas are enabled and enforced; users who exceed their quota limit will not be able to save additional data to the drive. When the value of the QuotaState property is set to 1, quotas will be enabled but not enforced. This means that users who exceed their quota limit will still be able to save data to the drive. When the value of the QuotaState property is set to 0, quotas are disabled.

When you disable quotas on a volume, you do not discard previous quota information. Instead, you simply stop the Windows 2000 operating system from enforcing disk quotas and tracking disk space usage.

For example, suppose you have a volume with the quota entries shown in Table 10.5.

Table 10.5   Sample Disk Quota Entries

Name	Quota Limit	Warning Level
KMeyer	100 MB	90 MB
PAckerman	200 MB	180 MB
RWilliams	400 MB	350 MB

If you disable disk quotas on this volume, these quota entries are not deleted. If you later decide to re-enable disk quotas, each of the entries shown in Table 10.5 is restored, along with the appropriate quota limit and warning level.

Scripting Steps

Listing 10.10 contains a script that enables disk quotas for drive C on a computer. To carry out this task, the script must perform the following steps:

1. Create a constant named ENABLE_QUOTAS and set the value to 2. This constant will be used to enable and enforce disk quotas on the volume.

2. Create an instance of the DiskQuota1 object.

3. Use the Initialize method to indicate that disk quotas should be enabled on drive C.

   The Initialize method requires the following two parameters:

   - The drive letter of the drive where disk quotas are being enabled (in this case, C).

   - The value True, indicating that the drive should be initialized for read/write access.

4. Set the value of the QuotaState property to 2, using the constant ENABLE_QUOTAS.

Listing 10.10   Enabling Disk Quotas

```
1  Const ENABLE_QUOTAS = 2
2  Set colDiskQuotas = CreateObject("Microsoft.DiskQuota.1")
3  colDiskQuotas.Initialize "C:\", True
4  colDiskQuotas.QuotaState = ENABLE_QUOTAS
```

Configuring Default Disk Quota Settings

As circumstances change, you might need to adjust the default quota settings on a volume. For example, you might initially give each user up to 100 MB of storage space on a volume. If your department hires new employees, you might have to lower this quota to ensure that all these additional users can store items on the disk. Alternatively, by purchasing a second file server for user data, you might be able to divide your users between the two servers, thus providing them with additional disk space.

Either way, you can use the DiskQuotaControl to change the default quota values for a volume. In addition to changing the quota and warning levels, you can also specify whether you want to record quota violations in the event log.

When you change the default disk quota settings, these new values apply only to new users; they are not applied to users who already have disk quota entries on the volume. For example, suppose you have a volume with the quota entries shown in Table 10.6.

Table 10.6 Sample Disk Quota Entries

Name	Quota Limit	Warning Level
KMeyer	100 MB	90 MB
PAckerman	200 MB	180 MB
RWilliams	400 MB	350 MB

If you change the default quota settings to a quota of 50 MB and a warning limit of 40 MB, those values are applied to any new user who saves a file or folder to the column. However, the quota settings for the three users shown in Table 10.6 do not change. The only way to change the quota settings for existing users is to individually bind to each quota entry and then change the value. For more information about this process, see "Modifying a Disk Quota Entry" later in this chapter.

Scripting Steps

Listing 10.11 contains a script that configures disk quota settings on a computer. To carry out this task, the script must perform the following steps:

1. Create an instance of the DiskQuota1 object.

2. Use the Initialize method to indicate that the default quota settings are being changed for drive C.

   The Initialize method requires the following two parameters:

   - The drive letter of the drive where the quota settings are being changed (in this case, C).

   - The value True, indicating that the drive should be initialized for read/write access. By setting this value to False, you can enumerate disk quota settings on the volume but you cannot make any changes (read-only).

3. Set the value of the DefaultQuotaLimit property to 10,000,000. This limits users to approximately 10 MB of disk space.

Listing 10.11 Configuring Disk Quota Settings

```
1  Set colDiskQuotas = CreateObject("Microsoft.DiskQuota.1")
2  colDiskQuotas.Initialize "C:\", True
3  colDiskQuotas.DefaultQuotaLimit = 10000000
```

Managing Disk Quotas for Individual Users

When you enable disk quotas on a volume and specify a quota, every user who stores data on that volume is automatically limited to the amount of disk space specified by the quota. For example, suppose you set a quota of 50 MB. As soon as users save their first bit of data to the volume, they are automatically assigned a quota of 50 MB. If you have users who require more (or less) than 50 MB of disk space, you can create individual quota entries for those users.

Determining Quota Limits

Disk quotas are based on the files and folders owned by a user. When determining disk quotas, consider the following factors:

- Disk quotas are based on file ownership. If a user modifies a file owned by another user, the disk space allocated for that file is charged to the file owner. This will typically be the user who initially created the file. However, some applications change the file owner based on the last person to modify the file. If a file is owned by User A and then modified by User B, some applications transfer ownership to User B. In that case, disk space is charged to User B.

- Disk quotas are based on the uncompressed size of a file. Compressing a file does not change the amount of disk space charged to the file owner.

- When disk quotas are enforced, the quotas change the amount of volume free space reported to a user. For example, suppose a user has been given a quota of 1 gigabyte (GB) on a volume that has 50 GB of free space. When the user checks free space on the volume, it reports only 1 GB minus whatever disk space is already used. The user does not know that there are actually 50 GB of free space available on the volume.

- By default, administrators have an unlimited amount of disk space on a volume. When you enable disk quotas, the Administrators group is automatically added to the quota table and given unlimited disk space. Do not change this default. If you remove the Administrators group or limit the disk space allocated to this group, you might limit the ability of administrators to manage the system.

 Note

The Administrators group owns all files created by any administrator.

Enumerating Disk Quotas

The DiskQuotaControl enables you to enumerate the quota entries for a particular volume. You can use this object to determine the quota and warning limit established for each user, the amount of disk space currently charged to the user, and whether the user has exceeded his or her quota level. Key user-related properties of the DiskQuotaControl are shown in Table 10.7.

Table 10.7 DiskQuotaControl Properties Related to Individual Users

Property	Description
AccountStatus	Status of the user account. Values are: 0 – Account is valid. 1 – Account information is unavailable. 2 – Account has been deleted. 3 – Account is invalid. 4 – Account cannot be found. 5 – Account information cannot be resolved.
DisplayName	Full name of the user associated with the quota entry (for example, Ken Myer). Values will be displayed only for local user accounts.
ID	Unique ID number assigned to the quota entry.
LogonName	User name of the user associated with the quota entry (for example, kmyer).
QuotaLimit	Quota limit (in bytes) set for this particular user. A value of -1 means that no limit has been set for the user.
QuotaThreshold	Warning limit (in bytes) set for this particular user. A value of -1 means that no limit has been set for the user.
QuotaUsed	Current number of bytes currently in use by this particular user.

Scripting Steps

Listing 10.12 contains a script that enumerates the disk quota entries on a computer. To carry out this task, the script must perform the following steps:

1. Create an instance of the DiskQuota1 object.

2. Use the Initialize method to indicate that the new quota entry should be added to drive C. This returns a collection of all users with disk quota entries on drive C.

    The Initialize method requires the following two parameters:

    -   The drive letter of the drive where quotas are being enumerated (in this case, C).

    -   The value True, indicating that the drive should be initialized for read/write access. By setting this value to False, you can enumerate disk quota entries on the volume but you cannot make any changes (read-only).

3. For each user in the collection of disk quota entries, echo the values of the LogonName, QuotaLimit, QuotaThreshold, and QuotaUsed properties.

Listing 10.12 Enumerating Disk Quotas

```
1  Set colDiskQuotas = CreateObject("Microsoft.DiskQuota.1")
2  colDiskQuotas.Initialize "C:\", True
3  For Each objUser in colDiskQuotas
4      Wscript.Echo "Logon name: " & objUser.LogonName
5      Wscript.Echo "Quota limit: " & objUser.QuotaLimit
6      Wscript.Echo "Quota threshold: " & objUser.QuotaThreshold
7      Wscript.Echo "Quota used: " & objUser.QuotaUsed
8  Next
```

Issuing Disk Quota Alerts

When a user reaches his or her quota warning level, an event is recorded in the System event log on the computer where the quota violation occurred. However, no notice of any kind is issued to the user. Users do not know that they are reaching their quota limit unless an administrator periodically scans the event log for quota violations and then issues a warning. Without such notices, users will find out they have reached their quota limit only when they attempt to save a file and are denied access because they have run out of disk space.

Because of this, you might want to create a script that periodically checks to see which users, if any, are over their warning limit and then issues an alert (such as an e-mail message).

Adding a New Disk Quota Entry

When disk quotas are enabled on a volume, the default quota and the default warning limit are automatically applied to any users who already have files stored on that volume. If a new user stores a file on the volume, a quota entry is created that grants that user the same default values. Administrators do not have to manually create new quota entries each time a new user saves a file on the volume.

However, you might want to assign some users a quota limit different from the default value. For example, you might want to allot graphic artists more disk space. If so, you can wait until a graphic artist has saved a file on the volume (and thus been assigned the default quotas) and then change his or her quota. Alternatively, you can create quota entries for each graphic artist in advance, before the user has saved any files to the volume, and give each of these users the desired quota value.

Scripting Steps

Listing 10.13 contains a script that adds a new entry to the disk quotas on a computer. To carry out this task, the script must perform the following steps:

1. Create an instance of the DiskQuota1 object.

2. Use the Initialize method to indicate that the new quota entry should be added to drive C.

    The Initialize method requires the following two parameters:

    -   The drive letter of the drive where the quota is added (in this case, C).

    -   The value True, indicating that the drive should be initialized for read/write access. By setting this value to False, you can enumerate disk quota entries on the volume but you cannot make any changes (read-only).

3. Use the AddUser method to create a quota entry for user jsmith from the fabrikam domain. If you are adding a quota entry for a domain user account, be sure to include the name of the domain (for example, fabrikam\jsmith). If you are adding a quota entry for a local user account, be sure to include the name of the computer where the entry is being added (for example, atl-dc-01\jsmith).

4. Use the Sleep method to pause the script for 5 seconds. This ensures that the new quota entry will be added before you attempt to connect to the new entry and modify the quota limit.

5. Use the FindUser method to query the quota entry for jsmith from the fabrikam domain.

6. Set the QuotaLimit for user jsmith from the fabrikam domain to 50,000,000 bytes.

Listing 10.13   Adding a New Disk Quota Entry

```
1  Set colDiskQuotas = CreateObject("Microsoft.DiskQuota.1")
2  colDiskQuotas.Initialize "C:\", True
3  Set objUser = colDiskQuotas.AddUser("fabrikam\jsmith")
4  Wscript.Sleep 5000
5  Set objUser = colDiskQuotas.FindUser("fabrikam\jsmith")
6  objUser.QuotaLimit = 50000000
```

Modifying a Disk Quota Entry

You can also use the DiskQuotaControl object to modify the quotas assigned to an existing user. By binding to the quota entry for a user, you can change both the maximum disk space allocated to that user (QuotaLimit) and the disk space usage that triggers a quota warning (QuotaThreshold).

Scripting Steps

Listing 10.14 contains a script that modifies the disk quota for a user. To carry out this task, the script must perform the following steps:

1. Create an instance of the DiskQuota1 object.

2. Use the Initialize method to indicate that the quota entry to be modified is on drive C.

   The Initialize method requires the following two parameters:

   - The drive letter of the drive where the quota resides (in this case, C).

   - The value True, indicating that the drive should be initialized for read/write access. By setting this value to False (read-only), you can enumerate disk quota entries on the volume but you cannot make any changes.

3. Use the FindUser method to query the quota entry for jsmith from the fabrikam domain.

4. Set the QuotaThreshold for user jsmith from the fabrikam domain to 90,000,000 bytes, and set the QuotaLimit to 100,000,000 bytes.

Listing 10.14   Modifying a Disk Quota Entry

```
1  Set colDiskQuotas = CreateObject("Microsoft.DiskQuota.1")
2  colDiskQuotas.Initialize "C:\", True
3  Set objUser = colDiskQuotas.FindUser("fabrikam\jsmith")
4  objUser.QuotaThreshold = 90000000
5  objUser.QuotaLimit = 100000000
```

Deleting a Disk Quota Entry

The DiskQuotaControl object includes a DeleteUser method that you can use to delete quota entries from a quota table. This method is useful for keeping your quota tables up to date. For example, if a user leaves the organization, you can remove his or her quota entry to ensure that the quota table reflects only valid users and user accounts.

It is important to note that deleting a quota entry does not deny the user the right to store files on the volume. If you delete a user's quota entry and the user attempts to store something on the volume, a brand-new quota entry is created for the user. You need to use NTFS permissions to deny a user permission to store files on a volume.

In addition, you cannot delete quota entries from the disk quota table as long as the user still owns any files or folders on the volume. If a user leaves the organization, you must perform one of the following actions before you can delete a user's quota entry:

- Move all the files or folders owned by the user to another volume.

- Take ownership of all the files or folders owned by the user.

Scripting Steps

Listing 10.15 contains a script that deletes the disk quota entry for a user. To carry out this task, the script must perform the following steps:

1. Create an instance of the DiskQuota1 object.

2. Use the Initialize method to indicate that the quota entry to be deleted is on drive C.

    The Initialize method requires the following two parameters:

    - The drive letter of the drive where the quota resides (in this case, C).

    - The value True, indicating that the drive should be initialized for read/write access. Setting this value to False allows you to enumerate disk quota entries on the volume but does not allow you to change the disk quota entries.

3. Use the FindUser method to query the quota entry for a user, (in this case, jsmith from the fabrikam domain).

4. Use the DeleteUser method to delete the quota entry for jsmith from the fabrikam domain.

Listing 10.15 Deleting a Disk Quota Entry

```
1  Set colDiskQuotas = CreateObject("Microsoft.DiskQuota.1")
2  colDiskQuotas.Initialize "C:\", True
3  Set objUser = colDiskQuotas.FindUser("fabrikam\jsmith")
4  colDiskQuotas.DeleteUser(objUser)
```

Managing File Systems

Disk drives can be likened to the mailrooms found in large organizations. These mailrooms typically consist of a huge array of mailboxes, each designed to hold information, such as a letter, a package, or an internal memo. For the most part, these mailboxes are identical, and nothing prevents you from storing a letter in mailbox A, mailbox B, or mailbox C. However, a mailroom must be organized in a way that makes it quick and easy to retrieve information. This is typically done by grouping mailboxes by employee name, by department, or by room number. This organization helps ensure that mailbox A contains only the mail intended for user A.

Disk drives are similar to an array of mailboxes. They provide a way to store information, but they do not impose any organizing scheme upon that information. If you want to quickly and easily retrieve information from a disk drive, you must use a file system, a component of the operating system that organizes and retrieves stored data.

Just as mailrooms can be set up differently, file systems can also be organized differently. For example, Windows operating systems support a number of different file systems, including NTFS, file allocation table (FAT), and FAT32. Each of these file systems has different capabilities; you must manage computers running the NTFS file system differently than you manage computers running the FAT file system. With Windows 2000, you can use scripts to help identify the file system in use on a computer and, at least in the case of NTFS, configure the properties of that file system to best fit the needs of that computer.

Identifying the File System Type

The type of file system installed on a volume determines the things you can and cannot do with that volume. For example, if you have a dual-boot computer and need to access a volume from Microsoft® Windows® Millennium Edition, you must format that volume using either FAT or FAT32; Windows Millennium Edition cannot access NTFS volumes. By contrast, if you need to enable disk quotas or use file and folder permissions, you must do this on an NTFS volume; neither capability is supported by FAT or FAT32.

The Win32_LogicalDisk class can be used to identify the file system installed on any logical drive on a computer.

Note

The Win32_LogicalDisk class does not distinguish between the versions of NTFS found in Microsoft® Windows NT® 4.0 or Windows 2000. Instead, it reports both as "NTFS," even though the versions differ in capabilities. In these cases, you might want to identify the operating system version as well as the type of file system installed. For more information about identifying the operating system version, see "Computer Assets" in this book.

Scripting Steps

Listing 10.16 contains a script that identifies the file system used on each logical disk on a computer. To carry out this task, the script must perform the following steps:

1. Create a variable to specify the computer name.

2. Use a GetObject call to connect to the WMI namespace root\cimv2, and set the impersonation level to "impersonate."

3. Use the ExecQuery method to query the Win32_LogicalDisk class.

   This returns a collection of all the logical disk drives installed on the computer.

4. For each logical disk drive in the collection, echo the device ID and the type of file system installed on the drive.

Listing 10.16   Identifying the File System Type

```
1   strComputer = "."
2   Set objWMIService = GetObject("winmgmts:" _
3       & "{impersonationLevel=impersonate}!\\" & strComputer & "\root\cimv2")
4   Set colDisks = objWMIService.ExecQuery _
5       ("SELECT * FROM Win32_LogicalDisk")
6   For Each objDisk in colDisks
7       Wscript.Echo "Device ID: " & objDisk.DeviceID
8       Wscript.Echo "File System: " & objDisk.FileSystem
9   Next
```

Enumerating NTFS Properties

NTFS properties play an important role in determining the optimal configuration of your file system. Despite that, few system administrators are aware of how these properties have been configured, largely because no graphical user tool for viewing NTFS properties is provided with the operating system. In fact, you can only view and configure these properties through the registry. You can find the registry entries that configure NTFS properties, shown in Table 10.8, in the subkey HKEY_LOCAL_MACHINE\System\CurrentControlSet\Control\FileSystem.

Note

Not all of these entries are present by default. Depending on your operating system and your setup, you might have to create these entries. For information on adding entries to the registry, see "Registry" in this book.

Table 10.8   Registry Entries for NTFS Properties

Registry Entry	Description
NtfsDisable8dot3NameCreation	Specifies whether NTFS automatically generates an 8.3 file name for each new file created on the volume. If MS-DOS or Microsoft® Windows® 3.x clients do not need access to the volume, enabling this property can speed up file system activity.
NtfsAllowExtendedCharacterIn8Dot3Name	Specifies whether you can use extended characters in short file names.
NtfsMftZoneReservation	Specifies the relative size of the master file table (MFT).
NtfsDisableLastAccessUpdate	Specifies whether NTFS updates the last-access timestamp on each directory when it lists the directories on an NTFS volume. This property is designed to prevent the NTFS log buffer in physical memory from becoming filled with timestamp update records. If you have an NTFS volume with a very large number of directories (in excess of 70,000) and the operating system does not respond quickly to **dir** commands, adding this entry to the registry might make directories list faster.
Win31FileSystem	Specifies whether the FAT file system uses long file names and extended timestamps. This entry limits the files stored on FAT volumes to using only features found in the FAT file system used in Windows 3.1 and earlier versions. Changing this entry does not change any files, but it does change how the FAT file system displays and manages the files.

You can use a tool such as Regedit.exe to view these registry entries and their values. Alternatively, you can retrieve this same information using a script. Scripts allow data retrieval to be carried out in an automated fashion. Furthermore, using WMI in the script allows you to retrieve these properties from remote computers as well as from the local computer.

 Caution

Changing the registry with a script can easily propagate errors. The scripting tools bypass safeguards, allowing settings that can damage your system, or even require you to reinstall Windows. Before scripting changes to the registry, test your script thoroughly and back up the registry on every computer on which you will make changes. For more information about scripting changes to the registry, see the Registry Reference on the *Microsoft Windows 2000 Server Resource Kit* companion CD or at http://www.microsoft.com/reskit.

Scripting Steps

Listing 10.17 contains a script that enumerates the properties of the NTFS file system that a computer uses. To carry out this task, the script must perform the following steps:

1. Create a constant named HKEY_LOCAL_MACHINE and set the value to &H80000002. This value is required by the Standard Registry Provider when connecting to the HKEY_LOCAL_MACHINE portion of the registry. (For more information about using the WMI Standard Registry Provider, see "Registry" in this book.)

2. Create a variable to specify the computer name.

3. Use a GetObject call to connect to the WMI namespace root\default:StdRegProv on the computer, and set the impersonation level to "impersonate."

4. Set the variable strValueName to the path within the HKEY_LOCAL_MACHINE portion of the registry. For each value being retrieved, the path is System\CurrentControlSet\Control\FileSystem.

5. Set the variable strValueName to the name of the first entry from which the value is being retrieved (NtfsDisable8dot3NameCreation).

6. Use the GetDWORDValue method to read the first registry value. This method requires the following parameters:

    -   **HKEY_LOCAL_MACHINE** — Constant required to access HKEY_LOCAL_MACHINE.

    -   **strKeyPath** — Registry path within HKEY_LOCAL_MACHINE.

    -   **strValueName** — Registry entry being read.

    -   **dwValue** — Out parameter that will be set to the registry value. For example, if NtfsDisable8dot3NameCreation is equal to 0, then dwValue is also be equal to 0.

7. Use an If Then construct to evaluate dwValue and echo the appropriate message. For example, if dwValue is 1, the message "No value set for disabling 8.3 file name creation" is echoed to the screen.

8. Repeat the process with the remaining registry values.

Listing 10.17   Enumerating NTFS Properties

```
1    Const HKEY_LOCAL_MACHINE = &H80000002
2
3    strComputer = "."
4    Set objRegistry = GetObject _
5        ("winmgmts:{impersonationLevel=impersonate}!\\" & _
6            strComputer & "\root\default:StdRegProv")
7
8    strKeyPath = "System\CurrentControlSet\Control\FileSystem"
9    strValueName = "NtfsDisable8dot3NameCreation"
10   objRegistry.GetDWORDValue _
11       HKEY_LOCAL_MACHINE,strKeyPath,strValueName,dwValue
12
13   If IsNull(dwValue) Then
14       Wscript.Echo "No value set for disabling 8.3 file name creation."
15   ElseIf dwValue = 1 Then
16       WScript.Echo "No 8.3 file names will be created for new files."
17   ElseIf dwValue = 0 Then
18       Wscript.Echo "8.3 file names will be created for new files."
19   End If
20
21   strValueName = "NtfsAllowExtendedCharacterIn8Dot3Name"
22   objRegistry.GetDWORDValue _
23       HKEY_LOCAL_MACHINE,strKeyPath,strValueName,dwValue
24
25   If IsNull(dwValue) Then
26       Wscript.Echo "No value set for allowing extended characters in " _
27           & " 8.3 file names."
28   ElseIf dwValue = 1 Then
29       WScript.Echo "Extended characters are permitted in 8.3 file names."
30   ElseIf dwValue = 0 Then
31       Wscript.Echo "Extended characters not permitted in 8.3 file names."
32   End If
33
34   strValueName = "NtfsMftZoneReservation"
35   objRegistry.GetDWORDValue _
36       HKEY_LOCAL_MACHINE,strKeyPath,strValueName,dwValue
37
38   If IsNull(dwValue) Then
39       Wscript.Echo "No value set for reserving the MFT zone."
40   ElseIf dwValue = 1 Then
41       WScript.Echo _
42           "One-eighth of the disk has been reserved for the MFT zone."
43   ElseIf dwValue = 2 Then
44       Wscript.Echo "One-fourth of the disk reserved for the MFT zone."
```

(continued)

Listing 10.17   Enumerating NTFS Properties *(continued)*

```
45  ElseIf dwValue = 3 Then
46      Wscript.Echo "Three-eighths of the disk reserved for the MFT zone."
47  ElseIf dwValue = 4 Then
48      Wscript.Echo "One half of the disk reserved for the MFT zone."
49  End If
50
51  strValueName = "NtfsDisableLastAccessUpdate"
52  objRegistry.GetDWORDValue _
53      HKEY_LOCAL_MACHINE,strKeyPath,strValueName,dwValue
54
55  If IsNull(dwValue) Then
56      Wscript.Echo "No value set for disabling the last access update " _
57          & "for files and folder."
58  ElseIf dwValue = 1 Then
59      WScript.Echo _
60          "The last access timestamp will not be updated on files " _
61              & "and folders."
62  ElseIf dwValue = 0 Then
63      Wscript.Echo "The last access timestamp updated on files and " _
64          & "folders."
65  End If
66
67  strValueName = "Win31FileSystem"
68  objRegistry.GetDWORDValue _
69      HKEY_LOCAL_MACHINE,strKeyPath,strValueName,dwValue
70
71  If IsNull(dwValue) Then
72      Wscript.Echo "No value set for using long file names and " _
73          & "timestamps."
74  ElseIf dwValue = 1 Then
75      WScript.Echo "Long file names and extended timestamps are used."
76  ElseIf dwValue = 0 Then
77      Wscript.Echo "Long file names and extended timestamps are not used."
78  End If
```

Modifying NTFS Properties

NTFS is a more sophisticated file system than either FAT or FAT32. Because NTFS tracks additional attributes, such as quota information, reparse points, and file and folder permissions, NTFS typically provides slower access to files and folders on small volumes (less than 1 GB). On larger volumes, however, the superior search algorithms used in NTFS often make NTFS faster than either FAT or FAT32.

However, unlike FAT or FAT32, NTFS allows you to modify the way the file system works. In some cases, this enables NTFS to work faster and more efficiently, thus negating the performance advantage FAT or FAT32 might have on some volumes. The NTFS properties are not exposed directly. However, you can configure the properties by modifying the registry entries shown in Table 10.9.

 Caution

Changing the registry with a script can easily propagate errors. The scripting tools bypass safeguards, allowing settings that can damage your system, or even require you to reinstall Windows. Before scripting changes to the registry, test your script thoroughly and back up the registry on every computer on which you will make changes. For more information about scripting changes to the registry, see the Registry Reference on the *Windows 2000 Server Resource Kit* companion CD or at http://www.microsoft.com/reskit.

Table 10.9   Registry Entries for NTFS Properties

Registry Entry/Data Type	Description
NtfsDisable8dot3NameCreation REG_DWORD	Do one of the following: ▪ Set the value to 0 to enable the creation of 8.3 file names. ▪ Set the value to 1 to disable the creation of 8.3 file names. You must restart the computer before this change takes effect.
NtfsAllowExtendedCharacterIn8Dot3Name REG_DWORD	Do one of the following: ▪ Set the value to 0 to limit 8.3 file names to the ASCII character set. ▪ Set the value to 1 to allow the use of extended characters in 8.3 file names.

(continued)

Table 10.9 Registry Entries for NTFS Properties *(continued)*

Registry Entry/Data Type	Description
NtfsMftZoneReservation REG_DWORD	Do one of the following: • Set the value to 1 to reserve one-eighth of the volume for the MFT. This is recommended for volumes with relatively few files. • Set the value to 2 to reserve one-fourth of the volume for the MFT. This is recommended for a volume with a moderate number of files. • Set the value to 3 to reserve three-eighths of the volume for the MFT. This is recommended for a volume with a moderate number of files. • Set the value to 4 to reserve one-half of the volume for the MFT. This is recommended for volumes with a large number of files.
NtfsDisableLastAccessUpdate REG_DWORD	Do one of the following: • Set the value to 0 to enable updating of the last access timestamp. • Set the value to 1 to disable updating of the last value timestamp. This is most effective for folders that contain 100,000 or more files.
Win31FileSystem REG_DWORD	Do one of the following: • Set the value to 0 to enable the use of long file names and extended timestamps. MS-DOS and Windows 3.x computers can access the files but cannot update the timestamps. • Set the value to 1 to disable the use of long file names and extended timestamps. Only those features of the FAT file system that are available to Windows 3.1 and earlier are used. You must restart the computer before this change takes effect.

Scripting Steps

Listing 10.18 contains a script that modifies the NTFS file system properties on a computer. To carry out this task, the script must perform the following steps:

1. Create a constant named HKEY_LOCAL_MACHINE and set the value to &H80000002. The Standard Registry Provider requires this value when connecting to the HKEY_LOCAL_MACHINE portion of the registry. (For more information about using the WMI Standard Registry Provider, see the "Registry" chapter in this book.)

2. Create a variable to specify the computer name.

3. Use a GetObject call to connect to the WMI namespace root\default:StdRegProv on the computer, and set the impersonation level to "impersonate."

4. Set the variable strValueName to the path within the HKEY_LOCAL_MACHINE portion of the registry (System\CurrentControlSet\Control\FileSystem).

5. Set the variable strValueName to the name of the entry being modified (Win31FileSystem).

6. Use the SetDWORDValue method to configure the new registry entry. This method requires the following parameters:

- **HKEY_LOCAL_MACHINE** — Constant required to access HKEY_LOCAL_MACHINE

- **strKeyPath** — Registry path within HKEY_LOCAL_MACHINE

- **strValueName** — Registry entry being modified

- **dwValue** — New value for Win31FileSystem

Listing 10.18   Modifying File System Properties

```
1   const HKEY_LOCAL_MACHINE = &H80000002
2   strComputer = "."
3
4   Set objRegistry = GetObject _
5       ("winmgmts:{impersonationLevel=impersonate}!\\" & _
6           strComputer & "\root\default:StdRegProv")
7
8   strKeyPath = "System\CurrentControlSet\Control\FileSystem"
9   strValueName = "Win31FileSystem"
10  dwValue = 1
11  objRegistry.SetDWORDValue _
12      HKEY_LOCAL_MACHINE,strKeyPath,strValueName,dwValue
```

Managing Page Files

The Windows 2000 operating system supports virtual memory. With virtual memory, a special file on a hard disk (known as a page file or a swap file) is used to supplement the physical memory installed on a computer. When a computer begins to run low on physical memory, data can be "swapped out" to the page file. This has the following advantages:

- It frees up physical memory.

- It makes it relatively fast and easy to retrieve the data, because the system knows exactly where to look for it.

Page files and virtual memory are extremely important to fast and effective computing. Without page files, computers would need double or triple the amount of physical memory in order to achieve the same level of performance.

System administrators need to review page file settings as part of a management routine that ensures that page files have been sized optimally and that each drive on a computer has its own page file. In addition, page file usage should be monitored on a regular basis; excessive paging often means that a computer has too little physical memory to carry out the tasks assigned to it.

WMI has several classes that can be used to help manage page files, including the Win32_PageFile class, which returns detailed information about each page file on a computer. Table 10.10 shows several of the key properties of this class.

Table 10.10   Win32_PageFile Properties

Property	Description
CreationDate	File creation date.
CSName	Name of the computer system.
Description	Description of the object.
Drive	Drive letter (including colon) of the file.
EightDotThreeFileName	MS-DOS–compatible file name for this file.
FileSize	Size of the file (in bytes).
InitialSize	Initial size of the page file, in megabytes.
InstallDate	Date the page file was created.
MaximumSize	Maximum size of the page file as set by the user. The operating system does not allow the page file to exceed this limit.
Name	File name of the page file.
Path	Path of the file. This includes leading and trailing backslashes.

Scripting Steps

Listing 10.19 contains a script that enumerates the properties of all the page files on a computer. To carry out this task, the script must perform the following steps:

1.   Create a variable to specify the computer name.

2.   Use a GetObject call to connect to the WMI namespace root\cimv2, and set the impersonation level to "impersonate."

3.   Use the ExecQuery method to query the Win32_PageFile class.

     This returns a collection of all the page files on the computer.

4.   For each page file in the collection, echo the values of such properties as the file name, current file size, initial file size, and maximum file size.

Listing 10.19   Enumerating Page File Properties

```
1   strComputer = "."
2   Set objWMIService = GetObject("winmgmts:" _
3       & "{impersonationLevel=impersonate}!\\" & strComputer & "\root\cimv2")
4   Set colPageFiles = objWMIService.ExecQuery _
5       ("SELECT * FROM Win32_PageFile")
6   For each objPageFile in colPageFiles
7       Wscript.Echo "Creation Date: " & objPageFile.CreationDate
8       Wscript.Echo "Description: " & objPageFile.Description
9       Wscript.Echo "Drive: " & objPageFile.Drive
10      Wscript.Echo "FileName: " & objPageFile.FileName
11      Wscript.Echo "FileSize: " & objPageFile.FileSize
12      Wscript.Echo "InitialSize: " & objPageFile.InitialSize
13      Wscript.Echo "InstallDate: " & objPageFile.InstallDate
14      Wscript.Echo "MaximumSize: " & objPageFile.MaximumSize
15      Wscript.Echo "Name: " & objPageFile.Name
16      Wscript.Echo "Path: " & objPageFile.Path
17  Next
```

Monitoring Page File Use

The Win32_PageFileUsage class enables you to obtain basic information about each page file on a computer, including the allocated file size, the current file size, and the largest size the file has reached since the computer started. This class is useful for routine monitoring of each page file.

As long as the maximum size of the file is less than 70 percent of the allocated size, it is generally safe to assume the page file is correctly configured.

Table 10.11 shows some of the key properties of the Win32_PageFileUsage class.

Table 10.11   Win32_PageFileUsage Properties

Property	Description
AllocatedBaseSize	Actual amount of disk space allocated for use with this page file. This value corresponds to the range established in Win32_PageFileSetting under the InitialSize and MaximumSize properties, set at system startup.
CurrentUsage	Amount of disk space currently used by the page file.
Description	Description of the object.
InstallDate	Date the page file was created.
Name	Path and file name of the page file.
PeakUsage	Highest use page file.

Scripting Steps

Listing 10.20 contains a script that monitors page file use on a computer. To carry out this task, the script must perform the following steps:

1. Create a variable to specify the computer name.

2. Use a GetObject call to connect to the WMI namespace root\cimv2, and set the impersonation level to "impersonate."

3. Use the ExecQuery method to query the Win32_PageFileUsage class.

    This returns a collection of statistics for each of the page files on the computer.

4. For each page file in the collection, echo the value of properties such as the current usage, the peak usage, and the file status.

Listing 10.20   Monitoring Page File Use

```
1   strComputer = "."
2   Set objWMIService = GetObject("winmgmts:" _
3       & "{impersonationLevel=impersonate}!\\" & strComputer & "\root\cimv2")
4   Set colPageFiles = objWMIService.ExecQuery _
5       ("SELECT * FROM Win32_PageFileUsage")
6   For each objPageFile in colPageFiles
7       Wscript.Echo "Allocated Base Size: " & objPageFile.AllocatedBaseSize
8       Wscript.Echo "CurrentUsage: " & objPageFile.CurrentUsage
9       Wscript.Echo "Description: " & objPageFile.Description
10      Wscript.Echo "InstallDate: " & objPageFile.InstallDate
11      Wscript.Echo "Name: " & objPageFile.Name
12      Wscript.Echo "PeakUsage: " & objPageFile.PeakUsage
13  Next
```

Configuring Page File Properties

When you install Windows on a computer, the operating system automatically sets up and configures a page file for you. In many cases, those settings will be adequate, and you will never need to reconfigure the page file.

In other cases, however, the settings might prove less than optimal. If a page file is too small, applications might run short on virtual memory. If a page file is too large, you might be wasting disk space that could be used for other purposes. In either case, you can reconfigure the page file settings in order to promote faster and more efficient computing.

You can use the Win32_PageFileSetting class to modify both the initial size and the maximum size of any page file on your computer. Table 10.12 describes the properties of the Win32_PageFileSetting class.

 Note

You must restart the computer before the new page file settings take effect.

Table 10.12 Win32_PageFileSetting Properties

Property	Description
InitialSize	Initial size of the page file, in megabytes.
MaximumSize	Maximum size of the page file, in megabytes.
Name	Path and file name of the page file.

Scripting Steps

Listing 10.21 contains a script that configures the page file properties on a computer. To carry out this task, the script must perform the following steps:

1. Create a variable to specify the computer name.

2. Use a GetObject call to connect to the WMI namespace root\cimv2, and set the impersonation level to "impersonate."

3. Use the ExecQuery method to query the Win32_PageFileSetting class.

    This returns a collection of all the page files on the computer.

4. For each page file in the collection, set the InitialSize to 300 MB and the MaximumSize to 600 MB.

5. Use the Put_ method to apply the changes and modify the page file settings.

Listing 10.21 Configuring Page File Properties

```
1   strComputer = "."
2   Set objWMIService = GetObject("winmgmts:" _
3       & "{impersonationLevel=impersonate}!\\" & strComputer & "\root\cimv2")
4   Set colPageFiles = objWMIService.ExecQuery _
5       ("SELECT * FROM Win32_PageFileSetting")
6   For Each objPageFile in colPageFiles
7       objPageFile.InitialSize = 300
8       objPageFile.MaximumSize = 600
9       objPageFile.Put_
10  Next
```

CHAPTER 11

Files and Folders

Files and folders are the lifeblood of any organization; this makes file system administration one of the more important responsibilities assigned to system administrators. Of course, file system administration is also one of the more difficult responsibilities to carry out, simply because files and folders are scattered on multiple hard disks and multiple computers throughout the organization. Scripts can help make file system management much easier, particularly when the files and folders to be managed are located on remote computers.

In This Chapter

Files and Folders Overview.. **768**

    Managing Files and Folders Using WMI 768

    Managing Files and Folders Using the Windows Shell Object 773

Folders and Folder Objects **775**

    Enumerating Folders and Folder Properties 778

    Managing Folders 794

Files and File Objects **804**

    Enumerating Files and File Properties 804

    Managing Files 813

Monitoring the File System **821**

Managing Shared Folders **825**

    Publishing Shared Folders in Active Directory 834

    Managing Published Folders 836

Files and Folders Overview

Scripts can automate many tasks associated with file and folder management, tasks that system administrators must perform on a regular basis. You can simplify the daily routine of system administrators by creating and running scripts that do such things as:

- Manage the folder structure to make files easy for users to locate.

- Ensure that the proper versions of specific files are installed and updated when necessary.

- Track files and folders, periodically culling files and folders that are no longer being used.

- Move files and folders from one location to another as circumstances dictate.

- Create and manage shared folders to provide access to files from anywhere within the organization.

Scripts are especially useful for organizations that must carry out file and folder management tasks simultaneously on multiple computers. For example, you can write scripts that copy the same set of templates to 100 different file servers, scripts that check the version of a particular .dll file on all your Domain Name System (DNS) servers, or scripts that delete outdated files from all your shared folders.

Aside from automating tasks, scripts can schedule these tasks to run off-hours, when the shuffling of files and folders does not inconvenience users, and when greater network bandwidth ensures that these tasks run as quickly as possible, without unduly affecting system resources.

Managing Files and Folders Using WMI

Scripts designed to help with file system management typically rely on the FileSystemObject. (For more information about the FileSystemObject, see "Script Runtime Primer" in this book.) For example, a popular Internet scripting site lists more than 100 scripts that carry out file system management tasks using the FileSystemObject, but none that use Windows Management Instrumentation (WMI). Despite the popularity of the FileSystemObject, however, there are several reasons why the primary scripting enabler for file system management should be WMI, and in particular, the Win32_Directory and CIM_Datafile classes.

To a large degree, the FileSystemObject and WMI have overlapping functionality: You can use either one to copy, delete, move, rename, or otherwise manipulate files and folders. However, WMI has two major advantages over the FileSystemObject. First, WMI works as well on remote computers as it does on the local computer. By contrast, the FileSystemObject is designed to work solely on the local computer; to use the FileSystemObject against a remote computer, you typically have to configure both computers to allow remote script execution using the WSHController Object.

Second, WMI can work with collections of files and folders across an entire computer. For example, using WMI you can delete all the .mp3 files on a computer by using a simple script that essentially says, "Locate all the .mp3 files on this computer, and then delete them." By contrast, the FileSystemObject is designed to work with a single folder at a time. To delete all the .mp3 files on a computer, you need to bind to each folder on the computer, check for the existence of .mp3 files, and then delete each one.

WMI does have some limitations, however. Enumerating files and folders using WMI can be slow, and processor-intensive. For example, on a Microsoft® Windows® 2000–based computer with approximately 80,000 files, the FileSystemObject returned a list of all files in less than 5 minutes. By contrast, WMI required over 30 minutes to return the same list. During that time, processor use averaged about 30 percent, often spiking above 50 percent. Although you would normally not need to retrieve a list of every single file on a computer, it is clearly not advisable to use WMI if you ever *do* need to perform this task.

Moreover, processor-intensive WMI queries cannot always be stopped simply by terminating the script. Suppose you start a query that returns a list of all the files on the file system. After a few minutes, you change your mind and terminate the script. There is a very good chance that the query will continue to run, using up memory and draining system resources, even though the script has been stopped. This is because the script and its query run on separate threads. To stop a query such as this, you typically have to stop and then restart the WMI service.

In addition, you cannot speed up a file or folder query by requesting only a subset of file or folder properties. On a computer running Windows 2000, this query, which returns all the properties for all the files, took about 30 minutes to complete:

```
"Select * From CIM_Datafile"
```

Although this query returns only the name property of the files, it required the same amount of time to complete:

```
"Select Name From CIM_Datafile"
```

Comparing WMI and the FileSystemObject

Administrators who write scripts to manage files and folders typically use the FileSystemObject rather than WMI. This is due more to familiarity than to anything else; most of the same core capabilities are available using either the FileSystemObject or WMI. The leads to an obvious question: when should you use the FileSystemObject, and when should you use WMI? Or does it even matter?

There is no simple answer to that question; instead, the best approach usually depends on what your script needs to accomplish. When choosing a method for managing files and folders, you should consider the impact of:

- Speed of execution.
- The ability to recover from errors.
- The ability to run against remote computers.
- Ease of use.

Speed

If your goal is to enumerate all the files on a hard disk, the FileSystemObject will be much faster. For example, on a Windows 2000 Server family–based test computer, with a relatively modest 21,963 files, the FileSystemObject required 68 seconds to return a list of all the files on drive C. By contrast, WMI took nearly 10 times as long (661 seconds) to complete the same operation.

With more targeted queries, however, WMI can be both faster and more efficient. For example, the FileSystemObject required 90 seconds to return a list of the 91 .bmp files on the Windows 2000–based test computer. It actually takes longer for the FileSystemObject to return a subset of files than it does to return the entire set of files; this is because the FileSystemObject does not allow you to use SQL-type queries. Instead, it uses recursion to return a list of all the files on the computer and then, in this case, individually checks each file to see whether the extension is .bmp.

Using a filtered query, WMI returned the list of .bmp files in 18 seconds. WMI is faster in this case because it can request a collection of all .bmp files without having to return the entire file set and then check the file name extension of each item in the collection.

Error Handling

The FileSystemObject sometimes provides a faster solution; it rarely, if ever, provides a more robust solution. The FileSystemObject provides no ability to recover from an error, even if your script includes the On Error Resume Next statement.

For example, suppose you have a script designed to delete 1,000 files from a computer. If an error occurs with the very first file, the script fails, and no attempt is made to delete any of the remaining files. If an error condition occurs, the FileSystemObject — and the script — immediately terminates. If an error occurs partway through an operation, you will have to manually determine which portions of the procedure succeeded and which portions did not.

WMI is better able to recover from a failed operation. If WMI is unable to delete the first of the 1,000 files, it simply reports an error condition and then attempts to delete the next file in the collection. By logging any errors that occur, you can easily determine which portions of a procedure succeeded and which ones did not.

 Note

You can log these individual errors because WMI treats each file operation separately; if you have 1,000 files, WMI treats this as 1,000 separate deletions. The FileSystemObject, by comparison, treats each file operation as one procedure, regardless of whether you have 1 file, 10 files, or 1,000 files.

WMI is also able to more intelligently deal with file and folder access permissions. For example, suppose you write a script to enumerate all the files on a hard drive. If WMI encounters a folder that you do not have access to, the script simply skips that folder and continues. The FileSystemObject, however, attempts to list the files in that folder. That operation will fail because you do not have access to the folder. In turn, the FileSystemObject, and your script, will also fail. This is a problem with Windows 2000–based computers because they typically include a System Volume Information folder that, by default, grants access only to the operating system. Without taking precautions to work around this folder, any attempt to enumerate all the files on a computer using the FileSystemObject is guaranteed to fail.

Remote Computers

One of the major benefits of WMI is that a script originally designed to run on the local computer can be easily modified to run on a remote computer. For example, this script sets the name of the computer (the variable strComputer) to a dot ("."). In WMI, specifying "." as the computer name causes the script to run against the local computer.

```
strComputer = "."
Set objWMIService = GetObject _
    ("winmgmts:" & "!\\" & strComputer & "\root\cimv2")
```

To run the script against a remote computer (for example, atl-dc-01), simply change the value of the variable strComputer:

```
strComputer = "atl-dc-01"
Set objWMIService = GetObject _
    ("winmgmts:" & "!\\" & strComputer & "\root\cimv2")
```

For most file and folder operations, this is the only change required to make a script work on a remote computer.

Working with remote computers using the FileSystemObject is more complicated. It is easy to access a shared folder using the FileSystemObject; simply connect to the folder using the Universal Naming Convention (UNC) path (for example, \\atl-dc-01\scripts). However, it is much more difficult to carry out such tasks as searching a remote computer for all files of a specified type. For the most part, there are only two ways to carry out this procedure:

- Configure an instance of the WSHController object, which allows you to run a script against a remote computer as if that script was running locally.

- Connect to the administrative shared folders of the remote computer (for example, using the path \\atl-dc-01\C$ to connect to drive C on the remote computer). This approach works, provided the administrative shared folders on the remote machines are not disabled.

Depending on the operation you are attempting, you might also have to determine what disk drives are installed on the remote computer. WMI can return all the files within the file system, regardless of the drive they are stored on. By contrast, the FileSystemObject can work only on a disk-by-disk basis. Before you can search a computer for files, you must first obtain a list of all the disk drives and then individually search each drive.

Ease of Use

WMI allows you to work with collections and to create queries that return a targeted set of items. This makes WMI easier to use for tasks that require you to do such things as identify all the read-only folders on a computer or delete all the .mp3 files in a file system; you issue a request, and WMI returns a collection of all those items, regardless of their physical location on the computer. This means that you can accomplish the task in far fewer lines of code than it would take to accomplish the same task using the FileSystemObject.

For example, this WMI query returns a collection of all the .mp3 files installed on all the disks on a computer:

```
"SELECT * FROM CIM_DataFile WHERE Extension = 'MP3'"
```

To achieve the same result using the FileSystemObject, you must write a script that:

1. Returns a list of all the disk drives on the computer.

2. Verifies that each disk drive is ready for use.

3. Recursively searches each drive in order to locate all the folders and subfolders.

4. Recursively searches each folder and subfolder to locate all the files.

5. Checks each extension to see whether the file is an .mp3 file.

6. Keeps track of each .mp3 file.

Managing Files and Folders Using the Windows Shell Object

The Windows operating system features another COM object, the Shell object, that includes a number of properties and methods useful in managing file systems. Because the Shell object offers capabilities not available using either the FileSystemObject or WMI, you should also consider it when writing scripts for file system management.

The Shell is the portion of the Windows operating system tasked with managing and providing access to such things as:

- Files and folders
- Network printers
- Other networked computers
- Control Panel applications
- The Recycle Bin

The Shell namespace provides a way to manage these objects in a tree-structured hierarchy. At the top of this hierarchy is the Desktop; directly below the Desktop are virtual folders such as My Computer, My Network Places, and Recycle Bin. Within each of these virtual folders are other items (such as files, folders, and printers) that can also be managed using the Shell. If you start Windows Explorer, you see a visual representation of the Shell, as shown in Figure 11.1.

Figure 11.1 The Shell Namespace

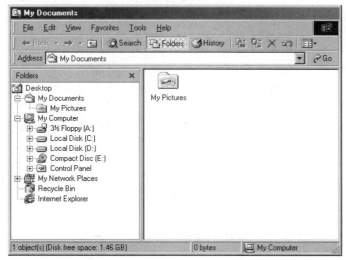

The Shell itself is composed largely of a series of COM objects, many of which can be accessed using VBScript. Included among these COM objects are folders. Within the Windows operating system, folders are individual COM objects that possess:

- Properties, such as a size and a creation date.

- Items (typically files stored within the folder).

- Methods (known as *verbs*), which represent actions — such as Copy and Delete — that can be carried out on the folder.

Folder objects — and all the properties, items, and methods belonging to those objects — can be accessed through the Shell object. The Shell object provides a way to programmatically reproduce all the features found in the Windows Shell. This means that file system management tasks — which typically involve working with files and folders — can be carried out using the Shell object.

Scripting the Shell object is not as intuitive as scripting with WMI or the FileSystemObject. For example, to bind to a file using a Shell object script, you must:

1. Create an instance of the Shell object.

2. Create an instance of a Folder object.

3. Create a collection of items in the folder.

4. Iterate through the collection until you find the desired file.

This is considerably more complicated than using the FileSystemObject or WMI. On the other hand, the Shell object does offer a number of capabilities not found in either WMI or the FileSystemObject, including the ability to:

- Retrieve extended properties for a file or folder (for example, the artist, album title, and track number for an audio file).

- Display a progress dialog box while copying or moving folders.

- Retrieve the locations of all the special folders on a computer.

- Carry out any of the commands found on the shortcut menu when you right-click a file or folder.

In this chapter, the Shell object is used whenever it provides a unique capability not available using either WMI or the FileSystemObject.

Folders and Folder Objects

Folders are file system objects designed to contain other file system objects. This does not mean that all folders are alike, however. Instead, folders can vary considerably. Some folders are operating system folders, which generally should not be modified by a script. Some folders are *read-only*, which means that users can access the contents of that folder but cannot add to, delete from, or modify those contents. Some folders are compressed for optimal storage, while others are hidden and not visible to users.

WMI uses the Win32_Directory class to manage folders. Significantly, the properties and methods available in this class are identical to the properties and methods available in the CIM_DataFile class, the class used to manage files. This means that after you have learned how to manage folders using WMI, you will, without any extra work, also know how to manage files.

Some of the more useful Win32_Directory class properties are shown in Table 11.1. These properties are identical to the properties found in the CIM_DataFile class.

Table 11.1 Win32_Directory Properties

Property	Description
Archive	Boolean value indicating whether the archive bit on the folder has been set. The archive bit is used by backup programs to identify files that should be backed up.
Compressed	Boolean value indicating whether or not the folder has been compressed. WMI recognizes folders compressed using WMI itself or using the graphical user interface; it does not, however, recognize .ZIP files as being compressed.
CompressionMethod	Method used to compress the file system object. Often reported simply as "Compressed."
CreationDate	Date that the file system object was created.
CSName	Name of the computer where the file system object is stored.
Drive	Drive letter of the drive where the file system object is stored.
EightDotThreeFileName	MS-DOS®-compatible name for the folder. For example, the **EightDotThreeFileName** for the folder C:\Program Files might be C:\Progra~1.
Encrypted	Boolean value indicating whether or not the folder has been encrypted.
EncryptionMethod	Method used to encrypt the file system object. Often reported simply as "Encryption."
Extension	File name extension for the file system object, not including the dot (.) that separates the extension from the file name.

(continued)

Table 11.1   Win32_Directory Properties *(continued)*

Property	Description
FileName	Name of the file system object, not including the extension.
FileSize	Size of the file system object, in bytes. Although folders possess a **FileSize** property, the value 0 is always returned. To determine the size of a folder, use the FileSystemObject or add up the size of all the files stored in the folder.
FileType	Type of file system object, based on the extension and the default registration for that extension. For example, an .mdb file is likely to have the file type Microsoft Access Application. An .htm file likely has the file type HTML Document. Folders are typically reported simply as Folder.
FSName	Type of file system (NTFS, FAT, FAT32) installed on the drive where the file or folder is located.
Hidden	Boolean value indicating whether the file system object is hidden.
LastAccessed	Date that the object was last accessed.
LastModified	Date that the object was last modified.
Name	Full path name of the file system object. For example: **c:\windows\system32\wbem**.
Path	Path for the folder. The path includes the leading and trailing backslashes, but not the drive letter or the folder name. For the folder c:\windows\system32\wbem, the path is **\windows\system32**. For the folder c:\scripts, the path is \.
Readable	Boolean value indicating whether you can read items in the folder.
System	Boolean value indicating whether the object is a system folder.
Writeable	Boolean value indicating whether you can write to the folder.

The relationship betweenthe Win32_Directory properties and the folder properties available through Windows Explorer is shown in Figure 11.2.

Figure 11.2   Win32_Directory and Windows Explorer

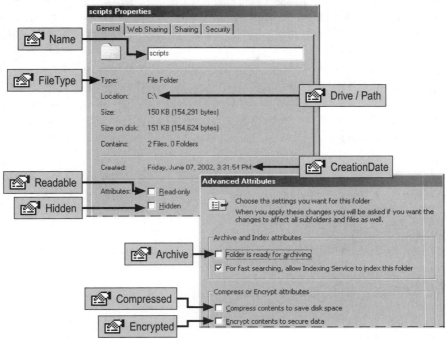

In addition, the Win32_Directory and CIM_DataFile classes share the same set of methods. Some of the more commonly used methods are shown in Table 11.2.

Table 11.1   Win32_Directory and CIM_DataFile Methods

Method	Description
Copy	Copies the file system object to a new location.
Rename	Renames the file system object.
Delete	Deletes the object from the file system.
Compress	Compresses a file system object using Windows compression.
Uncompress	Uncompresses a file system object that was compressed using Windows compression.

These methods return the values shown in Table 11.3. Because files and folders share the same set of methods, you can copy, delete, or rename both files and folders using the same approach. Similarly, you can easily add error handling to file and folder scripts; the code used to interpret error codes in one script is exactly the same as the code used to interpret error codes in any other file or folder management script.

Table 11.3   WMI File and Folder Return Values

Value	Description
0	Operation completed successfully.
2	Access denied.
8	An unspecified failure occurred.
9	Invalid name.
10	Object already exists.
11	The file system is not NTFS.
12	The platform is not Windows NT®, Windows 2000, or Windows® XP.
13	The drive is not the same.
14	The folder is not empty.
15	A sharing violation has occurred.
16	Invalid file.
17	The user does not have the rights required to perform this operation.
21	Invalid parameter.

In addition to the Win32_Directory class, the Win32_Subdirectory association class is also used to manage files and folders. The Win32_Subdirectory class relates a folder and its immediate subfolders. For example, in the folder structure C:\Scripts\Logs, Logs is a subfolder of Scripts, and Scripts is a subfolder of the root folder C:\. However, Logs is not considered a subfolder of C:\.

Enumerating Folders and Folder Properties

The primary advantage of using scripts for file system management is the fact that scripts can carry out tasks that would be too tedious and time-consuming to perform using either the graphical user interface or a command-line tool. For example, suppose you have 500 domain controllers, and a new organizational policy requires you to verify the following:

- A folder named Scripts exists on each of these domain controllers.
- The Scripts folder is hidden.

- The Scripts folder is marked as read-only.

- The Scripts folder is compressed.

It would take a significant amount of time to carry out this task using Windows Explorer or a command-line tool. By contrast, in about a half hour you can write a script that connects to each domain controller, performs the requisite checks, and logs the data. You can start this script before you go home, and when you return to work the next day, the verification will be complete.

Scripts can be used to carry out tasks such as these because, within the Windows shell, folders are actually COM objects. As COM objects, folders have properties that can be retrieved, properties that answer questions such as:

- Is this folder hidden?

- Is this folder read-only?

- Is this folder compressed?

You can retrieve the properties of any folder in the file system using the Win32_Directory class. The properties available using this class are shown in Table 11.1. To retrieve the properties for a single folder, construct a Windows Query Language (WQL) query for the Win32_Directory class, making sure that you include the name of the folder. For example, this query binds to the folder D:\Archive:

```
"SELECT * FROM Win32_Directory WHERE Name = 'D:\\Archive'"
```

When specifying a file or folder name in a WQL query, be sure you use two backslashes (\\) to separate path components.

Scripting Steps

Listing 11.1 contains a script that retrieves properties for the folder C:\Scripts. To carry out this task, the script must perform the following steps:

1. Create a variable to specify the computer name.

2. Use a GetObject call to connect to the WMI namespace root\cimv2, and set the impersonation level to "impersonate."

3. Use the ExecQuery method to query the Win32_Directory class.

   To limit data retrieval to a specified folder, a Where clause is included restricting the returned folders to those where Name equals C:\\Scripts. You must include both backslashes (\\) in the specified name.

4. For the single folder in the collection, echo the properties shown in Listing 11.1.

Listing 11.1   Retrieving Folder Properties

```
1    strComputer = "."
2    Set objWMIService = GetObject("winmgmts:" _
3        & "{impersonationLevel=impersonate}!\\" & strComputer & "\root\cimv2")
4    Set colFolders = objWMIService.ExecQuery _
5        ("SELECT * FROM Win32_Directory WHERE Name = 'c:\\Scripts'")
6    For Each objFolder in colFolders
7        Wscript.Echo "Archive: " & objFolder.Archive
8        Wscript.Echo "Caption: " & objFolder.Caption
9        Wscript.Echo "Compressed: " & objFolder.Compressed
10       Wscript.Echo "Compression method: " & objFolder.CompressionMethod
11       Wscript.Echo "Creation date: " & objFolder.CreationDate
12       Wscript.Echo "Encrypted: " & objFolder.Encrypted
13       Wscript.Echo "Encryption method: " & objFolder.EncryptionMethod
14       Wscript.Echo "Hidden: " & objFolder.Hidden
15       Wscript.Echo "In use count: " & objFolder.InUseCount
16       Wscript.Echo "Last accessed: " & objFolder.LastAccessed
17       Wscript.Echo "Last modified: " & objFolder.LastModified
18       Wscript.Echo "Name: " & objFolder.Name
19       Wscript.Echo "Path: " & objFolder.Path
20       Wscript.Echo "Readable: " & objFolder.Readable
21       Wscript.Echo "System: " & objFolder.System
22       Wscript.Echo "Writeable: " & objFolder.Writeable
23   Next
```

Enumerating All the Folders on a Computer

As demonstrated in the preceding script, WMI can be used to bind to and retrieve the properties from a specific file system folder. In addition, WMI can be used to retrieve the properties for all the folders in the file system, allowing you to easily map the layout of your disk drives. Although you probably do not need to enumerate all the folders on a regular basis, carrying out this task on occasion can help you spot anomalies in the file system, including such things as folders that:

- Should never have been created.
- Are no longer required.
- Do not adhere to your file system naming convention.

To retrieve a list of all the folders on a computer, use the following WQL query:

```
"SELECT * FROM Win32_Directory"
```

If you want to limit data retrieval to a single disk drive, include a Where clause specifying the drive letter. For example, this query returns a list of all the folders on drive C:

```
"SELECT * FROM Win32_Directory WHERE Drive = 'C'"
```

If you need to enumerate all the folders on a computer, be aware that this query can take an extended time to complete. For example, on a Windows 2000–based computer with 5,788 folders, a script that returns the name of each folder required 429 seconds to complete.

Scripting Steps

Listing 11.2 contains a script that returns a list of all of the folders on a computer. To carry out this task, the script must perform the following steps:

1. Create a variable to specify the computer name.

2. Use a GetObject call to connect to the WMI namespace root\cimv2, and set the impersonation level to "impersonate."

3. Use the ExecQuery method to query the Win32_Directory class.

    This returns a collection of all the folders on the computer.

4. For each folder in the collection, echo the folder name.

Listing 11.2   Enumerating All the Folders on a Computer

```
1  strComputer = "."
2  Set objWMIService = GetObject("winmgmts:" _
3      & "{impersonationLevel=impersonate}!\\" & strComputer & "\root\cimv2")
4  Set colFolders = objWMIService.ExecQuery("SELECT * FROM Win32_Directory")
5  For Each objFolder in colFolders
6      Wscript.Echo objFolder.Name
7  Next
```

Enumerating the Subfolders of a Folder

Instead of enumerating all the folders and subfolders on a computer, a more common task is examining the subfolders for a single folder. For example, you might have a folder named Users, and you might encourage your users to store their documents in this folder. Enumerating the subfolders within the Users folder can tell you which users have set up personal folders within that parent folder.

The Win32_Subdirectory class is an association class that allows you to associate a folder with its subfolders (or with its parent folder). Association classes typically have very few properties; their purpose is simply to derive the associations between objects. The Win32_Subdirectory class, for example, has only two properties:

- **GroupComponent.** Returns the parent folder of a folder.

- **PartComponent.** Returns the first-level subfolders of a folder.

To return a collection of subfolders for a folder, create an association query that sets the ResultRole to PartComponent. This indicates that all the items in the returned collection must play the role of a PartComponent, or subfolder, of the folder object. To return the parent folder for a folder, set the ResultRole to GroupComponent.

Figure 11.3 shows a sample folder structure. In this example, the associations for the folder Subfolder 1 are:

- **GroupComponent:** Scripts.

- **PartComponent:** Subfolder 1A; Subfolder 1B.

Figure 11.1   Sample Folder Structure

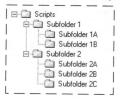

The Win32_Subfolder class works only on the file system level immediately above or immediately below the specified folder. If you retrieve the subfolders for the folder Scripts shown in Figure 11.3, the following two items are returned:

- Subfolder 1

- Subfolder 2

However, the subfolders of those subfolders (for example, Subfolder 1A and Subfolder 1B) are not included in the returned collection. This is because these folders are not directly contained within Scripts. To enumerate subfolders of subfolders, you need to create a recursive function that:

1. Returns a collection of subfolders.

2. Returns a collection of subfolders stored in each of those subfolders.

3. Returns a collection of subfolders stored in each of those sub-subfolders.

The recursion continues until every subfolder has been queried.

 Note

For information about creating recursive functions, see "VBScript Primer" in this book.

Scripting Steps

Listing 11.3 contains a script that returns a list of all subfolders within the folder C:\Scripts. To carry out this task, the script must perform the following steps:

1. Create a variable to specify the computer name.

2. Use a GetObject call to connect to the WMI namespace root\cimv2, and set the impersonation level to "impersonate."

3. Use the ExecQuery method and an Associators of query to return a collection of all the subfolders within the folder C:\Scripts. The Associators of query requires the following parameters:

- The source class, Win32_Directory, where Name equals C:\Scripts.

- The associated class, Win32_Subdirectory. This limits data retrieval to folders. Files are not included in the returned collection.

- The ResultRole, PartComponent, indicating that the items in the returned collection should be subfolders. Setting the ResultRole to GroupComponent would return the parent folder for C:\Scripts.

4. For each subfolder in the collection, echo the folder name.

Listing 11.3   Enumerating the Subfolders of a Folder

```
1  strComputer = "."
2  Set objWMIService = GetObject("winmgmts:" _
3      & "{impersonationLevel=impersonate}!\\" & strComputer & "\root\cimv2")
4  Set colSubfolders = objWMIService.ExecQuery _
5      ("ASSOCIATORS OF {Win32_Directory.Name='c:\scripts'} " _
6          & "WHERE AssocClass = Win32_Subdirectory " _
7              & "ResultRole = PartComponent")
8  For Each objFolder in colSubfolders
9      Wscript.Echo objFolder.Name
10 Next
```

Enumerating a Specific Set of Folders

The previous two topics — generating a list of all the folders on a computer, and generating a list of all the subfolders contained in a specified folder — illustrate basic forms of folder management. Unfortunately, real-world folder management does not always fall into such tidy categories. Instead, folder management often requires you to search through the entire file system looking for folders that meet specific criteria.

For example, you might need to return a list of all the encrypted folders or all the compressed folders on a computer, regardless of their physical location. With the FileSystemObject, this type of task can be achieved only by methodically retrieving each folder on each drive and then checking to see whether it meets the criteria.

WMI makes it much easier to return a list of folders meeting specific criteria; all you have to do is include the criteria within your WQL query. For example, this query returns a collection of all the compressed folders on a computer:

```
SELECT * FROM Win32_Directory WHERE Compressed = True
```

Scripting Steps

Listing 11.4 contains a script that returns a list of all the hidden folders on a computer. To carry out this task, the script must perform the following steps:

1. Create a variable to specify the computer name.

2. Use a GetObject call to connect to the WMI namespace root\cimv2, and set the impersonation level to "impersonate."

3. Use the ExecQuery method to query the Win32_Directory class.

   To limit data retrieval to hidden folders, a Where clause is included restricting the returned folders to those for which the Hidden property is True.

4. For each folder in the collection, echo the folder name.

Listing 11.4   Enumerating a Specific Set of Folders

```
1   strComputer = "."
2   Set objWMIService = GetObject("winmgmts:" _
3       & "{impersonationLevel=impersonate}!\\" & strComputer & "\root\cimv2")
4   Set colFiles = objWMIService.ExecQuery _
5       ("SELECT * FROM Win32_Directory WHERE Hidden = True")
6   For Each objFile in colFiles
7       Wscript.Echo objFile.Name
8   Next
```

Enumerating Folders by Date

Folder date properties — CreationDate, LastAccessed, and LastModified — are very useful in managing folders. For example, you might use the CreationDate property to return a list of all the folders created in the past week. O,r you might use the LastAccessed property to identify rarely used folders, folders that might be candidates for compression or for removal from the file system.

The primary complication in working with folder dates is the fact that WMI stores date and time information using the UTC (Universal Time Coordinate) format. In this format, dates are displayed as yyyymmddHHMMSS.xxxxxx±UUU, where:

- **yyyy** represents the year.

- **mm** represents the month.

- **dd** represents the day.

- **HH** represents the hour (in 24-hour format).

- **MM** represents the minutes.

- **SS** represents the seconds.

- **xxxxxx** represents the milliseconds.

- **±UUU** represents the difference, in minutes, between the current time zone and Greenwich mean time.

For example, in UTC format, a folder created on October 18, 2002, at 10:45:39 A.M. Pacific Standard Time returns this CreationDate value:

20021018104539.000000–480

This means that you cannot specify a standard date, such as 10/18/2002, in your search query; WMI will not be able to interpret this date. Instead, you will need to convert any dates used in your queries to UTC format. Your converted date should use the items in Table 11.4 in each character position in the 25-character UTC string.

Table 11.4   Converting a Date to UTC Format

Character Positions	Description	Sample Value
1–4	Four digits representing the year (such as 2001 or 2002).	2002
5–6	Two digits representing the month. For example, January is represented by the digits 01; November by the digits 11.	10
7–8	Two digits representing the day of the month. For example, the 5th day is represented by the digits 05; the 23rd day by the digits 23.	18
9–14	Six zeros representing the hours, minutes, and seconds of the day (in 24-hour format). If you prefer, you can specify values other than zero to create more finely-targeted searches. For example, to search for folders created after 1:47 P.M. on a given day, set these characters to 134700, where 13 represents the hours (1:00 P.M. in 24-hour format), 47 represents the minutes, and 00 represents the seconds.	000000
15	A period (.).	.
16–21	Six zeros representing the milliseconds.	000000
22–25	The number of minutes difference between your local time and Greenwich mean time.	–480

You can determine the offset from Greenwich mean time by using this script:

```
strComputer = "."
Set objWMIService = GetObject("winmgmts:" _
    & "{impersonationLevel=impersonate}!\\" & strComputer & "\root\cimv2")
Set colTimeZone = objWMIService.ExecQuery _
    ("SELECT * FROM Win32_TimeZone")
For Each objTimeZone in colTimeZone
    Wscript.Echo "Offset: "& objTimeZone.Bias
Next
```

To search for folders using the date October 18, 2002, you would use a value similar to this (depending on your time zone):

20021018000000.000000–480

Scripting Steps

Listing 11.5 contains a script that returns a list of all the folders on a computer that have been created since March 1, 2002. To carry out this task, the script must perform the following steps:

1. Create a variable named dtmTargetDate and set it to the value "20020301000000.000000–420." This value, which represents the target date, March 1, 2002, can be parsed as follows:

- **2002** —Year.

- **03** —Month (in two-digit format).

- **01** —Day (in two-digit format).

- **000000** —Hours, minutes, and seconds of the day.

- **.000000** —Milliseconds.

- **–480** —Offset (in minutes) from Greenwich mean time.

2. Use a GetObject call to connect to the WMI namespace root\cimv2, and set the impersonation level to "impersonate."

3. Use the ExecQuery method to query the Win32_Directory class.

To limit data retrieval to a specified set of folders, a Where clause is included restricting the returned folders to those with a CreationDate later than the target date of March 1, 2002.

4. For each folder in the collection, echo the folder name.

Listing 11.5 Enumerating Folders Using Dates

```
1   dtmTargetDate = "20020301000000.000000-420"
2   strComputer = "."
3   Set objWMIService = GetObject _
4       ("winmgmts:" & "!\\" & strComputer & "\root\cimv2")
5   Set colFolders = objWMIService.ExecQuery _
6       ("SELECT * FROM Win32_Directory WHERE CreationDate > '" & _
7           dtmtargetDate & "'")
8   For Each objFolder in colFolders
9       Wscript.Echo objFolder.Name
10  Next
```

Enumerating Special Folders

The Windows operating system includes a number of special folders, folders that have a well-defined purpose and are generally present on all computers. These special folders include virtual folders, such as My Documents and Recycle Bin, as well as physical file system folders such as Program Files and Fonts. Because of the importance of these folders, it is useful for a system administrator to be able to locate and, if necessary, manipulate these folders on any computer.

However, there are at least two problems with identifying special folders on a computer. First, the location of these folders can vary. Mary might have her My Documents folder on drive C, Ken might have his My Documents folder on drive D, while Mike might have his My Documents folder located on a network drive. In addition, there is no guarantee that these three folders are all named My Documents. Special folders can be renamed; Mary might retain the name My Documents for this folder, but Ken might have renamed his My Documents folder to Ken Myer's Personal Folder.

Fortunately, the operating system does not use physical locations or names to keep track of special folders. Instead, special folders are tracked using CSIDLs, a standard method for identifying these objects regardless of their name or location. For example, the CSIDL for the Recycle Bin is this:

{645FF040-5081-101B-9F08-00AA002F954E}

Other special folders have similar CSIDLs.

Windows Script Host (WSH) can be used to retrieve the location of many of these special folders, particularly those that have a physical location. WSH can retrieve these locations by specifying a folder mnemonic (StartMenu, MyDocuments, Fonts). However, WSH cannot retrieve the location of all the special folders, particularly virtual folders (such as My Network Places) that do not have a physical location. In addition, WSH can only return the location of special folders; it cannot be used to enumerate the items within those folders or to perform any action on those folders.

If you need to locate any special folder on the computer or if you need to perform an action on a particular special folder, you can use the Shell object instead. The Shell object includes a number of predefined constants that can be passed to the Namespace method and return a folder object for a special folder. For example, the constant &H21& represents the Cookies folder; this code returns a folder object for the Cookies folder:

```
Set objShell = CreateObject("Shell.Application")
Set objFolder = objShell.Namespace(&H21&)
```

A list of Shell special folder constants and their Windows Script Host equivalents (where applicable) is shown in Table 11.5. WSH has one advantage over the Shell object: the WSH mnemonics (Programs for the Programs folder, MyDocuments for the My Documents folder) are easier to use and easier to remember than the Shell object constants. However, the Shell object can enumerate many more special folders than WSH can.

Table 11.2   Special Folder Constants and Their WSH Equivalents

Constant	Special Folder	WSH Equivalent
&H1&	Internet Explorer	None
&H2&	Programs	Programs
&H3&	Control Panel	None
&H4&	Printers and Faxes	None
&H5&	My Documents	MyDocuments
&H6&	Favorites	Favorites
&H7&	Startup	Startup
&H8&	My Recent Documents	Recent
&H9&	SendTo	SendTo
&Ha&	Recycle Bin	None
&Hb&	Start Menu	StartMenu
&Hd&	My Music	None
&He&	My Videos	None
&H10&	Desktop	Desktop
&H11&	My Computer	None
&H12&	My Network Places	None
&H13&	NetHood	Nethood
&H14&	Fonts	Fonts
&H15&	Templates	Templates
&H16&	All Users Start Menu	AllUsersStartMenu
&H17&	All Users Programs	AllUsersPrograms
&H18&	All Users Startup	AllUsersStartup
&H19&	All Users Desktop	AllUsersDesktop
&H1a&	Application Data	None

(continued)

Table 11.5 Special Folder Constants and Their WSH Equivalents *(continued)*

Constant	Special Folder	WSH Equivalent
&H1b&	PrintHood	PrintHood
&H1c&	Local Settings\Application Data	None
&H19&	All Users Favorites	None
&H20&	Local Settings\ Temporary Internet Files	None
&H21&	Cookies	None
&H22&	Local Settings\History	None
&H23&	All Users Application Data	None
&H24&	Windows	None
&H25&	System32	None
&H26&	Program Files	None
&H27&	My Pictures	None
&H28&	User Profile	None
&H2b&	Common Files	None
&H2e&	All Users Templates	None
&H2f&	Administrative Tools	None
&H31&	Network Connections	None

Not all computers have each of the special folders shown in Table 11.5. However, even if a folder does not exist, the name and location of that folder are predefined by the operating system. As a result, a script that attempts to enumerate special folders does not fail even if some of these folders do not exist.

Scripting Steps

Listing 11.6 contains a script that returns the path to the My Pictures folder. To carry out this task, the script must perform the following steps:

1. Create a constant named MY_PICTURES and set the value to &H27&.

2. Create an instance of the Shell object.

3. Use the Namespace method to return a Folder object representing the My Pictures folder. This is done by passing the constant MY_PICTURES as the parameter for the Namespace method.

4. Use the Self method to return a FolderItems object for the My Pictures folder. This is required because only FolderItems objects possess the Path property, which allows you to resolve the actual path to the My Pictures folder. The Folder object returned in step 3 can return the name of the My Pictures folder but not the path.

5. Echo the name and path to the My Pictures folder.

Listing 11.6   Enumerating Special Folders

```
1  Const MY_PICTURES = &H27&
2  Set objShell = CreateObject("Shell.Application")
3  Set objFolder = objShell.Namespace(MY_PICTURES)
4  Set objFolderItem = objFolder.Self
5  Wscript.Echo objFolderItem.Name & ": " & objFolderItem.Path
```

Enumerating the Items in a Special Folder

After you have connected to a special folder, you can enumerate the items within the folder the same way you enumerate the files found in a standard file system folder. This allows you to do such things as identify the administrative tools or the control panel applications that are installed on a computer.

For example, Listing 11.7 contains a script that lists the administrative tools installed on a computer. To carry out this task, the script must perform the following steps:

1. Create a constant named ADMINISTRATIVE_TOOLS and set the value to &H2f&.

2. Create an instance of the Shell object.

3. Use the Namespace method to return a Folder object representing the Administrative Tools folder. This is done by passing the constant ADMINISTRATIVE_TOOLS as the parameter for the Namespace method.

4. Use the Items method to return the folder items (the installed administrative tools) within the folder.

5. Create a For Each loop to iterate all the folder items.

6. Echo the item name.

Listing 11.7   Enumerating Installed Administrative Tools

```
1  Const ADMINISTRATIVE_TOOLS = &H2f&
2  Set objShell = CreateObject("Shell.Application")
3  Set objFolder = objShell.Namespace(ADMINISTRATIVE_TOOLS)
4  Set colTools = objFolder.Items
5  For Each objTool in colTools
6      Wscript.Echo objTool
7  Next
```

Binding to a Folder by Using the Browse For Folder Dialog Box

Folder management scripts are often designed to work against any folder on a computer. Because of this, folder names and paths are typically not hard-coded into the script; instead, these values must be typed in as command-line arguments each time the script is run. This provides your script with the flexibility to work against any folder on a computer; however, it also requires you to know the exact location of each folder you want to manage and to correctly type that location before the script can run. This can be particularly cumbersome if the folder you want to manage has a name such as C:\System Administration\Administrator Tools\Diagnostics\Scripts\Network\IP Configuration.

If you are working with a single folder at a time, the Shell's Browse For Folder dialog box provides a graphical alternative to command-line arguments. Instead of requiring you to type in a folder path, the Browse For Folder dialog box (shown in Figure 11.4) allows you to select the folder from a standard Windows Explorer–like tree control.

Figure 11.4 Browse For Folder Dialog Box

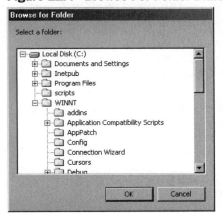

After you select a folder and click **OK**, your script is bound to the Folder object for the selected folder. If you are using a Shell object script, you can proceed to carry out the desired actions on that folder. If you want to pass the selected folder to the FileSystemObject or to WMI, your script can:

1. Use the Self method to return a FolderItems object for the selected folder.

2. Use the Path method to return the path to the folder (for example, C:\Scripts\Logs\Performance.vbs).

3. Use the Replace method to replace each backslash in the path with a pair of backslashes (for example, C:\\Scripts\\Logs\\Performance.vbs). This must be done if you are using WMI because WQL queries require you to use double backslashes in path names.

4. Pass the path to WMI or the FileSystemObject.

To display the Browse for Folder dialog box, use the Shell object's BrowseForFolder method along with the parameters shown in Table 11.6.

Table 11.6   BrowseForFolder Parameters

Parameter	Description
Window handle	Numeric ID to be assigned to the displayed dialog box. For scripts, this value should be 0.
Title	Text string to be displayed inside the dialog box. The title typically represents instructions to the user; in Figure 11.4, the title is "Select a folder to compress:"
Options	Optional values that can be used in constructing the dialog box. Two values are particularly useful in scripts: ■ &H10& (BIF_EDITBOX). Includes an edit box in the dialog box that allows you to type in a folder path. ■ &H4000& (BIF_BROWSEINCLUDEFILES). Shows files as well as folders in the dialog box. This allows you to bind to an individual file rather than an entire folder. To display the standard dialog box, set the Options to 0.
Root folder	Optional parameter specifying the root folder shown at the top of the dialog box. If the root folder is set to C:\Scripts\ADSI, the folder ADSI appears at the top of the dialog box, and neither C:\Scripts nor C:\ is accessible.

For example, the following code displays the Browse For Folder dialog box with these options:

■ A window handle of 0.

■ The title, "Select a folder to compress."

■ No options for adding an edit box or displaying files as well as folders.

■ The root folder D:\. Only folders on drive D are shown in the dialog box.

```
Set objFolder = objShell.BrowseForFolder _
    (0, "Select a folder to compress:", 0, "D:\")
```

Scripting Steps

Listing 11.8 contains a script that uses the Browse For Folder dialog box to return the path of a selected folder. To carry out this task, the script must perform the following steps:

1. Create a constant named WINDOW_HANDLE and set the value to 0. This constant is used to provide the handle to the dialog box window.

2. Create a constant named NO_OPTIONS and set the value to 0. This constant is used to indicate that the dialog box should be displayed without any special options.

3. Create an instance of the Shell object.

4. Use the BrowseForFolder method to display the Browse For Folder dialog box. The method uses the following values for the four parameters:

- **WINDOW_HANDLE**.

- **Select a folder to compress**.

- **NO_OPTIONS**.

- **C:\Scripts**.

5. Use the Self method to return a FolderItem object representing the folder selected in the dialog box.

6. Set the variable objPath to the path of the folder (for example, C:\Scripts\Network).

7. Use the VBScript Replace function to replace all single backslashes (\) in the path with double backslashes (\\). (For example, C:\Scripts\Network becomes C:\\Scripts\\Network.) The double backslashes are required by WMI any time you use a single backslash in a query.

8. Create a variable to specify the computer name.

9. Use a GetObject call to connect to the WMI namespace root\cimv2, and set the impersonation level to "impersonate."

10. Use the ExecQuery method to query the Win32_Directory class.

    To limit data retrieval to a specified folder, a Where clause is included restricting the returned folders to the folder selected from the Browse for Folder dialog box.

11. For the single folder in the collection, echo the value of the Readable property.

Listing 11.8   Using the Browse For Folder Dialog Box

```
1   Const WINDOW_HANDLE = 0
2   Const NO_OPTIONS = 0
3   Set objShell = CreateObject("Shell.Application")
4   Set objFolder = objShell.BrowseForFolder _
5       (WINDOW_HANDLE, "Select a folder:", NO_OPTIONS, "C:\Scripts")
6   Set objFolderItem = objFolder.Self
7   objPath = objFolderItem.Path
8   objPath = Replace(objPath, "\", "\\")
9   strComputer = "."
10  Set objWMIService = GetObject _
11      ("winmgmts:" & "!\\" & strComputer & "\root\cimv2")
12  Set colFiles = objWMIService.ExecQuery _
13      ("SELECT * FROM Win32_Directory WHERE Name = '" & objPath & "'")
14  For Each objFile in colFiles
15      Wscript.Echo "Readable: " & objFile.Readable
16  Next
```

Managing Folders

File systems are dynamic entities that evolve over time. For example, suppose you take a snapshot of your file system today and then compare that snapshot with your file system a year from now; the two will likely bear only a passing resemblance to each other. During the course of a year, file systems undergo many changes. New folders are created, and old folders are deleted. Some folders are copied to multiple locations, and other folders are moved to new locations. Folders are renamed, compressed, and uncompressed.

As a system administrator, it is up to you to carry out many of these activities. Fortunately, you can use scripts to help make the transition from the file system you have today to the file system you need tomorrow.

Renaming Folders

Standardization helps facilitate system administration. For example, having a standard set of folder names makes it easier to run scripts that verify that the proper set of files has been installed on a computer. With standard folder names, scripts such as these can simply connect to the desired folders without needing a list of unique folder names and locations for each individual computer.

Scripts can help you implement standardized naming schemes on computers throughout your organization. For example, the Win32_Directory class provides a Rename method that allows you to rename a folder. Thus, you can write a script that connects to all the domain controllers in your organization and renames the folder C:\Stuff to C:\Administrative Scripts.

To rename a folder, first bind to the folder in question and then call the Rename method. As the sole parameter to the method, pass the new name for the folder as a complete path name. For example, if the folder in the C:\Scripts\Logs\Backup is to be renamed C:\Scripts\Archive, you must pass C:\Scripts\Archive as the complete folder name. Passing only the folder name — Archive — results in an Invalid path error.

Scripting Steps

Listing 11.9 contains a script that binds to the folder C:\Scripts and renames the folder C:\Script Repository. To carry out this task, the script must perform the following steps:

1. Create a variable to specify the computer name.

2. Use a GetObject call to connect to the WMI namespace root\cimv2, and set the impersonation level to "impersonate."

3. Use the ExecQuery method to query the Win32_Directory class.

    To limit data retrieval to a specified folder, a Where clause is included restricting the returned folders to those with the name C:\\Scripts. You must include both backslashes (\\) in the name.

4. For the single folder in the returned collection, use the Rename method to rename the folder to C:\Script Repository.

5. Echo the results of the renaming procedure. A 0 indicates that the folder was successfully renamed.

Listing 11.9 Renaming Folders

```
1  strComputer = "."
2  Set objWMIService = GetObject("winmgmts:" _
3      & "{impersonationLevel=impersonate}!\\" & strComputer & "\root\cimv2")
4  Set colFolders = objWMIService.ExecQuery _
5      ("SELECT * FROM Win32_Directory WHERE Name = 'c:\\Scripts'")
6  For Each objFolder in colFolders
7      errResults = objFolder.Rename("C:\Script Repository")
8      Wscript.Echo errResults
9  Next
```

Moving Folders by Using the Rename Method

The Win32_Directory class does not provide a one-step method for moving folders. Instead, moving a folder generally involves two steps:

1. Copying the folder to its new location

2. Deleting the original folder

The one exception to this two-step process involves moving a folder to a new location on the same drive. For example, suppose you want to move C:\Temp to C:\Scripts\Temporary Files\Archive. As long as the current location and the new location are on the same drive, you can move the folder by simply calling the Rename method and passing the new location as the method parameter. This approach effectively allows you to move the folder in a single step. However, the script fails if the current drive and the new drive are different. An attempt to rename C:\Temp to D:\Temp fails with a "Drive not the same" error.

Scripting Steps

Listing 11.10 contains a script that moves the folder C:\Scripts to C:\Admins\Documents\Archive\VBScript. To carry out this task, the script must perform the following steps:

1. Create a variable to specify the computer name.

2. Use a GetObject call to connect to the WMI namespace root\cimv2, and set the impersonation level to "impersonate."

3. Use the ExecQuery method to query the Win32_Directory class.

   To limit data retrieval to a specified folder, a Where clause is included restricting the returned folders to those with the name C:\\Scripts. You must include both backslashes (\\) in the name.

4. For the single folder in the returned collection, use the Rename method to move the folder to C:\Admins\Documents\Archive\VBScript.

5. Echo the results of the procedure. A 0 indicates that the folder was successfully moved.

Listing 11.10   Moving Folders Using WMI

```
1   strComputer = "."
2   Set objWMIService = GetObject("winmgmts:" _
3       & "{impersonationLevel=impersonate}!\\" & strComputer & "\root\cimv2")
4   Set colFolders = objWMIService.ExecQuery _
5       ("SELECT * FROM Win32_Directory WHERE Name = 'c:\\Scripts'")
6   For Each objFolder in colFolders
7       errResults = objFolder.Rename("C:\Admins\Documents\Archive\VBScript")
8       Wscript.Echo errResults
9   Next
```

Copying Folders by Using WMI

Folders often need to be copied from one location to another. For example, you might copy a folder from one server to another to create a backup copy of that folder. Or you might have a templates folder that needs to be copied to user workstations, or a scripts folder that should be copied to all of your DNS servers.

The Win32_Directory Copy method enables you to copy a folder from one location to another, either on the same computer (for example, copying a folder from drive C to drive D) or on a remote computer. To copy a folder, you return an instance of the folder to be copied and then call the Copy method, passing as a parameter the target location for the new copy of the folder. For example, this line of code copies a folder to the Scripts folder on drive F:

```
objFolder.Copy("F:\Scripts")
```

WMI will not overwrite an existing folder when executing the Copy method. This means that the copy operation fails if the destination folder exists. For example, suppose you have a folder named Scripts and you attempt to copy that folder to a remote share named \\atl-fs-01\archive. If a folder named Scripts already exists on that share, the copy operation fails.

Scripting Steps

Listing 11.11 contains a script that copies the folder C:\Scripts to D:\Scripts. To carry out this task, the script must perform the following steps:

1. Create a variable to specify the computer name.

2. Use a GetObject call to connect to the WMI namespace root\cimv2, and set the impersonation level to "impersonate."

3. Use the ExecQuery method to query the Win32_Directory class.

To limit data retrieval to a specified folder, a Where clause is included restricting the returned folders to those with the name C:\\Scripts. You must include both backslashes (\\) in the name.

4. For the single folder in the returned collection, use the Copy method to copy the folder to D:\Archive. This procedure fails if the folder D:\Archive\Scripts already exists.

5. Echo the results of the renaming procedure. A 0 indicates that the folder was successfully renamed.

Listing 11.11 Copying Folders Using WMI

```
1  strComputer = "."
2  Set objWMIService = GetObject("winmgmts:" _
3      & "{impersonationLevel=impersonate}!\\" & strComputer & "\root\cimv2")
4  Set colFolders = objWMIService.ExecQuery _
5      "SELECT * FROM Win_32 Directory" WHERE Name = 'c:\\Scripts'")
6  For Each objFolder in colFolders
7      errResults = objFolder.Copy("D:\Archive")
8      Wscript.Echo errResults
9  Next
```

Copying Folders by Using the Shell Folder Object

WMI has several limitations when copying folders. For one, WMI provides no built-in method for tracking script progress. Although many system administration scripts have no user interface and are designed to run silently, there might be times when you would like to follow the progress of a script. For example, you might want to visually track a script that copies a large number of files and folders from one computer to another. That way, you can verify that the script is proceeding as expected.

A second limitation of the WMI Copy method is that a folder-copying script fails if the destination folder already exists. For example, you might want to periodically copy a folder named DiskPerformance to an archive folder named Monitoring. The first time you run the script, the copy operation will succeed. The next time you run the script, however, the folder Monitoring\DiskPerformance already exists. As a result, the copy operation fails unless you include extra code within the script to test for the existence of the DiskPerformance folder and then rename either that folder or the new folder being copied.

In addition, the WMI Copy method is an all-or-nothing method: It works only if the destination folder does not exist, and only if you copy over the entire source folder. WMI does not allow you to merge folders; that is, you cannot copy over new items without also deleting all the existing items in the destination folder.

The Shell Folder object includes a CopyHere method that allows you to overcome these limitations. First, the CopyHere method enables you to optionally display the Copying dialog box as the script runs. This dialog box is shown in Figure 11.5.

Figure 11.2   Copying Dialog Box

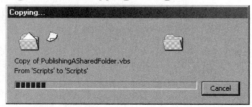

Another optional parameter allows you to copy a folder without overwriting the contents of the target folder. For example, suppose you have a target folder named E:\Scripts. You can copy a second folder named Scripts to that same location without losing the data in the original target folder. Instead, the new folder is automatically named Copy (1) of Scripts. If you copy another folder, it is named Copy (2) of Scripts. This allows you to copy folders from multiple computers without having to worry about providing those folders with unique names.

Finally, the CopyHere method supports merging folders. For example, suppose you have target and source folders with the file sets shown in Table 11.7.

Table 11.7   Sample File Sets Before Copying

Source Folder	Target Folder
SourceFile1	TargetFile1
SourceFile2	TargetFile2
SourceFile2	

When you copy the source folder to the target folder, the file sets are merged, and the new folder contents look like those shown in Table 11.8.

Table 11.8   Sample File Sets After Copying

Source Folder	Target Folder
SourceFile1	TargetFile1
SourceFile2	TargetFile2
SourceFile2	SourceFile1
	SourceFile2
	SourceFile2

> **Note**
> If the target folder already has files named SourceFile1 and SourceFile2, those files are replaced by the versions being copied from the source folder.

To copy a folder using the CopyHere method, you need to create an instance of the Shell object, and then use the Namespace method to bind to the target folder (the location where the folder will be copied). You then call the CopyHere method, passing the path of the source folder (the folder being copied) as a required parameter. In addition, you can pass one or more of the optional constants shown in Table 11.9.

Table 11.9 Shell Folder CopyHere Constants

Constant	Description
&H0&	Displays a progress dialog box that shows the name of each file being copied.
&H4&	Copies files without displaying a dialog box.
&H8&	Automatically creates a new folder name if a folder with that same name already exists.
&H10&	Automatically responds "Yes to All" to any dialog box that appears. For example, if you attempt to copy over existing files, a dialog box appears, asking whether you are sure you want to copy over each file. Selecting this option is identical to clicking **Yes to All** within that dialog box.
&H40&	Preserves undo information. After the script has completed, you can open Windows Explorer and select **Undo** from the **Edit** menu to undo the copy procedure.
&H100&	Displays a simple progress dialog box that does not show the name of each file being copied. Instead, it merely indicates that the copying procedure is in progress.

For example, this line of code copies the folder C:\Scripts while displaying a simple progress dialog box:

```
objFolder.CopyHere "C:\Scripts", &H100&
```

Scripting Steps

Listing 11.12 contains a script that copies a folder to a new location, displaying the Copying dialog box as it carries out the procedure. To carry out this task, the script must perform the following steps:

1. Create a constant named FOF_CREATEPROGRESSDLG and set the value to &H0&.

2. Create a variable named ParentFolder and set the value to D:\Archive. This variable is used to indicate where the folder should be copied to.

3. Create an instance of the Shell object.

4. Use the Namespace method to create a Folder object representing D:\Archive. This is done by passing the variable ParentFolder to the Namespace method. If the folder D:\Archive does not exist, the procedure fails.

5. Use the CopyHere method to copy C:\Scripts to D:\Archive. This creates a new folder, D:\Archive\Scripts, that contains the same files and subfolders as C:\Scripts. The CopyHere method uses two parameters:

   - The name of the folder being copied (C:\Scripts).

   - The optional constant FOF_CREATEPROGRESSDLG. This causes the Copying dialog box to be displayed as the contents of C:\Scripts are being copied.

Listing 11.12   Copying Folders Using the Shell Folder Object

```
1  Const FOF_CREATEPROGRESSDLG = &H0&
2  ParentFolder = "D:\Archive"
3  Set objShell = CreateObject("Shell.Application")
4  Set objFolder = objShell.NameSpace(ParentFolder)
5  objFolder.CopyHere "C:\Scripts", FOF_CREATEPROGRESSDLG
```

Moving Folders by Using the Shell Folder Object

The Shell method MoveHere is similar to the CopyHere method; the only difference is that MoveHere moves a folder from one location to another, whereas CopyHere copies the folder (resulting in two identical folders). Otherwise, MoveHere is called in the same manner as CopyHere and accepts the same set of optional parameters found in Table 11.9.

Scripting Steps

Listing 11.13 contains a script that moves a folder to a new location, displaying the Move Files dialog box as it carries out the procedure. To carry out this task, the script must perform the following steps:

1. Create a constant named FOF_CREATEPROGRESSDLG and set the value to &H0&.

2. Create a variable named TargetFolder and set the value to D:\Archive. This variable is used to indicate where the folder should be moved.

3. Create an instance of the Shell object.

4. Use the Namespace method to create a Folder object representing D:\Archive. This is done by passing the variable TargetFolder to the Namespace method. If the folder D:\Archive does not exist, the procedure fails.

5. Use the MoveHere method to move C:\Scripts to D:\Archive. This creates a new folder, D:\Archive\Scripts, that contains the same files and subfolders as originally found in C:\Scripts. The MoveHere method uses two parameters:

- The name of the folder being moved (C:\Scripts).

- The optional constant FOF_CREATEPROGRESSDLG. This causes the Move Files dialog box to be displayed as the contents of C:\Scripts are being moved.

Listing 11.13 Moving Folders Using the Shell Folder Object

```
1  Const FOF_CREATEPROGRESSDLG = &H0&
2  TargetFolder = "D:\Archive"
3  Set objShell = CreateObject("Shell.Application")
4  Set objFolder = objShell.NameSpace(TargetFolder)
5  objFolder.MoveHere "C:\Scripts", FOF_CREATEPROGRESSDLG
```

Deleting Folders

Folders are not necessarily permanent additions to a file system. At some point, folders might need to be deleted, perhaps because they are no longer required, because the role of the computer has changed, or because the folders were created by mistake.

The Win32_Directory class includes a Delete method that allows you to delete folders: you simply bind to the folder in question and then call the Delete method. After the Delete method is called, the folder is permanently removed from the file system; it is not sent to the Recycle Bin. In addition, no confirmation notice ("Are you sure you want to delete this folder?") is issued. Instead, the folder is immediately removed.

You cannot delete read-only folders using the FileSystemObject; however, this can be done using WMI. If your script uses WMI and you do not want to remove a read-only folder, you must use the Readable property to check the folder status before deleting it.

Scripting Steps

Listing 11.14 contains a script that deletes the folder C:\Scripts. To carry out this task, the script must perform the following steps:

1. Create a variable to specify the computer name.

2. Use a GetObject call to connect to the WMI namespace root\cimv2, and set the impersonation level to "impersonate."

3. Use the ExecQuery method to query the Win32_Directory class.

    To limit data retrieval to a specified folder, a Where clause is included restricting the returned folders to those with the name C:\\Scripts. You must include both backslashes (\\) in the name.

4. For the single folder in the collection, use the Delete method to delete the folder, and then echo the results of this operation. The value 0 indicates that the folder was successfully deleted.

Listing 11.14 Deleting Folders

```
1   strComputer = "."
2   Set objWMIService = GetObject("winmgmts:" _
3       & "{impersonationLevel=impersonate}!\\" & strComputer & "\root\cimv2")
4   Set colFolders = objWMIService.ExecQuery _
5       ("SELECT * FROM Win32_Directory WHERE Name = 'c:\\Scripts'")
6   For Each objFolder in colFolders
7       errResults = objFolder.Delete
8       Wscript.Echo errResults
9   Next
```

Compressing and Uncompressing Folders

Compression provides a way to free additional storage space on a disk drive without purchasing new hardware and without removing files or folders. Depending on the size of your hard disk and the type of files stored on that disk, you might be able to recover hundreds of megabytes of disk space and thus preclude the need to purchase a new hard drive and to take the computer offline until the new drive is installed.

The Win32_Directory class includes a Compress method that compresses all the files and subfolders within a specified folder. In addition, the class also includes an Uncompress method that removes compression from all the files and subfolders in a folder. Similar methods are also provided with the CIM_Datafile class. This allows you to selectively compress or uncompress specific files within a folder.

Because compression imparts a slight performance penalty, it is not recommended for files or folders that are accessed on a routine basis; for example, you probably do not want to compress database files, log files, or user profile folders. Better candidates for compression are files and folders that are not accessed very often. For example, you might write a script to return a collection of folders on a drive that have not been accessed for a month or more and then compress each of those folders.

The amount of disk space freed by compressing folders varies depending on the type of files stored in that folder. For example, .jpg files are already compressed, and further compression has little effect on the size of the file. With other file types, however, the savings can be considerable. For example, a new folder was created on a Windows 2000-based test computer, and 33 Microsoft Word documents, taking up a total of 15 megabytes (MB) of disk space, were copied into that folder. When the documents were compressed, the folder took up only 7 MB of disk space.

Scripting Steps

Listing 11.15 contains a script that compresses the folder C:\Scripts. To carry out this task, the script must perform the following steps:

1. Create a variable to specify the computer name.

2. Use a GetObject call to connect to the WMI namespace root\cimv2, and set the impersonation level to "impersonate."

3. Use the ExecQuery method to query the Win32_Directory class.

   To limit data retrieval to a specified folder, a Where clause is included restricting the returned folders to those with the name C:\\Scripts. You must include both backslashes (\\) in the name.

4. For the single folder in the collection, use the Compress method to compress the folder, and then echo the results of that operation. The value 0 indicates that the folder was successfully compressed.

Listing 11.15   Compressing Folders

```
1  strComputer = "."
2  Set objWMIService = GetObject("winmgmts:" _
3      & "{impersonationLevel=impersonate}!\\" & strComputer & "\root\cimv2")
4  Set colFolders = objWMIService.ExecQuery _
5      ("SELECT * FROM Win32_Directory WHERE Name = 'c:\\Scripts'")
6  For Each objFolder in colFolders
7      errResults = objFolder.Compress
8      Wscript.Echo errResults
9  Next
```

To uncompress a folder, follow exactly the same procedure, but call the Uncompress method rather than the Compress method. For example, the script shown in Listing 11.16 uncompresses the folder C:\Scripts.

Listing 11.16   Uncompressing Folders

```
1  strComputer = "."
2  Set objWMIService = GetObject("winmgmts:" _
3      & "{impersonationLevel=impersonate}!\\" & strComputer & "\root\cimv2")
4  Set colFolders = objWMIService.ExecQuery _
5      ("SELECT * FROM Win32_Directory WHERE Name = 'c:\\Scripts'")
6  For Each objFolder in colFolders
7      errResults = objFolder.Uncompress
8      Wscript.Echo errResults
9  Next
```

Files and File Objects

Files are the ultimate building blocks of any file system; neither disk drives nor folders serve much purpose unless they are used for storing files. Despite their importance, files are often considered beyond the scope of system administration; instead, in many organizations, users manage their own files. This might be a reasonable approach except that users often:

- Store files (such as files infected by viruses) that should not be on the network.

- Store large media files that serve no purpose other than using up hard disk space.

- Needlessly duplicate files and maintain those duplicates indefinitely.

- Store files that have not been accessed in years.

- Do not know how to perform file management activities such as compressing files to conserve disk space.

Because of this, it is a good idea for system administrators to keep track of the files stored within their file systems. Both WMI and the Shell object provide methods that enable you to identify a file or set of files and to return detailed information about that file (including such data as the file size and when the file was last used). In addition, both WMI and the Shell object allow you to carry out common administrative tasks such as copying, moving, renaming, and deleting files.

Enumerating Files and File Properties

In the NTFS file system, files are actually made up of two distinct parts. In addition to the file itself, such as the Microsoft Word document MyDocument.doc, NTFS files also contain "metadata" regarding the file. The file MyDocument.doc contains more than just the words typed into the document; MyDocument.doc also contains information about itself, including such things as file size, the date it was created, and whether it can be modified or is a read-only file.

The WMI CIM_Datafile class allows you to retrieve this metadata for any file on a computer. Using WMI, you can retrieve any of the file properties listed in Table 11.1 (file properties are the same as folder properties). To retrieve this information, simply bind to a file and then echo the appropriate properties.

The relationship between the CIM_DataFile class and Windows Explorer is shown in Figure 11.6.

Figure 11.6 CIM_DataFile and Windows Explorer

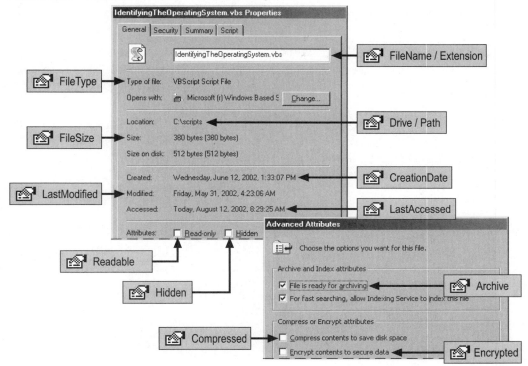

Scripting Steps

Listing 11.17 contains a script that returns the properties of the file C:\Scripts\Adsi.vbs. To carry out this task, the script must perform the following steps:

1. Create a variable to specify the computer name.

2. Use a GetObject call to connect to the WMI namespace root\cimv2, and set the impersonation level to "impersonate."

3. Use the ExecQuery method to query the CIM_Datafile class.

   To limit data retrieval to a specific file, a Where clause is included restricting the returned files to those with the name C:\\Scripts\\Adsi.vbs. You must include both backslashes (\\) in the name.

4. For the single file in the collection, echo a number of the properties shown in Table 11.1.

Listing 11.17   Retrieving File Properties

```
1   strComputer = "."
2   Set objWMIService = GetObject("winmgmts:" _
3       & "{impersonationLevel=impersonate}!\\" & strComputer & "\root\cimv2")
4   Set colFiles = objWMIService.ExecQuery _
5       ("SELECT * FROM CIM_Datafile WHERE Name = 'c:\\Scripts\\Adsi.vbs'")
6   For Each objFile in colFiles
7       Wscript.Echo "Access mask: " & objFile.AccessMask
8       Wscript.Echo "Archive: " & objFile.Archive
9       Wscript.Echo "Compressed: " & objFile.Compressed
10      Wscript.Echo "Compression method: " & objFile.CompressionMethod
11      Wscript.Echo "Creation date: " & objFile.CreationDate
12      Wscript.Echo "Computer system name: " & objFile.CSName
13      Wscript.Echo "Drive: " & objFile.Drive
14      Wscript.Echo "8.3 file name: " & objFile.EightDotThreeFileName
15      Wscript.Echo "Encrypted: " & objFile.Encrypted
16      Wscript.Echo "Encryption method: " & objFile.EncryptionMethod
17      Wscript.Echo "Extension: " & objFile.Extension
18      Wscript.Echo "File name: " & objFile.FileName
19      Wscript.Echo "File size: " & objFile.FileSize
20      Wscript.Echo "File type: " & objFile.FileType
21      Wscript.Echo "File system name: " & objFile.FSName
22      Wscript.Echo "Hidden: " & objFile.Hidden
23      Wscript.Echo "Last accessed: " & objFile.LastAccessed
24      Wscript.Echo "Last modified: " & objFile.LastModified
25      Wscript.Echo "Manufacturer: " & objFile.Manufacturer
26      Wscript.Echo "Name: " & objFile.Name
27      Wscript.Echo "Path: " & objFile.Path
28      Wscript.Echo "Readable: " & objFile.Readable
29      Wscript.Echo "System: " & objFile.System
30      Wscript.Echo "Version: " & objFile.Version
31      Wscript.Echo "Writeable: " & objFile.Writeable
32  Next
```

Retrieving Extended File Properties

When you right-click a file in Windows Explorer and select **Properties** from the shortcut menu, a dialog box displays basic properties for that file, including such things as file name, file size, and the file creation, last access, and last modification dates. In addition to these basic properties, the Windows operating system also tracks a number of extended file properties. These properties are typically hidden; to display them in Windows Explorer, you must click **View**, click **Choose Details**, and then select the desired properties from the resulting dialog box (shown in Figure 11.7).

Figure 11.7   Choose Details Dialog Box

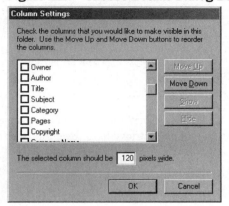

The Shell FolderItems object includes a GetDetailsOf method that allows you to access these extended properties. These properties, and their associated index numbers, are shown in Table 11.10.

Table 11.10   Retrieving Extended File Properties

Index	Property	Index	Property
0	Name	18	Year
1	Size	19	Track Number
2	Type	20	Genre
3	Date Modified	21	Duration
4	Date Created	22	Bit Rate
5	Date Accessed	23	Protected
6	Attributes	24	Camera Model
7	Status	25	Date Picture Taken
8	Owner	26	Dimensions
9	Author	27	Not used
10	Title	28	Not used
11	Subject	29	Not used
12	Category	30	Company
13	Pages	31	Description
14	Comments	32	File Version

(continued)

Table 11.10   Retrieving Extended File Properties *(continued)*

Index	Property	Index	Property
15	Copyright	33	Product Name
16	Artist	34	Product Version
17	Album Title		

To access any one of these properties, call the GetDetailsOf method, passing two parameters: the name of the file and the index number of the property to be retrieved. For example, the following code snippet echoes the Duration property for a media file:

```
Wscript.Echo objFolder.GetDetailsOf(strFileName, 21)
```

Scripting Steps

Listing 11.18 contains a script that retrieves all the extended properties for each file in the folder C:\Scripts. To carry out this task, the script must perform the following steps:

1. Create a one-dimensional array named arrHeaders, and set the size to 35. This array is used to hold the names of the extended properties.

2. Create an instance of the Shell object.

3. Use the Namespace method to return a Folder object representing the folder where the files are stored. In Listing 11.18, that folder is C:\Scripts.

4. Create a For Next loop to return the names of the extended properties. Because the first extended property has the index number 0, the loop runs from 0 to 34.

5. Use the GetDetailsOf method to retrieve the names of all 35 extended properties.

6. For each file in the folder, set up another For-Next loop running from 0 to 34.

7. For each file, echo the property name, and use the GetDetailsOf method to retrieve and echo the property value.

Listing 11.18   Retrieving Extended File Properties

```
1   Dim arrHeaders(35)
2   Set objShell = CreateObject("Shell.Application")
3   Set objFolder = objShell.Namespace("C:\Scripts")
4   For i = 0 to 34
5       arrHeaders(i) = objFolder.GetDetailsOf(objFolder.Items, i)
6   Next
7   For Each strFileName in objFolder.Items
8       For i = 0 to 34
9           Wscript.Echo i & vbtab & arrHeaders(i) _
10              & ": " & objFolder.GetDetailsOf(strFileName, i)
11      Next
12  Next
```

Enumerating All the Files on a Computer

The CIM_Datafile class provides access to all the files stored on a computer, including those stored on hard disks, floppy disks, and CD-ROM drives. This means that you can use WMI and the CIM_Datafile class to retrieve a list of all the files stored on a computer.

Admittedly, retrieving a list of all the files on a computer rarely has any practical value. Queries such as this can take an extremely long time to complete; on a large file server, for example, it might take several hours to return such a list; even then, the query will complete only if there is enough memory on the computer to carry out the request. This is due to the way standard WMI queries operate. As objects (such as files) are enumerated, they are queued in memory and then reported in batches. If too many objects are found, memory can exhausted before the entire list has been generated.

In addition, a query such as this typically returns far more information than is useful. After all, even a typical user workstation might contain some 50,000 files.

Although enumerating all the files on a computer might have little practical value, it does provide an introduction to the CIM_Datafile class and emphasizes the importance of using targeted queries when working with this class. Unlike many other WMI classes, some care must be taken when using CIM_Datafile. For example, when you return a list of services on a computer using WMI, a script completes in approximately the same time regardless of whether you return the entire set of services or some subset of services (for example, all the services currently running). This is not true of CIM_Datafile. Returning a list of all the files on a computer might take hours; returning a list of all the files with the .jpg extension might take just a few seconds.

Scripting Steps

Listing 11.19 contains a script that returns a list of all the files on a computer. To carry out this task, the script must perform the following steps:

1. Create a variable to specify the computer name.

2. Use a GetObject call to connect to the WMI namespace root\cimv2, and set the impersonation level to "impersonate."

3. Use the ExecQuery method to query the CIM_Datafile class.

   This returns a collection of all the files on the computer.

4. For each file in the collection, echo the file name.

Listing 11.19 Enumerating All the Files on a Computer

```
1   strComputer = "."
2   Set objWMIService = GetObject("winmgmts:" _
3       & "{impersonationLevel=impersonate}!\\" & strComputer & "\root\cimv2")
4   Set colFiles = objWMIService.ExecQuery _
5       ("SELECT * FROM CIM_Datafile")
6   For Each objFile in colFiles
7       Wscript.Echo objFile.Name
8   Next
```

Using an Asynchronous Query to Enumerate All the Files on a Computer

The script for enumerating all the files on a computer (as shown in Listing 11.19) works as long as there is sufficient memory to maintain a list of all the files on a computer. For example, on a Windows 2000–based computer with 128 MB of RAM and approximately 22,000 files, the enumeration script completed successfully. On a similar computer with approximately 82,000 files, however, the script exhausted available memory and failed.

With a standard query, data retrieval can tie up available memory and slow system performance. If you expect your file query to return a large amount of data, you might find it more expedient to use an *asynchronous query*, even if you are returning only a subset of files on a computer (for example, a query that returns several thousand .doc files from a file server). With an asynchronous query, objects are retrieved and reported one at a time. This allows the script to proceed with other tasks; equally important, it allows data retrieval to take place in the background, lessening the system load.

Scripting Steps

Listing 11.20 contains a script that uses an asynchronous query to return a list of all the files on a computer. To carry out this task, the script must perform the following steps:

1. Create a constant named POPUP_DURATION, and set the value to 120. This ensures that the popup message box remains on screen for 120 seconds, allowing enough time for the asynchronous query to begin returning data.

2. Create a constant named OK_BUTTON and set the value to 0. This constant is used in constructing the popup message box.

3. Create an instance of the Wscript Shell object.

4. Create a variable to specify the computer name.

5. Use a GetObject call to connect to the WMI namespace root\cimv2, and set the impersonation level to "impersonate."

6. Create an SWbemSink object named SINK_.

7. Use the ExecQueryAsync method to tie the SWbemSink object to the WQL query "SELECT * FROM CIM_Datafile". This query returns a list of all the files on the computer and sends that list, one file at a time, to the SWbemSink object.

8. As each file is returned to the SWbemSinkObject, display the file name.

Listing 11.20   Using an Asynchronous Query to Enumerate All the Files on a Computer

```
1   Const POPUP_DURATION = 120
2   Const OK_BUTTON = 0
3   Set objWSHShell = Wscript.CreateObject("Wscript.Shell")
4   strComputer = "."
5   Set objWMIService = GetObject("winmgmts:" _
6       & "{impersonationLevel=impersonate}!\\" & strComputer & "\root\cimv2")
7   Set objSink = WScript.CreateObject("WbemScripting.SWbemSink","SINK_")
8   objWMIService.ExecQueryAsync objSink, "SELECT * FROM CIM_DataFile"
9   objPopup = objWshShell.Popup("Starting event retrieval", _
10      POPUP_DURATION, "Event Retrieval", OK_BUTTON)
11  Sub SINK_OnObjectReady(objEvent, objAsyncContext)
12      Wscript.Echo objEvent.Name
13  End Sub
```

Enumerating All the Files in a Folder

Although it is possible to enumerate all the files on the computer, this procedure can be extremely slow, and typically yields far more information than you can make use of. A faster, and generally more useful, approach is to enumerate all the files in a particular folder. This allows you to do such things as verify that each of your servers has a Scripts folder containing a full set of system administration scripts. Likewise, you might want to connect to an application folder and verify the version number for each .dll file stored there.

To enumerate all the files in a folder, you can use a script similar to the one shown in Listing 11.19. The only difference is that you include a Where clause in your WQL query to restrict data retrieval to those files found in the specified folder.

Scripting Steps

Listing 11.21 contains a script that returns a list of all the files in the folder C:\Scripts. To carry out this task, the script must perform the following steps:

1. Create a variable to specify the computer name.

2. Use a GetObject call to connect to the WMI namespace root\cimv2, and set the impersonation level to "impersonate."

3. Use the ExecQuery method to query the CIM_Datafile class.

To limit data retrieval to the files in a specific folder, a Where clause is included restricting the returned files to those with the path \\Scripts\\. (You must include double backslashes [\\] before and after the path name.) Note that you do not have to include the drive letter provided the path is unique within the file system.

4. For each file in the collection, echo the file name and the file size.

Listing 11.21   Enumerating All the Files in a Folder

```
1   strComputer = "."
2   Set objWMIService = GetObject("winmgmts:" _
3       & "{impersonationLevel=impersonate}!\\" & strComputer & "\root\cimv2")
4   Set colFiles = objWMIService.ExecQuery _
5       ("SELECT * FROM CIM_DataFile WHERE Path = '\\Scripts\\'")
6   For Each objFile in colFiles
7       Wscript.Echo objFile.Name
8   Next
```

Enumerating a Specific Set of Files

One of the advantages of using WMI as a file management tool is the fact that WMI allows you to locate all the files that meet a specified set of criteria, regardless of the physical location of those files. For example, you can return a collection of all the files consisting of a particular file name extension, all the read-only files, or all the files created on a specified date. After these files are enumerated, you can carry out various operations on the entire collection, including copying, deleting, or renaming each of the files.

  Tip

If you want to limit your search to a particular drive, include the appropriate Where clause in your query. For example, the clause Where Drive = 'C' limits the search to files found on drive C.

Scripting Steps

Listing 11.22 contains a script that returns a set of all the files with a file size larger than 1,000,000 bytes. To carry out this task, the script must perform the following steps:

1. Create a variable to specify the computer name.

2. Use a GetObject call to connect to the WMI namespace root\cimv2, and set the impersonation level to "impersonate."

3. Use the ExecQuery method to query the CIM_Datafile class.

To limit data retrieval to a specific set of files, a Where clause is included restricting the returned files to those with a size of 1,000,000 bytes or more.

4. For each file in the collection, echo the file name and the file size.

Listing 11.22   Enumerating a Specific Set of Files

```
1   strComputer = "."
2   Set objWMIService = GetObject("winmgmts:" _
3       & "{impersonationLevel=impersonate}!\\" & strComputer & "\root\cimv2")
4   Set colFiles = objWMIService.ExecQuery _
5       ("SELECT * FROM CIM_DataFile WHERE FileSize > 1000000")
6   For Each objFile in colFiles
7       Wscript.Echo objFile.Name & " — " & objFile.FileSize
8   Next
```

Managing Files

Managing files by using scripts is similar to managing folders. WMI treats files and folders as if they were essentially the same type of object; in fact, the properties and methods of the Win32_Directory and CIM_DataFile classes are identical. Files and folders are also similar in that they are not static entities; when you create a new file named C:\Scripts\ScriptLog.txt, there is no guarantee that it will be in the same place, under the same name, a year from now.

Instead, files might be renamed or be given a new file name extension. Files might be copied to multiple servers, moved to new locations, or deleted altogether. All of these tasks — and more — can be carried out programmatically using WMI and the Shell object.

Renaming Files

It is not unusual for files to be given new names. Sometimes this is done to provide a file with a more descriptive name (for example, changing 03b4cast.xls to Budget Forecast for 2003.xls). At other times, this is done to ensure that data is not lost or that other operations can proceed. For example, you might have a script that backs up the Application event log to a file named ApplicationBackup.evt. If that file already exists, the backup operation fails. Consequently, you might want to rename the existing version of ApplicationBackup.evt before running the backup script. This, and any other renaming operation, can be carried out using the CIM_Datafile Rename method.

When renaming a file, you must specify the complete path name. For example, to rename a file in the C:\Scripts\Logs folder, you must include the entire path name as the parameter:

```
errResult = objFile.Rename("C:\Scripts\Logs\NewName.vbs")
```

Passing only the file name results in an error. For example, this line of code results in an "Invalid name" error:

```
errResult = objFile.Rename("NewName.vbs")
```

Scripting Steps

Listing 11.23 contains a script that renames a file. To carry out this task, the script must perform the following steps:

1. Create a variable to specify the computer name.

2. Use a GetObject call to connect to the WMI namespace root\cimv2, and set the impersonation level to "impersonate."

3. Use the ExecQuery method to query the CIM_DataFile class.

   To limit data retrieval to a specific file, a Where clause is included restricting the returned files to those with the file name c:\\scripts\\toggle_service.vbs. You must include both backslashes in the query.

4. For the single file in the collection, use the Rename method to rename the file c:\scripts\toggle_service.old, and then echo the results of that procedure. A 0 indicates that the file was successfully renamed.

Listing 11.23   Renaming Files

```
1   strComputer = "."
2   Set objWMIService = GetObject("winmgmts:" _
3       & "{impersonationLevel=impersonate}!\\" & strComputer & "\root\cimv2")
4   Set colFiles = objWMIService.ExecQuery _
5       ("SELECT * FROM Cim_Datafile WHERE Name = " _
6           & "'c:\\scripts\\toggle_service.vbs'")
7   For Each objFile in colFiles
8       errResult = objFile.Rename("c:\scripts\toggle_service.old")
9       Wscript.Echo errResult
10  Next
```

Changing File Name Extensions

Using a script to rename a single file is inefficient; usually, it is faster to carry out this task using Windows Explorer or a command-line tool. A more practical operation might be to use a script to change the extensions of all the files in a folder. For example, you might have a folder containing numerous log files on a computer, all with the extension .log. Using a script, you can change the extension for all of these .log files to .txt or .bkp or anything else. These repetitive tasks represent the kinds of things that scripts do best.

When changing file name extensions using WMI, it is important to keep in mind that the Rename method requires a complete path. This means that you cannot simply specify a new file name extension for the file. Instead, you must construct an entire path.

For example, suppose you have a file named Performance.log in the C:\Logs\MailServer folder. To rename this file to Performance.bkp, you need to pass C:\Logs\MailServer\Performance.bkp as the Rename parameter. This new path can be constructed by combining:

- The CIM_Datafile Drive property (**C:**).

- The Cim_Datafile Path property (**\Logs\MailServer**).

- The CIM_Datafile FileName property (**Performance**).

- A dot (**.**) to separate the file name and extension.

- **Bkp**, the new extension.

Scripting Steps

Listing 11.24 contains a script that changes the file name extensions of all the .log files in a specified folder to .txt. To carry out this task, the script must perform the following steps:

1. Create a variable to specify the computer name.

2. Use a GetObject call to connect to the WMI namespace root\cimv2, and set the impersonation level to "impersonate."

3. Use the ExecQuery method and an Associators of query to return a collection of all the files within the folder C:\Scripts. The Associators of query requires the following parameters:

   - The source class, Win32_Directory, where Name equals C:\Scripts.

   - The ResultClass, CIM_Datafile. This limits data retrieval to files, which are instances of the CIM_Datafile class. Subfolders are not included in the returned collection.

4. For each file in the collection, check the file name extension.

5. For each file in the collection with the file name extension .log, create a new file name using the following:

   - The folder path (C:\Scripts\).

   - The existing file name. (For example, for the file C:\Scripts\DiskPerformance.log, the FileName is DiskPerformance.)

   - A dot (used to separate the FileName from the file name extension).

   - txt (the new file name extension).

   Consequently, the file C:\Scripts\DiskPerformance.log is given a new path: C:\Scripts\DiskPerformance.txt.

6. Use the Rename method to rename the file, and then echo the results of that procedure. A 0 indicates that the file was successfully renamed.

Listing 11.24   Changing File Name Extensions

```
1   strComputer = "."
2   Set objWMIService = GetObject("winmgmts:" _
3       & "{impersonationLevel=impersonate}!\\" & strComputer & "\root\cimv2")
4   Set FileList = objWMIService.ExecQuery _
5       ("ASSOCIATORS OF {Win32_Directory.Name='c:\Scripts'} Where " _
6           & "ResultClass = CIM_DataFile")
7   For Each objFile In FileList
8       If objFile.Extension = "log" Then
9           strNewName = objFile.Drive & objFile.Path & _
10              objFile.FileName & "." & "txt"
11          errResult = objFile.Rename(strNewName)
12          Wscript.Echo errResult
13      End If
14  Next
```

Copying Files

In addition to copying entire folders, you often need to copy individual files or specific sets of files. For example, you might need to copy a particular template to each computer or copy all .vbs files to a new administrator workstation. The CIM_Datafile Copy method can be used to copy individual files or a set of files from one location to another.

This ability to copy individual files (as opposed to entire folders) is especially powerful when combined with WMI's ability to locate all the files of a specified type regardless of their location in the file system. This allows you to perform such tasks as automatically searching for all .log files and copying them to a central monitoring station, or searching for all Microsoft Word files and copying them to a document repository.

You can use the CIM_DataFile class and the Copy method to copy either a single file or a set of files to a new location.

Scripting Steps

Listing 11.25 contains a script that copies all the Microsoft® Windows Media® files on a computer to a specified folder. To carry out this task, the script must perform the following steps:

1.   Create a variable to specify the computer name.

2.   Use a GetObject call to connect to the WMI namespace root\cimv2, and set the impersonation level to "impersonate."

3.   Use the ExecQuery method to query the CIM_DataFile class.

   To limit data retrieval to Windows Media files, a Where clause is included restricting the returned files to those with the extension .wma.

4. For each file in the collection, set the value of the variable strCopy to the new path for the file. This value is a combination of the following items:

- The destination folder (C:\Media Archive\). You must include the trailing backslash.

- The file name. If the file is named Annual Meeting.wma, the file name is Annual Meeting.

- A period (.), used to separate the file name and the extension.

- The extension.

For example, if you have a file named D:\Finance\Annual Meeting.wma, the value of strCopy is C:\Media Archive\Annual Meeting.wma.

5. Use the Copy method to copy the file to the new file path.

Listing 11.25 Copying Files

```
1   strComputer = "."
2   Set objWMIService = GetObject("winmgmts:" _
3       & "{impersonationLevel=impersonate}!\\" & strComputer & "\root\cimv2")
4   Set colFiles = objWMIService.ExecQuery _
5       ("SELECT * FROM CIM_DataFile WHERE Extension = 'wma'")
6   For Each objFile in colFiles
7       strCopy = "C:\Media Archive\" & objFile.FileName _
8           & "." & objFile.Extension
9       objFile.Copy(strCopy)
10  Next
```

Deleting Files

Deleting files is as an integral part of file management. Files need to be deleted for many reasons: to free up disk space; to remove outdated files; to remove inappropriate files. WMI is a powerful tool for deleting files because it allows you to select a specified set of files (regardless of their physical location in the file system) and then delete all those files in a single operation.

For example, you might have a policy that prohibits users from storing media files on a particular file server. A WMI script can be scheduled to run each night, search for a specific set of files (for example, .mp3 or .wma files), and then delete all instances of that file type.

Unlike the FileSystemObject, the WMI Delete method automatically deletes read-only files. If you do not want to delete read-only files, you have to construct your query in such a way as to exclude these files from the returned collection (for example, by including the clause Where Readable = True).

Scripting Steps

Listing 11.26 contains a script that deletes all the Windows Media files from a computer. To carry out this task, the script must perform the following steps:

1. Create a variable to specify the computer name.

2. Use a GetObject call to connect to the WMI namespace root\cimv2, and set the impersonation level to "impersonate."

3. Use the ExecQuery method to query the CIM_DataFile class.

   To limit data retrieval to Windows Media files, a Where clause is included restricting the returned files to those with the extension .wma.

4. For each file in the collection, use the Delete method to delete the file.

Listing 11.26   Deleting Files

```
1   strComputer = "."
2   Set objWMIService = GetObject("winmgmts:" _
3       & "{impersonationLevel=impersonate}!\\" & strComputer & "\root\cimv2")
4   Set colFiles = objWMIService.ExecQuery _
5       ("SELECT * FROM CIM_DataFile WHERE Extension = 'wma'")
6   For Each objFile in colFiles
7       objFile.Delete
8   Next
```

Performing Actions on Files

When you right-click a Shell object in Windows Explorer, a shortcut menu appears showing actions that can be performed on that object. For example, when you right-click a VBScript file, you see such options as Open, Edit, Print, Create Shortcut, and Delete.

Within the Shell nomenclature, each of the commands that appear on a shortcut menu is known as a *verb*. A verb is a text string in the registry that specifies the command to be run when the menu item is clicked. Different objects have a different set of verbs. The Recycle Bin, for example, does not have a Print option, but it does have an Empty Recycle Bin option.

The FolderItem object features an InvokeVerbEx method that allows you to execute any of the verbs associated with an object. For example, this command opens the associated file:

```
objFile.InvokeVerbEx("Open")
```

Calling InvokeVerbEx without specifying a verb automatically invokes the default verb for the object. For example, with a Windows Media file, the default verb is Play; for a folder, the default verb is Open.

Be aware that verbs always function in exactly the same way they do when clicked in Windows Explorer. If you right-click a file and select **Open**, the file automatically opens. If you select **Delete**, however, a confirmation box is displayed before the file is deleted. This same confirmation box appears if you attempt to delete any object using InvokeVerbEx. For example, using the Delete verb on a file results in a dialog box similar to the one shown in Figure 11.8.

Figure 11.3   Confirmation Dialog Box

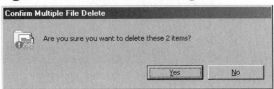

By comparison, right-clicking a file and selecting **Print** does not display a dialog box; instead, the file is automatically printed to the default printer. If you use InvokeVerbEx to print a file programmatically, that file is automatically printed to the default printer without displaying a dialog box of any kind.

Scripting Steps

Listing 11.27 contains a script that prints all the files in the folder C:\Logs. To carry out this task, the script must perform the following steps:

1. Create a variable named TargetFolder, and set the value to C:\Logs. This is the folder where the files to be printed are stored.

2. Create an instance of the Shell object.

3. Use the Namespace method to return a Folder object representing C:\Logs.

4. Use the Items method to return a collection of all the FolderItems within C:\Logs.

5. Create a For Each loop to iterate through all the collection of FolderItems.

6. For each item in the collection, use the InvokeVerbEx method to perform an action using one of the shortcut menu options for that item. In this script, that action is Print.

Listing 11.27   Performing Actions on Files

```
1  TargetFolder = "C:\Logs"
2  Set objShell = CreateObject("Shell.Application")
3  Set objFolder = objShell.Namespace(TargetFolder)
4  Set colItems = objFolder.Items
5  For Each objItem in colItems
6      objItem.InvokeVerbEx("Print")
7  Next
```

Identifying Shell Object Verbs

One potential problem with carrying out actions using Shell object verbs is knowing which verbs, and thus which actions, are available to you. Fortunately, each Shell object exposes its verbs as a collection that can be enumerated programmatically. To identify the verbs for a particular Shell object, obtain a FolderItem object and then use the Verbs method to return a collection of all the verbs for that object. You can then list each verb in the collection.

Scripting Steps

Listing 11.28 contains a script that returns a list of all the Shell Object verbs that can be used with the Recycle Bin. To carry out this task, the script must perform the following steps:

1. Create a constant named RECYCLE_BIN and set the value to &Ha&. This is the value used by the Namespace method to locate the Recycle Bin.

2. Create an instance of the Shell object.

3. Use the Namespace method to return a Folder object representing the Recycle Bin.

4. Use the Self method to return a FolderItems object for the Recycle Bin. This is required because only FolderItems objects possess the Verbs method. This method returns a list of Shell object verbs that can be used with the Recycle Bin.

5. Use the Verbs method to return a list of Shell object verbs that can be used with the Recycle Bin. Verbs are returned as an array, with the first verb assigned the index number 0.

6. Create a For Each loop to echo the name of each verb.

Listing 11.28   Identifying Shell Object Verbs

```
1   Const RECYCLE_BIN = &Ha&
2   Set objShell = CreateObject("Shell.Application")
3   Set objFolder = objShell.NameSpace(RECYCLE_BIN)
4   Set objFolderItem = objFolder.Self
5   Set colVerbs = objFolderItem.Verbs
6   For Each objVerb in colVerbs
7       Wscript.Echo objVerb
8   Next
```

Monitoring the File System

File systems are in a constant state of flux: New files are created, old files are deleted, and files are modified in various ways. This behavior is entirely expected, and most of it is of little interest to system administrators; system administrators do not need to be notified every time the operating system creates or deletes a temporary file, or every time a user makes a change to a Word document or a spreadsheet.

On the other hand, certain files and folders are very important to the organization. Because of that, you might want to keep a closer watch on these items. If someone adds a new file to a folder for proposed projects, you might want a notice to that effect sent to specified people. Likewise, these same people might want to be notified if a file is removed from that folder. If you have a file that prescribes the daily routine for all system administrators, you might want to be notified whenever that file is modified.

You can use the WMI event monitoring capabilities to monitor changes to the file system. If you choose to carry out such monitoring, it is highly recommended that you limit your monitoring to a specific file or folder. As noted previously, file systems are in a constant state of flux; attempting to monitor the entire file system on a computer is very slow, very processor intensive, and results in a huge quantity of data, most of which is of no interest to you. By limiting your monitoring to a specific file or folder, you can ensure that you are immediately notified of changes to the file system and that you are notified only of the changes that really matter to you.

Monitoring File Creation

At times, you might find it useful to know when a new file is added to the file system. For example, you might have a central repository for system administration scripts. Each time a new script is added to the repository, the script writer can be tasked with issuing an e-mail to other administrators. Alternatively, you can use a script to monitor the repository and automatically send an e-mail any time a new script is added. That way, administrators immediately know that a new script is available for use.

To keep track of newly created files, you need to write a script that includes two key elements. First, you need to monitor for new instances of the __InstanceCreationEvent class; new instances of this class are created each time a new managed object of any kind is created on the computer. Second, you need to limit data retrieval to new instances of the CIM_DirectoryContainsFile class.

CIM_DirectoryContainsFile is an association class that associates a specified folder with all the files contained within it. If you pass the name of a folder to CIM_DataContainsFile, it returns a collection of all the files in that folder. CIM_DataContainsFile has two components:

- **GroupComponent.** The path to the folder being monitored
- **PartComponent.** The individual files within that folder

Scripting Steps

Listing 11.29 contains a script that monitors the C:\Scripts folder and issues an alert whenever a new file is added to that folder. To carry out this task, the script must perform the following steps:

1. Create a variable to specify the computer name.

2. Use a GetObject call to connect to the WMI namespace root\cimv2, and set the impersonation level to "impersonate."

3. Use the ExecNotificationQuery method to monitor for new instances of the CIM_DirectoryContainsFile class, where the GroupComponent (the folder being monitored) is equal to "c:\\\\scripts". All four backslashes must be included in the query.

4. Create a Do Loop with no exit condition. This causes the loop to continue (and the script to run) indefinitely. The only way to stop the loop is to terminate the script process.

5. Create an object (objLatestEvent) to represent new instances of the CIM_DirectoryContainsFile class. Each time a new file is created in C:\Scripts, a new instance of objLatestEvent is created as well.

6. Echo the PartComponent of the objLatestEvent.TargetInstance. In the association between CIM_DirectoryContainsFile and Win32_Directory, the PartComponent represents the path name of the newly created file.

Listing 11.29   Monitoring File Creation

```
1   strComputer = "."
2   Set objWMIService = GetObject("winmgmts:" _
3       & "{impersonationLevel=impersonate}!\\" & strComputer & "\root\cimv2")
4   Set colMonitoredEvents = objWMIService.ExecNotificationQuery _
5       ("SELECT * FROM __InstanceCreationEvent WITHIN 10 WHERE " _
6           & "Targetinstance ISA 'CIM_DirectoryContainsFile' AND " _
7               & "TargetInstance.GroupComponent= " _
8                   & "'Win32_Directory.Name=""c:\\\\scripts""'")
9   Do
10      Set objLatestEvent = colMonitoredEvents.NextEvent
11      Wscript.Echo objLatestEvent.TargetInstance.PartComponent
12  Loop
```

Monitoring File Deletion

The CIM_DataContainsFile class can be used to keep track of the files within a specified folder. This means that CIM_DataContainsFile not only tracks which files are currently in a folder but can also keep track of changes to the contents of that folder. As shown in the preceding script, CIM_DataContainsFile can be used to identify new files added to a folder. It can also be used to identify files that are deleted from that folder.

Monitoring file deletion is similar to monitoring file creation; the only difference is that you must monitor for instances of the __InstanceDeletionEvent class. New instances of this class are created each time a managed object is deleted from the computer. By using the CIM_DataContainsFile class to limit data retrieval to deleted objects from a specific folder, you can be notified whenever a file is deleted from that folder.

Scripting Steps

Listing 11.30 contains a script that issues an alert whenever a file is deleted from the folder C:\Scripts. To carry out this task, the script must perform the following steps:

1. Create a variable to specify the computer name.

2. Use a GetObject call to connect to the WMI namespace root\cimv2, and set the impersonation level to "impersonate."

3. Use the ExecNotificationQuery method to monitor for deleted instances of the CIM_DirectoryContainsFile class, where the GroupComponent (the folder being monitored) is equal to "c:\\\\scripts". All four backslashes must be included in the query.

4. Create a Do Loop with no exit condition. This causes the loop to continue (and the script to run) indefinitely. The only way to stop the loop is to terminate the script process.

5. Create an object (objLatestEvent) to represent deleted instances of the CIM_DirectoryContainsFile class. Each time a file is deleted from C:\Scripts, a new instance of objLatestEvent is created.

6. Echo the PartComponent of the objLatestEvent.TargetInstance. In the association between CIM_DirectoryContainsFile and Win32_Directory, the PartComponent represents the path name of the newly deleted file.

Listing 11.30 Monitoring File Deletion

```
1   strComputer = "."
2   Set objWMIService = GetObject("winmgmts:" _
3       & "{impersonationLevel=impersonate}!\\" & strComputer & "\root\cimv2")
4   Set colMonitoredEvents = objWMIService.ExecNotificationQuery _
5       ("SELECT * FROM __InstanceDeletionEvent WITHIN 10 WHERE " _
6           & "Targetinstance ISA 'CIM_DirectoryContainsFile' AND " _
7               & "TargetInstance.GroupComponent= " _
8                   & "'Win32_Directory.Name=""c:\\\\scripts""'")
9   Do
10      Set objLatestEvent = colMonitoredEvents.NextEvent
11      Wscript.Echo objLatestEvent.TargetInstance.PartComponent
12  Loop
```

Monitoring File Modification

Some documents are far more important to an organization than others. Because of this, you might want to keep a closer watch on these documents and be notified whenever they change in some way. For example, you might have a manual that describes the roles and responsibilities for each of your Information Technology (IT) personnel. If this document is modified, you need to look at it immediately to see whether the changes affect your daily routine. Or, if the home page for your Web site is modified, you might want to know right away so you can quickly verify that this is a valid change, and not the result of an attack by a hacker.

You can use a WMI event notification query to issue an alert whenever a particular file is modified in any way.

Scripting Steps

Listing 11.31 contains a script that issues an alert anytime the file C:\Scripts\Index.vbs is modified. To carry out this task, the script must perform the following steps:

1. Create a variable to specify the computer name.

2. Use a GetObject call to connect to the WMI namespace root\cimv2, and set the impersonation level to "impersonate."

3. Use the ExecNotificationQuery method to monitor for any changes made to the file "C:\\Scripts\\Index.vbs". The two sets of double backslashes must be included in the file name.

4. Create a Do Loop with no exit condition. This causes the loop to continue (and the script to run) indefinitely. The only way to stop the loop is to terminate the script process.

5. Create an object (objLatestEvent) to represent new instances of the CIM_DirectoryContainsFile class. Each time the file C:\Scripts\Index.vbs is modified, a new instance of objLatestEvent is created as well.

6. Each time the file is modified, echo:

    - The file name.

    - The current size of the file (TargetInstance.FileSize).

    - The previous size of the file (PreviousInstance.File Size).

Listing 11.31 Monitoring File Modification

```
1   strComputer = "."
2   Set objWMIService = GetObject("winmgmts:" _
3       & "{impersonationLevel=impersonate}!\\" & strComputer & "\root\cimv2")
4   Set colMonitoredEvents = objWMIService.ExecNotificationQuery _
5       ("SELECT * FROM __InstanceModificationEvent WITHIN 10 WHERE " _
6           & "TargetInstance ISA 'CIM_DataFile' AND " _
7               & "TargetInstance.Name='c:\\scripts\\index.vbs'")
8
9   Do
10      Set objLatestEvent = colMonitoredEvents.NextEvent
11      Wscript.Echo "File: " & objLatestEvent.TargetInstance.Name
12      Wscript.Echo "New size: " & objLatestEvent.TargetInstance.FileSize
13      Wscript.Echo "Old size: " & objLatestEvent.PreviousInstance.FileSize
14  Loop
```

Managing Shared Folders

Computer networks evolved out of the need to share information while avoiding needless and confusing duplication. For example, suppose you have a task list that needs to be shared by a number of users. If you prefer, you can create the task list, copy it onto floppy disks, and give each user his or her own copy of the document. This works just fine, provided the task list never has to be changed.

But suppose User A completes a task, needs to add a new task, or otherwise must modify the document. User A not only has to modify his or her document but then has to copy the modified task list onto floppy disks, redistribute it, and hope that everyone else correctly updates the task list.

Needless to say, a system such as this will break down in a hurry. It is much easier, faster, safer, and more reliable to store a single copy of the task list in a central repository, and then provide users access to that document on an as-needed basis. In the Windows operating system, this central repository is typically a *shared folder*, a standard file system folder that is configured so that users can access it over the network.

Shared folders are an integral part of any Windows network. Therefore, it is important for system administrators to keep track of shared folders and to create new shares, modify existing shares, and delete old shares as needed. These tasks can all be carried out using WMI and the Win32_Share class. In addition, you can use Active Directory Service Interfaces (ADSI) to publish shared folders in the Active Directory® directory service, making these shares much easier for users and administrators to locate.

Enumerating Shared Folders

For the most part, you should not share out every single folder on your computer. After all, doing so exposes all your documents and all your data to anyone browsing the network. Likewise, it potentially allows anyone to make changes to critical or confidential files and folders.

To guard against the possible misuse of shared folders, it is a good idea to periodically review the shared folders on a computer and then decide whether those folders should be shared at all. You can use the Win32_Share class to return information about the shared folders on a computer. The shared folder properties available through this class are shown in Table 11.11.

Table 11.11   Win32_Share Properties

Property	Description
AllowMaximum	Indicates whether or not the number of users allowed to simultaneously access this folder has been limited. If True, the value in the MaximumAllowed property is ignored.
Caption	Description of the object.
MaximumAllowed	Limit on the maximum number of users allowed to use this resource concurrently. The value is valid only if the AllowMaximum property is set to False.
Name	Network name given to the shared folder.
Path	Local path of the shared folder.
Type	Type of resource being shared. Types include disk drives, print queues, interprocess communications (IPC), and general devices. Values are: 0 — Disk drive 1 — Print queue 2 — Device 3 — IPC 2147483648 — Disk drive (Administrative share) 2147483649 — Print queue (Administrative share) 2147483650 — Device (Administrative share) 2147483651 — IPC (Administrative share)

The relationship between the Win32_Share class and Windows Explorer is shown in Figure 11.9.

Figure 11.9 Win32_Share and Windows Explorer

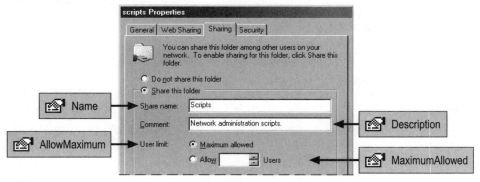

Scripting Steps

Listing 11.32 contains a script that enumerates the properties of all the shared folders on a computer. To carry out this task, the script must perform the following steps:

1. Create a variable to specify the computer name.

2. Use a GetObject call to connect to the WMI namespace root\cimv2, and set the impersonation level to "impersonate."

3. Use the ExecQuery method to query the Win32_Share class.

   This returns a collection of all the shared folders on the computer.

4. For each shared folder instance in the collection, echo the values for properties such as the shared folder name, the shared folder path, the maximum number of simultaneous connections allowed, and the shared folder type.

Listing 11.32 Enumerating Shared Folders

```
1   strComputer = "."
2   Set objWMIService = GetObject("winmgmts:" _
3       & "{impersonationLevel=impersonate}!\\" & strComputer & "\root\cimv2")
4   Set colShares = objWMIService.ExecQuery("SELECT * FROM Win32_Share")
5   For Each objShare in colShares
6       Wscript.Echo "Allow Maximum: " & vbTab &  objShare.AllowMaximum
7       Wscript.Echo "Caption: " & vbTab &  objShare.Caption
8       Wscript.Echo "Maximum Allowed: " & vbTab &  objShare.MaximumAllowed
9       Wscript.Echo "Name: " & vbTab &  objShare.Name
10      Wscript.Echo "Path: " & vbTab &  objShare.Path
11      Wscript.Echo "Type: " & vbTab &  objShare.Type
12  Next
```

Creating Shared Folders

Creating shared folders on the local computer is easy. In Windows Explorer, simply right-click a folder, select **Sharing and Security**, enter the desired share name, and click **OK**. If you prefer to use the command line, you can use the net share command to accomplish the same task.

Sharing folders on remote computers is a different story; neither Windows Explorer nor net share allows you to share out a folder on another computer. However, you can use WMI and the Win32_Share class to create a shared folder on remote computers as well as on the local computer.

To create a shared folder using WMI, you need to connect to the Win32_Share class and then call the Create method. The Create method requires you to specify the five parameters shown in Table 11.12.

Table 11.12   Shared Folder Parameters

Parameter	Description
Path	Local path to the folder being shared. This folder must already exist or the Create method fails.
Name	Share name used to access the folder over the network. To create a hidden share, append a $ at the end of the name (for example, MyShare$). A hidden share is not visible to users browsing in Network Neighborhood but remains available to anyone who knows that the share exists.
Type	Indicates the type of network share. This is typically one of two values: 0 – Standard network file share. These shared folders can be viewed by anyone on the network. However, you can use share permissions or NTFS permissions to limit access to the contents of the share. 2147483648 – Administrative share. For example, the Administrative share Admin$ resolves to the Windows folder on a computer. Only users with Administrative credentials can connect to these shared folders.
MaximumAllowed	Maximum number of users permitted to connect to the share at one time. If this parameter is left blank, an unlimited number of simultaneous connections to the share are permitted.
Description	Optional description displayed when users view the share in Network Neighborhood.

Values returned from calling the Create method are shown in Table 11.13.

Table 11.13   Network Share Return Values

Value	Description
0	The operation completed successfully.
2	The operation could not be completed because access was denied.
8	The operation could not be completed because of an unknown problem.
9	The operation could not be completed because an invalid name was specified.
10	The operation could not be completed because an invalid level was specified.
21	The operation could not be completed because an invalid parameter was specified.
22	The operation could not be completed because a share by this name already exists.
23	The operation could not be completed because this is a redirected path.
24	The operation could not be completed because the specified folder could not be found.
25	The operation could not be completed because the specified server could not be found.
Other	The operation could not be completed.

Scripting Steps

Listing 11.33 contains a script that creates a shared folder on a computer. To carry out this task, the script must perform the following steps:

1. Create two constants, FILE_SHARE (with the value 0) and MAXIMUM_CONNECTIONS (with the value 25). FILE_SHARE is used to indicate the type of share being created, and MAXIMUM_CONNECTIONS is used to limit the number of simultaneous connections to the share to 25.

2. Create a variable to specify the computer name.

3. Use a GetObject call to connect to the WMI namespace root\cimv2, and set the impersonation level to "impersonate."

4. Use the Get method to query the Win32_Share class.

5. Use the Create method to create a new share. The method is passed the following parameter values:

- **C:\Finance** — Local path of the folder being shared.

- **FinanceShare** — Network name to be assigned to the new share.

- **FILE_SHARE** — Constant indicating that the new share is a standard network file share.

- **MAXIMUM_CONNECTIONS** — Constant setting the maximum number of simultaneous connections to the new share to 25.

- **Public share for members of the Finance group** — Description available to users accessing the share through Network Neighborhood.

6. Echo the results.

Listing 11.33   Creating Shared Folders

```
1   Const FILE_SHARE = 0
2   Const MAXIMUM_CONNECTIONS = 25
3   strComputer = "."
4   Set objWMIService = GetObject("winmgmts:" _
5       & "{impersonationLevel=impersonate}!\\" & strComputer & "\root\cimv2")
6   Set objNewShare = objWMIService.Get("Win32_Share")
7   errReturn = objNewShare.Create _
8       ("C:\Finance", "FinanceShare", FILE_SHARE, _
9           MAXIMUM_CONNECTIONS, "Public share for the Finance group.")
10  Wscript.Echo errReturn
```

Mapping Shared Folders to Local Folders

Shared folders have properties — such as the maximum allowable connections — that are available through the Win32_Share class. It is easy to forget, however, that in addition to being virtual entities available over the network, shared folders are actual physical file folders on a computer hard disk. As physical file folders, shared folders have additional properties, such as the date the folder was last modified and whether or not the folder is compressed or encrypted, that are not available using the Win32_Share class.

If you need to retrieve the actual folder properties of a shared folder, you can use the Win32_ShareToDirectory class. Win32_ShareToDirectory is an association class that associates a shared folder with an actual file folder; you simply pass Win32_ShareToDirectory the name of a shared folder, and it returns a reference to the actual physical file folder. After you have that reference, you can retrieve all the properties available through the Win32_Directory class.

Scripting Steps

Listing 11.34 contains a script that maps a shared folder named Scripts to a local folder. To carry out this task, the script must perform the following steps:

1. Create a variable to specify the computer name.

2. Use a GetObject call to connect to the WMI namespace root\cimv2, and set the impersonation level to "impersonate."

3. Use an Associators of query to return a collection of local folders mapped to shared folders. To ensure that only the local folder that corresponds to the shared folder Scripts is returned, a clause is included limiting data retrieval to folders that have the share name Scripts.

4. For the single folder in the collection, echo the folder Name. This is not the share name, but the folder name as retrieved using the Win32_Directory class.

Listing 11.34 Mapping a Shared Folder to a Local Folder

```
1   strComputer = "."
2   Set objWMIService = GetObject("winmgmts:" _
3       & "{impersonationLevel=impersonate}!\\" & strComputer & "\root\cimv2")
4   Set colShares = objWMIService.ExecQuery _
5       ("ASSOCIATORS OF {Win32_Share.Name='Scripts'} WHERE " _
6           & "AssocClass=Win32_ShareToDirectory")
7   For Each objFolder in colShares
8       Wscript.Echo objFolder.Name
9   Next
```

You can also create a script that maps all the shared folders on a computer to their local counterparts. This requires you to do two things:

- Return a collection of all the shared folders on a computer.

- For each shared folder in that collection, use an Associators of query to determine the local folder.

Listing 11.35 contains a script that maps all the shared folders on a computer to their local equivalents. To carry out this task, the script must perform the following steps:

1. Create a variable to specify the computer name.

2. Use a GetObject call to connect to the WMI namespace root\cimv2, and set the impersonation level to "impersonate."

3. Use an ExecQuery call to return a collection of all the shared folders on the computer.

4. For each shared folder in the collection, use an Associators of query to return a collection consisting of the local folder mapped to the shared folder.

To determine the shared folder to be mapped, you use the share names returned by the Win32_Share class. For example, suppose three shared folders are returned:

- Share1

- Share2

- Share3

The first time the For Each loop is run, the name Share1 is passed to the Associators of query. On the next iteration, the name Share2 is passed to the query. This continues until each of the shared folder names has been used in the query.

5. For the single local folder in the new collection, echo the share name and the folder name.

Listing 11.35   Mapping All Shared Folders to Local Folders

```
1   strComputer = "."
2   Set objWMIService = GetObject("winmgmts:" _
3       & "{impersonationLevel=impersonate}!\\" & strComputer & "\root\cimv2")
4   Set colShares = objWMIService.ExecQuery _
5       ("SELECT * FROM Win32_Share")
6   For Each objShare in colShares
7       Set colAssociations = objWMIService.ExecQuery _
8           ("ASSOCIATORS OF {Win32_Share.Name='" & objShare.Name & "'} " _
9               & " WHERE AssocClass=Win32_ShareToDirectory")
10      For Each objFolder in colAssociations
11          Wscript.Echo objShare.Name & vbTab & objFolder.Name
12      Next
13  Next
```

Deleting Shared Folders

Shared folders provide a convenient way for users to access and share resources. This also means that shared folders are a potential security risk; anything that gives remote users access to your computer provides a method by which that computer can be exploited.

As a system administrator, you want to keep track of the folders being shared on your network (especially those shared on servers); folders should be shared only if there is a valid reason for them to be shared and only if the proper security precautions are in place. If neither of these criteria is true, the share should be removed, at least until the reason for the share is clear and security is correctly implemented.

The Win32_Share class includes a Delete method that can be used to delete shared folders. The Delete method does not remove the local folder or erase any of the files stored in that folder. It simply stops the folder from being shared over the network. If you later change your mind, you can use the Create method to reshare the folder.

Scripting Steps

Listing 11.36 contains a script that deletes the FinanceShare shared folder on a computer. To carry out this task, the script must perform the following steps:

1. Create a variable to specify the computer name.

2. Use a GetObject call to connect to the WMI namespace root\cimv2, and set the impersonation level to "impersonate."

3. Use the ExecQuery method to query the Win32_Share class.

Because only one shared folder is to be deleted, a Where clause is included to limit data retrieval to the shared folder with the name FinanceShare. This results in a collection consisting of a single folder.

To delete all the shared folders on a computer, leave out the Where clause. The resulting collection consists of all the shared folders on the computer.

4. For each shared folder in the collection, use the Delete method to remove the share.

Listing 11.36 Deleting Network Shares

```
1   strComputer = "."
2   Set objWMIService = GetObject("winmgmts:" _
3       & "{impersonationLevel=impersonate}!\\" & strComputer & "\root\cimv2")
4   Set colShares = objWMIService.ExecQuery _
5       ("SELECT * FROM Win32_Share WHERE Name = 'FinanceShare'")
6   For Each objShare in colShares
7       objShare.Delete
8   Next
```

Modifying Shared Folder Properties

As your network evolves, you might find it necessary to modify your shared folders. For example, you might need to limit the number of people who can connect to a shared folder at any one time. Alternatively, you might want to change the description of a shared folder, either to reflect a new use for that folder or to make it easier for users to identify the information stored in the folder.

The SetShareInfo method allows you to modify the maximum number of connections and the description of an existing shared folder. SetShareInfo accepts two parameters:

- **MaximumAllowed.** The maximum number of users that can be connected to the share at one time. To allow unlimited simultaneous connections, leave this parameter blank.

- **Description.** Comment describing the shared folder. This comment is visible to users who have enabled the Details view in My Network Places.

Scripting Steps

Listing 11.37 contains a script that modifies the properties of the FinanceShare shared folder on a computer. To carry out this task, the script must perform the following steps:

1. Create a variable to specify the computer name.

2. Use a GetObject call to connect to the WMI namespace root\cimv2, and set the impersonation level to "impersonate."

3. Use the ExecQuery method to query the Win32_Share class.

   To limit data retrieval to a specified share, a Where clause is included restricting the returned folders to those with the name FinanceShare. Without the Where clause, all the shared folders would be returned, and each shared folder would then have its properties modified.

4. For each shared folder in the collection, use the SetShareInfo method to set the MaximumAllowed and Description properties. The SetShareInfo method is passed two parameters:

   - **50** — Indicating that the share supports a maximum of 50 simultaneous connections.

   - **Public share for HR administrators and members of the Finance Group** — Description displayed to users accessing the share through My Network Places.

Listing 11.37   Modifying Network Share Properties

```
1   strComputer = "."
2   Set objWMIService = GetObject("winmgmts:" _
3       & "{impersonationLevel=impersonate}!\\" & strComputer & "\root\cimv2")
4   Set colShares = objWMIService.ExecQuery _
5       ("SELECT * FROM Win32_Share WHERE Name = 'FinanceShare'")
6   For Each objShare in colShares
7       errReturn = objShare.SetShareInfo(50, _
8           "Public share for HR administrators and the Finance Group.")
9   Next
10  Wscript.Echo errReturn
```

Publishing Shared Folders in Active Directory

One problem with shared folders is that each shared folder is tied to an individual computer. To access the resources on a shared folder, users must know not only the name of the shared folder itself but also the name of the computer where that shared folder is located. In a large organization, this can make it difficult to find resources.

One way to overcome this problem is to publish shared folders in Active Directory. When a shared folder is published in Active Directory, users can search for such a folder using Network Neighborhood.

You can also search for shared folders using ADSI scripts or Active Directory Users and Computers. Regardless of the tool you use, you can search for these resources based not only on name but also on description or keyword.

Shared folders are published in Active Directory by creating an instance of the Volume class that represents the shared folder. Some of the key attributes of the Volume class are listed in Table 11.14.

Table 11.14 Volume Class Attributes

Attribute	Description
CN	Common name. Name of the object as displayed in Active Directory Users and Computers. (This is typically the same name as the share name.) For example: FinanceShare
UNCName	UNC path of the shared folder. For example: \\Server1\FinanceShare
Description	Description of the share and its contents.
Keywords	Array of descriptive terms that can be used in searching for specific shared folders.
ManagedBy	Indicates the user responsible for the share.

Folders can be published in Active Directory either by using Active Directory Users and Computers or by using a custom ADSI script. An ADSI script can also be used to enumerate all the shared folders on a computer and then publish each one in Active Directory.

Scripting Steps

Listing 11.38 contains a script that publishes a shared folder in Active Directory. To carry out this task, the script must perform the following steps:

1. Use a GetObject call to bind to the organizational unit in Active Directory where the shared folder will be published.

2. Use the Create method to create the shared folder object. The Create method is passed two parameters:

    -   **Volume** — Indicates that the entity being created is a shared folder.

    -   **CN = FinanceShare** — Specifies the name of the published folder.

3. Use the Put method to specify the network path to the shared folder.

4. Use the Put method to specify a description of the shared folder.

    This description is available to anyone who accesses the shared folder in Active Directory Users and Computers. However, this description is not available to anyone accessing the shared folder by using Network Neighborhood, nor is this the same description as the one set using the WMI Win32_Share class.

5. Use the Put method to specify keywords that can be used when searching for this folder.

The Keywords property is a multiple-attribute property; that is, it can accept more than one value. To assign multiple keywords to the folder, the keywords are passed as parameters using the Array method.

6. Use the SetInfo method to apply the changes and publish the folder in Active Directory.

Listing 11.38   Publishing a Shared Folder in Active Directory

```
1   Set objComputer = GetObject _
2       ("LDAP://OU=Finance, DC=fabrikam, DC=com")
3   Set objShare = objComputer.Create("volume", "CN=FinanceShare")
4   objShare.Put "uNCName", "\\atl-dc-02\FinanceShare"
5   objShare.Put "Description", "Public share for users in the Finance group."
6   objShare.Put "Keywords", Array("finance", "fiscal", "monetary")
7   objShare.SetInfo
```

Managing Published Folders

Published folders are like any other object stored in Active Directory: After they have been created, they need to be managed. This management includes such tasks as:

- Enumerating all the published folders.
- Searching for published folders that meet specific criteria.
- Deleting published folders that should no longer be maintained in Active Directory.

All of these tasks can be carried out using ADSI scripts.

Enumerating Published Folders

Folders are published in Active Directory to make it easier to identify all the shares on your network. After a folder is shared and published, you can locate it using tools such as Active Directory Users and Computers.

In addition, ADSI can be used to retrieve a list of all the folders that have been published in Active Directory. This can be done by constructing a script that returns all instances of the Volume class.

Scripting Steps

Listing 11.39 contains a script that enumerates the shared folders published in Active Directory. To carry out this task, the script must perform the following steps:

1. Include the On Error Resume Next statement. Without this statement, the script fails if it is unable to find any published folders in Active Directory.

2. Create a constant named ADS_SCOPE_SUBTREE and set the value to 2. This is used to specify a search that begins in the Active Directory root and proceeds to search all the child containers as well.

3. Create an instance of the Active Directory connection object (ADODB.Connection).

4. Create an instance of the Active Directory command object (ADODB.Command).

   The command object allows you to issue queries and other database commands using the Active Directory connection.

5. Set the provider property of the connection object to the Active Directory provider (ADsDSOObject). This is the OLE database provider for ADSI.

6. Set the active connection to the Active Directory connection.

7. Set the command text for the Active Directory command object to the SQL query that retrieves all the published shared folders from fabrikam.com.

8. Specify values for time-out, search scope, and caching.

9. Execute the SQL query.

10. When the set of published shared folders is returned, use the MoveFirst method to move to the first share in the recordset.

11. For each share in the recordset, echo the share name, the UNC name, and the name of the user responsible for managing the share.

Listing 11.39 Enumerating Published Shared Folders

```
1   On Error Resume Next
2   Const ADS_SCOPE_SUBTREE = 2
3   Set objConnection = CreateObject("ADODB.Connection")
4   Set objCommand =    CreateObject("ADODB.Command")
5   objConnection.Provider = "ADsDSOObject"
6   objConnection.Open "Active Directory Provider"
7   Set objCOmmand.ActiveConnection = objConnection
8   objCommand.CommandText = "SELECT Name, unCName, ManagedBy FROM " _
9       & "'LDAP://DC=Fabrikam,DC=com' WHERE objectClass='volume'"
10  objCommand.Properties("Timeout") = 30
11  objCommand.Properties("Searchscope") = ADS_SCOPE_SUBTREE
12  objCommand.Properties("Cache Results") = False
```

(continued)

Listing 11.39   Enumerating Published Shared Folders *(continued)*

```
13   Set objRecordSet = objCommand.Execute
14   objRecordSet.MoveFirst
15   Do Until objRecordSet.EOF
16       Wscript.Echo "Share Name: " & objRecordSet.Fields("Name").Value
17       Wscript.Echo "UNC Name: " & objRecordSet.Fields("uNCName").Value
18       Wscript.Echo "Managed By: " & objRecordSet.Fields("ManagedBy").Value
19       objRecordSet.MoveNext
20   Loop
```

Searching for Published Folders in Active Directory

Retrieving a list of all the folders that are published in Active Directory is obviously useful. At the same time, in a large organization a list such as this might contain hundreds or even thousands of shares. Having to read through a list that large to find a particular folder or two would be very inefficient.

Fortunately, you can also search Active Directory for only those published folders that meet specific criteria. For example, you might search for a folder named FinanceShare, for all the folders managed by Ken Myer, or for all the folders that have "finance" as one of their keywords. By combining criteria, you can create targeted searches that help you quickly and easily locate only the published folders you are most interested in.

Scripting Steps

Listing 11.40 contains a script that searches for a published folder in Active Directory. To carry out this task, the script must perform the following steps:

1. Include the On Error Resume Next statement. Without this statement, the script fails if it is unable to find any published folders in Active Directory.

2. Create a constant named ADS_SCOPE_SUBTREE and set the value to 2. This is used to specify a search that begins in the Active Directory root and proceeds to search all the child containers as well.

3. Create an instance of the Active Directory connection object (ADODB.Connection).

4. Create an instance of the Active Directory command object (ADODB.Command).

   The command object allows you to issue queries and other database commands using the Active Directory connection.

5. Set the provider property of the connection object to the Active Directory provider (ADsDSOObject). This is the OLE database provider for ADSI.

6. Set the active connection to the Active Directory connection.

7. Set the command text for the Active Directory command object to the SQL query that retrieves all the published folders from fabrikam.com.

To limit data retrieval to a specific set of shared folders, a Where clause is included that restricts the returned collection to those shared folders that include the keyword "finance."

8. Specify values for time-out, search scope, and caching.

9. Execute the SQL query.

10. When the set of published shared folders is returned, use the MoveFirst method to move to the first share in the recordset.

11. For each share in the recordset, echo the share name, the UNC name, and the name of the user responsible for managing the share.

Listing 11.40 Searching for a Shared Folder in Active Directory

```
1    On Error Resume Next
2    Const ADS_SCOPE_SUBTREE = 2
3    Set objConnection = CreateObject("ADODB.Connection")
4    Set objCommand =   CreateObject("ADODB.Command")
5    objConnection.Provider = "ADsDSOObject"
6    objConnection.Open "Active Directory Provider"
7    Set objCOmmand.ActiveConnection = objConnection
8    objCommand.CommandText = "SELECT Name, unCName, ManagedBy FROM " _
9        & "'LDAP://DC=fabrikam,DC=com'" _
10           & " WHERE objectClass='volume' AND Keywords = 'finance*'"
11   objCommand.Properties("Timeout") = 30
12   objCommand.Properties("Searchscope") = ADS_SCOPE_SUBTREE
13   objCommand.Properties("Cache Results") = False
14   Set objRecordSet = objCommand.Execute
15   objRecordSet.MoveFirst
16   Do Until objRecordSet.EOF
17       Wscript.Echo "Share Name: " & objRecordSet.Fields("Name").Value
18       Wscript.Echo "UNC Name: " & objRecordSet.Fields("uNCName").Value
19       Wscript.Echo "Managed By: " & objRecordSet.Fields("ManagedBy").Value
20       objRecordSet.MoveNext
21   Loop
```

Deleting a Published Folder in Active Directory

Because a published folder is simply an Active Directory object, it can be deleted using an ADSI script: You bind to the object and then use the DeleteObject method to remove it from Active Directory.

Deleting a published folder does not delete the contents of that folder, nor does it stop the sharing of that folder. Instead, it merely removes the folder from Active Directory.

Scripting Steps

Listing 11.41 contains a script that deletes a published folder from Active Directory. To carry out this task, the script must perform the following steps:

1. Use a GetObject call to connect to the shared folder object in Active Directory.

2. Use the DeleteObject method to delete the shared folder.

   The DeleteObject method requires the parameter (0). This is currently the only parameter that can be used with this method.

Listing 11.41   Deleting a Published Folder in Active Directory

```
1   Set objContainer = GetObject("LDAP://CN=FinanceShare, " _
2       & "OU=Finance, DC=fabrikam, DC=com")
3   objContainer.DeleteObject (0)
```

CHAPTER 12

Logs

Record keeping is an important part of system administration. A record of the activities that have taken place on a computer can help you troubleshoot problems currently occurring on a computer; in addition, by searching for patterns and trends, you can often anticipate potential problems and take steps to ensure that those problems never arise. In the form of event logs and plain-text log files, Microsoft® Windows® 2000 operating systems perform much of this record keeping for you. As a system administrator, your job is to routinely manage and analyze these log files, tasks that can be greatly facilitated through the use of the scripting technologies in the Microsoft® Windows® 2000 family of operating systems.

In This Chapter

Logs Overview **842**
Managing Logs...**842**
    Managing Event Logs..844
    Querying Event Logs 857
    Writing Events to Event Logs...870
    Managing Plain-Text Logs..876

Logs Overview

Financial institutions typically keep detailed records of each transaction they undertake. This record keeping serves at least two purposes. First, it allows the institutions to know, without question, where the money has been and where it is going; if a problem occurs, troubleshooters can go through archived records and retrace every transaction that has taken place in the past few hours, the past few days, and even the past few months. Second, by routinely analyzing these records, institutions are often alerted to trouble before it occurs. Many instances of fraud or embezzlement have been prevented because auditors noticed patterns of activity that were out of the ordinary and were able to put a stop to abuses before it was too late.

The Windows operating system also keeps detailed records of the activity that takes place on a computer. These records, typically stored in the event logs, provide system administrators with the same capabilities financial records provide financial institutions: The event logs help you trace the activity that has taken place on a computer and help you identify potential problems before it is too late. Few activities are as useful to a system administrator as a regular audit and analysis of the event logs for a computer.

Despite the acknowledged value of event logs, however, few system administrators routinely audit and analyze these logs. This is largely because the primary tool provided for working with event logs — Event Viewer — limits you to working with a single event log from a single computer at a time. Although it is recommended that you periodically analyze all the event logs for all your domain controllers, in practice this is tedious and time-consuming using Event Viewer. As a result, administrators rarely undertake this kind of analysis except in organizations that have gone to the trouble and expense of purchasing and installing third-party tools for working with event logs.

Fortunately, scripting provides you with the same capabilities that these third-party tools have.

Managing Logs

Event logs provide a central repository for recording the activities that take place on a computer. Because many of the most meaningful of these events are recorded in one of the event logs, you can find a given event without having to search through a multitude of source-specific log files. On the other hand, because each event log contains events generated from many sources, it can be difficult to identify a set of related events. The advantages/disadvantages of the operating system's use of event logs reflect the problems inherent in managing one large data source versus the problems inherent in managing many smaller data sources.

Another advantage/disadvantage is that event logs are written using a proprietary binary data format and are designed to prevent modification of the contents of the log. This design provides a high level of security but also makes it more difficult to analyze the contents of the event log. Historically, this could be done only by using the Event Viewer snap-in and on only one computer at a time.

Fortunately, Windows 2000 includes a number scripting tools that make it easy to manage event logs across the enterprise.

Plain-Text Log Files

In addition to the event logs, the operating system also writes other events to plain-text log files, most of which are located in the %*windir*%\Debug folder. Plain-text log files are useful for operations that might generate thousands of events at a time. Because these operations generate so many events, it would be unwise to have them save events to an event log; the thousands of events generated by this single operation might completely fill the log, overwriting all the other events that have taken place on the computer.

For example, each time the File Replication service runs, the resulting log file might contain several thousand lines, depending on the amount of data replicated. Instead of each replication operation being written as an event log record, all the replicated data is recorded in a plain-text log file (%*windir*%\Debug\NtFrs.log).

One major advantage of these log files is that they are written as plain-text files, files that can be opened and viewed using any text editor. However, plain-text log files also have limitations:

- Plain-text log files can be easily modified by any user who has read-write access to the folder in which the logs are stored. For example, an unscrupulous administrator might open a log file, modify it to remove evidence of any activity he or she would prefer to keep secret, and then save the file.

- Plain-text log files are difficult to analyze by using automated analysis methods. This is due, in part, to the fact that plain-text log files in Windows can use any one of several formatting styles, including comma-separated values, fixed-width text, or free-form text. This makes it difficult to write a single script that can read and analyze multiple log files.

Managing Event Logs

The Event service is an integral part of Windows 2000. Each time a Windows 2000–based computer is started, the Event service automatically begins recording events in the appropriate event logs, even if no one is logged on to the computer. In fact, the first event in the System event log is always a record that the Event service has been started.

The Event service is so integral to the operating system that it cannot be stopped except by turning off the computer.

 Note

> The fact that the Event service cannot be stopped is a security measure: This prevents someone from stopping the service, carrying out an action, and then restarting the service. An administrator *could* carry out an action and then clear the event log, thus deleting all traces of that action, but the act of clearing the event log would be recorded as the first record in the new log.

The Event service is fully automated; you cannot stop it or start it, and you should never attempt to reconfigure it. Although the Event service is self-managing, at least two important management tasks are related to the event logs themselves: managing the size of event logs and backing up event logs.

Managing the Size of Event Logs

By default, event logs are configured for a maximum file size of 512 KB and are set to overwrite events that are older than seven days. When the log reaches its maximum size, any events older than seven days are overwritten to allow room for new records unless you reconfigure the maximum size of the log or the overwrite policy.

These default settings are adequate for user workstations and for small servers that conduct relatively little activity. However, these values might not be appropriate for servers such as domain controllers. For example, 512 KB is likely to be too small a log size based on the number of events that are recorded each day on a domain controller.

Backing Up Event Logs

To help maintain a historical record of events, you should back up your event logs on a regular schedule. However, you cannot back up event logs by using a standard backup process; this creates archived event logs that cannot be opened. Instead, to back up event logs, you must use a special backup procedure. Fortunately, this procedure is available through Windows Management Instrumentation (WMI).

Retrieving Event Log Properties

Knowing the properties of your event logs can be useful in planning management activities such as backing up and clearing the logs. For example, knowing both the maximum allowable size and the current size of an event log tells you how much space is available in the log. In turn, this helps you decide whether the log needs to be backed up and cleared.

In addition, tracking the number of records in each log is a simple metric that can often trigger alarms regarding potential problems. For example, suppose routine checks of the number of records in an event log show that a specific computer typically records 100 events a day. Today, however, this routine check shows that the computer has recorded 500 events. This might indicate a serious problem that warrants further investigation.

The WMI class Win32_NTEventLogFile can be used to retrieve the properties of any event log on a computer. Some of the most important event log properties you can retrieve by using WMI are shown in Table 12.1.

Table 12.1 Event Log Properties Available Through WMI

Property	Description
FileSize	Current size of the event log, in bytes.
LogFileName	"Friendly" name for the event log (for example, System).
	To return the actual path and file name of the event log (for example, C:\Windows\System32\Config\Sysevent.evt), use the Name property instead.
MaxfileSize	Maximum allowable size (in bytes) for the event log.
	Although event logs can be sized as large as 4 gigabytes, in practice they should be limited to no more than 300 megabytes. Event logs larger than that can be difficult to analyze because of the number of events contained within the log and because event logs are not optimized for data retrieval.
Name	Full path and file name for the event log.
NumberOfRecords	Number of records in the event log.

(continued)

Table 12.1 Event Log Properties Available Through WMI *(continued)*

Property	Description
OverwriteOutdated	Number of days after which a record can be overwritten should an event log reach its maximum size. Values are: **0** — Any record can be overwritten if necessary. If necessary, all existing events in the event log can be overwritten to make room for new events. **1-365** — Events older than the specified number of days can be overwritten as needed. If the event log does not contain any records older than the value specified, no new events will be recorded until the log has been cleared. **4294967295** — No records can be overwritten. If the log reaches its maximum size, no new events will be recorded until the log has been cleared.
OverwritePolicy	Current overwrite policy for the event log. Values are the following: **WhenNeeded** — Any record can be overwritten to make room for new records. **OutDated** — Records older than a specified number of days can be overwritten to make room for new records. **Never** — Old records are never overwritten.

The Event Log properties and methods available through WMI map to the event log properties as seen in Event Viewer. This relationship is shown in Figure 12.1.

Figure 12.1   Win32_NTEventLogFile Properties and Methods

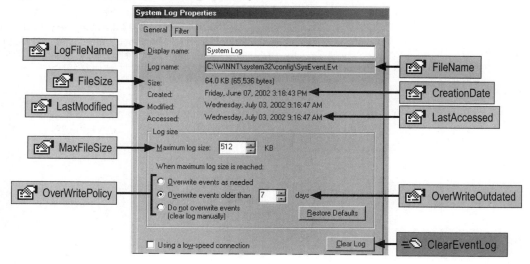

Scripting Steps

There are several ways to retrieve the properties of event logs. For example, you might want to:

- Retrieve the properties of multiple event logs.
- Retrieve the properties of a single event log.
- Retrieve the properties of the Security event log.

Retrieving the properties of multiple event logs

Listing 12.1 contains a script that retrieves the properties of multiple event logs on a single computer. To carry out this task, the script must perform the following steps:

1. Create a variable to specify the computer name.

2. Use a GetObject call to connect to the WMI namespace root\cimv2, and set the impersonation level to "impersonate."

3. Use the ExecQuery method to query the Win32_NTEventLogFile class.

   This returns a collection consisting of all the event logs on the computer, except the Security event log. The additional step required to return information from the Security event log is discussed later in this chapter.

4. For each event log in the collection, echo the event log properties LogFileName, MaxFileSize, and OverWriteOutdated.

   If you configure an event log so that it never overwrites events, you actually set the OverWriteOutdated property to 4294967295. If the value 4294967295 is returned, the script displays the string "Overwrite Outdated Records: Never." If the value 0 is returned, this means the log has been configured to overwrite records as needed. To make this clear, the script displays the message "Overwrite Outdated Records: As Needed."

Listing 12.1 Retrieving the Properties of Multiple Event Logs

```
1  strComputer = "."
2  Set objWMIService = GetObject("winmgmts:" _
3      & "{impersonationLevel=impersonate}!\\" & strComputer & "\root\cimv2")
4  Set objInstalledLogFiles = objWMIService.ExecQuery _
5      ("SELECT * FROM Win32_NTEventLogFile")
6  For Each objLogfile in objInstalledLogFiles
7      Wscript.Echo "Name: " &  objLogfile.LogFileName
8      Wscript.Echo "Maximum Size: " &  objLogfile.MaxFileSize
9      If objLogfile.OverWriteOutdated > 365 Then
10         Wscript.Echo "Overwrite Outdated Records: Never." & VbCrLf
11     ElseIf objLogfile.OverWriteOutdated = 0 Then
12         Wscript.Echo "Overwrite Outdated Records: As needed." & VbCrLf
13     Else
14         Wscript.Echo "Overwrite Outdated Records After: " & _
15             objLogfile.OverWriteOutdated & " days" & VbCrLf
16     End If
17  Next
```

Retrieving a property of a single event log

Listing 12.2 contains a script that retrieves the number of records in the System event log. To carry out this task, the script must perform the following steps:

1. Create a variable to specify the computer name.

2. Use a GetObject call to connect to the WMI namespace root\cimv2, and set the impersonation level to "impersonate."

3. Use the ExecQuery method to query the Win32_NTEventLogFile class.

   To limit the data returned to the System event log, include a Where clause specifying the LogFileName "System". This returns a collection of event logs with a single item: the System event log.

4. For the only event log in the collection, echo the value of the NumberOfRecords property.

Listing 12.2   Retrieving a Property in a Single Event Log

```
1   strComputer = "."
2   Set objWMIService = GetObject("winmgmts:" _
3       & "{impersonationLevel=impersonate}!\\" & strComputer & "\root\cimv2")
4   Set colLogFiles = objWMIService.ExecQuery _
5       ("SELECT * FROM Win32_NTEventLogFile WHERE LogFileName='System'")
6   For Each objLogFile in colLogFiles
7       Wscript.Echo objLogFile.NumberOfRecords
8   Next
```

Retrieving the properties of the Security event log

Scripts that retrieve information about the event logs on a computer do not retrieve information about the Security event log unless those scripts include the Security privilege. The ability to manipulate the Security event log is provided by the **Manage auditing and security logs** user right, which must be explicitly assigned. To manipulate the Security event log, you must include this privilege as part of the GetObject moniker, even if you are an administrator and have been assigned this right by default.

Note that the Security privilege does not grant you the ability to manage auditing and security logs. You must already possess this right (typically assigned through Group Policy), or the script will fail. To access information from or about the Security event log, you must possess the **Manage auditing and security logs** user right, and the script must include the Security privilege.

The results of querying event logs without including the Security privilege are shown inTable 12.2.

Table 12.2 Querying Event Logs Without Including the Security Privilege

If You Attempt to Access …	You Will Retrieve …
All the event logs on a computer	Data for all the event logs except the Security event log
Security event log plus a second event log	Data for only the second event log
Only the Security event log	No data

No special user rights are required to access any of the other event logs on a computer.

Listing 12.3 contains a script that retrieves the number of records in and the maximum file size of the Security event log. To carry out this task, the script must perform the following steps:

1. Create a variable to specify the computer name.

2. Use a GetObject call to connect to the WMI namespace root\cimv2, and set the impersonation level to "impersonate."

   Because special user rights are required to access the Security event log, the Security privilege must be included as part of the moniker.

3. Use the ExecQuery method to query the Win32_NTEventLogFile class.

   To limit the data returned to the Security event log, include a Where clause specifying the LogFileName as "Security." This returns a collection of event logs with a single item: the Security event log.

4. For the only item in the collection, echo the values for NumberOfRecords and MaxFileSize.

Listing 12.3 Retrieving the Properties of the Security Event Log

```
1  strComputer = "."
2  Set objWMIService = GetObject("winmgmts:" _
3     & "{impersonationLevel=impersonate,(Security)}!\\" & _
4        strComputer & "\root\cimv2")
5  Set colLogFiles = objWMIService.ExecQuery _
6     ("SELECT * FROM Win32_NTEventLogFile WHERE LogFileName='Security'")
7  For Each objLogFile in colLogFiles
8     Wscript.Echo objLogFile.NumberOfRecords
9     Wscript.Echo "Maximum Size: " &  objLogfile.MaxFileSize
10 Next
```

Configuring Event Log Properties

Depending on the role played by a computer, you might need to change the default event log settings for that computer. If the default settings remain unchanged for all the computers in an organization, a domain controller that records thousands of events each day will be configured exactly the same as a workstation that records only 15 or 20 events a day. As a result, the domain controller might fail to record a number of important events, either because its event logs fill up too quickly or because some events might be overwritten before they can be archived.

Event log properties have typically been configured by means of the Event Viewer, a graphical user utility that has two major limitations: Event Viewer can configure only one event log on a single computer at a time, and Event Viewer cannot automate the process of configuring event logs. Because manually configuring event logs on an individual basis can be very time-consuming, administrators often leave the default settings as-is, even if those settings are not optimal for the roles played by certain computers. In turn, this means important events might not be recorded, or might be overwritten before they can be archived.

WMI enables you to write scripts that can programmatically configure event log properties. Two of the most important properties are shown in Table 12.3.

Table 12.3   Event Log Properties Configurable with WMI

Property	Description
MaxfileSize	Maximum allowable size (in bytes) for the event log.
	Log files must be sized in increments of 64 KB to prevent file fragmentation. Although you can specify any size for the log file, this will automatically be resized to the nearest multiple of 64 KB. For example, if you specify a file size of 2,200 KB, the actual size will turn out to be 2,240 KB (35 x 64 KB).
OverwriteOutdated	Number of days after which a record can be overwritten when an event log reaches its maximum size. Values are the following:
	▪ 0 – any record can be overwritten if needed
	▪ 1–365 – events older than the specified number of days can be overwritten as needed
	▪ 4294967295 – no records can be overwritten

When you reconfigure an event log, the changes you make do not take effect until the event log has been cleared. If you want the reconfiguration to take effect immediately, create your script to first reconfigure and then to back up and clear the event log.

Scripting Steps

Listing 12.4 contains a script that configures the maximum size and the overwrite policy for all the event logs on a computer. To carry out this task, the script must perform the following steps:

1. Create a constant named wbemFlagUseAmendedQualifiers and set the value to &h2000.

   This constant is required when using the Put_ method to apply changes to an event log.

2. Create a variable to specify the computer name.

3. Use a GetObject call to connect to the WMI namespace root\cimv2, and set the impersonation level to "impersonate."

   The Security privilege is included in the moniker so that the script can access all the event logs, including the Security event log.

4. Use the ExecQuery method to query the Win32_NTEventLogFile class. This returns a collection consisting of all the event logs on the computer.

5. Retrieve the name of the first event log in the connection.

6. Set the maximum file size to 400 megabytes (approximately 4194304).

7. Set the overwrite policy so that all records older than 14 days are overwritten.

8. Use the Put_ method to write the changes to the event log. You must include the wbemFlagUseAmendedQualifiers flag, or the script will fail.

9. Repeat the process with the next event log in the collection.

Listing 12.4 Configuring Event Log Properties

```
1   Const wbemFlagUseAmendedQualifiers = &h20000
2   strComputer = "."
3   Set objWMIService = GetObject("winmgmts:" & _
4       "{impersonationLevel=impersonate,(Security)}!\\" & _
5       strComputer & "\root\cimv2")
6   Set colNTEventLogFiles = objWMIService.ExecQuery _
7       ("SELECT * FROM Win32_NTEventLogFile")
8   For each objNTEventLogFile in colNTEventLogFiles
9       objNTEventLogFile.MaxFileSize = 4194304
10      objNTEventLogFile.OverwriteOutDated = 14
11      objNTEventLogFile.Put_ wbemFlagUseAmendedQualifiers
12  Next
```

Backing Up and Clearing Event Logs

Event logs maintain a historical record of important events that occur on a computer. These records should be archived, at least temporarily, to help you carry out tasks such as troubleshooting problems (when did the first instance of X occur?) or capacity planning (how does the number of Ys occurring this month compare with the number of Ys that occurred last month?).

The most efficient way to archive event log records is to routinely back up and then clear these logs. Backing up the logs before clearing them ensures that the records will be available if you ever need them; clearing the event logs keeps those logs to a manageable size. Clearing the event logs also ensures that all events will be recorded. If you do not clear the event log before it reaches its maximum size, it either stops recording any new events or starts overwriting older events, depending on how the log has been configured. As a result, events will either be overwritten, and thus lost, or never recorded in the first place.

Note

When you clear an event log, the operating system does not delete the previous event log file. Instead, Windows creates a new 64 KB log file that replaces the old log file. (The new log file is placed on exactly the same sectors of the disk drive as the old log file.) Because the disk drive sectors are overwritten and filled with new information, you cannot retrieve records from a cleared event log using an undelete tool.

Before you clear an event log, it is a good idea to create a backup of that log. WMI provides a method for backing up event logs. However, this method comes with two important stipulations. For one, you must use the proprietary event log binary log format. To archive event logs in plain-text format, you need to create a query to extract the records and then write the extracted information to a text file.

In addition, you must make backups to the local computer; you cannot save a backup of the event logs on Computer A to Computer B. Backups are implemented by using the LocalSystem account, which does not have the network credentials necessary to access remote computers. If you want to save backups to a central repository, modify the script to first perform the backup, and then move the backup file to the central repository.

A technical note on backing up event logs

Event logs must be backed up separately from any other system files. Although a regular system backup can *copy* the event log files, the copied event log files will be unusable. If you attempt to open an event log file that has been copied or backed up by using any means other than the Event Log Backup Application Programming Interface (API), you receive an error message stating that the event log file is corrupt.

This error message is the result of a unique characteristic of event log files. When a computer starts, the Event service changes several bits in each event log file header. These changed bits indicate that the event log file is open, and they prevent applications, including backup programs, from accessing the event log file. If you copy an event log file by using the Copy command or a standard backup program, the copied event log file includes these changed bits. If you then try to open the copied file, you receive a message that the event log is corrupt.

Despite the changed bits, you can use Event Viewer to work with the event log files, but only because it does not try to open the event log file itself. Instead, Event Viewer uses the Event service and the Event Logging API to open the event log files.

However, this does not completely solve the problem. For better or worse, the Event service and Event Logging API can be used to open only actual event logs; they cannot open archived event log files. Instead, Event Viewer must directly access backup event log files. If the Event Log Backup API did not produce these backup event log files, these backup files will include the changed bits indicating that the file is open. In that case, any attempt to access the file will fail.

When you use the Event Log Backup method, these header bits are changed to indicate that the file is closed, giving Event Viewer access to the data.

Scripting Steps

There are multiple ways to back up and clear the event logs. For example, you might:

- Back up and clear an event log.
- Back up and clear an event log only if the log meets specific conditions.

Backing up and clearing an event log

Listing 12.5 contains a script that backs up and then clears the Application event log on a computer. To carry out this task, the script must perform the following steps:

1. Create a variable to specify the computer name.

2. Use a GetObject call to connect to the WMI namespace root\cimv2, set the impersonation level to "impersonate," and include the Backup privilege.

   To use the BackupEventLog method, you must include the Backup privilege as part of your connection string. Backup is a user right that must be explicitly assigned and included as part of the GetObject moniker.

3. Use the ExecQuery method to query the Win32_NTEventLogFile class.

   To limit data retrieval to the Application event log, include a Where clause specifying Application as the LogFileName. This returns a collection with a single item: the Application event log.

4. For the sole item in the collection, use the WMI BackupEventLog method to back up the event log, specifying the full path to the backup file when using this method. If the backup file does not exist, WMI will create a new backup file.

   However, if a backup file by that name already exists, the backup attempt will fail. The failure occurs because the BackupEventLog method does not allow you to overwrite an existing backup file or to append additional records to an existing backup file. This is another security measure, one that prevents anyone from modifying archived event logs. Without this provision, an unscrupulous administrator could back up and clear the event logs, open the backup files, and then remove any events he or she wanted to keep secret.

5. Use the WMI ClearEventLog method to clear the event log.

   In the script, this method will run only if the backup succeeded; if the BackupEventLog method returns anything other than 0, this means the backup failed. As a result, the message "The application event log could not be backed up" is echoed to the screen, and the event log is not cleared.

Listing 12.5   Backing Up and Clearing an Event Log

```
1   strComputer = "."
2   Set objWMIService = GetObject("winmgmts:" _
3       & "{impersonationLevel=impersonate,(Backup)}!\\" & _
4           strComputer & "\root\cimv2")
5   Set colLogFiles = objWMIService.ExecQuery _
6       ("SELECT * FROM Win32_NTEventLogFile WHERE LogFileName='Application'")
7   For Each objLogfile in colLogFiles
8       errBackupLog = objLogFile.BackupEventLog("c:\scripts\application.evt")
9       If errBackupLog <> 0 Then
10          Wscript.Echo "The Application event log could not be backed up."
11      Else
12          objLogFile.ClearEventLog()
13      End If
14  Next
```

You might want to run the script shown in Listing 12.5 as a scheduled task and thus back up and clear your event log on a regular basis.

Backing up and clearing an event log if the log meets specific conditions

If you wanted to, you could schedule the script in Listing 12.5 to run as a scheduled task each morning. The script would thus start up each day and then back up and clear each event log. At the end of the year, you would have 365 archive files for each event log. Although the data would be safely archived, dealing with scores of small event log files can be more complicated than dealing with a single large event log file.

As an alternative approach, you can create a script that backs up and clears an event log only if the log meets specific conditions.

Listing 12.6 contains a script that backs up and clears an event log only if the log is larger than 20 megabytes (approximately 20,000,000 bytes). If the log is smaller than 20 megabytes, the script exits without performing the backup. To carry out this task, the script must perform the following steps:

1. Create a variable to specify the computer name.

2. Use a GetObject call to connect to the WMI namespace root\cimv2 on the computer, and set the impersonation level to "impersonate."

3. Use the ExecQuery method to query the Win32_NTEventLogFile class.

    This returns a collection consisting of all the event logs on the computer, except the Security event log. To return the Security event log, you need to include the Security privilege as part of the WMI moniker. The Security event log is not included in this script simply because the Security event log is often managed separately from the other event logs (and often by a separate administrator).

4. For each event log in the collection, check the FileSize property to see whether the event log size is larger than 20 megabytes.

    ■   If the FileSize property returns a value greater than 20 megabytes, the event log is backed up to a file, using the name of the event log as the file name, and the event log is then cleared.

    ■   If the FileSize property returns a value less than 20 megabytes, the event log is not backed up and then cleared.

Listing 12.6 Backing Up and Clearing Event Logs If the Log Meets Specific Conditions

```
1   strComputer = "."
2   Set objWMIService = GetObject("winmgmts:" _
3       & "{impersonationLevel=impersonate, (Backup, Security)}!\\" _
4           & strComputer & "\root\cimv2")
5   Set colLogFiles = objWMIService.ExecQuery _
6       ("SELECT * FROM Win32_NTEventLogFile")
7   For Each objLogfile in colLogFiles
8       If objLogFile.FileSize > 20000000 Then
9           strBackupLog = objLogFile.BackupEventLog _
10              ("c:\scripts\" & objLogFile.LogFileName & ".evt")
11          objLogFile.ClearEventLog()
12      End If
13  Next
```

Creating Unique File Names When Backing Up Event Logs

Each time you back up an event log, you must create a new archive file; you cannot overwrite existing archive files nor can you append additional information to an existing file. Instead, you must either rename the existing archive file or ensure that the new file is given a different name.

For example, the first time you back up the System event log to C:\Scripts\SystemBackup.evt, the new file is created and the procedure succeeds. The second time you attempt the backup, however, the file SystemBackup.evt will already exist and the procedure will fail. To do a second backup, you must first rename or remove SystemBackup.evt.

To help overcome this problem, you can create a script to generate unique file names for each of your event log archives.

Scripting Steps

Listing 12.7 contains a script that uses the log name, date, and time to create unique file names when backing up an event log. To carry out this task, the script must perform the following steps:

1. Use the VBScript functions Day, Month, and Year to determine the day, month, and year of the current date.

2. Create a variable to specify the computer name.

3. Use a GetObject call to connect to the WMI namespace root\cimv2 on the computer, and set the impersonation level to "impersonate."

4. Use the ExecQuery method to query the Win32_NTEventLogFile class.

   To limit data retrieval to a single event log, a Where clause is used specifying that only the Application event log should be returned. The resulting collection will have a single item: the Application event log.

5. For the first (and only) item in the collection, use the LogFileName property to determine the name of the event log file being backed up.

6. Create a unique file name for the backup file.

   This is done by combining the LogFileName with the year, month, and day, separating each portion of the file name with underscores. The net result will be a file name similar to this: System_2002_12_20.evt, where:

   - **System** = The LogFileName.
   - **2002** = The year.
   - **12** = The month.
   - **20** = The day.
   - **.evt** = The file extension.

7. Use the Backup method to back up the event log, specifying the generated name as the file name.

8. Use the Clear method to clear the event log.

Listing 12.7   Creating Unique File Names When Backing Up Event Logs

```
1    dtmThisDay = Day(Now)
2    dtmThisMonth = Month(Now)
3    dtmThisYear = Year(Now)
4    strBackupName = dtmThisYear & "_" & dtmThisMonth & "_" & dtmThisDay
5    strComputer = "."
6    Set objWMIService = GetObject("winmgmts:" _
7        & "{impersonationLevel=impersonate,(Backup)}!\\" & _
8            strComputer & "\root\cimv2")
9    Set colLogFiles = objWMIService.ExecQuery _
10       ("SELECT * FROM Win32_NTEventLogFile WHERE LogFileName='Application'")
11   For Each objLogfile in colLogFiles
12       objLogFile.BackupEventLog("c:\scripts\" & strBackupName & _
13           "_application.evt")
14       objLogFile.ClearEventLog()
15   Next
```

Querying Event Logs

Although events are automatically recorded on a computer (except for security events, which must be enabled by using Group Policy), few administrators routinely analyze their event logs. This is due in part to the limitations inherent within Event Viewer and in part to the nature of how events are recorded throughout the enterprise. The impediments to routinely analyzing event logs include:

- **The large number of events typically stored in an event log.** Many of the events that take place on a computer are recorded to the event logs. The thousands of events recorded in the event logs on a domain controller make analysis extremely difficult.

- **Inability to save filtered records to a separate file.** Event Viewer allows you to filter a desired set of records but does not allow you to save just those records to a separate file. To analyze, graph, or otherwise work with a filtered set of records, you must export all the events from Event Viewer to a text file, open the file in another application, and then filter and save the events of interest.

- **Lack of printing capabilities.** Event Viewer provides no printing capabilities; records must be imported into another application before they can be printed.

- **Inability to record events on remote computers or on multiple computers.** Because events are recorded only on the computer where they occur, the only way to obtain enterprise-wide data has been to manually examine the event logs on every computer.

The WMI class Win32_NTLogEvent class can be used to extract records from an event log and either display the results of those queries or save them to a file. This enables you to automate the process of analyzing event logs by creating scripts that do such things as:

- Periodically return any instances of a particular event (for example, a failed logon or failed service).

- Run each morning and retrieve all the events that occurred on the previous day. These event records can then be copied into a database, where they can be easily sorted, filtered, analyzed, and printed.

Several key event properties that can be returned using WMI are shown in Table 12.4.

Table 12.4   Event Properties in WMI

Property	Description
Category	Classification of the event as determined by the source. Although primarily used when recording Security events, this property is available in other event logs as well. Common Security categories include Logon/Logoff, Account Management, and System Event.
ComputerName	Name of the computer on which the event occurred.
EventCode	Identification number for a particular kind of event. For example, a successful logoff is recorded in the Security log with the Event ID 538. However, Event IDs are not necessarily unique. It is possible that, when retrieving Event ID 538, you can get other kinds of events with ID 538. If this happens, you might need to filter by the source as well as ID.
Message	Event description.
RecordNumber	Record number for the event. Record numbers are always unique; they are not reset to 1 when an event log is cleared. As a result, the highest record number also indicates the number of records that have been written to the event log since the operating system was installed.
SourceName	Application that generated the event.

(continued)

Table 12.4 Event Properties in WMI *(continued)*

Property	Description
TimeWritten	Time that the record was written to the event log in the Universal Time Coordinate (UTC) format yyyymmddHHMMSS.xxxxxx-UUU, where: **yyyy** represents the year **mm** represents the month **dd** represents the day **HH** represents the hour (in 24-hour format) **MM** represents the minutes **SS** represents the seconds **xxxxxx** represents the milliseconds **UUU** represents the number of minutes to be subtracted from the current time in order to calculate Greenwich mean time For example, an event recorded on October 31, 2002, at 10:45:39 A.M. Pacific time looks like this: `20021031104539.000000-480`
Type	Error type. Values are: 1 = Error 2 = Warning 4 = Information 8 = Audit success 16 = Audit failure
User	User account under which the event occurred. Rather than storing the user account name, the event log stores the user's Security Identifier (SID). This means the user field will "disappear" if a user account is deleted and the SID is no longer valid. When you back up an event log, however, the actual user name (rather than the SID) is included in the backup file.

Designing Event Log Queries

The way an event log query is constructed can have a huge impact on how long it takes WMI to process the query and return the requested information. This is not necessarily true of other managed objects. For example, a query that returns all the properties for all the installed services on a typical Windows 2000–based computer takes about 2 seconds to complete. A filtered query that returns the properties of a single service takes about 1 second to complete, a difference of only 1 second.

However, query times for different types of event log queries can vary widely. The relative query times for several different types of event log queries run on a Windows 2000 Server–based test computer are listed in Table 12.5. The test computer had a total of 13,743 events recorded in its event logs, with 669 of these in the System event log. Retrieving all the events from all the event logs required over 2 hours to complete. When the query was modified so that it retrieved events from only the System event log, the process took just 4 minutes.

Table 12.5 Relative Event Log Query Times

Query Type	Query Time (hours:minutes:seconds)
Select all events from all event logs	2:06:15
Select events only from the System event log	0:04:03
Select events only from the System event log that have EventCode 1000	0:01:33
Select events only from the System event log that have EventCode 1000 and occurred on a specific day	0:00:17

Event log queries can also return a very large amount of information compared with queries for other WMI classes, such as Win32_Service. Retrieving the properties for all the services on the test computer and saving them to a text file resulted in a file that was less than 13 KB. Performing the same task with the event logs resulted in a text file of nearly 1 MB. Attempting to retrieve events from large event logs over the network could cause a script to take hours to run and might generate a huge amount of network traffic.

Because of the length of time it can take an event log query to run and the large amount of information that can be returned, it is important that you carefully design your queries for retrieving data from the event logs. Unless you need to return all the events from all the event logs on a computer, write your queries so that they do one or more of the following:

- **Specify a single event log.** If events are recorded in only one event log, there is no need to search the other logs for these records. For example, computer startup and shutdown events are recorded only in the System event log. If you are querying for these records, there is no reason to search the Application or DNS event logs.

- **Return only a subset of events.** When analyzing event logs, you rarely need to examine every event. The vast majority of records in a typical event log report the success of a particular operation. If you are interested only in operations that failed, there is no reason to examine hundreds of records that report operations that succeeded. Instead, you can focus on a subset of events: those records reporting an operation that failed.

- **Return only events that occurred on a particular day.** For most computers, this kind of query returns only a few hundred records, compared with thousands of records stored in a large event log. If you need to view only the event records for last Tuesday, construct your query so that only the records from that day are returned.

- **Asynchronouly return event records.** If a dataset is large, asynchronous queries will usually run faster than semi-synchronous queries.

- **Copy events to a database.** Unlike databases, event logs are not optimized for data retrieval and analysis. If you need to perform a number of queries on your event logs, or if you need to combine events from multiple event logs, you should copy those events to a database and then use the database and its tools to analyze the records. In addition to the speed differential, databases typically provide more sophisticated tools for analyzing data and calculating statistics than do event logs.

Querying a Specific Event Log

You can greatly speed up data queries by limiting your searches to a specific event log. It is very rare for events of a certain type, or events generated by a specific application, to be written to multiple event logs. Instead, operating system events are invariably written to the System event log, events generated by an application such as Microsoft Office are written to the Application event log, and so forth.

For example, if you are interested in the activities of the DNS service, any such events will be written to the DNS server event log. There is no reason to search the other event logs. A nonoptimized query that searches all the event logs instead of limiting the search to the DNS service log might search tens of thousands of events in the Security event log, even though no DNS service events will be recorded there.

Scripting Steps

Listing 12.8 contains a script that queries a specific event log and echoes the properties of all the records in that log. To carry out this task, the script must perform the following steps:

1. Create a variable to specify the computer name.

2. Use a GetObject call to connect to the WMI namespace root\cimv2 on the computer, and set the impersonation level to "impersonate."

3. Use the ExecQuery method to query the Win32_NTLogEvent class.

To limit data retrieval to the records in the System event log, a Where clause is included specifying that the Logfile must be equal to System. The resulting collection will contain only the events in the System event log.

4. For each event in the collection, echo the event properties.

Listing 12.8   Querying a Specific Event Log

```
1    strComputer = "."
2    Set objWMIService = GetObject("winmgmts:" _
3        & "{impersonationLevel=impersonate}!\\" & strComputer & "\root\cimv2")
4    Set colLoggedEvents = objWMIService.ExecQuery _
5        ("SELECT * FROM Win32_NTLogEvent WHERE Logfile = 'System'")
6    For Each objEvent in colLoggedEvents
7        Wscript.Echo "Category: " & objEvent.Category
8        Wscript.Echo "Computer Name: " & objEvent.ComputerName
9        Wscript.Echo "Event Code: " & objEvent.EventCode
10       Wscript.Echo "Message: " & objEvent.Message
11       Wscript.Echo "Record Number: " & objEvent.RecordNumber
12       Wscript.Echo "Source Name: " & objEvent.SourceName
13       Wscript.Echo "Time Written: " & objEvent.TimeWritten
14       Wscript.Echo "Event Type: " & objEvent.Type
15       Wscript.Echo "User: " & objEvent.User
16   Next
```

Querying an Event Log for a Subset of Events

Querying an event log for a specific set of events can greatly increase the speed and efficiency of your query. The following examples demonstrate two ways to construct a script for determining the number of improper shutdowns recorded in the System event log with Event ID 6008 one way that is fast and efficient, another way that is not:

- Retrieve all the events from the System event log, check each one to see whether the Event ID is 6008, and then report the total number of improper shutdown events found.

  On a Windows 2000–based test computer with approximately 700 events in the System event log, this process took more than 10 minutes.

- Retrieve only events from the System event log that have Event ID 6008, and report the number of records retrieved by this query.

  On the same test computer, this query took just 9 seconds. If you know exactly what you are looking for, you should create a targeted query that returns only this information. This reduces processing time and, when you are working with remote computers, limits the amount of data that must be transferred across the network.

Scripting Steps

Listing 12.9 contains a script that queries an event log and tallies all instances of a specific Event ID. To carry out this task, the script must perform the following steps:

1. Create a variable to specify the computer name.

2. Use a GetObject call to connect to the WMI namespace root\cimv2 on the computer, and set the impersonation level to "impersonate."

3. Use the ExecQuery method to query the Win32_NTLogEvent class.

    To limit data retrieval to specific events, include a Where clause specifying the System event log and EventCode 6008. The resulting collection will include only records from the System event log that have EventCode 6008.

4. Use the Count property to echo the number of records in the collection.

    Because a filter was applied as part of the GetObject call, the number of records in the collection equals the number of proper shutdowns recorded in the System event log.

Listing 12.9   Querying an Event Log for a Specific Event ID

```
1  strComputer = "."
2  Set objWMIService = GetObject("winmgmts:" _
3      & "{impersonationLevel=impersonate}!\\" & strComputer & "\root\cimv2")
4  Set colLoggedEvents = objWMIService.ExecQuery _
5      ("SELECT * FROM Win32_NTLogEvent WHERE Logfile = 'System' AND " _
6      & "EventCode = '6008'")
7  Wscript.Echo "Improper shutdowns: " & colLoggedEvents.Count
```

Retrieving Event Log Records from a Specified Day

When analyzing event logs, you will often want to review events that occurred only on a specific day or set of days. For example, if a computer had problems on August 15, 2002, you would want to review only the records from that date. At least for your initial investigation, you do not need records for the entire month of August.

The one complicating factor in retrieving events that occurred on a specific day is the fact that WMI stores dates using the Universal Time Coordinate (UTC) format. Because of this, you cannot use a standard date-time (such as 12/19/2002) in your queries. Instead, you have to use a UTC date-time format such as this:

```
20021219000000.000000-480
```

UTC dates and techniques for converting them to standard dates (and vice-versa) are discussed in detail in "WMI Scripting Primer" in this book.

Scripting Steps

Listing 12.10 contains a script that queries the event logs for all events that occurred on December 19, 2002. To perform this task, the script must carry out the following steps:

1. Create a variable named dtmStartDate, and set the value to 20021219000000.000000-480. This is a UTC date corresponding to the beginning of the day (hour 0) on December 19, 2002.

2. Create a variable named dtmEndDate, and set the value to 20021220000000.000000-480. This is a UTC date corresponding to the beginning of the day (hour 0) on December 20, 2002. Your query will search for all events that were recorded on or after dtmStartDate (the start of the day on December 19), but before dtmEndDate (the start of the day on December 20).

3. Create a variable to specify the computer name.

4. Use a GetObject call to connect to the WMI namespace root\cimv2 on the computer, and set the impersonation level to "impersonate."

5. Use the ExecQuery method to query the Win32_NTLogEvent class.

   To limit data retrieval to events that were recorded on December 19, 2002, include a Where clause specifying that the TimeWritten is both:

   - Greater than or equal to dtmStartDate
   - Less than dtmEndDate.

   Because no log file name is specified in the query, events will be returned from all the event logs except the Security event log.

6. For each event in the collection, echo the event properties.

Listing 12.10   Querying an Event Log for All Events From a Specified Day

```
1  dtmStartDate = "20021219000000.000000-480"
2  dtmEndDate = "20021220000000.000000-480"
3  strComputer = "."
4  Set objWMIService = GetObject("winmgmts:" _
5      & "{impersonationLevel=impersonate}!\\" & strComputer & "\root\cimv2")
6  Set colEvents = objWMIService.ExecQuery _
7      ("Select * from Win32_NTLogEvent Where TimeWritten >= '" _
8          & dtmStartDate & "' and TimeWritten < '" & dtmEndDate & "'")
```

(continued)

Listing 12.10   Querying an Event Log for All Events From a Specified Day *(continued)*

```
9    For each objEvent in colEvents
10       Wscript.Echo "Category: " & objEvent.Category
11       Wscript.Echo "Computer Name: " & objEvent.ComputerName
12       Wscript.Echo "Event Code: " & objEvent.EventCode
13       Wscript.Echo "Message: " & objEvent.Message
14       Wscript.Echo "Record Number: " & objEvent.RecordNumber
15       Wscript.Echo "Source Name: " & objEvent.SourceName
16       Wscript.Echo "Time Written: " & objEvent.TimeWritten
17       Wscript.Echo "Event Type: " & objEvent.Type
18       Wscript.Echo "User: " & objEvent.User
19       Wscript.Echo objEvent.LogFile
20    Next
```

Asynchronously Retrieving Event Log Statistics

WMI supports both asynchronous and semi-synchronous scripts. When retrieving events from the event logs, asynchronous scripts often retrieve this data much faster.

In an asynchronous script, a query is issued and control is immediately returned to the script. The query continues to process on a separate thread while the script begins to immediately act on the information that is returned. Asynchronous scripts are event driven: each time an event record is retrieved, the OnObjectReady event is fired. When the query has completed, the OnCompleted event will fire, and the script can continue based on the fact that all the available records have been returned.

In a semi-synchronous script, by contrast, a query is issued and the script then queues a large amount of retrieved information before acting upon it. For many objects, semi-synchronous processing is adequate; for example, when querying a disk drive for its properties, there might be only a split second between the time the query is issued and the time the information is returned and acted upon. This is due in large part to the fact that the amount of information returned is relatively small.

When querying an event log, however, the interval between the time the query is issued and the time that a semi-synchronous script can finish returning and acting on the information can take hours. On top of that, the script might run out of memory and fail on its own before completing.

For event logs with a large number of records, the difference in processing time can be considerable. On a Windows 2000–based test computer with 2,000 records in the event log, a semi-synchronous query that retrieved all the events and displayed them in a command window took 10 minutes 45 seconds. An asynchronous query that performed the same operation took one minute 54 seconds.

Scripting Steps

Listing 12.11 contains a script that asynchronously queries the event logs for all records. To perform this task, the script must apply the following steps:

1. Define two constants used to create a message box.

   - **POPUP_DURATION = 10** — Indicates that the message box will automatically dismiss itself after 10 seconds unless the user clicks the **OK** button.

   - **OK_BUTTON = 0** — Indicates that only an **OK** button will be displayed as part of the message box.

2. Create a variable to specify the computer name.

3. Use a GetObject call to connect to the WMI namespace root\cimv2 on the computer, and set the impersonation level to "impersonate."

4. Create an SWbemSink object named SINK_.

5. Retrieve the records in the event logs by using an InstancesOfAsync query, specifying Win32_NTLogEvent as the source of the query.

6. Display a Popup message box that dismisses itself after 10 seconds.

   Displaying the message box ensures that the query will have enough time to start before the last line of the script has been processed. Without this message box, the script might finish before the query starts; if the last line of the script is executed before the query can begin to return data, the script will terminate and no data will be returned. After the query begins to return data, however, the data retrieval will continue, even if the last line of the script has been executed.

7. Use a SINK_OnCompleted subroutine to indicate the code that runs when the query is complete. In this case, a message will be echoed to the screen.

8. Use a SINK_OnObjectReady subroutine to indicate the code that runs each time the query returns an object (in this case, an event record).

Listing 12.11 Asynchronously Querying an Event Log

```
1   Const POPUP_DURATION = 10
2   Const OK_BUTTON = 0
3   Set objWSHShell = Wscript.CreateObject("Wscript.Shell")
4   strComputer = "."
5   Set objWMIService = GetObject("winmgmts:" _
6       & "{impersonationLevel=impersonate}!\\" & strComputer & "\root\cimv2")
7   Set objSink = WScript.CreateObject("WbemScripting.SWbemSink","SINK_")
8   objWMIService.InstancesOfAsync objSink, "Win32_NTLogEvent"
9   errReturn = objWshShell.Popup("Retrieving events", POPUP_DURATION, _
10      "Event Retrieval", OK_BUTTON)
11  Sub SINK_OnCompleted(iHResult, objErrorObject, objAsyncContext)
12      WScript.Echo "Asynchronous operation is done."
13  End Sub
14  Sub SINK_OnObjectReady(objEvent, objAsyncContext)
15      Wscript.Echo "Category: " & objEvent.Category
16      Wscript.Echo "Computer Name: " & objEvent.ComputerName
17      Wscript.Echo "Event Code: " & objEvent.EventCode
18      Wscript.Echo "Message: " & objEvent.Message
19      Wscript.Echo "Record Number: " & objEvent.RecordNumber
20      Wscript.Echo "Source Name: " & objEvent.SourceName
21      Wscript.Echo "Time Written: " & objEvent.TimeWritten
22      Wscript.Echo "Event Type: " & objEvent.Type
23      Wscript.Echo "User: " & objEvent.User
24  End Sub
```

Copying Events to a Database

WMI provides a way to programmatically access the records in an event log. Although this is an extremely useful capability, WMI does have at least two limitations when it comes to querying large data sources such as event logs:

- The WMI Query Language (WQL) contains only a small subset of the keywords and commands in Structured Query Language (SQL).

  For example, you might want to tally frequency statistics for the events in an event log. (This would tell you that Event ID 1 has occurred X number of times, Event ID 2 has occurred Y number of times, and so forth.) This type of query can be constructed in SQL by using code similar to the following (assuming you have a database named EventLog):

```
SELECT Count(EventID) AS CountOfEventID, EventID FROM EventLog GROUP BY
CountOfEventID
```

  However, this kind of query cannot be constructed using WQL.

- Unlike a database, event logs are not optimized to process queries and rapidly return information.

  A query against an event log with a large number of records can take a long time to complete. On a Windows 2000–based test computer with an event log containing 12,000 records, a query that returned events with a specific Event ID required 48 seconds to complete. The same query run against an SQL database holding the exact same information completed in less than 1 second.

To carry out a regular and detailed analysis of your event logs, you might want to periodically extract the records from the event log and copy them to a database. Copying the records to a database enables you to create more sophisticated queries and greatly decreases the time it takes to run these queries.

Copying records to a database also allows you to combine the event logs from multiple computers. For example, you might combine all the DNS event logs from all your DNS servers into a single database. Using that database, you can easily construct queries that compare the events that occur on one DNS server with the events that occur on your other DNS servers.

Scripting Steps

You can periodically copy all the events from an event log to a database, clear the event log, and allow events to accumulate until you copy the events and clear the log again.

Listing 12.12 contains a script that retrieves all the events from an event log and copies them to a database. Before you create this script, you need to create the following:

- A database with the System Data Source Name (DSN) of EventLogs.

  For information about accessing databases by using scripts, see "Creating Enterprise Scripts" in this book.

- A table in the database named EventTable with field names equivalent to the field names used in the script:
  - Category
  - ComputerName
  - EventCode
  - Message
  - RecordNumber
  - SourceName
  - TimeWritten
  - Type
  - User

To carry out this task, the script must perform the following steps:

1. Create the following two objects:

   - ADODB.Connection, representing a connection to an Active Data Objects (ADO) database.

   - ADODB.Recordset, representing an ADO recordset.

2. Open the database with the System DSN of EventLogs.

3. Open the table EventTable, using the SQL query "Select * from EventTable."

4. Create a variable to specify the computer name.

5. Use a GetObject call to connect to the WMI namespace root\cimv2 on the computer, and set the impersonation level to "impersonate."

6. Use the ExecQuery method to query the Win32_NTLogEvent class.

   This query returns a collection consisting of all the events from all the event logs, except the Security event log.

7. For each event in the collection, use the AddNew command to add a new record to the database.

   The appropriate fields in the new record are then populated using the properties of the event record.

8. After the record has been populated, use the Update command to write the new data to the database.

9. Close the database connection and the recordset.

Listing 12.12 Copying Events to a Database

```
1   Set objConn = CreateObject("ADODB.Connection")
2   Set objRS = CreateObject("ADODB.Recordset")
3   objConn.Open "DSN=EventLogs;"
4   objRS.CursorLocation = 3
5   objRS.Open "SELECT * FROM EventTable" , objConn, 3, 3
6   strComputer = "."
7   Set objWMIService = GetObject("winmgmts:" _
8       & "{impersonationLevel=impersonate}!\\" & strComputer & "\root\cimv2")
9   Set colRetrievedEvents = objWMIService.ExecQuery _
10      ("SELECT * FROM Win32_NTLogEvent")
```

(continued)

Listing 12.12   Copying Events to a Database *(continued)*

```
11   For Each objEvent in colRetrievedEvents
12       objRS.AddNew
13       objRS("Category") = objEvent.Category
14       objRS("ComputerName") = objEvent.ComputerName
15       objRS("EventCode") = objEvent.EventCode
16       objRS("Message") = objEvent.Message
17       objRS("RecordNumber") = objEvent.RecordNumber
18       objRS("SourceName") = objEvent.SourceName
19       objRS("TimeWritten") = objEvent.TimeWritten
20       objRS("Type") = objEvent.Type
21       objRS("User") = objEvent.User
22       objRS.Update
23   Next
24   objRS.Close
25   objConn.Close
```

Writing Events to Event Logs

Windows operating systems do not automatically record every event that takes place on a computer. Many events of interest, including logon scripts that failed, software that could not be installed, and drives that could not be mapped, are not recorded in the event logs and are therefore not automatically available to anyone analyzing the event logs.

If your scripts carry out activities that should be logged (either because they succeeded or because they failed), you can use the Windows Script Host (WSH) LogEvent method to record events in the Application event log.

 Note

WMI does not provide a method for writing events to the event logs.

Limitations of the LogEvent method

Before you begin using the LogEvent method in your scripts, it is important to understand the limitations inherent in this method:

- The LogEvent method can record only events in the Application Log.

- You cannot specify a unique event ID or a unique Event Source when using this method.

   Instead, all events are logged with an event ID that corresponds to the event type (for example, all successful events will have an event ID of 0) and the Event Source *WSH*. This makes it impossible to search for events derived from a particular script unless you include the script name as part of the Event Description.

Writing to Event Logs

The LogEvent method in WSH allows you to write events to the Application Log. When writing these events, you can specify the information shown in Table 12.6.

Table 12.6 LogEvent Method Parameters

Specification	Description
Event type	Event types include the following: 0 – Success 1 – Error 2 – Warning 4 – Information 8 – Audit success (generally not used in the Application Log) 16 – Audit failure (generally not used in the Application Log)
Event description	Any text message describing the event.
Name of the computer to which the event will be recorded	If not specified, the event will be recorded to the Application Log on the computer on which the script is being run. If you prefer to record the event in the Application Log on a remote computer, enclose the Universal Naming Convention (UNC) name of the computer in quotation marks (for example, "\\PrimaryServer"). Before you attempt to record events to a remote computer, make sure the user running the script has permission to write events to the remote event log.

Scripting Steps

There are multiple ways to write an event to an event log. You can do this by:

- Writing an event to an event log on the local computer.
- Writing an event to an event log on a remote computer.

Writing an event to an event log on the local computer

Listing 12.13 contains a script that writes a Success event (event type 0) to the Application event log on the local computer. To carry out this task, the script must perform the following steps:

1. Create a constant EVENT_SUCCESS and set the value to 0.

2. Create an instance of the WSH Shell object.

3. Use the LogEvent method to write the record to the event log, specifying two parameters:

   - **EVENT_SUCCESS** — Constant that indicates the type of event.
   - **"Payroll application successfully installed."** — The event description.

Because this event will be written to the local computer, the computer name (an optional, third parameter) does not have to be specified.

Listing 12.13   Writing an Event to the Application Log

```
1  Const EVENT_SUCCESS = 0
2  Set objShell = Wscript.CreateObject("Wscript.Shell")
3  objShell.LogEvent EVENT_SUCCESS, _
4      "Payroll application successfully installed."
```

Writing an event to an event log on a remote computer

To record the event to the Application Log on a remote computer, add the UNC computer name as an optional, third, parameter to the LogEvent method. Listing 12.14 contains a script that writes the same event to the Application Log on the remote computer \\PrimaryServer.

Listing 12.14   Writing an Event to the Application Log on a Remote Computer

```
1  Const EVENT_SUCCESS = 0
2  Set objShell = Wscript.CreateObject("Wscript.Shell")
3  objShell.LogEvent EVENT_SUCCESS, _
4      "Payroll application successfully installed." , "\\PrimaryServer"
```

Creating Detailed Event Log Entry Descriptions

When your script writes an event to the event log, it can tap the capabilities of WMI to create more meaningful event descriptions, descriptions that can include information such as the amount of memory installed on a computer or the amount of available disk space on a computer.

For example, the event log might include an error event indicating that an application could not be installed on a computer. This particular application might require 15 MB of free disk space in order to be installed. If the event description includes the fact that the computer had only 10 MB of free disk space, you know at least one reason why the application could not be installed on that computer.

Scripting Steps

Listing 12.15 contains a script that adds WMI data to an event log entry. To carry out this task, the script must perform the following steps:

1. Create a constant EVENT_FAILED and set the value to 2.

   This indicates that an error occurred.

2. Create an instance of the WSH Shell object. This is required to use the LogEvent method.

3. Create a WSH Network object.

This object is used to return the name of the computer on which the installation was attempted, as well as the domain and user name of the person who attempted the installation.

4. Create a variable to specify the computer name.

5. Use a GetObject call to connect to the WMI namespace root\cimv2 on the computer, and set the impersonation level to "impersonate."

6. Use the ExecQuery method to query the Win32_ LogicalDisk class.

This query returns a collection consisting of all the logical disks installed on the computer.

7. For each logical disk in the collection, retrieve the free disk space by using the FreeSpace property.

8. Add the drive name, the amount of free space, and a carriage return (VbCrLf) to the variable strDrive Space.

After the script loops through the entire collection, this variable will contain a list of drives and the available space on each. For example:

```
A: 0
C: 152611
D: 5678322
```

9. Set the value of the variable strEventDescription to a string consisting of:

- The string "Payroll application could not be installed on ".

- The user domain, computer name, and user name.

- The string "Free space on each drive is: " and the variable strDriveSpace.

The final value for strEventDescription might look similar to this:

```
Payroll application could not be installed on FABRIKAM\atl-xp-pro-001
by user kmeyer. Free space on each drive is:
A: 0
C: 152611
D: 5678322
```

10. Use the LogEvent method to write the record to the event log, specifying the event type and the event description.

Listing 12.15   Adding WMI Data to an Event Log Entry

```
1   Const EVENT_FAILED = 2
2   Set objShell = Wscript.CreateObject("Wscript.Shell")
3   Set objNetwork = Wscript.CreateObject("Wscript.Network")
4   strComputer = "."
5   Set objWMIService = GetObject("winmgmts:" _
6       & "{impersonationLevel=impersonate}!\\" & strComputer & "\root\cimv2")
7   Set colDiskDrives = objWMIService.ExecQuery _
8       ("SELECT * FROM Win32_Logicaldisk")
9   For Each objDisk in colDiskDrives
10      strDriveSpace = strDriveSpace & objDisk.Name & " " & _
11          objDisk.FreeSpace & VbCrLf
12  Next
13  strEventDescription = "Payroll application could not be installed on " _
14      & objNetwork.UserDomain & "\" & objNetwork.ComputerName _
15          & " by user " & objNetwork.UserName & _
16              ". Free space on each drive is: " & VbCrLf & strDriveSpace
17  objShell.LogEvent EVENT_FAILED, strEventDescription
```

Creating Custom Event Logs

By default, Windows 2000–based computers have three event logs: System Log, Security Log, and Application Log. Depending on a computer's role and on the services hosted by the computer, you can have additional event logs, such as Directory Service Log, DNS Server Log, and File Replication Service Log.

Custom event logs, which can be created by adding a subkey to the registry, can make it easier for you to monitor specific applications or types of events. For example, you might create a custom event log named ScriptingEventLog and use this as a repository for any events written by one of your scripts. After the custom log has been created, it can be programmatically monitored and managed by using WMI.

One minor limitation of a custom event log is that no event sources are registered for the log. As a result, your event descriptions are prefaced with a notice informing you that no event source could be found for the event. An event description, recorded as "Drive X could not be mapped" and similar to the following, appears in Event Viewer:

```
The description for Event ID ( 100 ) in Source ( SCRIPTINGEVENTLOG ) cannot
be found. The local computer may not have the necessary registry information
or message DLL files to display messages from a remote computer. You may be able
to use the /AUXSOURCE= flag to retrieve this description; see Help and Support
for details. The following information is part of the event: Drive X could not
be mapped.
```

 Caution

Changing the registry with a script can easily propagate errors. The scripting tools bypass safeguards, allowing settings that can damage your system, or even require you to reinstall Windows. Before scripting changes to the registry, test your script thoroughly and back up the registry on every computer on which you will make changes. For more information about scripting changes to the registry, see the Registry Reference on the *Microsoft Windows 2000 Server Resource Kit* companion CD or at http://www.microsoft.com/reskit.

Scripting Steps

Listing 12.16 contains a script that creates a custom event log by adding a subkey to the registry. To carry out this task, the script must perform the following steps:

1. Create a constant named NO_VALUE and set the value to Empty. This constant is used to create an empty value for the new registry subkey.

2. Create an instance of the WSH Shell object.

3. Use the RegWrite method to create a new registry subkey and set its value to NO_VALUE. The new subkey is named HKLM\System\CurrentControlSet\Services\EventLog **ScriptingEventLog**\, which means that the new event log will be named ScriptingEventLog.

Listing 12.16 Creating a Custom Event Log

```
1  Const NO_VALUE = Empty
2  Set WshShell = WScript.CreateObject("WScript.Shell")
3  WshShell.RegWrite _
4  "HKLM\System\CurrentControlSet\Services\EventLog\ScriptingEventLog\", _
5     NO_VALUE
```

Managing Plain-Text Logs

In addition to the event logs, various Windows 2000 services record event information in plain-text log files. Plain-text logs are often used to store a large quantity of information that does not need to be (or perhaps should not be) stored in the event logs. For example, if the thousands of events generated each day by a Web server on an intranet were all recorded in event logs, the event logs would be far more difficult to filter and analyze. Because of this, it makes sense to log Internet Information Services events in a plain-text log instead of an event log.

A typical Windows 2000 domain controller might have 200 or more of these logs that store event information for such things as File Replication service replication, DHCP server activities, and Internet Information Services sessions. A partial list of Windows 2000 Server plain-text logs is shown in Table 12.7.

Table 12.7   Plain-Text Logs Used in Windows 2000 Server

Log Name	Format	Description
DCPromoUI.log	Fixed-width	Contains a detailed report of the Active Directory® directory service installation and removal process, including the name of the source domain controller used for replication and the directory partitions and number of items that were replicated.
DCPromo.log	Fixed-width	Records settings used during the promotion or demotion of a domain controller, including site name, location of Active Directory log and database files, and configuration of services and security settings.
Netsetup.log	Fixed-width	Records events that occur when joining a computer to a domain.
Netlogon.log	Fixed-width	Records errors that occur when the Net Logon service attempts to dynamically create a DNS record. If this log is blank, that means no errors have occurred.
Ntfrs.log	Fixed-width	Records events that occur each time the File Replication Service runs.
Userenv.log	Text	Records events that occur when a computer processes user profiles and Group Policy.
DHCPSrvLog	Comma-separated	Records DHCP server events.

Managing plain-text logs has always been difficult because of the large number of logs used on a computer and the large amount of information stored in each log. In addition, Windows 2000 Server log files can use different text formats: comma-separated values, fixed-width text, or a unique formatting scheme. It is difficult to import these files into a single application where the events can be filtered, sorted, and analyzed.

Scripts can help manage plain-text log files. A script can automatically parse a set of log files to extract and reformat the data or to search for a particular event. Because scripts can handle different log-file formats, they can also take data from disparate sources and combine this data in a central database.

Parsing Comma-Separated-Values Logs

A comma-separated-values (CSV) log consists of two primary components:

- A header line, which indicates the data fields used in the log.

- Record lines, containing the data for each record written to the log.

In both header and record lines, commas separate individual fields. By contrast, in a tab-separated-values (TSV) log, tab characters separate fields.

For example, in DHCPSrvLog.log, the header line and the first two record lines look something like the following:

```
ID Date,Time,Description,IP Address,Host Name,MAC Address
10,04/02/01,15:16:00,Assign,192.168.1.10,workstation1.fabrikam.com,0000F8083446,
10,04/02/01,15:16:00,Assign,192.168.1.11,workstation2.fabrikam.com,0000F8083447,
```

To parse a CSV log, the script needs to read in each line and then extract each field within the line. This can be done using the VBScript Split function, which splits a line into constituent parts based on the field delimiter (the character used to separate the individual fields). For example, this line:

```
Part 1,Part 2,Part 3,Part 4
```

Would be split into a four-item array, with the array consisting of the following elements:

- Part 1

- Part 2

- Part 3

- Part 4

Scripting Steps

Listing 12.17 contains a script that parses a CSV file. To carry out this task, the script must perform the following steps:

1. Create a constant (ForReading) to be used with the FileSystemObject.

2. Create an instance of the FileSystemObject.

3. Open the DHCP server Log for Monday (C:\Windows\System32\DHCP \DhcpSrvLog-Mon.log).

4.   Use the SkipLine method to move through the first 25 lines in the file.

The first 25 lines in a DHCP server log are always header information that is not required for this script. You must start at the beginning of the file and explicitly skip these lines, however, because the FileSystemObject always begins reading at the first line of the file. You cannot specify an alternative starting point, such as the 26th line of the file.

5.   Beginning with line 26, read each line by using the ReadLine method, and temporarily store the contents in the variable strNextLine.

6.   Use the VBScript Split function to split the line into 8 separate variables. (The comma is used as the split delimiter.)

Each variable (representing a comma-delimited field in the log) is stored in the array arrDHCPRecord.

7.   Echo the contents of arrDHCPRecord to the screen.

In a production script, you would probably either save selected variables to a database or take some action based on the value of one or more of those variables (for example, the Event ID).

Listing 12.17   Parsing a Comma-Separated-Values Log

```
1   Const ForReading = 1
2   Set objFSO = CreateObject("Scripting.FileSystemObject")
3   Set objTextFile = objFSO.OpenTextFile("C:\Windows\System32\DHCP\" _
4       & "DhcpSrvLog-Mon.log", ForReading)
5   Do While objTextFile.AtEndOfStream <> True
6       If inStr(objtextFile.Readline, ",") Then
7           arrDHCPRecord = split(objTextFile.Readline, ",")
8           Wscript.Echo "Event ID: " & arrDHCPRecord(0)
9           Wscript.Echo "Date: " & arrDHCPRecord(1)
10          Wscript.Echo "Time: " & arrDHCPRecord(2)
11          Wscript.Echo "Description: " & arrDHCPRecord(3)
12          Wscript.Echo "IP Address: " & arrDHCPRecord(4)
13          Wscript.Echo "Host Name: " & arrDHCPRecord(5)
14          Wscript.Echo "MAC Address: " & arrDHCPRecord(6)
15      Else
16          objTextFile.Skipline
17      End If
18      i = i + 1
19  Loop
20  objTextFile.Close
```

Parsing Fixed-Width Logs

Fixed-width text log fields are parsed differently from CSV log fields. In a comma-separated-values log, an individual field can contain any number of characters; by definition, a field contains all the characters that precede a comma. For example, the following are valid comma-separated-values fields, even though the fields consist of different field lengths:

```
Computer,Domain
WebServer,fabrikam.com
FinancialAccountingServer,finance.accounting.fabrikam.com
```

In a fixed-width text log, fields are delimited by length rather than by a comma or other character. The fields in any given record must be exactly the same size as fields in all the records.

For example, in NetSetup.log, there are three fields: date, time, and description. As shown in the following log excerpt, date begins with the first character, time with the seventh character, and description with the sixteenth character (numbers have been added to help indicate character positions):

```
12345678901234567890123456789012345678901234567890
08/16 11:50:49 NetpDoDomainJoin
08/16 11:50:49 NetpMachineValidToJoin: 'WINTEST'
08/16 11:50:49 NetpGetLsaPrimaryDomain: status: 0x0
08/16 11:50:49 NetpMachineValidToJoin: status: 0x0
```

When this log is parsed, the first record is split into these three fields:

- 08/16
- 11:50:49
- NetpDoDomainJoin

Scripting Steps

Listing 12.18 contains a script that parses the fixed-width-column log Netsetup.log. To carry out this task, the script must perform the following steps:

1. Create a constant (ForReading) to be used with the FileSystemObject.
2. Create an instance of the FileSystemObject.
3. Open the Netsetup log (C:\Windows\Debug\Netsetup.log).
4. Create a loop for reading each line in the file.
5. Read the first line, and temporarily store the contents in the variable strLineToParse.

6. Use the Mid function to parse the Date, Time, and Description from the variable.

   - Date represents the first six characters in the string.

   - Time begins at character position 7 and is nine characters long.

   - Description begins at character position 16 and makes up the remainder of the line.

7. Echo the values of the individual fields.

8. Repeat the loop with the next line in the log file.

9. Close the log file.

Listing 12.18   Parsing a Fixed-Width-Column Log

```
1   Const ForReading = 1
2   Set objFSO = CreateObject("Scripting.FileSystemObject")
3   Set objTextFile = objFSO.OpenTextFile("C:\Windows\Debug\Netsetup.log", _
4       ForReading)
5   Do While objTextFile.AtEndOfStream <> True
6       strLinetoParse = objTextFile.ReadLine
7       dtmEventDate = Mid(strLinetoParse, 1, 6)
8       dtmEventTime = Mid(strLinetoParse, 7, 9)
9       strEventDescription = Mid(strLinetoParse, 16)
10      Wscript.Echo "Date: " & dtmEventDate
11      Wscript.Echo "Time: " & dtmEventTime
12      Wscript.Echo "Description: " & strEventDescription & VbCrLf
13  Loop
14  objTextFile.Close
```

CHAPTER 13

Printing

Print management has always commanded a disproportionate share of system administration time. This is due both to the large number of documents that are printed in the typical organization, and to the fact that many printer administration tools are designed for monitoring and managing single printers rather than multiple printers located throughout the enterprise. Scripting can facilitate enterprise-wide print management in your organization.

In This Chapter

Printing Overview 882

Monitoring Printers, Print Queues, and Print Jobs 885

- Monitoring Printers 885
- Monitoring Printer Workloads 897
- Monitoring Print Jobs 899

Managing Printer Operations, Print Queues, and Print Jobs 906

- Managing Printer Operations 906
- Managing Print Queues 913
- Managing Print Jobs 914

Configuring Printers and Print Jobs 917

- Configuring Printer Properties 917
- Configuring Printer Availability 918
- Tracking Printer Locations 919
- Configuring Print Jobs 923

Managing Printer Connections on Client Computers 926

- Enumerating Printer Connections 927
- Adding and Deleting Printer Connections 928

Searching for Printers in Active Directory 930

- Enumerating All the Published Printers in a Domain 931
- Searching for Specific Printers in a Domain 932

Printing Overview

Print management is one of the most time-consuming of all system administration tasks in an enterprise. This is due to a number of factors:

- In large organizations, the number of pages printed each day might number in the tens of thousands. In addition, these print jobs take place on multiple printers located throughout the enterprise, complicating the logistics involved in monitoring and managing these devices.

- Printers, unlike many other peripheral devices, require daily maintenance: replenishing the paper trays, installing new toner cartridges, and carrying out other maintenance activities. Printers can also encounter problems, such as paper jams, that require a visit from a service technician.

- Unlike other services, the print service is typically engaged all day long, even during the so-called off hours. Administrators often schedule large print jobs to take place when most users have left for the day. As a result, the printers are continually busy, even when few users are physically present in the building.

- When a printer breaks down, a domino effect can occur. If not immediately fixed, this breakdown can create a huge backlog of stalled print jobs. This can place an enormous burden on Help desk personnel, who must not only fix the problem but also deal with user complaints and questions.

In addition to these challenges, print management has traditionally been carried out on a printer-by-printer basis and has required administrators to rely on the graphical user interface (GUI) to monitor printer status and modify printer configurations. While this approach is adequate in small organizations, it is far less effective in organizations with hundreds of printers, many at remote sites.

Microsoft® Windows® 2000 provides a number of scripting tools for managing printers, print queues, print jobs, and printer drivers. Enhancements to the Windows Management Instrumentation (WMI) and Active Directory Service Interfaces (ADSI) scripting technologies make it possible for administrators to write scripts that can automate much of the print management process.

 Note

There are times when WMI and ADSI offer similar functionality for managing printers, print queues, or print jobs. When the functionality overlaps, the WMI method is demonstrated. This is because WMI is the preferred method for managing computers, while ADSI is the preferred method for managing directory service objects. ADSI scripts are used only when there is no WMI equivalent.

Working with Multiple Printers

In large organizations, a single print server is likely to be responsible for scores of printers. Accessing all the printers managed by a print server, or all the print jobs currently in print queues on that print server, is easy when using WMI. By default, WMI retrieves collections consisting of multiple printers or print jobs; for example, the following query returns a collection consisting of all the printers managed by a print server:

```
SELECT * FROM Win32_Printer
```

If you want to access only a single printer, you need to include the printer name as part of your query:

```
SELECT * FROM Win32_Printer WHERE Name = 'ArtDepartmentPrinter'
```

ADSI, by comparison, requires you to individually bind to each printer on a print server. For example, to bind to the printer named ArtDepartmentPrinter on the print server atl-ps-01, you would use a code statement similar to the following:

```
Set objPrinter = GetObject("WinNT://atl-ps-01/ArtDepartmentprinter")
```

However, it is still possible to return a collection of all the printers on a print server, and without knowing the names of those printers. To do this, a script must:

1. Connect to the print server and return a list of all objects on that server.

2. Use an ADSI filter to limit the working data set to printQueue items.

3. For each printQueue item, use a GetObject call and the ADsPath property to individually bind to the printer.

For example, the script in Listing 13.1 returns a list of all the printers managed by the print server atl-ps-01, individually binds to each printer, and then echoes the printer name.

Listing 13.1   Using ADSI to Enumerate All the Printers on a Print Server

```
1   Set objComputer = GetObject("WinNT://atl-win2k-01,computer")
2   objComputer.Filter = Array("printQueue")
3   For Each objPrinter In objComputer
4       Set objPrintQueue = GetObject(objPrinter.ADsPath)
5       Wscript.Echo objPrintQueue.Name
6   Next
```

For educational purposes, the scripts in this chapter typically use ADSI to bind to a single printer on a print server. However, you can use the code shown in Listing 13.1 to modify those scripts and thus work with all the printers managed by a print server.

Print Terminology

The terminology used when discussing printing with Windows 2000–based systems sometimes differs from the terminology used when discussing printing in regular conversation. Table 13.1 lists some of the key terms, along with a brief definition of each term as it is used in this chapter.

Table 13.1   Print Terminology

Term	Definition
Print device	Also referred to as the *physical printer*, the print device is the physical device that produces printed pages. In Windows 2000, the term *printer* specifically refers to the logical printer, the software interface between a print device and the computers submitting documents for printing. In this chapter, the term *print device* is used only when there is possible confusion between the logical printer and the physical printer. Most of the time, the term *printer* or *physical printer* is used instead.
Printer	Also referred to as a *logical printer*, this is the software interface between a print device and computers submitting documents for printing.
Print server	The computer responsible for managing the print queues for a printer or group of printers. In a large organization, a single computer might manage 200 or more printers.
Printer driver	The software that allows applications to communicate with specific printers. Printer drivers translate print commands sent to a computer into the print language understood by a particular printer. Because printers vary in their capabilities and print language, separate printer drivers might be needed for each printer installed on a computer.
Print job	Any document sent to a printer. Print jobs are assigned both a unique job ID and a priority (0–99). Higher-priority jobs are printed before lower-priority jobs.
Print queue	The collection of print jobs waiting to be printed by a specified printer.
Printer port	The interface through which the logical printer communicates with the physical printer. For physical printers directly attached to computers, the port will typically be a parallel port such as LPT1 or a Universal Serial Bus (USB) port. For printers directly attached to the network (that is, using their own network adapter), the port will typically be a TCP/IP port. Printers can be attached directly to a print server using a local printer port. However, local ports such as LPT1 are much slower than TCP/IP printer ports.
Print spooler	Software that accepts a document sent to a printer and then stores it on disk or in memory until the printer is ready for it. The spooler receives, processes, schedules, and distributes documents for printing. In Windows 2000, spooling is carried out by the Print Spooler service (usually called the *print service*). If this service is stopped, you cannot print until the service has restarted.

Monitoring Printers, Print Queues, and Print Jobs

Monitoring is an important part of print management: It allows you to be notified of problems as soon as they occur and enables you to spot potential problems *before* they occur (for example, noticing that one printer is receiving all the print jobs while other printers sit idle).

In addition to the administrative benefits, monitoring also helps minimize disruptions for users. With an effective monitoring strategy, printing problems (such as paper jams and low toner) can often be identified and corrected before they have an adverse effect on users. Monitoring enables you to better distribute print resources, ensuring that some printers do not sit idle while others are unable to keep up with the printing demands made on them.

Monitoring can even be important for economic reasons. If invoices cannot be printed, customers cannot be billed and revenue cannot be collected. If proposals cannot be printed, deadlines might be missed and job opportunities lost. Because printed documents are a crucial component in day-to-day business transactions, it is important for administrators to ensure that printers are available and that those printers are being used appropriately.

In Windows 2000, several WMI classes, such as Win32_Printer and Win32_PrintJob, can be used to monitor various aspects of the printing infrastructure.

Monitoring Printers

Even the most mechanically sound printer stops working or needs maintenance from time to time: Printers run low on toner, run out of paper, or get jammed — unavoidable situations that prevent users from printing their documents.

Unfortunately, when a printer stops working, no notice is sent to users; in addition, users can still send print jobs to the printer. If the problem is not identified and corrected, those jobs will continue to accumulate as long as the printer is unavailable.

For these reasons, monitoring the printers in your organization is an important part of print management. With a well-designed monitoring strategy in place, you can receive timely notification whenever a printer stops functioning and take immediate steps to either get the printer back online or transfer print jobs to a different printer.

Printer status can be monitored by using the Win32_Printer class. A number of the Win32_Printer class properties relevant to status monitoring are shown in Table 13.2.

 Note

Not all printers support each of the properties listed in Table 13.2. If a printer does not support a particular property, the value Null will be returned as the value of that property.

Table 13.2 Win32_Printer Properties

Property	Description
Availability	Availability and status of the printer. Values are returned as integers and indicate the following conditions: 1 – Other 2 – Unknown 3 – Running/Full Power 4 – Warning 5 – In Test 6 – Not Applicable 7 – Power Off 8 – Offline 9 – Off Duty 10 – Degraded 11 – Not Installed 12 – Install Error 13 – Power Save-Unknown 14 – Power Save-Low Power Mode 15 – Power Save-Standby 16 – Power Cycle 17 – Power Save-Warning
Description	Description of the printer.
Location	Physical location of the printer.
Name	Label by which the printer is known.
PrinterStatus	Status information for a printer beyond that specified in the Availability property. Values are returned as numbers and indicate conditions as follows: 1 – Other. This value usually indicates that an error has occurred and that the print device has stopped printing. 2 – Unknown 3 – Idle 4 – Printing 5 – Warming up
ServerName	Name of the server that controls the printer.

Monitoring Printer Status

The best way to minimize the impact of a printer that is no longer working or accessible is to identify the problem and restore the printer functionality as quickly as possible. Even if this functionality cannot be restored (for example, the printer might have experienced a hardware problem that you are unable to repair), it is still important that printer problems be identified as quickly as possible; at the very least, this allows you to notify users that they should reroute their documents and not print anything to the "broken" printer.

You can use the Win32_Printer class to retrieve a status report for all the printers managed by a given print server.

Scripting Steps

Listing 13.2 contains a script that monitors the status of all the printers on a computer. To carry out this task, the script must perform the following steps:

1. Create a variable to specify the computer name.

2. Use a GetObject call to connect to the WMI namespace root\cimv2, and set the impersonation level to "impersonate."

3. Use the ExecQuery method to query the Win32_Printer class.

   This query returns a collection consisting of all the printers installed on the computer.

4. For each printer in the collection, echo values such as printer share name, printer location, and the current printer status.

   Because printer status is returned as an integer, a series of Select Case statements is used to convert the integer to a recognizable text string. For example, if PrinterStatus is 4, the value "Printing" is echoed to the screen.

Listing 13.2   Monitoring the Status of All the Printers on a Computer

```
1   strComputer = "."
2   Set objWMIService = GetObject("winmgmts:" _
3       & "{impersonationLevel=impersonate}!\\" & strComputer & "\root\cimv2")
4   Set colInstalledPrinters =  objWMIService.ExecQuery _
5       ("SELECT * FROM Win32_Printer")
6   For Each objPrinter in colInstalledPrinters
7       Wscript.Echo "Name: " & objPrinter.Name
8       Wscript.Echo "Location: " & objPrinter.Location
9       Select Case objPrinter.PrinterStatus
10          Case 1
11              strPrinterStatus = "Other"
12          Case 2
13              strPrinterStatus = "Unknown"
14          Case 3
15              strPrinterStatus = "Idle"
16          Case 4
17              strPrinterStatus = "Printing"
18          Case 5
19              strPrinterStatus = "Warmup"
20      End Select
21      Wscript.Echo   "Printer Status: " & strPrinterStatus
22      Wscript.Echo   "Server Name: " & objPrinter.ServerName
23      Wscript.Echo   "Share Name: " & objPrinter.ShareName
24      Wscript.Echo
25  Next
```

Monitoring Printer Status in Real Time

The script shown in Listing 13.2 is probably best run as a scheduled task; otherwise, it will simply run once and then stop; it will not display the most current status unless you manually rerun it. By scheduling the script to run on a periodic basis (for example, every 15–20 minutes), you will be able to routinely view the current printer status in a command window. After you have viewed these results, you can close the command window and wait for the script to run again.

This script is less useful, however, if you want to have a real-time display of printer status, with a single window that periodically updates itself and shows the current printer status. This is due in large part to limitations on displaying output within a command window. Because there is no way to clear the command window programmatically, you cannot simply replace an old data set with a new data set. Instead, any updated printer status must be appended to the bottom of the old data set, resulting in a confusing display, particularly for print servers that manage scores of printers.

If you prefer to have a real-time display of printer status, you can display status information in a Web page rather than in a command window. There are several advantages to displaying results in a Web page:

- It is easy to print or save the results: Simply use the Save or Print function built into your Web browser. The command window does not provide such a straightforward method for saving or printing data.

- It is possible to create formatted output that provides visual cues regarding printer status. For example, you might use a green icon for a running printer and a red icon for a stopped printer. Formatting of this kind is impossible inside a command window.

- It is easy to update the results. At the end of five minutes, the script can erase the previous status information and write the update status information in its place.

You can create a Web page to display printer status by combining WMI methods and VBScript functions with HTML tags. The best way to do this is by creating a Hypertext Application (HTA), a Web page saved with the .HTA file name extension rather than the more standard .HTM file name extension.

Although functionally equivalent to a Web page, HTAs are not bound by the tight security restrictions imposed by Microsoft® Internet Explorer. For example, if you attempt to run a WMI query from a standard .HTM Web page, you will receive a message informing you that WMI has not been marked as "safe for scripting" and asking whether you want to proceed. You can avoid this message and run the query without any problem simply by changing the file name extension from .HTM to .HTA.

Scripting Steps

Listing 13.3 contains the HTML tags and script code required to display printer status in a Web page. The code shown in this listing should be typed in Notepad or another text editor and then saved with the .HTA file name extension.

To carry out its task, the HTA must perform the following steps:

1. Create a <SCRIPT> tag specifying VBScript as the scripting language.

2. Create a window_onLoad procedure.

   Code in the window_onLoad procedure will automatically run whenever the window is loaded (either through initial startup, or by clicking the browser **Refresh** button).

3. Use the setInterval method to create a timer that will update printer status every 60 seconds.

The setInterval method requires three parameters:

- **GetInfo**. The name of the procedure called by the timer.

- **60000**. Number of milliseconds between calls (60,000 milliseconds equals 60 seconds). The timer will call the GetInfo subroutine, wait 60 seconds, and then call the procedure again.

- **VBScript**. Scripting language used by the GetInfo script.

The setInterval method provides functionality similar to Wscript.Sleep: It allows the script to pause for a specified amount of time and then resume processing. This method must be used instead of Wscript.Sleep because Windows Script Host (WSH) methods cannot be called from within Internet Explorer.

4. Create a subroutine named GetInfo that retrieves the current list of installed printers and displays status information in a table.

To do this, the GetInfo subroutine must first delete the current version of the table (if one exists), re-create the table header, retrieve the list of printers, and then display the printer status in the table. It is easier to delete and re-create the table than to update individual rows within the table.

5. Create a loop that deletes all the rows in the existing table (with the Table ID of objTable).

Deleting the current table has the effect of wiping the page clean, allowing the latest status information to be displayed.

The loop works backward from the last row in the table (Rows.Length — 1) to the first row in the table (row 0). If there are three rows in the table, row 2 will be deleted first, then row 1, and then row 0.

6. Create the table header. To do this, the script must:

a. Use the InsertRow method to insert a new row in the table.

b. Use the InsertCell method to insert a new cell in the table.

c. Use the InnerText method to set the contents of the new cell to **Name**.

d. Use the same procedures to insert cells labeled **Location** and **Status**.

7. Create a variable to specify the computer name.

8. Use a GetObject call to connect to the WMI namespace root\cimv2, and set the impersonation level to "impersonate."

9. Use the ExecQuery method to query the Win32_Printer class.

This query returns a collection consisting of all the printers installed on the computer.

10. For each printer in the collection, create a new table row with three cells:

   - one cell to display the printer name
   - one cell to display the printer location
   - one cell to display the printer status

   Because printer status is returned as an integer, a Select Case statement is used to convert the value to a recognizable text string. For example, if the printer status is returned as 3, the word **Idle** will be displayed in the Web page.

11. Use a <TABLE> tag with the ID objTable; this tag indicates the location of the table on the Web page. The Border = 1 parameter is included to place a border around each cell in the table.

12. Use a <TBODY> tag with the ID objTableBody to represent the body of the table.

13. Use the </TBODY> and </TABLE> tags to mark the end of the table.

Listing 13.3 Displaying Printer Status in a Web Page

```
1   <SCRIPT LANGUAGE = "VBScript">
2   Sub window_onLoad
3       GetInfo
4       iTimerID = window.setInterval("GetInfo", 60000, "VBScript")
5   End Sub
6   Sub GetInfo
7       For i = (objTable.Rows.Length - 1) to 0 Step -1
8           myNewRow = Document.All.objTable.deleteRow(i)
9       Next
10      Set objRow = objTableBody.InsertRow()
11      objRow.Style.fontWeight = "bold"
12      Set objCell = objRow.InsertCell()
13      objCell.InnerText = "Name"
14      Set objCell = objRow.InsertCell()
15      objCell.InnerText = "Location"
16      Set objCell = objRow.InsertCell()
17      objCell.InnerText = "Status"
18      strComputer = "."
19      Set objWMIService = GetObject("winmgmts:" _
20          & "{impersonationLevel=impersonate}!\\" & _
21              strComputer & "\root\cimv2")
22      Set colPrinters =  objWMIService.ExecQuery _
23          ("SELECT * FROM Win32_Printer")
```

(continued)

Listing 13.3   Displaying Printer Status in a Web Page *(continued)*

```
24      For Each objPrinter in colPrinters
25          Set objRow = objTableBody.InsertRow()
26          Set objCell = objRow.InsertCell()
27          objCell.InnerText = objPrinter.Name
28          Set objCell = objRow.InsertCell()
29          objCell.InnerText = objPrinter.Location
30          Set objCell = objRow.InsertCell()
31          Select Case objPrinter.PrinterStatus
32              Case 1
33                  strPrinterStatus = "Other"
34              Case 2
35                  strPrinterStatus = "Unknown"
36              Case 3
37                  strPrinterStatus = "Idle"
38              Case 4
39                  strPrinterStatus = "Printing"
40              Case 5
41                  strPrinterStatus = "Warming up"
42          End Select
43          objCell.InnerText = strPrinterStatus
44      Next
45  End Sub
46  </SCRIPT>
47  <TABLE ID = "objTable" border = "1" >
48  <TBODY ID = "objTableBody">
49  </TBODY>
50  </TABLE>
```

Filtering Printer Status Displays

When carrying out routine printer monitoring, you are likely to be concerned only with printers that are experiencing problems. Because of this, you might want to write a script that displays only printers that are not functioning correctly. For example, a print server in a large organization might handle 100 or more printers. If you return the status of every printer, you might have to search through 99 printers that are working in order to identify the single printer that has stopped responding. This not only wastes a considerable amount of time, but also increases the odds that you will overlook the one printer that is not working and thus not take immediate steps to correct the problem.

One of the prime benefits of WMI is that you can fine-tune the information returned. Instead of returning a list of all 100 printers, you can create a query that returns only a list of printers that are not responding. This makes it much faster and easier to identify the printers that are in need of immediate attention.

Scripting Steps

Listing 13.4 contains a script that issues a notification when a printer stops responding. To carry out this task, the script must perform the following steps:

1. Create a variable to specify the computer name.

2. Use a GetObject call to connect to the WMI namespace root\cimv2, and set the impersonation level to "impersonate."

3. Use the ExecQuery method to query the Win32_Printer class.

   To limit data retrieval to printers that have stopped, use a Where clause to restrict the collection to printers with a printer status equal to 1 (Other) or 2 (Unknown).

4. Use the Count property to check for the number of printers in the collection.

   - If the Count is 0, that means no stopped printers were discovered. In that case, echo a message stating that all printers are functioning correctly.

   - If the Count is greater than 0, then for each printer in the collection echo the name of the printer along with the message that the printer has stopped responding.

Listing 13.4   Receiving Notification When a Printer Stops

```
1   strComputer = "."
2   Set objWMIService = GetObject("winmgmts:" _
3       & "{impersonationLevel=impersonate}!\\" & strComputer & "\root\cimv2")
4   Set colInstalledPrinters =  objWMIService.ExecQuery _
5       ("SELECT * FROM Win32_Printer WHERE PrinterStatus = 1" _
6           & "OR PrinterStatus = 2")
7   If colInstalledPrinters.Count = 0 Then
8       Wscript.Echo "All printers are functioning correctly."
9   Else
10      For Each objPrinter in colInstalledPrinters
11          Wscript.Echo "Printer " & objprinter.Name & " is not responding."
12      Next
13  End If
```

Monitoring Printer Status by Using a Temporary Event Subscription

Monitoring scripts typically check printer status, pause for a predetermined interval (for example, 10 minutes), and then check printer status again. This is done to minimize the processing power and network bandwidth required to monitor printers, and is usually based on an acceptable response time (as determined by your organization) for responding to printer problems. If your users are not severely impacted by a printer that might be out of commission for 10 minutes before support personnel are notified of the problem, then using a standard monitoring script that verifies printer status every 10 minutes is an acceptable approach.

However, for high-volume printers or for printers that print critical business documents (such as invoices), administrators might want immediate notification of any printer problem. For these printers, you can use a temporary event subscription that constantly monitors their status and immediately notifies you the moment one of these printers changes status (for example, a printer that *was* printing but is now jammed).

Scripting Steps

Listing 13.5 contains a script that monitors printer status by using a temporary event subscription. To carry out this task the script must perform the following steps:

1. Create a variable to specify the computer name.

2. Use a GetObject call to connect to the WMI namespace root\cimv2, and set the impersonation level to "impersonate."

3. Use an ExecNotificationQuery to register for notification each time there is an instance modification (that is, each time an instance within the namespace changes in some way).

   Because the script monitors only changes to printers, include a Where clause that limits data retrieval to instance modifications involving the Win32_Printer class. The additional clause (within 30) causes the script to check every 30 seconds to see whether there has been a change in status. Therefore, status changes will not last longer than 30 seconds before being reported. In theory, a printer could stop and restart in less than 30 seconds. If that happened, the instance modification would go unreported.

4. Use a loop that allows the script to run indefinitely.

   To stop monitoring, terminate the process the script is running in.

5. se the NextEvent method to retrieve the properties of each event when it occurs.

   These properties are retrieved from an event object known as the TargetInstance. Each time a printer is modified in some way, the script checks to see whether the current printer status differs from the previous printer status. If it does not, the script resumes looping. This check is performed by comparing the status property of the TargetInstance with the status property of the PreviousInstance, an event object representing the state of the printer prior to the last instance modification.

   Comparing the previous state with the current state enables you to identify whether the modification involved a change in printer status (for example, going from Idle to Printing). If the previous and current states are the same, the modification did not involve printer status but instead reflects a change to some other property of the printer (for example, a change in the printer location).

   Because printer status is returned as an integer, a pair of Select Case statements is used to convert the current status and the previous status to a more recognizable text string. For example, if the printer status is returned as 3, the word **Idle** will be displayed as part of the event notification message.

6. If the printer states differ, echo the printer name, its current state, and its previous state.

Listing 13.5   Monitoring Printer Status Using a Temporary Event Subscription

```
1   strComputer = "."
2   Set objWMIService = GetObject("winmgmts:" _
3       & "{impersonationLevel=impersonate}!\\" & strComputer & "\root\cimv2")
4   Set colPrinters = objWMIService. _
5       ExecNotificationQuery("SELECT * FROM __instancemodificationevent " _
6           & "WITHIN 30 WHERE TargetInstance ISA 'Win32_Printer'")
7   i = 0
8   Do While i = 0
9       Set objPrinter = colPrinters.NextEvent
10      If objPrinter.TargetInstance.PrinterStatus <> _
11          objPrinter.PreviousInstance.PrinterStatus Then
12          Select Case objPrinter.TargetInstance.PrinterStatus
13              Case 1 strCurrentState = "Other"
14              Case 2 strCurrentState = "Unknown"
15              Case 3 strCurrentState = "Idle"
16              Case 4 strCurrentState = "Printing"
17              Case 5 strCurrentState = "Warming Up"
18          End Select
19          Select Case objPrinter.PreviousInstance.PrinterStatus
20              Case 1 strPreviousState = "Other"
21              Case 2 strPreviousState = "Unknown"
22              Case 3 strPreviousState = "Idle"
23              Case 4 strPreviousState = "Printing"
24              Case 5 strPreviousState = "Warming Up"
25          End Select
26          Wscript.Echo objPrinter.TargetInstance.Name _
27              & " is " & strCurrentState _
28                  & ". The printer previously was " & strPreviousState & "."
29      End If
30  Loop
```

Verifying the Status of the Print Service

In Windows 2000, printing is controlled by the Print Spooler service (usually called the *print service*). If this service is stopped, printing cannot take place. Because printing requires the Print Spooler service, any attempt to diagnose printer problems should include a check to ensure that this service is still running.

Checking the status of the Print Spooler service is especially important because the error messages presented to users when a printing problem occurs can be misleading. For example, if the Print Spooler service stops on the local computer, a user attempting to print a document receives this message:

```
Before you can perform printer-related tasks such as page setup or printing a
document, you need to install a printer. Do you want to install a printer now?
```

If the user clicks **Yes**, this message is displayed:

```
Operation could not be completed.
```

Needless to say, this will leave the typical user helpless, and the problem might even be difficult for a support technician to initially diagnose and correct.

Likewise, if the Print Spooler service stops on a remote print server, a user attempting to print a document receives this cryptic message:

```
The RPC server is unavailable.
```

To programmatically check the status of the Print Spooler service, use the Win32_Service class.

Scripting Steps

Listing 13.6 contains a script that verifies the status of the print service. To carry out this task, the script must perform the following steps:

1. Create a variable to specify the computer name.

2. Use a GetObject call to connect to the WMI namespace root\cimv2, and set the impersonation level to "impersonate."

3. Use the ExecQuery method to query the Win32_Service class.

   To limit data retrieval to the print service, use a Where clause that targets only the service with the name Spooler.

4. For each service in the collection, echo the service name and the current service status.

Listing 13.6   Verifying the Status of the Print Service

```
1   strComputer = "."
2   Set objWMIService = GetObject("winmgmts:" _
3       & "{impersonationLevel=impersonate}!\\" & strComputer & "\root\cimv2")
4   Set colRunningServices = objWMIService.ExecQuery _
5       ("SELECT * FROM Win32_Service WHERE Name = 'Spooler'")
6   For Each objService in colRunningServices
7       Wscript.Echo objService.DisplayName & ": " & objService.State
8   Next
```

This script only returns the status of the Print Spooler service. In a production script, you might first check the status of the Print Spooler service and then attempt to restart the service if it has stopped. If the script is unable to restart the service, an administrative alert of some kind can then be issued. For more information about starting services by using WMI, see "Services" in this book.

Monitoring Printer Workloads

It is as important to monitor the workloads on print servers as it is to simply ensure that these print servers are running. By monitoring individual print queues, you can gain a better understanding of how the printing load is being distributed among your printers. In turn, this allows you to make better decisions regarding the distribution of printing resources. For example, if you know that a printer in one department is being underutilized, you might transfer that device to a department where the only printer is experiencing an extremely heavy workload.

Printer workloads are monitored by checking individual print queues for such things as:

- Number of print jobs in the queue.

- Size of the print jobs in the queue.

- Amount of time print jobs spend in the queue before being printed.

These items can be monitored by using WMI and the Win32_PrintJob class.

Reporting Print Queue Statistics

Monitoring the number of jobs in a print queue can provide a rough estimate of the printer workload. However, the number of jobs in a print queue can be misleading. For example, a single document of 250 pages ties up a printer longer than 100 single-page documents. Likewise, a pair of 10-page documents filled with intricate graphics might take longer to print than that same 250-page, all-text print job.

Unless your users tend to print the same type of document over and over (for example, an all-text document no more than a few pages long), you might need to use a more precise metric when monitoring print queues. In a situation such as that, you can use the Win32_PrintJob class to tally not only the number of jobs in the queue but also the number of pages scheduled to be printed or the total number of bytes still in the queue.

Neither the total number of pages to be printed nor the total number of bytes in the queue is provided as a Win32_PrintJob property. Instead, you must retrieve the number of pages and number of bytes for each print job and then add these values to determine the total number of pages and total number of bytes to be printed. This provides more comprehensive data than merely reporting the number of jobs in a queue. For example, the script can also calculate such values as the largest print job in the queue and the average number of pages per print job.

Scripting Steps

Listing 13.7 contains a script that reports cumulative print queue statistics for a specific print server. To carry out this task, the script must perform the following steps:

1. Create a variable to specify the computer name.

2. Use a GetObject call to connect to the WMI namespace root\cimv2, and set the impersonation level to "impersonate."

3. Use the ExecQuery method to query the Win32_PrintJob class.

   This query returns a collection consisting of all the print jobs on the computer.

4. For each print job in the collection, do the following:

   a. Increment the total number of print jobs (intTotalJobs) by 1. Print jobs are incremented in this fashion to illustrate how calculations can be performed within a script. However, you can also use the WMI Count property to report the number of print jobs in the collection.

   b. Add the number of pages in the print job to the total number of pages for all the active print jobs (intTotalPages).

   c. If the total number of pages in the print job is greater than the value intMaxPrintJob, replace the value of intMaxPrintJob with the number of pages in the current print job. The variable intMaxPrintJob will thus store the size of the largest print job in the queue (based on page count).

5. Echo the values for total print jobs, total number of pages for the print jobs in the print queues, and the largest print job in the queue.

Listing 13.7 Reporting Print Queue Statistics

```
1   strComputer = "."
2   Set objWMIService = GetObject("winmgmts:" _
3       & "{impersonationLevel=impersonate}!\\" & strComputer & "\root\cimv2")
4   Set colPrintJobs = objWMIService.ExecQuery _
5       ("SELECT * FROM Win32_PrintJob")
6   For Each objPrintJob in colPrintJobs
7       intTotalJobs = intTotalJobs + 1
8       intTotalPages = intTotalPages + objPrintJob.TotalPages
9       If objPrintJob.TotalPages > intMaxPrintJob Then
10          intMaxPrintJob = objPrintJob.TotalPages
11      End If
12  Next
13  Wscript.Echo "Total print jobs in queue: " & intTotalJobs
14  Wscript.Echo "Total pages in queue: " & intTotalPages
15  Wscript.Echo "Largest print job in queue: " & intMaxPrintJob
```

Note

The TotalPages property does not always reflect the number of pages to be printed. Most software applications (including the Microsoft® Office applications) correctly report the number of pages to be printed. However, some applications do not. For example, Notepad always reports a document as being a single page in length, regardless of the actual number of printed pages that will result from printing that document. If your organization uses software that does not correctly report total pages, you might want to measure the size of the print jobs instead.

Monitoring Print Jobs

In general, monitoring is limited to printers and print queues; as an administrator, your primary concerns are that printers remain available and that print queues are up and running. Sometimes, however, it is useful to monitor each print job sent to a printer. This kind of monitoring can catch conditions such as:

- Documents that get stuck in a print queue — that is, documents that for some reason do not get printed, even though other documents in the queue do get printed.

- Large documents that monopolize printer time. Depending on the size, a single document can delay the printing of scores of other documents.

- Workload that is inequitably distributed among printers. For example, Printer A might print 100 documents each hour, while Printers B and C, with the same capabilities and located in the same room, print only 5 or 10 documents an hour.

Print jobs can be monitored using the Win32_PrintJob class. Some of the Win32_PrintJob properties useful in monitoring print jobs are shown in Table 13.3.

Table 13.3   Win32_PrintJob Properties for Monitoring Print Jobs

Property	Description
Caption	Short description of the printer. Typically, the caption is the name of the printer followed by the print job ID. For example: `printer1, 171`
Document	Name of the print job; equivalent to the file name of the document being printed. The user sees this name when viewing the set of documents in a print queue.
HostPrintQueue	Name of the computer on which the print job was created.
JobId	Identifier assigned to the print job.
JobStatus	String representing the job's status. Common status values include: **Printing** **Error** **Degraded** — Indicates that a print job is paused.
Notify	User to be notified upon job completion or failure.
Owner	User that submitted the job.
PagesPrinted	Number of pages that have been printed. This value might be 0 if the print job does not contain page-delimiting information.
Priority	Urgency or importance of execution of a job, with a range of 0 to 99. Higher-priority jobs are printed before lower-priority jobs.
Size	Size of the print job (in bytes).

(continued)

Table 13.3   Win32_PrintJob Properties for Monitoring Print Jobs *(continued)*

Property	Description
StatusMask	Bitmap of the possible status conditions relating to this print job. Values include the following: 1 — Paused 2 — Error 3 — Deleting 4 — Spooling 5 — Printing 6 — Offline 7 — Paperout 8 — Printed 9 — Deleted 10 — Blocked_DevQ 11 — User_Intervention_Req 12 — Restart For more information about working with bitmap values, see "Script Runtime Primer" in this book.
TimeSubmitted	Time that the job was submitted.
TotalPages	Number of pages in the job. This value might be 0 if the print job does not contain page-delimiting information.
UntilTime	Time after which the job is invalid or should be stopped. For example, you can specify that if the document is not printed by 5:00 P.M., it should not be printed at all.

A comparison of Win32_PrintJob properties and the print job properties seen in the GUI is shown in Figure 13.1.

Figure 13.1   Win32_PrintJob Properties

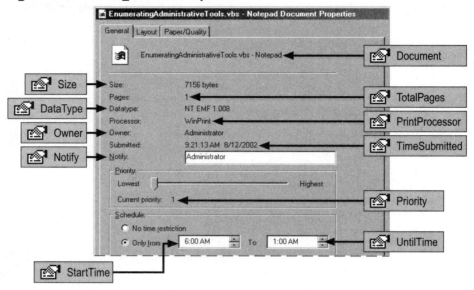

In addition to the Win32_PrintJob class, the IADsPrintJob interface can be used to monitor print jobs. Properties available through the IADsPrintJob interface are shown in Table 13.4. Many of these properties can be configured by using scripts; those that cannot be are denoted as read-only.

Table 13.4   IADsPrintJob Properties

Property	Description
Description	Name of the document and the application used to print that document. For example, the description for the document Budget.xls printed using Excel would be "Budget — Excel".
HostPrintQueue (read-only)	ADsPath of the print queue (for example, WinNT:// atl-ps-01/ArtDepartmentPrinter).
Notify	Logon name of the user to be notified when the print job has finished printing.
Priority	Priority assigned to the print job, ranging from 1–99. Print jobs with higher priorities are printed before those with lower priorities.
Size (read-only)	Size of the print job, in bytes.
StartTime	Earliest time when the print job can begin printing.

(continued)

Table 13.4 IADsPrintJob Properties *(continued)*

Property	Description
TimeSubmitted (read-only)	Date and time that the print job was submitted.
TotalPages (read-only)	Total number of pages in the print job.
UntilTime	Latest time that the print job can be printed.
User (read-only)	Logon name of the user who submitted the print job.

Monitoring Print Job Status

Monitoring individual print jobs allows you to retrieve detailed information about each print job on a print server. In turn, this information allows you to:

- Verify that documents are moving through the print queue at the expected rate.

- Identify unusually large documents that might monopolize the printer.

- Identify users who print an excessive number of documents.

- Assist users with printing problems.

  For example, a user might call the Help desk complaining that a document has not been printed. By examining the print job status, a technician might notice that the document has been paused or that it has a low priority compared with other documents in the queue. In the latter case, this means that the document will not be printed until all the higher-priority jobs have completed.

You can use the Win32_PrintJob class to retrieve detailed information about every print job on a print server.

Scripting Steps

Listing 13.8 contains a script that monitors print job status. To carry out this task, the script must perform the following steps:

1. Create a variable to specify the computer name.

2. Use a GetObject call to connect to the WMI namespace root\cimv2, and set the impersonation level to "impersonate."

3. Use the ExecQuery method to query the Win32_PrintJob class.

   This query returns a collection consisting of all the print jobs on the computer.

4. Echo the column headers Print Queue, Job ID, Owner, and Total Pages.

5. For each print job in the collection, echo the name of the printer where the job is queued, the job ID number, the person who submitted the print job, and the total number of pages in the print job.

The Name property is a combination of the name of the printer where the job is queued and the ID number assigned to the print job. For example, a print job assigned ID number 522 on the printer ColorPrinter would have the following name:

```
ColorPrinter, 522
```

The VBScript Split function is used to split the printer name and the print job ID into an array. In this script, the Split function uses the following parameters:

- **objPrintJob.Name** — Print job name (for example, ColorPrinter, 522). This is the value being split into the array.

- **,** — Delimiter used to separate fields in the string.

- **−1** — Indicates that all substrings of the array should be returned.

- **1** — Indicates that a text comparison should be performed. To perform a binary comparison, enter 0 as the parameter.

When the Split function is called, the print job name will be split into an array with two elements: Element 0 will contain the name of the printer, and element 1 will contain the job ID. To reference the printer name, simply specify element 0 in the array. For example:

```
Wscript.Echo strPrinter(0)
```

Listing 13.8   Monitoring Print Job Status

```
1   strComputer = "."
2   Set objWMIService = GetObject("winmgmts:" _
3       & "{impersonationLevel=impersonate}!\\" & strComputer & "\root\cimv2")
4   Set colPrintJobs =  objWMIService.ExecQuery _
5       ("SELECT * FROM Win32_PrintJob")
6   Wscript.Echo "Print Queue, Job ID, Owner, Total Pages"
7   For Each objPrintJob in colPrintJobs
8       strPrinter = Split(objPrintJob.Name,",",-1,1)
9       Wscript.Echo strPrinter(0) & ", " & _
10          objPrintJob.JobID & ", " &  objPrintJob.Owner & ", " _
11              & objPrintJob.TotalPages
12  Next
```

Monitoring the Time Print Jobs Spend in a Print Queue

One way to measure how well the workload is distributed among your printers is to track the amount of time documents spend in the print queue. Users can generally expect to receive their printed output within minutes after submitting a print job. If they do not, this could be the result of a single large job monopolizing the printer or of an extremely large print queue.

To help ensure that print jobs are being printed at the expected rate, you can periodically check to see whether any documents have been in the queue longer than a baseline rate established for a particular printer. For example, you might determine that all documents sent to printer A should be printed no later than 15 minutes after they have been submitted. If documents take longer than that to print, then:

- Users might be printing too many documents to the printer.

- Users might be printing large documents not intended for that printer.

- The printer might be experiencing problems.

To determine the amount of time a print job has been in the print queue, use the IADsPrintJob property TimeSubmitted. This property indicates the time the print job was sent to the printer. You can subtract the submitted time from the current time to determine how long a document has been in the print queue.

Scripting Steps

Listing 13.9 contains a script that lists print jobs that have spent 15 minutes or more in the print queue. To carry out this task, the script must perform the following steps:

1. Use a GetObject call to bind to the printer ArtDepartmentPrinter on the print server atl-ps-01.

2. Use the PrintJobs method to assign a value to the variable colPrintJobs.

   This variable will now contain a collection consisting of all the print jobs in the ArtDepartmentPrinter print queue.

3. For each print job in the collection, use the DateDiff function to determine the number of minutes that the job has been in the print queue and assign this value to the variable dtmTimeInQueue.

   The DateDiff function requires the following three parameters:

   - **"n"** — Used by DateDiff to indicate that the time differential should be returned in minutes.

   - **objPrintJob.TimeSubmitted** — Date and time that the print job was submitted.

   - **Now** — Current date and time. The difference between the current date and time and the time the print job was submitted represents the amount of time that the job has been in the print queue.

4. If dtmTimeInQueue is greater than 15, echo a message indicating the name of the document being printed and the number of minutes that this document has been in the print queue.

Listing 13.9   Monitoring the Time Print Jobs Spend in a Print Queue

```
1   Set objPrinter = GetObject("WinNT://atl-ps-01/ArtDepartmentPrinter")
2   Set colPrintJobs = objPrinter.PrintJobs
3   For Each objPrintJob in colPrintJobs
4       dtmTimeInQueue = DateDiff("n", objPrintJob.TimeSubmitted, Now)
5       If dtmTimeInQueue > 15 Then
6           Wscript.Echo objPrintJob.Description, dtmTimeInQueue
7       End If
8   Next
```

Managing Printer Operations, Print Queues, and Print Jobs

For the most part, print management is a hands-off activity. Other than routine maintenance, such as adding paper and replacing toner cartridges, not much management work is usually required. From time to time, however, you do have to carry out tasks such as:

- Taking inventory of your printers and their capabilities.
- Pausing and resuming printers to do routine maintenance.
- Pausing and resuming individual print jobs.

You can use a combination of WMI and ADSI scripting to help you manage printers, print queues, and print jobs across the enterprise.

Managing Printer Operations

Like most management activities, print management requires a detailed understanding of the capabilities of each element in the infrastructure. As an administrator, you must ensure that users have access to printers, and to the right kind of printers. Graphic artists, for example, have very different printing needs than word processor operators. Users who prepare large monthly reports likely require a much faster printer than users who occasionally print a memo or two.

When planning the distribution of print resources to meet these needs, you must take into account the capabilities of those resources. For example, printers that cannot collate and staple documents should not be placed in locations where collating and stapling are required.

You can use two WMI classes, Win32_Printer and Win32_PrinterConfiguration, to return information about all the printers installed on a given print server. This information includes the subset of Win32_Printer properties shown in Table 13.5.

Table 13.5   Win32_Printer Properties

Property	Description
Capabilities	Array of printer capabilities. Values include the following: 0 – Unknown 1 – Other 2 – Color Printing 3 – Duplex Printing 4 – Copies 5 – Collation 6 – Stapling 7 – Transparency Printing 8 – Punch 9 – Cover 10 – Bind 11 – Black and White Printing 12 – One Sided 13 – Two Sided Long Edge 14 – Two Sided Short Edge 15 – Portrait 16 – Landscape 17 – Reverse Portrait 18 – Reverse Landscape 19 – Quality High 20 – Quality Normal 21 – Quality Low
CapabilityDescriptions	Array of free-form strings providing more detailed explanations for any of the printer features indicated in the Capabilities array. Each entry in this array is related to the entry in the Capabilities array that is located at the same index.
Description	Description of the printer.
DeviceID	Unique identifier of the printer, used to distinguish it from other devices on the system.
DriverName	Name of the printer driver.
Location	Physical location of the printer.

(continued)

Table 13.5   Win32_Printer Properties *(continued)*

Property	Description
Name	Label by which the printer is known.
PortName	Port that can be used to transmit data to the printer. If a printer is connected to more than one port, the names of the ports are separated by commas.
SeparatorFile	Name of the file used to create a separator page.
ServerName	Name of the server that controls the printer.
ShareName	Share name of the printer.
StartTime	Earliest date and time the printer can print a job (if the printer has been configured to print only at certain times). This value is expressed as time elapsed since 12:00 A.M. GMT (Greenwich mean time).
TimeOfLastReset	Date and time this printer was last reset.
UntilTime	Latest date and time the printer can print a job (if the printer has been limited to print only at certain times). This value is expressed as time elapsed since 12:00 A.M. GMT (Greenwich mean time).

Additional properties available through the Win32_PrinterConfiguration class are listed in Table 13.6. Many of these properties represent the default values that are assigned to all print jobs sent to the printer. For example, if the Copies property is set to 2, by default the printer will print two copies of each print job. Users can override these default values by changing the appropriate options in the **Print** dialog box each time they print a document.

Table 13.6   Win32_PrinterConfiguration Properties

Property	Description
Collate	Boolean value indicating whether the pages that are printed should be collated. This property is ignored if the printer driver does not support collation.
Color	Method used by a color printer to print a black-and-white document. Some color printers have the capability to print using true black instead of a combination of cyan, magenta, and yellow (CMY). This usually creates darker and sharper text for documents. This option is useful only for color printers that support true black printing. Values include the following: 1 — Monochrome (true black) 2 — Color (CMY)
Copies	Number of copies to be printed.
DeviceName	Friendly name of the printer.

(continued)

Table 13.6 Win32_PrinterConfiguration Properties *(continued)*

Property	Description
DriverVersion	Version number of the printer driver. Version numbers are created and maintained by the driver manufacturer.
Duplex	Boolean value indicating whether printing is done on both sides (True) or only one side of the medium (False).
HorizontalResolution	Print resolution in dots per inch for the width of the print job. This value is set only when the PrintQuality property is positive.
Name	Name of the printer.
Orientation	Printing orientation of the paper. Values include the following: 1 – Portrait 2 – Landscape
PaperLength	Length of the paper (in tenths of a millimeter). To determine the size of the paper in inches, divide this value by 254.
PaperSize	Size of the paper.
PaperWidth	Width of the paper (in tenths of a millimeter). To determine the size of the paper in inches, divide this value by 254.
PrintQuality	One of four quality levels of the print job. If a positive value is specified, the quality is measured in dots per inch. Values include the following: 1 – Draft 2 – Low 3 – Medium 4 – High
Scale	Factor by which the printed output is to be scaled. For example, a scale of 75 reduces the print output to 3/4 its original height and width.
SpecificationVersion	Version number of the initialization data for the device associated with the printer.
TTOption	Indicates the manner in which TrueType fonts should be printed. Values include the following: 1–Bitmap – Prints TrueType fonts as graphics. This is the default action for dot-matrix printers. 2–Download – Downloads TrueType fonts as soft fonts. This is the default action for printers that use the Printer Control Language (PCL). 3–Substitute – Substitutes device fonts for TrueType fonts. This is the default action for PostScript printers.
VerticalResolution	Print resolution for the height of the print job. This value is set only when the PrintQuality property is positive.

The IADsPrintQueue interface can also return information about a printer. Selected properties, all of which are read/write, available through this interface are shown in Table 13.7.

Table 13.7   IADsPrintQueue Properties

Property	Description
BannerPage	Local path to the page used to separate print jobs. If this value is Null, a separator page is not used for this printer.
Description	Description of the printer. This description is available to anyone accessing the printer over the network.
Location	Physical location of the printer.
Model	Model name of the printer (for example, HP LaserJet 6).
Priority	Priority assigned to the printer (and to print jobs).
StartTime	Earliest time that the printer can begin printing documents.
UntilTime	Latest time that the printer can continue printing documents.

Enumerating Printers and Print Capabilities

Before you can determine how to best distribute and use your printing resources, you must have a detailed knowledge of those resources. For example, Department A might have only three printers compared with five printers in Department B. However, if the printers in Department A can print 20 pages per minute and the printers in Department B can print only 5 pages per minute, users in Department A actually have more printing capacity. Without knowing the detailed capabilities of these printers, you might erroneously conclude that Department A is short on printing capacity and thus purchase additional printers that end up going unused.

WMI includes two classes, Win32_Printer and Win32_PrinterConfiguration, which can be used to return detailed information about all the printers installed on a computer.

Scripting Steps

Listing 13.10 contains a script that retrieves printer information. To carry out this task, the script must perform the following steps:

1. Create a variable to specify the computer name.

2. Use a GetObject call to connect to the WMI namespace root\cimv2, and set the impersonation level to "impersonate."

3. Use the ExecQuery method to query the Win32_PrinterConfiguration class.

    This query returns a collection consisting of configuration information for all the printers installed on the computer.

4. For each printer in the collection, echo the specified properties.

Many of these property values are returned as integers or as other values that might be difficult to interpret. Because of this, the script converts the following property values to recognizable values:

- **Orientation.** If the value 1 is returned, the orientation is Portrait mode. Otherwise, the orientation is Landscape mode.

- **Paper length.** Paper length is returned in tenths of a millimeter. To convert the value to inches, divide the length by 254. For example, if the value 2,794 is returned, the length is divided by 254, converting 2,794 tenths of a millimeter to 11 inches.

- **Paper width.** Paper width is returned in tenths of a millimeter. To convert the value to inches, divide the width by 254. For example, if the value 2,159 is returned, width length is divided by 254, converting 2,159 tenths of a millimeter to 8.5 inches.

- **TrueType option.** If the value is 1, the string "Print TrueType fonts as graphics" is echoed. If the value is 2, the string "Download TrueType fonts as soft fonts" is echoed. If the value is anything other than 1 or 2, the string "Substitute device fonts for TrueType fonts" is echoed.

Listing 13.10 Enumerating Printers and Printer Capabilities

```
1   strComputer = "."
2   Set objWMIService = GetObject("winmgmts:" _
3       & "{impersonationLevel=impersonate}!\\" & strComputer & "\root\cimv2")
4   Set colInstalledPrinters =  objWMIService.ExecQuery _
5       ("SELECT * FROM Win32_PrinterConfiguration")
6   For Each objPrinter in colInstalledPrinters
7       Wscript.Echo "Name: " & objPrinter.Name
8       Wscript.Echo "Collate: " & objPrinter.Collate
9       Wscript.Echo "Copies: " & objPrinter.Copies
10      Wscript.Echo "Driver Version: " & objPrinter.DriverVersion
11      Wscript.Echo "Duplex: " & objPrinter.Duplex
12      Wscript.Echo "Horizontal Resolution: " & _
13          objPrinter.HorizontalResolution
14      If objPrinter.Orientation = 1 Then
15          strOrientation =  "Portrait"
16      Else
17          strOrientation = "Landscape"
18      End If
19      Wscript.Echo "Orientation : " & strOrientation
20      Wscript.Echo "Paper Length: " & objPrinter.PaperLength / 254
21      Wscript.Echo "Paper Width: " & objPrinter.PaperWidth / 254
22      Wscript.Echo "Print Quality: " & objPrinter.PrintQuality
23      Wscript.Echo "Scale: " & objPrinter.Scale
```

(continued)

Listing 13.10   Enumerating Printers and Printer Capabilities *(continued)*

```
24      Wscript.Echo "Specification Version: " & _
25          objPrinter.SpecificationVersion
26      If objPrinter.TTOption = 1 Then
27          strTTOption = "Print TrueType fonts as graphics."
28      ElseIf objPrinter.TTOption = 2 Then
29          strTTOption = "Download TrueType fonts as soft fonts."
30      Else
31          strTTOption = "Substitute device fonts for TrueType fonts."
32      End If
33      Wscript.Echo "True Type Option: " & strTTOption
34      Wscript.Echo "Vertical Resolution: " & objPrinter.VerticalResolution
35  Next
```

Pausing Printers

Physical printers and logical printers are not irrevocably tied to one another. If you turn off the physical printer, this will not affect the logical printer in any way. Instead, the logical printer will still appear to be functioning, even though the physical printer is no longer available.

Among other things, this means that anytime a physical printer is removed from the network (for example, to undergo routine maintenance), the logical printer representing that device should be paused. If the physical printer is removed from the network and the logical printer is not paused, the print server will periodically attempt to print the first job in the print queue, even though the printer is no longer available. As a result, the print server uses up processing power in an attempt to complete a task that cannot be completed. When the logical printer is paused, print jobs simply remain in the queue, and no attempt is made to print them until the logical printer is resumed.

Logical printers can be paused by using the Pause method of the IADsPrintQueueOperations interface.

Scripting Steps

Listing 13.11 contains a script that pauses a printer. To carry out this task, the script must perform the following steps:

1. Use a GetObject call to bind to the printer ArtDepartmentPrinter on the print server atl-ps-01.

2. Use the Pause method to pause the printer.

Listing 13.11   Pausing a Single Printer

```
1   Set objPrinter = GetObject("WinNT://atl-ps-01/ArtDepartmentPrinter")
2   objPrinter.Pause
```

Resuming Printers

After a printer has been paused, it must be resumed. This is because the paused state is a property of the logical printer and is controlled by the print server. You cannot resume a logical printer simply by turning the physical printer on and off.

Instead, printers must be resumed manually by using the Printers control panel or programmatically by using the Resume method of the IADsPrintQueueOperations interface. Until a printer has been resumed, no documents can be printed using that printer. Users will be able to submit print jobs, but those jobs will remain in the queue until the printer has been resumed.

Scripting Steps

Listing 13.12 contains a script that resumes a printer. To carry out this task, the script must perform the following steps:

1. Use a GetObject call to bind to the printer ArtDepartmentPrinter on the print server atl-ps-01.

2. Use the resume method to resume printing.

Listing 13.12   Resuming a Printer

```
1  Set objPrinter = GetObject("WinNT://atl-ps-01/ArtDepartmentPrinter")
2  objPrinter.Resume
```

Managing Print Queues

Print queues are nothing more than the documents waiting to be printed by a specified printer. Although print queues require little management activity other than routine monitoring, sometimes a printer breaks down or becomes inaccessible while there are documents in its print queue. When this occurs, documents remain in the print queue until the physical printer is restored to the network. This can create problems for the users who submitted the print jobs: The print queue will still show their documents as being in line to be printed, even though it might be days before the printer is restored to the network.

In these cases, you might need to delete all the documents from the print queue, a process typically referred to as *purging* the print queue. (If you do this, you might also want to notify users that their documents have been deleted and must be reprinted.)

Purging Print Queues

Purging a print queue provides a fast and easy way to remove all the print jobs from a specified print queue.

For example, if you need to remove a printer from the network, you can purge the print queue and thus delete all the existing print jobs. If you do not, users will assume their documents are still in line to be printed because they will still see them in the print queue. This is because the existence of a logical printer is not dependent on the availability of a physical printer: Removing the physical printer will not also remove the logical printer. Because the logical printer still exists, the print queue, and any documents in it, continue to exist as well.

The IADsPrintQueueOperations interface includes a method, Purge, that can be used to purge print jobs on a printer or group of printers.

Scripting Steps

Listing 13.13 contains a script that purges a print queue. To carry out this task, the script must perform the following steps:

1. Use a GetObject call to bind to the printer ArtDepartmentPrinter on the print server atl-ps-01.

2. Use the Purge method to delete all the documents in the print queue.

Listing 13.13   Purging a Print Queue

```
1  Set objPrinter = GetObject("WinNT://atl-ps-01/ArtDepartmentPrinter")
2  objPrinter.Purge
```

Managing Print Jobs

There might be times when you need to pause a print job after it has been sent to a printer. For example, a user might accidentally click the Print button and send a 300-page job to the printer that he or she does not want to be printed at the moment. You might allow such large print jobs but prefer that documents like this be printed when there is less demand for the printer and fewer users will be inconvenienced by waiting for the job to finish. In this case, you might want to monitor the print queue and then temporarily pause the printing of any large documents.

The IADsPrintJob interface includes two methods, Pause and Resume, that enable you to manage the printing of individual documents within a print queue.

Pausing Print Jobs

On occasion, you might need to pause a print job or set of print jobs and then resume printing those documents later. For example, if you have one document that needs to be printed immediately, you can pause all the other print jobs on a printer. As soon as that document begins to print, you can resume the paused print jobs.

Alternatively, you might have a very large document that takes a long time to print. In that case, you can pause the large document and wait until the print queue is empty before printing it.

In practice, you can pause only print jobs that are waiting in the queue. Although you can pause the document currently being printed, this usually has no practical benefit. Except for extremely large documents, the entire print job is sent to the printer buffer. Because the printer continues printing until the buffer is empty, the pause command might have no effect. If the entire print job is in the buffer, the entire print job will print. If you pause all the print jobs in the queue, those jobs will not print. However, any new documents sent to the printer will print as expected.

You can pause print jobs by using the Pause method of the IADsPrintJobOperations interface.

Note

The Pause method is best used for pausing only those documents in the queue that meet a specified condition. If you want to pause all the print jobs on a specific printer, you can pause the printer rather than pausing each individual print job. For more information, see "Pausing Printers" earlier in this chapter.

Scripting Steps

Listing 13.14 contains a script that pauses all the print jobs in a print queue that are over 400,000 bytes in size. To carry out this task, the script must perform the following steps:

1. Use a GetObject call to bind to the printer ArtDepartmentPrinter on the print server atl-ps-01.

2. Use the PrintJobs method to set the value of the variable colPrintJobs.

    This variable will now contain a collection consisting of all the print jobs in the ArtDepartmentPrinter print queue.

3. For each print job in the collection, check to see whether the size of the document being printed is greater than 400,000 bytes.

4. For each print job larger than 400,000 bytes, use the Pause method to pause the job.

Listing 13.14   Pausing Print Jobs

```
1  Set objPrinter = GetObject("WinNT://atl-ps-01/ArtDepartmentPrinter")
2  Set colPrintJobs = objPrinter.PrintJobs
3  For Each objPrintJob in colPrintJobs
4      If objPrintJob.Size > 400000 Then
5          objPrintJob.Pause
6      End If
7  Next
```

Resuming Print Jobs

After a print job has been paused, that job must be resumed before the document will be printed. You can resume the print job programmatically by using the Resume method of the IADsPrintJobOperations interface.

For the most part, the Resume method works only on print jobs that were paused before they started printing. If you pause a print job while it is printing, it is likely that the document will not actually be paused but will continue printing. If the document is larger than the print buffer, however, it is possible that only part of the document will be printed and then the print job will be paused. If a document has printed partway and then paused, resuming the print job will not cause printing to pick up where it left off. Instead, the entire document will be reprinted.

Scripting Steps

Listing 13.15 contains a script that resumes all the print jobs on a computer. To carry out this task, the script must perform the following steps:

1. Use a GetObject call to bind to the printer ArtDepartmentPrinter on the print server atl-ps-01.

2. Use the PrintJobs method to set the value of the variable colPrintJobs.

    This variable will now contain a collection consisting of all the print jobs in the ArtDepartmentPrinter print queue.

3. For each print job in the collection, use the Resume method to resume printing the document.

Listing 13.15   Resuming Print Jobs

```
1  Set objPrinter = GetObject("WinNT://atl-ps-01/ArtDepartmentPrinter")
2  Set colPrintJobs = objPrinter.PrintJobs
3  For Each objPrintJob in colPrintJobs
4      objPrintJob.Resume
5  Next
```

Configuring Printers and Print Jobs

Both printers and print jobs expose a number of properties that can be configured by using scripts. For example, after a printer has been installed, you can use scripting to change printer properties such as Location and Priority or to schedule the hours when a printer actually processes print jobs. This allows you to dynamically manage the printing infrastructure, thus making the printing process easier for both you and your users.

You can use ADSI to change the properties of print jobs already in the print queue. These properties include such things as the job priority and the time at which the job is printed. In turn, this provides you with the ability to print specific documents as needed. For example, large documents can be rescheduled to print after hours, while important documents can be reassigned a higher priority and printed immediately, even if other documents are in the queue ahead of them.

Configuring Printer Properties

Most of the IADsPrintQueue properties can be configured by using ADSI. These configurable properties provide a way for you to dynamically change your printing infrastructure as needed. For example, you can assign a higher priority to a particular printer, thereby ensuring that documents sent to that printer are printed first. Alternatively, you might want to share a printer over the network or use a script to modify the location or the availability of a printer.

Scripting Steps

Listing 13.16 contains a script that configures the priority of a printer. To carry out this task, the script must perform the following steps:

1. Use a GetObject call to bind to the printer ArtDepartmentPrinter on the print server atl-ps-01.

2. Set the Priority to 2.

3. Use the SetInfo method to apply the new priority to the logical printer.

Listing 13.16   Configuring Printer Priority

```
1  Set objPrinter = GetObject("WinNT://atl-ps-01/ArtDepartmentPrinter")
2  objPrinter.Priority = 2
3  objPrinter.SetInfo
```

Note that changing the priority of a printer is meaningless unless multiple logical printers are targeted to the same physical printer. For example, you might have a single physical printer that has two logical printers configured as follows:

- Printer A, with a priority of 2

- Printer B, with a priority of 1

In this case, any documents sent to Printer A print before documents sent to Printer B. Why? Because Printer A has a higher priority. If the physical printer has only one logical printer, documents will print in the order in which they are submitted, regardless of the priority assigned to the printer. This is because all print jobs will have the same priority.

Configuring Printer Availability

Print management commonly includes the scheduling of printer availability. For example, many organizations limit the hours during which print jobs can be printed. This is often done to prevent users from printing personal documents after the close of regular business hours. It also provides an opportunity for support personnel to perform routine maintenance without the fear of interrupting a submitted print job.

Alternatively, printer scheduling might be used to allow users to submit print jobs during business hours and have those print jobs automatically printed late at night, when the printing will not interfere with other documents.

For example, suppose a user routinely prints a 300-page document for use the next day. You can create a logical printer for that user and schedule the printer to print only between the hours of 2:00 A.M. and 6:00 A.M. The user sends the print job to this custom printer each time the document is printed. The job queues but does not begin printing until 2:00 A.M. Therefore, it does not monopolize the printer during regular working hours.

Printer availability can be configured by modifying the IADsPrintQueue properties StartTime and UntilTime.

Scripting Steps

Listing 13.17 contains a script that configures the availability of a printer. To carry out this task, the script must perform the following steps:

1. Use a GetObject call to bind to the printer ArtDepartmentPrinter on the print server atl-ps-01.

2. Set the value of the StartTime property to 6:00 A.M. To ensure that the correct data type is used when setting StartTime, use the VBScript TimeValue function.

3. Set the value of the UntilTime property to 1:00 A.M. To ensure that the correct data type is used when setting StartTime, use the VBScript TimeValue function.

4. Use the SetInfo method to apply the changes to the logical printer.

Listing 13.17 Configuring Printer Availability

```
1  Set objPrinter = GetObject("WinNT://atl-ps-01/ArtDepartmentPrinter")
2  objPrinter.StartTime = TimeValue("6:00 AM")
3  objPrinter.UntilTime = TimeValue("1:00 AM")
4  objPrinter.SetInfo
```

Tracking Printer Locations

The printer location tracking mechanism introduced in Windows 2000 helps users find hardware devices by allowing you to store the location of these devices in the Active Directory® directory service.

Among other things, this makes it easy for users to locate printers that are within close physical proximity (that is, in the same building, on the same floor, in the same wing, and so forth). When printer location tracking is enabled, a user who opens the **Find Printers** dialog box finds the location of his or her computer automatically inserted into the **Location** box, as shown in Figure 13.2.

Figure 13.2 Find Printers Dialog Box

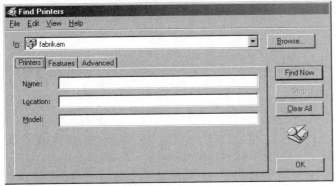

A user who clicks the **Find Now** button can then view a list of all the printers available in that location.

Alternatively, the user can click **Browse** and then choose any other location to search for printers (Figure 13.3). This is especially useful for mobile users who routinely log on from various locations within the organization. Rather than having to know the names of the printers located in each building, users can allow printer location tracking to locate nearby printers for them.

Figure 13.3   Browse for Location Dialog Box

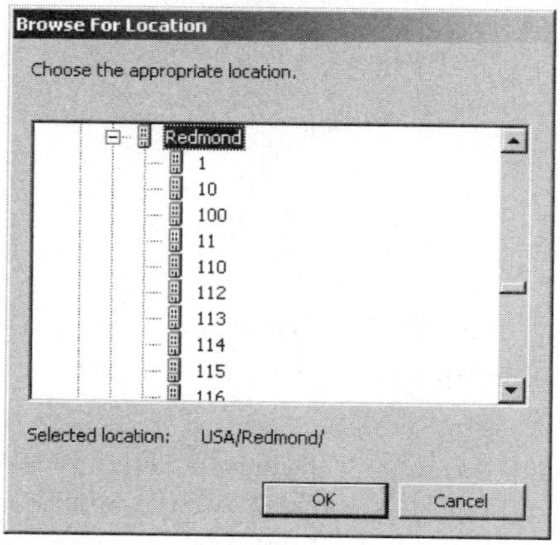

Enabling Printer Location Tracking

To enable printer location tracking, you must do the following:

1. Develop a naming scheme for your organization.

    Typically, naming schemes in large organizations use the format Country/City/Building/Floor: for example, USA/Redmond/Building 37/Floor 3. Although you can use any naming scheme, the scheme must match the physical layout of your subnets. If a particular subnet spans two floors in your building (for example, floors 3 and 4), your naming scheme must reflect this: USA/Redmond/Building 37/Floors 3 and 4.

2. Associate each subnet in your organization with a location, using your chosen naming scheme.

    For example, suppose you have two subnets (192.168.1 and 192.168.2) and two locations (Building 1/Floor 1 and Building 1/Floor2). In **Active Directory Sites and Services**, set the location of subnet 192.168.1 to Building 1/Floor 1 and the location of subnet 192.168.2 to Building 1/Floor 2.

3. Set the location attribute for your printers and your computers using the naming scheme previously developed.

    You must use the same naming scheme to set the locations for both printers and computers. If you do not, printer location tracking either fails completely or provides misleading results.

4. Enable (at the domain level) the Group Policy setting **Pre-populate printer search location text.**

This is located under Computer Configuration\Administrative Templates\Printers.

When developing a naming scheme, keep the following in mind:

- You must use the forward slash (/) character to divide the sections of a name. USA/Redmond/Building 37/Floor 3 is a valid name; USA-Redmond-Building 37-Floor 3 is not.

- Each name section is limited to 32 characters, and a location is limited to a total of 260 characters. Each name section represents the portion of a name between the / characters. For example, the name USA/Redmond/Building 37 has three name sections:

    - USA

    - Redmond

    - Building 37

- Searches are based on the locations given to subnets. For example, if you have a subnet with the location USA/Redmond/Building 37, your searches can resolve only to the Building level. In a situation such as this, you cannot search for printers on individual floors within a building. These searches are possible only if your subnet locations map to floor numbers.

To make the process of finding a printer easier for your users, however, you can include additional information as part of a printer location, even if that information is ignored when a search is performed. For example, if the subnet location is USA/Redmond/Building 37/Floor 3, you can make it easier for users to pinpoint the location of a printer by adding extra identifying information to the location string for those devices. Thus, you might have a printer with the location USA/Redmond/Building 37/Floor 3/Mail Room or USA/Redmond/Building 37 /Floor 3/Room 351 near the back wall. Although you can only search for a particular building, users finding all the printers in Building 37 will be able to view the full description and can then manually select the nearest printer.

Configuring Printer Locations

Printer location tracking requires printer locations to reflect the actual physical location of the printer in question. If a printer moves from one building to another, the location attribute must be changed to reflect this move. If the naming scheme is changed, printer locations must be changed accordingly. If a building is renamed, printer locations must, again, be modified to reflect the change.

You can modify printer locations by binding to the printer object in Active Directory and then changing the Location attribute. This is useful if you need to change the location for an entire group of printers, such as all the printers in the Finance organizational unit.

Scripting Steps

You can use printer location configuration in several ways:

- Configuring initial printer locations.
- Updating a set of printer locations.

Configuring initial printer locations

Listing 13.18 contains a script that configures printer locations. To carry out this task, the script must perform the following steps:

1. Use a GetObject call to bind to the Finance organizational unit in Active Directory.
2. Set the Filter property to "printQueue" to ensure that only printer objects are returned.

   This prevents you from inadvertently changing the location for a computer or a user account.
3. For each printer in the Finance organizational unit (OU), use the Put_ method to specify the location. This method requires two parameters:
   - **Location** —The attribute to be changed.
   - **USA/Redmond/Finance Building** — The new value for the attribute.
4. Use the SetInfo method to apply the changes to each printer object.

Listing 13.18   Configuring Printer Locations

```
1  Set objOU = GetObject("LDAP://OU = Finance, DC = fabrikam, DC = com")
2  objOU.Filter = Array("printQueue")
3  For Each objPrintQueue In objOU
4      objPrintQueue.Put "Location" , "USA/Redmond/Finance Building"
5      objPrintQueue.SetInfo
6  Next
```

Updating a set of printer locations

If you are configuring the location of a single printer only, there is no need to write a script; it is probably faster and easier to make this change using the graphical user interface. In other cases, however, you might need to make a similar change to a large number of printers. In those situations, a script will prove faster and more efficient.

For example, suppose your initial naming scheme includes only the building number and the floor number (such as Building 37/Floor 2). As your organization expands, a branch office might be opened in a new city. In that case, you should modify your naming scheme to reflect the fact that different buildings are in different cities.

Listing 13.19 contains a script that updates printer locations. To carry out this task, the script must perform the following steps:

1. Use a GetObject call to bind to the Finance organizational unit in Active Directory.
2. Set the Filter property to "printQueue" to ensure that only printer objects are returned.

   This prevents you from inadvertently changing the location for a computer or user account.

3.   Set the variable strNewLocation to Redmond/ plus the current printer location. For example, if the printer is currently in Building 37/Room 4, the new location will be Redmond/Building 37/Room 4.

4.   For each printer in the Finance OU, use the Put_ method to specify the location. This method requires two parameters:

   ▪   **Location** — The attribute to be changed.

   ▪   **StrNewLocation** — The new value for the attribute.

5.   Use the SetInfo method to apply the changes to each printer object.

Listing 13.19   Updating Printer Locations

```
1   Set objOU = GetObject("LDAP://OU=Finance, DC=fabrikam, DC=com")
2   objOU.Filter = Array("printQueue")
3   For Each objPrintQueue In objOU
4       strNewLocation = "Redmond/" & objPrintQueue.Location
5       objPrintQueue.Put "Location" , strNewLocation
6       objPrintQueue.SetInfo
7   Next
```

Configuring Print Jobs

From time to time you might need to modify the properties of a print job after it is in the print queue. For example, you might want to reschedule a print job to print at a specified time. This enables you to print a large print job after hours, when it will not prevent other documents from being printed. Furthermore, you can do this while the print job is in the print queue, without requiring the user to cancel and then resubmit the print job.

To configure print jobs, you can use ADSI and the IADsPrintJob interface (available through the WinNT provider). Some of the print job properties available through this interface are shown in Table 13.8. Properties that cannot be configured using a script are denoted as read-only.

Table 13.8   IADsPrintJob Properties

Property	Description
Description	Name of the document (for example, Readme.doc).
Priority	Priority placed on the print jobs. Jobs with a higher priority are always printed first, regardless of the time they were sent to the print queue.
StartTime	Earliest time that the document can begin printing. Regardless of the document's position in the print queue, it will not begin printing until the StartTime.

(continued)

Table 13.8   IADsPrintJob Properties *(continued)*

Property	Description
UntilTime	Sets the time after which the document will not be printed. For example, suppose you set the UntilTime to 9:00 A.M. If the document has not been printed by 9:00 A.M., it will be suspended and will not be resumed (and thus will not move up in the queue) until the StartTime has been reached again.
Notify	User name of the user to be notified when the print job is finished.
NotifyPath	ADsPath value for the user to be notified when the job is finished.
HostPrintQueue (read only)	AdsPath name for the print queue processing the print job. Because you must use the WinNT provider (the IADSPrintJob interface is not supported by the LDAP provider), path names will look similar to this: `WinNT://FABRIKAM/PRINTSERVER1/financeprinter` where FABRIKAM represents the domain name, PRINTSERVER1 the print server name, and financeprinter the printer name.
User (read-only)	User name of the user who submitted the print job.
Userpath (read-only)	ADsPath name for the user who submitted the print job.
TimeSubmitted (read-only)	Date and time the print job was submitted. The date and time will look similar to this: `12/21/2001 2:04:32 PM.`
TotalPages (read-only)	Total number of pages in the print job.
Size (read-only)	Size of the print job in bytes. To determine the size of the print job in kilobytes, divide this number by 1,024.

Configuring Print Job Properties

The IADsPrintJob interface can be used to configure print job properties while those print jobs are in the print queue. Typically, this is done to control the order in which documents, especially large documents that might monopolize printer time, are printed.

For example, suppose you have several large (more than 400 KB) print jobs in the print queue, along with a number of smaller print jobs. You might want the small print jobs to print first so that those users do not have to wait for the larger jobs to finish. In this scenario, you want jobs to print in this order:

1.   Any existing jobs less than 400 KB.

2.   Any existing jobs greater than 400 KB.

3.   Any new jobs added to the queue.

In this case, pausing the larger print jobs will not suffice. After all, while those jobs are paused, any new jobs added to the print queue will move ahead of them in the queue.

Instead, you can change the priority of each print job. For example, jobs less than 400 KB can be given a priority of 3. Because higher-priority jobs print first, these jobs will immediately move to the head of the print queue. Print jobs greater than 400 KB can be given a priority of 2. Any new jobs that are sent to the print queue will have the default priority of 1. As a result, they will not be printed until after the larger print jobs have finished.

You must use the WinNT provider to bind to and configure print jobs; the LDAP provider does not support the IADsPrintJob interface. This means your script has to bind to a specific printer on a specific print server using a format similar to the following:

```
Set objPrinter = GetObject("WinNT://printserver1/financeprinter")
```

Scripting Steps

You can control the order in which a job prints in several ways. For example:

- You can change the priority of a print job.
- You can change the start time of a print job.

Changing the priority of a print job

Listing 13.20 contains a script that changes the priority of a print job. To carry out this task, the script must perform the following steps:

1. Use a GetObject call to bind to the printQueue object on the print server.

   Because the LDAP provider does not support binding to print jobs, you must use the WinNT provider and bind to a specific printer on a specific print server.

2. For each print job in the print queue, check the size of the print job. If the size is greater than 400,000 bytes, set the job priority to 2. If the job size is less than this, set the job priority to 3.

   Job priorities are set using the Put method and the following two parameters:

   - The name of the attribute to be configured (Priority).
   - The value to be assigned the attribute (either 2 or 3).

3. After configuring the priority, use the SetInfo method to write the changes to the print job.

Listing 13.20 Changing Print Job Priority

```
1   Set objPrinter = GetObject _
2       ("WinNT://atl-ps-01/ArtDepartmentPrinter ")
3   For each objPrintJob in objPrinter.PrintJobs
4       If objPrintJob.Size > 400000 Then
5           objPrintJob.Put "Priority" , 2
6           objPrintJob.SetInfo
7       Else
8           objPrintJob.Put "Priority" , 3
9           objPrintJob.SetInfo
10      End If
11  Next
```

Changing the start time of a print job

Another way to postpone the printing of large documents is to change the start time for that print job. For example, the script shown in Listing 13.21 changes the start time for all documents greater than 400,000 bytes to 2:00 A.M. To carry out this task, the script must perform the following steps:

1. Use a GetObject call to bind to the printQueue object on the print server.

   Because the LDAP provider does not support binding to print jobs, you must use the WinNT provider and bind to a specific printer on a specific print server.

2. For each print job in the print queue, check the size of the print job. If the size is greater than 400,000 bytes, set the start time to 2:00 A.M. If the job size is less than this, do nothing.

   Job priorities are set by using the Put method and the following two parameters:

   - The name of the attribute to be configured (StartTime).

   - The value to be assigned the attribute (2:00:00 AM). To ensure that the start time is passed in the correct date and time format, use the VBScript TimeValue function, which converts a string expression (such as 2:00:00 AM) to a datetime value.

3. After configuring the start time, use the SetInfo method to write the changes to the print job.

Listing 13.21   Changing the Start Time of a Print Job

```
1   Set objPrinter = GetObject _
2       ("WinNT://atl-ps-01/ArtDepartmentPrinter")
3   For each objPrintQueue in objPrinter.PrintJobs
4   If objPrintQueue.Size > 400000 Then
5       objPrintQueue.Put "StartTime" , TimeValue("2:00:00 AM")
6       objPrintQueue.SetInfo
7   End If
8   Next
```

Managing Printer Connections on Client Computers

In addition to monitoring and managing print servers and the printers they host, it is important to keep track of print resources on client computers. For example, adding new printers can reduce the load on existing printers, but only if users actually print to these new devices. Because of this, it is very useful to know which users have created connections to which printers, and which of these printers has been configured as the default print device. It is also useful to be able to reconfigure printer connections as needed.

WSH and WMI allow you to manage print resources on client computers by:

- Enumerating printer connections
- Adding and deleting printer connections
- Configuring the default printer

Enumerating Printer Connections

Enumerating the printer connections on client computers can help you better understand why print resources are (or are not) being used. For example, there could be a number of reasons why Printer A attracts twice the workload of Printer B:

- Printer A might be faster than Printer B.
- Printer A might be more reliable than Printer B.
- Printer A might be more conveniently located than Printer B.

On the other hand, Printer A might receive a disproportionate amount of the workload simply because twice as many users have configured Printer A to be their default printer. In a case such as this, you can facilitate the printing process by changing the default printer for some of your users. Before you can do this, however, you must know which printers have been connected to which computers. This information can be obtained by using the Win32_Printer class.

 Note

The WSH method EnumPrinterConnections can also be used to enumerate the printer connections on a computer. However, any script using EnumPrinterConnections must be run on the local computer. By contrast, WMI can be used to enumerate printer connections on remote computers.

Scripting Steps

Listing 13.22 contains a script that enumerates printer connections. To carry out this task, the script must perform the following steps:

1. Create a variable to specify the computer name.
2. Use a GetObject call to connect to the WMI namespace root\cimv2, and set the impersonation level to "impersonate."

3. Use the ExecQuery method to query the Win32_Printer class.

This query returns a collection consisting of all the printers installed on the computer.

4. For each printer in the collection, echo the printer name and location, and whether the printer is the default printer.

Listing 13.22   Enumerating Printer Connections

```
1  strComputer = "."
2  Set objWMIService = GetObject("winmgmts:" _
3      & "{impersonationLevel=impersonate}!\\" & strComputer & "\root\cimv2")
4  Set colInstalledPrinters =  objWMIService.ExecQuery _
5      ("SELECT * FROM Win32_Printer")
6  For Each objPrinter in colInstalledPrinters
7      Wscript.Echo "Name: " & objPrinter.Name
8      Wscript.Echo "Location: " & objPrinter.Location
9  Next
```

Adding and Deleting Printer Connections

Using WSH methods as part of a logon script can ensure that the printer connections are properly configured for each user. Several WSH methods, including AddWindowsPrinterConnection and RemovePrinterConnection, can be used to manage printer connections on client computers.

These methods are typically used in logon scripts, and for two reasons:

- WSH methods do not normally work against remote computers (although you can use the WshController object to run scripts remotely). To manage printer connections by using these methods, the script must be run locally.

- Printers are configured independently for each user and are stored in the user profile. When you enumerate printers using WSH or WMI, you actually enumerate them on a per-user basis rather than a per-computer basis. Using the WSH methods as part of a logon script ensures that the printer connections are properly configured for each user.

Including the methods in a logon script enables you to dynamically adjust printer connections each time a user logs on. For example, if you install a new printer for a department, you can add code to the logon script for each user in the department that creates a new connection to a printer. If you delete a printer, you can add code that automatically removes any connections to that printer. This prevents the problems that can arise from users attempting to print to a printer that no longer exists.

Adding a Printer Connection by Using WSH

The WSH AddWindowsPrinterConnection method provides a quick and easy way to add a printer connection to the local computer. (To add a printer connection to a remote computer, you will need to run the WSH script using the WSHController object.)

The AddWindowsPrinterConnection method requires only a single parameter: the UNC path to the network printer. For example, this line of code adds a connection to the printer named ColorPrinter managed by the print server atl-ps-001:

```
objNetwork.AddWindowsPrinterConnection "\\atl-ps-001\ColorPrinter"
```

After a printer connection has been created, you can optionally use the SetDefaultPrinter method to configure the new connection to be the default printer. SetDefaultPrinter also requires only one parameter: the UNC path to the network printer.

Scripting Steps

Listing 13.23 contains a script that adds a printer connection on the local computer. To carry out this task, the script must perform the following steps:

1. Create an instance of the WSH Network object.

2. Use the AddWindowsPrinterConnection method to add a connection to the printer Xerox300 on the print server atl-ps-01.

3. Use the SetDefaultPrinter method to configure the printer Xerox300 on the print server atl-ps-01 as the default printer.

Listing 13.23   Adding a Printer Connection

```
1  Set objNetwork = CreateObject("Wscript.Network")
2  objNetwork.AddWindowsPrinterConnection "\\atl-ps-01\Xerox300"
3  objNetwork.SetDefaultPrinter "\\atl-ps-01\Xerox300"
```

Removing a Printer Connection

To remove a printer connection, use the RemovePrinterConnection method, along with the Universal Naming Convention (UNC) path to the printer. RemovePrinterConnection can be used only to remove printer connections from the local computer. If you want to remove a printer connection on a remote computer, you will need to run the script using the WSHController object.

Scripting Steps

Listing 13.24 contains a script that removes a printer connection. To carry out this task, the script must perform the following steps:

1. Create an instance of the WSH Network object.

2. Use the RemovePrinterConnection method to delete the connection to the printer Xerox300 on the print server atl-ps-01.

Listing 13.24   Removing a Printer Connection

```
1  Set objNetwork = CreateObject("Wscript.Network")
2  objNetwork.RemovePrinterConnection "\\atl-ps-01\xerox3006"
```

Searching for Printers in Active Directory

The print service and Active Directory are closely integrated. By default, shared printers hosted by a print server are published in Active Directory. When a printer is published, a printQueue object is placed in the print server's computer object in Active Directory.

Administrators can use Active Directory Users and Computers to identify the printers managed by a print server and to access information regarding each of these printers. Equally important, administrators (and users) can search for these printQueue objects.

Because of this, users can easily locate printers within close physical proximity or printers that meet specific criteria (for example, color printers). At the same time, administrators can easily enumerate all the shared printers within their domain and compile a list of properties for each of those printers.

Enumerating All the Published Printers in a Domain

Publishing printers in Active Directory is a convenience for users: They can easily locate printers, especially if printer location tracking is enabled. However, publishing printers in Active Directory can also be a convenience for administrators: Administrators can retrieve a list of shared printers simply by searching for these printers in Active Directory, by using GUI tools or by using a script that searches Active Directory.

To enumerate all the published printers, you can search Active Directory by using the Active Directory OLE DB provider.

Scripting Steps

Listing 13.25 contains a script that enumerates all the printers published in Active Directory. To carry out this task, the script must perform the following steps:

1. Insert an On Error Resume Next Statement. This prevents the script from failing if no printers can be found in Active Directory.

2. Create a constant named ADS_SCOPE_SUBTREE and set the value to 2. This will be used to specify a search that begins in the Active Directory root and proceeds to search all the child containers as well.

3. Create an instance of the Active Directory connection object (ADODB.Connection).

   This allows you to connect to Active Directory.

4. Set the provider property of the connection object to the Active Directory provider (ADsDSOObject). This is the OLE database provider for ADSI.

5. Set the active connection to the Active Directory connection.

6. Set the command text for the Active Directory command object to the SQL query that retrieves all the printers from fabrikam.com.

   To ensure a quicker search, include only the attributes printerName and serverName in the SQL query.

7. Specify values for page size, time-out, search scope, and caching.

8. Execute the SQL query.

9. When the set of printers is returned, use the MoveFirst method to move to the first printer in the recordset.

10. For each printer in the recordset, echo the printer name and the print server name.

Listing 13.25   Enumerating All the Published Printers in Active Directory

```
1    On Error Resume Next
2    Const ADS_SCOPE_SUBTREE = 2
3    Set objConnection = CreateObject("ADODB.Connection")
4    Set objCommand = CreateObject("ADODB.Command")
5    objConnection.Provider = "ADsDSOObject"
6    objConnection.Open "Active Directory Provider"
7    Set objCommand.ActiveConnection = objConnection
8    objCommand.CommandText = "SELECT printerName, serverName FROM " _
9        & " 'LDAP://DC=fabrikam,DC=com'  WHERE objectClass='printQueue'"
10   objCommand.Properties("Page Size") = 1000
11   objCommand.Properties("Timeout") = 30
12   objCommand.Properties("Searchscope") = ADS_SCOPE_SUBTREE
13   objCommand.Properties("Cache Results") = False
14   Set objRecordSet = objCommand.Execute
15   objRecordSet.MoveFirst
16   Do Until objRecordSet.EOF
17       Wscript.Echo "Printer Name: " & objRecordSet.Fields("printerName").Value
18       Wscript.Echo "Server Name: " & objRecordSet.Fields("serverName").Value
19       objRecordSet.MoveNext
20   Loop
```

Searching for Specific Printers in a Domain

In addition to enumerating all the printers in a domain, you can search for specific printers. To do this, you simply search for printers that have one or more of the attributes of the printQueue object in Active Directory.

For example, to find all the color printers in the domain, you would search for all printers for which the printsColor attribute is True. To find printers that support stapling, you would search for all printers for which the printStaplingSupported attribute is True.

The printQueue object attributes are shown in Table 13.9.

Table 13.9   Attributes for the printQueue Object

Attribute	Friendly Name	Description
cn	Directory Service Name	Name of the printer as viewed in Active Directory Users and Computers.
uNCName	Network Name	UNC path of the printer. This attribute is populated by the print spooler when the printQueue object is created.
assetNumber	Asset Number	Asset number assigned to the printer. This attribute can be configured by using ADSI.
contactName	Contact	Name of the person to contact regarding the printer. This attribute can be configured by using ADSI.
description	Comment	Description of the printer. This is derived from the printer object at the time the printQueue object is created.
driverName	Model	Model of the printer. This is derived from the printer driver at the time the printQueue object is created.
location	Location	Physical location of the printer. This attribute can be configured by using ADSI.
portName	Port	Name of the port(s) supporting this printer. This attribute is populated by the print spooler when the printQueue object is created.
printBinNames	Input Trays	Input tray names. This attribute is populated by the printer driver when the printQueue object is created.
printCollate	Supports Collation	Indicates whether or not the printer supports collation. This attribute is populated by the printer driver when the printQueue object is created.
printColor	Supports Color Printing	Indicates whether or not this is a color device. This attribute is populated by the printer driver when the printQueue object is created.
printDuplexSupported	Supports Double-sided Printing	Indicates whether or not this device can print on both sides of the paper. This attribute is populated by the printer driver when the printQueue object is created.

(continued)

Table 13.9   Attributes for the printQueue Object *(continued)*

Attribute	Friendly Name	Description
printerName	Name	Name of the printer. This attribute is populated by the print object when the printQueue object is created.
printLanguage	Printer Language	Page description language used by the printer. This attribute is populated by the printer driver when the printQueue object is created.
printMaxResolutionSupported	Maximum Resolution	Maximum resolution (in DPI). This attribute is populated by the printer driver when the printQueue object is created.
printMediaReady	Paper Available	Paper types loaded in the device at the present time. This attribute is populated by the printer driver when the printQueue object is created.
printMediaSupported	Paper Types Supported	Media types that the printer supports. This attribute is populated by the printer driver when the printQueue object is created.
printMemory	Installed Memory	Amount of installed memory. This attribute is populated by the printer driver when the printQueue object is created.
printOwner	Owner Name	Name of the person or group that owns the printer. This attribute can be configured by using ADSI.
printRate	Speed	Speed of the device. This attribute is populated by the printer driver when the printQueue object is created.
printRateUnit	Speed Units	Units that the printer speed is measured in. This attribute is populated by the printer driver when the printQueue object is created.
printPagesPerMinute	Pages per Minute	Printer speed normalized to pages per minute. This attribute is populated by the printer driver when the printQueue object is created.
printShareName	Share Name	Share name of the printer. This attribute is populated by the print object when the printQueue object is created.
printStaplingSupported	Supports Stapling	Indicates whether or not the device can staple. This attribute is populated by the printer driver when the printQueue object is created.

(continued)

Table 13.9 Attributes for the printQueue Object *(continued)*

Attribute	Friendly Name	Description
serverName	Server Name	Name of the server supporting the printer. This attribute is populated by the print spooler when the printQueue object is created.
url	Web Page Address	URL of the printer's Web page. This attribute is populated by the print spooler when the printQueue object is created.
versionNumber	Object Version	Internal version number of the printer object. This attribute is populated by the print spooler when the printQueue object is created.

Scripting Steps

Listing 13.26 contains a script that searches for specific printers in Active Directory. To carry out this task, the script must perform the following steps:

1. Insert an On Error Resume Next statement. This prevents the script from failing if no printers can be found in Active Directory.

2. Create a constant named ADS_SCOPE_SUBTREE and set the value to 2. This will be used to specify a search that begins in the Active Directory root and proceeds to search all the child containers as well.

3. Create an instance of the Active Directory connection object (ADODB.Connection).

   The connection object allows you to connect to Active Directory.

4. Create an instance of the Active Directory command object (ADODB.Command).

   The command object allows you to issue queries and other database commands using the Active Directory connection.

5. Set the provider property of the connection object to the Active Directory provider (ADsDSOObject). This is the OLE database provider for ADSI.

6. Set the active connection to the Active Directory connection.

7. Set the command text for the Active Directory command object to the SQL query that retrieves printer data from fabrikam.com.

   To limit data retrieval to printers with a priority of 2, add the statement "and Priority = 2" to the Where clause. To ensure a quicker search, include only the attributes printerName and serverName in the SQL query.

8. Specify values for page size, time-out, search scope, and caching.

9. Run the SQL query.

10. When the set of printers is returned, use the MoveFirst method to move to the first printer in the recordset.

11. For each printer in the recordset, echo the printer name and the print server name.

Listing 13.26 Searching for Specific Printers in Active Directory

```
1   On Error Resume Next
2   Const ADS_SCOPE_SUBTREE = 2
3   Set objConnection = CreateObject("ADODB.Connection")
4   Set objCommand = CreateObject("ADODB.Command")
5   objConnection.Provider = "ADsDSOObject"
6   objConnection.Open "Active Directory Provider"
7   Set objCOmmand.ActiveConnection = objConnection
8   objCommand.CommandText = "SELECT printerName, serverName FROM " _
9       & "'LDAP://DC=fabrikam,DC=com'  WHERE objectClass='printQueue' AND " _
10          & " Priority = 2 "
11  objCommand.Properties("Page Size") = 1000
12  objCommand.Properties("Timeout") = 30
13  objCommand.Properties("Searchscope") = ADS_SCOPE_SUBTREE
14  objCommand.Properties("Cache Results") = False
15  Set objRecordSet = objCommand.Execute
16  objRecordSet.MoveFirst
17  Do Until objRecordSet.EOF
18      Wscript.Echo "Printer Name: " & objRecordSet.Fields("printerName").Value
19      Wscript.Echo "Server Name: " & objRecordSet.Fields("serverName").Value
20      objRecordSet.MoveNext
21  Loop
```

Processes

Everything that takes place on a computer is somehow connected to a process — a running instance of an application or executable file. Because processes underlie all the activities on a computer, it is important that you routinely monitor and manage processes and process performance. Doing so provides a window into how a computer is being used, enables you to quickly correct software-related problems, and even allows you to anticipate trouble before it occurs. These activities can be greatly facilitated by the scripting technologies available in the Microsoft® Windows® 2000 family of operating systems.

In This Chapter

Processes Overview **938**

Managing Processes **940**

    Monitoring Processes 940

    Enumerating Additional Process Properties 954

    Creating and Terminating Processes...959

Processes Overview

Users tend to think of software in terms of shrink-wrapped boxes bought at the local computer store. System administrators tend to think of software as something that needs to be installed, upgraded, and, on occasion, removed. Few people think of software as a dynamic entity that needs to be monitored and managed in the same way you need to monitor and manage such things as printers, disk drives, or services.

Managing software that is actually running, as opposed to software that is simply waiting to be installed, upgraded, or removed, is a very important, yet often overlooked, system administration task. This type of management (often referred to as process management) helps ensure that your computers run efficiently and effectively, and that they run legally as well. Software that is not running as expected might use up a disproportionate amount of system resources; in fact, a single errant process could exhaust all available memory and bring a computer to a halt. Unlicensed (and thus illegal) software running on a system might have ramifications that go much further.

Scripting can be used to help keep track of the software running on a computer, to help ensure that this software runs efficiently, and to stop and start software as needed. All of these activities fall under the umbrella of process management.

What Is a Process?

A process is a running instance of an application or executable file, along with all the system resources that have been allocated to that instance. In general, a process is equivalent to a single application or service; for example, Microsoft® Word runs in the Winword.exe process.

 Note

> A script is not equivalent to a process. Instead, each script runs in an instance of the scripting host process; each time you run a VBScript script, an instance of either Wscript.exe or Cscript.exe is started. If you start five scripts, the Task Manager lists five instances of Wscript.exe. It does not list the names of the individual scripts running in each of these processes.

To a user, a process appears as a single entity (such as Winword.exe). The operating system, however, takes a very different view of processes. It is this view that helps explain how processes work and, equally important, what happens when they do not work.

How Processes Work

Each process is composed of a set of threads. A thread is a unit of work that runs simultaneously with other units of work on the computer; each process must have at least one thread.

Threads represent the basic unit of execution in the Windows 2000. When a thread starts, the Windows 2000 Memory Manager allocates enough physical memory and page file space to allow the thread to run. While a thread is running, it can request additional memory to enable it to complete its task. When a thread ends, it releases the memory it was using back to the Memory Manager for reallocation.

Memory is also allocated based on the number of threads spawned by each process. For example, consider a computer running two processes. Process A has 5 threads, and Process B has 15 threads. Assuming the two processes have equal priority, Process A is allocated 25 percent (5 / 20) of the memory being used and Process B is allocated 75 percent (15 / 20) of the memory being used.

This method of thread allocation helps ensure that applications receive the memory they need. However, this same method can also result in memory leaks. A memory leak occurs when an application receives an increasing amount of memory but does not relinquish that memory back to the Memory Manager. This typically happens when a process creates threads but does not destroy those threads when they have finished their work. This disrupts memory allocation in two ways:

- Each thread that is created is allocated a certain amount of memory. If the thread is not destroyed, that memory is retained by the process and is not reallocated.

- The number of threads created by a process determines how much memory is allocated to the process. If a process continually creates threads without destroying them, the number of threads owned by that process keeps increasing and the process receives a disproportionate share of memory.

If left unchecked, a single process can eventually exhaust the supply of available memory, causing the system to fail. This alone provides an important reason for carefully monitoring and managing the processes running on your computers.

Managing Processes

Processes underlie almost everything that happens on a computer. In fact, the root cause of most computer problems can be traced to processes; for example, too many processes might be running on a computer (and contending for a finite set of resources), or a single process might be using more than its share of resources.

These factors make it important to keep a close watch on the processes running on a computer. Process monitoring, the main activity in process management, allows you to determine what a computer actually does, what applications the computer runs, and how those applications are affected by changes in the computing environment.

Process monitoring helps you:

- Optimize your system to account for peak demands.

  For example, you can ensure that a backup service runs only at night, when the high network utilization does not adversely affect users.

- Identify and react to potential problems.

  Monitoring memory use can help you identify memory leaks and enable you to take action before an application can monopolize system resources and bring the computer to a halt.

- Ensure that computers are being used properly.

  For example, by monitoring the processes running on a computer, you know whether an administrator has started a resource-intensive application on a Domain Name System (DNS) server.

In addition to monitoring processes, process management also includes such tasks as creating processes, terminating processes, and configuring process priority.

Processes can be managed by using the graphical user utility Windows Task Manager. However, Task Manager returns information only about the processes running on the local computer and cannot be used as part of an automated management strategy. Fortunately, the Windows Management Instrumentation (WMI) Win32_Process class can retrieve much of the same information and carry out many of the same tasks as Task Manager. A comparison of selected Win32_Process classes and methods and the Windows Task Manager is shown in Figure 14.1.

Figure 14.1   Win32_Process and Windows Task Manager

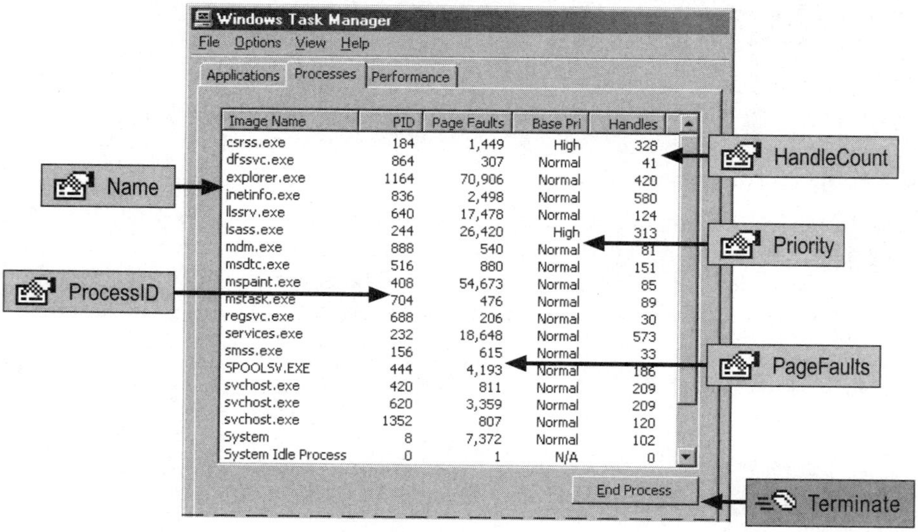

Monitoring Processes

Monitoring processes on a regular basis helps you ensure that a computer runs at peak efficiency and that it carries out its appointed tasks as expected. For example, by monitoring processes you can be notified immediately of any application that has stopped responding, and then take steps to end that process. In addition, process monitoring enables you to identify problems before they occur. For example, by repeatedly checking the amount of memory used by a process, you can identify a memory leak. You can then stop the process before the errant application uses all of the available memory and brings the computer to a halt.

Process monitoring also helps minimize the disruptions caused by planned outages for upgrades and maintenance. For example, by checking the status of a database application running on client computers, you can determine the impact of taking the database offline in order to upgrade the software.

Process monitoring can be divided into three general categories:

- **Monitoring process availability.** Measures the percentage of time that a process is available.

  Availability is typically monitored by use of a simple probe, which reports whether the process is still running. By keeping track of the results of each probe, you can calculate the availability of the process. For example, a process that is probed 100 times and responds on 95 of those occasions has an availability of 95 percent.

  This type of monitoring is typically reserved for databases, mail programs, and other applications that are expected to run at all times. It is not appropriate for word processing programs, spreadsheets, or other applications that are routinely started and stopped several times a day.

- **Monitoring process reliability.** Measures how frequently a process fails, and the amount of time required to restart a failed process.

  Reliability is calculated by dividing the time the process is functioning by the total number of days in a year. For example, a process that experiences a total downtime of 2 days during the course of a year is 99.5 percent reliable (363 days of availability divided by 365 days in a year).

  This type of monitoring is also reserved for databases, mail programs, and other applications that are expected to run at all times. It is not appropriate to measure reliability for word processing programs, spreadsheets, or other applications that are routinely started and stopped several times a day.

- **Monitoring process performance.** Measures whether the process runs in the expected manner.

  Performance monitoring is typically done by tracking memory use and threads. In general, a process should show a pattern of being allocated additional memory as needed and then releasing that memory when it is no longer needed. Likewise, a process should continually be creating and destroying threads. If memory is allocated but not released, or threads are created but not destroyed, this is usually an indication of a memory leak or another problem. Performance should be a series of peaks and valleys rather than a steady incline.

Monitoring Processes for Availability

Availability is the simplest form of process monitoring: with this approach, you simply ensure that the process is running. When you monitor for process availability, you typically retrieve a list of processes running on a computer and then verify that a particular process is still active. If the process is active, it is considered available. If the process is not active, it is not available.

The Win32_Process class enables you to create scripts that identify the processes currently running on any computer in your organization.

Scripting Steps

Listing 14.1 contains a script that monitors process availability by checking the list of processes running on a computer and issuing a notification if the Database.exe process is not found. To carry out this task, the script must perform the following steps:

1. Create a variable to specify the computer name.

2. Use a GetObject call to connect to the WMI namespace root\cimv2 on the computer, and set the impersonation level to "impersonate."

3. Use the ExecQuery method to query the Win32_Process class.

    To restrict data retrieval to a single process, a WHERE clause is used to limit data retrieval to the process with the name Database.exe.

4. Use the Count method to determine the number of processes retrieved.

    The Count method provides a quick way to determine whether Database.exe is running. If Count is equal to 1, that means one instance of Database.exe is running on the computer. If Count is equal to 0, no instances of Database.exe are running on the computer.

5. If no instances of Database.exe are detected, a message to that effect is echoed to the screen. Otherwise, the script echoes the fact that Database.exe is running.

Listing 14.1 Monitoring Process Availability

```
1   strComputer = "."
2   Set objWMIService = GetObject("winmgmts:" _
3       & "{impersonationLevel=impersonate}!\\" & strComputer & "\root\cimv2")
4   Set colProcesses = objWMIService.ExecQuery _
5       ("SELECT * FROM Win32_Process WHERE Name = 'Database.exe'")
6   If colProcesses.Count = 0 Then
7       Wscript.Echo "Database.exe is not running."
8   Else
9       Wscript.Echo "Database.exe is running."
10  End If
```

Monitoring Processes for Reliability

Reliability measures the mean time between failures for an application; that is, how long an application runs before it fails. For many applications, attempting to measure this type of reliability is irrelevant. For example, Microsoft Word typically runs only as long as a user needs it. When finished, the user closes Word. The fact that Word might be running only for a few minutes does not necessarily tell you anything about the reliability of the application. Instead, it typically indicates only that the user simply did something — such as open a document and print it — and then closed Word.

Other applications, such as many database applications, are designed to run continuously. For these applications, reliability measurements are much more meaningful. You can use WMI event subscriptions to help monitor the reliability of those processes.

Event subscriptions can notify you any time a process is created or deleted on a computer. This allows you to carry out reliability monitoring: you can record the time each process is created and the time each process is deleted, and then calculate the reliability of the application (the amount of time that elapsed between process creation and deletion).

Monitoring process creation and deletion also provides a rudimentary but useful way to monitor software use in your organization. You can use this approach to keep track of the number of times software applications are started and to determine the length of a typical application session. This provides you with a rough estimate of which programs are used most often, and for how long.

You can also use process creation monitoring to help control the services and applications that run on a computer. For example, in an enterprise setting, servers are typically dedicated to single tasks, such as allocating IP addresses or managing print queues. By monitoring process creation, you can be notified immediately any time a different service or application starts on one of these servers.

In addition to keeping track of each time a process is created, you can use WMI to keep track of each time a process is deleted. Monitoring process deletion helps you ensure that critical applications remain running at all times. For example, you might write a script that monitors a database application on a computer. If the application fails, the process is deleted. The script can identify the fact that the database process no longer exists and automatically restart the application.

 Note

> By monitoring process deletion, you can determine that an application has finished running. However, you cannot determine whether the application finished running because a user closed it or because it failed.

Scripting Steps

The scripts for monitoring process creation and process deletion are similar.

Monitoring process creation

Listing 14.2 contains a script that monitors process creation using a temporary event consumer. To carry out this task, the script must perform the following steps:

1. Create a variable to specify the computer name.

2. Use a GetObject call to connect to the WMI namespace root\cimv2 on the computer and set the impersonation level to "impersonate."

3. Use the ExecNotificationQuery method to register for notification each time there is an instance creation (each time a new instance is created within the namespace).

   To restrict data retrieval to processes, a WHERE clause is included to limit data retrieval to instance creations involving the Win32_Process class (WHERE TargetInstance ISA 'Win32_Process').

4. Create a loop that allows the script to run indefinitely.

   To stop monitoring, you need to either log off the computer or terminate the process the script is running in.

5. Use the NextEvent method to retrieve the properties of each event when it occurs.

6. Each time a process is created, echo the name of that process and the current time (Now). The current time indicates the time the process was created.

Listing 14.2   Monitoring Process Creation

```
1   strComputer = "."
2   Set objWMIService = GetObject("winmgmts:" _
3       & "{impersonationLevel=impersonate}!\\" & strComputer & "\root\cimv2")
4   Set colMonitoredProcesses = objWMIService. _
5       ExecNotificationQuery("SELECT * FROM __InstanceCreationEvent " _
6           & "WITHIN 10 WHERE TargetInstance ISA 'Win32_Process'")
7   i = 0
8   Do While i = 0
9       Set objLatestProcess = colMonitoredProcesses.NextEvent
10      Wscript.Echo objLatestProcess.TargetInstance.Name, Now
11  Loop
```

Monitoring process deletion

To monitor process deletion, use a script similar to Listing 14.2 but substitute
__InstanceDeletionEvent for __InstanceCreationEvent in the ExecNotificationQuery,
as shown in Listing 14.3.

Listing 14.3   Monitoring Process Deletion

```
1   strComputer = "."
2   Set objWMIService = GetObject("winmgmts:" _
3       & "{impersonationLevel=impersonate}!\\" & strComputer & "\root\cimv2")
4   Set colMonitoredProcesses = objWMIService. _
5       ExecNotificationQuery("SELECT * FROM __InstanceDeletionEvent " _
6           & "WITHIN 1 WHERE TargetInstance ISA 'Win32_Process'")
7   i = 0
8   Do While i = 0
9       Set objLatestProcess = colMonitoredProcesses.NextEvent
10      Wscript.Echo objLatestProcess.TargetInstance.Name, Now
11  Loop
```

Monitoring Processes for Performance

Performance monitoring is typically directed at entire systems; for example, administrators
often monitor such things as the available bytes of memory or total processor use on a computer.
This kind of monitoring is extremely useful because it identifies problems, such as rapid
diminution of available memory, that can have a detrimental effect on the performance of the
computer itself. However, monitoring performance of the system as a whole typically does not
indicate *why* memory is diminishing. To help answer that question, you can monitor the
performance of individual processes.

Monitoring the performance of individual processes is particularly useful when you are trying to identify memory leaks. To help diagnose memory leaks in Windows 2000, you can monitor several process properties, including:

- **Threads and pool space.** If a process is leaking memory, the number of threads owned by the process and the amount of pool space used increase in a stair-step pattern. The usage of both threads and pool space remain flat for a while, jump dramatically, and then remain flat again. This pattern can repeat indefinitely, with threads and pool space both increasing over time. If a process releases threads and pool space appropriately, these totals remain relatively stable over time.

- **Working set size.** The working set is the amount of physical memory assigned to a process. If the working set is too small, the process incurs a high number of page faults as it repeatedly accesses the disk drive to locate data not currently in memory. If the working set is too large, fewer page faults occur, but the process retains memory that it no longer needs, and which might be required by other processes. A steady increase in the size of the working set can mean that the process is not releasing memory appropriately.

- **Page file bytes.** Page file bytes typically correspond to memory consumption. Memory leaks often cause a similar increase in both the working set size and the page file bytes.

- **Processor use.** Processor use is determined in part by the number of threads allocated to a process. A process that is not destroying threads receives a disproportionate amount of processor time.

All of these key indicators of process performance can be monitored by using WMI. A list of important process properties available through the Win32_Process class is shown in Table 14.1.

Table 14.1 WMI Win32_Process Properties

Property	Description
ExecutablePath	Local path to the executable file.
ExecutionState	Current status of the process. Valid values are: 0 — Unknown 1 — Other 2 — Ready 3 — Running 4 — Blocked 5 — Suspended Blocked 6 — Suspended Ready
KernelModeTime	Kernel mode usage, in milliseconds.

(continued)

Table 14.1   WMI Win32_Process Properties *(continued)*

Property	Description
Name	Name of the executable file responsible for the process, equivalent to the Image Name property in Task Manager. The name is hard-coded into the application itself and is not affected by changing the file name. For example, even if you rename Calc.exe, the name Calc.exe will still appear in Task Manager and in any WMI scripts that retrieve the process name.
PageFaults	Number of page faults generated by the process.
PageFileUsage	Amount of page file space (in kilobytes) currently used by the process.
PeakWorkingSetSize	Maximum size of the working set (in kilobytes) used by the process since it was created.
Priority	Scheduling priority of the process. Priorities range from 0 (lowest priority) to 31 (highest priority).
ProcessID	Numeric identifier used to distinguish one process from another. ProcessIDs are valid from process creation time to process termination. Upon termination, that same numeric identifier can be applied to a new process. This means that you cannot use ProcessID alone to monitor a particular process. For example, an application could have a ProcessID of 7, and then fail. When a new process is started, the new process could be assigned ProcessID 7. A script that checked only for a specified ProcessID could thus be "fooled" into thinking that the original application was still running.
QuotaNonPagedPoolUsage	Quota of nonpaged pool usage available to the process.
QuotaPagedPoolUsage	Quota of paged pool usage available to the process.
ThreadCount	Number of active threads associated with a process. Each process must have at least one thread.
UserModeTime	User mode usage (in milliseconds).
WorkingSetSize	Amount of memory (in bytes) the process needs to execute efficiently. If adequate memory is not available, "disk thrashing" occurs. (Disk thrashing refers to those times when the operating system must repeatedly access the hard disk.)

Scripting Steps

Process performance can be monitored in several different ways, including:

- Monitoring process performance information (memory use, page file use, and threads created) for each individual process.

- Monitoring processor use by process.

Monitoring process performance information

Listing 14.4 contains a script that monitors process performance information. To carry out this task, the script must perform the following steps:

1. Create a variable to specify the computer name.

2. Use a GetObject call to connect to the WMI namespace root\cimv2 on the computer, and set the impersonation level to "impersonate."

3. Use the ExecQuery method to query the Win32_Process class. This returns a collection consisting of all the processes running on the computer.

4. For each process in the collection, echo the following information:

   - Process name

   - Process ID

   - Thread count

   - Page file use

   - Total page faults

   - Current working set size

Listing 14.4   Monitoring Process Performance

```
1   strComputer = "."
2   Set objWMIService = GetObject("winmgmts:" _
3       & "{impersonationLevel=impersonate}!\\" & strComputer & "\root\cimv2")
4   Set colProcessList = objWMIService.ExecQuery _
5       ("SELECT * FROM Win32_Process")
6   For Each objProcess in colProcessList
7       Wscript.Echo "Process: " & objProcess.Name
8       Wscript.Echo "Process ID: " & objProcess.ProcessID
9       Wscript.Echo "Thread Count: " & objProcess.ThreadCount
10      Wscript.Echo "Page File Size: " & objProcess.PageFileUsage
11      Wscript.Echo "Page Faults: " & objProcess.PageFaults
12      Wscript.Echo "Working Set Size: " & objProcess.WorkingSetSize
13  Next
```

The script shown in Listing 14.4 is designed to display process information once and then terminate. Alternatively, you might want to view process performance over time. To do this, include a For-Next loop in your script, and use the Wscript.Sleep command to pause the script for the appropriate interval. For example, the script shown in Listing 14.5 runs 10 times, displaying the current process data each time, and pauses 60 seconds (60,000 milliseconds) before retrieving updated process information.

Listing 14.5 Monitoring Process Performance Over Time

```
1   strComputer = "."
2   Set objWMIService = GetObject("winmgmts:" _
3       & "{impersonationLevel=impersonate}!\\" & strComputer & "\root\cimv2")
4   For i = 1 to 10
5   Set colProcessList = objWMIService.ExecQuery
6       ("SELECT * FROM Win32_Process")
7       For Each objProcess in colProcessList
8           Wscript.Echo "Process: " & objProcess.Name
9           Wscript.Echo "Process ID: " & objProcess.ProcessID
10          Wscript.Echo "Thread Count: " & objProcess.ThreadCount
11          Wscript.Echo "Page File Size: " & objProcess.PageFileUsage
12          Wscript.Echo "Page Faults: " & objProcess.PageFaults
13          Wscript.Echo "Working Set Size: " & objProcess.WorkingSetSize
14      Next
15      Wscript.Echo
16      Wscript.Sleep 60000
17  Next
```

Monitoring processor use

Listing 14.6 contains a script that monitors processor use by process. To carry out this task, the script must perform the following steps:

1. Create a variable to specify the computer name.

2. Use a GetObject call to connect to the WMI namespace root\cimv2 on the computer, and set the impersonation level to "impersonate."

3. Use the ExecQuery method to query the Win32_Process class. This returns a collection consisting of all the processes running on the computer.

4. For each process in the collection, calculate the total processor use.

   a. Add the values for KernelModeTime and UserModeTime.

      Together, KernelModeTime and UserModeTime tell you the total amount of processor time allocated to a process. To ensure that these values are added and not concatenated, use the VBScript function CSng to convert the variant data to the single data type.

   b. Divide the combined value by 10,000,000.

      Processor use times are reported in 100-nanosecond increments. (A nanosecond is one-billionth of a second; 100 nanoseconds equal one ten-millionth of a second.) This calculation results in processor use being reported in seconds.

5.   Echo the process name and total processor use.

Listing 14.6   Monitoring Processor Use by Process

```
1   strComputer = "."
2   Set objWMIService = GetObject("winmgmts:" _
3       & "{impersonationLevel=impersonate}!\\" & strComputer & "\root\cimv2")
4   Set colProcesses = objWMIService.ExecQuery _
5       ("SELECT * FROM Win32_Process")
6   For Each objProcess in colProcesses
7       sngProcessTime = (CSng(objProcess.KernelModeTime) + _
8           CSng(objProcess.UserModeTime)) / 10000000
9       Wscript.Echo objProcess.Name & VbTab & sngProcessTime
10  Next
```

Displaying Current Process Performance Data

Although many system administration scripts run in a command window, the command window is not always suitable for displaying process performance data. Within a command window, there are few options for formatting data: you are limited to a single nonproportional font, with each character the same size and color. In addition, data within the command window cannot be cleared by using a script. Neither Windows Script Host (WSH) nor VBScript provides methods for clearing the screen; although you can call the command-line utility cls from within a script, instead of the current command window being cleared a second command window opens, and the cls command is carried out there.

The inability to clear a command window has important implications for scripts that monitor process status or process performance. You cannot display the current process status, wait a few minutes, and then erase that data and replace it with updated status information. Instead, each time you retrieve process information, the new data is appended to the end of the existing data. While this large collection of data might be useful for viewing process performance over time, it is far less useful if you simply want to view the current state of each process running on a computer.

As an alternative to displaying process performance in a command window, you can use a hypertext application (HTA) that allows you to display process information on a Web page. Displaying process data in an HTA offers the following advantages:

- You can clear the page each time the latest set of data is retrieved so that the page displays only the current process information.

- You can use additional formatting to highlight important items. For example, you might use a different font color to indicate a process that has a working set size greater than a specified amount.

An HTA is a Web page that has the file name extension .HTA. HTAs are useful for script writers because they can use Automation objects that have not been marked as safe for scripting. This allows you to use WMI within a Web page.

For more information about HTAs, see "Creating Enterprise Scripts" in this book.

Scripting Steps

Listing 14.7 contains the HTML tags and VBScript code required to create an HTA that displays process performance information on a Web page. Type this information into a text editor, and then save it with the .HTA file name extension.

To carry out the task of displaying process performance information on a Web page, the HTA must perform the following steps:

1. Create a <SCRIPT> tag specifying VBScript as the scripting language.

2. Create a constant named USE_COMMAS.

   This constant is used to format the working set value for each process.

3. Create a window_onLoad subroutine.

   Code in the window_onLoad subroutine automatically runs whenever the window is loaded (either through initial startup or by clicking the browser Refresh button).

4. Use the setInterval method to create a timer that updates the list of running processes every 10 seconds.

   The setInterval method requires three parameters:

   - **GetInfo.** The name of the subroutine called by the timer.

   - **10000.** Number of milliseconds between calls. The timer calls the GetInfo subroutine, waits 10 seconds, and then calls the subroutine again.

   - **VBScript.** Scripting language used by the GetInfo script.

   The setInterval method provides functionality similar to Wscript.Sleep: It allows you to pause the script for a specified amount of time and then resume processing. This method must be used instead of Wscript.Sleep because Windows Script Host (WSH) methods cannot be called from Internet Explorer.

5. Create a subroutine named GetInfo that retrieves the current set of processes and displays the process information in a table.

   To do this, the GetInfo subroutine must first delete the current version of the table (if one exists), create the table header, retrieve the process information, and then display the process information in the table.

6. Create a loop that deletes all the rows in the existing table (with the Table ID of objTable).

   Deleting the current table has the effect of wiping the page clean, allowing the latest process information to be displayed.

   The loop works backward from the last row in the table (Rows.Length — 1) to the first row in the table (row 0). If there are three rows in the table, row 2 is deleted first, then row 1, and then row 0.

7. Create the table header.

   To do this, the script must:

   - Use the InsertRow method to insert a new row in the table.

   - Use the InsertCell method to insert a new cell in the table.

   - Use the InnerText method to set the contents of the new cell to **Process ID**.

   - Use the same procedures to insert cells labeled **Process Name** and **Working Set Size**.

8. Create a variable to specify the computer name.

9. Use a GetObject call to connect to the WMI namespace root\cimv2 on the computer, and set the impersonation level to "impersonate."

10. Use the ExecQuery method to query the Win32_Process class. This query returns a collection consisting of all the processes running on the computer.

11. For each process in the collection, create a new row with three cells to display the following: process ID, process name, and working set size.

    The FormatNumber function is used to insert comma delimiters in the working set values. By using this function, numbers are displayed with thousands separators, such as 3,456,789 rather than 3456789. The FormatNumber function requires the following parameters:

    - **StrProcess.WorkingSetSize.** Value to be formatted.

    - **0.** Indicates the number of digits displayed after the decimal point. A 0 indicates that the decimal point should not be used.

    - **Empty.** Used to display a leading 0 for fractional values. Not applicable for this script.

    - **Empty.** Used to place parentheses around negative values. Not applicable for this script.

    - **USE_COMMAS.** Constant that indicates whether numbers are grouped using the group delimiter specified in Control Panel. For U.S. English, this is typically the comma. You can find the default delimiter for a computer by opening the Regional and Language Options Control Panel, clicking the **Numbers** tab, and then checking the value in the **Digit grouping symbol** box.

12. Create a <TABLE> tag with the ID objTable. In addition, include the Border = 1 parameter to place a border around each cell in the table.

13. Create a <TBODY> tag with the ID objTableBody.

This tag is used to represent the actual body of the table.

Listing 14.7   Displaying Process Performance on a Web Page

```
1   <SCRIPT LANGUAGE = "VBScript">
2   Sub window_onLoad
3       iTimerID = window.setInterval("GetInfo", 10000, "VBScript")
4   End Sub
5   Sub GetInfo
6       For i = (objTable.Rows.Length - 1) to 0 Step -1
7           myNewRow = document.all.objTable.deleteRow(i)
8       Next
9       Set objRow = objTableBody.InsertRow()
10      objRow.Style.fontWeight = "bold"
11      Set objCell = objRow.InsertCell()
12      objCell.InnerText = "Process ID"
13      Set objCell = objRow.InsertCell()
14      objCell.InnerText = "Process Name"
15      Set objCell = objRow.InsertCell()
16      objCell.InnerText = "Working Set Size"
17      strComputer = "."
18      Set objWMIService = GetObject("winmgmts:" _
19          & "{impersonationLevel=impersonate}!\\" & strComputer & "\root\cimv2")
20      Set colProcesses = objWMIService.ExecQuery _
21          ("SELECT * FROM Win32_Process")
22      For Each strProcess in colProcesses
23          Set objRow = objTableBody.InsertRow()
24          Set objCell = objRow.InsertCell()
25          objCell.InnerText = strProcess.ProcessID
26          Set objCell = objRow.InsertCell()
27          objCell.InnerText = strProcess.Name
28          Set objCell = objRow.InsertCell()
29          objCell.InnerText = FormatNumber(strProcess.WorkingSetSize,0,,,-1)
30      Next
31  End Sub
32  </SCRIPT>
33  <TABLE ID = "objTable">
34  <TBODY ID = "objTableBody">
35  </TBODY>
36  </TABLE>
```

The finished HTA appears similar to Figure 14.2. Every 10 seconds, the display is replaced with updated process information.

Figure 14.2   Process Performance Data Displayed on a Web Page

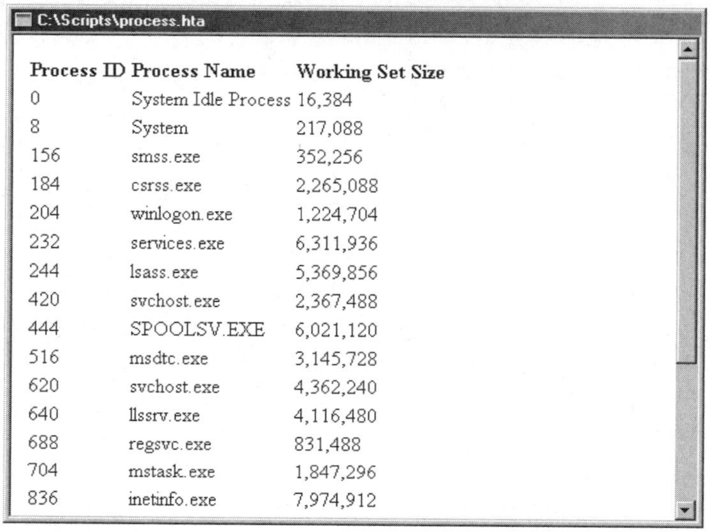

C:\Scripts\process.hta

Process ID	Process Name	Working Set Size
0	System Idle Process	16,384
8	System	217,088
156	smss.exe	352,256
184	csrss.exe	2,265,088
204	winlogon.exe	1,224,704
232	services.exe	6,311,936
244	lsass.exe	5,369,856
420	svchost.exe	2,367,488
444	SPOOLSV.EXE	6,021,120
516	msdtc.exe	3,145,728
620	svchost.exe	4,362,240
640	llssrv.exe	4,116,480
688	regsvc.exe	831,488
704	mstask.exe	1,847,296
836	inetinfo.exe	7,974,912

Enumerating Additional Process Properties

In addition to basic process properties such as executable path name and working set size, WMI scripts can retrieve additional properties for each process. These additional properties include such things as:

- Information about the process owner (the account name under which the process is running).
- Information about each thread in the process.

Although rarely needed for routine monitoring, these properties can be useful in diagnosing problems. Monitoring each thread in a process can help verify that an application is leaking memory. Knowing who owns a process tells you who is running an application on a computer. This information can also be useful when helping remote users terminate processes. Users can terminate only those processes that run under their user account; if a user is unable to stop a process on his or her computer, it might be because the process is running under a different account.

Determining Process Owners

Because processes represent such things as software applications or services, they need to carry out actions on a computer. For example, a process might write data to a particular folder, modify a specific registry key, or connect to a remote computer. The ability of a process to carry out these actions depends on the security context under which the action is attempted. Processes generally run under the security context of the user who started the process. (This user is known as the *process owner*.) If the user account that owns the process has the appropriate access rights, the action succeeds; if it does not, the action fails.

By identifying the owner of a process, you can tell which account the process is running under. This information can help you:

- Identify users who have remotely created processes on a computer.

- Determine whether a specific user can terminate a specific process. By default, users can terminate only those processes that they themselves have started.

- Create scripts that automatically terminate all the processes owned by a specified user.

To retrieve the owner of a process, use the Win32_Process class GetOwner method. GetOwner returns the user account name for the process owner as well as the domain for that user account.

Scripting Steps

Listing 14.8 contains a script that determines the owner of each process running on a computer. To carry out this task, the script must perform the following steps:

1. Create a variable to specify the computer name.

2. Use a GetObject call to connect to the WMI namespace root\cimv2 on the computer, and set the impersonation level to "impersonate."

3. Use the ExecQuery method to query the Win32_Process class. This returns a collection consisting of all the processes running on the computer.

4. For each process in the collection, use the GetOwner method to determine the user name and domain for the process.

5. Echo the name of the process and its owner by using the following format:

```
Process Winword.exe is owned by Fabrikam\kmyer.
```

Listing 14.8   Determining Process Ownership

```
1   strComputer = "."
2   Set objWMIService = GetObject("winmgmts:" _
3       & "{impersonationLevel=impersonate}!\\" & strComputer & "\root\cimv2")
4   Set colProcessList = objWMIService.ExecQuery _
5       ("SELECT * FROM Win32_Process")
6   For Each objProcess in colProcessList
7       colProperties = objProcess.GetOwner(strNameOfUser,strUserDomain)
8       Wscript.Echo "Process " & objProcess.Name & " is owned by " _
9           & strUserDomain & "\" & strNameOfUser & "."
10  Next
```

Monitoring Threads

For routine day-to-day monitoring, there is usually little reason to have a detailed list of threads and their associated properties. Computers create and delete thousands of threads during the course of a day, and few of these creations or deletions are meaningful to anyone but the developer who wrote the software.

However, when you are troubleshooting problems with an application, tracking the individual threads for a process allows you to identify when threads are created and when (or if) they are destroyed. Because threads that are created but not destroyed cause memory leaks, tracking individual threads can be useful information for support technicians. Likewise, identifying thread priorities can help pinpoint threads that, by running at an abnormally high priority, are preempting CPU cycles needed by other threads and other processes.

For occasions such as this, you can use the Win32_Thread class to return information about all the threads on a computer. Some of the more useful properties of the Win32_Thread class are shown in Table 14.2.

Table 14.2   Win32_Thread Properties

Property	Description
ElapsedTime	Total execution time, in milliseconds, allotted to this thread since its creation.
Handle	Identifier assigned by the operating system to the thread.
KernelModeTime	Kernel-mode time used by the thread, in 100-nanosecond increments.
Priority	Dynamic priority of the thread.
	Each thread has a dynamic priority that the scheduler uses to determine which thread to execute. Initially, a thread's dynamic priority is the same as its base priority. The operating system can raise and lower the dynamic priority to ensure that the computer remains responsive (guaranteeing that no threads are starved for processor time).

(continued)

Table 14.2   Win32_Thread Properties *(continued)*

Property	Description
PriorityBase	Current base priority of a thread. The operating system can raise the thread's dynamic priority above the base priority if the thread is handling user input, or lower it toward the base priority as needed. The PriorityBase property can have a value between 0 and 31.
ProcessHandle	Process ID for the process that spawned the thread. This is the only way to tie an individual thread to its parent process.
ThreadState	Current execution state for the thread. Values include: 1 – Initialized 2 –Ready 3 – Running 4 –Standby 5 – Terminated 6 – Waiting 7 – Transition 8 – Unknown
UserModeTime	User-mode time used by the thread, in 100-nanosecond increments.

As implied in the preceding table, the Win32_Thread class does not report the name of the process under which each thread runs. Instead, it reports the ID of the process under which the thread runs. To return the name of a process and a list of all its threads, your script must:

1. Connect to the Win32_Process class and return the list of processes and their process IDs.

2. Temporarily store this information in an array or Dictionary object.

3. For each process ID, return the list of threads for that process, and then display the process name and the list of threads.

Scripting Steps

Listing 14.9 contains a script that monitors the threads running on a computer. To carry out this task, the script must perform the following steps:

1. Create a Dictionary object that is used to store process names and IDs.

2. Create a variable to specify the computer name.

3. Use a GetObject call to connect to the WMI namespace root\cimv2 on the computer, and set the impersonation level to "impersonate."

4. Use the ExecQuery method to query the Win32_Process class. This returns a collection consisting of all the processes running on the computer.

5. For each process in the collection, add the process ID and process name to the Dictionary. As a result, the Dictionary will contain entries such as these:

```
Clisvcl.exe    564

Crss.exe    168

Explorer.exe    1728
```

6. Use the ExecQuery method to retrieve the list of running threads from the Win32_Thread class. This returns a collection consisting of all the threads running on the computer.

7. For each thread in the collection, retrieve the ProcessHandle.

   The ProcessHandle represents the process ID of the process that created the thread. This is used to identify the threads that belong to each process. Because the process IDs are stored in the Dictionary as integers, the VBScript function CInt is used to ensure that the ProcessHandle is stored in the variable intProcessID as an integer.

8. Use the variable intProcessName to query the Dictionary and return the name of the process corresponding to that process ID.

   This step is required because the Win32_Thread class maintains only the ID of the process that created the thread; it does not maintain information about the name of the process. Including this step allows you to determine the threads that are running under processes such as Winword.exe rather than threads that are running under a process ID such as 599.

9. Echo the name of the process, the process ID, the thread ID, and the current thread state.

Listing 14.9   Monitoring Threads

```
1   Set objDictionary = CreateObject("Scripting.Dictionary")
2   strComputer = "."
3   Set objWMIService = GetObject("winmgmts:" _
4       & "{impersonationLevel=impersonate}!\\" & strComputer & "\root\cimv2")
5   Set colProcesses = objWMIService.ExecQuery _
6       ("SELECT * FROM Win32_Process")
7   For Each objProcess in colProcesses
8       objDictionary.Add objProcess.ProcessID, objProcess.Name
9   Next
10  Set colThreads = objWMIService.ExecQuery _
11      ("SELECT * FROM Win32_Thread")
12  For Each objThread in colThreads
13      intProcessID = CInt(objThread.ProcessHandle)
14      strProcessName = objDictionary.Item(intProcessID)
15      Wscript.Echo strProcessName & VbTab & objThread.ProcessHandle & _
16          VbTab & objThread.Handle & VbTab & objThread.ThreadState
17  Next
```

Creating and Terminating Processes

To develop a complete process management system using WMI, you must be able to create and terminate processes. Among other things, this allows you to create scripts that:

- Monitor for process availability and, if necessary, restart a process that has abnormally terminated.

- Monitor for process performance and terminate a process that has exceeded specified thresholds.

- Start a program on a remote computer and, when finished, terminate the program.

The Win32_Process class contains two methods, Create and Terminate, that can be used to create and terminate processes.

Creating Processes

The WMI Win32_Process Create method allows you to create processes on either the local computer or a remote computer. This is similar to Windows Script Host (WSH) version 5.6, which also allows you to create processes on either the local computer or a remote computer (using the WSHController object).

For the most part, WSH provides a simpler approach for starting processes on the local computer. For example, these two lines represent all the code needed to start a hypothetical application named Database.exe:

```
Set objShell = CreateObject("Wscript.Shell")
objShell.Run "database.exe"
```

When you need to create a process on remote computers, however, Win32_Process Create has the following advantages:

- The Win32_Process Create method works on any computer running any version of WMI. By contrast, WSH requires you to configure both computers to allow for the use of the WSHController object, and it works only if WSH 5.6 has been installed on both computers.

- You can create the process using a single script. WSH, by contrast, needs two scripts to start a remote process: a script on the remote computer that starts the process and a script on the local computer that starts the remote script.

- You can retrieve the process ID for the created process; this allows you to monitor the process and, if necessary, terminate it. By contrast, WSH can monitor and terminate only the script that launched the new process, not the process itself.

- You can specify additional options (such as priority and window style) when starting an application.

Scripting Steps

Listing 14.10 contains a script that creates a process on a remote computer. To carry out this task the script must perform the following steps:

1. Create a variable to specify the computer name.

2. Use a GetObject call to connect to the WMI namespace root\cimv2 on the computer, and set the impersonation level to "impersonate."

   By specifying the class name as part of the call, the script is connected directly to the Win32_Process class on the remote computer.

3. Use the Create method to create a new process on the remote computer, and specify the following parameters:

   - **Database.exe.** Name of the executable file to be started. If the file is in the computer's path, only the name must be specified; otherwise, you must specify the entire path name relative to the computer where the process runs. To start a script remotely, as opposed to an executable file, specify the script host as part of the name (for example, "Wscript.exe MyScript.vbs").

   - **USE_SAME_STARTUP_FOLDER.** Constant indicating the startup folder for the new process. The value Null is assigned to this constant to indicate that the new process should use the same startup folder as the script that created the process. This parameter is typically used for command-line applications and scripts that must reference a particular drive or folder when starting.

   - **NO_STARTUP_OPTIONS.** Constant indicating that there are no special startup options for the process. For more information about these options, see Modifying Process Startup Options later in this chapter.

   - **intProcessID.** If the Create method succeeds, the value of this variable is set to the process ID assigned to the remote process.

4. Return an error code of 0 if the process is successfully created, and echo the process ID assigned to the new process.

5. Return an error code other than 0 if the process could not be created, and echo that error code.

Listing 14.10 Creating a Process on a Remote Computer

```
1   strComputer = "webserver"
2   Set objWMIService = GetObject("winmgmts:" _
3       & "{impersonationLevel=impersonate}!\\" & strComputer & _
4           "\root\cimv2:Win32_Process")
5   errReturn = objWMIService.Create("database.exe", null, null, intProcessID)
6   If errReturn = 0 Then
7       Wscript.Echo "Database.exe was started with a process ID of " _
8           & intProcessID & "."
9   Else
10      Wscript.Echo "Database.exe could not be started due to error " & _
11          errReturn & "."
12  End If
```

Modifying Process Startup Options

The Win32_Process Create method enables you to configure startup options for any new process running on a computer. For example, you can configure a process so that it starts in a "hidden" window, which prevents a user from seeing, and possibly interrupting, it. If the process runs in a command window, you can configure the size, title, and foreground and background colors of the window.

Startup options are configured using the Win32_ProcessStartup class. Win32_ProcessStartup is a Method Type class; the Method Type class exists solely to pass information to a method. In this case, all the properties of an instance of Win32_ProcessStartup are passed to an instance of Win32_Process.

To configure a startup option by using Win32_ProcessStartup:

1. Create an instance of Win32_ProcessStartup.

2. Configure the properties of the new instance.

3. Include the instance as part of the Win32_Process Create method.

For example, if you have created a Win32_ProcessStartup instance named objConfig, you would pass the object name in the Create method as follows:

```
errReturn = objProcess.Create("Database.exe", null, objConfig, intProcessID)
```

A partial list of startup options that can be configured using the Win32_ProcessStartup class is shown in Table 14.3.

Table 14.3   Process Startup Properties Available Through the Win32_ProcessStartup Class

Startup Option	Description
FillAtrribute	Initial text and background colors if the process runs in a command window. These values are ignored in graphical user interface (GUI) applications. Valid values are: 1 — Foreground blue 2 — Foreground green 4 — Foreground red 8 — Foreground intensity 16 — Background blue 32 — Background green 64 — Background red 128 — Background intensity To specify both foreground and background colors, add the values together. For example, to have red type (4) on a blue background (16), set the FillAttribute to 20.
PriorityClass	Priority class of the new process (used to determine the scheduling priorities of the threads in the process). Values are: 32 — Normal 64 — Low 128 — High 16384 — Below Normal 32768 — Above Normal
ShowWindow	State of the window as it appears to the user. Valid values are: 1 — Window is shown minimized 3 — Window is shown maximized 5 — Window is shown in normal view 12 — Window is hidden and not displayed to the user
Title	Text to be displayed in the title bar of a command window where the process runs. If not specified, the name of the executable file is used as the window title instead. This property is ignored by processes that do not create a new command window.

(continued)

Table 14.3   Process Startup Properties Available Through the Win32_ProcessStartup Class *(continued)*

Startup Option	Description
XCountChars	Screen buffer width in character columns. This property is used for processes that create a command window but is ignored in GUI processes.
XSize	Width, in pixels, of the window, if a new window is created.
YCountChars	Screen buffer height in character rows. This property is used for processes that create a command window but is ignored in GUI processes.
YSize	Height, in pixels, of the window if a new window is created.

Scripting Steps

You can use the Win32_ProcessStartup class to configure various startup options for a process. These options include, but are not limited to, such things as creating a process in a hidden window and creating a higher-priority process.

Creating a process in a hidden window

Listing 14.11 contains a script that creates a process in a hidden window. To carry out this task, the script must perform the following steps:

1. Create a constant named HIDDEN_WINDOW, and set the value to 12. This is the value required to start a process in a hidden window.

2. Create a variable to specify the computer name.

3. Use a GetObject call to connect to the WMI namespace root\cimv2 on the computer, and set the impersonation level to "impersonate."

4. Get an instance of the Win32_ProcessStartup class.

5. Use the SpawnInstance_ method to create a new, "blank" instance of Win32_ProcessStartup. The new instance, named objConfig, stores the startup properties of the process to be created.

6. Set the ShowWindow property of the new instance to HIDDEN_WINDOW.

7. Use a second GetObject call to get an instance of Win32_Process.

8. Create the new process using the CreateProcess method.

   The first three parameters in the method specify the name of the executable file (such as Database.exe), the name of the startup folder (specifying Null gives the new process the same startup folder as the script that called the process), and the startup properties previously stored in objConfig.

   The fourth parameter (intProcessID) is a variable that represents the Process ID assigned to the new process. You can use this ID to monitor and, if necessary, terminate the process programmatically. This is especially useful for a process that runs in a hidden window and thus provides no visual cue to indicate that it is still running.

Listing 14.11   Creating a Process in a Hidden Window

```
1   Const HIDDEN_WINDOW = 12
2   strComputer = "."
3   Set objWMIService = GetObject("winmgmts:" _
4       & "{impersonationLevel=impersonate}!\\" & strComputer & "\root\cimv2")
5   Set objStartup = objWMIService.Get("Win32_ProcessStartup")
6   Set objConfig = objStartup.SpawnInstance_
7   objConfig.ShowWindow = HIDDEN_WINDOW
8   Set objProcess = GetObject("winmgmts:root\cimv2:Win32_Process")
9   errReturn = objProcess.Create _
10      ("Notepad.exe", null, objConfig, intProcessID)
```

Creating a higher-priority process

Listing 14.12 contains a script that creates a higher-priority process. To carry out this task, the script must perform the following steps:

1. Create a constant named ABOVE_NORMAL, and set the value to 32768. This is the value required to start a process with a priority of Above Normal.

2. Create a variable to specify the computer name.

3. Use a GetObject call to connect to the WMI namespace root\cimv2 on the computer, and set the impersonation level to "impersonate."

4. Get an instance of the Win32_ProcessStartup class.

5. Use the SpawnInstance_ method to create a new, "blank" instance of Win32_ProcessStartup. The new instance, which is used to store the startup properties of the process to be created, is named objConfig.

6. Set the PriorityClass property of the new instance to ABOVE_NORMAL.

7. Use a second GetObject call to get an instance of Win32_Process.

8. Create the new process using the CreateProcess method.

   The first three parameters in the method specify the name of the executable file (Database.exe), the name of the startup folder (specifying Null gives the new process the same startup folder as the script that called the process), and the startup properties previously stored in objConfig.

   The fourth parameter (intProcessID) is a variable that represents the Process ID assigned to the new process. You can use this ID to monitor and, if necessary, terminate the process programmatically.

Listing 14.12   Creating a Higher-Priority Process

```
1   Const ABOVE_NORMAL = 32768
2   strComputer = "."
3   Set objWMIService = GetObject("winmgmts:" _
4       & "{impersonationLevel=impersonate}!\\" & strComputer & "\root\cimv2")
5   Set objStartup = objWMIService.Get("Win32_ProcessStartup")
6   Set objConfig = objStartup.SpawnInstance_
7   objConfig.PriorityClass = ABOVE_NORMAL
8   Set objProcess = GetObject("winmgmts:root\cimv2:Win32_Process")
9   objProcess.Create "Database.exe", Null, objConfig, intProcessID
```

Terminating Processes

Computer problems are often due to a process that is no longer working as expected. For example, the process might be leaking memory, or it might have stopped responding to user input. When problems such as these occur, the process must be terminated. Although this might seem like a simple enough task, terminating a process can be complicated by several factors:

- The process might be hung and therefore no longer responds to menu or keyboard commands for closing the application. This makes it all but impossible for the typical user to dismiss the application and terminate the process.

- The process might be orphaned. For example, a script might create an instance of Word and then exit without destroying that instance. In effect, Word remains running on the computer, even though no user interface is visible. Because there is no user interface, there are no menu or keyboard commands available to terminate the process.

- You might not know which process needs to be terminated. For example, you might want to terminate all programs that are exceeding a specified amount of memory.

- Because Task Manager allows you to terminate only those processes that you created, you might not be able to terminate a process, even if you are an administrator on the computer.

Scripts enable you to overcome all of these potential obstacles, providing you with considerable administrative control over your computers. For example, if you suspect users are playing games that have been prohibited in your organization, you can easily write a script to connect to each computer, identify whether the game is running, and immediately terminate the process.

Scripting Steps

You can terminate a process by:

- Terminating a process that is currently running. For example, you might need to terminate a diagnostic program running on a remote computer. If there is no way to control the application remotely, you can simply terminate the process for that application.

- Preventing a process from running in the first place. By continuously monitoring process creation on a computer, you can identify and instantly terminate any process as soon as it starts. This provides one method of ensuring that certain applications (such as programs that download large media files over the Internet) are never run on certain computers.

Note

Group Policy can also be used to restrict the programs that run on a computer. However, Group Policy can restrict only the programs run using either the **Start** menu or Windows Explorer; it has no effect on programs started using other means, such as the command line. By contrast, WMI can prevent a process from running regardless of how the process was started.

Terminating a process that is currently running

Listing 14.13 contains a script that terminates the process in which the application Diagnose.exe is currently running. To carry out this task, the script must perform the following steps:

1. Create a variable to specify the computer name.

2. Use a GetObject call to connect to the WMI namespace root\cimv2 on the computer, and set the impersonation level to "impersonate."

3. Use the ExecQuery method to query the Win32_Process class.

   To restrict data retrieval to instances of Diagnose.exe, a WHERE clause is included that filters out all processes except those named Diagnose.exe.

4. For each process in the collection, use the Terminate method to end the process.

Listing 14.13 Terminating a Process

```
1  strComputer = "."
2  Set objWMIService = GetObject("winmgmts:" _
3      & "{impersonationLevel=impersonate}!\\" & strComputer & "\root\cimv2")
4  Set colProcessList = objWMIService.ExecQuery _
5      ("SELECT * FROM Win32_Process WHERE Name = 'Diagnose.exe'")
6  For Each objProcess in colProcessList
7      objProcess.Terminate()
8  Next
```

Terminating a process as soon as it starts

Listing 14.14 contains a script that uses a temporary event consumer to terminate a process as soon as it starts. To carry out this task, the script must perform the following steps:

1. Create a variable to specify the computer name.

2. Use a GetObject call to connect to the WMI namespace root\cimv2 on the computer, and set the impersonation level to "impersonate."

3. Use the ExecNotificationQuery method to register for notification each time there is an instance creation (each time an instance is created within the namespace).

    To restrict data retrieval to the process named Download.exe, include a WHERE clause to filter out all instance creations that do not involve Download.exe.

4. Create a loop that allows the script to run indefinitely.

    To stop monitoring, you need to either log off the computer or terminate the process in which the script runs.

5. Use the NextEvent method to retrieve the properties of each event when it occurs.

6. If Download.exe is created, use the Terminate method to terminate the new instance.

Listing 14.14   Preventing a Process from Running

```
1   strComputer = "."
2   Set objWMIService = GetObject("winmgmts:" _
3       & "{impersonationLevel=impersonate}!\\" & strComputer & "\root\cimv2")
4   Set colMonitoredProcesses = objWMIService. _
5       ExecNotificationQuery("SELECT * FROM __InstanceCreationEvent " _
6           & " WITHIN 1 WHERE TargetInstance IS 'Win32_Process'")
7   i = 0
8   Do While i = 0
9       Set objLatestProcess = colMonitoredProcesses.NextEvent
10      If objLatestProcess.TargetInstance.Name = "Download.exe" Then
11          objLatestProcess.TargetInstance.Terminate()
12      End If
13  Loop
```

C H A P T E R   1 5

Services

Many of the more important activities performed by a Windows-based computer are carried out using services, specialized applications that can run without the need for user intervention. Because services perform so many important tasks, service management — including monitoring services, configuring service properties, changing service passwords, and starting and stopping services — is an important part of system administration. Scripting can help facilitate the management of services throughout your organization.

In This Chapter

Services Overview 971
Monitoring Services..973
    Monitoring Service Availability 974
    Monitoring Service Reliability...976
Retrieving Service Properties 978
    Enumerating Service Properties 980
    Identifying the Services Running in a Process....................................983
Changing Service State 987
    Determining Which Services Can Be Stopped or Paused...................989
    Stopping or Pausing Services...990
    Starting or Resuming Services...991
Enumerating Dependent and Antecedent Services 993
    Enumerating Dependent Services..994
    Enumerating Antecedent Services 997
    Stopping and Starting Dependent Services 998
Configuring Services..1001
    Configuring Service Start Options..1003
    Configuring Error Control Codes for Autostart Services 1004

Managing Service Accounts and Service Account Passwords **1006**

    Configuring Service Accounts..1007

    Configuring Service Account Passwords 1009

Installing and Removing Services **1010**

    Installing Services 1011

    Removing Services..1013

Services Overview

Services are an important part of the Microsoft® Windows® 2000 operating system. A service, which is similar to the daemons used in the UNIX operating system, is an application that can communicate with and be administered by the Service Control Manager (SCM). In addition, a service can:

- Automatically start each time a computer starts.

- Run when no user is logged on to the computer. In fact, services can run even if no user ever logs on to the computer.

- Respond to requests without human intervention.

- Be configured to automatically restart if it fails.

These capabilities not only make services vitally important to the way computers function, but also make system administration viable. For example, without the DHCP service, an administrator would have to manually configure each computer's IP address. Without the DNS service, an administrator would have to manually configure and maintain Hosts or Lmhosts files. Without the automated capabilities of services, these tasks simply could not be performed in an enterprise setting.

Because services play such an important role in an organization's computing infrastructure, service management is a crucial part of any system administrator's job. If a service stops functioning, it affects the computer on which the service runs. Depending on the service, however, it could also adversely affect many users and their computers. If the DHCP service fails, computers are not given IP addresses, and users lose network connectivity. If the DNS service fails, the Active Directory® directory service is unavailable, and users cannot locate domain resources.

Managing services helps ensure that:

- Computers can fill their roles as workstations, domain controllers, mail servers, and database servers. For example, if the mail service stops, a mail server cannot carry out its assigned function.

- Users have access to resources both on the local computer and throughout the network.

- Disruptions to the workplace are minimized. By monitoring services, you can be alerted the moment a problem occurs. For example, if the mail service stops, the service failure can be immediately detected and the mail service restarted, even before users begin to experience problems.

How Services Work

Services, like other applications, are run from executable files. For example, the DNS service runs in an instance of *systemroot*\system32\dns.exe, and Internet Information Services runs in an instance of *systemroot*\ system32\inetsrv\inetinfo.exe.

However, services are a special type of application. Unlike the executable files for most applications, the executable file for a service includes code that enables it to perform the special functions of a service and to communicate with the SCM.

To run an application as a service, the following components (some part of the operating system, some part of the individual service) must be present.

- **Service Control Manager.** Communicates with services by forwarding commands that request a service to start, stop, pause, or resume. The SCM also monitors the status of each installed service and carries out specific actions if a service fails. (A failure is defined as any time a service stops without first sending the appropriate stop code to the SCM.)

  The SCM provides a unified means for configuring and managing services. In particular, the SCM does the following:

  - Maintains a database of all services.

  - Starts services either during system startup or on demand.

  - Enumerates installed services.

  - Maintains status information for all services.

  - Transmits commands (control requests) to services.

  - Locks and unlocks the service database.

- **Executable file for each service.** Includes code that enables the service to respond to commands from the SCM and to communicate its status to the SCM. This requirement precludes most applications from running as a service; Notepad, for example, cannot run as a service because the developers did not include code that enables Notepad to communicate with the SCM.

- **Service control program.** Allows a user to communicate with the SCM, which in turn communicates with an individual service. For example, to modify a service, you use a service control program (SCP) to send the modification commands to the SCM. In turn, the SCM relays those commands to the service, and the appropriate modifications are made.

  The Services snap-in to the Microsoft Management Console (MMC) is an example of a service control program, as are Sc.exe and the Net Start and Net Stop commands. Windows Management Instrumentation (WMI) scripts can also function as service control programs.

Running Services in Windows 2000

When a Windows 2000–based computer starts, the executable file for SCM (Services.exe) begins running before the logon dialog box appears. This allows autostart services to start before any user logs on.

After Services.exe starts, the SCM scans the contents of the registry subkey HKEY_LOCAL_MACHINE\SYSTEM\CurrentControlSet\Services. For each service listed in the registry, the SCM creates a corresponding entry in the services database. It establishes channels for communicating with service control programs and then starts the autostart services.

When a service starts, it initializes a minimum of two threads. One thread is used to communicate with the SCM and the other is used to respond to requests from client applications. For example, a Web server service creates a TCP "listen socket" and waits for inbound HTTP requests. When such a request is received, the thread becomes active, processes the request, and then suspends itself until the next request arrives. An application that initializes only a single thread cannot run as a service.

Monitoring Services

Many of the important operations that take place on a computer (especially on servers) run as services. This makes it imperative that you carefully monitor the services running on the computers in your network. Many services (such as DNS and DHCP) are so critical that a failure on a single server could adversely affect hundreds or even thousands of users, preventing them from logging on to the network or accessing network-based resources.

In general, there are three forms of service monitoring:

- **Monitoring service availability.** Measures the percentage of time that a service is available.

  The exact definition of availability depends on the expectations for each service. If a database service must be available to users from 8:00 A.M. to 6:00 P.M. Monday through Friday, it can be considered completely available as long as the service is running during those times. If the service fails on a Saturday, or at 2:00 A.M. on Tuesday, this does not affect availability. It does, however, affect service reliability.

- **Monitoring service reliability.** Measures how frequently a service fails and the amount of time required to restore a failed service to full functionality.

  Reliability is calculated by dividing the time the service is functioning by the total number of days in a year. For example, a service that experiences a total downtime of 2 days during the course of a year is 99.5 percent reliable (363 days of availability divided by 365 days in a year).

- **Monitoring service performance.** Measures whether the service carries out its tasks in the expected manner (for example, whether the service handles the expected number of requests in the expected amount of time). Although it is possible to use WMI to monitor the performance of some operating system services in Windows 2000, a complete discussion of this type of monitoring is beyond the scope of this chapter.

Monitoring Service Availability

When you monitor a service for availability, you verify only that the service is running. If you need to know whether the service is running at peak efficiency, you need to use a more in-depth type of monitoring (such as performance monitoring). Although relatively simple, availability monitoring is extremely important; other questions, such as whether the service is performing at the expected level, are meaningless if the service is not even running.

Availability monitoring generally involves a probe that returns the status of a service. By saving the results of each probe to a database, you can calculate the availability of a service. For example, if you issue 100 probes and the service responds 99 times, the service has an availability of 99 percent.

Availability is often expressed as the amount of time during a year that the service was not available. For example, a service with an availability of 99 percent means the service was unavailable for a total of 3.7 days. This could be the result of one outage of 3.7 days or several outages that, combined, add up to 3.7 days.

To increase the availability of a service, you can do one of two things:

- Increase the mean time between failures.

  Unfortunately, a service failure is often the result of a bug, either in the service or in the operating system. Unless you wrote the code for both the service and the operating system, it might be difficult for you to increase the mean time between failures.

- Decrease the time it takes to restart the service.

  If you manually restart the service each time it fails, the service does not return to full functionality unless you are available to restart it. To increase availability, you can write a script that monitors the service state periodically and restarts the service automatically each time it fails.

Scripting Steps

Reporting on the availability of services can be done by:

- Reporting the status of all services.

- Reporting on services that are in a specific state (for example, services that are running or services that are not running).

Reporting the state of all services

Listing 15.1 contains a script that monitors service availability; it does this by querying the list of services installed on a computer and reporting the current state of each service. To carry out this task, the script must perform the following steps:

1. Create a variable to specify the target computer name.

2. Use a GetObject call to connect to the WMI namespace root\cimv2 on the target computer, and set the impersonation level to "impersonate."

3. Use the ExecQuery method to query the Win32_Service class. This returns a collection consisting of all the services installed on the computer.

4. For each service in the collection, echo the service display name and the current state of each service.

Listing 15.1   Monitoring Service Availability

```
1   strComputer = "."
2   Set objWMIService = GetObject("winmgmts:" & _
3       "{impersonationLevel=Impersonate}!\\" & strComputer & "\root\cimv2")
4   Set colServices = objWMIService.ExecQuery("SELECT * FROM Win32_Service")
5   For Each objService in colServices
6       Wscript.Echo objService.DisplayName & " = " & objService.State
7   Next
```

Reporting on services that are not running

Listing 15.2 contains a script that monitors service availability; it does this by querying the list of services installed on a computer and reporting on all services that are not running. To carry out this task, the script must perform the following steps:

1. Create a variable to specify the target computer name.

2. Use a GetObject call to connect to the WMI namespace root\cimv2 on the target computer, and set the impersonation level to "impersonate."

3. Use the ExecQuery method to query the Win32_Service class. To restrict data retrieval to the set of services that are not running, the query includes a Where clause that limits the return to services with a state that does not equal "Running."

Unlike the WMI Query Language WQL statement in Listing 15.1 that retrieved all the properties for every service, the query in Listing 15.2 retrieves only the values of the display name and state properties. This minimizes the amount of data that must be sent across the network.

4. For each service in the collection, echo the service display name and the service state.

Listing 15.2   Monitoring Inactive Services

```
1  strComputer = "."
2  Set objWMIService = GetObject("winmgmts:" & _
3      "{impersonationLevel=Impersonate}!\\" & strComputer & "\root\cimv2")
4  Set colStoppedServices = objWMIService.ExecQuery _
5   ("SELECT DisplayName,State FROM Win32_Service WHERE State <> 'Running'")
6  For Each objService in colStoppedServices
7      Wscript.Echo objService.DisplayName & " = " & objService.State
8  Next
```

An attempt to echo a Win32_Service property other than display name and state would result in an error based on the property list defined in the WQL query.

Monitoring Service Reliability

Reliability monitoring enables you to track the mean time between service failures. The mean time between failures tells you the amount of time you can expect a service to run before it fails. A service with a mean time between failures of 1000 hours is expected to run approximately 1000 hours before encountering problems.

Knowing the mean time between failure can help you prevent problems before they occur. For example, you might have a service that fails every 10 days because of a memory leak. Rather than wait for the service to fail (perhaps at a highly inconvenient time for your users), you might periodically schedule the service to stop and restart at a time that minimizes the impact on users, on other services, and on other parts of the computing environment.

Reliability monitoring can also tell you how long it takes for a service to be restored in the event that it does fail. For example, your reliability statistics might show that it takes 6 hours to fully restore a particular service. This information can help you plan routine service maintenance: If you need to upgrade or reconfigure the service, schedule this maintenance during a 6-hour block that minimally disrupts users.

You can create an event subscription that notifies you each time a service changes state (for example, goes from running to stopped). By saving these state changes to a database, you can calculate the mean time between failures and the time required to restore full functionality.

Scripting Steps

Listing 15.3 contains a script that uses a temporary event subscription to monitor changes in service state. To carry out this task, the script must perform the following steps:

1. Create a variable to specify the target computer name.

2. Use a GetObject call to connect to the WMI namespace root\cimv2 on the target computer, and set the impersonation level to "impersonate."

3. Use the ExecNotificationQuery method to register for notification each time there is an instance modification (each time an instance within the namespace changes in some way).

   Because the script monitors only changes to services, a Where clause is included to limit monitoring and data retrieval to instance modifications that involve the Win32_Service class.

4. Create a loop that allows the script to run indefinitely.

   To stop monitoring, you need to terminate the script.

5. Use the NextEvent method to retrieve each event when it occurs.

6. Each time a service is modified in some way, the script checks to see whether the current state of the service differs from the previous state of the service. If it does not, the script resumes by waiting for the next event.

   Comparing the previous state with the current state enables you to identify whether the modification involved a change in service state. For example, a change in service state would be indicated by a service that was started when last monitored but is now stopped. If the previous and current states are the same, the modification did not involve service state but instead reflects a change to some other property of the service (such as changing the start mode from manual to autostart).

7. If the service states differ, echo the display name of the service, its current state, and its previous state.

Listing 15.3   Monitoring Changes in Service Status by Using a Temporary Event Subscriber

```
1   strComputer = "."
2   Set objWmiService = GetObject("winmgmts:" & _
3       "{impersonationLevel=impersonate}!\\" & strComputer & "\root\cimv2")
4   Set objWmiEventSource = objWMIService.ExecNotificationQuery _
5       ("SELECT * FROM __InstanceModificationEvent " & _
6           "WITHIN 30 WHERE TargetInstance ISA 'Win32_Service'")
7   Do
8       Set objService = objWmiEventSource.NextEvent
9       If objService.TargetInstance.State <> _
10          objService.PreviousInstance.State Then
11              Wscript.Echo objService.TargetInstance.DisplayName & _
12                  " is " & objService.TargetInstance.State & _
13                      ". The service previously was " & _
14                          objService.PreviousInstance.State & "."
15      End If
16  Loop
```

Retrieving Service Properties

To effectively manage services in your organization, you need a detailed understanding of the properties of those services. You need to know which services are configured to automatically start whenever a computer is started, and which services need to be manually restarted. You also need to know the user account under which each service is running and whether the service runs as part of a service group.

You can use the WMI Win32_Service class to retrieve the properties of all the services installed on all the computers on your network. Some of the important service properties available through the Win32_Service class are listed in Table 15.1.

Table 15.1   Service Properties Available from the Win32_Service Class

Property	Description
AcceptPause	Indicates whether the service can be paused.
AcceptStop	Indicates whether the service can be stopped.
Description	Description of the service.
DesktopInteract	Indicates whether the service can create or communicate with windows on the desktop, and thus interact in some way with a user. Interactive services must run under the Local System account. Most services are not interactive; that is, they do not communicate with the user in any way.

(continued)

Table 15.1 Service Properties Available from the Win32_Service Class *(continued)*

Property	Description
DisplayName	Name of the service as viewed in the Services snap-in. Note that the display name and the service name (which is stored in the registry) are not always the same. For example, the DHCP Client service has the service name Dhcp but the display name DHCP Client.
ErrorControl	Action to be taken if a service fails during startup. Values and their associated actions include: • Ignore — User is not notified. • Normal — Message box displays notifying the user of the problem. • Severe — Computer restarts with last-known good configuration. • Critical — Computer attempts to restart with a good configuration. If the service fails to start a second time, startup fails.
ExitCode	Error code defining any problems that were encountered when starting or stopping a service. If a service is able to properly start or stop, this value is set to 0 (no error).
Name	Unique name of the service as stored in the registry.
PathName	Fully qualified path to the executable file responsible for implementing the service.
ProcessID	Process identifier assigned to the service during startup.
ServiceType	Valid service types include: • Kernel Driver • File System Driver • Adapter • Recognizer Driver • Own Process • Win32 Share Process • Interactive Process
Started	Indicates whether or not the service is started.
State	Valid states include: • Stopped • Start Pending • Stop Pending • Running • Continue Pending • Pause Pending • Paused • Unknown
SystemName	Name of the computer where the service is installed. This property is useful in scripts that retrieve service status from multiple computers.

The service properties available through Win32_Service are similar to the service properties available through the Services snap-in, as shown in Figure 15.1.

Figure 15.1 Win32_Service Properties

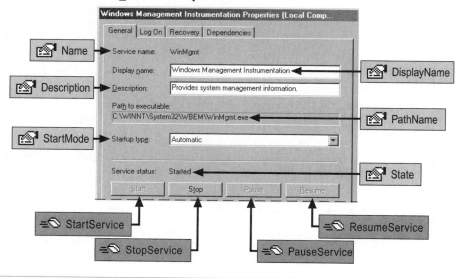

Enumerating Service Properties

In an enterprise setting, you often want services to be configured consistently. This facilitates service management, because you do not have to guess how a particular service is configured on a particular computer. Instead, you can be sure that the DHCP service is configured exactly the same on all your DHCP servers.

By using WMI, you can create a script that retrieves the properties of all the services on all your computers and saves that information to a file or database. You can then analyze the information in the file to determine which services, if any, need to be reconfigured in order to bring them in line with organization standards. In fact, the script can even carry out the reconfiguration for you.

Scripting Steps

Listing 15.4 contains a script that retrieves the properties of all the services on a computer and then saves those properties to a text file. To carry out this task, the script must perform the following steps:

1. Create a constant ForAppending and set the value to 8. This constant is used when opening the text file where the service properties are written.

2. Create an instance of the FileSystemObject.

3. Open the text file C:\Scripts\Service_list.csv.

   If the file does not exist, it is created.

4. Write a list of field headers to the file.

    Because the data is being saved in comma-separated-values format, field headers are separated by commas.

5. Create a variable to specify the computer name.

6. Use a GetObject call to connect to the WMI namespace root\cimv2, and set the impersonation level to "impersonate."

7. Use the ExecQuery method to query the Win32_Service class. This returns a collection consisting of all the services installed on the computer.

8. For each service in the collection, write the service properties to the text file, separating the properties using commas. After all the properties for a service are written to the text file, write a carriage return (WriteLine) so that the properties for the next service are written on a new line in the file.

9. Close the text file.

Listing 15.4 Retrieving Service Properties

```
1   Const ForAppending = 8
2   Set objFSO = CreateObject("Scripting.FileSystemObject")
3   Set objLogFile = objFSO.OpenTextFile("c:\scripts\service_list.csv", _
4       ForAppending, True)
5   objLogFile.Write _
6       ("System Name,Service Name,Service Type,Service State,Exit " _
7           & "Code,Process ID,Can Be Paused,Can Be Stopped,Caption," _
8           & "Description,Can Interact with Desktop,Display Name,Error " _
9           & "Control,Executable Path Name,Service Started," _
10          & "Start Mode,Account Name ")
11  objLogFile.Writeline
12  strComputer = "."
13  Set objWMIService = GetObject("winmgmts:" _
14      & "{impersonationLevel=impersonate}!\\" & strComputer & "\root\cimv2")
15  Set colListOfServices = objWMIService.ExecQuery _
16          ("SELECT * FROM Win32_Service")
17  For Each objService in colListOfServices
18      objLogFile.Write(objService.SystemName) & ","
19      objLogFile.Write(objService.Name) & ","
20      objLogFile.Write(objService.ServiceType) & ","
21      objLogFile.Write(objService.State) & ","
22      objLogFile.Write(objService.ExitCode) & ","
23      objLogFile.Write(objService.ProcessID) & ","
24      objLogFile.Write(objService.AcceptPause) & ","
25      objLogFile.Write(objService.AcceptStop) & ","
```

(continued)

Listing 15.4   Retrieving Service Properties (continued)

```
26      objLogFile.Write(objService.Caption) & ","
27      objLogFile.Write(objService.Description) & ","
28      objLogFile.Write(objService.DesktopInteract) & ","
29      objLogFile.Write(objService.DisplayName) & ","
30      objLogFile.Write(objService.ErrorControl) & ","
31      objLogFile.Write(objService.PathName) & ","
32      objLogFile.Write(objService.Started) & ","
33      objLogFile.Write(objService.StartMode) & ","
34      objLogFile.Write(objService.StartName) & ","
35      objLogFile.Writeline
36   Next
37   objLogFile.Close
```

The resulting text file looks similar to the following when opened in a text editor such as
Notepad:

```
System Name,Service Name,Service Type,Service State, Exit Code,Process ID,Can Be
Paused,Can Be Stopped,Caption,Description,Can Interact with Desktop,Display
Name,Error Control, Executable Path Name,Service Started,Start Mode,Account Name
Computer1,Alerter,Share
Process,Stopped,1077,0,False,False,Alerter,Alerter,False,Alerter,Normal,C:\Window
s\System32\services.exe,False,Manual,LocalSystem,\
```

As you can see, a text editor is not the optimal choice for reviewing the data. Because of this, you
might want to create a script that uses the Tabular Data Control to display service properties
within Internet Explorer. This allows you to display data using multiple fonts, multiple colors, or
any other formatting style available through HTML. By using the Tabular Data Control, you can
also display the data in table form without having to write the HTML code required to create a
table for a Web page.

Note

For more information about the Tabular Data Control, see "Creating
Enterprise Scripts" in this book.

For example, you might create a Web page similar to the one shown in Figure 15.2.

Figure 15.2   Displaying Service Properties in a Web Page

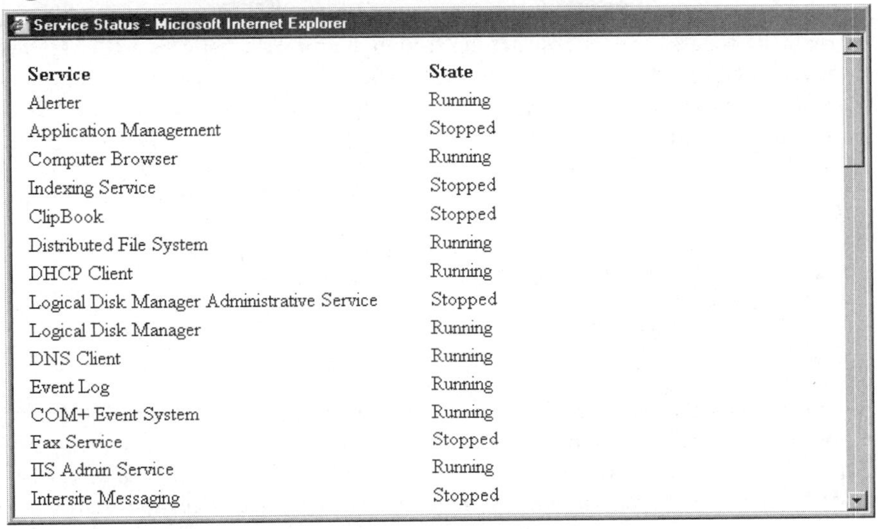

Service	State
Alerter	Running
Application Management	Stopped
Computer Browser	Running
Indexing Service	Stopped
ClipBook	Stopped
Distributed File System	Running
DHCP Client	Running
Logical Disk Manager Administrative Service	Stopped
Logical Disk Manager	Running
DNS Client	Running
Event Log	Running
COM+ Event System	Running
Fax Service	Stopped
IIS Admin Service	Running
Intersite Messaging	Stopped

Identifying the Services Running in a Process

Windows 2000 allows services to run in a shared process. This means a single executable file can be responsible for running multiple services, an approach that helps conserve system resources. In Windows 2000, each new process is given a minimum working set (memory size) of 800 kilobytes (KB). If you are running five services in separate executable files, that adds up to 4 megabytes (MB) of working set space. By running the five services from a single executable file, you might be able to limit memory use to the 800 KB minimum required for a single executable file.

This is possible if the memory required by each of the services totals 800 KB or less. For example, if each service requires 100 KB of memory, the total memory required by the five services running under a single executable file is 500 KB. In this case, the single executable file is then assigned the minimum 800 KB of memory. If you run each service as a separate executable file, each is assigned the minimum 800 KB, and the five services combined thus use 4 MB of memory.

The reduction in memory use represents the advantage of running multiple services in a single process. The disadvantage is the fact that this can complicate system administration in at least two ways:

- When services share a process, the failure of any one service in that process results in the failure of all the services in the process.

  For example, if 10 services share a process and Service 1 fails, Services 2 through 10 also fail.

- Determining which services are running in which process is difficult.

  This is especially true for the operating system application Svchost.exe. Svchost.exe is a generic host process for services running from dynamic-link libraries (DLLs). On a typical Windows 2000–based computer, multiple copies of Svchost.exe are running, each hosting a different set of services. For example, the Netsvcs group hosts four services: Netman, Rasman, Rasauto, and RemoteAccess.

> **Note**
>
> During system startup, Svchost.exe checks the registry for the set of services to load together in a shared process. The Svchost.exe groups and the services hosted by each group are identified in the registry subkey HKEY_LOCAL_MACHINE\SOFTWARE\Microsoft \Windows NT\CurrentVersion\Svchost.

Knowing the services that run in a given process provides important information when you are troubleshooting computer problems. For example, if an instance of Svchost.exe appears to be leaking memory, you need to know which services are affected if you stop that process. If an instance of Svchost.exe stops running, you need to know which services to restart.

You can use WMI to determine which services are running in a given process. You can do this by retrieving the service path name (for example, C:\Windows\System32\Services.exe) and then enumerating all the services that share that path.

Scripting Steps

You can display services running in shared processes by doing the following:

- Displaying the services running in a single shared process
- Displaying the services running in all processes

Displaying the services running in a single shared process

Listing 15.5 contains a script that displays the services running in a single shared process, Services.exe. To carry out this task, the script must perform the following steps:

1. Create a variable to specify the computer name.

2. Use a GetObject call to connect to the WMI namespace root\cimv2, and set the impersonation level to "impersonate."

3. Use the ExecQuery method to query the Win32_Service class. This returns a collection consisting of all the services installed on the computer.

4. For each service in the collection, check to see whether the PathName is C:\Windows\System32\Services.exe. (The path name indicates the executable file responsible for the service.) If True, echo the service display name.

Listing 15.5   Displaying the Services Running in a Specified Process

```
1  strComputer = "."
2  Set objWMIService = GetObject("winmgmts:" _
3     & "{impersonationLevel=impersonate}!\\" & strComputer & "\root\cimv2")
4  Set colListOfServices = objWMIService.ExecQuery("SELECT * FROM Win32_Service")
5  For Each objService in colListOfServices
6      If objService.PathName = "c:\windows\system32\services.exe" Then
7          Wscript.Echo objService.DisplayName
8      End If
9  Next
```

Displaying the services running in all processes

The script shown in Listing 15.5 works well for services running in a standard executable file such as Services.exe. However, it is less useful for services running in Svchost.exe because several instances of Svchost.exe are probably running on your computer. A script that enumerates services by using the path name lists all the services running under all the instances of Svchost.exe as if they were all part of the same process.

However, you can use the ProcessID property to determine which services are running in a given process: retrieve the list of process IDs corresponding to active services, and then query each ID to determine the individual services sharing that process.

Listing 15.6 contains a script that displays the services running in all the processes on a computer. To carry out this task, the script must perform the following steps.

1. Create a Dictionary object.

    This is used to temporarily store the unique process ID for each service.

2. Create a variable to specify the computer name.

3. Use a GetObject call to connect to the WMI namespace root\cimv2, and set the impersonation level to "impersonate."

4. Use the ExecQuery method to query the Win32_Service class. Because process IDs are valid only for services that are running, a Where clause is included to limit data retrieval to those services that are not stopped.

5. For each service in the collection, retrieve the process ID and then check to see whether that ID has been stored in the Dictionary object.

    This generates a list of unique process IDs. If the ID is already in the Dictionary, the script simply proceeds; this ensures that no duplicate IDs are added to the Dictionary. If the process ID is not in the Dictionary, the script adds the ID.

6. Retrieve the list of all Dictionary items (the unique process IDs).

7. Create a loop that cycles through all the items in the Dictionary.

   The loop must begin at 0 because the first item in the Dictionary is assigned item 0. This also means that the loop must end at the number of items minus 1. For example, if the Dictionary has 5 items, the loop would be from 0 to 4 because the Dictionary would contain items 0, 1, 2, 3, and 4.

8. For each Dictionary item (process ID), use a GetObject call to retrieve the list of services from the Win32_Service class that have that same process ID.

9. Echo the process ID.

10. Echo the display name for each service running in that process.

Listing 15.6   Displaying the Services Running in All Processes on a Computer

```
1   set objIdDictionary = CreateObject("Scripting.Dictionary")
2   strComputer = "."
3   Set objWMIService = GetObject("winmgmts:" _
4       & "{impersonationLevel=impersonate}!\\" & strComputer & "\root\cimv2")
5   Set colServices = objWMIService.ExecQuery _
6       ("Select * from Win32_Service Where State <> 'Stopped'")
7   For Each objService in colServices
8       If objIdDictionary.Exists(objService.ProcessID) Then
9       Else
10          objIdDictionary.Add objService.ProcessID, objService.ProcessID
11      End If
12  Next
13  colProcessIDs = objIdDictionary.Items
14  For i = 0 to objIdDictionary.Count - 1
15      Set colServices = objWMIService.ExecQuery _
16          ("SELECT * FROM Win32_Service WHERE ProcessID = '" & _
17              colProcessIDs(i) & "'")
18      Wscript.Echo "Process ID: " & colProcessIDs(i)
19      For Each objService in colServices
20          Wscript.Echo VbTab & objService.DisplayName
21      Next
22  Next
```

When the script in Listing 15.6 is run using Cscript.exe, output similar to the following is displayed in the command window:

```
Process ID: 1332
        Windows Installer
Process ID: 228
        Net Logon
        IPSEC Policy Agent
        Security Accounts Manager
Process ID: 676
        Remote Registry Service
```

Changing Service State

You can use WMI to automatically start and stop services based on certain conditions. This enables you to create scripts that can query the services on multiple computers and then either start or stop specific services based on the criteria specified in the script.

For example, if you have a service with a known memory leak, you might need to periodically stop the service, wait a few minutes, and then restart it. Instead of doing this manually, you can schedule a WMI script to run at a specified interval (for example, every 72 hours) and stop and restart the service.

Alternatively, you can create a script that continuously monitors the memory usage of the process responsible for the service and then automatically stops and restarts the service if memory use exceeds a specified threshold.

The approach you take depends on the nature of the problem. If the service consistently runs for 72 hours without a problem, a scheduled script is the optimal solution: It can stop and restart the service before the memory leak occurs. If the memory leak occurs at more random intervals, continuous monitoring can enable you to identify the problem and fix it immediately, without having to wait until the next time the script is scheduled to run.

In addition to starting and stopping services, WMI can be used to pause services and to resume services that have been paused. The difference between a stopped service and a paused service depends on how the service is created. In general, a stopped service quits functioning and disconnects all users currently using the service. A paused service no longer accepts new connections but continues to support users already connected to the service.

When you control services by using WMI, an error code is returned indicating the success or failure of the operation. These error codes are shown in Table 15.2.

Table 15.2   Service Method Error Codes

Value	Description
0	The request was accepted.
1	The request is not supported.
2	The user did not have the necessary access.
3	The service cannot be stopped because other services that are running are dependent on it.
4	The requested control code is not valid, or it is unacceptable to the service.
5	The requested control code cannot be sent to the service because the state of the service (Win32_BaseService State property) is equal to 0, 1, or 2.

(continued)

Table 15.2   Service Method Error Codes *(continued)*

Value	Description
6	The service has not been started.
7	The service did not respond to the start request in a timely fashion.
8	Unknown failure when starting the service.
9	The directory path to the service executable file was not found.
10	The service is already running.
11	The database to add a new service is locked.
12	A dependency this service relies on has been removed from the system.
13	The service failed to find the service needed from a dependent service.
14	The service has been disabled from the system.
15	The service does not have the correct authentication to run on the system.
16	This service is being removed from the system.
17	The service has no execution thread.
18	The service has circular dependencies when it starts.
19	A service is running under the same name.
20	The service name has invalid characters.
21	Invalid parameters have been passed to the service.
22	The account under which this service runs is either invalid or lacks the permissions to run the service.
23	The service exists in the database of services available from the system.
24	The service is currently paused in the system.

Determining Which Services Can Be Stopped or Paused

Not all services can be stopped, and even fewer services can be paused. The capability of being stopped or paused must be coded into the service itself; without this code, the service does not respond to stop or pause requests. In particular, services that run as part of Services.exe (the process that is also responsible for running the SCM) can be neither stopped nor paused. If Services.exe could be stopped, that would stop the SCM. Without the SCM, all other services on the computer would be unable to function.

You can query the WMI AcceptStop and the AcceptPause properties to determine which services can be paused and which services can be stopped. For example, of the 88 services installed on a particular Windows 2000 domain controller, 54 were capable of being stopped, but only 17 were capable of being paused.

Scripting Steps

The scripts for determining which services can be stopped or which services can be paused are similar.

Determining which services can be stopped

Listing 15.7 contains a script that displays a list of services that can be stopped. To carry out this task, the script must perform the following steps.

1. Create a variable to specify the computer name.

2. Use a GetObject call to connect to the WMI namespace root\cimv2, and set the impersonation level to "impersonate."

3. Use the ExecQuery method to query the Win32_Service class. To restrict data retrieval to those services that can be stopped, a Where clause is included that returns only services for which the AcceptStop property is True.

4. For each service in the collection, echo the service display name.

Listing 15.7   Determining Which Services Can Be Stopped

```
1  strComputer = "."
2  Set objWMIService = GetObject("winmgmts:" _
3      & "{impersonationLevel=impersonate}!\\" & strComputer & "\root\cimv2")
4  Set colServices = objWMIService.ExecQuery _
5      ("SELECT * FROM Win32_Service WHERE AcceptStop = True")
6  For Each objService in colServices
7      Wscript.Echo objService.DisplayName
8  Next
```

Determining which services can be paused

To determine which services can be paused, you can use a script similar to Listing 15.7 but substitute the AcceptPause property for the AcceptStop property in the Where clause, as shown in Listing 15.8. The output displayed in the command window lists the services that can be paused instead of those that can be stopped.

Listing 15.8   Determining Which Services Can Be Paused

```
1  strComputer = "."
2  Set objWMIService = GetObject("winmgmts:" _
3      & "{impersonationLevel=impersonate}!\\" & strComputer & "\root\cimv2")
4  Set colServices = objWMIService.ExecQuery _
5      ("SELECT * FROM Win32_Service WHERE AcceptPause = True")
6  For Each objService in colServices
7      Wscript.Echo objService.DisplayName
8  Next
```

Stopping or Pausing Services

After you have determined which services can be stopped or paused, you can use the StopService and PauseService methods to stop and pause services. The decision to stop a service rather than pause it, or vice versa, depends on several factors, including the following:

- Is the service capable of being paused? If not, your only option is the stop the service.

- Do you need to continue handling client requests for anyone already connected to the service? If so, pausing a service typically allows it to handle existing clients while denying access to new clients. By contrast, when you stop a service, all clients are immediately disconnected.

- Do you need to reconfigure a service and have the changes take effect immediately? Although service properties can be changed while a service is paused, most of them do not take effect until the service is actually stopped and restarted.

The scripting code required to stop a service is almost identical to the code required to pause the service.

Scripting Steps

The scripts for stopping services and pausing services are similar.

Stopping services

Listing 15.9 contains a script that stops all the services running under a specified user account. To carry out this task, the script must perform the following steps:

1. Create a variable to specify the computer name.

2. Use a GetObject call to connect to the WMI namespace root\cimv2, and set the impersonation level to "impersonate."

3. Use the ExecQuery method to query the Win32_Service class. To limit data retrieval to a specific set of services, a Where clause is included restricting the collection to those services with the StartName .\\Netsvc.

4. For each service in the collection, stop the service using the StopService method.

   The return code for the StopService method is stored in the errReturnCode variable. In a production script, it is a good idea to check the value of that variable to ensure that the method was successfully applied.

Listing 15.9   Stopping Services Running Under a Specified Account

```
1   strComputer = "."
2   Set objWMIService = GetObject("winmgmts:" _
3       & "{impersonationLevel=impersonate}!\\" & strComputer & "\root\cimv2")
4   Set colServices = objWMIService.ExecQuery _
5       ("SELECT * FROM win32_Service WHERE StartName = '.\\Netsvc'")
6   For Each objService in colServices
7       errReturnCode = objService.StopService()
8   Next
```

Pausing services

To pause services, use a script similar to Listing 15.9 but substitute the PauseService method for the StopService method, as shown in Listing 15.10.

Listing 15.10   Pausing Services Running Under a Specified Account

```
1   strComputer = "."
2   Set objWMIService = GetObject("winmgmts:" _
3       & "{impersonationLevel=impersonate}!\\" & strComputer & "\root\cimv2")
4   Set colProcesses = objWMIService.ExecQuery _
5       ("SELECT * FROM Win32_Service WHERE StartName = '.\\Netsvc'")
6   For Each objService in colServices
7       errReturnCode = objService.PauseService()
8   Next
```

Starting or Resuming Services

Although there might appear to be no practical difference between a service that is stopped and a service that is paused, the two states appear differently to the SCM. A stopped service is a service that is not running and must go through the entire service start procedure. A paused service, however, is still running but has had its functioning is suspended. Because of this, a paused service does not need to go through the entire service start procedure but needs a different procedure to resume functioning.

You must use the proper method to start a service that has been stopped or to resume a service that has been paused. The Win32_Service methods StartService and ResumeService should be used in the following situations:

- If a service is currently stopped, you must use the StartService method to restart it; ResumeService cannot start a service that is currently stopped.

- If a service is paused, you must use ResumeService. If you use the StartService method on a paused service, you receive the message, "The service is already running." However, the service remains paused until the resume service control code is sent to it.

Scripting Steps

The scripts for starting services that are stopped or resuming services that are paused are similar.

Starting automatic services that are stopped

Listing 15.11 contains a script that starts all automatic services that have been stopped. To carry out this task, the script must perform the following steps:

1. Create a variable to specify the computer name.

2. Use a GetObject call to connect to the WMI namespace root\cimv2, and set the impersonation level to "impersonate."

3. Use the ExecQuery method to query the Win32_Service class. To restrict data retrieval to a subset of services, the query includes a Where clause that limits data retrieval only to autostart services that are currently stopped.

4. For each service in the collection, use the StartService method to start the stopped service.

Listing 15.11   Starting Automatic Services That Are Stopped

```
1   strComputer = "."
2   Set objWMIService = GetObject("winmgmts:" _
3       & "{impersonationLevel=impersonate}!\\" & strComputer & "\root\cimv2")
4   Set colListOfServices = objWMIService.ExecQuery _
5       ("SELECT * FROM Win32_Service WHERE State = 'Stopped' and StartMode = " _
6           & "'Auto'")
7   For Each objService in colListOfServices
8       objService.StartService()
9   Next
```

Resuming automatic services that are paused

To resume services that have been paused, use a script similar to Listing 15.12 but substitute the Paused property for the Stopped property in the Where clause and the ResumeService method for the StartService method, as shown in Listing 15.12.

Listing 15.12 Resuming Automatic Services That Are Paused

```
1  strComputer = "."
2  Set objWMIService = GetObject("winmgmts:" _
3      & "{impersonationLevel=impersonate}!\\" & strComputer & "\root\cimv2")
4  Set colListOfServices = objWMIService.ExecQuery _
5      ("SELECT * FROM Win32_Service WHERE State = 'Paused' and StartMode = " _
6          & "'Auto'")
7  For Each objService in colListOfServices
8      objService.ResumeService()
9  Next
```

Enumerating Dependent and Antecedent Services

Service management is complicated by service dependencies. For example, many Internet services — including the FTP Publishing Service, the World Wide Web Publishing Service, and the Simple Mail Transfer Protocol (SMTP) Service — are dependent upon the Internet Information Services (IIS) Admin Service. If the IIS Admin Service is not available, none of these dependent services can run.

Conversely, you cannot stop the IIS Admin Service without first stopping the dependent services. If this were allowed, stopping the IIS Admin Service would cause all its dependent services to fail because those services cannot run unless IIS Admin Service is also running. The IIS Admin Service is therefore antecedent to its dependent services.

The relationship between the dependent and antecedent roles is as follows:

- **Antecedent**. If Service X is antecedent to Service Y, Service X must be running before you can run Service Y.

- **Dependent**. If Service X is dependent on Service Y, Service Y must be running before you can run Service X.

Figure 15.3 maps these service roles to the Dependencies property page found in the Services snap-in.

Figure 15.3   Dependent and Antecedent Roles

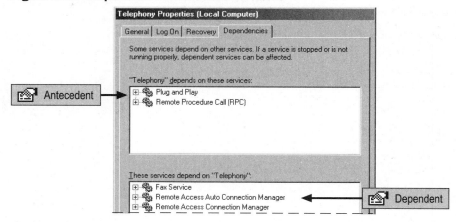

To determine service dependencies, you need a script that specifies the service to be enumerated and its role. The Win32_DependentService class provides a means to identify the particular role played by that service.

 Note

Win32_DependentServices is an association class, a special type of class that specifies a relationship between two WMI objects. For more information about Association classes, see "WMI Scripting Primer" in this book.

For example, to list all the services that depend on the Remote Access Connection Manager, you need to create a script that:

1.   Retrieves all services associated with the Remote Access Connection Manager.

2.   Filters the list so it displays only those associated services for which the Remote Access Connection Manager is the antecedent.

Enumerating Dependent Services

As noted earlier, dependent services are those services that cannot start unless the antecedent service is running. Likewise, you cannot stop an antecedent service if one of its dependents is still running.

These dependencies can complicate service management, particularly if you are creating automated methods for starting and stopping services. Because of this, identifying service dependencies is an important part of service management.

Scripting Steps

You can enumerate dependent services by doing the following:

- Enumerating dependent services for a single service. This approach is useful if you are creating an automated script for starting or stopping a particular service.

- Enumerating dependent services for all the services on a computer. This approach is useful if you would like to view the dependency relationships for all your services.

Enumerating dependent services for a single service

Listing 15.13 contains a script that enumerates the dependent services for the Remote Access Connection Manager service. To carry out this task, the script must perform the following steps:

1. Create a variable to specify the computer name.

2. Use a GetObject call to connect to the WMI namespace root\cimv2, and set the impersonation level to "impersonate."

3. Use the ExecQuery method to query the Win32_Service class.

   You must use an Associators of query and specify the following information:

   - The instance of the service on which the query is performed (Win32_Service.Name = 'Rasman').

   - The name of the Association class (AssocClass = Win32_DependentService). If the class name is not specified, the query returns all associated classes and their instances.

   - The role played by the Rasman service. In this case, Rasman is antecedent to the services to be returned by the query.

   This query returns a collection of all the services dependent on Remote Access Connection Manager.

4. For each service in the collection, echo the service display name.

Listing 15.13   Enumerating Dependent Services for a Single Service

```
1  strComputer = "."
2  Set objWMIService = GetObject("winmgmts:" _
3      & "{impersonationLevel=impersonate}!\\" & .strComputer & "\root\cimv2")
4  Set colServiceList = objWMIService.ExecQuery("ASSOCIATORS OF " _
5      & "{Win32_Service.Name='rasman'} WHERE " _
6          & "AssocClass=Win32_DependentService " & "Role=Antecedent" )
7  For Each objService in colServiceList
8      Wscript.Echo objService.DisplayName
9  Next
```

Enumerating dependent services for all the services on a computer

Listing 15.14 contains a script that enumerates the dependents for all the services installed on a computer. To carry out this task, the script must perform the following steps:

1. Create a constant ForAppending, and set the value to 8.

   This constant is used when opening the text file where the service dependency information is written.

2. Create an instance of the FileSystemObject.

3. Open the text file C:\Scripts\Service_dependencies.csv.

   If the file does not exist, it is created automatically.

4. Write the file header "Service Dependencies" to the text file.

5. Create a variable to specify the computer name.

6. Use a GetObject call to connect to the WMI namespace root\cimv2, and set the impersonation level to "impersonate."

7. Use the ExecQuery method to query the Win32_Service class. This returns a collection consisting of all the services installed on the computer.

8. For each service in the collection, use the ExecQuery method to retrieve the list of dependent services.

   This query must use an Associators of query and specify the following information:

   - The instance of the service on which the query is performed. In this script, the service name is stored in the variable strServiceRegistryName.

   - The name of the Association class (AssocClass = Win32_DependentService). If the class name is not specified, the query returns all associated classes and their instances.

   - The role played by the individual service. In this case, the service is Antecedent to the services to be returned by the query.

9. Use the Count method to check the number of dependent services returned by the query.

   If Count = 0, the service has no dependents, and the display name of the service and the value "None" are written to the text file.

   If Count > 0, the display name of the service and the display name of its dependents are written to the text file.

10. Close the text file.

Listing 15.14   Enumerating Dependent Services for All the Services on a Computer

```
1   Const ForAppending = 8
2   Set objFSO = CreateObject("Scripting.FileSystemObject")
3   Set objLogFile = _
4       objFSO.OpenTextFile("c:\scripts\service_dependencies.csv", _
5           ForAppending, True)
6   objLogFile.Write("Service Dependencies")
7   objLogFile.Writeline
8   strComputer = "."
9   Set objWMIService = GetObject("winmgmts:" _
10      & "{impersonationLevel=impersonate}!\\" & strComputer & "\root\cimv2")
11  Set colListOfServiceS = objWMIService.ExecQuery _
12      ("SELECT * FROM Win32_Service")
13  For Each objService in colListofServices
14      objServiceRegistryName = objService.Name
15      objServiceDisplayName = objService.DisplayName
16      Set colServiceList = GetObject("winmgmts:").ExecQuery _
17          ("ASSOCIATORS OF {Win32_service.Name='" _
18              & objServiceRegistryName & _
19                  "'} WHERE AssocClass=Win32_DependentService Role=Antecedent" )
20      If colServiceList.Count = 0 then
21          objLogFile.Write(objServiceDisplayName) & ", None"
22          objLogFile.Writeline
23      Else
24          For Each objDependentService in colServiceList
25              objLogFile.Write(objServiceDisplayName) & ","
26              objLogFile.Write(objDependentService.DisplayName)
27              objLogFile.Writeline
28          Next
29      End If
30  Next
31  objLogFile.Close
```

Enumerating Antecedent Services

Antecedent services are services that must be running before dependent services can start. This information is extremely valuable for anyone writing scripts that automatically start services. By enumerating the antecedent services, you can ensure that all required services are already running before you attempt to start a dependent service. Alternatively, by enumerating antecedent services, you can also determine which dependent services you might not want to start. When you start a dependent service, its antecedent services automatically start; in some cases, you might prefer to leave those services inactive.

Antecedent services can be enumerated by using a script similar to the one used to enumerate dependent services. If you set the service role to Dependent in your WMI script, it lists the antecedents for a particular service.

Scripting Steps

Listing 15.15 contains a script that enumerates the antecedents of the Fax service. To carry out this task, the script must perform the following steps:

1. Create a variable to specify the computer name.

2. Use a GetObject call to connect to the WMI namespace root\cimv2, and set the impersonation level to "impersonate."

3. Use the ExecQuery method to query the Win32_Service class.

   This query must use an Associators of query and specify the following information:

   - The instance of the service on which the query is performed (Win32_Service.Name = 'Fax').

   - The name of the Association class (AssocClass = Win32_DependentService). If the class name were not specified, the query would return all associated classes and their instances.

   - The role played by the Fax service. In this case, Fax is dependent on the services the query returns.

   This returns a collection consisting of all the services for which the Fax service is a dependent.

4. For each service in the collection, echo the service display name.

Listing 15.15   Enumerating Antecedent Services

```
1  strComputer = "."
2  Set objWMIService = GetObject("winmgmts:" _
3      & "{impersonationLevel=impersonate}!\\" & strComputer & "\root\cimv2")
4  Set colServiceList = objWMIService.ExecQuery _
5      ("ASSOCIATORS OF {Win32_Service.Name='fax'} WHERE " _
6          & "AssocClass=Win32_DependentService Role=Dependent" )
7  For Each objService in colServiceList
8      Wscript.Echo objService.DisplayName
9  Next
```

Stopping and Starting Dependent Services

Service dependencies are especially important when you try to stop services. To stop an antecedent service, you must first stop the dependent services. For example, if you attempt to stop the IIS Admin Service without first stopping dependent services such as FTP, SMTP, and World Wide Web Publishing Service, you receive an error message, and all the services continue to run.

Dependencies also affect the order in which services start. To start a dependent service, the antecedent service must start first. If you are starting a dependent service such as FTP, the antecedent service (IIS Admin) automatically starts first. Only after IIS Admin starts does the FTP service start.

However, starting the antecedent service first does not cause a dependent service to start. If you start the IIS Admin Service, that service itself starts, but its dependent services (such as FTP) do not automatically start at the same time.

In other words, stopping and restarting an antecedent service sometimes involves stopping and restarting a number of dependent services. You could do this manually — coding all the dependencies within your script. The difficulty with this approach is twofold. First, you must determine all the dependencies and manually add them to the script. Second, if those dependencies ever change (because of a service or operating system upgrade), your script must be modified to reflect these changes.

Alternatively, you can use WMI to enumerate the dependencies, and then stop and restart the appropriate services in the appropriate order. By using WMI, you avoid the problems of hard-coding service dependencies: you do not have to determine these dependencies beforehand, and you do not have to be concerned that changes to the operating system affect these dependencies. Instead, WMI determines the appropriate dependencies each time the script runs.

Scripting Steps

The scripts for stopping and starting dependent services perform similar steps but in the opposite order.

Stopping dependent services

Listing 15.16 contains a script that stops the IIS Admin Service and all its dependents. To carry out this task, the script must perform the following steps:

1. Create a variable to specify the computer name.

2. Use a GetObject call to connect to the WMI namespace root\cimv2, and set the impersonation level to "impersonate."

3. Use the ExecQuery method to query the Win32_Service class.

    This query must use an Associators of query and specify the following information:

    -   The instance of the service on which the query is performed (Win32_Service.Name = 'IISAdmin').

    -   The name of the Association class (AssocClass = Win32_DependentService). If the class name is not specified, the query returns all associated classes and their instances.

    -   The role played by the IISAdmin Service. In this case, IISAdmin is Antecedent to the services to be returned by the query.

    The query returns a collection consisting of all the services dependent on the IIS Admin Service.

4. For each service in the collection, use the StopService method to stop the service.

5. After a stop control has been sent to each dependent service, pause for 60 seconds (60,000 milliseconds) to give the SCM time to stop each service.

6. Use a the ExecQuery method to retrieve the instance of the IISAdmin Service.

7. Use the StopService method to stop the IISAdmin Service.

Listing 15.16   Stopping a Service and Its Dependents

```
1   strComputer = "."
2   Set objWMIService = GetObject("winmgmts:" _
3       & "{impersonationLevel=impersonate}!\\" & strComputer & "\root\cimv2")
4   Set colServiceList = objWMIService.ExecQuery _
5       ("ASSOCIATORS OF {Win32_Service.Name='iisadmin'} WHERE " _
6           & "AssocClass=Win32_DependentService Role=Antecedent" )
7   For Each objService in colServiceList
8       errReturn = objService.StopService()
9   Next
10  Wscript.Sleep 60000
11  Set colServiceList = objWMIService.ExecQuery _
12      ("SELECT * FROM Win32_Service WHERE Name='iisadmin'")
13  For Each objService in colServiceList
14      errReturn = objService.StopService()
15  Next
```

Starting dependent services

To start a service and all its dependents, simply reverse the process for stopping a service and its dependents: start the antecedent service, obtain a list of dependent services, and start each one. Listing 15.17 contains a script that starts the IIS Admin Service and all its dependents.

Listing 15.17   Starting Dependent Services

```
1   strComputer = "."
2   Set objWMIService = GetObject("winmgmts:" _
3       & "{impersonationLevel=impersonate}!\\" & strComputer & "\root\cimv2")
4   Set colServiceList = objWMIService.ExecQuery _
5       ("SELECT * FROM Win32_Service WHERE Name='iisadmin'")
6   For Each objService in colServiceList
7       errReturn = objService.StartService()
8   Next
9   Wscript.Sleep 60000
10  Set colServiceList = objWMIService.ExecQuery _
11      ("ASSOCIATORS OF {Win32_Service.Name='iisadmin'} WHERE " _
12          & "AssocClass=Win32_DependentService Role=Antecedent" )
13  For Each objService in colServiceList
14      objService.StartService()
15  Next
```

Configuring Services

Although services generally require little hands-on administration, there will be times when you need to reconfigure a service. For example, you might want to configure a service so that it starts automatically each time the computer starts. Alternatively, you might want to change the display name of a service, making the service and its function more obvious to administrators working in the Services snap-in. Management tasks such as these can be carried out using WMI.

The WMI Win32_Service Change method is especially useful for changing selected service properties on multiple computers throughout the enterprise. The Change method accepts 11 parameters, each representing a service property that can be modified. When passing these parameters, it is important to maintain the correct order. For example, PathName is the second parameter in the set of 11 parameters. To change this property, the new value for PathName must be the second item in the parameters passed to the Change method.

This means you must pass a value of some kind for DisplayName, the first item in the parameter list. If you do not want to change the current value of DisplayName, you can insert a comma for that value. For example, the following code changes just the PathName:

```
errReturn = strService.Change( , "c:\windows\services\new_name.exe")
```

Because these single commas might be confusing to someone editing your script, you can instead insert the keyword Null or use a constant with the value Null. For example, you might create a constant named SAME_DISPLAYNAME, set it to Null, and then insert the constant into the parameter string as follows:

```
Const SAME_DISPLAYNAME  = Null
errReturn = strService.Change _
    (SAME_DISPLAYNAME , "c:\windows\services\new_name.exe")
```

This makes it clearer that you are keeping the same display name and changing only the service path.

Table 15.3 provides a complete list of the service properties exposed to the Change method, as well as their ordinal position. The items that can be changed by using WMI represent only a subset of a service's full property set and do not include some properties, such as service description.

Table 15.3   Service Properties Exposed to the WMI Change Method

Position	Property
1	**DisplayName** – Name of the service as displayed in the Services snap-in.
2	**PathName** – Full path to the service's executable file.
3	**ServiceType** — Type of service. Most services are type 4: services that run in their own process. Valid services types include the following: 1 — Kernel driver 2 — File system driver 3 — Adapter 4 — Own process 5 — Win32 shared process
4	**ErrorControl** — Action to be taken if a service fails during startup. Valid error controls include the following: 0 — Ignore 1 — Normal 2 — Severe 3 — Critical
5	**StartMode** — Method used to start the service. Most service start modes are either Auto or Manual. Valid start modes include the following: ▪ **Boot.** This start mode is reserved for device drivers. ▪ **System.** This start mode is reserved for device drivers. ▪ **Auto.** Services automatically start each time the computer starts. ▪ **Manual.** Services must be explicitly started, either by using the Services snap-in or by using a script. ▪ **Disabled.** Services cannot be started until the start mode has been changed to either Auto or Manual.
6	**DesktopInteract** — Indicates whether the service can create or communicate with windows on the desktop. DesktopInteract can be set to either TRUE or FALSE. Interactive services must run under the LocalSystem account.
7	**StartName** — Account name under which the service runs. If not specified, the service runs under the LocalSystem account.
8	**StartPassword** — Password for the account name specified by StartName. Use an empty string ("") to specify no password and NULL to indicate that you are not changing the current password.

(continued)

Table 15.3   Service Properties Exposed to the WMI Change Method (*continued*)

Position	Property
9	**LoadOrderGroup** — Load-ordered group to which the service belongs. When you start services as part of the computer start process, those that belong to load-ordered groups start first, services that belong to groups (but not load-ordered groups) start next, and services that do not belong to groups of any kind start last.
10	**LoadOrderGroupDependencies** — Set of load-ordered groups that must be running before this service can start.
11	**ServiceDependencies** — Services that must be running before this service can start.

Configuring Service Start Options

One key aspect of service management is determining when or if services run. The three options for configuring service start options are shown in Table 15.4.

Table 15.4   Service Start Options

Option	Description
Auto	Service is started automatically by the SCM during system startup. Autostart services start before a user logs on to the computer and run even if no user logs on to the computer.
Manual	Service is started by the SCM when a process calls the StartService method. Although manual services must be specifically started by a user (or by a script), they continue to run even if the user logs off. Manual services are often referred to as on-demand services.
Disabled	Service that can no longer be started. To start a disabled service, you must first change the startup option to either Auto or Manual.

Start options are often changed in order to accomplish one of the following:

- Ensure that a service automatically restarts when a computer restarts.

  Services set to Manual startup can be started only if a user logs on and either manually starts the service or runs a script to start the service. If the power fails, manual services do not automatically restart when the computer restarts.

- Prevent Power Users from starting a service.

  Although you can use Group Policy to prevent Power Users from starting a service, you can also set the service start mode to Disabled. A disabled service cannot start unless it is reconfigured as either Manual or Auto. Because Power Users do not have the right to change service configurations, disabling a service also prevents these users from starting that service.

Scripting Steps

Listing 15.18 contains a script that disables all the on-demand services on a computer. To carry out this task, the script must perform the following steps:

1. Create a variable to specify the computer name.

2. Use a GetObject call to connect to the WMI namespace root\cimv2, and set the impersonation level to "impersonate."

3. Use the ExecQuery method to query the Win32_Service class. To restrict data retrieval to a subset of services, a Where clause is used to limit data retrieval only to those services for which the StartMode property is equal to "Manual."

4. For each service in the collection, use the Change method to set StartMode to "Disabled."

   With the Change method, the StartMode property must be the fifth parameter in the list of arguments supplied. Because of this, four empty arguments (represented by the four commas) must precede the new value for StartMode.

   If the service is currently running, StartMode is changed to Disabled. However, the service continues to run until it is stopped. If you want to immediately disable a service, your script can first stop the service and then change StartMode to Disabled. That both stops the service and prevents it from being restarted.

Listing 15.18   Configuring Service Start Options

```
1  strComputer = "."
2  Set objWMIService = GetObject("winmgmts:" _
3      & "{impersonationLevel=impersonate}!\\" & strComputer & "\root\cimv2")
4  Set colServiceList = objWMIService.ExecQuery _
5      ("Select * from Win32_Service where StartMode = 'Manual'")
6  For Each objService in colServiceList
7      errReturnCode = objService.Change( , , , , "Disabled")
8  Next
```

Configuring Error Control Codes for Autostart Services

When a computer starts, all the autostart services also start. On occasion, one of these services might fail to start along with the computer. When a service fails during system startup, the computer takes action based on the value of the service error control code. These codes and the corresponding actions are listed in Table 15.5.

Also listed in the table are the values that must be used to configure the error control code. Admittedly, this can be a bit confusing. Although error control codes are reported as strings (such as Ignore), you must configure these codes using integers. For example, this line of code sets an error control code to Critical:

```
errReturn = objService.Change( , , , 3)
```

Regardless of the error control code, all startup failures are recorded in the System Event Log.

Table 15.5 Service Error Control Codes

Error code	Value	Description
Ignore	0	Startup continues. No notification is given to the user that the service failed.
Normal	1	Startup continues. Before the user logs on, the user receives the notification, "At least one service or device failed during startup."
Severe	2	Computer attempts to restart with last-known good configuration. If the service fails again, startup continues and notification is given to the user.
Critical	3	Computer attempts to restart with last-known good configuration. If the service fails again, startup stops.

Most Windows 2000 services are installed using the Normal error control code. A few of the exceptions, which are installed using the Ignore error code, include:

- File Replication Service
- Smart Card
- Secondary Logon
- WMI

For the services installed using the Ignore error code, no notification is given to the user that the service has failed. If you prefer on-screen notification that a service could not start, you can use WMI to change the error control code.

Error control codes apply only to computer startup; error control codes are not used if you stop and then attempt to restart a service after the computer is running.

Scripting Steps

Listing 15.19 contains a script that changes the error control code to Normal for all services that currently have the error control code Ignore. To carry out this task, the script must perform the following steps:

1. Create a variable to specify the computer name.
2. Use a GetObject call to connect to the WMI namespace root\cimv2, and set the impersonation level to "impersonate."

3. Use the ExecQuery method to query the Win32_Service class. To restrict data retrieval to a subset of services, a Where clause is used to limit data retrieval only to those services for which the ErrorControl property is equal to Manual.

4. For each service in the collection, use the Change method set ErrorControl to Normal.

    With the Change method, the ErrorControl property must be the fourth parameter in the list of arguments supplied. Because of this, three empty arguments (represented by the three commas) must precede the new value for ErrorControl.

Listing 15.19   Configuring Service Error Control Codes

```
1   Const NORMAL = 1
2   strComputer = "."
3   Set objWMIService = GetObject("winmgmts:" _
4       & "{impersonationLevel=impersonate}!\\" & strComputer & "\root\cimv2")
5   Set colServiceList = objWMIService.ExecQuery _
6       ("SELECT * FROM Win32_Service WHERE ErrorControl = 'Ignore'")
7   For Each objService in colServiceList
8       errReturn = objService.Change( , , , NORMAL)
9   Next
```

Managing Service Accounts and Service Account Passwords

Services must run under a user account. When the SCM starts a service, it logs on to the account that is associated with the service. If the logon is successful, the service process is given an access token. This token identifies the service in any subsequent interactions with securable objects (objects that have a security descriptor attached to them). For example, if the service attempts to access a remote computer, the token is used for authentication. If authentication fails, the service is denied access to the resource.

In Windows 2000, most operating system services run under the LocalSystem account, a special account that is granted all possible privileges to the local computer on which it resides. (Even administrators do not have all privileges granted to them by default.) LocalSystem is often used as a service account because it already has all privileges and does not require special privileges to ensure that the service runs.

Although the LocalSystem account has full access to the local computer, it is never validated by Active Directory. In fact, no password is associated with the LocalSystem account, and you cannot interactively log on as LocalSystem. Because it has no domain credentials, the LocalSystem account has limited access to resources outside the local computer.

Although most services use the LocalSystem account by default, it is recommended that you not run services under this account, especially on domain controllers.

 Caution

The LocalSystem account has access to all resources on the local computer. If the local computer is a domain controller, this means the account has access to everything in Active Directory as well. If someone compromises a service running under LocalSystem, that person then has full Administrator access to every resource on the computer. To avoid this potential security problem, run services under an account other than LocalSystem whenever possible.

Configuring Service Accounts

On occasion, you might need to change the account under which a given service runs. For example, you might run a service under an administrative account. Because this can create a security vulnerability, you might switch the service to an account with fewer privileges. Alternatively, you might have services running under an account that is about to be deleted, or you might want to ensure that, on all your servers, certain services run under certain accounts.

You can use the Win32_Service Change method to configure services to run under a specified user account. When selecting an account, keep in mind the following:

- The account being used as a service account must have the right to log on as a service. This right can be granted by using Group Policy.

- The account being used as a service account should not be a member of a local, domain, or enterprise Administrators group.

- Each instance of a service should run under a unique user account. This provides additional security, and enables the auditing of individual service instances.

- If the service is interactive, then the service must run under the LocalSystem account.

   LocalSystem is required because only one window station (WinSta0) can be visible and interactive at a time. If a service runs under an account other than LocalSystem, it runs in the Service-0x03e7$\Default window station, which is an invisible window. Services running in this window station cannot receive input or display output.

Win32_Service properties and methods related to service accounts are shown in Figure 15.4.

Figure 15.4   Win32_Service Account Properties and Methods

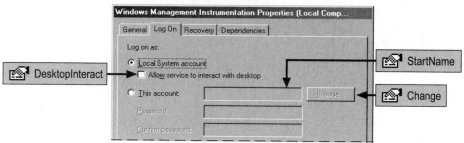

Scripting Steps

Listing 15.20 contains a script that changes the service account for services from running under a specified user account to LocalSystem. To carry out this task, the script must perform the following steps:

1. Create a variable to specify the computer name.

2. Use a GetObject call to connect to the WMI namespace root\cimv2, and set the impersonation level to "impersonate."

3. Use the ExecQuery method to query the Win32_Service class.

   To limit data retrieval to a specific set of services, a Where clause is included that restricts the collection to those services with a ServiceName of .\Netsvc.

   The period and backslash (.\) preceding the account name indicate that the account is a local user account (a second backslash is required whenever a single backslash is used in a query). If the service is running under a domain account, the period is replaced by the domain name (for example, fabrikam\\Netsvc).

4. For each service in the collection, use the Change method to switch the account to LocalSystem.

   Because StartName must be the seventh parameter passed to the Change method, the new account name is preceded by six empty arguments (represented by the six commas). Following StartName, an empty string ("") is used to indicate that the LocalSystem account does not use a password. If LocalSystem did use a password, the password for the account would be listed following StartName.

Listing 15.20 Switching Service Accounts to LocalSystem

```
1  strComputer = "."
2  Set objWMIService = GetObject("winmgmts:" _
3      & "{impersonationLevel=impersonate}!\\" & strComputer & "\root\cimv2")
4  Set colServiceList = objWMIService.ExecQuery _
5      ("SELECT * FROM Win32_Service WHERE StartName = '.\\NetSvc'")
6  For Each objService in colServices
7      errServiceChange = objService.Change _
8          ( , , , , , , ".\LocalSystem" , "")
9  Next
```

Configuring Service Account Passwords

When you assign an account to a service, the SCM requires the correct password for that account before it makes the assignment. If you supply an incorrect password, the SCM rejects the account. If you configure a service account using the LocalSystem, LocalService, or NetworkService account, you do not need to supply an account password because these accounts do not have passwords.

The SCM stores the account password in the services database. After the password is assigned, however, the SCM does not ensure that the password stored in the services database and the password assigned to the user account in Active Directory continue to match. Consequently, a situation similar to the following could occur:

1. You configure a service to run under a particular user account.

2. The service starts up under that account by using the current account password.

3. You change the password for the user account.

4. The service continues to run. However, if the service stops, you cannot restart it because the SCM continues to use the old, invalid password. Changing the password in Active Directory does not change the password stored in the services database.

If you run services under regular user accounts, you need to update those service passwords each time the user account password changes. This can be particularly time-consuming if you are not sure which services are running under that account or which computers have services running under that account.

Fortunately, you can use WMI to check the service accounts on all your computers and, if necessary, change the service account password.

Scripting Steps

Listing 15.21 contains a script that changes the service account password for all scripts running under Netsvc. To carry out this task, the script must perform the following steps:

1. Create a variable to specify the computer name.

2. Use a GetObject call to connect to the WMI namespace root\cimv2, and set the impersonation level to "impersonate."

3. Use the ExecQuery method to query the Win32_Service class. To limit data retrieval to a specific set of services, a Where clause is included that restricts the collection to those services with the ServiceName .\\Netsvc (a second backslash is required whenever a single backslash is used in a query).

4. For each service in the collection, use the Change method to change the password to "password".

   When using the Change method, the password must be the eighth parameter passed to the method. Because of this, the password is preceded by seven empty arguments (represented by the seven commas). Unless you are using a variable, the password must be enclosed in quotation marks.

Listing 15.21   Changing a Service Account Password

```
1  strComputer = "."
2  Set objWMIService = GetObject("winmgmts:" _
3      & "{impersonationLevel=impersonate}!\\" & strComputer & "\root\cimv2")
4  Set colServiceList = objWMIService.ExecQuery _
5      ("SELECT * FROM Win32_Service WHERE StartName = '.\\NetSvc'")
6  For Each objservice in colServiceList
7      errReturn = objService.Change( , , , , , , , "password")
8  Next
```

Installing and Removing Services

WMI provides methods that allow you to install and remove services programmatically. These methods work best for installing and removing third-party services rather than services that are part of the operating system. It is difficult (or impossible) to install operating system services using WMI, if for no other reason than the fact that you are unlikely to have a detailed list of the executable files and the service accounts required for each service.

And while it *is* possible to remove operating system services using WMI, this is not recommended. This is because the service removal will be incomplete: for example, the service will no longer function, but it will still be listed as **Installed** in **Windows Components**. If you need a command-line method for installing or removing operating system services, you can use Sysocmgr.exe instead; however, Sysocmgr.exe is designed to work on the local computer and not on remote computers.

Although it is somewhat limited in scope, WMI can be useful in the following situations:

- You need to install an in-house service on multiple computers.

- You need to replace a third-party service previously used in your organization.

    For example, your script could check for the presence of this service on each computer in your organization and, if found, stop and remove the service. The script could then install the replacement service.

Installing Services

Services are generally installed in one of two ways: either as a part of the operating system installation or by using an installation program provided by the service developer. However, some services, particularly those created in-house, might not have an installation program. In those instances, you can use the Win32_Service Create method to programmatically install services.

Despite the name, the Create method does not actually create a service; it merely installs an existing service. To use this command, you need to copy the service executable file to a computer and then use Win32_Service Create to install the service.

The Create method is similar to the Change method. In both cases, the properties of the service are passed as parameters to the method. As with the parameters used with the Change method, the order in which these parameters are passed is very important. You must pass the parameters in the order shown in Table 15.6.

A complete list of the service properties exposed to the Win32_Service Create method are shown in Table 15.6. For more information about each property, see "Retrieving Service Properties" earlier in this chapter.

Note
The ordinal positions of the service properties exposed to the Create method differ slightly from those exposed to the Change method. Make sure you use the values shown in Table 15.6 when installing a service.

Table 15.6 Service Properties Exposed to the WMI Create Method

Position	Property
1	Name — Name of the service as stored in the registry.
2	DisplayName — Name of the service as displayed in the Services snap-in.
3	PathName — Full path to the service's executable file.
4	ServiceType — Type of service.

(continued)

Table 15.6   Service Properties Exposed to the WMI Create Method *(continued)*

Position	Property
5	ErrorControl — Action to be taken should a service fail during startup.
6	StartMode — Method used to start the service.
7	DesktopInteract — Indicates whether the service can create or communicate with windows on the desktop.
8	StartName — Account name under which the service runs.
9	StartPassword — Password for the account name specified by StartName.
10	LoadOrderGroup — Load-ordered group to which the service belongs.
11	LoadOrderGroupDependencies — Set of load-ordered groups that must be running before this service can start.
12	ServiceDependencies — Services that must be running before this service can start.

Scripting Steps

Listing 15.22 contains a script that installs a service named DbService. To carry out this task, the script must perform the following steps:

1. Create a constant named OWN_PROCESS, and set the value to 16.

   This constant is used to specify that the service must run in its own process.

2. Create a constant named NOT_INTERACTIVE, and set the value to True.

   This constant indicates that the service does not interact with the desktop.

3. Create a variable to specify the computer name.

4. Use a GetObject call to connect to the WMI namespace root\cimv2, and set the impersonation level to "impersonate."

5. Get an instance of the Win32_BaseService class, the parent class for Windows services.

6. Use the Create method to create (install) a new service.

   To create the service, include the following parameters:

   - **DbService.** Name of the service as it is stored in the registry.
   - **Personnel Database Service.** "Friendly" name of the service, as viewed in the Services snap-in.
   - **C:\Windows\System32\Db.exe.** Local path to the executable file for the service.
   - **OWN_PROCESS.** Service runs in its own process.
   - **Normal.** Error control code for the service.

- **Auto.** Service startup type.

- **NOT_INTERACTIVE.** Service does not interact with the desktop.

- **.\LocalService.** Account name under which the service runs. (Two backslashes are not required in the name, because the name, and its single backslash, is not being used in a query.)

  You must specify a valid account name when installing a service. If the SCM cannot locate the specified account, installation fails.

- **"".** Empty string indicating that the LocalService account does not use a password.

  If you specify an incorrect password, installation continues because the SCM does not verify passwords when installing a service. However, if the password is incorrect, the service fails when you try to start it.

Listing 15.22 Installing a Service

```
1   Const OWN_PROCESS = 16
2   Const NOT_INTERACTIVE = True
3   strComputer = "."
4   Set objWMIService = GetObject("winmgmts:" _
5       & "{impersonationLevel=impersonate}!\\" & strComputer & "\root\cimv2")
6   Set objService = objWMIService.Get("Win32_BaseService")
7   errReturn = objService.Create ("DbService", "Personnel Database", _
8    "c:\windows\system32\db.exe", OWN_PROCESS ,2 ,"Automatic" , _
9       NOT_INTERACTIVE ,".\LocalSystem" ,"")
```

Removing Services

As your organization changes, you might decide to remove certain services from certain computers. In-house and third-party services can be removed by using WMI, while operating system services can be removed by using Sysocmgr.exe.

When preparing to remove services, keep the following information in mind:

- Services must be stopped before you remove them.

  If the service is running when you issue the delete command, the service is marked for deletion, but it continues to run until it stops and all open handles are closed. If the service is never stopped, that service will never be deleted.

- Removing a service does not remove the service's executable file.

  Removing a service by using WMI deletes the related registry entries under HKEY_LOCAL_MACHINE\SYSTEM\CurrentControlSet\Services. As a result, the service is no longer installed and is not available through the Services snap-in. However, WMI does not delete the executable file, meaning you could easily reinstall the service. To delete the executable file, you must retrieve the path name and then delete the file.

- Removing a base Windows 2000 service (for example, DHCP) by using WMI deletes the registry entries for that service but does not remove the shortcut from the **Administrative Tools** menu or remove the service from the **Windows Components Wizard**. This can confuse anyone trying to determine how the computer has been configured.

  For example, if you remove the DHCP service by using a WMI script, the DHCP service is no longer listed in the Services snap-in. However, a nonfunctioning shortcut to the DHCP console remains in the **Administrative Tools** menu, and if you start the **Windows Component Wizard**, it indicates that the DHCP service is installed.

  Because of this, you should always use Sysocmgr.exe to programmatically remove Windows 2000 services.

Scripting Steps

Listing 15.23 contains a script that removes a service named DbService. To carry out this task, the script must perform the following steps:

1. Create a variable to specify the computer name.

2. Use a GetObject call to connect to the WMI namespace root\cimv2, and set the impersonation level to "impersonate."

3. Use the ExecQuery method to query the Win32_Service class. To restrict data retrieval to a single service, a Where clause is included to limit data retrieval only to the service named DbService. This ensures that the correct service is retrieved because service names must be unique.

4. For the single service in the collection, use the StopService method to stop the service.

5. Use the Delete method to delete the service.

Listing 15.23   Removing a Service

```
1   strComputer = "."
2   Set objWMIService = GetObject("winmgmts:" _
3       & "{impersonationLevel=impersonate}!\\" & strComputer & "\root\cimv2")
4   Set colListOfServices = objWMIService.ExecQuery _
5       ("SELECT * FROM Win32_Service WHERE Name = 'DbService'")
6   For Each objService in colListOfServices
7       objService.StopService()
8       objService.Delete()
9   Next
```

Registry

The registry is an integral part of the Microsoft® Windows® 2000 operating system, containing configuration settings for both the operating system and the applications and services that run under Windows. Scripts that use the Windows Management Instrumentation (WMI) Registry Provider offer a flexible solution for managing the registries of computers across an enterprise.

In This Chapter

Registry Overview **1016**

Managing the Registry **1024**

Backing Up the Registry 1025

Reading Entry Values and Types 1026

Changing String-valued and DWORD-valued Entries 1033

Creating Registry Subkeys and Entries 1035

Enumerating Keys, Subkeys, and Entries 1041

Deleting Subkeys and Entries 1045

Checking Registry Subkey Access Rights 1047

Monitoring the Registry **1050**

Registry Overview

The registry is the centralized configuration database for the Windows operating system and for applications and services running under Windows. As such, it plays a vital role as the repository for computer system configuration data. The registry stores a wide range of configuration settings, from boot parameters to user desktop settings. Because these settings play a crucial role in determining how — and sometimes even if — a computer runs, managing the registry is an important aspect of Windows system administration.

You might not be aware of it, but if you manage Windows-based systems you spend a significant amount of your time reading and modifying settings in the registry. Many of the Control Panel applets, command-line tools, and Microsoft Management Console (MMC) plug-ins that you use each day perform some of their functions by reading, changing, or adding registry subkeys or entries. These tools offer a more user-friendly interface for working with the registry and provide a safeguard against misconfiguring a registry value. When you use these tools, you might not be aware that you are actually modifying the registry.

In most cases, you can use system tools to indirectly modify registry settings. However, occasionally you need to work with the registry directly, especially if you do not have system tools available that can manage those settings across an enterprise. When you need to manage registry settings across an enterprise and no system tool is available to do this, you can use scripts that leverage the WMI Registry Provider.

 Note

Windows Script Host also provides methods for working with the registry. However, these methods represent only a subset of the capabilities found in the Registry Provider. In addition, the Registry Provider makes it as easy to work with the registry on a remote computer as it does to work with the registry on the local computer. WSH, by contrast, is designed to work only on the local computer.

Regardless of whether you use the registry editors or a script, when you edit the registry directly, you must determine which entries or subkeys to modify and how to modify them. In contrast, if you use a system tool to modify the entries or subkeys, the tool will determine which items you can modify and will ensure that you can make only valid modifications. For example, if only 0 and 1 are valid values for a registry entry, these tools will typically not allow you to set the value of the entry to 2 or 3. Before you decide to write a script or otherwise edit the registry directly, research the use of the following configuration management alternatives:

- Group Policy
- Scriptable COM objects
- Command-line tools

Given how critical the registry is to the proper functioning of the operating system and your applications, it is imperative that you back it up regularly. You should be especially diligent about backing up the registry immediately before editing it — directly or indirectly.

This chapter demonstrates how to use the WMI Registry Provider in your scripts to automate the examination, modification, and deletion of subkeys and entries in the registry. The chapter does not explain the meaning and effect of the various entries in the registry. To make use of the scripting techniques demonstrated, you must already be knowledgeable about certain subkeys or entries. Otherwise, begin by consulting a reliable source of information such as the Registry Reference on the *Microsoft Windows 2000 Server Resource Kit* companion CD, or on the Web at http://www.microsoft.com/reskit.

The Registry Reference contains detailed information about where in the registry specific configuration settings are stored, what values the settings can have, and what the values mean. The Registry Reference also includes a "Change Method" section for many of the entries; these sections describe system tools that manage the entry so that you can avoid editing it directly.

 Caution

Changing the registry with a script can easily propagate errors. The scripting tools bypass safeguards, allowing settings that can damage your system, or even require you to reinstall Windows. Before scripting changes to the registry, test your script thoroughly and back up the registry on every computer on which you will make changes. For more information about scripting changes to the registry, see the Registry Reference on the *Windows 2000 Server Resource Kit* companion CD or at http://www.microsoft.com/reskit.

Registry Editor

The registry editors Regedit.exe and Regedt32.exe are the GUI-based system tools for managing the registry. They present a view of the registry that looks similar to the Windows Explorer view of the file system.

Although you can use the registry editors to connect to and manage the registry on a remote computer, they do not provide an easy way to make the same changes across multiple registries. If you need to make such enterprise-wide changes, you should first investigate other means, such as Group Policy. If you find no other alternative, try scripts like the ones presented in this chapter.

▶ **To open the registry editor Regedit.exe**

- In the **Run** dialog box, type **regedit**, and then click **OK**.

Figure 16.1 shows the registry editor Regedit.exe.

Figure 16.1   Registry Editor Regedit.exe

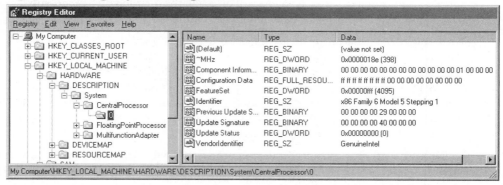

Note

In Windows 2000, there are two registry editors Regedit.exe and Regedt32.exe. Each provides a different view of the information in the registry and includes useful features not available in the other. Regedit.exe, for instance, provides powerful search capabilities, while Regedt32.exe enables the viewing and changing of access permissions.

Registry Structure

The registry, as it appears in Regedit.exe, has a hierarchical organization. Figure 16.2 identifies the elements in the hierarchy as they are displayed in the registry editors: subtrees, keys, subkeys, and the components of a registry *entry*. This hierarchy looks similar to the system drive letters, folders, and subfolders you find in Windows Explorer.

Figure 16.2   Registry Elements

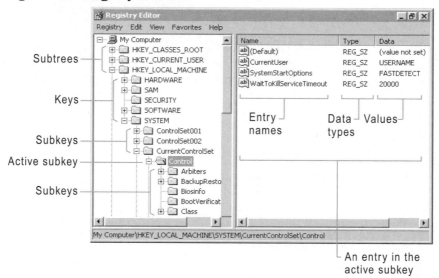

When you view the registry in a registry editor, you see the hierarchy in a tree control in the left section of the window and the registry entries in the right section of the window. When you are using a registry editor, you typically navigate through the keys and subkeys of a given subtree until you find the entry you are interested in and then edit that entry. You rarely need to edit the subkeys themselves.

Subtrees

Subtrees make up the first or *root* level of the registry hierarchy. If you compare the elements of the registry hierarchy to the elements of the file system hierarchy, registry subtrees correspond to file system drive letters. Each subtree contains a particular category of keys, subkeys, and entries. The HKEY_LOCAL_MACHINE subtree, for instance, contains computer-specific settings, while the HKEY_CURRENT_USER subtree contains user-specific settings. Many of the changes you make to the registry involve entries contained within one of these two subtrees.

Table 16.1 lists all the subtrees in the registry along with descriptions and commonly used abbreviations. (In registry documentation, for example, you will typically see HKEY_CURRENT_USER referred to as HKCU.)

Table 16.1   Registry Subtrees

Subtree	Description	Abbreviation
HKEY_CLASSES_ROOT	Symbolic link to HKEY_LOCAL_MACHINE \SOFTWARE\Classes Clicking on the HKEY_CLASSES_ROOT subtree takes you to the same place you would reach by navigating to HKEY_LOCAL_MACHINE\SOFTWARE\Classes	HKCR
HKEY_CURRENT_USER	Symbolic link to a key under HKEY_USERS representing the current user	HKCU
HKEY_LOCAL_MACHINE	Information about the local computer	HKLM
HKEY_USERS	Information about users	HKU
HKEY_CURRENT_CONFIG	Symbolic link to the key of the current hardware profile under HKEY_LOCAL_MACHINE\SYSTEM\CurrentControlSet \Control\IDConfigDB\Hardware Profiles	HKCC
HKEY_PERFORMANCE_DATA	Information about performance. Not accessible using the registry editors	No commonly used abbreviation

Keys and subkeys

Keys make up the second level of the registry hierarchy. They correspond to top-level folders located in the root directory of a file system. Keys can contain other folder-like elements known as subkeys. Keys do not normally contain registry entries other than the default entry (to be discussed later in this chapter).

Subkeys are analogous to subfolders. They can contain other subkeys as well as registry entries.

Entries

Registry entries correspond to files in a file system. Unlike subtrees, keys, and subkeys, entries are designed to store configuration data, not to categorize it. An entry consists of a name, a data type (which defines the length and format of data that the entry can store), and a field known as the *value* of the entry. Configuration data is stored in the value field of a registry entry.

Table 16.2 lists all of the data types that can be used in registry entries. The first four are the ones most commonly used in scripts.

Table 16.2   Registry Entry Data Types

Data Type	Description
REG_SZ	A string (series of characters) that ends with a null character. Strings that end with a null character are known as null-terminated strings. The Z in REG_SZ refers to the null (or *zero*) character.
REG_DWORD	A number that can range from 0 to 4,294,967,295.
	DWORD refers to the fact that 32 bits are allocated for storing the value. Because 16 bits of storage space is known as a word, 32 bits is known as a double word (DWORD).
REG_MULTI_SZ	An array of null-terminated strings that is itself terminated by two successive null characters. This enables you to store multiple values in a single registry entry, similar to the way arrays enable you to store multiple values within a single variable.
REG_EXPAND_SZ	A null-terminated string that contains unexpanded references to environment variables (%PATH%, for example).
REG_BINARY	Binary data in any form.
REG_DWORD_LITTLE_ENDIAN	A number that can range from 0 to 4,294,967,295 and is stored in a format known as little-endian. (Little-endian means that the most significant byte is located on the right end of the word.)
REG_DWORD_BIG_ENDIAN	A 32-bit number in big-endian format. (Big-endian means that the most significant byte is located on the left end of the word.)
REG_QWORD	A 64-bit number.
REG_QWORD_LITTLE_ENDIAN	A 64-bit number in little-endian format (same as REG_QWORD).
REG_RESOURCE_LIST	A device driver resource list.

(continued)

Table 16.2 Registry Entry Data Types *(continued)*

Data Type	Description
REG_FULL_RESOURCE_DESCRIPTOR	A list of hardware resources that a physical device is using. The system detects the resources and writes the list into the \HardwareDescription tree.
REG_RESOURCE_REQUIREMENTS_LIST	A device driver's list of possible hardware resources that it or one of the physical devices it controls can use. The system writes a subset of this list into the \ResourceMap tree.
REG_LINK	A Unicode symbolic link. Used internally; not used by applications.
REG_NONE	No defined value type.

Each registry subtree, key, and subkey has a *default* entry. Default entries are of the string data type, which is denoted REG_SZ. If a default entry does not contain a value, a registry editor displays the value as *(value not set)*. When you create a subkey, a default entry with *(value not set)* is automatically added. You can change the value of the default entry using the methods of the Registry Provider. Note that, in contrast, the RegWrite method of the WshShell object does not allow you to modify the value of the default entry.

Registry files

The registry is composed of several sources of data. These sources include some of the files in the folder *systemroot*\System32\config. Each file that houses some portion of the registry is known as a *hive*. The list of hive files is stored in the registry itself.

 Note

> The registry editors hide some portions of the registry, including a subtree related to performance counters. These items are not accessible because you should never directly modify them. Incorrectly configuring these values could seriously degrade the performance of your computer.

Listing 16.1 contains a script that displays the locations of the registry hive files. It retrieves the information from registry entries in the HKEY_LOCAL_MACHINE\SYSTEM \CurrentControlSet\Control\hivelist subkey. The techniques used in this script are explained later in this chapter.

Listing 16.1 Listing the Files That Make Up the Registry

```
1  Const HKEY_LOCAL_MACHINE = &H80000002
2  strComputer = "."
3
4  Set objReg=GetObject("winmgmts:{impersonationLevel=impersonate}!\\" & _
5      strComputer & "\root\default:StdRegProv")
6  strKeyPath = "System\CurrentControlSet\Control\hivelist"
```

(continued)

Listing 16.1   Listing the Files That Make Up the Registry *(continued)*

```
7   objReg.EnumValues HKEY_LOCAL_MACHINE, strKeyPath, _
8       arrValueNames, arrValueTypes
9
10  For i=0 To UBound(arrValueNames)
11      Wscript.Echo "File Name: " & arrValueNames(i)
12      objReg.GetStringValue HKEY_LOCAL_MACHINE,strKeyPath, _
13          arrValueNames(i),strValue
14      Wscript.Echo "Location: " & strValue
15  Next
```

When the preceding script runs under CScript on a Microsoft® Windows® 2000 Professional–based computer, information similar to the following appears in the command window:

```
File Name: \REGISTRY\MACHINE\SECURITY
Location: \Device\HarddiskVolume1\WINDOWS\system32\config\SECURITY
File Name: \REGISTRY\MACHINE\SOFTWARE --
Location: \Device\HarddiskVolume1\WINDOWS\system32\config\SOFTWARE
File Name: \REGISTRY\MACHINE\SYSTEM
Location: \Device\HarddiskVolume1\WINDOWS\system32\config\SYSTEM
File Name: \REGISTRY\USER\.DEFAULT
Location: \Device\HarddiskVolume1\WINDOWS\system32\config\DEFAULT
File Name: \REGISTRY\MACHINE\SAM
Location: \Device\HarddiskVolume1\WINDOWS\system32\config\SAM
File Name: \REGISTRY\USER\S-1-5-20
```

Note that there are no file extensions on the file names.

Constants Commonly Used in WMI-based Registry Scripts

Most of the scripts in this chapter use the WMI Registry Provider, and many use constants that specify a subtree or an entry data type. These constants are expressed as hexadecimal values for subtrees or as integer values for entry data types.

Hexadecimal values for subtrees

Many of the Registry Provider methods require, as the first parameter, a hexadecimal value indicating the registry subtree that the method should act upon. Table 16.3 lists the registry subtrees and the hexadecimal values used to represent them within Registry Provider methods.

Table 16.3 Registry Subtrees and Corresponding Hexadecimal Values

Subtree	Value
HKEY_CLASSES_ROOT	&H80000000
HKEY_CURRENT_USER	&H80000001
HKEY_LOCAL_MACHINE	&H80000002
HKEY_USERS	&H80000003
HKEY_CURRENT_CONFIG	&H80000005

In your scripts, you can use either the hexadecimal values or a constant that has been set to the appropriate value. For example, you might set a constant named HKEY_USERS to &H80000003:

```
Const HKEY_USERS = &H80000003
```

In your scripts, you would then use the constant to access the subtree rather than the hexadecimal value. The constant HKEY_USERS is likely to be more meaningful for someone reading and maintaining your script than the value &H80000003 would be.

Integer values for registry entry data types

When you use Registry Provider methods that work with the data types of registry entries, you have to translate between the common string representation of the data type, such as REG_SZ, and the integers that the Registry Provider uses to refer to the data types. Table 16.4 lists the registry data types and the corresponding integers that you need within your scripts.

Table 16.4 Registry Data Types and Corresponding Values

Registry Data Type	Value
REG_SZ	1
REG_EXPAND_SZ	2
REG_BINARY	3
REG_DWORD	4
REG_MULTI_SZ	7

In other words, when you query a registry entry for its value type, WMI will return one of the integers shown in the preceding table. If you want to display the value as a string, you will have to do the conversion yourself. For example:

```
If intDataType = 1 Then
    strDataType = "REG_SZ"
End If
```

Managing the Registry

Most of the time, managing the registry involves little more than backing it up on a regular basis. Although the registry is constantly being accessed and modified, both the Windows operating system and Windows applications typically take care of these activities for you; you will rarely need to directly manipulate the contents of the registry.

However, you might need to occasionally work directly with the contents of the registry: reading, changing, creating, enumerating, and deleting entries and subkeys. This is due to the fact that the registry stores important configuration information that affects so many components of Windows itself (as well as applications and services running under Windows). For example:

- You might read a Knowledge Base article that describes how changing a registry entry can provide a solution to a problem you have encountered.

- You might know that a certain application you uninstalled left behind a number of registry entries, and you would like to delete those entries, and for a large number of computers.

- You might be working with support personnel, and they ask you to find out the value of a registry entry or to determine whether or not a certain subkey exists.

- You might have learned a great deal about how a certain component of Windows works, and you want to optimize the configuration of this component. As it turns out, you can do this only by modifying the values of its registry entries.

- You have been informed by an application vendor that you need to change a certain registry entry to improve performance of the application on your particular system.

Do not try to memorize configuration settings stored in the registry. Instead, try to develop a sense for the types of things that you can expect to manage by modifying values in the registry. The best sources of information about registry settings are: the Resource Kit Registry Reference, MSDN® Web site, and Knowledge Base articles. Although many third-party sources provide information about the registry, do not rely on the accuracy of third-party information when it comes to the registry. If you find a registry entry referenced in a third-party source, try to verify the information provided by consulting the Resource Kit Registry Reference or another source available from Microsoft.

 Caution

Changing the registry with a script can easily propagate errors. The scripting tools bypass safeguards, allowing settings that can damage your system, or even require you to reinstall Windows. Before scripting changes to the registry, test your script thoroughly and back up the registry on every computer on which you will make changes. For more information about scripting changes to the registry, see the Registry Reference on the *Windows 2000 Server Resource Kit* companion CD or at http://www.microsoft.com/reskit.

Backing Up the Registry

With the proper precautions, you can edit the registry without creating unrecoverable problems. Nevertheless, it is possible to make changes to the registry that will prevent Windows from loading, and force you to reinstall the operating system. However, if you are careful about making backups, a number of recovery options will be available to you should a problem arise.

Assuming you have a proven backup procedure in place, however, making registry changes is no more dangerous than installing new hardware devices. If you replace your video card and Windows will not start, you can simply remove the new video card and reinstall the old card. Likewise, if you make a change to the registry and Windows will not start, you can simply remove the new registry and reinstall the old registry.

Back up regularly

Back up your current working registry regularly. One incorrect or conflicting value can create many problems, even preventing the operating system from starting.

Saving a backup of the registry on removable media or in secure shared folders can help you restart a computer even if an error prevents you from accessing files on your hard disk.

Back up before direct editing

The Registry Provider methods bypass standard safeguards, allowing settings that can degrade performance, damage your system, or even require you to reinstall the operating system. Some settings are incompatible with others, forcing you to reload your original settings to restore system performance. Unless you have backed up the correct settings, restoring them can prove very difficult, especially if you have made other changes to the registry or if some changes are preventing you from starting Windows.

It should be noted that there is nothing inherently harmful with the Registry Provider; the caution is warranted simply because the Registry Provider requires you to know, in advance, the acceptable values for a registry entry. For example, proper computer operation could depend on a registry entry whose value is set to either 0 or 1. A command-line or graphical configuration tool would typically allow you to set this entry only to 0 or 1. The Registry Provider, by contrast, might allow you to set this to 2, a value that might create problems.

Back up before installing new hardware or software

Back up your registry before you install new hardware or software, and before you remove old hardware or software. This precaution allows you to restore the system to its previous configuration if the changes conflict or degrade performance.

You can create scripts that use the Reg.exe tool (which ships as part of the Windows 2000 Support Tools) to generate backups of the registry and to restore those backups. To make your changes effective after restoring the registry, restart your computer.

Before relying on your registry backup process, perform a practice backup and restore on a noncritical system.

Scripting Steps

Listing 16.2 contains a script backs up the registry. To carry out this task, the script performs the following steps:

1. Use the CreateObject method to create a WshShell object and store a reference to the object in a variable.

2. Use the Exec method of the WshShell object to invoke the Reg.exe tool to back up HKLM/System to a file named sw.hiv.

Listing 16.2   Backing Up the Registry

```
1   Set objShell = CreateObject("WScript.Shell")
2   objShell.Exec "%comspec% /k reg.exe SAVE HKLM/System sw.hiv"
```

You can use the Reg.exe command-line tool itself instead of invoking it within a script. The advantage of writing a script is that you can then write a second script that uses the WshController object (see "WSH Primer") to run the backup script on computers throughout your enterprise. If necessary, you can use the Reg.exe command-line tool to restore a saved registry hive.

Reading Entry Values and Types

The registry is filled with interesting and useful information about Windows-based computer systems, including a wealth of information about the services and applications installed on those systems.

In many cases, you can use system administration tools such as MMC plug-ins to browse registry values. These tools use registry values as the source of much of the information they provide, and thus allow you to read registry values indirectly.

There are, however, a number of useful registry values that cannot be viewed using the system administration tools included with Windows 2000. In addition, even when a tool allows you to view the registry values you are interested in, the tool might not allow you to easily view those same values across a large number of computers. For example, a security bulletin might alert you to a registry entry on servers that, if not configured properly, could leave your network vulnerable. Using a script to verify this registry value on all your servers would be much faster than attempting to verify the value one computer at a time using an application such as Regedit.

Although you can script the reading of registry values in a number of ways, a powerful approach is to use the WMI Registry Provider. The Registry Provider includes five different methods for reading registry values, with each method used to read a different data type. These five methods include:

- GetBinaryValue
- GetDWORDValue

- GetExpandedStringValue

- GetMultiStringValue

- GetStringValue

Each of these methods will be demonstrated in this section of the chapter.

Using the Registry Provider to Read Registry Entries

The fact that there are five different methods for reading the registry might seem a bit daunting at first. Fortunately, each of these methods uses the same four parameters:

- The subtree (such as HKEY_LOCAL_MACHINE) that contains the value being read. This must be set to one of the hexadecimal values shown in Table 16.3.

- The path to the registry entry (for example, CurrentControlSet\Services).

- The name of the value being read. Specify an empty string ("") to read the default value.

- An "out" parameter, a variable that contains the value read from the registry. To display the returned value on screen, simply echo this variable.

In this chapter, variables and constants are configured for use as the method parameters. This is done to reduce the size of individual lines of code, particularly those that require long registry paths. For example, a constant for the subtree and variables for the path and value name might be configured within a script similar to this:

```
Const HKEY_LOCAL_MACHINE = &H80000002
strKeyPath = "SOFTWARE\Microsoft\Windows Script Host\Settings"
strEntryName = "TrustPolicy"
```

The resulting call to the GetDWORDValue method thus looks like this, with the call fitting on a single line:

```
objReg.GetStringValue HKEY_LOCAL_MACHINE, strKeyPath, strEntryName, strValue
```

Without using variables and constants to represent the parameter values, this same method would look like this, requiring at least two lines of code:

```
objReg.GetStringValue &H8000000, _
    "SOFTWARE\Microsoft\Windows Script Host\Settings" , "TrustPolicy" ,strValue
```

Reading String-valued and DWORD-valued Entries

The majority of registry values that hold useful information for a system administrator are made up of either alphanumeric characters (REG_SZ) or numbers (REG_DWORD). String values in the registry are often clearly interpretable words, such as the name of a component manufacturer. Registry values of other types, like binary values, cannot be interpreted quite so readily.

You can read REG_SZ and REG_DWORD values by using the GetStringValue and the GetDWORDValue methods, respectively.

Scripting Steps

Listing 16.3 contains a script that retrieves both a string value and a DWORD value from the registry. To carry out this task, the script performs the following steps:

1. Create constants that hold the hexadecimal numbers corresponding to the HKEY_CURRENT_USER and HKEY_LOCAL_MACHINE registry subtrees.

2. Create a variable and set it to the name of the computer where the script will run.

3. Use a GetObject call to connect to the WMI namespace root\default, and set the impersonation level to "impersonate."

4. Create a variable and set it to the path of the registry subkey in which the value is located.

5. Create a variable and set it to the name of the entry.

6. Use the GetDWORDValue method to retrieve the value of the entry. The value is returned in the dwValue variable that is passed to the method. GetDWORDValue is used because the data type of the value of the entry, **Console**, is REG_DWORD.

7. Display the value retrieved using the Echo method.

8. Repeat steps 4 through 7, substituting the GetStringValue method for GetDWORDValue in step 6. You must use the GetStringValue method rather than the GetDWORDValue method to retrieve the value of the second entry, **TrustPolicy**. This is because the data type of the value is REG_SZ (string).

Listing 16.3   Reading String and DWORD Registry Values

```
1   Const HKEY_CURRENT_USER = &H80000001
2   Const HKEY_LOCAL_MACHINE = &H80000002
3   strComputer = "."
4
5   Set objReg=GetObject("winmgmts:{impersonationLevel=impersonate}!\\" & _
6       strComputer & "\root\default:StdRegProv")
7
8   strKeyPath = "Console"
9   strEntryName = "HistoryBufferSize"
10  objReg.GetDWORDValue HKEY_CURRENT_USER,strKeyPath,strEntryName,dwValue
11  Wscript.Echo "Current History Buffer Size: " & dwValue
12
13  strKeyPath = "SOFTWARE\Microsoft\Windows Script Host\Settings"
14  strEntryName = "TrustPolicy"
15  objReg.GetStringValue HKEY_LOCAL_MACHINE,strKeyPath,strEntryName,strValue
16  Wscript.Echo "Current WSH Trust Policy Value: " & strValue
```

Reading a Multistring-valued Entry

A multistring value stores a list of strings. A typical use of a multistring value is demonstrated by the Autorecover MOFs entry in the HKEY_LOCAL_MACHINE\SOFTWARE \Microsoft\WBEM\CIMOM subkey. This entry holds a list of .mof files that are used to autorecover the CIM repository. The list could have been held in a series of string-valued entries, all stored under a single Autorecover MOFs subkey. However, using a multistring value is more compact and makes programmatic retrieval of the values more convenient. With a multistring entry, there is only one registry entry to read, which makes it more likely that you will retrieve every value. By contrast, storing each value in a separate registry entry requires you to individually read each of those entries. In turn, that increases the likelihood of you missing a value.

Figure 16.3 shows how a registry editor displays a multistring value. You can see that it is simply a list of strings contained under the single Autorecover MOFs entry.

Figure 16.3 Multistring Value as Displayed by a Registry Editor

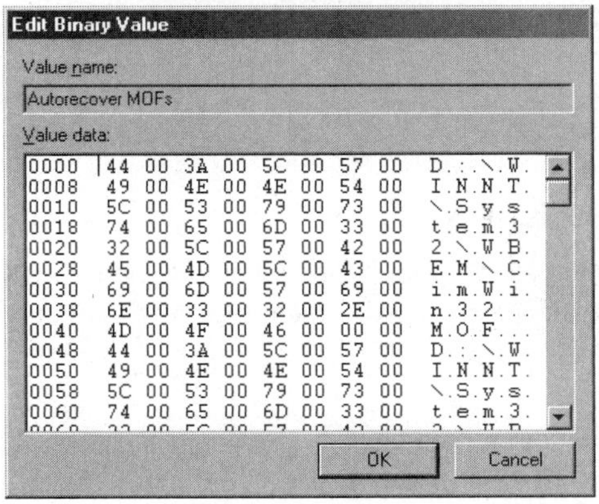

You use the GetMultiStringValue method to retrieve a multistring value. The method takes as one of its parameters a variable that holds the set of strings retrieved. The strings are returned in an array, so you must use a For Each loop in your script to enumerate each of the individual strings in the array.

Scripting Steps

Listing 16.4 contains a script that retrieves a multistring value from the registry. To carry out this task, the script must perform the following steps:

1. Create a constant that holds the hexadecimal number corresponding to the HKEY_LOCAL_MACHINE subtree.

2. Create a variable and set it to the computer name.

3. Use a GetObject call to connect to the WMI namespace root\default, and set the impersonation level to "impersonate."

4. Create a variable and set it to the path of the registry subkey in which the value is located.

5. Create a variable and set it to the name of the entry.

6. Use the GetMultiStringValue method to retrieve the array of string values.

7. For each string value in the array, echo the value to the screen.

Listing 16.4   Reading a Multistring-valued Entry

```
1    Const HKEY_LOCAL_MACHINE = &H80000002
2    strComputer = "."
3
4    Set objReg=GetObject("winmgmts:{impersonationLevel=impersonate}!\\" & _
5        strComputer & "\root\default:StdRegProv")
6
7    strKeyPath = "SOFTWARE\Microsoft\WBEM\CIMOM"
8    strValueName = "Autorecover MOFs"
9    objReg.GetMultiStringValue HKEY_LOCAL_MACHINE,strKeyPath, _
10        strValueName,arrValues
11
12   For Each strValue In arrValues
13       Wscript.Echo  strValue
14   Next
```

Reading an Expanded String-valued Entry

Registry values of the expanded string type are strings that include items that are evaluated only when the string value is actually used. For instance, a typical expanded string value is the one that holds the location of the TEMP directory:

```
%USERPROFILE%\Local Settings\Temp
```

The \Local Settings\Temp component of the string is treated literally, but the value of the %USERPROFILE% component can be determined only when it is actually accessed. This is because the value is dependent upon the user accessing the entry. If you look at the registry entry in Regedit.exe, you will see the value %USERPROFILE%\Local Settings\Temp. However, when you retrieve the value of the entry, the value will be something like this: C:\Documents and Settings\jsmith.REDMOND\Local Settings\Temp. In other words, the environment variable %USERPROFILE% is replaced with the folder (in this case, jsmith.REDMOND) that contains the user profile.

The components of expanded string types that appear between percent symbols (%) correspond to environment variables and are dependent either on the aspects of the particular user or the current configuration of the computer.

You use the GetExpandedStringValue method to retrieve expanded string values. The method takes, as one of its parameters, a variable in which the retrieved value is stored. In the retrieved value, the components of the string that appear between percent symbols are automatically evaluated. This means your script will echo a value similar to C:\Documents and Settings\jsmith.REDMOND\Local Settings\Temp rather than a value like %USERPROFILE%\Local Settings\Temp.

Scripting Steps

Listing 16.5 contains a script that retrieves an expanded string value from the registry. To carry out this task, the script must perform the following steps:

1. Create a constant that holds the hexadecimal number corresponding to the HKEY_LOCAL_MACHINE registry subtree.

2. Create a variable and set it to the computer name.

3. Use a GetObject call to connect to the WMI namespace root\default, and set the impersonation level to "impersonate."

4. Create a variable and set it to the path of the registry subkey in which the value is located.

5. Create a variable and set it to the name of the entry.

6. Use the GetExpandedStringValue method to retrieve the value.

7. Echo the value to the screen.

Listing 16.5 Reading an Expanded String-valued Entry

```
1   Const HKEY_LOCAL_MACHINE = &H80000002
2   strComputer = "."
3
4   Set objReg=GetObject("winmgmts:{impersonationLevel=impersonate}!\\" & _
5       strComputer & "\root\default:StdRegProv")
6
7   strKeyPath = "SOFTWARE\Microsoft\Windows Scripting Host\Locations"
8   strEntryName = "CScript"
9   objReg.GetExpandedStringValue HKEY_LOCAL_MACHINE,strKeyPath, _
10      strEntryName,strValue
11
12  Wscript.Echo  "The location of the cscript host is: " & strValue
```

Reading a Binary-valued Entry

Binary registry values are very cryptic, and difficult for humans to make sense of. However, there is useful information in the registry that is stored in binary format. As an advanced system administrator, you might find yourself interested in understanding, and possibly even editing, certain binary entries.

For example, services are organized in groups. The GroupOrderList subkey stores information about the order in which groups of services are loaded when Windows boots. This information looks similar to the following:

```
17 0 0 0 14 0 0 0 1 0 0 0 2 0 0 0 3 0 0 0 4 0 0 0 5 0 0 0 6 0 0 0 7 0 0 0 8 0 0 0
9 0 0 0 10 0 0 0 11 0 0 0 12 0 0 0 13 0 0 0 15 0 0 0 16 0 0 0 17 0 0 0
```

> ### Tip
> If you are interested in better understanding this example of binary registry values usage, consult the Registry Reference on the *Windows 2000 Server Resource Kit* companion CD (or on the Web at http://www.microsoft.com/reskit).

Although this type of information is rarely useful to a system administrator, it can be important to support personnel troubleshooting computer problems. If support personnel need to know the value of a binary registry entry, you can use scripts to retrieve this information.

The caution about manipulating registry entries directly is even more relevant with binary entry values. For one thing, they are cryptic, with no obvious meaning. Along the same lines, they are difficult to remember in case you need to restore their original values. Although there is no harm in reading one of these values, be very careful about modifying the value in any way.

The Registry Provider includes the GetBinaryValue method to enable you to work with binary entry values. The method takes, as one of its parameters, a variable that is used to store the retrieved value. The value is returned as an array of bytes. Therefore, to extract the value, you need to loop through the array, extracting a single byte with each pass.

Scripting Steps

Listing 16.6 contains a script that retrieves a binary value from the registry. To carry out this task, the script must perform the following steps:

1. Create a constant that holds the hexadecimal number corresponding to the HKEY_LOCAL_MACHINE registry subtree.

2. Create a variable and set it to the computer name.

3. Use a GetObject call to connect to the WMI namespace root\default, and set the impersonation level to "impersonate."

4. Create a variable and set it to the path of the registry subkey in which the entry is located.

5. Create a variable and set it to the name of the entry.

6. Use the GetBinaryValue method to retrieve the value of the entry as an array of bytes.

7. Use a For Next loop to iterate through each byte value in the array, arrValue, displaying it using the StdOut.Write method. StdOut.Write is used instead of the WScript Echo method to avoid displaying new line characters after each byte value. Using StdOut enables you to display the value on a single line, similar to this:

   ```
   17 0 0 0 14
   ```

   By contrast, Wscript.Echo would display each byte value on a separate line:

   ```
   17
    0
    0
    0
   14
   ```

Listing 16.6   Reading a Binary Registry Value

```
1    Const HKEY_LOCAL_MACHINE = &H80000002
2    strComputer = "."
3
4    Set objReg=GetObject("winmgmts:{impersonationLevel=impersonate}!\\" & _
5       strComputer & "\root\default:StdRegProv")
6
7    strKeyPath = "SYSTEM\CurrentControlSet\Control\GroupOrderList"
8    strEntryName = "Base"
9    objReg.GetBinaryValue HKEY_LOCAL_MACHINE,strKeyPath, _
10      strEntryName,arrValue
11
12   For Each byteValue in arrValue
13      WScript.StdOut.Write byteValue & " "
14   Next
```

Changing String-valued and DWORD-valued Entries

Changing the values of registry entries is a common registry management task. The most challenging aspect of that task is determining which entries you need to change, and to which values they must be changed. After you have this information, you must choose the appropriate Registry Provider methods for making the change.

To change a string value (REG_SZ), you use the SetStringValue method; to change a numeric value (DWORD), you use the SetDWORDValue method. Each of these methods takes four parameters:

- A constant that specifies the subtree in which the value being changed is located.

- The path to the subkey in which the value is located.

- The name of the entry with the value to be changed.

- The new value.

These parameters are similar to the parameters used to read registry entries. The only difference is that when registry entries are read, the fourth parameter represents the value read from the registry; when registry entries are configured, the fourth parameter represents the new value being written to the registry.

Be certain to investigate whether other methods of configuration are available before deciding to script direct changes to the registry.

 Caution

Regardless of where you obtain your information, always back up the registry before modifying it in any way.

Scripting Steps

Listing 16.7 contains a script that changes the values of both a DWORD and a String value in the registry. To carry out this task, the script must perform the following steps:

1. Create a constant that holds the hexadecimal number corresponding to the HKEY_LOCAL_MACHINE registry subtree.

2. Create a variable and set it to the computer name.

3. Use a GetObject call to connect to the WMI namespace root\default, and set the impersonation level to "impersonate."

4. Create a variable and set it to the path of the registry subkey in which the entry is located.

5. Create a variable and set it to the name of the entry.

6. Use the SetDWORDValue method to set the value of the HistoryBufferSize registry entry to the value stored in the dwValue variable (300).

7. Set the values of the variables holding the entry name and value to use in setting the string-valued entry.

8. Use the SetStringValue method to set the value of the FaceName registry entry to the value (Lucida Console) stored in the strValue variable.

Listing 16.7   Changing Registry String and DWORD Values

```
1   Const HKEY_CURRENT_USER = &H80000001
2   strComputer = "."
3
4   Set objReg = GetObject("winmgmts:{impersonationLevel=impersonate}!\\" & _
5       strComputer & "\root\default:StdRegProv")
6
7   strKeyPath = "Console"
8   strEntryName = "HistoryBufferSize"
9   dwValue = 300
10  objReg.SetDWORDValue HKEY_CURRENT_USER, strKeyPath, strEntryName, dwValue
11
12  strEntryName = "FaceName"
13  strValue = "Lucida Console"
14  objReg.SetStringValue HKEY_CURRENT_USER, strKeyPath, _
15      strEntryName, strValue
```

Creating Registry Subkeys and Entries

Managing computer system configuration by directly editing the registry usually involves changing the value of certain entries, not creating new ones. However, some registry subkeys, entries, and values can be used to affect the configuration of a computer, even though these items are not automatically created when the operating system is installed.

For example, to use the WshController object, you must first create an entry named **Remote** in the HKLM\SOFTWARE\Microsoft\Windows Script Host\Settings subkey on the remote computer on which you want to run scripts. The **Remote** entry is not created by default, yet the WshController object cannot be used until the entry has been added and its value set to 1. This means you must create this entry and set the value before you will be able to run remote scripts either from or against a given computer.

Fortunately, you can use scripts to create both registry subkeys and registry entries.

Creating a Subkey

You rarely need to create a registry subkey. However, in some circumstances the solution to a problem — as described in a Knowledge Base article or a security bulletin — requires the addition of a subkey. If you need to create a subkey on a large number of computers, the best solution might very well be a script. After all, a single script can be used to create the subkey on every computer affected by the problem.

The Registry Provider's CreateKey method enables you to add a new subkey. It takes two parameters: a constant indicating the subtree to which the new subkey will be added and the path of the new subkey.

Scripting Steps

Listing 16.8 contains a script that creates a subkey in the SOFTWARE key under the subtree HKEY_LOCAL_MACHINE in the registry. To carry out this task, the script must perform the following steps:

1. Create a constant to hold the hexadecimal number corresponding to the HKEY_LOCAL_MACHINE registry subtree.

2. Create a variable and set it to computer name.

3. Use a GetObject call to connect to the WMI namespace root\default, and set the impersonation level to "impersonate."

4. Create a variable and set it to the path of the registry subkey to create.

5. Use the CreateKey method to create the new subkey.

Listing 16.8   Creating a Subkey

```
1   Const HKEY_LOCAL_MACHINE = &H80000002
2   strComputer = "."
3
4   Set objReg=GetObject("winmgmts:{impersonationLevel=impersonate}!\\" & _
5       strComputer & "\root\default:StdRegProv")
6
7   strKeyPath = "SOFTWARE\System Admin Scripting Guide"
8   objReg.CreateKey HKEY_LOCAL_MACHINE,strKeyPath
```

Figure 16.4 shows the newly created subkey in a registry editor.

Figure 16.4   Viewing a Newly Created Subkey Using a Registry Editor

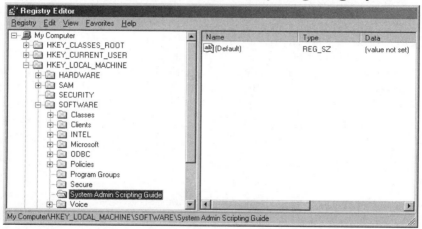

Creating String-valued and DWORD-valued Entries

The Registry Provider's SetStringValue and SetDWORDValue methods enable you to create string and DWORD-valued registry entries. Each of the methods accepts the same four parameters: a constant corresponding to the subtree in which the entry will be created, the path to the subkey in which the entry will be created, the name of the entry, and the value of the entry.

Note that the subkey must already exist. If the subkey does not exist, the script cannot create it for you. Because no location is available for the entry, the script will fail.

Be careful to use the method that corresponds to the data type of the value you want to create. If you want to create an entry with the DWORD value 8 and you mistakenly use the SetStringValue method and pass it the value 8, the method will interpret the 8 as the string "8" without warning you. This could incorrectly configure the registration, and lead to any number of problems..

Scripting Steps

Listing 16.9 contains a script that creates two entries in the System Admin Scripting Guide subkey, one having a string value and the other a DWORD value, in the subkey created by the script in Listing 16.8. Before running this script, run the script in Listing 16.8 to create the subkey SOFTWARE\System Admin Scripting Guide.

To carry out this task, the script must perform the following steps:

1. Create a constant that holds the hexadecimal number corresponding to the HKEY_LOCAL_MACHINE subtree.

2. Create a and set it to the computer name.

3. Use a GetObject call to connect to the WMI namespace root\default, and set the impersonation level to "impersonate."

4. Create variables and set them to the following:

   ■ Subkey in which the entries will be created

   ■ Name of the string-valued registry entry being created

   ■ String value of the registry entry being created

5. Use the SetStringValue method to create the new string value.

6. Create variables and set them to the following:

   ■ Name of the DWORD-valued registry entry being created

   ■ DWORD value of the registry entry being created

7. Use the SetDWORDValue method to create the new DWORD value.

Listing 16.9 Creating Registry String-valued and DWORD-valued Entries

```
1   Const HKEY_LOCAL_MACHINE = &H80000002
2   strComputer = "."
3
4   Set objReg = GetObject("winmgmts:{impersonationLevel=impersonate}!\\" & _
5       strComputer & "\root\default:StdRegProv")
6
7   strKeyPath = "SOFTWARE\System Admin Scripting Guide"
8
9   strEntryName = "String Value Name"
10  strValue = "string value"
11  objReg.SetStringValue HKEY_LOCAL_MACHINE,strKeyPath,strEntryName,strValue
12
13  strEntryName = "DWORD Value Name"
14  dwValue = 82
15  objReg.SetDWORDValue HKEY_LOCAL_MACHINE,strKeyPath,strEntryName,dwValue
```

Figure 16.5 shows the newly created string and DWORD-valued entries in a registry editor.

Figure 16.5   Viewing Newly Created Entries Using a Registry Editor

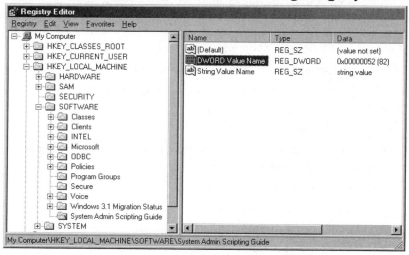

Creating Multistring-valued Entries

Multistring-valued registry entries are relatively rare in the registry. The Registry Provider does, however, provide the SetMultiStringValue method to enable you to create these entries as needed. Because a multistring can store a list of strings, the SetMultiStringValue method accepts an array of strings as the parameter that determines the values of the entry.

Note that if you use the SetMultiStringValue method to append to an existing multistring-valued entry rather than create a new one, you have to first use the GetMultiStringValue method to retrieve the existing list of strings. This is because SetMultiStringValue overwrites any existing value. For example, suppose you have a multistring value consisting of the following strings:

A
B
C
D

If you use the SetMultiStringValue method, you cannot pass the string "E" as the sole parameter; if you do, the A, B, C, and D strings will be replaced, and the entry will contain this value:

E

To append "E" as an additional string within the value, you must pass an array containing the initial string values as well as the new value:

```
arrStringValues = Array("A", "B", "C", "D", "E")
objReg.SetMultiStringValue HKEY_LOCAL_MACHINE,strKeyPath, _
    strEntryName,arrStringValues
```

Scripting Steps

Listing 16.10 contains a script that creates a multistring-valued entry in the registry subkey created by the script in Listing 16.8. To carry out this task, the script must perform the following steps:

1. Create a constant that holds the hexadecimal number corresponding to the HKEY_LOCAL_MACHINE subtree.

2. Create a variable and set it to the computer name.

3. Use a GetObject call to connect to the WMI namespace root\default, and set the impersonation level to "impersonate."

4. Create a variable and set it to the subkey in which the entries will be created.

5. Create a variable and set it to the name of the string-valued registry entry being created.

6. Create an array variable in which to specify the multiple strings that will make up the multistring value of the registry entry being created.

7. Use the SetMultiStringValue method to create the new multistring-valued entry.

Listing 16.10 Creating Registry Multistring-valued Entries

```
1   Const HKEY_LOCAL_MACHINE = &H80000002
2   strComputer = "."
3
4   Set objReg=GetObject("winmgmts:{impersonationLevel=impersonate}!\\" & _
5       strComputer & "\root\default:StdRegProv")
6
7   strKeyPath = "SOFTWARE\System Admin Scripting Guide"
8   strEntryName = "Multi String Value Name"
9   arrStringValues = Array("first string", "second string", _
10    "third string", "fourth string")
11
12  objReg.SetMultiStringValue HKEY_LOCAL_MACHINE,strKeyPath, _
13      strEntryName,arrStringValues
```

Figure 16.6 shows the newly created multistring-valued entry in a registry editor.

Figure 16.6   Newly Created Multistring-valued Entry

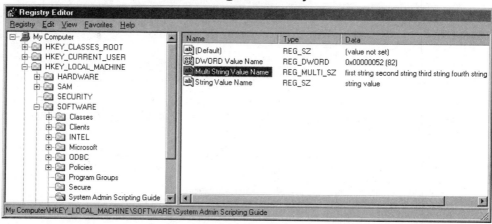

Creating Expanded String-valued Entries

Expanded strings are strings that can include variables; these variables are resolved when an application or a service uses the value. For example, the value of an entry that references a file might include the variable %systemroot%. When a service, such as the Event Log, references the entry, the %systemroot% variable is replaced by the name of the directory containing the Windows system files (for example, C:\Windows). On a different computer, one with Windows installed on drive D, this same registry value might be replaced by D:\Windows.

If you need to create an entry that includes a value that might change, such as the path environment variable or the location of the current user's profile, you can use the SetExpandedStringValue method.

Scripting Steps

Listing 16.11 contains a script that creates an expanded string-valued registry entry in the System Admin Scripting Guide subkey created by the script in Listing 16.8. To carry out this task, the script must perform the following steps:

1. Create a constant that holds the hexadecimal number corresponding to the HKEY_LOCAL_MACHINE subtree.

2. Create a variable and set it to the computer name.

3. Use a GetObject call to connect to the WMI namespace root\default, and set the impersonation level to "impersonate."

4. Create variables in which to specify the following:

- Subkey in which the entries will be created.

- Name of the expanded string-valued registry entry being created.

- Expanded string value of the registry entry being created.

5. Use the SetExpandedStringValue method to create the new entry with the expanded string value.

Listing 16.11 Creating Expanded String-valued Entries

```
1   Const HKEY_LOCAL_MACHINE = &H80000002
2   strComputer = "."
3
4   Set objReg=GetObject("winmgmts:{impersonationLevel=impersonate}!\\" & _
5       strComputer & "\root\default:StdRegProv")
6
7   strKeyPath = "SOFTWARE\System Admin Scripting Guide"
8   strValueName = "Expanded String Value Name"
9   strValue = "%PATHEXT%"
10
11  objReg.SetExpandedStringValue _
12      HKEY_LOCAL_MACHINE,strKeyPath,strValueName,strValue
```

Enumerating Keys, Subkeys, and Entries

Enumeration is the process of listing the contents of a container. Just as you might open a folder and inspect its subfolders and files, you might want to inspect the child subkeys within a subkey or the entries within a subkey. For example, the script in Listing 16.1 retrieves the location of the registry hive files by listing all of the entries in the HKEY_LOCAL_MACHINE\SYSTEM\CurrentControlSet\Control\hivelist subkey. The only way to determine all the registry hive files is to enumerate each entry within this subkey.

Enumeration is also used when troubleshooting configuration problems with the operating system or with an application. When a particularly stubborn problem occurs with an application, support personnel might ask you to provide a list of all the registry subkeys, entries, and values for that application. Retrieving these items programmatically is obviously much faster and easier than retrieving them using the GUI, especially if the same information must be obtained from multiple computers.

Enumerating Subkeys of a Key or Subkey

In some instances, useful configuration information is stored as the names of a set of subkeys. In the following sample script, for instance, the subkey names represent the services on a computer. In a case such as this, simply listing the names of the subkeys provides useful information.

The EnumKey method enables you to return the subkeys of a registry key or subkey. Note that the EnumKey method returns only the immediate subkeys of a key or subkey; it does not return any subkeys that might be contained within those top-level subkeys. For example, suppose you run the EnumKey method against the Control subkey shown in Figure 16.7. In this case, EnumKey will return an array consisting of the subkeys AGP, Arbiters, and BackupRestore. However, that array will not include the subkeys of those subkeys (such as AllocationOrder and DllPaths).

Figure 16.7   Sample Registry Subkeys

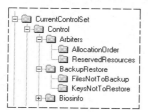

To return the subkeys of Arbiters and BackupRestore, you need to use a recursive function. For more information about recursive functions, see "VBScript Primer" in this book.

Scripting Steps

Listing 16.12 contains a script that enumerates the subkeys of a registry subkey. To carry out this task, the script must perform the following steps:

1. Create a constant that holds the hexadecimal number corresponding to the HKEY_LOCAL_MACHINE subtree.

2. Create a variable and set it to the computer name.

3. Use a GetObject call to connect to the WMI namespace root\default, and set the impersonation level to "impersonate."

4. Create a variable and set it to the subkey to be enumerated.

5. Use the EnumKey method to enumerate the subkeys, storing the results in the arrSubKeys variable.

6. For each of the subkey names stored in the array arrSubKey, use the Echo method to display the values.

Listing 16.12   Enumerating Subkeys of a Subkey

```
1   Const HKEY_LOCAL_MACHINE = &H80000002
2   strComputer = "."
3
4   Set objReg=GetObject("winmgmts:{impersonationLevel=impersonate}!\\" & _
5       strComputer & "\root\default:StdRegProv")
6
7   strKeyPath = "SYSTEM\CurrentControlSet\Services"
8   objReg.EnumKey HKEY_LOCAL_MACHINE, strKeyPath, arrSubKeys
9
10  For Each Subkey in arrSubKeys
11      Wscript.Echo Subkey
12  Next
```

Enumerating Entry Names, Values, and Data Types

Registry subkeys group entries with related information, and it is often useful to display that related information. Unfortunately, this is not necessarily a straightforward procedure; after all, you cannot read a registry value unless you use the appropriate method. But how can you call the appropriate method if you do not know the data type of the value being read?

Fortunately, you can accomplish this task by using the Registry Provider EnumValues method to retrieve an array containing the entry names and an array containing the data type of each entry. After you know the entry name and its data type, you can select the appropriate method to retrieve and display the value of each entry.

Scripting Steps

Listing 16.13 contains a script that displays the name, data type, and value of all the entries within a registry subkey. To carry out this task, the script must perform the following steps:

1. Create a constant that holds the hexadecimal number corresponding to the HKEY_LOCAL_MACHINE subtree.

2. Create constants that correspond to the various registry entry data types (lines 2–6).

3. Create a variable and set it to the computer name (line 8).

4. Use a GetObject call to connect to the WMI namespace root\default, and set the impersonation level to "impersonate."

5. Create a variable and set it to the subkey to be enumerated (line 13).

6. Use the EnumValues method to enumerate the entry names and data types, storing the results in the variables arrEntryNames and arrValueTypes.

7. Use For Next to loop through each of the entry names stored in the arrEntryNames variable, displaying each entry name and using the corresponding data type in a Select Case statement to display a message identifying the data type (thus determining which method needs to be called to display the value of the entry). For details about each individual Get method, refer to "Reading Entry Values and Types" in this chapter.

Listing 16.13   Enumerating Entries and Data Types

```
1   Const HKEY_LOCAL_MACHINE = &H80000002
2   Const REG_SZ = 1
3   Const REG_EXPAND_SZ = 2
4   Const REG_BINARY = 3
5   Const REG_DWORD = 4
6   Const REG_MULTI_SZ = 7
7
8   strComputer = "."
9   Set objReg=GetObject("winmgmts:{impersonationLevel=impersonate}!\\" & _
10      strComputer & "\root\default:StdRegProv")
11  strKeyPath = "SYSTEM\CurrentControlSet\Control\Lsa"
12  objReg.EnumValues HKEY_LOCAL_MACHINE,_
13      strKeyPath,arrEntryNames,arrValueTypes
14
15  For i=0 To UBound(arrEntryNames)
16      Wscript.Echo "Entry Name: " & arrEntryNames(i)
17      Select Case arrValueTypes(i)
18      Case REG_SZ
19          Wscript.Echo "Data Type: String"
20          objReg.GetStringValue HKEY_LOCAL_MACHINE, _
21              strKeyPath, arrEntryNames(i),strValue
22          Wscript.Echo "Value: " & strValue
23      Case REG_EXPAND_SZ
24          Wscript.Echo "Data Type: Expanded String"
25          objReg.GetExpandedStringValue HKEY_LOCAL_MACHINE _
26              strKeyPath, arrEntryNames(i),estrValue
27          Wscript.Echo "Value: " & estrValue
28      Case REG_BINARY
29          Wscript.Echo "Data Type: Binary"
30          objReg.GetBinaryValue HKEY_LOCAL_MACHINE, _
31              strKeyPath, arrEntryNames(i),arrValue
32          WScript.StdOut.Write "Value: "
33          For Each byteValue in arrValue
34              WScript.StdOut.Write byteValue & " "
35          Next
36          WScript.StdOut.Write vbCRLF
```

(continued)

Listing 16.13   Enumerating Entries and Data Types *(continued)*

```
37    Case REG_DWORD
38        Wscript.Echo "Data Type: DWORD"
39        objReg.GetDWORDValue HKEY_LOCAL_MACHINE, _
40           strKeyPath, arrEntryNames(i),dwValue
41        Wscript.Echo "Value: " & dwValue
42    Case REG_MULTI_SZ
43        Wscript.Echo "Data Type: Multi String"
44        objReg.GetMultiStringValue HKEY_LOCAL_MACHINE, _
45           strKeyPath, arrEntryNames(i),arrValues
46        For Each strValue in arrValues
47            Wscript.Echo strValue
48        Next
49    End Select
50 Next
```

Deleting Subkeys and Entries

For the most part, you should be very careful about deleting anything from the registry. Despite that caution, however, there will likely be times when you must delete registry subkeys or entries. For example, you might discover, after adding an entry to modify the behavior of a system component, that the component is not working. Should that happen, you will likely want to revert to your previous configuration, which means removing the newly added registry entry. Another possibility is that you read a Knowledge Base article that describes a security issue whose temporary fix involves the deletion of a certain subkey.

The Registry Provider provides two methods for deleting elements of the registry: DeleteValue and DeleteKey. The DeleteValue method takes three parameters:

- A constant representing the subtree where the entry being deleted is located.

- The path to the subkey that contains the entry.

- The name of the entry.

The DeleteKey method accepts two parameters: a constant representing the subtree where the subkey being deleted is located and the path of the subkey to be deleted.

Deleting Registry Entries

The DeleteValue method deletes a registry entry. (If you are wondering why the name is DeleteValue rather than DeleteEntry, it is because a number of different terms are used to refer to registry entries, including *values*). The script in Listing 16.14 deletes all registry entries added by the scripts in the "Creating Registry Subkeys and Entries" section of this chapter. Run those scripts before running this one — otherwise, there will be no entry for this demonstration script to delete.

Scripting Steps

Listing 16.14 contains a script that deletes entries from the registry. To carry out this task, the script must perform the following steps:

1. Create a constant that holds the hexadecimal number corresponding to the HKEY_LOCAL_MACHINE subtree.

2. Create a variable and set it to the computer name.

3. Use a GetObject call to connect to the WMI namespace root\default, and set the impersonation level to "impersonate."

4. Create a variable and set it to the subkey from which the entries will be deleted.

5. Create variables and set it to the names of the entries being deleted.

6. Use the DeleteValue method to delete the various registry entries.

Listing 16.14   Deleting Registry Entries

```
1   Const HKEY_LOCAL_MACHINE = &H80000002
2   strComputer = "."
3
4   Set objReg=GetObject("winmgmts:{impersonationLevel=impersonate}!\\" & _
5       strComputer & "\root\default:StdRegProv")
6
7   strKeyPath = "SOFTWARE\System Admin Scripting Guide"
8   strDWORDValueName = "DWORD Value Name"
9   strExpandedStringValueName = "Expanded String Value Name"
10  strMultiStringValueName = "Multi String Value Name"
11  strStringValueName = "String Value Name"
12
13  objReg.DeleteValue HKEY_LOCAL_MACHINE,strKeyPath,strDWORDValueName
14  objReg.DeleteValue _
15     HKEY_LOCAL_MACHINE,strKeyPath,strExpandedStringValueName
16  objReg.DeleteValue HKEY_LOCAL_MACHINE,strKeyPath,strMultiStringValueName
17  objReg.DeleteValue HKEY_LOCAL_MACHINE,strKeyPath,strStringValueName
```

Deleting a Registry Subkey

You can use the DeleteKey method to delete a registry subkey. The script in Listing 16.15 deletes the subkey HKLM\SOFTWARE\System Admin Scripting Guide, added by the script in Listing 16.8. If you have not already run Listing 16.8, you should do so before running the following script. Otherwise, there will be no subkey for this demonstration script to delete.

Scripting Steps

Listing 16.15 contains a script that deletes the HKLM\SOFTWARE\System Admin Scripting Guide subkey created by the script in Listing 16.8. To carry out this task, the script must perform the following steps:

1. Create a constant that holds the hexadecimal number corresponding to the HKEY_LOCAL_MACHINE subtree.

2. Create a variable and set it to the computer name.

3. Use a GetObject call to connect to the WMI namespace root\default, and set the impersonation level to "impersonate."

4. Create a variable and set it to the subkey to be deleted.

5. Use the DeleteKey method to delete the subkey.

Listing 16.15 Deleting a Registry Key

```
1   Const HKEY_LOCAL_MACHINE = &H80000002
2   strComputer = "."
3
4   Set objReg=GetObject("winmgmts:{impersonationLevel=impersonate}!\\" & _
5       strComputer & "\root\default:StdRegProv")
6   strKeyPath = "SOFTWARE\System Admin Scripting Guide"
7
8   objReg.DeleteKey HKEY_LOCAL_MACHINE, strKeyPath
```

Checking Registry Subkey Access Rights

You can use a registry editor to check and modify the access rights assigned to registry subkeys and entries. Although a registry editor allows you to connect to and manage the registry of a remote computer, it allows you to manage only one computer at a time. If you need to check the access rights of registry subkeys or entries on a large number of computers, a script that uses the Registry Provider is a far better solution.

The Registry Provider CheckAccess method allows you to determine whether the user of a script has a particular access right on a registry subkey or entry. The Registry Provider does not provide a way to list all of the access rights on a given subkey or entry, or to make any changes to the access rights.

When you use the Registry Provider CheckAccess method to determine access rights, you must use hexadecimal values that refer to the particular rights you are interested in. Table 16.5 lists those hexadecimal values and the access rights to which they correspond.

Table 16.5   Registry Key Access Permissions and Corresponding Values

Access Right	Value
KEY_QUERY_VALUE	&H0001
KEY_SET_VALUE	&H0002
KEY_CREATE_SUB_KEY	&H0004
KEY_ENUMERATE_SUB_KEYS	&H0008
KEY_NOTIFY	&H0010
KEY_CREATE_LINK	&H0020
DELETE	&H00010000
READ_CONTROL	&H00020000
WRITE_DAC	&H00040000
WRITE_OWNER	&H00080000

The CheckAccess method will return a Boolean value: True if the user possesses the access right, False if the user does not.

Scripting Steps

Listing 16.6 contains a script that checks whether the user account under which the script is running has various access rights to a registry subkey. The script reports whether the user account has those rights on the subkey. To carry out this task, the script must perform the following steps:

1. Create the constants that hold the hexadecimal numbers corresponding to the various access rights.

2. Create a constant that holds the hexadecimal number corresponding to the HKEY_LOCAL_MACHINE subtree.

3. Create a variable and set it to the computer name.

4. Use a GetObject call to connect to the WMI namespace root\default, and set the impersonation level to "impersonate."

5. Use the Registry Provider CheckAccess method to determine whether the user account under which the script is running has the KEY_QUERY_VALUE access right on the subkey.

6. Use the Registry Provider CheckAccess method to determine whether the user account under which the script is running has the KEY_SET_VALUE access right on the subkey.

7. Use the Registry Provider CheckAccess method in a similar manner to check KEY_CREATE_SUBKEY and DELETE access rights.

Listing 16.16 Checking Registry Key Access Rights

```
1    Const KEY_QUERY_VALUE = &H0001
2    Const KEY_SET_VALUE = &H0002
3    Const KEY_CREATE_SUB_KEY = &H0004
4    Const DELETE = &H00010000
5    Const HKEY_LOCAL_MACHINE = &H80000002
6
7    strComputer = "."
8
9    Set objReg=GetObject("winmgmts:{impersonationLevel=impersonate}!\\" & _
10       strComputer & "\root\default:StdRegProv")
11
12   strKeyPath = "SYSTEM\LastKnownGoodRecovery"
13
14   objReg.CheckAccess HKEY_LOCAL_MACHINE, strKeyPath, KEY_QUERY_VALUE, _
15       bHasAccessRight
16   If bHasAccessRight = True Then
17       Wscript.Echo "Have Query Value Access Rights on Key"
18   Else
19       Wscript.Echo "Do Not Have Query Value Access Rights on Key"
20   End If
21
22   objReg.CheckAccess HKEY_LOCAL_MACHINE, strKeyPath, KEY_SET_VALUE, _
23       bHasAccessRight
24   If bHasAccessRight = True Then
25       Wscript.Echo "Have Set Value Access Rights on Key"
26   Else
27       Wscript.Echo "Do Not Have Set Value Access Rights on Key"
28   End If
29
30   objReg.CheckAccess HKEY_LOCAL_MACHINE, strKeyPath, KEY_CREATE_SUB_KEY, _
31       bHasAccessRight
32   If bHasAccessRight = True Then
33       Wscript.Echo "Have Create SubKey Access Rights on Key"
34   Else
35       Wscript.Echo "Do Not Have Create SubKey Access Rights on Key"
36   End If
37
38   objReg.CheckAccess HKEY_LOCAL_MACHINE, strKeyPath, DELETE, bHasAccessRight
39   If bHasAccessRight = True Then
40       Wscript.Echo "Have Delete Access Rights on Key"
41   Else
42       Wscript.Echo "Do Not Have Delete Access Rights on Key"
43   End If
```

Monitoring the Registry

The registry contains a great deal of sensitive data, so it is worth the effort to ensure that it is secure. You secure the registry by setting appropriate access rights on the various subkeys and entries in much the same way that you secure files and folders.

You cannot, however, completely lock down the registry. After all, users and programs must be allowed access to certain areas. Because you must allow at least limited access to the registry, it is sometimes useful to be able to monitor what users are doing when they exercise this access. In certain situations, this might enable you to immediately spot potential problems.

This is especially true in light of the fact that settings in the registry can directly affect the security of your computers. WSH, for example, uses the registry entry HKEY_LOCAL_MACHINE\SOFTWARE\Microsoft\Windows Script Host\Settings **TrustPolicy** in deciding whether to verify that a script is digitally signed before running it. Clearly, the value of this key needs to be secured from unauthorized modification. On certain servers, you might not want anyone, including administrators, to have the ability to run remote WSH scripts.

Because of this, you might want to periodically run a script that checks the value of the entry. If you find that the value of the entry is being changed, you can write a script that monitors the subkey and, upon detecting activity, logs information that might be useful in identifying who made the unauthorized change.

Monitoring the registry is also useful when troubleshooting computer problems. For example, a user might complain that the settings of an application are not being saved. If you know those settings are supposed to be saved in the registry, you can troubleshoot the problem by writing a script that monitors the appropriate subkey. Such a script can help you determine whether the registry is actually being changed any time the user reconfigures the application.

Monitoring Subtree-Level Events

Because subtrees receive a great deal of activity, you typically would not want to monitor an entire subtree (such as HKEY_LOCAL_MACHINE). However, this can be useful if you want to generate statistical data about registry use. For example, you might notice a large amount of disk activity when configuring an application. To help pinpoint the cause of this, you can monitor a registry subtree to see whether the disk activity is the result of a large number of changes being made to the registry.

To monitor a subtree, subscribe to the RegistryTreeChangeEvent, specifying the particular subtree you are interested in monitoring. An event will be generated only when an actual modification takes place within the subtree. No event is fired when the subtree is accessed without being modified. (For example, you will not be notified anytime an application reads a registry entry.) The event does not include information about the change that took place; it simply provides notification that a change has occurred. You cannot use the event to determine who made the change or what change was made.

In scripts that monitor the registry, you will typically use the GetObjectText_ method to echo the fact that a change has been made. This is the only information about the change that is available to you. The output from the scripts used in this section of the chapter will look similar to this:

```
Received Registry Change Event
------------------------------

instance of RegistryTreeChangeEvent
{
        Hive = "HKEY_LOCAL_MACHINE";
        RootPath = "";
        TIME_CREATED = "126746045405872087";
};
```

The script in Listing 16.17 subscribes to the RegistryTreeChangeEvent for the HKEY_USERS subtree. You can modify the script to monitor a different subtree by changing HKEY_USERS to HKEY_LOCAL_MACHINE or any other registry subtree.

Scripting Steps

The script in Listing 16.17 monitors and reports on events in the HKEY_USERS subtree, displaying messages regarding each detected event. To carry out this task, the script must perform the following steps:

1. Use the GetObject method to connect to the WMI service.

2. Use the CreateObject method to create an event sink.

3. Use ExecNotificationQuery to register for the event.

4. Put the script in sleep mode while waiting on the event.

5. Implement the event handler as a subroutine that uses the Echo method to display a message indicating that a registry change event was received.

Listing 16.17   Monitoring Events at the Subtree Level

```
1    strComputer = "."
2    Set objReg=GetObject("winmgmts:{impersonationLevel=impersonate}!\\" & _
3        strComputer & "\root\default")
4
5    Set wmiSink = WScript.CreateObject("WbemScripting.SWbemSink", "SINK_")
6
7    wmiServices.ExecNotificationQueryAsync wmiSink, _
8        "SELECT * FROM RegistryTreeChangeEvent WHERE Hive='HKEY_USERS'" _
9            & " AND RootPath=''"
10
11   Wscript.Echo "Listening for Registry Change Events ..." & vbCrLf
12
13   Do While(1)
14       Wscript.Sleep 1000
15   Loop
16
17   Sub SINK_OnObjectReady(wmiObject, wmiAsyncContext)
18       Wscript.Echo "Received Registry Change Event" & vbCrLf & _
19           "-------------------------------" & vbCrLf & _
20               wmiObject.GetObjectText_()
21   End Sub
```

Monitoring Subkey-Level Events

You might want to monitor an entire subkey if you are interested in changes happening to a group of related registry entries. For instance, if you are troubleshooting an application that does not seem to save user customization data and you know the data should be stored in the registry, you can monitor the registry subkey of the program where the configuration settings are stored, in an effort to understand what is going wrong.

To monitor a subkey, subscribe to the RegistryKeyChangeEvent, specifying the subtree where the subkey you are interested in monitoring is located as well as the path of the subkey you want to monitor. Like the RegistryTreeChangeEvent, the RegistryKeyChangeEvent is fired when a modification is made to the subkey being monitored and the event does not provide any information beyond the fact that a modification has taken place.

Scripting Steps

The script in Listing 16.18 monitors and reports on events in the subkey. To carry out this task, the script must perform the following steps:

1. Use the GetObject method to connect to the WMI service.

2. Use the CreateObject method to create an event sink.

3. Use ExecNotificationQuery to register for the event.

4. Put the script in sleep mode while waiting on the event.

5. Implement the event handler as a subroutine that uses the Echo method to display a message indicating that a registry change event was received.

Listing 16.18   Monitoring Events at the Subkey Level

```
1   strComputer = "."
2   Set objReg=GetObject("winmgmts:{impersonationLevel=impersonate}!\\" & _
3       strComputer & "\root\default")
4
5   Set wmiSink = WScript.CreateObject("WbemScripting.SWbemSink", "SINK_")
6
7   wmiServices.ExecNotificationQueryAsync wmiSink, _
8       "SELECT * FROM RegistryKeyChangeEvent WHERE Hive= " _
9           & "'HKEY_LOCAL_MACHINE' AND " _
10                  & "KeyPath='SOFTWARE\\Microsoft\\Windows NT\\CurrentVersion'"
11
12  Wscript.Echo "Listening for Registry Change Events ..." & vbCrLf
13
14  Do While(1)
15      Wscript.Sleep 1000
16  Loop
17
18  Sub SINK_OnObjectReady(wmiObject, wmiAsyncContext)
19      Wscript.Echo "Received Registry Change Event" & vbCrLf & _
20          "----------------------------" & vbCrLf & _
21              wmiObject.GetObjectText_()
22  End Sub
```

Monitoring Entry-Level Events

There are likely to be times when you want to monitor changes to specific registry entries. For example, certain registry entries are used to configure system security and are therefore potential targets for anyone trying to compromise the computer. You can create a script to monitor these entries to be sure that they are not being altered.

To monitor an entry, subscribe to the RegistryValueChangeEvent class, specifying the subtree, the subkey, and the name of the entry to be monitored. As with the other registry change events, the RegistryValueChangeEvent is fired when a modification is made to the entry being monitored, and the event does not provide any information beyond the fact that a modification has taken place.

Scripting Steps

Listing 16.19 contains a script that monitors events at the registry entry level. To carry out this task, the script must perform the following steps:

1. Use the GetObject method to connect to the WMI service.

2. Use the CreateObject method to create an event sink.

3. Use ExecNotificationQuery to register for the event.

4. Put the script in sleep mode while waiting on the event.

5. Implement the event handler as a subroutine that uses the Echo method to display a message indicating that a registry change event was received.

Listing 16.19   Monitoring Events at the Registry Entry Level

```
1   strComputer = "."
2   Set objReg=GetObject("winmgmts:{impersonationLevel=impersonate}!\\" & _
3       strComputer & "\root\default")
4
5   Set wmiSink = WScript.CreateObject("WbemScripting.SWbemSink", "SINK_")
6
7   wmiServices.ExecNotificationQueryAsync wmiSink, _
8       "SELECT * FROM RegistryValueChangeEvent WHERE Hive= " _
9           & "'HKEY_LOCAL_MACHINE' AND KeyPath= " _
10              & "'SOFTWARE\\Microsoft\\Windows NT\\RegisteredOwner' AND " _
11                  & "ValueName='CSDVersion'"
12
13  Wscript.Echo "Listening for Registry Change Events ..." & vbCrLf
14
15  Do While(1)
16      WScript.Sleep 1000
17  Loop
18
19  Sub SINK_OnObjectReady(wmiObject, wmiAsyncContext)
20      Wscript.Echo "Received Registry Change Event" & vbCrLf & _
21          "-------------------------------" & vbCrLf & _
22              wmiObject.GetObjectText_()
23  End Sub
```

Scripting for the Enterprise

Administrators in an enterprise setting face different challenges than the ones faced by system administrators in a small office. In the enterprise, system administrators typically must manage hundreds of computers, many of them situated in remote locations. Likewise, administrators in enterprise settings typically must share resources, such as system administration scripts, that follow approved standards. Part 3 of this book provides ways to deal with these challenges, demonstrates how scripts can be tailored to run against multiple computers, and offers guidelines that make it easier for scripts to be shared within an organization.

In This Part

Creating Enterprise Scripts 1057
Scripting Guidelines 1147

Creating Enterprise Scripts

Administrators in enterprise settings face a number of added challenges when writing scripts. They must configure scripts to run against different computers at different times, they must track script progress, and they must maintain the security of the administrator password when running scripts that require administrative privileges. In addition, administrators need options to collect, save, and report the data returned by their scripts. The scripting techniques presented in this chapter help administrators meet the unique challenges of using scripts in an enterprise setting.

In This Chapter

Enterprise Scripts Overview **1059**

Retrieving Arguments **1060**

    Retrieving Arguments from a Text File 1061

    Retrieving Arguments from a Database 1067

    Retrieving Arguments from an Active Directory Container 1070

Displaying Output **1072**

    Displaying Tabular Script Output in a Command Window 1073

    Displaying Data by Using Internet Explorer 1077

    Working with HTML Applications 1087

    Displaying Script Output by Using the Tabular Data Control 1092

Working with Databases **1103**

    Connecting to a Database 1105

    Adding New Records to a Database 1107

    Finding Records in a Recordset 1109

    Updating Records in a Database 1112

    Deleting Selected Records from a Database 1114

    Deleting All Records in a Database Table 1116

Masking Passwords **1117**

    Masking Passwords by Using Internet Explorer 1118

Sending E-Mail **1120**

    Sending E-Mail from a Script.. 1122

    Sending E-Mail Without Installing the SMTP Service 1123

Tracking Script Progress.. **1125**

    Tracking Script Progress by Using Internet Explorer 1126

    Tracking Dynamic Script Progress by Using Internet Explorer.................... 1128

    Tracking Script Progress in a Command Window....................................... 1133

Managing Scheduled Tasks **1135**

    Enumerating Scheduled Tasks 1137

    Creating Scheduled Tasks... 1140

    Deleting Scheduled Tasks... 1144

Enterprise Scripts Overview

In some ways, the notion of an "enterprise-enabled" script is a misnomer. In most cases, a script written to run on a single stand-alone computer can run unchanged in an enterprise setting. The fact that the script runs on the only computer you manage or that it runs on one of the thousands of computers you manage is irrelevant.

The question, however, is whether you *want* that script to run unchanged in an enterprise setting. Suppose you have an inventory script that needs to run regularly on a number of computers. You can choose to place a copy of that script on each computer and then run the script locally. Typically, the script will run faster; after all, anything run locally runs faster than the same item run remotely. However, running separate copies of a script, one on each computer, can lead to logistical problems. For example, how will you deploy the script to each computer? What happens if you need to modify the script? How will you make sure you modified every copy? How can you ensure that each script runs as scheduled? If something goes wrong, whom do you notify, and how do you notify them?

As an alternative to running separate copies of the script, one on each computer, you can run your script from a central workstation, successively connecting to each computer, retrieving the inventory information, and then connecting to the next computer. This approach eliminates many logistical problems; for example, it is easy to deploy and modify the script because only a single copy of the script exists. At the same time, however, this approach creates a different set of problems. How do you configure a script so that it can run against multiple computers? What happens if the script needs to run against one set of computers on Monday and another set on Tuesday? If all your scripts run from a central workstation, how do you know which scripts are active at any given time?

Although this might appear to be a no-win situation, a number of simple scripting techniques are available to help you meet the challenges of using scripts in an enterprise setting. These challenges include the need to:

- Retrieve arguments for running the same script against different computers at different times.

- Create alerts that can be directed to the appropriate administrator, even if that administrator is not physically near the computer experiencing the problem.

- Collect and save large quantities of data.

- Sort, filter, and display data in a manner that lets you spot potential problems at a glance.

- Identify the scripts that are running at any given moment and determine how (or even if) those scripts are progressing.

- Maintain the security of administrative passwords for scripts that require administrative privileges.

This chapter presents possible solutions to each of these challenges.

Retrieving Arguments

In an enterprise setting, it is common to have a generic script that is designed to run at different times against different computers. For example, you might have a script that backs up and then clears the event logs on a computer. You might run this script every Monday against your domain controllers, every Tuesday against your Dynamic Host Configuration Protocol (DHCP) servers, and every Wednesday against your print servers.

To carry out this task, you might create separate scripts, one for the domain controllers, one for the DHCP servers, and so on. On Monday, you run the domain controller script, on Tuesday you run the DHCP script (which is identical to the domain controllers script except for the set of computers it runs against), and so on.

This works fine as long as you do not have to modify the script. However, what happens if you decide to have the script extract selected records to a text file before backing up and clearing the event logs? In that case, you will need to modify each version of the script, a process that is both time consuming and error prone.

Instead of creating separate scripts, each one with the computer names hard-coded, you might type in the appropriate command-line arguments each time you run a script. For example, to run the script against three mail servers, you could use a command similar to this:

```
cscript Backuplogs.vbs MailServer1 MailServer2 MailServer3
```

Assuming that your script has the code for parsing command-line arguments, this approach lets you run the script against a different set of computers any time you want.

Or at least you can do this as long as you have no more than two or three computers being passed as command-line arguments. But what if you need to run the script against 50 mail servers? In that case, you have to type in the names of all 50 computers anytime you run the script. What if you need to run the script against 85 print servers? Trying to pass all these computer names as command-line arguments will be extremely tedious, highly susceptible to typing mistakes, and likely exceed the maximum number of characters allowed in a command-line command.

Instead of typing command-line arguments, you can retrieve these arguments from a text file, a database, or even the Active Directory® directory service. By separating the arguments from the script, you can overcome the problems inherent in using command-line arguments: You do not have to worry about the time required to type 100 server names, you do not have to worry about typographical errors, and you do not have to be concerned with the maximum number of characters allowed in a command-line command.

In addition, this approach lets you add or delete computer names simply by editing the outside data source. Modifying a script requires someone with scripting knowledge and scripting experience; it is much easier to find someone capable of opening a text file and deleting the name of a computer recently decommissioned.

Using the Dictionary Object

Many of the sample scripts in this chapter work by retrieving arguments from an outside data source (for example, a text file or a database), storing those arguments in a Dictionary object, and then looping through the elements in the Dictionary and running the script by using each argument.

This is done for primarily for the sake of efficiency. As an alternative, the scripts could instead:

1. Connect to the outside data source.

2. Retrieve the first argument.

3. Run the script by using the first argument.

4. Connect to the outside data source again, retrieve the next argument, and so on.

Although this approach works, it requires repeated calls to the data source. If the data source resides on a second computer, located across the network, the script will have to make continual calls across the network. This leaves the computer, and your script, prone to any number of network-related difficulties. For example, the remote computer where the data source resides could temporarily lose network connectivity, meaning that the script could no longer retrieve the computer names.

To avoid this issue, the scripts in this chapter make a single call to retrieve all the command-line arguments, and then store these arguments in a Dictionary object. The Dictionary, which is stored in local memory, is then used as the argument repository. (For more information about the Dictionary object, see "Script Runtime Primer" in this book.)

Retrieving Arguments from a Text File

To run a single script against multiple computers you can include each computer name as a command-line argument. For example, this command runs the script Monitor.vbs against Server1, Server2, and Server3:

```
Cscript Monitor.vbs Server1 Server2 Server3
```

This works fine for a script that runs against two or three computers, but it is far less effective for scripts that need to run against scores of computers. For scripts that must run against more than a handful of computers, you will likely find it much more efficient to store the list of computer names in a text file; your script can then open the text file, read in each computer name, and then run against each of these computers. Not only is this efficient, but your text file need be no more complicated than this:

```
atl-dc-01
atl-dc-02
atl-dc-03
atl-dc-04
```

You can read arguments into a script by using the FileSystemObject. In the script shown in Listing 17.1, the FileSystemObject is used to read a list of server names from a text file; each name is then stored as a key-item pair with a Dictionary. This demonstration script then successively runs against each name in the Dictionary, connecting to the computer and reporting the number of services installed on that computer.

 Note

This might not be the most practical use of an enterprise script; you rarely need to know how many services are installed on a computer. However, the actual activity performed by the script is irrelevant; the important aspect is how the script reads server names from a text file and then connects to each computer. A trivial task such as reporting the number of services installed was chosen simply to keep the focus on connecting to multiple computers and not on the activity carried out after each connection is made.

Scripting Steps

Listing 17.1 contains a script that retrieves arguments from a text file. To carry out this task, the script must perform the following steps:

1. Create a constant ForReading, and set the value to 1.

   This constant will be used to open the text file in read-only mode. Opening the file in read-only mode ensures that the script cannot inadvertently overwrite the contents of that file.

2. Create an instance of the Dictionary object.

   The Dictionary object will be used to store server names as those names are read from the text file.

3. Create an instance of the FileSystemObject.

4. Use the OpenTextFile method to open the text file.

   You must specify two parameters when opening a text file: the path to the file and the mode in which to open the file. In this script, the path is C:\Scripts\Servers.txt, and the file is opened in read-only mode.

5. Set the counter variable i to 0.

   The counter variable will be used as the key to each element in the Dictionary. The name of the server will be used as the item associated with each key. For more information about Dictionary keys and items, see "Script Runtime Primer" in this book.

   The counter is initially set to 0 because, in VBScript, the first element in an array is element 0. Although any value can be used as a Dictionary key, setting the first element to 0 gets you used to the notion of working with 0 as the first number instead of 1.

6. Create a Do Until loop that continues until each line of the text file has been read.

   You can identify the end of the text file by looping until the property AtEndOfStream is True. When this property is True, that means the entire file has been read. The script will then automatically exit the loop.

7. Use the ReadLine method to read the first line in the text file and store the value in strNextLine.

Because each line of the text file consists of a server name, strNextLine will contain the name of a server. If the first line in the text file is atl-dc-01, the value of strNextLine will also be atl-dc-01.

8. Use the Add method to add the counter variable i and the value of strNextLine to the Dictionary.

9. Increment the value of i.

10. Repeat the process with the next line in the text file. After the last line of the text file has been read, the Dictionary will consist of a set of items equivalent to the lines in that text file. For example, suppose the text file contains the following lines:

```
atl-dc-01
atl-dc-02
atl-dc-03
atl-dc-04
```

In that case, the Dictionary will consist of the following key-item pairs:

```
0        atl-dc-01
1        atl-dc-02
2        atl-dc-03
3        atl-dc-04
```

11. Set the value of the variable strComputer to the value of the first item in the Dictionary (for example, atl-dc-01). The variable strComputer will then represent the name of the first computer the script must connect to.

12. Use a GetObject call to connect to the WMI namespace root\cimv2 on the remote computer (as specified by strComputer), and set the impersonation level to "impersonate."

13. Use the ExecQuery method to query the Win32_Service class.

This query returns a collection consisting of all the services installed on the computer.

14. For each server the script connects to, use the Count property to echo the server name and the number of installed services.

15. Repeat the process using each item in the Dictionary.

Listing 17.1   Retrieving Arguments from a Text File

```
1  Const ForReading = 1
2  Set objDictionary = CreateObject("Scripting.Dictionary")
3  Set objFSO = CreateObject("Scripting.FileSystemObject")
4  Set objTextFile = objFSO.OpenTextFile _
5      ("c:\scripts\servers.txt", ForReading)
6  i = 0
```

(continued)

Listing 17.1   Retrieving Arguments from a Text File *(continued)*

```
7   Do Until objTextFile.AtEndOfStream
8       strNextLine = objTextFile.Readline
9       objDictionary.Add i, strNextLine
10      i = i + 1
11  Loop
12  For Each objItem in objDictionary
13      StrComputer = objDictionary.Item(objItem)
14      Set objWMIService = GetObject("winmgmts:" _
15      & "{impersonationLevel=impersonate}!\\" & strComputer& "\root\cimv2")
16      Set colServices = objWMIService.ExecQuery _
17          ("SELECT * FROM Win32_Service")
18      Wscript.Echo strComputer, colServices.Count
19  Next
```

Using a Text File as a Command-Line Argument

It is not unusual to have a script that needs to run against a different set of computers at different times. For example, you might have a monitoring script that occasionally runs against your Domain Name System (DNS) servers. At other times, you might run this same script against your DHCP servers. To ensure that the script runs against the correct set of computers, you can have separate text files, one containing the list of DNS servers and the other containing the list of DHCP servers. In this case, simply having the script read in the contents of a particular text file will not suffice; after all, the name of the text file to be read might change each time the script is run.

One way to have the same script run against a different set of computers at different times is to use the appropriate text file name as a command-line argument. To run the script against your DNS servers, you pass the script the name of the text file (for example, Dns_servers.txt) that contains the list of DNS servers. To run the script against the DHCP servers, use a different text file name (for example, Dhcp_servers.txt) as the command-line argument. In either case, the script opens the text file, reads in the computer names, and then runs against each of those computers.

For example, if you are running a script under Cscript, you can include the appropriate text file name as part of the command string that starts the script:

```
cscript monitor.vbs dns_servers.txt
```

Alternatively, you can use My Computer or Windows Explorer to drag the icon for the text file onto the icon for the script file. Any time you drag and drop a file onto a script file, the script file uses the dropped file name as an argument.

To illustrate how this works, this two-line script snippet echoes the path name for any file that is dragged onto the script file in Windows Explorer. If you drag a file onto the icon for this script, a message box appears, echoing the path of the file name:

```
Set objArgs = Wscript.Arguments
Wscript.Echo objArgs(0)
```

To use a file name as an argument, you need to make two minor modifications to the script shown in Listing 17.1. First, you need to create an instance of the WSH Arguments collections; this requires a single line of code:

```
Set objArgs = WScript.Arguments
```

Second, you need to modify the portion of the script that actually opens the text file. In Listing 17.1, the file path is hard-coded into the script:

```
Set objTextFile = objFSO.OpenTextFile _
    ("c:\scripts\servers.txt", ForReading)
```

In the script shown in Listing 17.2, the file path is not hard-coded. Instead, the script opens the file supplied as the command-line argument:

```
Set objTextFile = objFSO.OpenTextFile(objArgs(0), ForReading)
```

Scripting Steps

Listing 17.2 contains a script that uses a text file as a command-line argument. To carry out this task, the script must perform the following steps:

1. Create an instance of the Wscript Arguments collection.

2. Create a constant ForReading, and set the value to 1.

   This constant will be used when the text file is opened in read-only mode.

3. Create an instance of the Dictionary object.

   The Dictionary object will be used to store server names as those names are read from the text file.

4. Create an instance of the FileSystemObject.

5. Use the OpenTextFile method to open the text file.

You must specify two parameters when opening a text file: the path to the file and the mode in which to open the file. In this script, the path is not hard-coded (for example, C:\Scripts\Myservers.txt). Instead, the path is designated by the variable objArgs(0), which represents the first element in the arguments collection.

This argument could have been supplied either by typing the file path at the command line or by using drag and drop to drop the icon for the text file on the icon for the script file. For example, if your script is named Monitor.vbs and you type the following command at the command prompt, objArgs(0) will be equal to C:\Scripts\ServerNames.txt:

```
cscript Monitor.vbs C:\Scripts\ServerNames.txt
```

As indicated by the second parameter, ForReading, the file is opened in read-only mode.

If you want to use multiple text files as command-line arguments, you need to modify the script so that it loops through the entire Arguments collection. For more information on looping through the Arguments collection, see "WSH Primer" in this book.

6. Set the counter variable i to 0.

The counter variable will be used as the key to each element in the Dictionary. The name of the server will be used as the item associated with each key.

7. Create a Do Until loop that will continue until each line of the text file has been read.

You can identify the end of the text file by looping until the property AtEndOfStream is True.

8. Use the ReadLine method to read the first line in the text file and store the value in strNextLine.

Because each line of the text file consists of a server name, strNextLine will contain the name of a server.

9. Use the Add method to add the counter variable i and the value of strNextLine to the Dictionary.

10. Increment the value of i.

11. Repeat the process with the next line in the text file.

12. Set the value of the variable strComputer to the value of the first item in the Dictionary (for example, atl-dc-01). The variable strComputer will then represent the name of the first computer the script must connect to.

13. Use a GetObject call to connect to the WMI namespace root\cimv2 on the remote computer (as specified by strComputer), and set the impersonation level to "impersonate."

14. Use the ExecQuery method to query the Win32_Service class.

This query returns a collection consisting of all the services installed on the computer.

15. For each server the script connects to, echo the server name and the number of installed services.

16. Repeat the process using each item in the Dictionary.

Listing 17.2   Using a Text File as a Command-Line Argument

```
1    Set objArgs = WScript.Arguments
2    Const ForReading = 1
3    Set objDictionary = CreateObject("Scripting.Dictionary")
4    Set objFSO = CreateObject("Scripting.FileSystemObject")
5    Set objTextFile = objFSO.OpenTextFile(objArgs(0), ForReading)
6    i = 0
7    Do While objTextFile.AtEndOfStream <> True
8        strNextLine = objTextFile.Readline
9        objDictionary.Add i, strNextLine
10       i = i + 1
11   Loop
12   For Each objItem in objDictionary
13       StrComputer = objDictionary.Item(objItem)
14       Set objWMIService = GetObject("winmgmts:" _
15       & "{impersonationLevel=impersonate}!\\" & strComputer& "\root\cimv2")
16       Set colServices = objWMIService.ExecQuery _
17           ("SELECT * FROM Win32_Service")
18       Wscript.Echo strComputer, colServices.Count
19   Next
```

Retrieving Arguments from a Database

Databases are especially useful if you have scripts whose arguments might vary each time the script is run. For example, you might have a script that backs up a separate set of computers each day. Although this information can be stored in a text file, you would need to parse the entire text file each time the script ran, picking out the computers of interest. By contrast, you can construct a database query that will retrieve only the computers scheduled to be backed up on a given day. This approach is more efficient than reading through and parsing a text file.

Table 17.1 shows a simple database listing computer names and the day of the week each computer is scheduled for a full backup.

Table 17.1   Sample Backup Schedule Database

ComputerName	BackupDay
Server1	Monday
Server2	Wednesday
Server3	Friday
Server4	Monday

To create a script that runs against the appropriate computers on the appropriate days, you simply include code that limits data retrieval to a specific day. For example, this SQL query returns only the set of computers designated for backup on Thursday:

```
"SELECT * FROM Computers WHERE BackupDay = 'Thursday'"
```

By including additional fields within the table, you can construct an all-purpose database that contains the arguments for many of your scripts. For example, additional fields might indicate the date to back up and clear event logs, the dates and times for performance monitoring, or the list of services to be checked on a routine basis.

 Note

Databases are discussed in more detail later in this chapter.

Scripting Steps

Listing 17.3 contains a script that retrieves arguments from a database. (The database and the database table must exist before this script can run.) To carry out this task, the script must perform the following steps:

1. Create three constants — adOpenStatic, adLockOptimistic, and adUseClient — and set the value of each to 3.

    These constants will be used to configure the CursorLocation, CursorType, and LockType for the connection.

2. Create an instance of the ADO Connection object (ADODB.Connection).

    The Connection object makes it possible for you to issue queries and other database commands.

3. Create an instance of the ADO Recordset object (ADODB.Recordset).

    The Recordset object stores the data returned from your query.

4. Use the Connection object Open method to open the database with the Data Source Name Inventory.

    Be sure to append a semicolon (;) to the Data Source Name.

5. Set the CursorLocation to 3 (client side) by using the constant adUseClient.

6. Use the Recordset object Open method to retrieve all the records from the ServerList table.

    The Open method requires four parameters:

    - The SQL query ("SELECT * FROM ServerList")
    - The name of the ADO connection being used (objConnection)
    - The cursor type (adOpenStatic)
    - The lock type (adLockOptimistic)

7. Use the MoveFirst method to move to the first record in the recordset.

8. Set the value of the variable strComputer to the value of the ComputerName field in the recordset. The variable strComputer will then represent the name of the first computer that the script must connect to.

9. Use a GetObject call to connect to the WMI namespace root\cimv2 on the remote computer (as specified by strComputer), and set the impersonation level to Impersonate.

10. Use the ExecQuery method to query the Win32_Service class.

    This query returns a collection consisting of all the services installed on the computer.

11. Echo the server name and the number of installed services (determined by using the Count property).

12. Use the MoveNext method to move to the next record in the recordset, and repeat the process until the end of the recordset has been reached.

13. Close the recordset.

14. Close the connection.

Listing 17.3 Retrieving Arguments from a Database

```
1   Const adOpenStatic = 3
2   Const adLockOptimistic = 3
3   Const adUseClient = 3
4   Set objConnection = CreateObject("ADODB.Connection")
5   Set objRecordset = CreateObject("ADODB.Recordset")
6   objConnection.Open "DSN=Inventory;"
7   objRecordset.CursorLocation = adUseClient
8   objRecordset.Open "SELECT * FROM ServerList" , objConnection, _
9       adOpenStatic, adLockOptimistic
10  objRecordSet.MoveFirst
11  Do While Not objRecordSet.EOF
12      strComputer = objRecordSet("ComputerName")
13      Set objWMIService = GetObject("winmgmts:" _
14      & "{impersonationLevel=impersonate}!\\" & strComputer& "\root\cimv2")
15      Set colServices = objWMIService.ExecQuery _
16          ("SELECT * FROM Win32_Service")
17      Wscript.Echo strComputer, colServices.Count
18      objRecordSet.MoveNext
19  Loop
20  objRecordset.Close
21  objConnection.Close
```

Retrieving Arguments from an Active Directory Container

Large organizations typically have more than one system administrator. In addition, those administrators generally are not responsible for managing the entire network; instead, they most likely have been delegated control over some subset of the network. For example, Administrator A might be responsible for managing users and computers in the Finance department, while Administrator B might be responsible for managing users and computers in the Human Resources department.

To facilitate system administration, Active Directory is often designed to mimic these management areas. Instead of placing all computer accounts in the Computers container, computer accounts might be put in organizational units (OUs) that correspond to these management areas. Thus all the accounts for computers belonging to the Finance department would be placed in the Finance OU, and all the accounts for computers belonging to the Human Resources department would be placed in the Human Resources OU.

Structuring Active Directory in this fashion not only facilitates system administration but also of benefits script writers. For example, suppose you need to write a script that takes a hardware inventory or checks the service pack version for all the computers under your control. If those computer accounts — and only those computer accounts — are stored in the same Active Directory container, you do not have to create a text file or database from which to extract computer names. Instead, you can simply bind to the appropriate Active Directory container and retrieve all the computer names from there.

Binding to Active Directory also ensures that you will have the most up-to-date list of computers, without having to do additional work to maintain a text file or database containing computer names.

To retrieve a list of computer names from Active Directory, use Active Directory Service Interfaces (ADSI) and:

1. Bind to the desired container.

2. Set the Filter property to Computers. This ensures that the query will return only computer accounts.

3. Use a For-Each loop to return the common name (CN) of each computer that has an account in the Active Directory container. The returned list might look similar to the following, depending on the common names of the computers:

```
atl-dc-01
atl-dc-02
atl-dc-03
atl-dc-04
```

Scripting Steps

Listing 17.4 contains a script that retrieves arguments from an Active Directory container. To carry out this task, the script must perform the following steps:

1. Create an instance of the Dictionary object.

   The Dictionary object will be used to store server names as those names are read from Active Directory.

2. Set the counter variable i to 0.

   The counter variable will be used as the key to each element in the Dictionary. The name of the server will be used as the item associated with each key.

3. Bind to the Computers container in Active Directory.

   Because Computers is a container, you must use the syntax CN=Computers. If you were binding to an OU (for example, the Finance OU), you would use the syntax OU=Finance OU.

4. Use the Filter property to limit data retrieval to computer accounts.

   This prevents the script from attempting to run against user accounts or any other noncomputer objects that might be stored in this container.

5. For each computer in the Computers container, use the Add method to add the counter variable i and the common name of the computer to the Dictionary.

6. Increment the value of i.

7. Repeat the process with the next computer in the container.

8. Set the value of the variable strComputer to the value of the first item in the Dictionary (for example, atl-dc-01). The variable strComputer will then represent the name of the first computer that the script must connect to.

9. Use a GetObject call to connect to the WMI namespace root\cimv2 on the remote computer (specified by strComputer), and set the impersonation level to "impersonate."

10. Use the ExecQuery method to query the Win32_Service class.

    This query returns a collection consisting of all the services installed on the computer.

11. For each server the script connects to, echo the server name and the number of installed services (determined by using the Count property).

12. Repeat the process using each server name stored in the Dictionary.

Listing 17.4   Retrieving Arguments from an Active Directory Container

```
1  Set objDictionary = CreateObject("Scripting.Dictionary")
2  i = 0
3  Set objOU = GetObject("LDAP://CN=Computers, DC=fabrikam, DC=com")
4  objOU.Filter = Array("Computer")
```

(continued)

Listing 17.4   Retrieving Arguments from an Active Directory Container *(continued)*

```
5   For Each objComputer in objOU
6       objDictionary.Add i, objComputer.CN
7       i = i + 1
8   Next
9   For Each objItem in objDictionary
10      StrComputer = objDictionary.Item(objItem)
11      Set objWMIService = GetObject("winmgmts:" _
12      & "{impersonationLevel=impersonate}!\\" & strComputer& "\root\cimv2")
13      Set colServices = objWMIService.ExecQuery _
14          ("SELECT * FROM Win32_Service")
15      Wscript.Echo strComputer, colServices.Count
16  Next
```

Displaying Output

One limitation of both Microsoft® Visual Basic® Scripting Edition (VBScript) and Windows Script Host (WSH) is the fact that neither language has any built-in functions for displaying output in anything but the most basic of formats. Because of this, script output is typically displayed in a command window by using a series of Wscript.Echo commands. This is acceptable for scripts that display a single item of information per line; for example, you might have a script that reports the name of each service installed on a computer:

```
Alerter
Application Management
Ati HotKey Poller
Computer Browser
Indexing Service
```

However, Wscript.Echo is far less than useful for scripts that display multiple items on a single line. For example, the following output displays three separate service-related properties: service display name, service start mode, and service state. Unfortunately, these properties and their values are difficult to distinguish from one another because of the way they are displayed:

```
Alerter Auto Running
Application Management Manual Running
Ati HotKey Poller Auto Stopped
Computer Browser Auto Running
Indexing Service Manual Stopped
```

If you have scripts that display a large amount of data, you might not want to simply echo values to the command window; instead, you might prefer to use one of the following techniques to help make your script output easier to read and understand:

- Display script output in table form in a command window.

- Display script output in a browser window, taking advantage of the formatting capabilities available using HTML.

- Use the tabular data control to display script output in a table within a browser window.

Displaying Tabular Script Output in a Command Window

Although the command window offers little in the way of formatting options, it is possible to at least align output in table format. Simply displaying multiple properties one after another, all on the same line, usually results in confusion; who really knows what to make of a command window display such as this:

```
Alerter Auto Running
Application Management Manual Running
Ati HotKey Poller Auto Stopped
Computer Browser Auto Running
Indexing Service Manual Stopped
```

However, that same data, displayed in the same command window, is remarkably easy to read and interpret when displayed in tabular format:

```
Alerter                     Auto        Running
Application Management       Manual      Running
Ati HotKey Poller           Auto        Stopped
Computer Browser            Auto        Running
Indexing Service            Manual      Stopped
```

To display data in tabular format, you need to use fixed-width columns. With fixed-width columns, you determine in advance the number of characters that will be displayed in each column in the table. In the preceding example, the following column widths — based on a command window 80 characters wide — are used:

- Column 1: 50 characters

- Column 2: 17 characters

- Column 3: 13 characters

After you decide on the widths for each column, you must then ensure that each item displayed in the table takes up the requisite number of spaces. This is done by using the following procedure on each item of data:

1. Determine the number of characters in the item. The Len function is used to return the number of characters in a string. For example, the code `Len("dog")` returns the value 3 because there are three characters in the word *dog*.

2. Subtract the number of characters in the string from the predetermined column width. This tells you how many additional character spaces must be added to the string to fill out the column. For example, if the word *dog* is to be displayed in a column 10 characters wide, you subtract the number of characters in *dog* (3) from the column width (10).

3. Use the Space function to append blank spaces to the end of the string, expanding the string to fill the entire column. In the example shown in step 2, you need to append seven spaces to the end of the word *dog*. Because blank spaces count as characters, adding seven spaces makes the string ten characters long: the letters *d*, *o*, and *g*, and the seven blank spaces.

The net result is that each item of data expands to fill the column width, even if many of the characters in that item are blank spaces. For example, the word *dog* expands to 10 characters (the underscores represent blank spaces in the string):

d o g -------

A subset of VBScript functions that can be used to format data for display in the command window are shown in Table 17.2. In addition to the functions listed in the table, VBScript also includes functions you can use to display numbers and dates in a specific manner. For more information about these functions (such as FormatNumber, FormatDate, and FormatPercent), see "VBScript Primer" in this book. The discussion of formatting output used in the "VBScript Primer" chapter is similar to the discussion in this chapter.

Table 17.2   VBScript String Formatting Functions

Function	Description

Len	Returns the number of characters in a string. For example, this code returns the value 15, because "This is a test." contains 15 characters:
	
	```strTestString = "This is a test."```
	```intCharacters = Len(strTestString)```
	```Wscript.Echo intCharacters```

Left	Returns the number of specified characters beginning from the left of a string. For example, this code returns the string "This is", the first seven characters in the test string:
	
	```strTestString = "This is a test."```
	```strCharacters = Left(strTestString, 7)```
	```Wscript.Echo strCharacters```

(continued)

Table 17.2   VBScript String Formatting Functions *(continued)*

Function	Description
Right	Returns the number of specified characters beginning from the right of a string and working backward. For example, this code returns the string " a test.", the last seven characters in the test string: ``` strTestString = "This is a test." strCharacters = Right(strTestString, 7) Wscript.Echo strCharacters ```
Space	Appends the specified number of spaces to the end of the string. For example, this code returns the string "This is a test.---------------", with the hyphens representing the 15 blank spaces appended to the end of the string: ``` strTestString = "This is a test." strCharacters = strTestString & Space(15) Wscript.Echo strCharacters ```

Scripting Steps

Listing 17.5 contains a script that displays formatted script output in a command window. To carry out this task, the script must perform the following steps:

1. Create a variable to specify the computer name.

2. Use a GetObject call to connect to the WMI namespace root\cimv2, and set the impersonation level to "impersonate."

3. Use the ExecQuery method to query the Win32_Service class.

    This query returns a collection consisting of all the services installed on the computer.

4. For each service in the collection, determine the number of spaces that must be appended to the service display name to ensure that the name takes up 50 spaces.

    This is done by setting the variable intPadding to 50 (the number of spaces in the first column of the display) minus the length of the service display name (determined by using the Len function). For example, if the service display name contains 23 characters, intPadding is equal to 27 (50–23).

5. Determine the number of spaces that must be appended to the service start mode to ensure that the name takes up 17 spaces.

    This is done by setting the variable intPadding2 to 17 (the number of spaces in the second column of the display) minus the length of the service start mode (determined by using the Len function). For example, if the start mode contains 4 characters (such as a start mode of Auto), intPadding is equal to 13 (17–4).

6. Set the variable strDisplayName to the service display name plus enough blank spaces to make the display name take up 50 characters.

    To do this, set strDisplayName to the display name of the service, and then use the Space function to add the proper number of blank spaces. The proper number of blank spaces is configured by using intPadding as the parameter for the Space function.

    The net result of using the Space function will be similar to this (the hyphens indicate blank spaces added to the service name):

    ```
    Application Management

    Application Management----------------------------
    ```

7. Set the variable strStartMode to the service start mode, plus enough blank spaces to make the start mode occupy 17 characters.

8. Echo strDisplayName, strStartMode, and the service state.

Listing 17.5   Displaying Tabular Output in a Command Window

```
1   strComputer = "."
2   Set objWMIService = GetObject("winmgmts:" _
3       & "{impersonationLevel=impersonate}!\\" & strComputer& "\root\cimv2")
4   Set colServices = objWMIService.ExecQuery _
5       ("SELECT * FROM Win32_Service")
6   For Each objService in colServices
7       intPadding = 50 - Len(objService.DisplayName)
8       intPadding2 = 17 - Len(objService.StartMode)
9       strDisplayName = objService.DisplayName & Space(intPadding)
10      strStartMode = objService.StartMode & Space(intPadding2)
11      Wscript.Echo strDisplayName & strStartMode & objService.State
12  Next
```

When the script runs under CScript, it displays formatted output similar to the following:

```
Alerter                                              Auto        Running

Application Management                               Manual      Running

Ati HotKey Poller                                    Auto        Stopped

Computer Browser                                     Auto        Running

Indexing Service                                     Manual      Stopped
```

Displaying Data by Using Internet Explorer

By using the various string manipulation functions found in VBScript, you can display data in tabular format within the command window. This makes the data easier to analyze but only partly compensates for the limitations found in the command window. For example, no VBScript function lets you use multiple fonts and multiple colors within the command window. Likewise, no VBScript method lets you easily print data from within the command window. Instead, you must copy the entire data set (assuming that the data does not exceed the command window display buffer), paste the data into another application, and then print the data.

If you prefer to use formatting that goes beyond a tabular display or if you would like the ability to print the returned data, you might consider outputting information to Internet Explorer rather than the command window. Unlike the command window, Internet Explorer lets you use multiple fonts and multiple colors; you can even include graphics within your output. In addition, you can use the Print function of the browser to print the data, without having to copy and paste it into another application.

In the examples that follow, you do not create a Web page (that is, an .HTM file). Instead, you use VBScript to instantiate an instance of Internet Explorer, and you then use VBScript commands to control that instance of the browser. This is possible because Internet Explorer provides an Automation object model that can be controlled from within a script. You can use this object model to create an instance of Internet Explorer and then do such things as:

- Configure the user interface (for example, hide or display the address bar or set the window size).
- Open a specific file or navigate to a specific URL.
- Dynamically show or hide the browser window based on specified conditions.
- Write data to the page displayed in the browser window.

In fact, nearly all the functionality of Internet Explorer is exposed through the Automation object model. Some of the properties and methods especially useful to script writers are shown in Table 17.3.

Table 17.3   Internet Explorer Properties and Methods

Property/Method	Description

Application	Used with the CreateObject method to return an instance of Internet Explorer. For example:
	
	```Set objExplorer = _```
	``` CreateObject("InternetExplorer.Application")```

(continued)

Table 17.3   Internet Explorer Properties and Methods *(continued)*

Property/Method	Description
Busy	Returns a Boolean value indicating whether Internet Explorer is still loading or performing some other activity. This is often used at the start of a script to ensure that Internet Explorer is fully loaded before any other script actions take place. Your script might check the Busy status and, if True, pause for a specified amount of time and then check again. As soon as Busy is False, the script can proceed. For example: ``` Do While (objExplorer.Busy) Wscript.Sleep 250 Loop ```
FullScreen	Boolean value that sets the Internet Explorer window mode. If True, the window is maximized, and the status bar, toolbar, menu bar, and title bar are hidden.
Height	Sets the height of the Internet Explorer window in pixels.
Width	Sets the width of the Internet Explorer window in pixels.
Left	Sets the position of the Internet Explorer window relative to the left side of the screen. For example, this command positions the window 200 pixels from the left side of the screen: ``` objExplorer.Left = 200 ```
Top	Sets the position of the Internet Explorer window relative to the top of the screen. For example, this command positions the window 100 pixels from the top of the screen: ``` objExplorer.Top = 100 ```
MenuBar	Toggles the display of the menu bar on or off. If 0, the menu bar is not visible; if 1, the menu bar is displayed.
StatusBar	Toggles the display of the status bar on or off. If 0, the status bar is not visible; if 1, the status bar is displayed.
StatusText	Sets the text in the status bar.
ToolBar	Toggles the display of the toolbar on or off. If 0, the toolbar is not visible; if 1, the toolbar is displayed.
Visible	Determines whether Internet Explorer is visible on the screen. Any instance of Internet Explorer you create will not be visible until you set this property to 1. To hide a running instance of Internet Explorer, set the value to 0.

(continued)

Table 17.3   Internet Explorer Properties and Methods (continued)

Property/Method	Description
Navigate	Loads the specified document in the Internet Explorer window.
	To load a blank document
	Set the property to "about:blank". For example:
	`ObjExplorer.Navigate "about:blank"`
	To load a file
	Specify the file name, prefacing the path with the file:// designator. For example:
	`ObjExplorer.Navigate "file://c:\scripts\service_data.htm"`
	To load a Web page from a URL
	Specify the URL, prefacing the path with the http:// designator. For example
	`ObjExplorer.Navigate "http://www.fabrikam.com"`
Quit	Closes Internet Explorer and terminates the object instance.
Refresh	Updates the Internet Explorer instance.

Internet Explorer also exposes several other objects that let you not only control the behavior of the browser but also dynamically control the contents of the browser window. For example, you might create an instance of Internet Explorer and open a blank Web page. You can then use the Document object to dynamically change the contents of that Web page.

This has nothing to do with creating pages for the World Wide Web. In fact, you still create files with the .vbs file name extension; you do not create Web pages with the .htm file name extension. Instead, you use a script to open Internet Explorer and then use a combination of scripting code and HTML tags to redirect the script output to the browser window.

Creating an Instance of Internet Explorer

You can use Internet Explorer as a display device by creating an instance of the browser and then issuing the appropriate commands to:

- Configure the user interface.
- Navigate to the desired pages.
- Write information to the document that is currently loaded.

To create an instance of Internet Explorer, use the CreateObject method and the ProgID InternetExplorer.Application. For example, this line of code creates an instance of Internet Explorer and assigns it to the object variable objExplorer:

```
Set objExplorer = CreateObject("InternetExplorer.Application")
```

After the object has been created, you can control it by using the object variable assigned to that instance of Internet Explorer. For example, this command will hide the toolbar:

```
objExplorer.ToolBar = 0
```

Any commands you issue will affect only the instance of Internet Explorer you created. If you have multiple copies of the browser running, a command to hide the toolbar will hide only the toolbar in the instance of Internet Explorer under the control of your script. The toolbar will remain visible in any other instances of Internet Explorer that are running.

Scripting Steps

Listing 17.6 contains a script that creates an instance of Internet Explorer. To carry out this task, the script must perform the following steps:

1. Create an instance of Internet Explorer.

2. Use the Navigate method to open a blank Web page.

    This is done by using "about:blank" as the method parameter. You can also open a URL or a file by passing the appropriate path to the Navigate method. For example, you can open the file C:\Scripts\Service_data.htm by using this code:

```
objExplorer.Navigate "file://c:\scripts\service_data.htm"
```

3. Configure various Internet Explorer properties, such as the height and width of the window, and hide items such as the toolbar and status bar.

4. Set the Visible property to 1 to display the instance on the screen. Internet Explorer will not appear on the screen unless you set the Visible property to 1.

Listing 17.6   Creating an Instance of Internet Explorer

```
1   Set objExplorer = CreateObject("InternetExplorer.Application")
2   objExplorer.Navigate "about:blank"
3   objExplorer.ToolBar = 0
4   objExplorer.StatusBar = 0
5   objExplorer.Width = 300
6   objExplorer.Height = 150
7   objExplorer.Left = 0
8   objExplorer.Top = 0
9   objExplorer.Visible = 1
```

When the script in Listing 17.6 is run, you will see a blank Web page similar to that shown in Figure 17.1.

Figure 17.1   A Blank Web Page in Internet Explorer

Displaying Data in a Web Page

Web pages provide an alternative to displaying script output in the command window. Unlike the command window, Web pages support a wide array of formatting options, including color, fonts, and graphics. This lets you display script output in a manner that is much easier to decipher at a glance than output displayed in the command window. For example, you might use red to format the status of any services that are stopped. That way, an administrator can verify that all services are up and running without having to stop and read through the entire display. Figure 17.2 shows a simple example of how you might display service status information.

Figure 17.2   Data Displayed in a Web Page

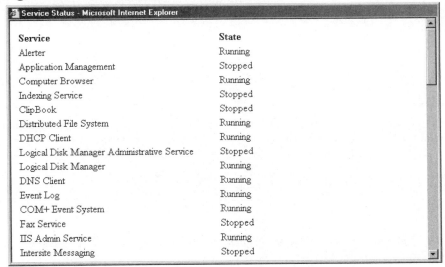

Perhaps the easiest way to display real-time data is to use the WriteLn method. With this method, you can use a script to open a blank Web page and then send HTML code to the page. Each time you send information to the Web page by using WriteLn, that information is appended to the end of the page. For example, this code writes the numbers 1 through 5 to a Web page, without any formatting of any kind:

```
objDocument.Writeln "1"
objDocument.Writeln "2"
objDocument.Writeln "3"
objDocument.Writeln "4"
objDocument.Writeln "5"
```

The resulting Web page will look like this:

12345

To place each number on a separate line, include the HTML tag <BR> as part of the WriteLn parameter:

```
objDocument.Writeln "1<BR>"
objDocument.Writeln "2<BR>"
objDocument.Writeln "3<BR>"
objDocument.Writeln "4<BR>"
objDocument.Writeln "5<BR>"
```

The revised Web page will look like this:

1

2

3

4

5

You can include any HTML tags as part of the WriteLn parameter; in that regard, dynamically creating a Web page is no different than using a text editor to write an .htm file. For example, to write text formatted with the <H2> heading level, use code similar to this:

```
objDocument.Writeln "<H2>This is an H2 heading</H2>"
```

Scripting Steps

Listing 17.7 contains a script that displays data in a Web page. To carry out this task, the script must perform the following steps:

1.   Create an instance of Internet Explorer.

2.   Open a blank Web page by navigating to "about:blank".

3.   Configure various Internet Explorer properties, such as the width and height of the window, and hide items such as the toolbar and status bar.

4. Set the Visible property to 1 to display the instance on the screen.

5. Create an object reference to the Document object.

6. Prepare the Web page for writing by opening the Document object (objDocument.Open).

7. Use HTML tags to:

   - Set the page title.

   - Set the background color (bgcolor) to white.

   - Insert a table that fills 100% of the document width.

   - Create the initial table row with two columns: one labeled **Service** and the other labeled **State**.

8. Create a variable to specify the computer name.

9. Use a GetObject call to connect to the WMI namespace root\cimv2, and set the impersonation level to "impersonate."

10. Use the ExecQuery method to query the Win32_Service class.

    This query returns a collection consisting of all the services installed on the computer.

11. For each service in the collection, create a new row in the table. Each row has two columns, one containing the service name and the other containing the service state.

12. Use HTML tags to mark the end of the table, the document body, and the document head.

Listing 17.7   Displaying Data in a Web Page

```
1   Set objExplorer = CreateObject("InternetExplorer.Application")
2   objExplorer.Navigate "about:blank"
3   objExplorer.ToolBar = 0
4   objExplorer.StatusBar = 0
5   objExplorer.Width = 800
6   objExplorer.Height = 570
7   objExplorer.Left = 0
8   objExplorer.Top = 0
9   objExplorer.Visible = 1
10
11  Do While (objExplorer.Busy)
12  Loop
13
14  Set objDocument = objExplorer.Document
15  objDocument.Open
16
17  objDocument.Writeln "<html><head><title>Service Status</title></head>"
18  objDocument.Writeln "<body bgcolor='white'>"
19  objDocument.Writeln "<table width='100%'>"
20  objDocument.Writeln "<tr>"
21
```

(continued)

Listing 17.7 Displaying Data in a Web Page (continued)

```
22  objDocument.Writeln "<td width='50%'><b>Service</b></td>"
23  objDocument.Writeln "<td width='50%'><b>State</b></td>"
24  objDocument.Writeln "</tr>"
25
26  strComputer = "."
27  Set objWMIService = GetObject("winmgmts:" _
28      & "{impersonationLevel=impersonate}!\\" & strComputer& "\root\cimv2")
29  Set colServices = objWMIService.ExecQuery _
30      ("SELECT * FROM Win32_Service")
31
32  For Each objService in colServices
33      objDocument.Writeln "<tr>"
34      objDocument.Writeln "<td width='50%'>" & objService.DisplayName & "</td>"
35      objDocument.writeln "<td width='50%'>" & objService.State & "</td>"
36      objDocument.Writeln "</tr>"
37  Next
38
39  objDocument.Writeln "</table>"
40  objDocument.Writeln "</body></html>"
41  objDocument.Write()
42  objDocument.Close
```

Clearing a Web Page

The WriteLn method allows you to add information to a Web page: Each time you call the WriteLn method, the new data is appended to the bottom of the page. This works fine in many situations. For example, if you want to extract a particular set of records from an event log, you can display those records in a Web page by using WriteLn. The fact that WriteLn appends these records one right after the other is no problem — in fact, that is exactly what you want it to do.

In other cases, however, you might want to periodically clear the screen to make room for new information. For example, if you have a script that monitors printer status every 15 minutes, you want the initial printer status displayed in the Web page. When the printer status is resampled, you probably do not want the second set of data to be appended to the end of the first set. Instead, you want to clear the browser screen and display only the current set of data.

One quick way to clear the browser screen is to create a TextRange object that encompasses the entire document and then set the Text property of that object to nothing. A TextRange object represents text within an HTML element; these elements include the document body, a button, a text box, and any other element that has a Text property.

For example, this code creates a TextRange object that encompasses the entire body of the document and then clears that object by setting the Text property to an empty string (""):

```
Set objTextRange = objDocument.body.CreateTextRange()
objTextRange.Text = ""
```

Stopping a Script When Internet Explorer Is Closed

Although Internet Explorer provides an excellent alternative to displaying script output in a command window, you can encounter a problem if the browser window is closed before your script finishes running. For example, you might have a script that creates an instance of Internet Explorer and then writes service information to the document window. If Internet Explorer is closed before you finish writing the service information, the script will fail; this occurs because the script is attempting to write to an instance of the browser that no longer exists.

To avoid this problem, you can configure your script to respond to Internet Explorer events. When Internet Explorer is closed, the browser triggers an onQuit event. Your script can watch for this event and take the appropriate action when it occurs. For example, the script might create a new instance of Internet Explorer, or it might use the Wscript.Quit method to terminate itself.

When creating this instance of Internet Explorer, you must use the Wscript CreateObject method; this is the only way to add event handling to a script. To enable event handling, CreateObject requires two parameters: the ProgID "InternetExplorer.Application" and a second argument consisting of a name to be given to the event handler. This name typically bears some relation to the created object followed by an underscore. For example, this code assigns the name IE_ to the entity responsible for handling Internet Explorer events:

```
Set objExplorer = WScript.CreateObject("InternetExplorer.Application", "IE_")
```

Although you do not have to follow this naming convention, it does make it easier for someone to read your script and understand how it works.

The event handler then watches for events triggered by Internet Explorer. When an event occurs, the event handler checks the script to see whether any procedures should run in response to that event. For example, this procedure causes the script to terminate itself any time the onQuit event is detected:

```
Sub IE_onQuit()
    Wscript.Quit
End Sub
```

In other words, any time the browser window is closed (thus triggering the onQuit event), the script will terminate itself. The script will thus automatically quit any time Internet Explorer quits.

You can create other procedures to respond to other events as well. For example, to respond to the onLoad event fired by Internet Explorer, create a procedure named IE_onLoad().

 Note

Event handling will not work with all scripts. WSH scripts automatically terminate themselves when the last line of code is run; in some cases, therefore, the script will terminate itself before the Internet Explorer event can be fired. If this is a problem, you might have to use Wscript.Sleep to pause the script for a specified amount of time, or you might have to create a loop that keeps the script running until a particular event is detected.

Scripting Steps

Listing 17.8 contains a script that terminates itself when the browser window closes. To carry out this task, the script must perform the following steps:

1. Use the Wscript CreateObject method to create an instance of Internet Explorer, and assign the name IE_ to the event handler responsible for monitoring Internet Explorer events.

2. Open a blank Web page by navigating to "about:blank".

3. Configure various Internet Explorer properties, such as the width and height of the window, and hide items such as the toolbar and status bar.

4. Set the Visible property to 1 to display the instance on the screen.

5. Create an object reference to the Document object.

6. Prepare the Web page for writing by opening the Document object (objDocument.Open).

7. Create a variable to specify the computer name.

8. Use a GetObject call to connect to the WMI namespace root\cimv2, and set the impersonation level to "impersonate."

9. Use the ExecQuery method to query the Win32_Service class.

   This query returns a collection consisting of all the services installed on the computer.

10. For each service in the collection, use the WriteLn method to write the service display name and a carriage return/linefeed (<BR>) to the browser window.

    Because this is a demonstration script, a two-second pause (Wscript.Sleep 2000) is inserted after each service name is written to the browser. This ensures that the script will continue running long enough for you to close the browser window.

11. Create a subroutine named IE_onQuit(). This subroutine will be called whenever Internet Explorer is closed.

12. If the subroutine is called (meaning Internet Explorer has been closed), use the Wscript.Quit method to terminate the script.

To demonstrate how the script responds to Internet Explorer events, start the script and then close the browser window before all the service names have been written. When the browser window closes, the script will automatically terminate itself without generating an error.

Listing 17.8   Stopping a Script When Internet Explorer Closes

```
1   Set objExplorer = WScript.CreateObject _
2       ("InternetExplorer.Application", "IE_")
3   objExplorer.Navigate "about:blank"
4   objExplorer.ToolBar = 0
5   objExplorer.StatusBar = 0
6   objExplorer.Width = 400
7   objExplorer.Height = 250
8   objExplorer.Left = 0
9   objExplorer.Top = 0
10  objExplorer.Visible = 1
11  Set objDocument = objExplorer.Document
12  objDocument.Open
13  strComputer = "."
14  Set objWMIService = GetObject("winmgmts:" _
15      & "{impersonationLevel=impersonate}!\\" & strComputer& "\root\cimv2")
16  Set colServices = objWMIService.ExecQuery _
17      ("SELECT * FROM Win32_Service")
18  For Each objService in colServices
19      objDocument.Writeln objService.DisplayName & "<BR>"
20      Wscript.Sleep 2000
21  Next
22  Sub IE_onQuit()
23     Wscript.Quit
24  End Sub
```

Working with HTML Applications

Although you can control Internet Explorer from a separate script, you will have to include code to repeatedly ensure that the browser is still running. If you do not, you will encounter problems such as:

- The browser is closed, and an error occurs when the script attempts to update a browser instance that no longer exists.

- The browser is closed, but the script continues to run. (Without additional coding, closing the browser will not stop the script.) This can be confusing, especially if you restart the script and now have two copies of the same script running in parallel.

Embedding the script code inside a Web page enables you to overcome these problems. When you embed the code, the Web page and the script are linked together; closing the Web page will also terminate the script. However, this introduces a new set of problems. Because Internet Explorer is designed for use over the Internet, it has a number of built-in security precautions that prevent Web sites from harming the local computer in any way. For example, if you include Windows Management Instrumentation (WMI) or another ActiveX® control in a Web page, a message box similar to the one shown in Figure 17.3 will appear when the script is run.

Figure 17.3   Unsafe for Scripting Message Box

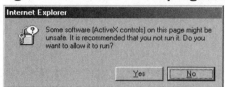

In turn, the script will suspend itself until you click **Yes**. This means you cannot create a Web page that can refresh itself (for example, a Web page that periodically updates the status of all the printers on a print server). Each time the page queries the WMI service, the "unsafe for scripting" message box will appear and the script will pause until you click **Yes**.

One way to work around the security issues inherent in Internet Explorer is to embed your script within a hypertext application (HTA) rather than an HTML file. In its simplest form, an HTA is nothing but a Web page with the .hta file name extension rather than the .htm file name extension. In fact, you can convert any Web page to an HTA just by changing the file name extension.

However, HTAs run in a different process (Mshta.exe) than do HTML files. This allows HTAs to bypass Internet Explorer security. (Of course, HTAs still respect such things as operating system security and the NTFS file system security.) HTAs are fully trusted applications, meaning that you will not receive any security warnings when using objects such as WMI or the FileSystemObject.

Although HTAs respond to the same commands that can be issued to an instance of Internet Explorer, a number of additional attributes are available through the HTA object model. Several of these attributes are listed in Table 17.4.

Table 17.4   HTA Object Model

Attribute	Description
ApplicationName	Sets the name of the HTA.
Border	Sets the type of border used for the HTA window. Values include: **Thick.** Creates a resizeable window. **Thin.** Creates a window that cannot be resized.

(continued)

Table 17.4   HTA Object Model *(continued)*

Attribute	Description
BorderStyle	Sets the style of the content border in the HTA window. Values are: **Normal.** Standard Windows border style. This is the default value. **Raised.** Raised three-dimensional border. **Sunken.** Sunken three-dimensional border. **Complex.** Combines sunken and raised styles. **Static.** Three-dimensional border typically used for windows that do not allow user input.
Caption	Yes/No value specifying whether the HTA displays a title bar. The default value is Yes.
Icon	Sets the path name of the icon that appears in the upper-left corner of the HTA window. The icon can be either a .ico or a .bmp file. If not specified, a generic application icon is used.
ID	Sets the identifier for the <HTA:Application> tag. This property is required if you need to write a script that returns the attributes of the HTA.
MaximizeButton	Yes/No value specifying whether the HTA displays a Maximize button in the title bar. The default value is Yes.
MinimizeButton	Yes/No value specifying whether the HTA displays a Minimize button in the title bar. The default value is Yes.
ShowInTaskbar	Yes/No value specifying whether the HTA is shown in the Windows taskbar. Regardless of the value set for this property, the HTA will always appear in the list of applications that are accessible when you press ALT+TAB. The default value is Yes.
SingleInstance	Yes/No value specifying whether more than one instance of this HTA can be active at any given time. For this property to take effect, you must also specify the ApplicationName attribute. The default value is Yes.
SysMenu	Yes/No value specifying whether the HTA displays the System menu in the title bar. The System menu is displayed in the upper-left corner of the HTA window and provides access to menu items such as Minimize, Maximize, Restore, and Close. The default value is Yes.
WindowsState	Sets the initial size of the HTA window. Values are: Normal Minimize Maximize

HTML applications require no special coding; you can create an HTA simply by changing the .htm file extension of a Web page to .hta. However, by adding the <HTA:Application> tag to the Web page code, you can gain additional control over how the HTA will be displayed on the screen and which elements of the user interface will be available. To configure any of these elements, include the <HTA:Application> tag and the appropriate elements within the Web page <HEAD> tag.

For example, the following code snippet prevents the HTA from being displayed in the taskbar:

```
<HTA:Application
    ShowInTaskbar = No
>
```

Scripting Steps

Listing 17.9 contains HTML tags for creating a sample HTA file. Type this code into a text editor, and then save it with the .hta file name extension.

To create an HTA file, you must:

1. Insert the beginning <HTML> and <HEAD> tags.

2. Insert the <HTA:Application> tag. Within this tag, set the configuration options for the HTA file. In this example, these options include setting Border to Thick and BorderStyle to Complex.

3. Insert the ending </HEAD> tag.

4. Insert the <BODY> tag, and then insert the body of the Web page, using standard HTML tags.

5. Insert the </BODY> and </HEAD> tags.

Listing 17.9   Creating an HTA File

```
1    <HTML>
2    <HEAD>
3    <HTA:Application
4        Border = Thick
5        BorderStyle = Complex
6        ShowInTaskBar = No
7        MaximizeButton = No
8        MinimizeButton = No
9    >
10   </HEAD>
11   <BODY>
12   This is a sample HTA.
13   </BODY>
14   </HTML>
```

A sample HTA that displays service information is shown in Listing 17.10. In this script, the code to retrieve service information and to write that data to the browser window is included in a window_onLoad procedure. This procedure automatically runs anytime the Web page is loaded. As a result, service information will be displayed anytime you start (or refresh) the HTA.

Listing 17.10   Using an HTA to Display Service Information

```
1   <HTML>
2   <HEAD>
3   <HTA:Application
4       Border = Thick
5       BorderStyle = Complex
6       ShowInTaskBar = No
7       MaximizeButton = No
8       MinimizeButton = No
9   >
10  <SCRIPT LANGUAGE="VBScript">
11  Sub window_onLoad
12      Set objDocument = self.Document
13      objDocument.open
14      strComputer = "."
15      Set objWMIService = GetObject("winmgmts:" _
16          & "{impersonationLevel=impersonate}!\\" & strComputer & "\root\cimv2")
17      Set colServices =  objWMIService.ExecQuery _
18          ("SELECT * FROM Win32_Service")
19      For Each objService in colServices
20          objdocument.WriteLn objService.DisplayName & "<br>"
21      Next
22  End Sub
23  </SCRIPT>
24  </HEAD>
25  <BODY>
26  </BODY>
27  </HTML>
```

Displaying Script Output by Using the Tabular Data Control

The script shown in Listing 17.10 provides a quick and easy way to display data. Like most standard Web pages, however, it does not allow you to manipulate that data in any way. The data cannot be sorted; instead, it is displayed in the order it is returned by WMI. Sorting is not the only limitation of this script; in addition, you cannot retrieve information for all the services on a computer and then choose to display only those services that are running. To filter the data display, you would need to edit and rerun the script so that it returns only the services that are running. To again look at all the services, you would need to re-edit and rerun the script.

The tabular data control (an ActiveX control that is installed with Internet Explorer) provides a way to display data in tabular format. But the tabular data control does more than just make it quick and easy to display data in a table. By adding a few lines of code, you can sort this data any way that you want; for example, you can sort a list of services by name, by status, by the service account under which they run, or by any other property in your data set. Likewise, you can also filter the data dynamically; for example, you can show all the services, dynamically hide all the services that are not running, and then dynamically show all the services again. This can all be done without having to refresh the page or requery the data set.

With the tabular data control, you do the following:

1. Save the data to be displayed to a text file (typically a comma-separated values file). The first row in the text file is the field headers; subsequent rows represent the field data for a record.

   For example, a text file containing service information might look like this:

   ```
   Service Name,Service Type,Service State

   Alerter,Share Process,Running

   AppMgmt,Share Process,Running

   Ati HotKey Poller,Own Process,Stopped
   ```

2. Insert the tabular data control in the Web page. As part of this process, indicate the path to the text file containing the data to be displayed. The code for inserting the tabular data control looks similar to this (the individual parameters are explained in Table 17.5):

   ```
   <OBJECT id="serviceList" CLASSID="clsid:333C7BC4-460F-11D0-BC04-
   0080C7055A83">
       <PARAM NAME="DataURL" VALUE="c:\scripts\service_list.csv">
       <PARAM NAME="UseHeader" VALUE="True">
       <PARAM NAME="TextQualifier" VALUE=",">
   </OBJECT>
   ```

3. Create the header row for the table.

4. Create the initial data row for the table. Instead of inserting data into this row, you set the Datafld (data field) property for each cell to correspond to a particular field in the text file. If your text file includes the field headers Service Name, Service Type, and Service State, you would set the Datafld property for the first cell in the table to Service Name, the Datafld property for the second cell to Service Type, and the Datafld property for the third cell to Service State.

The actual HTML code might look like this:

```
<TR>
<TD><DIV datafld="Service Name"></DIV></TD>
<TD><DIV datafld="Service Type"></DIV></TD>
<TD><DIV datafld="Service State"></DIV></TD>
</TR>
```

After you have created the initial row, all subsequent rows in the table are created dynamically when the text file is read. Setting up one row in the table results in multiple rows (one for each line in the text file) being displayed when the Web page is opened.

You can also use other HTML formatting in creating your table. For example, if you want to display the Service Name in bold, you can insert the HTML tag for bold (<B>):

```
<TD><B><DIV datafld="Service Name"></DIV></B></TD>
```

The tabular data control supports the properties shown in Table 17.5.

Table 17.5 Tabular Data Control Properties

Property	Description
DataURL	Specifies the location of the data file. This can be either a URL or a file path. For example, this parameter sets the DataURL to C:\Scripts\Service_List.csv: `<PARAM NAME="DataURL" VALUE="c:\scripts\service_list.csv">`
FieldDelim	Identifies the *field delimiter*, the character used to mark the end of a field in the data file. By default, this is the comma. To set the field delimiter to another character, use the HTML value for that character. This example sets the field delimiter to the tab character: `<PARAM NAME = FieldDelim VALUE = "&#09">`
TextQualifier	Specifies characters that might surround data fields in a text file. For example, in this file, the field delimiter is the comma, and the text qualifier is the quotation mark: `Ken, Myer, "Human Resources"`

(continued)

Table 17.5   Tabular Data Control Properties *(continued)*

Property	Description
RowDelim	Identifies the character used to mark the end of each row of data. The default value is the newline character (NL), which simply means that new lines are denoted by pressing ENTER at the end of the previous line.
UseHeader	Specifies whether the first line of the data file contains field headers. The default value is False.
Sort	Specifies the sort order for the table. For more information, see "Sorting Data by Using the Tabular Data Control" later in this chapter.
Filter	Provides the ability to display a subset of records based on specific criteria. For more information, see "Filtering Data by Using the Tabular Data Control" later in this chapter.

Scripting Steps

Listing 17.11 contains a Web page that displays script output by using the tabular data control. To carry out this task, the Web page must include the following:

1. The starting <HTML> and <BODY> tags.

2. An <OBJECT> tag used to insert the tabular data control. You must specify an id for the control as well as this CLASSID:

    clsid:333C7BC4-460F-11D0-BC04-0080C7055A83.

    In addition, specify the following parameters:

    - DataURL, along with the path to the comma-separated-values file.

    - UseHeader, indicating that the first row in the comma-separated-values file contains header information.

    - TextQualifier, indicating that the comma is used to separate items within each row of the text file.

3. An <H2> tag used to provide a heading for the page.

4. A table, with the datasrc set to #serviceList (the id assigned to the tabular data control, prefaced by the pound sign [#]). This means that the table will derive its data from the tabular data control. If your id is serviceInformation, the datasrc is set to #serviceInformation.

5. A <THEAD> and <TR> tag to mark the first row in the table. Three <TD> tags are used to indicate individual columns in the table:

    - Computer

    - Service

    - Status

6. A <TBODY> and <TROW> tag used to delineate the data columns. Each column must specify a datafld used in the header row of the text file:

- System Name

- Display Name

- Service State

7. Ending tags for the table, body, and HTML.

Listing 17.11 Displaying Data by Using the Tabular Data Control

```
1   <HTML>
2   <BODY>
3   <OBJECT id="serviceList" CLASSID="clsid:333C7BC4-460F-11D0-BC04-0080C7055A83">
4      <PARAM NAME="DataURL" VALUE="c:\scripts\service_list.csv">
5      <PARAM NAME="UseHeader" VALUE="True">
6      <PARAM NAME="TextQualifier" VALUE=",">
7   </OBJECT>
8   <H2>Current Service Status</H2>
9   <table border='1' width='100%' cellspacing='0' datasrc=#serviceList>
10  <THEAD><TR>
11  <TD>Computer</TD>
12  <TD>Service</TD>
13  <TD>Status</TD>
14  </TR>
15  </THEAD>
16  <TBODY>
17  <TR>
18  <TD><B><DIV datafld="System Name"></DIV></B></TD>
19  <TD><DIV datafld="Display Name"></DIV></TD>
20  <TD><DIV datafld="Service State"></DIV></TD>
21  </TR>
22  </TBODY>
23  </TABLE>
24  </BODY>
25  </HTML>
```

Sorting Data by Using the Tabular Data Control

One limitation of WMI and the WMI Query Language is that you cannot sort by a particular item. For example, when you retrieve information about the print queues installed on a computer, the returned data is always sorted by print queue name. There is no way to sort by the number of items currently in the queue or by the number of jobs that have been printed.

One way to work around this limitation is to save the data to a comma-separated-values file and then use the tabular data control to display the data. Using the tabular data control, you can specify any sort order you want. This is done by including the SortColumn parameter and specifying the column name (as it appears in the text file header) as the parameter value. For example, adding this line of code to Listing 17.11 sorts the service information by service state:

```
<PARAM NAME="SortColumn" VALUE="Service State">
```

To sort by multiple columns (for example, sorting first by service state and then by display name), set the value to the appropriate column names, separating the names with semicolons:

```
<PARAM NAME="SortColumn" VALUE="Service State;Display Name">
```

By default, data is sorted in ascending order (A through Z, 0 through 9). To sort in descending order (Z through A, 9 through 0), prefix a minus sign (–) to the column name. For example:

```
<PARAM NAME="SortColumn" VALUE="-Service State">
```

To ensure that data is sorted correctly, you can also specify the field type within the text-file header. If you do not specify the field type, all data will be sorted as if it consists of text strings. That means numeric data will be sorted like this:

1
11
2
27
3

Field types recognized by the tabular data control are shown in Table 17.6.

Table 17.6   Field Types Recognized by the Tabular Data Control

Field Type	Description
String	Text data. This is the default value if a field type is not specified.
Date	Date values. The Date type can be optionally followed by a space and the letters D, M, and Y in any order. These indicate how the date has been formatted. For example, if the date is formatted Day/Month/Year (22/10/2001), you use DMY as the optional parameter.

(continued)

Table 17.6 Field Types Recognized by the Tabular Data Control *(continued)*

Field Type	Description
Boolean	True/False or Yes/No values. For True, you can use any of the following: Yes True 1 –1 Any nonzero number For False, you can use any of the following: No False 0
Int	Integer (positive or negative) value.
Float	Number (positive or negative) values containing a decimal point. The decimal separator used by the float type is determined by the Language property of the operating system.

To specify field types within the text file header, append a colon and the field type to each field name. For example:

```
Service Name:Text,Local Service:Boolean,Install Date:Date MDY
```

Scripting Steps

Listing 17.12 contains a Web page that displays script output by using the tabular data control. In this example, the output is sorted by Service State. To carry out this task, the Web page must include the following:

1. The starting <HTML> and <BODY> tags.

2. An <OBJECT> tag used to insert the tabular data control. You must specify an id for the control as well as the CLASSID

   clsid:333C7BC4-460F-11D0-BC04-0080C7055A83.

   In addition, specify the following parameters:

   - DataURL, along with the path to the comma-separated-values file.

   - UseHeader, indicating that the first row in the comma-separated-values file contains header information.

   - TextQualifier, indicating that the comma is used to separate items within each row of the text file.

   - SortColumn, which specifies the datafld to be sorted on (Service State).

3. An <H2> tag used to provide a heading for the page.

4. A table, with the datasrc set to #serviceList, the id assigned to the tabular data control. This means that table will derive its data from the tabular data control.

5. A <THEAD> and <TR> tag to mark the first row in the table. Three <TD> tags are used to indicate individual columns in the table:

   - Computer

   - Service

   - Status

6. A <TBODY> and <TROW> tag used to delineate the data columns. The three columns must specify a datafld used in the header row of the text file:

   - System Name

   - Display Name

   - Service State

7. Ending tags for the table, body, and HTML.

Listing 17.12 Displaying Sorted Data by Using the Tabular Data Control

```
1   <HTML>
2   <BODY>
3   <OBJECT id="serviceList" CLASSID="clsid:333C7BC4-460F-11D0-BC04-0080C7055A83">
4       <PARAM NAME="DataURL" VALUE="c:\scripts\service_list.csv">        <PARAM
5   NAME="UseHeader" VALUE="True">
6       <PARAM NAME="TextQualifier" VALUE=",">
7       <PARAM NAME="SortColumn" VALUE="Service State">
8   </OBJECT>
9   <H2>Current Service Status</H2>
10  <table border='1' width='100%' cellspacing='0' datasrc=#serviceList>
11  <THEAD><TR>
12  <TD>Computer</TD>
13  <TD>Service</TD>
14  <TD>Status</TD>
15  </TR>
16  </THEAD>
17  <TBODY>
18  <TR>
19  <TD><B><DIV datafld="System Name"></DIV></B></TD>
20  <TD><DIV datafld="Display Name"></DIV></TD>
21  <TD><DIV datafld="Service State"></DIV></TD>
22  </TR>
23  </TBODY>
24  </TABLE>
25  </BODY>
26  </HTML>
```

Filtering Data by Using the Tabular Data Control

Data can also be filtered by using the tabular data control. This capability can help administrators quickly spot items of interest. For example, if an administrator is interested only in services that are currently stopped, he or she can use a filter to display only those services. In this way, a single data source can serve multiple purposes. Otherwise, you might have to save information about stopped services to one text file and information about paused services to another text file.

To create a filter for the tabular data control, set the value for the Filter parameter to the name of the column to be filtered, and set the criteria for which records are to be included or excluded. For example, this line of code creates a filter that will limit data retrieval to those records for which the Service State is Stopped:

```
<PARAM NAME="Filter" VALUE="Service State = Stopped">
```

 Note

Although it is beyond the scope of this chapter to demonstrate, both filtering and sorting can be done interactively. For example, you might configure your Web page so that each time you click a column heading, the data is sorted by that column.

Scripting Steps

Listing 17.13 contains a Web page that displays script output by using the tabular data control. In this example, a filter is applied so that only services that are stopped are displayed. To carry out this task, the Web page must include the following:

1. The starting <HTML> and <BODY> tags.

2. An <OBJECT> tag used to insert the tabular data control. You must specify an id for the control as well as the CLASSID:

   clsid:333C7BC4-460F-11D0-BC04-0080C7055A83.

   In addition, specify the following parameters:

   - DataURL, along with the path to the comma-separated-values file.

   - UseHeader, indicating that the first row in the comma-separated-values file contains header information.

   - TextQualifier, indicating that the comma is used to separate items within each row of the text file.

   - Filter, which specifies the datafld and value to be filtered on (ServiceState = 'Stopped').

3. An <H2> tag used to provide a heading for the page.

4. A table, with the datasrc set to #serviceList, the id assigned to the tabular data control. This means that table will derive its data from the tabular data control.

5. A <THEAD> and <TR> tag to mark the first row in the table. Three <TD> tags are used to indicate individual columns in the table:

- Computer

- Service

- Status

6. A <TBODY> and <TROW> tag used to delineate the data columns. The three columns must specify a datafld used in the header row of the text file:

- System Name

- Display Name

- Service State

7. Ending tags for the table, body, and HTML.

Listing 17.13   Displaying Filtered Data by Using the Tabular Data Control

```
1   <HTML>
2   <BODY>
3   <OBJECT id="serviceList" CLASSID="clsid:333C7BC4-460F-11D0-BC04-0080C7055A83">
4      <PARAM NAME="DataURL" VALUE="c:\scripts\service_list.csv">
5      <PARAM NAME="UseHeader" VALUE="True">
6      <PARAM NAME="TextQualifier" VALUE=",">
7      <PARAM NAME="Filter" VALUE="Service State = Stopped">
8   </OBJECT>
9   <H2>Current Service Status</H2>
10  <table border='1' width='100%' cellspacing='0' datasrc=#serviceList>
11  <THEAD><TR>
12  <TD>Computer</TD>
13  <TD>Service</TD>
14  <TD>Status</TD>
15  </TR>
16  </THEAD>
17  <TBODY>
18  <TR>
19  <TD><B><DIV datafld="System Name"></DIV></B></TD>
20  <TD><DIV datafld="Display Name"></DIV></TD>
21  <TD><DIV datafld="Service State"></DIV></TD>
22  </TR>
23  </TBODY>
24  </TABLE>
25  </BODY>
26  </HTML>
```

Sorting Data by Using a Disconnected Recordset

As noted previously, one of the major limitations of the WMI Query Language (WQL) is the fact that you cannot specify a sort order of any kind; all you can do is request a collection of data and then display the data in the order in which WMI returns it. For example, service instances are always returned in alphabetical order. You cannot modify your WQL query to instead sort the data by service state or by the user account under which the service runs.

If you want to display data in an alternative fashion (and if you do not want to use the tabular data control), you will have to write code that can sort and then display the data. Traditionally, script writers have done this by placing the data in an array and then using sorting algorithms (such as the "bubble sort", an algorithm that iterates through a list of elements, swapping adjacent pairs that are out of order) to sort the data.

Unfortunately, these sorting algorithms can become quite complicated, particularly if the data set contains a number of fields (service name, service status, service account, and so forth). A much easier way to sort information is to place this information in a disconnected recordset and then use a single line of code to sort the information.

A disconnected recordset is essentially a database that exists only in memory; it is not tied to a physical database. You create the recordset, add records to it, and then manipulate the data, just like any other recordset. The only difference is that the moment the script terminates, the recordset, which is stored only in memory, disappears as well.

To use a disconnected recordset to sort data, you must first create the recordset, adding any fields needed to store the data. After you have created the fields, you then use the AddNew method to add new records to the recordset, using the same process used to add new records to a physical database. After the recordset has been populated, a single line of code can then sort the data on the specified field. For example, this line of code sorts the recordset by the field ServiceAccountName:

```
DataList.Sort = "ServiceAccountName"
```

Scripting Steps

Listing 17.14 contains a script that sorts data by using a disconnected recordset. To carry out this task, the script must perform the following steps:

1. Create constants named adVarChar (value = 200) and MaxCharacters (value = 255). These constants are used when creating fields for the disconnected recordset; they set the data type to variant and the maximum number of characters to 255.

2. Create an instance of the ADO Recordset object.

3. Use the Fields.Append method to add two fields to the recordset: ServiceName and ServiceState.

4. Open the recordset.

5. Use a GetObject call to connect to the WMI namespace root\cimv2, and set the impersonation level to "impersonate."

6. Use the ExecQuery method to query the Win32_Service class.

    This query returns a collection consisting of all the services installed on the computer.

7. For each service in the collection, use the AddNew method to add a new record to the recordset. For each new record:

    - Set the value of the ServiceName field to the name of the service.

    - Set the value of the ServiceState field to the state (running, stopped, paused, resuming) of the service.

8. Use the Update method to update the recordset with the new record.

9. After all the records have been added, use the Sort method to sort the recordset by ServiceState.

10. Use the MoveFirst method to move to the first record in the recordset.

11. For each record in the recordset, echo the service name and the service state. The output will be sorted by service state.

Listing 17.14   Sorting Data by Using a Disconnected Recordset

```
1   Const adVarChar = 200
2   Const MaxCharacters = 255
3   Set DataList = CreateObject("ADOR.Recordset")
4   DataList.Fields.Append "ServiceName", adVarChar, MaxCharacters
5   DataList.Fields.Append "ServiceState", adVarChar, MaxCharacters
6   DataList.Open
7   strComputer = "."
8   Set objWMIService = GetObject("winmgmts:" _
9       & "{impersonationLevel=impersonate}!\\" & strComputer& "\root\cimv2")
10  Set colServices = objWMIService.ExecQuery _
11      ("SELECT * FROM Win32_Service")
12  For Each Service in colServices
13      DataList.AddNew
14      DataList("ServiceName") = Service.Name
15      DataList("ServiceState") = Service.State
16      DataList.Update
17  Next
18  DataList.Sort = "ServiceState"
19  DataList.MoveFirst
20  Do Until DataList.EOF
21      Wscript.Echo DataList.Fields.Item("ServiceName") _
22          & vbTab & DataList.Fields.Item("ServiceState")
23  DataList.MoveNext
24  Loop
```

Working with Databases

System administrators often find themselves working with large amounts of data. For example, consider a simple task such as inventorying computer hardware. If you have 10,000 computers in your organization, this task will result in an enormous amount of data. Although this data can be stored in a text file, your ability to view, modify, and analyze that data will be limited, to say the least. Instead, it is typically better to store large amounts of data in a database.

Most databases have an import feature that allows you to import data stored in other formats (such as text files). Because of this, you can save retrieved data as a text file and then open your database application and import the data. Needless to say, it would be much faster and much easier if your scripts could directly interact with a database. Using ActiveX Data Objects, scripts can do just that.

ActiveX Data Objects (ADO) are part of the Universal Data Access (UDA) technology that provides access to information across the enterprise. Like its predecessor, Open Database Connectivity (ODBC), UDA provides a common interface for communicating with SQL databases. However, UDA goes beyond database connectivity to provide access to information that is not stored in relational databases; for example, you can access information stored as part of an e-mail service, a file system, or a hierarchical database such as Microsoft Indexing Service.

Note

ADO is sometimes referred to as ADO/OLE DB (OLE Database). This is because ADO serves as the scripting and application-level programming interface, while OLE DB serves as the system-level programming interface. ADO is required when working with scripting languages; system-level programming languages such as C++ can bypass ADO and work directly with OLE DB.

Although a complete discussion of the ADO object model is beyond the scope of this book, two objects are particularly important to administrators who need to connect to databases when writing scripts. These two objects, the Connection object and the Recordset object, are explained in more detail in Table 17.7.

Table 17.7   ADO Objects

Object	Description
Connection	Manages the connection between your script and the database. The Connection object is used to open the database but does not return any data. The Recordset object is used to return data.
Recordset	Contains the data returned by your query. The data is contained in rows (referred to as records) and columns (referred to as fields). Each column is stored in a Field object in the Recordset Fields collection.
	Recordsets are returned by using SQL commands such as "SELECT * FROM Hardware". A recordset can represent all the records in a database or a subset, depending on how you construct your SQL queries.

Using a DSN

To connect to a database by using ADO, you must have an OLE DB data provider; this data provider serves as the mechanism that connects you to a particular type of database (SQL Server, Microsoft Access, Active Directory, and so on). Although you can connect directly to a database by including the provider name and the path to the database as part of the connection string, a simpler method of connecting to a database is to create a data source name (DSN) for the database.

A DSN stores all the information required to connect to a database. If you create a DSN for a database, you can connect to that database by using a single line of code (for example, `objConnection.Open "DSN=Inventory;"`), without having to know the provider name or the physical path to the database. If you change the path to the database (for example, by moving the database to a faster hard disk), you can change the DSN rather than modifying all the scripts that connect to that database.

▶ **To create a DSN**

1. Open **Administrative Tools**, and then click **Data Source (ODBC)**.

2. On the **System DSN** tab in the **ODBC Data Source Administrator** dialog box, click **Add**.

3. In the Create New Data Source wizard, follow the prompts to create a DSN for your database. The steps will vary depending on the type of database. (For example, the steps required to create a DSN for a SQL Server database are different from those required to create a DSN for a Microsoft Access database.)

When you connect to the database in a script, you will make the connection by using the DSN you create with this wizard, not the name of the database itself. The ADO examples used in this chapter connect to the database by using a DSN.

Connecting to a Database

To connect to a database by using ADO, you follow the same standard procedure regardless of the type of database to which you are connecting. Your script must:

1. Create instances of the Connection and Recordset objects.

2. Use the Connection object Open method to connect to the DSN for the database.

3. Use the Recordset object Open method to retrieve data from the desired table within the database.

When using the Recordset object Open method, include both a standard SQL command (for example, "SELECT * FROM Inventory") and parameters specifying CursorLocation, CursorType, and LockType. These parameters are described in more detail in Table 17.8.

Table 17.8 Parameters for the Recordset Object Open Method

Property	Description
CursorLocation	Data structure that holds the results of any query you make. Cursors can be stored either on the server or on the client. In general, it is better to store the cursor on the client; this tends to improve performance (because the data is stored locally) and places less strain on the database server.
	To set the CursorLocation to the client, set the value of the constant adUseClient to 3.
CursorType	Allows you to browse a recordset in different ways: some cursors allow you to move backward and forward in a recordset, while other cursors limit you to moving forward only.
	If you set the CursorLocation to the client, you must set the CursorType to adOpenStatic (value = 3). This type supports scrolling forward and backward in the recordset but does not show changes made by other users. This is because the cursor is operating on data cached on the client computer rather than directly from the database.
LockType	Determines how (and if) a recordset can be updated. Recordsets can be set to read-only, or they can be configured to allow updates. For most scripts, the LockType can be set to adLockOptimistic (value = 3). With this setting, the record being edited is not locked (that is, no restrictions are placed on another user accessing that record) until you call the Update method.

When you are finished with the database connection and the recordset, use the Close method to close both objects.

Scripting Steps

Listing 17.15 contains a script that creates an ADO connection. To carry out this task, the script must perform the following steps:

1.   Create three constants — adOpenStatic, adLockOptimistic, and adUseClient — and set the value of each to 3.

   These constants will be used to configure the CursorLocation, CursorType, and LockType for the connection.

2.   Create an instance of the ADO Connection object (ADODB.Connection).

   The Connection object makes it possible for you to issue queries and other database commands.

3.   Create an instance of the ADO Recordset object (ADODB.Recordset).

   The Recordset object stores the data returned from your query.

4.   Use the Connection object Open method to open the database with the DSN Inventory.

   Be sure to append a semicolon (;) to the DSN name.

5.   Set the CursorLocation to 3 (client side) by using the constant adUseClient.

6.   Use the Recordset object Open method to retrieve all the records from the Hardware table.

   The Open method requires four parameters:

   - The SQL query ("SELECT * FROM Hardware")
   - The name of the ADO connection being used (objConnection)
   - The cursor type (adOpenStatic)
   - The lock type (adLockOptimistic)

7.   Close the recordset.

   In an actual production script, of course, you would probably do something with a recordset besides just opening and closing it.

8.   Close the connection.

Listing 17.15   Connecting to an ADO Database

```
1   Const adOpenStatic = 3
2   Const adLockOptimistic = 3
3   Const adUseClient = 3
4   Set objConnection = CreateObject("ADODB.Connection")
5   Set objRecordset = CreateObject("ADODB.Recordset")
6   objConnection.Open "DSN=Inventory;"
7   objRecordset.CursorLocation = adUseClient
8   objRecordset.Open "SELECT * FROM Hardware" , objConnection, _
9       adOpenStatic, adLockOptimistic
10  objRecordset.Close
11  objConnection.Close
```

Adding New Records to a Database

Many enterprise scripts are designed to take data from multiple sources (for example, all the event logs on all your domain controllers) and then combine that information into a single database. This is typically done for two reasons: It creates a central repository for this data, and it makes it possible for you to use database tools to analyze the data.

To copy information to a database, your script must create a new record for each piece of information retrieved. (For example, a new record must be added to the database for each event retrieved from an event log.)

You use the AddNew method to add new records to a database. After you have opened a connection to a database and a recordset, do the following:

1. Call the AddNew method.

2. Specify the name of each field and the value for the new record. For example, if the database includes a field named ComputerName and you want to add a new computer named WebServer, use code similar to the following:

```
objRecordset("ComputerName") = "WebServer"
```

3. Use the Update method to write the new record to the database. The AddNew method by itself does not save the new record.

You can use the AddNew method only if the recordset can be updated. If you opened the recordset in read-only mode, any attempt to add a new record will fail.

Scripting Steps

Listing 17.16 contains a script that adds a new record — the name of a sound card — to a database. To carry out this task, the script must perform the following steps:

1. Create three constants — adOpenStatic, adLockOptimistic, and adUseClient — and set the value of each to 3.

    These constants will be used to configure the CursorLocation, CursorType, and LockType for the connection.

2. Create an instance of the ADO object (ADODB.Connection).

    The Connection object makes it possible for you to issue queries and other database commands.

3. Create an instance of the ADO Recordset object (ADODB.Recordset).

    The Recordset object stores the data returned from your query.

4. Use the Connection object Open method to open the database with the DSN Inventory.

    Be sure to append a semicolon (;) to the DSN name.

5. Set the CursorLocation to 3 (client side) by using the constant adUseClient.

6. Use the Recordset object Open method to retrieve all the records from the Hardware table.

    The Open method requires four parameters:

    -   The SQL query ("SELECT * FROM Hardware")
    -   The name of the ADO connection being used (objConnection)
    -   The cursor type (adOpenStatic)
    -   The lock type (adLockOptimistic)

7. Use a GetObject call to connect to the WMI namespace root\cimv2, and set the impersonation level to "impersonate."

8. Use the ExecQuery method to query the Win32_SoundDevice class.

    This query returns a collection consisting of all the sound cards installed on the computer.

9. For each sound card in the collection, use the AddNew method to create a record for that sound card in the database.

10. For each sound card, use the values obtained from the Win32_SoundDevice class to update the database fields ComputerName, Manufacturer, and ProductName.

11. Use the Update method to write the new record to the database.

12. Close the recordset.

13. Close the connection.

Listing 17.16   Adding New Records to a Database

```
1   Const adOpenStatic = 3
2   Const adLockOptimistic = 3
3   Const adUseClient = 3
4   Set objConnection = CreateObject("ADODB.Connection")
5   Set objRecordset = CreateObject("ADODB.Recordset")
6   objConnection.Open "DSN=Inventory;"
7   objRecordset.CursorLocation = adUseClient
8   objRecordset.Open "SELECT * FROM Hardware" , objConnection, _
9       adOpenStatic, adLockOptimistic
10  strComputer = "."
11  Set objWMIService = GetObject("winmgmts:" _
12      & "{impersonationLevel=impersonate}!\\" & strComputer& "\root\cimv2")
13  Set colSoundCards = objWMIService.ExecQuery _
14      ("SELECT * FROM Win32_SoundDevice")
15  For Each objSoundCard in colSoundCards
16      objRecordset.AddNew
17      objRecordset("ComputerName") = objSoundCard.SystemName
18      objRecordset("Manufacturer") = objSoundCard.Manufacturer
19      objRecordset("ProductName") = objSoundCard.ProductName
20      objRecordset.Update
21  Next
22  objRecordset.Close
23  objConnection.Close
```

Finding Records in a Recordset

Many enterprise scripts require you to perform an action on multiple records in the database. For example, you might have a script that updates the hardware inventory for a set of computers. The script needs to connect to the database, locate the record for the first computer, and apply any required updates. The script must then repeat the process for each computer being inventoried.

It is possible to create an SQL query that returns only the name of computer being updated (for example, "SELECT * FROM Inventory WHERE ComputerName = 'WebServer'"). However, if your script must update 100 computers, this would require 100 separate SQL queries being passed to the database server, one for each computer being updated. A more efficient approach might be to download the entire set of computers and then use the Recordset object Find method to locate each computer as needed.

The Find method requires two steps:

1. Set the criteria for the method. For example, to find a computer named WebServer, set the criteria as follows:

```
strSearchCriteria = "ComputerName = 'WebServer'"
```

2. Apply the method. For example:

```
objRecordSet.Find strSearchCriteria
```

You can use the Recordset object EOF (end-of-file) property to determine whether a record was found. If EOF is True, this means the recordset has been searched from beginning to end and no record was found. This is important because your script will fail if it attempts to take action on a record that does not exist. For example, you might use the Find method to locate a particular record and then use the Delete method to delete that record. If the record does not exist, however, both the Delete method and your script will fail.

Using the Find method also helps you eliminate duplicate records within a database. For example, when creating an inventory of your computers, you probably want one record per computer; you do not want multiple records for the computer WebServer. To prevent the possibility of creating duplicate records, follow a procedure similar to this:

1. Take the inventory on a computer (for example, WebServer).

2. Search the recordset for a computer named WebServer.

    - If a computer named WebServer is found, update the record with the current inventory information.

    - If a computer named WebServer is not found, use the AddNew method to create a record for WebServer.

Scripting Steps

Listing 17.17 contains a script that finds a record in a recordset. To carry out this task, the script must perform the following steps:

1. Create three constants — adOpenStatic, adLockOptimistic, and adUseClient — and set the value of each to 3.

    These constants will be used to configure the CursorLocation, CursorType, and LockType for the connection.

2. Create an instance of the ADO Connection object (ADODB.Connection).

    The Connection object makes it possible for you to issue queries and other database commands.

3. Create an instance of the ADO Recordset object (ADODB.Recordset).

    The Recordset object stores the data returned from your query.

4. Use the Connection object Open method to open the database with the DSN Inventory.

    Be sure to append a semicolon (;) to the DSN name.

5. Set the CursorLocation to 3 (client side) by using the constant adUseClient.

6. Use the Recordset object Open method to retrieve all the records from the Hardware table.

   The Open method requires four parameters:

   - The SQL query ("SELECT * FROM Hardware")
   - The name of the ADO connection being used (objConnection)
   - The cursor type (adOpenStatic)
   - The lock type (adLockOptimistic)

7. Set the variable strSearchCriteria to ComputerName = 'WebServer'.

   The variable strSearchCriteria will serve as the search criteria for the Find method.

8. Use the Find method to locate the computer named WebServer.

9. Use the EOF property to verify whether the record can be found:

   - If the record cannot not be found (because EOF = True), echo the string, "Record cannot be found."
   - If the record is found (because EOF = False), echo the string, "Record found."

10. Close the recordset.

11. Close the connection.

Listing 17.17   Finding Records in a Recordset

```
1   Const adOpenStatic = 3
2   Const adLockOptimistic = 3
3   Const adUseClient = 3
4   Set objConnection = CreateObject("ADODB.Connection")
5   Set objRecordset = CreateObject("ADODB.Recordset")
6   objConnection.Open "DSN=Inventory;"
7   objRecordset.CursorLocation = adUseClient
8   objRecordset.Open "SELECT * FROM Hardware" , objConnection, _
9       adOpenStatic, adLockOptimistic
10  strSearchCriteria = "ComputerName = 'WebServer'"
11  objRecordSet.Find strSearchCriteria
12  If objRecordset.EOF Then
13      Wscript.Echo "Record cannot be found."
14  Else
15      Wscript.Echo "Record found."
16  End If
17  objRecordset.Close
18  objConnection.Close
```

Updating Records in a Database

Scripts often need to update existing records rather than add new records to a database. For example, with an inventory script you do not want to add a new record each time the script is run. If you did, you would end up with multiple records for the same computer. Instead, you want to update the existing record for each computer, replacing the old inventory data with the newly retrieved data.

To update a record by using ADO, do the following:

1. Connect to the recordset.

2. Connect to the appropriate record. This is typically done by using the Find method to locate an individual record.

3. Set the new values as needed.

4. Use the Update method to apply the changes to the database.

Scripting Steps

Listing 17.18 contains a script that updates a record in a database. To carry out this task, the script must perform the following steps:

1. Create three constants — adOpenStatic, adLockOptimistic, and adUseClient — and set the value of each to 3.

   These constants will be used to configure the CursorLocation, CursorType, and LockType for the connection.

2. Create an instance of the ADO Connection object (ADODB.Connection).

   The Connection object makes it possible for you to issue queries and other database commands.

3. Create an instance of the ADO Recordset object (ADODB.Recordset).

   The Recordset object stores the data returned from your query.

4. Use the Connection object Open method to open the database with the DSN Inventory.

   Be sure to append a semicolon (;) to the DSN name.

5. Set the CursorLocation to 3 (client side) by using the constant adUseClient.

6. Use the Recordset object Open method to retrieve all the records from the Hardware table.

   The Open method requires four parameters:

   - The SQL query ("SELECT * FROM Hardware")

   - The name of the ADO connection being used (objConnection)

   - The cursor type (adOpenStatic)

   - The lock type (adLockOptimistic)

7.   Set the variable strSearchCriteria to ComputerName = 'WebServer'.

The variable strSearchCriteria will serve as the search criteria for the Find method.

8.   Use the Find method to locate the computer named WebServer.

9.   Use a GetObject call to connect to the WMI namespace root\cimv2, and set the impersonation level to "impersonate."

10.   Use the ExecQuery method to query the Win32_SoundDevice class.

This query returns a collection consisting of all the sound cards installed on the computer.

11.   For each sound card in the collection, use the values obtained from the Win32_SoundDevice class to update the database fields ComputerName, Manufacturer, and ProductName.

12.   Use the Update method to write the new record to the database.

13.   Close the recordset.

14.   Close the connection.

Listing 17.18   Updating Records in a Database

```
1    Const adOpenStatic = 3
2    Const adLockOptimistic = 3
3    Const adUseClient = 3
4    Set objConnection = CreateObject("ADODB.Connection")
5    Set objRecordset = CreateObject("ADODB.Recordset")
6    objConnection.Open "DSN=Inventory;"
7    objRecordset.CursorLocation = adUseClient
8    objRecordset.Open "SELECT * FROM Hardware" , objConnection, _
9        adOpenStatic, adLockOptimistic
10   strSearchCriteria = "ComputerName = 'WebServer'"
11   objRecordSet.Find strSearchCriteria
12   strComputer = "."
13   Set objWMIService = GetObject("winmgmts:" _
14       & "{impersonationLevel=impersonate}!\\" & strComputer& "\root\cimv2")
15   Set colSoundCards = objWMIService.ExecQuery _
16       ("SELECT * FROM Win32_SoundDevice")
17   For Each objSoundCard in colSoundCards
18       objRecordset("ComputerName") = objSoundCard.SystemName
19       objRecordset("Manufacturer") = objSoundCard.Manufacturer
20       objRecordset("ProductName") = objSoundCard.ProductName
21       objRecordset.Update
22   Next
23   objRecordset.Close
24   objConnection.Close
```

Deleting Selected Records from a Database

There will undoubtedly be times when you want to delete a record or set of records from a database. For example, you might decommission the DNS Server service on a computer; in turn, you will then need to delete that computer from the database table that contains the names of your DNS servers. Or suppose you maintain three months of performance monitoring information in a database. Each month you will need to delete some of the old data to make room for the new data. For example, in April you will need to delete the data for January. After you add the April data, the database will again contain data for three months: February, March, and April.

To delete a record by using ADO, do the following:

1.   Connect to the recordset.

2.   Connect to the appropriate record. This is typically done by using the Find method to locate an individual record.

3.   Use the Delete method to delete the record.

When you use the Delete method to delete a record, the record will be deleted as soon as the method is called. You do not need to use the Update method to apply the changes. No warning of any kind will be issued before the record is deleted.

Scripting Steps

Listing 17.19 contains a script that deletes a record from a database. To carry out this task, the script must perform the following steps:

1.   Create three constants — adOpenStatic, adLockOptimistic, and adUseClient — and set the value of each to 3.

   These constants will be used to configure the CursorLocation, CursorType, and LockType for the connection.

2.   Create an instance of the ADO Connection object (ADODB.Connection).

   The Connection object makes it possible for you to issue queries and other database commands.

3.   Create an instance of the ADO Recordset object (ADODB.Recordset).

   The Recordset object stores the data returned from your query.

4.   Use the Connection object Open method to open the database with the DSN Inventory.

   Be sure to append a semicolon (;) to the DSN name.

5.   Set the CursorLocation to 3 (client side) by using the constant adUseClient.

6. Use the Recordset object Open method to retrieve all the records from the Hardware table.

The Open method requires four parameters:

- The SQL query ("SELECT * FROM Hardware")
- The name of the ADO connection being used (objConnection)
- The cursor type (adOpenStatic)
- The lock type (adLockOptimistic)

7. Set the variable strSearchCriteria to ComputerName = 'WebServer'.

The variable strSearchCriteria will serve as the search criteria for the Find method.

8. Use the Find method to locate the computer named WebServer.

9. Use the Delete method to delete the record for the computer named WebServer.

10. Close the recordset.

11. Close the connection.

Listing 17.19   Deleting Selected Records from a Database

```
1    Const adOpenStatic = 3
2    Const adLockOptimistic = 3
3    Const adUseClient = 3
4    Set objConnection = CreateObject("ADODB.Connection")
5    Set objRecordset = CreateObject("ADODB.Recordset")
6    objConnection.Open "DSN=Inventory;"
7    objRecordset.CursorLocation = adUseClient
8    objRecordset.Open "SELECT * FROM Hardware" , objConnection, _
9        adOpenStatic, adLockOptimistic
10   strSearchCriteria = "ComputerName = 'WebServer'"
11   objRecordSet.Find strSearchCriteria
12   objRecordset.Delete
13   objRecordset.Close
14   objConnection.Close
```

Deleting All Records in a Database Table

There will also be times when you need to clear a database table, deleting all the records. For example, suppose at the end of each month you import event log records into a database and then run a series of statistical analyses on that data. At the end of the next month, you might want to clear the table; that way, the next set of records imported into the database will not commingle with any previous records.

Although you can clear a database by finding and deleting each record individually, a better and faster approach is to use an SQL Delete query to delete all the records in a single operation.

Scripting Steps

Listing 17.20 contains a script that deletes all the records in a database table. To carry out this task, the script must perform the following steps:

1. Create three constants — adOpenStatic, adLockOptimistic, and adUseClient — and set the value of each to 3.

   These constants will be used to configure the CursorLocation, CursorType, and LockType for the connection.

2. Create an instance of the ADO Connection object (ADODB.Connection).

   The Connection object makes it possible for you to issue queries and other database commands.

3. Create an instance of the ADO Recordset object (ADODB.Recordset).

   The Recordset object stores the data returned from your query.

4. Use the Connection object Open method to open the database with the DSN Inventory.

   Be sure to append a semicolon (;) to the DSN name.

5. Set the CursorLocation to 3 (client side) by using the constant adUseClient.

6. Use the Recordset object Open method to delete all the records from the Hardware table.

   The Open method requires four parameters:

   - The SQL query ("DELETE * FROM Hardware"). The exact query used to delete all the records will vary depending on your database. Some SQL databases use "DELETE FROM Hardware", without the asterisk, instead.

   - The name of the ADO connection being used (objConnection).

   - The cursor type (adOpenStatic).

   - The lock type (adLockOptimistic).

7. Close the connection.

Listing 17.20   Deleting All Records in a Database Table

```
1    Const adOpenStatic = 3
2    Const adLockOptimistic = 3
3    Const adUseClient = 3
4    Set objConnection = CreateObject("ADODB.Connection")
5    Set objRecordset = CreateObject("ADODB.Recordset")
6    objConnection.Open "DSN=Inventory;"
7    objRecordset.CursorLocation = adUseClient
8    objRecordset.Open "DELETE * FROM Hardware" , objConnection, _
9        adOpenStatic, adLockOptimistic
10   objConnection.Close
```

Masking Passwords

As a security precaution, administrators are encouraged to log on to computers by using a typical user account, one without administrative privileges. This means that administrators must supply alternate security credentials (in the form of a user name and a password) to run scripts that require administrative privileges. Although this is good advice, it does have at least possible two drawbacks:

- If you hard-code the administrator password within the script itself, the password is visible to anyone who has access to the script.

- If you type the administrator password in response to a prompt (either at the command line or in a VBScript Input box), the password is not masked in any way. This means that the password you type on the screen will be clearly visible to anyone looking at the monitor.

In turn, this creates a dilemma for system administrators. On the one hand, they are discouraged from logging on to a computer by using the administrator account. On the other hand, neither VBScript nor WSH provides a method for masking passwords as they are entered. As a result, typing a password can be considered as big a security hole as logging on as an administrator.

Fortunately, both VBScript and WSH support COM automation. As a result, you can tap the capabilities found in Internet Explorer to provide password masking for your scripts.

Masking Passwords by Using Internet Explorer

You can use Internet Explorer as a way to enter passwords. To mask passwords using Internet Explorer, you need to:

1. Create a Web page to use as the form. The Web page must contain, at a minimum:

   - A password box for entering the password.

   - An OK button, to be clicked after a password has been entered.

   - A hidden text field. When the OK button is clicked, the value of the hidden text field is changed. The script used to open the Web page monitors this text field for changes. Because the value will change only when the OK button is clicked, the script will pause until this change is detected.

   For example, the HTML coding might look like this:

```
<SCRIPT language="VBScript">
    <!--
        Sub OKButton_OnClick
            OkClicked.Value = 1
        End Sub
    '-->
</SCRIPT>
<BODY>
Please enter your password: <INPUT TYPE=password Name = "PasswordBox"
size="20">
<P>
<INPUT NAME="OKButton" TYPE="BUTTON" VALUE="OK" >
<P>
<input type="hidden" name="OKClicked" size="20">
</BODY>
```

2. Create a script that opens the Web page and waits for the password to be entered.

3. Provide a mechanism for the script to identify the password that was typed in the password box.

Scripting Steps

Listing 17.21 contains a script that masks passwords entered in Internet Explorer. (To actually use the script, you will have to create the file C:\Scripts\Password.htm.) To carry out this task, the script must perform the following steps:

1. Use the Wscript CreateObject method to create an instance of Internet Explorer, and assign the name IE_ to the event handler responsible for monitoring Internet Explorer events.

2. Use the Navigate method to open the Web page C:\Scripts\Password.htm.

3. Configure various Internet Explorer properties, such as width and height, and hide items such as the toolbar and the status bar.

4. Set the Visible property to 1 to display Internet Explorer, opened to the correct page and properly configured.

5. Use a Do loop to pause the script until the **OK** button in Internet Explorer has been clicked.

   This is done by periodically checking the value of a hidden text field named OKClicked. If this text box is empty, the script sleeps for 250 milliseconds and then checks again. When the **OK** button is clicked, the value of this text box is set to 1. At that point, the script exits the loop.

6. Set the value of the variable strPassword to the value of the PasswordBox text box. This is the name of the text box in Internet Explorer where the user typed the password.

7. Use the Quit method to close Internet Explorer.

8. Pause for 250 milliseconds.

9. Echo the value of strPassword. In a production script, you would probably not echo the value of strPassword but instead would use it to connect to a resource of some kind.

Listing 17.21 Masking Passwords in Internet Explorer

```
1   Set objExplorer = WScript.CreateObject _
2       ("InternetExplorer.Application", "IE_")
3   objExplorer.Navigate "file:///c:\scripts\password.htm"
4   objExplorer.ToolBar = 0
5   objExplorer.StatusBar = 0
6   objExplorer.Width = 400
7   objExplorer.Height = 250
8   objExplorer.Left = 0
9   objExplorer.Top = 0
10  objExplorer.Visible = 1
11  Do While (objExplorer.Document.All.OKClicked.Value = "")
12      Wscript.Sleep 250
13  Loop
14  strPassword = objExplorer.Document.All.PasswordBox.Value
15  objExplorer.Quit
16  Wscript.Sleep 250
17  Wscript.Echo strPassword
```

The script shown in Listing 17.22 shows how a masked password can be retrieved from Internet Explorer, and then used to connect to a remote computer and install a software package. In line 10, the variable strPassword, which contains the value typed by the user, is used to connect to the remote computer. This is done rather than hard-coding the password in the script.

Listing 17.22   Using a Password Masked in Internet Explorer

```
1    Const wbemImpersonationLevelDelegate = 4
2
3    Set objExplorer = WScript.CreateObject _
4        ("InternetExplorer.Application", "IE_")
5    objExplorer.Navigate "file:///c:\scripts\password.htm"
6    objExplorer.ToolBar = 0
7    objExplorer.StatusBar = 0
8    objExplorer.Width = 400
9    objExplorer.Height = 250
10   objExplorer.Left = 0
11   objExplorer.Top = 0
12   objExplorer.Visible = 1
13   Do While (objExplorer.Document.All.OKClicked.Value = "")
14       Wscript.Sleep 250
15   Loop
16   strPassword = objExplorer.Document.All.PasswordBox.Value
17   objExplorer.Quit
18
19   Set objWbemLocator = CreateObject("WbemScripting.SWbemLocator")
20   Set objConnection = objwbemLocator.ConnectServer _
21       ("WebServer", "root\cimv2", "fabrikam\administrator", _
22           strPassword")
23   Set objSoftware = objConnection.Get("Win32_Product")
24   errReturn = objSoftware.Install("\\atl-dc-02\scripts\1561_lab.msi",,True)
```

Sending E-Mail

E-mail is one of the most important avenues of communication within large organizations, and for good reason. E-mail is not dependent on time or place; messages can be sent at any time of the day or night, and they can be accessed from practically anywhere. The fact that it might be after hours or that you do not know the physical location of the recipient is no deterrent to sending information via e-mail.

For that matter, the fact that no human being is present is also no deterrent to sending information via e-mail. You can include code that enables your scripts to send e-mail in response to a specified event. For example, a monitoring script can be coded so that it sends an e-mail message anytime disk space begins to run low on a server. An inventory script can retrieve information and then, instead of saving that information to a file, e-mail it to the appropriate administrator.

You can use the Collaboration Data Objects (CDO) technology to incorporate e-mail messaging within a script. CDO includes a COM component (Cdosys.dll) that can be used to send e-mail messages by using either the SMTP or the NNTP protocol. These messages can be sent even if the SMTP or NNTP service is not installed locally; you can use CDO to send messages as long as the SMTP or NNTP service is installed somewhere on your network.

The CDO automation library defines a number of objects, including the Message object, which represents a complete e-mail message. In turn, the Message object has a number of interfaces, including the IMessage interface. This interface is used to perform such tasks as addressing, adding content to, and sending a message.

Some of the key properties of the IMessage interface are shown in Table 17.9.

Table 17.9   IMessage Interface Properties

Property/Method	Description
AddAttachment	Enables you to add an attached file to the message. As the AddAttachment parameter, specify the full path name of the file to be attached.
From	E-mail address of the primary author of the message. This property is optional; if left blank, the From property will be set to the value of the Sender property, assuming a value for this property has been configured. If neither the From property nor the Sender property is configured, the script will fail.
ReplyTo	E-mail address or addresses that replies should be sent to.
Sender	E-mail address of the person who actually sent the message. This does not have to be the same address as the From property. If the From and Sender properties refer to the same person, you do not need to configure the Sender property.
Subject	Specifies the subject line for the e-mail message.
TextBody	Plain-text representation of the actual e-mail message.
To	Specifies recipients of the message.

Sending E-Mail from a Script

Enabling a script to send automated e-mail messages provides a way for your script to send real-time alerts whenever a particular event occurs (for example, when the script runs, when the script finishes, or when the script encounters a problem of some kind). Alerts are commonly used in system administration scripting, but these notices are typically displayed either by using pop-up message boxes or by recording an event in the event log. Although both of these techniques are useful, they require someone to either physically sit at the computer where the message box is displayed or continually monitor the event log for the occurrence of new events.

By contrast, e-mail alerts can be directed to a particular administrator or group of administrators regardless of their physical location; administrators can receive these alerts even if they are off-site. Because most administrators read their e-mail more often than they read event logs, there is a greater chance that they will respond quickly to the e-mail alert. With the new generation of PDAs and cell phones that can be used to check e-mail, the ability to programmatically send alerts using this technology becomes even more valuable.

E-mail can be sent from any Microsoft® Windows® 2000–based computer by using CDO.

Scripting Steps

Listing 17.23 contains a script that sends an e-mail message by using CDO. To carry out this task, the script must perform the following steps:

1.   Create an instance of a CDO e-mail message.

2.   Set the values for the From, To, Subject, and TextBody properties of the message.

3.   Use the Send method to send the message.

For this script to work, the SMTP service must be installed on the computer where the script is being run.

Listing 17.23   Sending E-Mail from a Script

```
1   Set objEmail = CreateObject("CDO.Message")
2   objEmail.From = "monitor1@fabrikam.com"
3   objEmail.To = "admin1@fabrikam.com"
4   objEmail.Subject = "Atl-dc-01 down"
5   objEmail.Textbody = "Atl-dc-01 is no longer accessible over the network."
6   objEmail.Send
```

Sending E-Mail Without Installing the SMTP Service

The script shown in Listing 17.23 can be used as long as the SMTP service is installed on the computer where the script is running. Obviously, this poses a problem: Most likely, you do not want the SMTP service to be installed and running on every one of your computers.

Even if the SMTP service is not installed on the computer, you can still send e-mail from a script as long as the SMTP service is installed somewhere on your network. To do this, your script must include code that specifies the properties of the computer and the SMTP service that will be used to send the message.

Each e-mail Message object has an associated Configuration object that defines configuration settings for sending the message. These settings are stored as fields within the Configuration object; each field is a Uniform Resource Identifier (URI) that contains information for the configuration setting. The three URIs required to send an SMTP e-mail message are shown in Table 17.10.

Table 17.10 Required URIs for Sending SMTP E-Mail Messages

Configuration Field	Description
SendUsing	Indicates how the message is to be sent. Values are:
	1 – Send messages by using the locally installed SMTP service. Use this value if the SMTP service is installed on the computer where the script is running.
	2 – Send messages by using the SMTP service on the network. Use this value if the SMTP service is not installed on the computer where the script is running.
	The full name for this field is:
	http://schemas.Microsoft.com/cdo/configuration/sendusing
SmtpServer	DNS name or IP address of the SMTP server through which messages are sent.
	The full name for this field is:
	http://schemas.Microsoft.com/cdo/configuration/smtpserver
SmtpServerPort	The port on which the SMTP server listens for connections. This is typically port 25.
	The full name for this field is:
	http://schemas.Microsoft.com/cdo/configuration/smtpserverport

Scripting Steps

Listing 17.24 contains a script that sends e-mail from a computer that is not running the SMTP service. To carry out this task, the script must perform the following steps:

1. Create an instance of a CDO e-mail message.

2. Set the values for the From, To, Subject, and TextBody properties of the message.

3. Specify the configuration properties for the remote SMTP server. In this script, those properties and their values are:

   - **SendUsing.** This property is set to 2, meaning that the SMTP service is not installed on this computer. Messages must instead be sent by using the computer specified in the SMTPServer property.

   - **SMTPServer.** This property is set to MySMTPHost, the name of the SMTP server on this hypothetical network. If the name of your SMTP server is MailServer1, set this property to MailServer1.

   - **SMTPServerPort.** This property is set to 25, the default SMTP port for most computers.

4. Use the Send method to send the message.

Listing 17.24   Sending E-Mail Without Installing the SMTP Service

```
1   Set objEmail = CreateObject("CDO.Message")
2   objEmail.From = "admin1@fabrikam.com"
3   objEmail.To = "admin2@fabrikam.com"
4   objEmail.Subject = "Server down"
5   objEmail.Textbody = "Server1 is no longer accessible over the network."
6   objEmail.Configuration.Fields.Item _
7       ("http://schemas.microsoft.com/cdo/configuration/sendusing") = 2
8   objEmail.Configuration.Fields.Item _
9       ("http://schemas.microsoft.com/cdo/configuration/smtpserver") = _
10          "MySMTPHost"
11  objEmail.Configuration.Fields.Item _
12      ("http://schemas.microsoft.com/cdo/configuration/smtpserverport") = 25
13  objEmail.Configuration.Fields.Update
14  objEmail.Send
```

Tracking Script Progress

System administration scripts typically run without displaying a user interface of any kind. This is due to the nature of many of these scripts. For example, you might have a script that runs at 4 A.M., checks the size of all your event logs, and — if necessary — backs up and clears the logs that are nearly full. Not only would you have little need for a user interface with a script like this, but, even if you provided one, no one would be present to view it.

Many scripts have no need to display a user interface for other reasons as well:

- Users are not distracted by a user interface. Scripts can run in the background, and users can continue doing their work without interruption.

- Users cannot easily stop a script from running. Without a user interface, the only way to stop a script from running is to terminate the script process.

- Many scripts complete their tasks so quickly that a user interface would be superfluous. For example, a script that does nothing but verify that a particular service is still running can probably complete its job in one or two seconds. There is little need to construct a user interface for a script that will display that interface for only a second or two.

On the other hand, at times the lack of a user interface can be a disadvantage:

- It is difficult to tell what scripts, if any, are running on a computer. Even Task Manager is of little use in this regard: Task Manager will report how many instances of WScript or CScript are running on a computer, but it cannot tell you which scripts are running in those instances.

- It is impossible to tell how much progress, if any, a script is making. In fact, it is sometimes difficult to tell whether a script is even running or if it has become hung. For example, Task Manager reports how much CPU time a script is using, but even 0 percent does not mean a script has stopped responding; it might mean the script is waiting for data to arrive over the network.

In an enterprise setting, it is useful to know which scripts are running on a computer. For example, you might have a script that copies events from an event log. Depending on how the script has been written, it might take an hour or more to complete its task. If so, you probably do not want to inadvertently start a second copy of the script.

Likewise, if the script has stopped responding, you need to know that as soon as possible. That way, you can terminate the process and restart the script. Otherwise, you might wait for over an hour only to discover that the script has failed and must be restarted.

Although scripting languages provide little in the way of user interface elements, you can still track script progress either by taking advantage of Internet Explorer or by using the standard output capabilities of CScript.

Tracking Relative Progress

It is difficult to track absolute script progress — that is, to report that a script is 63 percent complete. Although this is possible in some cases, usually too many variables are involved to enable you to accurately predict when a script will finish. For example, anything from increased network traffic to a new process starting on the local computer can increase the amount of time required to complete a script.

Because of this, the progress indicators used in this chapter do one of two things: They simply note that a script is currently running, or they report relative progress. For example, the progress indicator might note that a connection is being made to a remote computer; after the connection is made, the indicator might note that data is being retrieved. However, no effort is made to estimate how long it will be before data retrieval is complete. Although it is possible to create progress indicators that do this, the code required for the progress indicator would be longer and more complex than the code required to carry out the primary function of the script.

Tracking Script Progress by Using Internet Explorer

If you feel that a script needs a progress indicator, it is recommended that you use a graphical progress indicator; after all, if visual cues are important, your progress indicator should be visually compelling. Perhaps the easiest way to add a graphical progress indicator to your scripts is to use Internet Explorer.

By the way, this is true even if the script runs in a command window under CScript; Internet Explorer can be instantiated and used as a progress indicator even if the script is running from the command line.

One way to indicate progress by using Internet Explorer is to display a message in the browser. In some cases, you might want to display a single message ("Please wait ….") and then have the message disappear when the script is finished. Alternatively, you might want to periodically change the message to reflect whatever the script is doing. For example, if you have a script that stopped a service, waited two minutes, and then restarted the service, you might display these messages in the browser:

- Stopping service….
- Waiting two minutes before restarting service….
- Restarting service….

Regardless of the number or the type of messages you choose to display, you can display custom messages within Internet Explorer by configuring the InnerHTML property of the document body. This replaces the entire document body with the specified text. For example, this code clears the document and displays the message, "Service retrieval in progress.":

```
objExplorer.Document.Body.InnerHTML = "Service retrieval in progress."
```

You can also use standard HTML tags to include formatting when setting the InnerHTML property. For example, this code uses the < B> tag to display the message in bold:

```
objExplorer.Document.Body.InnerHTML = "<B>Service information retrieved.</B>"
```

There are two important points to keep in mind when using Internet Explorer as a progress indicator:

- Closing Internet Explorer will not necessarily terminate the script. However, it is possible to code your script so that closing Internet Explorer will stop the script from running.

- If Internet Explorer is closed and your script attempts to manipulate the nonexistent object, an error will occur.

To prevent this, use On Error Resume Next statement within the script. Anytime you attempt to manipulate Internet Explorer, check the error number. If the error number is anything other than 0, that means a problem occurred, and it is likely that Internet Explorer is no longer available. In that case, you must decide whether you want your script to terminate itself, continue without a progress indicator, or generate a new instance of Internet Explorer.

For information about a way to overcome these problems, see "Stopping a Script When Internet Explorer Is Closed" in this chapter.

Scripting Steps

Listing 17.25 contains a script that tracks script progress by using Internet Explorer. To carry out this task, the script must perform the following steps:

1. Create an instance of Internet Explorer.

2. Open a blank Web page by navigating to "about:blank".

3. Configure the user interface settings, and then show Internet Explorer by setting the Visible property to True.

4. Set the InnerHTML property of the document to the message "Retrieving service information. This might take several minutes to complete."

5. Use a GetObject call to connect to the WMI namespace root\cimv2, and set the impersonation level to "impersonate."

6. Use the ExecQuery method to query the Win32_Service class.

    This query returns a collection consisting of all the services installed on the computer.

7. For each service in the collection, pause for 200 milliseconds. This is done simply to ensure that the progress indicator remains on the screen long enough for you to view it.

8. Set the InnerHTML property of the document to the message "Service information retrieved."

9. Pause for 3 seconds (3,000 milliseconds). This pause is inserted simply to give the user a chance to see the message that service information has been retrieved.

10. Use the Quit method to dismiss Internet Explorer.

Listing 17.25   Tracking Script Progress by Using Internet Explorer

```
1   Set objExplorer = CreateObject("InternetExplorer.Application")
2   objExplorer.Navigate "about:blank"
3   objExplorer.ToolBar = 0
4   objExplorer.StatusBar = 0
5   objExplorer.Width = 400
6   objExplorer.Height = 200
7   objExplorer.Left = 0
8   objExplorer.Top = 0
9   Do While (objExplorer.Busy)
10      Wscript.Sleep 200
11  Loop
12  objExplorer.Visible = 1
13  objExplorer.Document.Body.InnerHTML = "Retrieving service information. " _
14      & "This might take several minutes to complete."
15  strComputer = "."
16  Set objWMIService = GetObject("winmgmts:" _
17      & "{impersonationLevel=impersonate}!\\" & strComputer& "\root\cimv2")
18  Set colServices = objWMIService.ExecQuery _
19      ("SELECT * FROM Win32_Service")
20  For Each objService in colServices
21      Wscript.Sleep 200
22  Next
23  objExplorer.Document.Body.InnerHTML = "Service information retrieved."
24  Wscript.Sleep 3000
25  Wscript.Quit
```

Tracking Dynamic Script Progress by Using Internet Explorer

The script shown in Listing 17.26 displays a message when the script starts and then displays a second message when the script ends. To create a more dynamic progress bar, you might want to do something to indicate the intermediate steps taken by the script. This can be as simple as displaying an asterisk (*) inside the browser window each time a service is retrieved and acted upon.

To create a dynamic progress indicator, you can use the WriteLn method to write information to the browser each time the script takes a particular action. As a result, you end up with a progress indicator similar to the one shown in Figure 17.4. Each time a service is retrieved and acted upon, another asterisk is added to the browser window.

Figure 17.4 Tracking Dynamic Script Progress by Using Internet Explorer

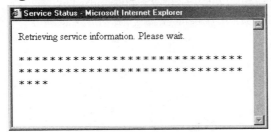

 Tip

By using different fonts, you can create a progress indicator that uses solid bars or dots rather than asterisks. For example, the letter "n" in the Wingdings font looks like this: ■.

Scripting Steps

Listing 17.26 contains a script that tracks script progress dynamically by using Internet Explorer. To carry out this task, the script must perform the following steps:

1. Create an instance of Internet Explorer.

2. Open a blank Web page by navigating to "about:blank".

3. Configure the user interface settings, and then show Internet Explorer by setting the Visible property to True.

4. Create a reference to the Internet Explorer Document object, and then use the Open method to make a connection to the Document object. This allows your script to use commands such as WriteLn to write information to the browser window.

5. Use the WriteLn method to create a title for the page, set the background color (bgcolor) to white, and create the message "Retrieving service information. Please wait." In addition to the message text, the HTML paragraph tag (<p>) is included. This ensures that the "progress bar" will be written on a separate line.

6. Use a GetObject call to connect to the WMI namespace root\cimv2, and set the impersonation level to "impersonate."

7. Use the ExecQuery method to query the Win32_Service class.

   This query returns a collection consisting of all the services installed on the computer.

8. For each service in the collection, use the WriteLn method to write an asterisk (*) in the browser window.

9. Use the WriteLn method to write the message "Service information retrieved" to the browser window.

10. Pause for 4 seconds (4,000 milliseconds). This pause is inserted simply to give the user a chance to see the message that service information has been retrieved.

11. Close the Document object, and use the Quit method to dismiss Internet Explorer.

Listing 17.26   Tracking Dynamic Script Progress by Using Internet Explorer

```
1   Set objExplorer = CreateObject("InternetExplorer.Application")
2   objExplorer.Navigate "about:blank"
3   objExplorer.ToolBar = 0
4   objExplorer.StatusBar = 0
5   objExplorer.Width = 400
6   objExplorer.Height = 200
7   objExplorer.Left = 0
8   objExplorer.Top = 0
9   objExplorer.Visible = 1
10
11  Do While (objExplorer.Busy)
12  Loop
13
14  Set objDocument = objExplorer.Document
15  objDocument.Open
16  objDocument.Writeln "<html><head><title>Service Status</title></head>"
17  objDocument.Writeln "<body bgcolor='white'>"
18  objDocument.Writeln "Retrieving service information. Please wait. <p>"
19
20  strComputer = "."
21  Set objWMIService = GetObject("winmgmts:" _
22      & "{impersonationLevel=impersonate}!\\" & strComputer& "\root\cimv2")
23  Set colServices = objWMIService.ExecQuery _
24      ("SELECT * FROM Win32_Service")
25
26  For Each objService in colServices
27      objDocument.Writeln "*"
28  Next
29
30  objDocument.Writeln "<br>Service information retrieved."
31  objDocument.Writeln "</body></html>"
32  Wscript.Sleep 4000
33  objDocument.Close
34  objExplorer.Quit
```

Changing the Mouse Pointer

If you are using Internet Explorer as a progress indicator, you might want to change the mouse pointer to an hourglass; this will help emphasize the fact that an operation is in progress. The mouse pointer can be configured by setting the cursor style to one of the values shown in Table 17.11.

Table 17.11   MousePointer Values

Value	Description
Crosshair	Simple crosshair.
Default	Platform-dependent default cursor; usually an arrow.
Hand	Hand with the first finger pointing up, as when the user moves the pointer over a link.
Help	Arrow with question mark, indicating that help is available.
Wait	Hourglass or watch, indicating that the program is busy and the user must wait.

To change the mouse pointer, create a reference to the Internet Explorer Document object, and then set the cursor style to the appropriate value. For example, to display an hourglass while the script runs, use this code:

```
Set objDocument = objIE.Document
objDocument.body.style.cursor = "wait"
```

To reset the cursor later in the script, use this code:

```
objDocument.body.style.cursor = "default"
```

Tracking Script Progress by Using an Animated .GIF

Because it is often difficult to report absolute script progress (for example, to note that a script is 37 percent complete), an alternative approach is to display a pseudo progress indicator that simply informs the user that an operation is in progress. For example, in Figure 17.5 an instance of Internet Explorer is used to note that a script operation is in progress. Instead of tracking the percentage of the operation that is complete, however, the dialog box merely displays a ticking clock and the message, "Please wait while service information is retrieved. This might take several minutes to complete."

Figure 17.5   Tracking Script Progress by Using an Animated .GIF

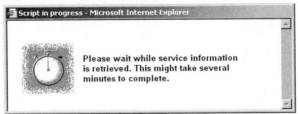

To use this type of progress indicator, start by creating an HTML file that includes both an animated GIF (for example, a ticking clock or a moving hourglass) and any other message you want the user to see. In your script, you create an instance of Internet Explorer and then use the Navigate method to open the HTML file. When the script completes, you then use the Quit method to close Internet Explorer.

Scripting Steps

Listing 17.27 contains a script that tracks script progress by displaying a pseudo progress indicator. This progress indicator is simply a Web page that includes an animated .GIF and a message asking the user to please wait. (The assumption is that you have already created this Web page.) To carry out this task, the script must perform the following steps:

1. Create an instance of Internet Explorer.

2. Open the HTML page by navigating to "file://c:\scripts\progress.htm".

3. Configure the user interface settings, and then show Internet Explorer by setting the Visible property to True.

4. Create a reference to the Internet Explorer Document object.

5. Set the cursor style to wait.

6. Pause for 5 seconds (5,000 milliseconds). This is done simply to keep the browser window open long enough for you to see the progress indicator.

7. Use the Quit method to dismiss Internet Explorer.

Listing 17.27   Using an Animated .GIF as a Progress Indicator

```
1   Set objIE = CreateObject("InternetExplorer.Application")
2   objIE.navigate "file://c:\scripts\progress.htm"
3   objIE.left=200
4   objIE.top=200
5   objIE.height=175
6   objIE.width=450
7   objIE.menubar=0
8   objIE.toolbar=0
9   objIE.addressbar=0
10  objIE.statusbar=0
11  objIE.visible=1
12  Do While (objIE.Busy)
13      Wscript.Sleep 200
14  Loop
15
16  Set objDocument = objIE.Document
17  objDocument.body.style.cursor = "wait"
18  Wscript.Sleep 5000
19  objIE.Quit
```

Tracking Script Progress in a Command Window

Running a script in a command window does not preclude you from using Internet Explorer as a way to track script progress; an Internet Explorer instance can be created and controlled from CScript in the same way it can be created and controlled from WScript.

At the same time, however, it is unusual for a command-line utility to generate a graphical progress indicator. Users might not recognize that the script running in the command window is tied to the progress indicator running in Internet Explorer. Because of this, you might want progress to be tracked in the same command window where the script is running.

Although you can track progress in a command window, there are at least two limitations:

- There are few formatting options available to you beyond using blank spaces and a mixture of lowercase and uppercase letters.

- You cannot erase the contents of the command window. For example, you might want to display a message such as, "Now completing Step 1 of 5." When this step is finished, you might want to erase the window and display, "Now completing Step 2 of 5." This cannot be done from a script. Even the **cls** command cannot be called from within a script; the command will run, but it will run within a new window that is automatically spawned. It will not clear the command window in which the script is running.

Of course, you can use Wscript.Echo to periodically display progress messages in a command window. For example, you might have script output that looks similar to this:

```
C:\Scripts>cscript services.vbs
Now completing Step 1 of 5.
Now completing Step 2 of 5.
Now completing Step 3 of 5.
Now completing Step 4 of 5.
```

Another approach commonly used with command-line utilities is to display a series of dots (periods) as a script progresses:

```
C:\Scripts>cscript services.vbs
Retrieving service information. This might take several minutes.
.........................................................................
```

Each time the script performs a subtask, a new dot is written to the command window. However, this cannot be done by using Wscript.Echo. Each time you call Wscript.Echo, the value is written to a new line. Because of this, your progress indicator would look like this:

```
C:\Scripts>cscript services.vbs
Retrieving service information. This might take several minutes.
.
.
.
.
```

To append text to the command window, you must instead use the Wscript.StdOut.Write method and write each new value to the standard output stream.

 Important

You can write to the standard output stream only if the script is running under CScript. If a script running under WScript attempts to write to the standard output stream, an "invalid handle" error will result.

Scripting Steps

Listing 17.28 contains a script that tracks script progress in a command window. To carry out this task, the script must perform the following steps:

1.   Echo the message, "Processing service information. This might take several minutes."

2.   Create a variable to specify the computer name.

3.   Use a GetObject call to connect to the WMI namespace root\cimv2, and set the impersonation level to "impersonate."

4.   Use the ExecQuery method to query the Win32_Service class.

     This query returns a collection consisting of all the services installed on the computer.

5.   For each service in the collection, use the Write method to write a period (.) to the standard output stream.

     A production script would probably do additional processing during this stage (for example, saving service information to a database). In this sample script, service information is retrieved but no additional action is taken.

6.   Use the WriteLine method to write a blank line to the standard output.

7.   Echo the message, "Service information processed."

Listing 17.28   Tracking Script Progress in a Command Window

```
1   Wscript.Echo "Processing information. This might take several minutes."
2   strComputer = "."
3   Set objWMIService = GetObject("winmgmts:" _
4       & "{impersonationLevel=impersonate}!\\" & strComputer& "\root\cimv2")
5   Set colServices = objWMIService.ExecQuery _
6       ("SELECT * FROM Win32_Service")
7   For Each objService in colServices
8       Wscript.StdOut.Write(".")
9   Next
10  Wscript.StdOut.WriteLine
11  Wscript.Echo "Service information processed."
```

Managing Scheduled Tasks

Scheduled tasks (also referred to as scheduled jobs) provide a way to schedule activities to run on a computer at specific days and at specific times. Because scheduled tasks are run by the Task Scheduler service, these tasks can be run regardless of whether a user is logged on to the computer.

Scheduled tasks are useful in several ways:

- They help ensure that important activities are carried out on a regular basis.

   If you need to run an inventory script every week, you can schedule the script to run automatically every Friday instead of sending out weekly reminders to users and relying on them to manually run the script.

- They help minimize disruptions to users and to the network.

   A backup program can require a considerable amount of processing power on a computer and use a considerable amount of network bandwidth. To minimize the impact of this program, you can schedule it to run late at night, when network traffic is at a minimum. Scheduled tasks will run even if no one is logged on to the computer.

- They are persistent.

   When you create a scheduled task, you create a file stored in a special folder (*systemroot*\Tasks). These files are not deleted unless you specifically delete them. As a result, scheduled tasks persist regardless of how many times a computer is restarted.

Comparing Win32_ScheduledJobs and the Task Scheduler

Working with scheduled tasks is complicated by the fact that Windows 2000 includes two sets of task-scheduling APIs:

- Task Scheduler APIs, used by the Scheduled Tasks wizard. These tasks cannot be scripted.
- AT APIs, used by At.exe. These tasks can be scripted using the WMI class Win32_ScheduledJob.

A comparison of the two kinds of task-scheduling APIs is shown in Table 17.12.

Table 17.12   Task-Scheduling APIs

Task Scheduler APIs	AT APIs
Tasks can run under any valid user account; you specify the account name and the password when you create the task.	Tasks must run under the same account as the scheduler service. By default, this is the LocalSystem account, although you can configure the service to run under a different account.
Tasks can be scheduled to start at logon, at system startup, or whenever the system is idle.	Tasks can be run only at specific times (for example, 3:00 P.M. every Tuesday).
Task durations can be specified. For example, you can schedule a task to run for one hour and then stop. This is useful for monitoring scripts: they can be scheduled to run for a specified amount of time, and then be shut down.	Task durations cannot be specified. To run a task for a specific amount of time (for example, one hour) you must include code within the task itself that will terminate the script at the appointed time.
Tasks can be given any file name (for example, Compact Database.job).	Tasks are automatically assigned a name that uses the format Atx.job, with x representing consecutive integers (At1.job, At2.job, At3.job, and so forth).
Tasks created using the Task Scheduler APIs are invisible to the Win32_ScheduledJob class.	Tasks created using the AT APIs can be opened and modified using Scheduled Tasks.

You cannot modify a task created using the AT APIs. Instead, you need to delete the task and then create a new one in its place. For example, to change a task scheduled to run on every Tuesday so that it instead runs every Friday, you need to delete the Tuesday task and then re-create the task, making sure that it is scheduled to run on Fridays.

You can use Scheduled Tasks to modify a task created by using the AT APIs. If you do this, however, that task will no longer be available to the Win32_ScheduledJob class. The task will still run, but you will not be able to enumerate or delete it by using WMI because the Scheduled Tasks tool adds properties to the job that are not supported by the AT APIs. The task will also "disappear" from WMI if you give it a name with any format other than At*x*.job.

Enumerating Scheduled Tasks

Scheduled tasks can save a great deal of work for administrators, especially if these tasks are well coordinated for minimal impact on users, computers, and the network. However, poorly planned scheduled tasks can cause a number of problems.

For example, if multiple tasks are scheduled to run at the same time, some tasks might interfere with other tasks. Likewise, CPU-intensive or network-intensive tasks scheduled to run at inopportune times might negatively affect users or the network.

To help ensure that tasks are carried out on a regular basis, but without adversely affecting users or the network, it is important for administrators to know which tasks are scheduled to run on their computers and when they are scheduled to run. Enumerating your scheduled tasks can help you minimize the impact of these activities on an individual computer and on the network as a whole.

The Win32_ScheduledJob class can be used to enumerate the following items about the scheduled tasks on a computer:

- Which task is scheduled to run.

- When the task is scheduled to run.

- What happened the last time the task was scheduled to run. (That is, did the task run as expected, or did it fail?)

Scheduled task properties available through the Win32_ScheduledJob class are shown in Table 17.13.

Table 17.13   Win32_ScheduledJob Properties

Property	Description
Caption	Short description (one-line string) of the task.
Command	Name of the command, batch program, or binary file (along with command-line arguments) that the schedule service will use to invoke the job. Example: "defrag /q /f"
DaysOfMonth	Days of the month when the job is scheduled to run. If a job is to run on multiple days of the month, these values can be joined in a logical OR. For example, if a job is to run on the 1st and 16th of each month, the value of the DaysOfMonth property will be 1 OR 32768. Values include: 1 – 1st 2 – 2nd 4 – 3rd 8 – 4th 16 – 5th 32 – 6th 64 – 7th 128 – 8th 256 – 9th 512 – 10th 1024 – 11th 2048 – 12th 4096 – 13th 8192 – 14th 16384 – 15th 32768 – 16th 65536 – 17th 131072 – 18th 262144 – 19th 524288 – 20th 1048576 – 21st 2097152 – 22nd 4194304 – 23rd 8388608 – 24th 16777216 – 25th 33554432 – 26th 67108864 – 27th 134217728 – 28th 268435456 – 29th 536870912 – 30th 1073741824 – 31st
Description	Description of the object.

(continued)

Table 17.13   Win32_ScheduledJob Properties *(continued)*

Property	Description
ElapsedTime	Length of time that the job has been executing.
InstallDate	Date the job was created.
InteractWithDesktop	Boolean value indicating that the specified job is interactive (meaning a user can give input to a scheduled job while it is executing).
JobID	Identifier number of the scheduled task.

JobStatus	Status of execution the last time this job was supposed to run. Values are:
	    Success
	    Failure

Notify	User to be notified upon job completion or failure.
Owner	User that submitted the job.
Priority	Urgency or importance of execution of a job.
RunRepeatedly	Scheduled job should run repeatedly on the days that the job is scheduled. If FALSE, the job is run once.

StartTime	UTC time to run the job, in the format:
	YYYYMMDDHHMMSS.MMMMMM±UUU
	Where YYYYMMDD must be replaced by ********.
	The replacement is necessary because the scheduling service allows jobs to be configured to run only once or to run on a day of the month or week. A job cannot be run on a specific date.
	For example, ********123000.000000–420 means that the task should run at 12:30 P.M. Pacific time with daylight saving time in effect.
	In the Universal Time Coordinate (UTC) format:
	    yyyy represents the year.
	    mm represents the month.
	    dd represents the day.
	    HH represents the hour (in 24-hour format).
	    MM represents the minutes.
	    SS represents the seconds.
	    xxxxxx represents the milliseconds.
	    ±UUU represents the number of minutes difference between the current time zone and Greenwich mean time.

TimeSubmitted	Time that the job was created.
UntilTime	Time after which the job is invalid or should be stopped.

Scripting Steps

Listing 17.29 contains a script that enumerates the scheduled tasks on a computer. To carry out this task, the script must perform the following steps:

1. Create a variable to specify the computer name.

2. Use a GetObject call to connect to the WMI namespace root\cimv2 on the computer, and set the impersonation level to "impersonate."

3. Use the ExecQuery method to query the Win32_ScheduledJob class.

   This query returns a collection consisting of all the scheduled tasks created for the computer.

4. For each scheduled task in the collection, echo the task properties.

Listing 17.29   Enumerating Scheduled Tasks

```
1    strComputer = "."
2    Set objWMIService = GetObject("winmgmts:" _
3        & "{impersonationLevel=impersonate}!\\" & strComputer & "\root\cimv2")
4    Set colScheduledJobs = objWMIService.ExecQuery _
5        ("SELECT * FROM Win32_ScheduledJob")
6    For Each objJob in colScheduledJobs
7        Wscript.Echo "Caption: " & objJob.Caption
8        Wscript.Echo "Command: " & objJob.Command
9        Wscript.Echo "Days Of Month: " & objJob.DaysOfMonth
10       Wscript.Echo "Days Of Week: " & objJob.DaysOfWeek
11       Wscript.Echo "Description: " & objJob.Description
12       Wscript.Echo "Elapsed Time: " & objJob.ElapsedTime
13       Wscript.Echo "Install Date: " & objJob.InstallDate
14       Wscript.Echo "Interact with Desktop: " & objJob.InteractWithDesktop
15       Wscript.Echo "Job ID: " & objJob.JobID
16       Wscript.Echo "Job Status: " & objJob.JobStatus
17       Wscript.Echo "Name: " & objJob.Name
18       Wscript.Echo "Notify: " & objJob.Notify
19       Wscript.Echo "Owner: " & objJob.Owner
20       Wscript.Echo "Priority: " & objJob.Priority
21       Wscript.Echo "Run Repeatedly: " & objJob.RunRepeatedly
22       Wscript.Echo "Start Time: " & objJob.StartTime
23       Wscript.Echo "Status: " & objJob.Status
24       Wscript.Echo "Time Submitted: " & objJob.TimeSubmitted
25       Wscript.Echo "Until Time: " & objJob.UntilTime
26   Next
```

Creating Scheduled Tasks

To run a program or script at a specified time on a specified date, you must create a scheduled task that contains the following information:

- Path to the program or script to be run.

- Days of the week on which the program or script is to be run.

- Time of day at which the program or script is to be run.

Scheduled tasks can be created on local computers by using the Scheduled Task Wizard. However, this wizard cannot be used to schedule tasks on remote computers (or to simultaneously schedule tasks on more than one computer). If you need to create scheduled tasks on remote or multiple computers, you can use the command-line tool At.exe or create a custom script by using the WMI class Win32_ScheduledJob.

The Win32_ScheduledJob Create method can be used to create scheduled tasks on a computer. The Create method requires the parameters shown in Table 17.14. Parameters not required for a specific task should be left blank.

Table 17.14   Win32_ScheduledJob Properties Available to the Create Method

Property	Description
Command	Name of the executable program, batch file, or script to be run.
StartTime	UTC time to run the job. This is of the form YYYYMMDDHHMMSS.MMMMMM(+-)000, where YYYYMMDD must be replaced by ********. Example: ********123000.000000-420, which implies 12:30 P.M. Pacific time with daylight saving time in effect.
RunRepeatedly	Indicates whether the scheduled job should run repeatedly on the days that the job is scheduled. The default is FALSE. This parameter is optional.
DaysOfWeek	Days of the week when the task should be run. Values are: 1 – Monday 2 – Tuesday 4 – Wednesday 8 – Thursday 16 – Friday 32 – Saturday 64 – Sunday To run the task on multiple days, use a logical OR to combine values. For example, to run a task on Tuesday, Thursday, and Saturday, use the following code: `2 OR 8 OR 32` To run a task on multiple days, you must set the RunRepeatedly parameter to True.
DaysOfMonth	Days of the month when the job is scheduled to run; used only when the RunRepeatedly parameter is True. This parameter is optional.

(continued)

Table 17.14   Win32_ScheduledJob Properties Available to the Create Method *(continued)*

Property	Description
InteractWithDesktop	Indicates whether the specified job should be interactive (meaning that a user can give input to the scheduled job while it is executing). The default is False. This parameter is optional and is rarely set to True. In general, the reason to use a scheduled task is to allow a task to be carried out without any user interaction.
JobID	Identifier number of the job. This parameter is a handle to the job being scheduled on this computer.

When a scheduled task is created, one of the error codes shown in Table 17.15 is returned, indicating the success or failure of the procedure.

Table 17.15   Win32_ScheduledJob Error Codes

Error Code	Description
0	The scheduled task was successfully created.
1	The request is not supported.
2	The user did not have the necessary access.
8	Interactive Process.
9	The directory path to the service executable file was not found.
21	Invalid parameters have been passed to the service.
22	The account under which this service is to run either is invalid or lacks the permissions to run the service.

Scripting Steps

Listing 17.30 contains a script that schedules a task on a computer. To carry out this task, the script must perform the following steps:

1. Create the constant RUN_REPEATEDLY and set the value to True.

    This constant will be used to indicate that the scheduled task should run repeatedly. If set to False, the scheduled task will run once and then never run again.

2. Create the constants MONDAY, WEDNESDAY, and FRIDAY and set the respective values to 1, 4, and 16.

    These constants represent the days of the week when the script is scheduled to run.

3. Use a GetObject call to connect to the WMI service.

4. Retrieve an instance of the Win32_ScheduledJob class.

5. Call the Create method, specifying the following:

- Name of the executable file or script to be scheduled.

  In this example, the file is Monitor.exe.

- The time that the task is scheduled to run (12:30 P.M.) in UTC format. The eight asterisks indicate that the year, month, and day are irrelevant. Only the time itself (123000, meaning 12:30:00) is important.

- Whether the job should run repeatedly or just once.

  The constant RUN_REPEATEDLY, with the value True, means that the job should run repeatedly.

- The days of the week on which the job should run.

  The constants MONDAY, WEDNESDAY, and FRIDAY indicate the days of the week when the task should run.

- The days of the month on which the job should run.

  This parameter is left blank because the job is scheduled to run on specific days of the week.

- Whether the task needs to interact with the user.

  This parameter is left blank because the task does not need to interact with the user.

- The variable name (JobID) that will hold the identification number assigned to the new job.

6. If the operation succeeded, echo the Job ID assigned to the new task.

Listing 17.30   Scheduling a Task

```
1   strComputer = "."
2   Set objService = GetObject("winmgmts:" & strComputer)
3   Set objNewJob = Service.Get("Win32_ScheduledJob")
4   errJobCreated = objNewJob.Create _
5       ("Monitor.exe", "********123000.000000-420", _
6           True , 1 OR 4 OR 16, , , JobID)
7   If Err.Number = 0 Then
8       Wscript.Echo "New Job ID: " & JobID
9   Else
10      Wscript.Echo "An error occurred: " & errJobCreated
11  End If
```

Deleting Scheduled Tasks

When a scheduled task is no longer needed on a computer, it should be deleted. If a task is not deleted, it will continue to run as scheduled. This can create problems that might be a minor irritant (running a monitoring program whose data is no longer needed) or that might be extremely destructive (deleting files and folders that should not be deleted).

Scheduled tasks can be deleted using the Win32_ScheduledJob Delete method. There are two ways to delete scheduled tasks:

- **Delete a single scheduled task.** To delete a single scheduled task, your script needs to connect to the specific task (using the JobID as a unique identifier) and then call the Delete method.

- **Delete all the scheduled tasks on a computer.** To delete all the scheduled tasks on a computer, your script needs to retrieve a list of all the scheduled tasks, connect to each one, and then individually delete each task.

Scripting Steps

There are multiple ways to delete scheduled tasks:

- Deleting a single scheduled task.
- Deleting all the scheduled tasks on a computer.

Deleting a single scheduled task

Listing 17.31 contains a script that deletes a scheduled task on a computer. To carry out this task, the script must perform the following steps:

1. Use a GetObject call to connect to the WMI service.

2. Retrieve the instance of the Win32_ScheduledJob class where the JobID = 1.

   JobID is a unique identifier for the specific task. The file name in this case is At1.job.

3. Use the Delete method to delete the job.

Listing 17.31   Deleting a Single Scheduled Task

```
1  strComputer = "."
2  Set objService = GetObject("winmgmts:\\" & strComputer)
3  Set objInstance = objService.Get("Win32_ScheduledJob.JobID=1")
4  objInstance.Delete
```

Deleting all the scheduled tasks on a computer

Listing 17.32 contains a script that deletes all the scheduled tasks on a computer. To carry out this task, the script must perform the following steps:

1. Use a GetObject call to connect to the WMI service.

2. Use a second GetObject call to connect to the Win32_ScheduledJob class.

3.   For each scheduled job, store the JobID in the variable intJobID.

4.   Connect to the individual job, specifying the value of intJobID as the JobId.

Because the Delete method will not work on a collection, you must individually connect to each scheduled task and then use the Delete methods to remove the tasks one by one.

5.   Use the Delete method to delete the scheduled task.

Listing 17.32   Deleting All the Scheduled Tasks on a Computer

```
1    strComputer = "."
2    Set objService = GetObject("winmgmts:\\" & strComputer)
3    Set colScheduledTasks = objService.ExecQuery _
4        ("SELECT * FROM Win32_ScheduledJob")
5    For Each objTask in colScheduledTasks
6        intJobID = objTask.JobID
7        Set objInstance = objService.Get_
8            ("Win32_ScheduledJob.JobID=" & intJobID & "")
9        objInstance.Delete
10   Next
```

Scripting Guidelines

Many system administrators who write scripts work as part of a team. This means it is important that the code they write follow accepted standards and conventions, making it easy to read and understand. By following a defined set of scripting guidelines, you can write clean, consistent code that your team can easily read, understand, and maintain. The standards presented in this chapter help you create high-quality scripts to use on the Microsoft® Windows® 2000 family of operating systems.

In This Chapter

Overview of Scripting Guidelines 1148
Using Naming Conventions 1148
Constructing Scripts 1157
Formatting Code 1165
    Commenting Scripts 1175
Debugging and Troubleshooting Scripts 1184
Testing Scripts 1188

Overview of Scripting Guidelines

When you write a script, you should always consider how the script might be used in the future. Some scripts are disposable by design: they are written once, they are run once, and then they are never used again. These scripts might resolve unique situations, or be so short and easy to write that there is no need to maintain them. Should the need arise again, you can easily re-create the script. This is one of the benefits of scripting: you can make the process as formal or as informal as needed.

Other scripts might be run repeatedly or be copied and used by other administrators. These administrators might need to modify the scripts to fit their own needs. At the very least, they will probably want to view the script code so they can better understand what the script actually does, and how. In these situations, it is a good idea if your scripts follow accepted organizational standards for such things as commenting, formatting, and naming; following these standards makes it easier for others to read, modify, and maintain the scripts.

As you read this chapter, keep in mind that everything suggested here is just that: a suggestion. You need not implement each guideline in every script; after all, a two-line script that maps a network drive probably does not need a 12-line script header and multiline comments. The first rule of script writing is: Never make things more complicated than they need to be.

Preparing for Visual Basic .NET

The scripts used in this chapter are written in Microsoft® Visual Basic® Scripting Edition (VBScript). Throughout this chapter, you will find notes that compare VBScript with the .NET programming languages (in particular, Microsoft® Visual Basic® .NET). If you plan to move to Visual Basic .NET, keep these notes in mind when you choose scripting guidelines for your organization, Although the scripts you write now cannot be copied as is into Visual Basic .NET, it is easier to manually convert scripts if you adopt the .NET standards now.

Using Naming Conventions

In many organizations, names of assets — whether they are buildings, computers, printers, or some other asset — follow a standardized convention. For example, a computer name might consist of the name of the primary user followed by the user department. These conventions provide at least two advantages. First, the name alone gives you important information about the item; by itself, the computer name kenmeyer-finance tells you that this computer belongs to Ken Meyer in the Finance department. Second, this convention takes the guesswork out of naming new assets; when Pilar Ackerman in Accounting gets a new computer, coming up with a name for this computer requires very little effort.

Scripts are no different than these other assets; it can be advantageous to use standard, consistent, and meaningful names for scripts and for the variables, constants, functions, and procedures used in those scripts. These naming conventions help make your scripts easier to read, understand, and maintain.

Table 18.1 contains a brief overview of naming conventions in scripting. These conventions are discussed in more detail later in this chapter.

Table 18.1 Naming Conventions in Scripting

Item	Naming Convention	Example
Script file name	As short as practicable, with no spaces or special characters in the name. Capitalize the first letter of each word in the name.	CreateOU.vbs
Variable	Meaningful name that reflects the purpose of the variable and the data it stores. The first word in the name should be a prefix indicating the type of data stored in the variable. The prefix should begin with a lowercase letter, and all subsequent words should begin with an uppercase letter.	intNumberOfFileServers
Constant	All uppercase letters. Separate individual words with underscores, except for constants that are intrinsic to a language or to an automation object. In those cases, follow the naming convention used by the language or the automation object. For example, use VbTab rather than VB_TAB.	DOMAIN_NAME
Function or Procedure	Verb followed by the noun that the verb acts upon. Capitalize all words in the name.	DeleteBackupFiles

Naming Scripts

If you are like most people, you consider the 8.3 naming convention (file names consisting of no more than 8 letters, followed by a three-letter file extension) to be a bygone relic of the distant past. Admittedly, there is probably no need to limit file names to the 8.3 naming convention; however, there are good reasons for keeping file names as short as possible and for not including spaces or special characters in those names. Although the name "Create an Exchange mailbox for a new user.vbs" clearly indicates the purpose of the script, long file names can create problems for system administrators who actually use the script. For example, to run a script named "NewMailbox.vbs" from the command line, you need only type the following:

```
newmailbox.vbs
```

By contrast, it takes more time to type a long file name such as the following:

```
"create an exchange mailbox for a new user.vbs"
```

Not only does this require additional typing, but using spaces in the name requires you to enclose the command in quotation marks. This can make it difficult for an administrator with limited command shell experience to run the script; he or she might not know that the file name must be enclosed in quotation marks. If the script requires arguments that must also be enclosed in quotation marks, the command-line string becomes even more complicated, and the chances of making an error are even greater.

Tip

Because long command-line strings are difficult to remember, and even more difficult to type in correctly, you should also limit command-line arguments to single letters. Typing a command such as **sample.vbs /?** is easier and faster than typing **sample.vbs /help**. Similarly, use standard command-line arguments such as **sample.vbs /?**. Do not invent for your own "standard," such as **sample.vbs /more_info**.

File or path names with spaces also make calling scripts and batch files from Windows Script Host (WSH) more difficult. As shown in the following code sample, starting a second script from WSH is easy when the path name does not contain spaces.

```
Const VbNormalFocus = 1
Set objShell = Wscript.CreateObject("Wscript.Shell")
intApplicationStarted = objShell.Run("C:\Scripts\CreateUsers.vbs", _
    vbNormalFocus, True)
```

This same call is more difficult when there is a space in the path name because the Run method requires you to enter the path exactly as you would from the command prompt. When entering commands from the command prompt, you must enclose path names that include spaces in double quotation marks as follows:

```
"c:\scripts\create users.vbs"
```

Because the Run method also requires double quotation marks around the path name, you must use *three* sets of double quotation marks to start the application. This makes the statement more difficult to write and more difficult to maintain:

```
Const VbNormalFocus = 1
Set objShell = Wscript.CreateObject("Wscript.Shell")
intApplicationStarted = objShell.Run("""C:\Scripts\Create Users.vbs""", _
    vbNormalFocus, True)
```

As you might expect, it is also a good idea to avoid using spaces in folder names and to keep scripts in top-level folders whenever possible. Typing **C:\Scripts\CreateUsers.vbs** is much faster and easier than typing **"C:\Program Files\Administrative Tools \Domain Admins\Scripts\Active Directory\User Management\Create Users.vbs."**

Naming Variables

If you were writing a novel, it is unlikely that you would give every character the same name. Although the storyline would not change, the plot in such a novel would be very difficult, if not downright impossible, to follow. That is at least one reason why novelists give their characters unique — and sometimes very meaningful — names.

In the same way, the use of unique and meaningful variable names can make your scripts much easier for others to read and understand. For example, the following script snippet includes a mathematical equation. You cannot easily tell if this equation is correct because the script uses variables named x and y. To make things even more confusing, the variable x is used not only as one of the items in the equation but also to represent the end result of the equation. This is allowed in VBScript but not recommended; reusing variables often causes confusion for people maintaining a script.

```
x = 2
y = 4
x = x * y
```

Compare the preceding script to the following script snippet. Although the scripts perform the identical function, meaningful variable names greatly improve readability. Furthermore, each variable represents only one item. As a result, it is very easy to look at this script and verify that the equation is correct.

```
Length = 2
Width = 4
Area = Length * Width
```

The preceding script uses variable names that clearly indicate what each variable represents. Keep in mind that even a variable with a name such as UserInfo can cause confusion because it does not indicate what kind of data should be stored in it. More descriptive names, such as UserMonthlySalary, UserIDNumber, and UserLastName, are less likely to cause confusion.

Using Hungarian Notation

It is also helpful if variable names indicate the type of data stored in the variable. Variable names such as strUserLastName indicate not only that the variable stores the user's last name but also that this name is made up of string data. This type of naming scheme is commonly referred to as *Hungarian Notation*.

 Note

The term "Hungarian notation" was coined in honor of former Microsoft Distinguished Engineer Charles Simonyi, who first proposed this method of naming variables. The term was chosen both in deference to Simonyi's Hungarian nationality and to the fact that resulting variable names — such as strUserLastName — did not always resemble English. The Hungarian Notation used in this chapter has been slightly modified from the original version to better meet the needs of script writers.

Hungarian notation is based on the premise that the name of a variable should tell you everything you need to know about that variable. In addition to describing the purpose of the variable, variable names have a prefix that indicates the type of data that the variable holds. This is especially important with VBScript because VBScript is a *typeless* language: VBScript variables can hold any type of data, making it easy to inadvertently store the wrong data in a variable.

For example, by looking at the variable named UserID, you cannot tell whether a value such as ACCT-1005 is a valid ID. If UserID can contain string data, ACCT-1005 might be valid. If UserID can contain only numeric data, however, ACCT-1005 is not valid.

By adding a prefix that indicates the type of data stored in the variable, you can more easily identify problems that occur when the wrong type of data is stored in a variable. Because VBScript is a typeless language, nothing prevents you from storing an improper value in the variable. However, when you are debugging a script that is not working properly, noticing that a variable named intUserID has the value ACCT-1005 immediately provides at least one reason why the script is not working. Assigning improper data types to a variable also causes problems when dealing with databases, which typically require the correct data type, and when carrying out mathematical equations, date conversions, or other functions that require specific kinds of data.

When naming variables using Hungarian Notation, format the variable names using *Camel casing*. With Camel casing, the first part of the variable name (the prefix that indicates the data type) should begin with a lowercase letter. All subsequent words in the name then begin with an uppercase letter. Consequently, variables have names such as intUserID and strUserLastName rather than IntUserID or struserlastname.

Table 18.2 lists various data subtypes recognized by VBScript, as well as the recommended prefix for variables designed to store each kind of data.

Table 18.2   Recommended Prefixes for VBScript Data Subtypes

Subtype	Description	Prefix	Example
Empty	Variable is not initialized. Value is 0 for numeric variables or a zero-length string ("") for string variables.		
Null	Variable intentionally contains no valid data.		
Boolean	Contains either True or False.	bln	blnIsUSCititzen
Byte	Contains an integer in the range 0 to 255.	byt	bytDepartmentNumber
Integer	Contains an integer in the range –32,768 to 32,767.	int	intNumberOfDirectReports
Currency	–922,337,203,685,477.5808 to 922,337,203,685,477.5807.	cur	curAnnualSalary
Long	Contains an integer in the range -2,147,483,648 to 2,147,483,647.	lng	lngSalesByDepartment
Single	Contains a single-precision floating-point number in the range –3.402823E38 to -1.401298E–45 for negative values; 1.401298E–45 to 3.402823E38 for positive values.	sng	sngHourlyPayRate
Double	Contains a double-precision floating-point number in the range -1.79769313486232E308 to – 4.94065645841247E–324 for negative values; 4.94065645841247E–324 to 1.79769313486232E308 for positive values.	dbl	dblMeritPayMulitplier
Date (Time)	Contains a date between January 1, 100 and December 31, 9999.	dtm	dtmHireDate
String	Contains a variable-length string. Strings can be made up of any alphanumeric characters.	str	strUserLastName
Object	Contains an object reference. An object variable represents an Automation object.	obj	objExcelSpreadsheet

(continued)

Table 18.2   Recommended Prefixes for VBScript Data Subtypes *(continued)*

Subtype	Description	Prefix	Example
Error	Contains an error number.	err	errFindFile
Array	Contains an array of variables. Because arrays are designed to hold multiple objects, array names should always be plural. To maintain consistency with the other naming conventions, arrays should have two prefixes: **arr** to indicate the array, and a second prefix to indicate the data type.	arr	arrstrUserAccountNames
Collection	Technically, a collection is not a variable subtype. However, it is listed in this table because you should use the **col** prefix to indicate collections. Collections are used extensively in system administration scripting.	col	colInstalledApplications

Guidelines for Naming Variables

Both Hungarian notation and Camel casing provide basic rules for creating variable names. In addition to these fundamental principles, some other suggested guidelines for naming variables in VBScript are listed in Table 18.3.

Table 18.3   Naming Guidelines for VBScript Variables

Variable Property	Guidelines
Length	Can be a maximum of 255 characters. However, variable names should be considerably shorter (32 characters or less). Shorter names are easier to read and easier to maintain. (Among other things, they take up less space on each line of code.)
First character	Must begin with an alphabetic character. A variable name such as User5 is allowed; a variable name such as 5User is not.
Special characters	Must not contain periods or spaces. Characters used in variable names should be limited to the following: a–z A–Z 0–9 In addition, variable names should start with one of the lowercase alphabetic characters (a–z).
Case sensitivity	Not case sensitive. intUserID and INTUSERID refer to the same variable value. However, it is recommended that you use Camel casing for all your variable names.

(continued)

Table 18.3 Naming Guidelines for VBScript Variables *(continued)*

Variable Property	Guidelines
Uniqueness	Must be unique in the scope in which they are declared. VBScript allows you to use the same variable name more than once, provided the variables have different scopes (for example, they are declared within separate procedures or in separate scripts used as part of a library). You must, however, use unique global variable names throughout a script.
Consistency	Many scripts require the same variables; for example, every Windows Management Instrumentation (WMI) script requires an object variable that represents the WMI service. Whenever possible, these names should be consistent among scripts; if you use the variable name objWMIService in the first WMI script you write, use that same variable name in any subsequent WMI scripts.

Reusing Variables

For the most part, you should not reuse variables during the execution of a script; each variable should represent only one item. For example, the following script code is valid. However, using the variable strName to represent, at various times, the user's first name, the user's middle initial, and the user's last name causes confusion.

```
strName = "Robert"
strName = "M."
strName = "Smith"
```

To lessen confusion, use separate variables to represent each piece of data, as shown in the following script snippet. The code is easier to read and maintain, and there is no appreciable performance penalty for using three separate variables as opposed to reusing the same variable.

```
strFirstName = "Robert"
strMiddleInitial = "M."
strLastName = "Smith"
```

Theoretically, reusing variables can help conserve memory. In the preceding script snippet, the variables strFirstName, strMiddleInitial, and strLastName must all be held in memory at the same time, even if they are used just once and then discarded. However, the amount of memory saved by reusing the same variable as opposed to using three separate variables is negligible. Memory conservation is usually not an issue in system administration scripts.

Loop variables, such as those in a For-Next loop, are an exception to this rule about never reusing variable names. Many script writers use **i** as the primary loop variable in scripts; additional, nested, loop variables take the values **j**, **k**, **l**, **m**, and so on. For example, the following script code includes two separate loops, both of which use **i** as the loop variable:

```
For i = 1 to 10
    Wscript.Echo i
Next

For i = 1 to 10
    intTotalCount = intTotalCount + i
Next
Wscript.Echo intTotalCount
```

Naming Constants

Constants provide meaningful names for values that cannot be changed while a script runs. User-defined constants are typically named using all uppercase letters, with underscores separating individual words in the constant (for example, NUMBER_OF_DEPARTMENTS or STATE_SALES_TAX). This formatting convention indicates that NUMBER_OF_DEPARTMENTS is a constant and thus cannot be changed at any point during the running of a script. Trying to change the value of a constant while a script is running results in an error. Because constants are not the same thing as variables, it makes sense to format their names in a different manner.

Scripting languages, automation objects, type libraries and other similar entities typically include intrinsic constants as well. For those intrinsic constants, follow the naming convention used in the language or object's documentation. For example, VBScript includes such intrinsic constants as VbGeneralDate (used in formatting dates) and VbAbortRetryIgnore (used in constructing message boxes). You should use these names rather than names such as VB_GENERAL_DATE.

Naming Functions and Procedures

Functions and procedures are sections of code that carry out specific actions; in most cases, functions and procedures are employed because these actions must be carried out repeatedly during the running of the script. For example, you might have a script that needs to connect to the WMI service on several different computers. Instead of repeating that same code over and over again, you might place this code in a function or procedure. Each time you need to connect to the WMI service on a new computer, you simply call the function or procedure, passing along the name of the computer as a parameter.

Because functions and procedures carry out actions, the names given to these elements should begin with a verb that indicates the action to be performed. This verb should then be followed by a noun representing the object on which the action occurs. For example, CalculateMeritPay indicates the action that is taken (Calculate) and the object that is acted upon (MeritPay).

It is recommended that you use *Pascal casing*, in which each word begins with an uppercase letter, to help distinguish functions and procedures from variables and constants. Thus, use ConvertToKilograms rather than convertToKilograms.

Constructing Scripts

One of the strengths of the telephone directory is that no user manual is required to read and use it; this is because the telephone directory is laid out in a consistent and logical manner. In most U.S. communities, for example, telephone directories have a set of blue pages that contain information about schools and government agencies. These directories always feature a set of white pages that contain residential phone numbers. Phone numbers are sorted by the name of the resident, and are presented in alphabetical order, from A to Z. Telephone directories also contain a set of yellow pages that include business listings, this time ordered by the business category (Hairdressers, Sporting Goods, and so forth). No matter how big the directory, you can find phone numbers with relative ease, because you know exactly where to look for that information. Unlike, say, mystery novels, telephone directories are specifically designed to keep the suspense to a minimum.

To make your scripts easy to read and maintain, consider using a similarly consistent and logical structure. Although scripts vary depending on their nature and complexity, longer scripts might include the following sections:

- **Initialization section.** Used for declaring variables and defining constants, the initialization section should always come first in a script.

   This section might also be needed to parse command-line arguments and to ensure that the script is running under the proper script host. If necessary, these actions should always occur before the script does anything else. If your script requires three command-line arguments and cannot complete successfully without all three, the script should verify the existence of those arguments before doing anything else. Never carry out half the functions in a script before verifying whether the script can complete successfully.

- **Main body.** To perform the primary actions of the script, some scripts include lines of code in the main body. Other scripts might use the main body as a starting point to call procedures and functions that perform the primary actions of the script. This approach is typically used for long scripts that carry out many activities.

- **Procedures and functions.** It is useful to place blocks of code used repeatedly to perform specific actions (for example, creating a user account or converting Fahrenheit temperatures to Celsius) in a function or procedure. That way, the script writer does not have to write the same code multiple times in a script.

It is also a good idea to list procedures and functions in the same order in which they are called. This is not required; placing a procedure in one location rather than another does not affect performance. In fact, before a script is run, the script host checks the file and identifies the location of all functions and procedures. As a result, the script host can find each function and procedure regardless of its location in the script, and regardless of the order in which the functions and procedures are called. However, placing procedures strategically makes it much easier for others to read and maintain your script.

Choosing a Script Construction

Although scripts often include an initialization section, a main body, and a set of functions and procedures, you can arrange those elements in different ways. As you might expect, some of these arrangements are better than others, depending on the length and complexity of the script. For example, scripts that span hundreds of lines and need to use the same code over and over benefit from a construction in which repeated code is placed in individual functions. By contrast, functions and procedures can needlessly complicate shorter scripts that perform only a single task. For example, placing the following code in a function does nothing to help the performance of the script and only makes a simple script much more complex:

```
Wscript.Echo AddTwoNumbers
Function AddTwoNumbers
    AddTwoNumbers=2+2
End Function
```

This same script can be written as follows:

```
Wscript.Echo 2+2
```

Table 18.4 lists advantages and disadvantages of several different scripting formats.

Table 18.4 Advantages and Disadvantages of Various Scripting Formats

Script Construction	Advantages	Disadvantages
Scripts that do not call any functions or procedures	<ul><li>Easiest way to write a script</li><li>Good choice for small scripts (less than 100 lines) that do not repeatedly call the same functions or procedures</li></ul>	<ul><li>Difficult to identify key components of the script</li><li>Can result in needless duplication if the same lines of code are used repeatedly</li><li>Difficult to create script libraries because there are no procedures in the script</li></ul>
Scripts that scatter functions and procedures throughout the script	<ul><li>None</li></ul>	<ul><li>Results in code that is extremely difficult to read and maintain</li><li>Not recommended under any circumstances</li></ul>
Scripts constructed as follows: 1. Initialization section 2. Main body of the script 3. All functions and procedures	<ul><li>Easy to read and understand</li><li>Script logically organized</li></ul>	<ul><li>Requires readers to flip back and forth between the main body and called functions or procedures</li><li>Might not be needed in shorter scripts unless a function or procedure is called multiple times</li></ul>
Scripts constructed as follows: 1. Initialization section 2. All functions and procedures 3. Main body of the script.	<ul><li>Makes it easy to identify the primary operations that are carried out by the script</li></ul>	<ul><li>Can be difficult to follow the scripting logic; anyone reading the script needs to search for the main body</li></ul>
Scripts constructed as follows: 1. Initialization section 2. A single statement calling the procedure Main (which contains the main body of the script) 3. Remaining functions and procedures	<ul><li>Follows the formatting conventions used in many programming languages, including the Visual Basic .NET languages</li></ul>	<ul><li>Requires readers to flip back and forth between the main body and called functions or procedures</li></ul>

Creating a Script Template

Templates provide a framework for entering data. When you order office supplies, you probably fill out a form of some kind. Rather than obligate you to guess at the information, and the format, required, the form will be presented to you as a template, a framework that tells you what information is required and where this information must be placed.

Script writers also need to know what information is required when they write a script, and they need to know to know how this information must be presented. A script template can help script writers adhere to organizational standards.

A script template contains placeholders predefined to fit a standard format. For example, your template might include placeholders for the script header, the initialization section, the parsing of command-line arguments, and other key sections. You might create several different templates for various script types. For example, you might have a template for Active Directory Service Interfaces (ADSI) scripts that includes all the predefined constants and procedures required to connect to your directory service.

The following is a sample script template:

```
'***********************************************************************
'* Microsoft Windows 2000 Scripting Guide
'* Chapter Name:     CHAPTER_NAME_GOES_HERE
'* Sample Listing:   CHAPTER_NUMBER_GOES_HERE.LISTING_NUMBER_GOES_HERE
'* File:             NAME_OF_SCRIPT_FILE_GOES_HERE
'* Purpose:          This script demonstrates ADDITIONAL_DESCRIPTION_GOES_HERE
'* Usage:            COMMAND_LINE_USAGE_GOES_HERE
'* Version:          1.0 (MONTH_GOES_HERE 2002)
'* Technology:       VBSCRIPT_WMI_ADSI_ETC._GOES_HERE
'* Requirements:     Windows 2000
'*                   Windows Script Host 5.6 - CSCRIPT.EXE_OR_WSCRIPT.EXE
'* Copyright (C) 2002 Microsoft Corporation
'* History:
'***********************************************************************


Option Explicit


'********************
'* Define Constants
'********************


'********************
'* Declare variables
'********************
```

These templates are particularly useful when they are available through the context menu in Windows Explorer. In Windows Explorer, you can right-click a blank area in the window, point to **New**, and then choose from various predefined document types (including **Text Document**, **Bitmap Image**, and **Wave Sound**). When you click one of these document types, a new, blank document of that type is created for you; for example, if you click **Text Document**, a new text-only document named **New Text Document.txt** is created for you.

By creating a script template and adding it to the Windows Explorer context menu, you can create a new script, based on the template, simply by clicking a blank area within Windows Explorer, pointing to **New**, and then clicking the template. By making a template readily, and universally, accessible, you make it more likely that system administrators and other script writers within your organization will use it.

To create a template and add it to the Windows Explorer context menu:

1. Develop the format in Notepad, and then save the file in the *systemroot*\ShellExt folder. In the example shown, the file is saved as C:\Windows\System32\ShellExt\Template.vbs.

2. After you save the file, add the template to the New context menu. When the template is added to the New context menu, you can create a new VBScript file based on the template by right-clicking anywhere inside a folder, pointing to **New**, and then clicking **VBScript Script File**.

3. To add your template to the context menu, create a new registry entry referencing the template you just created, as shown in Listing 18.1.

Listing 18.1 Creating a Registry Entry

```
1  Set objShell = CreateObject("WScript.Shell")
2  objShell.RegWrite "HKCR\.VBS\ShellNew\FileName","template.vbs"
```

Using Functions and Procedures

Many shorter scripts (those with fewer than 100 lines) are written without using any functions or procedures. Instead, the actions carried out by the script are performed in linear fashion in the main body of the script. This is the recommended way to write short scripts; needlessly wrapping code in a function that is called only once merely makes the script longer, more difficult to read, and harder to maintain.

When working with longer scripts, however, you should place your code in separate functions and procedures whenever possible, and for the following reasons:

- **Functions and procedures easily identify the tasks performed by the script.** Without functions and procedures, you must read each line of code just to determine the actions carried out by the script. By using procedures and functions, it is easier to skim through the code and pick out the major tasks.

- **Functions and procedures prevent needless duplication of code.** If you find yourself repeating the same lines of code in a script, encapsulate them in a function or procedure. Needless duplication of code creates extra work and can lead to problems if you revise the code and miss one of the instances where the code is used in the script.

- **Functions and procedures make your code portable and reusable.** After you write code that successfully performs a task, it is likely to be copied and used in other scripts in your organization. Placing your code in a function or procedure makes the relevant statements easier to identify and copy.

- **Functions and procedures allow your code to be encapsulated in code libraries.** *Include files* are blocks of code that are imported into a script at run time. These files can be referenced in WSH scripts through the use of Windows Script Files.

  Include files enable you to create *scripting libraries*, collections of code snippets that carry out particular tasks. For example, you might have code that parses command-line arguments. The next time you write a script that requires command-line arguments, you can write a single statement that calls the appropriate script in the code library. Writing the initial code as a function or procedure makes it easier to remove the code from the script itself, place it in a code library, and make it readily available to other scripts and script writers.

- **Functions and procedures make your code easier to test, troubleshoot, and debug.** Functions and procedures help you control the lines of code that are actually run during testing. For example, if you suspect your script is encountering problems with a certain block of code, you can comment out calls to other functions and procedures and then test only that block of code.

Calling Functions and Procedures

VBScript provides multiple ways to call functions and procedures. Some require parentheses around parameters; others do not. This is important, because improperly called functions and procedures can either result in errors within the script or, perhaps worse, cause subtle changes that affect the data returned by the script.

Valid ways of calling functions and procedures and passing parameters are shown in Table 18.5. For more information about passing parameters by value and by reference, see "VBScript Primer" in this book.

Table 18.5 Calling Functions and Procedures by Passing Parameters

Passing Mechanism	Syntax
By reference	<ul><li>MyProcedure strVariable</li><li>MyProcedure strVariable, intVariable</li><li>Call MyProcedure (strVariable)</li><li>Call MyProcedure (strVariable, intVariable)</li><li>Return = MyProcedure(strVariable)</li><li>Return = MyProcedure (strVariable, intVariable)</li></ul>

(continued)

Table 18.5 Calling Functions and Procedures by Passing Parameters *(continued)*

Passing Mechanism	Syntax
By value	<ul><li>MyProcedure (strVariable)</li><li>MyProcedure ((strVariable))</li><li>Call MyProcedure ((strVariable))</li><li>Return = MyProcedure((strVariable))</li></ul>
First parameter by reference, second parameter by value	<ul><li>MyProcedure (strVariable), intVariable</li><li>Call MyProcedure((strVariable), intVariable)</li><li>Return = MyProcedure((strVariable), intVariable)</li></ul>

Note

Preparing for Visual Basic .NET. As shown in Table 18.5, the Call statement can be used with VBScript. Because Call is optional in VBScript, and because it cannot be used in Visual Basic .NET, it is recommended that you not use this statement when calling functions and procedures.

Calling functions and procedures in multiple ways can lead to considerable confusion and errors within the script. For example, an error occurs if you use a syntax that inadvertently passes a parameter by value when you intend to pass it by reference (or vice versa). To prevent problems with function and procedure calls, explicitly indicate the passing mechanism when writing the function or procedure. For example, the function shown in the following script snippet makes it clear that the parameter is being passed by value:

```
Function ConvertToFahrenheit(ByVal sngDegreesCelsius)
    ConvertToFahrenheit = (sngDegreesCelsius * (9/5)) + 32
End Function
```

As a general rule, pass parameters by value rather than by reference. Passing a parameter by value ensures that your function will not inadvertently change the value of that parameter. This is especially important if the parameter is required elsewhere in the script.

Note

Preparing for Visual Basic .NET. If you do not specify ByVal or ByRef when passing a parameter in Visual Basic .NET, the parameter is automatically passed by reference. This is different from previous versions of Visual Basic, in which the default mechanism for passing parameters is by value. To help make your intention clear, explicitly indicate the passing mechanism for all functions and procedures.

Formatting Code

Because scripts are written as plaintext files with the use of a simple text editor such as Notepad, you might not think that correctly formatting your scripts would be much of an issue; besides, Notepad does not provide you with many options for formatting text. However, while such things as font size and font color might be irrelevant when writing scripts, the way you format your scripts is still important. Although formatting does not affect the efficiency, robustness, or memory required to run a script, it can improve the ease with which others can read, understand, maintain, and modify the script.

Script formatting involves a number of important considerations, including the following:

- **The use of white space.** White space helps delineate the key sections on a page and provides relief for eyes easily strained by a page of otherwise solid text.

- **The length of statements.** Long lines, particularly those that scroll off the screen, are difficult to read and modify. Several different techniques can be employed to help limit the length of each line of code in your script.

Using White Space

White space, achieved with blank lines, blank spaces, and character indentation, provides visual cues that help delineate and identify program flow and program sections. Because white space does not affect performance, use it whenever and wherever it is required. For instance, consider the following script, with a file size of 75 bytes.

```
For i = 1 to 100
    intTotal = intTotal + i
Next
Wscript.Echo intTotal
```

As an experiment, insert 10,000 blank lines before and after each of the lines in the script. This increases the file size to 98 KB, most of it white space. When you run the revised version of this script, there is no appreciable performance difference between the 98-KB version and the 75-byte version. Because performance is not affected, you can insert as many blank lines or blank spaces as needed to improve readability. For example, you might want to use blank spaces:

- Before and after operators.

- In parameter lists.

- To indent control structures, functions, and procedures.

Using Blank Spaces Before and After Operators

A blank space before and after each operator makes your code more readable. In most scripting languages, scripts run regardless of whether or not you put spaces before or after operators; however, the additional blank spaces generally make the script easier to read. For example, in the following line of VBScript code, notice how the *k* in the variable *intCheck* tends to run together with the >= sign and the <> sign. In addition, it is hard to separate the >= sign from the – sign that precedes the 3.

```
If intCheck>=-3 and intCheck<>7 then
```

Adding spaces before and after each operator makes the code easier to read and understand:

```
If intCheck >= -3 and intCheck <> 7 then
```

To further enhance readability, you might also enclose the If Then criteria in parentheses. In addition to enhancing readability, parentheses help enforce the order of precedence when using a conditional statement; the parentheses ensure that these statements are properly evaluated before the script takes any further action. Although parentheses are not required, they also make it easier to see the conditions being evaluated:

```
If (intCheck >= -3) and (intCheck <> 7) then
```

Using Blank Spaces in Parameter Lists

System administration scripts, including many WMI scripts that either create new items or reconfigure existing items, require you to supply parameters in a specific order. In many cases, this poses no problem. For example, in this hypothetical script, it is clear that the first parameter is "Large", the second parameter "Heavy", and the third parameter "Red":

```
objThing.Change("Large","Heavy","Red")
```

But what if you want to change only the third parameter? In a situation such as that, you typically leave the first two parameters blank. When you do that, you must include two commas, making "Red" the third parameter:

```
objThing.Change(,,"Red")
```

When constructing parameter lists such as this, it is a good idea to put blank spaces before or after commas. In the following script, it is difficult to tell how many commas precede the value True. This is important in this example because each comma represents a placeholder for a service parameter, and True must be the sixth item in the list.

```
Set objServiceList = GetObject("winmgmts:").InstancesOf("Win32_Service")
For Each strService in objServiceList
    Return = strService.Change(,,,,,True,,,,,,)
Next
```

The commas are easier to count when separated by blank spaces, as shown in the following script snippet:

```
Set objServiceList = GetObject("winmgmts:").InstancesOf("Win32_Service")
For Each strService in objServiceList
    Return = strService.Change( , , , , , True , , , , , , )
Next
```

Indenting Control Structures, Functions, and Procedures

Control structures are coding conventions that determine the flow of a script. For example, If Then is a control structure because the flow of the script hinges on this structure: If the condition is True, the script branches in one direction; if it is False, the script branches in another direction.

Indentation is commonly used with control structure statements such as If Then and For Next. For example, the syntax shown in the following snippet is valid, but it is difficult to understand what the script is doing without reading the code several times and mentally tracing the program flow.

```
For Each strEvent in objInstalledLogFiles
If (strEvent.EventCode >= "529") and (strEvent.EventCode <= "539") Then
If (strEvent.EventCode <> "538") Then
intEventTotal = intEventTotal +1
End If
End If
Next
```

Compare that with the revised code shown in the following script snippet. This is the same code, but each new control structure statement is indented four spaces.

```
For Each Event in InstalledLogFiles
    If (strEvent.EventCode >= "529") and (strEvent.EventCode <= "539") Then
        If (strEvent.EventCode <> "538") Then
            intEventTotal = intEventTotal +1
        End If
    End If
Next
```

The indentation makes it easier to understand when each block of code runs. In the preceding example, you can see that the first If Then section runs only for events with an EventCode of 529 through 539. The nested If Then statement, which adds up the total number of events, runs only if the EventCode does not equal 538. Thus, the script tallies all the events with the EventCode 529, 530, 531, 532, 533, 534, 535, 536, 537, or 539. An event with the EventCode 538 is not included in the tally.

It is also recommended that you use indentation in all major sections in your scripts, including functions and procedures. As a rule of thumb, use four spaces for each indent; in some cases, identifying passages indented less than four spaces is difficult, while indenting more than four spaces usually creates more empty space than needed. For example, indent a function as follows:

```
Function ConvertToMiles(ByVal sngKilometers)
    ConvertToMiles = sngKilometers * 2.2
End Function
```

When formatting control structure code, be sure that you align all the control structure statements (such as Do and Loop). In the following example, the If, ElseIf, Else, and End If statements are all aligned. Alignment clearly indicates that three possible values for the variable strState are being evaluated.

```
If (strState = "WA") Then
    intStateIDNumber = 1
ElseIf (strState = "OR") Then
    intStateIDNumber = 2
Else
    intStateIDNumber = 3
End If
```

In addition, use spaces rather than tabs when indenting statements. Some text editors use different tab formats than others; as a result, your carefully aligned code might look quite different when viewed by someone using a different editor.

Setting Statement Breaks

Text editors allow you to create lines of seemingly infinite length (for example, you can type 1,024 characters on a single line in Notepad); in theory, you could type an entire script — and a reasonably lengthy one at that — on a single line in Notepad. There might be some advantage to creating long lines of code; nevertheless, it is strongly recommended that you limit the length of any statement in a script to a maximum of 80 characters. This is suggested for at least two reasons.

- 80 characters is the default setting for the command shell. Unless you change this setting, a statement longer than 80 characters forces you to scroll horizontally as well as vertically to view all parts of the statement. Without scrolling horizontally, the following statement is cut off:

```
Set colServiceList = GetObject("winmgmts:").ExecQuery("Select * from
32_Servi
```

Statements that require a user to scroll back and forth are more difficult to read and modify.

In addition, many system administrators use programs such as Edit.exe for editing scripts. With many of these editors, lines are always wrapped at the 80th character, regardless of the screen resolution.

- Notepad is often used for printing scripts. Notepad is not designed to work with lines with more than 80 characters. In fact, lines that exceed 80 characters are printed in the following fashion:

```
Set colServiceList = GetObject("winmgmts:").ExecQuery("Select * from
Win32_Servi
ce Where State = 'Stopped' And StartMode = 'Auto' ")
```

If a statement has more than 80 characters, pick a logical spot to split the line, insert a statement break, and then continue the statement on the next line:

```
Set colServiceList = GetObject("winmgmts:").ExecQuery("Select * from " _
    & "Win32_Service Where State = 'Stopped' And StartMode = 'Auto' ")
```

Limiting Each Line to a Single Statement

Although many scripting languages allow you to place multiple statements on a single line, this can be confusing to anyone reading your script and should be avoided. For example, using VBScript you can place multiple statements on a single line by separating each statement with a colon. The following code sample shows four statements included on a single line of code:

```
For i = 1 to 100 : intTotal = intTotal + i : Next : Wscript.Echo intTotal
```

This code is valid, but the purpose of the script is not readily apparent. In fact, although it appears far more complicated, this script merely adds the integers from 1 to 100 and then echoes the result. The purpose is more apparent when each statement is placed on a separate line and formatted according to previous recommendations:

```
For i = 1 to 100
    intTotal = intTotal + i
Next
Wscript.Echo intTotal
```

Avoiding Single-Line If Then Statements

VBScript allows you to place If Then statements on a single line, a shortcut method that can save a few keystrokes when writing a script. However, the time saved writing the script could result in additional time required for someone editing your script, because single-line If Then statements are often hard to read. For example, determining the purpose and possible variable values is difficult in this line of code:

```
If (intDept = 1) Then strDepartment = "Accounting" Else strDepartment = "Other"
```

By comparison, the multiline If Then statement in the following script snippet clearly shows the purpose of the script: check the value of the variable intDept, and use that result to set the value of the variable strDepartment.

```
If (intDept = 1) Then
    strDepartment = "Accounting"
Else
    strDepartment = "Other"
End If
```

By avoiding single-line If Then statements, you also facilitate using statement blocks such as If End If and Do Loop. One common scripting mistake is to start a statement block but then fail to end it, such as using an opening statement like For i = 1 to 100 without using a closing statement such as Next.

 Note

Preparing for Visual Basic .NET. Single-line If-Then statements are not allowed in Visual Basic .NET. In Visual Basic .NET, you must use multiple-line If-Then statements.

Limiting Your Scripts to a Single Language

To help other administrators who maintain or modify your scripts, limit each individual script to a single scripting language. Windows Script Files provide a way to use multiple scripting languages within a single script; for example, you can write a script that carries out one function in VBScript, a second function in JScript®, and a third in any other registered ActiveX® scripting language. Although this provides considerable flexibility, anyone who maintains your script must be proficient in each of these languages. Use additional languages only if you cannot perform those operations any other way.

 Note

Preparing for Visual Basic .NET. Windows Script Files can be used with Visual Basic .NET, but only if all the jobs specified in the file use the same scripting language. Windows Script Files using multiple languages are not allowed.

Creating Scripts That Are Easier to Read

Most people think of scripts as something that you run, not something that you read. However, scripts are actually read far more than you might think. Obviously the original author of the script needs to read the code from time to time; however, so do others charged with maintaining and modifying the code, people hoping to learn something about scripting from reading the code, and system administrators who want to know more about the script before they begin using it.

A readable script, using consistent, predictable, and complete code, is easier to maintain and adapt to other uses. Readability might not be important for scripts that are designed to be run once and then discarded. However, if you expect a script to be used repeatedly, and if you expect that other administrators might need to modify your script, readability becomes a concern.

To make your scripts easier to read and understand:

- Use the proper case for VBScript keywords.
- Phrase If Then statements positively.
- Order If Then and Select Case statements logically.
- Use Boolean expressions rather than literal values in conditional statements.
- Use parentheses in mathematical expressions.
- Specify default properties.

Using the Proper Case

VBScript is a case-insensitive language; this means that you can type keywords and statements in uppercase, lowercase, or any combination without generating a syntax error. For example, the four case styles shown in the following are all syntactically equivalent:

```
wsCRIpt.EchO "This is a valid VBScript statement."
wSCRIPt.eCHo "This is a valid VBScript statement."
WSCRIPT.ECHO "This is a valid VBScript statement."
Wscript.Echo "This is a valid VBScript statement."
```

Although the four styles are syntactically equivalent, some are definitely easier to read than others, and the combination of the four different styles results in a document that is difficult to read. To enhance readability, type VBScript keywords, statements, and other elements using Pascal casing. To use Pascal casing, begin each individual word with an uppercase letter, and type remaining letters in lowercase. This is not only easier to read but also helps distinguish the VBScript elements from the rest of the text.

In the following script snippet, Pascal casing is used to distinguish keywords from variables and constants:

```
Const MANAGER_JOB_TITLE_ID = 100
Select Case
Case strDepartment = "Accounting"
    If intJobTitle = MANAGER_JOB_TITLE_ID Then
        intRatingScale = 1
    Else
        intRatingScale = 2
    End If
Case strDepartment = "Administration"
    intRatingScale = 1
Case Else
    intRatingScale = 2
End Select
```

Phrasing If Then Statements

Compared with programming languages such as C and C++, the syntax of scripting languages is almost conversational. Scripting languages allow you to write your script in a fashion somewhat similar to ordinary speech. You should take advantage of this when writing scripts and try to mimic typical conversational patterns and syntax whenever possible. This makes your scripts easier to read and understand because the code appears more like ordinary language than computer programming.

 Note

Brian Kernighan, author of a number of books on programming style and programming conventions, refers to this as the "telephone test." He believes you should attempt to read your code to someone over the telephone. If the person on the other end does not understand what you are talking about, then you need to rewrite your code.

For example, consider the phrasing of If Then statements in your scripts. In conversation, people generally phrase these statements positively. Suppose that stores in the state of Washington charge a special sales tax to residents of the state but not to residents of other states. If you are a store owner in Washington, you would likely to explain your store's sales tax policy by saying, "If the customer is from Washington state, then we charge them sales tax. Otherwise, we do not."

Your If Then statements should use a similar syntax. For example, the following script uses valid VBScript syntax but is awkward to read (try reading it out loud):

```
If (Not State = "WA") Then
    SngSalesTax = 0
End If
```

A grammatical construction such as **If Not State Equals Washington** causes confusion. Instead of testing for the negative condition, test for the positive condition, as shown in the following snippet. Read this script aloud, and notice that it sounds less awkward.

```
If (State = "WA") Then
    SngSalesTax = .065
End If
```

Or you might use the does not equal (<>) operator:

```
If (State <> "WA") Then
    SngSalesTax = 0
End If
```

Using Boolean Expressions in Conditional Statements

When checking the value of a Boolean (True/False) expression, script writers often use a syntax such as this:

```
If blnIsUSCitizen = True Then
    Wscript.Echo "This person is a citizen."
Else
    Wscript.Echo "This person is not a citizen."
End If
```

On the surface, this statement appears to pose no problems. In reality, however, a statement like this can return the value False even when the expression is actually True. This is because VBScript sets the value of True to –1, while most programming languages set the value of True to 1. As a result, the following situation can occur:

- Someone saves the value 1 (True) to a database using a Visual Basic program.

- Someone else uses VBScript to check the value. The statement If blnIsUSCitizen = True can be translated to read, "If blnUSCitizen equals –1" with –1 representing the value of True in VBScript.

- Because the value in this case is actually 1 rather than –1, the script decides that blnIsUSCitizen is False, even though it is actually True.

To avoid this problem, use syntax similar to that shown in the following script snippet. In this case, the statement "If blnIsUSCitizen Then" is used as the condition. This statement translates as, "If blnIsUSCitizen equals anything other than 0." Because 1 is not 0, the condition is correctly interpreted as being True.

```
If blnIsUSCitizen Then
    Wscript.Echo "This person is a citizen."
Else
    Wscript.Echo "This person is not a citizen."
End If
```

By contrast, False is always assigned 0. When you check for a False value, you can look for either False or for 0. For the sake of consistency, however, it is generally best to test for False as shown in the following snippet:

```
If blnIsUSCitizen = False Then
    Wscript.Echo "This person is not a citizen."
Else
    Wscript.Echo "This person is a citizen."
End If
```

Using Parentheses in Mathematical Expressions

Parentheses serve two purposes in mathematical equations: they force the order of arithmetic precedence, and they enhance readability. These two functions are illustrated in the following script snippet. This script works as expected: It multiplies the regular price of an item by the tax rate, multiplies the standard discount rate by a preferred customer rate, and then subtracts the total discount from the total regular price. However, the equation is somewhat difficult to read, and the fact that it works is, in part, an accident: The different terms and operators used in the equation just happen to be arranged in a way that respects the order of precedence.

```
RegPrice = 100
Discount = 5
SalesTax = 1.05
PreferredCustomer = 2
Wscript.Echo RegPrice * SalesTax - Discount * PreferredCustomer
```

Although the equation works as expected, someone editing the script might have difficulty understanding how the calculation works. If so, he or she might try to group the items within parentheses. If those parentheses are misplaced, the equation yields unexpected results. For example, one placement produces a correct answer, but another placement produces an incorrect answer:

- **Correct**: $(100 * 1.05) - (5 * 2) = 95$

- **Incorrect**: $100 * (1.05 - 5) * 2 = -790$

To avoid problems such as this, always use parentheses when performing calculations that have the following characteristics:

- Have three or more elements

- Use more than one type of operator (for example, an equation that includes both addition and division)

A revised version of the script, which groups the items into logical sets, is shown in the following snippet:

```
RegPrice = 100
Discount = 5
SalesTax = 1.05
PreferredCustomer = 2
Wscript.Echo (RegPrice * SalesTax) - (Discount * PreferredCustomer)
```

Specifying Default Properties in Statements

Automation objects often have default properties associated with them. A default is simply the property that is used unless a different property is specified. For example, in WSH the Arguments object has the default property Item. In VBScript, you can omit the property name when working with the default property of an item. Thus, you can write the following script to cycle through the arguments passed to that script:

```
Set objArgs = WScript.Arguments
For i = 0 to objArgs.Count - 1
    WScript.Echo objArgs(i)
Next
```

Although VBScript allows you to omit default properties, it is a good idea to always include the default property name as part of your script. This makes your code easier to read and understand, especially if you are working with an automation object whose default property is not widely known. To ensure that there is no doubt as to which property is being employed, you should use code similar to this, which clearly specifies the default property Item:

```
Set objArgs = WScript.Arguments
For i = 0 to objArgs.Count - 1
   WScript.Echo objArgs.Item(i)
Next
```

Note

Preparing for Visual Basic .NET. Default properties are not supported in Visual Basic .NET. In Visual Basic .NET, you must always specify the property name.

Commenting Scripts

Comments provide clarification or additional information about a script and the script's purpose. Comments serve a function similar to that of a narrator in a movie: The narrator tells you what the characters in the movie are thinking; comments tell you what the script writer was thinking when he or she wrote the code. Without comments, readers must guess at the script's purpose and why it uses one approach rather than another. Comments improve a reader's understanding of the script.

It is generally a good idea to comment all scripts except scripts that are used once and then discarded. At a minimum, you should comment the following:

- The script itself, in the form of a script header.

- Procedures and functions.

- Large control structures that are not part of a procedure or function. For example, if your script connects to a directory service, comment the section of the script where you actually connect to the directory service, even if it is not encapsulated in a function or procedure.

- Any line of the script that needs clarification. When in doubt, it is better that a script have too many comments than too few.

Adding comments

A good narrator tries to avoid the obvious and to tell you only what you might not be able to determine for yourself. If the main character in a movie is seen walking along a river, the narrator will rarely say something like, "And then the main character walked along the river." Instead, the narrator might tell you *why* the main character is walking along the river, but only if the reason behind this might not be obvious, and only if this narration helps to clarify what is happening.

Comments should be added only in similar circumstances; that is, only if the reason for using the code is not obvious, and only if the comment helps clarify what happens within the script. You might consider these guidelines when adding comments to a script:

- **Comments should describe the general purpose of the script.** Comments need not provide a step-by step description of what happens in the script and should not provide a primer in scripting; someone who does not understand what the Wscript.Echo method does should not be editing your script. Reserve comments for those items that need further clarification. Commenting every statement leads to two problems. First, you need to write the script twice — once for each statement and again for each comment. Second, you risk obscuring the important comments if you include too many unneeded comments. The following type of comment should be avoided:

```
' Echo the date
Wscript.Echo Date
```

In addition, be careful not to editorialize when commenting the code. Comments should explain what the code does, not offer judgments as to the quality of that code. Raise quality issues in a different forum. The following type of comment does little to assure the reader that this is a script worth running:

```
' Echo the date even though it seems silly to echo the date at this point
Wscript.Echo Date
```

- **Comments are not a solution for a poorly constructed script.** If a section of your script is too complicated to summarize in a few sentences, consider rewriting that section. As a general rule, well-written code requires minimal commenting. If you find yourself having to explain over and over why you wrote a particular section of code in a particular way, you might stop and think about whether there is a better way to carry out the same function.

- **Use complete sentences, and proofread for spelling and grammar.** Do not add terse and cryptic comments to your code. A comment such as "Get user info" adds no value. Instead, use a comment that gives the reader useful information. The following comment makes it clear user information is being retrieved:

```
'    Retrieve the account name, department, and job title for each user.
```

  You should also ensure that comments are grammatically correct and spelled correctly. Poor grammar and spelling not only make the code harder to read, but do little to inspire confidence in your professionalism, and to offer assurance that the code has been properly checked and tested.

- **Write comments as you write the script.** Although it is customary to write comments after the code is complete, this approach can lead to the following problems:

  - Finding time to go back and add the comments is difficult. After a script is working, it is usually more important to begin using that script than it is to delay its implementation while you add comments. If you save comments until the end, you are less likely to add them.

  - You might forget what the code does. Comments not only help other people understand your code, they also help you understand your own code. For example, if you copy a procedure from another source and fail to comment it, you might not remember what the procedure does, and why you included it.

  - Comments added after a script is written are often included as an afterthought and do little to improve the readability of the script. Comments that do not enhance the clarity of the code can be worse than no comments; they can be a distraction to anyone trying to read and understand the script.

  Interestingly enough, some script writers actually write comments before writing code. This enables them to record their thoughts and forces them to construct a logical flow for the program before writing code on a line-by-line basis.

- **Comments should not contradict the script.** Because comments clarify your script, ensure that the comments and the script do not conflict. For example, the following script snippet reveals a conflict between the comments and the script itself. According to the script, the variable strUserLocationIdentifier is based on the user's home state; according to the comments, however, the value of this variable is based on the user's home city:

```
'* Set the location identifier for the user based on the user's home city
If strUserHomeState = "WA" Then
    strUserLocationIdentifier = "Local"
Else
    strUserLocationIdentifier = "Off-site"
End If
```

  Contradictions like this often occur when a section of a script is modified but the accompanying comments are not. Any time you make a change in your script, make sure that the comments are still valid.

Adding Comments to a Script

Comments are statements that are ignored by the script host when the script runs. To ensure that the script host does not attempt to interpret a comment as a command, you must preface each comment with a comment delimiter. VBScript allows two delimiters: the single quotation mark (') and the REM statement. For example, both of the following lines of code are valid comments:

```
' This is a comment using a single quote delimiter.
REM This is a comment using the REM statement as a delimiter.
```

Although most script writers use the single quotation mark, you might consider following the single quotation mark with an asterisk when commenting your code:

```
'* This is another comment.
```

This approach has two advantages over the single quotation mark alone. First, it makes the comment stand out from the rest of the text; a single quotation mark by itself can be difficult to see at times. Second, the single quotation mark is a valid VBScript character that has uses beyond delimiting comments. This can be a problem if you use an automated procedure to extract comments from a script; such a procedure might also retrieve items that are not comments. Because you are less likely to use '* anywhere else in your script, it makes a good delimiter.

Always include comments on separate lines except for comments that accompany the declaration of a variable. Comments included on the same line as a VBScript statement (end-of-the-line comments) are valid but can be difficult to read. For example, compare the two commenting styles in the following script snippet; in the first half of the script, comments are placed on the same line as a VBScript statement, while in the second half of the script, the comments are placed on separate lines. Most people find it easier to quickly identify the comments used in the second half of the script.

```
On Error Resume Next
Set WshNetwork = WScript.CreateObject("WScript.Network")
WshNetwork.MapNetworkDrive "Z:", "\\RemoteServer\Public" '* Map drive Z.
If Err.Number <> 0 Then '* Check to make sure the operation succeeded.
    Err.Clear
    Wscript.Echo "The drive could not be mapped."
End If

'* Map drive Z.
WshNetwork.MapNetworkDrive "Z:", "\\RemoteServer\Public"

'* Check to make sure the operation succeeded.
If Err.Number <> 0 Then
    Err.Clear
    Wscript.Echo "The drive could not be mapped."
End If
```

Formatting Comments

In many scripting books, comments are set off from the rest of the text by use of a frame (typically a box drawn with asterisks). These frames make it easy to identify the comments; however, the frames themselves can be difficult to maintain. For example, consider the frame used to surround the comments in this script snippet:

```
'*****************************************************************
'*    This is a comment enclosed within a frame. These frames might look    *
'*    nice, but they can be difficult to maintain.                          *
'*****************************************************************
```

Although the frame might have a certain aesthetic appeal, if you edit the comment, the line lengths will change and the frame might look like this:

```
'*****************************************************************
'*    This is a comment enclosed within a frame. Frames might look    *
'*    nice, but they are difficult to maintain.                   *
'*****************************************************************
```

If you like the idea of clearly delineating comments, you might want to use only a top and bottom border instead of a complete frame, as shown in the following snippet. The comments are still easy to identify, but the frame requires less maintenance.

```
'*****************************************************************
'*    If you feel the need to include a frame of some kind, just use a
'*    border on the top and bottom. This is much easier to maintain.
'*****************************************************************
```

Creating Script Headers

Whenever you document something, it is a good idea to make clear what you are documenting; do not require readers to read the entire manual to determine whether this really is the information they are looking for. The same is true of scripts. If your scripts are shared with others, it is strongly recommended that you include information about the script, and that you include it at the very beginning of the script in the form of a script header.

Script headers are a collection of comments that explain the purpose and history of a script. Script headers detail such things as:

- The name of the script.
- The date the script was created.
- The author of the script.
- The purpose of the script.
- A history of revisions made to the script.

For example, an organization might use the following standard script header:

```
'*    Script name:    NewUsers.vbs
'*    Created on:     8/15/2000
'*    Author:         Ken Myer
'*    Purpose:        Creates new user accounts and new Exchange 2000 mailboxes.
'*                    Adds new users to security groups based on job title and
'*                    department.
'*    History:        Pilar Ackerman 10/15/2000
'*                    Modified to reflect new area code.
```

Simply by reading the header, you can tell what a script does, when it was written, how often it has been modified, and who to contact if you have questions about the script or the script code.

Creating Function and Procedure Headers

Each function and procedure in a script should also have a header that describes the purpose of that function or procedure. Information typically included in a function or procedure header is shown in Table 18.6.

Table 18.6   Function and Procedure Headers

Header Item	Description
Name	Label applied to the function or procedure within the script. Follow the guidelines described in "Naming Scripts" earlier in this chapter.
Purpose	General explanation of the task performed by the function or procedure.
Arguments supplied	Data (usually in the form of variables) passed to the function or procedure.
Return value	Result returned from the function or procedure.
Function is called by	Name of the function or procedure that calls this section of the script. Omit if called from within the main body of the script.
Function calls	Name of any functions or procedures that are called from within this section of the script. Omit if no such calls are made. Both this header item and the preceding header item help you to trace program flow.

A sample function header might look like this:

```
'*    Function Name:          CalculateTotalPay()
'*    Purpose:                Calculates total pay for an employee based on
'*                            current salary plus merit increase.
'*    Arguments supplied:     intUserIDNumber, curCurrentSalary, intMeritRank
'*    Return Value:           curRevisedSalary
'*    Function is called by:  SalaryAdjustment
'*    Function calls:         ConvertMeritRank
```

Creating Script Documentation by Using Comments

Scripts are often short pieces of code designed to carry out a single function. Because of this, formal documentation is not always required; the script comments usually provide sufficient information for anyone using the script. For longer scripts, however, it might be useful to provide separate documentation rather than requiring users to read through the script, searching for comments.

Well-commented scripts can actually help you write the documentation for your scripts. By including comments such as who wrote the script, when it was written, why it was written, and the purpose of procedures and functions, you already have much of the written documentation for the script as well. You only need to copy those comments from the script to the script documentation.

One way to create separate documentation for a script is to use an automated procedure to extract the comments. These comments can then serve as the basis for the written documentation. For example, the script shown in Listing 18.2 extracts comments by doing the following:

- Opens a script file (C:\Scripts\SystemMonitor.vbs).

- Reads through each line of the script, looking for comments. These are readily identifiable because the script uses a unique identifier ('*) to delineate comments.

- Saves the line to a text file (C:\Scripts\Comments.txt) if the line is a comment. If the line is not a comment, the script proceeds to the next line of the script file. This process continues until all the lines in SystemMonitor.vbs are read and processed.

Listing 18.2 Extracting Comments

```
1   Const ForReading = 1
2   Const ForWriting = 2
3   Set objFSO = CreateObject("Scripting.FileSystemObject")
4   Set objScriptFile = objFSO.OpenTextFile _
5       ("c:\scripts\Service_Monitor.vbs", ForReading)
6   Set objCommentFile = objFSO.OpenTextFile("c:\scripts\Comments.txt", _
7       ForWriting, TRUE)
8   Do While objScriptFile.AtEndOfStream <> TRUE
9       strCurrentLine = objScriptFile.ReadLine
10      intIsComment = Instr(1,strCurrentLine,"'*")
11      If intIsComment > 0 Then
12          objCommentFile.Write strCurrentLine & VbCrLf
13      End If
14  Loop
15  objScriptFile.Close
16  objCommentFile.Close
```

Using Comments as a Debugging Aid

If you have ever written a lengthy report or memorandum, you might have found it useful to type notes to yourself as you worked on the document. For example, you might have typed something such as, "Need to add a section here about the budget problems from a year ago" or "These two paragraphs need to be rewritten." Notes such as these are useful reminders and also serve as a sort of status report, letting you know what is and is not working, and how you are progressing.

Comments allow you to put this same type of status report in scripts still in development. For example, suppose you are working on a script and you encounter a problem. If you are unable to immediately solve the problem, insert a comment labeled BUG to indicate that this section of code needs further work. The next time you work on that script, search for BUG to locate any sections of the code that are not working properly. If you are able to fix the problem, remove the BUG comment.

For example, you might use the following comment labels:

- BUG. Indicates code that is not working correctly.

- INCOMPLETE. Indicates code that is not yet finished.

- PERFORMANCE. Indicates code that works but whose performance might be improved.

- REVIEW. Indicates lines of code that need further review to ensure they are working correctly.

The following script snippet illustrates comments used as a debugging aid.

```
'* BUG (DMS 3/10/02)     This should loop through all 100 sales districts,
'* BUG (DMS 3/10/02)     calling the function RetrieveInformation for each one,
'* BUG (DMS 3/10/02)     but it only does the first 90 sales districts and then
'* BUG (DMS 3/10/02)     stops.

For i = 1 to 100
    RetrieveInformation(i)
Next
```

The debugging comments in the preceding snippet include the reviewer's initials and the date the comment was added. This facilitates communication between the script writer and the reviewer. In addition, it helps ensure that no unneeded comments are left in the finished code; a debugging comment added years earlier is unlikely to still be valid and should be deleted.

Removing Debugging Comments

To ensure that you remove all debugging comments from a script, you can use a second script to remove them. The script shown in Listing 18.3 removes debugging comments by doing the following:

- Opens the script C:\Scripts\CreateUser.vbs.

- Reads each line in the file and checks for the presence of the string '* BUG anywhere in the line. If the string is found, the line is discarded as a debugging comment. If the string is not found, the line is retained as part of the variable strSavedLines.

- Overwrites the existing version of the script using the variable strSavedLines, which contains all the non-debug lines in the script.

Listing 18.3 Removing Debugging Comments

```
1   Const ForReading = 1
2   Const ForWriting = 2
3   Set objFSO = CreateObject("Scripting.FileSystemObject")
4   Set objTextFile = objFSO.OpenTextFile("C:\Scripts\CreateUser.vbs", ForReading)
5   Do While objTextFile.AtEndOfStream <> true
6       strNextLine = objTextFile.Readline
7       intCheckForBugComment = Instr(strNextLine, "'* BUG")
8       If intCheckForBugComment = 0 Then
9           strSavedLines = strSavedLines & strNextLine & VbCrLf
10      End If
11  Loop
12  Set objTextFile = objFSO.OpenTextFile _
13      ("c:\scripts\CreateUser.vbs" , ForWriting)
14  objTextFile.Write strSavedLines
15  objTextFile.Close
```

Debugging and Troubleshooting Scripts

Debugging code can be a long and tedious process. This is especially true with scripts because most scripts are written in text editors that do include a debugger. However, you can employ several techniques to facilitate debugging and troubleshooting.

 Note

You can also use the Microsoft Script Debugger or third-party debugging tools to troubleshoot scripts.

Adding a Trace Routine to a Script

Trace routines allow you to track a program as it runs and help you identify lines of code that produce unexpected results. You can add a rudimentary trace routine to your scripts by having the script periodically report its status.

For example, you might echo the value of your variables each time those variables are changed in some way. This enables you to identify any spot in the script where a variable is not assigned the correct value (a common cause of run-time errors). Or you might display a message each time you enter a procedure or function. If a message does not appear, you know that the function or procedure was not called.

The following script projects the number of support calls to a help desk by doing the following:

- Requests the total number of calls for two weeks.

  Assume that there are 93 calls in the first week and 96 in the second week.

- Adds the number of calls for the first two weeks together.

  The total of calls for the first two weeks is 189.

- Multiplies the two-week total by 26, giving a projection of the total number of support calls for the next year (52 weeks).

- Divides the total number of calls by 8 support technicians to determine the anticipated number of calls each technician will need to handle in the coming year.

```
intWeekOneCalls = InputBox("Enter the number of support calls for Week 1:")
intWeekTwoCalls = InputBox("Enter the number of support calls for Week 2:")
intTotalCalls = intWeekOneCalls + intWeekTwoCalls
intProjectedNumberOfCalls = intTotalCalls * 26
sngCallsPerTechnician = intProjectedNumberOfCalls / 8
Wscript.Echo  sngCallsPerTechnician
```

The script returns a value of 30,537 as the number of calls each technician can expect to handle. Unfortunately, the correct answer is 614.25.

To make matters worse, determining where the problem lies is difficult, because no error messages are returned, and both the scripting syntax and mathematical formulas appear correct.

One solution is to insert a trace routine that periodically reports the value of the variables used in the script. For example, the following revised script uses the Echo statement to display the value of a variable each time that value changes.

```
intWeekOneCalls = InputBox("Enter the number of support calls for Week 1:")
Wscript.Echo intWeekOneCalls
intWeekTwoCalls = InputBox("Enter the number of support calls for Week 2:")
Wscript.Echo intWeekTwoCalls
intTotalCalls = intWeekOneCalls + intWeekTwoCalls
Wscript.Echo intTotalCalls

intProjectedNumberOfCalls = intTotalCalls * 26
Wscript.Echo intProjectedNumberOfCalls

sngCallsPerTechnician = intProjectedNumberOfCalls / 8
Wscript.Echo  sngCallsPerTechnician
```

When this script runs, you will see that the sum of the week 1 and week 2 totals (93 + 96) does not equal 189. Instead, VBScript returns the value 9396. Why? B intWeekTwoCalls ecause it is treating the two variants as string variables rather than integers. As a result, the variables are concatenated (93 & 96 = 9396) and not added (93 + 96 = 189). You have now located the problem.

To solve this problem, you can use the data type features in VBScript to cast these two variables as integers, as shown in the following code snippet:

```
intWeekOneCalls = InputBox("Enter the number of support calls for Week 1:")
intWeekTwoCalls = InputBox("Enter the number of support calls for Week 2:")
intTotalCalls = Cint(intWeekOneCalls) + Cint(intWeekTwoCalls)
Wscript.Echo intTotalCalls

intProjectedNumberOfCalls = Cint(intTotalCalls) * 26
Wscript.Echo intProjectedNumberOfCalls

sngCallsPerTechnician = Cint(intProjectedNumberOfCalls) / 8
Wscript.Echo  sngCallsPerTechnician
```

Tip

You can also have your script periodically write trace information to a log file. This enables you to run the script without interruption and then later read the log file and determine whether the script ran as expected.

Incrementally Running a Script

Suppose you woke up this morning and discovered that your car would not start. How would you handle this situation? You could call a tow truck and have the car towed to the nearest mechanic. Or, if you are a do-it-yourselfer, you could immediately take the engine apart and begin looking for broken or worn-out items.

Of course, both those approaches might be a bit extreme; after all, what if the car is simply out of gas? Instead of taking the entire cart apart, you are likely to take a a step-by-step approach to trying to figure out what it wrong. For example, you might check whether there is gas in the gas tank or whether the battery is still charged. Most likely, your diagnosis and troubleshooting will involve incremental steps, identifying possible problems, and then investigating each one in turn.

This same technique can be used for debugging scripts. Rather than read through each line of code, trying to determine where the problem might be, you might instead run part of the script and then quit. This can help you determine the exact location where the problem occurs. For example, you might run half the script and then quit; if the script runs without errors, you can generally assume that the problem is in the second half of the script. You can then continue to run a selected portion of the script until you finally locate the problem.

To run only part of a script, insert a **Wscript.Quit** statement at the point where you want the script to stop running. For example, the following script snippet creates a new organizational unit and then adds a new user to it. To troubleshoot the script, first verify that the section that creates the organizational unit works as expected. To ensure that only this portion of the script is run, insert **Wscript.Quit** at the end of this section.

```
Set objRootDSE = GetObject("LDAP://RootDSE")
objDomain=rootDSE.Get("DefaultNamingContext")
strOUName = "Accounting"
Set objContainer = GetObject("LDAP://" & objDomain)
Set objOU = objContainer.Create("organizationalUnit", "OU=" & strOUName)
objOU.SetInfo

Wscript.Quit

strUserAccountName = "rsmith"
strSAMAccountName = "rsmith"
set objUser = objOU.Create("user", "cn=" & strUserAccountName )
objUser.Put "samAccountName", strSAMAccountName
objUser.SetInfo
```

After creating the organizational unit, the script stops before creating any user accounts. If the organizational unit is not created, you can then focus your debugging efforts on that section of the script before moving on to the section that creates user accounts.

The Wscript.Quit method also allows you to check the syntax of your script without actually running that script. To check syntax without running the script, insert **Wscript.Quit** as the first line. When you run the script, the script host checks the syntax and reports any errors. If the script host discovers no syntax errors, it attempts to run the script. Because the first command is Wscript.Quit, it runs only that line and then stops.

Turning Off Error Handling as a Debugging Tool

The primary advantage of error handling is that it allows a script to proceed from start to finish without displaying any error messages, and without abruptly terminating if an error condition occurs. At the same time, the primary *disadvantage* of error handling is that error handling allows a script to proceed from start to finish without displaying any error messages, and without abruptly terminating if an error condition occurs. After all, without seeing an error message, you will not know where the error occurred in your script. In fact, you might not even know that an error *did* occur.

Because of this, it is often a good idea to turn off error handling when writing and debugging a script. For example, the following script sample creates a new organizational unit and then adds user to it. If the script is run by a user who does not have the right to create a new organizational unit, nothing happens: neither the new organizational unit nor the new user is created, nor does an error message appear.

```
On Error Resume Next
Set objRootDSE = GetObject("LDAP://RootDSE")
ObjDomain = rootDSE.Get("DefaultNamingContext")
strOUName = "Accounting"
Set objContainer = GetObject("LDAP://" & objDomain)
Set objOU = objContainer.Create("organizationalUnit", "OU=" & strOUName)
objOU.SetInfo
strUserAccountName = "rsmith"
strSAMAccountName = "rsmith"
set objUser = objOU.Create("user", "cn=" & strUserAccountName )
objUser.Put "samAccountName", strSAMAccountName
objUser.SetInfo
```

This script is difficult to troubleshoot because it is syntactically correct; under the right circumstances, this script works every time. In this case, the script is correct; the failure occurs not because of a defect in the code, but because the user is not authorized to create a new organizational unit. This problem can be very difficult to identify; when a script fails to work, the usual assumption is that there is something wrong with the script code.

To catch run-time errors such as this, comment out the **On Error Resume Next** statement. When you run the script without error handling enabled, you immediately receive an error message such as the following:

```
C:\Scripts\NewOU.vbs(6, 1) Microsoft VBScript runtime error: Object required:
'rootDSE'
```

This error message tells you that the script failed because it could not return a reference to the rootDSE object. This means that either the domain does not exist or the user is not authorized to bind to the domain root. With error handling enabled, this problem is more difficult to diagnose.

Testing Scripts

When you buy a new car, you have some assurance that you will not turn the key and have the back end of the car burst into flames. This is because cars are thoroughly tested before they are placed into production and before they are sold to consumers. No car maker would last long if it simply slapped a new car together and then sold it to consumers on a "use at your own risk" basis.

Admittedly, it is unlikely that any of your scripts will burst into flames the first time they are run. On the other hand, scripts are powerful tools for system administration; this means they can do a number of good things if written correctly, and a number of bad things if written incorrectly. To make sure your scripts are working properly, and to make sure there are no surprises when you use them in a production environment, always test your scripts before deploying them. Although a complete guide to software testing is beyond the scope of this chapter, you can benefit from following these general guidelines:

- **Test in iterative fashion.** Do not wait until your script is finished before you begin testing it. For example, suppose you have a script that:

  - Reads in a Microsoft Excel spreadsheet containing information about new users in your domain.

  - Creates new user accounts based on that information.

  - Creates new Microsoft Exchange mailboxes based on that information.

  - Adds the new users to the appropriate security groups.

  - Creates custom logon scripts based on the security groups the users belong to.

If the script is written in this same order, you should test the code as soon as the procedure to read the Excel spreadsheet is written. If that procedure does not work, the rest of the script fails as well. After you have written and debugged the procedure for reading in the Excel spreadsheet, move on to the procedure for creating new user accounts.

In addition, test any new statements added to your script before the script is released. Never assume that the new statements work and thus require no testing.

- **Cover all possibilities when testing.** Always test whether the script can be made *not* to work. For example, suppose your script requests that the user enter an ID number. What happens if the user enters an ID number that does not exist, or an ID number that contains an invalid character? What happens if the user doesn't even enter an ID number but merely presses ENTER? What happens if the user clicks **Cancel** instead? Make sure your testing accounts for all these possibilities.

- **Verify that the output you receive is correct.** Sometimes the problem with a script is subtle and difficult to detect. For example, suppose you have a script that retrieves user information from Active Directory. You enter a user name, and the script responds by showing you the person's address, phone number, and job title. Do not assume that the script is working just because you received information of some kind; what if the script returns the address, phone number, and title of someone other than the person requested? Double-check the returned information against some other source, such as the form originally filled out by the employee.

- **Have someone else test your script.** As much as possible, you should avoid testing scripts that you write, simply because you know what kind of input the script expects at any given time. As a result, you tend to do the expected. If the script requires you to enter a drive letter, you are likely to type a valid drive letter using a valid format (for example, C:). Someone who does not know how the script works might type something else, perhaps an invalid drive (6:), or the wrong format (C). This provides a more realistic test of how the script will actually be used.

- **Test your scripts on multiple platforms.** You should test your scripts on each platform used in your organization. For example, the Microsoft® Windows XP® family includes a different version of WSH than the version that shipped with Windows 2000. Unless you upgrade WSH on the Windows 2000–based computers, you might discover that scripts that work on Windows XP development computers do not work anywhere else. Likewise, there are differences between WMI on Microsoft® Windows NT® and WMI on Windows 2000 or the Windows XP family. Do not assume that just because each of these platforms contains a WMI class named Win32_OperatingSystem the properties and methods of these classes are identical. Because of differences between platforms, a script that works on one platform might not work on others.

Because of such differences, you might need to design scripts only for a specific platform. In that case, your script should include code that verifies that it is running on the correct platform. The WMI script shown in Listing 18.4 retrieves the operating system platform.

Listing 18.4 Retrieving the Operating System Platform

```
1  strComputer = "."
2  Set objWMIService = GetObject("winmgmts:" _
3      & "{impersonationLevel=impersonate}!\\" & strComputer & "\root\cimv2")
4  Set colOS = objWMIService.ExecQuery _
5      ("SELECT * FROM Win32_OperatingSystem")
6  For Each objOS in colOS
7      Wscript.Echo objOS.Caption & ", " & objOS.Version
8  Next
```

If you do not have WMI installed on all the computers in your organization, the VBScript shown in Listing 18.5 can query the registry and return the operating system.

Listing 18.5   Querying the Registry and Returning the Operating System

```
1  Set WshShell = WScript.CreateObject("WScript.Shell")
2  Set WshSysEnv = WshShell.Environment("SYSTEM")
3  strOS = WshSysEnv("OS")
4  strVersionNumber = WshShell.RegRead("HKLM\Software\Microsoft\" _
5     & "Windows NT\CurrentVersion\CurrentVersion")
6  strBuildNumber = WshShell.RegRead("HKLM\Software\Microsoft\" _
7     & "Windows NT\CurrentVersion\CurrentBuildNumber")
8  strActualOS = strOS & ", " & strVersionNumber & ", " & strBuildNumber
9  Wscript.Echo strActualOS
```

- **Test your scripts on all relevant computers.** If your script must run on computers with different hardware, make sure you test it on each of those hardware platforms. Depending on the task you are trying to perform, differences in computer hardware, such as processor speed, memory, hard disk speed, and network adapters can affect the operation of the script. Scripts typically do not depend on hardware, but it is better to test for the exceptional situation.

- **Record problems you encounter and their resolution.** Keep track of common coding problems and how they are resolved; it is likely that someone else might encounter this same problem. Methods of recording this information range from the formal, such as storing problems and solutions in a database, to the informal, such as creating a Frequently Encountered Problems Web page.

Index

Special Characters

#...# (pound signs), VBScript date literals 61

% (percentage symbols), environment variables 201

& (ampersand), concatenating strings 29

( ) (parentheses)

   enclosing If-Then statements 1165

   in mathematical expressions 1174

   operator precedence, VBScript 83

* (multiplication operator), VBScript operator precedence 82–83

. (dot notation)

   Automation objects, calling methods 21

   Automation objects, retrieving properties 22

   binding to current folder 250

.. (dot-dot notation), binding to root folder 250

/ (division operator), VBScript operator precedence 82–83

/ (forward slash), in named arguments 164, 170

: (colon), in named arguments 164, 170

\ (backslash), binding to root folder 250

_ (underscore), VBScript line continuation character 48–49

+ (addition operator), VBScript operator precedence 82–83

= (equals sign), initializing VBScript variables 52

> character, redirecting script output to text files 145

>> characters, redirecting script output to text files 145

8.3 naming convention 1149

88 classes, Active Directory 399

.csv files

   converting to arrays, VBScript 101–102

   log files, parsing 877

   saving script output for use with tabular data control 1092, 1096

.dll files, WMI providers 438–439

.exe files See executable files

.gif files, showing script progress with 1131

.hta files See HTAs

.htm files, converting to .hta files 1090

.js files, WSH-compliant scripting languages 137

.lnk files 191

.mof files

   method definitions in 469

   overview 467

   property definitions in 469

   retrieving class definition in 477–478

.pls files, WSH-compliant scripting languages 136

.txt files See text files

.vbs files, WSH-compliant scripting languages 137

A

abstract classes, Active Directory 399

abstract classes, WMI 450, 465

Abstract qualifier, WMI 465, 470

AcceptPause property, Win32_Service class 978–980, 989

AcceptStop property, Win32_Service class 978–980, 989

Access denied (error) 284

Access Denied error message 662–663

access rights

   See also permissions

   to registry subkeys, administering 1047–1048

Accesses property, Win32_SoftwareFeature class 658–659

accessing databases with enterprise scripts 1103

accountDisabled attribute, Computer class 691

accounts

   computer See computer accounts

   LocalSystem account 1006–1007

   service account passwords 1009–1010

   service accounts 1006–1008

   user See user accounts

AccountStatus property, DiskQuotaControl object 748–749

Active Directory

   See also directory service objects

   Active Directory store 393

   Active Directory-specific computer roles 716

   architecture *See* Active Directory architecture

   as a database 1104

   as managed resource 436

   attributes *See* attributes, Active Directory

   binding to 1070

   classes *See* Active Directory classes

   computer accounts *See* computer accounts

   Computer class 691–693

   Configuration partition 406

   containers *See* Active Directory containers

   domain controllers, enumerating 716–717

   Domain Directory partition 406

   global catalog servers, enabling and disabling 723–724

   global catalog servers, identifying 722

   locating resources *See* searching in Active Directory

   objects *See* directory service objects

   operations master roles, identifying 719–721

   partitions 406

   printer location tracking 919–922

   published folders, administrative tasks 836

   published folders, deleting 839–840

   published folders, enumerating 836–837

   published folders, searching for 838

   publishing shared folders 834–835

   replication *See* Active Directory replication

   Schema partition 406

   schema *See* Active Directory schema

   searching *See* searching in Active Directory

   snap-ins *See* snap-ins

   user accounts *See* user accounts

Active Directory architecture

   See also Active Directory

   attributes 395

Active Directory architecture *(continued)*

   classes 395

   Database Layer 393

   Directory System Agent 393

   Extensible Storage Engine 393

   forests 394

   LDAP 393

   logical structure 394–413

   physical architecture 393

   schemas 395

   trees 394

Active Directory classes

   See also Active Directory

   attributes replicated to Global Catalog 407, 410

   categorization 398–403

   class list, Active Directory Schema Snap-in 403

   in Active Directory architecture 395

   indexed attributes 409, 410

   inheritance 398–403

   instantiation 395

   mandatory attributes 396–398

   objectClassCategory attribute 399

   operational attributes 412

   optional attributes 396–398

   parent classes 403

   subClassOf attribute 403

   systemAuxiliaryClass attribute 401

   systemMayContain attribute 396

   systemMustContain attribute 396

Active Directory containers

   configuration container, binding to 392

   enterprise scripts and 1070–1072

   enumerating contents 386

   enumerating contents to perform tasks on 387

   enumerating objects of specific types 388

   enumeration, managing user accounts 613–614

   retrieving computer names from 1070–1072

   schema container, binding to 392

   searching for attributes 593, 596, 598

   selecting for user account creation 556

Active Directory objects *See* directory service objects

Active Directory provider, WMI 438–439

Active Directory replication

    attributes replicated to Global Catalog 407, 410

    full replicas 406

    overview 406

    partial replicas 406

Active Directory schema

    Active Directory Schema Snap-in 403

    ADSI Edit snap-in 405

    in Active Directory architecture 395

Active Directory Schema Snap-in 403

Active Directory searches *See* searching in Active Directory

Active Directory store 393

ActiveScriptEventConsumer class 545

ActiveState ActivePerl

    See also Perl

    WMI and 430

ActiveX controls

    HTAs and 1088

    tabular data control *See* tabular data control

ActiveX Data Object interfaces, searching in Active Directory 589

ActiveX Data Objects *See* ADO

Add method, Dictionary object 298–299

addition operator (+), VBScript operator precedence 82–83

additional information about scripting 8

AddNew method

    DataList object 1101

    Recordset object, ADO 1107

add-on providers, WMI 438

AddPrinterConnection method, WshNetwork object 224

AddWindowsPrinterConnection method, WshNetwork object 224, 928, 929

Administrative Tools folder

    See also special folders

    locating special folders 788

administrator credentials required to run WMI scripts 443

administrator passwords, masking 1117–1120

Administrators group

    disk quotas 748

    WMI security and 444

ADO

    adding records 1107–1109

    ADO object model 1103

    connecting to databases 1105–1107

    deleting all records 1116–1117

    deleting selected records 1114–1116

    finding records 1109–1112

    in Active Directory searches 358

    overview 1103–1104

    updating records 1112–1114

ADO interfaces, searching in Active Directory 589

ADO objects, in Active Directory searches 358

ADS_UF_ACCOUNTDISABLE flag 568–569

ADS_UF_PASSWD_NOTREQD flag 696

ADS_UF_WORKSTATION_TRUST_ACCOUNT flag 696

ADS_USER_FLAG_ENUM enumeration 562

ADSI

    See also Active Directory

    Active Directory, searching *See* searching in Active Directory

    administrative credentials required 14

    ADsPaths *See* ADsPaths

    binding to Automation objects using VBScript 20

    binding to configuration container 392

    binding to current domain 391

    binding to directory service objects 320–325, 333

    binding to root domain 392

    binding to schema container 392

    choosing a scripting language 12–13

    committing changes to Active Directory 331

    compared to WSH 148, 226

    computer accounts, copying 350

    containers, enumerating contents 386

    containers, enumerating contents to perform tasks on 387

    containers, enumerating objects of specific types 388

    copying directory service objects 350–353

ADSI *(continued)*

Create method 310–313, 326, 327–328

creating directory service objects 310–313, 327–328

Delete method 317–318, 326, 330

deleting directory service objects 317–318, 330

directory service management overview 309

Get method 315–317, 326, 330, 346–347

GetEx method 344–345, 347

GetInfo method 346, 347–348

GetInfoEx method 346, 348–349

groups, creating 311

groups, deleting 318

groups, modifying attributes 314

groups, moving between containers 356

groups, reading attributes 316

history of 7

installed components 415

interfaces *See* ADSI interfaces

LDAP provider vs. WinNT provider 693

local property cache 326, 346–349

modifying directory service objects 313–315, 329, 334

MoveHere method 354–358

moving directory service objects between domains 354–355, 357

moving directory service objects 354–358

multiple scripting tasks 332–334

object model 414–415

object references, creating 325

OUs, creating 310

OUs, deleting 318

OUs, modifying attributes 313

OUs, moving between domains 357

OUs, reading attributes 315

overview 308–309

paths to directory service objects 322–325

production scripts 332–334

providers *See* ADSI providers

Put method 313–315, 326, 329

PutEx method 337–339

ADSI *(continued)*

reading attributes of directory service objects 315–317, 330, 334, 346–349

renaming directory service objects 356

results of searches, performing operations on 382–385

rootDSE 390–392

searching in Active Directory *See* searching in Active Directory

serverless binding 390

SetInfo method 331

steps in ADSI scripts 320–331, 332–334

user accounts, copying 352

user accounts, creating 311

user accounts, deleting 318

user accounts, modifying attributes 314

user accounts, reading attributes 315

ADSI architecture

ADSI object model 414–415

ADSI-enabled applications 420

directory namespace 417

installed components 415

interfaces 414, 421–425

layers 416–420

local property cache 420

providers 417–420

router 420

ADSI Edit snap-in 405

ADSI interfaces

categorization of interfaces 422

implementation by providers 421

overview 414, 421

ADSI object model 414–415

ADSI OLE DB provider 418

ADSI providers

implementation of interfaces 421

in ADsPaths 323

interfaces supported by 423–425

list of providers 418

overview 417

ADSI router 420

ADSI scripts

    printers and print management 882–883

    published folders, enumerating 836–837

    publishing shared folders in Active Directory 835

ADSI-enabled applications 420

ADsPath property, IADs interface 423

ADsPaths

    ADSI providers 323, 419

    distinguished names 323–325

    overview 322

    rootDSE 390–392

ADSystemInfo object 693

alerts

    disk quota alerts, issuing 750

    file creation events, monitoring 821–822

    file deletion events, monitoring 822–823

    file modification, monitoring 824

    in e-mail See e-mail messages, sending from scripts

Alias (file attribute) 275

all records, deleting from databases 1116–1117

all scheduled tasks, deleting 1144

All Users Application Data folder

    See also special folders

    locating special folders 788

All Users Desktop folder

    See also special folders

    locating special folders 788

    special folder identifiers 195

All Users Favorites folder

    See also special folders

    locating special folders 788

All Users Programs folder

    See also special folders

    locating special folders 788

    special folder identifiers 195

All Users Start Menu

    See also special folders

    locating special folders 788

    special folder identifiers 195

All Users Startup folder

    See also special folders

    locating special folders 788

    special folder identifiers 195

All Users Templates folder

    See also special folders

    locating special folders 788

AllocatedBaseSize property, Win32_PageFileUsage class 764–765

AllowMaximum property, Win32_Share class 826

AllUsers parameter, Install method 661

AllUsersDesktop (special folder identifier) 195

AllUsersPrograms (special folder identifier) 195

AllUsersStartMenu (special folder identifier) 195

AllUsersStartup (special folder identifier) 195

ALT key, SendKeys representation 206

ampersand (&), concatenating strings 29

AND keyword

    in WMI queries 512

    WMI event notifications and 540

AND operator, VBScript conditional statements 92

animated .gif files, showing script progress with 1131

Anonymous impersonation, WMI 496

antecedent services

    enumerating 997–998

    overview 993

APIs

    task-scheduling APIs 1136–1137

    WMI providers and 437–438

AppActivate method, WshShell object 209

appending to text files

    See also text files

    ForAppending mode 283, 292, 295

    overview 295

    redirecting script output 145

Application Center

    managing with WMI scripts 430

    WMI consumer 443

    WMI provider 438

Application Data folder

    See also special folders

    locating special folders 788

Application event log
    writing events to 870–872
    writing to, WSH 201–202
Application property, Internet Explorer object 1077–1079
ApplicationName property, HTA object 1088–1090
applications
    See also processes
    ADSI-enabled applications 420
    automating See COM
    auto-start programs 673–674
    COM components See COM
    ensuring applications are active 209
    running from within scripts 184–187
    sending keystrokes to See keystrokes, sending to
        applications
    setting focus 210
    without COM object model, automating 206–210
Architecture property, Win32_Processor class 620–621
architecture, Active Directory
    See also Active Directory
    attributes 395
    classes 395
    Database Layer 393
    Directory System Agent 393
    Extensible Storage Engine 393
    forests 394
    LDAP 393
    logical structure 394–413
    physical architecture 393
    schemas 395
    trees 394
architecture, WMI
    See also WMI
    managed resources 436
    overview 434–436
    security 443–444
    security, DCOM 445–446
    security, namespace-level 444–445
    security, operating system 446
    WMI consumers 443
    WMI infrastructure 437–442

architecture, WSH 135–139
Archive attribute
    file attribute 275
    folder attribute 258
Archive property, Win32_Directory class 775–776
archiving event logs
    event log backup files 852–855
    overview 852
    unique file names for backup files 856
arguments
    See also parameters
    command-line See command-line arguments
    for enterprise scripts See enterprise scripts
    user input 41–42
Arguments property
    WScript object 167
    WshShortcut object 192
arithmetic operators, VBScript operator precedence 82–83
arr (variable name prefix) 1153–1154
Array (data subtype) 1153–1154
Array function, VBScript 98
Array of Strings data type (WSH), corresponding registry
    and VBScript data types 204
arrays
    See also collections; Dictionary object
    alternatives to arrays 103
    Array function 98
    assigning data to, VBScript 99
    creating, VBScript 98
    declaring, VBScript 98
    delimited strings, converting to arrays, VBScript 101–102
    Dim statement 98
    dynamic arrays, VBScript 100
    index numbers 40
    overview 39–41
    parsing data files, VBScript 102
    ReDim Preserve statement, VBScript 100
arrow mouse pointer in Internet Explorer 1130
ASPScriptDefaultNamespace property, Win32_WMISetting
    class 647–649, 651–652

ASPScriptDefaultNamespace property, Win32_WMISetting object 454

asset management

enumerating installed hot fixes 645

identifying chassis type 634–636

identifying installed service packs 643–644

installing software 660–663

inventorying computer hardware 629–636

inventorying software 654–659

logging off users 682

monitoring power status changes 686–688

operating system name and version number 637–638

operating system properties 639–641

overview 617–618

recovery options 675–682

restarting computers 685–686

retrieving BIOS information 623–626

retrieving SMBIOS information 628–629

retrieving system information 619–621

shutting down computers 682–685

startup commands 673–674

startup options 667–673

System Information snap-in 619–620

uninstalling software 666

upgrading software 664–665

WMI settings 646–652

asset tag numbers, retrieving 628–629

assetNumber attribute, printQueue object 933–935

assigning data to arrays, VBScript 99

assigning values to variables, VBScript 52

association classes, WMI 450, 466

Association qualifier, WMI 466, 470

AssociatorsOf method, SWbemServices object 487, 490

asynchronous methods, SWbemServices object 488

asynchronous mode, SWbemServices object 489

Asynchronous property, Command object (ADO) 380

asynchronous queries, enumerating files 810

asynchronous scripts, event log queries 865–866

AT APIs 1136–1137

At.exe 1136

AtEndOfLine property, StdIn stream 160

AtEndOfStream property, StdIn stream 160

attribute list, Active Directory Schema Snap-in 403

attributes

See also attribute-value pairs; names of specific classes and objects; properties

Active Directory See attributes, Active Directory

bitmap values 259–260

computer account attributes 701–703

configuring 261–262

directory service objects See attributes, directory service objects

file attributes 275–277

folder attributes 258–262

indexed attributes 409, 410

mandatory attributes 313, 329, 396, 398

multivalued See multivalued attributes, directory service objects; multivalued attributes, user accounts

null-value attributes 701–702

operational attributes 347, 412

password attributes See attributes, passwords

user account attributes See attributes, user accounts

Attributes property

Folder object 256–257

Win32_SoftwareFeature class 658–659

attributes, Active Directory

attribute list, Active Directory Schema Snap-in 403

attributes replicated to Global Catalog 407, 410

in Active Directory architecture 395

indexed attributes 409, 410

isMemberOfPartialAttributeSet attribute 407

mandatory attributes 396–398

operational attributes 412

optional attributes 396–398

searchFlags attribute 409

attributes, directory service objects

attribute names 329

lDAPDisplayNames 329

mandatory attributes 313, 329

modifying in multiple objects 382

attributes, directory service objects *(continued)*

   modifying 313–315, 329, 334

   multivalued attributes 336

   multivalued attributes, appending 340

   multivalued attributes, clearing 339, 342

   multivalued attributes, deleting entries 341

   multivalued attributes, modifying 336–343

   multivalued attributes, PutEx method 337–339

   multivalued attributes, reading 344–345

   multivalued attributes, updating 339, 342

   operational attributes 347

   reading 315–317, 330, 334, 346–349

   searching in Active Directory, referral chasing 367–369

   searching in Active Directory, specifying attributes 362

attributes, passwords

   See also passwords

   list of attributes 561–562

   userAccountControl attribute, changing flag values 565

   userAccountControl attribute, displaying values 562

   userAccountControl attribute, flag values 563

attributes, user accounts

   See also searching in Active Directory

   attributes to be returned by searches, specifying 592

   attributes without values, searching for 603

   available on General properties page 571–573

   characteristics of attributes 570

   clearing 580

   copying user accounts 581–583

   data type considerations 570

   empty attribute values, searching for 601–605

   lDAPDisplayNames, determining 570

   identification attributes 553

   managing, IADs interface vs. IADsUser interface 570

   multivalued attributes, adding entries to 578

   multivalued attributes, clearing 580

   multivalued attributes, modifying 577–580

   multivalued attributes, reading 573–575

attributes, user accounts *(continued)*

   multivalued attributes, removing entries from 579

   multivalued attributes, searching for 608

   multivalued attributes, writing 576–577

   multivalued vs. single-valued attributes 570

   optional attributes, default settings 555

   reading 573–575

   sAMAccountName attribute, verifying uniqueness 600

   searching for in containers 593, 596

   searching for in subcontainers 598

   security principal naming attributes 554

   single-valued attributes, clearing 580

   single-valued attributes, reading 573–575

   single-valued attributes, writing 576–577

   verifying uniqueness in forests 600

   writing 576–577

attribute-value pairs

   See also attributes, directory service objects

   attribute types, distinguished names 324

   attributes, modifying 313–315, 329, 334

   directory service objects, modifying 329

   distinguished names 323–325

   mandatory attributes 313, 329

authentication

   authenticationLevel setting, WMI 497

   authority setting, WMI 498

   identifying current domain controller 718–719

authority setting, WMI moniker 498

Auto (service start option) 1003

automated e-mail messages *See* e-mail messages, sending from scripts

AutomaticResetBootOption property, Win32_ComputerSystem class 669

AutomaticResetCapability property, Win32_ComputerSystem class 669

Automation object model of Internet Explorer 1077

Automation objects

   See also COM objects

   applications without COM object model, automating 206–210

Automation objects *(continued)*

binding to, VBScript 19–20

calling object methods 21–22

collections *See* collections

default properties 1175

dot notation 21

monikers 20, 124

object references *See* object references

overview 122

retrieving object properties 22

VBScript and 18–19

WMI scripting library 480–483

WSH support for 131

AutoReboot property, Win32_OSRecoveryConfiguration class 676–677

AutoRecoverMOFs property, Win32_WMISetting class 647–649

auto-start programs

enumerating 673–674

Win32_StartupCommand class 674

auto-start services

configuring start options 1003–1004

error control codes 1004–1005

running 973

auxiliary classes, Active Directory 399, 401

availability

increasing service availability 974

monitoring process availability 941, 942

monitoring service availability 973, 974–975

availability of classes, WMI 471, 479

availability of printers, scheduling 918

Availability property, Win32_Printer class 885–887

available disk space

See also disk quotas

disk quotas and 748

enumerating by user 739–740

enumerating 738

monitoring in real time 740–741

AvailableSpace property, FileSystemObject 245–247

AvailableVirtualMemory property, Win32_OperatingSystem class 620–621

B

background processing *See* asynchronous queries, enumerating files

backing up files

event logs 844, 852–856

registry data, backing up before editing 1025–1026

backslash (\), binding to root folder 250

BACKSPACE key, SendKeys representation 206

BackupInterval property, Win32_WMISetting class 647–649, 651–652

BackupLastTime property, Win32_WMISetting class 647–649

Bad file mode (error) 285

BannerPage property, IADsPrintQueue interface 910

base option, Active Directory search scope 370, 592

batch files, moving beyond shell scripting 11

batch mode, running WSH scripts 143

batch scripts, compared to WSH scripts 133, 184

binary mode, Dictionary object 297–298

Binary Value data type (WSH), corresponding registry and VBScript data types 204

binary-tree index file, CIM repository 442

binary-valued registry entries

overview 1031–1032

reading 1032

REG_BINARY data type 1020, 1023

binding

early binding 124

late binding 124

serverless binding 390

to Active Directory 1070

to COM objects 19–20, 124

to configuration container 392

to current domain 391

to directory service objects 320–325, 333

to disk drives 245

to files 266–267

to folders 249–250

to resources, WMI 502

to root domain 392

to schema container 392

BIOS
overview 623
retrieving BIOS information 623–626
SMBIOS specification 623, 628–629
BIOSCharacteristics property, Win32_BIOS class 624–626
bit fields 562–563
bitmap values
configuring attributes 261–262
file attributes 275–277
folder attributes 260
overview 259–260
blank lines
See also white space in scripts
including in script output 157
bln (variable name prefix) 1153–1154
BlockSize property, Win32_DiskPartition class 730–732
blue screen See stop messages
Boolean (data subtype) 1153–1154
boolean expressions
readability of code 1173
testing for True and False 1173
Boolean values
in WHERE clauses, WMI queries 509
sorting with tabular data control 1096
Boot loader section, Boot.ini file 671
Boot.ini file 671
Bootable property, Win32_DiskPartition class 730–732
BootDevice property, Win32_OperatingSystem class 639–641
booting computers, startup options See startup options
BootPartition property, Win32_DiskPartition class 730–732
BootupState property, Win32_ComputerSystem class 669
Border property, HTA object 1088–1090
BorderStyle property, HTA object 1088–1090
BREAK key, SendKeys representation 206
Browse for Folder dialog box 791–792
BrowseForFolder method, Shell object 792
browsers, Internet Explorer See Internet Explorer
btree index file, CIM repository 442
build numbers, WSH, retrieving 179

Build property, WScript object 179
BuildNumber property
Win32_BIOS class 624–626
Win32_OperatingSystem class 639–641
BuildType property, Win32_OperatingSystem class 639–641
BuildVersion property, Win32_WMISetting class 647–649
built-in providers, WMI 438–439
Busy property, Internet Explorer object 1077–1079
ByRef keyword, VBScript 119
byt (variable name prefix) 1153–1154
Byte (data subtype) 1153–1154
Byte values, VBScript, CByte type conversion function 58
BytesPerSector property, Win32_DiskDrive class 726–728
ByVal keyword, VBScript 119

C

Cache Results property, Command object (ADO) 380
cache, local properties See local property cache, ADSI
Camel casing, variable names 1152
Cannot Change Password setting 561
canonicalName attribute, Computer class 691
Capabilities property
Win32_DiskDrive class 726–728
Win32_Printer class 907–908
CapabilityDescriptions property, Win32_Printer class 907–908
CAPS LOCK key, SendKeys representation 206
Caption property
HTA object 1088–1090
Win32_OperatingSystem class 638, 639–641
Win32_PrintJob class 900–902
Win32_Product class 656
Win32_ScheduledJob class 1137–1140
Win32_Share class 826
Win32_SoftwareFeature class 658–659
carriage return, VBScript statement breaks 47
carriage return/linefeed, appending to script output 157
case
See also case sensitivity
Camel casing 1152

case *(continued)*

    case styles, and code readability 1171

    modifying in VBScript script output 81–82

    Pascal casing 1157, 1171

case sensitivity

    See also case

    CompareMode property, Dictionary object 297–298

    variable names 1154–1155

Case statement, VBScript 96

casting type values 57

categorization

    Active Directory classes 398–403

    ADSI interfaces 422

Category property, Win32_NTLogEvent class 858–859

CBool function, VBScript 58

CByte function, VBScript 58

CCur function, VBScript 58

CDate function, VBScript 58

CDbl function, VBScript 58

CDO, e-mail messaging and 1121

Cdosys.dll 1121

CD-ROM (System Information category), equivalent WMI class 630

Change method, Win32_Service class 1001–1003, 1007

ChangePassword method, IADsUser interface 558, 560

changing values of registry entries

    DWORD-valued entries 1033–1034

    string-valued entries 1033–1034

Character property, WshRemoteError object 232

characters

    allowed in variable names 1154–1155

    case *See* case

    modifying character case, VBScript 81–82

    proportional vs. non-proportional fonts 78–79

    reading text files character-by-character 290–292

    SendKeys representations of keyboard characters 206–207

Chase Referrals property, Command object (ADO) 367

chassis type, identifying 634–636

CheckAccess method, Registry Provider 1047–1048

child classes, WMI 463–465

child namespaces 445, 457

choosing a scripting language 12–13

CIM class definitions

    accessing using SWbemObject 461

    managed resource class definition structure 467

    relationship to WMI scripting library Automation objects 480

    retrieving using SWbemObject GetObjectText_ method 477–478

    retrieving using SWbemObject properties 472–477

CIM classes

    See also CIM class definitions; WMI classes

    availability of 471–472

    blueprint of WMI-managed environment 449–450

    categories of classes 458

    components of classes 466–467

    core and common classes 459–460

    extension classes 460–461

    hierarchy and inheritance 463–465

    importance of 446

    listing classes in a namespace 461–463

    methods 469

    namespaces *See* namespaces

    overview 441–442

    properties 467–469

    qualifiers 469–471

    retrieving class definitions 472–478

    system classes 458–459

    types of classes 465–466

    WMI Tester and 471

CIM Object Manager *See* CIMOM

CIM repository

    as component of WMI infrastructure 435–436

    blueprint of WMI-managed environment 449–450

    browsing in, tools for 479

    classes *See* CIM classes

    event subscriptions stored in 543

    location 442

    namespaces *See* namespaces

    overview 441–442, 446–449

    queries *See* WMI queries

    registering consumer classes in 545

CIM repository *(continued)*

  relationship to WMI scripting library Automation
    objects 480

  security 444

  WMI provider registration 440

CIM Studio 479, 536

Cim.rep 442

CIM_DataFile class

  Copy method 816

  Delete method 817, 529

  dynamic classes 460

  methods 776–778

  properties available in Windows Explorer
    interface 804

  Rename method 813

CIM_DirectoryContainsFile class 460

  file creation events, monitoring 821

  file deletion events, monitoring 822

CIM_LogicalElement class 463

CIM_ManagedSystemElement class 463

CIM_ProcessExecutable class 460

CIM_Service class 463

CIM_VideoControllerResolution class 460

CIMOM

  as component of WMI infrastructure 435–436

  connecting to, remote access 440

  overview 439–440

  processing consumer requests 440

CIMType qualifier, WMI 470

cimv2 namespace 442, 450, 453

Cimwin32.dll 438–439

Cimwin32.mof 477

CInt function, VBScript 58

clarifying code See comments

Class argument, Create method, IADsContainer
  interface 557

class definitions, CIM See CIM class definitions

class list, Active Directory Schema Snap-in 403

Class property, IADs interface 423

class qualifiers, WMI 470

class store, CIM repository 441, 449

classes

  Active Directory See Active Directory classes

  CIM See CIM classes

  WMI See WMI classes

__ClassOperationEvent class 536, 537

Clear method, VBScript 46

clearing event logs 852–855

clearing script output from Internet Explorer 1084

client-side network settings, managing with WMI
  scripts 430

CLng function, VBScript 58

Close method

  Connection object, ADO 1105

  FileSystemObject 285

  Recordset object, ADO 1105

closing text files 284–285

CLSID, WMI 494

Cmd.exe, compared to WSH scripts 133

CN attribute type, distinguished names 324

CN attribute, Volume class 835

cn argument, Create method, IADsContainer interface 557

cn attribute

  Computer class 691

  printQueue object 933–935

  user accounts 553

code

  See also scripts

  formatting See formatting code

  readability See readability of code

CodeSet property, Win32_OperatingSystem class 639–
  641

coercion See type coercion

col (variable name prefix) 1153–1154

Collaboration Data Objects See CDO, e-mail messaging
  and

Collate property, Win32_PrinterConfiguration class 908–
  910

Collection (data subtype) 1153–1154

collections

  See also arrays

  Count property 33

collections *(continued)*

    determining number of items 33

    For Each statement 31–32

    iterating, VBScript 31–32

    of installed drives, returning 244

    overview 30–31

    with zero items 33–34

    WMI scripting vs. FileSystemObject 772

colon (:), in named arguments 164, 170

Color property, Win32_PrinterConfiguration class 908–910

colors in script output 1077, 1081–1084

columns in tabular script output

    filtering data using tabular data control 1099

    fixed-width columns in command window 1073

    sorting data using tabular data control 1096

COM

    Automation objects *See* Automation objects

    Automation *See* COM Automation

    COM clients 122

    COM servers 122

    in-process servers 122

    objects *See* COM objects

    out-of-process servers 122

    overview 121

    registration of COM servers 122

    WSH support for 131

COM Automation

    Automation objects *See* Automation objects

    password masking and 1117

    WMI and 430

COM clients 122

COM objects

    See also Automation objects

    applications without COM object model, automating 206–210

    binding to 124

    binding to using WScript object 150

    CreateObject method, VBScript 124

    CreateObject method, WSH vs. VBScript 153

    creating 123

    creating new instances of, WSH 151–152

COM objects *(continued)*

    dissociating object references 128

    early binding 124

    Embedded mode 123

    error handling, VBScript 110–111

    event-handling capabilities 153

    GetObject method, VBScript 124

    GetObject method, WSH vs. VBScript 153

    interactions with WScript library 140

    late binding 124

    making applications visible 124

    methods, calling 152

    Nothing keyword, VBScript 128

    object references *See* object references

    properties, accessing 152

    references *See* object references

    remote object creation 153

    Server mode 123

    unloading from memory 127–128

    using previously instantiated objects, WSH 152

    VBScript and 18–19

    verifying object references 126

    within Shell object 774

    WSH support for 131, 139

    WshController object *See* WshController object

    WshNetwork object *See* WshNetwork object

    WshShell object *See* WshShell object

COM servers 122

command line

    See also command window

    arguments *See* command-line arguments

    running WSH scripts 142–145

    tools *See* command-line tools

Command object, ADO

    Asynchronous property 380

    Cache Results property 380

    Chase Referrals property 367

    CommandText property 589

    in Active Directory searches 358

    optimizing Active Directory searches 380

    Page Size property 380

    searching in Active Directory 589

Command object, ADO *(continued)*

  Size Limit property 380

  Sort On property 371

  Time Limit property 380

  Timeout property 380

Command property

  Win32_ScheduledJob class 1137–1140, 1141–1142

  Win32_StartupCommand class 674

command window

  accepting user input 159–162

  clearing 950

  displaying data 950

  displaying script output 154–159, 1072–1076

  messages, displaying 159

  StdErr stream *See* StdErr stream

  StdIn stream *See* StdIn stream

  StdOut stream *See* StdOut stream

  streams *See* streams, input and output

  tracking script progress 1133–1135

  WScript Echo method 154–157

command-line arguments

  accessing 167–168

  Arguments property, WScript object 167

  double quotation marks 164

  filtering by WSH 164–165

  for enterprise scripts, limitations of 1060

  for enterprise scripts, text files as 1064

  named and unnamed arguments in same script 172

  named arguments 164, 170–171

  naming 1150

  overview 162

  storage by WSH 164–165

  storing in Dictionary object 296

  unnamed arguments 164, 168–170

  verifying correct number of arguments 172–173

  verifying presence of required arguments 174–175

  white space 164

  WshArguments collection 164, 166–168

  WshNamed collection 164, 170–171

  WshUnnamed collection 164, 165, 168–170

command-line processor, specifying on command line 188–189

command-line tools

  moving beyond shell scripting 11

  parameters, spaces in 189–190

  running from within scripts 132, 188–189

CommandLineEventConsumer class 545

CommandText property, Command object 589

comma-separated-value files

  converting to arrays, VBScript 101–102

  log files, parsing 877

  saving script output for use with tabular data control 1092, 1096

comments

  See also documenting code

  comment delimiters 1178

  extracting for script documentation 1181

  formatting 1179

  function and procedure headers 1180

  general guidelines 1176–1178

  overview 1175

  removing debugging comments 1183

  script headers 1179–1180

  used as debugging aid 1182

common classes, WMI

  See also WMI classes

  overview 459–460

  structure of CIM repository 450

Common Files folder

  See also special folders

  locating special folders 788

Common Information Model repository *See* CIM repository

Common-Name attribute, Computer class 691

company attribute, Computer class 691

CompareMode property, Dictionary object 297–298

Component Object Model *See* COM

Compress method

  CIM_DataFile class 776–778

  Win32_Directory class 776–778, 802

Compressed attribute

  files 275

  folders 258

Compressed property
    Win32_Directory class 775-776
    Win32_LogicalDisk class 733-734
compressing folders 802-803
compression, and disk quotas 748
CompressionMethod property
    Win32_Directory class 775-776
    Win32_DiskDrive class 726-728
computer accounts
    See also computer roles
    attributes, Computer class 691-693
    attributes, configuring 703
    attributes, enumerating 701-702
    computer information, retrieving 693-694
    copying 350
    creating 695-697
    current domain controller, identifying 718-719
    deleting 698
    deleting specified accounts 699
    enabling 696
    enumerating 709
    locating based on attributes 710-711
    logon information, retrieving 693-694
    Microsoft Windows operating systems and 694-695
    moving between OUs 705
    overview 690
    passwords, resetting 706-707
    renaming 704-705
    searching for in Active Directory 707-711
    structuring in Active Directory 1070
computer assets, managing See asset management
Computer class 691, 693
computer configuration, determining
    BIOS information 623-626
    chassis type 634-636
    installed hot fixes 645
    inventorying computer hardware 629-636
    latest installed service pack 643-644
    operating system name and version number 637-638
    operating system properties 639-641
    SMBIOS information 628-629
    system information 619-621

computer hardware See hardware
computer information
    See also system information
    retrieving in WSH scripts 226
computer roles
    See also computer accounts
    Active Directory-specific roles 716
    computer accounts See computer accounts
    current domain controller 718-719
    domain controllers, enumerating 716-717
    DomainRole property, Win32_ComputerSystem class 713
    global catalog servers 722, 723-724
    identifying 713-714
    identifying based on installed services 715
    operations master roles 719-721
    overview 689, 712
ComputerName attribute, ADSystemInfo object 693
ComputerName property
    Win32_NTLogEvent class 858-859
    WshNetwork object 226
computers
    accounts See computer accounts
    as managed resources 436
    listing in databases 1067
    listing in text files 1061
    logging off users 682-685
    managing with WMI scripts 430
    monitoring power status changes 686-688
    multiple computers, running scripts on See enterprise scripts
    recovery See disaster recovery
    remote See remote computers, managing recovery options
    restarting 685-686
    retrieving names from Active Directory 1070
    roles See computer roles
    shutting down 682-685
    specifying physical location 703
    startup commands See startup commands
    startup options See startup options
    system requirements 13-14
    trusting for delegation 663

COMSPEC (environment variable) 198

%comspec% environment variable 188–189

concatenating strings, VBScript 29–30

concatenating text files 288

conditional statements, VBScript

    Case statement 96

    If...Then...ElseIf statement 93–95

    If...Then statement 37

    If...Then...Else statement 38–39

    logical AND operator 92

    logical OR operator 93

    Select Case statements 96–97

    testing multiple conditions 92–97

conditions (loop conditions), checking 89–90

configuration container, binding to 392

Configuration object, CDO 1123

Configuration partition, Active Directory 406

configuring services

    See also services

    error control codes 1004–1005

    parameters for service properties 1001–1003

    service account passwords 1009–1010

    specifying service accounts 1007–1008

    start options 1003–1004

    Win32_Service Change method 1001

connecting to CIMOM, remote access 440

connecting to databases

    data source names (DSNs) 1104

    scripting steps 1105–1107

connecting to namespaces 452–454, 484, 486

connecting to WMI

    CIMOM security 440

    namespace-level security 444

    SWbemLocator object 484

    SWbemServices object 486

    WMI moniker 493

Connection object, ADO

    Close method 1105

    described 1103

    in Active Directory searches 358, 589

    Open method 1105

connections, printer See printer connections

consistency of variable names 1154–1155

constants

    assigning strings to 26

    compared to literal values 53

    defining, VBScript 54

    intrinsic constants, VBScript 54–56

    naming conventions 1149, 1156

    overview 25–26, 53

    WMI Registry Provider, built-in constants 1022

    WMI Registry Provider, method parameters 1027

consumer classes, WMI 545

Consumer property, __FilterToConsumerBinding class 546

consumers, WMI

    See also WMI scripts

    as layer of WMI architecture 435–436

    overview 443

    request processing by CIMOM 440

Contact user account 553

contactName attribute, printQueue object 933–935

containers, Active Directory

    configuration container, binding to 392

    enterprise scripts and 1070–1072

    enumerating contents 386

    enumerating contents to perform tasks on 387

    enumerating objects of specific types 388

    enumeration, managing user accounts 613–614

    retrieving computer names from 1070–1072

    schema container, binding to 392

    searching for attributes 593, 596, 598

    selecting for user account creation 556

context menu, Windows Explorer

    adding script templates 1161

    running WSH scripts 146

continuously-running scripts 89

CONTROL key, SendKeys representation 206

Control Panel folder

    See also special folders

    locating special folders 788

control structure statements, indenting for readability 1166–1167 controller scripts

    See also remotely running scripts

    overview 227

converting dates

    standard to UTC 519–522, 784–786

    UTC to standard 517

Cookies folder

    See also special folders

    locating special folders 788

Copies property, Win32_PrinterConfiguration class 908–910

Copy method

    CIM_DataFile class 776–778, 816

    Win32_Directory class 776–778, 796

CopyFile method, FileSystemObject 270–271

CopyFolder method, FileSystemObject 252–254

CopyHere method, Shell Folder object 798–799

copying

    computer accounts 350

    directory service objects 350–353

    files 270–271, 816

    folders and folder contents 252–254

    folders using Shell Folder object 797–799

    folders using WMI 796

    folders with same name 798

    user accounts 352, 581–583

Copying dialog box, displaying 798, 799

core classes, WMI

    overview 459–460

    structure of CIM repository 450

core interfaces, ADSI 422

correctness, testing scripts for 1188

Count method

    verifying correct number of arguments 172

    WshArguments collection 166

    WshNamed collection 165

    WshUnnamed collection 165

Count property

    collections 33

    Dictionary object 299

    SWbemObjectSet collection 491

counters, as managed resources 436

CountryCode property, Win32_OperatingSystem class 639–641

Create method

    ADSI 310–313, 326, 327–328

    IADsContainer interface 557

    Win32_Process class 959–960

    Win32_ScheduledJob class 1141–1142

    Win32_Service class 1011–1012

    Win32_Share class 828–829

    WMI classes 528

CreateFolder method, FileSystemObject 250, 251

CreateKey method, Registry Provider 1035

CreateObject method

    Internet Explorer object 1077–1079

    VBScript 20, 123, 124

    WMI objects 483

    Wscript object 1085

    WScript object 150, 151, 153

    WSH compared to VBScript 153

CreateScript method, WshController object 230

CreateShortcut method

    WshShortcut object 192

    WshUrlShortcut object 193

CreateTextFile method, FileSystemObject 280–281

creating directory service objects

    See also directory service objects

    binding to containers 312

    committing changes to Active Directory 331

    Create method parameters 327–328

    creating objects 312

    groups 311

    mandatory attributes 313

    object references 328

    OUs 310

    selecting object for binding 320–322

    setting attribute values 313

    user accounts 311

creating enterprise scripts *See* enterprise scripts

creating files, monitoring file creation events 821–822

creating processes
  event subscriptions 943
  monitoring 943–944
  startup options 961–964
  Win32_Process Create method 959–960
creating resources, WMI 528, 538, 542
creating scheduled tasks 1140–1143
creating scripts
  See also scripts
  introduction to scripting 3–6
creating user accounts
  changing passwords 560
  configuring passwords 558–560
  Create method, IADsContainer interface 557
  overview 555
  scripting steps 311
  selecting containers for account creation 556
  setting passwords 559
  specifying paths 556
  verifying name uniqueness in domains 556
CreationDate property
  Win32_Directory class 775–776, 784
  Win32_PageFile class 763
credentials
  coding into WMI scripts 485
  impersonation See impersonation levels
  required to run WMI scripts 443
Critical (error control code) 1004
crosshair mouse pointer, Internet Explorer 1130
crossRefContainer class, identifying operations master roles 719–721
CScript host
  See also script hosts, WSH; WScript host; WSH scripts
  command-line options 143–145
  compared to WScript host 137–138
  default script host, setting 143
  determining current script host 180
  input to scripts, accepting 159–162
  logo, displaying or suppressing in script output 143

CScript host (continued)
  output from scripts, displaying 156–159
  running scripts from command line 143–145
  StdErr stream See StdErr stream
  StdIn stream See StdIn stream
  StdOut stream See StdOut stream
  streams See streams, input and output
  WScript Echo method 156–157
CSIDLs, identifying special folders 787
CSName property
  Win32_Directory class 775–776
  Win32_PageFile class 763
  Win32_QuickFixEngineering class 645
CSng function, VBScript 58
CStr function, VBScript 58
CSV files
  converting to arrays, VBScript 101–102
  log files, parsing 877
  saving script output for use with tabular data control 1092, 1096
cur (variable name prefix) 1153–1154
Currency (data subtype) 1153–1154
Currency values, VBScript, CCur type conversion function 58
current domain, binding to 391
current folder, binding to 250
current working directory, changing for scripts 211
CurrentDirectory property, WshShell object 211
CurrentLanguage property, Win32_BIOS class 624–626
CurrentUsage property, Win32_PageFileUsage class 764–765
cursor styles, mouse pointer in Internet Explorer 1130
CursorLocation property, Recordset object, ADO 1105
CursorType property, Recordset object, ADO 1105
custom event logs 874–875

D

data model, WMI 449
data provider, OLE DB 1104
data source names 1104
data type interfaces, ADSI 422

data types
    casting type values 57
    data subtypes 1153-1154
    Empty variables, VBScript 58-59
    Null variables, VBScript 58-59
    of registry entries 1020
    of registry entries, enumerating 1043
    of registry entries, integer values for 1023
    registry types, WSH and VBScript 204
    strongly-typed languages 56
    type coercion, VBScript 57-58
    type conversion functions, VBScript 58
    typeless languages 56
    variable name prefixes 1153-1154
Database Layer, Active Directory 393
DatabaseDirectory property, Win32_WMISetting
    class 647-649
databases
    about database and script interaction 1103
    adding records to 1107-1109
    ADO and 1103-1104
    connecting to 1105-1107
    copying events to 867-869
    data source names (DSNs) 1104
    deleting all records from 1116-1117
    deleting selected records from 1114-1116
    finding records in 1109-1112
    retrieving arguments from 1067-1070
    updating records in 1112-1114
DataList object
    AddNew method 1101
    Sort method 1101
DataURL property, tabular data control 1093-1094
Date (Time) (data subtype) 1153-1154
Date function, VBScript 60, 70
date values See dates and date values
Date values, VBScript
    See also dates and date values
    CDate type conversion function 58
DateAdd function, VBScript 70
DateCreated property, Folder object 256-257

DateDiff function, VBScript 68-69
DateLastAccessed property, Folder object 256-257
DateLastModified property, Folder object 256-257
DatePart function, VBScript 62-66
dates and date values
    converting to standard format, WMI scripts 517
    converting to UTC format 784-786
    converting to UTC format, WMI scripts 519-522
    date arithmetic, VBScript 68-70
    date formats, system settings and 61
    date literals, VBScript 61
    first week of the year, configuring in VBScript 65-66
    folder date properties 784
    formatting day names, VBScript 72-73
    formatting month names, VBScript 72-73
    formatting, VBScript 70-73
    importance of in system administration 59
    intervals between, determining, VBScript 68-69
    projecting based on specified interval, VBScript 70
    retrieving specific parts of, VBScript 62-67
    retrieving, VBScript 60-61
    sorting with tabular data control 1096
    standard format 517
    UTC format 515, 519-522, 784-786
    verifying values are dates, VBScript 61-62
Day function, VBScript 66-67
days
    formatting day names, VBScript 72-73
    intervals between, determining, VBScript 69
    retrieving from date and time values 62-64, 66-67
DaysOfMonth property, Win32_ScheduledJob
    class 1137-1140, 1141-1142
DaysOfWeek property, Win32_ScheduledJob class 1137-
    1140, 1141-1142
dbl (variable name prefix) 1153-1154
DC attribute type, distinguished names 324
DCOM security, WMI 445-446, 496-498
DCPromo.log 876
DCPromoUI.log 876
debug files See memory dump files
Debug property, Win32_OperatingSystem class 639-641

debugging scripts

    comments as debugging aid 1182

    disabling error handling 1187-1188

    running scripts incrementally 1186-1187

    syntax checking 1187

    testing scripts 1188

    trace routines 1184-1185

DebugPathFile property, Win32_OSRecoveryConfiguration class 676-677

decimal point, formatting numbers 84, 86-87

declaring arrays 98

declaring variables, VBScript

    explicit declaration 50-51

    implicit declaration 49-50

default mouse pointer, Internet Explorer 1130

default namespace

    retrieving 454

    root\default namespace 452, 453

    setting 452-455

default operating system, configuring 670

default printer, setting 226

default properties

    See also properties

    of automation objects 1175

default registry entries 1021

default script host, setting 143

default values, VBScript variables 51-52

defaultNamingContext attribute, rootDSE 391

DefaultQuotaLimit property, DiskQuotaControl object 744

DefaultQuotaThreshold property, DiskQuotaControl object 744

DEL or DELETE key, SendKeys representation 206

Delegate impersonation, WMI 445, 496-497

delegation, trusting users and computers for 663

DELETE (registry subkey access right) 1048

Delete method

    ADSI 317-318, 326, 330

    CIM_DataFile class 776-778, 817

    IADsContainer interface 588

    Recordset object, ADO 1110, 1114

    SWbemServices object 487-488

Delete method (continued)

    Win32_Directory class 776-778, 801

    Win32_ScheduledJob class 1144

    Win32_Share class 832

    WMI classes 529

Delete query, SQL 1116

DeleteFile method, FileSystemObject 269-270

DeleteFolder method, FileSystemObject 251

DeleteKey method, Registry Provider 1045, 1046

DeleteObject method, IADsDeleteOps interface 698-699

DeleteValue method, Registry Provider 1045-1046

deleting

    computer accounts 698-699

    database records See deleting records from databases

    directory service objects See deleting directory service objects

    file deletion events, monitoring 822-823

    files 268-270, 817-818

    folders 251-252, 801

    network shares 832-833

    printer connections 928-929, 930

    processes 943, 944, 945

    published folders 839-840

    read-only folders 801

    records See deleting records from databases

    registry entries 1045-1046

    registry subkeys 1045, 1046

    resources, WMI 529, 538, 542

    scheduled tasks 1144-1145

    shared folders 832-833, 839-840

    shortcuts 194

    text files 284

    user accounts 588

deleting directory service objects

    See also directory service objects

    committing changes to Active Directory 331

    Delete method parameters 330

    groups 318

    OUs 318

    overview 317-318, 330

    user accounts 318

deleting records from databases
    all records 1116-1117
    selected records 1114-1116
delimited strings, converting to arrays, VBScript 101-102
delimiters, comments 1178
demonstration scripts See tasks
department attribute, Computer class 691
dependent services
    enumerating for all services 995, 996
    enumerating for single service 995
    overview 993, 994
    starting 998-999, 1000
    stopping 998, 999
description attribute
    Computer class 691
    printQueue object 933-935
    user accounts 572
    Volume class 835
Description parameter
    Create method (Win32_Share class) 828
    SetShareInfo method (Win32_Share class) 833
Description property
    IADsPrintJob interface 902-903, 923-924
    IADsPrintQueue interface 910
    Win32_DiskDrive class 726-728
    Win32_PageFile class 763
    Win32_PageFileUsage class 764-765
    Win32_Printer class 885-887, 907-908
    Win32_Processor class 620-621
    Win32_Product class 656
    Win32_QuickFixEngineering class 645
    Win32_ScheduledJob class 1137-1140
    Win32_Service class 978-980
    Win32_SoftwareFeature class 658-659
    Win32_StartupCommand class 674
    WshRemoteError object 232
    WshShortcut object 192
Desktop folder
    See also special folders
    locating special folders 788
    special folder identifiers 195

Desktop, in Shell namespace hierarchy 773
DesktopInteract property, Win32_Service class 978-980, 1001-1003, 1011-1012
device drivers, as managed resources 436
DeviceID property
    Win32_DiskDrive class 726-728
    Win32_DiskPartition class 730-732
    Win32_LogicalDisk class 733-734
    Win32_Printer class 907-908
DeviceName property, Win32_PrinterConfiguration class 908-910
devices, as managed resources 436
DHCPSrvLog 876
Dictionary object
    See also arrays
    Add method 298-299
    adding key-item pairs 298-299
    alternatives to arrays 103
    binary mode 297-298
    CompareMode property 297-298
    Count property 299
    creating 296
    determining number of key-item pairs 299
    displaying value of specific item 301
    enterprise scripts and 1061
    enumerating keys and items 300-301
    Exists method 301
    inadvertently adding keys 298
    Item method 301
    Items method 300
    Keys method 300
    modifying items 302-303
    overview 296
    Remove method 303-304
    RemoveAll method 303, 305
    removing all key-item pairs 303-304
    removing specific key-item pair 304-305
    verifying existence of specific key 301
digitally signing scripts 235-238
Dim statement, VBScript 51, 98

directories

    See also folders and folder management

    current working directory, changing for scripts 211

    rootDSE 390–392

Directory (folder attribute) 258

directory namespace, ADSI 417

directory service management

    ADSI *See* ADSI

    directory service objects *See* directory service objects

    overview 309

directory service objects

    ADsPath 322–325

    attributes *See* attributes, directory service objects

    binding to 320–325, 333

    committing changes to Active Directory 331

    computer accounts, copying 350

    containers, enumerating contents 386

    containers, enumerating contents to perform tasks on 387

    containers, enumerating objects of specific types 388

    copying 350–353

    creating 310–313, 327–328

    deleting 317–318, 330

    distinguished names 323–325

    groups, creating 311

    groups, deleting 318

    groups, modifying attributes 314

    groups, moving between containers 356

    groups, reading attributes 316

    instantiation of classes 395

    local property cache 326, 346–349

    modifying 313–315, 329, 334

    moving 354–358

    moving, cross-domain moves 354–355, 357

    object references, creating 325

    OUs, creating 310

    OUs, deleting 318

    OUs, modifying attributes 313

    OUs, moving between domains 357

    OUs, reading attributes 315

    paths to 322–325

    renaming 356

directory service objects *(continued)*

    results of searches, performing operations on 382–385

    rootDSE 390–392

    searching for *See* searching in Active Directory

    steps in ADSI scripts 320–331, 332–334

    user accounts, copying 352

    user accounts, creating 311

    user accounts, deleting 318

    user accounts, modifying attributes 314

    user accounts, reading attributes 315

Directory System Agent 393

Disabled (service start option) 1003

disabling error handling for script debugging 1187–1188

disabling privileges, WMI settings 500

disabling user accounts 568

disaster recovery, managing recovery options 679–675

disconnected recordsets

    See also arrays

    alternatives to arrays 103

    sorting script output 1101–1103

disk drive management

    access to drives from scripts 243–244

    binding to disk drives 245

    disk drive properties 245–247

    drive letter formats 245

    ensuring drives are ready 248

    enumerating disk drive properties 247

    returning collection of installed drives 244

disk drives

    See also file systems

    drive types, verifying 735

    free disk space, enumerating 738

    free disk space, enumerating by user 739–740

    free disk space, monitoring in real time 740–741

    logical *See* logical drives

    overview 726

    partitions, enumerating 730–732

    physical *See* physical disks

    quotas *See* disk quotas

    volume names, changing 737

    Win32_DiskDrive class properties 726–728

disk partitions See partitions

disk quota alerts, issuing 750

disk quota entries

    adding 750–751

    deleting 752–753

    enumerating 748–749

    modifying 752

disk quotas

    Administrators group 748

    alerts, issuing 750

    default settings, configuring 746–747

    DiskQuotaControl object 743–744, 748–749

    enabling and disabling 745–746

    entries See disk quota entries

    file compression and 748

    file ownership and 748

    for individual users 748–749

    free disk space and 748

    free disk space, enumerating by user 739–740

    on NTFS volumes 742–743

    overview 742–743, 748

    settings, enumerating 744

    warning levels 750

disk space

    See also disk quotas

    disk quotas and 748

    enumerating by user 739–740

    free disk space, enumerating 738

    monitoring in real time 740–741

DiskIndex property, Win32_DiskPartition class 730–732

DiskQuotaControl object 743, 744, 748–749

disks, as managed resources 436

Display (System Information category), equivalent WMI class 630

displaying data

    hypertext applications (HTAs) 950–954

    in command window 950

    process performance data 951–954

    script output See output from scripts

    tabular data control See tabular data control

displaying script output See output from scripts

displayName attribute, user accounts 572

DisplayName property

    DiskQuotaControl object 748–749

    Win32_Service class 978–980, 1001–1003, 1011–1012

distinguished names 323–325, 327, 390–392

distinguishedName attribute

    Computer class 691

    user accounts 553

Distributed Management Task Force, WMI and 429

division attribute, Computer class 691

division operator (/), VBScript operator precedence 82–83

DLLs, WMI providers 438–439

dMD class, identifying operations master roles 719–721

DMTF, WMI and 429

DNs 323–325, 327, 390–392

DNS, managing with WMI scripts 430

dnsHostName attribute, Computer class 691, 718

Do loops

    checking loop condition 89–90

    Do Until loops 88

    Do While loops 88

    endless loops 89

    exiting, VBScript 90–91

    VBScript 88–89

Do Until loops 88

Do While loops 88

Document object

    changing mouse pointer cursor style 1131

    changing Web page contents 1079

Document property, Win32_PrintJob class 900–902

documenting code

    See also comments

    extracting comments from scripts 1181

domain controllers

    enumerating 716–717

    identifying current domain controller 718–719

Domain Directory partition, Active Directory 406

domain naming master role 719–721

domainDNS class, identifying operations master roles 719–721

DomainDNSName attribute, ADSystemInfo object 693

DomainRole property, Win32_ComputerSystem class 713

domains

　　See also domain controllers

　　binding to current domain 391

　　binding to root domain 392

　　moving user accounts between 584–585, 586

DomainShortName attribute, ADSystemInfo object 693

dot (.) notation

　　Automation objects, calling methods 21

　　Automation objects, retrieving properties 22

　　binding to current folder 250

dot-dot (..) notation, binding to root folder 250

Double (data subtype) 1153–1154

double quotation marks (") 164, 189, 190

Double values, VBScript, CDbl type conversion function 58

DOWN ARROW key, SendKeys representation 206

drag-and-drop

　　dragging text files onto scripts 1064

　　running WSH scripts 146

drive letters

　　compared to volume names 737

　　formats 245

　　logical drives compared to physical disks 733

Drive not ready (error) 248

Drive property

　　Folder object 256–257

　　Win32_Directory class 775–776

　　Win32_PageFile class 763

drive types, verifying for installed disk drives 735

DriveLetter property, FileSystemObject 245–247, 248

driverName attribute, printQueue object 933–935

DriverName property, Win32_Printer class 907–908

drivers, as managed resources 436

DriverVersion property, Win32_PrinterConfiguration class 908–910

drives *See* disk drive management; disk drives; logical drives; physical disks

Drives (System Information category), equivalent WMI class 631

DriveType property

　　FileSystemObject 245–247, 248

　　Win32_LogicalDisk class 733–734

DSA 393

DSNs 1104

Dsprov.dll 438–439

dtm (variable name prefix) 1153–1154

dump files *See* memory dump files

Duplex property, Win32_PrinterConfiguration class 908–910

DWORD-valued registry entries

　　changing 1033–1034

　　creating 1036–1038

　　overview 1027

　　reading 1027–1028

　　REG_DWORD data type 1020, 1023

dynamic arrays, VBScript 100

dynamic classes, WMI

　　overview 466

　　structure of CIM repository 450

dynamic link libraries, WMI providers 438–439

dynamic object interfaces, ADSI 422

Dynamic qualifier, WMI 465, 466, 470

dynamic resources, CIM repository and 441

dynamic tracking of script progress with Internet Explorer

　　changing mouse pointer 1130–1131

　　overview 1128–1130

　　using animated .gif files 1131

E

Echo method, Wscript object

　　limitations of 1072

　　overview 154

　　showing script progress with 1133

EightDotThreeFileName property

　　Win32_Directory class 775–776

　　Win32_PageFile class 763

ElapsedTime property

　　Win32_ScheduledJob class 1137–1140

　　Win32_Thread class 956–957

e-mail messages, sending from scripts

　　CDO and 1121

　　overview 1120–1122

　　scripting steps 1122

　　without installing SMTP service 1123–1125

Embedded mode, COM objects 123

embedding script code in Web pages, drawbacks of 1088

Empty (data subtype) 1153–1154

empty attribute values, searching for 601–605

empty text files 286–287

Empty variables, VBScript 51–52, 58–59

EnableEvents property, Win32_WMISetting class 647–649, 651–652

enabling privileges, WMI settings 498–500

enabling user accounts 568

Encrypted property, Win32_Directory class 775–776

EncryptionMethod property, Win32_Directory class 775–776

End event, WshRemote object 231

END key, SendKeys representation 206

endless loops 89

end-of-file property, Recordset object, ADO 1110

engines, scripting language
    interactions with script hosts 139
    overview 138
    specifying for individual scripts 143

ENTER key, SendKeys representation 206

enterprise scripts
    See also tasks
    challenges of using enterprise scripts 1059
    command-line arguments, limitations of 1060
    command-line arguments, text files as 1064
    database operations See databases
    Dictionary object and 1061
    displaying script output 1072
    displaying script output, in Internet Explorer 1077–1087
    displaying script output, in tabular format in command window 1073–1076
    displaying script output, using HTAs 1087–1091
    displaying script output, using tabular data control 1092–1095
    e-mail alerts 1120–1122
    e-mail alerts, scripting steps 1122
    e-mail alerts, without SMTP service installed 1123–1125

enterprise scripts (continued)
    filtering script output, using tabular data control 1099–1101
    overview 1059
    password masking 1117–1120
    retrieving arguments 1060
    retrieving arguments, from Active Directory containers 1070–1072
    retrieving arguments, from databases 1067–1070
    retrieving arguments, from text files 1061–1067
    scheduled tasks See scheduled tasks
    sorting script output, using disconnected recordsets 1101–1103
    sorting script output, using tabular data control 1095–1099
    tracking progress See tracking script progress

entries, registry
    binary-valued entries, reading 1031–1032
    changing 1033–1034
    creating 1035, 1036–1040
    data types 1020
    data types, enumerating 1043
    data types, integer values 1023
    default entries 1021
    deleting 1045–1046
    DWORD-valued entries, changing 1033–1034
    DWORD-valued entries, creating 1036–1038
    DWORD-valued entries, reading 1027–1028
    enumerating 1041, 1043
    expanded string-valued entries, creating 1040
    expanded string-valued entries, reading 1030–1031
    monitoring modifications to 1053
    multistring-valued entries, creating 1038–1040
    multistring-valued entries, reading 1029
    overview 1020
    reading values 1026–1027
    string-valued entries, changing 1033–1034
    string-valued entries, creating 1036–1038
    string-valued entries, reading 1027–1028
    values, enumerating 1043

EnumClasses.vbs 479

enumeration
    Filter property, IADsContainer interface 613
    Hints property, IADsContainer interface 613
    managing user accounts 613
enumerators, forward-only, in WMI queries 513–514
EnumInstances.vbs 479
EnumKey method, Registry Provider 1042
EnumNameSpaces subroutine 457
EnumNetworkDrives method, WshNetwork object 223
EnumPrinterConnections method, WshNetwork
    object 225
EnumValues method, Registry Provider 1043
Environment property, WshShell object 197
environment variables
    creating 199–200
    expanding 200–201
    modifying 200
    overview 197
    registry locations 197
    retrieving 197–199
    values of environment variables 201
    variables available to WSH (list) 198
environment, scripting runtime See scripting runtime
    environment
EOF property, Recordset object, ADO 1110
equals sign (=), initializing VBScript variables 52
equations See mathematical equations
err (variable name prefix) 1153–1154
Err object, VBScript 44–46
Error (data subtype) 1153–1154
error codes
    service control operations 987–989
    Win32_ScheduledJob class 1142
error control codes, auto-start services 1004–1005
Error event, WshRemote object 231
error handling
    See also errors
    Clear method, VBScript 46
    COM object errors, handling in VBScript 110–111
    disbling for script debugging 1187–1188
    Err object, VBScript 44–46

error handling (continued)
    FileSystemObject vs. WMI scripting 770–771
    ignoring errors, VBScript 105, 106–107
    in MapNetworkDrive method, WshNetwork object 222
    On Error GoTo 0 statement, VBScript 108–109
    On Error Resume Next statement, VBScript 43–46,
        106–109
    options, VBScript 105–106
    overview 43
    remotely running scripts 232
    resetting Err object, VBScript 46
    responding to errors, VBScript 105, 106, 107–108
    return values, WMI file and folder operations 778
    runtime errors, VBScript 104–105
    syntax errors, VBScript 104
    toggling, VBScript 108–109
ErrorControl property, Win32_Service class 978–980,
    1001–1003, 1011–1012
errors
    See also error handling
    "Access denied" 284
    "Bad file mode" 285
    "Drive not ready" 248
    "File exists" 251
    "Path not found" 250
ESC key, SendKeys representation 206
ESE 393
__Event class 536
event classes, WMI See WMI event classes
event consumers
    See also event subscriptions, monitoring
    free disk space, monitoring in real time 740
event handling
    for COM objects 153
    in WSH scripts 181
    Internet Explorer events 1085–1087
    remotely running scripts 231
    WMI See WMI event notifications
Event IDs See EventCode property, Win32_NTLogEvent
    class

Event Log provider, WMI 437, 438–439, 452

event log queries

asynchronous queries 865–866

query design 859–860, 862

retrieving specific date's events 863–864

retrieving specific event logs 861

retrieving specific event types 862–863

event logs

See also logs and log files; plain text log files

analyzing 857–858

Application log See Application event log

as managed resources 436

backing up 844, 852–856

clearing 852–855

configuring 850–851

copying events to databases 867–869

custom event logs 874–875

detailed event descriptions 872

Event IDs See EventCode property, Win32_NTLogEvent class

Event service 844

file header bits 853

LogEvent method 870–872

managing with WMI scripts 430

maximum file size 844, 851

overview 842–843

overwrite policy 851

querying See event log queries

retrieving properties 845–849

Security event log properties 848–849

System Event log See System Event log, querying for stop events

unique file names for backup files 856

Win32_NTEventLogFile class properties 845–846

Win32_NTLogEvent class properties 858

writing events to Application log 870–872

writing to, WSH 201–202

event monitoring, WMI See WMI event notifications

event notifications, WMI See WMI event notifications

Event service 844

event subscriptions, monitoring

printer status 893–894

process reliability 943

registry, entry-level events 1053

registry, subkey-level events 1052

registry, subtree-level events 1051

service reliability 976–977

WMI See WMI event subscriptions

Event Viewer

events in custom event logs 875

limitations of 842, 857

Win32_NTEventLogFile class properties 846

Win32_NTLogEvent class properties 859

EventCode property, Win32_NTLogEvent class 858–859

__EventConsumer class 544, 545–546

__Event-derived classes 536

__EventFilter class 544, 546

events

See also event logs

analyzing event logs 857–858

copying to databases 867–869

detailed event descriptions 872

Event IDs See EventCode property, Win32_NTLogEvent class

event monitoring, WMI See WMI event notifications

event notifications, WMI See WMI event notifications

handling See event handling

in custom event logs 874–875

LogEvent method 870–872

logging, WshShell object 201–202

querying See event log queries

subscriptions See event subscriptions, monitoring

Win32_NTLogEvent class properties 858

writing to Application log 870–872

EventType property, Win32_PowerManagementEvent class 687

Everyone group, WMI security and 444

example scripts See tasks

Exchange Server, managing with WMI scripts 430

Exec method, WshShell object 184–185, 188–189

ExecMethod method, SWbemServices object 487–488

ExecNotificationQuery method 487, 488, 824

ExecQuery method, SWbemServices object 487–488, 490

ExecQueryAsync method 810

executable files

    inventorying software 654

    removing services 1013

    running applications as services 972

ExecutablePath property, Win32_Process class 946–948

Execute method, WshRemote object 230

ExecutionState property, Win32_Process class 946–948

Exists method

    Dictionary object 301

    WSH named collection 165, 171, 174

Exit Do statement, VBScript 90–91

ExitCode property, Win32_Service class 978–980

exiting loops, VBScript 90–91

Expandable String data type (WSH), corresponding registry and VBScript data types 204

expanded string-valued registry entries

    creating 1040

    overview 1030

    reading 1030–1031

    REG_EXPAND_SZ data type 1020, 1023

ExpandEnvironmentStrings method, WshShell object 201

expanding environment variables 200–201

explicit declaration of variables, VBScript 50–51

Explorer, Internet See Internet Explorer

Explorer, Windows See Windows Explorer

extended partitions 730

Extensible Storage Engine 393

extension classes, WMI

    overview 460–461

    structure of CIM repository 450

extension interfaces, ADSI 422

Extension property, Win32_Directory class 775–776

extensions, file name See file name extensions

extrinsic events, WMI event classes 540

__ExtrinsicEvent class 540

F

failed processes See reliability

failed services See reliability

False (boolean value), integer value of 1173

Favorites folder

    See also special folders

    locating special folders 788

    special folder identifiers 195

FieldDelim property, tabular data control 1093–1094

fields

    Configuration object, CDO 1123

    disconnected recordsets 1101

    in comma-separated-value logs 877

    in fixed-width logs 879

    Recordset object, ADO 1103

    types recognized by tabular data control 1096

file compression, disk quotas and 748

File exists (error) 251

file name extensions

    changing 814–815

    non-standard extensions, running scripts with 143

    WSH-compliant scripting languages 137

file name generator 281–282

file names

    8.3 naming convention 1149

    script names 1149–1150

    spaces in names 1149–1150

    unique, creating in scripts 281–282

    unique, event log backup files 856

file ownership, disk quotas and 748

file size, verifying 286–287

file systems

    accessing from scripts See Script Runtime library

    administrative tasks 821

    as managed resources 436

    file creation events, monitoring 821–822

    file deletion events, monitoring 822–823

    file modification, monitoring 824

    file system type, identifying 754–755

    files See files and file management

file systems *(continued)*

folders *See* folders and folder management

managing with WMI scripts 430

monitoring changes to file system 821

NTFS *See* NTFS file system

overview 754

shared folders *See* shared folders

FileExists method, FileSystemObject 267–268

FileName property, Win32_Directory class 775–776

files

as managed resources 436

managing *See* files and file management

files and file management

See also file systems; folders and folder management

administrative tasks 768, 804, 813

binding to files 266–267

compressing folders 802–803

copying files 270–271, 816

deleting files 268–270, 817–818

deleting files with WMI scripts 529

enumerating files 809

enumerating all files in a folder 262–263, 811

enumerating files using asynchronous queries 810

enumerating specified sets of files 812

extended properties, retrieving 806–808

file access on remote computers 771–772

file access permissions 771

file attributes 275–277

file creation events, monitoring 821–822

file deletion events, monitoring 822–823

file modification, monitoring 824

file name extensions, changing 814–815

file properties 273–275

files as managed resources 436

moving files 272

overview 266

path names 277–278

performing actions on files 818–819

properties, retrieving 804–805

renaming files 272–273, 813–814

return values, WMI 778

files and file management *(continued)*

scripting overview 768

Shell object *See* Shell object

text files *See* text files

uncompressing folders 802–803

verbs, executing 818–819

verifying file existence 267–268

version numbers, retrieving 279

WMI scripting vs. FileSystemObject 768–772

Files property, Folder object 256–257, 262

files, registry

See also files and file management; registry

locations of, displaying 1021

overview 1021

FileSize property

Win32_Directory class 775–776

Win32_NTEventLogFile class 845–846

Win32_PageFile class 763

FileSystem property

FileSystemObject 245–247

Win32_LogicalDisk class 733–734

FileSystemObject

Close method 285

collections, working with 772

compared to Shell object 774

compared to WMI 243, 768–772

CopyFile method 270–271

CopyFolder method 252–254

CreateFolder method 250, 251

CreateTextFile method 280–281

DeleteFile method 269–270

DeleteFolder method 251

disk drive properties 245–247

drive management *See* disk drive management

error-handling capabilities 770–771

file management *See* files and file management

FileExists method 267–268

folder management *See* folders and folder management

Folder object properties 256–257

folder paths, browsing for 791–792

FileSystemObject *(continued)*

    FolderExists method 250

    GetAbsolutePathName method 278

    GetBaseName method 278

    GetDrive method 245

    GetExtensionName method 278

    GetFile method 266–267

    GetFileName method 278

    GetFileVersion method 279

    GetFolder method 249–250

    GetParentFolderName method 278

    GetTempName method 281–282

    HTAs and 1088

    MoveFile method 272–273

    MoveFolder method 254–255, 255

    OpenTextFile method 283, 292

    overview 243

    Read method 286, 291

    ReadAll method 286, 287–288

    reading arguments into scripts 1062

    ReadLine method 286, 288, 289

    remote file and folder access 771–772

    Skip method 286, 291

    SkipLine method 286, 291

    speed of query processing 770

    text files *See* text files

    Write method 292

    WriteBlankLines method 292

    WriteLine method 292, 295

FileType property, Win32_Directory class 775–776

FillAttribute property, Win32_ProcessStartup class 962–963

Filter property

    __FilterToConsumerBinding class 546

    IADsContainer interface 424, 613

    tabular data control 1093–1094, 1099

filtered searches, Active Directory

    See also filters, Active Directory searches; searching in Active Directory

    locating computer accounts 710–711

    overview 707–708, 708

filtering command-line arguments, WSH 164–165

filtering event log queries

    by date 863–864

    by event log 861

    by event type 862–863

filtering printer status data 892–893

filtering script output using tabular data control 1099–1101

filters, Active Directory searches

    See also filtered searches, Active Directory; searching in Active Directory

    not present operator, search filters 602

    objectCategory property 591–592

    objectClass property 591–592

    overview 591

    wildcards in search filters 606–607

__FilterToConsumerBinding class 546

Find method, Recordset object, ADO 1109, 1112

finding classes, WMI 462

finding more information about scripting 8

finding records in databases 1109–1112

Findstr.exe 462

fixed-width columns in tabular script output 1073

fixed-width logs, parsing 879

flags in UserAccountControl password attribute

    changing flag values 565

    displaying attribute values 563

    flag values 563

flat-file databases *See* text files

flexible single master operation roles *See* operations master roles

float type values, sorting with tabular data control 1096

focus, setting on applications 210

Folder object

    See also Shell object

    CopyHere method 798–799

    copying folders 797–799

    MoveHere method 800

    moving folders 800

FolderExists method, FileSystemObject 250

FolderItems object

    See also Shell object

    GetDetailsOf method 807–808

    InvokeVerbEx method 818

folders

as managed resources 436

managing See folders and folder management

folders and folder management

See also files and file management

administrative tasks 768, 778, 794

binding to folders 249–250

Browse for Folder dialog box 791–792

CIM_DataFile class 776–778

compressing folders 802–803

copying folders and folder contents 252–254

copying folders using Shell Folder object 797–799

copying folders using WMI 796

copying multiple folders with same name 798

creating folders 250–251

creating folders on remote computers 251

current folder, specifying 250

date properties 784

deleting folders 251–252, 801

deleting folders with WMI scripts 529

enumerating all files in a folder 262–263, 811

enumerating folder properties 257

enumerating folders 780–781

enumerating folders based on date properties 784–786

enumerating specified sets of folders 783–784

enumerating subfolders 263–264, 781–782

enumerating subfolders within subfolders 264–266

folder access on remote computers 771–772

folder access permissions 771

folder attributes 258–262

Folder object properties 256–257

folder paths, browsing for 791–792

folder paths, passing to scripts 791

folders as managed resources 436

merging folders 798

moving folders and folder contents 254–255

moving folders using Shell Folder object 800

moving folders using WMI 795

network shares, creating 828–829

network shares, deleting 832–833

folders and folder management (continued)

network shares, modifying properties 833–834

overview 249

overwriting folders 253

parent folder, specifying 250

parent folders, returning 781

properties, retrieving 779

published folders, administrative tasks 836

published folders, deleting 839–840

published folders, enumerating 836–837

published folders, searching for 838

publishing in Active Directory 834–835

read-only folders, deleting 801

renaming folders 255, 794

return values, WMI 778

root folder, specifying 250

scripting overview 768, 778

shared folders, administrative tasks 825

shared folders, as managed resources 436

shared folders, creating 828–829

shared folders, deleting 832–833, 839–840

shared folders, deleting with WMI scripts 529

shared folders, enumerating 836–837

shared folders, enumerating properties 826–827

shared folders, managing with WMI scripts 430

shared folders, mapping to local folders 830–831

shared folders, modifying properties 833–834

shared folders, publishing in Active Directory 834–835

shared folders, searching for in Active Directory 838

Shell object 773–774

short names 256

special folders, enumerating items in 790

special folders, retrieving location of 787–789

uncompressing folders 802–803

verfying folder existence 250

virtual folders in Shell object 773

Win32_Directory class 775–778

Win32_Subdirectory class 778, 781–782

WMI scripting vs. FileSystemObject 768–772

folders, shared See shared folders

fonts

    See also characters

    modifying character case, VBScript 81–82

    proportional vs. non-proportional fonts 78–79

Fonts folder

    See also special folders

    locating special folders 788

    special folder identifiers 195

fonts in script output 1077, 1081–1084

For Each statement, VBScript 31–32

For Next loops, VBScript 34–36

ForAppending mode, text files 283, 292, 295

Force parameter, DeleteFile method 269, 270

ForestDNSName attribute, ADSystemInfo object 693

forests, in Active Directory architecture 394

FormatNumber function, VBScript 85

FormatPercent function, VBScript 86–87

formatting code

    See also comments

    boolean expressions 1173

    case styles 1171

    default properties of automation objects 1175

    indentations 1166–1167

    limiting lines to single statements 1168–1169

    line length 1168

    multiple-language scripts 1170

    overview 1164

    parentheses enclosing If-Then statements 1165

    parentheses in mathematical expressions 1174

    phrasing If-Then statements 1172

    readability *See* readability of code

    single-line If-Then statements 1169

    spaces in parameter lists 1165–1166

    spaces surrounding operators 1165

    statement breaks 1168–1169

    white space 1164–1167

formatting comments 1179

formatting date and time values, VBScript 70–73

formatting numbers

    percentages, formatting in VBScript 86–87

    VBScript 84–87

    VBScript script output 24

formatting script output

    in command window 1073–1076

    in Internet Explorer 1077, 1081–1084

    using tabular data control 1093

formatting string data

    for message boxes, VBScript 78–79

    overview 74–76

    proportional vs. non-proportional fonts 78–79

    string manipulation functions, VBScript 76–77

    tabular output, VBScript 77–78

ForReading mode, text files 283

forward slash (/), in named arguments 164, 170

forward-only enumerators in WMI queries 513–514

forward-only SWbemObjectSet collections 489

ForWriting mode, text files 283, 292, 294

frames, surrounding comments in code 1179

free disk space

    See also disk quotas

    disk quotas and 748

    enumerating 738

    enumerating by user 739–740

    monitoring in real time 740–741

FreePhysicalMemory property, Win32_OperatingSystem class 620–621

FreeSpace property

    FileSystemObject 245–247

    Win32_LogicalDisk class 733–734

From property, IMessage interface, CDO Message object 1121

FSMO roles *See* operations master roles

FSName property, Win32_Directory class 775–776

FSO *See* FileSystemObject

full replicas, Active Directory 406

FullName property

    WScript object 179, 180

    WshShortcut object 192

FullScreen property, Internet Explorer object 1077–1079

function keys, SendKeys representation 206

functions

    calling 1162–1163

    function headers 1180

    indenting for readability 1167

functions *(continued)*

  naming conventions 1149, 1156–1157

  overview 112, 114–115, 1161

  passing parameters by reference, VBScript 118–119

  passing parameters by value, VBScript 119

  passing parameters, Script Runtime library 1162–1163

  passing parameters, VBScript 115–118

  recursion, VBScript 120–121

  return values, VBScript 114–115

  script structure and organization 1157

G

GC moniker, in Active Directory searches 590

GC provider 418, 419

General properties page, user account attributes available 571–573

generic scripts, running on multiple computers *See* enterprise scripts

Get method

  ADSI 315–317, 326, 330, 346–347

  Computer class 701–702

  SWbemServices object 477, 487–488, 491, 544

GetAbsolutePathName method, FileSystemObject 278

GetBaseName method, FileSystemObject 278

GetBinaryValue method, Registry Provider 1026–1027, 1032

GetDetailsOf method, FolderItems object 807–808

GetDrive method, FileSystemObject 245

GetDWORDValue method, Registry Provider 1026–1027

GetEx method, ADSI 344–345, 347

GetExpandedStringValue method, Registry Provider 1026–1027, 1030

GetExtensionName method, FileSystemObject 278

GetFile method, FileSystemObject 266–267

GetFileName method, FileSystemObject 278

GetFileVersion method, FileSystemObject 279

GetFolder method, FileSystemObject 249–250

GetInfo method, ADSI 346, 347–348

GetInfoEx method, ADSI 346, 348–349

GetMulitStringValue method, Registry Provider 1029

GetObject function, WMI objects 483

GetObject method

  VBScript 20, 123, 124

  WScript object 150, 152, 153

  WSH compared to VBScript 153

GetObjectText_ method, SWbemObject 477–478

GetParentFolderName method, FileSystemObject 278

GetStringValue method, Registry Provider 1026–1027, 1027

GetTempName method, FileSystemObject 281–282

getting started

  about scripting 3–6

  about scripts used in this book 11–12

  about this book 8–11

  administrative credentials required 14

  choosing a scripting language 12–13

  finding more information 8

  history of scripting 6

  system requirements 13–14

GIF files, showing script progress with 1131

givenName attribute, user accounts 572

Global Catalog

  attributes replicated to Global Catalog 407, 410

  optimizing Active Directory searches 381

  specifying in Active Directory search base 366–367

global catalog servers

  enabling and disabling 723–724

  identifying 722

GMT, determining offset from 519

granting privileges, WMI settings 498–500

graphics, including in script output in Internet Explorer 1077, 1081–1084

Greenwich Mean Time

  converting dates to UTC format 784–786

  determining offset from 519

GroupComponent property

  CIM_DirectoryContainsFile class 821

  Win32_Subdirectory class 781

groups

    creating 311

    deleting 318

    modifying attributes 314

    moving between containers 356

    multivalued attributes, appending 340

    multivalued attributes, clearing 342

    multivalued attributes, deleting entries 341

    multivalued attributes, reading 344

    multivalued attributes, updating 339

    reading attributes 316

groups of servers, running enterprise scripts on 1064

groups, SAM, as managed resources 436

GUID property, IADs interface 423

guidelines, scripting See scripting guidelines

H

hand mouse pointer, Internet Explorer 1130

Handle property, Win32_Thread class 956–957

handling events

    for COM objects 153

    in WSH scripts 181

    Internet Explorer events 1085–1087

    remotely running scripts 231

hard disks See disk drives

hardware

    identifying chassis type 634–636

    inventorying 629–636

    WMI classes equivalent to hardware components (table) 631

    WMI classes equivalent to System Information categories (table) 630

header bits, event logs 853

headers

    function and procedure headers 1180

    script headers 1179–1180

health monitoring, WMI scripts for 430

Height property, Internet Explorer object 1077–1079

HELP key, SendKeys representation 206

help mouse pointer, Internet Explorer 1130

Hidden attribute

    files 275

    folders 258

Hidden property, Win32_Directory class 775–776

hidden windows, creating processes in 963

hierarchical organization of registry 1018–1022

HighThresholdOnClientObjects property, Win32_WMISetting class 647–649, 651–652

HighThresholdOnEvents property, Win32_WMISetting class 647–649, 651–652

Hints property, IADsContainer interface 613

history of scripting 6

hive files

    See also registry

    locations of, displaying 1021

    overview 1021

HKEY_CLASSES_ROOT subtree 123, 151, 1019, 1022

HKEY_CURRENT_CONFIG subtree 1019, 1022

HKEY_CURRENT_USER subtree 1019, 1022

HKEY_LOCAL_MACHINE subtree 1019, 1022

HKEY_PERFORMANCE_DATA subtree 1019

HKEY_USERS subtree 1019, 1022

HOME key, SendKeys representation 206

HOMEDRIVE (environment variable) 198

HOMEPATH (environment variable) 198

HorizontalResolution property, Win32_PrinterConfiguration class 908–910

HostPrintQueue property

    IADsPrintJob interface 902–903, 923–924

    Win32_PrintJob class 900–902

hosts See script hosts, WSH

hot fixes 645

HotFixID property, Win32_QuickFixEngineering class 645

HotKey property, WshShortcut object 192

Hour function, VBScript 66–67

hourglass mouse pointer, Internet Explorer 1130

hours

    intervals between, determining, VBScript 69

    retrieving from date and time values 62–64, 66–67

HTAs
 converting .htm files to 1090
 creating, samples 1090-1091
 displaying printer status 888-889
 displaying process performance data 951-954
 displaying script output 1087-1091
 HTA object model 1088-1090
 overview 1088
HTM files, converting to .hta files 1090
HTML coding
 hypertext applications See HTAs
 script output 1082-1084
 script progress messages 1127
 tabular data control and 1093
Hungarian notation, variable names 1152-1154
hypertext applications See HTAs

I

IADs interface
 ADsPath property 423
 Class property 423
 compared to IADsUser interface 570
 GUID property 423
 interface categories 422
 managing user account attributes 570
 Name property 423
 Parent property 423
 Schema property 423
IADsAccessControlEntry interface 422
IADsAccessControlList interface 422
IADsADSystemInfo interface 693
IADsClass interface 422
IADsContainer interface
 Create method 557
 Delete method 588
 enumeration, managing user accounts 613
 Filter property 424, 613
 Hints property 613
 interface categories 422
IADsDeleteOps interface
 DeleteObject method 698-699
 interface categories 422

IADsExtension interface 422
IADsGroup interface 422
IADsLargeInteger interface 422
IADsLocality interface 422
IADsMembers interface 422
IADsNamespaces interface 422
IADsO interface 422
IADsObjectOptions interface 422
IADsOpenDSObject interface 422
IADsOU interface 422
IADsPathname interface 422
IADsPrinteQueue interface 422
IADsPrintJob interface 902-903, 923-924
IADsPrintJobOperations interface
 Pause method 915
 Resume method 916
IADsPrintQueue interface
 printer properties, configuring 917-918
 properties (list) 910
IADsPrintQueueOperations interface
 interface categories 422
 Pause method 912
 Purge method 914
 Resume method 913
IADsProperty interface 422
IADsPropertyEntry interface 422
IADsPropertyList interface 422
IADsPropertyValue interfaces 422
IADsSecurityDescriptor interface 422
IADsSyntax interface 422
IADsUser interface
 ChangePassword method 558, 560
 compared to IADs interface 570
 interface categories 422
 PasswordLastChanged property 564
 SetPassword method 558, 559
Icon property, HTA object 1088-1090
IconLocation property, WshShortcut object 192
ID property
 DiskQuotaControl object 748-749
 HTA object 1088-1090
IDAPDisplayNames 329

identification attributes, user accounts 553

Identify impersonation, WMI 496

IdentifyingNumber property

    Win32_Product class 656

    Win32_SoftwareFeature class 658–659

IDirectoryObject interface 422

IDirectorySearch interface 422

If...Then...ElseIf statement, VBScript 93–95

If...Then...Else statement, VBScript 38–39

If-Then statements

    enclosing with parentheses 1165

    phrasing for readability 1172

    single-line If-Then statements 1169

    VBScript 37

Ignore (error control code) 1004

IIS provider 418, 419

IIS, WMI provider 438

IMessage interface, CDO Message object 1121

Impersonate impersonation, WMI 496–497

impersonation levels

    WMI DCOM security 445–446

    WMI moniker settings 496–497

Implemented qualifier, WMI 471

implicit declaration of variables, VBScript 49–50

incremental running of scripts 1186–1187

indentations, formatting code 1166–1167

index numbers, arrays 40

Index property

    Win32_DiskDrive class 726–728

    Win32_DiskPartition class 730–732

Index.btr 442

Index.map 442

indexed attributes 409, 410

Indexing Service, UDA and 1103

indicators, script progress See tracking script progress

information about computers See system information

Infrared (System Information category), equivalent WMI class 630

infrastructure master role 719–721

infrastructure, WMI See WMI infrastructure

infrastructureUpdate class, identifying operations master roles 719–721

inheritance

    Active Directory 398–403

    CIM classes 463–465

    WMI classes 463–465

    WMI permissions 445

initialization section of scripts 1157

initializing variables, VBScript 51–52

initials attribute, user accounts 572

InitialSize property

    Win32_PageFile class 763

    Win32_PageFileSetting class 765–766

InnerHTML property, Internet Explorer object 1127

in-process servers

    See also COM objects

    overview 122

input stream

    See also StdIn stream

    overview 157

input to scripts

    See also command-line arguments

    accepting under CScript host 159–162

    input stream See StdIn stream

    StdIn stream See StdIn stream

    user input 41–42

    WSH compared to VBScript 154

INS or INSERT key, SendKeys representation 206

Install method, Win32_Product class 660–661

InstallableLanguages property, Win32_BIOS class 624–626

InstallDate property

    Win32_OperatingSystem class 639–641

    Win32_PageFile class 763

    Win32_PageFileUsage class 764–765

    Win32_QuickFixEngineering class 645

    Win32_ScheduledJob class 1137–1140

    Win32_SoftwareFeature class 658–659

InstallDate2 property, Win32_Product class 656

InstalledBy property, Win32_QuickFixEngineering class 645

installing services

    Create method 1011–1012

    operating system services 1010

installing software, WMI scripts 653–654, 659, 660

InstallLocation property, Win32_Product class 656

InstallState property

Win32_Product class 656

Win32_SoftwareFeature class 658–659

__InstanceCreationEvent class 537, 538, 542, 821

__InstanceDeletionEvent class 534, 537, 538, 542, 823

__InstanceModificationEvent class 534, 537, 538, 542

__InstanceOperationEvent class 534, 536, 537, 542

instances of Internet Explorer, creating 1079–1081

instances, WMI classes

See also managed resources

defined 436

monitoring See WMI event notifications

queries about See WMI queries

uniquely identifying with key properties 502

InstancesOf method, SWbemServices object 455, 487–488, 490

Instance-Type attribute, Computer class 691

instantiation of classes 395

InStr function, VBScript 80–81

int (variable name prefix) 1153–1154

Integer (data subtype) 1153–1154

Integer data type (VBScript), corresponding registry and WSH data types 204

integer values

sorting with tabular data control 1096

VBScript, CInt type conversion function 58

InteractWithDesktop property, Win32_ScheduledJob class 1137–1140, 1141–1142

interfaces, ADSI

categorization of interfaces 422

implementation by providers 421

overview 414, 421

InterfaceType property, Win32_DiskDrive class 726–728

Internet Explorer

Automation object model 1077

creating an instance of 1079–1081

displaying script output in See redirecting script output to Internet Explorer

event handling 1085–1087

methods and properties (table) 1077

password masking with 1118–1120

Internet Explorer (continued)

tabular data control See tabular data control

tracking script progress in 1126–1128

tracking script progress in, changing mouse pointer 1130–1131

tracking script progress in, dynamic tracking 1128–1130

tracking script progress in, with animated .gif files 1131

Internet Explorer folder

See also special folders

locating special folders 788

intervals between date and time values

determining in VBScript 68–69

projecting date and time based on specified interval, VBScript 70

intrinsic constants

from other scripting languages, using 55–56

VBScript 54–56

intrinsic events, WMI event classes 537–538

introduction

about scripting 3–6

about scripts used in this book 11–12

about this book 8–11

administrative credentials required 14

choosing a scripting language 12–13

finding more information 8

history of scripting 6

system requirements 13–14

inventorying hardware

identifying chassis type 629–636

overview 629

taking inventory 632–633

WMI classes equivalent to hardware components (table) 631

WMI classes equivalent to System Information categories (table) 630

inventorying software

enumerating installed software 655–656

enumerating installed software features 658–659

listing executable files 654

Win32_Product class 655, 656

Win32_SoftwareFeature class 655, 658

InvokeVerbEx method, FolderItems object 818

ISA keyword, WMI notification queries and 531, 536

IsDate function, VBScript 61

isMemberOfPartialAttributeSet attribute, Active Directory 407

IsNativeMode attribute, ADSystemInfo object 693

IsNull function 702

IsNull method, VBScript 59

IsObject function, VBScript 126

IsReady property, FileSystemObject 245–247, 248

IsRootFolder property, Folder object 256–257

Item method, Dictionary object 301

Item property

    WshArguments collection 166, 168

    WshNamed collection 165

items (Dictionary object)

    adding key-item pairs 298–299

    determining number of key-item pairs 299

    displaying value of specific item 301

    enumerating keys and items 300–301

    key-item pairs 296

    modifying items 302–303

    removing all key-item pairs 303–304

    removing specific key-item pair 304–305

Items method, Dictionary object 300

iterating collections

    See also collections

    For Each statement 31–32

iterative testing of scripts 1188

J

JobID property

    Win32_PrintJob class 900–902

    Win32_ScheduledJob class 1137–1140, 1141–1142, 1144

jobs, scheduled See scheduled tasks

JobStatus property

    Win32_PrintJob class 900–902

    Win32_ScheduledJob class 1137–1140

JS files, WSH-compliant scripting languages 137

JScript

    choosing a scripting language 12–13

    history of 7

    WMI and 430

K

Kerberos authentication, WMI setting for 498

KernelModeTime property, Win32_Process class 946–948, 949

KernelOnlyDump property, Win32_OSRecoveryConfiguration class 676–677

Kernighan, Brian 1172

key properties, WMI 478, 502–503

Key qualifier, WMI 470–471, 478

KEY_CREATE_LINK (registry subkey access right) 1048

KEY_CREATE_SUB_KEY (registry subkey access right) 1048

KEY_ENUMERATE_SUB_KEYS (registry subkey access right) 1048

KEY_NOTIFY (registry subkey access right) 1048

KEY_QUERY_VALUE (registry subkey access right) 1048

KEY_SET_VALUE (registry subkey access right) 1048

Keyboard (System Information category), equivalent WMI class 630

keyboard characters, SendKeys representations 206–207

keyboard input

    See also input to scripts

    keystrokes, sending to applications 206–210

    StdIn stream See StdIn stream

key-item pairs

    See also Dictionary object

    adding to Dictionaries 298–299

    determining number of pairs 299

    displaying value of specific item 301

    enumerating keys and items 300–301

    inadvertently adding keys 298

    modifying items 302–303

    overview 296

    removing all key-item pairs 303–304

    removing specific key-item pair 304–305

    verifying existence of specific key 301

keys (Dictionary object)

    adding inadvertently 298

    adding key-item pairs 298–299

    binary mode vs. text mode 297–298

    determining number of key-item pairs 299

    displaying value of specific item 301

    enumerating keys and items 300–301

    key-item pairs 296

    removing all key-item pairs 303–304

    removing specific key-item pair 304–305

    verifying existence of specific key 301

Keys method, Dictionary object 300

keys, registry

    default entries 1021

    enumerating 1041

    overview 1019

keystrokes, sending to applications

    controlling applications 207

    ensuring applications are active 209

    limitations of SendKeys method 208–209

    SendKeys method, WshShell object 206–207

    setting focus on apps 210

Keywords attribute, Volume class 835

L

language settings

    date and time formats 61, 70–73

    number formats 84

languages

    multiple-language scripts 1170

    scripting language engines 138, 139, 143

    WSH-compliant scripting languages 136

LastAccessed property, Win32_Directory class 775–776, 784

LastModified property, Win32_Directory class 775–776, 784

LastUse property, Win32_SoftwareFeature class 658–659

layers, ADSI architecture 416–420

LCase function, VBScript 82

LDAP

    See also LDAP provider; LDAP search dialect

    in Active Directory architecture 393

LDAP moniker, in Active Directory searches 590

LDAP provider

    ADSI providers 418, 419

    in ADsPath 323

    interfaces supported by 423–425

    vs. WinNT provider 693

LDAP search dialect

    See also searching in Active Directory

    attributes to be returned by searches, specifying 592

    attributes without values, searching for 603

    attributes, searching for in containers 593

    IsNull function, VBScript 603

    not present operator, search filters 602

    sAMAccountName attribute, verifying uniqueness 600

    search base 590

    search filters 591–592, 602, 606–607

    search results, limiting to user account types 596

    search scope 592

leading zero, formatting numbers, VBScript 84

leaks *See* memory leaks

LEFT ARROW key, SendKeys representation 206

Left function, VBScript 76–77, 1074–1075

Left property, Internet Explorer object 1077–1079

Len function, VBScript 76–77, 1074–1075

Length property

    WshArguments collection 166

    WshNamed collection 165

    WshUnnamed collection 165

Lightweight Directory Access Protocol *See* LDAP

line breaks, in VBScript statement breaks 47–49

line continuation character, VBScript 48–49

Line property, WshRemoteError object 232

lines in code

    limiting lines to single statements 1168–1169

    line length 1168

    single-line If-Then statements 1169

    statement breaks 1168–1169

literal values

    See also constants

    assigning to constants, VBScript 54

    compared to constants 25–26, 53

lng (variable name prefix) 1153–1154

LNK files 191

LoadOrderGroup property, Win32_Service class 1001–1003, 1011–1012

LoadOrderGroupDependencies property, Win32_Service class 1001–1003, 1011–1012

local computers
    See also remote computers
    installing software 660–661

local folders, mapping network shares to 830–831

local property cache, ADSI
    attribute values, retrieving 346–347
    Get method 346
    GetEx method 347
    GetInfo method 347–348
    GetInfoEx method 348–349
    in ADSI architecture 420
    overview 326
    refreshing and loading 347–349

Local Settings\Application Data folder
    See also special folders
    locating special folders 788

Local Settings\History folder
    See also special folders
    locating special folders 788

Local Settings\Temporary Internet Files folder
    See also special folders
    locating special folders 788

Locale property, Win32_OperatingSystem class 620–621

LocalName argument, MapNetworkDrive method 221

LocalSystem account 1006–1007

locating printers *See* printer location tracking

locating resources *See* searching in Active Directory

location attribute
    Computer class 691, 703
    printQueue object 933–935

location of special folders, retrieving 196

Location property
    IADsPrintQueue interface 910
    Win32_Printer class 885–887, 907–908
    Win32_StartupCommand class 674

locking workstations from command line 682

LockType property, Recordset object, ADO 1105

LogEvent method
    limitations of 870–871
    parameters 871
    writing to local computers 871
    writing to remote computers 872
    WshShell object 201

LogFileEventConsumer class 545

LogFileName property, Win32_NTEventLogFile class 845–846

LoggingDirectory property, Win32_WMISetting class 647–649, 651–652

LoggingLevel property, Win32_WMISetting class 647–649, 651–652

logical AND operator, VBScript conditional statements 92

logical drives
    See also physical disks
    compared to physical disks 733
    file system type, identifying 754–755
    overview 733
    quotas *See* disk quotas
    volume names, changing 737
    Win32_LogicalDisk class properties 733–734

logical OR operator, VBScript conditional statements 93

logical printers
    pausing printers 912
    purging print queues 914
    resuming printers 913
    scheduling printer availability 918

logo, displaying or suppressing in script output 143

logon information, retrieving 693–694

logon scripts, printer connections, adding and removing 928

LogonName property, DiskQuotaControl object 748–749

LogQuotaLimit property, DiskQuotaControl object 744

LogQuotaThreshold property, DiskQuotaControl object 744

logs and log files
    See also text files
    analyzing 857–858
    Application Log *See* Application event log
    comma-separated-value logs 877
    event logs *See* event logs

logs and log files *(continued)*

  fixed-width logs 879

  overview 842

  plain text log files *See* plain text log files

  System event log *See* System Event log, querying for stop results

  TSV logs 877

Long (data subtype) 1153–1154

Long values, VBScript, CLng type conversion function 58

loop condition, checking 89–90

loop variables 1156

loops

  checking loop condition 89–90

  Do Until loops 88

  Do While loops 88

  endless loops 89

  exiting 90–91

  For Next loops 34–36

  terminating scripts 541

  VBScript 88–89

lowercase characters, modifying character case 81–82

LowThresholdOnClientObjects property, Win32_WMISetting class 647–649, 651–652

LowThresholdOnEvents property, Win32_WMISetting class 647–649, 651–652

LTrim function, VBScript 76–77

M

mail attribute, user accounts 572

main body of scripts 1157

Managed Object Format files *See* MOF files

managed resources

  as layer of WMI architecture 435–436

  availability of classes for 471–472

  binding to 502

  changing scripts to manage different resources 447

  CIM classes and 442

  CIM repository and 441

  CIMOM security 440

  class definitions, retrieving using SWbemObject GetObjectText_ method 477–478

  class definitions, retrieving using SWbemObject properties 472–477

managed resources *(continued)*

  class definitions, structure 467

  creating, event notification 538

  creating, script template 528

  defined 429

  deleting, event notification 538

  deleting, script template 529

  displaying all properties, script template 524

  displaying specified properties, script template 523

  event notifications *See* WMI event notifications

  modifying, event notification 538

  monitoring *See* WMI event notifications

  multiple types, handling in scripts 542

  object paths *See* WMI object paths

  overview 436

  SWbemObject and 483

  writing properties, script template 525

ManagedBy attribute, Volume class 835

Management Information Base data, as managed resource 436

mandatory attributes 313, 329, 396, 398

Manual (service start option) 1003

Manufacturer property

  Win32_BIOS class 624–626

  Win32_ComputerSystem class 620–621

  Win32_DiskDrive class 726–728

  Win32_OperatingSystem class 620–621

MapNetworkDrive method, WshNetwork object 221, 222

mapping network drives 221–222, 227

masking passwords 1117–1120

mathematical equations

  Null variables vs. Empty variables, VBScript 59

  operator precedence, VBScript 82–83

  type coercion, VBScript 57

mathematical expressions, parentheses in 1174

MaxfileSize property, Win32_NTEventLogFile class 845–846, 850

MaximizeButton property, HTA object 1088–1090

MaximumAllowed parameter

  Create method (Win32_Share class) 828

  SetShareInfo method (Win32_Share class) 833

MaximumAllowed property, Win32_Share class 826

MaximumComponentLength property, Win32_LogicalDisk class 733-734

MaximumSize property

    Win32_PageFile class 763

    Win32_PageFileSetting class 765-766

MaxLogFileSize property, Win32_WMISetting class 647-649, 651-652

MaxWaitOnClientObjects property, Win32_WMISetting class 647-649, 651-652

MaxWaitOnEvents property, Win32_WMISetting class 647-649, 651-652

mean time between failures See reliability

MediaType property

    Win32_DiskDrive class 726-728

    Win32_LogicalDisk class 733-734

memory

    dump files See memory dump files

    leaks See memory leaks

    management See memory management

    page files 762-766

memory dump files

    See also recovery options

    configuring 679

    generating stop events manually 681-682

    overview 675

memory leaks

    diagnosing 946-948

    monitoring process performance 948-949

    monitoring service reliability 976

    overview 939

memory management

    See also memory leaks

    thread allocation 938-939

memory resources

    enumerating files 809

    enumerating files using asynchronous queries 810

memory use, limiting using shared processes 983

MenuBar property, Internet Explorer object 1077-1079

merging folders 798

message boxes

    See also command window

    displaying script output 154-157

    formatting text for, VBScript 78-79

    WScript Echo method 154-157

Message object, CDO

    Configuration object and 1123

    described 1121

    IMessage interface 1121

Message property, Win32_NTLogEvent class 858-859

messages

    See also message boxes; output from scripts

    displaying in command window 159

    e-mail See e-mail messages, sending from scripts

    script progress See tracking script progress

metadata, retrieving WSH environment information 179-180

method qualifiers, WMI 471

methods

    See also functions

    CIM classes 442

    in ADSI interfaces 421

    of COM objects, calling 152

    WMI classes 469, 471, 527

Methods_property, SWbemObject 472, 475

MIB data, as managed resources 436

Microsoft Access databases

    See also databases

    connecting to 1104

Microsoft Internet Explorer See Internet Explorer

Microsoft Windows operating system, names and version numbers 638

Mid function, VBScript 76-77

MiniDumpDirectory property, Win32_OSRecoveryConfiguration class 676-677

MinimizeButton property, HTA object 1088-1090

Minute function, VBScript 66-67

minutes

    intervals between, determining, VBScript 69

    retrieving from date and time values 62-64, 66-67

MMC snap-ins
    Active Directory Schema Snap-in 403
    ADSI Edit snap-in 405
Model property
    IADsPrintQueue interface 910
    Win32_ComputerSystem class 620-621
    Win32_DiskDrive class 726-728
Modem (System Information category), equivalent WMI class 630
modifying directory service objects
    See also directory service objects
    attributes, clearing 339
    committing changes to Active Directory 331
    groups 314
    multivalued attributes 336-343
    multivalued attributes, appending 340
    multivalued attributes, clearing 339, 342
    multivalued attributes, deleting entries 341
    multivalued attributes, PutEx method 337-339
    multivalued attributes, updating 339, 342
    OUs 313
    overview 313, 334
    Put method parameters 329
    user accounts 314
modifying scripts, to run on multiple computers See enterprise scripts
MOF files
    method definitions in 469
    overview 467
    property definitions in 469
    retrieving class definition in 477-478
MOFSelfInstallDirectory property, Win32_WMISetting class 647-649
monikers
    binding to Automation objects 20, 124
    in query strings, Active Directory searches 590
    WMI See WMI moniker
monitoring availability
    process availability 941, 942
    service availability 973, 974-975
monitoring file creation events 821-822
monitoring file deletion events 822-823

monitoring file modification 824
monitoring print jobs
    See also print jobs
    IADsPrintJob interface 902-903
    overview 885, 899
    print job status 903
    time spent in print queue 905
    Win32_PrintJob class 900-902
monitoring print queues
    See also print queues
    overview 885, 897
    reporting queue statistics 897-898
monitoring print service status 896-897
monitoring printer status
    See also printers and print management
    displaying status in Web pages 888-889
    filtering status data 892-893
    in real time 888-889
    monitoring all printers on a computer 887-888
    overview 885
    using event subscriptions 893-894
    Win32_Printer class 885-887
monitoring printers
    See also printers and print management
    overview 885
    printer status See monitoring printer status
monitoring processes See process monitoring
monitoring registry access 1050-1053
monitoring reliability
    process reliability 941, 943-945
    service reliability 973, 976-977
monitoring script progress
    in command window 1133-1135
    in Internet Explorer 1126-1128
    in Internet Explorer, changing mouse pointer 1130-1131
    in Internet Explorer, dynamic tracking 1128-1130
    in Internet Explorer, with animated .gif files 1131
    overview 1125-1126
monitoring script running time 69
monitoring service performance 973
monitoring threads 956-957

Month function, VBScript 66–67

MonthName function, VBScript 72–73

months

formatting month names, VBScript 72–73

intervals between, determining, VBScript 69

retrieving from date and time values 62–64, 66–67

mouse pointer in Internet Explorer, changing to show script progress 1130–1131

Move Files progress dialog box, displaying 800

MoveFile method, FileSystemObject

moving files 272

renaming files 272–273

MoveFolder method, FileSystemObject

moving folders 254–255

renaming folders 255

MoveHere method, ADSI

moving computer accounts between OUs 705

overview 354–358

renaming computer accounts 704–705

MoveHere method, IADsContainer interface 584–585

MoveHere method, Shell Folder object 800

moving

directory service objects 354–358

directory service objects, moving between domains 354–355, 357

files 272

folders and folder contents 254–255

folders, moving using Shell Folder object 800

folders, moving using WMI 795

groups, moving between containers 356

OUs, moving between domains 357

user accounts, between containers 585, 586

user accounts, between domains 584–585, 586

MS-DOS-based printer connections

adding 224

removing 225

MS-DOS-style names 256

Mshta.exe 1088

Msiprov.dll 438–439

multi-hop security, installing software on remote computers 662–663

multi-language scripting environments 138

multiple computers, running scripts on See enterprise scripts

multiple operating systems, Windows 2000 Service Pack 2 and 14

multiple-language scripts 1170

multiplication operator (*), VBScript operator precedence 82–83

multistring-valued registry entries

creating 1038–1040

overview 1029

reading 1029

REG_MULTI_SZ data type 1020, 1023

multivalued attributes, directory service objects

appending 340

clearing 339, 342

deleting entries 341

duplicate entries 338

modifying 336–343

overview 336

PutEx method 337–339

reading 344–345

returning from Active Directory searches 374–378

updating 339, 342

multivalued attributes, user accounts

adding entries to 578

clearing 580

modifying 577–580

reading 573–575

removing entries from 579

searching for 608

writing 576–577

My Computer folder

See also special folders

in Shell namespace hierarchy 773

locating special folders 788

My Documents folder

See also special folders

locating special folders 788

special folder identifiers 195

My Music folder

See also special folders

locating special folders 788

My Network Places folder

   See also special folders

   in Shell namespace hierarchy 773

   locating special folders 788

   published folders, searching for 834

My Pictures folder

   See also special folders

   locating special folders 788

My Recent Documents folder

   See also special folders

   locating special folders 788

My Videos folder

   See also special folders

   locating special folders 788

N

name attribute

   Computer class 691

   user accounts 553

Name parameter, Create method (Win32_Share class) 828

Name property

   Folder object 256–257

   IADs interface 423

   Win32_BIOS class 624–626

   Win32_ComputerSystem class 620–621

   Win32_Directory class 775–776

   Win32_DiskDrive class 726–728

   Win32_DiskPartition class 730–732

   Win32_LogicalDisk class 733–734

   Win32_NTEventLogFile class 845–846

   Win32_OperatingSystem class 620–621

   Win32_OSRecoveryConfiguration class 676–677

   Win32_PageFile class 763

   Win32_PageFileSetting class 765–766

   Win32_PageFileUsage class 764–765

   Win32_Printer class 885–887, 907–908

   Win32_PrinterConfiguration class 908–910

   Win32_Process class 946–948

   Win32_Product class 656

   Win32_Service class 978–980, 1011–1012

Name property *(continued)*

   Win32_Share class 826

   Win32_SoftwareFeature class 658–659

   Win32_StartupCommand class 674

   WScript object 179

named command-line arguments

   See also command-line arguments

   name and value format 164, 170

   overview 164

   using with unnamed arguments in same script 172

   WshNamed collection 165, 170–171

Named property, WshArguments collection 166

names

   conventions *See* naming conventions

   data source names (DSNs) 1104

   file names *See* file names

   listing in databases 1067

   listing in text files 1061

   of selected Microsoft Windows operating systems 638

   operating system name, retrieving 637–638

   printer location naming schemes 920–921

   retrieving from Active Directory 1070

   short names of folders 256

   user accounts, name uniqueness in domains 556

__NAMESPACE class 455, 458

__NamespaceOperationEvent class 536, 537

namespaces

   ADSI 417

   classes in, listing 461–463

   connecting to 452–454

   default namespace 452–455

   default WMI namespace 649

   in object paths *See* WMI object paths

   introduction 442

   listing 455–458

   namespace-level security 444–445

   nesting of 450

   overview 450–452

   structure of CIM repository 450

   target namespaces 454

naming conventions
 Camel casing 1152
 constant names 1149, 1156
 function names 1149, 1156–1157
 Hungarian notation 1152–1154
 overview 1148–1149
 Pascal casing 1157
 procedure names 1149, 1156–1157
 script names 1149–1150
 variable names 1149, 1151–1156
naming schemes, printer location naming schemes 920–921
Navigate property, Internet Explorer object 1077–1079
NDS provider 418, 419
negative numbers, formatting, VBScript 84
nesting of WMI namespaces 450
net.exe tool, and WshNetwork object 219
NetHood (special folder identifier) 195
NetHood folder
 See also special folders
 locating special folders 788
Netlogon.log 876
Netsetup.log 876
Network Adapter (System Information category), equivalent WMI class 630
Network Connections folder
 See also special folders
 locating special folders 788
network drives
 See also WshNetwork object
 enumerating 223
 mapping 221–222
 mapping according to user domain 227
 overview 221
 unmapping 222–223
network printers
 See also WshNetwork object
 default printer, setting 226
 MS-DOS-based printer connections, adding 224
 overview 224
 printer connections, enumerating 225
 printer connections, removing 225
 Windows-based printer connections, adding 224

network shares
 See also published folders; shared folders
 creating 828–829
 deleting 832–833
 mapping to local folders 830–831
 properties, modifying 833–834
networking components, as managed resources 436
networks, managing with WMI scripts 430
NewPassword argument
 ChangePassword method 560
 SetPassword method 559
Next statement, VBScript 34
NextEvent method 531, 541
NNTP service, e-mail messaging 1121
non-automation interfaces, ADSI 422
non-proportional fonts 78–79
Normal (error control code) 1004
Normal (file attribute) 275
NOT operator (!), search filters 605
NOT PRESENT operator, search filters 602
Nothing keyword, VBScript 128
notifications, event, WMI See WMI event notifications
Notify property
 IADsPrintJob interface 902–903, 923–924
 Win32_PrintJob class 900–902
 Win32_ScheduledJob class 1137–1140
NotifyPath property, IADsPrintJob interface 923–924
Now function, VBScript 60, 70
Ntds.dit 393
nTDSDSA object class 717
NTEventLogEventConsumer class 545
Ntevet.dll 438–439
Ntfrs.log 876
NTFS file system
 See also file systems
 properties, enumerating 755–757
 properties, modifying 760–761
NTFS permissions, WMI and 446
NTFS volumes, disk quotas 742–743
NtfsAllowExtendedCharacterIn8Dot3Name (registry entry) 755, 760
NtfsDisable8Dot3NameCreation (registry entry) 755, 760

NtfsDisableLastAccessUpdate (registry entry) 755, 760

NtfsMftZoneReservation (registry entry) 755, 760

NTML authentication, WMI setting for 498

NT-Security-Descriptor attribute, Computer class 691

Null (data subtype) 1153–1154

Null variables, VBScript 58–59

null-value attributes 701–702

NUM LOCK key, SendKeys representation 206

Number data type (WSH), corresponding registry and VBScript data types 204

Number property, WshRemoteError object 232

NUMBER_OF_PROCESSORS (environment variable) 198

NumberOfBlocks property, Win32_DiskPartition class 730–732

NumberOfLicensedUsers property, Win32_OperatingSystem class 639–641

NumberOfRecords property, Win32_NTEventLogFile class 845–846

numbers and numerical data

See also mathematical equations

formatting percentages, VBScript 86–87

formatting, VBScript 24, 84–87

operator precedence, VBScript 82–83

numbers in WHERE clauses, WMI queries 509

NWCOMPAT provider 418, 419

O

obj (variable name prefix) 1153–1154

Object (data subtype) 1153–1154

object models

ADO 1103

ADSI 414–415

applications without COM object model, automating 206–210

Automation object model, Internet Explorer 1077

Component Object Model See COM

HTA 1088

WMI scripting library 480–483

WSH 140

WshController object 227

WshNetwork object 219–220

WshShell object 181

object paths, WMI

format of 502

key properties 502–503

overview 501

object references

assigning to variables, VBScript 21

creating in VBScript 20

directory service objects, creating 325, 328

dissociating from COM objects 128

storing using WSH 151

verifying 126

object repository, CIM 441

Object-Category attribute, Computer class 691

objectCategory property, search filters 591–592

Object-Class attribute, Computer class 691

objectClass property, search filters 591–592

objectClassCategory attribute, Active Directory classes 399

objectGUID attribute, user accounts 553

objects

Automation See Automation objects

COM See COM objects

directory service See directory service objects

references See object references

WSH See WSH objects

Objects.data 442

Objects.map 442

objectSID attribute, user accounts 554

ODBC

data source names (DSNs) 1104

replaced by UDA 1103

OEMEventType property, Win32_PowerManagementEvent class 687

OldPassword argument, ChangePassword method 560

OLE DB 1103

On Error GoTo 0 statement, VBScript 108–109

On Error Resume Next statement, VBScript 43–46, 106–109

onelevel option, Active Directory search scope 370, 592

onLoad event, Internet Explorer, handling in scripts 1086

onQuit event, Internet Explorer, handling in scripts 1085

Open Database Connectivity *See* ODBC

Open method

    Connection object, ADO 1105

    Recordset object, ADO 1105

opening text files

    See also text files

    ForAppending mode 283, 292, 295

    ForReading mode 283

    ForWriting mode 283, 292, 294

    overview 282–283

OpenTextFile method, FileSystemObject 283, 292

operating system requirements 13–14

operating system services, installing and removing 1010, 1013

operating systems

    configuring startup options 670–673

    default operating system 670

    determining code base 643

    enumerating installed hot fixes 645

    identifying latest installed service pack 643–644

    identifying name and version number 637–638

    managing with WMI scripts 430

    names and version numbers of selected Microsoft Windows operating systems 638

    overview 637

    retrieving operating system properties 639–641

    subsystems as managed resources 436

    system startup delay 670

Operating systems section, Boot.ini file 671

operatingSystem attribute, Computer class 691

operatingSystemServicePack attribute, Computer class 691

operatingSystemVersion attribute, Computer class 691

operational attributes 347, 412

Operations Manager

    managing with WMI scripts 430

    WMI consumer 443

    WMI provider 438

operations master roles

    associated ADSI object classes 719

    identifying 719–721

operator precedence, VBScript 82–83

optimization *See* performance monitoring; process monitoring

optimizing Active Directory searches

    Command object properties 380

    consolidating query strings 379

    result set, limiting 379

    using Global Catalog 381

Option Explicit statememt, VBScript 51

optional attributes, Active Directory classes 396–398

Options parameter

    Install method 661

    Upgrade method 664

options parameter, BrowseForFolder method 792

OR keyword

    in WMI queries 512

    WMI event notifications and 540, 543

OR operator, in conditional VBScript statements 93

order of operations, VBScript operator precedence 82–83

Organization property, Win32_OperatingSystem class 639–641

organizational units *See* OUs

Orientation property, Win32_PrinterConfiguration class 908–910

OS (environment variable) 198

OSLanguage property, Win32_OperatingSystem class 639–641

OSProductSuite property, Win32_OperatingSystem class 639–641

OSType property, Win32_OperatingSystem class 639–641

otherTelephone attribute, user accounts 572

OU attribute type, distinguished names 324

OUs

    creating 310

    deleting 318

    enterprise scripts and 1070–1072

    modifying attributes 313

    moving between domains 357

    moving computer accounts between OUs 705

    reading attributes 315

    retrieving computer names from 1070–1072

out-of-process servers
    overview 122
    unloading from memory 127–128
output from scripts
    accessing from other scripts 184–185
    blank lines, including in output 157
    carriage return/linefeed, appending 157
    clearing Internet Explorer window 1084
    displaying 1072
    displaying in Internet Explorer 1077–1087
    displaying in tabular format in command
        window 1073–1076
    displaying under CScript host 156–159
    displaying under WScript host 156–157
    displaying, using HTAs 1087–1091
    displaying, using tabular data control 1092–1095
    echoing values to command window 1072
    filtering using tabular data control 1099–1101
    HTML coding 1082–1084
    input stream 157
    logo, displaying or suppressing under CScript 143
    output streams 157–159
    redirecting to text files 145–146
    sorting using disconnected recordsets 1101–1103
    sorting using tabular data control 1095–1099
    StdErr stream 157
    StdOut stream See StdOut stream
    WScript Echo method 154–157
    WSH compared to VBScript 154
output of running programs, accessing 190–191
output streams
    overview 157
    StdErr See StdErr stream
    StdOut See StdOut stream
overriding privileges, WMI settings 498–500
Overwrite parameter
    CopyFile method 270
    CopyFolder method 253
overwrite policy, event logs 851

OverWriteExistingDebugFile property,
    Win32_OSRecoveryConfiguration class 676–677
OverwriteOutdated property, Win32_NTEventLogFile
    class 845–846, 850
OverwritePolicy property, Win32_NTEventLogFile
    class 845–846
overwriting text files 145, 280–281, 294
Owner property
    Win32_PrintJob class 900–902
    Win32_ScheduledJob class 1137–1140
ownership
    file ownership and disk quotas 748
    process owners, identifying 955

P

PackageCache property, Win32_Product class 656
PackageLocation parameter
    Install method 661
    Upgrade method 664
PAGE DOWN key, SendKeys representation 206
page file bytes, diagnosing memory leaks 946
page files
    monitoring usage 764–765
    overview 762–763
    properties, configuring 765–766
    Win32_PageFile class properties 763
    Win32_PageFileSetting class properties 765–766
Page Size property, Command object (ADO) 380
PAGE UP key, SendKeys representation 206
PageFaults property , Win32_Process class 946–948
PageFileUsage property, Win32_Process class 946–948
PagesPrinted property, Win32_PrintJob class 900–902
PaperLength property, Win32_PrinterConfiguration
    class 908–910
PaperSize property, Win32_PrinterConfiguration
    class 908–910
PaperWidth property, Win32_PrinterConfiguration
    class 908–910
Parallel Ports (System Information category)
    equivalent WMI class 630

parameters

   See also arguments

   passing by reference, Script Runtime library 1162–1163

   passing by reference, VBScript 118–119

   passing by value, Script Runtime library 1162–1163

   passing by value, VBScript 119

   passing to functions, VBScript 115–118

   spaces in parameter lists 1165–1166

   user input 41–42

parent classes

   Active Directory 403

   WMI 463–465

parent folder

   binding to 250

   returning 781

Parent property, IADs interface 423

ParentFolder property, Folder object 256–257

parentheses (( ))

   enclosing If-Then statements 1165

   in mathematical expressions 1174

   operator precedence, VBScript 83

parsing file paths 277–278

PartComponent property

   CIM_DirectoryContainsFile class 821

   Win32_Subdirectory class 781

partial replicas, Active Directory 406

partitions

   Active Directory partitions 406

   extended partitions 730

   overview 730

   primary partitions 730

   system partitions 730

   Win32_DiskPartition class properties 730–732

Partitions property, Win32_DiskDrive class 726–728

PartNumber property, Win32_SystemEnclosure class 628

Pascal casing 1157, 1171

passing parameters to functions

   by reference, Script Runtime library 1162–1163

   by reference, VBScript 118–119

   by value, Script Runtime library 1162–1163

   by value, VBScript 119

   VBScript 115–118

Password argument, MapNetworkDrive method 221

Password Expired setting 561

Password Last Changed setting 561

Password Never Expires setting 561

PasswordLastChanged property, IADsUser interface 564

passwords

   coding into WMI scripts 485

   LocalSystem account 1006

   masking 1117–1120

   resetting computer account passwords 706–707

   secure channel passwords 706

   user accounts *See* passwords, user accounts

passwords, user accounts

   See also passwords

   attributes 561–563

   change password at next logon requirement 566

   changing 560

   date last set, determining 564

   overview 558–559

   setting 559

   userAccountControl attribute, changing flag values 565

   userAccountControl attribute, displaying values 563

   userAccountControl attribute, flag values 563

PATH (environment variable) 198

path names

   binding to files 266, 267

   binding to folders 249

   parsing file paths 277–278

   short path names 256

   spaces in names 1150

Path not found (error) 250

Path parameter, Create method (Win32_Share class) 828

Path property
 FileSystemObject 245-247
 Folder object 256-257
 Win32_Directory class 775-776
 Win32_PageFile class 763
 Win32_Share class 826
 WScript object 179
Path_ property, SWbemObject 461
PATHEXT (environment variable) 198
PathName property, Win32_Service class 978-980, 1001-1003, 1011-1012
paths
 ADSI providers 323
 ADsPath See ADsPaths
 directory service object paths 322-325
 distinguished names 323-325
 folder paths, browsing for 791-792
 folder paths, passing to scripts 791
 of currently-running script, retrieving 179
 specifying for user account creation 556
 to databases, specifying in data source names 1104
 to script host folder, retrieving 179
Pause method, IADsPrintJobOperations interface 915
Pause method, IADsPrintQueueOperations interface 912
paused services, resuming 992, 993
PauseService method, Win32_Service class 990, 991
pausing
 print jobs 915
 printers 912
 scripts 176-177
 services 987, 989, 990, 991
PDC emulator role 719-721
PDCRoleOwner attribute, ADSystemInfo object 693
PeakUsage property, Win32_PageFileUsage class 764-765
PeakWorkingSetSize property, Win32_Process class 946-948
percentage symbols (%), environment variables 201
Performance Counter provider, WMI 438-439, 452
performance counters
 See also performance monitoring
 as managed resources 436

performance monitoring
 displaying process performance data 950-954
 memory leaks, diagnosing 946
 monitoring process performance 948-949
 monitoring processor usage 949
 monitoring service performance 973
 overview 941, 945
 performance counters as managed resources 436
 process properties 946-948
peripheral devices, as managed resources 436
Perl
 choosing a scripting language 12-13
 WMI and 430
permissions
 See also access rights
 NTFS permissions and WMI 446
 required to run WMI scripts 443
 stored in CIM repository 444
 WMI scripting vs. FileSystemObject 771
 WMI 444-445
persistent object interfaces, ADSI 422
physical architecture, Active Directory 393
physical disks
 See also logical drives
 compared to logical drives 733
 free disk space, enumerating by user 739-740
 free disk space, enumerating 738
 free disk space, monitoring in real time 740-741
 overview 726
 partitions, enumerating 730-732
 quotas See disk quotas
physical folders, mapping network shares to 830-831
physical location of computers, specifying 703
physical memory
 See also memory
 page files See page files
physical printers
 See also printers and print management
 pausing 912
physicalDeliveryOfficeName attribute, user accounts 572
PhysicalMemory property, Win32_ComputerSystem class 620-621

plain text log files
> See also event logs
> comma-separated-value logs 877
> fixed-width logs 879
> overview 843, 876–877
> tab-separated-value logs 877

plain-text files
> See also text files
> script files, WSH 136–137

PLS files 136

PNPDeviceID property, Win32_DiskDrive class 726–728

pointer, mouse, changing to show script progress 1130–1131

Pointing Device (System Information category), equivalent WMI class 630

pool space, diagnosing memory leaks 946

portName attribute, printQueue object 933–935

PortName property, Win32_Printer class 907–908

pound signs (#...#), VBScript date literals 61

power status, monitoring changes 686–688

pre-built consumer classes, WMI 545

precedence, operators, VBScript 82–83

prefixes, Hungarian notation 1152–1154

PreviousInstance object 535

primary domain controllers, PDC emulator role 719–721

primary partitions 730

Primary property, Win32_OperatingSystem class 639–641

PrimaryBIOS property, Win32_BIOS class 624–626

PrimaryPartition property, Win32_DiskPartition class 730–732

print devices
> See also printers and print management
> definition 884–885

print jobs
> See also printers and print management
> definition 884–885
> IADsPrintJob interface 902–903, 923–924
> modifying in print queues 923–926
> monitoring 885, 899–902
> monitoring status 903
> monitoring time spent in print queue 905

print jobs (continued)
> overview 914
> pausing 915
> priority, changing 924–925
> resuming 916
> start time, changing 926
> Win32_PrintJob class 900–902

print management See printers and print management

print queues
> See also printers and print management
> definition 884–885
> modifying print jobs in queues 923–926
> monitoring 885, 897
> monitoring print job time in queues 905
> overview 913
> purging 914
> reporting queue statistics 897–898

PRINT SCREEN key, SendKeys representation 206

print servers
> See also printers and print management
> definition 884–885

print service, monitoring 896–897

Print Spooler service, monitoring 896–897

print spoolers 884–885

printBinNames attribute, printQueue object 933–935

printCollate attribute, printQueue object 933–935

printColor attribute, printQueue object 933–935

printDuplexSupported attribute, printQueue object 933–935

printer capabilities
> See also printers and print management
> enumerating 910
> IADsPrintQueue interface properties 910
> Win32_Printer class properties 907–908
> Win32_PrinterConfiguration class properties 908–910

printer connections
> See also printers and print management; WshNetwork object
> adding 928–929
> default printer, setting 226
> enumerating 225, 927

printer connections *(continued)*

>MS-DOS-based printer connections, adding 224

>overview 224

>removing 225, 928–929, 930

>Windows-based printer connections, adding 224

printer drivers 884–885

printer location tracking

>*See also* printers and print management

>configuring locations 921–922

>location naming schemes 920–921

>overview 919–920

>updating locations 922

printer ports 884–885

printerName attribute, printQueue object 933–935

printers

>as managed resources 436

>definition 884–885

>managing with WMI scripts 430

>managing *See* printers and print management

Printers (System Information category), equivalent WMI class 630

Printers and Faxes folder

>*See also* special folders

>locating special folders 788

printers and print management

>ADSI vs. WMI scripting 882–883

>availability of printers, scheduling 918

>default printer, setting 226

>IADsPrintJob interface 902–903, 923–924

>IADsPrintQueue interface properties 910

>multiple printer management 883

>overview 881–885

>print jobs, changing priority 924–925

>print jobs, changing start time 926

>print jobs, configuring 923–926

>print jobs, monitoring status 903

>print jobs, monitoring time in print queues 905

>print jobs, monitoring 885, 899–902

>print jobs, pausing 915

>print jobs, resuming 916

>print queues, monitoring 885, 897–898

printers and print management *(continued)*

>print queues, purging 914

>print service, monitoring status 896–897

>printer capabilities 906, 910

>printer connections, adding 224, 928–929

>printer connections, enumerating 225, 927

>printer connections, removing 225, 928–929, 930

>printer location tracking 919–922

>printer properties 907–910

>printer properties, configuring 917–918

>printer status data, filtering 892–893

>printer status, displaying in Web pages 888–889

>printer status, monitoring 887–894

>printers with specified attributes, locating 932–935

>printers, monitoring 885

>printers, pausing 912

>printers, resuming 913

>priority of printers, configuring 917–918

>published printers, enumerating 931

>published printers, renaming 356

>scheduling printer availability 918

>searching in Active Directory for printers 930–935

>terminology (table) 884–885

>Win32_Printer class properties 907–908

>Win32_Printer class 885–887

>Win32_PrinterConfiguration class properties 908–910

>Win32_PrintJob class 900–902

PrinterStatus property, Win32_Printer class 885–887

PrintHood folder

>*See also* special folders

>locating special folders 788

>special folder identifiers 195

printing, managing *See* printers and print management

printLanguage attribute, printQueue object 933–935

printMaxResolutionSupported attribute, printQueue object 933–935

printMediaReady attribute, printQueue object 933–935

printMediaSupported attribute, printQueue object 933–935

printMemory attribute, printQueue object 933–935

printOwner attribute, printQueue object 933–935

printPagesPerMinute attribute, printQueue object 933–935

PrintQuality property, Win32_PrinterConfiguration class 908–910

printQueue object 933–935

printRate attribute, printQueue object 933–935

printRateUnit attribute, printQueue object 933–935

printShareName attribute, printQueue object 933–935

printStaplingSupported attribute, printQueue object 933–935

priority
  creating higher-priority processes 964
  of print jobs, changing 924–925
  of printers, configuring 917–918

Priority property
  IADsPrintJob interface 902–903, 923–924, 925
  IADsPrintQueue interface 910
  Win32_PrintJob class 900–902
  Win32_Process class 946–948
  Win32_ScheduledJob class 1137–1140
  Win32_Thread class 956–957

PriorityBase property, Win32_Thread class 956–957

PriorityClass property, Win32_ProcessStartup class 962–963

privilege overrides, WMI moniker 498–500

Privileges qualifier, WMI 470, 471

privileges, setting in WMI scripts 498–500

procedures
  calling, Script Runtime library 1162–1163
  calling, VBScript 112–113
  functions, passing parameters by reference 118–119
  functions, passing parameters by value 119
  functions, passing parameters to, VBScript 115–118
  functions, return values, VBScript 114–115
  functions, VBScript 112, 114–115
  indenting for readability 1167
  naming conventions 1149, 1156–1157
  overview 111–112, 113, 1161
  passing parameters, Script Runtime library 1162–1163
  procedure headers 1180
  recursion, VBScript 120–121

procedures (continued)
  script structure and organization 1157
  subroutines, VBScript 112, 113

process availability
  monitoring 942
  overview 941

process creation
  event subscriptions 943
  monitoring process creation 943–944
  startup options 961–964
  Win32_Process Create method 959–960

process deletion
  event subscriptions 943
  monitoring 943–944, 945

Process environment variables, registry locations 197

process management
  See also process monitoring
  overview 939–940
  Windows Task Manager 940

process monitoring
  availability monitoring 941, 942
  identifying process owners 955
  overview 940, 941
  performance data, displaying 950–954
  performance monitoring 941, 945–949
  process creation monitoring 943–944
  process deletion monitoring 943–944, 945
  reliability monitoring 941, 943–945
  WMI event notification 530, 542

process reliability
  monitoring 943–945
  overview 941, 943

process termination
  newly started processes 967
  overview 965–966
  running processes 966

processes
  See also services; threads
  as managed resources 436
  availability 941, 942
  compared to scripts 938

processes *(continued)*

 creating in hidden windows 963

 creating with higher priorities 964

 creating *See* process creation

 deleting *See* process deletion

 identifying running processes 942

 identifying services running in processes 983-986

 listing threads 957

 managing with WMI scripts 430

 memory allocation 939

 memory leaks 939, 946-949

 monitoring *See* process monitoring

 overview 938-939

 performance *See* performance monitoring

 process owners, identifying 955

 reliability 941, 943-945

 shared processes 983-986

 startup options 961-964

 terminating 965-967

 Win32_Process class properties 946-948

ProcessHandle property, Win32_Thread class 956-957

ProcessID property

 Win32_Process class 946-948

 Win32_Service class 978-980

processor use

 See also processes

 diagnosing memory leaks 946

 monitoring 949

PROCESSOR_ARCHITECTURE (environment variable) 198

PROCESSOR_IDENTIFIER (environment variable) 198

PROCESSOR_LEVEL (environment variable) 198

PROCESSOR_REVISION (environment variable) 198

production scripts, ADSI 332-334

ProductName property, Win32_SoftwareFeature class 658-659

ProgIDs

 COM objects, creating with WSH 151, 152

 COM objects, registering 123

 WshController object 228

Program Files folder

 See also special folders

 locating special folders 788

programs

 See also applications; processes

 ADSI-enabled applications 420

 applications without COM object model, automating 206-210

 automating *See* COM

 auto-start programs 673-674

 COM components *See* COM

 ensuring applications are active 209

 running from within scripts 184-187

 sending keystrokes to *See* keystrokes, sending to applications

 setting focus 210

Programs folder

 See also special folders

 locating special folders 788

progress of scripts, tracking

 in command window 1133-1135

 in Internet Explorer 1126-1128

 in Internet Explorer, changing mouse pointer 1130-1131

 in Internet Explorer, dynamic tracking 1128-1130

 in Internet Explorer, with animated .gif files 1131

 overview 1125-1126

PROMPT (environment variable) 198

properties

 See also attributes; names of specific classes

 CIM classes 442

 default properties of automation objects 1175

 extended file properties, retrieving 806-808

 File object 273-274

 file properties, retrieving 804-805

 in ADSI interfaces 421

 of COM objects, accessing 152

 WMI classes 433, 467-469

 WMI classes, examining using WMI Tester 471

 WMI classes, in WMI object paths 502-503

 WMI classes, querying *See* WMI queries

Properties_ property, SWbemObject 472, 474

property cache interfaces, ADSI 422

property cache, local *See* local property cache, ADSI

property qualifiers, WMI 470

proportional fonts 78–79

__Provider class 458

Provider qualifier, WMI 470

providers, ADSI

    implementation of interfaces 421

    in ADsPaths 323

    interfaces supported by 423–425

    list of providers 418

    overview 417

providers, WMI *See* WMI providers

published folders

    administrative tasks 836

    deleting 839–840

    enumerating 836–837

    publishing in Active Directory 834–835

    searching for 838

    Volume class 835

published printers

    enumerating 931

    renaming 356

Purge method, IADsPrintQueueOperations interface 914

purging print queues 914

_Put method 526, 544

Put method, ADSI 313–315, 326, 329, 571

PutEx method, ADSI 337–339, 571

pwdLastSet attribute, user accounts 555, 561

Q

qualifiers, WMI

    class qualifiers 470

    examining using WMI Tester 471

    method qualifiers 471

    overview 469

    property qualifiers 470

Qualifiers_ property, SWbemObject 472, 476

quarters

    intervals between, determining, VBScript 69

    retrieving from date and time values 62–64

queries

    Active Directory *See* searching in Active Directory

    event logs *See* event log queries

    WMI *See* WMI queries

query processing speeds, WMI vs. FileSystemObject 770

Query property, __EventFilter class 544

query strings, Active Directory searches

    See also searching in Active Directory

    attributes to be returned by searches 592

    filters 591

    search base 590

    search scope 592

question mark mouse pointer, Internet Explorer 1130

Quick Fix Engineering group *See* hot fixes

Quick Launch buttons, creating 194

Quit method

    Internet Explorer object 1077–1079

    Wscript object 1085

    WScript object 178

quitting scripts 177–178

quota warning levels 750

QuotaLimit property, DiskQuotaControl object 748–749

QuotaNonPagedPoolUsage property, Win32_Process class 946–948

QuotaPagedPoolUsage property, Win32_Process class 946–948

quotas *See* disk quotas

QuotaState property, DiskQuotaControl object 744, 745–746

QuotaThreshold property, DiskQuotaControl object 748–749

quotation marks, comment delimiters 1178

QuotaUsed property, DiskQuotaControl object 748–749

R

Read method

    FileSystemObject 286, 291

    StdIn stream 160

Read qualifier, WMI 470–471

READ_CONTROL (registry subkey access right) 1048

readability of code

See also comments

boolean expressions 1173

case styles 1171

default properties of automation objects 1175

limiting lines to single statements 1168–1169

line length 1168

overview 1170

parentheses in mathematical expressions 1174

phrasing If-Then statements 1172

single-line If-Then statements 1169

statement breaks 1168–1169

telephone test 1172

white space 1164–1167

Readable property, Win32_Directory class 775–776

ReadAll method

FileSystemObject 286, 287–288

StdIn stream 160

reading directory service object attributes

See also directory service objects

Get method parameters 330

groups 316

OUs 315

user accounts 315

reading from text files

character-by-character 290–292

entire file 287–288

file reading methods 286

ForReading mode 283

from bottom to top 289–290

line-by-line 288–289

overview 285

reading values of registry entries

binary-valued entries 1031–1032

DWORD-valued entries 1027–1028

expanded string-valued entries 1030–1031

multistring-valued entries 1029

overview 1026–1027

string-valued entries 1027–1028

ReadLine method

FileSystemObject 286, 288, 289

StdIn stream 160, 161

Read-only (file attribute) 275

read-only files, deleting 269

read-only folders, deleting 801

Reboot method, Win32_OperatingSystem class 685

Recent (special folder identifier) 195

record-keeping See logs and log files

RecordNumber property, Win32_NTLogEvent class 858–859

records

adding 1107–1109

adding to disconnected recordsets 1101

deleting all records 1116–1117

deleting selected records 1114–1116

finding 1109–1112

updating 1112–1114

Recordset object, ADO

See also recordsets

AddNew method 1107

Close method 1105

Delete method 1110, 1114

described 1103

EOF property 1110

Find method 1109, 1112

in Active Directory searches 358, 589

Open method 1105

Update method 1112

recordsets

See also arrays; databases; Recordset object, ADO

disconnected recordsets 103, 1101–1103

recovery options

configuring 679

enumerating 677–678

stop messages 675

Win32_OSRecoveryConfiguration class 676–677

recursion and recursive functions

enumerating subfolders within subfolders 264–266

recursive procedures, VBScript 120–121

Recycle Bin folder

    See also special folders

    in Shell namespace hierarchy 773

    locating special folders 788

ReDim Preserve statement, VBScript 100

redirecting script output to Internet Explorer

    clearing Web pages 1084

    creating an instance of Internet Explorer 1079–1081

    event handling 1085–1087

    formatting using HTML coding 1082–1084

    HTAs and 1087–1091

    Internet Explorer closed, handling 1085–1087

    overview 1077–1079

    tabular data control *See* tabular data control

redirecting script output to text files, WSH scripts 145–146

reference, passing parameters by

    Script Runtime library 1162–1163

    VBScript 118–119

ReferencesTo method, SWbemServices object 487–488, 490

referral chasing 367, 369, 407

Refresh method, Internet Explorer object 1077–1079

Reg.exe tool 1025

REG_BINARY data type

    See also binary-valued registry entries

    corresponding WSH and VBScript data types 204

    description of 1020

    integer values of registry data types 1023

REG_DWORD data type

    See also DWORD-valued registry entries

    corresponding WSH and VBScript data types 204

    description of 1020

    integer values of registry data types 1023

REG_DWORD_BIG_ENDIAN data type 1020

REG_DWORD_LITTLE_ENDIAN data type 1020

REG_EXPAND_SZ data type

    See also expanded string-valued registry entries

    corresponding WSH and VBScript data types 204

    description of 1020

    integer values of registry data types 1023

REG_FULL_RESOURCE_DESCRIPTOR data type 1020

REG_LINK data type 1020

REG_MULTI_SZ data type

    See also multistring-valued registry entries

    corresponding WSH and VBScript data types 204

    description of 1020

    integer values of registry data types 1023

REG_NONE data type 1020

REG_QWORD data type 1020

REG_QWORD_LITTLE_ENDIAN data type 1020

REG_RESOURCE_LIST data type 1020

REG_RESOURCE_REQUIREMENTS_LIST data type 1020

REG_SZ data type

    See also string-valued registry entries

    corresponding WSH and VBScript data types 204

    description of 1020

    integer values of registry data types 1023

RegDelete method, WshShell object 205

regedit.exe 1017

regedit32.exe 1017

regional settings

    date and time formats 61, 70–73

    number formats 84

RegisteredUser property, Win32_OperatingSystem class 639–641

registering consumer classes in CIM repository 545

registration, WMI providers 440

registry

    adding values to 681

    administrative tasks 1016–1017, 1024, 1050

    alternative configuration management tools 1016

    as managed resource 436

    backing up before editing 1025–1026

    data types, WSH and VBScript 204

    default entries 1021

    entries *See* registry entries

    environment variables, locations of 197

    files *See* registry files

    hierarchical organization 1018–1022

    hives *See* hive files

    keys *See* registry keys

registry *(continued)*

managing with WMI scripts 430

monitoring entry-level events 1053

monitoring registry access 1050

monitoring subkey-level events 1052

monitoring subtree-level events 1050–1051

namespace definitions 452

overview 1016–1017

reading entries *See reading values of registry entries*

Reg.exe tool 1025

Registry Editor overview 1017

Registry Provider *See WMI Registry Provider*

remotely running scripts, configuring environment
for 229

Shell object verbs 818

structure 1018–1022

subkeys *See registry subkeys*

subtrees *See registry subtrees*

updating using WSH 203–205

WMI Registry Provider *See WMI Registry Provider*

Registry Editor 1017

registry entries

binary-valued entries, reading 1031–1032

changing 1033–1034

changing, WSH 205

creating 1035, 1036–1040

creating, WSH 205

data types 1020

data types, enumerating 1043

data types, integer values 1023

default entries 1021

deleting 1045–1046

deleting, WSH 205

DWORD-valued entries, changing 1033–1034

DWORD-valued entries, creating 1036–1038

DWORD-valued entries, reading 1027–1028

enumerating 1041, 1043

expanded string-valued entries, creating 1040

expanded string-valued entries, reading 1030–1031

monitoring modifications to 1053

multistring-valued entries, creating 1038–1040

multistring-valued entries, reading 1029

registry entries *(continued)*

NTFS properties 755–757, 760–761

overview 1020

reading values 1026–1027

reading, WSH 203–205

string-valued entries, changing 1033–1034

string-valued entries, creating 1036–1038

string-valued entries, reading 1027–1028

values, enumerating 757, 1043

values, modifying 760–761

registry files

locations of, displaying 1021

overview 1021

registry hives *See hive files*

registry keys

default entries 1021

enumerating 1041

overview 1019

Registry Provider *See WMI Registry Provider*

Registry Reference 1017

registry subkeys

access rights, administering 1047–1048

creating 1035

default entries 1021

deleting 1045, 1046

enumerating 1041, 1042

monitoring modifications to 1052

overview 1019

registry subtrees

abbreviations 1019

constants, WMI Registry Provider 1022

default entries 1021

list of subtrees 1019

monitoring modifications to 1050–1051

overview 1019

RegistryKeyChangeEvent 1052

RegistryTreeChangeEvent 1051

RegistryValueChangeEvent 1053

RegRead method, WshShell object 203

RegWrite method, WshShell object 205

relational databases

See also databases

UDA and 1103

ReleaseDate property, Win32_BIOS class 624–626

reliability

    monitoring process reliability 941, 943–945

    monitoring service reliability 973, 976–977

REM statement 1178

remote access through CIMOM 440

remote computers

    See also local computers

    COM objects, creating 153

    installing software 662–663

    running scripts on *See* remotely running scripts

    security and remote connections 663

    shared folders *See* network shares

remote file access, WMI scripting vs. FileSystemObject 771–772

remote WSH *See* remotely running scripts

remotely running scripts

    configuring environment for 229

    controller scripts 227

    error handling 232

    event handling 231

    limitations of remote WSH 234

    monitoring status of 231

    overview 227

    running scripts 230

    worker scripts 227, 230

RemoteName argument, MapNetworkDrive method 221

Remove method, Dictionary object 303–304

RemoveAll method, Dictionary object 303, 305

RemoveNetworkDrive method, WshNetwork object 222

RemovePrinterConnection method, WshNetwork object 225, 928, 930

removing

    See also deleting

    scheduled tasks 1144–1145

    services 1010, 1013–1014

Rename method

    CIM_DataFile class 776–778, 813

    Win32_Directory class 776–778, 794, 795

renaming

    computer accounts 704–705

    directory service objects 356

    files 272–273, 813–814

    folders 255, 794

    user accounts 586

replication, Active Directory

    attributes replicated to Global Catalog 407, 410

    full replicas 406

    overview 406

    partial replicas 406

ReplyTo property, IMessage interface, CDO Message object 1121

repository, CIM *See* CIM repository

request routing, CIMOM 440

rereading text files 284

resetting mouse pointer in Internet Explorer 1131

Resource Kit, WMI scripts for browsing CIM 479

resources

    See also asset management

    managing with WMI scripts 436

resources, monitoring

    print jobs *See* monitoring print jobs

    print queues *See* monitoring print queues

    printers *See* monitoring printers

restarting

    computers 685–686

    stopped services 987, 992, 998–999, 1000

result sets, Active Directory searches

    See also searching in Active Directory

    limiting 379

    modifying user accounts using 611

    performing operations on 382–385

    running *See* searching in Active Directory

    sorting 610

Resume method

    IADsPrintJobOperations interface 916

    IADsPrintQueueOperations interface 913

ResumeService method, Win32_Service class 992, 993

resuming

    print jobs 916

    printers 913

    services 992, 993

return values

    VBScript functions 114–115

    WMI file and folder operations 778

reuse of variable names 1155–1156

revoking privileges, WMI settings 498–500

RID master role 719–721

rIDManager class, identifying operations master roles 719–721

RIGHT ARROW key, SendKeys representation 206

Right function, VBScript 76–77, 1074–1075

rights, WMI 444–445

roles See computer roles

Root Directory Service Entry See rootDSE

root domain, binding to 392

root folder parameter, BrowseForFolder method 792

root folder, binding to 250

rootDSE

    binding to configuration container 392

    binding to current domain 391

    binding to root domain 392

    binding to schema container 392

    defaultNamingContext attribute 391

    identifying computer's current domain controller 718–719

    overview 390

    using in scripts 391

RootFolder property, FileSystemObject 245–247

router, ADSI 420

routing (request routing), CIMOM 440

RowDelim property, tabular data control 1093–1094

RTrim function, VBScript 76–77

Run method, WshShell object 184–185, 186–187, 188–189

running processes, identifying 942

running queries, WMI See WMI queries

running scripts

    See also scripts

    in enterprise settings See enterprise scripts

    introduction to scripting 3–6

    on multiple computers See enterprise scripts

running WSH scripts

    from command line 142–145

    from context-sensitive menus 146

    from Windows Explorer 146

    on remote computers 146

    overview 140–142

    scheduling script execution 146

    using drag-and-drop 146

RunRepeatedly property, Win32_ScheduledJob class 1137–1140, 1141–1142

runtime errors

    See also error handling

    Clear method, VBScript 46

    COM object errors, handling in VBScript 110–111

    Err object, VBScript 44–46

    error handling 43

    error handling options, VBScript 105–106

    ignoring, VBScript 105, 106–107

    On Error GoTo 0 statement, VBScript 108–109

    On Error Resume Next statement, VBScript 43–46, 106–109

    overview, VBScript 104–105

    resetting Err object, VBScript 46

    responding to, VBScript 105, 106, 107–108

S

SAM users and groups, as managed resources 436

sAMAccountName attribute

    Computer class 691

    user accounts 554, 556, 600

sample scripts See tasks

Save method

    WshShortcut object 192

    WshUrlShortcut object 193

Scale property, Win32_PrinterConfiguration class 908–910

Scheduled Task Wizard 1136, 1137, 1141

scheduled tasks

creating 1140–1143

database storage of task information 1067

deleting 1144–1145

deleting with WMI scripts 529

enumerating 1137–1140

managing with WMI scripts 430

overview 1135–1137

task-scheduling APIs 1136–1137

WSH scripts, scheduling execution 146

scheduling printer availability 918

schema container, binding to 392

schema interfaces, ADSI 422

schema master role 719–721

Schema partition, Active Directory 406

Schema property, IADs interface 423

schema, Active Directory

Active Directory Schema Snap-in 403

ADSI Edit snap-in 405

in Active Directory architecture 395

schema, WMI See CIM repository

SchemaRoleOwner attribute, ADSystemInfo object 693

Schtasks.exe 1141

SCM

overview 972, 973

service account passwords 1009

scope of Active Directory searches 369–371, 708

Script Debugger, running WSH scripts 143

script files, WSH

interactions with script hosts 139

overview 136–137

script hosts, WSH

command-line options 143–145

CScript See CScript host

default script host, setting 143

determining current script host 180

interactions with script files 139

interactions with scripting language engines 139

overview 137–138

running scripts from command line 143–145

WScript See WScript host

script input See input to scripts

script output See output from scripts

Script Runtime library

compared to WMI 243

drive management See disk drive management

file management See files and file management

folder management See folders and folder management

overview 242

ScriptFullName property, WScript object 179

scripting guidelines

comments See comments

debugging See debugging scripts

formatting See formatting code

in enterprise settings See enterprise scripts

naming See naming conventions

overview 1147–1148

readability See readability of code

running scripts on multiple computers See enterprise scripts

script structure and organization 1157–1159

scripting language engines

interactions with script hosts 139

overview 138

specifying for individual scripts 143

scripting languages

about scripting 3–6

choosing 12–13

engines See scripting language engines

history of scripting 6

multiple-language scripts 1170

WSH-compliant languages (list) 136

scripting runtime environment

See also WSH

Cmd.exe, compared to WSH scripts 133

script files, WSH 136–137, 139

script hosts See script hosts, WSH

scripting language engines See scripting language engines

scripting languages 136

WSH capabilities 130–133

WSH components, interaction of 139–140

scripting steps See tasks

ScriptingStandardConsumerSetting class 545

ScriptName property, WScript object 179

scripts

    See also Script Runtime library

    about scripting 3–6

    about scripts used in this book 11–12

    about system requirements 13–14

    about this book 8–11

    access to file system from scripts *See* Script Runtime library

    administrative credentials required 14

    ADSI *See* ADSI

    auto-start programs 673–674

    choosing a scripting language 12–13

    command-line tools, running from within scripts 188–189

    comments *See* comments

    compared to processes 938

    continuously running with endless loops 89

    database operations *See* databases

    debugging *See* debugging scripts

    disabling error handling 1187–1188

    documentation 1181

    embedding code in Web pages, drawbacks of 1088

    enterprise-enabled scripts *See* enterprise scripts

    error handling *See* error handling

    event handling *See* event handling

    examples *See* tasks

    for system administration tasks *See* tasks

    formatting *See* formatting code

    guidelines *See* scripting guidelines

    history of scripting 6

    in enterprise settings *See* enterprise scripts

    input from users *See* input to scripts

    monitoring progress *See* tracking script progress

    monitoring running time 69

    multiple-language scripts 1170

    naming conventions 1149–1150

    output from *See* output from scripts

    pausing 176–177

    programs, running from within scripts 184–187

scripts *(continued)*

    quitting 177–178

    readability *See* readability of code

    running incrementally 1186–1187

    running on multiple computers *See* enterprise scripts

    running on remote computers *See* remotely running scripts

    running scripts from within scripts 184–187

    scheduled tasks *See* scheduled tasks

    script headers 1179–1180

    streams, input and output, accessing 184–185

    structure and organization 1157–1159

    syntax checking 1187

    templates 1160–1161

    terminating 177–178

    testing 1188

    time-out values 178

    trace routines 1184–1185

    tracking progress *See* tracking script progress

    user input *See* input to scripts

    VBScript *See* VBScript

    Visual Basic .NET *See* Visual Basic .NET

    white space 1164–1167

    WMI *See* WMI scripts

    WSH *See* WSH scripts

SCROLL LOCK key, SendKeys representation 206

SCSI (System Information category), equivalent WMI class 630

SCSIBus property, Win32_DiskDrive class 726–728

SCSILogicalUnit property, Win32_DiskDrive class 726–728

SCSIPort property, Win32_DiskDrive class 726–728

SCSITargetID property, Win32_DiskDrive class 726–728

search base, LDAP search dialect 590

search filters *See* filters, Active Directory searches

search scope

    LDAP search dialect 592

    limiting in Active Directory searches 369–371

searchFlags attribute, Active Directory 409

searching

    in Active Directory *See* searching in Active Directory

    searching strings for text, VBScript 79–81

searching for classes, WMI 462
searching in Active Directory
    ADO interfaces 589
    ADO objects used in search scripts 358
    attributes to be returned, specifying 362, 592
    attributes without values, searching for 603
    attributes, searching for in containers 593, 596
    attributes, searching for in subcontainers 598
    attributes, verifying uniqueness in forests 600
    Command object properties 380
    consolidating query strings 379
    containers, searching for attributes 593, 596
    empty attribute values, searching for 601–605
    enumerating all computer accounts 709
    filtered searches 707–708, 710–711
    filters, LDAP search dialect 591–592, 602
    Global Catalog, specifying in search base 366–367
    IsNull function, VBScript 603
    LDAP search dialect *See* LDAP search dialect
    limiting number of attributes retrieved 708
    limiting results to user account types 596
    multivalued attributes 608
    multivalued attributes, returning 374–378
    not present operator, search filters 602
    optimizing searches 378–381
    overview 707–708
    printers 930–935
    printers with specified attributes 932–935
    published printers 931
    queries, specifying using CommandText property 589
    range limits 376–378
    referral chasing 367–369, 407
    result sets, expanding using referral chasing 367–369
    result sets, limiting 379
    result sets, modifying user accounts using 611
    result sets, performing operations on 382–385
    result sets, sorting 610
    scope of searches 708
    search base, LDAP search dialect 590
    search results page size 708
    search scope, controlling 369–371
    search scope, LDAP search dialect 592

searching in Active Directory *(continued)*
    simple search script 360–362
    sorting search results 371–373
    steps in search scripts 359
    subcontainers, searching for attributes 598
    time-out value 708
    tips for effective searching 708
    type of object to be returned, specifying 364–365
    using Global Catalog 381
    wildcards in search filters 606–607
Second function, VBScript 66–67
seconds
    intervals between, determining, VBScript 69
    retrieving from date and time values 62–64, 66–67
SectorsPerTrack property, Win32_DiskDrive class 726–728
secure channel passwords 706
security
    Access Denied error message 662–663
    CIMOM and 440
    connecting to remote computers 663
    installing software on remote computers 662–663
    managing with WMI scripts 430
    multi-hop security 662–663
    password masking 1117–1120
    registry, monitoring 1050–1053
    single-hop security 662
    WMI *See* WMI security
    WSH *See* WSH security
Security event log, retrieving properties 848–849
security interfaces, ADSI 422
Security parameter, managing Security event log 848–849
security principal naming attributes, user accounts 554
Select Case statements, VBScript 96–97
Select queries, WMI 505, 506, 508
semi-synchronous mode, SWbemServices object 489
SendAdminAlert property, Win32_OSRecoveryConfiguration class 676–677
Sender property, IMessage interface, CDO Message object 1121
sending e-mail messages from scripts
    CDO and 1121
    overview 1120–1122

sending e-mail messages from scripts *(continued)*

    scripting steps 1122

    without installing SMTP service 1123–1125

sending script output to Internet Explorer

    clearing Web pages 1084

    creating an instance of Internet Explorer 1079–1081

    event handling 1085–1087

    formatting using HTML coding 1082–1084

    HTAs and 1087–1091

    Internet Explorer closed, handling 1085–1087

    overview 1077–1079

    tabular data control *See* tabular data control

SendKeys method, WshShell object

    ensuring applications are active 209

    limitations of 208–209

    overview 206

    representations of keyboard characters 206–207

    sending keystrokes to applications 207

    setting focus on apps 210

SendTo folder

    See also special folders

    creating shortcuts in 196

    locating special folders 788

    special folder identifiers 195

SendUsing property, Configuration object, CDO 1123

SeparatorFile property, Win32_Printer class 907–908

serial numbers, retrieving 628–629

Serial Ports (System Information category), equivalent WMI class 630

SerialNumber property

    FileSystemObject 245–247

    Win32_BIOS class 624–626

    Win32_OperatingSystem class 639–641

    Win32_SystemEnclosure class 628

Server mode, COM objects 123

serverless binding 390

serverName attribute

    printQueue object 933–935

    rootDSE 718

ServerName property, Win32_Printer class 885–887, 907–908

servers

    listing in databases 1067

    listing in text files 1061

    multiple servers, running scripts on *See* enterprise scripts

    retrieving names from Active Directory 1070

    structuring in Active Directory 1070

service accounts

    LocalSystem account 1006–1007

    overview 1006

    passwords 1009–1010

    specifying 1007–1008

Service Control Manager *See* SCM

service control programs 972

service dependencies

    antecedent services 993, 997–998

    dependent services 993, 994–996, 998–1000

    enumerating dependencies 995–996, 997–998

    overview 993

    starting dependent services 998–999, 1000

    stopping dependent services 998, 999

service packs

    identifying latest installed service pack 644

    overview 643–644

service start options 1003–1004

ServiceDependencies property, Win32_Service class 1001–1003, 1011–1012

ServicePackMajorVersion property, Win32_OperatingSystem class 620–621

ServicePackMinorVersion property, Win32_OperatingSystem class 620–621, 644

services

    See also processes

    antecedent services 993, 997–998

    Auto (start option) 1003

    auto-start services 973, 1003–1004, 1004–1005

    base Windows 2000 services 1013

    computer roles and installed services 715

    configuring 1001–1005

    dependencies *See* service dependencies

    dependent services 993, 994–996, 998–1000

    Disabled (start option) 1003

    error codes (table) 987–989

services *(continued)*
    error control codes 1004–1005
    event logs *See* event logs
    identifying services running in processes 983–986
    increasing availability 974
    installed services, enumerating 715
    installing 1010–1012
    managing with WMI scripts 430
    Manual (start option) 1003
    monitoring availability 973, 974–975
    monitoring performance 973
    monitoring reliability 973, 976–977
    monitoring, WMI event notification 532, 542
    operating system services 1010, 1013
    overview 971–972
    pausing 987, 989, 990, 991
    preventing startup by Power Users 1003–1004
    properties 978–982, 1001–1003
    removing 1010, 1013–1014
    reporting on not-running services 975
    reporting on service states 975
    required components 972–973
    restarting automatically 1003
    resuming 992, 993
    running in Windows 2000 973
    service account passwords 1009–1010
    service accounts 1007–1008
    shared processes 983–986
    start options 1003–1004
    starting 987, 992, 998–999, 1000
    stopping 987, 989, 990, 991, 998, 999
    threads initialized by 973
ServiceType property, Win32_Service class 978–980, 1001–1003, 1011–1012
Set keyword, VBScript 21, 249, 266, 325
SetDefaultPrinter method, WshNetwork object 226
SetDWORDValue method, Registry Provider 1033, 1036
SetExpandedStringValue method, Registry Provider 1040
SetInfo method, ADSI 331
SetMultiStringValue method, Registry Provider 1038
SetPassword method, IADsUser interface 558, 559
SetShareInfo method, Win32_Share class 833
SetStringValue method, Registry Provider 1033, 1036

Severe (error control code) 1004
shared folders
    administrative tasks 825
    as managed resources 436
    deleting with WMI scripts 529
    managing with WMI scripts 430
    mapping to local folders 830–831
    network shares, creating 828–829
    network shares, deleting 832–833
    number of connections allowed, specifying 828
    properties, enumerating 826–827
    properties, modifying 833–834
    published folders, administrative tasks 836
    published folders, deleting 839–840
    published folders, enumerating 836–837
    published folders, searching for 838
    publishing in Active Directory 834–835
    Volume class 835
    Win32_Share class 826
shared processes
    listing services running in 984–986
    overview 983–984
ShareName property
    FileSystemObject 245–247, 248
    Win32_Printer class 907–908
Shell Folder object *See* Folder object
Shell FolderItems object *See* FolderItems object
Shell namespace hierarchy 773
Shell object
    Browse for Folder dialog box 791–792
    BrowseForFolder method 792
    copying folders 797–799
    Folder object *See* Folder object
    FolderItems object *See* FolderItems object
    moving folders 800
    overview 773–774
    scripting, vs. WMI and FileSystemObject 774
    Shell namespace hierarchy 773
    special folder constants 787–789
    verbs, enumerating for specified objects 820
    verbs, executing 818–819

shells *See* scripting runtime environment

    Shell object *See* Shell object

SHIFT key, SendKeys representation 206

short names of folders 256

shortcut menus, executing Shell object verbs 818–820

shortcuts

    creating in special folders 196

    deleting 194

    overview 191–192

    Quick Launch buttons, creating 194

    standard shortcuts 191, 192–193

    URL shortcuts 191, 193, 194

ShortName property

    Folder object 256–257

ShortPath property

    Folder object 256–257

ShowInTaskbar property, HTA object 1088–1090

ShowUsage method, WshArguments collection 166

ShowWindow property, Win32_ProcessStartup class 962–963

shutting down computers 682–685

Signature property, Win32_DiskDrive class 726–728

signed scripts 235–238

Simonyi, Charles 1152

Single (data subtype) 1153–1154

single quotation marks, comment delimiters 1178

Single values, VBScript, CSng type conversion function 58

single-hop impersonation, WMI DCOM security 446

single-hop security, installing software on remote computers 662

SingleInstance property, HTA object 1088–1090

SiteName attribute, ADSystemInfo object 693

size

    file size, verifying 286–287

    maximum size of event logs 844, 851

Size Limit property, Command object (ADO) 380

Size property

    Folder object 256–257

    IADsPrintJob interface 902–903, 923–924

    Win32_DiskDrive class 726–728

    Win32_DiskPartition class 730–732

    Win32_LogicalDisk class 733–734

    Win32_PrintJob class 900–902

SizeStoredInPagingFiles property, Win32_OperatingSystem class 620–621

Skip method

    FileSystemObject 286, 291

    StdIn stream 160

SkipLine method

    FileSystemObject 286, 291

    StdIn stream 160

SKU property, Win32_SystemEnclosure class 628

SKUNumber property, Win32_Product class 656

Sleep method, WScript object 176–177, 1086

SMBIOS specification

    overview 623

    retrieving SMBIOS information 628–629

SMBIOSAssetTag property, Win32_SystemEnclosure class 628

SMBIOSMajorVersion property, Win32_BIOS class 624–626

SMBIOSMinorVersion property, Win32_BIOS class 624–626

SMBIOSPresent property, Win32_BIOS class 624–626

SMBIOSVersion property, Win32_BIOS class 624–626

SMS

    managing with WMI scripts 430

    WMI consumer 443

    WMI provider 438

SMTP service

    e-mail messaging when service not installed 1123–1125

    e-mail messaging 1121

SMTPEventConsumer class 545

SmtpServer property, Configuration object, CDO 1123

SmtpServerPort property, Configuration object, CDO 1123

sn attribute, user accounts 572

snap-ins

    Active Directory Schema Snap-in 403

    ADSI Edit snap-in 405

sng (variable name prefix) 1153–1154

SNMP MIB data, as managed resources 436

SNMP provider, WMI 438–439

SNMP-enabled devices, managing with WMI scripts 430

Snmpincl.dll 438–439

software
> *See also* processes
> enumerating installed software features 658–659
> enumerating installed software 655–656
> installing 653–654, 659–660
> installing on local computers 660–661
> installing on remote computers 662–663
> inventorying *See* inventorying software
> maintaining 653–654
> uninstalling 653–654, 659–660, 666
> upgrading 653–654, 659–660, 664–665

software features, enumerating installed features 658–659

Software Installation and Maintenance 653–654

Sort method, DataList object 1101

Sort On property, Command object (ADO) 371

Sort property, tabular data control 1093–1094

SortColumn parameter, tabular data control 1096

sorting
> script output 1095–1099, 1101–1103
> search results, Active Directory searches 371–373, 610

Sound Device (System Information category), equivalent WMI class 630

Source property, WshRemoteError object 232

SourceName property, Win32_NTLogEvent class 858–859

SourceText property, WshRemoteError object 232

Space function, VBScript 76–77, 1074–1075

spaces
> *See also* white space in scripts
> in command-line arguments 164
> in parameters for command-line tools 189–190
> in path names 1150
> in script file names 1149–1150
> indenting code for readability 1167

spacing tabular script output 1074

SpawnInstance_ method
> creating resources 528
> __EventFilter class and 544

special folders
> creating shortcuts in 196
> enumerating items in 790
> identifying 787
> retrieving location of 196, 787–789
> Shell object constants 787–789
> special folder identifiers 195
> WScript SpecialFolders collection 195
> WSH mnemonics 787–789

SpecialFolders collection 195

SpecificationVersion property, Win32_PrinterConfiguration class 908–910

speed of query processing, WMI vs. FileSystemObject 770

speed of WMI queries, increasing using forward-only enumerators 513–514

SQL databases
> *See also* databases
> connecting to 1104
> UDA and 1103

SQL functions supported by WQL 504

SQL Server
> managing with WMI scripts 430
> WMI provider 438

SQL syntax, searching for attributes in containers 595

standard providers, WMI 438–439

standard shortcuts
> creating 192–193
> overview 191

Start event, WshRemote object 231

Start Menu folder
> *See also* special folders
> locating special folders 788

start options 1003–1004

start time of print jobs, changing 926

Started property, Win32_Service class 978–980

starting services 987, 992, 998–999, 1000

starting WMI service 440

StartingOffset property, Win32_DiskPartition class 730–732

StartMenu (special folder identifier) 195

StartMode property, Win32_Service class 978-980, 1001-1003, 1011-1012

StartName property, Win32_Service class 978-980, 1001-1003, 1011-1012

StartPassword property, Win32_Service class 1001-1003, 1011-1012

StartService method, Win32_Service class 992

StartTime property
    IADsPrintJob interface 902-903, 923-924, 926
    IADsPrintQueue interface 910
    Win32_Printer class 907-908
    Win32_ScheduledJob class 1137-1140, 1141-1142

Startup (special folder identifier) 195

Startup and Recovery Page
    Win32_ComputerSystem class properties 672
    Win32_OSRecoveryConfiguration class properties 677

startup commands
    enumerating 673-674
    Win32_StartupCommand class 674

Startup folder
    See also special folders
    locating special folders 788

startup options
    configuring 670-673
    default operating system 670
    enumerating 668
    modifying 963-964
    overview 667-668
    system startup delay 670
    Win32_ComputerSystem class properties 669, 671
    Win32_ProcessStartup class properties 962-963
    Windows startup process 668

State property, Win32_Service class 978-980

statement breaks, VBScript 47-49

static classes, WMI 450, 465

status of scripts, tracking
    in command window 1133-1135
    in Internet Explorer 1126-1128
    in Internet Explorer, changing mouse pointer 1130-1131

status of scripts, tracking (continued)
    in Internet Explorer, dynamic tracking 1128-1130
    in Internet Explorer, with animated .gif files 1131
    overview 1125-1126

Status property, WshRemote object 231

status, monitoring
    print jobs See monitoring print jobs
    print queues See monitoring print queues
    print service 896-897
    printers See monitoring printer status

StatusBar property, Internet Explorer object 1077-1079

StatusMask property, Win32_PrintJob class 900-902

StatusText property, Internet Explorer object 1077-1079

StdErr stream
    accessing from scripts 184-185
    belonging to running programs, accessing 190-191
    overview 157

StdIn stream
    accessing from scripts 184-185
    AtEndOfLine property 160
    AtEndOfStream property 160
    belonging to running programs, accessing 190-191
    overview 157, 159-162
    Read method 160
    ReadAll method 160
    ReadLine method 160, 161
    Skip method 160
    SkipLine method 160

StdOut stream
    accessing from scripts 184-185
    belonging to running programs, accessing 190-191
    overview 157
    Write method 157, 161, 1134
    WriteBlankLines method 157
    WriteLine method 157

Stdprov.dll 438-439

StdRegProv class 460

stop errors See stop messages

stop events
    See also stop messages
    generating manually 681-682
    querying System Event log for 680-681

stop messages
  See also stop events
  configuring recovery options 679
  enumerating recovery options 677-678
  overview 675
  querying System Event log for stop events 680-681
  Win32_OSRecoveryConfiguration class 676-677
stopped services, restarting 987, 992
stopping scripts when Internet Explorer closes 1085-1087
stopping services 987, 989, 990, 991, 998, 999
stopping WMI service 440
StopService method, Win32_Service class 527, 990
Store password using reversible encryption (setting, password attributes) 561
store, Active Directory 393
str (variable name prefix) 1153-1154
strComputer variable 453, 523
streams, input and output
  accessing from scripts 184-185
  belonging to running programs, accessing 190-191
  overview 157
  StdErr *See* StdErr stream
  StdIn *See* StdIn stream
  StdOut *See* StdOut stream
String (data subtype) 1153-1154
String data type (VBScript), corresponding registry and WSH data types 204
String data type (WSH), corresponding registry and VBScript data types 204
string data *See* strings and string data
string values, sorting with tabular data control 1096
String values, VBScript, CStr type conversion function 58
strings and string data
  See also string-valued registry entries
  assigning to constants 26
  assigning to variables, VBScript 26-28
  concatenating, VBScript 29-30
  delimited strings, converting to arrays, VBScript 101-102
  formatting 74-76

strings and string data *(continued)*
  formatting for message boxes, VBScript 78-79
  in WHERE clauses, WMI queries 509
  modifying character case, VBScript 81-82
  overview 73-74
  registry entries *See* string-valued registry entries
  searching strings for text, VBScript 79-81
  string manipulation functions, VBScript 76-77
  tabular output, VBScript 77-78
strings *See* strings and string data
string-valued registry entries
  See also strings and string data
  changing 1033-1034
  creating 1036-1038
  overview 1027
  reading 1027-1028
  REG_SZ data type 1020, 1023
strongly-typed languages, compared to typeless languages 56
structural classes, Active Directory 399
SubClassesOf method, SWbemServices object 461, 487-488, 490
subClassOf attribute, Active Directory classes 403
subcontainers, searching for attributes 598
subfolders
  See also folders and folder management
  enumerating subfolders within subfolders 264-266
  enumerating 263-264, 781-782
  Win32_Subdirectory class 778
SubFolders property, Folder object 256-257, 263
Subject property, IMessage interface, CDO Message object 1121
subkeys, registry
  access rights, administering 1047-1048
  creating 1035
  default entries 1021
  deleting 1045, 1046
  enumerating 1041, 1042
  monitoring modifications to 1052
  overview 1019

subroutines, VBScript
    calling 113
    overview 112
    recursion 120–121
subscriptions, event See event subscriptions, monitoring
subscriptions, WMI event See WMI event subscriptions
subsystems, as managed resources 436
subtraction operator (-), VBScript operator
    precedence 82–83
subtree option, Active Directory search scope 370, 592
subtrees, registry
    abbreviations 1019
    constants, WMI Registry Provider 1022
    default entries 1021
    list of subtrees 1019
    monitoring modifications to 1050–1051
    overview 1019
SupportsFileBasedCompression property,
    Win32_LogicalDisk class 733–734
Svchost.exe 439, 983–984, 985
SWbemEventSource object 486
SWbemLastError object 483
SWbemLocator object 483, 484–485
SWbemMethod object 475
SWbemMethodSet collection 475
SWbemNamedValueSet collection 483
SWbemObject
    accessing class definitions 461
    accessing properties 468
    as multiple-identity object 483
    calling methods 469
    creating with GetObject function 483
    GetObjectText_ method 477–478
    Methods_ property 472, 475
    Path_ property 461
    Properties_ property 472, 474
    Qualifiers_ property 472, 476
    retrieving class definitions from MOF files 477–478
    retrieving class information 472–477
    returned by SWbemServices 486
SWbemObjectPath object 483
SWbemObjectSet collection 486, 489, 491–492

SWbemProperty object 474
SWbemPropertySet collection 474
SWbemQualifier object 476
SWbemQualifierSet collection 476
SWbemSecurity object 483
SWbemServices object
    creating with GetObject function 483
    described 483
    Get method 477
    overview 486–491
    SubClassesOf method 461
SWbemSink object 483
synchronous mode, SWbemServices object 488
synchronous scripts, event log queries 865
syntax checking 1187
syntax errors
    See also error handling
    VBScript 104
SysMenu property, HTA object 1088–1090
Sysocmgr.exe 1013
system administration
    about scripting 3–6
    about scripts used in this book 11–12
    about this book 8–11
    administrative credentials required 14
    choosing a scripting language 12–13
    history of scripting 6
    scripts for system administration tasks See tasks
System attribute
    files 275
    folders 258
system classes, WMI 450, 458, 459
System environment variables, registry locations 197
System Event log, querying for stop events 680–681
system information
    retrieving BIOS information 623–628
    retrieving SMBIOS information 628–629
    retrieving with WMI scripts 620–621
    System Information snap-in 619–620
System Information snap-in, equivalent WMI classes and
    properties 620–621, 630
System Management BIOS See SMBIOS specification

system partitions 730

System property, Win32_Directory class 775–776

system requirements 13–14

system settings

date and time formats 61, 70–73

number formats 84

system startup delay, configuring 670, 672

System32 folder

See also special folders

locating special folders 788

systemAuxiliaryClass attribute, Active Directory classes 401

__SystemClass class 458

SYSTEMDRIVE (environment variable) 198

systemMayContain attribute, Active Directory classes 396

systemMustContain attribute, Active Directory classes 396

SystemName property

Win32_DiskDrive class 726–728

Win32_DiskPartition class 730–732

Win32_LogicalDisk class 733–734

Win32_Service class 978–980

SYSTEMROOT (environment variable) 198

Systems Management Server

managing with WMI scripts 430

WMI consumer 443

WMI provider 438

SystemStartupDelay property, Win32_ComputerSystem class 669, 671–672

SystemStartupOptions property, Win32_ComputerSystem class 669

SystemStartupSetting property, Win32_ComputerSystem class 669, 671–672

T

tab character, inserting using VbTab constant 293

TAB key, SendKeys representation 206

tab-separated-data files 293

tab-separated-value logs 877

tabular data control

See also tabular script output

displaying data from scripts 982

displaying script output 1092–1095

tabular data control (continued)

filtering script output 1099–1101

properties (table) 1093–1094

sorting script output 1095–1099

tabular script output

See also tabular data control

displaying in command window 1073–1076

VBScript 77–78

target namespaces 454

targeted queries, WMI 504, 512, 540

TargetInstance object 535, 538, 543

TargetPath property, WshShortcut object 192

Task Manager 940

Task Scheduler

See also scheduled tasks

APIs compared to AT APIs 1136–1137

tasks

access rights to registry subkeys, checking 1048

Active Directory classes, determining parent classes 403

Active Directory classes, listing auxiliary classes 401

Active Directory classes, reading categories 399

Active Directory user accounts, changing passwords 560

Active Directory user accounts, creating 557

Active Directory user accounts, setting passwords 559

ADSI providers, displaying 419

alerts, sending in e-mail 1122, 1124

antecedent services, enumerating 998

appending data to text files 295

applications, sending keystrokes to 207, 210

arguments, retrieving from Active Directory containers 1071

arguments, retrieving from databases 1068

arguments, retrieving from text files 1062

arrays, converting delimited strings to 102

asynchronous event log queries 866

attribute values, configuring 262

attributes replicated to Global Catalog, determining 407, 410

attributes, computer accounts, configuring 703

attributes, computer accounts, enumerating 702

attributes, directory service objects, modifying 382

tasks (continued)

attributes, indexed, determining 409, 410

attributes, operational, determining 412

attributes, searching for in containers 593, 595, 596

attributes, user accounts, adding entries to 578

attributes, user accounts, clearing 580

attributes, user accounts, copying between users 582

attributes, user accounts, reading 573–575

attributes, user accounts, removing entries from 579

attributes, user accounts, searching in
containers 593, 595, 596

attributes, user accounts, searching in
subcontainers 598

attributes, user accounts, verifying uniqueness in
forests 600

attributes, user accounts, writing 576–577

auxiliary classes, listing 401

backing up event logs 853–855

backing up registry data before editing 1026

binary-valued registry entries, reading 1032

binding to configuration container 392

binding to current domain 391

binding to directory service objects 320–325

binding to disk drives 245

binding to files 267

binding to folders 249

binding to root domain 392

binding to schema container 392

BIOS information, retrieving 626

Browse For Folder dialog box 792

categories of Active Directory classes, reading 399

chassis type, identifying 636

classes, reading attributes 396

clearing event logs 853–855

closing text files 285

command window, displaying messages 159

command-line arguments, verifying correct number of
arguments 172

command-line arguments, verifying presence of
required arguments 174

comma-separated-value log files, parsing 877

CompareMode property, Dictionary object,
configuring 297

tasks (continued)

computer account information, retrieving 694

computer accounts, copying 350

computer accounts, creating 696–697

computer accounts, deleting specified accounts 699

computer accounts, deleting 698

computer accounts, enumerating 709

computer accounts, locating 711

computer accounts, moving between OUs 705

computer accounts, renaming 705

computer roles, identifying based on installed
services 715

computer roles, identifying 714

computers, restarting 686

configuration container, binding to 392

configuring file attributes 276–277

containers, enumerating contents 386

containers, enumerating contents to perform tasks
on 387

containers, enumerating objects of specific types 388

containers, searching for attributes 593, 595, 596

copying events to databases 869

copying files 271

copying folders and folder contents 253

current domain controller, identifying 719

current domain, binding to 391

current working directory, changing for scripts 211

data types of registry entries, enumerating 1043

databases, adding records to 1108

databases, connecting to 1106

databases, deleting all records from 1116

databases, deleting selected records from 1114

databases, finding records in 1110

databases, updating records in 1112

date values, retrieving specific parts of 64

dates, converting to standard format 519

dates, converting to UTC format 521

default disk quota settings, configuring 747

delimited strings, converting to arrays 102

dependent services, enumerating 995–996

dependent services, starting 1000

dependent services, stopping 999

tasks *(continued)*

   desktop shortcuts, creating 193, 194

   Dictionary items, echoing value of non-existent items 299

   Dictionary items, modifying 302–303

   directories, changing script's working directory 211

   directory service objects, binding to 320–325

   directory service objects, copying 350–353

   directory service objects, creating 310–313, 327–328

   directory service objects, deleting 317–318, 330

   directory service objects, modifying 313–315, 329, 334

   directory service objects, moving 354–358

   directory service objects, moving between domains 354–355, 357

   directory service objects, multivalued attributes, appending 340

   directory service objects, multivalued attributes, clearing 339, 342

   directory service objects, multivalued attributes, deleting entries 341

   directory service objects, multivalued attributes, reading 344–345

   directory service objects, multivalued attributes, updating 339, 342

   directory service objects, reading attributes 315–317, 330, 334

   directory service objects, renaming 356

   disk drive properties, enumerating 247

   disk drives, binding to 245

   disk drives, ensuring readiness 248

   disk drives, enumerating properties 728

   disk quota entries, adding 751

   disk quota entries, deleting 753

   disk quota entries, enumerating 749

   disk quota entries, modifying 752

   disk quota settings, configuring defaults 747

   disk quota settings, enumerating 744

   disk quotas, enabling and disabling 746

   domain controllers, enumerating 717

   drive types, verifying for installed disk drives 735

   DWORD-valued registry entries, creating 1037–1038

   DWORD-valued registry entries, reading 1028, 1034

   dynamic arrays, creating in VBScript 100

tasks *(continued)*

   e-mail messages, sending 1122, 1124

   ensuring that a drive is ready 248

   enumeration, managing user accounts 614

   environment variables, creating 200

   environment variables, expanding 201

   environment variables, modifying 200

   environment variables, retrieving 198

   error control codes, configuring 1005

   error handling, remotely running scripts 233

   event handling, remotely running scripts 231

   event log properties, retrieving 847–849

   event logs, backing up 853–855

   event logs, clearing 853–855

   event logs, configuring 851

   event logs, custom, creating 875

   events, copying to databases 869

   events, logging 202

   expanded string-valued registry entries, creating 1040

   expanded string-valued registry entries, reading 1031

   extended file properties, retrieving 808

   file attributes, configuring 276–277

   file attributes, enumerating 275

   file creation events, monitoring 822

   file deletion events, monitoring 823

   file existence, verifying 268

   file modification, monitoring 824

   file name extensions, changing 815

   file paths, parsing 278

   file properties, enumerating 274–275

   file properties, retrieving 805, 808

   file size, verifying 287

   file system type, identifying 755

   file version numbers, retrieving 279

   files in folders, enumerating 262

   files, binding to 267

   files, copying 271, 816

   files, deleting 268, 270, 818

   files, enumerating 809

   files, enumerating in a folder 811

   files, enumerating specified sets 812

   files, enumerating using asynchronous queries 810

tasks *(continued)*

files, executing Shell object verbs 819

files, moving 272

files, opening files specified in command line 1065

files, opening text files 283

files, renaming 273, 814

folder existence, verifying 250

folder paths, browsing for 792

folder properties, enumerating 257

folder properties, retrieving 779

folders and folder contents, copying 253

folders and folder contents, moving 255

folders, binding to 249

folders, compressing 803

folders, copying using Shell Folder object 799

folders, copying using WMI 796

folders, creating 250

folders, deleting 801

folders, enumerating 781

folders, enumerating based on date properties 786

folders, enumerating specified sets 784

folders, moving using Shell Folder object 800

folders, moving using WMI 795

folders, publishing in Active Directory 835

folders, renaming 255, 794

folders, uncompressing 803

free disk space, enumerating 738

free disk space, enumerating by user 740

free disk space, monitoring in real time 741

global catalog servers, disabling 724

global catalog servers, enabling 723

global catalog servers, identifying 722

Global Catalog, determining attributes replicated to 407, 410

groups, appending multivalued attributes 340

groups, clearing multivalued attributes 342

groups, creating 311

groups, deleting 318

groups, deleting multivalued attributes 341

groups, modifying attributes 314

groups, moving between containers 356

groups, reading attributes 316

tasks *(continued)*

groups, reading multivalued attributes 344

groups, updating multivalued attributes 339

hardware, inventorying 633

hive files, displaying locations of 1021

hot fixes, enumerating installed fixes 645

HTAs, creating 1090

IADs interface properties, displaying 424

indexed attributes, determining 409, 410

installed ADSI providers, displaying 419

installed drives, returning collection of 244

installing services 1012

installing software on local computers 661

installing software on remote computers 663

Internet Explorer, creating an instance of 1080

Internet Explorer, terminating script on closure of 1086

inventorying computer hardware 633

items, Dictionary, enumerating 300

key-item pairs, determining number of in Dictionaries 299

key-item pairs, removing from Dictionaries 303–304, 305

keys, Dictionary, enumerating 300

keystrokes, sending to applications 207, 210

local property cache, loading 347, 349

logging events 202

logical drives, enumerating properties 734

managed resources, creating 528

managed resources, deleting 529

managed resources, displaying all properties 524

managed resources, displaying specified properties 523

managed resources, writing properties 525

mandatory attributes, reading 396

mapping network drives according to user domain 227

mapping network drives 222

messages, displaying in command window 159

MS-DOS-based printer connections, adding 224

MS-DOS-based printer connections, removing 225

multistring-valued registry entries, creating 1039–1040

tasks *(continued)*

multistring-valued registry entries, reading 1029

multivalued attributes, appending 340

multivalued attributes, clearing 342

multivalued attributes, deleting entries 341

multivalued attributes, reading 344–345

multivalued attributes, searching for 608

multivalued attributes, updating 339, 342

namespaces, listing 455

namespaces, listing classes in 461–463

namespaces, listing recursively 457

namespaces, retrieving default 454

namespaces, setting default 455

network drives, enumerating 223

network drives, mapping according to user domain 227

network drives, mapping 222

network drives, unmapping 223

network printers, adding 224

network printers, enumerating 225

network printers, removing 225

network printers, setting default printers 226

network shares, creating 829

network shares, deleting 833

network shares, mapping to local folders 831

network shares, modifying properties 834

NTFS properties, enumerating 757

NTFS properties, modifying 761

objectClassCategory attribute, reading 399

operating systems, identifying name and version number 638

operating systems, retrieving properties 641

operational attributes, determining 412

operations master roles, identifying 721

optional attributes, reading 396

OUs, creating 310

OUs, deleting 318

OUs, modifying attributes 313

OUs, moving between domains 357

OUs, reading attributes 315

overwriting existing data in text files 294

page files, configuring properties 766

tasks *(continued)*

page files, enumerating properties 763

page files, monitoring use 765

parent classes, determining 403

parsing comma-separated-value log files 877

parsing data files, VBScript 102

parsing file paths 278

parsing fixed-width log files 879

partitions, enumerating 732

password attribute values, displaying 563

password masking using Internet Explorer 1118

passwords, change password at next logon requirement 566–567

passwords, changing 560

passwords, changing UserAccountControl attribute values 565

passwords, determining date last set 564

passwords, resetting for computer accounts 707

passwords, setting for user accounts 559

paused services, restarting 993

pausing scripts 177

pausing services 991

power status changes, monitoring 688

print job status, monitoring 903

print jobs, changing priority 925

print jobs, monitoring time in print queues 905

print jobs, pausing 915

print jobs, resuming 916

print queues, monitoring 898

print queues, purging 914

print service, monitoring 897

printer availability, scheduling 918

printer capabilities, retrieving 910

printer connections, adding 224, 929

printer connections, enumerating 225, 927

printer connections, removing 225, 930

printer connections, setting default printer 226

printer locations, configuring 922

printer locations, updating 922

printer status data, filtering 893

printer status, displaying in Web pages 889

printer status, monitoring 888

tasks *(continued)*

printer status, monitoring in real time 889

printer status, monitoring using event
  subscriptions 894

printers with specified attributes, locating 935

printers, enumerating 910

printers, pausing 912

printers, resuming 913

priority of printers, configuring 917–918

process availability, monitoring 942

process creation, monitoring 944

process deletion, monitoring 945

process owners, identifying 955

process performance, monitoring 948–949

process reliability, monitoring 944–945

process startup options, configuring 963–964

processes, creating 960

processes, displaying performance data 951–954

processes, terminating 966–967

processor use, monitoring 949

programs, running using Run method 186

providers, displaying 419

published folders, deleting 840

published folders, enumerating 837

published folders, searching for 838

published printers, enumerating 931

publishing folders in Active Directory 835

querying for specific event types 863

querying for specified day's events 864

querying specific event logs 861

querying System Event log for stop events 681

Quick Launch buttons, creating 194

reading entire text files 288

reading text files character-by-character 291–292

reading text files from bottom to top 290

reading text files line-by-line 289

recovery options, configuring 679

recovery options, enumerating 678

registry data, backing up before editing 1026

registry entries, creating 205, 1037–1038, 1039–
  1040

registry entries, deleting 205, 1046

tasks *(continued)*

registry entries, enumerating 1043

registry entries, modifying 761

registry entries, monitoring modifications to 1053

registry entries, reading 204

registry entry values, changing 1034

registry entry values, enumerating 757

registry entry values, reading 1028, 1029, 1031,
  1032

registry subkeys, checking access rights 1048

registry subkeys, creating 1035

registry subkeys, deleting 1047

registry subkeys, enumerating 1042

registry subkeys, monitoring modifications to 1052

registry subtrees, monitoring modifications to 1051

remotely running scripts, configuring environment
  for 229

remotely running scripts, error handling 233

remotely running scripts, event handling 231

remotely running scripts, running worker scripts 230

reporting on not-running services 975

reporting on service states 975

resetting computer account passwords 707

restarting computers 686

restarting stopped services 992

result sets, modifying user accounts using 612

result sets, performing operations on 382–385

result sets, sorting 610

resuming paused services 993

root domain, binding to 392

Run method, running programs 186

running processes, identifying 942

scheduled tasks, creating 1142

scheduled tasks, deleting all tasks 1144

scheduled tasks, deleting selected tasks 1144

scheduled tasks, enumerating 1140

schema container, binding to 392

script output, displaying in Internet Explorer 1082

script output, displaying using tabular data
  control 1094

script output, filtering using tabular data control 1099

script output, formatting in command window 1075

tasks *(continued)*

script output, formatting in Internet Explorer 1082

script output, sorting using disconnected
   recordsets 1101

script output, sorting using tabular data control 1097

script progress, tracking in command window 1134

script progress, tracking in Internet Explorer 1127,
   1129, 1132

scripts, pausing 177

search results, limiting to user account types 596

searching in Active Directory 359–362

searching in Active Directory, attributes in
   containers 593, 595, 596

searching in Active Directory, attributes in
   subcontainers 598

searching in Active Directory, limiting search
   scope 369–371

searching in Active Directory, modifying user
   accounts 612

searching in Active Directory, multivalued
   attributes 608

searching in Active Directory, optimizing
   searches 378–381

searching in Active Directory, referral chasing 367–
   369

searching in Active Directory, returning multivalued
   attributes 374–378

searching in Active Directory, sorting result sets 610

searching in Active Directory, sorting results 371–373

searching in Active Directory, specifying
   attributes 362

searching in Active Directory, specifying Global
   Catalog 366–367

searching in Active Directory, specifying object
   type 364–365

searching in Active Directory, using range limits 376–
   378

searching in Active Directory, verifying attribute
   uniqueness 600

searching in Active Directory, wildcards in search
   filters 606

Security event log, managing 849

sending e-mail alerts 1122, 1124

service account passwords, configuring 1010

service accounts, specifying 1008

service availability, monitoring 975

tasks *(continued)*

service packs, identifying installed packs 644

service properties, enumerating 980–982

service reliability, monitoring 977

service start options, configuring 1004

services running in shared processes,
   displaying 984–986

services, determining ability to be paused 990

services, determining ability to be stopped 989

services, enumerating antecedent services 998

services, installing 1012

services, pausing 991

services, removing 1014

services, stopping 990

shared folders, creating on remote computers 829

shared folders, deleting 833, 840

shared folders, enumerating 837

shared folders, enumerating properties 827

shared folders, mapping to local folders 831

shared folders, modifying properties 834

shared folders, publishing in Active Directory 835

shared folders, searching for in Active Directory 838

Shell object verbs, enumerating for specified
   objects 820

Shell object verbs, executing 819

shortcuts, creating 193, 194

shortcuts, creating in special folders 196

shortcuts, deleting 194

shutting down computers 684–685

SMBIOS information, retrieving 629

software features, enumerating 659

software, enumerating installed software 656

software, installing on local computers 661

software, installing on remote computers 663

software, uninstalling 666

software, upgrading 665

special folders, creating shortcuts in 196

special folders, enumerating items in 790

special folders, locating 789

special folders, retrieving location of 196, 789

startup commands, enumerating 674

startup options, enumerating 669

tasks *(continued)*

    stopped services, restarting 992

    string-valued registry entries, creating 1037–1038

    string-valued registry entries, reading 1028, 1034

    subClassOf attribute, reading 403

    subcontainers, searching for attributes 598

    subfolders within subfolders, enumerating 264–266

    subfolders, enumerating 263, 782

    subkeys, creating in registry 1035

    subkeys, enumerating for registry key or subkey 1042

    subtrees, monitoring modifications to 1051, 1052

    system information, retrieving 626

    system startup delay, configuring 672

    systemAuxiliaryClass attribute, reading 401

    tabular output, generating in VBScript 77–78

    terminating processes 966–967

    terminating when browser window closes 1086

    text files as command-line arguments 1065

    text files, appending data to 295

    text files, creating 280–281

    text files, opening 283

    text files, overwriting existing data 294

    text files, reading 288

    text files, reading character-by-character 291–292

    text files, reading from bottom to top 290

    text files, reading line-by-line 289

    threads, monitoring 957

    time values, retrieving specific parts of 64

    time-out values for scripts, setting 178

    tracking script progress in command window 1134

    tracking script progress in Internet Explorer 1127, 1129, 1132

    uninstalling software 666

    unique file names for event log backup files 856

    unique file names, creating in scripts 281–282

    unmapping network drives 223

    upgrading software 665

    URL shortcuts, creating 194

    user account attributes, adding entries to 578

    user account attributes, clearing 580

    user account attributes, copying between users 582

    user account attributes, reading 573–575

tasks *(continued)*

    user account attributes, removing entries from 579

    user account attributes, writing 576–577

    user accounts, changing passwords 560

    user accounts, copying 352, 582

    user accounts, creating 311, 557

    user accounts, deleting 318, 588

    user accounts, determining whether enabled or disabled 569

    user accounts, disabling 568

    user accounts, enabling 568

    user accounts, managing using enumeration 614

    user accounts, modifying attributes 314

    user accounts, modifying using search results 612

    user accounts, moving between containers 585, 586

    user accounts, moving between domains 586

    user accounts, reading attributes 315

    user accounts, reading multivalued attributes 345

    user accounts, renaming 586

    user accounts, setting passwords 559

    user accounts, updating multivalued attributes 342

    values of registry entries, enumerating 1043

    verbs, enumerating for specified objects 820

    verbs, executing 819

    verifying existence of specific Dictionary key 301

    verifying file existence 268

    verifying file size 287

    verifying folder existence 250

    volume names, changing 737

    Windows-based printer connections, adding 224

    Windows-based printer connections, removing 225

    WMI classes, listing 461–463

    WMI methods, calling 527

    WMI queries, all properties of all instances of a class 506

    WMI queries, all properties of selected instances of a class 507

    WMI queries, selected properties of all instances of a class 506

    WMI queries, selected properties of selected instances of a class 512

    WMI queries, targeted queries using AND or OR 512

    WMI queries, using forward-only enumerators 513

    WMI settings, configuring 652

tasks *(continued)*

WMI settings, enumerating 649

worker scripts, running 230

working directories, changing for scripts 211

writing detailed event descriptions 872

writing events to Application Log 871–872

WSH environment, displaying information about 180

tasks, scheduled

creating 1140–1143

database storage of task information 1067

deleting with WMI scripts 529

deleting 1144–1145

enumerating 1137–1140

managing with WMI scripts 430

overview 1135–1137

task-scheduling APIs 1136–1137

task-scheduling APIs 1136–1137

telephone test 1172

telephoneNumber attribute, user accounts 572

TEMP (environment variable) 198

templates

adding to Windows Explorer context menu 1161

script templates 1160–1161

WMI script templates 523

Templates folder

See also special folders

locating special folders 788

special folder identifiers 195

terminating processes

newly started processes 967

overview 965–966

running processes 966

terminating scripts

when Internet Explorer closes 1085–1087

WMI scripts 541

WSH scripts 177–178

testing scripts 1188

text

See also strings and string data

formatting for message boxes 78–79

proportional vs. non-proportional fonts 78–79

searching strings for text 79–81

text files

appending new data 283, 295

appending script output 145

as command-line arguments 1064

closing 284–285

concatenating 288

creating 280–281

deleting 284

dragging onto scripts in Windows Explorer or My Computer 1064

empty files 286–287

for enterprise scripts 1061–1067

modifying specific lines 294

opening 282–283

overview 280

overwriting existing data 280–281, 294

overwriting with script output 145

reading character-by-character 290–292

reading entire file 287–288

reading from bottom to top 289–290

reading from 283, 285–286

reading line-by-line 288–289

redirecting WSH script output 145–146

rereading 284

retrieving arguments from 1061–1067

saving script output for use with tabular data control 1092, 1096

storing computer names in 1061

storing contents in a variable 287–288

unique file names, creating in scripts 281–282

verifying file size 286–287

writing to 283, 292–295

text mode, Dictionary object 297–298

Text property, TextRange object 1084

text values, sorting with tabular data control 1096

TextBody property, IMessage interface, CDO Message object 1121

TextQualifier property, tabular data control 1093–1094

TextRange object, Text property 1084

TextStream object 282

ThreadCount property, Win32_Process class 946–948

threads
    See also processes
    diagnosing memory leaks 946
    initialized by services 973
    listing for a process 957
    memory allocation 939
    memory leaks 939
    monitoring 956-957
    overview 938-939
    Win32_Thread class properties 956-957
ThreadState property, Win32_Thread class 956-957
Time function, VBScript 60, 70
Time Limit property, Command object (ADO) 380
time values
    date and time arithmetic, VBScript 68-70
    date literals, VBScript 61
    formatting, VBScript 70-73
    importance of in system administration 59
    intervals between, determining, VBScript 68-69
    projecting based on specified interval, VBScript 70
    retrieving specific parts of, VBScript 62-67
    retrieving, VBScript 60-61
    time formats, system settings and 61
    verifying values are dates, VBScript 61-62
    WMI scripts 515
    WMI scripts, converting to standard format 517
    WMI scripts, converting to UTC format 519-522
TimeOfLastReset property, Win32_Printer class 907-908
timeout option, WSH scripts 143
Timeout property
    Command object (ADO) 380
    WScript object 178
time-out values, limiting Active Directory search times 708
time-out values, WSH scripts 178
timer events, WMI event classes 536
TimeSubmitted property
    IADsPrintJob interface 902-903, 923-924
    Win32_PrintJob class 900-902
    Win32_ScheduledJob class 1137-1140
TimeWritten property, Win32_NTLogEvent class 858-859
TimeZone property, Win32_ComputerSystem class 620-621

title parameter, BrowseForFolder method 792
Title property, Win32_ProcessStartup class 962-963
TMP (environment variable) 198
To property, IMessage interface, CDO Message object 1121
ToolBar property, Internet Explorer object 1077-1079
tools, WMI 479
Top property, Internet Explorer object 1077-1079
TotalCylinders property, Win32_DiskDrive class 726-728
TotalHeads property, Win32_DiskDrive class 726-728
TotalPages property
    IADsPrintJob interface 902-903, 923-924
    Win32_PrintJob class 900-902
TotalPhysicalMemory property, Win32_LogicalMemoryConfiguration class 430-431
TotalSectors property, Win32_DiskDrive class 726-728
TotalSize property, FileSystemObject 245-247
TotalTracks property, Win32_DiskDrive class 726-728
TotalVirtualMemory property
    Win32_LogicalMemoryConfiguration class 431
    Win32_OperatingSystem class 620-621
trace routines 1184-1185
tracking script progress
    in command window 1133-1135
    in Internet Explorer 1126-1128
    in Internet Explorer, changing mouse pointer 1130-1131
    in Internet Explorer, dynamic tracking 1128-1130
    in Internet Explorer, with animated .gif files 1131
    overview 1125-1126
TracksPerCylinder property, Win32_DiskDrive class 726-728
transaction control files, CIM repository 442
trees, in Active Directory architecture 394
Trim function, VBScript 76-77
troubleshooting scripts *See* debugging scripts
True (boolean value), integer value of 1173
trusting users and computers for delegation 663
TSV logs 877
TTOption property, Win32_PrinterConfiguration class 908-910
turning on computers, startup options *See* startup options
TXT files *See* text files

type casting, VBScript 57

type coercion

   See also data types

   Empty variables, VBScript 58–59

   VBScript 57–58

Type parameter, Create method (Win32_Share class) 828

Type property

   Folder object 256–257

   Win32_DiskPartition class 730–732

   Win32_NTLogEvent class 858–859

   Win32_Share class 826

typeless languages, compared to strongly-typed languages 56

types of servers, running enterprise scripts on 1064

types *See* data types

U

UCase function, VBScript 82

UDA 1103

UNC attribute, Volume class 835

uNCName attribute, printQueue object 933–935

Uncompress method

   CIM_DataFile class 776–778

   Win32_Directory class 776–778, 802

uncompressing folders 802–803

underscore (_), VBScript line continuation character 48–49

unicodePwd attribute, user accounts 558

Uninstall method, Win32_Product class 666

uninstalling software 653–654, 659–660, 666

uniqueness

   attributes in forests 600

   user account names 556

   variable names 1154–1155

Universal Data Access 1103

Universal Time Coordinate format *See* UTC date-time format

unmapping network drives 222–223

unnamed command-line arguments

   See also command-line arguments

   overview 164

   using with named arguments in same script 172

   WshUnnamed collection 165, 168–170

Unnamed property, WshArguments collection 166

UntilTime property

   IADsPrintJob interface 902–903, 923–924

   IADsPrintQueue interface 910

   Win32_Printer class 907–908

   Win32_PrintJob class 900–902

   Win32_ScheduledJob class 1137–1140

UP ARROW key, SendKeys representation 206

Update method, Recordset object, ADO 1107, 1112

UpdateProfile argument, MapNetworkDrive method 221

updating records in databases 1112–1114

Upgrade method, Win32_Product class 664–665

upgrading software 653–654, 659–660, 664–665

UPN attribute, user accounts 554

uppercase characters, modifying character case 81–82

url attribute

   printQueue object 933–935

   user accounts 572

URL files 191

.url files 191

URL shortcuts

   creating 193

   overview 191

   Quick Launch buttons, creating 194

USB (System Information category), equivalent WMI class 630

UseHeader property, tabular data control 1093–1094

User account 553

user accounts

   attributes *See* attributes, user accounts

   Contact user account 553

   copying 352, 581–583

   creating 311, 555

   creating, changing passwords 560

   creating, configuring passwords 558–560

   creating, Create method, IADsContainer interface 557

   creating, selecting containers for account creation 556

   creating, setting passwords 559

   creating, specifying paths 556

   creating, verifying name uniqueness 556

   deleting 318, 588

user accounts *(continued)*

    description attribute 572

    determining whether enabled or disabled 569

    disabling 568

    displayName attribute 572

    enabling 568

    givenName attribute 572

    identification attributes 553–554

    initials attribute 572

    mail attribute 572

    managing using enumeration 613–614

    modifying attributes 314

    modifying using search result sets 611

    moving between containers 585, 586

    moving between domains 584–585, 586

    multivalued attributes, reading 345

    multivalued attributes, updating 342

    name uniqueness 556

    otherTelephone attribute 572

    overview 551–552

    passwords *See* passwords, user accounts

    physicalDeliveryOfficeName attribute 572

    reading attributes 315

    renaming 586

    searching for *See* searching in Active Directory

    security principal naming attributes 554

    sn attribute 572

    telephoneNumber attribute 572

    types of user accounts 552–553

    url attribute 572

    User account 553

    user accounts 552

    wWWHomePage attribute 572

User environment variables, registry locations 197

user information, retrieving in WSH scripts 226

user input

    command-line *See* command-line arguments

    to scripts *See* input to scripts

user interfaces for scripts, disadvantages of 1125

User must change password at next logon (option), configuring 566

User Profile folder

    See also special folders

    locating special folders 788

User property

    IADsPrintJob interface 902–903, 923–924

    Win32_NTLogEvent class 858–859

    Win32_StartupCommand class 674

userAccountControl attribute, user accounts

    ADS_UF_ACCOUNTDISABLE flag 568–569

    default settings 555

    enabling computer accounts 696

    flags and flag values 562, 563

    user account settings 561

UserDomain property, WshNetwork object 226

Userenv.log 876

UserModeTime property

    Win32_Process class 946–948, 949

    Win32_Thread class 956–957

UserName argument, MapNetworkDrive method 221

UserName attribute, ADSystemInfo object 693

UserName property, WshNetwork object 226

Userpath property, IADsPrintJob interface 923–924

userPrincipalName attribute, user accounts 554

users, SAM, as managed resources 436

users, trusting for delegation 663

UTC date-time format

    See also dates and date values

    converting standard dates to 519–522, 784–786

    converting to standard date-time format 517

    overview 515

utility interfaces, ADSI 422

V

value, passing parameters by

    Script Runtime library 1162–1163

    VBScript 119

ValueMap qualifier, WMI 471

values of registry entries

    changing DWORD-valued entries 1033–1034

    changing string-valued entries 1033–1034

    default entries 1021

    enumerating 1043

    reading 1026–1027

    reading binary-valued entries 1031–1032

    reading DWORD-valued entries 1027–1028

    reading expanded string-valued entries 1030–1031

    reading multistring-valued entries 1029

    reading string-valued entries 1027–1028

variable names

    Camel casing 1152

    Hungarian notation 1152–1154

    loop variables 1156

    reuse of 1155–1156

    script readability 1151

    suggested guidelines 1154–1155

variables

    See also Dictionary object

    assigning strings to, VBScript 26–28

    assigning values to, VBScript 52

    data subtypes 1153–1154

    default values, VBScript 51

    Empty variables, VBScript 51–52, 58–59

    explicit declaration, VBScript 50–51

    implicit declaration, VBScript 49–50

    in WHERE clauses, WMI queries 510–511

    initializing, VBScript 51–52

    naming conventions 1149, 1151–1156

    Null variables, VBScript 58–59

    overview, VBScript 23

    return values of functions 114–115

    reuse of variable names 1155–1156

    VBScript 49–52

    WMI naming conventions 483

VBArray of Integers data type (VBScript), corresponding registry and WSH data types 204

VBArray of Strings data type (VBScript), corresponding registry and WSH data types 204

VbCrLf constant, VBScript 55

VBS files, WSH-compliant scripting languages 137

VBScript

    ADSI, binding to 20

    Array function 98

    arrays 39–41

    arrays, alternatives to 103

    arrays, assigning data to 99

    arrays, converting delimited strings to 101–102

    arrays, creating 98

    arrays, declaring 98

    arrays, dynamic 100

    Automation objects *See* Automation objects

    ByRef keyword 119

    ByVal keyword 119

    choosing a scripting language 12–13

    Clear method 46

    collections 30–31

    collections with zero items 33–34

    collections, determining number of items 33

    collections, iterating 31–32

    COM *See* COM

    COM object creation, compared to WSH 153

    COM objects *See* COM objects

    compared to WScript object 148

    compared to WSH 148, 153

    concatenating strings 29–30

    conditional statements 37–39, 92–97

    constants 25–26, 53, 54

    constants, intrinsic 54–56

    continuously-running scripts 89

    CreateObject method 20, 123, 124

    data types 56

    data types, type coercion 57–58

    data types, type conversion functions 58

    Date function 60, 70

    DateAdd function 70

    DateDiff function 68–69

    DatePart function 62–66

    dates, arithmetic using 68–70

    dates, determining interval between 68–69

    dates, first week of the year 65–66

    dates, formatting 70–73

    dates, formatting day names 72–73

VBScript *(continued)*

    dates, formatting month names 72–73

    dates, projecting based on specified interval 70

    dates, retrieving 60–61

    dates, retrieving specific parts of 62–67

    dates, verifying values as dates 61–62

    Day function 66–67

    delimited strings, converting to arrays 101–102

    Dim statement 51, 98

    Do loops 88–89

    Do Until loops 88

    Do While loops 88

    dynamic arrays 100

    Empty variables 51–52, 58–59

    endless loops 89

    Err object 44–46

    error handling 43–46, 104–111

    Exit Do statement 90–91

    For Each statement 31–32

    For Next loops 34–36

    FormatNumber function 84

    FormatPercent function 86–87

    formatting numerical output 24

    functions 112, 114–119

    GetObject method 20

    GetObject method, COM objects 123, 124

    history of 7

    Hour function 66–67

    InStr function 80–81

    intrinsic constants 54–56

    IsDate function 61

    IsNull method 59

    IsObject function 126

    LCase function 82

    Left function 76–77

    Len function 76–77

    line continuation character 48–49

    loops 34–36, 88–91

    LTrim function 76–77

    Mid function 76–77

    Minute function 66–67

    Month function 66–67

VBScript *(continued)*

    MonthName function 72–73

    Next statement 34

    Nothing keyword 128

    Now function 60

    Now function, formatting output 70

    Null variables 58–59

    numbers, formatting 84–87

    object references, verifying 126

    On Error GoTo 0 statement 108–109

    On Error Resume Next statement 106–109

    On Error Resume Next statement 43–46

    Option Explicit statment 51

    overview 17–18

    parameters, passing by reference 118–119

    parameters, passing by value 119

    parameters, passing to functions 115–118

    percentages, formatting 86–87

    procedures 111–112, 113

    procedures, calling 112–113

    recursive procedures 120–121

    ReDim Preserve statement 100

    registry data types, corresponding to WSH types 204

    Right function 76–77

    RTrim function 76–77

    runtime errors, handling 43–46, 104–111

    Second function 66–67

    Set keyword 21, 325

    Space function 76–77

    statement breaks 47–49

    string data 73–74

    string data, converting to arrays 101–102

    string data, formatting 74–76

    string data, formatting for message boxes 78–79

    string data, modifying character case 81–82

    string data, searching for text 79–81

    string data, tabular output 77–78

    string manipulation functions 76–77

    strings, assigning to variables 26–28

    strings, concatenating 29–30

    subroutines 112

VBScript *(continued)*
   syntax errors 104
   Time function 60
   Time function, formatting output 70
   time values, arithmetic 68–70
   time values, determining interval between 68–69
   time values, formatting 70–73
   time values, projecting based on specified interval 70
   time values, retrieving 60–61
   time values, retrieving specific parts of 62–67
   time values, verifying 61–62
   Trim function 76–77
   type coercion 57–58
   type conversion functions 58
   UCase function 82
   variables 23
   variables, assigning values to 52
   variables, default values 51–52
   variables, explicit declaration 50–51
   variables, implicit declaration 49–50
   variables, initializing 51–52
   VbCrLf constant 55
   VbTab constant 55, 293
   Weekday function 66–67
   WeekdayName function 72–73
   WMI and 430
   WMI, binding to 20
   WSH, binding to 20
   Year function 66–67
VbTab constant, VBScript 55, 293
Vendor property
   Win32_Product class 656
   Win32_SoftwareFeature class 658–659
verbs, Shell object
   enumerating for specified objects 820
   executing 818–819
verifying command-line arguments
   correct number of arguments 172–173
   presence of required arguments 174–175
verifying script correctness 1188

version numbers
   file version numbers, retrieving 279
   of selected Microsoft Windows operating systems 638
   operating system version numbers, retrieving 637–638
   overview 279
Version property
   Win32_BIOS class 620–626
   Win32_OperatingSystem class 620–621, 638, 639–641
   Win32_Product class 656
   Win32_SoftwareFeature class 658–659
   WScript object 179
versionNumber attribute, printQueue object 933–935
versions, WSH
   version 5.6 compared to earlier versions 134
   version number, retrieving 179
   version required for scripts in this book 13
VerticalResolution property, Win32_PrinterConfiguration class 908–910
virtual folders, in Shell namespace hierarchy 773
virtual memory
   See also memory
   page files 762–766
Visible property, Internet Explorer object 1077–1079
Visual Basic .NET
   calling functions and procedures 1162–1163
   default properties of automation objects 1175
   migrating scripts to 1148
   multiple-language scripts 1170
   script file formats 1161
   single-line If-Then statements 1169
Volatile environment variables, registry locations 197
Volume class 835
volume names
   changing 737
   compared to drive letters 737
VolumeName property
   FileSystemObject 245–247
   Win32_LogicalDisk class 733–734

volumes

    names *See* volume names

    quotas *See* disk quotas

VolumeSerialNumber property, Win32_LogicalDisk
class 733–734

W

wait mouse pointer, Internet Explorer 1130

watch mouse pointer, Internet Explorer 1130

WBEM

    See also Wbemtest.exe

    WMI and 429

WBEM_E_INVALID_CLASS error 453

Wbemcntl.exe 444

Wbemdisp.dll *See* WMI scripting library

wbemFlagForwardOnly flag 489, 513

wbemFlagReturnImmediately flag 489, 513

Wbemperf.dll 438–439

Wbemtest.exe

    examining components of classes 471

    overview 479

WDM device drivers, as managed resources 436

WDM provider, WMI 438–439

Web pages

    clearing script output from 1084

    displaying script output in 1081–1084

    embedding script code in, drawbacks 1088

    HTAs *See* HTAs

    password masking with 1118–1120

    tracking script progress in *See* tracking script
    progress

Web-Based Enterprise Management

    See also Wbemtest.exe

    WMI and 429

Weekday function, VBScript 66–67

WeekdayName function, VBScript 72–73

weekdays

    intervals between, determining, VBScript 69

    retrieving from date and time values 62–64, 66–67

weeks of year

    first week of the year, configuring in VBScript 65–66

    intervals between, determining, VBScript 69

    retrieving from date and time values 62–64

whenChanged attribute, Computer class 691

whenCreated attribute, Computer class 691

WHERE clauses, WMI queries

    Boolean values used in 509

    enhancements 540

    in targeted queries 512

    numbers used in 509

    strings used in 509

    syntax 508

    variables used in 510–511

white space in scripts

    See also spaces

    indentations 1166–1167

    overview 1164

    spaces in parameter lists 1165–1166

    spaces surrounding operators 1165

width of columns in tabular script output 1073

Width property, Internet Explorer object 1077–1079

wildcard characters

    binding to folders 250

    copying folders and folder contents 254

    copying sets of files 271

    deleting files 269–270

    deleting sets of folders 252

    moving sets of files 272

    verifying file existence 268

wildcards in search filters 606–607

Win31FileSystem (registry entry) 755, 760

Win32 APIs, and WMI providers 437–438

Win32 extension classes 460–461

Win32 provider, WMI 438–439, 452, 460

Win32_Baseboard class 631

Win32_BaseService class 460, 463

Win32_BIOS class

  properties equivalent to System Information
    fields 620–621

  properties 624–626

Win32_Bus class 631

Win32_CDRomDrive class 630

Win32_ComputerSystem class

  DomainRole property 713

  Microsoft extension classes 460

  properties (table) 669, 671–672

  properties displayed in Startup and Recovery
    Page 672

  properties equivalent to System Information
    fields 620–621

Win32_DependentService class 994

Win32_DesktopMonitor class 631

Win32_Directory class

  Compress method 802

  Copy method 796

  Delete method 529, 801

  methods 776–778

  properties available in Windows Explorer
    interface 776

  properties 775–776

  Rename method 794, 795

  Uncompress method 802

Win32_DiskDrive class

  inventorying computer hardware 630

  properties 726–728

Win32_DiskPartition class 730–732

Win32_Fan class 631

Win32_InfraredDevice class 630

Win32_Keyboard class 630

Win32_LogicalDisk class 733–734

Win32_LogicalDiskDrive class 436

Win32_LogicalMemoryConfiguration class 430–431

Win32_NetworkAdapter class 630

Win32_NTEventLogFile class

  properties available on Event Viewer 846

  properties 845–846

Win32_NTEventLogfile class 527

Win32_NTLogEvent class

  properties displayed in Event Viewer 859

  properties 858–859

Win32_NTLogEventLog class 470

Win32_OperatingSystem class

  properties (table) 639–641

  properties equivalent to System Information
    fields 620–621

  properties 638

  Reboot method 685

  retrieving operating system information 447

  Win32Shutdown method 682, 684

Win32_OSRecoveryConfiguration class

  properties (table) 676–677

  properties displayed in Startup and Recovery
    Page 677

Win32_PageFile class 763

Win32_PageFileUsage class 764–765

Win32_ParallelPort class 630

Win32_PhysicalMemory class 631

Win32_PNPEntity class 631

Win32_POTSModem class 630

Win32_PowerManagementEvent class 686–687

Win32_Printer class

  inventorying computer hardware 630

  properties (list) 885–887, 907–908

Win32_PrinterConfiguration class 908–910

Win32_PrintJob class 900–902

Win32_Process class 534, 538

  compared to Windows Task Manager 940

  Create method 959–960

  properties (table) 946–948

Win32_Processor class

  inventorying computer hardware 631

  properties equivalent to System Information
    fields 620–621

Win32_ProcessStartup class

  configurable startup options 962–963

  modifying startup options 961, 963–964

Win32_Product class
  enumerating installed software 655
  Install method 660–661
  installing software on remote computers 662–663
  properties (table) 656
  Uninstall method 666
  Upgrade method 664–665
Win32_QuickFixEngineering class 645
Win32_ScheduledJob class
  compared to Task Scheduler APIs 1136–1137
  Create method 1141–1142
  creating scheduled tasks 1141
  Delete method 529, 1144
  enumerating scheduled tasks 1137
  error codes 1142
  properties (table) 1137
Win32_SCSIController class 630
Win32_SerialPort class 630
Win32_Service class
  Change method 1001–1003, 1007
  Create method 1011–1012
  inheritance 463
  installed services, enumerating 715
  methods 527
  Microsoft Extension classes 460
  monitoring print service 897
  PauseService method 990, 991
  properties 466, 989, 1001–1003
  properties (table) 978–980
  ResumeService method 992, 993
  StartService method 992
  StopService method 527, 990
  use of in scripts 433
Win32_Share class
  Create method 828–829
  Delete method 529, 832
  properties 826
  properties available in Windows Explorer interface 827
  SetShareInfo method 833
Win32_ShareToDirectory class 830

Win32_SoftwareFeature class
  enumerating installed software 655
  properties (table) 658–659
Win32_SoundDevice class 630
Win32_StartupCommand class 674
Win32_Subdirectory class 778
Win32_SystemEnclosure class
  chassis type values (table) 635
  properties 628
Win32_SystemServices class 460, 466
Win32_Thread class 956–957
Win32_TSSessionSetting class 462
Win32_USBController class 630
Win32_VideoController class 630
Win32_WMISetting class
  configurable WMI settings (table) 651–652
  properties (table) 647–649
  use of in scripts 454
Win32_Provider class 458
Win32Shutdown method, Win32_OperatingSystem class 682, 684
WINDIR (environment variable) 198
window handle parameter, BrowseForFolder method 792
window style, programs run from within scripts 186
Windows 2000 Resource Kit, WMI scripts for browsing CIM 479
Windows 2000 Service Pack 2 14
Windows 2000 services, removing 1013
Windows 2000 system requirements 13–14
Windows Driver Model device drivers, as managed resources 436
Windows Explorer
  adding script templates to context menu 1161
  CIM_Datafile class properties available in Explorer interface 804
  extended file properties, displaying 806
  running WSH scripts 146
  shortcut menus and Shell object verbs 818–819
  Win32_Directory class properties available in Explorer interface 776
  Win32_Share class properties available in Explorer interface 827

Windows folder

See also special folders

locating special folders 788

Windows Installer

as managed resource 436

enumerating installed software 655, 656

Windows Installer provider, WMI 438–439, 452

Windows Management Instrumentation See WMI

Windows NT Directory Services Directory Information Tree file 393

Windows Query Language queries See WQL queries

Windows Script Host See WSH

Windows Script Technologies, history of 7

Windows Shell object See Shell object

Windows Shell process

See also WshShell object

environment variables 197–201

Windows XP system requirements 13–14

windows, hidden, creating processes in 963

Windows-based printer connections

adding 224

removing 225

WindowsDirectory property, Win32_OperatingSystem class 620–621

WindowsState property, HTA object 1088–1090

WindowStyle property, WshShortcut object 192

Winmgmt.exe 439

winmgmts prefix, WMI moniker 494–495

WinNT provider 323, 418, 419, 693

WITHIN keyword, WMI event notification queries and 531, 534–535

WMI

See also WMI scripting library; WMI scripts

administrative credentials required 14

architecture See WMI architecture

binding to Automation objects using VBScript 20

capabilities of 430–433

choosing a scripting language 12–13

CIM repository See CIM repository

classes See WMI classes

collections, working with 772

compared to FileSystemObject 243

WMI (continued)

compared to WSH 148

consumers See WMI consumers

event notifications See WMI event notifications

event subscriptions See WMI event subscriptions

history of 7

HTAs and 1088

infrastructure See WMI infrastructure

managed resources See managed resources

moniker See WMI moniker

namespaces See namespaces

object paths See WMI object paths

operating system support for 427

overview 429–433

permissions 444–445

providers See WMI providers

queries See WMI queries

repository See CIM repository

security See WMI security

WMI architecture

managed resources 436

overview 434–436

security 443–444

security, DCOM 445–446

security, namespace-level 444–445

security, operating system 446

WMI consumers 443

WMI infrastructure 437–442

WMI classes

See also CIM repository; managed resources; names of specific classes

availability of 471–472, 479

categories of classes 458

CIM classes 441

components of classes 466–467

core and common classes 459–460

equivalent to hardware components (table) 631

equivalent to System Information fields 620–621, 630–631

event classes See WMI event classes

extension classes 460–461

hierarchy and inheritance 463–465

WMI classes *(continued)*

    instances of, defined 436

    listing classes in a namespace 461–463

    methods 469

    properties 467–469

    qualifiers 469–471

    queries *See* WMI queries

    retrieving class definitions 472–478

    searching for using findstr.exe 462

    structure of CIM repository 450

    system classes 458–459

    types of classes 465–466

    WMI Tester and 471

WMI consumers

    See also WMI scripts

    as layer of WMI architecture 435–436

    overview 443

    request processing by CIMOM 440

WMI Control snap-in 444

WMI event classes

    extrinsic events 540

    hierarchy 536

    intrinsic events 537–538

    notification queries and 534

    overview 536

WMI event notifications

    basic script steps 533

    CIMOM issuance of 440

    enhancements 540

    enhancements, __EventConsumer classes 545

    enhancements, __EventFilter class 544

    enhancements, __FilterToConsumerBinding class 546

    enhancements, multiple events 541

    enhancements, multiple types of events 542

    enhancements, multiple types of managed
       resources 542

    enhancements, permanent event subscriptions 543

    enhancements, targeting resources 540

    event classes 536

    extrinsic events 540

WMI event notifications *(continued)*

    health monitoring and 430

    intrinsic events 537–538

    overview 530–532

    queries 531, 533–536

WMI event subscriptions

    CIMOM processing of 440

    health monitoring and 430

    permanent event subscriptions 543

WMI infrastructure

    as layer of WMI architecture 435–436

    browsing the CIM repository 479

    CIM repository 441–442

    CIMOM 439–440

    overview 437

    security 443–444

    security, DCOM 445–446

    security, namespace-level 444–445

    security, operating system 446

    WMI providers 437–439

    WMI scripting library *See* WMI scripting library

WMI moniker

    overview 493

    security settings 495–500

    winmgmts prefix 494–495

    WMI object paths 501–503

WMI namespaces *See* namespaces

WMI object paths

    format of 502

    key properties 502–503

    overview 501

WMI providers

    add-on providers 438

    as component of WMI infrastructure 435–436

    finding more information 439

    list 438–439

    namespace locations 452

    overview 437–439

    registration 440

WMI queries
  all properties, all instances of a class 505–506
  all properties, selected instances of a class 507–511
  CIMOM processing of 440
  event notification queries 531, 533–536
  overview 503–505
  selected properties, all instances of a class 506–507
  selected properties, selected instances of a class 512
  speeding up with forward-only enumerators 513–514
  targeted queries 504
  targeted queries using AND or OR 512
  terminating 769
WMI Query Language queries See WMI queries
WMI Registry Provider
  backing up registry data before using 1025–1026
  binary-valued entries, reading 1031–1032
  CheckAccess method 1047–1048
  class definition storage location 452
  constants, built-in 1022–1023
  constants, method parameters 1027
  CreateKey method 1035
  data types, enumerating 1043
  DeleteKey method 1045, 1046
  DeleteValue method 1045–1046
  DWORD-valued entries, changing 1033–1034
  DWORD-valued entries, creating 1036–1038
  DWORD-valued entries, reading 1027–1028
  entries, changing 1033–1034
  entries, creating 1035, 1036–1040
  entries, enumerating 1043
  entries, reading 1026, 1027–1032
  enumerating entries 1043
  enumerating subkeys 1042
  enumerating values 1043
  EnumKey method 1042
  EnumValues method 1043
  expanded string-valued entries, creating 1040
  expanded string-valued entries, reading 1030–1031
  GetBinaryValue method 1026–1027, 1032
  GetDWORDValue method 1026–1027, 1027
  GetExpandedStringValue method 1026–1027, 1030
  GetMultiStringValue method 1026–1027, 1029

WMI Registry Provider (continued)
  GetStringValue method 1026–1027
  integer values of registry data types 1023
  multistring-valued entries, creating 1038–1040
  multistring-valued entries, reading 1029
  overview 438–439
  reading entries 1026, 1027–1032
  SetDWORDValue method 1033, 1036
  SetExpandedStringValue method 1040
  SetMultiStringValue method 1038–1040
  SetStringValue method 1033, 1036
  string-valued entries, changing 1033–1034
  string-valued entries, creating 1036–1038
  string-valued entries, reading 1027–1028
  subkeys, creating 1035
  subkeys, enumerating 1042
  values of registry entries, enumerating 1043
WMI repository See CIM repository
WMI schema See CIM repository
WMI scripting library
  as component of WMI infrastructure 435–436
  Automation objects and class definitions 480
  naming conventions 483
  object model 480–483
  overview 480
  SWbemLocator object 484–485
  SWbemObjectSet collection 491–492
  SWbemServices object 486–491
  WMI moniker See WMI moniker
WMI scripts
  See also managed resources; WMI consumers; WMI
    scripting library
  basic steps 482, 492, 533
  calling WMI methods 527
  changing resource managed by 447
  compared to FileSystemObject 768–772
  compared to Shell object 774
  creating resources 528
  dates and times 515\dates and times, converting to
    standard format 517
  dates and times, converting to UTC format 519–522
  deleting resources 529

WMI scripts *(continued)*

displaying all managed resource properties 524

displaying specified managed resource properties 523

error-handling capabilities 770–771

event notifications *See* WMI event notifications

folder paths, browsing for 791–792

limitations of 769, 797

monitoring resources *See* WMI event notifications

multi-hop security support 662

overview 430–433, 492–493

printers and print management 882–883

queries *See* WMI queries

remote file and folder access 771–772

return values, file and folder operations 778

speed of query processing 770

templates 523

terminating loops 541

WMI moniker *See* WMI moniker

writing managed resource properties 525

WMI security

authentication level 497

authority setting 498

DCOM security 445–446

impersonation level 496–497

moniker settings 495, 500

namespace-level security 444–445

overview 443–444

privilege overrides 498–500

Windows operating system security 446

WMI service

See also WMI settings

as component of WMI infrastructure 435–436

connecting to, remote access 440

default namespace 649

overview 439–440

processing consumer requests 440

WMI settings

See also WMI service

configuring 651–652

enumerating 649

Win32_WMISetting class 646–649

WMI Tester

examining components of classes 471

overview 479

Wmimgmt.msc 444

Wmiprov.dll 438–439

WMISetting object, ASPScriptDefaultNamespace property 454

worker scripts

See also remotely running scripts

overview 227

running 230

working directory, changing for scripts 211

working set size, diagnosing memory leaks 946

WorkingDirectory property, WshShortcut object 192

WorkingSetSize property, Win32_Process class 946–948

workstations, locking from command line 682

WQL queries

See also WMI queries

folder properties, retrieving 779

folders, enumerating 780

Write method

FileSystemObject 292

StdOut stream 157, 161

WScript object 1134

Write qualifier, WMI 470–471

WRITE_DAC (registry subkey access right) 1048

WRITE_OWNER (registry subkey access right) 1048

Writeable property, Win32_Directory class 775–776

WriteBlankLines method

FileSystemObject 292

StdOut stream 157

WriteDebugInfo property, Win32_OSRecoveryConfiguration class 676–677

WriteLine method

FileSystemObject 292, 295

StdOut stream 157

WriteLn method

sending script output to Internet Explorer 1082–1084

tracking script progress in Internet Explorer 1129

WriteToSystemLog property, Win32_OSRecoveryConfiguration class 676–677

writing scripts
  See also scripts
  an introduction to scripting 3–6
writing scripts, WMI See WMI scripts
writing to text files
  appending new data 295
  file writing methods 292
  ForAppending mode 292, 295
  ForWriting mode 283, 292, 294
  modifying specific lines 294
  overview 292
  overwriting existing data 294
WScript host
  See also script hosts, WSH; WScript object; WSH
  command-line options 143–145
  compared to CScript 137–138
  default script host, setting 143
  determining current script host 180
  output from scripts, displaying 156–157
  running scripts from command line 143–145
WScript library, interactions with COM objects 140
WScript object
  See also WScript host; WSH
  accessing in scripts 150
  Arguments property 167
  binding to COM objects 150
  Build property 179
  capabilities 150
  COM object creation, compared to VBScript 153
  COM object methods, calling 152
  COM object properties, accessing 152
  COM object references See object references
  COM objects, creating 151–152
  COM objects, using previously instantiated objects 152
  command-line arguments See command-line arguments
  compared to VBScript 148
  CreateObject method 150, 151, 153, 1085
  Echo method 154, 1072, 1133
  FullName property 179, 180
  functionality 150

WScript object (continued)
  GetObject method 150, 152, 153
  in WSH object model 140
  input See input to scripts
  metadata properties 179–180
  Name property 179
  output See output from scripts
  overview 148–150
  Path property 179
  properties and methods 149–150
  Quit method 178, 1085
  ScriptFullName property 179
  ScriptName property 179
  Sleep method 176–177, 1086
  StdOut.Write method 1134
  Timeout property 178
  user input See input to scripts
  Version property 179
  Write method 1134
  WScript Echo method 156–157
  WSH environment information, retrieving 179–180
  WshArguments collection See WshArguments collection
  WshNamed collection See WshNamed collection
  WshUnnamed collection See WshUnnamed collection
WScript SpecialFolders collection 195
Wscript.Quit statement, running scripts incrementally 1186–1187
WSH
  architecture overview 135–139
  Automation objects, WSH support for 131
  batch files, compared to WSH scripts 133
  choosing a scripting language 12–13
  Cmd.exe, compared to WSH scripts 133
  COM object references See object references
  COM objects See COM objects
  COM, WSH support for 131
  command-line tools, running 132
  compared to ADSI 148
  compared to batch scripts 183–184
  compared to VBScript 148
  compared to WMI 148

WSH *(continued)*

   components, diagram 135–136

   components, interaction of 139–140

   connecting to using VBScript 20

   disabling 239–240

   environment variables (list) 198

   history of 7

   input facilities 154

   input to scripts *See* input to scripts

   object model 140

   objects *See* WSH objects

   output facilities 154

   output from scripts *See* output from scripts

   overview 130–134

   registry data types, corresponding to VBScript types 204

   script files 136–137, 139

   script hosts *See* script hosts, WSH

   scripting language engines 138, 139, 143

   scripting runtime environment *See* scripting runtime environment

   scripts *See* WSH scripts

   special folder mnemonics 787–789

   version 5.6 compared to earlier versions 134

   version required for scripts in this book 13

   WMI and 430

   WScript library, interactions with COM objects 140

   WSH-compliant scripting languages 136

   WshController object *See* WshController object

   WshNetwork object *See* WshNetwork object

   WshShell object *See* WshShell object

WSH architecture 135–139

WSH objects 147, 148

WSH scripts

   See also WSH

   accessing command-line output 185

   command-line arguments *See* command-line arguments

   command-line options, script hosts 143

   command-line tools, running from within scripts 188–189

   compared to ADSI 226

WSH scripts *(continued)*

   compared to batch scripts 183–184

   computer information, retrieving 226

   current working directory, changing 211

   ensuring applications are active 209

   environment variables 197–198

   environment variables, creating 199–200

   environment variables, expanding 200–201

   environment variables, modifying 200

   environment variables, retrieving 198

   event handling 181

   input *See* input to scripts

   keystrokes, sending to applications 206–210

   logging events 201–202

   logo, displaying or suppressing in script output 143

   MS-DOS-based printer connections, adding 224

   network drives, enumerating 223

   network drives, mapping 221–222

   network drives, unmapping 222–223

   network printers, adding 224–225

   network printers, default printer 226

   network printers, enumerating 225

   network printers, removing 225

   output *See* output from scripts

   pausing 176–177

   printer connections, adding 224–225

   printer connections, default printer 226

   printer connections, enumerating 225

   printer connections, removing 225

   programs, running from within scripts 184–187

   quitting 177–178

   redirecting output to text files 145–146

   registry entries, creating 205

   registry entries, deleting 205

   registry entries, modifying 205

   registry entries, reading 203–205

   remotely running scripts 227, 230

   remotely running scripts, configuring environment for 229

   remotely running scripts, error handling 232

   remotely running scripts, event handling 231

WSH scripts *(continued)*

remotely running scripts, limitations of remote WSH 234

remotely running scripts, monitoring status of 231

remotely running scripts, running worker scripts 230

running 140–142

running from command line 142–145

running from context-sensitive menus 146

running from Windows Explorer 146

running in batch mode 143

running on remote computers 146

running using drag-and-drop 146

running with Script Debugger 143

scheduling script execution 146

scripting language engines, specifying 143

scripting runtime *See scripting runtime environment*

scripts, running from within scripts 184–187

streams, input and output, accessing 184–185

terminating 177–178

timeout option 143

time-out values 178

user account information, retrieving 226

Windows-based printer connections, adding 224

WSH security

digitally signing scripts 235–238

disabling Windows ScriptHost 239–240

enforcing signed scripts 236

overview 234–235

restricting ability to run scripts 238–240

signing scripts 237

verifying signed scripts 237–238

WshArguments collection

command-line argument storage 164, 166–168

Count method 166

Item property 166, 168

Length property 166

Named property 166

properties and methods 149–150

ShowUsage method 166

Unnamed property 166

WshController object

accessing 228

capabilities 229

COM objects, WSH support for 139

CreateScript method 230

in WSH object model 140

methods, properties, and events 229

object model 227

overview 227

ProgID naming convention 228

WshEnvironment collection 197

WshNamed collection

Exists method 171

methods and properties 149–150, 165

storing named arguments 164, 170–171

WshNetwork object

See also network drives; network printers

AddPrinterConnection method 224

AddWindowsPrinterConnection method 224

COM objects, WSH support for 139

ComputerName property 226

EnumNetworkDrives method 223

EnumPrinterConnections method 225

in WSH object model 140

MapNetworkDrive method 221, 222

methods and properties 219–220

object model 219–220

RemoveNetworkDrive method 222

RemovePrinterConnection method 225

retrieving logon information 693

SetDefaultPrinter method 226

UserDomain property 226

UserName property 226

WshRemote object

capabilities 229

End event 231

Error event 231

Execute method 230

Start event 231

Status property 231

WshRemoteError object 229, 231, 232

WshShell object
  AppActivate method 209
  applications without COM object model, automating 206–210
  capabilities 183
  COM objects, WSH support for 139
  CurrentDirectory property 211
  Environment property 197
  Exec method 184–185, 188–189
  ExpandEnvironmentStrings method 201
  in WSH object model 140
  LogEvent method 201
  methods and properties 183
  object model 181
  overview 181
  programs, running 183–191
  RegDelete method 205
  RegRead method 203
  RegWrite method 205
  Run method 184–185, 186–187, 188–189
  SendKeys method 206–210
  special folders 195–196
WshShortcut object
  Arguments property 192
  CreateShortcut method 192
  Description property 192
  FullName property 192
  HotKey property 192
  IconLocation property 192
  Save method 192
  TargetPath property 192
  WindowStyle property 192
  WorkingDirectory property 192

WshUnnamed collection
  properties and methods 149–150, 165
  storing unnamed arguments 164, 168–170
WshUrlShortcut object
  CreateShortcut method 193
  Save method 193
wWWHomePage attribute, user accounts 572

X

XCountChars property, Win32_ProcessStartup class 962–963
XOR bitwise operator, changing flag values 565
Xsize property, Win32_ProcessStartup class 962–963

Y

YCountChars property, Win32_ProcessStartup class 962–963
Year function, VBScript 66–67
years
  See also dates and date values
  first week of the year, configuring in VBScript 65–66
  intervals between, determining, VBScript 69
  retrieving from date and time values 62–64, 66–67
Ysize property, Win32_ProcessStartup class 962–963

Z

zero, leading, formatting numbers 84

Faucet-Handle Puller

Faced with a gummed-up and frozen faucet handle, many homeowners will throw up their hands in despair or reach for a pair of vise grips, which can scratch the faucet handle. In this situation, the wise homeowner reaches for a **faucet-handle puller**, a tool built like a corkscrew that can lift a stuck handle off its stem without damaging its finish. Simply slide the handle-puller's shaft into the hole on the faucet handle and position the puller's arms under the base of the handle. Then tighten the screw, and the puller's arms easily lift the handle free of its stem.

At Microsoft Press, we use tools to illustrate our books for software developers and IT professionals. Tools very simply and powerfully symbolize human inventiveness. They're a metaphor for people extending their capabilities, precision, and reach. From simple calipers and pliers to digital micrometers and lasers, these stylized illustrations give each book a visual identity, and a personality to the series. With tools and knowledge, there's no limit to creativity and innovation. Our tagline says it all: *the tools you need to put technology to work.*

Ready
solutions
for the
IT administrator

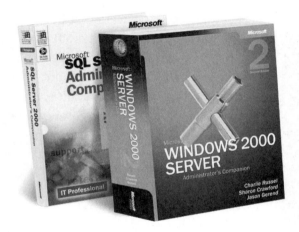

Keep your IT systems up and running with the ADMINISTRATOR'S COMPANION series from Microsoft. These expert guides serve as both tutorials and references for critical deployment and maintenance of Microsoft products and technologies. Packed with real-world expertise, hands-on numbered procedures, and handy workarounds, ADMINISTRATOR'S COMPANIONS deliver ready answers for on-the-job results.

Microsoft® SQL Server™ 2000 Administrator's Companion

U.S.A. $59.99
Canada $86.99
ISBN   0-7356-1051-7

Microsoft Exchange 2000 Server Administrator's Companion

U.S.A. $59.99
Canada $86.99
ISBN   0-7356-0938-1

Microsoft Windows® 2000 Server Administrator's Companion, Second Edition

U.S.A. $ 69.99
Canada $ 107.99
ISBN   0-7356-1785-6

Microsoft Systems Management Server 2.0 Administrator's Companion

U.S.A. $59.99
Canada $92.99
ISBN   0-7356-0834-2

microsoft.com/mspress

Comprehensive
information and tools—
straight from the
Windows 2000 Server team!

Deploy, manage, and optimize Microsoft Windows 2000 Server with expertise from those who know the technology best—the Windows 2000 Server product team. These five powerhouse guides—also available as part of the WINDOWS 2000 RESOURCE KIT—provide thousands of pages of technical details and hundreds of tools and utilities on CD. They give you everything you need to maximize the power of your enterprise server systems and reduce your ownership and support costs!

Microsoft® Windows® 2000 Server Deployment Planning Guide
U.S.A.   **$49.99**
Canada $72.99
ISBN: 0-7356-1794-5

Microsoft Windows 2000 Server Distributed Systems Guide
U.S.A.   **$59.99**
Canada $86.99
ISBN: 0-7356-1795-3

Microsoft Windows 2000 Server Operations Guide
U.S.A.   **$39.99**
Canada $57.99
ISBN: 0-7356-1796-1

Microsoft Windows 2000 Server Internetworking Guide
U.S.A.   **$49.99**
Canada $72.99
ISBN: 0-7356-1797-X

Microsoft Windows 2000 Server TCP/IP Core Networking Guide
U.S.A.   **$49.99**
Canada $72.99
ISBN: 0-7356-1798-8

Microsoft
microsoft.com/mspress

Get a **Free**
e-mail newsletter, updates,
special offers, links to related books,
and more when you

register on line!

Register your Microsoft Press® title on our Web site and you'll get a FREE subscription to our e-mail newsletter, *Microsoft Press Book Connections.* You'll find out about newly released and upcoming books and learning tools, online events, software downloads, special offers and coupons for Microsoft Press customers, and information about major Microsoft® product releases. You can also read useful additional information about all the titles we publish, such as detailed book descriptions, tables of contents and indexes, sample chapters, links to related books and book series, author biographies, and reviews by other customers.

Registration is easy. Just visit this Web page and fill in your information:

http://www.microsoft.com/mspress/register

***Microsoft*®**

- -

MICROSOFT LICENSE AGREEMENT

Book Companion CD

IMPORTANT—READ CAREFULLY: This Microsoft End-User License Agreement ("EULA") is a legal agreement between you (either an individual or an entity) and Microsoft Corporation for the Microsoft product identified above, which includes computer software and may include associated media, printed materials, and "online" or electronic documentation ("SOFTWARE PRODUCT"). Any component included within the SOFTWARE PRODUCT that is accompanied by a separate End-User License Agreement shall be governed by such agreement and not the terms set forth below. By installing, copying, or otherwise using the SOFTWARE PRODUCT, you agree to be bound by the terms of this EULA. If you do not agree to the terms of this EULA, you are not authorized to install, copy, or otherwise use the SOFTWARE PRODUCT; you may, however, return the SOFTWARE PRODUCT, along with all printed materials and other items that form a part of the Microsoft product that includes the SOFTWARE PRODUCT, to the place you obtained them for a full refund.

SOFTWARE PRODUCT LICENSE

The SOFTWARE PRODUCT is protected by United States copyright laws and international copyright treaties, as well as other intellectual property laws and treaties. The SOFTWARE PRODUCT is licensed, not sold.

1. **GRANT OF LICENSE.** This EULA grants you the following rights:

    a. **Software Product.** You may install and use one copy of the SOFTWARE PRODUCT on a single computer. The primary user of the computer on which the SOFTWARE PRODUCT is installed may make a second copy for his or her exclusive use on a portable computer.

    b. **Storage/Network Use.** You may also store or install a copy of the SOFTWARE PRODUCT on a storage device, such as a network server, used only to install or run the SOFTWARE PRODUCT on your other computers over an internal network; however, you must acquire and dedicate a license for each separate computer on which the SOFTWARE PRODUCT is installed or run from the storage device. A license for the SOFTWARE PRODUCT may not be shared or used concurrently on different computers.

    c. **License Pak.** If you have acquired this EULA in a Microsoft License Pak, you may make the number of additional copies of the computer software portion of the SOFTWARE PRODUCT authorized on the printed copy of this EULA, and you may use each copy in the manner specified above. You are also entitled to make a corresponding number of secondary copies for portable computer use as specified above.

    d. **Sample Code.** Solely with respect to portions, if any, of the SOFTWARE PRODUCT that are identified within the SOFTWARE PRODUCT as sample code (the "SAMPLE CODE"):

    i. **Use and Modification.** Microsoft grants you the right to use and modify the source code version of the SAMPLE CODE, *provided* you comply with subsection (d)(iii) below. You may not distribute the SAMPLE CODE, or any modified version of the SAMPLE CODE, in source code form.

    ii. **Redistributable Files.** Provided you comply with subsection (d)(iii) below, Microsoft grants you a nonexclusive, royalty-free right to reproduce and distribute the object code version of the SAMPLE CODE and of any modified SAMPLE CODE, other than SAMPLE CODE, or any modified version thereof, designated as not redistributable in the Readme file that forms a part of the SOFTWARE PRODUCT (the "Non-Redistributable Sample Code"). All SAMPLE CODE other than the Non-Redistributable Sample Code is collectively referred to as the "REDISTRIBUTABLES."

    iii. **Redistribution Requirements.** If you redistribute the REDISTRIBUTABLES, you agree to: (i) distribute the REDISTRIBUTABLES in object code form only in conjunction with and as a part of your software application product; (ii) not use Microsoft's name, logo, or trademarks to market your software application product; (iii) include a valid copyright notice on your software application product; (iv) indemnify, hold harmless, and defend Microsoft from and against any claims or lawsuits, including attorney's fees, that arise or result from the use or distribution of your software application product; and (v) not permit further distribution of the REDISTRIBUTABLES by your end user. Contact Microsoft for the applicable royalties due and other licensing terms for all other uses and/or distribution of the REDISTRIBUTABLES.

2. **DESCRIPTION OF OTHER RIGHTS AND LIMITATIONS.**

    - **Limitations on Reverse Engineering, Decompilation, and Disassembly.** You may not reverse engineer, decompile, or disassemble the SOFTWARE PRODUCT, except and only to the extent that such activity is expressly permitted by applicable law notwithstanding this limitation.

    - **Separation of Components.** The SOFTWARE PRODUCT is licensed as a single product. Its component parts may not be separated for use on more than one computer.

    - **Rental.** You may not rent, lease, or lend the SOFTWARE PRODUCT.

- **Support Services.** Microsoft may, but is not obligated to, provide you with support services related to the SOFTWARE PRODUCT ("Support Services"). Use of Support Services is governed by the Microsoft policies and programs described in the user manual, in "online" documentation, and/or in other Microsoft-provided materials. Any supplemental software code provided to you as part of the Support Services shall be considered part of the SOFTWARE PRODUCT and subject to the terms and conditions of this EULA. With respect to technical information you provide to Microsoft as part of the Support Services, Microsoft may use such information for its business purposes, including for product support and development. Microsoft will not utilize such technical information in a form that personally identifies you.

- **Software Transfer.** You may permanently transfer all of your rights under this EULA, provided you retain no copies, you transfer all of the SOFTWARE PRODUCT (including all component parts, the media and printed materials, any upgrades, this EULA, and, if applicable, the Certificate of Authenticity), **and** the recipient agrees to the terms of this EULA.

- **Termination.** Without prejudice to any other rights, Microsoft may terminate this EULA if you fail to comply with the terms and conditions of this EULA. In such event, you must destroy all copies of the SOFTWARE PRODUCT and all of its component parts.

3. **COPYRIGHT.** All title and copyrights in and to the SOFTWARE PRODUCT (including but not limited to any images, photographs, animations, video, audio, music, text, SAMPLE CODE, REDISTRIBUTABLES, and "applets" incorporated into the SOFTWARE PRODUCT) and any copies of the SOFTWARE PRODUCT are owned by Microsoft or its suppliers. The SOFTWARE PRODUCT is protected by copyright laws and international treaty provisions. Therefore, you must treat the SOFTWARE PRODUCT like any other copyrighted material **except** that you may install the SOFTWARE PRODUCT on a single computer provided you keep the original solely for backup or archival purposes. You may not copy the printed materials accompanying the SOFTWARE PRODUCT.

4. **U.S. GOVERNMENT RESTRICTED RIGHTS.** The SOFTWARE PRODUCT and documentation are provided with RESTRICTED RIGHTS. Use, duplication, or disclosure by the Government is subject to restrictions as set forth in subparagraph (c)(1)(ii) of the Rights in Technical Data and Computer Software clause at DFARS 252.227-7013 or subparagraphs (c)(1) and (2) of the Commercial Computer Software—Restricted Rights at 48 CFR 52.227-19, as applicable. Manufacturer is Microsoft Corporation/One Microsoft Way/Redmond, WA 98052-6399.

5. **EXPORT RESTRICTIONS.** You agree that you will not export or re-export the SOFTWARE PRODUCT, any part thereof, or any process or service that is the direct product of the SOFTWARE PRODUCT (the foregoing collectively referred to as the "Restricted Components"), to any country, person, entity, or end user subject to U.S. export restrictions. You specifically agree not to export or re-export any of the Restricted Components (i) to any country to which the U.S. has embargoed or restricted the export of goods or services, which currently include, but are not necessarily limited to, Cuba, Iran, Iraq, Libya, North Korea, Sudan, and Syria, or to any national of any such country, wherever located, who intends to transmit or transport the Restricted Components back to such country; (ii) to any end user who you know or have reason to know will utilize the Restricted Components in the design, development, or production of nuclear, chemical, or biological weapons; or (iii) to any end user who has been prohibited from participating in U.S. export transactions by any federal agency of the U.S. government. You warrant and represent that neither the BXA nor any other U.S. federal agency has suspended, revoked, or denied your export privileges.

DISCLAIMER OF WARRANTY

NO WARRANTIES OR CONDITIONS. MICROSOFT EXPRESSLY DISCLAIMS ANY WARRANTY OR CONDITION FOR THE SOFTWARE PRODUCT. THE SOFTWARE PRODUCT AND ANY RELATED DOCUMENTATION ARE PROVIDED "AS IS" WITHOUT WARRANTY OR CONDITION OF ANY KIND, EITHER EXPRESS OR IMPLIED, INCLUDING, WITHOUT LIMITA-TION, THE IMPLIED WARRANTIES OF MERCHANTABILITY, FITNESS FOR A PARTICULAR PURPOSE, OR NONINFRINGEMENT. THE ENTIRE RISK ARISING OUT OF USE OR PERFORMANCE OF THE SOFTWARE PRODUCT REMAINS WITH YOU.

LIMITATION OF LIABILITY. TO THE MAXIMUM EXTENT PERMITTED BY APPLICABLE LAW, IN NO EVENT SHALL MICROSOFT OR ITS SUPPLIERS BE LIABLE FOR ANY SPECIAL, INCIDENTAL, INDIRECT, OR CONSEQUENTIAL DAM-AGES WHATSOEVER (INCLUDING, WITHOUT LIMITATION, DAMAGES FOR LOSS OF BUSINESS PROFITS, BUSINESS INTERRUPTION, LOSS OF BUSINESS INFORMATION, OR ANY OTHER PECUNIARY LOSS) ARISING OUT OF THE USE OF OR INABILITY TO USE THE SOFTWARE PRODUCT OR THE PROVISION OF OR FAILURE TO PROVIDE SUPPORT SERVICES, EVEN IF MICROSOFT HAS BEEN ADVISED OF THE POSSIBILITY OF SUCH DAMAGES. IN ANY CASE, MICROSOFT'S ENTIRE LIABILITY UNDER ANY PROVISION OF THIS EULA SHALL BE LIMITED TO THE GREATER OF THE AMOUNT ACTUALLY PAID BY YOU FOR THE SOFTWARE PRODUCT OR US$5.00; PROVIDED, HOWEVER, IF YOU HAVE ENTERED INTO A MICROSOFT SUPPORT SERVICES AGREEMENT, MICROSOFT'S ENTIRE LIABILITY REGARDING SUPPORT SERVICES SHALL BE GOVERNED BY THE TERMS OF THAT AGREEMENT. BECAUSE SOME STATES AND JURISDICTIONS DO NOT ALLOW THE EXCLUSION OR LIMITATION OF LIABILITY, THE ABOVE LIMITATION MAY NOT APPLY TO YOU.

MISCELLANEOUS

This EULA is governed by the laws of the State of Washington USA, except and only to the extent that applicable law mandates govern-ing law of a different jurisdiction.

Should you have any questions concerning this EULA, or if you desire to contact Microsoft for any reason, please contact the Microsoft subsidiary serving your country, or write: Microsoft Sales Information Center/One Microsoft Way/Redmond, WA 98052-6399.

System Requirements

To use the *Microsoft Windows 2000 Scripting Guide* companion CD, you need a computer equipped with the following minimum configuration:

- Pentium-compatible 133-MHz or higher processor

- Microsoft Windows 2000 Server operating system (the latest service pack is recommended)

- 128 MB of RAM (256 MB is recommended)

- 2-GB hard disk with a minimum of 1-GB free space (additional free hard disk space is required if you are installing over a network)

- CD-ROM drive

- Microsoft Internet Explorer 5.5 or later

- Mouse or compatible pointing device

Actual requirements will vary based on your system configuration and the elements on the CD that you choose to install.

NOTE: Windows Script 5.6 (Scripten.exe) runs only on Windows 2000 Server operating systems; Windows Script 5.6 is already included in Microsoft Windows XP operating systems.